THE LAW OF INTERNATIONAL FINANCE

THE LAW OF
INTERNATIONAL
FINANCE

ANDREW MCKNIGHT

OXFORD
UNIVERSITY PRESS

OXFORD

UNIVERSITY PRESS

Great Clarendon Street, Oxford OX2 6DP

Oxford University Press is a department of the University of Oxford.
It furthers the University's objective of excellence in research, scholarship,
and education by publishing worldwide in

Oxford New York

Auckland Cape Town Dar es Salaam Hong Kong Karachi
Kuala Lumpur Madrid Melbourne Mexico City Nairobi
New Delhi Shanghai Taipei Toronto

With offices in

Argentina Austria Brazil Chile Czech Republic France Greece
Guatemala Hungary Italy Japan Poland Portugal Singapore
South Korea Switzerland Thailand Turkey Ukraine Vietnam

Oxford is a registered trade mark of Oxford University Press
in the UK and in certain other countries

Published in the United States
by Oxford University Press Inc., New York

British Library Cataloguing in Publication Data

Data available

Library of Congress Cataloging in Publication Data

Data available

Typeset by Cepha Imaging Private Ltd, Bangalore, India
Printed in Great Britain
on acid-free paper by
CPI Antony Rowe

ISBN 978-0-19-924471-3

1 3 5 7 9 10 8 6 4 2

This book is dedicated
to Tom, Unee and Liz

FOREWORD

It is a privilege to be asked to write the Foreword to this outstanding book, which represents a major and ground-breaking contribution in the field of international financial law.

This work is concerned with transactions in the London financial markets under which finance is arranged in those markets for those who require finance, whether they are based here or overseas. The legal issues that arise are examined from the perspective of English law, including English conflict of laws rules. English commercial law in this field is based on general principles of English law as applied to and reflecting the practice of the relevant markets. Andrew McKnight brings to bear in this book the knowledge and experience of a leading academic lawyer who also practises extensively in the field and therefore knows and understands the way the relevant markets work. Practitioners, parties to transactions in the London financial markets and students of the subject will all find this work of enormous value.

Any understanding of the law of international finance would be incomplete without an account of banking regulation, loan facilities, conflict of laws, cross-border insolvencies, jurisdiction issues, sovereign immunity and legal opinions. Andrew McKnight considers these and related issues in turn comprehensively and from a practical viewpoint. By way of example the specimen legal opinions illuminate the analysis in the text.

If one pauses to reflect on the size, volume and value of London financial market transactions every year, the central importance of this book becomes apparent. Syndicated loans, bond issues, derivative transactions, loan transfers, securitisation, structured finance and project finance are all carefully and fully examined. The use of diagrams to explain derivative transactions is particularly helpful. The treatment of secured transactions, equipment finance and guarantees is equally thorough and extensive. The book concludes with a consideration of the Law Commission's proposals in 2005 for reform of the law concerning transactions involving corporate security and sales of receivables.

English law in this field has had and continues to have an enormous influence on most international transactions of a similar nature. There is a need for clarity and certainty in commercial law. This is particularly so in relation to composite and specialised financing transactions and secured transactions, equipment finance and guarantees. Andrew McKnight has made a formidable contribution to clarity and certainty in setting out and explaining the law in relation to transactions in these fields and thus to the development of English and international law.

Peter Cresswell
Gray's Inn
June 2008

PREFACE

In writing this book I have tried to wear my two hats as a practising solicitor and an academic and so combine the experience that I have gained from both of those areas of interest. After all, the development of the law in a common law system is, essentially, an intellectual pursuit which should be guided and, perhaps, tempered by legal research, as well as by experience gained from the real world of legal practice and the needs of those who are served by legal practitioners. Similarly, academic work can be enhanced through knowledge provided by a connection with legal practice. That connection should also be useful in giving a practical and systematic focus to teaching and legal education, as well as research and legal writing. In my own experience as a teacher and a practitioner, I have also gained much from discussions with students and the searching questions that they have often raised. Rather sadly, and in contrast to the approach that I have followed, the disciplines of legal practice and academic work have often been seen as separate and remote from each other, although the attitudes that engendered such views are changing, as is evident from the discussions that now take place between academics and practitioners, the reference to academic views in court judgments and the presence of some (but not yet enough) practitioners on the teaching staffs of academic institutions. As an aside on a related matter, I should also like to make a plea to the institutions where law students are taught, which is that the academics in those institutions should devote at least as much of their commitment and enthusiasm to teaching as they do to research, legal writing and parading around at academic conferences. In their defence, it must be admitted that the system in the UK for assessing and funding academic institutions is skewed towards research at the expense of teaching. That imbalance should be corrected.

At the time of writing, the crisis in the international financial markets, which began in the second part of 2007, continues almost unabated. The longer term consequences of the crisis have yet to be revealed in full, but it is clear that the excesses in the years that led up to it must be understood and reined in for the good of the future. The participants in the financial markets and the regulators who oversee them also need to gain a better understanding of the areas of risk that have been exposed by the crisis and they must put in place mechanisms to meet and temper those risks. I hope that this book might assist in that endeavour, by providing an explanation of the practical and legal bases for the financial transactions that take place in the financial markets and the consequences of such transactions. It may also assist those who have the unenviable task of clearing up the mess that has been left by the crisis.

I am very grateful to the friends and colleagues that I have consulted in writing this book, who have given me their time and advice so generously. It would be unfair to single out any particular person above the others, so I trust that a general acknowledgement will suffice. I would, however, like to thank Sir Peter Cresswell for so kindly providing the Foreword to this book and for all the help and support that he has given me over the years. I should also like to express my thanks to Salans, which is the international law firm where I have practised in recent years. The firm has been very kind in providing me with resources that have assisted me in my writing. Finally, I must thank my wife, Liz, for all of her help and understanding, which has enabled me to get on with the task of writing the book.

The law is stated at 1 June 2008.

Andrew McKnight

CONTENTS—SUMMARY

PART D: SECURED TRANSACTIONS, EQUIPMENT FINANCE, AND GUARANTEES

CONTENTS

2. Banking Regulation

PART B: CONFLICT OF LAWS AND CROSS-BORDER ISSUES

4. Conflict of Laws in Transactional Matters

Contents

PART D: SECURED TRANSACTIONS, EQUIPMENT FINANCE, AND GUARANTEES

14. Secured Transactions

15. Equipment Finance

TABLE OF CASES

AUSTRALIA

BELGIUM

BRITISH VIRGIN ISLANDS

CANADA

EUROPEAN COURT OF JUSTICE AND COURT OF FIRST INSTANCE

Alphabetical

Chronological

ICSID Arbitral Tribunal

Netherlands

New Zealand

United Kingdom

United States of America

TABLE OF LEGISLATION

INTERNATIONAL

UNITED STATES OF AMERICA

PART A

INTRODUCTORY AND GROUND
LEVEL MATTERS

Chapter 1 provides a brief general introduction to this book. As contracts lie at the heart of the finance transactions with which this book is concerned, the chapter then goes on to examine various legal issues of a general nature that relate to contracts, particularly those that might concern finance transactions.

Chapter 2 deals with the prudential and supervisory regulation of banking activities, because of its relevance to finance transactions that are effected through the auspices of the London financial markets.

Chapter 3 examines loan facilities. It is included in this section of the book because much of what is discussed in the chapter is also of relevance to the more specialised forms of finance that are discussed in other parts of this book.

1

INTRODUCTORY MATTERS

1.1 Preliminary Points

This book is concerned with transactions in the London financial markets under **1.1.1** which finance is arranged in those markets for provision to those who require the finance, whether they be located in the UK or abroad. It will examine the legal issues that arise concerning such transactions, which it will do from the perspective of English law, including the application of its conflict of laws rules.

There are a number of ways in which finance may be raised in the London mar- **1.1.2** kets, ranging from finance provided by loan facilities of various different types, to capital markets issues of bonds and notes and structured finance in the form of a securitisation. Derivatives transactions may also be a relevant part of the way in which a financial package is structured. Finance may also be raised by a receivables or debt purchase transaction or through an equipment finance facility, in the latter case, by leasing, hire-purchase, and conditional sale. Sometimes a supplier (which may, in fact, be a financier) may be prepared to extend credit by giving time to pay, or a purchaser may be prepared to make an advance payment. In addition, finance may be raised by other methods such as through the issuance of share capital. Project finance utilises one or more methods of raising finance for the development of large-scale asset-based projects. A number of those various methods of raising finance in the London markets will be addressed in this book.

1.1.3 The structure and costs of a financing transaction may be affected by regulatory matters which concern the bank or banks that provide the finance. It is therefore relevant, in that connection, to consider banking regulation, which will be done in a separate chapter.

1.1.4 Because of the cross-border nature of international finance and the associated issues that may arise under the laws of different jurisdictions, the subject of conflict of laws will be important in any consideration of such transactions. The conflict of laws position must be analysed as a preliminary matter, as the application of the relevant conflicts rules will indicate the domestic system or systems of law which should be applied in determining the structure and effect of a transaction, and, indeed, if it is possible for the transaction and its various constituent elements to be recognised and enforced in each relevant jurisdiction. This will concern the transactional and proprietary issues that may arise, the resolution of disputes and enforcement of judgments or awards, sovereign immunity, and the effect of the insolvency of a party which is a participant in the transaction. A word of caution must be sounded at this point. Whilst there has been some limited standardisation as between different jurisdictions of their conflicts rules (for instance, under EC law or by international treaties and conventions), the general position is that each jurisdiction has its own conflicts rules and so there can be no guarantee that the conflicts analysis under the rules of one jurisdiction will be the same as that which is applied in a different jurisdiction. A practical consequence of this is that it may be necessary to obtain legal advice in each jurisdiction that has a connection with a transaction, or with those who are involved in it or may be affected by it, so as to determine how the transaction will be viewed, and whether it will be acknowledged and enforced, in that jurisdiction. Due to its importance, the subject of conflict of laws, and the subjects that are associated with it, are dealt with in a separate section of this book.

1.1.5 A perennial problem that must be faced by those who provide credit is the possibility of suffering a default in repayment of the indebtedness that has been incurred in utilising the credit. If it has not become apparent beforehand, the problem will do so when the entity that has obtained the credit becomes insolvent. To guard against this problem, or at least to mitigate against its effect, credit protection may be sought in various different ways. Once again, a conflict of laws analysis will be important in considering the methods of protection that may be available and, of course, the commercial adequacy of what is available will also have to be assessed. The possible methods to achieve credit protection will include taking security over assets of the debtor, use of the techniques of set-off or netting of claims, holding proprietary claims against assets that are used by the debtor or generated by its business or by obtaining the commitment of a third party to be answerable for the debtor's default by way of a suretyship obligation, which may itself be protected by taking security over the surety's assets, or using one of the other techniques that have just been mentioned. Equipment finance is a subject that is related to the techniques for holding proprietary protection in assets. These various matters are covered in a separate section of the book.

This book is laid out in the following way. Part A consists of this chapter, which **1.1.6** deals with general issues of a legal nature that might affect financing transactions. It includes a chapter on banking regulation, as that is relevant to the structure of transactions and the regulatory costs of transactions. It also contains a chapter on loan facilities, as many of the matters that are dealt with in that chapter are also relevant to the other types of financing transactions that are mentioned in this book. Part B contains chapters covering conflict of laws, the resolution of disputes across borders, international insolvency, sovereign immunity and state default, and legal opinions. Part C contains chapters on specialised and composite transactions, including syndicated lending, bond issues, derivatives transactions, loan transfers, securitisations, and structured finance, and project finance. Part D addresses the subject of proprietary transactions and credit protection and contains chapters on guarantees, secured transactions (including some transactions that have an equivalence to security), and equipment financing. It also contains a chapter on reform of the law of secured transactions.

It is now relevant to turn to a consideration of various general issues of a legal **1.1.7** nature that might concern a transaction (particularly as to contractual matters), which will occupy the remainder of this chapter. Reference should also be made to Chapter 3 on loan facilities, as the discussion in that chapter of various issues relating to the extension of loan credit is likely to be relevant to most types of transaction and not just to loan facilities.

1.2 Contractual Issues

From a legal perspective, the law of contract lies at the heart of most types of **1.2.1** finance transaction. What follows explores contractual issues that may arise under English law and which are of particular relevance to finance transactions. Similar issues are likely to arise under any other system of law that may be connected with a transaction, although the analysis and outcome may be different. It is not possible to provide a treatise on the whole of the law of contract, so the discussion will cover some of the particular contractual issues that may arise in the context of the provision of finance.

1.2.2 Some contractual prerequisites

Generally speaking, English law does not prescribe any formal requirements that must be fulfilled in entering into contracts, although it should always be remembered that a contract must be supported by consideration or be made by way of a deed.[1] Accordingly, a contract may be reduced to writing, be oral, be evidenced by conduct, or be a mixture of those things. In a limited number of instances, however, the law (principally statutory law) does prescribe certain formal requirements.[2]

1.2.2.1 By way of example, a guarantee must be in writing or evidenced by a note or memorandum which is in writing and the guarantee or the note or memorandum must be signed by or on behalf of the guarantor.[3] A contract for the disposition of an interest in land must be in writing, signed by both parties.[4] A disposition of an equitable interest in an asset must be in writing and signed by the disponor or his agent.[5] A conveyance of land or an interest in land must be by way of deed if it is to convey or create a legal estate in the land.[6] A power of attorney must be in the form of a deed.[7] A dealing with a patent (including the grant of a security interest) must be in writing.[8] An absolute (or legal) assignment of a chose in action must be in writing under the hand of (signed by) the assignor and written notice must be given to the debtor.[9] The principal statutory enforcement remedies for security only apply if the security was made by deed.[10] A further requirement arises in

---

[1] As to the requirements for making a deed, see s 1 of the Law of Property (Miscellaneous Provisions) Act 1989 and *HSBC Trust Co (UK) Ltd v Quinn* [2007] EWHC 1543 (Ch). As to execution of a deed, see that section, ss 44 and 46 of the Companies Act 2006 (replacing ss 36 to 36AA of the Companies Act 1985) and ss 74, 74A, and 76 of the Law of Property Act 1925.

[2] The view taken by the Law Commission in its paper *Electronic Commerce: Formal Requirements in Commercial Contracts* (2001) was that the requirements for writing and signatures that are required by statutory provisions in relation to commercial contracts can be satisfied by electronic means and that there was no need for English law to take any legislative steps by way of further implementation of the EC Directive on electronic commerce (EC 2000/31 OJ L178/1 17/7/2000) or the EC Directive on electronic signatures (EC 1999/93 OJ L13/12 19/1/2000). See also the Electronic Communications Act 2000 and the Signatures Regs 2002 (SI 2002/318).

[3] See Chap 16.

[4] S 2 of the Law of Property (Miscellaneous Provisions) Act 1989.

[5] S 53(1)(c) of the Law of Property Act 1925, but this is subject to Reg 4(1)(2) of the Financial Collateral Arrangements (No 2) Regs 2003 (SI 2003/3226).

[6] S 52 of the Law of Property Act 1925.

[7] S 1(1) of the Powers of Attorney Act 1971.

[8] S 30(6)(a) of the Patents Act 1977.

[9] S 136 of the Law of Property Act 1925, but this is subject to Reg 4(1)(3) of the Financial Collateral Arrangements (No 2) Regs 2003 (SI 2003/3226).

[10] S 101 of the Law of Property Act 1925.

relation to contracts which the law requires to be in writing or evidenced in writing. An amendment or variation of such a contract must also be in writing, otherwise it will be ineffective.[11]

It is also important to remember that equity requires value to have been given, in a real and substantial sense, before it is prepared to enforce an agreement to carry out a proprietary transaction.[12] Hence, a proprietary transaction that would be ineffective at law, and so, if it is to be enforced, will have to rely on the assistance of equity, may require value before that assistance will be available. The question of value (and a similar question concerning unfair benefit) may also raise its head when the validity of a transaction is reconsidered in the context of an insolvency, such as in relation to a transaction at an undervalue, a transaction that amounts to a preference, an extortionate credit transaction, the avoidance of a floating charge, or a transaction to defraud creditors.[13]

1.2.2.2

1.2.3 Corporate entities and other legal persons

Where a legal person, that is, an entity other than a natural person, wishes to enter into a transaction, it must possess the constitutional power to do so under the law that governs it, and those who purport to make decisions for it and act on its behalf must be duly authorised to do so. There may be formal processes that must be undertaken internally before it can enter into the transaction. These matters raise conflict of laws questions that are addressed elsewhere in this book.[14] As a matter of English law, a person who deals with an English company (strictly speaking, a company incorporated under one of the Companies Acts) enjoys various protections against the consequences if it transpires that the company lacked the corporate capacity to enter into the transaction or if it was not properly sanctioned by the directors.[15]

1.2.4 Intention to contract and certainty of agreement

There must be an intention on the part of both parties to enter into a legally binding contractual relationship, and there must be certainty as to the essential terms of their agreement, before there can be a valid agreement between them.

Thus, a document which makes it clear that a party does not intend to undertake a binding obligation or which simply sets out a non-binding statement of intention

1.2.4.1

---

[11] *McCausland v Duncan Lawrie Ltd* [1997] 1 WLR 38.

[12] As opposed to recognising the consequences of a completed transaction. Two recent cases which have examined the subject are *T Choithram International SA v Pagarani* [2001] 1 WLR 1 and *Pennington v Waine* [2002] EWCA Civ 227, [2002] 1 WLR 2075.

[13] For English law in a corporate context under, respectively, ss 238, 239, 244, 245, and 423 of the Insolvency Act 1986.

[14] See Chap 4.

[15] Ss 39 and 40 of the Companies Act 2006 (ss 35 and 35A of the Companies Act 1985).

will not give rise to a contract which is enforceable against that party, as has been evident in various cases concerning so called 'comfort letters' issued in lieu of giving a guarantee.[16] In similar vein, there have been cases where there has been no evidence that an alleged guarantor ever agreed to give a guarantee or any other type of commitment.[17] A document that has the appearance of being a contract but which is expressed to be 'subject to contract' will mean that there is no binding agreement until such later stage as the parties then agree that the contract is binding, or unless they subsequently conduct themselves so as to indicate that they have entered into an agreement on the terms of the earlier document.[18] On the other hand, the mere fact that it is envisaged that an earlier document or understanding will be superseded or replaced by a later and more formal document does not, of itself, mean that the earlier arrangement might not constitute a binding agreement.[19] As to the enforceability of a preliminary arrangement, it will depend upon whether the parties had the necessary intention to contract at the earlier stage and if there was sufficient certainty as to the essentials of what they had agreed. As stated below, on the question of intention, the matter will be judged objectively, by reference to whether a reasonable man, versed in the business of the nature involved, would have understood the exchanges between the parties as sufficient to indicate an intention on the part of both parties to enter into a binding contract.

1.2.4.2   Another of the prerequisites to a valid contract is the requirement as to the certainty of its essential terms.[20] 'There can be no contract without some terms, express or implied. If the express terms that are pleaded are significant, but are too uncertain and vague to be legally enforceable, there can be no concluded and binding agreement . . .'[21] Thus, a supposed agreement between the parties that they will negotiate so as to conclude a contract, even if expressed to be an agreement to negotiate in good faith, is unenforceable and will fail for uncertainty[22] because it will amount to nothing more than an unenforceable agreement to agree. On the other hand, a 'lock out' agreement, by which a person agrees not to enter into negotiations concerning a specified subject matter with third parties for a defined period, may be enforceable.[23] Certainty can be achieved where the contract refers to an external and independent criterion for fixing a matter (as, for instance,

---

[16] See the discussion on this point at Chap 16.

[17] For instance, *Carlton Communications PLC v The Football League* [2002] EWHC 1650 (Comm) and *Manches LLP v Freer* [2006] EWHC 991 (QB).

[18] *Rugby Group Ltd v Proforce Recruit Ltd* [2005] EWHC 70 (QB). The case was subject to an appeal, but not on this point: [2006] EWCA Civ 69.

[19] *Pagnan SpA v Feed Products Ltd* [1987] 2 Lloyd's Rep 601, at 619; *Bear Stearns Bank PLC v Forum Global Equity PLC* [2007] EWHC 1576 (Comm).

[20] *May and Butcher Ltd v R* [1934] 2 KB 17.

[21] Per Mummery LJ in *Cayzer v Beddow* [2007] EWCA Civ 644, at [57].

[22] *Walford v Miles* [1992] AC 128.

[23] Ibid and *Pitt v PHH Asset Management Ltd* [1993] 1 WLR 327.

is often done in loan facilities where the interest rate is fixed by reference to a Libor rate) or by reference to an objective criterion, such as a standard of reasonableness,[24] provided the court can determine what that criterion should be.[25] Certainty can also be achieved by the use of a master agreement, by which the parties agree that future dealings between them should be subject to the terms as contained in the master agreement. Such a mechanism will only be effective, however, if it can be certain when the parties deal that they meant to do so by reference to the master agreement and not independently of it.

The courts generally work on the basis of seeking to uphold bargains rather than finding them to be of no effect, particularly where one or both of the parties have acted on the agreement, and so the courts will sometimes be prepared to uphold an agreement which omits certain matters or leaves them to be agreed at a later time by finding ways to fill in the gaps,[26] such as by reference to established customs of trade or usage,[27] or previous dealings between the parties, or by the implication of a term, such as to act reasonably. In the words of Lord Goff, speaking extra-judicially: **1.2.4.3**

> We are there to help businessmen, not to hinder them; we are there to give effect to their transactions, not to frustrate them; we are there to oil the wheels of commerce, not to put a spanner in the works, or even grit in the oil.[28]

Generally speaking, a term may be implied if it is not contrary to the express terms of the contract[29] and it is considered to be so obvious that the parties would have thought it unnecessary to state it if asked by an 'officious bystander'[30] or if the term should be implied so as to give business efficacy to the contract.[31] A term will not be implied if the contract works perfectly well without it.[32] It is also necessary that **1.2.4.4**

---

[24] *Hillas & Co Ltd v Arcos Ltd* (1932) 147 LT 503.

[25] *Baird Textile Holdings Ltd v Marks & Spencer PLC* [2001] EWCA Civ 274, [2002] 1 All ER (Comm) 737.

[26] *Hillas & Co Ltd v Arcos Ltd* (1932) 147 LT 503; *Foley v Classique Coaches Ltd* [1934] 2 KB 1; *Scammell v Ouston* [1941] AC 251; *British Bank of Foreign Trade v Novimex Ltd* [1949] 1 KB 623; *F&G Sykes (Wessex) Ltd v Fine Fare Ltd* [1967] 1 Lloyd's Rep 53; *Sudbroke Trading Estate Ltd v Eggleton* [1983] 1 AC 444; *G Percy Trentham Ltd v Archital Luxfer Ltd* [1993] 1 Lloyd's Rep 25; *Mamidoil-Jetoil Greek Petroleum Co SA v Okta Crude Oil Refinery AD* [2001] EWCA Civ 406, [2001] 2 Lloyd's Rep 76.

[27] However, incorporation of terms by usage and custom can only take place if the usage or custom is notorious, certain, and reasonable, not just if there is a mere trade practice: *Bear Stearns Bank PLC v Forum Global Equity PLC* [2007] EWHC 1576 (Comm).

[28] *Commercial Contracts and the Commercial Court* [1984] LMCLQ 382, at 391, quoted with approval by Lord Steyn in *Homburg Houtimport BV v Agrosin Private Ltd, The Starsin* [2003] UKHL 12; [2004] 1 AC 715, at [57].

[29] *Duke of Westminster v Guild* [1985] QB 688, at 700.

[30] Per MacKinnon LJ in *Shirlaw v Southern Foundries (1926) Ltd* [1939] 2 KB 206, at 227 (affd [1940] AC 701).

[31] *The Moorcock* (1889) LR 14 PD 64.

[32] See, for instance, Lord Scott in *Concord Trust v Law Debenture Trust Corp PLC* [2005] UKHL 27; [2005] 1 WLR 1591, at [37].

the implied term is capable of clear expression[33] and it must properly reflect what the court feels the parties must have intended. The court will more willingly imply a term in cases where, typically, the express terms are brief, such as relating to the use of care and skill in a services contract, but it will not be so ready to imply terms to deal with a matter that was not expressly covered in a complex written contract where it may not be clear what the parties might have intended.[34] In other situations, statutory law may fill the gap by providing for implied terms.[35]

1.2.4.5   Whilst it was not meant to be a definitive guide, the general position as to finding certainty and filling gaps was succinctly summarised by Rix LJ in *Mamidoil-Jetoil Greek Petroleum Co SA v Okta Crude Oil Refinery AD*[36] as follows:

> In my judgment the following principles...can be deduced from [the] authorities, but this is intended to be in no way an exhaustive list. (i) Each case must be decided on its own facts and on the construction of its own agreement. Subject to that, (ii) where no contract exists, the use of an expression such as 'to be agreed' in relation to an essential term is likely to prevent any contract coming into existence, on the ground of uncertainty. This may be summed up by the principle that you 'cannot agree to agree'. (iii) Similarly, where no contract exists, the absence of agreement on essential terms of the agreement may prevent any contract coming into existence, again on the ground of uncertainty. (iv) However, particularly in commercial dealings between parties who are familiar with the trade in question, and particularly where the parties have acted in the belief that they had a binding contract, the courts are willing to imply terms, where that is possible, to enable the contract to be carried out. (v) Where a contract has once come into existence, even the expression 'to be agreed' in relation to future executory obligations is not necessarily fatal to its continued existence. (vi) Particularly in the case of contracts for future performance over a period, where the parties may desire or need to leave matters to be adjusted in the working out of their contract, the courts will assist the parties to do so, so as to preserve rather than destroy bargains, on the basis that what can be made certain is itself certain. Certum est quod certum reddi potest. (vii) This is particularly the case where one party has either already had the advantage of some performance which reflects the parties' agreement on a long-term relationship, or has had to make an investment premised on that agreement. (viii) For these purposes, an express stipulation for a reasonable or fair measure or price will be a sufficient criterion for the

---

[33] See Lord Simon, giving the advice of the Privy Council, in *BP Refinery (Westernport) Pty Ltd v The President etc of the Shire of Hastings* (1978) 52 ALJR 20, at 26, where a useful summary is provided of the circumstances in which a term will be implied.

[34] See Rix LJ in *Socimer International Bank Ltd v Standard Bank London Ltd* [2008] EWCA Civ 116, at [105] to [106].

[35] In addition to the examples given by Rix LJ in the passage from the *Mamidoil-Jetoil* case that follows, the following (which is not an exhaustive list) further implied terms might be mentioned: ss 12–15 of the Sale of Goods Act 1979 (implied terms as to title, description, quality and fitness and samples), together with several other provisions of that Act and provisions of the Supply of Goods (Implied Terms) Act 1973 and of the Supply of Goods and Services Act 1982 (including s 13 as to a duty of care and skill in a contract for the supply of services) and the implied covenants for title contained in the Law of Property (Miscellaneous Provisions) Act 1994.

[36] [2001] EWCA Civ 406; [2001] 2 Lloyd's Rep 76, at [69].

courts to act on. But even in the absence of express language, the courts are prepared to imply an obligation in terms of what is reasonable. (ix) Such implications are reflected but not exhausted by the statutory provision for the implication of a reasonable price now to be found in S. 8(2) of the Sale of Goods Act 1979 (and, in the case of services, in S. 15(1) of the Supply of Goods and Services Act 1982). (x) The presence of an arbitration clause may assist the courts to hold a contract to be sufficiently certain or to be capable of being rendered so, presumably as indicating a commercial and contractual mechanism, which can be operated with the assistance of experts in the field, by which the parties, in the absence of agreement, may resolve their dispute.

One area where the issue as to certainty arises is in relation to contracts where a party is given a discretion which affects its own rights and obligations or the rights and obligations of the other party. This is particularly relevant to finance documentation and is discussed further below.   **1.2.4.6**

The requirements that there should be a mutual intention to contract and certainty as to the essential terms of the supposed agreement will usually be conflated and are likely often to arise in market-based transactions that are concluded between dealers or brokers by exchanges over the telephone or by telexes, emails, or faxes, particularly where the transaction is not subsequently set down in a detailed written agreement between the parties. The considerations that are relevant in determining if a binding agreement has arisen in such circumstances were summarised by Lloyd LJ in *Pagnan SpA v Food Products Ltd*,[37] which was a case concerning a transaction that was concluded by an exchange of telexes, but the same principles will also apply to telephone conversations and the other types of exchanges: **1.2.4.7**

1. In order to determine whether a contract has been concluded in the course [of the exchanges], one must first look to the [exchanges] as a whole . . .
2. Even if the parties have reached agreement on all of the terms of the proposed contract, nevertheless they may intend that the contract shall not become binding until some further condition has been fulfilled. That is the ordinary 'subject to contract' case.
3. Alternatively, they may intend that the contract shall not become binding until some further term or terms have been agreed . . .
4. Conversely, the parties may intend to be bound forthwith even though there are some further terms still to be agreed or some further formality to be fulfilled . . .
5. If the parties fail to reach agreement on such further terms, the existing contract is not invalidated unless the failure to reach agreement on such further terms renders the contract as a whole unworkable or void for uncertainty.

---

[37] [1987] 2 Lloyd's Rep 601, at 619, which was followed in *Manatee Towing Co v Oceanbulk Maritime SA* [1999] 2 All ER (Comm) 306 and in *Bear Stearns Bank PLC v Forum Global Equity PLC* [2007] EWHC 1576 (Comm), the latter being a case involving a contract that was concluded between dealers over the telephone.

6. It is sometimes said that the parties must agree on the essential terms and that it is only matters of detail which can be left over. This may be misleading, since the word 'essential' in that context is ambiguous. If by 'essential' one means a term without which the contract cannot be enforced then the statement is true: the law cannot enforce an incomplete contract. If by 'essential' one means a term which the parties have agreed to be essential for the formation of a binding contract, then the statement is tautologous. If by 'essential' one means only a term which the Court regards as important as opposed to a term which the Court regards as less important or a matter of detail, the statement is untrue. It is for the parties to decide whether they wish to be bound and, if so, by what terms, whether important or unimportant. It is the parties who are, in the memorable phrase coined by the Judge [Bingham J], 'the master of their contractual fate'. Of course, the more important the term is the less likely it is that the parties will have left it for future decision. But there is no legal obstacle which stands in the way of the parties agreeing to be bound now while deferring important matters to be agreed later. It happens every day when parties enter into so-called 'heads of agreement'.

In applying those tests in a later case to determine if there had been a mutual intention to enter into a binding contract in the case of a transaction purportedly entered into between brokers over the telephone, it was said that the matter will be judged objectively, by reference to whether a reasonable man, versed in the business of the nature involved, would have understood the exchanges between the parties as sufficient to indicate an intention on the part of both parties to enter into a binding contract.[38]

1.2.5 Good faith and fairness

There is no general doctrine in English law which imposes an obligation on a party to act in good faith when negotiating and entering into a contract, such as by disclosing facts that might be relevant to another party in deciding if it wishes to contract.[39]

1.2.5.1 However, a misrepresentation (as opposed to mere silence[40]) that is made by a party in the course of such negotiations may be actionable,[41] a unilateral mistake by one party may make a contract voidable where the other was aware of it,[42] and

---

[38] Per Andrew Smith J in *Bear Stearns Bank PLC v Forum Global Equity PLC* [2007] EWHC 1576 (Comm), at [171].

[39] *Walford v Miles* [1992] AC 128. See also Bingham LJ in *Interfoto Picture Library Ltd v Stiletto Visual Programmes Ltd* [1989] 1 QB 433, at 439 and the review conducted by Morgan J in *Berkeley Community Villages Ltd v Pullen* [2007] EWHC 1330 (Ch), at [91]–[97].

[40] *Hamilton v Allied Domecq PLC* [2007] UKHL 33.

[41] Depending on the facts, in the tort of deceit as a fraudulent misrepresentation, in negligence for a negligent misrepresentation or under s 2 of the Misrepresentation Act 1967. It may also be possible to bring a claim based upon a collateral contract and, if the recipient acts expeditiously (but subject to s 2(2) of the Misrepresentation Act 1967), it may be able to rescind the contract.

[42] See, for instance, *Associated Japanese Bank (International) Ltd v Credit du Nord SA* [1989] 1 WLR 255, which also discusses the concept of a common mistake that will make a contract void at common law.

there are particular situations where there is an obligation of good faith as, for instance, the obligation of good faith and disclosure that is inherent in entering into an insurance contract and the equitable obligations that arise out of a fiduciary relationship and under the law as to the exertion of undue influence where the necessary relationship of influence exists.

Nor is there any general concept of striking down contracts or contract terms that are unfair as, for instance, because of an inequality of bargaining power,[43] although there has been some very limited statutory amelioration of this by the Unfair Contract Terms Act 1977 and, more generally in relation to contracts entered into by business suppliers with consumers, by the Unfair Terms in Consumer Contracts Regulations 1999.[44] In addition, the courts have imposed obligations of fair dealing in the context of a fiduciary relationship or where the situation involved a relationship of undue influence. The courts have also imposed notice requirements in relation to particularly onerous terms that appear in a party's printed terms and conditions of business, which are beyond what the other party (which is adversely affected by them) might reasonably expect.[45]   **1.2.5.2**

Similarly, there is no general duty of good faith or reasonableness that is owed by a party in exercising its rights under a contract,[46] as the party is entitled to consider its own interests but, again, this is qualified by restrictions that are placed by equity in relation to the enforcement of penalties, the duties of a fiduciary towards its beneficiaries and the obligation of good faith and clean hands that is imposed on a party seeking equitable relief. In addition, an obligation to act in good faith may arise under an express term of a contract and it may also be implied where a party has an apparently unfettered discretion under a contract[47] or where it has the power to prevent the performance of the contract.   **1.2.5.3**

1.2.6 The parties to a contract: mistake

Something similar to the requirement for certainty raises its head in relation to the identification of the parties to a contract. The consequence of a mistake by one party as to the identity of the other, particularly if that other is a rogue who has

---

[43] *Pao On v Lau Yiu Long* [1980] AC 614; *National Westminster Bank PLC v Morgan* [1985] AC 686.

[44] SI 1999/2083.

[45] See the review on this subject by the Court of Appeal in *Interfoto Picture Library Ltd v Stiletto Visual Programmes Ltd* [1989] 1 QB 433.

[46] This may be contrasted with the obligation of good faith and fair dealing which arises under New York law in relation to the performance of a contract and the exercise of disputes and remedial action: see §1-203 of the New York Uniform Commercial Code and, in relation to the exercise of a right to accelerate a payment obligation, §1-208 of that Code. For a general commentary, see Summers, 'Good Faith in Contract Law and the Sales Provisions of the Uniform Commercial Code' (1968) 54 Virginia Law Review 195.

[47] See at para 1.2.10 below.

misled the mistaken party, was finally settled by the House of Lords in *Shogun Finance Ltd v Hudson*.[48] The majority[49] followed the previous case law, which had tended to distinguish between oral contracts concluded face to face and contracts entered into in writing. In the former situation, the courts took the view that, prima facie, the parties meant to deal with the person physically before them,[50] so that a mistake as to the identity of another contracting party would only make the contract voidable and not void. A voidable contract remains valid until it is rescinded by the wronged party or is set aside by the court, so that title may have passed or rights have accrued which could be passed on to, or relied upon by, third parties. In the second situation, however, the courts were prepared to take the view that the only contract that could have existed would have been between the named parties so that the fictitious identity of one of the parties would nullify it from the outset.[51] Under a void contract, no legal relationship will arise between the parties. The majority of the House of Lords declined to adopt the more general approach favoured by the minority,[52] that in all cases (whether the contract was in writing or oral) the contract should be considered as being only voidable and so valid and enforceable until such time as it was avoided.

1.2.7 Mistake as to the subject matter of a contract

In passing, it is also worth mentioning that a common mistake by the parties as to the existence or essential character of the subject matter of a supposed contract, where the contract does not expressly make provision for the consequences of the mistake, will mean that the contract does not exist and is void.[53] If only one of the parties was mistaken, the contract is voidable at the instance of that party where the other party was aware of the mistake when the contract was made.[54] Whereas previously the courts only granted relief in cases involving a mistake

---

[48] [2003] UKHL 62, [2004] 1 AC 919.

[49] Lords Hobhouse, Phillips, and Walker.

[50] See, for instance, *Phillips v Brooks* [1919] 2 KB 243 and *Lewis v Avery* [1972] 1 QB 198, although a different conclusion was reached in *Ingram v Little* [1961] 1 QB 31.

[51] See, for instance, *Cundy v Lindsay* (1878) 3 App Cas 459 and *Hector v Lyons* (1988) 58 P&CR 156. In *King's Norton Metal Co Ltd v Deridge, Merrett & Co Ltd* (1897) 14 TLR 98, a different result was reached but that was because the relevant contracting party was using an alias and its identity was not a material concern to the other party.

[52] Lords Nicholls and Millett.

[53] *Bell v Lever Bros Ltd* [1932] AC 161. See also *Associated Japanese Bank (International) Ltd v Credit du Nord SA* [1989] 1 WLR 255. The Court of Appeal in *Great Peace Shipping Ltd v Tsavliris Salvage (International) Ltd, The Great Peace* [2002] EWCA Civ 1407, [2003] QB 679 said that there was no jurisdiction in equity to grant rescission of a contract on the ground that the contract was voidable for common mistake where the common law would not have regarded the contract as void, thereby overruling its previous decision in *Solle v Butcher* [1950] 1 KB 671, as having been given in error.

[54] *Garrard v Frankel* (1862) 30 Beav 445; *Thomas Bates & Son Ltd v Wyndham's (Lingerie) Ltd* [1981] 1 WLR 505; *Commission for the New Towns v Cooper (Great Britain) Ltd* [1995] Ch 259.

of fact, the courts will now grant relief as well in cases involving a mistake of law.[55]

1.2.8 Privity of contract

A similar issue to that concerning the identity of the contracting parties concerns the effect of a contract which purports to extend the benefit of the contract (such as a right to receive a payment, the benefit of warranties or covenants, or the benefit of an exclusion clause) to third parties, including unrelated parties and the servants or agents of a contracting party. There was previously a real difficulty at general law in achieving this as the doctrine of privity of contract would intervene to prevent the third party, which was not a party to the contract, from relying upon the provision or being able to enforce it.[56] If a contracting party sought to recover damages for the benefit of the third party, because the other party had failed to perform in favour of the third party, the contracting party would be met by the defence that it had suffered no loss, so it could not recover anything further than nominal damages.

There were, however, certain circumstances in which the contract might be   **1.2.8.1**
enforced for the benefit of a third party as, for instance, where an agent or trustee had contracted for the benefit of the third party (particularly in the case of enforcing an exclusion clause for the benefit of a third party),[57] where a party could obtain an order for specific performance of the contract on the basis that damages would be an inadequate remedy because only nominal damages were recoverable,[58] where a party assigned its rights under the contract to the third party,[59] where the benefit of the contract was novated in favour of the third party, or where the case fell within the circumstances of agency mentioned in the

---

[55] *Kleinwort Benson Ltd v Lincoln City Council* [1999] 2 AC 349.

[56] See, for instance, *Scruttons Ltd v Midland Silicones Ltd* [1962] AC 446; *Cosgrove v Horsfall* (1945) 62 TLR 140; and *Genys v Matthews* [1966] 1 WLR 758.

[57] See *New Zealand Shipping Co Ltd v AM Satterthwaite & Co Ltd (The Eurymedon)* [1975] AC 154 and *Port Jackson Stevedoring Pty Ltd v Salmond and Spraggon (Australia) Pty Ltd (The New York Star)* [1981] 1 WLR 138. Clauses under which a party to a contract acts as an agent in obtaining protection for a third party, when used in a contract for the carriage of goods by sea, are often referred to as 'Himalaya clauses' after the name of the vessel that was involved in *Adler v Dickson* [1955] 1 QB 158.

[58] *Beswick v Beswick* [1968] AC 58.

[59] But an assignment is subject to equities, including that the assignee should not recover from the debtor or obligor to any greater extent than the rights that were vested in the assignor and could have been recovered by it: *Dawson v Great Northern & City Ry Co.* [1905] 1 KB 260 (but see also *Technotrade Ltd v Larkstore Ltd* [2006] EWCA Civ 1079, [2006] 1 WLR 2926). Hence, the purported assignment of all of the rights of a lender under a facility agreement will include the right to receive payment of principal and interest but not the benefit of clauses that are purely personal to the circumstances of the assignor, such as under an increased costs clause which relates to the personal position of the assignor. Having transferred its commitment, it will not be exposed to the risks against which such a clause is intended to protect.

next paragraph. A contract may also contain a promise by a party not to sue the servants or agents of the other party and the latter should be able to prevent the promisor from breaching the contract by suing the servants or agents.[60]

1.2.8.2 It should be noted that at common law, two parties to a contract cannot impose the burden of a contract upon a third party that is a stranger to the contract, although an agent can bind its principal because the contract is really between the principal and the other contracting party.

1.2.8.3 The courts have also fashioned a particular exception to the operation of the doctrine of privity of contract (and the associated concept that a claimant should only recover for its own loss) in cases that involved a contract to do work or perform services relating to property. This exception was developed to ensure that a contract breaker should not escape liability because the other party had sold its interest in the property to which the contract related. The exception was applied initially to enable damages to be recovered against a contract breaker by the other contracting party where that party had disposed of the property and suffered no loss and the contract had prohibited the assignment of the benefit of the contract. In *St Martins Property Corp Ltd v Sir Robert McAlpine Ltd*[61] the House of Lords held that a previous owner of real property could recover substantial damages against a contractor that it had employed to do work relating to the property even though it had sold the property and had suffered no loss. In effect, it would be allowed to recover on behalf of the transferee, on the supposition that the claimant would be treated as having entered into the contract with the contractor on behalf of itself and the transferee because it was contemplated at the time of contracting that the property would be sold. The House of Lords arrived at that result by extending a principle that had previously been applied in the case of the carriage of goods, in situations where it was contemplated at the time of contracting that the goods might be sold to a third party after the time of contracting but before the contract of carriage was completed.[62] The principle was further extended by the Court of Appeal in *Darlington Borough Council v Wiltshire Northern Ltd*,[63] which was approved by the House of Lords in *Alfred McAlpine Construction Ltd v Panatown Ltd*,[64] so that it would apply despite the lack of a prohibition against assignment of the contract or any contemplation when the contract was entered into that the property might be transferred. In the *Panatown* case, however, the House of Lords refused to apply the principle where the transferee had been given direct claims against the contractor.

---

[60] *Snelling v John G Snelling Ltd* [1973] QB 87.
[61] [1994] 1 AC 85.
[62] *Dunlop v Lambert* (1839) 6 Cl&F 600.
[63] [1995] 1 WLR 68.
[64] [2001] 1 AC 518.

In similar vein, in *Technotrade Ltd v Larkstore Ltd*[65] the Court of Appeal allowed   **1.2.8.4**
an assignee of the benefit of a contract for the performance of services relating to
an asset to recover substantial damages for breach of the contract by the other
contracting party. The breach had occurred prior to the date of the assignment,
but the assignor had disposed of the asset to the assignee prior to the loss becoming
apparent and consequent damage being suffered. It did not matter that the assignor
had itself suffered no loss in that it had disposed of the asset to the assignee for full
value and without any responsibility for the loss to the asset that later became
apparent. The court distinguished the position in this case from the general rule
that an assignment is subject to equities and that the assignee cannot recover for a
claim or loss that would not have been recoverable under the contract by the
assignor.[66] This was done on the basis that it was the cause of action (as opposed
to the manifestation and suffering of the loss arising from the breach) that was
assigned, and that had accrued prior to the date of the assignment. As a matter of law,
the cause of action was complete when the breach occurred, even though the consequences of the breach were not manifested, and the consequential loss was not
suffered, until a later time. To have found otherwise would have permitted a legal
'black hole' to arise into which the claim would have disappeared, with the result
that the defendant would have escaped liability for its breach of the contract.

The position at general law regarding privity of contract was substantially modi-   **1.2.8.5**
fied by the Contracts (Rights of Third Parties) Act 1999,[67] although the Act does
not detract from any right that a third party may have at general law.[68] Accordingly,
if the third party cannot avail itself of the Act, it might still be able to fall back on
one of the limited exceptions that applied at general law to the doctrine of privity
of contract.[69] The Act provides that a third party which is intended to benefit from
a provision of a contract[70] will be able to enforce the contract in its own right,

---

[65] [2006] EWCA Civ 1079, [2006] 1 WLR 2926.

[66] *Dawson v Great Northern & City Railway Co* [1905] 1 KB 260.

[67] Which applies, generally speaking, to contracts made after 11 May 2000 (s 10(2) of the Act),
but see also s 10(3) of the Act.

[68] S 7(1).

[69] In addition, in *Nisshin Shipping Co Ltd v Cleaves & Co Ltd* [2003] EWHC 2602 (Comm),
[2004] 1 Lloyd's Rep 38 it was held that a third party could avail itself of the Act even though at
general law the contract might have been enforceable for its benefit under a trust in its favour of the
contractual benefit.

[70] I.e., it is expressly named as being entitled to enforce the provision, it is a member of an identified class of intended beneficiaries, or if it answers a particular description, even if it was not in
existence at the time of the contract: s 1(3). See the discussion on this point in *Avraamides v Colwill*
[2006] EWCA Civ 1533, [2007] BLR 76. See also *Prudential Assurance Co Ltd v Ayres* [2007]
EWHC 775 (Ch), in which it was held that a third party will be treated as entitled to benefit from a
contractual term even if the intention that it should do so was not the predominant purpose of the
term or that the term was also intended to benefit a contracting party or another person. Although
the actual decision in the *Prudential Assurance* case was overturned on appeal ([2008] EWCA Civ
52, [2008] 1 All ER 1266), the appeal was not concerned with this issue.

unless on a proper construction of the contract it is apparent that the third party was precluded by the contract from doing so.[71] The Act makes it clear that the third party has the right to enforce an exclusion or limitation clause that was intended for its benefit[72] but that right is itself subject to any restriction on the operation of such a clause that might arise by virtue of other legislation, such as the Unfair Contract Terms Act 1977.[73] However, if a third party wishes under the Act to enforce a positive obligation in its favour in the contract, its right to do so will be subject to any limitations on that right which are imposed by the contract, such as a limitation or exclusion of liability for breach of the contract that is contained in the contract for the benefit of the promisor.[74]

1.2.9 The interpretation of a contract

It is surprising how frequently what was thought to be a well crafted contractual document turns out to be ambiguous and not to be as clear as previously imagined. Different interpretations can be put on the same words by those with opposing interests, particularly when something has gone wrong and it is necessary to determine which party should bear the responsibility or suffer the resulting loss. Agreements that have not been carefully prepared are even more susceptible to ambiguity. It is appropriate, therefore, to consider the approach that the courts take to the construction or interpretation of the express provisions of a contract. This is a different exercise from deciding if terms should be implied to fill in any gaps which appear in the express provisions of the contract.

1.2.9.1　The modern principles by which the courts undertake the process of construction of contractual documents were summarised by Lord Hoffmann in *Investors Compensation Scheme Ltd v West Bromwich Building Society*[75] as follows:

> (1) Interpretation is the ascertainment of the meaning which the document would convey to a reasonable person having all the background knowledge which

---

[71] S 1(2). In *Nisshin Shipping Co Ltd v Cleaves & Co Ltd* [2003] EWHC 2602 (Comm), [2004] 1 Lloyd's Rep 38 it was held that the third party will be entitled to enforce the term for its own benefit unless the right to do so was contrary to the intention of the parties in the contract. Thus, if the contract is neutral on the point, s 1(2) will not operate against the third party. In *Laemthong International Lines Co Ltd v Abdullah Mohammed Fahem & Co* [2005] EWCA Civ, [2005] 1 Lloyd's Rep 688 the Court of Appeal quoted with approval from the opinion of the Law Commission (*Privity of Contract* Report No. 242 of 31/7/1996, para 7.18) that the proper construction of a term for the purposes of s 1(2) of the Act would include taking account of the surrounding circumstances in making the contract, such as industry practice relating to that type of contract.

[72] S 1(6).

[73] S 3(6).

[74] Ss 3(1)–3(5). It would also appear that the provisions of the Unfair Contract Terms Act 1977 (except for s 2(1)) would not affect the rights of the promisor under ss 3(1)–3(5).

[75] [1998] 1 WLR 896, at 912–913. His Lordship made it clear that he had drawn his summary from the approach previously enunciated by Lord Wilberforce in *Prenn v Simmonds* [1971] 1 WLR 1381 and in *Reardon Smith Line Ltd v Hansen-Tangen* [1976] 1 WLR 989.

would reasonably have been available to the parties in the situation in which they were at the time of the contract.

(2) The background was famously described by Lord Wilberforce[76] as the 'matrix of fact', but this phrase is, if anything, an understated description of what the background may include. Subject to the requirement that it should have been reasonably available to the parties and to the exception to be mentioned next, it includes absolutely anything which would have affected the way in which the language of the document would have been understood by a reasonable man.

(3) The law excludes from the admissible background the previous negotiations of the parties and their declarations of subjective intent. They are admissible only in an action for rectification. The law makes this distinction for reasons of practical policy and, in this respect only, legal interpretation differs from the way we would interpret utterances in ordinary life. The boundaries of this exception are in some respects unclear. But this is not the occasion on which to explore them.

(4) The meaning which a document (or any other utterance) would convey to a reasonable man is not the same thing as the meaning of its words. The meaning of words is a matter of dictionaries and grammars; the meaning of the document is what the parties using those words against the relevant background would reasonably have been understood to mean. The background may not merely enable the reasonable man to choose between the possible meanings of words which are ambiguous but even (as occasionally happens in ordinary life) to conclude that the parties must, for whatever reason, have used the wrong words or syntax (see *Mannai Investment Co. Ltd v Eagle Star Life Assurance Co. Ltd*[77]).

(5) The 'rule' that words should be given their 'natural and ordinary meaning' reflects the commonsense proposition that we do not easily accept that people have made linguistic mistakes, particularly in formal documents. On the other hand, if one would nevertheless conclude from the background that something must have gone wrong with the language, the law does not require judges to attribute to the parties an intention which they plainly could not have had. Lord Diplock made this point more vigorously when he said in *Antaios Cia Naviera SA v Salen Rederierna AB, The Antaios*,[78] 'if detailed semantic and syntactical analysis of words in a commercial contract is going to lead to a conclusion that flouts business common sense, it must be made to yield to business common sense'.

In his opinion in the later case of *Bank of Credit and Commerce International SA v Ali*,[79] Lord Hoffmann explained that the starting point of the analysis should always be the wording that has been used as interpreted in accordance with conventional usage and that it should not be too readily accepted that people will make linguistic mistakes, particularly in formal documents. Subject to that point, the relevant background that could be considered was that which a reasonable

1.2.9.2

---

[76] In *Reardon Smith Line Ltd v Hansen-Tangen* [1976] 1 WLR 989.
[77] [1997] AC 749.
[78] [1985] AC 191, at 201.
[79] [2001] UKHL 8; [2002] 1 AC 251, at [39].

man would consider to be relevant, rather than material which such a person would not consider to be relevant. The relevant background might include not just the factual background but also the parties' understanding of the law or the facts, even if that understanding was mistakenly held.

1.2.9.3   The importance of giving a commercially sensible interpretation to the construction of contracts, rather than taking a strict and literalistic approach, was emphasised by Lord Steyn in *Mannai Investment Co Ltd v Eagle Star Life Assurance Co Ltd*[80] and in *Sirius International Insurance Co (Publ) v FAI General Insurance Ltd*.[81] In making this point, his Lordship was echoing what had been said by Lord Diplock in *Antaios Cia Naviera SA v Salen Rederierna AB, The Antaios*.[82]

1.2.9.4   The third point in Lord Hoffmann's summary reflects what was said by Lord Wilberforce in *Prenn v Simmonds*[83] and is sometimes referred to as the 'exclusionary principle'. It also partly reflects the so-called parol evidence rule,[84] by which extrinsic evidence was inadmissible to add to or subtract from the contents or meaning of a written agreement or instrument. The principle is subject to a number of exceptions and qualifications, such as where the written document was not intended to contain the whole agreement,[85] where another document is incorporated by reference into the agreement or where there is a collateral contract,[86] where there is a claim for misrepresentation, where evidence is admitted as to the validity of the agreement[87] or that it is a sham,[88] where a term may be implied in the agreement, and where there is a claim for rectification of the document because it does not represent the true agreement between the parties.

1.2.9.5   It has also been held that evidence of the prior negotiations between the parties will be admitted to prove the meaning of an unusual expression that was used in the contract and which was commonly understood between the parties in their negotiations to have a particular meaning[89] and that evidence of prior negotiations may be admitted to establish the intended contents of an obvious omission on the face of the document.[90] Evidence of prior negotiations may be admitted to

---

80   [1997] AC 749, at 771.
81   [2004] UKHL 54; [2004] 1 WLR 3251, at [18]–[19].
82   [1985] AC 191, at 201.
83   [1971] 1 WLR 1381, at 1383–1385.
84   *Goss v Lord Nugent* (1833) 5 B&Ad 58.
85   *Allen v Pink* (1838) 4 M&W 140.
86   *Mann v Nunn* (1874) 30 LT 526.
87   *Clever v Kirkman* (1876) 33 LT 672.
88   *AG Securities v Vaughan* [1990] 1 AC 469.
89   *Proforce Recruit Ltd v The Rugby Group Ltd* [2006] EWCA Civ 69.
90   *Caterpillar Financial Services Ltd v Goldcrest Plant and Groundworks Ltd* [2007] EWCA Civ 272. As to the ability of the court to interpolate missing words into a written contract, see Lord Bingham in *Homburg Houtimport BV v Agrosin Private Ltd* [2003] UKHL 12; [2004] 1 AC 715, at [23].

prove the subject matter of the contract.[91] Evidence of a prior agreement between the parties can also be admitted.[92]

For similar reasons, but subject to much the same exceptions, evidence of the conduct of the parties after the making of a contract is not admissible in construing the contract.[93] Nonetheless, such conduct may be admissible to prove that the contract had been varied by subsequent agreement[94] or to raise an estoppel.[95] It may also now be relevant to take into account the subsequent conduct of the parties in determining the true nature or character of a transaction, so as to ascertain if the transaction (and its mechanics) as provided for in the contract was carried into effect, or if, in reality, it was something else because the transaction represented by the agreement was not operated in the manner provided for in the contract. Lord Millett, in giving the advice of the Privy Council in *Agnew v Commissioner of Inland Revenue*,[96] made that point in relation to determining whether a charge over book debts should be characterised as a fixed or floating charge. His approach was approved by the House of Lords in *National Westminster Bank PLC v Spectrum Plus Ltd*.[97]

1.2.9.6

To reinforce the effect of the exclusionary principle and the parol evidence rule and to prevent reference to implied terms, other agreements (including collateral contracts and earlier agreements), and other matters, a contract may contain an 'entire agreement' clause along the following lines:

1.2.9.7

> This Agreement constitutes the entire contract between the parties and supersedes all prior or collateral representations, agreements, negotiations or understandings, whether oral or in writing.

Depending upon the wording that is used, such a clause should be effective to exclude consideration of a collateral contract and an earlier agreement, as well as an attempt to include terms, such as implied terms, that were not expressly set out in the contract.[98] However, if the clause does not refer to pre-contractual

---

[91] *Macdonald v Longbottom* (1859) 1 E&E 977.

[92] Rix LJ in *HIH Casualty and General Insurance Ltd v New Hampshire Insurance Co* [2001] 2 Lloyd's Rep 161, at [81]–[84], although his Lordship doubted the value of such evidence. The Court of Appeal did find an earlier agreement useful in *KPMG LLP v Network Rail Infrastructure Ltd* [2007] EWCA Civ 363, as the earlier agreement provided for the form of the later agreement, which erroneously omitted a significant matter which the court was able to correct as a matter of construction of the later document.

[93] *James Miller & Partners v Whitworth Street Estates (Manchester) Ltd* [1970] AC 583, at 603 (Viscount Dilhorne) and 606 (Lord Wilberforce); *L Schuler AG v Wickman Machine Tool Sales Ltd* [1974] AC 325.

[94] *McCausland v Duncan Lawrie Ltd* [1997] 1 WLR 38.

[95] *James Miller & Partners v Whitworth Street Estates (Manchester) Ltd* [1970] AC 583.

[96] [2001] UKPC 28; [2001] 2 AC 710, at [48].

[97] [2005] UKHL 41, [2005] 2 AC 680. See, in particular, Lord Walker at [140].

[98] *Inntrepreneur Pub Co v East Crown Ltd* [2000] 2 Lloyd's Rep 611.

representations then it cannot exclude consideration of them.[99] It has also been held that wording along the lines quoted above would not prevent the court from considering the pre-contractual negotiations between the parties to ascertain the meaning of an uncommon expression that was used in the contract and which the parties had agreed between them in those negotiations.[100]

1.2.10 Contractual discretions

A lender or financier is often given a measure of discretion in a facility as to what may be required of the borrower and the extent of the rights and obligations of the borrower under the facility. Such a discretion may go to matters such as setting interest rates, determining if conditions precedent have been fulfilled before the facility will be available for drawing, the extent of performance or observance of restrictions by the borrower that is required under the covenants and undertaking provisions of the facility, and the basis on which the lender will give consents when requested by the borrower. Sometimes the discretion has the appearance of being unlimited, in the sense of it being entirely within the will of the lender. The question that arises is whether any limitation should be implied in such a case as to the factors that the lender should take into account and the grounds upon which it would be entitled to make a determination or take other action within its discretion.

1.2.10.1 Whilst it may appear to be in the lender's interest that there should be no such limitation, there is a risk that a limitless discretion which goes to a fundamental matter under the contract may mean that there has been a failure to agree on an essential element of the contract and, in consequence, the contract may be unenforceable and fail for uncertainty for the reasons previously discussed. For example, an entirely unfettered discretion that is vested in the lender as to charging and setting the interest rate in a term loan facility might have the result that there was lack of certainty and agreement concerning a matter going to the heart of the contract, namely, as to the price payable by the borrower for the use of the money borrowed under the facility.[101] In a different vein, some limitation may be thought

---

99 *Thomas Witter Ltd v TBP Industries Ltd* [1996] 2 All ER 573, at 595–596. In any event, as that case explained, an attempt to exclude or restrict reference to (and thus liability for) a misrepresentation will be subject to s 3 of the Misrepresentation Act 1967. This should be distinguished from the effect of a 'non-reliance' clause, by which a party confirms that it did not rely upon any representation in deciding to enter into the contract: contrast the approach in *Thomas Witter Ltd v TBP Industries Ltd*, at 596–597 with that taken in *Watford Electronics Ltd v Sanderson CFL Ltd* [2001] EWCA Civ 317; [2001] 1 All ER (Comm) 696, at [38] to [41]. The approach taken on this latter point in the *Thomas Witter* case may now also be seen as being inconsistent with that taken by the Court of Appeal in *IFE Fund SA v Goldman Sachs International* [2007] EWCA Civ 811.

100 *Proforce Recruit Ltd v The Rugby Group Ltd* [2006] EWCA Civ 69.

101 The same conclusion would not arise under an overdraft facility as, from a legal perspective, it is considered to be a contract from day to day, with each party being able to terminate at any time.

desirable where the lender appears to be given in a facility agreement a completely unfettered discretion in determining whether the borrower had fulfilled the conditions precedent for it to draw down under the facility (particularly if some of the conditions were within the lender's own control) or where no parameters are prescribed expressly as to the grounds upon which the lender may determine that a material adverse change has arisen that would entitle it to determine that an event of default has occurred.

There have been a number of Court of Appeal decisions[102] that have concerned this issue in relation to a variety of different contracts. They have addressed the issue by seeing if a term could be implied into the contract as to the extent of, and the manner in which, the discretion should be exercised and, if so, what the term should be. In summary, the following propositions may be drawn from the cases.   **1.2.10.2**

First, it is a matter of interpretation of the contract and, to the extent permitted by   **1.2.10.2.1** ordinary contractual rules, the implication of a term (which is required to give business efficacy to the contract or which would be obvious on the 'officious bystander test') to determine if there is a fetter placed on the scope of the discretion and how it should be exercised. This should be done in the context of the contract as a whole. Unless the parties have otherwise provided, the contract should be interpreted in accordance with current law and not by the law as it was understood at the time of contracting.[103] If the relevant provision in the contract is plain and the contract works perfectly well without the necessity for such an implied term, then the contract should be applied on its own, without implying anything further.[104] However, a court will usually be prepared to imply terms along the lines next mentioned, unless there is an express provision that is contrary to them.[105]

Thus, the lender theoretically is treated as proposing an interest rate each day, which the borrower accepts by maintaining its borrowing or rejects by repaying the outstanding amount. In a term loan, however, the legal mechanics are different as the contract is intended to endure for the term of the facility and thus the borrower is meant to be bound as to the payment of interest for the term.

[102] *Abu Dhabi National Tanker Co v Product Star Shipping Ltd, The Product Star (No 2)* [1993] 1 Lloyd's Rep 397; *Gan Insurance Co Ltd v Tai Ping Insurance Co Ltd* [2001] EWCA Civ 1047, [2001] 2 All ER (Comm) 299; *Paragon Finance PLC v Nash & Staunton* [2001] EWCA Civ 1466, [2002] 1 WLR 685; *Paragon Finance PLC v Pender* [2005] EWCA Civ 760, [2005] 1 WLR 3412; *Lymington Marina Ltd v Macnamara* [2007] EWCA Civ 151; *Socimer International Bank Ltd v Standard Bank London Ltd* [2008] EWCA Civ 116.

[103] In general, the effect of a court decision on the common law is retrospective and not just prospective: see *National Westminister Bank v Spectrum Plus Ltd* [2005] UKHL 41, [2005] 2 AC 680. However, a change to the parties' understanding of the law that is brought about by a later court decision might be grounds for termination of the contract and a restitutionary claim based upon a mistake of law: see *Kleinwort Benson Ltd v Lincoln City Council* [1999] 2 AC 349.

[104] *Lymington Marina Ltd v Macnamara* [2007] EWCA Civ 151.

[105] See Rix LJ in *Socimer International Bank Ltd v Standard Bank London Ltd* [2008] EWCA Civ 116, at [66] and [106].

1.2.10.2.2   Secondly, where a term is to be implied, it should be the minimum that is necessary to meet the tests for its implication. It would appear that, if a term is to be
implied, the minimum that might be implied would include an obligation to act
in good faith, on the basis of the facts or the available material, with perhaps some
obligation to review the adequacy of that material and seek further information if
the material was obviously deficient.[106] In addition, it might be implied that the
discretion should not be exercised capriciously, arbitrarily, or for a collateral purpose which was outside the legitimate scope of the contract.[107] It is uncertain
whether an obligation to refrain from acting capriciously or arbitrarily would also
encompass an obligation to refrain from acting in a way in which no other person
in a similar position, acting reasonably, would act (the *Wednesbury* unreasonableness test[108]). There is authority that this requirement would exist as part of the
minimum that should be implied.[109]

1.2.10.2.3   Thirdly, except in the unusual case where the court would imply an obligation to
act in an entirely objective and reasonable fashion, the discretion may still be exercised in the commercial interests of the person exercising the discretion and, where
appropriate (e.g. in setting an interest rate), by taking into account matters more
generally relating to its business and its customers than just the particular circumstances of the other party to the contract, even if that meant that the other party

---

[106] Contrast the approach of Arden LJ in *Lymington Marina Ltd v Macnamara* [2007] EWCA
Civ 151, at [42] and [43] with that of Pill LJ in that case, at [71] and of Mance LJ in *Gan Insurance
Co Ltd v Tai Ping Insurance Co Ltd* [2001] EWCA Civ 1047; [2001] 2 All ER (Comm) 299, at
[76].

[107] *Lymington Marina Ltd v Macnamara* [2007] EWCA Civ 151. An example provided by
Paragon Finance PLC v Nash & Staunton [2001] EWCA Civ 1466, [2002] 1 WLR 685 would be
where a lender had a discretion in setting the interest rate payable by a borrower and set an unduly
high rate beyond what the lender knew the borrower could afford simply to force the borrower to
repay because the borrower was a nuisance and the lender wished to be rid of the borrower. It should
be noted that in *Sterling Credit Ltd v Rahman* [2002] EWHC 3008 (Ch) it was held that a lender
would not be obliged to exercise its discretion and reduce the rate it charged the borrower.

[108] After the test formulated by Lord Greene MR in *Associated Provincial Picture Houses Ltd v
Wednesbury Corp* [1948] 1 KB 223, at 233–234, that should be applied in administrative law.

[109] See Leggatt LJ in *Abu Dhabi National Tanker Co v Product Star Shipping Ltd, The Product Star
(No 2)* [1993] 1 Lloyd's Rep 397, at 404 and Dyson LJ in *Paragon Finance PLC v Nash & Staunton*
[2001] EWCA Civ 1466, [2002] 1 WLR 685. In relation to the point as to not acting in a way in
which no other person in that position, acting reasonably, would act, Dyson LJ had referred, at [38],
and without disapproval in its application in a contractual context, to the analogous *Wednesbury* test
of unreasonableness in administrative law. Dyson LJ did, however, emphasise that this was a much
more restricted approach than a general concept of unreasonableness based on objective market
standards of what was reasonable. The approach taken by Dyson LJ was referred to with approval
by the Court of Appeal in *Paragon Finance PLC v Pender* [2005] EWCA Civ 760, [2005] 1 WLR
3412. However, Arden LJ in *Lymington Marina Ltd v Macnamara* [2007] EWCA Civ 151, at [37],
had eschewed the application of any *Wednesbury* type of test. Pill LJ, at [69]–[70] in the same case,
whilst saying that a test along those lines might be appropriate, felt it was undesirable to make a
direct reference to an administrative law concept in a contractual context. See also Rix LJ in *Socimer
International Bank Ltd v Standard Bank London Ltd* [2008] EWCA Civ 116, at [66] and [106], who
was firm that a *Wednesbury* unreasonableness test would be relevant.

had to pay more under the contract than the remaining customers of the person exercising the discretion.[110]

It is not every situation, however, in which a lender's discretion will be fettered. As is clear from the first of the propositions stated above, a term will be implied only if it is necessary to do so. If the contract works perfectly well without implying a term then the contract will be left in its original state. One particular area where it is submitted that a lender's discretion would be left unfettered is in relation to the determination by a lender of whether it wishes to make demand for repayment and enforce its security. For a commercial facility that is expressed to be repayable on demand, assuming that such a stipulation has not been waived or abrogated by the lender, the authorities have consistently allowed the lender to decide if and when it wishes to make demand, without having to ascribe any reason for doing so.[111] However, the Court of Appeal has also made it clear that the lender must be acting within its right to make a demand under the terms of the facility; that is, that the facility is expressed to be repayable on demand[112] or the demand is made in accordance with a provision which permits the demand to be made following the occurrence of an event of default.[113] Subject to that particular point, the view that a lender's discretion in deciding if it wishes to make demand is unlimited is reinforced by the freedom of a creditor at general law[114] to decide entirely within its discretion whether and how it will enforce its security or a guarantee it holds, as exemplified by the decision of the Privy Council in *China & South Sea Bank Ltd v Tan*.[115]

1.2.10.3

1.2.11 Best endeavours and reasonable endeavours

The expressions 'best endeavours' and 'reasonable endeavours' are frequently used in contracts. They are used to qualify what would otherwise be an absolute and

---

[110] *Paragon Finance PLC v Nash & Staunton* [2001] EWCA Civ 1466, [2002] 1 WLR 685 and *Paragon Finance PLC v Pender* [2005] EWCA Civ 760, [2005] 1 WLR 3412. In the first of those cases, Dyson LJ said that a lender was free to raise the interest rate payable by a borrower because of financial difficulties suffered by the lender or to set a rate which provided a subsidy to compensate for what it received from other customers.

[111] See *Bank of Baroda v Panessar* [1987] Ch 335. The Court of Appeal has indicated that it might on some future occasion be prepared to consider if the borrower should be allowed time to find the funds to make repayment following the making of a demand upon it: see *Lloyds Bank PLC v Lampert* [1999] 1 All ER (Comm) 161.

[112] See *Cryne v Barclays Bank PLC* [1978] BCLC 548.

[113] See *The Angelic Star* [1988] 1 Lloyd's Rep 122. If, within the particular terms of the wording of an event of default, the lender is given an apparently unfettered discretion to make a determination, as for instance in determining (without any express limitation) if an adverse change has occurred, then there may be scope for the implication of a term as to the manner in which the lender may make its determination.

[114] To which there are statutory exceptions, such as under the Consumer Credit Act 2006 and under provisions regulating possession proceedings concerning residential land.

[115] [1990] AC 536.

unqualified contractual obligation that a party would have under the contract, so that the relevant party undertakes to use its best endeavours, or its reasonable endeavours, to achieve a stated object, rather than undertaking an unqualified obligation to do so.[116] Given their frequent use, it is surprising that there has been only a limited amount of case law on the meaning of the two expressions and there is little precision as to their construction. It is apparent, however, that there is a distinction between an obligation to use best endeavours and an obligation to use reasonable endeavours and that the latter is less stringent than the former.[117]

1.2.11.1 It has been said that best endeavours does not mean second-best endeavours and, broadly speaking, that no stone should be left unturned in seeking to achieve the desired result: *Sheffield District Ry Co v Great Central Ry Co*.[118] Somewhat less stridently, the Court of Appeal said in *IBM United Kingdom Ltd v Rockware Glass Ltd*[119] that an obligation placed upon a party to use its best endeavours meant that the party should take all of the possible steps that a prudent and determined person would take, if he were acting in his own interests and wished to obtain or achieve the stated objective. This would include incurring reasonable expenditure. In *Terrell v Mabie Todd & Co*[120] it was said that the obligor could have regard to the likely commercial success of the steps to be taken as well as its own financial and commercial position. By way of further qualification, in another case it was held that an obligation on a company and its merchant bank advisers to use their best endeavours to obtain the approval of the company's shareholders to a transaction did not extend to recommending the transaction if there had been an intervening event which would make the transaction disadvantageous to the company and its shareholders, as to have given the recommendation in such circumstances would have amounted to giving bad advice to the shareholders and contrary to the obligors' duties to the shareholders.[121]

1.2.11.2 An obligation to use reasonable endeavours does not require a party to sacrifice its commercial interests and the obligation must come to an end at the point when the party has exhausted the avenues available to it, although account had to be taken of events as they occurred, including extraordinary events. In deciding upon the available avenues, the obligor was entitled to consider the likelihood of success

---

116 An agreement to use best endeavours to achieve a stated result, which is an enforceable obligation, has been contrasted with an unenforceable agreement to negotiate: see Lord Ackner in *Walford v Miles* [1992] AC 128, at 138.

117 See Rougier J in *UBH (Mechanical Services) v Standard Life Assurance Co* (unreported, The Times 13/11/1986), Kim Lewison QC, sitting as a deputy High Court judge, in *Jolley v Carmel Ltd* [2000] 2 EGLR 154 and Julian Flaux QC, sitting as a Deputy High Court judge, in *Rhodia International Holdings Ltd v Huntsman International LLC* [2007] EWHC 292 (Comm).

118 (1911) 27 TLR 451.

119 [1980] FSR 335.

120 (1952) 69 RPC 234, affirmed by the Court of Appeal (1953) 70 RPC 97.

121 *Rackham v Peek Foods Ltd* [1990] BCLC 895.

in achieving the desired result. However, if the contract actually specifies that certain steps must be taken as part of the endeavours then they must be taken, even if that would involve the party in sacrificing its commercial interests.[122] Subject to such a specific requirement as to the steps to be taken, it would appear that the party is entitled to have regard to its own financial interests in deciding upon what is required of it: *Phillips Petroleum Co UK Ltd v Enron Europe Ltd.*[123]

It has been said that, as a matter of language and business common sense, an obligation to use reasonable endeavours should only require a party to take one reasonable course of action, whereas an obligation to use best endeavours should require the party to take all reasonable courses that he can take.[124] Thus, an obligation to take 'all reasonable endeavours' probably equates to an obligation to use best endeavours.[125]

1.2.11.3

1.3 Illegality

Illegality is a subject that might raise its head when considering the validity and enforceability of a finance transaction. The law as to the effect of illegality on a transaction is not terribly clear and what follows is an attempt to summarise a rather difficult area.[126] Illegality in this sense means unlawfulness under statute or at common law, the latter including contracts to commit a crime or a tort and contracts which offend against morals or public policy. Illegality may affect a transaction where the entry into or the performance of the transaction is unlawful in itself, where the intended purpose or use of the subject matter of the transaction is unlawful, or where some related transaction is unlawful so that it taints the principal transaction. The illegality is likely to be raised as an objection to reliance on the transaction or as a defence against a claim for non-performance of one or more putative obligations under it.

1.3.1

Examples of instances where it may (although not necessarily would) be unlawful to enter into or perform a transaction would include a contract where one or both

1.3.1.1

---

[122] Lewison J in *Yewbelle v London Green Developments* [2006] EWHC 3166 (Ch), at [122]–[123], which was approved on appeal by the Court of Appeal ([2007] EWCA Civ 475), although a different conclusion was reached on the application of the principle to the facts. See also *Rhodia International Holdings Ltd v Huntsman International LLC* [2007] EWHC 292 (Comm).

[123] [1997] CLC 329.

[124] *Rhodia International Holdings Ltd v Huntsman International LLC* [2007] EWHC 292 (Comm).

[125] See also Mustill J in *Overseas Buyers v Granadex SA* [1980] 2 Lloyd's Rep 608, at 613, Buckley LJ in *IBM United Kingdom Ltd v Rockware Glass Ltd* [1980] FSR 335, at 343 and *UBH (Mechanical Services) Ltd v Standard Life Assurance Co*, n 117 above.

[126] For a more detailed review, see Part II of the Consultation Paper issued by the Law Commission (No 154 of 1999) entitled *Illegal Transactions: the Effect of Illegality on Contracts and Trusts.* The recommendations that were made by the Law Commission for reform of the law in this area have not been adopted.

of the parties requires a statutory licence or permission before it or they may enter into the contract or carry out an activity contemplated by the contract,[127] a contract to hire goods for an unlawful purpose,[128] a contract to carry goods in a manner that is unlawful,[129] or a loan that did not comply with statutory requirements.[130] An example of where the intended purpose or use of the subject matter of a transaction may be unlawful would be where moneys were borrowed with the intention that the proceeds should be used for some unlawful purpose.[131] An example of a transaction which may be affected or tainted by a related unlawful transaction would be an agreement under which moneys were borrowed to repay an existing unlawful loan[132] or where there was an agreement to pay the outstanding price owing under an earlier illegal contract[133] or a contract to finance such a payment.

1.3.1.2 The discussion that follows will commence by examining the effect of illegality under statute and then turn to unlawfulness at common law. It will go on to examine the situations where title in property may pass notwithstanding an illegal contract and the right of a party to an illegal contract to bring a restitutionary claim to recover benefits it has conferred on the other party under the contract, before concluding with the approach that the courts should take in considering pleadings or evidence which concern illegality.

1.3.2 Statutory illegality

As a preliminary matter, a distinction should be drawn between the effect of an illegality that existed under statute at the time the contract was made and supervening illegality under legislation that came into force after that time. In the latter situation, it is likely that the contract will be frustrated[134] unless the illegality affects the contract in some minor way that is irrelevant to the main purpose or fulfilment of the contract[135] or if it arises in consequence of an earlier default of the relevant party.[136]

---

127 As in *Cope v Rowlands* (1836) 2 M&W 149, *Re Mahmoud and Ispahani* [1921] 2 KB 716, and *Chai Sau Yin v Liew Kwee Sam* [1962] AC 304.

128 *JM Allan (Merchandising) Ltd v Cloke* [1963] 2 QB 340.

129 *Ashmore Benson Pease & Co Ltd v Dawson Ltd* [1973] 1 WLR 828.

130 As, for instance, under the Moneylenders Acts 1900 and 1927 (repealed by s 192(4) of the Consumer Credit Act 1974). For a recent example of the application of similar legislation in other parts of the Commonwealth, see the decision of the Privy Council in *Palmer v Cornerstone Investments & Finance Co Ltd* [2007] UKPC 49.

131 As was examined in *Anglo Petroleum Ltd v TFB (Mortgages) Ltd* [2007] EWCA Civ 456, where it was alleged that moneys borrowed under a loan were employed in giving unlawful financial assistance in breach of s 151 of the Companies Act 1985.

132 *Spector v Ageda* [1973] Ch 30.

133 *Fisher v Bridges* (1854) 3 El & Bl 643.

134 *Wynn v Shropshire Union Railways and Canal Co* (1850) 5 Exch 420.

135 As, for instance, in *Cricklewood Property and Investment Trust Ltd v Leighton's Investment Trust Ltd* [1945] AC 221.

136 *Ocean Tramp Tankers Corp v V/O Sovfracht, The Eugenia* [1964] 2 QB 226.

It would appear that the effect of a supervening illegality is not a matter for which the parties can expressly provide in the contract so as to preclude the contract from being frustrated,[137] unlike the position in most other situations that would otherwise give rise to a frustration of a contract.

Where the unlawfulness is proscribed from the outset by statute then the legislation may itself provide for the consequences of the unlawfulness as, for instance, is the case in relation to transactions that are made in breach of the general prohibition contained in section 19 of the Financial Services and Markets Act 2000[138] and the fact that contracts and promises that were made in breach of section 18 of the Gaming Act 1845 or section 1 of the Gaming Act 1892 were void.[139] In such cases, the statute may provide that the transaction remains valid or that it is rendered unenforceable by both parties or only by the party that is in breach of the statutory requirement. The statute may also provide for restitutionary remedies that would be available to the parties. In other cases, the effect of the legislation will be less clear and will depend upon whether the transaction is rendered unenforceable by an implication to be drawn from the legislation and, if so, whether both parties are affected or only the party which is in breach of the statutory requirement. It follows that not every breach of a statutory requirement that relates to the entry into the transaction or its performance will lead to a transaction being unenforceable.[140] On the other hand, the unlawfulness may render a transaction unenforceable even though a defendant may thereby gain a purely fortuitous and commercially unmeritorious defence to a claim brought against it under the transaction.[141] The unlawfulness does not have to involve the commission of a criminal offence,[142] although it will often do so.

1.3.2.1

Various considerations have been put forward in determining the intended effect of a statute on transactions, although none of them provides a conclusive test that can be applied in all situations and there is more than an element of contradiction between them. The following things have been said. The intended effect should

1.3.2.2

---

[137] *Ertel Bieber & Co v Rio Tinto Co Ltd* [1918] AC 260.

[138] See ss 26–29 of the Act.

[139] Those two sections were repealed by s 334 of the Gambling Act 2005, as to contracts entered into after the date of the repeal (1/9/2007). Prior to that repeal, s 412 of the Financial Services and Markets Act 2000 provided that certain contracts (i.e. contracts relating to investments that met prescribed criteria) were not avoided or rendered unenforceable by those sections.

[140] As, for instance, in *St John Shipping Corp v Joseph Rank Ltd* [1957] 1 QB 267; *Archbolds (Freightage) Ltd v Spanglett Ltd* [1961] 1 QB 374; *Yango Pastoral Co Pty Ltd v First Chicago Ltd* (1978) 139 CLR 410; and *Hughes v Asset Managers PLC* [1995] 3 All ER 669.

[141] As was the case in *Re Mahmoud and Ispahani* [1921] 2 KB 716 and *Chai Sau Yin v Liew Kwee Sam* [1962] AC 304.

[142] For instance, the avoidance of gaming and wagering contracts by s 18 of the Gaming Act 1845 and of supporting activities by s 1 of the Gaming Act 1890 did not involve any prohibition of gaming or wagering per se, nor did it make them criminal acts.

be gauged by asking, first, if the statute intended any prohibition of transactions at all and, if so, whether the particular transaction under consideration belonged to the class of transactions that the statute intended to prohibit.[143] The matter should be tested against the mischief at which the statute is aimed, the language it uses, the scope and purpose of the statute, the consequences to the parties (particularly to an innocent party) should the transaction be found to be unenforceable, and any other relevant considerations.[144] A transaction will be void, and so unenforceable, if it infringes a statute which is intended to protect the public interest and which proscribes the activity contemplated by the contract.[145] A statute which intends to protect the public will affect a transaction which involves a breach of the statute, in contrast to a statute which primarily acts as a means of raising revenue for the state.[146] A statute which imposes penalties by reference to individual acts done in breach of the prohibition is more likely to affect a transaction involving the commission of such acts than a statute which imposes a general penalty for carrying out a proscribed activity without making reference to the consequences in individual instances where the activity occurs.[147] A statute is unlikely to affect a transaction whose purpose is lawful and which could therefore be performed and carried out lawfully but where one of the parties chooses (without the encouragement of the other party) to perform in a manner which involves a breach of a statute dealing with some peripheral or incidental matter.[148]

1.3.2.3 If the transaction is affected by statutory illegality, the next question is to ascertain if the illegality affects both parties, even if one of them is entirely innocent, or only the party which is in breach of the statute. Where the latter applies, the transaction will remain enforceable by the innocent party which is not in breach and was unaware of the other party's unlawful conduct.[149] Once again, the matter may be addressed specifically by the statute but in other cases it will be necessary to determine the issue by the implication that should be drawn from the statute. In some cases, the courts have held that the illegality should only affect the party that was

---

[143] Per Devlin J in *St John Shipping Corp v Joseph Rank Ltd* [1957] 1 QB 267, at 287–288.

[144] Per Kerr LJ in *Phoenix General Insurance Co of Greece SA v Halvanon Insurance Co Ltd* [1988] QB 216, at 273.

[145] *Mohamed v Alaga* [2000] 1 WLR 1815.

[146] *Cope v Rowlands* (1836) 2 M&W 149, but contrast with *Smith v Mawhood* (1845) 14 M&W 452 and *Shaw v Groom* [1970] 2 QB 504.

[147] *Victorian Daylesford Syndicate Ltd v Dott* [1905] 2 Ch 624 and *Yango Pastoral Co Pty Ltd v First Chicago Ltd* (1978) 139 CLR 410.

[148] *St John Shipping Corp v Joseph Rank Ltd* [1957] 1 QB 267; *Archbolds (Freightage) Ltd v Spanglett Ltd* [1961] 1 QB 374.

[149] Even in cases where a party had knowledge of the other party's unlawful activity, it may still be able to argue that it was unaffected by mere knowledge which did not amount to 'participation' in the unlawfulness, along the same lines as are discussed below in connection with participation in an unlawfulness that affects contracts at common law.

in breach of the statute,[150] particularly if the innocent party was a member of a class which the statute intended to protect, so that the transaction should remain enforceable by the innocent party.[151] However, that approach is not universal and there are other cases where the affected transaction has been held to be unenforceable by both parties to it, even though one of them was innocent, ignorant of the unlawfulness of the other's conduct, and might have fallen within the class of those whom the statute intended to protect.[152]

That last point was discussed by Kerr LJ in *Phoenix General Insurance Co of Greece SA v Halvanon Insurance Co Ltd*,[153] in which his Lordship said that a contract of insurance entered into by an unauthorised insurer in breach of the Insurance Companies Act 1974 would be void and so unenforceable by both parties, even though the statutory obligation to be authorised was placed upon the insurer and was intended to protect the public, including the insured, against the activities of unauthorised insurers. This was because the statute prohibited the entry into and carrying out of contracts of insurance, rather than just entering into such contracts, although it is submitted that the distinction is not easy to follow.[154] All will not be entirely lost in such a situation, however, as the innocent party should be able to recover moneys that it has paid in purported pursuance of the contract (such as premiums under an insurance policy) under a restitutionary remedy based upon a mistake of fact by the innocent party (that the other party was duly authorised)[155]

1.3.2.4

---

[150] See, for instance, the explanations provided in the Court of Appeal in *Marles v Philip Trant & Sons Ltd* [1954] 1 QB 29, at 32 (Singleton LJ) and 36 (Denning LJ) as to its earlier decision in *Anderson Ltd v Daniel* [1924] 1 KB 138.

[151] As, for instance, in *Hughes v Asset Managers PLC* [1995] 3 All ER 669. See also *Mistry Amar Singh v Kulubya* [1964] AC 142, in which the plaintiff was held by the Privy Council, relying upon *Browning v Morris* (1778) 2 Cowp 790 and *Kearley v Thomson* (1890) 24 QBD 742, to be a member of the class for whose benefit the statute had been introduced, so that his claim should not be defeated by the statute. In *Kasumu v Baba-Egbe* [1956] AC 539, a lender under an unlawful money lending transaction was precluded from enforcing its security but the borrower was held by the Privy Council to be entitled to plead the illegality of the transaction and recover his security without being obliged to repay the moneys that had been borrowed, as the borrower was a member of a class that the statute intended to protect.

[152] *Re Mahmoud and Ispahani* [1921] 2 KB 716 and *Chai Sau Yin v Liew Kwee Sam* [1962] AC 304.

[153] [1988] QB 216, at 267–277.

[154] The judgment on this point was obiter, as it was held that the insurer was authorised. However, the statement of principle enunciated by Kerr LJ was followed in *Re Cavalier Insurance Co Ltd* [1989] 2 Lloyd's Rep 430, *Overseas Union Insurance Ltd v Incorporated General Insurance Ltd* [1992] 1 Lloyd's Rep 439, and *DR Insurance Co v Seguros America Banamex* [1993] 1 Lloyd's Rep 120. The statutory provision (subsequently contained in s 2 of the Insurance Companies Act 1982) was replaced by s 132 of the Financial Services Act 1986, which gave the insured the right to enforce the policy against an unauthorised insurer. The Insurance Companies Act 1982 and the Financial Services Act 1986 were, in turn, repealed by Art 3 of the Financial Services and Markets Act 2000 (Consequential Amendments and Repeals) Order 2001 (SI 2001/3649). The matter is now governed by ss 26–28 of the Financial Services and Markets Act 2000.

[155] *Oom v Bruce* (1810) 12 East 225.

or of law[156] or that the innocent party was not the person primarily responsible for the mistake.[157]

1.3.3 Unlawfulness at common law

It is now convenient to consider the position at common law as to the effect of unlawfulness on a transaction.[158] This covers transactions which involve (in their formation, their performance, or in the use to which their subject matter will be put) the commission of a crime or a tort or which offend against morals or public policy.[159] A related matter that will also be discussed concerns the enforceability of transactions that, taken in isolation, could be valid and enforceable but which are linked to or tainted by some other unlawful transaction.

1.3.3.1 With respect to the intended purpose or manner of performance of the immediate transaction between the parties, if both parties from the outset are fully aware and complicit in the facts giving rise to the illegality,[160] albeit ignorant of the legal consequences, the transaction will be unenforceable by either of them against the other.[161] However, where one party in entering into the transaction relied upon a representation or undertaking by the other that the transaction was lawful or that the other would obtain the necessary permissions so that the transaction could be carried out lawfully, the first of those parties may have a claim which it can assert

---

[156] In reliance upon the decision of the House of Lords in *Kleinwort Benson Ltd v Lincoln City Council* [1999] 2 AC 349.

[157] *Re Cavalier Insurance Co Ltd* [1989] 2 Lloyd's Rep 430.

[158] To some extent, the analysis on this issue will overlap with that set out above concerning the effect of statutory illegality, as a contract which involves a breach of a statute could be seen as a contract to commit a crime and as being against public policy. There may also be an overlap, on the facts of a particular case, between this area and those concerning the tort of conspiracy to commit a crime or to injure a third party (see *Belmont Finance Corp v Williams Furniture Ltd (No 2)* [1980] 1 All ER 383), claims for dishonest assistance in a breach of trust (see *Agip (Africa) Ltd v Jackson* [1990] 1 Ch 265; *Royal Brunei Airlines v Tan* [1995] 2 AC 378; *Twinsectra Ltd v Yardley* [2002] UKHL 12, [2002] 2 AC 164; *Barlow Clowes International Ltd v Eurotrust International Ltd* [2005] UKPC 37, [2006] 1 WLR 1476; and *Abou-Rahmah v Abacha* [2006] EWCA Civ 1492, [2007] 1 Lloyd's Rep 115), and claims for knowing receipt of trust property (see *Agip (Africa) Ltd v Jackson* [1990] 1 Ch 265; *El Ajou v Dollar Land Holdings PLC* [1994] 2 All ER 685; and *Heinl v Jyske Bank (Gibraltar) Ltd* [1999] Lloyd's Rep 511).

[159] An example of a contract that may be against public policy is an 'influence' or 'lobbying' contract, which involves the payment of a commission to a middleman for procuring government orders or concessions. Whilst lobbying per se may be acceptable, it has been held unacceptable for the intermediary to receive a payment, particularly a large payment, where the payment was undisclosed to the government or official that was to be influenced: *Lemenda Trading Co Ltd v African Middle East Petroleum Co Ltd* [1988] 1 QB 448; *Tekron Resources Ltd v Guinea Investment Co Ltd* [2003] EWHC 2577 (QB); *Donegal International Ltd v Republic of Zambia* [2007] EWHC 197 (Comm).

[160] For instance, because the very purpose of the contract binds them into carrying out an unlawful activity.

[161] *JM Allan (Merchandising) Ltd v Cloke* [1963] 2 QB 340; *Ashmore Benson Pease & Co Ltd v Dawson Ltd* [1973] 1 WLR 828.

against the other in deceit, or for fraudulent misrepresentation,[162] or for a breach of a collateral contract or in negligent misrepresentation.[163]

Where one of the parties (the 'innocent party') was unaware of the facts which made the transaction unlawful, or if the innocent party was unaware of the other party's intention to perform it in an unlawful manner, in a situation where the transaction could otherwise have been entered into and performed lawfully, the innocent party will be entitled to enforce the transaction with respect to rights that had accrued in its favour up to the time the unlawfulness was discovered,[164] but the party which intended to enter into the transaction for a purpose which was unlawful or which intended from the outset to perform it in a manner which was unlawful will be unable to enforce the transaction.[165] It may also be the case that a party which enters into a transaction whose purpose is lawful and with an intention to perform lawfully, but which breaches the law in performing the transaction, may still be entitled to enforce it, at least where the unlawful performance was merely incidental to the main purpose and intent of the transaction.[166]

1.3.3.2

A transaction which may appear to be valid in itself may, nonetheless, be unenforceable if it is tainted by an illegality or impropriety that affects a connected transaction.[167] Before the illegality or impropriety will affect the transaction, there must be a relevance in the connection between it and the other transaction that is sufficiently substantial to taint it,[168] rather than a more distant connection which is merely collateral or peripheral to the transaction and the claim that is made to enforce it.[169]

1.3.3.3

The question arises as to the extent or degree to which a party's awareness of the other party's intended unlawful behaviour (in entering into the transaction, in its

1.3.3.4

---

[162] *Shelley v Paddock* [1980] QB 348; *Saunders v Edwards* [1987] 1 WLR 1116. Such a claim was refused in *Parkinson v College of Ambulance Ltd and Harrison* [1925] 2 KB 1 because of the claimant's own turpitude.

[163] *Strongman (1945) Ltd v Sincock* [1955] 2 QB 525.

[164] *Clay v Yates* (1856) 1 H&N 73.

[165] *Archbolds (Freightage) Ltd v Spanglett Ltd* [1961] 1 QB 374.

[166] *Wetherell v Jones* (1832) 3 B&Ad 221; *St John Shipping Corp v Joseph Rank Ltd* [1957] 1 QB 267; *Coral Leisure Group Ltd v Barnett* [1981] ICR 503.

[167] *Fisher v Bridges* (1854) 3 El & Bl 643 (a separate deed of covenant was held to be unenforceable as it constituted an undertaking by a purchaser to pay part of the purchase price of land that remained outstanding under an earlier illegal contract of sale). See also *Spector v Ageda* [1973] Ch 30 (the borrower's obligation to repay a loan was held to be unenforceable as the loan had been advanced to provide the funds to pay off an earlier unlawful loan that had been made to the borrower by a third party) and *Mansouri v Singh* [1986] 1 WLR 1393 (which discussed the enforceability of a cheque or other negotiable instrument given in pursuance of a transaction which is made unenforceable by the Bretton Woods Agreement).

[168] *Tinsley v Milligan* [1994] 1 AC 340 and *Standard Chartered Bank v Pakistan National Shipping Corp* [2000] 1 Lloyd's Rep 218.

[169] *Sweetman v Nathan* [2003] EWCA Civ 115, [2004] PNLR 89; *Hewison v Meridian Shipping Services Pte Ltd* [2002] EWCA Civ 1821; *Donegal International Ltd v Republic of Zambia* [2007] EWHC 197 (Comm).

manner of performance, in the intended use of the subject matter of the transaction, or in its connection with a related transaction that is tainted by illegality) will be taken to amount to a sufficient knowledge of that unlawfulness, so as to prevent the first of those parties from being able to rely upon and enforce the transaction. Where, on the facts, the essence of the transaction is to engage in an unlawful activity or there is an obvious shared intention to engage in such an activity,[170] the parties will be equally complicit and neither will be able to enforce the transaction. In one early case it was held that mere knowledge on its own would amount to a sufficient participation in the other party's unlawful activities so as to deny the right to enforce the contract,[171] but in another case (which was decided a few months later) the court came to the opposite conclusion.[172] The approach that developed over time has been to see the issue as a matter of the degree of a party's involvement or 'participation' in the unlawfulness, rather than judging it in absolute terms.[173] The question is whether the parties had a common design or a shared intention so that they each participated in the unlawfulness. It is not always easy to draw the line, and the effect of the relevant unlawfulness will depend upon the facts of the particular case. The law in this area is based on public policy, and public policy may sometimes be better served by enforcing transactions rather than seeing them avoided.[174]

1.3.3.5 If a party actively participates and assists in the other party's scheme, that will mean that it cannot enforce the transaction.[175] Similarly, if a party to what might be a lawful transaction knows of, or deliberately shuts its eyes to, the unlawful purpose for which the other party has entered into the transaction or of the unlawful purpose for which that party intends to use the subject matter of the transaction, the first party will be unable to enforce the transaction.[176] On the other

---

[170] As there was in *JM Allan (Merchandising) Ltd v Cloke* [1963] 2 QB 340 and *Ashmore Benson Pease & Co Ltd v Dawson Ltd* [1973] 1 WLR 828.

[171] *Langton v Hughes* (1813) 1 M&S 593.

[172] *Hodgson v Temple* (1813) 5 Taunt 181.

[173] See the review of this subject by Toulson LJ in *Anglo Petroleum Ltd v TFB (Mortgages) Ltd* [2007] EWCA Civ 456, at [70]–[83].

[174] On the public policy point, Toulson LJ in *Anglo Petroleum Ltd v TFB (Mortgages) Ltd* referred to what Lord Wright had said in *Vita Food Product Inc v Unus Shipping Co Ltd* [1939] AC 277, at 293.

[175] *Biggs v Lawrence* (1789) 3 TR 454 and *Weymell v Reed* (1794) 5 TR 599, which were cases where goods were sold in a form made ready for smuggling by the other party.

[176] *Pearce v Brooks* (1866) LR 1 Exch 213 (the case concerned the sale of an 'ornamental' brougham to a known prostitute, who plied her trade in it. The seller was denied its claim for the price of the goods). By contrast, in *Appleton v Campbell* (1826) 2 C&P 347 a contract to let a room to a prostitute who practised her occupation elsewhere was held to be valid. Similarly, in *Lloyd v Johnson* (1798) 1 B&P 340 a washerwoman who washed the clothes of a prostitute at normal rates was entitled to recover payment. Lord Denning MR suggested in *JM Allan (Merchandising) Ltd v Cloke* [1963] 2 QB 340, at 348, that tradesmen who supplied ordinary goods at normal commercial rates to such a person would not usually be taken to be assisting them in an unlawful or immoral purpose.

hand, if a party to what could be a lawful transaction innocently assists the other party in pursuing some unlawful purpose but without realising the unlawful intention of the other party, the first party should be entitled to enforce the transaction.[177]

1.3.4 Passing of title under an unlawful transaction

Notwithstanding the unlawfulness of a transaction which affects a party to it, title[178] in an asset may pass under the transaction and be recognised in favour of such a party where the tainted obligation to effect the conveyance has been fulfilled so that it is no longer executory and in need of assistance by the court.[179] This will not be the case, however, if the illegality arises under a statute and the statute (either expressly or by implication) prevents the passing of title under the impugned transaction.[180] It has also been held that the grant of a limited interest in property under an unlawful transaction that affects the grantor will not prevent the recovery of the property by the grantor upon the determination of that interest,[181] provided that the grantor does not need to rely on the unlawful transaction to prove its ownership[182] (although it may rely on the transaction to prove that the limited interest has ceased[183]). It has also been held in the case of statutory illegality that the grantor of a limited interest in property (for instance, a grant by way of security or by way of a tenancy) may recover the full ownership of the property if it was in a class of persons that the statute was intended to protect.[184]

1.3.5 Restitutionary claims

A party to a transaction that is unenforceable because of illegality may also have a restitutionary claim to recover benefits it has conferred on the other party in pursuance of the transaction, such as for money it has paid. The claim may be based

---

On the other hand, if the price was inflated, that would be evidence of participation in the unlawful or immoral purpose. His Lordship also distinguished *Waugh v Morris* (1873) LR 8 QB 202 on the grounds that in *Waugh v Morris* there was no common design nor any participation in an unlawful activity.

[177] *Fielding & Platt Ltd v Najjar* [1969] 1 WLR 357; *Anglo Petroleum Ltd v TFB (Mortgages) Ltd* [2007] EWCA Civ 456.

[178] Including equitable title: *Tinsley v Milligan* [1994] 1 AC 340.

[179] *Singh v Ali* [1960] AC 167; *Belvoir Finance Co. Ltd v Stapleton* [1971] 1 QB 210.

[180] In *Mistry Amar Singh v Kulubya* [1964] AC 142 the Privy Council held that a leasehold interest in land could not have been created in contravention of the relevant statute.

[181] *Bowmakers Ltd v Barnet Instruments Ltd* [1945] KB 65; *Mistry Amar Singh v Kulubya* [1964] AC 142.

[182] *Taylor v Chester* (1869) LR 4 QB 309; *Bowmakers Ltd v Barnet Instruments Ltd* [1945] KB 65.

[183] Ibid.

[184] *Kasumu v Baba-Egbe* [1956] AC 539; *Mistry Amar Singh v Kulubya* [1964] AC 142.

upon a mistake of fact[185] or of law[186] giving rise to the illegality or, more generally, that the claimant was misled by the other party in entering into the transaction,[187] was compelled by the duress of the other party in entering into it[188] or was not the person primarily responsible for the mistake.[189] However, if the claimant was the instigator of the illegality or was otherwise at fault then it will not be permitted to recover the benefits it has conferred under the transaction, at least in relation to restitutionary claims based on a total failure of consideration.[190] It has been held that the court may award interest, including compound interest, as part of a restitutionary award.[191]

1.3.6 Pleadings and evidence concerning illegality

The approach that the courts should take in considering pleadings or evidence which concern illegality was addressed in *North Western Salt Co Ltd v Electrolytic Alkali Co*,[192] *Edler v Auerbach*,[193] and *Snell v Unity Finance Co Ltd*.[194] They were summarised as a set of propositions by Lord Mance in giving the advice of the Privy Council in *Morrell v Workers Savings & Loan Bank*[195] as follows:

> First, where a contract is ex facie illegal, the court will not enforce it, whether the illegality is pleaded or not; secondly, where the contract is not ex facie illegal, evidence of surrounding circumstances tending to show that it has an illegal object should not be admitted unless the circumstances are pleaded; thirdly, where unpleaded facts, which taken by themselves show an illegal object, have been revealed in evidence (because, perhaps, no objection was raised or because they were adduced for some other purpose), the court should not act on them unless it is satisfied that the whole of the surrounding circumstances are before it; but, fourthly, where the court is satisfied that all the relevant facts are before it and it can see clearly from them that the contract had an illegal object, it may not enforce the contract, whether the facts were pleaded or not.

---

[185] *Oom v Bruce* (1810) 12 East 225.

[186] *Kleinwort Benson Ltd v Lincoln City Council* [1999] 2 AC 349.

[187] *Hughes v Liverpool Victoria Friendly Society* [1916] 2 KB 482.

[188] *Smith v Cuff* (1817) 6 M&S 160; *Davies v London and Provincial Marine Insurance Co* (1878) 8 ChD 469.

[189] *Kiriri Cotton Co Ltd v Dewani* [1960] AC 192; *Re Cavalier Insurance Co Ltd* [1989] 2 Lloyd's Rep 430.

[190] *Parkinson v College of Ambulance Ltd and Harrison* [1925] 2 KB 1; *Berg v Sadler and Moore* [1937] 2 KB 158. Contrast the position in those cases with *Mohamed v Alaga & Co* [2000] 1 WLR 1815, in which the Court of Appeal allowed a *quantum meruit* claim for services provided under an unlawful contract because the claimant was less blameworthy than the defendants, who were in a much better position to realise the unlawfulness of the transaction and who had, nonetheless, knowingly entered into the contract in disregard of the unlawfulness.

[191] *Sempra Metals Ltd v HM Commissioners of Inland Revenue* [2007] UKHL 34.

[192] [1914] AC 461.

[193] [1950] 1 KB 359.

[194] [1964] 2 QB 203.

[195] [2007] UKPC 3, at [35].

1.4 Frustration of Contract and *Force Majeure* Clauses

English law does not recognise the civil law concept of *force majeure*, by which a party's   **1.4.1**
obligations may be adjusted or terminated as a matter of law (and without the need
to make express provision in the contract) in consequence of an adverse change in
circumstances which makes it uneconomic or more difficult or onerous to perform
the contract. The precise parameters of the doctrine of *force majeure* will depend upon
the laws of the particular civil law jurisdiction which governs the contract.

By contrast, the English law doctrine of frustration of contract is much stricter in   **1.4.2**
its application and more narrow in the circumstances in which it will operate.
Under it, the whole contract is automatically terminated and each of the parties
to it is discharged from having to make further performance. A contract will be
frustrated if the relevant event is external (i.e. outside the control of one of the
parties) and it is so fundamental as to affect the very basis of the contract, provided
that the contract did not provide for one of the parties to bear the consequences
thereof and the possibility of the relevant event was not foreseen by the parties.
Unless those requirements are met, the contract will continue under English law
despite the fact that its performance might have become more burdensome to one
or other of the contracting parties.[196] If the contract is frustrated then a restitutionary remedy may lie to enable a party to recover moneys paid before it was frustrated, and to obtain compensation for benefits conferred under the contract,
pursuant to the Law Reform (Frustrated Contracts) Act 1943.[197]

Nonetheless, English law does permit the parties in their contract to provide for   **1.4.3**
the consequences of events which the contract stipulates will have the effect of

---

[196] The foregoing statement as to frustration is a summary of a large body of case law, including
Wynn v Shropshire Union Railways and Canal Co (1850) 5 Exch 420 (supervening illegality. see also
1.3.2 above); *Taylor v Caldwell* (1863) 3 B&S 826 (destruction of the subject matter of the contract);
Krell v Henry [1903] 2 KB 740 (change in the fundamental basis of the contract); *Bank Line Ltd v Arthur
Capel & Co* [1919] AC 433 (government requisition of the subject matter of the contract); *Hirji Mulji
v Cheong Yue SS Co* [1926] AC 497 (the self executing effect of frustration); *Davis Contractors Ltd v
Fareham UDC* [1956] AC 696 (the requisite nature of a fundamental change in the basis of the contract,
as opposed to a contract where performance has been delayed or become more onerous); *Peter Cassidy
Steel Co Ltd v Osuustukkukauppa* [1957] 1 Lloyd's Rep 25 (a party could not plead frustration where it
had assumed responsibility under the contract for the risk of the occurrence of the relevant events, in
that case for obtaining an export licence); *Tsakiroglou & Co Ltd v Noblee Thorl GmbH* [1962] AC 93
(contract made more onerous and performance delayed but contract not frustrated); *National Carriers
Ltd v Panalpina (Northern) Ltd* [1981] AC 675 (similar in its analysis to the *Davis Contractors* case);
J Lauritzan AS v Wijsmuller BV, The Super Servant Two [1990] 1 Lloyd's Rep 1 (a party could not plead
frustration where it was 'self-induced' or the party could have prevented the event from occurring).

[197] The Act was reviewed by Goff J in *BP Exploration Co. (Libya) Ltd v Hunt* [1979] 1 WLR 783
(upheld at [1983] 2 AC 352). Recovery was possible at common law if there had been a total failure
of consideration but not if there had only been a partial failure: *Fibrosa Spolka Akcyjina v Fairbairn
Lawson Combe Barbour Ltd* [1943] AC 32.

modifying or discharging their responsibilities. Such clauses are often referred to, if somewhat confusingly, as '*force majeure* clauses'. They may comprehend matters that might fall within the civil law concept of *force majeure* or the more fundamental matters required before the common law doctrine of frustration could be invoked. Typically, such a clause will provide a list of possible events and then define the consequences thereof, which may include some or all of a temporary suspension of a party's obligations, an adjustment in the contract price, an extension of time to perform, restitution of moneys paid and compensation for work or services already performed, or a complete discharge from the obligation to make further perform-ance of the contract. The list of events may include matters such as labour strikes and similar industrial action, external blockades and embargoes, war, terrorist attacks, civil commotion, and acts of God.[198] Another typical event is political risk and other governmental intervention which prevents or impedes performance.

1.4.4 Such provisions are often to be found in project, construction, development, and supply contracts, which contracts themselves will sometimes provide the basis for a financing. In such a case, it is essential for the financier to understand the circum-stances in which the clause may operate in the underlying commercial contract and its consequences, both in relation to that contract and the financing arrangements.

1.4.5 In *Mamidoil-Jetoil Greek Petroleum Company SA v Okta Crude Oil Refinery AD*[199] Aikens J made a number of observations concerning the operation of such a clause, as follows. In general and unless they provide otherwise, *force majeure* clauses are concerned to excuse performance of contracts where the relevant events are out-side the control of the party claiming to be excused and their effect could not have been avoided or mitigated by reasonable steps taken by that party.[200] The eviden-tial burden was upon the party relying upon the clause to establish that the facts fell within the terms of the clause. The alleged *force majeure* event had to be the effective cause of the failure to perform, rather than the real cause for such failure arising for some other reason.

1.5 Enforcement and Recovery upon Breach of Contract

1.5.1 This matter concerns the remedies that are available to a party to a contract (the 'innocent party') where the other party (the 'defendant') has breached the con-tract, always assuming that the contract is (and remains) valid and enforceable.

---

[198] The author has always felt that if one believes in a benevolent God (whichever version of the deity that might be) then He receives a rather bad press in this regard. Surely, it would be more cor-rect to refer to 'acts of the Devil'. In polytheistic systems, the expression might be 'acts of the gods'.

[199] [2002] EWHC 2210 (Comm), [2003] 1 Lloyd's Rep 1 (upheld on appeal at [2003] EWCA Civ 1031, [2003] 2 Lloyd's Rep 635).

[200] See *Channel Island Ferries Ltd v Sealink UK Ltd* [1988] 1 Lloyd's Rep 323.

Needless to say, it is a complex area of law upon which there is a vast amount of case law. All that can be provided here is a summary. In particular cases, questions of waiver, estoppel, and acquiescence may arise as a defence to an innocent party's claim, which are beyond the scope of this book. The reader is referred to the standard texts on contract law for a fuller analysis. The discussion that follows will deal with breaches of contract in general, before examining the separate position concerning liquidated claims in debt.

1.5.2 The general position

Breaches of contract, and their consequences, come in all shapes and sizes and this is recognised by English law. Some breaches are of such significance that they obviously go to the heart or root of the contract. Other breaches are comparatively minor. In between, there are breaches which initially may be regarded as minor but which, by continuance or repetition, build up to such a stage that they become significant as indicating an unwillingness on the part of the defendant to perform the contract. In addition, some terms of the contract (called 'conditions', as opposed to the other terms of the contract, which are called 'warranties') may be considered as being of such significance that a breach of such a term will automatically be considered as going to the heart of the contract. On the other hand, a term of the contract may initially appear to be of neutral significance but a breach of it may, in fact, be of considerable significance. The parties may expressly provide that a particular term should be regarded as a condition as, for instance, by declaring that the term is of the essence of the contract,[201] but it may be necessary to show that the parties really meant to ascribe such a status to the term, especially where it would lead to an unreasonable result.[202] Otherwise, the status of the term must be determined by the language that the parties have used in the contract and the surrounding circumstances.

The consequence of these distinctions goes to the remedies that will be available to an innocent party upon the occurrence of a breach of contract. A breach of contract by the defendant which goes to the heart of the contract, or which shows that the defendant no longer wishes to be bound by the contract, is called a repudiatory breach. The innocent party may treat such a breach as entitling it to terminate the contract and sue for damages for general loss of its bargain. In addition, if it becomes apparent to the innocent party before the time for performance by

1.5.2.1

---

201 *Lombard North Central PLC v Butterworth* [1987] QB 527. But a mere right that is expressly given to an innocent party in a contract to terminate the contract for a breach does not mean that the provision that has been breached should always be treated as a condition of the contract or that the breach is so serious as otherwise to amount to a repudiatory breach of the contract: see *Financings Ltd v Baldock* [1963] QB 104 and *Capital Finance Co Ltd v Donati* (1977) 121 SJ 270.

202 See Lord Reid in *L Schuler AG v Wickman Machine Tool Sales Ltd* [1974] AC 235, at 251–252.

the defendant of an essential obligation that the defendant will be unable or unwilling to perform the obligation, the innocent party may anticipate the breach (thus called an 'anticipatory breach'), terminate the contract, and sue for damages.[203] A termination of the contract for (or in anticipation of) a repudiatory breach is only prospective; it does not effect a rescission of the contract *ab initio*.[204] The consequences of termination in such circumstances are discussed elsewhere in this book.[205]

1.5.2.2 As an alternative to terminating the contract in consequence of a repudiatory breach, the innocent party may elect to continue with the contract by holding the defendant to it. However, where a repudiatory breach has occurred, the innocent party may find its hands tied if it is apparent that the defendant is no longer able or otherwise completely unwilling to perform the contract. Because of its duty to mitigate its loss and seek substituted performance from another source before it can claim damages, the innocent party must not unreasonably delay in terminating the contract and seeking to mitigate its loss once it realises that the contract is lost, as, otherwise, it will suffer a reduction in its claim for damages arising from the breach and termination of the contract.[206] If it is reasonable for the innocent party to try and persuade the defendant to resile from its unwillingness to perform, the innocent party is entitled to defer terminating the contract and taking action to mitigate whilst so attempting to continue with the contract, until such time as it should realise that the contract is lost.[207]

1.5.2.3 In cases of a breach which do not amount to a repudiatory breach of the contract, the innocent party will have a claim for damages for the loss that arises specifically from the breach, but it may not terminate the contract in consequence of the breach, nor will it have a claim in damages for loss of the benefit of the whole contract, as it would have been able to advance in a case where the contract had been terminated following a repudiatory breach. There is, however, a qualification to that statement. The contract may expressly provide the innocent party with a right to terminate the contract upon the occurrence of a non-repudiatory breach by the defendant. If such a breach occurs, the innocent party may terminate the

---

[203] This may be a dangerous strategy because if an incorrect assessment of the situation was made and the other party was, in fact, ready and willing to perform, then the party which wrongly purported to terminate will, by doing so, have committed a repudiatory breach of the contract and the tables will be turned upon it.

[204] For the effect of a termination in these circumstances, see Lord Diplock in *Moschi v Lep Air Services Ltd* [1973] AC 331, at 350.

[205] See Chap 3.

[206] See Lord Wilberforce in *Johnson v Agnew* [1980] AC 367, at 400, such question of reasonableness being relevant in assessing the time at which the buyer's duty to mitigate had arisen, as explained by Oliver J in *Radford v De Froberville* [1977] 1 WLR 1262, at 1285. See also *Bear Stearns Bank PLC v Forum Global Equity PLC* [2007] EWHC 1576.

[207] Ibid.

contract in pursuance of its express right to do so but it will not have a claim in damages for general loss of bargain, although it will be able to claim damages that relate specifically to the breach that occurred.[208]

Generally speaking, a breach of the contract by the defendant does not entitle the innocent party to withhold its own performance, unless the contract has been terminated in consequence of the breach.[209] However, the innocent party may be relieved of its own obligation to perform by the express terms of the contract or by the fact that the defendant has impeded it from performing, such as where the innocent party's performance was dependent upon the prior performance by the defendant.[210]

1.5.2.4

Subject to the rules of remoteness, as referred to below, the general principle[211] governing the assessment of the quantum of damages in a claim for breach of contract is that the damages should compensate the innocent party, as the victim of the breach, for the loss it has suffered,[212] but it is up to the innocent party to prove its loss[213] and it has a duty to take reasonable steps to mitigate its loss (for instance, by finding an alternate source of performance). In assessing damages, the innocent party is entitled to be placed, so far as money can do it, in the position it would have been in had the contract been performed.[214] The starting point is that damages should usually be assessed as at the date of breach,[215] although the tribunal which makes the assessment will, inevitably, be hearing the case at a later date; the tribunal must therefore perform its task in assessing the starting position retrospectively.

1.5.2.5

---

208 *Financings Ltd v Baldock* [1963] QB 104 and *Capital Finance Co Ltd v Donati* (1977) 121 SJ 270.

209 See Lord Ackner in *Fercometal SARL v Mediterranean Shipping Co SA, The Simona* [1989] AC 788, at 805. See also *DRC Distribution Ltd v Ulva Ltd* [2007] EWHC 1716 (QB).

210 *Bulk Oil (Zug) AG v Sun International Ltd* [1984] 1 Lloyd's Rep 531.

211 The House of Lords indicated in *Attorney General v Blake* [2001] 1 AC 268 that, in exceptional circumstances where normal remedies were inadequate to compensate for a breach of contract, the court may be prepared to order the defendant to account for the profits it had received or to which it was entitled. The difficulties that ensue from this are demonstrated by the subsequent decisions of the Court of Appeal in *Experience Hendrix LLC v PPX Enterprises Inc* [2003] EWCA Civ 323, [2003] 1 All ER (Comm) 830 and *World Wide Fund for Nature v World Wrestling Federation Entertainment Inc* [2007] EWCA Civ 286. In the first of those two cases, the Court of Appeal did not grant an account of profits but it did order the payment of a reasonable sum to compensate for an unauthorised breach of contract, even though no actual loss could be demonstrated. In the second case, the court refused (on a procedural issue concerning the case) to grant a remedy on those lines but acknowledged that an award could be made where it was not possible to demonstrate identifiable financial loss.

212 See Parke B in *Robinson v Harman* (1848) 1 Exch 850, at 855 and the review conducted by Lord Scott in *Golden Strait Corp v Nippon Yussen Kubishika Kaisha* [2007] UKHL 12, at [29]–[36].

213 See Lord Nicholls in *Sempra Metals Ltd v HM Commissioners of Inland Revenue* [2007] UKHL 34, at [95]–[96].

214 See Lord Atkinson in *Wertheim v Chicoutini Pulp Co* [1911] AC 301, at 307.

215 See Lord Bingham in *Golden Strait Corp v Nippon Yussen Kubishika Kaisha* [2007] UKHL 12, at [11].

If the contract stipulated for performance of the contract over a period of time and it had been terminated early in consequence of a repudiatory breach, the assessment should take into account the possibility that, had it not been terminated, some later event might have occurred (i.e. an event occurring after the date of termination) which may have brought the contract to an end before its final contractual date, so that the innocent party would not have enjoyed all of the benefit of the contract had it run its full course. That possibility may range from the improbable to something that was distinctly possible and will depend upon the particular case. If the event has actually occurred prior to the date on which the tribunal makes its decision concerning the assessment, it must be taken into account.[216] In addition, and as previously mentioned, if it is reasonable for the innocent party to mitigate its loss by finding a replacement contract, it must do so as soon as is reasonably possible; its failure to do so will be taken into account in the assessment of damages.[217]

1.5.2.6 The recoverable loss for which damages are sought must also fall within the rules as to remoteness,[218] that is to say, that the loss which is claimed must be of a type that could naturally be expected to arise or was foreseeable within the knowledge of the parties at the time of contracting. This matter is explained more fully in the chapter on loan facilities.[219]

1.5.2.7 Under the rules that used to apply relating to privity of contract (as described earlier in this chapter), only a party to the contract (or its agent, trustee, or assignee) may enforce the contract, so that in general a third party could not enforce the contract for its own benefit. If the contracting party sought to enforce the contract for the benefit of a third party, the contracting party (unless it was the agent or trustee of the other person) was likely to be met by a defence that it had suffered no loss and so was only entitled to receive nominal damages. The Contracts (Rights of Third Parties) Act 1999 has overcome much of the problems associated with the privity rule, but the operation of the Act may be excluded or restricted and, in such cases, the rule will continue to be relevant.

1.5.3 Equitable remedies

An innocent party may not be happy to be confined to a claim for damages. It may want the contract to be performed by the defendant and so it may wish to obtain a mandatory order from the court to compel the defendant to perform

---

[216] Per Lords Scott, Carswell, and Brown (Lords Bingham and Walker dissenting) in *Golden Strait Corp v Nippon Yussen Kubishika Kaisha* [2007] UKHL 12.

[217] See Lord Bingham and Lord Carswell in ibid, at [10] and [57], respectively.

[218] I.e. the rule in *Hadley v Baxendale* (1854) 9 Exch 341.

[219] See the discussion in Chap 3.

its bargain.[220] Such orders are not readily available. Exceptionally, however, the court may make an equitable order requiring performance of the contract, by way of an order for specific performance or the grant of a mandatory injunction, but such a remedy is discretionary, the applicant for equitable relief must come to the court with clean hands (i.e. its own conduct in relation to the contract and its relationship with the defendant must be of a high standard), the court will not (save in exceptional circumstances) order performance of a contract for the performance of personal services,[221] and there must be something exceptional or unique in the subject matter of the contract to warrant the intervention of the court in this manner, so that damages would not be an adequate remedy. Subject again to the exercise of its discretion, a court may be prepared to grant a prohibitory injunction to restrain a threatened breach or the continuance of a breach of a negative stipulation in a contract.[222]

1.5.4 Liquidated claims

The situation that has been described so far concerns contracts where the innocent party's claim for damages is an unliquidated claim where the loss has to be assessed by the court. The position is different where the innocent party as claimant sues for non-payment by the defendant of a monetary sum, a liquidated sum, that has fallen due for payment under the contract, as for instance for the repayment of a debt (including where the obligation for repayment has been accelerated in pursuance of a contractual right[223]) or for the price of goods or services that have been sold or supplied.[224] In such a case, the claimant sues for that sum and does not have to prove its loss, is not subject to any rule as to remoteness,[225] nor (in the case of recovery of a debt) has it any obligation to mitigate its loss. However, if the claimant also sues for other damage or loss that it has suffered (for instance, for interest on the unpaid sum[226]) then it will have to meet the usual rules before

---

[220] Subject to the rules as to laches, there may be a benefit in seeking equitable relief by way of an order for specific performance, as the limitation period that applies to an ordinary claim at common law may not apply to such an equitable claim: *P&O Nedlloyd BV v Arab Metals Co, The UB Tiger* [2006] EWCA Civ 1717, [2007] 2 All ER (Comm) 401.

[221] *Johnson v Shrewsbury and Birmingham Ry Co* (1853) 3 De M&G 358, *The Scraptrade* [1983] 2 AC 694, at 700–701, *LauritzenCool AB v Lady Navigation Inc* [2005] EWCA Civ 579, [2005] 1 WLR 3686.

[222] *Lumley v Wagner* (1852) 1 De GM&G 604; *Doherty v Allman* (1878) 3 App Cas 709; *LauritzenCool AB v Lady Navigation Inc* [2005] EWCA Civ 579, [2005] 1 WLR 3686. See also the discussion of Briggs J on this point and on the point concerning the enforcement of contracts for personal services in *Akai Holdings Ltd v RSM Robson Rhodes LLP* [2007] EWHC 1641 (Ch).

[223] See Chap 3.

[224] This should, however, be distinguished from contracts, such as hire-purchase and lease contracts, where the claim relates to loss of the bargain to receive future contractual payments, as the claim in those situations will be an unliquidated claim for damages for the loss of the bargain. See Chap 15 and see also Chap 11.

[225] *Jervis v Harris* [1996] Ch 195.

[226] See *Sempra Metals Ltd v HM Commissioners of Inland Revenue* [2007] UKHL 34.

it can recover that loss. Care must also be taken to distinguish between a genuine liquidated damages clause and a clause which amounts to a penalty. Whilst the former is enforceable, the latter is not and will be struck down.[227]

1.5.5 Part payment

In accordance with the rule in *Pinnel's* case,[228] part payment of a debt that has accrued due for payment will not amount to a discharge of the debtor and a promise by the debtor to pay part of the debt provides no consideration for the release of the debt; nor does either thing provide consideration for the creditor to give up its other remedies for non-payment or later payment, such as foregoing interest on a judgment debt. All the debtor has done is to perform or promise to perform part of an existing obligation, and that can provide no consideration in itself that can bind the creditor.[229]

1.5.5.1 There are various ways, however, in which an agreement to compromise the debt can be made binding on the creditor. The agreement may be made by deed or the debtor may provide fresh consideration, such as by agreeing to pay early,[230] by agreeing to pay in a different currency to the currency in which the debt was originally payable, by agreeing to make payment together with the delivery of some other asset or benefit,[231] or by agreeing to forebear in the enforcement of a cross-claim. It has also been held that part payment of a debt by a third party, if accepted by the creditor, will release the debtor, and that this does not depend upon an agreement to which the debtor is a party.[232] In that regard, it is easy to see that the third party may enter into an agreement which it could enforce against the creditor, by preventing the creditor from suing the debtor, but, prior to the Contracts (Rights of Third Parties) Act 1999, it is difficult to understand how the debtor might have benefited directly from such an agreement.

1.5.5.2 In similar vein, a debtor can enter into an enforceable agreement with its creditors, by which they all agree with the debtor to accept a compromise of their respective claims.[233] This has been extended by the provisions of the Insolvency Act 1986 concerning voluntary arrangements. In addition, under section 62 of the Bills of Exchange Act 1882, an unconditional renunciation in writing by the holder of a bill, at or after maturity of the bill, of the liability of the acceptor under the bill will amount to a discharge of the acceptor[234] and (if specified) other parties to the bill,

---

227 See the discussion at Chap 3.
228 (1602) 5 Co Rep 117a.
229 *Foakes v Beer* (1884) 9 App Cas 605, *D&C Builders Ltd v Rees* [1966] 2 QB 617.
230 *Pinnel's* case (1602) 5 Co Rep 117a.
231 Ibid.
232 *Welby v Drake* (1825) 1 C&P 557, *Cook v Lister* (1863) 13 CB (NS) 543.
233 *Good v Cheesman* (1831) 2 B&Ad 328, *Boyd v Hind* (1857) 1 H&N 938.
234 As against the acceptor, the renunciation can also be achieved by delivering the bill to the acceptor.

and an earlier written renunciation by the then holder of the bill will bind the holder but not a subsequent holder in due course who took without notice.

1.5.6 Equitable forbearance

There is also the difficult concept of equitable forbearance (also called promissory estoppel), whose parameters are not certain. In *Hughes v Metropolitan Ry Co*[235] it was held that it would be inequitable to allow a contracting party to enforce its strict contractual rights when by its conduct it could be taken clearly and unequivocally to have agreed (albeit voluntarily) not to do so, where the other party had acted in reliance on that promise and altered its position. Generally speaking, it has been taken that the effect of this is that the rights are suspended and can be revived upon giving reasonable notice,[236] although there have been cases where, because of the passage of time, the occurrence of subsequent events or the debtor incurring other liabilities in reliance on the promise, it has been held that it would also be impossible or inequitable to require any further performance of the original obligation.[237] It is respectfully submitted, however, that, contrary to the view expressed by Denning J in *Central London Property Trust Ltd v High Trees House Ltd*,[238] the application of the principle does not generally mean that the creditor will be taken to have given up its rights altogether and cannot sue for payment of an accrued debt after giving reasonable notice.

---

[235] (1877) 2 App Cas 439. See also *Birmingham and District Land Co v London and North Western Ry Co* (1888) 40 ChD 268 and *Ajayi v RT Briscoe (Nigeria) Ltd* [1964] 1 WLR 1326.

[236] *Tool Metal Manufacturing Co Ltd v Tungsten Electric Co Ltd* [1955] 1 WLR 761.

[237] See the third point mentioned by Lord Hodson in *Ajayi v RT Briscoe (Nigeria) Ltd* [1964] 1 WLR 1326, at 1330 and, for instance, *Ogilvy v Hope-Davies* [1976] 1 All ER 683 and *Maharaj v Chand* [1986] AC 898.

[238] [1947] KB 130, at 134.

2

BANKING REGULATION

2.1 Introduction

2.1.1 The purpose of this chapter is to describe the prudential and supervisory regulation of banking activities, particularly as that matter is relevant to the structure and cost of transactions that take place in the London banking and financial markets. In nearly every situation that can be imagined, a bank which is operating in the London markets will be subject to the regulation of its activities by virtue of various rules and requirements that are imposed upon it in either the UK or the state in which it is established (or both). One consequence of this is that there will be costs to a bank in having a licence to carry on its business and in its participation in the London markets. This will include costs associated with its entry into and participation in individual transactions (even before a single penny has been advanced or paid). Such costs will be referable, in large part, to the regulatory treatment of the transactions in which it is involved[1] and the way it conducts its business, which will include capital and other costs (such as liquidity costs) associated with compliance by the bank in meeting regulatory requirements. These costs may be calculated by reference to the amount or the volume of its activities. In an extreme case, a bank may find that it is unable to enter into or maintain a transaction or a line of business because it cannot meet the regulatory requirements that are imposed upon it.

2.1.2 Banking regulation is usually derived from legislation and rules made by the supervisory authorities in pursuance of powers granted to them by the legislation. It is also likely that a large measure of discretion will be conferred upon the authorities in the ways in which they exercise their supervisory powers. A bank operating

---

[1] An example of such a cost is to be found in the concept of the 'Mandatory Cost' of a loan transaction (and the formula that accompanies it), as set out in most forms of Libor-based loan documentation used in the London commercial loan market.

in the markets in London will be faced with regulatory requirements that are imposed by the UK authorities, or, if the bank is established in another EC or EEA State (for convenience, collectively referred to in this chapter as the EEA), by the authorities in that State,[2] although the common source on which both the UK and other EEA authorities base most of their supervisory powers is derived from EC legislation. A bank may also be subject to regulation by the authorities in other states outside the EEA if it is established or has a presence in such states.

Of principal relevance to the discussion in this chapter, in terms of the regulatory treatment of transactions, are the rules concerning capital adequacy, large exposures, maintenance of liquidity, and consolidated supervision when a bank is part of a group. Such matters will be examined by reference to the position as it applies in the UK. Before proceeding to address those particular matters, it is relevant to set the overall picture and to give a more general description of the regulatory system as it relates to banks and their activities. **2.1.3**

2.2 The Themes of Banking Regulation

There are a number of themes that traditionally have been present in the objectives of banking regulation. To a large extent, the themes overlap and build upon each other. Some of the more important of them are as follows. **2.2.1**

First, it is thought to be desirable that banks should be licensed and required to establish their credentials as suitable institutions to carry on a banking business, so that the rotten apples are not part of the banking system or let loose on the unsuspecting public or the financial marketplace. As a condition to the granting and continued maintenance of the licence, the bank and those connected with it (including its major shareholders, its directors, and its senior management) should meet certain standards of fitness and competence. This, in turn, involves proper disclosure to the regulatory authorities of information concerning such persons and the business of the bank. **2.2.1.1**

Secondly, there is the wish to provide protection against sharp practice or misleading conduct and to lay down certain minimum standards that should apply to the way in which banks conduct themselves and the transactions into which they enter, albeit that such minimum standards are usually set fairy highly. These requirements are likely to be imposed more severely in relation to transactions that concern consumers and small businesses than with respect to a bank's relationships and transactions with large enterprises and active participants in the financial markets, although some standards will still apply in the latter situations. **2.2.1.2**

---

[2] In addition, a branch of an EEA bank operating in the UK will have to comply with the UK's liquidity requirements, as referred to below.

2.2.1.3 Thirdly, there is the desire to achieve deposit protection, so that persons placing deposits with a bank can be reasonably assured that they will be repaid their deposits and not suffer should the bank fail.[3]

2.2.1.4 Fourthly, there is the aim of ensuring that a bank has sufficient resources to prevent it from collapsing or, should it collapse, that its ordinary creditors (including its depositors) will be reasonably protected. If this is looked at in terms of the two general tests of insolvency, namely the relationship between liabilities and assets as one test, and whether there is enough cash and liquid assets and other resources available to meet liabilities as they fall due[4] as the other test, a bank should be required to hold sufficient capital to meet anticipated losses in the short and longer term arising in its business and the consequential diminution in the value of its assets, and it should have sufficient liquidity, in terms of available cash and other readily realisable and available assets, to meet its liabilities to its ordinary creditors as they arise or are expected to arise due for payment. The purpose of the regimes to ensure the capital adequacy of banks (as described more fully below) has been to meet the first of those goals.[5] Unfortunately, the second of those goals has tended to receive less prominence and attention. This difficulty was sorely tested in the UK in the second part of 2007, with the liquidity crisis that enveloped the British mortgage bank Northern Rock PLC. The bank found itself in difficulties in obtaining funds to support its lending, as it had been heavily dependent on the interbank lending market and the capital markets for access to funding. Those sources of funding had become restricted as a consequence of the turmoil in the financial markets that had been prompted by the downturn in the sub-prime mortgage market in the USA.

2.2.1.5 Fifthly, to meet the objective just mentioned, it is essential that the bank and its regulators should have a proper understanding of its business, its funding, its liabilities, its commitments to provide facilities (both commitments that are legally binding and those of a moral or commercially persuasive nature), and its assets.

---

[3] Small business and private individuals are given some partial protection against a loss of their deposits arising upon the failure of a bank by the Financial Services Compensation Scheme established under Part XV of the Financial Services and Markets Act 2000. The maximum compensation that is payable was set at £35,000 in October 2007 (which the UK Government indicated would be increased). This serves to implement in the UK the EC Deposit Guarantee Scheme Directive (94/19/EEC OJ L135/5). The scheme is currently under review: see the review conducted by HM Treasury in its Discussion Paper *Banking Reform—Protecting Depositors* (Oct 2007, ISBN 13-978-84532-360-8).

[4] As to which, see *Re Cheyne Finance plc* [2007] EWHC 2402 (Ch).

[5] Included in this is the necessity of recognising the true extent of the assets of a bank and the risks of default and non-performance associated with those assets. This involves, for instance, a proper determination of the point at which it can be said that a bank has ceased to have an association with an asset (i.e. a claim for payment) which it has purported to transfer to a third party (in both a legal and economic sense, as well as with respect to any 'moral hazard' that it may have because of its former connection with the asset).

In particular, they should understand the risks to which it may be exposed, including the risks to its assets through a depreciation in the value of the assets (e.g. because of default and non-performance in payment by its customers and its counterparties), the expenditures to which it is committed, the risks to its liquidity (e.g. because one or more of its sources of funding might diminish or become unavailable), and the risks that might arise in its management and the general operation of its affairs which could lead to unintentional losses. Allied to this is the desire that sufficient information should be available publicly, so that people who wish to deal with it can make an informed decision before they enter into transactions with it.

Sixthly, in the event that a bank does become insolvent and collapses, it is sometimes thought desirable that it should be subject to a special insolvency regime that is suitable for banks, rather than simply being wound up and liquidated in the same manner that applies generally to companies. Such a regime may be tailored to allow for a temporary continuance of a bank's affairs and a transfer of its engagements to another bank or to an entity that will arrange for an orderly winding up. This may be particularly important for a bank which conducts retail activities, because of the disruption to the affairs of its customers if it suddenly ceases business, leaving customers stranded because they cannot obtain access to their accounts, payments may be frozen and so forth. Some jurisdictions have special insolvency regimes for failed banks. The UK presently does not have any special insolvency procedures for banks.[6] **2.2.1.6**

Seventhly, there is the necessity to guard against the risk to a bank of 'having too many eggs in the one basket', where it may be adversely affected by a collapse in a geographic or sectoral market in which there is a concentration of its business,[7] or where it may have too much exposure to one customer or group of connected customers.[8] **2.2.1.7**

Eighthly, a bank should be protected against any adverse consequences that might otherwise arise because of its connection with other companies in the same group. That connection may relate to its reputation or its resources if there is a financial connection between it and other members of the group. It may, therefore, be necessary to restrict the ambit and nature of such connections or to restrict financial dealings between the bank and other members of the group. It may also be necessary to assess the financial position not just of the bank but of the whole group. **2.2.1.8**

---

[6] See the review conducted by HM Treasury in its Discussion Paper *Banking Reform—Protecting Depositors* (Oct 2007, ISBN 13-978-84532-360-8).

[7] This is dealt with in the UK as part of the general on-going supervisory review process of banks by the Financial Services Authority including, for instance, under Supervisory Review and Assessment Process (SREP).

[8] This aspect in the UK falls within the requirements as to large exposures (or concentration risks).

2.2.1.9 Ninthly, the banking system as a whole should be protected from the contagion that could occur in consequence of a collapse of any individual bank or number of banks, sometimes described as systemic risk. This is important because of the relationships that exist between banks in the transactions that take place between them through the marketplace in which they operate. For instance, in the London interbank market the same bank is likely at any particular time and through multiples of transactions to be both a borrower and lender. The collapse of that bank would mean that it was unable to repay on the due date the banks which had lent it money, and those banks may, in consequence, be adversely affected in meeting their own obligations to other banks in the market. In addition, the payments systems may be affected if one or more banks collapsed and were unable to meet their obligations, particularly if there was a delay in settlement of payments. The methods that are likely to be employed to guard against the consequences of systemic risk will relate to ensuring overall liquidity and the adequacy of capital, the proper conduct and testing by banks of their activities and systems to safeguard the payment and settlement systems, as well as the possibility, in some countries, of central bank support and intervention to prevent a bank from ceasing its business. The advent of real time gross settlement in payment systems and special rules to deal with the insolvency of participants in financial markets has mitigated against some of the risks of default by banks in meeting their obligations within payment systems and financial markets.

2.2.1.10 Tenthly, there is the international and cross-border element of banking activities and the extent to which that is relevant in the context of banking regulation. It is like a two-sided coin. One side is concerned with the extent to which the regulation of a bank in one country, particularly the country in which it has its head office and the centre of its operations (usually referred to as its 'home' country), should take into account transactions in which the bank engages in other countries. It is desirable that such activities should be taken into account, particularly if they might have adverse consequences on the bank's solvency and its ability to meet its commitments. The other side of the coin involves the question of whether a foreign bank should be subject to local licensing and regulation in a country in which it has local operations (a 'host' country) or if such matters should be left to the licensing and regulatory authorities in its home country. Within the EEA, the system that now applies confers licensing and supervisory authority upon the home authorities and a bank which is licensed or authorised by its home authorities enjoys a 'passport' to deal with customers in other EEA States or to conduct its activities in other EEA States.[9]

2.2.1.11 Finally, in consequence of meeting the various objectives already mentioned, it is hoped that there will be confidence in banks and the overall financial system so as to mitigate against crises in confidence which could lead to a collapse for entirely

---

[9] See Title III of EC Directive 2006/48/EC (OJ L177/1 30/6/2006).

irrational reasons, including a so-called 'run on the banks'. The crisis that involved Northern Rock in 2007 also provides a salutary lesson of what can happen when there is a lack of confidence in a bank. The queues of the bank's depositors outside its branches, waiting to withdraw their savings, provided an embarrassing example of what can happen.

The crisis in the financial markets in the second part of 2007 exposed a new concern that had not been present in the earlier analysis of banking regulation. It became apparent that a great deal of the liquidity in the financial markets had been derived from activities in the secondary debt markets, in which dealings in debt and debt instruments had taken place. In essence, much of the debt that had been originated by banks and through bond issues had been passed on to investors, often through being packaged and re-packaged in various forms of structured finance. Various different structures had been developed to achieve this, including the use of structured investment vehicles (SIVs) and packaging vehicles, which issued short-term debt to investors and used the funds raised to purchase longer term debt instruments. Doubts as to the creditworthiness of the assets held by such vehicles led to the value of their portfolios declining rapidly, although it was uncertain how their values should be assessed. That, in turn, led to investors suffering large losses and withdrawing from the markets, with the consequence that new schemes could not be funded and existing short-term instruments could not be re-financed. This left many banks exposed, including banks that held such investments and banks that were connected with the vehicles concerned, through exposures under stand-by and liquidity facilities and because they had sponsored the establishment of the vehicles. It also meant that banks could not use these secondary markets as sources to fund existing lending that they wished to sell on or to fund new lending. **2.2.2**

The resulting uncertainties had not been anticipated by banking regulators, who had concentrated on the traditional model of banking, by which banks lent money using funds raised by deposits and through the interbank markets. Under that model, the risks faced by banks were connected with the creditworthiness of their borrowers and other obligors, rather than the newer types of risks, particularly to liquidity and through connection with the vehicles and structures that had been used, which became apparent in consequence of the financial crisis. Clearly, future banking regulation must address the new concerns as they relate to banks and, indeed, the wider financial system. **2.2.2.1**

2.3 The Historical Approach to Banking Regulation

At one time, the regulation of banks was thought to be such a specialist area that it was kept separate from other areas of regulation. In the UK, for instance, the regulation of banks was principally undertaken by the Bank of England in pursuance **2.3.1** of powers granted to it under the Banking Acts of 1979 and 1987. The Bank of England was responsible for the licensing and supervision of banks as deposit takers, and it imposed liquidity requirements upon them. If the same entity carried on other types of activity, it was likely to be subject to separate regulation in pursuance of other legislation, such as under the Financial Services Act 1986. In the USA, an even stricter approach was taken, as it was thought undesirable that banks should engage in types of activity that were not strictly of a banking nature, for fear that the soundness of their banking operations might be compromised by adverse associations with, and losses in, other areas. Thus, the Glass-Stegall Act 1933 prevented national banks from carrying on non-banking activities.

2.3.2   Over time, however, attitudes have changed. The Gramm-Leach-Bliley Act 1999 removed the restrictions from carrying on non-banking activities that had existed in the USA under the 1933 legislation. In the UK, the licensing and supervision of banks was transferred to the Financial Services Authority (the FSA) in consequence of the Bank of England Act 1998. Shortly afterwards, the regulation of virtually the whole of the financial services sector was consolidated into the hands of the FSA as a result of the Financial Services and Markets Act 2000, although the Bank of England retained some limited responsibility in relation to the imposition of deposit and similar requirements for liquidity purposes, and the Office of Fair Trading remained responsible for much of the system of licensing of the providers of consumer credit and the associated protection of consumers.[10] It remains to be seen whether it was sensible to remove the supervision of banks from the hands of the Bank of England by placing it in the hands of the FSA. A consequence of this has been that the Bank of England, which is at the centre of the financial and monetary system, does not have the same level of knowledge of the banks and their activities as it would have if it were also their regulator. This means that it may be impeded in providing timely support and advice to a bank which may find itself in difficulties.

2.4   The UK Requirement for Authorisation

2.4.1   The expression that is used in the UK for the process of licensing a bank or other entity is 'authorisation'. A bank is an authorised person if it has been granted a permission by the FSA to carry on regulated activities or if it is an EEA regulated firm which is entitled to carry on such activities by virtue of a passport under EC legislation.

2.4.2   As just mentioned, the statutory requirement for the authorisation of banks in the UK and the continuing supervision of their activities, except in relation to

---

[10] Under the Consumer Credit Acts of 1974 and 2006.

consumer credit transactions and certain of the liquidity requirements, now falls within the ambit of the Financial Services and Markets Act 2000 (FSMA). That Act, and secondary legislation made under it, is the method by which the relevant EC legislation[11] is implemented in the UK.

In actual fact, there is no explicit requirement to be authorised simply as a bank   **2.4.3**
or, for that matter, as a simple lender of money;[12] rather, the requirements for authorisation relate to the various regulated activities in which a bank (or any other type of entity) may engage, as amplified in secondary legislation made under FSMA, principally in the Financial Services and Markets Act 2000 (Regulated Activities) Order 2001[13] (the Regulated Activities Order). A bank (or any other provider or arranger of, or adviser upon, financial services) is required to obtain permission in respect of each such activity that it undertakes. In the field of banking, the principal regulated activity that requires authorisation is that of accepting deposits,[14] which will be examined in further detail below. Other regulated activities in which a bank typically engages and which would require authorisation include issuing electronic money,[15] being concerned in derivatives transactions,[16] engaging in or advising upon transactions involving debt and equity securities, entering into regulated mortgage contracts,[17] and managing investments[18] or advising on them.[19] Effecting and carrying out contracts of insurance is also an activity that requires authorisation.[20] There are also limited exclusions that may apply with respect to the necessity of obtaining permission to carry on those various activities, depending upon the facts.

Section 19 of FSMA provides that no person may carry on a regulated activity in   **2.4.4**
the United Kingdom (which is given an extended meaning by virtue of section 418 of FSMA[21]) unless he has been authorised under the Act or is exempted from

---

[11] So far as concerns most banking activities, previously consolidated in the Directive relating to the taking up and pursuit of the business of credit institutions (2000/12/EC OJ L126/1 26/5/2000) and now recast in a new Directive (2006/48/EC OJ L177/1 30/6/2006). In relation to the issuance of electronic money, FSMA implements the Directive on the taking up, pursuit of, and prudential supervision of the business of electronic money institutions (2000/46/EC OJ L275/39 27/10/2000).

[12] Except in pursuance of the Consumer Credit Acts of 1974 and 2006.

[13] SI 2001/544, as amended.

[14] Art 5 of SI 2001/544.

[15] Art 9B of SI 2001/544.

[16] By virtue of Arts 14, 21, and 25, and 83–85 and, as relevant thereto, Art 89 of SI 2001/544. See further the commentary on this aspect at Chap 11.

[17] Art 61 of SI 2001/544.

[18] Art 37 of SI 2001/544.

[19] Art 53 of SI 2001/544.

[20] Art 10 of SI 2001/544.

[21] For instance, s 418(5) provides that a person whose head office is outside the UK, but who carries on the regulated activity from an establishment he maintains in the UK, is to be treated as carrying on the relevant business in the UK.

the need to be authorised. By section 22 a regulated activity is an activity of a specified kind which is carried on by way of business and which relates to an investment of a specified kind. For present purposes, the specified activities and the specified investments will be found in the Regulated Activities Order. A breach of section 19 is an offence. There is also a restriction on financial promotion by an unauthorised person (section 21).

2.5 Unauthorised Activities (Except Unauthorised Deposit Taking)

2.5.1 By section 26 of FSMA, an agreement made by a person in breach of the prohibition upon him under section 19 (except if the breach concerns accepting deposits[22]) is unenforceable by him against the other party and the latter is entitled to the return of any money paid or transferred by him under the agreement and compensation (assessed under section 28(2)), but subject to the obligation imposed on that other party by section 28(7) to return any money or property that he received. Section 27 imposes similar consequences where an authorised person enters into an agreement in consequence of something said or done by an unauthorised person. Section 28(3) provides, however, that the court may allow the agreement affected by sections 26 or 27 to be enforced or that such money or property paid to the person in breach should be retained if the court is satisfied that it is just and equitable so to allow.[23] Section 28(4)–(6) makes provision for the matters to be taken into account under section 28(3).

2.5.2 Section 28(9) of FSMA limits the further civil consequences of a breach of the requirement for authorisation. In consequence, the innocent counterparty to an unauthorised transaction can elect to perform it and enforce it against the defaulting unauthorised party. This is in contrast, for instance, to the position that was formerly thought to have applied in relation to insurance policies issued by an unauthorised insurer in breach of the prohibition contained in section 2 of the Insurance Companies Act 1982 (which was repealed by FSMA), and its predecessor legislation, under which an innocent insured might find that he could not enforce the policy against the insurer because the policy was rendered illegal and therefore unenforceable by either party.[24]

---

[22] S 26(4) of FSMA.

[23] In *CR China Trading Ltd v China National Sugar & Alcohol Group Corp* [2003] EWHC 79 (Comm), [2003] 1 Lloyd's Rep 279, David Steel J noted the point, but did not decide it, as to whether the reference in s 29(3) to the 'court' included an arbitrator before whom an issue of invalidity under ss 26 or 27 had arisen.

[24] See Kerr LJ in *Phoenix General Insurance Co of Greece SA v Administratia Asigurarilor de Stat* [1988] QB 216, at 267–277. S 2 was amended by s 132 of the Financial Services Act 1986 to give the insured the right to enforce the contract.

2.6 The Regulation of Deposit Taking

The acceptance of deposits by way of business is a regulated activity in the UK for **2.6.1** which authorisation is required. Section 29 of FSMA provides for the civil consequences of accepting deposits in breach of the prohibition in section 19. If a depositor does not have a contractual right to recover the deposit without delay, section 29(2) provides that he may apply to the court for an order to that effect. However, section 29(3) then provides that the court need not make such an order if it is satisfied that it would not be just and equitable to order the return of the deposit, having regard, under section 29(4), to whether the deposit-taker reasonably believed that in contracting to take the deposit he was not contravening the prohibition.

Given its importance to the business carried on by banks, it is now appropriate to **2.6.2** examine in some detail the method by which the acceptance of deposits by way of business is treated as a regulated activity in the UK for which authorisation is required.

Section 22 of FSMA provides that a regulated activity is (1) an activity of a speci- **2.6.2.1** fied kind, (2) which is carried on by way of business, and (3) which relates to an investment of a specified kind. By Article 74 of the Regulated Activities Order, a deposit (the definition of which is set out below) is a specified kind of investment. By Article 5(1), accepting deposits is a specified kind of activity, if:

(a) money received by way of deposit is lent to others; or
(b) any other activity of the person accepting the deposit is financed wholly, or to a material extent, out of the capital of or interest on money received by way of deposit.

Paragraphs (a) and (b) classically describe the ways in which a bank operates. It uses (at least in large part) the funds placed with it on deposit to lend money to its borrowers. No doubt, it may also finance other types of activity from such deposits or from interest it earns by redeploying the deposits.

Nonetheless, accepting deposits is only a regulated activity if it is done by way of **2.6.2.2** business. In that regard, it is separately provided[25] that a person should not be regarded as accepting deposits by way of business if:

(a) he does not hold himself out as accepting deposits on a day to day basis; and
(b) any deposits which he accepts are accepted only on particular occasions, whether or not involving the transfer of any securities.

---

[25] By Art 2(1) of the Financial Services and Markets Act 2000 (Carrying on Regulated Activities by Way of Business) Order 2001 (SI 2001/1177) (as amended). The Order was made in pursuance of s 419 of FSMA.

It is further provided that in determining if deposits are only accepted on particular occasions for the purposes of paragraph (b), 'regard should be had to the frequency of those occasions and to any characteristics distinguishing them from each other'.[26] In *SCF Finance Co Ltd v Masri (No 2)*[27] the Court of Appeal held, in relation to similar wording in the Banking Act 1979[28] that the holding out of a willingness to accept deposits on a day-to-day basis involved the deposit taker in holding itself out, either explicitly or implicitly, as being generally willing on any normal working day to accept deposits from those invited to place them if they wished to make deposits. The wording did not cover the situation where payments were demanded and received by the recipient in pursuance of a contractual right to require the payments to be made by way of margin payments. The court also held, on the wording in the 1979 Act, that it did not matter if there were numerous such occasions, as it might be possible that each could still be considered as being a 'particular' occasion. That latter point would now be subject to the more recently imposed requirement, recited above, that regard should be had in determining if deposits were only accepted on particular occasions, to the frequency of the occasions, and if there were any characteristics distinguishing between them.

2.6.2.3 A 'deposit' is defined in Article 5(2) of the Regulated Activities Order to mean a sum of money, other than one excluded by any of Articles 6 to 9A of that Order, which is paid on terms:

    (a) under which it will be repaid, with or without interest or premium, and either on demand or at a time or in circumstances agreed by or on behalf of the person making the payment and the person receiving it; and

    (b) which are not referable to the provision of property (other than currency) or services or the giving of security.

Article 5(3) provides that, for the purposes of Article 5(2)(b), 'money is paid on terms which are referable to the provision of property or services or the giving of security if, and only if':

    (a) it is paid by way of advance or part payment under a contract for the sale, hire or other provision of property or services, and is repayable only in the event that the property or services is or are not in fact sold, hired or otherwise provided;

    (b) it is paid by way of security for the performance of a contract or by way of security in respect of loss which may result from the non-performance of a contract; or

    (c) without prejudice to sub-paragraph (b), it is paid by way of security for the delivery up or return of any property, whether in a particular state or repaid or otherwise.

---

[26] Art 2(2) of SI 2001/1177.
[27] [1987] QB 1002.
[28] S 1(3).

In *SCF Finance Co Ltd v Masri (No 2)*[29] the Court of Appeal also considered the equivalent provisions to Article 5(3) which had been contained in the Banking Act 1979.[30] The case essentially concerned the taking of margin payments by a dealer in commodities and financial futures transactions, such margin payments having been made to it by its customer pursuant to a contractual requirement that the customer should pay a margin to the dealer from time to time. The margin was calculated by reference to the amount of the customer's outstanding positions on contracts it had entered into with the dealer. The dealer had replicated the transactions by entering into equivalent contracts with participants in the relevant markets. The court pointed out that a payment could only fall within the paragraphs of Article 5(3) if it was made exclusively for the purpose identified in the relevant paragraph. Hence, a margin payment could not fall within paragraph (a) if the dealer had supplied any services or property to which the payment related. However, the court was prepared to hold that the payment of margin fell within paragraph (b). The payment was made to protect the dealer against the risk of the customer's default in paying for any property that might have been delivered (should the customer have opted for physical delivery) and for the provision of the dealer's contractual services to the customer, by which it had entered into the equivalent contracts in the markets so as to satisfy the customer's orders, it had extended credit to the customer for the outstanding contract amounts payable by the customer and it had undertaken risk and exposure to its market counterparties.

2.6.2.4   Articles 6 to 9A of the Regulated Activities Order contain exclusions from the definition of 'deposit'. Article 6 relates to sums paid to the recipient by certain specified persons, including those authorised to accept deposits or authorised insurers, those whose business is primarily that of being money lenders, companies within the same group, and money paid by close relatives; Article 7 relates to money received by legal practitioners; Article 8 relates to money received by certain types of authorised persons; Article 9 exempts money subscribed for debt securities; and Article 9A concerns money paid in immediate exchange for electronic money.

2.7 The UK System of Authorisation and Supervision of Banks

2.7.1   The statutory basis for the authorisation of banks as deposit takers (and for other regulated activities) is to be found in Parts III and IV of FSMA. Part III provides for the persons who are authorised to carry on regulated activities. This includes those to whom the FSA has granted a permission under Part IV and those persons established and authorised in other EEA states who are entitled to carry on

29 [1987] QB 1002.
30 S 1(6).

'passported' activities in the UK. Part IV sets out the requirements upon which the FSA may grant permission to be authorised, and for the variation, restriction, and removal of such a permission. Of particular relevance are the threshold conditions that are set out in Schedule 6 to FSMA, as well as the various requirements relating to authorisation in the FSA's Handbook. Part XII is also relevant, as it provides for the FSA's ability to monitor and approve those who control a bank or are able to influence it. The FSA has a wide amount of discretion in deciding upon whether it should grant a permission to be authorised and as to the scope of any such permission.

2.7.2   At the heart of the supervisory regime are the FSA's Principles for Business, which are set out in PRINC 2.1 in the FSA's Handbook. Of the eleven principles, the following (which do not contain the principles relating to the relationship between a bank and its customers, although they are also of importance) are the most important in the context of the present discussion:

1. Integrity: a firm must conduct its business with integrity.
2. Skill, care and diligence: a firm must conduct its business with due skill, care and diligence.
3. Management and control: a firm must take reasonable care to organise and control its affairs responsibly and effectively, with adequate risk management systems.
4. Financial prudence: a firm must maintain adequate financial resources.
5. Market conduct: a firm must observe proper standards of market conduct.
. . .
11. Relations with regulators: a firm must deal with its regulators in an open and co-operative way, and must disclose to the FSA appropriately anything relating to the firm of which the FSA would reasonably expect notice.[31]

The Code of Market Conduct, issued by the FSA under section 119 of FSMA, is important to banks that are active in the financial markets and in dealing in financial instruments. It implements the Market Abuse Directive[32] within the UK and deals with misuse of information, creating a false or misleading impression, and market distortion.

2.7.3   Part X of FSMA provides for the FSA's powers to make rules and guidance as to the continuing business of authorised persons. It is under section 138 (which is in Part X of FSMA) that the prudential supervision rules for authorised persons are made. In relation to banks and other types of authorised entities, they appear in the GENPRU block of the Prudential Sourcebooks (themselves contained in the

---

[31] It follows from this principle that a bank must be full and frank in its dealings with the FSA and not attempt to engage in 'cat and mouse' activities.
[32] 2003/6/EC OJ L096/16 12/4/2003.

FSA's Handbook), with particular requirements for, inter alia, banks in the BIPRU block of the Prudential Sourcebooks. The prudential supervision rules are supported by the FSA's investigatory powers under Part XI and its disciplinary powers that appear in various parts of FSMA.

Amongst the various rules concerning prudential supervision of banks in the UK are those that relate to capital adequacy, large exposures, liquidity, and consolidated supervision, which are also relevant in terms of their effect upon transactions into which a bank may engage (including as to the resultant cost of the transaction), and to which attention will now turn.

2.8.4

2.8 Capital Adequacy: The Basel, EC, and UK Requirements

One of the most important of the prudential supervisory requirements concerns capital adequacy, by which a bank is required to maintain sufficient capital to support its activities. This follows from the fourth of the FSA's Principles for Business referred to above. The capital adequacy requirements for banks established in the UK are imposed under the GENPRU and BIPRU block of the Prudential Sourcebooks in the FSA's Handbook.[33] It is also important to understand that the continuing requirements as to capital adequacy are imposed in addition to the requirement as to initial capital in order to secure authorisation.[34]

2.8.1

The capital adequacy requirements (and the large exposures and consolidated supervision requirements) contained in the FSA's Handbook implement, in turn, the requirements of the EC's so-called Capital Requirements Directive (the CRD). In fact, the CRD is comprised of two directives. The CRD in its application to banks (credit institutions) is to be found in EC Directive 2006/48/EC[35] (the Banking Consolidation Directive or BCD). The other part of the CRD applies to investment firms and is contained in EC Directive 2006/49/EC,[36] which applies various parts of the BCD to investment firms. The CRD is the means by which the EC has adopted, in very large part, the Basel Capital Accord of 2004 entitled, *International Convergence of Capital Standards—A Revised Framework* (Basel 2), but with the significant difference that the BCD is intended to apply to all banks that are established in EU Member States and not, as Basel 2 contemplates in a more restricted fashion, just banks that partake in the business of international banking. In addition, the CRD is intended (by virtue of EC Directive 2006/49/EC)

2.8.2

---

[33] See also the Capital Requirements Regs 2006 (SI 2006/3221) which give powers to the FSA to deal with co-operation between the FSA and other regulators, particularly with respect to consolidated supervision and approval of External Credit Assessment Institutions.

[34] Set at €5m by Art 9 of EC Directive 2006/48/EC OJ L177/1 30/6/2006.

[35] OJ L177/1 30/6/2006.

[36] OJ L177/201 30/6/2006.

to apply to investment firms as well as banks. It is interesting to note that the European Court of Justice has held, in relation to the predecessor EC legislation to the BCD, that the legislation did not confer rights on depositors of a bank against a Member State's regulatory bodies, in the event that such bodies had failed to supervise a bank correctly in accordance with the requirements of such legislation and the depositors had suffered loss in consequence of such a failure. Accordingly, a provision of a national law which precluded a depositor from pursuing a claim against a regulatory body did not infringe Community law.[37]

2.8.3 By way of historical background, the Basel[38] Committee on Banking Supervision was established in 1974 by the governors of the central banks of the G10 countries. It meets under the aegis of the Bank for International Settlements. It has no statutory basis and its pronouncements and publications do not have any binding force of their own volition. They have tended, however, to be adopted and generally observed by the banking regulatory authorities in many countries around the world and have come to be regarded as minimum standards that should be observed by banks that are active in the business of international banking. The first of the Committee's standards was the *Basel Concordat* of 1975, which dealt with principles concerning consolidated supervision of banking groups and the exchange of information between supervisory authorities. In 1988, the Committee published the *Capital Accord* (Basel 1), which was intended to achieve minimum capital standards for banks across the world, with the intention that the regulatory authorities should impose in each country at least the same minimum capital standards for banks, so that the banks of any one country would not enjoy a competitive advantage by having a weaker capital requirement than might be required in another country; this was intended to achieve the so-called 'level playing field'. In 1995, the Basel Committee published the *Market Risk* amendment to Basel 1, which incorporated capital requirements for the market risk associated with the trading and banking book activities of banks; essentially, the market risk attached to equity and debt instruments held by banks. Following proposals originally published in 1999, the Committee published Basel 2 in 2004 as its new capital accord, with the intention that it should begin to be adopted from the beginning of 2007.

2.8.4 Prior to the BCD, the position in the EC with respect to the regulation of banks was laid down by an earlier Banking Consolidation Directive[39] (which consolidated

---

[37] *Paul & Ors v Federal Republic of Germany* Case C-222/02, ECR I-9425. The ECJ made a similar finding with respect to the failure of the Member State to implement the requirements of the EC's Deposit Scheme Guarantee Directive (94/19/EEC OJ L135/5).

[38] Originally, the French spelling of the town was preferred, but this later changed to the German spelling, which will be used in this chapter.

[39] 2000/12/EC.

a number of earlier instruments, including the Own Funds Directive,[40] the Solvency Ratio Directive,[41] and the Second Banking Directive[42]) and by two Capital Adequacy Directives.[43] Amongst other things, those instruments reflected much of Basel 1 and the amendments to it that were introduced by the Market Risk amendment in 1995.

The BCD had to be implemented by the EEA Member States by 1 January 2007, but its application could be delayed at the discretion of national authorities until 1 January 2008. The BCD has very largely been adopted in the UK in a 'copyout' approach, that is, with little variation. For that reason and for ease of reference, the provisions of the BCD, together with the provisions of GENPRU and BIPRU, will be referred to as the sources of reference for the text that follows relating to the implementation of the BCD in the UK.

2.8.5

2.9 The Approach under Basel 1

In general terms, Basel 1 laid down a fairly simple set of capital requirements in relation to banks and their banking activities, which were amended in 1995 to introduce capital requirements in relation to the market risk that banks bore concerning their trading and banking books.[44] Put in very simple terms, Basel 1 recognised four things. First, that in the event of a bank's insolvency its ordinary unsecured creditors (e.g. its depositors, suppliers of interbank funding, and other ordinary unsecured creditors) should have a claim on its assets, represented by its capital, which ranked ahead of the claims of its shareholders and the holders of quasi-capital that it had issued. Secondly, that there should be a consensus as to the items that could comprise capital, reflecting the fact that, in an economic sense, the capital of a bank could include more than just ordinary share capital. Thirdly, so as to have a buffer available to meet the claims of its ordinary unsecured creditors, that such capital of a bank should be of at least a minimum amount, when calculated by reference to the value of its banking assets, such assets being represented by the claims to payment that the bank had against those with whom it had done business, being its counterparties. Fourthly, that in determining the value of such assets, account should be taken of the risk that the bank may not be paid in full because of default by its counterparties, so that an adjustment or weighting (a 'risk weighting') should be ascribed to the value of each asset to reflect the likelihood and consequences of the occurrence of such a default.

2.9.1

---

40 89/229/EEC OJ L124/16 5/5/1989.
41 89/647/EEC OJ L386/14 30/12/1989.
42 89/646/EEC OJ L386/1 30/11/1989.
43 93/6/EC OJ L141/1 11/6/1993 and 98/31/EC.
44 For ease of explanation, the capital requirements for market risk will be examined separately.

2.9.2   At the heart of Basel 1, in relation to banking activities, was the requirement that banking regulators in individual countries should impose a minimum require-ment upon the banks they supervised, namely, that such banks should maintain capital of at least 8 per cent of the aggregate of their risk weighted assets. The regu-lators were free to set higher requirements if they so wished, but they should not set any lower requirement. The requirement could be expressed as:

> Capital ≥ 8% of total risk weighted assets.

The Accord specified both the acceptable components of capital and the method for determining the risk weighting of assets, with some variance permitted in cer-tain instances.

2.9.3 Capital

The concept of capital in this context relates to the paid up resources that will be available, particularly in a winding up, to satisfy the obligations of a bank to its ordinary creditors ahead of being available for distribution to its shareholders and others who rank behind ordinary creditors in a winding up. Basel 1 recognised that in addition to the traditional concept of ordinary paid up share capital, there were other types of capital, quasi-capital, or reserves that might be available to a bank and which could be treated as capital or as a proxy for capital in a winding up. However, it also required that a bank should have a minimum of core capital which had the characteristics normally ascribed to the holders of ordinary share capital, namely, as being the last to receive any entitlement to a distribution in a winding up, after all other claimants had been paid (in that sense, subordinated and 'perpetual'), and which did not have any cumulative entitlement to unpaid income.

2.9.3.1   To achieve the distinction between the different types and characteristics of acceptable capital, Basel 1 distinguished between three tiers of capital, with a fur-ther differentiation between the components in the tiers of capital. Tier one cap-ital, being core capital, had to amount to at least 50 per cent of all the available capital that could be taken into account in assessing a bank's acceptable capital for capital adequacy purposes. The balance could be made up of acceptable capital or quasi-capital falling within Tier two or, in assessing capital requirements for the trading book of a bank, quasi-capital that fell within Tier three.

2.9.3.2   The definition and components of capital under Basel 1 continued to apply under Basel 2 and have remained largely unaffected by the changes that are made in other areas, particularly in the methods for assessment of credit risk.[45]

---

[45] The present provisions as to acceptable regulatory capital are referred to in section 1 of Directive 2006/48/EC. See also GENPRU 2.2 and Annex 2 to GENPRU 2.

In tabular form, the following sets out in a simplified manner the types of capital that may be taken into account:

Tier 1 ('Core capital'), being at least 50 per cent of required regulatory capital: capital or hybrid instruments that are subordinated + perpetual + non-cumulative.

E.g. ordinary share capital, perpetual non-cumulative preference shares and retained earnings (credited to reserves or held as capitalised dividends).

No more than 15 per cent of Tier 1 capital to be capital raised indirectly through SPVs.

Tier 2 ('Supplementary capital').

Upper Tier 2 (at least 50 per cent of Tier 2): other capital or instruments of a perpetual nature.

E.g. perpetual cumulative subordinated debt, perpetual cumulative preference shares, general provisions, and revaluation reserves.

Lower Tier 2: redeemable capital or instruments.

E.g. dated cumulative preference shares, repayable subordinated debt > 5 years at issue (with a straight line amortisation during the period of 4 years to retirement of the debt and various other conditions).

Tier 3 ('Ancillary capital').

Only relevant for the trading book.

E.g. repayable subordinated debt > 2 years (subject to similar conditions as for Lower Tier 2 subordinated debt).

Note: there are various deductions that must be made from capital. E.g.:

From Tier 1: the value of holdings of own shares, goodwill and other intangibles, current year unpublished losses and recapitalisation of property revaluation reserves after 1/1/92 (which may, instead, be included in Upper Tier 2 capital).

From Tiers 1 and 2 (pro rata): the value of investments in unconsolidated subsidiaries and associates, connected lending of a capital nature (e.g. capital guarantees), holdings in capital instruments issued by credit and financial institutions and some others (e.g. in connection with some holdings of debt, credit enhancement, and liquidity facilities in a securitisation).

2.9.4 Risk weighting of assets

The other component of capital adequacy in Basel 1 concerned the calculation of the aggregate of a bank's risk weighted assets. The method for determining the risk weighting of assets under Basel 1 was fairly simple and straightforward. It involved a determination, in accordance with prescribed categories, of a set of risk factors relating to (i) the type of counterparty to a transaction which was liable to the bank for payment (or, if there was a guarantee given by an acceptable guarantor with a better counterparty risk factor, the guarantor, being the party ultimately liable and therefore the party against whom the risk of default should be assessed);

(ii) the amount of the transaction (being the total face amount of the bank's actual and potential exposure to the counterparty); and (iii) whether the transaction or position was on- or off-balance sheet (in the case of off-balance sheet transactions or positions there were credit conversion factors to achieve an equivalence to an on-balance sheet risk weighting).

2.9.4.1 Generally speaking, Basel 1 made no allowance in the risk weighting of assets for the benefit to a bank of holding security over assets or other credit risk mitigation techniques, except for guarantees given by certain types of guarantor, mortgages of residential property, security over government securities, and the benefit to a bank of legally recognised techniques of netting and set-off in its favour. As the factors relating to counterparty risk were set by a pre-ordained list depending on the type of counterparty involved, there was no possibility of varying those factors to take account of the real risk of default by a counterparty, the bank's own assessment of risk was not relevant, and there was no allowance for the consequences of a default once it had occurred. The prescribed factors also failed to take account of the different perceptions of risk that might arise as between counterparties that were in the same or in different categories; nor did they allow for changes in the perception of risk that might occur during the life of a transaction. Thus, for instance, all corporate borrowers were assessed as having the same possible risk of default, no matter how solvent or otherwise they might have been. There was no encouragement to a bank to hold better quality assets within the same category of risk-weighted assets, as it would be subject to the same risk weighting for risks associated with similar counterparties, no matter whether they were, in fact, a good or bad credit risk.

2.9.4.2 By way of example, the determination of the risk weighting of assets in typical types of banking transaction under Basel 1 was as follows:

1. 'On-balance sheet' activities.

Formula: Principal amount of the exposure × risk weighting for the counterparty (or, for mortgages of residential property or exposures secured by government or central bank securities, type of asset exposure).

E.g.

Exposures to Zone A Governments and Central Banks	0%
Exposures guaranteed by Zone A Governments and Central Banks	0%
Exposures secured by cash collateral/netted	0%
Exposures secured by Zone A Govt/CB securities	0–20%
Exposures to or guaranteed by Zone A banks	20%
Exposures to or guaranteed by Zone B banks < 1 year	20%
Exposures to financing of and secured by residential property	50%
General exposures	100%

Zone A countries: the OECD countries and one or two others (e.g. Saudi Arabia).

Note: for derivatives and similar types of risk, there were special rules.

2. Credit conversion factors (CCF) for 'off-balance sheet' risks to calculate the relevant risk weightings.

Formula: Nominal amount of facility × CCF × risk weighting for counterparty.

E.g.

100% CCF—direct credit substitutes (e.g. guarantees of indebtedness and acceptances)

50% CCF—Commitments to lend > one year, performance bonds

20% CCF—Trade related contingent items (e.g. letters of credit)

0% CCF—Commitments < one year (or cancellable at any time).

2.10 Basel 2 and the Banking Consolidation Directive

2.10.1 The three Pillars

The framework of Basel 2 is based upon three principles or 'Pillars'.

The first Pillar deals with the setting and calculation of minimum capital require-   2.10.1.1
ments, covering an evaluation of a bank's counterparty credit risks and, for the
first time, an evaluation of the operational risks in a bank's business and its
operations.

The second Pillar relates to the on-going supervisory review process of banks by   2.10.1.2
their regulators, which is relevant generally as a matter of prudential supervision
and, more specifically, in gaining approval for the use of the more sophisticated
and beneficial methods in measuring a bank's exposure risks under the Internal
Ratings Based approach, and also in relation to the advanced measurement
approach to ascertaining operational risks. In the UK, this will be reflected by, for
instance, the Supervisory Review and Assessment Process (SREP) and the
Individual Capital Adequacy Assessment Process (ICAAP).[46] The effectiveness of
these processes and the way they were carried into effect might be questioned in
light of the crisis that hit Northern Rock in the UK in the second half of 2007. The
bank had expanded its mortgage lending rapidly in the preceding period, which it
had funded largely by raising funds in the interbank and the capital markets. Both
of those sources of funding became suddenly restricted because of market conditions. One might question the wisdom of a rapid expansion of business which was
so dependent on those sources of funding, especially as there was not a commensurate expansion in the bank's deposit base, which would have been a more traditional source of funding for mortgage lending.

---

[46] See BIPRU 2.2.

2.10.1.3 The third Pillar is concerned with market discipline and public awareness through extensive public disclosure of information by banks, including information concerning a bank's capital structure and the adequacy of its capital, its credit risks, market and interest rate risks, and its operational risks. Whilst the matters that are dealt with under the second and third Pillars are of undoubted importance to banks, it is the first Pillar that is relevant in the context of capital adequacy, as discussed in this chapter.

2.10.1.4 A criticism that might be levelled at the approach taken by Basel 2 (and, indeed, of Basel 1 as well) is that because of the emphasis that it places on capital adequacy and the risks associated with asset quality, it fails to allow for a proper appreciation of another significant risk of failure that a bank may suffer due to a lack of liquidity and a failure in the continued availability of funding. Whilst that matter does fall within the considerations that should be taken into account under the second Pillar, there is no detailed treatment of the risks associated with those problems in the Basel approach. It may now be appropriate for the Basel Committee to consider if this matter should be given more attention.

2.10.1.5 As indicated at paragraph 2.2.2, it will also be necessary for greater attention to be paid to the sources of liquidity that banks obtain by selling on debt through loan sales, securitisation, and other forms of structured finance. The financial crisis in the second part of 2007 demonstrated the risks that banks face if such sources of liquidity cease to be available.

2.10.1.6 A further note of caution must be sounded. The approach to the assessment of risk under Basel 2 (and, indeed, Basel 1) proceeds on the basis of assessing risk exposures that have been incurred by a bank and commitments which a bank may have which might lead it to incur an actual exposure. More study may be needed of the risks that are associated with exposures to the secondary debt markets and structured finance schemes, via holdings of debt, investments in the schemes, and connections with the vehicles involved. It has been almost impossible to arrive at proper assessments of such exposures. It will also be necessary to assess the 'moral hazard' that banks may face in such cases, that is, where a bank is under no legal obligation to provide a facility or other accommodation but may feel itself under some moral or reputational duty to do so.

2.10.1.6.1 In the financial crisis of 2007, a number of banks found themselves facing large losses (which were difficult to quantify) through their holdings in debt instruments and investments in such schemes. They also felt themselves to be under a duty to support so-called 'structured investment vehicles', conduits, and hedge funds with which they had an association (e.g. by involvement in the establishment of the relevant vehicle or fund). When such entities ran out of funds to support the investments they had made, the banks with which they were associated felt obliged to take over the positions held by the vehicles or to provide facilities, being mindful of the damage their own reputations might suffer if the entities collapsed, as well as the overall adverse effects that such a collapse might have on the financial markets, which were already in a state of some turmoil.

2.10.2 Adoption in the EEA

The approach taken in Basel 2 has been largely adopted within the EEA by the CRD although, as previously noted, it applies (via the BCD) to all banks that are established in EEA States and not just to banks engaged in international business. In relation to the measurement of credit risks under the first Pillar, the Standardised and Foundation IRB approaches under Basel 2 (which are explained further below) were available for use by banks from the beginning of 2007, although they might be permitted to continue with the old Basel 1 regime until the beginning of 2008. The Advanced IRB approach will become available for banks who qualified to use it as from the beginning of 2008. Out of an abundance of caution, for the first three years of the use of Basel 2 in the EEA, the BCD requires that banks should maintain risk capital at not less than the following percentage levels of their previous Basel 1 capital adequacy requirements: for 2007, 95 per cent; for 2008, 90 per cent; and for 2009, 80 per cent.[47]

2.10.3 Assessment of capital and risk

In overall terms, whilst Basel 2 kept the minimum capital requirement that could be set at a percentage figure of 8 per cent and preserved the definition of capital as it had been formulated under Basel 1, Basel 2 effected substantial changes in the methods for the assessment and calculation of the credit risk associated with a bank's transactional exposures, and, in addition, it brought in a requirement for the inclusion of operational risk in the measurement of required capital (operational risk is referred to separately below). Apart from anything else, Basel 2 required that the assessment of risk would be 'dynamic', in the sense that the assessment should be continuous, so as to reflect improvements or adverse changes in the perceived risk associated with a counterparty or a transaction. Basel 2 also introduced an 'evolutionary' approach to the methods of evaluating credit risk. At its simplest or basic level, the approach to measuring risk (the Standardised Approach) would be based upon set parameters, under which transactions would, in general, be ascribed risk weightings based upon external assessments of risk relevant to the counterparty. With the permission of a bank's regulator (dependent upon a satisfactory outcome of the supervisory review process under Pillar 2),

---

[47] Art 152 of Directive 2006/48/EC.

risk assessment in a number of categories of exposures could, however, evolve to an approach based, either partly or wholly, on a bank's own assessment of risk, called the Internal Ratings Based approach (the IRB Approach).

2.10.3.1 The financial crisis in the second part of 2007 raised doubts as to the soundness of risk assessments under the Basel 2 approach, whether the assessments were based on credit ratings issued by external ratings agencies or on a bank's own internal assessments. Quite clearly, the evaluations of risk by applying either method to the preceding period had serious flaws, as evidenced by the failure to perceive the problems associated with sub-prime lending and the problems that were disguised or obfuscated by the complexities employed in structured finance transactions, as well as the difficulties in assessing the true value of investments associated with such transactions (e.g. the worth of investments held in structured investment vehicles). It may be necessary to re-consider the wisdom of the approach to risk assessment that is taken under the Basel 2 models, or, at least, it may be sensible to consider if some additional factors should be taken into account, which would allow for a greater degree of caution. What follows will address the system as represented by Basel 2, but these concerns must be borne in mind for the future.

2.10.4 It is likely that banks that are active in the capital markets will apply the IRB Approach and that relatively few banks of any size will use the Standardised Approach. Nonetheless, it is instructive to consider the Standardised Approach before moving to discuss the IRB Approach, as the Standardised Approach provides a useful introduction to the new methods of assessing credit risk.

2.11 The Standardised Approach to the Assessment of Credit Risk

2.11.1 Under the Standardised Approach,[48] there is a series of 'risk buckets' or 'credit quality steps', based largely on external assessments, for evaluating the credit risk associated with exposures to sets of stipulated counterparties and thus the appropriate risk weighting to be given to a transaction, with some additional risk categories being dealt with separately. The evaluation of risk is also subject to the use of permitted credit risk mitigation techniques that are wider in scope than had been available under Basel 1. The external assessments are those ascribed by External Credit Assessment Institutions (ECAIs) or, as an alternative in the case

---

[48] The provisions relating to the Standardised Approach will be found in Chapter 2, Section 3, Subsection 1 of and Annex VI to Directive 2006/48/EC and in BIPRU 3.

of sovereign risk, by export credit agencies. There is a separate process for recognition of ECAIs for this purpose.[49]

Put in tabular form, the Standardised Approach may be seen as follows: **2.11.2**

2.11.2.1 *Claims on sovereigns/central banks and some public sector entities (PSEs)*

Risk buckets:

AAA to AA−	A+ to A−	BBB+ to BBB−	BB+ to B−	Below B−	Unrated
0%	20%	50%	100%	150%	100%

E.g. a loan of £1m to a sovereign with an ECAI rating of AAA would attract a 0% risk weighting, so it would have no capital consequences. If, however, the sovereign was rated at below B−, the loan would attract a 150% risk weighting. Assuming the bank's capital requirement was at 8%, the loan would attract an associated capital requirement for the bank of £120,000.

Notes: An alternative to ratings for sovereigns is the risk scoring system of the export credit agencies: 1, 2, 3, 4−, 6, and 7.

PSEs may be treated as sovereigns or in a similar way to banks within national discretion.

2.11.2.2 *Claims on multilateral development banks and international organisations:*

0%

Multilateral Development Banks, e.g.: IBRD and IFC, ADB, AfDB, IADB, EIB, EBRD, NIB, CDB, and CEDB.[50]

International organisations: The EC, IMF, and BIS.[51]

2.11.2.3 *Claims on banks, some investment firms and some PSEs*

Two alternatives:

Option 1:

One risk bucket worse than ascribed to the home country of the bank

But if the home country is rated at BB+ to BB− or below, the same as for the home country and if the home country is unrated then capped at 100%.

---

[49] See Art 81 of Directive 2006/48/EC, and Part 2 of Annex VI to that Directive and, as well, in the case of the rating of positions in securitisations, Art 97 of and Part 3 of Annex IX to that Directive. See also the Capital Requirements Regs 2006 (SI 2006/3221) which give powers to the FSA to deal with approval of ECAIs. The role of the ECAIs and their methods of assessment of risk has come into question in both the EC and the USA.

[50] Respectively, the International Bank for Reconstruction and Development (the World Bank); the International Finance Corporation; the Asian Development Bank; the African Development Bank; the Inter-American Development Bank; the European Investment Bank; the European Bank for Reconstruction and Development; the Nordic Investment Bank; the Caribbean Development Bank; and the Council of Europe Development Bank.

[51] Respectively, the European Communities; the International Monetary Fund; and the Bank for International Settlements.

Option 2:

Six risk buckets based on the bank's ECAI rating with two alternative methods:

	AAA to AA–	A+ to A–	BBB+ to BBB–	BB+ to BB–	Below BB–	Unrated
Method 1: everything	20%	50%	50%	100%	150%	50%
Method 2: > 3 mths:	20%	50%	50%	100%	150%	50%
< 3 mths:	20%	20%	20%	50%	150%	20%

Notes:

A consistent approach is required within each country.

No unrated bank should be treated worse than its home country.

2.11.2.4 Claims on corporates

(unless supervisor treats all as unrated)

Five risk buckets

AAA to AA–	A+ to A–	BBB+ to BB–	Below BB–	Unrated
20%	50%	100%	150%	100% (unless the home country is worse)

2.11.2.5 Other risk categories

At 150–100%: claims over 90 days in default (net of specific provisions)

At 75%: retail exposures to individuals and small and medium-sized entities (i.e. claims, including amongst connected customers, of €1m or less, of a widely diversified nature)

At 50%: claims secured on some commercial property transactions

At 35%: claims secured on residential property

At 100%: other claims.

2.11.2.6 Off-balance sheet items

Direct credit substitutes at 100%. Otherwise generally to be at 50% or otherwise essentially the same as under Basel 1 for credit conversion factors, but a 20% CCF for exposures of under one year unless unconditionally cancellable (in which case, 0%).[52]

2.11.2.7 Others

There are special provisions for exposures in securitisation transactions (see below) and for the assessment of the exposure values of derivatives and similar instruments[53] (see below).

---

[52] See Art 78 of and Annex II to Directive 2006/48/EC and BIPRU 3.7.2.
[53] See Art 78(2) of Directive 2006/48/EC.

2.11.3 Credit risk mitigation

The subject matter of credit risk mitigation under the Standardised Approach is wider than was available under Basel 1, but the availability and applicable treatment for the various types of mitigation are subject to various requirements, as set out in the BCD,[54] including the necessity for proper documentation and procedures, the enforceability of the relevant arrangements in all relevant jurisdictions, including in the insolvency of the customer or other relevant counterparty providing the risk mitigation (backed, in some cases, by supporting legal opinions), and a low correlation of the relevant mitigation technique with the bank's customer itself. For master netting agreements within (e) below, there are specific requirements relating to termination and close-out netting and the ascertainment of a single netted amount.

In principle, claims against the following are available to be taken into account as an acceptable mitigation of risk: **2.11.3.1**

(a) Gold, cash on deposit with the bank itself, debt securities issued by central governments or central banks rated at BB+ to BB– or better, debt securities issued by banks rated at BBB+ to BBB– or better, other debt securities rated (short term) at BBB+ to BBB– or better, equities and convertible bonds which are included in a main index, some collective investment units.

(b) Equities and convertible bonds listed on a recognised exchange but not included in the main index.

(c) Guarantees issued by governments and central banks, regional governments, multilateral development banks, other international organisations with a 0 per cent risk weighting, public sector entities, banks, other corporates with a rating of A+ to A– or better.

(d) Credit derivatives by way of credit default swaps, total return swaps and credit linked notes (for the latter, to the extent they are cash funded).

(e) On-balance sheet netting restricted to claims and deposits with the bank itself and under master netting agreements.

There are two methods used for taking account of credit risk mitigation. One is the 'simple' method, which is available for the types of collateral included in (a) above. Under this method, a credit exposure should be divided into two parts. One part is that covered by the collateral, which is assigned a risk weight taking into account the market value of the collateral. A risk weight of 0 per cent is available for cash deposits, certain government securities, and transactions subject to a daily market valuation with a daily margin call. Otherwise, the risk weights are ranged from 20 per cent upwards. The other part (if any) is treated as an unsecured exposure with a risk weight normally given to such an exposure.   **2.11.3.2**

---

[54] See Arts 90–93 of Directive 2006/48/EC, and Annex VIII to that Directive, as well as BIPRU 5.

2.11.3.3 The second method for taking account of credit risk mitigation is the 'comprehensive' method under which the original risk weighting for the main counterparty is adjusted to take account of the risk mitigation technique that is used, such adjustment including 'haircuts' (negative adjustments) to take account of potential volatility and mismatches between the maturity of the underlying exposure and the maturity of the relevant risk mitigation instrument. This method must be used for each of the methods of risk mitigation other than those within (a) above.

2.12 The Internal Ratings Based Approach to the Assessment of Credit Risk

2.12.1 The IRB Approach[55] permits a bank to make its own assessment, through internal modelling, of some or all of the factors that may be relevant to assess credit risk in certain categories. A bank will only be allowed to use the IRB Approach, and to progress within it from the Foundation IRB Approach to the Advanced IRB Approach, with the permission (in the UK called a 'waiver') of its regulator, based upon demonstrating that the bank's systems for the management and rating of risk exposures are sound and implemented with integrity.[56] Permission may only be given if the bank has been using broadly equivalent risk assessment systems and methods for at least three years. Without that permission, a bank must remain using the Standardised Approach or, if it already has permission to do so, the Foundation IRB Approach. In addition, a bank may not regress to a less sophisticated approach without the permission of its regulator, although there are certain circumstances where a regulator may permit a bank to use the Standardised Approach for certain types of exposure where the bank only has a limited total number of such exposures.[57]

2.12.2 Phraseology

There are some important concepts or phrases that are relevant to the IRB Approach, the meanings of which are outlined below:

'Default': an obligor is unlikely to pay its credit obligations to the bank in full, without recourse to security (if held) or the obligor is past due by more than 90 days on any material credit obligation.

'Probability of default' (PD): the probability of default by an obligor within the ensuing 12 months.

---

[55] Set out in Chapter 2, Section 3, Subsection 2 of and Annex VII to Directive 2006/48/EC and BIPRU 4.
[56] See Art 84 of Directive 2006/48/EC.
[57] See Art 89 of Directive 2006/48/EC.

'Loss': economic loss, including material discount effects, and material direct and indirect costs associated with recovering outstanding obligations.

'Loss given default' (LGD): the ratio of the loss on an exposure due to the default of the counterparty to the outstanding amount at default.

'Exposure at default' (EAD): the amount of the total exposure that the bank expects to have to its customer at the time of default. It must therefore take account of amounts remaining available to be drawn by the customer. It can be seen that under the IRB Approach, off-balance sheet items are taken into account as part of the relevant factors in assessing likely exposure. There are conversion factors to do this.[58]

'Maturity' (M): (only relevant to the corporate class) generally speaking, the weighted average of the remaining and expected exposure of the bank to the customer over various assumed periods.

2.12.3 The approaches

Under each of the IRB Approaches, a bank will calculate its own estimate of PD for claims (including contingent claims) against certain classes of counterparties, being sovereigns, banks and investment firms, and corporates (including specialised lending linked to the financing and operation of physical assets, e.g. project, asset, commodity, and real estate finance). Under the Foundation IRB Approach, the regulator then supplies its own components for calculating LGD, EAD, and (for the corporate class of exposures) M. Under the Advanced IRB Approach, the bank uses its own determination of those additional factors. There is a common regime applicable to the assessment of credit risks for exposures to retail claims, equity claims, and other claims. There are special rules as to exposures in a securitisation (see below) and to the assessment of the exposure values of derivatives and similar instruments[59] (see below).

2.12.4 Credit risk mitigation

There is a distinction in relation to the availability and use of credit risk mitigation techniques between the Foundation IRB Approach and the Advanced IRB Approach. For the latter, most types of technique are available, which will then be taken into account by the bank in the calculation of EAD and LGD or, for guarantees and credit derivatives, PD and LGD.

2.12.4.1 For the Foundation IRB Approach, the same credit risk mitigation techniques are available (subject to the same conditions) as in the Standardised Approach, together with access to commercial receivables (which access is subject to the fulfilment of

---

58 Set out in Part 3, Annex VII to Directive 2006/48/EC.
59 See point 5 of Part 3 of Annex VII to Directive 2006/48/EC.

certain conditions, including that the receivables have a maturity of one year or less, that they are not within a securitised portfolio or the subject of a credit derivative and that they are not owed by a person which is affiliated to the bank's customer) and other types of liquid and readily marketable physical collateral, such as commodities. Only the comprehensive method (as mentioned above) is available to take the relevant risk mitigation technique into account. The regulator then assigns specific LGD percentages that must be met; for instance, that the value of the collateral exceeds a minimum percentage of the total exposure (including the unsecured portion of such exposure) to which it relates and that the collateral must exceed a percentage of the exposure against which it is effectively held.

2.12.4.2 By way of example:

Type of collateral	Minimum percentage of total exposure	Minimum percentage of excess over exposure effectively secured
Residential real estate	30%	140%
Receivables	0%	125%
Other physical collateral	30%	140%

2.13 Capital Requirements for Market Risk

2.13.1 In 1995, the Basel Committee published the *Market Risk* amendment to Basel 1, which was intended to incorporate capital requirements for the market risk associated with the trading book and banking book activities of banks; essentially, the market risk attached to marketable equity and debt instruments and foreign exchange and commodity positions held by banks. This was because of the risk of loss to a bank arising from a fall in the market prices for such holdings. Within the EC, the requirements were laid down by two Capital Adequacy Directives.[60] The capital requirement applied to all positions in a bank's trading book and its commodity and foreign exchange positions in its banking book, as well as its merchant banking investments, equity stakes in hedge funds, and real estate holdings. The trading book comprises all positions in financial instruments, foreign exchange, and commodities held either with trading intent or in order to hedge other trading book positions.

2.13.2 In a way that foreshadowed the alternative approaches that would become available under Basel 2 in calculating credit risk for capital adequacy purposes, a bank was required to calculate its Position Risk Requirement (PRR) for such positions. There were three possible approaches in doing this, the second and third of which would only be available with the regulator's approval. First, by the use of a set of

---

[60] 93/6/EC OJ L141/1 11/6/1993 and 98/31/EC.

standard rules, using a building block approach (based upon a sensitivity analysis) for assessing market risk and specific position related risk. Secondly, by use of the so-called 'CAD 1' model, to calculate all or part of the PRR, based on a set of models specified by the regulator. This allowed for a more sophisticated capital treatment for options and interest rate aggregation. Thirdly, under the 'CAD 2' model, using a bank's internal value at risk (VAR) models, which employed on a daily basis statistical measures to predict ranges in the movements of profit and loss in positions and associated confidence levels.

The capital requirements for market risk broadly continued to apply in the EC 2.13.3 and EEA after the adoption of Basel 2 and, for the UK, are to be found in BIPRU 7, 13, and 14.

2.14 Credit Risks Associated with Derivative Instruments, Repo Transactions, Securities and Commodities Lending/ Borrowing, Long Settlement, and Margin Lending

There are special rules for the assessment of credit risks for exposures of a bank to 2.14.1 counterparties in these types of transactions, which are contained in Annex III to the BCD and in BIPRU 13 and 14 (for trading book positions). There are alternative methods to determine the exposure value and counterparty credit risks of an outstanding instrument, with certain criteria applicable to their use. The methods are the mark-to-market method, the standardised method, and the internal model method, after taking into account the effect of netting.[61] There are further rules where a credit derivative hedges an exposure.[62] The value of an exposure to a clearing house or other central counterparty may be set at zero where that counterparty fully collateralises its arrangements with its participants on a daily basis.[63] The rules involve the application of mathematical formulae that are beyond the abilities of the writer, so they will be discussed very briefly.

Under the mark-to-market method, risk weighting is calculated by obtaining the 2.14.2 current replacement cost of a contract (if positive), to which a stipulated adjustment is made for potential future credit exposure. Under the standardised method, a set of tabulated calculations is made that relate to types of transaction or instrument, risk positions, exposures, notional values, and payment obligations. Under the internal model method, a bank will use its own internal models to calculate the exposure value for counterparty credit risk in a transaction.

---

[61] BIPRU 13.3.8. See also BIPRU 13.4.16–13.4.19.
[62] BIPRU 13.3.14.
[63] BIPRU 13.12 and 13.3.13.

2.15 Credit Risks Associated with Securitisations

2.15.1 There are special rules for the assessment of credit risks for exposures of banks that are associated with a securitisation, which are to be found in Articles 94 to 101 of, and Annex IX to, the BCD.[64] Those rules displace the rules that might otherwise apply for the determination of such credit risks[65] but a bank will be entitled to take into account the benefit of credit risk mitigation techniques for such exposures.[66] The rules relate both to the effect of a transfer of the risks associated with the underlying pool or portfolio of receivables by an originator into a securitisation and the assessment of the exposures of banks that have positions in the securitisation, such as by holding debt instruments issued by the securitisation vehicle or by extending credit enhancement[67] or liquidity facilities to it.[68] However, exposures arising from derivatives and similar instruments should be assessed in accordance with the special rules referred to above.

2.15.2 Traditional securitisations

An originator bank (that is, a bank which incepted the underlying pool of receivables that are to be the subject of a securitisation or which purchased them for that purpose[69]) that transfers the significant credit risk associated with a portfolio of receivables via a 'traditional securitisation' may treat the transfer as relieving it of that risk and hence it may exclude the exposures associated with the receivables

---

[64] See also BIPRU 9.

[65] Art 94 of Directive 2006/48/EC.

[66] Art 96(3) of Directive 2006/48/EC.

[67] Defined in Art 4(43) of Directive 2006/48/EC.

[68] Before the application of the BCD in the UK, the position in the UK was governed by the chapter (SE) on *Securitisation and Asset Transfers* in the part of the FSA's Handbook containing the *Interim Prudential Sourcebook for Banks*. That chapter set down rules addressing the requirements that had to be met before an asset transfer by a bank or a securitisation by a bank could be treated as effectively removing the underlying assets from the bank's exposures in calculating its risk-weighted capital requirements and its large exposures positions. One significant difference between that chapter and the BCD and BIPRU 9 is that the chapter in the *Interim Prudential Sourcebook for Banks* applied to both single transfers and transfers of whole portfolios into a securitisation, whereas the BCD and BIPRU 9 are only addressed to securitisations. A second important difference is that the BCD and BIPRU 9 also address the assessment of risk weightings for any bank, whether an originator or not, which has a securitisation position, that is, an exposure relating to the securitisation and the securitised assets, such as by holding securities issued by the securitisation vehicle or by providing credit enhancement or a liquidity facility. GENPRU 1.3.4 and 1.3.6 address the approach that should be taken in assessing the consequences to a transferor bank of a transfer of a single asset. The effect of the transfer should be assessed in the same way as would be used under normal accounting requirements in determining if the transfer had resulted in the underlying asset being derecognised in the transferor's balance sheet, so that the transferor bank should only treat the asset as removed from its risk weighted exposures if the transfer would result in a derecognition of the exposure from its balance sheet.

[69] An 'originator' is defined in Art 4(41) of Directive 2006/48/EC.

from its risk asset weighting requirements. A traditional securitisation[70] is one where the originator bank has, by a transfer of ownership or by a sub-participation, transferred the receivables from an economic standpoint to a special purpose vehicle (called a 'securitisation special purpose entity' or SSPE) and under which the SSPE issues securities which do not represent payment obligations of the originator bank. The SSPE must be established for and limited to carrying on one or more securitisations, its obligations must be isolated from those of the originator bank, and the holders of the beneficial interests in it must have the right to pledge or exchange those interests without restriction.[71]

It should be noted that the requirements under Basel 2 and the BCD for recogni- **2.15.2.1** tion of the effectiveness of a transfer within a securitisation are not expressed in the same way as are the requirements under IAS 39 to achieve derecognition in a balance sheet for accounting purposes. It is possible, therefore, that an originator bank may be successful in removing the risk of its exposure to the underlying pool of receivables for the purposes of achieving a nil risk asset weighting under Basel 2 and the BCD, but find that it has not been successful in having those exposures removed from its balance sheet for accounting purposes, and vice versa.

A traditional securitisation will be regarded as having effected a transfer of **2.15.2.2** the significant credit risk of an originator bank associated with the underlying pool of receivables for risk asset weighting purposes if it meets the following criteria:[72]

(a) The documentation for the securitisation must reflect the economic substance of the transaction.

(b) The transfer must effect a complete divestment of the originator bank's interest in the receivables, such that they are put beyond the reach of the originator bank and its creditors, including in its insolvency. This must be supported by a legal opinion from duly qualified lawyers.

(c) The securities that are issued by the SSPE must not represent payment obligations of the originator bank.

(d) The transferee must be an SSPE.

(e) The originator bank must not retain direct or indirect control over the receivables. It will be considered to have retained such control if it has the right to repurchase the receivables so as to realise their benefits or if it is obliged to re-assume the transferred risk. It is provided, however, that the performance of a servicing function by the originator bank will not of itself constitute indirect control over the receivables. As there is a separate reference

---

[70] Defined in Art 4(37) of Directive 2006/48/EC.
[71] See the definition in Art 4(44) of Directive 2006/48/EC.
[72] As set out in Part 2 of Annex IX to Directive 2006/48/EC.

(mentioned below) to the possibility that the originator bank may have an option to make a clean-up call, it must be assumed that the presence of such an option would not be considered as a method of retaining control of the portfolio.

(f) A clean-up call option must only be exercisable at the discretion of the originator bank, it may only be exercised if 10 per cent or less of the original value of the transferred receivables remains outstanding, and it may not be structured to avoid allocating losses to credit enhancement positions or other positions held by investors; nor may it be structured to provide credit enhancement.

(g) The securitisation documentation may not contain provisions which have the effect of requiring (i) the originator bank to improve other parties' positions in the securitisation (other than in the case of an early amortisation), such as by altering the underlying credit exposures or increasing the yield payable to investors if there is a deterioration in the credit quality of securitised exposures, nor (ii) of increasing the yield payable to holders of positions in the securitisation in response to a deterioration in the credit quality of the underlying pool of receivables.

2.15.3 Synthetic securitisations

An originator bank (the same definition applies to 'originator bank' as for a traditional securitisation) which transfers the significant credit risk associated with a portfolio of receivables via a 'synthetic securitisation' will be treated as having a securitisation exposure position calculated by taking into account the protection it receives from credit derivatives and guarantees granted to it in the securitisation, whether that protection is funded (i.e. backed by assets or cash or which can be netted[73]) or, subject as mentioned below, unfunded (i.e. merely contractual, such as under a guarantee or an unsecured derivative instrument[74]). Such position will be risk weighted in accordance with the risk weighting for securitisation positions as set out in Annex IX to the BCD. A synthetic securitisation is defined as being a securitisation where the transfer of risk is achieved by the use of credit derivatives or guarantees but where the pool of receivables remains on the balance sheet of the originator bank.[75]

2.15.3.1 A synthetic securitisation will be regarded, from a regulatory point of view, as having transferred the significant credit risk of an originator bank associated with a portfolio of receivables if it meets the following requirements:

(a) The documentation for the securitisation must reflect the economic substance of the transaction.

---

73 See the definition in Art 4(31) of Directive 2006/48/EC.
74 See the definition in Art 4(32) of Directive 2006/48/EC.
75 Art 4(40) of Directive 2006/48/EC.

(b) The credit protection by which the risk is transferred meets the eligibility and other requirements under the BCD for credit risk mitigation techniques (see above). For this purpose, a special purpose vehicle will be regarded as ineligible to provide unfunded credit protection (e.g. an SSPE in a securitisation cannot simply provide to the originator bank an unfunded credit derivative or guarantee).

(c) The instruments by which the credit protection is provided must not contain provisions which (i) impose significant materiality thresholds before the protection is triggered if a credit event occurs, (ii) allow for the termination of the protection if there is a deterioration of the credit quality in the underlying portfolio of receivables, (iii) (other than in the case of early amortisation) require positions in the securitisation to be improved by the originator bank, or (iv) impose an increase in the cost of the protection or in the yield payable to holders of positions in the securitisation in consequence of a deterioration in the credit quality of the underlying portfolio of receivables.

(d) A legal opinion must be obtained from duly qualified lawyers confirming the enforceability of the credit protection in all relevant jurisdictions (e.g. including that of the provider of the protection).

2.15.4 Failure by the originator to meet the requirements

If the originator bank fails to meet the requirements to achieve regulatory recognition of the securitisation as set out above, it must continue to risk weight in full its exposures to the underlying pool of receivables, but it need not separately or additionally risk weight any other exposures that it may have in the securitisation.[76] An originator bank which does achieve regulatory recognition of the effect of the securitisation must not (with a view to reducing potential or actual losses to the investors in the securitisation) provide any support to the securitisation beyond its contractual obligations in the transfer. A transgression of the prohibition has severe consequences as, if it does provide such support, an originator bank will retain or re-acquire the full risk weighting for the receivables and it must make a public disclosure of the fact that it has done so and of the associated regulatory impact to it.[77]

2.15.5 Revolving exposures

Where there is a securitisation of revolving exposures (e.g. credit card receivables) which is subject to a provision providing for early amortisation by the originator bank (i.e. which requires early redemption of the securities issued in the securitisation

---

[76] Art 95 of Directive 2006/48/EC.
[77] Art 101 of Directive 2006/48/EC.

on the occurrence of defined events) an additional risk weighted exposure amount must be calculated to take account of the increased credit risk to which the originator bank is exposed because of the risk of the occurrence of the defined events.[78] The additional requirements are set out in Sub-parts 2.5 and 3.7 of Annex IX to the BCD. They do not apply for events that are unrelated to the performance of the securitised assets or the originator bank, such as changes in tax law.[79]

2.15.6 Securitisation positions

Article 94 of the BCD requires that for its 'securitisation positions', a bank must calculate its risk-weighted exposure amounts in accordance with the provisions of Annex IX to the BCD, rather than in accordance with the ordinary rules under the Standardised or IRB Approaches. A securitisation position is any exposure that a bank may have in a securitisation,[80] such as that of an originator bank under a synthetic securitisation with respect to the protection it receives from credit derivatives and guarantees granted to it in the securitisation; an originator bank which has a first or some other junior loss position in the tranches of debt securities issued in a securitisation; a sponsor which establishes an asset backed programme or securitisation scheme; or a bank which has provided credit enhancement or a liquidity facility.

2.15.6.1 Annex IX provides different rules for calculating risk-weighted exposures depending upon whether it is a bank which normally uses the Standardised Approach or which normally uses the IRB Approach. Nonetheless, there are some general rules that apply whichever approach a bank normally uses. First, the exposure value of a securitisation position arising from a derivative instrument is to be determined in accordance with Annex III to the BCD, which applies generally to banks using either the Standardised Approach or the IRB Approach.[81] Secondly, where a securitisation position is subject to funded credit protection (i.e. backed by assets or cash or which can be netted[82]), the exposure value of that position may be modified in accordance with the rules for credit risk mitigation under Annex VIII to the BCD.[83] In the case of banks which normally use the IRB Approach, this benefit is extended to some unfunded credit protection as well.[84] Thirdly, if a bank has overlapping positions in a securitisation (i.e. they represent an exposure to the same risk so that there is really a single exposure) then, to the extent of the overlap,

---

[78] Art 100 of Directive 2006/48/EC.
[79] Point 21 of Part 4 of Annex IX to Directive 2006/48/EC.
[80] Art 4(40) of Directive 2006/48/EC.
[81] Point 3 of Part 4 of Annex IX to Directive 2006/48/EC.
[82] See the definition in Art 4(31) of Directive 2006/48/EC.
[83] Point 4 of Part 4 of Annex IX to Directive 2006/48/EC.
[84] Point 61 of Part 4 of Annex IX to Directive 2006/48/EC.

the position will be assessed singly by reference to the higher of the risk-weighted exposure amounts for those positions.[85]

For a bank which normally uses the Standardised Approach, if the securitisation position is rated by an ECAI, its risk weighting will be as follows:

2.15.6.2

Short-term credit assessments:

AAA to AA–	A+ to A–	BBB+ to BBB–	Others
20%	50%	100%	1,250%

Other credit assessments:

AAA to AA–	A+ to A–	BBB+ to BBB–	BB+ to B–	Below B–
20%	50%	100%	350%	1,250%

If a position is unrated: 1,250%.

As an alternative to a weight of 1,250%, a bank may deduct the exposure from its capital, in accordance with Article 66(2) of the BCD.

For originator banks and sponsors: an alternative is permitted, by which the same risk weighting is used as would have applied had the positions not been securitised.

For unrated liquidity facilities (subject to conditions): 20% for a facility of one year or less and 50% for the remainder. Further provisions apply to liquidity facilities that may only be drawn in the event of a general market disruption and for cash advance facilities.[86]

There are special requirements for revolving exposures with early amortisation provisions.

For a bank which normally uses the IRB Approach, there is a hierarchy of methods that may be used to assess the risk weightings of securitised positions. One is a Ratings Based Approach, which should be used where the relevant securitisation position has an external rating given to it by an ECAI or an equivalent to a rating can be inferred from the fact that the position ranks ahead of a rated position.[87] Under this method, an exposure will be given a risk weighting which depends upon a combination of the relevant external rating of the position (or that from which it is inferred), the ranking of the exposure, and the number of receivables that comprise the pool that has been securitised. For unrated positions, there is a Supervisory Formula Method, which uses special formulas for securitisation positions.[88] Except for originator banks and sponsors, the use of this method is subject to regulatory approval.[89] There is also, with permission, an internal ratings capital

2.15.6.3

---

[85] Point 5 of Part 4 of Annex IX to Directive 2006/48/EC.
[86] Points 14 and 15 of Part 4 of Annex IX to Directive 2006/48/EC.
[87] Point 38 of Part 4 of Annex IX to Directive 2006/48/EC.
[88] Point 39 of Part 4 of Annex IX to Directive 2006/48/EC.
[89] Point 40 of Part 4 of Annex IX to Directive 2006/48/EC.

calculation method known as the Internal Assessments Approach for use in relation to unrated positions in asset-backed commercial paper programmes.[90] In substitution to the foregoing, an originator bank is permitted to ascribe the risk weighting to its securitisation positions on the same basis as if it had not securitised the receivables.[91]

2.16 Operational Risk

2.16.1 As previously mentioned, Basel 2 introduced the additional requirement for inclusion of operational risk in the measurement of required capital.[92] Operational risk is defined as 'the risk of loss resulting from inadequate or failed internal processes, people and systems or from external events, and includes legal risk'.[93] It does not include strategic or reputational risk. There are three possible methods to the measurement of operational risk, as follows.

2.16.2 First method

The first method is the Basic Indicator Approach, under which the capital requirement is assessed as 15 per cent of the average of a bank's banking book income (both from interest and other sources and before deducting provisions and operating expenses, but excluding income from extraordinary items and income derived from insurance) over a period of three years.

2.16.3 Second method

The second method is the Standardised Approach, under which the capital requirement is the sum of the different capital requirements for various business lines of the bank (by use of varying percentages, depending upon the nature of the relevant business line and ranging from 12 per cent to 18 per cent), each taken as the average over three years. The Standardised Approach is subject to the bank meeting certain criteria and is only available to a bank whose activities are overwhelmingly concentrated in retail or commercial banking activities, or a combination thereof.

2.16.4 Third method

The third method, which only became available as from 1 January 2008, is to use the Advanced Measurement Approach, based upon a bank's own internal assessment

---

[90] Points 29, 43, and 44 of Part 4 of Annex IX to Directive 2006/48/EC.
[91] Point 45 of Part 4 of Annex IX to Directive 2006/48/EC.
[92] Operational risk is dealt with in Section 4 of Directive 2006/48/EC (Arts 102–105) and in Annex X to that Directive. See also BIPRU 6.
[93] Art 4(22) of Directive 2006/48/EC.

of operational risk. Its use is subject to prior approval of the regulator, which will only be granted if a set of qualitative and quantitative criteria are met by the bank.

2.17 Large Exposures

Whilst it is separate from the concept of capital adequacy, the subject of large **2.17.1** exposures is an important part of banking regulation and is dealt with under the BCD, so it is relevant to mention it here. The requirements as to large exposures (or 'concentration risks') reflect a concern that a bank's business should be widely dispersed and so should not be concentrated in a small number of customers (including their connected entities). If such concentrations were permitted then a bank might be at a disproportionate degree of risk from the failure of any one customer to meet its obligations to the bank. In colloquial terms, the policy is aimed at preventing a bank from having too many eggs in one basket. The requirements (which were previously laid down by earlier EC legislation) now spring from Section 5 of the BCD, which covers Articles 106 to 119 and Annex VI to the BCD, and are reflected in BIPRU 10.

2.17.2 The requirements

In outline, the large exposure requirements are as follows:

(a) any large exposure of a Bank must be reported to the bank's regulator;[94]
(b) a bank may not incur an exposure to a customer or group of connected customers which exceeds 25 per cent of the bank's regulatory capital;[95] and
(c) a bank may not incur large exposures which in aggregate amount exceed 800 per cent of its regulatory capital.[96]

2.17.3 Definition

A large exposure is defined as a situation where a bank's exposure to a customer or a group of connected customers is equal to or exceeds 10 per cent of the bank's regulatory capital.[97] An exposure includes on-balance sheet claims in both the banking and the trading books, guarantees and other contingent claims in the banking book, and undrawn facilities in the banking book.[98] For the purpose of

---

[94] Art 110 of Directive 2006/48/EC.
[95] Art 111(1) of Directive 2006/48/EC.
[96] Art 111(3) of Directive 2006/48/EC.
[97] Art 108 of Directive 2006/48/EC. Regulatory capital for these purposes is essentially Tier 1 and Tier 2 capital (after deductions), with some allowance for Tier 3 capital for trading book limits: see BIPRU 10.5.3–10.5.5.
[98] Art 106 of Directive 2006/48/EC, by reference to Arts 78 et seq of that Directive.

calculating exposures, risk weights are not applied, so that the exposure is measured as the gross amount although, for derivatives contracts, the exposure is assessed as a credit equivalent amount, calculated by the replacement cost method.

2.17.4 Exemptions

Certain exemptions (within limits) are allowed in calculating exposures. They include claims on governments, central banks, international organisations and multilateral development banks, claims on banks and investment firms of one year or less, claims secured by cash deposited with, or CDs issued by, the bank, exposures guaranteed by a bank's parent or where the parent gives an undertaking to increase the bank's capital to cover the exposure, exposures secured by certain types of collateral within accepted credit risk mitigation techniques, mortgages on residential property, and 50 per cent of the value of certain mortgages of commercial property.[99] There is also an exemption for exposures to entities within the same integrated UK group as the bank, where the exposure requirements are judged in relation to the consolidated capital of the group and the consolidated exposures of the group to external customers of the UK group's members.[100] If the last mentioned exemption does not apply, there are special rules as to the position where the bank is a member of a wider group.

2.18 Liquidity

2.18.1 Liquidity is also a subject that falls within the broader spectrum of banking regulation and should be mentioned because of its relevance to the context of the matters under discussion. It is an area of national regulatory competence rather than falling within the Basel requirements or the BCD. As previously remarked, this may be a deficiency in the Basel system, which concentrates on the risk to banks that might result from a decline in asset values and an inadequacy of capital, without giving equal prominence to the risk that might arise because of a deficiency in liquidity and adequate cash resources. At present, it is a matter for national regulators to decide on what liquidity policies should be adopted with respect to the banks that they regulate. In light of the difficulties that were experienced in the interbank and capital markets in the second half of 2007, it might be time for the Basel Committee to consider this issue, with a view to establishing a set of uniform minimum rules for the proper measurement and maintenance of liquidity and access to cash resources.

---

[99] Art 113 of Directive 2006/48/EC. See also BIPRU 10.6.
[100] BIPRU 10.8.

There are two sets of liquidity requirements in the UK that relate to banks. The **2.18.2** first and principal set of obligations are the prudential requirements that are imposed by the FSA. The second set of obligations (which may be seen more as a fee mechanism) are the requirements which relate to the maintenance of liquidity and reserves and they are imposed by the Bank of England.

2.18.2.1 The FSA's requirements

The FSA's requirements[101] are both qualitative and quantitative, and they apply to UK banks, as well as the UK branches of EEA[102] and other foreign banks. The qualitative aspect of the requirements is to the effect that a bank should have a prudent liquidity policy and adequate systems and controls to manage liquidity risks. There are two different approaches to the quantitative aspect of the require-ments. For most banks, the requirements involve the setting of mismatch limits on projected cash flows over the future. This involves a measurement of the difference (or mismatch) between expected inflows and outflows of cash in various time bands (i.e. deducting outflows from inflows). The measurements are taken on a net cumu-lative basis, as a percentage of total deposit liabilities, with limits being set for the maximum mismatch percentages. Those limits will vary according to the circum-stances of an individual bank. For banks with a large retail deposit base, the other approach to the requirements will apply, based on an assessment of sterling stock liquidity. Under this approach, a bank should hold a sufficient reserve of high quality liquid assets (e.g. cash, gilts, and EC or EEA government/central bank instru-ments) which is sufficient to service the bank's anticipated obligations for five work-ing days without the need to renew maturing wholesale sterling funding and on the assumption that it will suffer a net reduction of 5 per cent of its retail deposits.

2.18.2.2 The Bank of England's requirements

The Bank of England's requirements are imposed pursuant to section 6 of and Schedule 2 to the Bank of England Act 1998 and statutory instruments made thereunder.[103] A bank to which the requirements relate (i.e. a UK bank or build-ing society and the UK branches of EEA and other foreign banks) is required to place non-interest bearing cash ratio deposits with the Bank of England, calcu-lated as a percentage of the amount of the bank's 'eligible liabilities' (i.e. its sterling interbank and deposit based funding). In addition, the Bank of England reserves the right, which is currently not imposed, to require particular banks to meet

---

101 Which are to be found in Chapters entitled 'Mismatch Liquidity' and 'Sterling Stock Liquidity' in the *Interim Prudential Sourcebook for Banks* contained in the FSA's Handbook.

102 Recital 21 to and Art 41 of Directive 2006/48/EC recognise the right of the UK, as the host state, to impose liquidity requirements on the UK branches of banks established in other EEA States.

103 Currently SIs 1998/1130 and 2004/1270.

additional requirements to place special deposits and to meet further liquidity requirements. At the beginning of 2008 the amount of cash-ratio deposits that a bank must make was calculated at zero on the first £500 million of eligible liabilities and 0.15 per cent of the amount of eligible liabilities above £500 million. In August 2007, HM Treasury published a proposal that the ratio should be reduced from 0.15 per cent to 0.11 per cent.[104]

2.19 Consolidated Supervision

2.19.1 Consolidated supervision involves an evaluation of the strengths and weaknesses of a group in which a bank is a member and relates to both capital adequacy and large exposures. Consolidated supervision is thought to be desirable because of the perceived risks to a bank that may arise from its membership of the group. Those risks include the possibility that ventures undertaken by other members of the group could undermine the bank and the group as a whole, that the bank may be exposed to the risk of default by other group members in the performance of obligations they owe to it, such as through defaulting in repayment of intra-group lending, and the more general risk to a bank's reputation by its association with the group and its other members.

2.19.2 The requirement for consolidated supervision is likely to arise where a bank is a parent undertaking or a subsidiary undertaking[105] in relation to other entities and, either alternatively or in addition, where the bank or another member of the group holds a 'participation' in another entity (i.e. an interest of 20 per cent or more of its share capital or the control of a similar percentage of the voting rights of its members). Each of those matters must be judged by taking into account both direct and indirect holdings, including holdings that may be held by an intermediate entity which would have been a member of the group save for the fact that it falls outside the description of the types of entity that must be included in the consolidation. Save in the case of 'solo consolidation' (which is discussed separately below), consolidated supervision is additional to the supervisory requirements relating to the bank itself. In overall effect, this means that the requirements relating to capital adequacy and large exposures will be assessed (using the same capital adequacy ratio that is set for the bank and treating the consolidated group as one entity in assessing exposures to third parties) at both the group level and at the individual level of the bank. The requirements for consolidated supervision

---

[104] Consultation Paper, *Review of the Cash Ratio Deposit Scheme* (ISBN 978-84532-326-4). This has since been effected pursuant to the Cash Ratio Deposits (Value Bands and Ratios) Order 2008 (SI 2008/1344), which came into force on 2 June 2008.

[105] The meaning of the expressions 'parent undertaking' and 'subsidiary undertaking' is the same as those found in s 1162 of the Companies Act 2006.

spring from Articles 71, 73, 125, 126, 127, 133, and 134 of the BCD, which are implemented in the UK by BIPRU 8.

The requirements for consolidated supervision under BIPRU 8 apply where a **2.19.3** bank that is established in the UK is a member of a 'UK consolidation group' or where, additionally, it is a member of a 'non-EEA sub-group'. The consolidation (or sub-consolidation in the case of a non-EEA sub-group) is made by reference to the whole of the relevant group or sub-group (excepting entities whose activities fall outside the relevant categories). Neither concept is easily explained, and what follows below contains an attempt to provide a rather basic simplification.[106] It should be noted that a UK bank may fall within a consolidation group that is supervised in another EEA Member State,[107] and this may be in addition to being a member of a consolidated group or sub-group under UK requirements. To the extent that one UK consolidation group forms part of a larger UK consolidation group, the smaller group is eliminated.[108] A little differently, if a larger non-EEA sub-group contains the same (and no other) non-EEA members as a smaller non-EEA sub-group, the smaller group is eliminated,[109] but such elimination cannot occur if there is not that precise matching of non-EEA members.[110] It is possible that a bank may find itself in both a UK consolidation group and an identical non-EEA sub-group. Technically speaking, it would have to comply with the consolidated supervision requirements for both groups but, in practice, it is unlikely that this would result in any greater burden.[111]

2.19.4 A UK consolidation group

A UK consolidation group will arise in the following circumstances:[112]

(1) Where a UK bank is a parent undertaking in relation to one or more other 'relevant entities' (for the purposes of this chapter being as defined below) or if it holds a participating interest in one or more such relevant entities (a 'participant') and irrespective of whether the bank is itself a subsidiary undertaking of another entity. In such a case, the UK consolidation group will comprise the UK bank and each relevant entity that is its subsidiary undertaking or participant

---

[106] A useful set of diagrammatic examples is given in BIPRU 8 Annex 2 (for determining a UK consolidation group) and Annex 3 (for determining a non-EEA sub-group).

[107] For instance, where the UK bank is a subsidiary undertaking of a bank established in another EEA Member State or where it has a fellow subsidiary undertaking that is a bank in another Member State and each of them is a subsidiary of a financial holding company established in that other Member State (see Arts 125(1), 125(2), and 126(1)(1) of Directive 2006/48/EC).

[108] BIPRU 8.2.5.

[109] BIPRU 8.3.18.

[110] BIPRU 8.3.21.

[111] BIPRU 8.3.22 and 8.3.23.

[112] This is derived from Arts 125 and 126 of Directive 2006/48/EC.

(wherever established), together with any 'financial holding company' (i.e. not a bank, whose subsidiaries are wholly or mainly banks or are engaged in banking and finance or investment types of activities) of the UK bank if that holding company is established in the UK or another EEA Member State.

(2) Where a UK bank has no relevant entities that are subsidiary undertakings or participants of it but it is a subsidiary undertaking of a financial holding company incorporated in the UK or another EEA Member State and either there are no other banks or investment firms being subsidiary undertakings or participants of that holding company incorporated in another Member State or, if there are such subsidiary undertakings or participants, none of them is incorporated in the same State as the holding company and the UK bank has the largest balance sheet. In such a case, the UK consolidation group will comprise the holding company, the UK bank and the other subsidiary undertakings, and participants of the holding company that are relevant entities.

(3) Where a UK bank has no relevant entities that are subsidiary undertakings or participants of it, but it is a subsidiary undertaking of an intermediate financial holding company incorporated in the UK or another EEA Member State and there are one or more other intermediate financial holding companies established in other EEA Member States with subsidiary undertakings or participants that are banks or investment firms which are established in the same States, and the UK bank has the largest balance sheet. In such a case, the UK consolidation group will comprise the UK bank, each of the intermediate financial holding companies and their subsidiary undertakings, and participants that are relevant entities.

2.19.4.1 It is not every entity within a group that must be taken into account for inclusion in a UK consolidated group. In essence, the consolidation will include the following types of entities, which are ascertained by reference to their activities[113] (for ease of reference, referred to herein as 'relevant entities'): financial holding companies of a bank that are established within the UK or another EEA Member State (i.e. holding companies established in an EEA Member State whose subsidiary undertakings include at least one bank established in a Member State); banks; investment firms; entities that engage in other types of banking and financial activities (such as lending money, the provision of credit or other financial facilities, equipment leasing and receivables purchase facilities, money broking and transmission, and derivatives and foreign exchange trading); entities which carry on the activity of asset management; and subsidiary entities which provide ancillary services to a bank. A significant omission from the list is insurers.[114] It should be

---

[113] BIPRU 8.5.

[114] This follows the approach taken by Basel 2: see para 24 (and n 5) in Part 1, 'Scope of Application' in *International Convergence of Capital Standards—A Revised Framework*.

noted that an entity which falls within the list and which is a subsidiary undertaking within the overall group or in which a participating interest is held by a member of the group but whose shares (or such a participation) are held by a company that is not in the list, will still fall within the consolidation.[115]

2.19.5 A non-EEA sub-group

A non-EEA sub-group[116] will arise where a UK bank (referred to hereunder as the 'UK sub-group bank'), which is a member of a UK consolidation group, is a subsidiary undertaking of another UK bank or of a financial holding company established in the UK or another EEA Member State and the UK sub-group bank or the financial holding company has one or more subsidiary undertakings or holds a participating interest in one or more entities that are established in a non-EEA Member State, being an undertaking or entity that carries on the business of banking, banking services, investment services, or asset management (referred to hereunder as a 'relevant non-EEA entity'). However, if such a non-EEA sub-group in the UK would also be a non-EEA sub-group in another EEA country and each sub-group contains only the same relevant non-EEA entities then the UK position will be eliminated if the connection between the non-EEA entities is closer to a regulated entity in that other EEA country.[117] If there is a non-EEA sub-group in the UK, it will comprise the UK sub-group bank, the financial holding company, and any subsidiary undertakings or participants of the UK sub-group bank that are relevant entities or relevant non-EEA entities.

2.19.6 The consolidation

Where consolidation is required, the bank must ensure that the capital adequacy ratio that is set for it is also met on consolidation, or sub-consolidation in the case of a non-EEA sub-group, by the relevant group. This involves determining, on the one side, the consolidated capital of the group, and, on the other side, the sum of the consolidated risk components against which the adequacy of the consolidated capital is measured. With certain adjustments and permitted variations, the consolidation of capital[118] is achieved by a consolidation in full[119] of the capital of the group members to the extent that such capital would qualify, within the relevant tierings, as acceptable banking regulatory capital for capital adequacy purposes.[120] However, where only a participating interest is held in a group member, only a proportion of its capital is included, representing the extent of the participating

---

[115] BIPRU 8.5.2 and 8.5.3.
[116] BIPRU 8.3.
[117] BIPRU 8.3.24.
[118] BIPRU 8.6.
[119] BIPRU 8.5.4.
[120] BIPRU 8.6.7.

interest in relation to the whole of its issued capital.[121] With respect to the sum of the consolidated risk components, the consolidation is achieved (by either a line by line approach across the group or by first calculating the components for each member of the group and adding them together[122]) by addition of the consolidated operational risk requirement, the consolidated credit risk requirement, and the consolidated market risk requirement of the group members.[123] Intra-group transactions may be excluded.[124] There are provisions for using risk components for other EEA and non-EEA regulators, provided (in the case of the latter) that the components set by the relevant regulators meet acceptable criteria.[125]

2.19.7 Large exposures

Similarly, a bank must ensure that the large exposure requirements ('concentration risk requirements') are applied on a consolidated basis as if the UK consolidated group or the non-EEA sub-group were a single undertaking.[126] There are special provisions as to the treatment of exposures that are within an integrated group.

2.20 Solo Consolidation

2.20.1   Where permission is given by the FSA (a 'solo consolidation waiver'),[127] solo consolidation[128] permits a bank to treat itself and certain of its subsidiaries as if they were one entity for on-going capital adequacy and large exposures purposes,[129] so that the bank does not report its own individual position separately from the consolidated position for it and such subsidiaries. In essence, such treatment will only be available where the bank holds at least 75 per cent of the shares and voting rights in the subsidiaries, the material exposures and liabilities of the subsidiaries are to the bank, they have such a close relationship with the bank that it would be possible to wind up each subsidiary rapidly and repatriate its capital to the bank (which must be demonstrated on an acceptable legal basis), and they are not a potential source of weakness to the bank.

---

[121] BIPRU 8.5.5 and 8.5.6.
[122] BIPRU 8.7.8.
[123] BIPRU 8.7.
[124] BIPRU 8.7.29.
[125] BIPRU 8.7.34, 8.7.35, 8.7.37, and 8.7.38.
[126] BIPRU 8.9.
[127] BIPRU 2.1.3.
[128] Which is dealt with in BIPRU 2.1, which implements Arts 70 and 118 of Directive 2006/48/EC.
[129] But not for its base capital resources requirement (i.e. its minimum initial capital for authorisation): BIPRU 2.1.15.

3

LOAN FACILITIES

3.1 Introduction

3.1.1 There are various types of loan facility that might be offered to a borrower, ranging from a bilateral facility between a single lender and a single borrower, to a facility offered by a single lender to a group of borrowers, and finally a syndicated facility between a group of lenders and one or more borrowers. Any of those facilities might be a term facility, under which the facility is granted for a definite period, or it might be an uncommitted facility (such as an overdraft facility) which could be terminated at any time. The facility might be a fixed facility, under which the moneys that have been borrowed remain outstanding until they are repaid but the repayment is final in the sense that what has been repaid cannot be re-borrowed under the facility. Alternatively, the facility may be a revolving facility under which a facility limit or ceiling is set with the borrower having the right from time to time to borrow and repay all or part of what has been borrowed but so that the aggregate outstanding amount at any one time may not exceed the limit. The classic example of a revolving facility is the overdraft facility, by which a bank permits its customer to make withdrawals that are debited to its current account (such as by drawing a cheque or by another payment instruction that the customer gives to its bank) and to which are credited any payments into the account that are made by the customer or collected on its behalf. A facility may be extended in one currency only, as a single currency facility, or it may be a multi-currency facility, under which the borrower is given a choice of the currencies in which it may borrow, with the possibility that borrowings may be outstanding at any one time in more than one currency and with the right to change between one currency and another during the period of the facility. For the purpose of setting the facility limit and for making other calculations, one currency will be specified as the base currency in a multi-currency facility.

3.1.2 This chapter concentrates on loan facilities but there are many ways of raising finance other than simply under a loan facility. In terms of banking facilities, a customer may raise finance by an acceptance credit facility, under which the bank permits the customer to draw bills of exchange (each with a fixed period to its maturity) on the bank, which the bank will accept and then discount on the customer's behalf.[1] The proceeds that are received will be passed to the customer, which has the obligation under the facility to put the bank in funds on the maturity of a bill (to the amount of the face value of the bill), so that the bank can meet its own obligations as the acceptor of the bill. The customer will often meet the obligation by drawing another bill on the bank, with the proceeds of the discounting of the new bill being used to provide the funds for payment of the old bill. In that sense, it can be seen that this is another type of revolving facility. Other banking facilities include letters of credit and bonding and guarantee issuance facilities. A customer may be offered more than one type of facility within the framework of an overall facility arrangement, which is sometimes referred to as a multi-option facility.

Outside the compass of banking facilities, funds can also be raised in various other ways, such as through the capital markets, by a bond issue,[2] or by raising capital via an issue of shares. Finance can also be raised by receivables or debt purchase facilities and through equipment finance facilities, by leasing, hire-purchase, and conditional sale. Sometimes a supplier may be prepared to extend credit by giving time to pay or, at the opposite end of the scale, a purchaser may provide credit by making an advance payment before the time at which delivery of the relevant goods or services is to be made.   **3.1.3**

This chapter discusses the structure and content of loan facility agreements. The chapter will proceed in the main by reference to bilateral loan facilities. Nonetheless, the discussion will be equally relevant to matters that are material to other types of transaction, including syndicated facilities and bond issues.   **3.1.4**

3.2 Heads of Terms

Before turning to the structure and content of loan facility agreements, it is relevant to examine the nature and legal effect, if any, of documents that might be described as 'heads of terms', 'term sheets', or 'heads of agreement'. It is not unusual in the discussions between a bank and a potential borrower that precede the granting of a facility for the bank to produce an initial document that bears one of those labels (which mean much the same thing). The bank is likely to do this once   **3.2.1**

---

[1] In the UK, if the bank is an 'eligible bank' then bills that it accepts ('eligible bills') are eligible for re-discount at the Bank of England, which means that the Bank of England will be prepared to purchase its bills, thereby giving the discount market a form of quasi-guarantee that if the bank fails before the maturity of a bill, a holder of the bill will be able to sell it to the Bank of England. There are various conditions that are imposed as to the types of bill that will qualify as eligible bills.

[2] See Chap 10.

the commercial basis of the transaction has been discussed and settled. Such a document is intended to provide, in summary form, an outline of what should be covered by the proposed facility, with the intention that a more detailed and formal document will be entered into by the parties, perhaps after further negotiation of its detailed terms. The initial document will summarise matters such as the purpose, term, nature, currency and amount of the facility, the interest rate and similar financial or commercial matters, and a summary of other provisions, such as the conditions precedent to the right to borrow, the representations and warranties to be given by the borrower, the covenants that will be undertaken by the borrower, and the events of default upon the occurrence of which the bank will have the right to call in early repayment of the facility.

3.2.2 The question may arise as to whether such a document might constitute a binding agreement in its own right.[3] If the document clearly states that it is not intended to have any binding effect then, in itself, it will not be binding, but it should be remembered that a later binding agreement, based on the provisions of the document, may be found to have come into effect if the parties have conducted themselves as if they were bound by what was contained in the document.[4] Without the expressed caveat that the document was not meant to constitute a binding agreement, the question would come down to whether the contents of the document evidenced a sufficient consensus and certainty as to the essential matters agreed between the parties as to be sufficient to constitute a binding agreement, bearing in mind that the mere fact that the parties contemplated that an initial document might subsequently be superseded by a more formal and detailed agreement will not necessarily deprive the earlier document of contractual effect and the court may be prepared to fill in the gaps by implying terms.[5]

3.2.3 Even where such a document states that it is not intended to create a binding obligation on the part of the bank to provide the facility, it may seek to impose certain subsidiary obligations that it states are to be binding. In particular, it may state that the borrower will be obliged to meet the bank's legal costs and other expenses in entering into negotiations with the borrower, in proceeding to arrange the facility, and in preparing the facility documentation, even if a facility agreement is not concluded. It may also seek to impose a confidentiality undertaking on the bank with respect to any information that was provided by the borrower to the bank. If a bank is to enforce the first of those purported obligations, it will need to show that it provided consideration in support of the borrower's agreement and some

---

[3] In this regard, see further the discussion at Chap 1.

[4] As, for instance, in *The Rugby Group Ltd v ProForce Recruit Ltd* [2005] EWHC 70 (QB) (reversed, but not on this point, at [2006] EWCA Civ 69).

[5] It is worth noting that Lloyd LJ in *Pagnan SpA v Feed Products Ltd* [1987] 2 Lloyd's Rep 601, at 619 expressly referred to 'heads of agreement' as being capable of constituting a binding contract.

element of certainty as to what was to be done; a nebulous statement of purpose on the part of the bank would not be sufficient. As to the confidentiality undertaking, the borrower should be able to argue that it reflects the position at general law[6] and thus it should be enforceable against the bank, at least to the extent that it reflects the position at general law.

3.3 The Overall Structure and Contents of a Loan Facility Agreement

On some occasions, the terms of the agreement may be set out in a facility letter, **3.3.1** which is a letter from the bank addressed to the borrower, that is accepted by the borrower by its counter-signature on a copy of the letter, which it then returns to the bank. A facility letter may be used where there is only a single bank that is providing the facility (e.g. a term loan facility, an overdraft facility, or an acceptance credit facility), but it is very unlikely that such a document would be used for any other type of facility. Even in the case of a single bank facility a more formal form of agreement may be used. Save in cases where a facility letter is used (or in the very unlikely event that the agreement will be oral or founded upon a term sheet), the agreement will be encapsulated in a formal agreement between the parties, with each party retaining a signed copy for its own purposes. There is no particular requirement as to the structure of such an agreement but, generally speaking, the pattern that is used and the order of the provisions are as follows.

In its overall structure and layout, the agreement will commence with a descrip- **3.3.2** tion of the parties, which may be followed by recitals setting out background information and that the parties have agreed to enter into the agreement so that the bank will provide the facility to the borrower, subject to the provisions contained in the agreement. Those provisions (which are described further below) will then follow. After they have been set out, the agreement may contain schedules which address various mechanical and technical matters, a list of the conditions precedent, the documentary procedures for transfer of the facility and for the addition and removal of borrowers (if that is contemplated), the forms of notices and statements that might be required of the borrower and its officers during the life of the facility, and similar matters. Finally, there will be the signature page or pages, which will be signed by the representatives of the parties to evidence their acceptance of the agreement as contained in the document.

---

[6] Either as a matter of the equitable principles relating to the receipt of confidential information (see Lord Goff in *Attorney-General v Guardian Newspapers Ltd (No 2)* [1990] 1 AC 109, at 281 to 282) or as a part of the banker's duty of confidence to its customer (*Tournier v National Provincial and Union Bank of England* [1924] 1 KB 461) but, with respect to the latter, there may be an issue as to whether the relationship of banker and customer had come into existence sufficiently for the duty to arise.

3.3.3 The list of conditions precedent will contain references to various other documents that have to be provided or entered into as part and parcel of the overall transaction. Such documentation may include, for instance, security documents and guarantees that are to be given in support of the borrower's obligations under the facility. In that sense, the conditions precedent have a structural role, as they are the means by which that additional documentation is brought into the overall compass of the transaction. Further reference will be made to conditions precedent later in this chapter.

3.3.4 By way of overview and for the purposes of explanation, the provisions within the body of the loan agreement may conveniently be described within the following broad categories, although the categories should not be seen as having any formal recognition. Many of them will be explored in further detail later in this chapter.

3.3.4.1 The first category, in terms of the usual layout of a loan agreement, contains the interpretative provisions of the agreement, relating to the definitions of expressions that are used in the agreement and matters going to its interpretation.

3.3.4.2 The next set of provisions will describe the facility and set out its purpose. In a syndicated facility, these provisions will also set out matters relating to the contractual relationship of the syndicate members as between themselves and as between themselves and the borrower, to emphasise the several nature of their rights and obligations.

3.3.4.3 The financial and operative provisions of a loan agreement include the clauses that cover the mechanics and procedures for drawing and utilisation of the facility, repayment, and interest.

3.3.4.4 Allied to those last mentioned provisions are the clauses that are designed to protect the lender's financial position and its rate of return on its financial commitment in the facility, the funds it has employed in granting the facility, and the amounts it is to receive under the facility.

3.3.4.5 The monitoring and minding provisions cover the representations and warranties that are given by the borrower to the lender to induce it to enter into and maintain the facility, as well as the covenants and undertakings by which the borrower agrees to the things it will do and those it will not do, with respect to itself, its business, assets, and affairs, during the life of the facility.

3.3.4.6 The enforcement provisions cover, principally, the events of default and the circumstances in which the lender can accelerate the borrower's obligation for repayment.

3.3.4.7 If the facility is guaranteed then the guarantee may be contained within the loan agreement (in which case the guarantor will have to be a party to the agreement) or it may be contained in a separate document.

Transfer provisions may occasionally be found in a straightforward bilateral facil- **3.3.4.8**
ity, but they are much more common in syndicated facilities. Both a bilateral
facility and a syndicated facility may contain provisions that deal with the addition and subtraction of borrowers.

The so-called 'boilerplate' provisions deal with matters such as the giving of **3.3.4.9**
notices, the effect of waivers, the effect on the remainder of the agreement if one
of its provisions is found to be unenforceable, the intention not to have a partnership, and so on. They are given that name because they appear in most types of
formal agreements and cover fairly standard matters which might otherwise burst
forth and cause a difficulty, particularly to the lender.

Finally, the law and jurisdiction clauses provide for the choice of the law which is **3.3.4.10**
to govern the agreement and the courts (or arbitral tribunal) which may hear disputes that arise under the agreement.

3.4 The Interpretative Provisions

These provisions relate to the definitions of terms that are used in the agreement **3.4.1**
and to matters going to its interpretation. There is a certain correlation between
the matters of interpretation and construction that are dealt with in these provisions and some of the boilerplate provisions that are contained later in the
agreement.

3.4.2 Definitions

The definitions clause contains those expressions which are used frequently in the
remainder of the agreement. They tend to have a technical meaning that is ascribed
in view of the purpose and commercial context of the facility and its mechanics of
operation. Using a single defined word or phrase avoids the necessity of setting out
the whole meaning each time it is needed in the remainder of the agreement. By
way of example, an expression that is frequently used in a loan facility agreement
is 'Libor', which is an abbreviation of the phrase 'London interbank offered rate'.
There is no single or universal rate as such, so the means of ascertaining the rate
for the purposes of the facility will be set out more fully in the definition of that
expression as contained in the definitions clause. Sometimes the definitions can
be extremely technical and laborious, and care needs to be taken in ensuring that
the meaning is properly understood. There is an unfortunate practice that sometimes occurs in a document, by which one or more of the definitions goes further
than simply defining a technical meaning, so that it becomes of dispositive effect.
This should be avoided, as the substance of what is agreed should be dealt with in
the main body of the agreement and not in the definitions clause.

3.4.3 Interpretation

The clause concerning interpretation deals with words and phrases that are used in general speech and which are given a meaning for the purposes of the agreement, so as to avoid possible uncertainty or confusion. The clause also gives a guide to matters going to the construction and interpretation of the agreement. In relation to fixing upon a meaning for an expression, the clause may adopt one of several possible meanings, it may choose a meaning that is set out in legislation, or it may expand upon a more restricted meaning than that which is used generally.

3.4.3.1 An example of the first type of usage concerns the concept of a month, which is usually given a precise meaning when used in a facility agreement. An example of the second of those usages would be the meanings ascribed to the words 'subsidiary', 'holding company', 'subsidiary undertaking', and 'parent undertaking', each of which is given a specific meaning in the Companies Act 2006. Those meanings are commonly adopted by facility agreements. An example of the latter usage would be the meaning given to the word 'person' which is usually defined in a facility agreement to mean not just a natural person but also a legal or other incorporated entity, a partnership and other collection of persons, or entities and States and administrative bodies. Another example will be the word 'bank', 'lender', or 'party' which will be defined to include the bank's, lender's, or party's successors and permitted assigns.

3.4.3.2 For the purpose of construing the agreement, the interpretation clause should state that clause headings that are used in the text of the document, and the index to the document, are not to be taken into account in determining the meaning of any of the provisions in the agreement.

3.5 The Description and Purpose of the Facility

3.5.1 The provisions in this section of the agreement provide an overall description of the facility and set out the purpose for which it is to be provided. The description will include the type and the amount or the limit of the facility. In a syndicated facility, these provisions will also set out matters relating to the contractual relationship of the syndicate members as between themselves and as between themselves and the borrower, to emphasise the several nature of their rights and obligations.[7]

3.5.2 In most cases, the purpose of the facility is likely to be described in general terms, such as for the provision of working capital, or for the general corporate purposes of the borrower. Sometimes the purpose may be more specific. If the purpose is

---

[7] See further Chap 9.

described with sufficient particularity and, following disbursement but prior to their use for the agreed purpose, the funds remain identifiable, the lender may be able to argue (within the applicable confines of English law) that, pending their use for the relevant purpose, the lender has the benefit of a resulting trust over the funds so that if they are not so used the lender has a proprietary claim for their return. This argument would be based upon the decision of the House of Lords in *Barclays Bank Ltd v Quistclose Investments Ltd*[8] and the line of authority which has come after it.[9] This matter is dealt with in more detail elsewhere in this book.[10]

3.6 The Financial and Operative Provisions

The financial and operative provisions of a loan agreement include the clauses that cover the mechanics and procedures for drawing and utilisation of the facility, repayment, cancellation and termination of the facility, the charging and payment of interest and fees, and the making of payments. Each of those matters will be examined. Before doing so, however, it is important to describe the sources of funding that may be available to a lending bank, as a great deal of the arrangements in a facility depend upon the relevant source of funds and the procedures or conventions that govern it. It is also important to understand the conventions that apply. Underlying this, of course, is the principle that banks borrow the funds that they then lend on to their own borrowers. Thus, a bank will be a borrower in one capacity and a lender or creditor in the other capacity. The bank makes its profit by the difference between the cost to it of borrowing funds and the return that it receives in lending the funds, always assuming that the latter is higher than the former and that the bank does not suffer excessively from defaults by its own borrowers.

3.6.1

3.6.2 Sources of funding

Traditionally, the two principal sources of funds for a bank have been retail deposits that are placed with it by its customers (in other words, which it borrows from its customers[11]) and wholesale funds that it borrows from other banks in the interbank market.[12] The crisis in the financial markets in the second part of 2007 has served to question the continued viability of the interbank market. Banks have

---

8 [1970] AC 567.

9 Particularly the decision of Lord Millett in *Twinsectra Ltd v Yardley* [2002] UKHL 12, [2002] 2 AC 164.

10 See Chap 14.

11 *Foley v Hill* (1848) 2 HLC 28.

12 Less significant sources of funding (in most cases) would be through the issuance of certificates of deposit and capital markets issues in the bond markets.

shown an unwillingness to lend to other banks for periods that previously were normal for interbank lending. Where funds have been provided, the funding has tended to be only for very short periods, such as overnight lending. This reflects widespread fears about the financial soundness, liquidity, and solvency of banks, and the uncertainty that has resulted from those fears. At the time of writing, it remained to be seen if this was only a temporary problem or if it heralded a more long-term change in the pattern of the markets and of dealings between banks. If it does signify a more permanent re-adjustment then the whole basis on which banks fund their lending activities will have to change (assuming that banks are able to find an alternative), particularly in relation to larger commercial facilities in non-domestic currencies. As it is not possible to predict where this may lead, what follows (especially as it relates to interbank funding) will describe the position as it had developed before the financial crisis occurred.

3.6.2.1.   Retail deposits are mainly denominated in the local currency of the place where they are held.[13] They tend to be held on a relatively short-term basis, often being repayable without notice at the customer's request. They normally bear interest at a rate that is referable to a domestic benchmark floating rate that is set from time to time by the bank. In the UK, such a benchmark rate for sterling is called a bank's 'base rate'. In the USA, for dollars, it is called the bank's 'prime rate'. Whilst in theory each bank sets its own base rate, in practice all the major banks in the UK set a similar rate which follows the rate set by the Bank of England. Banks tend to use such deposits to fund lending to domestic customers on a relatively short-term or immediately cancellable basis (such as under an overdraft), so that the bank may require repayment at any time. In the UK, base rate is calculated on the number of days that have elapsed in a relevant period and on a per annum basis by reference to a year of 365 or 366 days. As a facility based on retail funds is pretty much confined to the domestic context, it will not be examined further in this chapter.

3.6.2.2   For nearly every other type of loan facility, it is most likely that the facility will be predicated on wholesale funding by the bank through the interbank market. Such wholesale funding involves a bank borrowing the funds from one or more other banks in that market. The market in London is called the London interbank market and (with the exception of the European interbank market in relation to funding in euros) it is that market to which further market-based concepts of funding will refer in this chapter. The types of funds that are available in the London interbank market are not restricted to sterling but include most major currencies that are freely available and transferable, including US and Canadian dollars,

---

[13] This is not a universal rule, as deposits in foreign currencies may be held by a bank in London, as was discussed in *Libyan Arab Foreign Bank v Bankers Trust Co* [1989] QB 728.

Swiss francs, and Japanese yen. In theory, the interest rate ('Libor') that is charged to a bank when it borrows funds in the market will reflect its own credit standing. In practice, there are published composite rates (called screen rates, as they are available electronically) which reflect an average of the rates that apply for the time being in the interbank market, from which the calculation of Libor is usually derived for the purposes of charging interest under a loan facility. By way of exception, the interest rate that is charged for borrowing in euros, as reflected in facility documents, refers to the Euribor rate that applies in the European interbank market.

3.6.3 Interbank funding conventions

There are certain conventions that apply in the London interbank market which will be mirrored in the documentation for a facility based on interbank funding. With some adaptation, the same conventions apply for lending in euros based upon the European interbank market. The conventions are as follows.

The market in London operates on the basis of borrowing funds, in neatly rounded amounts, for definite periods, being overnight, one week, one month, three months, and six months. Other periods and amounts may be available on an ad hoc basis. A day reflects the period from one day to the next. **3.6.3.1**

Except in the case of sterling, which is available daily, other funds are borrowed on two business days' notice. Dealings are agreed as at 11.00am (London time) on the day that sterling is to be made available or, for other currencies, 11.00am (London time or, for a euro-denominated transaction, Brussels time) two business days prior to the funds being made available. **3.6.3.2**

Payments are made on the basis that the funds will be freely available to the recipient for value on the day of intended receipt. Payments are made by transfers between bank accounts; in the case of sterling, between accounts in London and, for other currencies, between accounts in the principal financial centre of the currency concerned (or, for euros, to an account in the financial centre of a participating state in the eurozone or in London). **3.6.3.3**

The period of a month ends on the same numerical day in the next month as the day on which it began (and so on for other periods of months), unless there is no such day at the end of the period, or it is not a banking business day in both London and the place for payment (or, in the case of a payment in euros, a day on which the TARGET system[14] is in operation), in which case the month will end **3.6.3.4**

---

[14] The Trans-European Automated Real-time Gross Settlement Express Transfer payment system, that operates for payments across the eurozone.

on the immediately preceding such business day. Otherwise, payments that fall due on a day which is not a business day will be made on the next business day.

3.6.3.5 For the purpose of making per annum interest calculations, interest is calculated on the actual number of days that have elapsed in a period, divided by a year of 360 days (or 365/366 in the case of sterling). Interest calculations and payments of interest conform to the foregoing, as do most other types of fees and commissions referable to a per annum basis of calculation.

3.6.4 Funding rollover

In loan facilities based upon interbank funding, the lender funds itself during the life of the loan by making successive borrowings in the interbank market for periods that are available in the market. The lender tends to be funding itself short and lending long. During the life of the facility, it repays a borrowing that it has made in the interbank market on the last day of the period of that borrowing by using the funds it has obtained for the next period, which commences simultaneously with the ending of the previous period (this is the concept of 'rollover' of funding). The interest that the borrower pays under the facility is used by the lender to pay the interest that is due on its own funding. The interest periods and interest payment dates in the facility therefore have to correlate with the periods for which funds are borrowed in the interbank market. When the facility is repaid, the merry-go-round will stop and the lender will use the repayment it receives from the borrower, together with the interest payment made by the borrower, to retire its final position in the interbank market.

3.6.5 Market disruption

As the underlying intention of the transaction is that the lender should fund itself in the interbank market, it will be necessary for the loan facility agreement to cater for the possibility that funds may not be available at some point in the life of the facility because of a disruption in the market arising from events that are outside the lender's control. Examples of such events are the storms that swept through southern England in October 1987 and the tragic events that occurred in New York in September 2001. Some facility agreements provide that the borrower may not draw whilst such an event is continuing, but this is not a common restriction on the borrower's rights. Nearly all facility agreements contemplate that the lender will fund itself during the period of disruption from such sources as are available to it, and that the calculation of interest will be based on the cost of such funding to the lender, unless the borrower and the lender can agree to some other arrangement. In the case of multi-currency facilities, it is also common to provide that the borrower may not draw in a currency other than the base currency of the facility and that the facility will be sourced and maintained by the lender in the base currency during the period of any disruption that affected the lender's ability to obtain funds in other currencies.

3.7 **Borrowing under the Facility**

There are a number of expressions (which are largely interchangeable) that are **3.7.1** used to refer to the process of borrowing or utilising a facility, including 'drawing', 'draw down', 'utilisation', 'advance', and 'disbursement'. For ease of reference, the expressions 'borrowing' and 'drawing' will be used in this chapter.

A facility might provide that it may be borrowed in one single amount or it might **3.7.2** provide for borrowings by one or more amounts until the facility limit has been reached. Normally, there will be a period that is prescribed in which the borrowing may take place, called an 'availability' or 'commitment' period. If the facility is a revolving facility, the borrower may draw, repay (wholly or partially), and redraw (on any number of occasions) during such a period, provided that the maximum amount borrowed and outstanding at any time does not exceed the prescribed facility limit. The borrower will signify its intention to make a drawing by providing a notice to the lender in the form that is prescribed by the facility agreement.

The facility agreement will usually specify that certain requirements must be met **3.7.3** before the borrower is entitled to borrow. The most important of these are the conditions precedent that must be satisfied before a borrowing can take place, which are mentioned separately below. In addition, the facility agreement will normally state that the lender may suspend, or even cancel, the borrower's entitlement to draw under the facility if an event of default has occurred or if it is likely that such an event will occur (for instance, because the borrower is about to default on one of its obligations under the facility agreement or because the borrower will be unable to make a representation and warranty on the next date on which it is to be made, as required under the representations and warranties clause). It should be noted that in facilities to finance a takeover bid and in certain other types of acquisition finance, where certainty of funding is a pre-requisite for a transaction to be announced publicly and to proceed, the lender might be required to remove such requirements from the facility agreement or to agree that the borrower may draw under the facility notwithstanding the occurrence of an event of default or some other technical ground on which the facility might otherwise be unavailable. By contrast, if the facility is an uncommitted (as opposed to a committed) facility, the lender will not have any obligation to make any advance at any time under the facility and the borrower must take its chances that the funds will be provided when it makes a request to borrow. For obvious reasons, a lender will charge less to provide an uncommitted facility and there will also be regulatory benefits to a lender if it has the right at any time to terminate and cancel the facility.[15]

---

[15] See, for instance, Art 78 of and Annex II to Directive 2006/48/EC (OJ L177/1 30/6/2006) and para 3.7.2 of the BIPRU block of the Financial Services Authority's *Handbook*.

3.7.4 In the case of revolving facilities that are predicated on interbank funding, the borrower will be permitted to borrow drawings during the commitment or availability period, each of which will be for the duration of an interest period. The borrower will be required to repay a drawing at the end of the interest period to which it relates, but with the right to re-draw immediately if it so wishes, so that the proceeds of the new drawing can be used to fund the repayment of the previous drawing. Alternatively, the borrower may have other funds that it may wish to use to make the repayment.

3.7.5 Multi-currency facilities are usually structured on a model that is similar to that just described for revolving facilities. The borrower is permitted to make a drawing in a permitted currency (being, basically, a currency that is freely available to the lender in the interbank market) for the duration of an interest period, at the end of which it is obliged to repay that drawing. It may choose to fund that repayment from the proceeds of a new drawing in the same currency or from other sources that it may have, in which case it may decide to make a new drawing in another currency. The borrower will usually be permitted to maintain drawings in more than one currency at the same time, with some limit on the number to meet administrative requirements. The interest periods need not be the same. An alternative, but less usual, structure to that just described is that drawings which are made by the borrower are not treated as being repaid at the end of each interest period, but the borrower is given the right to have them re-denominated in another currency at the end of each such period if it so wishes, with payments being made between the borrower and the lender to reflect the choice that the borrower has made. At the conclusion of the facility, the borrower will repay in the currency or currencies in which the facility is then outstanding. Whichever method is used, it is necessary to have a measuring stick against which the value of amounts drawn can be assessed, so that the overall facility amount is not exceeded. This is achieved by one currency being nominated as the base currency, in which the total amount of the facility is expressed. Drawings in other currencies are then notionally valued back against the base currency (usually at the beginning of each interest period), and adjusting payments may have to be made by the borrower, so as to ensure that the facility amount is not exceeded.

3.8 A Wrongful Refusal to Lend

3.8.1 The question arises as to the borrower's rights in a situation where the lender was contractually obliged to lend but has wrongly refused to make an advance, even though the borrower may have fulfilled all the requirements to entitle it to borrow. Lord Scott in *Concord Trust v Law Debenture Trust Corporation PLC*[16] agreed with

---

[16] [2005] UKHL 27; [2005] 1 WLR 1591, at [41].

a suggestion that such a lender might be at risk of incurring a liability in damages for breach of contract. It is unlikely, however, that the borrower could obtain a mandatory order against the lender for performance of the contract, such as by way of an order for specific performance.[17] The borrower would thus be left to consider what other remedies might be available to it.

3.8.2 Repudiatory breach

Given its seriousness, the breach might be considered as constituting a repudiatory breach of contract by the lender. The borrower may then elect to treat the contract as at an end, with the consequence, in broad terms, that its own obligations for future performance would also be terminated. As will be seen below, the contract is not treated as terminated ab initio, nor does it mean that the parties are discharged for all purposes by the termination. The borrower would also be entitled to claim damages for the loss it has suffered in consequence of the breach and termination of the contract (see further below).

3.8.3 The obligation to repay after termination

It is an interesting question as to whether the borrower would be entitled to claim, in consequence of its election to bring the contract to an end, that it was relieved of its liability to repay any money that had already been advanced to it before the termination, where the facility agreement had provided for repayment at some future date or dates.

At first blush, support for such a view might be drawn from what Lord Diplock   3.8.3.1
said in *Moschi v Lep Air Services Ltd*.[18] He said that the election by the innocent party to bring the contract to an end:

> Puts an end to the primary obligations of the party not in default to perform any of his contractual promises which he has not already performed by the time of [the termination]. It deprives him of any right as against the other party to continue to perform them. It does not give rise to any secondary obligation [on his part] in substitution for a primary obligation which has come to an end. The primary obligations of the party in default to perform any of the promises made by him and remaining unperformed likewise come to an end as does his right to continue to perform them. But for his primary obligations there is substituted by operation of law a

---

[17] See *South African Territories Ltd v Wallington* [1898] AC 309, but contrast with the position under s 740 of the Companies Act 2006 (previously s 195 of the Companies Act 1985) in relation to a contract to subscribe for debentures to be issued by a company. In *Battlebridge Group Ltd v Amala Equity Ltd* [2006] EWHC 2982 (Comm), David Steel J ordered a lender to furnish the funds to a borrower which the lender had wrongly refused to lend. It would appear, however, that *South African Territories Ltd v Wallington* was not cited to the judge and the lender did not dispute that such an order could be made against it.

[18] [1973] AC 331, at 350.

secondary obligation to pay to the other party a sum of money to compensate him for the loss he has sustained as a result of the failure to perform the primary obligations. The secondary obligation is just as much an obligation arising from the contract as are the primary obligations that it replaces . . .

3.8.3.2 There are, however, limits on the apparent width of that statement. In the first place, as Lord Diplock explained in *Moschi*, matters which are of an ancillary or secondary nature to the main purpose of the contract will survive the termination of the parties' primary obligations. It is a matter of construing the contract to determine which provisions the parties intended should be regarded as falling within that category so that they will continue to apply.[19] It has been held that provisions relating to choice of law and jurisdiction and arbitration clauses could survive the termination of the contract.[20] It is submitted that a number of the other provisions in a loan agreement, such as those dealing with set-off and the various 'boiler-plate' provisions, might fall into this category as well.

3.8.3.3 Secondly,[21] the election by the innocent party to terminate the contract does not have the effect of discharging the rights, and the corresponding obligations, of either party which have accrued or been 'unconditionally acquired' prior to the date of termination. This was succinctly expressed by Sir Owen Dixon in the High Court of Australia in *McDonald v Dennys Lascelles Ltd*,[22] when he said:

> When a party to a simple contract, upon a breach by the other contracting party of a condition of the contract, elects to treat the contract as no longer binding upon him, the contract is not rescinded as from the beginning. Both parties are discharged from further performance of the contract, but rights are not divested or discharged which have been unconditionally acquired. Rights and obligations which arise from partial execution [i.e. partial performance] of the contract and causes of action which have accrued from its breach alike continue unaffected.

That statement was expressly approved by Lord Wilberforce in *Johnson v Agnew*.[23] It was followed by Lord Brandon in *Bank of Boston Connecticut v European Grain & Shipping Ltd*.[24] It might well be argued that the obligation of the borrower to repay the amount already advanced to it under the loan agreement, albeit that the date for repayment had not fallen due, should be seen as a right that had vested in the lender prior to the termination of the contract and which therefore should survive the election by the borrower to terminate the contract. This is demonstrated by the *Bank of Boston* case. That case concerned a charterparty where the

---

[19] *Duffen v Frabo SpA* [2000] 1 Lloyd's Rep 180, at 194.

[20] *Heyman v Darwins Ltd* [1942] AC 356; *Yasuda Fire & Marine Ins Co of Europe Ltd* [1995] QB 174.

[21] The author is indebted to John Whittle SC of the NSW Bar for his illuminating insight on this point.

[22] (1933) 48 CLR 457, at 476–477.

[23] [1980] AC 367, at 396.

[24] [1989] AC 1056, at 1098–1099.

voyage had commenced. The charterer had an obligation under the contract to pay the freight, but the date for payment had not arisen prior to the date when the charterer terminated the contract because of the owner's default during the voyage. The House of Lords held that the right to be paid the freight had been 'unconditionally acquired' before the termination of the contract, even though the date for payment was postponed in the contract to a later date and so had not arisen. Lord Brandon said[25] that, 'The postponement of payment was an incident attaching to the right acquired, but it was not a condition of its acquisition.' A similar approach was taken by Rix LJ in *Explora Group plc v Hesco Bastion Ltd*[26] in relation to commission earned under an agency agreement prior to the termination of the agreement due to the agent's repudiatory breach of the agreement.

3.8.4 Set-off claim

The borrower, as the innocent party, should be entitled to assert as an equitable set-off against any amount so payable by it to the defaulting party, the value of its entitlement to damages for the consequences of the repudiatory breach. This entitlement would be subject to any provision in the contract which prevented the claim to set-off from arising, although that, in turn, would depend upon whether the provisions of the contract dealing with set-off had survived the termination of the contract, as referred to above.

3.8.5 Damages

It is now appropriate to consider the borrower's claim for damages for the loss it has suffered in consequence of the lender's breach of contract,[27] particularly for loss of credit in not having the funds that it expected to be made available to it and for damage to its business reputation. It may also wish to claim more generally for economic loss, such as for the loss of profit on a transaction that was to be funded by the facility, damages it may have to pay if it defaulted on that transaction, and the loss of the opportunity to gain further business. In general, damages for breach of contract are awarded in English law to compensate for the loss of its contractual bargain that was suffered by the innocent party in consequence of the breach.[28] To succeed in such a claim, a number of hurdles have to be overcome. The innocent party must prove the loss it has suffered, it has a duty to mitigate its loss and,

---

25 At 1098–1099.

26 [2005] EWCA Civ 646, at [82]–[90].

27 See further the discussion on remedies for breach and claims for damages at Chap 1.

28 The House of Lords indicated in *Attorney General v Blake* [2001] 1 AC 268 that, in exceptional circumstances where normal remedies were inadequate to compensate for a breach of contract, the court may be prepared to order the defendant to account for the profits it had received or to which it was entitled.

as mentioned below, the recoverable loss for which damages are sought must fall within the rule as to remoteness.

3.8.5.1 In establishing its claim for damages, the borrower must bring itself within the rule as to remoteness, as set down originally by *Hadley v Baxendale*[29] (thus often referred to as the rule in *Hadley v Baxendale*). There are two limbs to the rule, which is applied as at the time of contracting and relates to the type of loss that could have been envisaged as at the time of contracting. Under the first limb of the rule, a claimant will be able to claim damages for the type of loss that could reasonably be expected to have arisen in the normal course of things. Under the second limb of the rule, the claimant may claim for those losses which may reasonably be supposed to have been in the contemplation of the parties, at the time they made the contract, as would probably result from the breach. The discussion that follows will begin by looking at the position before the decision of the House of Lords in *Sempra Metals Ltd v HM Commissioners of Inland Revenue*[30] and then by discussing how the decision in that case may have changed the approach that might be taken in this type of situation.

3.8.5.2 In *Kpohraror v Woolwich Building Society*,[31] the Court of Appeal awarded damages, within the first limb of the rule, for loss of perceived credit worthiness and damage to business reputation[32] that was suffered by a bank's customer in consequence of the bank having wrongly bounced the customer's cheque when there were funds available in the customer's account to meet the cheque. Although that case concerned a situation where the customer had a sufficient credit balance in his current account to meet the cheque, the same conclusion should have been reached if the cheque could have been met within an agreed facility which had not been terminated. By analogy, similar considerations should apply when a bank wrongly refuses to make funds available to a borrower under a committed banking facility with the consequence that a third party is not paid by the borrower when it should have been paid.

3.8.5.3 It is not clear, however, if the borrower could claim under the first limb of the rule in its traditional application for more general economic loss, although the House

---

[29] (1854) 9 Exch 341. See the discussion of the rule in *Jackson v Royal Bank of Scotland plc* [2005] UKHL 3, [2005] 1 WLR 377.

[30] [2007] UKHL 34.

[31] [1996] 4 All ER 119.

[32] The computation of a claim for such a loss is problematic. In *Kpohraror*, the Court of Appeal said that there was a presumption that some damage to reputation arose, but it is not clear how the amount that was awarded was calculated, other than that 'some allowance, though not very great' was made for the loss to the claimant's reputation. In *Anglo-Continental Holidays Ltd v Typaldos Lines (London) Ltd* [1967] 2 Lloyd's Rep 61, the Court of Appeal allowed an award of damages for loss of goodwill and business reputation. Lord Denning MR (with whom Davies LJ agreed) was prepared to uphold the award that the judge had made, as it was permitted to award a 'reasonable sum as damages' without proof of specific loss. Russell LJ felt there was proof of specific loss on the facts to justify the sum that the judge had awarded.

of Lords allowed a claim under the first limb for loss of the customer's profit on future transactions (which were cancelled in consequence of the bank's wrongful actions) in *Jackson v Royal Bank of Scotland plc*,[33] but the facts were rather different in that case. Generally speaking, however, the courts have been unwilling in the past to award substantial damages under the first limb of the rule for a failure to make funds available because the loss is treated as being too remote from what was foreseeable at the time of contracting. The assumption has been that an intended recipient of funds is not impecunious and that alternative facilities should be available from another provider of finance.

Assuming that the type of loss that the borrower wished to claim did not fall within the first limb of the rule, as it was traditionally applied, the borrower would have had to establish its claim for more general loss under the second limb of the rule in *Hadley v Baxendale*. To do this, it would need to show that the defendant bank was aware, when it granted the facility, of special circumstances relating to the borrower and its business which gave rise to the loss claimed. For instance, the borrower would have to show that the lender was aware, when it contracted, that the borrower was dependent upon the facility, that finance was not readily available from elsewhere within applicable time limits, and that the borrower would suffer substantial loss if the funds were not provided as agreed under the contract.[34] Although it would not be an easy task, it may have been possible that the borrower could show this, given that most lenders undertake extensive investigations before they agree to provide facilities and would be aware of the borrower's actual circumstances, its plans for the future, and its reliance on the facility that is to be provided.

3.8.5.4

It is now relevant to consider if the borrower's task might be any easier in light of the decision of the House of Lords in *Sempra Metals Ltd v HM Commissioners of Inland Revenue*.[35] It is submitted that that task has been made easier. Lord Nicholls, who delivered the leading opinion of the majority in the case, made it clear[36] that the usual principles relating to damages for breach of contract would apply where the breach consisted in the failure to pay money or in the late payment of money. The ordinary remoteness rules would apply and there was no special rule which would deny a claimant the opportunity to recover its losses simply because of this type of breach. The losses that were claimed must have been reasonably foreseeable and the court would not presume what was foreseeable but, subject to that and the rule as to mitigation, it would always be open to the claimant to plead and prove its actual loss. His Lordship envisaged that such loss could include interest,

3.8.5.5

---

[33] [2005] UKHL 3, [2005] 1 WLR 377.
[34] See, by analogy, *Trans Trust SPRL v Danubian Trading Co Ltd* [1952] 2 QB 297 and *Wadsworth v Lydell* [1981] 1 WLR 598.
[35] [2007] UKHL 34.
[36] At [92]–[96].

including compound interest, for the loss of the use of the money. In addition, in his Lordship's words,[37] it might be:

> the loss of an opportunity to invest the promised money. Here again, where the circumstances require, the investment loss may need to include a compound element if it is to be a fair measure of what the [claimant] lost by the late [or non-existent] payment. Or the loss flowing from the [default] may take some other form. Whatever form the loss takes the court will, here as elsewhere, draw from the proved or admitted facts such inferences as are appropriate . . . There are no special rules for the proof of facts in this area of the law.

3.9 Conditions Precedent

3.9.1 A loan facility agreement usually specifies a number of conditions precedent that must be satisfied before the borrower is entitled to draw under the facility. They are required for the benefit of the lender and it is often stated that they must be fulfilled 'in form and substance' to the satisfaction of the lender. If extensive, the list of requirements will probably be set out in one of the schedules to the agreement, which requirements are incorporated by virtue of a reference to them in one of the clauses of the agreement. Sometimes, there may be conditions precedent to be fulfilled at intervals during the life of the facility, before further drawings can take place, as may be the case in a facility which is intended to provide the finance in stages for a construction, engineering, or infrastructure project.

3.9.2 The list

The list of conditions precedent usually relates to documentary evidence and other matters that must be produced to the lender, such as copies of resolutions of the directors and shareholders of the borrower approving the transaction and the relevant documentation, the provision of guarantees and security in support of the borrower's obligations, other documentation that is relevant in the context of the transaction, certificates that might be required as to factual matters, information that the lender requires for regulatory purposes, including money laundering and knowledge of customer checks, and legal opinions confirming the enforceability of the transaction.

3.9.3 Conditions precedent and conditions subsequent

As a matter of general contract law, a distinction is drawn between conditions precedent and conditions subsequent.[38] The latter concern events that might

---

[37] At [95].

[38] See, for instance, the discussion in *Total Gas Marketing Ltd v Arco British Ltd* [1998] 2 Lloyd's Rep 209.

occur after the contract has become binding upon the parties and which the contract contemplates would have the effect of discharging the parties from the obligation to make further performance under the contract after the event has occurred. The former are conditions that the contract lays down and which must be satisfied before one or other, or both, of the parties is obliged to perform under the contract, let alone be bound by it. In the context of a loan facility agreement, the conditions precedent are intended to be requirements that must be satisfied by the borrower before the lender is obliged to advance funds under the agreement, although it is also normally intended that, irrespective of whether or not the conditions are satisfied, the borrower will have certain secondary obligations that it must meet, such as in the payment of fees to the lender.

The agreement will also normally provide that the lender is to be the arbiter of   3.9.4
whether the conditions precedent have been met. It is also worth making the point that as the conditions precedent are intended to be for the benefit of the lender, it is always free to waive any one or more of the conditions, so that the borrower is then permitted to draw under the facility. Alternatively, the lender might agree with the borrower that the fulfilment of a condition might become a condition subsequent, so that the borrower would be permitted to draw under the facility but be required to repay if the condition was not met by some later date.

Questions might arise in relation to the apparent width of a lender's discretion in   3.9.5
determining if the borrower has satisfied the conditions precedent.

One question concerns the limits, if any, that might be imposed upon the lender   3.9.5.1
in making its determination that the conditions precedent have been met to its satisfaction, in the absence of some explicit requirement that the lender should act reasonably or in some other objective manner. As mentioned above, the agreement will often state almost the opposite to any objective requirement, by stating that the conditions precedent must be met in a manner which, in form and substance, is satisfactory to the lender within its own discretion. It might be argued that some limit should be implied on the apparent width of such a discretion. This could be done by arguing that there was an implied term of the agreement to that effect. At the least, it might be said that the discretion should be exercised in good faith and not capriciously, arbitrarily, or for a collateral purpose which was outside the legitimate scope of the contract.[39] Nonetheless, this would leave quite a measure of subjective decision making in the hands of the lender.

It might also be said that, by implication, the lender should not act in a way which   3.9.5.2
deliberately prevented the conditions precedent from being met[40] or that it would

---

[39] See the discussion on this point in Chap 1.
[40] See *Blake & Co v Sohn* [1969] 1 WLR 1412.

not wrongfully impede them from being met,[41] particularly in relation to matters that were within its own control as, for instance, in approving legal opinions from its own lawyers.[42] This draws upon a concept that has been advanced in a number of cases, which is in turn based upon the supposition that parties enter into contracts that they wish to perform, that a term might be implied that neither party will prevent the other from being able to perform the contract and enjoy its rights under the contract.[43] There are cases, however, where attempts at arguing for even such mild forms of limitation have failed.[44]

3.9.5.3 In the end, it comes down to the construction of the agreement and whether a court would be prepared to imply a term, but it is always possible to prevent the implication of a term by a provision to the contrary in the agreement.[45] It is submitted that this can be achieved by using the formula referred to above, which is that meeting the conditions precedent is subject to the lender being satisfied with the materials presented to it, both as to form and substance. This must be subject to the reservation that a lender would probably have an implied duty to act in good faith and that it should not act capriciously, arbitrarily, or for a collateral purpose which was outside the legitimate scope of the contract.

3.9.5.4 If the lender does have some type of obligation as to the way in which it acts concerning the conditions precedent and is found to be in breach of that obligation, there will then be an issue as to the remedy that should be granted to the borrower. It is very unlikely that a mandatory order (for instance, an order for specific performance or for an injunction) would be made against the lender, given that such an order would not be made requiring it to lend even when it was in breach of a clear obligation to do so. On the other hand, and for the reasons already discussed, the borrower may have difficulty in proving a recoverable loss should it seek damages.

3.9.5.5 Another question is whether the secondary obligations of the borrower (to pay fees and the like) can be enforced where the lender is given a wide and unrestricted element of discretion in its right to make its determination, at least in the period before the lender has confirmed its complete satisfaction and, consequently, that the facility has become available for drawing by the borrower. It might be argued that the lender has, in effect, a right of veto upon the borrower's enjoyment of the

---

[41] See *Thompson v ASDA-MFI Group PLC* [1988] Ch 241.

[42] Bearing in mind that it is very unlikely, if not unheard of, for a legal opinion to give merely positive assurances and contain no qualifications.

[43] *Stirling v Maitland* (1864) 5 B&S 840; *Southern Foundries (1926) Ltd v Shirlaw* [1940] AC 701; *Schindler v Northern Raincoat Co Ltd* [1960] 1 WLR 1038.

[44] *Lee-Parker v Izzet (No 2)* [1972] 1 WLR 775; *Astra Trust Ltd v Adams and Williams* [1969] 1 Lloyd's Rep 81; *Stabilad Ltd v Stephens & Carter Ltd (No 2)* [1999] 2 All ER (Comm) 651.

[45] See *Micklefield v SAC Technology Ltd* [1990] 1 WLR 1002; *BNP Paribas SA v Yukos Oil Company* [2005] EWHC 1321 (Ch).

facility and that, until it gives its confirmation, it has not undertaken any binding commitment on its own part, with the consequence that there cannot be an effective and binding contract between the parties.

3.9.6 Role of the borrower

It is now relevant to consider the role of the borrower and whether it has any obligation to bring about the satisfactory achievement of the conditions precedent. An obvious point to make is that the borrower can hardly be expected to undertake that it will meet whatever the lender happens eventually to decide might be required within its own unfettered discretion. In other situations, it will be a question of whether a term might be implied under which such an obligation is undertaken by the borrower; for instance, that the borrower will use its reasonable endeavours to meet and satisfy the conditions precedent. Such a term has been implied in cases involving contracts for the sale of an asset where the sale has been subject to the fulfilment of a condition, with one of the parties being responsible for seeking to bring it about.[46] It is submitted that a court would be unlikely to imply such a term in relation to a loan facility agreement, because it is not necessary to give efficacy to the contract, which can work perfectly well without the term. If the borrower fails to satisfy the conditions precedent then the lender has no obligation to lend. Subject to the fulfilment of any pre-existing secondary obligations on the part of the borrower, the contract will simply fall away.

3.10 Repayment

3.10.1 Limited and non-recourse lending

In most cases, the obligation of the borrower to repay will relate to the full amount that has been lent to it, so that the borrower undertakes an unqualified covenant for repayment. It is possible, however, for the obligation to repay to be limited or qualified,[47] so that it is made conditional upon certain circumstances being met (e.g. prescribed cash flow requirements).[48] The borrowing may even be expressed as being without recourse to the borrower, in that it is limited to the proceeds of

---

[46] *Re Anglo-Russian Merchant Traders and John Butt & Co (London) Ltd* [1917] 2 KB 679; *Hargreaves Transport Ltd v Lynch* [1969] 1 WLR 215.

[47] As opposed to being entirely negated, as it would then cease to be a loan and would be a gift. The negation of any stipulation for repayment of a loan (as opposed to a gift) would equate to a proviso that was wholly repugnant to a loan: *Williams v Hathaway* (1877) 6 ChD 544.

[48] An example is the so-called 'flawed asset' provision which limits the obligation of a bank to repay a deposit: see *Re Bank of Credit and Commerce International SA (No 8)* [1996] Ch 245, at 262–263 (CA) and [1998] AC 214, at 225 (HL).

realisation of an asset or the income derived from that asset.[49] Hence, the liability of a trustee for moneys it borrows can be limited to the funds available to it from the trust assets and, in any event, expressed only to apply to the trustee of the trust for the time being so that a person who occupied that position will have no liability once it has ceased to be trustee.[50] The same points may be made in relation to other types of payment obligation, including as to interest, fees, or commission. The following discussion will be based on the assumption that the borrower has a full personal obligation to make payment.

3.10.2 Repayment on demand

The obligation to repay may be expressed to be an obligation to repay on demand. An overdraft facility is a typical example of a facility that normally is repayable on demand.

3.10.2.1 Generally speaking, the underlying principle in contract law is that it is not necessary to make a demand upon a debtor before commencing proceedings to recover a debt that was expressed to be payable on demand.[51] However, there is an exception to that underlying principle in the case of the relationship between banker and customer, which is that (in the absence of agreement to the contrary, as, for instance, in the case of a term deposit or a term loan) a demand is necessary before either is entitled to require payment from the other, although the issuance of proceedings will normally serve as a sufficient demand if an express demand has not already been made.[52]

3.10.2.2 Under English law as it currently stands, the right of the lender to make demand (where the facility gives it that right) is exercisable at any time and without reason.[53] The borrower must repay without delay; it is not entitled to any more time than is necessary to allow for the mechanics of making payment.[54] The Court of Appeal, however, has left open the possibility that the law might be changed so that a debtor

---

[49] *Mathew v Blackmore* (1857) 1 H&N 762; *De Vigier v IRC* [1964] 1 WLR 1073; *Levett v Barclays Bank PLC* [1995] 1 WLR 1260, at 1271–1272.

[50] *Williams v Hathaway* (1877) 6 ChD 544.

[51] *Bradford Old Bank Ltd v Sutcliffe* [1918] 2 KB 833.

[52] As to deposits made by the customer with its bank, see *Joachimson v Swiss Bank Corp* [1921] 3 KB 110. As to overdrafts granted by the bank to its customer, see *Cripps v Wickenden* [1973] 1 WLR 944; *Williams and Glyn's Bank Ltd v Barnes* [1981] Com LR 205; *Lloyds Bank PLC v Lampert* [1999] 1 All ER (Comm) 161; and *Bank of Ireland v AMCD (Property Holdings) Ltd* [2001] 2 All ER (Comm) 894.

[53] *Williams and Glyn's Bank v Barnes* [1981] Comm LR 205; *Bank of Baroda v Panessar* [1987] Ch 335; *Lloyd's Bank PLC v Lampert* [1999] 1 All ER (Comm) 161; *Bank of Ireland v AMCD (Property Holdings) Ltd* [2001] 2 All ER (Comm) 894. There may be a question as to whether the facility is repayable on demand as a matter of construction of the facility agreement and the conduct of the parties: *Titford Property Co Ltd v Cannon Street Acceptances Ltd* (unreported, 22/5/1975); *Bank of Ireland v AMCD (Property Holdings) Ltd.*

[54] *Bank of Baroda v Panessar* [1987] Ch 335. In *Sheppard & Cooper Ltd v TSB Bank PLC* [1996] 2 All ER 654, it was said that some minimum time should be allowed, unless the debtor admits

which is able to raise funds from another lender to enable it to make the repayment should be given a reasonable time to do so.[55] There is no special wording that must be used in making the demand for repayment, so long as it clearly requires repayment,[56] and the demand need not specify the precise amount that is due.[57]

3.10.3 Term facilities

A term facility is a facility where the date or (if repayment is to be made by instalments) dates for repayment are fixed by the facility agreement. In such a situation, there is no inherent right upon the lender to demand earlier repayment[58] unless the facility specifically provides for such a right, as through the operation of an events of default clause[59] or in other defined circumstances.[60] If the whole debt is repayable on one date, it is sometimes colloquially referred to as a 'bullet' repayment. Where the debt is repayable by instalments, the debt is said to amortise over the period for the payment of the instalments.

3.10.4 No agreed date for repayment

If there is no agreement as to the date for repayment of a debt and (in the case of a loan by a bank) it has not been agreed that it should be repayable on demand, then the debt will treated as having become repayable immediately after it was incurred.[61] This may give rise to problems in recovering the debt as the limitation period under the Limitation Act 1980 will begin to run from the date the debt was incurred.

3.10.5 Cloggs on the equity of redemption

In equity, it is not permitted to prevent a secured borrower from redeeming its security; for instance, by providing that the security may never be redeemed. The debtor is entitled to redeem its security on payment of the secured obligations

---

that it cannot repay. In that case, one hour was held to be sufficient where the demand was made in business hours.

[55] *Lloyd's Bank PLC v Lampert* [1999] 1 All ER (Comm) 161.

[56] *Re Colonial Finance Mortgage Investment and Guarantee Corp Ltd* (1905) 6 SRNSW 6, approved in *In Re A Company* [1985] BCLC 37.

[57] *Bunbury Foods Pty Ltd v National Bank of Australasia Ltd* (1984) 153 CLR 491; *Bank of Baroda v Panessar* [1987] Ch 335.

[58] *Cryne v Barclays Bank PLC* [1987] BCLC 548.

[59] See further below.

[60] For instance, by the operation of an illegality clause, which is a clause which purports to give the lender the right to demand early repayment if it becomes unlawful for the lender to maintain the facility in a relevant jurisdiction. It has also become common in facility agreements for the lender to have the right to require the borrower to make early repayment where there has been a substantial change in the ownership of the borrower or of its parent company, usually referred to as a change of control.

[61] *Bradford Old Bank Ltd v Sutcliffe* [1918] 2 KB 833; *Longstaff International Ltd v Evans* [2001] All ER (D) 283 (Jul).

and a provision which is intended to prevent that entitlement (called a 'clogg on the equity of redemption') is void and unenforceable.[62] The parties may agree that the right of redemption should be postponed for the period of the facility,[63] provided that is not an unreasonably long period.[64] The position has been changed by legislation in relation to companies, which can issue perpetual debentures.[65]

3.10.6 Early repayment

Failing a provision in the agreement which allows it to make early repayment, a debtor has no right to make early repayment of a term facility.[66] The lender is entitled to rely on the contract and its right to earn interest for the full term. If the debtor does make early repayment it will be in breach of contract and liable in damages for the loss the lender suffers, but the lender will be obliged to mitigate its loss by re-deploying the funds. For this reason, it is common for a borrower to negotiate a right in the contract to make early repayment of the whole or part of the loan that has been advanced to it, usually referred to as a 'prepayment'. The borrower will usually be given, as well, a right to cancel the whole or part of the facility so as to defray any commitment charges that would otherwise accumulate on the undrawn portion of the facility. The agreement will probably provide that if repayment is made otherwise than at the end of the relevant interest period, the borrower will compensate the lender for any loss it suffers which is not covered by its redeployment of the funds it receives on repayment.

3.11 Interest

3.11.1 Almost without exception, commercial loan transactions that take place in western cultures will be expressed to bear interest. The position relating to Islamic finance, and the alternative ways of structuring financial transactions to meet Sharia law, is examined separately below.

3.11.2 Interest is a charge for the use of money over time. It is usually calculated at a rate per cent per annum and accrues for each day on which a loan is outstanding. Most

---

[62] *Noakes & Co Ltd v Rice* [1902] AC 24; *Krelinger v New Patagonia Merat and Cold Storage Co Ltd* [1914] AC 25; *Jones v Morgan* [2001] EWCA Civ 995, [2002] 1 EGLR 125.

[63] *Teevan v Smith* (1882) 20 ChD 724; *Williams v Morgan* [1906] 1 Ch 804. As to the relationship between a contractual provision for redemption and the equitable right to redeem, especially in the context of contingent and future liabilities due to the mortgagee, see *Re Rudd and Son Ltd* (1986) 2 BCC 98,955 and *Law Debenture Trust Corp PLC v Concord Trust* [2007] EWHC 1380 (Ch).

[64] *Morgan v Jeffreys* [1910] 1 Ch 620.

[65] S 739 of the Companies Act 2006, (previously s 193 of the Companies Act 1985). See *Knightsbridge Estates Trust Ltd v Byrne* [1940] AC 613.

[66] *Hyde Management Services Pty Ltd v FAI Insurance* [1979] HCA 22, (1979) 144 CLR 541, quoting, inter alia, Luxmoor J in *Knightsbridge Estates Trust Ltd v Byrne* [1938] Ch 741.

facilities provide for interest to be paid periodically on interest payment dates which are the last days of successive interest periods. As previously explained, those periods and payment dates correlate with the funding arrangements that the lender has entered into in the interbank market. The borrower is given some say in the process, as the facility agreement will provide that it may choose the length of each interest period (and thereby it also chooses the length of the relevant funding period that the lender will obtain in the interbank market), so long as its choice conforms with the normal practices in the interbank market and certain other mechanical and practical requirements are met (e.g. as to conforming the last day of an interest period with a repayment date for principal).

3.11.3 Agreement to pay interest

The traditional position at common law (which has recently changed in relation to interest on amounts in default, as mentioned below) is that interest is not payable on a loan or a debt unless it had been agreed between the parties or arose under a course of dealing or custom.[67] Such an agreement should normally be express but it will be implied in the case of an overdraft.[68] The agreement can cover the position both before and (subject to it not amounting to a penalty) after default. To prevent the covenant for payment of interest merging in any judgment that the creditor might obtain should the debtor default in making payment, the obligation to pay interest at the contractual rate should be expressed as being payable 'after as well as before any judgment'.[69]

3.11.4 Rates of interest

In commercial agreements not involving consumers, there is very little restriction upon the interest rate that the parties may choose as the rate of interest that the borrower can agree to pay for the period prior to default. The usury laws were repealed in the middle of the nineteenth century[70] and subsequent legislation in the form of the Moneylenders Acts 1900 and 1927 has also been repealed.[71] There remains, however, the provision concerning 'extortionate credit transactions' in section 244 of the Insolvency Act 1986, which gives a liquidator or administrator

---

[67] *Page v Newman* (1829) 9 B&C 378; *London Chatham & Dover Ry Co v South Eastern Ry Co* [1893] AC 429; *President of India v La Pintada Compania Navegacion SA* [1985] AC 104.

[68] *Lloyds Bank PLC v Voller* [2000] 2 All ER (Comm) 978; *Emerald Meats (London) Ltd v AIB Group (UK) PLC* [2002] EWCA Civ 460. But see also *Financial Institutions Services Ltd v Negril Holdings Ltd* [2004] UKPC 40.

[69] *Economic Life Assurance Soc v Usborne* [1902] AC 147. See also *Director General of Fair Trading v First National Bank PLC* [2001] UKHL 52, [2002] 1 AC 481 (as to the use of such a clause in consumer lending).

[70] Usury Laws Repeal Act 1854.

[71] Repealed by s 192(4) of the Consumer Credit Act 1974. An example of the application of such legislation in other parts of the Commonwealth is provided by the decision of the Privy Council in *Palmer v Cornerstone Investments & Finance Co Ltd* [2007] UKPC 49.

the power to challenge such a transaction if it was entered into within a period of three years preceding the onset of the relevant insolvency proceedings.[72]

3.11.5 Interest as a share of profits

It should be noted that if the loan agreement provides that the lender is to receive a share of the borrower's profits or that the interest on the loan is to vary dependent upon those profits, the claim of the lender for repayment of the loan will be subordinated in the borrower's insolvency behind the claims of its unsecured creditors.[73] However, to the extent that the loan is secured, the lender may have recourse to its security and so it will not be affected by such a subordination.[74] It is submitted that if the lender holds share capital in the borrower separately from its loan, and the loan is expressed to carry interest in the normal way, the lender's rights under the loan will not be subordinated, as the relevant legislation specifically provides that it is the loan contract which must contain the profit sharing agreement, although this must be subject to the overall arrangement not being seen as a sham to disguise the true nature of the loan.

3.11.6 Interest for default in payment

Traditionally (but subject as explained below), interest was not normally awarded by way of damages at common law for failure to pay a debt on the due date with respect to the period from the due date to the date of judgment.[75] However, interest could be awarded on the unpaid amount where interest was agreed to be paid on the loan, even though it was not expressly agreed that interest would continue to accrue after default, although it may not have been awarded at the contract rate.[76] Furthermore, interest might be awarded under the second limb of the rule in *Hadley v Baxendale*[77] as damages if it was in the reasonable contemplation of the

---

[72] The meaning of the expression 'extortionate credit transaction' was considered in *Paragon Finance plc v Staunton* [2001] EWCA Civ 1466, [2002] 1 WLR 685, in which the Court of Appeal quoted from Goode, *Consumer Law and Practice*, para 47.26, that: 'the concepts of extortion and unconscionability are very similar. "Extortionate", like "harsh and unconscionable", signifies not merely that the terms of the bargain are stiff, or even unreasonable, but that they are so unfair as to be oppressive. This carries with it the notion of morally reprehensible conduct on the part of the creditor in taking grossly unfair advantage of the debtor's circumstances.'

[73] S 3 of the Partnership Act 1890, which is of general application and applies in the administration or winding up of companies, as well as in bankruptcy: see Rule 12.3(2A)(c) of the Insolvency Rules 1986. See also *Re Theo Garvin Ltd* [1969] 1 Ch 624, which concerned a related point under s 317 of the Companies Act 1948. It does not matter if the loan was made under a written or an oral agreement: *Re Fort, ex p Schofield* [1897] 2 QB 495.

[74] *Re Lonergan, ex p Sheil* (1877) 4 ChD 789; *Badeley v Consolidated Bank* (1888) 38 ChD 238, which concerned the predecessor of s 3 that was found in s 5 of Bovill's Act 1865.

[75] *London Chatham & Dover Ry Co v South Eastern Ry Co* [1893] AC 429.

[76] *Cook v Fowler* (1874) LR 7 HL 27.

[77] (1854) 9 Exch 341.

defendant at the time of contracting that the creditor would itself suffer an interest charge if the debt was not paid on the due date.[78]

The rule at common law was partially relaxed by statute. Under section 35A of the Supreme Court Act 1981,[79] the High Court has power to award simple interest on an unpaid debt provided that the debt remained unpaid at the time that proceedings were commenced for its recovery.[80] The courts are prepared to award such interest at a commercial rate.[81] There is also an entitlement to interest under various other statutory provisions, such as that under the Late Payment of Debts (Interest) Act 1998 relating to the late payment on debts arising for the supply of goods or services,[82] where the purchaser and supplier are both acting in the course of a business.

      3.11.6.1

In *Sempra Metals Ltd v HM Commissioners of Inland Revenue*[83] the House of Lords changed the law and held that interest may be awarded at common law as damages for late payment of a debt within the first limb of the rule in *Hadley v Baxendale*,[84] subject to the usual rule in awarding damages that the claimant must prove its loss. Furthermore, it held that compound interest could be awarded at common law within such damages, as that is consistent with everyday practice in the lending of money. It also held that interest, including compound interest, could be awarded on a tortious claim and, by majority,[85] that such interest could be awarded upon a restitutionary claim for money paid under a mistake.[86]

      3.11.6.2

It might be argued that the decision in the *Sempra Metals* case was obiter dicta, in so far as it related to contractual damages for an unpaid debt. The case concerned

      3.11.6.3

---

   [78] *Wadsworth v Lydell* [1981] 1 WLR 598, approved by the House of Lords in *President of India v La Pintada Compania Navegacion SA* [1985] AC 104.

   [79] See also the Judgment Act 1838, s 74 of the County Courts Act 1984, and s 49 of the Arbitration Act 1996. The latter also permits an award of compound interest to be made.

   [80] See Lord Brandon in *President of India v La Pintada Compania Navegacion SA* [1985] AC 104.

   [81] *Tate & Lyle Food Distribution Ltd v Greater London Council* [1982] 1 WLR 149, at 154; *Kuwait Airways Corp v Kuwait Insurance Co SAK (No 2)* [2000] 1 All ER (Comm) 972.

   [82] Financial services, such as lending money, would not be considered the supply of a service: see Lord Goff in *R v Preddy* [1996] AC 815, at 840.

   [83] [2007] UKHL 34.

   [84] (1854) 9 Exch 341.

   [85] Lords Hope, Nicholls, and Walker. Lord Scott and Lord Mance dissented on this point. Lord Scott said that such interest should only be awarded to the extent that it could be shown that the defendant had been unjustly enriched by itself receiving interest on the amount mistakenly paid to it. Lord Mance said there should be no entitlement to interest on such a claim but, if there were, it should be on the basis put forward by Lord Scott.

   [86] Thereby overruling the position, as to compound interest, as it had applied since the earlier decision of the House of Lords in *Westdeutsche Landesbank Girozentrale v Islington LBC* [1996] AC 669. Their Lordships were divided as to whether a restitutionary award of interest would arise in equity or at common law (compare Lords Nicholls and Hope, who would award such interest as a matter of the common law, with Lord Walker, who would award it within the court's equitable jurisdiction. Lord Scott and Lord Mance would also have confined it to a jurisdiction at common law).

a claim for interest as damages in tort or as a restitutionary award. However, the decision on the contractual issue was unanimous and their Lordships felt that it was necessary to deal with that issue as it was part of the background to the conclusions that they reached on the tortious and restitutionary claims.

3.11.7 Interest in equity

In certain circumstances interest might be awarded in equity despite there being no agreement for payment of interest. For instance, equity will award interest on a mortgage debt,[87] a surety is entitled to interest under its indemnity from the principal debtor,[88] a fiduciary may be liable to pay interest on funds of its beneficiary that are in its hands,[89] a trustee may have to pay compound interest on any wrongful profit it makes for itself,[90] and interest is payable on fraudulently obtained money.[91]

3.11.8 Compound interest

The right to charge compound interest will arise either by agreement or by custom, such as by the practice of bankers.[92] As mentioned above, in the *Sempra Metals* case the House of Lords held that compound interest may also be awarded as damages for late payment of a debt, for a tortious claim, or upon a restitutionary claim for payment made under a mistake or pursuant to an unlawful demand. Compound interest is interest that is charged on unpaid interest, which is usually achieved by capitalising the unpaid interest (adding it to principal) so that it becomes part of the principal on which interest is charged. It is not yet clear how frequently the practice of bankers would apply the 'rests', being the dates for capitalising of interest.[93] The right of a banker to compound interest continues until payment, notwithstanding that the banker has made demand for repayment.[94]

3.12 Penalties

3.12.1   Fairly typically, a loan facility agreement will provide for an additional rate of interest to be payable on any amount that is in default of payment; that is, a rate which is additional to the normal contractual rate that applied prior to default.

---

[87] *Re Kerr's Policy* (1869) LR 8 Eq 331; *Al Wazir v Islamic Press Agency Inc* [2001] EWCA Civ 1276, [2002] 1 Lloyd's Rep 410.

[88] *Re Fox Walker & Co* (1880) 15 ChD 400.

[89] *Brown v IRC* [1965] AC 244.

[90] *Attorney-General v Alford* (1855) 4 De GM & G 843, at 851.

[91] *Johnson v The King* [1904] AC 817, at 822.

[92] *National Bank of Greece SA v Pinios Shipping Co* [1990] AC 637.

[93] Quarterly rests were conceded in *National Bank of Greece SA v Pinios Shipping Co.* [1990] AC 637 and were permitted in *Kitchen v HSBC Bank PLC* [2000] 1 All ER (Comm) 787.

[94] Ibid.

Such a rate is often referred to as the 'default rate'. A different category of contract may provide for some other type of additional amount to be payable if there has been a breach, sometimes called a 'liquidated damages clause'. Such provisions, however, run the risk that they might be struck down by the courts as being an unenforceable penalty.[95] In such a case, the court will make its own assessment of the damages to which the claimant will be entitled in consequence of the default that has occurred, based upon the normal rules for the assessment of damages, including the rules as to remoteness.

A provision will be characterised as being a penalty if it was intended to deter a **3.12.2** breach of contract from occurring.[96] However, it will not be a penalty if it can be shown that the provision was a genuine pre-estimate[97] by the parties, at the time of contracting, of the likely loss or the additional risk that they contemplated would be suffered in consequence of the breach.[98] In looking at this issue, the courts have been reluctant to interfere in commercial contracts where a provision had a commercially justifiable reason other than mere deterrence.[99]

The tests that will be applied by the courts in determining whether a provision **3.12.3** amounts to a penalty were set out by Lord Dunedin in *Dunlop Pneumatic Tyre v New Garage*,[100] which may be summarised as follows. First, if the sum expressed to be payable is extravagant and unconscionable in comparison with the greatest loss that could conceivably result from the breach, it will be a penalty.[101] Secondly, if the breach only relates to non-payment and the stipulated amount is greater than the amount that should have been paid, it will be a penalty. Thirdly, as a rebuttable presumption, it will be a penalty if the same amount is payable for both trivial and serious breaches. Fourthly, if the parties anticipate when contracting

---

95 Most commentaries on this subject begin with the speech of Lord Dunedin in *Dunlop Pneumatic Tyre Co Ltd v New Garage & Motor Co Ltd* [1915] AC 79, particularly at 87–88. See also more recently *Export Credits Guarantee Department v Universal Oil Products Co* [1983] 1 WLR 399; *The Angelic Star* [1988] 1 Lloyd's Rep 122; *Workers Trust & Merchant Bank Ltd v Dojap Investments Ltd* [1993] AC 573; *Philips Hong Kong Ltd v The Attorney General of Hong Kong* (1993) 61 BLR 41; *Lordsvale Finance Ltd v Bank of Zambia* [1996] QB 752; *Jeancharm v Barnet Football Club* [2003] EWCA Civ 58, (2003) 92 Con LR 26; Mance LJ in *Cine Bes Filmcilik Ve Yapimcilik v United International Pictures* [2003] EWCA Civ 1669, [2004] 1 CLC 401, at [9]–[21]; and *Murray v Leisureplay* [2005] EWCA Civ 963, [2005] IRLR 946.

96 The modern approach is to refer to whether the clause is intended to deter a breach from occurring, rather than the older formulation of whether it was intended to act 'in terrorem': see Colman J in *Lordsvale Finance Ltd v Bank of Zambia* [1996] QB 752, at 762.

97 I.e. on objective grounds, a reasonable attempt: see Arden LJ in *Murray v Leisureplay* [2005] EWCA Civ 963; [2005] IRLR 946 at [55].

98 In *Murray v Leisureplay* [2005] EWCA Civ 963, [2005] IRLR 946 Buxton LJ, at [111], with whom Clarke LJ agreed, thought that unless it could be shown that the clause was intended to have a deterrent effect, it could not be a penalty.

99 See Colman J in *Lordsvale Finance Ltd v Bank of Zambia* [1996] QB 752, at 763–764.

100 [1915] AC 79, particularly at 87–88.

101 In *Murray v Leisureplay* the Court of Appeal emphasised that the amount had to be 'extravagant and unconscionable', not just a generous overpayment.

that it will not be possible to make a precise quantification of the loss, that is likely to mean that it was a genuine attempt by the parties to pre-estimate the loss and it will not be a penalty.[102]

3.12.4 Each case will depend on its facts,[103] so a provision that may be acceptable in the circumstances of one contract may not work in the circumstances of another. For instance, it was held in one case that a 'modest increase' of 1 per cent per annum above the normal pre-default rate, which was payable during the period of default, could be justified.[104] Care must be taken in placing too much reliance on that particular outcome. Whilst an additional 1 per cent per annum might be considered to be a modest increase over a normal contractual rate of 12 to 15 per cent per annum, it would look disproportionate if the normal contractual rate was only 3 or 4 per cent per annum.

3.12.5 Various situations have been examined by the courts in relation to the approach that should be taken, including the following.

3.12.5.1 A practice that has traditionally been used in mortgages is to provide for a normal rate which will be reduced for prompt payment. In effect, the mortgage provides that the normal rate will be x per cent per annum but if the mortgagor pays an instalment of interest on or before the due date, the mortgagee will accept a payment equal to a lower specified rate. Despite the apparent artificiality of such an arrangement, it has been upheld as not amounting to a penalty, because the mortgagor is not being charged an extra amount in consequence of a default but is being allowed a concessionary benefit for paying on time. Hence, the full or higher rate may be legitimately charged if the mortgagor defaults in due and punctual payment.[105] There is no reason why this approach should be confined to mortgages; it could be applied to other types of credit or finance arrangements.[106]

3.12.5.2 An obligation on a party to a principal contract to indemnify a third party for a payment due by the third party under a guarantee or a bond is not a penalty, even though the guarantee or bond relates to the indemnifier's own breach of its contractual obligations under the principal contract. This is because the obligation under the indemnity is not one arising due to a breach of the indemnity.[107]

---

102 See Diplock LJ in *Robophone Facilities Ltd v Blank* [1966] 1 WLR 1428, at 1447.

103 See Clarke LJ in *Murray v Leisureplay* at [106], point (vi).

104 *Lordsvale Finance Ltd v Bank of Zambia* [1996] QB 752, in which it was held that an additional 1% pa over the normal pre-default contractual rate payable by the borrower under that loan agreement would not be a penalty.

105 See Lord Hatherley in *Wallingford v Mutual Society* (1880) 5 App Cas 685, at 702.

106 *Lordsvale Finance Ltd v Bank of Zambia* [1996] QB 752, at 762.

107 *Export Credits Guarantee Department v Universal Oil Products Co* [1983] 1 WLR 399.

A premium or fee that is payable by a contracting party if it wishes to exercise a right of early termination of the contract is not a penalty. It is regarded as the legitimate consideration that is payable for the exercise of a contractual right.[108]

3.12.5.3

It has also been held that a right to accelerate the repayment of a loan on the occurrence of an event of default and to receive payment of the interest that had accrued up to the date of payment does not amount to a penalty.[109] Similarly, a right to terminate a hire purchase or equipment lease agreement for breach by the hirer or lessee will not be a penalty.[110] However, it would be a penalty if a loan agreement additionally provided for the lender to receive all of the interest to which it would have been entitled had the loan run its full course.[111] It may be a penalty if a hire purchase or equipment lease agreement purports to legislate for the amount payable by the hirer or lessee on termination.[112]

3.12.5.4

It has been held that a compromise agreement is enforceable[113] if the creditor agrees to forgo payment of the whole of a debt should the debtor pay a lesser sum but that if such lesser sum is not paid the whole debt will be payable. The revived obligation to pay the whole debt is not regarded as a penalty but merely as a reservation of the creditor's pre-existing right to be paid the whole debt.[114] The same principle will apply where the stipulated residual or revived amount represents a bona fide calculation of what would have been due, even if it was not the precise amount.[115] However, the principle will not apply if the creditor acquired new or additional rights under the settlement agreement that it did not have previously.[116]

3.12.5.5

3.13 Islamic Finance

It is well known that the principles of Islam and Sharia law prohibit the charging and payment of interest ('riba'), although it is permissible to obtain a return on funds which has been earned as a profit derived from a commercial risk that the lender has undertaken. Similarly, certain types of speculation which does not

3.13.1

---

108 *Bridge v Campbell Discount Co Ltd* [1962] AC 600. As that case demonstrates, a court may strain to find that the relevant party did not intend to exercise its right to terminate but, instead, indicated its unwillingness to be bound by the contract if such a finding would result in a lesser amount being payable by way of damages than under the exercise of the contractual right.

109 *The Angelic Star* [1988] 1 Lloyd's Rep 122.

110 *Transag Haulage Ltd v Leyland Daf Finance PLC* [1994] 2 BCLC 88. For the position concerning conditional sale, see ss 48(3) and (4) of the Sale of Goods Act 1979.

111 *The Angelic Star* [1988] 1 Lloyd's Rep 122; *County Leasing Ltd v East* [2007] EWHC 2907 (QB).

112 *Bridge v Campbell Discount Co Ltd* [1962] AC 600; *Lombard North Central PLC v Butterworth* [1987] QB 527.

113 Subject, of course, to being supported by consideration or being made by way of a deed.

114 *Thompson v Hudson* (1869) 4 HL 1.

115 *Society of Lloyd's v Twinn* (The Times 4/4/2000).

116 *Donegal International Ltd v Republic of Zambia* [2007] EWHC 197 (Comm).

involve productive effort, contracts which give rise to an unfair gain, and contracts that involve uncertainty in their subject matter, such as conventional insurance, are prohibited. In consequence, fairly typical types of western financial transactions, including lending, derivatives transactions, and the issuance of debt securities, are likely to infringe Islamic principles. This has deterred participation in such transactions by those who wish to observe Islamic principles.

3.13.2   In recent times, various transactions have been developed in consultation with Islamic scholars, which were intended to meet the principles of Sharia law, although there is always a risk that divergent views may be taken by different scholars and traditions within the Islamic world, and difficulties remain in dealing with the treatment of compensation for overdue amounts. Indeed, more development of this market is needed before it will be fully established and understood in its sophistication. Banks which offer transactions that are intended to comply with Sharia principles will often have a special board or committee of scholars who review proposed transactions so as to decide if they meet acceptable principles. Various regulatory, accounting, and fiscal issues have arisen as to the treatment of these types of transaction. For instance, the UK Finance Act 2007 made a number of changes that were favourable to the tax treatment of such transactions.

3.13.3   There follows a brief description of transactions or techniques that are commonly put forward (sometimes involving a combination of them) as being in conformity with Sharia principles, although it must be emphasised that there is not unanimity in the acceptance of the methods that are used.

3.13.3.1   'Sukuk' involves the issuance of a negotiable certificate which entitles the holder to an economic return based upon a proportionate interest in an asset or a portfolio of assets that is held by the issuer which conforms to Islamic principles. It may be compared with a western style of bond or similar debt instrument but it does not carry interest. As it is intended to be negotiable, it should be tradeable in a secondary capital market.

3.13.3.2   'Ijara' resembles a form of leasing of assets, which carries an agreed return in the rental stream. If title is to pass to the lessee at the end of the rental period, the transaction will be structured as 'ijara wa-iktina', by which the lessee is given an option to purchase the asset. This is not dissimilar to the English concept of hire purchase.

3.13.3.3   'Murabaha' is a transaction by which the financier purchases an asset from a supplier and sells it to the customer at an agreed mark up. The customer may pay the price immediately or it may be deferred. This type of transaction may be used to finance infrastructure projects and asset-based financings. 'Reverse Murabaha' or 'Tawarruq' goes a step further and involves the customer (which is paying the financier by deferred terms) selling on the asset to a third party for immediate payment and delivery. The third party may be the original seller or a party linked to it.

'Istisn'a' is useful in providing advance financing of projects and large assets such as ships or aircraft. The financier pre-pays the supplier and takes title to the asset on delivery, which it then sells (perhaps on deferred terms) or leases to the customer.

3.13.3.4

'Bai Al Inah' involves the sale and re-purchase of an asset. The financier purchases the asset from its customer and sells it back at a higher price.

3.13.3.5

'Salam' or 'Bai salam' is a form of forward financing, under which the financier pays in advance for assets which will be delivered at a later date. The payment may involve the financier paying a discounted price for the asset which it may then sell on at delivery of the asset, or the financier may enter into a back-to-back salam with a third party purchaser.

3.13.3.6

'Musharaka' is an equity investment or profit and loss sharing arrangement. It can be used to provide equity or venture capital funding. Under such an arrangement, a financier and an investor provide their investments in a project in agreed proportions, which may include the contribution of cash or a contribution in kind. The arrangement will prescribe how the profits or losses of the project will be shared between them. If a party provides services, such as management or technical services, it may also receive a fee for its services.

3.13.3.7

'Mudaraba' involves a fund contributed by investors, which is managed and invested on their behalf by a fund manager in acceptable businesses or investments that might include, for instance, financing provided to its customers by the fund manager or other types of investments. The manager will charge a fee for its services, and the profits or losses on the fund will be shared by the investors in agreed proportions.

3.13.3.8

3.14 Payments under a Loan Facility Agreement

A finance transaction involves payments as between the lender and the borrower, not infrequently involving international payments between different jurisdictions. The lender disburses the drawing to the borrower and the borrower makes payment of principal, interest, and other amounts to the lender. Various questions may arise that relate to such payments, including the method and finality of making payment, the effect of rights of set-off, and the conclusiveness of the lender's determination of amounts that are payable by the borrower. The common law rules relating to those matters will be addressed in the following paragraphs.[117]

3.14.1

---

[117] The EC Directive on payment services (2007/64/EC OJ L319/1 5/12/2007) may affect some of the rules as they had been developed at common law. The Directive must be implemented by the Member States by 1/11/2009. It has relevance to electronic payments and payment systems throughout the EC and the EEA. It deals with matters such as the authorisation of entities that may

Conflict of laws issues may also arise relating to the currency of account for calculating the obligations of the parties, the currency of payment in which payments should be made, the requirements for effecting performance, and the effect of illegality in a place that is relevant to performance and payment. The conflict of laws issues are addressed elsewhere in this book.[118] It should also be noted that damages may be awarded under English law for currency exchange losses that arise in consequence of making late payment.[119]

3.14.2 Methods of payment

The common methods for making a payment (or the equivalent to making a payment) are by cash, by cheque, bill of exchange, promissory note or similar instrument, by a barter through the exchange of goods or by some other method of payment in kind,[120] by netting and set-off of liabilities, or by transfers between bank accounts. For practical purposes, payments in cash are unlikely to occur in transactions of any size[121] and payments by cheque or a similar instrument are also unlikely to occur in commercial finance transactions. Barter transactions and payments in kind are confined to specialist transactions that are outside the scope of the present discussion. Set-off and netting will be referred to separately below.

3.14.3 The most likely method of payment in finance transactions, being that which is commonly stipulated in loan facility agreements, is by payment to the credit of a bank account which will probably involve payment transfers across the accounts of different banks. For instance, a payment in US dollars by a payer situated in London to a payee whose account is in New York will probably be effected by the payer instructing its bank in London to effect the payment, if necessary after having converted sterling into US dollars. That bank will instruct its correspondent bank in New York[122] (or its own branch in New York) to make the payment to the payee's bank in New York,[123] which, on receipt, will credit the payment to the

---

provide payment services, transparency, and the provision of information relating to payments, the rights and obligations of users and providers of payment services, and liabilities for incorrectly executed payment orders.

[118] Chap 4.

[119] *President of India v Lips Maritime Corp* [1988] 1 AC 395.

[120] For instance, by the provision of services, by issuing equity or further debt, or by off-taking or transferring products, rights, or benefits that might have been generated by, or resulted from, the subject matter of the financing.

[121] Although they may be available when other methods of payment cannot be used: see *Libyan Arab Foreign Bank v Bankers Trust Co* [1989] QB 728.

[122] E.g. by sending an instruction through the SWIFT system (the Society for Worldwide Interbank Financial Telecommunications).

[123] Unless agreed otherwise between the payer and its bank, the latter is entitled to determine the method of transfer and to make payment within a reasonable time, although it does owe the payer a duty of care and skill in carrying out the payer's instruction: *Royal Products Ltd v Midland Bank Ltd* [1981] 2 Lloyd's Rep 194. See also *Dovey v Bank of New Zealand* [2000] NZLR 641. Generally

payee's account. Whilst commercially the various steps are seen as payments, in fact they do not involve any physical payments of money but, instead, involve a series of successive credits and debits to bank accounts, each representing debtor–creditor relationships. Thus, the receipt of payment by the payee will be constituted by a credit entry on its account with its bank, which represents a debt due by that bank to the payee. The payment to the payee's bank will be represented by debit and credit entries in the payment system to which the correspondent bank and the payee's bank are members, the payment effected by the payer's bank to the correspondent bank will be effected on the accounts between them, and the whole process will be begun by the payer's bank debiting the payer's account with the amount it has been instructed to pay.

3.14.4 Effectiveness of payment

Under English law, an obligor with a payment obligation is obliged to make payment in cash (i.e. legal tender by the use of notes and coins) unless the parties have agreed to another method of payment or the payee accepts an alternative method of payment.[124] Where the contract specifically provides for a different method of payment (e.g. by a transfer to a specified bank account) that will constitute effective payment if it is made in accordance with the requirements (e.g. as to time) of the contract.[125] If such a method is the only method of payment that is permitted by the contract then payment must be made by the contractually agreed method. Otherwise, a debtor is entitled to pay in cash in addition to any alternative method specified by the contract; indeed, the debtor may be obliged to pay in cash if the alternative method is unavailable.[126] In other cases, the debtor must tender payment but payment will not be effective unless the tender is accepted by the creditor or its authorised agent. If a tender of payment is rejected, the tenderer can protect itself if it is subsequently sued by paying the money into court and raising a defence of tender.[127] In cases of money transfers that are not made pursuant to, and in conformity with, an agreed requirement in the contract between the payer and payee, the payee's bank may not be authorised as agent to accept payment (e.g. where the payment is late) so as to bind its customer and prevent the customer from rejecting the purported payment and exercising its rights arising in consequence of late payment.[128] Accordingly, there is no general authorisation for

---

speaking, the payer's bank owes no duty to the payee, nor does the correspondent bank owe a duty to either the payer or the payee: *Royal Products Ltd v Midland Bank Ltd.*

[124] *Libyan Arab Foreign Bank v Bankers Trust Co* [1989] QB 728, at 764.

[125] *TSB Bank of Scotland v Welwyn Hatfield DC* [1993] 2 Bank LR 267, at 272; *Royal Products Ltd v Midland Bank PLC* [1981] 2 Lloyd's Rep 194, at 198; *Hosni Tayeb v HSBC Bank PLC* [2004] EWHC 1529 (Comm); [2004] 4 All ER 1024, at [80]–[82].

[126] *Libyan Arab Foreign Bank v Bankers Trust Co* [1989] QB 728, at 764.

[127] *HM Customs & Excise v National Westminster Bank PLC* [2002] EWHC 2204 (QB), at [9].

[128] *Mardorf Peach & Co Ltd v Attica Sea Carriers Corp, The Laconia* [1977] AC 850.

a bank to accept payment on behalf of its customer where the customer has not agreed to the receipt,[129] either in the contract between the payer and the customer or as between the customer and the bank (for instance, in the bank's mandate, as will often be the case). An unauthorised payment by a third party will not bind the debtor unless it is ratified.[130]

3.14.5 Receipt of payment

Where a payment is received by the payee's bank and it is received within the bank's mandate, payment is treated (as between the payee and its bank and also as between the payer and payee) as received by the payee, and cannot be countermanded, when its account is credited with the payment, unless it is merely credited conditionally (e.g. a cheque awaiting clearance of funds), in which case it will be treated as finally received when the condition has been satisfied; effective receipt by the payee in accordance with the foregoing is not dependent upon the bank notifying the receipt to the payee.[131] Where a conditional payment is accepted by a payee pending clearance (e.g. a cheque), the payment will be treated, as between payer and payee, as being effective from the date of receipt of the conditional payment, provided clearance is effected.[132] If such a payment is received by the payee but it fails to seek clearance of the payment, it will not be able to claim it has not received payment.[133] Where a conditional payment is received pending clearance and clearance fails, the payment is ineffective (unless it was agreed that it would be an absolute payment).[134]

3.14.6 Drafting

A loan facility agreement should take account of the issues outlined above, as well as the associated conflict of laws issues. Subject to one point that arises in consequence of the experience in the *Libyan Arab Foreign Bank* litigation,[135] the agreement

---

[129] *TSB Bank of Scotland v Welwyn Hatfield DC* [1993] 2 Bank LR 267; *HM Customs & Excise v National Westminster Bank PLC* [2002] EWHC 2204 (QB).

[130] *Owen v Tate* [1976] QB 402.

[131] *The Brimnes, Tenax SS Co Ltd v The Brimnes (Owners)* [1975] QB 929; *Mardorf Peach & Co Ltd v Attica Sea Carriers Corp, The Laconia* [1976] QB 835, (reversed by HL on other grounds); *Momm v Barclays Bank International Ltd* [1977] QB 790; *Libyan Arab Foreign Bank v Manufacturers Hanover Trust Co (No 2)* [1989] 1 Lloyd's Rep 608; *Hosni Tayeb v HSBC Bank PLC* [2004] EWHC 1529 (Comm). The *Hosni Tayeb* case contains an interesting discussion of the workings of the UK CHAPS payment system, which is a real time gross settlement payment system.

[132] *Holmes v Smith* [2000] Lloyd's Rep Bank 139.

[133] *Fusion Interactive Communication Solutions Ltd v Venture Investment Placement Ltd* [2005] EWHC 736 (Ch), [2006] BCC 187.

[134] *Re Romer & Haslam* [1893] 2 QB 286; *Bolt & Nut Co (Tipton) Ltd v Rowlands Nicholls & Co Ltd* [1964] 2 QB 10.

[135] *Libyan Arab Foreign Bank v Bankers Trust Co* [1989] QB 728 and *Libyan Arab Foreign Bank v Manufacturers Hanover Trust Co (No 2)* [1989] 1 Lloyd's Rep 608.

should provide for all calculations and payments to be made in the relevant currency or currencies of account, to be made unconditionally for value on the due date and that the payments should be made to nominated bank accounts. As payments have to be settled by transfers via the relevant payments systems, they should be made for settlement in the principal financial centre of the relevant currency (or, in the case of payments in euros, in a financial centre of a participating Member State in the eurozone or in London). The point raised by the exception is that it would be sensible for the contract expressly to give the lender the right to direct that payments by the borrower (and, perhaps, by the lender) should be made in an equivalent amount in a different currency to the currency of account and in a different place if it becomes unlawful or impossible for them to be made in the normal way. Otherwise, a borrower under an agreement governed by English law might be excused from having to make a payment if it becomes unlawful for it to make the payment under the law stipulated by the agreement as the place of payment.[136]

3.14.7 Unlawfulness

Such unlawfulness or, indeed, illegality on a broader scale may mean that it is not feasible for the lender to continue with the facility. For instance, the lender's regulator or other authorities in its home jurisdiction may prohibit it from maintaining the facility or having dealings with the borrower. Strictly speaking, if all of those dealings and any payments it has to make take place outside its home jurisdiction, so that the transaction is not unlawful in its intended place of performance, the lender may not be excused by English law from its contractual obligations under the facility,[137] unless it could argue that the contract had been frustrated.[138] To cover the possibility that the lender may be at risk in such circumstances, the agreement should contain a provision which gives the lender the right to terminate the facility and call for repayment of any amounts that it might have lent in the event that it becomes unlawful for it to maintain the facility.

3.14.8 Conclusive evidence clauses

Loan facility agreements, security documents, and the like often contain a provision to the effect that a certificate provided by the creditor or one of its officers as to the amount due by the borrower at any time should be treated as conclusive evidence of that fact, save for any error that is manifest on the face of the certificate. Similar provisions will also be found in guarantees with respect to the amount of the guaranteed liabilities. It has been held that such a certificate will be binding

---

[136] See the discussion in Chap 4.
[137] Ibid.
[138] See Chap 1.

upon the borrower or the guarantor and cannot be challenged in proceedings to enforce payment of the amount of the relevant liability.[139] On the other hand, it has been held that a clause in a bank's terms and conditions with its customer, by which the customer agreed that any statement of account produced by the bank would be binding upon the customer and that the bank would not be responsible for any loss suffered by the customer if it contained any error, unless the customer queried the statement within a defined period after it received the statement, should be construed as only relating to areas of computation. It was designed as a form of release by the customer of the bank for claims for consequential loss that the customer might suffer as a result of a customer being misinformed about its financial position. It did not serve to validate items wrongly debited to the account, such as an invalid interest charge.[140]

3.14.9 Set-off provisions

One of the ways in which a party's liabilities may be settled is through the operation of netting or set-off. Those matters are dealt with substantively elsewhere in this book.[141] For present purposes, it is relevant to observe that under English law rights of set-off may be enhanced or restricted[142] by contract. However, set-off is mandatory in the insolvency of either of the parties between whom there have been mutual dealings and it is not possible to contract out of set-off in insolvency.[143] Contractual provisions which advance and restrict rights of set-off are frequently to be found in a loan facility agreement. The rights are enhanced in favour of the lender, so that it can set-off any liability it may have to the borrower against the borrower's obligations to it, such as by the application of a credit balance in the borrower's favour against the borrower's liability under the loan agreement. The right of the borrower to assert a claim to set-off is restricted. This rather unevenly handed approach may appear to be unfair. The justification from the lender's perspective is that it relies upon receiving payments from the borrower to meet its own obligations for payment in the interbank market with respect to the funding it has obtained for the purposes of the facility. Precluding a right of set-off

---

[139] *Bache & Co (London) Ltd v Banque Vernes et Commerciale de Paris SA* [1973] 2 Lloyd's Rep 437, which was a case concerning a guarantee. See also *Van Der Merwe v IIG Capital LLC* [2008] EWCA Civ 542.

[140] *Financial Institutions Services Limited v Negril Holdings Limited* [2004] UKPC 40.

[141] See Chap 14.

[142] *Coca-Cola Financial Corp v Finsat International Ltd* [1998] QB 43, but this is subject to the possible operation of the Unfair Contract Terms Act 1977 and the Unfair Terms in Consumer Contracts Regs 1999 (SI 1999/2083): see *Stewart Gill Ltd v Horatio Meyer & Co Ltd* [1992] QB 600; *Governor & Co of the Bank of Scotland v Singh* (unreported 17/6/2005, HHJ Kershaw QC sitting in the High Court in Manchester).

[143] *National Westminster Bank Ltd v Halesowen Presswork & Assemblies Ltd* [1972] AC 785; *Re Maxwell Communications Corp PLC (No 2)* [1993] 1 WLR 1402; *Re West End Networks Ltd* [2004] UKHL 24, [2004] 2 AC 506.

does not mean that the counter claim on which it would have been based is lost. The counter claim can still be pursued independently but the cash-flow advantage of the set-off is lost, as the debt must be paid in full and the counterclaim sought elsewhere and probably paid at a later date.

3.14.10 Payments made by mistake[144]

It is relevant to consider, briefly, the position under English law where a payment is made in consequence of a mistake held by the payer concerning a matter of fact[145] or of law.[146] The payer has a prima facie right to recover the payment from the recipient, even if the mistake is only held by the payer and is not shared by the payee.[147] The claim for recovery may fail, however, if the payer intends that the payee should have the money at all events.[148] It may also fail if the payment was made for good consideration, in particular if the money is paid to discharge a debt owed to the payee (or the payee's principal on whose behalf the payee is authorised to receive payment), such debt being due by the payer (or the payer's principal in a case where the principal had authorised the payment).[149] In addition, the right to recovery will fail if the payee has changed its position in good faith, or is deemed in law to have done so,[150] even if the payee had paid away the money voluntarily, provided it did so in good faith.[151] A change of position defence (e.g. that the payee had paid away the money it had received from the payer) will not be available if the payee had acted in bad faith, for instance, if it paid away the money with knowledge of the mistake, or if the payment it made was for expenditure that it would have incurred in any event.[152] Nor will the defence be available to the extent that the payee had retained the benefit of its expenditure of the money.[153] It would appear that a defence of change of position can only apply where the change occurred after the receipt by the payee of the money.[154]

---

[144] These matters may be affected by the implementation in the UK of the EC Directive on payment services (2007/64/EC OJ L319/1 5/12/2007), which concerns electronic payments within the EU and the EEA. It contains provisions relating to obligations on a payment service provider to give refunds for incorrectly executed payment orders and payments executed without consent.

[145] *Barclays Bank Ltd v WJ Simms Son & Cooke (Southern) Ltd* [1980] QB 677.

[146] *Kleinwort Benson Ltd v Lincoln City Council* [1999] 2 AC 349.

[147] *National Westminster Bank Ltd v Barclays Bank International Ltd* [1975] QB 654; *Barclays Bank Ltd v WJ Simms Son & Cooke (Southern) Ltd* [1980] QB 677.

[148] Ibid.

[149] Ibid; *Lloyds Bank PLC v Independent Insurance Co Ltd* [2000] QB 110.

[150] *Gowers v Lloyds and National and Provincial Bank Ltd* [1938] 1 All ER 766; *Barclays Bank Ltd v WJ Simms Son & Cooke (Southern) Ltd* [1980] QB 677.

[151] *Lipkin Gorman v Karpnale & Co* [1991] 2 AC 548.

[152] Ibid.

[153] *Scottish Equitable PLC v Derby* [2001] EWCA Civ 369; *National Westminster Bank PLC v Somer International (UK) Ltd* [2001] EWCA Civ 970, [2002] QB 1286.

[154] *South Tyneside Metropolitan BC v Svenska International PLC* [1995] 1 All ER 545.

3.14.10.1 It has been held that if a paying bank which has paid by mistake (e.g. it made the payment without authority) is unable to recover payment from the payee, it may be entitled to recover from its own customer where the payment it made had the effect of discharging a genuine liability that the customer owed to the payee or its principal. This was on the basis that the paying bank should be treated as being subrogated to the claim of the payee (or its principal) against the customer.[155] This has been doubted in later cases, except where it could be said that the customer had ratified the payment.[156]

3.15 Protecting the Lender's Financial Position and its Rate of Return

3.15.1 As previously explained, in most cases a bank will obtain the money to provide a facility by borrowing the funds that are required from other banks in the inter-bank market or from retail deposits that have been placed with it by its customers, for which it must bear a cost. It agrees to lend to the borrower on the basis of making a rate of return calculated by reference to that cost. As has also been seen, the bank expects to receive full payment from the borrower of interest during the life of the loan and (at the due date for repayment) principal, so that the bank can meet its own obligations to pay interest and, ultimately, to repay its own funding. The borrower benefits from this as the cost to the bank of obtaining the funds reflects the bank's own financial standing and the fine rate that it can usually obtain for the funds provided to it.[157] If something occurs which increases the bank's cost base and the underlying cost of funds to the bank, which would have the result of eroding the return that the bank has bargained to receive or which would mean that the bank does not receive in full on the due date the gross amount of interest and principal that it expects to receive from the borrower, then the bank will expect the borrower to meet the extra cost or to make up the diminished return or amount.

3.15.2 Matters along those lines might typically arise in consequence of regulatory or liquidity costs or fees that may be imposed on a bank in connection with a facility or its funding of the facility. They may also arise because of withholding taxes on interest payments that are made or in consequence of a default by the borrower or due to a currency loss that the bank suffers in enforcement proceedings against the borrower.

---

[155] *B Liggett (Liverpool) Ltd v Barclays Bank Ltd* [1928] 1 KB 48.
[156] *Re Cleadon Trust Ltd* [1939] Ch 286; *Crantrave Ltd v Lloyds Bank PLC* [2000] QB 917.
[157] The position was sorely tested in the crisis that enveloped the financial markets in the second part of 2007, in which interbank lending rates exceeded domestic deposit rates.

3.15.3 Mandatory and increased costs

In facilities that are based upon interbank funding in London, the loan facility agreement will contain provisions which require the borrower to compensate the bank for a diminution that it might suffer in its rate of return. Such provisions will be found as a part of the mechanism for calculating and charging interest, where the 'Mandatory Cost' element of the interest rate reflects the continuing regulatory and liquidity fees that are charged to the bank from the inception of the facility and which are referable to the facility.[158] They will also be found in the 'Increased Costs' clause, which covers additional costs or diminished returns to the bank (or an entity affiliated with the bank) arising after it has entered into the facility agreement (except for those included in the calculation of the Mandatory Cost). An example of an increased cost would be where a bank lender or an affiliate of the bank[159] suffers an increased regulatory capital cost because of an adverse change during the life of a facility in the capital adequacy treatment of the facility.[160] There may be some negotiation of what should be covered by the Increased Costs clause when the facility documentation is being prepared, and a number of exceptions may be made which limit its scope.[161]

In a facility funded through retail deposits where interest is charged to the borrower with reference to the bank's base rate, the cost to the bank of such matters is averaged out across all of the bank's borrowers. It is taken into account as a component in arriving at the bank's base rate, so it is not separately and individually charged to the borrower under specific provisions of the facility agreement.

3.15.4

3.15.5 Third party issues

Traditionally, difficulties arose at general law when it was sought to apply the benefit of an Increased Costs clause in favour of a person other than the original lender, such as an assignee of the loan or an affiliate of the lender.[162] In the case of the former, if the assignee sought to enforce the benefit of the agreement as assignee, it might be met by an argument that the clause only applied to the personal circumstances of the assignor, being the original lender.[163] By force of the assignment, the assignor was no longer in the position where it would suffer the costs and impositions covered by the clause. An assignee could not be in a better position than the assignor, nor should the borrower be required to meet claims

---

[158] In most loan facility agreements, the Mandatory Cost is calculated by reference to a formula which is set out in one of the Schedules to the agreement.

[159] For instance, as may arise under consolidated supervision of the bank and the affiliate.

[160] For a description of such matters, see Chap 2.

[161] For instance, as to the implementation of the revised capital standards under Basel 2.

[162] See generally the discussion on these issues in Chap 1.

[163] Of course, if a claim under the clause had already accrued in favour of the original lender, it could assign the right to be paid.

that did not relate to the rights of the original lender.[164] If the assignee tried, in the alternative, to argue that the clause was intended to benefit it personally and not just as an assignee seeking to assert the assignor's rights, it might be met by a privity of contract point; that is, that it was seeking to enforce the contract in that regard as a stranger to the contract. A privity of contract point might also be raised against an affiliate which sought on its own behalf to enforce the contract. It was a stranger to the contract with no right to enforce it for its own benefit (unless, of course, it was a contracting party to the contract).

3.15.5.1 In an attempt to defeat those arguments, the original lender might seek to enforce the contract itself on behalf of those persons. If it did so, it would be met by an argument that it was seeking to enforce the agreement for the benefit of a non-contracting party so that the loss it suffered if the borrower failed to pay was merely a nominal loss. One possible counter to this, although it seems rather far-fetched, would be for the contracting party to obtain an equitable mandatory order requiring the payment to be made because damages would clearly be an inadequate remedy.[165] Another possibility would be for the original lender to argue that it had contracted, with respect to the benefit of the provision, as the agent or trustee of such other persons, although such a role is not commonly acknowledged in loan facility agreements. Another way around the problem from the perspective of a potential assignee would be to novate the facility agreement in favour of the assignee/transferee, so that it would obtain a direct contractual relationship with the borrower, as is commonly done in the case of syndicated facilities.

3.15.5.2 The problems as just described can now be overcome. Under the Contracts (Rights of Third Parties) Act 1999, it is possible for a third party which was intended to benefit under a contract to enforce the intended benefit of the contract in its own right, provided that the application of the Act has not been disapplied by the contract and the other requirements of the Act have been met. This means that it is now possible for a person in the position of an assignee or an affiliate of the lender to enforce a clause like an Increased Costs clause for its own benefit, so long as it can be demonstrated that the clause was not intended to be solely for the benefit of the original lender.[166]

3.15.6 Grossing up clauses

To protect the lender against the effect of the imposition of withholding taxes (and similar types of mandatory deductions from payments that are to be made by

---

[164] *Dawson v Great Northern & City Ry Co* [1905] 1 KB 260.

[165] *Beswick v Beswick* [1968] AC 58.

[166] See further Chap 1. A similar analysis and outcome may also be relevant in the case of the Grossing Up clause that is discussed below.

the borrower), the agreement will contain a 'Grossing Up' clause, to which further reference is made below. The expression 'withholding tax' is used to describe a requirement that is imposed by law on a person that makes a payment (typically a payment of a revenue nature, such as an interest payment). The payer is required to deduct from the payment an amount being a tax charge referable to the amount payable to the recipient of the payment. The amount deducted is then paid over by the payer to the relevant taxing authority. A withholding tax is usually imposed by the country in which the payer is resident or from which it is to make the payment. In effect, the payer is acting as the tax collection agent of the relevant country. The nature and incidence of withholding taxes differs from one jurisdiction to the next but, in some instances, the charge may be imposed without reference to the taxable status, residence, or affairs of the recipient. In other cases, the incidence of a withholding tax charge can be avoided, such as by reference to the residence and status of the recipient (e.g. the recipient has a tax residence in the relevant country and so is subject to its normal tax rules) or through the operation of a double tax treaty between the country where the deduction would have to be made and the country of residence of the recipient.

In the UK, the relevant statutory provisions dealing with the equivalent of withholding tax on interest payments are to be found in section 874 of the Income Tax Act 2007 (ITA 2007). It imposes a withholding or deduction obligation on the payer with respect to 'yearly interest' (basically, interest on a loan which may exist for more than a year), if the payer is a company or a partnership of which a company is a member, or if the recipient's usual place of residence is outside the UK. The interest must have a UK source or the payer must be subject to UK tax. Where such a deduction is required then the payer must account to HM Revenue & Customs for the amount so withheld. There are a number of exceptions to the withholding requirement. One exception applies to interest that is payable on an advance from a UK bank,[167] where the person beneficially entitled to receive it (which could be an assignee of the UK bank which advanced the loan) is within the UK charge to tax with respect to the interest.[168] Another set of exceptions[169] applies to interest paid by a local authority, a company, or a partnership which includes a company to a payee that is either UK tax resident or which carries on a trade in the UK through a permanent establishment in the UK and brings the interest into its UK tax account or which meets certain other criteria. Yet another exception applies to interest that is paid by a UK bank in the ordinary course of its business.[170] There are also exceptions that will apply in consequence of double tax treaties between the UK and other countries.

3.15.6.1

---

[167] As defined by s 991 of ITA 2007.
[168] S 879 of ITA 2007.
[169] Ss 933–937 of ITA 2007.
[170] S 878 of ITA 2007.

3.15.6.2   A Grossing Up clause is to the effect that if the borrower is required by the law of any relevant jurisdiction to make a deduction from any amount payable to the lender, it will pay to the lender a total sum which comprises both the original amount as so reduced and such an additional amount (after taking account of any further deduction that might be attracted to the grossed up amount) as will ensure that the lender receives in total the full gross amount it would have received had such a deduction not been required. It can be seen that, from the borrower's perspective, the effect of having to gross up the payment is that the borrower will find that it has to pay far more than the original amount, as it will have to pay the deducted amount to the relevant tax authority and it will have to pay an additional amount to the lender so as to ensure that the lender receives the full amount it should have received without the deduction.

3.15.6.3   A well advised borrower may seek certain qualifications to the operation of a Grossing Up clause, particularly to reflect the scope of statutory exceptions that would normally be available to a lender had it met the relevant criteria as, for instance, outlined above under UK legislation. The borrower may also seek a right of reimbursement from any additional amount that it has paid to the lender where the lender obtains a tax credit referable to the amount that was withheld and paid over to a taxing authority. In theory, the amount withheld and paid over to the tax authority should be applied as a credit against the lender's own tax liability; in effect, it amounts to a pre-payment of the lender's tax liability. Most lenders will concede the point in principle but hedge it about with various conditions; for instance, that the concession should only apply if the lender would normally be subject to tax in the relevant jurisdiction and that its application should not prejudice the freedom of the lender to arrange its tax affairs in the manner it wishes, such as by the utilisation of other credits available to the lender. In practice, it is difficult for the borrower to gain much advantage from the point.

3.15.7 Indemnity provisions

A loan facility agreement is also likely to contain indemnity provisions in favour of the lender which apply in relation to a default by the borrower or a currency loss that the bank suffers in enforcement proceedings against the borrower. The provisions concerning default usually apply to cover losses that the lender may suffer because it does not receive a payment on its due date or where an anticipated drawing does not proceed. The type of losses will include losses on funding that the lender has obtained or contracted to obtain and which cannot be recouped. Where the facility contemplates that the lender will enter into hedging arrangements with respect to currency or interest rate exposures associated with the facility, the indemnity will extend to cover associated losses that the lender may suffer if the borrower fails to fulfil its obligations under the facility; for instance, because the lender has to break or retire the hedging arrangements ahead of their normal expiry date.[171] Currency losses may be suffered by the lender where it has to convert a claim into a local currency for the purposes of bringing a claim or enforcing a judgment or so as to lodge a proof in an insolvency of the borrower.[172]

3.16 The Monitoring and Minding Provisions in a Loan Facility Agreement

The description of clauses in a loan facility agreement as the 'monitoring and minding' provisions of the agreement is used here merely for convenience to describe the clauses of the agreement which, together with the events of default clause, relate to the legal and commercial circumstances and state of affairs of the borrower (and, often, those affiliated with it) and its or their financial affairs, business, assets, and legal status. The relevant provisions comprise the representations and warranties clause and the covenants or undertaking clauses. The former contains the representations and warranties that are stated as being given by the borrower so as to induce the lender to grant and maintain the facility. The latter sets out the 'do's' and 'don'ts' of what the borrower (and its affiliates) will do and will not do during the course of the facility so as to preserve and maintain the economic, commercial, and legal state of affairs, and the flow of information relating to the borrower (and its affiliates) that the lender expects to receive for the duration of the facility. There is often some degree of overlap in the subject matter of the provisions (particularly as between the subject matter of the representations and warranties, on the one hand, and the covenants and undertakings, on the other) and it is necessary to ensure that the overlap does not lead to any inconsistency between them.

3.16.1

As just indicated, the provisions are likely to refer to both the borrower and those that are affiliated within the same corporate group as the borrower. A group in this sense will probably fall within much the same definition as a consolidated group for accounting purposes, although it may also be relevant to include other companies or entities in which a member of the group has a participating interest or which, for purely technical reasons, may not fall within the consolidation. Although as a strict matter of law a borrower is regarded as a separate legal entity from the other members of its group (assuming, that is, that the borrower is a corporation or other form of separate legal entity), as a matter of economic and commercial reality, it is likely that there will be some fairly close degree of connection and inter-dependence between them. The relationship may be reflected explicitly if

3.16.2

---

[171] For an example of the type of loss that may be suffered, see the Scottish case of *Bank of Scotland v Dunedin Property Investment Co Ltd* [1999] SLT 470.

[172] See the discussion in Chap 4.

other members of the group are to give a guarantee or security for the borrower's obligations under the facility. Even without that formal recognition, it is likely that the connection will be important in relation to the borrower's business, assets, and resources. For instance, if the borrower is the holding company of a group of companies, their affairs are of immediate relevance to it. Similarly, there may be a trading or financial dependence between the members of the group, they may share or supply assets or stock to each other, and so forth. Exceptions may be made for companies that are entirely irrelevant to the fortunes of the borrower, such as non-trading companies with no assets. If the borrower is not the parent company of the group, it might be felt to be more appropriate that the parent should make statements and give undertakings about the group members and their affairs, in which case the parent will need to be a party to the loan facility agreement, or its involvement will have to be incorporated in some other legally binding manner.

3.16.3 These provisions fit in with the remainder of the agreement in that the agreement will provide that if they are breached or not observed (or, indeed, if such a state of affairs is likely to occur) the borrower may be denied the right to avail itself of the facility or the remainder of it that has not been drawn. If a breach actually occurs the same may also constitute an event of default which entitles the lender to suspend or terminate the facility and accelerate the borrower's obligation to repay the total amount that has been drawn, although sometimes the borrower may be given a second chance if it can rectify the position before the lender has taken the step of terminating the facility. The borrower may also be required to certify its proper observance of these provisions before it may make a drawing and at various times during the life of the facility. Because of their importance in the context of the agreement and the availability of the facility and the effect that they will have on the continuing affairs of the borrower and its affiliates during the life of the facility, the monitoring and minding provisions of the agreement, together with the events of default clause, usually give rise to most of the contentious discussion that may take place during the negotiations that lead to settling the wording of the agreement.

3.16.4 As previously noted, in facilities to finance a takeover bid and in certain other types of acquisition finance, where certainty of funding is a pre-requisite for a transaction to be announced and to proceed, the lender might be required to permit a drawing to take place and so to provide funds even if there has been a breach of the representations and warranties clause or a default in the borrower's observance of the covenants and undertaking.

3.16.5 Due to their importance and content, the representations and warranties clause, on the one hand, and the provisions containing the covenants and undertakings, on the other, will be examined separately.

3.17 Representations and Warranties

3.17.1 Preliminary observations

In traditional legal analysis, a representation is a statement of fact (rather than opinion) that is made prior to the making of a contract; it is made by one party to the other party so as to induce that other party to enter into the contract. In this context, a warranty is a statement to similar effect that has become a term of the contract. Prior to the Misrepresentation Act 1967, the making of a misrepresentation (whether fraudulently, negligently, or innocently made) gave rise to a right in the recipient to rescind the contract, provided it could show that the representation was substantially untrue and that it had relied on the representation in deciding whether it should enter into the contract, but that right was easily lost. There was no claim for damages available to the recipient of an innocent misrepresentation. A breach of a warranty gave rise to a claim for damages but there was no right to rescind. The deficiencies in the law concerning innocent misrepresentations and warranties were largely rectified by sections 1 and 2 of the Act, although section 2(1) does give the representor a defence to a claim for damages for a misrepresentation if it can show that it was not negligent in making the representation and section 2(2) gives the court the power to award damages in lieu of a right to rescind. On the other hand, if the representation was made fraudulently or negligently, there was a claim for damages at general law, as a claim in deceit or for a negligent misrepresentation, which right remained after the passing of the Act.[173]

Such legal niceties are not of great importance to the lender in the context of the representations and warranties clause of a loan facility agreement. The lender is not really very interested in having a claim for damages or, more tenuously, a claim for rescission. Nor is the lender likely to be interested in the distinction between matters of fact (for which the law gives remedies if they were incorrectly represented) and matters of opinion (for which no remedy is available[174]). What the lender needs, and what a well drafted agreement should provide, is the right to refuse to make advances to the borrower if the terms of the clause (whether relating strictly to factual matters or concerning matters of opinion) have been breached or if such a breach is likely to occur (which right will usually be found in the provisions relating to drawings). In addition, the lender will wish to have the right, where the clause has been breached, to suspend or terminate the facility and to demand repayment of any amounts already advanced to the borrower, perhaps with some opportunity being afforded to the borrower to rectify the breach before 3.17.2

---

[173] See further the discussion of these matters in Chap 9.

[174] With the rather fine distinction that a statement of opinion might be taken to imply the fact that the maker genuinely held the opinion: see *Edgington v Fitzmaurice* (1885) 29 ChD 459.

the lender takes such drastic action. Such a right is conferred by the events of default clause.

3.17.3 To achieve those aims, the clause also departs from a traditional legal analysis by providing that the statements that are made by the borrower under it are stated as being made not just as at the time of the signing of the agreement but are also to be treated as being repeated at various intervals during the life of the facility. So as to keep the statements that are made by the borrower up to date, the clause will provide that each repetition will be expressed to be by reference to the facts and circumstances prevailing at the time of the repetition, with specific exceptions being provided in the clause for matters that the borrower was only prepared to warrant at the date the agreement was signed.

3.17.4 It follows that the role of the representations and warranties clause in a facility agreement is partly preliminary to the facility being made available and, in that sense, acts as an inducement to the lender to enter into the agreement and provide the facility, and partly continuing as to the availability of drawings during the commitment or availability period of the facility and as to the continuance of the facility once the drawings have been made. From a practical perspective, the pro- posed wording of the clause also has another role even before the agreement is signed. Once the wording of the clause has been produced in the negotiations prior to the signing of the agreement, it should flush out any potential difficulties that then exist or which may be anticipated, as the borrower should be encouraged to indicate those matters where it cannot accurately give the statements that the wording requires. It is always far better that these matters are brought out into the open and addressed at that stage (perhaps by providing for exceptions by reference to a statement of disclosures that is made by the borrower), rather than giving rise to difficulties because of a breach occurring later on.

3.17.5 Types of provision

For explanatory purposes, the representations and warranties may be divided into two categories. The description that follows refers to the borrower but the same issues will also concern other members of the borrower's group, particularly those that might be giving guarantees or security for the transaction, where reference is made to them in the clause.

3.17.5.1 The first category concerns matters relating to legal issues, such as:

(1) the due existence, status, powers, and authority to contract of the borrower and those who act on its behalf;[175]

---

[175] As a matter of English law, a company may be unable to give a representation that it has power to enter into a transaction when it lacked the corporate capacity to enter into that transaction: see Aldous LJ in *British and Commonwealth Holdings PLC v Barclays Bank PLC* [1996] 1 WLR 1, at 24.

(2) the legal validity and enforceability of the documentation and the transaction overall;

(3) the ranking of the lender's rights as a creditor;

(4) the tax treatment of the transaction (particularly as to payments to be made under the facility);

(5) that the transaction will not contravene the rights of third parties;

(6) that the borrower has all the necessary consents and permits that are required for it to own its assets and carry on its business; and

(7) that the borrower intends and will use the proceeds of the facility for lawful and legitimate purposes.[176]

The second category concerns commercial and factual matters, such as: **3.17.5.2**

(1) the absence of litigation which might adversely affect the borrower, its business or assets and its ability to perform its obligations under the facility;

(2) that no events of default have occurred under the facility and that no similar events have occurred under other transactions to which the borrower is a party;

(3) that the financial and accounting statements that it has supplied to the lender give a true and fair view of it and its assets as at the date and for the period to which they relate, do not omit any matters that were material and had been prepared in accordance with the requisite accounting standards;

(4) that there has been no material adverse change in the circumstances of the borrower and its assets since the date of those statements;

(5) that other information which has been supplied to the lender was true and accurate and did not omit any material matters; and

(6) that opinions that have been expressed to the lender concerning the borrower and its affairs were held on reasonable grounds.

There may also be additional representations and warranties relating to matters that are specific to the borrower's business and its assets (for instance, as to environmental matters if that is relevant to the business), the facility, and the use of the finance provided under it.

3.17.6 Negotiating points

Needless to say, a well advised borrower will scrutinise the wording that has been presented to it as part of the negotiating process before the agreement is signed and seek to ameliorate the strictness represented by that wording before it is

---

[176] The last of these representations and warranties may be helpful to the lender in resisting an argument that it knowingly participated (by providing the finance) in an unlawful scheme or activity in which the borrower was engaged. Of course, if the lender was aware of the facts, the representation and warranty will be of no avail.

prepared to proceed. Qualifications to the wording that may be sought might be along the following lines:

(1) where the representations and warranties concern other members of its group, the borrower may seek to exclude references to companies that are not directly involved in the transaction and are of no material significance to the group taken as a consolidated whole;

(2) it may seek to qualify the statements concerning legal matters by reference to the types of qualification that appear in legal opinions. A lender needs to be careful in accepting such a qualification where it relates to matters that concern questions of reasonableness, that an opinion is genuinely held (for instance, that a default interest clause represents a genuine pre-estimate of loss) or that a certain factual situation existed when the facility was signed;

(3) in relation to the commercial and factual statements contained in the representations and warranties, the borrower might wish to qualify them by reference to a test of materiality and the likely effect that such matters may have on the lender's rights and the borrower's state of health and its ability to perform its obligations under the facility. After all, no business is run perfectly and many events may occur which have no significance to its long-term operations and viability; and

(4) as previously indicated, the borrower might also seek exceptions to the statements by reference to specific disclosures that it has made to the lender.

3.18 Covenants and Undertakings

3.18.1 Preliminary observations

The words 'covenants' and 'undertakings' these days are used interchangeably, although a traditionally trained English lawyer would prefer to see the use of the word 'covenant' confined so that it describes obligations that are created by deed. In a loan facility agreement, the covenants and undertakings clause (sometimes there is more than one clause in the agreement dealing with this subject) contains the obligations undertaken by the borrower in favour of the lender relating to what the borrower will do and will not do during the period of the facility. From the lender's perspective, the intention behind the clause is to require that the economic, commercial, and legal state of affairs of the borrower should be preserved and maintained for the duration of the facility, as well as to provide for a flow of information relating to the borrower that the lender expects to receive in that period. Essentially, the covenants and undertakings reflect the agreement between the parties that the state of affairs concerning the borrower on which the lender made its decision to proceed with the facility should be maintained by the borrower for the duration of the facility (or even improved), as well as to provide the lender with relevant information so that it can asses and check the position from time to time. As previously mentioned, these provisions may extend to cover the affairs of other members of the borrower's group. If the borrower wishes to depart from the legislated position as it was agreed in the facility agreement then it must seek the lender's consent.

As with the position concerning the representations and warranties clause, a lend- **3.18.2** er's objective in relation to a breach by the borrower of the covenants and undertakings is not to pursue the remedies that might be available at general law,[177] but, rather, that it should have the right to refuse to make advances to the borrower if the clause has been breached or if such a breach is likely to occur (which right will usually be found in the provisions relating to drawings). This should be viewed together with the right of the lender (under the events of default clause), where the clause has been breached, to suspend or terminate the facility and to demand repayment of any amounts already advanced to the borrower, perhaps with some opportunity being afforded to the borrower to rectify the breach before the lender takes such drastic action. Of course, no sensible lender would enter into an agreement with a borrower if it thought it likely that the borrower would default under its obligations or, worse, deliberately breach those obligations. The whole point of the undertakings and covenants is to lay down a set of rules which the borrower is able and willing to observe, which can only be achieved as a result of a sensible negotiation between the parties before the agreement is signed. It also means that the parties should act sensibly during the currency of the agreement in an attempt to overcome difficulties that may arise before they turn into insuperable problems.

In recent years it became fashionable to limit the extent of the covenants and **3.18.3** undertakings in high yield[178] facilities granted to borrowers with lower credit ratings who were raising more risky finance under so-called 'covenant light' (or worse, 'cov lite'[179]) facilities, particularly in facilities designed to finance the activities of private equity groups and such like. To some extent, this trend reflected the easy flow of credit that had become available and the fact that a great deal of the debt arising under such facilities was held by creditors which were not banks (such debt often having been acquired by a process of transfer in the secondary markets after the debt was advanced). Whilst the relevant loan facility agreements retained some of the obligations and restrictions traditionally imposed upon borrowers, they also relaxed the more traditional restrictions on the potential activities of

---

[177] Such as by way of a claim for damages and, perhaps, a claim to terminate the agreement for a repudiatory breach of contract. The one exception to this may be where the lender might seek an injunction to restrain a threatened breach by the borrower of the negative pledge clause or the clause which limits the disposal of assets, as discussed further below.

[178] I.e. bearing a higher rate of interest than would apply for a less risky transaction.

[179] Which expression is reminiscent of fizzy drinks and cigarettes.

borrowers in matters such as those relating to acquisitions and disposals of assets and the granting of security. In addition, they contained a relaxation of the usual forms of financial covenants. They also made provision for processes under which a borrower might be assisted in obtaining consents and waivers if it wished to depart from the requirements of the remaining undertakings and covenants in an agreement, as well as procedures for dissenting creditors to be removed from the facility and replaced by more compliant successors. Time will tell if there was wisdom in the pursuit of that fashion, but it is difficult to escape from the impression that there was a 'wild west' environment generated by easy access to credit in the financial markets.

3.18.4 Shadow directors

At the opposite end of the scale, there is a risk that a bank which becomes too closely involved in the affairs of its borrower and which has the effective power to control or direct its activities and its decision-making processes, may find itself accused of being in the position of a 'shadow director' of the borrower. This is a particular concern in a situation where a borrower might be in financial difficulties, in pursuance of which the lender might have imposed strict conditions as to the conduct of the borrower's business, as well as onerous monitoring and supervision of the borrower, as a requirement for its continued support of the borrower. Under English law, the consequences to a lender of being found to be a shadow director are serious. It may, for instance, find itself exposed to disqualification proceedings under the Company Directors Disqualification Act 1986[180] or to misfeasance proceedings under the Insolvency Act 1986,[181] and such circumstances might also be relevant to the continuance of its authorisation under the Financial Services and Markets Act 2000 (FSMA) and any licence that it may hold under the Consumer Credit Act 2006. In addition, transactions between a borrower and a shadow director may require the observance of the special procedures provided for transactions with directors and related parties under Chapter 3 and Chapter 4 of Part 10 of the Companies Act 2006.[182] Any such transaction may also attract the additional disadvantages that are relevant to connected persons who have entered into transactions with the borrower in a period before the onset of insolvency under the Insolvency Act 1986.[183] There may also be adverse consequences under tax and environmental legislation.

---

[180] See s 6(3C) of the Act.

[181] For instance, for fraudulent trading under s 213 of the Act (where, strictly speaking, it is not necessary for the liquidator to prove that the person knowingly concerned in the fraudulent carrying on of the company's business was a shadow director of the insolvent company) or for wrongful trading under s 214 of the Act.

[182] See ss 187 and 223 of the Act.

[183] Under ss 238, 239, and 245 of the Act.

A 'shadow director' of a company is defined[184] to mean: **3.18.4.1**

> a person in accordance with whose directions or instructions the directors of the company are accustomed to act (but so that a person is not deemed a shadow director by reason only that the directors act on advice given by him in a professional capacity).

It had been said that for the definition to apply there must have been an element of subservience by the directors to the will of the other person; such a person should be like a puppet master pulling the strings behind the curtain.[185] Accordingly, it used to be thought that if the lender did not engage in active intervention in the borrower's day-to-day affairs, but simply imposed conditions in the contract between it and the borrower which the borrower had to observe if it wished the lender to continue providing its facilities, that would not make the lender a shadow director. The borrower could decide whether it wished to accept the terms of the facility or decline to use the facility, even where there was financial dependency of the borrower on the lender for the borrower's continued existence.[186]

The position is now less certain in view of the decision of Morritt LJ in *Secretary* **3.18.4.2** *of State for Trade and Industry v Deverell.*[187] His Lordship made a number of observations as to the meaning of the concept of shadow directorship, which could mean that third parties, such as banks, might be held to be shadow directors. His Lordship said that the definition should not be construed narrowly but, rather, in the normal way in light of an intention to protect the public against the consequences of directors acting on the directions or instructions of a shadow director. There was no need for the person to have been 'in the shadows'; his involvement could be public and obvious. It was not necessary to show that the directors acted in a subservient role or that they surrendered all of their discretions to that person. Such a person should be shown to have real influence over the affairs of the company but it need not be over the whole field of its activities. It was necessary to ascertain objectively whether the person's words or conduct amounted to directions or instructions, but it was not necessary to prove any understanding or expectation on the part of the giver or recipients of those directions and instructions that they would be followed. Although the definition excludes advice given in a professional capacity, non-professional advice could be caught.

---

[184] By s 251 of the Insolvency Act 1986. Similar definitions are to be found in s 22(5) of the Company Directors Disqualification Act 1986 and in s 251 of the Companies Act 2006.

[185] *Re Unisoft Group Ltd (No 3)* [1994] 1 BCLC 609, at 620.

[186] *Re PFRZM Ltd* [1995] BCC 280. See also Sir Peter Millett, 'Shadow Directorships—A real or imagined threat to the banks' [1991] Insolvency Practitioner 14.

[187] [2001] Ch 340, at [24]–[36]. See also the judgment of Finn J in the Australian case of *Australian Securities Commission v AS Nominees Ltd* (1995) 133 ALR 1.

3.18.4.3 It is submitted that in light of those observations, a lender should be very careful before it becomes too involved in the affairs of a borrower, such as in a situation where it might wish to monitor the borrower closely, particularly if the borrower is in financial difficulties. The imposition of covenants and undertakings along the usual lines in a loan facility agreement is a normal fact of life and should not lead to any difficulties in this area. However, if the agreement is too prescriptive so that it has the effect of controlling to a large degree the conduct of the affairs and activities of the borrower, that could be a problem, particularly if there was a dependence upon the lender for the continued survival of the borrower. It would be even more damning if the lender had actively become involved in the conduct of the business, such as where the borrower was required to obtain the lender's consent before it could make payments and deal with everyday matters.

3.18.5 Having made those preliminary observations, it is now relevant to examine the types of covenants and undertakings that will usually be found in a loan facility agreement.

3.18.6 Information undertakings

The undertakings to provide information to the lender usually relate to matters along the following lines:

(1) an obligation to furnish accounting information at specified intervals during the life of the facility, together with obligations as to the manner in which that information will be compiled and presented, reflecting the consistent application of relevant accounting standards, as well as the necessity for at least the yearly accounts to be audited by auditors of repute. There might also be some further stipulation as to the identity or suitability of the auditors;

(2) a requirement that the lender should be sent the same information as is supplied to the borrower's creditors and shareholders or which is disclosed to stock exchanges and the like;

(3) an obligation to provide information that the lender may require for the purpose of meeting regulatory requirements that are imposed upon the lender, including information that is relevant to the assessment of risk weightings for capital adequacy purposes and information to meet customer knowledge and money laundering requirements;

(4) the borrower may be required to produce other information that may be relevant to the affairs of the borrower and other relevant entities, either when it becomes known to the borrower[188] or when requested by the lender;[189]

---

[188] See the discussion as to the attribution to a corporate borrower of knowledge that was held by one of its directors in *Jafari-Fini (Mohammad) v Skillglass Ltd* [2007] EWCA Civ 261.

[189] See the discussion of such a requirement in *Milner Laboratories Ltd v Citibank NA* (unreported, Morison J 18/12/2001).

(5) the borrower may be obliged to provide information relating to the occurrence of an event of default or the likelihood of such an event occurring; and

(6) the borrower may be required to supply certificates at various times, signed by its directors, confirming compliance by the borrower with the covenants and undertakings in the agreement.

3.18.7 Financial covenants

Financial covenants are intended to regulate and preserve the financial and economic position of the borrower (and, where relevant, its group). By them, the lender wishes to be assured that, provided the borrower observes the covenants, the borrower will have sufficient resources to meet its obligations to the lender as they become due for payment. These types of covenant have the effect of requiring the borrower to ensure the maintenance and, perhaps, the improvement of that position during the life of the facility. If the borrower has difficulty in meeting the covenants, or breaches them, that should serve as a warning that all is not well, although the value of such a warning mechanism is open to doubt, for the reasons mentioned below. Some of the covenants relate to successive periods and provide that during such periods, a certain state of affairs will be maintained. Other covenants speak of the circumstances as at the end of each such period, because they relate to the cumulative position at the end of the period. The formulation and measurement of the covenants and what they require is based upon the financial statements of the borrower (and its group), including the profit and loss account and the balance sheet, but it is common for the loan facility agreement to provide for adjustments to be made to what is contained in those financial statements, so as to take into account additional material or to ignore certain other matters. Such financial statements will normally include the annual audited accounts, as well as half yearly accounts and, not infrequently, quarterly and monthly accounts.

As a method of monitoring the borrower's observance of the covenants, the loan facility agreement will almost invariably provide for certificates to be provided by the borrower at the end of each of the relevant periods. The certificates are intended to confirm that the borrower has complied with the covenants for the period and as at the date to which the certificate relates or, alternatively, state that it has been unable to do so and give an explanation of the reasons for the failure to comply. The certificates should be signed by one or more of the directors of the borrower on its behalf. Sometimes a loan facility agreement may also require that the auditors of the borrower should confirm the accuracy of what is stated by reference to the borrower's audited accounts, although auditors are increasingly reluctant to undertake such a task because of the responsibilities that might be associated with such a role.[190]

3.18.7.1

---

[190] For instance, it might be argued that they have accepted responsibility towards the lender for the accuracy of what is stated in such a way that the lender may argue that they owed it a duty of care

It should also be remembered that such certificates speak historically so that the grounds for a breach of the covenants may already have occurred or be accumulating prior to the date on which the certificate is to be provided. In such a case, the borrower would probably have been obliged to alert the lender to the looming problem in pursuance of its obligations under the fifth of the obligations to provide information (as to actual or potential defaults) as set out above. Whether it did so, of course, is another matter, which may well have depended upon its appreciation of the significance of the potential problem.

3.18.7.2 Some of the traditional types of financial covenant that are contained in a loan facility agreement are as follows:

(1) there may be a requirement that the worth or balance sheet value of the borrower (and its group) will be maintained at not less than a certain stated amount in each of the periods. The requirement may be expressed to vary (usually upwards) from one period to a later period. Adjustments may be required in ascertaining the amount of such worth by ignoring the value (if any) ascribed in the accounts to intangible assets, such as intellectual property[191] and goodwill, by adjusting the value of holdings in companies that are not wholly owned and by moderating or ignoring upwards revaluations of assets (particularly if they cannot be justified on objective grounds), in which case the covenant will relate to the tangible net worth of the borrower. An adjustment in the opposite direction may permit subordinated debt to be treated as if it were equity share capital, where that debt is subordinated in right of payment behind the debt due to the lender under the loan facility agreement;

(2) there may be a gearing covenant, which limits the amount of financial indebtedness of the borrower when compared with its worth or tangible net worth at any time in each of the periods. The concept of financial indebtedness is usually drafted widely, to encompass all of the various ways in which debt or credit may be raised and remain outstanding, including debt or credit arising under or concerning borrowing facilities, acceptance credit and other types of banking facilities, debt instruments, the deferred price for the provision of goods and services, advance payment arrangements, redeemable capital, recourse receivables purchase facilities, certain types of derivatives

---

in the tort of negligence on the basis of claim under *Hedley Byrne & Co Ltd v Heller & Partners Ltd* [1964] AC 465. If there were such an acceptance of responsibility, the position of the auditors in *Caparo Industries plc v Dickman* [1990] 2 AC 605 would be overcome (see, for instance, the approach taken by the Outer House of the Court of Session in *Royal Bank of Scotland v Bannerman Johnstone Maclay* [2003] SLT 181 and compare with *Al Saudi Banque v Clarke Pixley* [1990] 1 Ch 313).

191 The valuation of these matters has always been difficult and often ignored in preparing financial statements. However, if the borrower's business is reliant upon intellectual property, such as trade marks, patents, design rights, and copyright, there may be a strong commercial case to recognise their value in determining the worth of the borrower.

transactions and option arrangements, equipment finance facilities, and suretyship obligations;

(3) there may be an interest cover covenant, under which the amount of interest payable by the borrower for a period is compared against its earnings for the period. Interest is defined widely to include all payments in the nature of interest, howsoever called. Earnings is taken as the bottom line figure on the profit and loss account, after ignoring any interest earned for the period and adding back any deductions for interest and taxation[192] and (sometimes) adding back the amount referable to any depreciation or amortisation of assets;[193]

(4) there may be a cash flow cover covenant, which measures outgoings (including some or all of debt service costs for interest and principal, tax payments and other expenditure) over a period against earnings and movements in working capital for that period;

(5) there may be restrictions on capital expenditure in each of the periods; and

(6) if security is to be given, there may be a security cover covenant, by which the value of the secured assets must exceed a certain multiple of the amount of principal and interest outstanding under the facility.

3.18.8 Other covenants and undertakings

The remaining undertakings and covenants in a loan facility agreement impose various restrictions on the scope of the borrower's activities during the period of the facility, and are also designed to maintain and preserve the position of the lender vis-a-vis the other creditors of the borrower. There may also be particular obligations that are undertaken by the borrower with respect to the particular purpose or project for which the facility has been provided which will be of relevance, for instance, in the financing of construction and infrastructure projects and in acquisition finance. The discussion that follows will refer to the covenants and undertakings that are normally found in loan facility agreements and which concern changes in the nature and scope of the borrower's business, the ranking of the lender's claims as against those of the other creditors of the borrower, and the negative pledge and anti-disposals clauses.

3.18.9 Maintenance of business

The borrower will undertake to carry on its business as it was undertaken at the commencement of the facility and that it will not vary the nature of its business. The point behind this covenant is that the lender will have made its decision to grant the facility to the borrower on the strength of the borrower's business as it

---

192 Often referred to as 'EBIT'.
193 Often referred to as 'EBITDA'.

existed when the decision was made. If the borrower undertakes a different type of business, that may expose it to risks that it does not understand and which may imperil its financial position. Allied to this, there may be a covenant to maintain all agreements, licences, and consents that are necessary for that business and the holding and use of its assets. There will probably also be an undertaking to maintain adequate insurance in connection with such business and assets.

3.18.10 Ranking

The lender will be concerned as to its ranking as a creditor of the borrower, particularly in an insolvency of the borrower. This concern will be manifested in two sets of undertakings by the borrower. The first, which is particularly relevant if the lender is providing the facility on an unsecured basis, will be that the borrower should ensure that the lender's claims will rank in an insolvency of the borrower *pari passu*[194] with the claims of all of the other unsecured creditors of the borrower, except for those mandatorily preferred by law.[195] Whilst that is the general position under English law,[196] there are some jurisdictions where it is possible for an unsecured creditor's claim to gain priority in an insolvency over the claims of other unsecured creditors by following certain procedures. If the lender is taking security then the clause should provide that, to the extent of the security, the lender's claims will have a first claim on such security (assuming that is intended to be the case) and, otherwise, that its residual unsecured claim will rank *pari passu* with the claims of the other unsecured creditors.

3.18.11 Negative pledge and disposals of assets

The second set of undertakings relating to the lender's position as a creditor is contained in the negative pledge clause and, allied to that, the clause against disposals of assets.[197] These clauses are designed to ensure that, to the maximum

---

[194] I.e. rateably in proportion that each claim bears to the total. It has sometimes been argued that a *pari passu* clause prevents the borrower from making any payment to another creditor, even before the onset of insolvency, unless it is in a position to make payment to the lender under the facility. It is submitted that this is an incorrect interpretation of the purpose of such a clause, which is to provide for the position upon insolvency. Of course, the interpretation of the clause will depend upon its drafting but a well advised borrower should ensure that the effect of a *pari passu* clause is confined in the manner suggested. The position as to payments to other creditors outside insolvency should be dealt with, if at all, in other provisions (e.g. in the financial covenants) that are specifically tailored to meet a particular objective.

[195] Under English law, the statutorily preferred claims in a liquidation are referred to in s 175 of, and are set out in Schedule 6 to, the Insolvency Act 1986. As to the ranking of liquidation expenses ahead of the claims of floating charge holders and other claims, see s 176ZA of the Insolvency Act 1986 and Rules 4.180 and 4.218 of the Insolvency Rules 1986.

[196] S 107 of the Insolvency Act 1986 (voluntary winding up), s 328(3) of that Act (bankruptcy), and Rule 4.181 of the Insolvency Rules 1986 (compulsory winding up).

[197] For a fuller discussion of this subject, see the author's article, 'Restrictions on Dealing with Assets in Financing Documents' [2002] JIBL 193.

extent possible, the borrower's assets will be available to meet the claims of its unsecured creditors (including that of the lender) in an insolvency of the borrower. If the lender is taking security, the clauses serve the alternate function of seeking to preserve the rights of the lender in the secured assets ahead of others seeking to assert a proprietary interest (whether by way of security, purchase, or other disposition) in the assets. As a matter of English law, if the lender wishes to assert that it has taken fixed security, rather than a floating charge, it is also important to have the clauses so as to prevent the borrower from having the right to deal with the assets which are the subject of the lender's security (again, by way of security, purchase, or other disposition) as it could do under a floating charge.[198]

The negative pledge clause is an undertaking by the borrower not to create security (or permit security to subsist[199]) in its assets in favour of a third party. The concept of security is usually extended, for this purpose, to include quasi-security and other devices which have the effect of conferring upon a creditor a preferred right in an asset of the borrower or a right to apply the asset in discharge of a liability of the borrower. It is intended, therefore, to address traditional concepts of security under English law, such as mortgages, charges, and possessory security (liens and pledges), as well as rights under title finance and rights of set-off, and similar concepts under other systems of law. A clause against the disposition of assets is intended to apply to methods of outright disposal of assets and more limited forms of divestment of possession or title, such as by way of lease or the grant of an equitable interest. **3.18.11.1**

A well advised borrower will seek various exceptions to the restrictions contained in these clauses. For instance, it will seek exceptions from the negative pledge clause to cover rights of set-off that arise by operation of law,[200] or in the ordinary course of carrying on its business,[201] or which arise in favour of its bankers, repairers' liens, and other liens arising by operation of law,[202] or in the ordinary course of its business, security over assets which it acquires or security granted by a company **3.18.11.2**

---

[198] *Agnew v Commissioner of Inland Revenue* [2001] UKPC 28, [2001] 2 AC 710; *National Westminster Bank PLC v Spectrum Plus Ltd* [2005] UKHL 41, [2005] 2 AC 680.

[199] This is important because the borrower may acquire an asset that is already subject to security or an asset may be subject to a statutory charge or the security may arise by operation of law, such as under an equitable lien.

[200] Such as under Rules 2.85 and 4.90 of the Insolvency Rules 1986.

[201] Care needs to be taken when considering the concept of the ordinary course of business, given the wide construction given to it by the courts in relation to the inherent liberty to deal with assets in the ordinary course of business under a floating charge: see the review in *Ashborder BV v Green Gas Power Ltd* [2004] EWHC 1517 (Ch), at [192]–[227].

[202] Such as an equitable lien: see *Re Molton Finance Ltd* [1968] Ch 325; *London & Cheshire Insurance Co Ltd v Laplagrene Property Co Ltd* [1971] Ch 499; *Burston Finance Ltd v Speirway Ltd* [1974] 1 WLR 1648; *Orakpo v Manson Investments Ltd* [1978] AC 95; *International Finance Corp v DSNL Offshore Ltd* [2005] EWHC 1844 (Comm), [2007] 2 All ER (Comm) 305.

which it acquires (usually subject to the security being discharged within a certain period after the acquisition), security that is given in connection with non-recourse lending where repayment of the lending will be taken from the sale of the secured assets and not by recourse to a personal covenant of the borrower,[203] security as disclosed when the loan facility agreement was signed, security up to a certain level of secured obligations during the term of the loan facility agreement, and other security which is likely to arise in the context of its business.[204] Exceptions to the disposals clause would be intended to allow the borrower to make payments and to acquire and dispose of assets in the ordinary course of trading, as well as being able to do other things that a business might ordinarily undertake.

3.18.11.3 The question arises as to the remedies that might be available to the lender if the negative pledge or disposals clauses are breached. In this instance, the lender might not be content to rely upon its usual rights to suspend the facility and demand repayment under the events of default clause in the loan facility agreement. If it learns of a threatened breach, it may seek an injunction to restrain the borrower from proceeding with the threatened breach[205] but it is unlikely that the lender would find out before the breach occurred. More importantly, the lender might wish to prevent the third party from benefiting from the borrower's breach of contract and relying upon the rights it has gained in the borrower's assets in consequence of the breach. Accordingly, the lender might seek an injunction against the third party, so as to prevent it from relying upon the interest it has gained in the assets[206] (although, if the lender is merely an unsecured creditor, this will not have the result in itself of giving the lender an interest in those assets). To do so, the lender would need to show that it had a cause of action against the third party for the tort of inducing or procuring a breach of contract, and to do that it would need to establish the following:[207]

(1) that there had been a breach by the borrower of the contract between it and the lender, which may be difficult to establish if there is a broad spectrum of exceptions to the restrictions in the clause;

(2) the third party must have known that it was inducing a breach by the borrower of its contract with the lender. It is not enough that the third party ought reasonably to have appreciated the likely effect nor that it should

---

[203] If such an exception is agreed then there is an argument that the value of the asset and the amount of the borrowing should be ignored in the constituent elements of the gearing covenant.

[204] For instance, margin payments that may be required under commodities and derivatives contracts or pledges over imported goods that have been paid for under a letter of credit.

[205] Under the principle propounded by Lord Cairns LC in *Doherty v Allman* (1878) 3 App Cas 709.

[206] As discussed by Browne-Wilkinson J in *Swiss Bank Corp v Lloyds Bank Ltd* [1979] Ch 548.

[207] The requisite elements of the tort, as set out here, are taken from the review of the tort conducted by Lord Hoffmann in *OBG Ltd v Allan; Douglas v Hello! Ltd; Mainstream Properties Ltd v Young* [2007] UKHL 21.

have realised, but did not, that the act done by the borrower would, as a matter of law or construction of the contract, amount to a breach of its contract with the lender. The issue is purely subjective;

(3) there is the question of what would amount to sufficient knowledge on the part of the third party of the contract, its terms and their breach, apart from actual knowledge. Actual knowledge is sufficient and a reckless indifference to the facts could constitute a sufficient degree of knowledge.[208] Negligence, even gross negligence, such as by negligently making the wrong enquiries, would not be sufficient to ground the tort. It is also submitted that merely having constructive knowledge would be insufficient knowledge for these purposes, when taken in conjunction with the second of the matters that must be established.[209] Furthermore, it has been held that constructive knowledge of the existence of a charge by virtue of its registration in the Companies Registry, does not give constructive knowledge of the contents of the charge instrument;[210]

(4) the third party must possess an intention to procure the breach of contract. If the breach of contract is merely a foreseeable consequence of some other intended action and is not in itself the end or intended consequence of the action taken by the third party, nor the means of achieving some other intended consequence, then there will not be an intention on its part to cause the breach of contract. Furthermore, if the third party, knowing of the contract, has been assured by the borrower that it will not be breaching its contract with the lender because it has the lender's consent or because an exception applies, and the third party honestly believes that answer, it will lack the necessary intention.[211]

Taking those various requirements together, the lender may find that it has an uphill struggle in making out its claim against the third party. If it cannot prevail against the third party then the latter will be able to assert its interest in the relevant assets despite the objections of the lender. If the lender is unsecured, it will be unable to prevent the third party resorting to its security.   **3.18.11.4**

With those difficulties in mind, an unsecured lender may wish to provide in the loan facility agreement that the borrower would be obliged to create equivalent   **3.18.11.5**

---

[208] As, for instance, was held to be the case by Sir John Donaldson MR in *Merkur Island Shipping Corpn v Laughton* [1983] 2 AC 570 at 591 (whose judgment was approved on appeal by Lord Diplock in the same case, at 608–609), when he held that 'almost certain knowledge' of the existence of the contract, its relevant terms and the breach thereof would amount to sufficient knowledge.

[209] *Swiss Bank Corp v Lloyds Bank Ltd* [1979] Ch 548.

[210] See Slade J in *Siebe Gorman & Co Ltd v Barclays Bank Ltd* [1979] 2 Lloyd's Rep 142, at 160 and the cases therein mentioned. This may change if details of a negative pledge contained in a floating charge (or in an instrument relating to it) become registrable, pursuant to a legislative change foreshadowed in a draft statutory instrument that was circulated at the end of 2007 by the Department for Business, Enterprise and Regulatory Reform.

[211] These were the facts in *Mainstream Properties Ltd v Young* [2007] UKHL 21.

security in favour of the lender if the borrower granted security to a third party (sometimes referred to as 'springing security'). To avoid an argument that the provision failed at the outset for uncertainty, it would be essential that the provision was drafted so that there could be no doubt at the time the provision came into effect as to which assets were to be the subject of the agreement, the type of security that was to be given, and how it was to rank. Even so, there would be considerable obstacles under English law in enforcing such a provision, which may be summarised as follows, not to mention the difficulties that might also arise under the laws of other relevant jurisdictions:

(1) it has been said that such a provision is registrable under Part 25 of the Companies Act 2006[212] as an agreement to give a floating charge.[213] Failure to meet the registration requirements would mean that the agreement was void as against a liquidator, administrator, or secured creditors of the borrower;

(2) the borrower may be unable to co-operate in giving the security because of a negative pledge in the third party's or some other creditor's documentation and they may intervene;

(3) if the borrower does give the security to the lender, the security may be vulnerable to attack under the avoidance provisions of the Insolvency Act 1986[214] or similar enactments and claw-back provisions under the laws of other jurisdictions;

(4) if the security is over future property, it may fail because it is not supported by valuable consideration provided at the time or subsequent to its creation;[215]

(5) if the borrower failed to co-operate in giving the security once the relevant circumstances had arisen, it is very unlikely that the lender would be able to obtain recognition of the original agreement as having the automatic effect of giving it the security. The lender would be seeking recognition in equity, on the basis that the borrower should be treated as having done that which it promised to do. The reasons why it would be unable to gain such recognition would be that, in the first place, the original agreement was conditional upon the will of the borrower in creating the circumstances under which the agreement took effect. Equity will not enforce such conditional arrangements. Secondly, to enforce the agreement the lender must show that it provided new value in return for its reliance on the security. Whilst it may have provided

---

212 Previously Part XII of the Companies Act 1985.
213 See Lord Scott in *Smith (Administrator of Cosslett (Contractors) Ltd) v Bridgend CBC* [2001] UKHL 58; [2002] AC 336, at [59]–[64].
214 Particularly ss 127, 238, 239, and 245 of the Act. See also Art 4(2)(m) of the EC Insolvency Regulation (1346/2000/EC OJ L160/1 30/6/2000).
215 See Lord Macnaughten in *Tailby v Official Receiver* (1888) 13 App Cas 523. Such value could include a realistic agreement by the lender to forebear from taking enforcement action against the borrower: *Glegg v Bromley* [1912] 3 KB 474.

value when it made its advances, that will have been spent by the time it claims that its proprietary rights arose under the security. Thirdly, the same problems may arise under the Insolvency Act 1986 as already mentioned.

3.19 Events of Default and Acceleration

As explained earlier in this chapter, a lender under a term loan does not have an **3.19.1** inherent right to demand early repayment of its loan.[216] It can only do so if the loan facility agreement gives it that right.[217] This will normally be done in accordance with the provisions of a clause in the agreement, usually referred to as the 'events of default' clause, under which a series of possible events will be specified.[218] Such a clause provides that if any of the stated events occurs, the lender will have the right to suspend or terminate the facility and demand repayment. It has been held that such a clause is enforceable and will not amount to a penalty, so long as it does not also provide for the payment of amounts of interest and such like that would have accrued due in the future, had the facility run its normal course[219] (provided, of course, it can establish that an event of default has occurred). For the reasons expressed elsewhere in this book, it is submitted that there is no other fetter on the ability of the lender to determine if it wishes to exercise its rights under the clause.[220] This might be contrasted with the position under New York law, where there is an obligation of good faith and fair dealing in determining if a power to accelerate payment should be exercised.[221]

The making of such a demand is said to 'accelerate' the repayment obligation of **3.19.2** the borrower and the process is referred to as 'acceleration' of the loan. The decision of a lender that an event of default has occurred is sometimes referred to as a 'declaration of default'. The expression 'events of default' is a bit of a misnomer. Some of the events specified in the clause are in the nature of defaults but others of them may arise in other circumstances, they may relate to different persons, and they may even be outside the control of the borrower. For instance, in cross-border and international lending, it may be relevant for the clause to refer to the circumstances of the country in which the borrower is incorporated or established. As with the monitoring and minding provisions of the agreement, the events of default clause is normally the product of negotiation between the parties before its final form is settled.

---

216 *Cryne v Barclays Bank PLC* [1987] BCLC 548.

217 *The Angelic Star* [1988] 1 Lloyd's Rep 122.

218 There may be other clauses as well which give rise to a right to require early repayment, such as those described at para 3.14.7 above.

219 *The Angelic Star* [1988] 1 Lloyd's Rep 122.

220 See Chap 1.

221 See § 1-208 of the New York Uniform Commercial Code.

3.19.3 The events

The list of events of default typically includes the occurrence of matters along the following lines (references to the borrower might be extended to include other members of its group):

(1) non-payment on the due date of amounts falling due under the agreement (perhaps with a period of grace in which the position may be rectified, particularly if it has arisen because of difficulties in the mechanics for transmission of payment);

(2) other breaches of the agreement or defaults by the borrower, such as under the representations and warranties clause or the covenants and undertakings (perhaps with a period of grace to allow the breach or default to be cured);

(3) a cross-default concerning payment due by the borrower to another creditor;

(4) enforcement action against the borrower by other creditors under security or by enforcement of judgment;

(5) insolvency events relating to the borrower;

(6) the loss of security or of a guarantee relating to the facility;

(7) events relating to third parties which are relevant to the circumstances of the facility or the borrower; and

(8) an adverse change in the borrower's circumstances.

Two of those provisions (often called 'clauses') call for further comment, namely the cross-default clause and the material adverse change clause.

3.19.4 Cross-default

A cross-default clause is likely to be along the following lines (with alternative wording placed in squared brackets):

(i) Any [Financial] Indebtedness of the Borrower [or any other member of its Group] [in an amount cumulatively exceeding []] is not paid when due (taking into account any applicable grace period); or (ii) any such Indebtedness is [validly] declared to be or otherwise becomes due and payable prior to its originally stated date of maturity (except in consequence of the exercise of a voluntary right of the Borrower [or such other member of its Group] to make early payment of it) [;or (iii) the creditor to whom such Indebtedness is due becomes entitled to declare it to be due and payable prior to its stated date of maturity in consequence of an event of default (howsoever described)].

3.19.4.1 The clause relates to defaults in payment, whether on the due date or in consequence of acceleration, by the borrower (or other members of its group) to other creditors, particularly financial creditors (as opposed to trade suppliers). The idea behind the clause is that if another such creditor has not been paid, it may take action against the borrower to recover its debt, either by formal proceedings or by exerting pressure. If so, the lender under the present facility wishes to be in the same position to make recovery as that other creditor. Otherwise, the other creditor may be paid, leaving little or nothing available for the lender when it does eventually have the right to pursue its remedies against the borrower.

A problem from the borrower's perspective is that the operation of the clause, in conjunction with similar clauses in its other financial agreements, may cause its collapse because all of its financial creditors may pursue it at the same time, should it fail to pay any one of its financial creditors, whether on normal maturity or because of acceleration of that creditor's debt. Similarly, such a provision has the effect of allowing the borrower's creditors to take advantage of more onerous terms in one creditor's agreement with the borrower, even if such terms are not contained in their own agreements or are expressed differently.

3.19.4.2

Given those disadvantages, a borrower would be well advised to resist an attempt to extend the operation of a cross-default clause (such an extension being represented by paragraph (iii) in the example given above) to a situation where another creditor has obtained a right to accelerate (for instance, because an event of default has occurred under its agreement) but has not yet done so. After all, that other creditor may be content to let the matter rest for the time being and not accelerate the borrower's payment obligations. In addition, a well-advised borrower should seek to include the word 'validly' where it is shown in the above example, to prevent an argument that even a wrongful attempt at acceleration by another creditor might lead to the triggering of the right to accelerate under the cross-default clause.

3.19.4.3

3.19.5 Material adverse change

A material adverse change clause in a loan agreement is likely to be along the following lines (with alternative wording placed in squared brackets):

> Any event or series of events occurs, whether or not related (including, without limitation, an adverse change in the business, revenues, profits, assets or other financial condition of the borrower [or any other member of its Group]) which [would] [might][in the [reasonable]opinion of the lender] affect [materially and] adversely the ability of the Borrower [or the Guarantor] to comply with its [respective] obligations under this Agreement [or the Guarantee] or the rights of the Lender hereunder [or under the Guarantee].

An extended version of the clause will be found in a subscription agreement for a capital markets issuance. That version will give the managers the right to terminate their obligations to subscribe for the issue if an event relating to economic conditions or market events should occur before the Closing which may impede the successful offering and distribution of the issue to the secondary market.[222]

3.19.5.1

---

[222] See the discussion in Chap 10.

3.19.5.2 The clause is rather general in its wording. Given its apparent generality, it might be thought that the courts would approach a material adverse change clause rather sceptically and read it down within the context of the events of default clause overall, particularly as the other provisions in most events of default clauses are extensive and should cover nearly anything that could go wrong. It might be said that it was difficult to envisage adverse events which might occur that would not cause one of those other provisions to be triggered or, alternatively, that the parties did not contemplate that any further events that were not so specified might be considered as having a material effect. On that basis, the *ejusdem generis* rule might be applied in construing the material adverse change clause, under which the more general wording of the material adverse change clause would be restricted to things of the same nature as the more specific matters dealt with in the events of default clause. However, when a material adverse change clause has come before them, the courts have followed a more independent approach. They have considered the clause on its own merits and, taking a practical approach, have determined whether the events that occurred fell within the wording of the clause taken in its literal terms.[223] Nonetheless, for the reasons mentioned in relation to paragraph 1.2.10.3, it is at least arguable that if the lender has an apparently unfettered discretion in determining whether an adverse change has occurred, some limitation might be implied as to the manner in which it might exercise that discretion, along the lines that it should not be exercised arbitrarily, capriciously, for some unwarranted collateral purpose, or in a way that no comparable lender, acting reasonably, would act.

3.19.6 Construction of the events of default clause

Such an approach in reading separately the various provisions within an events of default clause and giving them a literal effect was reflected in the judgment of Hart J in *Law Debenture Trust Corporation PLC v Elecktrim Finance BV*.[224] The judgment is of interest in relation to two provisions in the events of default clause that his Lordship considered. Whilst the case concerned the conditions of a bond issue, there is no reason to believe that the same approach to construction would not have been taken in construing the similar provisions of a loan facility agreement.

3.19.6.1 The first of those provisions was in the following terms:

> All or any part of the undertaking, assets or revenues of the Guarantor, the Issuer or [any material subsidiary of the Guarantor] is condemned, seized or otherwise

---

[223] *BNP Paribas SA v Yukos Oil Company* [2005] EWHC 1321 (Ch); *Pan Foods Company Importers & Distributors Pty Ltd v Australia & New Zealand Banking Group Ltd* [2000] HCA 20, (2000) 74 ALJR 791.

[224] [2005] EWHC 1999 (Ch).

appropriated by any person acting under the authority of any national, regional or local government or any political sub-division thereof.

The tax authorities of the relevant country, Poland, had carried out an execution against the bank accounts of such a material subsidiary to satisfy alleged substantial tax liabilities. The validity of the execution was being contested before the courts in Poland. It was argued by the issuer and the guarantor that an event within the wording above had not occurred on essentially two grounds. First, it was said that any such seizure etc. had to be material when taken in the context of the undertaking and assets of the whole group which, it was said, was not the case on the facts. Although there was no direct reference to such a requirement of materiality in the wording, it was claimed that this was imported from the wording of another provision in the events of default clause which was apt to refer to the same events but which was qualified by the materiality test. Secondly, it was argued that the wording should be construed as if it was intended to catch only lawful seizures etc. As the execution was being contested, its lawfulness was in doubt and so it was not possible to proceed on the basis that an event within the wording had occurred. His Lordship rejected both arguments. There was nothing in the wording to suggest that it should be qualified on either basis. It was perfectly possible that the same set of facts might fall within separate provisions in the events of default clause and there was nothing in the clause to indicate that one provision should be read down so as to conform with the wording of another provision. Each provision depended upon its own wording. Furthermore, the wording as set out above did not justify any conclusion that the seizure etc. had to be lawful to fall within the compass of the provision.

The other provision which is relevant for present purposes provided as follows: **3.19.6.2**

> If . . . proceedings shall have been initiated against . . . the Guarantor under any applicable bankruptcy, reorganisation or insolvency law.

An application for the bankruptcy of the guarantor had been filed before the courts in Poland, which was then contested by the guarantor. The application was subsequently withdrawn without any order being made against the guarantor. The expert evidence as to Polish law showed that such a filing on its own had no legal implications upon the guarantor's contractual relations with third parties, and that such a filing was only a preliminary step in bankruptcy proceedings and had no legal significance where it had been withdrawn. Nonetheless, Hart J held that the fact of the filing fell within the wording of the paragraph and so an event of default had occurred. The proceedings had been initiated. The subsequent withdrawal of the filing did not detract from the fact that proceedings had been initiated.

The conclusion to be drawn from these findings is that an issuer or a borrower   **3.19.6.3**
should ensure that the wording of each provision within an events of default

clause contains qualifications to give protection against the harshness of the operation of the provisions in circumstances such as those that have been described. It would also be sensible to provide that action against the issuer or the borrower can only be taken in reliance upon the occurrence of an event of default if the relevant circumstances are still present and continuing at the time that the relevant creditors, or their representatives, purport to take the action.

3.19.7 An invalid declaration of default

Notwithstanding the apparent liberality of the courts in construing an events of default clause in favour of the lender, there may still be circumstances in which a lender purports to declare that an event of default has occurred on incorrect grounds or where no grounds exist at all. The case law indicates that if the lender specifies the wrong grounds for its declaration, but other valid grounds did exist, the declaration will be valid and the lender will be entitled to exercise its right to accelerate the borrower's obligations and enforce any security that it may hold.[225] The position is more complicated if no grounds existed on which the declaration might have been based.[226]

3.19.7.1   In the leading case in the House of Lords, *Concord Trust v Law Debenture Trust Corp PLC*,[227] it was held that, in the absence of an explicit provision by which a creditor undertook not to make an invalid declaration of default, there was no term that should be implied by which the relevant creditor undertook such an obligation. The contract worked perfectly well on its own, so it was unnecessary to imply such a term. As there was no such term, an invalid declaration would simply be a nullity and of no effect; it could not give rise to a breach of contract by the creditor. The case concerned the events of default clause in the conditions of a bond issue and an assumed invalid declaration of default by the trustee for the bond holders, but the same consequence would apply with respect to a loan facility agreement.[228]

3.19.7.2   It is submitted that a borrower which was faced with such a situation could obtain a declaration from the court that the lender's purported determination was invalid

---

[225] *Byblos Bank SAK v Al Khudhairy* (1986) 2 BCC 99549; *Anglo Petroleum Ltd v TFB (Mortgages) Ltd* [2003] EWHC 3125 (QB) at [42]; *Brampton Manor (Leisure) Ltd v McClean* [2006] EWHC 2983 (Ch).

[226] For a fuller discussion than that which follows, see the note written by the author at [2006] JIBLR 117–124.

[227] [2005] UKHL 27, [2005] 1 WLR 1591. Lord Scott gave the leading judgment, which was supported by the four other members of the House who sat on the appeal.

[228] Jonathan Parker LJ had arrived at the same conclusion when considering the position under a bilateral loan facility agreement in *Bournemouth & Boscombe AFC Ltd v Lloyds TSB Bank plc* [2003] EWCA Civ 1755, at [49]–[50]. Evans-Lombe J in *BNP Paribas SA v Yukos Oil Company* [2005] EWHC 1321 (Ch) applied the decision of the House of Lords in *Concord Trust v Law Debenture Trust Corp PLC* in relation to a syndicated loan facility agreement, as did the Court of Appeal in relation to a bilateral loan facility agreement in *Jafari-Fini (Mohammad) v Skillglass Ltd* [2007] EWCA Civ 261.

and an injunction to restrain the lender from taking further action in pursuance of its invalid determination. It could also plead the matter by way of a defence if the lender brought proceedings against it. If the lender was holding security, particularly over goods or land, and purported to enforce the security following upon an invalid demand then the creditor (or a receiver appointed by it) may be exposed to an action in conversion or for trespass. Such an action in conversion could not be brought for wrongful interference with the borrower's contractual rights,[229] and, in the absence of proof of a subjective intention to cause the borrower harm, it is doubtful if any other claim in tort would be available to the borrower.[230] If the lender, in reliance upon its wrongful determination, refused to make further advances to the borrower, the borrower may have rights against the lender, along the lines previously discussed.[231]

It was also held in *Concord Trust v Law Debenture Trust Corp PLC*[232] that the trustee did not owe any duty of care in the tort of negligence towards the issuer and so there could be no liability for any loss (for example, commercial or financial loss) that the issuer might have suffered in consequence of the invalid declaration of default. The position of a trustee for the bond holders is different from that of a lender under a loan facility, as the trustee has explicit fiduciary duties towards the bond holders which might well be inconsistent with any alleged duty of care towards the issuer.[233] A bank may owe its customer a duty of care in consequence of the contractual relationship[234] and there is no reason why a duty of care may not also arise in tort.[235] Whether the duty would extend to the circumstances under discussion is another matter and would have to be tested in accordance with established rules.[236] It might be argued that the immediacy of the relationship between the parties and the foreseeability of loss supported the existence of the duty.

3.19.7.3

---

[229] *OBG Ltd v Allan; Douglas v Hello! Ltd; Mainstream Properties Ltd v Young* [2007] UKHL 21.

[230] Ibid.

[231] See 3.8 above.

[232] [2005] UKHL 27, [2005] 1 WLR 1591.

[233] A similar view could be taken concerning the position of an agent bank in a syndicated facility. The agent acts on behalf of the syndicate of lenders and its duties towards them would be inconsistent with an assertion that it had a duty of care towards the borrower. The same could not be said, however, of the lenders themselves, on whose behalf the agent acted, particularly if the lenders had instructed the agent to act. If they had not instructed it, they might (depending upon the facts) be able to argue that the agent had acted outside the scope of its authority and they were not liable for its actions.

[234] See s 13 of the Supply of Goods and Services Act 1982 and *Selangor United Rubber Estates Ltd v Cradock (No 3)* [1968] 1 WLR 1555, at 1592–1610.

[235] See Lord Goff in *Henderson v Merrett Syndicates Ltd* [1995] 2 AC 145, at 184–194, in which he approved the decision of Oliver J in *Midland Bank Trust Co Ltd v Hett Stubbs & Kemp* [1979] Ch 384 and disapproved the decision of the Privy Council in *Tai Hing Cotton Mill Ltd v Liu Chong Hing Bank Ltd* [1986] AC 80.

[236] In particular, those discussed by the House of Lords in *Commissioners of Customs and Excise v Barclays Bank PLC* [2006] UKHL 28, [2007] 1 AC 181.

On the other hand, in entering into the agreement the parties acted on their own behalf and they clearly had divergent interests. In deciding to act, the lender was entitled to have regard to its own interests. If the borrower wanted protection, it could have stipulated for it by insisting upon an explicit term in the contract under which the lender undertook not to make an invalid declaration of default.

PART B

CONFLICT OF LAWS AND CROSS-BORDER ISSUES

Chapter 4 is concerned with conflict of laws in transactional matters. After a general introduction to the subject of conflict of laws, it examines the method by which the issues in a transaction should be characterised by an English court so as to apply the appropriate conflicts rule and thereby find the law or laws that should be applied in determining the issues. It then deals with the English conflicts rules for determining the governing law for issues that have been so characterised as concerning corporate matters, agency, contractual obligations, tort, proprietary rights, and trusts. It also examines the effect upon a transaction of unlawfulness under a foreign law, the circumstances in which an English court may refuse to give recognition or effect to a foreign law, the role of public policy, and the effect of foreign exchange controls.

Chapter 5 is concerned with cross-border insolvency, where an insolvent entity may have a presence or assets in more than one jurisdiction and be subject to the possibility of insolvency proceedings in more than one jurisdiction. It examines the approach that an English court will take in determining jurisdiction in such an insolvency, in recognising foreign proceedings, and in assisting those proceedings.

Chapter 6 is concerned with jurisdiction and the resolution of disputes where there is a foreign element. It examines the basis on which an English court may have jurisdiction to hear such a dispute, the circumstances where it may decline to hear the dispute, and the position where a dispute is the subject of proceedings in more than one jurisdiction. It then examines arbitration as an alternative method for resolving disputes and the recognition of foreign arbitral awards.

Chapter 7 is concerned with disputes involving foreign States and international organisations and the position where a State cannot pay its debts and defaults in its obligations to its external creditors. Accordingly, it deals with the subjects of sovereign immunity, the immunity conferred on international organisations, and the problems associated with insolvent States.

Chapter 8 concerns the use of legal opinions in financial transactions. It describes the situations where such opinions are given and the matters which they address.

4

CONFLICT OF LAWS IN TRANSACTIONAL MATTERS

4.1 Introduction

Conflict of laws or, for the purists, private international law, looms large in the **4.1.1** international or cross-border context of financing transactions and in the resolution of disputes concerning such transactions. Conflict of laws considerations will be present from the outset in the very nature of transactions where it is contemplated that the parties will be in different countries or where the subject matter of the transaction or any other matters related to the transaction will involve elements in more than one jurisdiction. It is also possible that such considerations may become apparent at a later stage, during the life of the transaction or when it falls apart, because some extra-jurisdictional consideration has arisen, such as where an asset has been moved from one place to another or a relevant party in a transaction has moved to a different place. In addition, it is important to consider (as will be done in later chapters) the effect of the insolvency of a party to a transaction, and how and where disputes may be resolved when the parties are in different places or where enforcement action is contemplated against persons or assets in another jurisdiction.

4.1.2 The relationship with public international law

The study of conflict of laws, or private international law, should be distinguished from the study of public international law. The latter is concerned with relations between States and a cynic may sometimes be tempted to feel that it is often involved more with the politics of international relations than matters of law, whereas the former relates to rights in private law. Nonetheless, public international law does have a part to play in private law matters. This is because some of the rules in conflict of laws are laid down by international treaties and conventions

and some treaties, particularly those relating to arbitration and bilateral investment, provide for the resolution of disputes involving private law rights.

4.1.2.1 Instances of international conventions that already affect private law rights or may
do so in the future include the Rome Convention of 1980 on the law applicable to
contractual obligations,[1] the UNCITRAL Convention of 2004 on the assignment of
receivables in international trade,[2] the UNIDROIT Convention of 2001 on international interests in mobile equipment (the Cape Town Convention),[3] the Hague
Convention of 1986 on the law applicable to trusts and their recognition,[4] the Hague
Convention of 2002 on certain rights in respect of securities held with an intermediary,[5] and the UNCITRAL Model Law on cross-border insolvency.[6] Examples of
international conventions that have the effect of conferring rights in the areas of arbitration and bilateral investments are the Convention on the recognition and enforcement of foreign arbitral awards of 1958 (the New York Convention),[7] the Convention
on the settlement of investment disputes between States and nationals of other States
of 1965, and various bilateral investment treaties which contain provisions for the
resolution of disputes by arbitration involving private persons and States, so that arbitration awards are given recognition in pursuance of the New York Convention or
pursuant to the Arbitration (International Investment Disputes) Act 1966.

4.1.2.2 The distinction between public and private international law is illustrated by the
attitude that the English courts take concerning international treaties and agreements between States. There is a basic principle that the English courts will not
adjudicate upon the transactions of foreign sovereign States. It is a matter of judicial self-restraint and is a principle of English law.[8] In addition, the courts of
England generally have no power to interpret or enforce treaties between foreign
sovereign States which have not been incorporated in English domestic law, nor
may such courts pronounce on the legal results that flow from a treaty.[9] The
parties to a dispute cannot by consent agree to oust the principle.[10] There are,

---

[1] Given effect in the UK by virtue of the Contracts (Applicable Law) Act 1990. This may be
replaced by an EC Regulation, commonly referred to as 'Rome I', as referred to later in this chapter.

[2] Not yet ratified by or applied in the UK.

[3] Not yet ratified by or applied in the UK.

[4] Given effect in the UK by virtue of the Recognition of Trusts Act 1987.

[5] Which it is intended should be ratified by the European Union on behalf of its Member States.

[6] Given effect in Great Britain by the Cross-border Insolvency Regs 2006 (SI 2006/1030),
pursuant to s 14 of the Insolvency Act 2000.

[7] Given effect in English law by Part III of the Arbitration Act 1996.

[8] See *Buttes Gas & Oil Co v Hammer* [1982] AC 888 and *JH Rayner (Mincing Lane) Ltd v
Department of Trade & Industry* [1990] 2 AC 418.

[9] See Lord Oliver in ibid, at 476–477, 480, and 499–500 and *Westland's Helicopters Ltd v Arab
Organisation for Industrialisation* [1995] QB 282.

[10] See Mance LJ in *Republic of Ecuador v Occidental Exploration and Production Co* [2005] EWCA
Civ 1116; [2005] 2 Lloyd's Rep 707, at [57].

however, exceptions to the concept of non-justiciability. It was recognised by the House of Lords in *Kuwait Airways Corp v Iraqi Airways Co (Nos 4 and 5)*[11] that an English court is required to respect international obligations that are imposed by a resolution of the UN Security Council. In *R v Prime Minister of the UK, ex p Campaign for Nuclear Disarmament*,[12] the Divisional Court recognised that it might be necessary for an English court to interpret a treaty for the purpose of determining private rights and obligations under domestic law. In *Republic of Ecuador v Occidental Exploration and Production Co*[13] the Court of Appeal held that, in the context of a bilateral investment treaty, the States that were party to that treaty might confer private rights to seek arbitration in the determination of a dispute, and the court was entitled to consider the treaty and its purpose to ascertain if that was intended to be the case.[14]

4.1.3 The role of external sources in English law

Reverting now to private international law, the traditional approach to the study of the subject is that each jurisdiction has evolved its own conflict of laws rules, which meant that the same set of facts could give rise to varying approaches in different jurisdictions. Gradually, there has been some standardisation with the intention of achieving a measure of uniformity of approach between jurisdictions, although significant areas remain where this has not yet occurred. So far as English law is concerned, standardisation of the rules applied in England and elsewhere has been achieved by virtue of the application of international treaties and conventions, as mentioned above, and within the European Union by the intervention of EC legislation. The study that follows will be concerned with the rules as they are applied by the English courts. Those rules, which will be referred to as the English rules, are made up of the rules evolved at common law, as modified by statute, including statues that implement international treaties and conventions, and by EC legislation.

4.1.4 *Dicey, Morris & Collins*

The most influential source in the development of this subject in English law has been the work originally done by Dicey, in what has become *Dicey, Morris & Collins on the Conflict of Laws* (*Dicey, Morris & Collins*), the general editor of the fourteenth edition of which is Sir Lawrence Collins.[15] Reference is frequently

---

[11] [2002] AC 883.

[12] [2002] EWHC 2777 (QB).

[13] [2005] EWCA Civ 1116, [2005] 2 Lloyd's Rep 707.

[14] For a more general review, see Sir Andrew Morritt C in *In the matter of AY Bank Ltd; AY Bank Ltd v Bosnia and Herzegovina and ors* [2006] EWHC 830 (Ch), [2006] 2 All ER (Comm) 463.

[15] Sweet & Maxwell, London, 2006.

made to that work by the judges when deciding cases and reference will also be made to it during the course of this chapter. It is recommended as essential reference material to anyone who wishes to gain a more detailed insight into the subject than can be given in this book.

4.1.5 Chapter and subject plan

This chapter is concerned with the role of conflict of laws in transactional matters, particularly in financial transactions. The first subject to be considered in this chapter is the approach that is taken in characterising an issue, so as to determine the English conflict of laws rule that should be applied, so as to ascertain the appropriate governing or applicable law to resolve the issue. The chapter will then progress by examining the conflict of laws rules under English law as they apply to find the governing or applicable laws relating to the issues that arise in the governance of commercial relationships and transactions, and, in particular, those that apply in relation to issues concerning corporations, the authority of an agent to bind its principal, contractual obligations, tort, proprietary rights, and trusts. In that connection, it will also be relevant to examine the effect on a transaction where performance is unlawful under a foreign law, the effect of public policy, the circumstances in which an English court will refuse to recognise or enforce a foreign law, and the effect of foreign exchange control legislation.

4.1.5.1 In the chapters that follow, the discussion will move to a consideration of cross-border insolvency issues, jurisdiction and the resolution of disputes with a foreign element, sovereign or State immunity, the immunity of international organisations, and the consequences of State default or insolvency. Finally, there is a chapter that addresses the use of legal opinions in financing transactions.

4.2 The English Method of Classifying or Characterising Legal Issues, Ascertaining the Conflict of Laws Rules that are Relevant to those Issues, and Applying those Rules to Determine the Applicable or Governing Law

4.2.1 Under the English approach, when considering the consequences of a transaction or some other state of affairs from the perspective of a possible conflict of laws, it is first necessary to characterise or classify the relevant issue or issues that may be involved, so as to ascertain which conflict of laws rules should be applied to that issue or those issues. The relevant conflicts rule would indicate the applicable or governing law which would then be applied to determine the outcome for the issue concerned. This process and the English approach to characterisation was described by Mance LJ in *Raiffeisen Zentralbank Osterreich AG v Five Star General*

Trading LLC.[16] An English court would apply the *lex fori* and thus English concepts would be used in determining how an issue should be characterised, so that a conflicts rule could be allocated to it. His Lordship pointed out, however, that this should be done in an internationalist manner with reference to the substance of the issue rather than by applying a purely mechanistic formula that might apply in a domestic setting, bearing in mind that the court should strive to identify the most appropriate law to govern the relevant issue.[17]

The process of characterisation of an issue may, for instance, lead to the conclusion that the issue involves matters relating to powers of a corporation to enter into a transaction, the authority of an agent to bind its principal, the rights and obligations of a party under a contract, or that it involves a tortious or a restitutionary claim. Alternatively, it may be that the issue concerns proprietary rights or a priority dispute between rival claimants in the same asset. This process of characterisation and ascertaining the appropriate governing or applicable law should be applied separately to each issue and each head of claim, even if they were based on the same facts.[18]

4.2.2

4.2.3 Characterising non-contractual civil claims

Under the law as it currently stands, there is some uncertainty as to how the various non-contractual claims for civil wrongs should be characterised. Many of those doubts will be resolved when the EC Regulation known as 'Rome II'[19] comes into force on 11 January, 2009, as it will require a wide spectrum of civil wrongs to be characterised as non-contractual civil wrongs to which its conflicts rules will apply.[20] Until that time, however, the English approach will continue. Indeed, Rome II will only apply to claims that concern events that occurred after it came into force, so the English approach will continue to have relevance for some time after Rome II comes into force, with respect to claims that are founded on events that occurred beforehand.[21]

---

[16] [2001] EWCA Civ 68; [2001] QB 825, at [26]–[33]. See also the Court of Appeal in *Macmillan Inc v Bishopsgate Investment Trust PLC (No 3)* [1996] 1 WLR 387, at 391–392, 407, and 418, Neuberger J in *Re Harvard Securities Ltd; Holland v Newbury* [1998] BCC 567, and Aikens J in *Trafigura Beheer BV v Kookmin Bank Co* [2006] EWHC 1450 (Comm), [2006] 2 Lloyd's Rep 455.

[17] Aikens J said in ibid, at [68], that s 9(2) of the Private International Law (Miscellaneous Provisions) Act 1995, which applies to claims in tort, directed that the task of characterisation, whilst being carried out in accordance with the legal concepts, as understood by the *lex fori*, should take a broad internationalist view of legal concepts, including those that might apply in another system of law that was relevant to the circumstances under consideration.

[18] See Tuckey LJ in *Base Metal Trading Ltd v Shamurin* [2004] EWCA Civ 1316; [2005] 1 WLR 1157, at [32]–[35].

[19] 2007/864/EC OJ L199/40 31/7/2007.

[20] See the discussion on Rome II below.

[21] It is arguable that there may be an element of back dating as to the effect of the Regulation. Art 31 provides that the Regulation will apply to events giving rise to damage which occur after the

4.2.3.1   So far as the English approach is concerned, Aikens J in *Trafigura Beheer BV v Kookmin Bank Co*[22] took the view that in light of section 9(1) and (2) of the Private International Law (Miscellaneous Provisions) Act 1995, any non-contractual civil wrong that gives rise to a remedy should be characterised as a claim relating to a tortious issue. On that basis, a non-proprietary claim for a restitutionary remedy might be considered as a claim relating to an issue in tort. This might include, for instance, a claim for compensation for breach of an alleged fiduciary duty in which there was not a demand for the return of mis-applied or misappropriated assets, as could be the case in claims relating to a conflict of interests, a breach of a duty of confidence, or for a failure by the fiduciary to exercise proper care and skill.

4.2.3.2   Such an approach is inconsistent with that taken in other cases, although they have not, as amongst themselves, produced a consistent approach. In *A-G for England & Wales v R*[23] the New Zealand Court of Appeal said that where the claim arose from a contractual relationship, the claim would characterised as one relating to a contract. On the other hand, in *Base Metal Trading Ltd v Shamurin*[24] the Court of Appeal in England was concerned with a case involving a claim that a director of a foreign company had breached his fiduciary duty towards the company. It would appear from that case that an English court would determine the underlying basis of the relationship on which it was alleged that the duty arose and then it would apply the law that governed that relationship to determine the nature and extent of any duty that might arise from it, as well as the consequences of any breach of that duty.

4.2.3.3   In the *Base Metal Trading* case it was held that the claim against a director of a company for an alleged breach of his fiduciary duty as a director to exercise proper care and skill was a claim concerning issues relating to a company matter and so was governed by the law of the place of incorporation of the company. That law governed the relationship between a company and its directors, being inherently a matter of company law. Even though the alleged facts raised the possibility of concurrent claims for breach of the director's contract of employment or in tort, neither the law which governed the contract nor the law of the tort was applicable in determining the law which governed the claim for breach of the fiduciary duty. It was also held that it would be a matter for the law of the place of incorporation, being that which governed the fiduciary duty, to determine if the nature or scope of that duty could be modified by the contract of employment.

'entry into force' of the Regulation. Art 32 provides (with one minor exception) that the Regulation is to apply from 11 January 2009. However, the Regulation itself became law as an EC instrument on 20 August 2007, being 21 days after its publication in the Official Journal, so it may be argued that 20 August 2007 is the date that the Regulation entered into force.

22   [2006] EWHC 1450 (Comm), [2006] 2 Lloyd's Rep 455.

23   [2002] 2 NZLR 91 (affd by the Privy Council on other grounds at [2003] UKPC 22, [2003] EMLR 24).

24   [2004] EWCA Civ 1316, [2005] 1 WLR 1157.

Having looked at the method for classifying or characterising an issue, it is now **4.2.4**
appropriate to examine the conflicts rules that apply for different types of issues.

4.3 The Rules for Issues Concerning a Corporation

The issues concerning a corporation will go to matters such as the existence and **4.3.1**
status of the corporation, its capacity and powers, how it makes its decisions and
how it is bound, its internal organisation, the appointment of its officers, the
rights and liability of its members and officers, and the issuance of its share capital.
The basic conflicts rule for such issues is that they will be governed, in the first
instance, by the law of the place of incorporation or establishment of the corporation,[25] which is sometimes referred to in the alternative as the law of its place of
domicile.[26] It has been held that the same rule applies in determining the effect of
a merger of two corporations in the context of the civil law concept of universal
succession[27] and the duties of a director to his corporation, including whether
those duties could be modified or abrogated by contract.[28] It has also been suggested that the rule will govern the right of a shareholder to bring a derivative
action.[29] In so far as it might be said that such issues may also involve contractual
matters, they are likely to fall within the specific exclusion from the scope of the
Rome Convention which is contained in Article 1(2)(e) of the Convention.[30]
However, the effect of insolvency proceedings brings in further complications
and will depend upon the law which governs the proceedings and their effect, as
described in Chapter 5.

---

[25] See Millett J in *Arab Bank plc v Mercantile Holdings Ltd* [1994] 2 Ch 71, at 82–83; Cresswell J in
Sierra Leone Telecommunications Co Ltd v Barclays Bank plc [1998] 2 All ER 821, at 827; and Cresswell J
in *Merrill Lynch Capital Services Inc v The Municipality of Piraeus* [1997] 6 Bank LR 241, at 250–251.

[26] See the use of that expression by Longmore J in *Eurosteel v Stinnes AG* [2000] 1 All ER (Comm)
964, at 969, relying upon *National Bank of Greece and Athens SA v Metliss* [1958] AC 509, at
529. Care should be taken not to confuse the use of the word 'domicile' in this context, where the
expression is used to denote the place of incorporation or establishment, being the place of the legal
system to which it owes its corporate existence, with the use of the expression 'domicile' in the EC
Regulation on jurisdiction and judgments (EC 44/2001 OJ L12/1 16/1/2001). In Art 60 of the
Regulation, there is a definition of 'domicile' in relation to corporations and other legal persons and
associations. It provides for three alternatives that may constitute the entity's domicile, being the
place of its statutory seat, its central administration, or its principal place of business.

[27] *Eurosteel v Stinnes AG* [2000] 1 All ER (Comm) 964.

[28] *Base Metal Trading Ltd v Shamurin* [2004] EWCA Civ 1316; [2005] 1 WLR 1157.

[29] *Konamaneni v Rolls-Royce Industrial Power (India) Ltd* [2002] 1 WLR 1269, at [50], although
the point was strictly obiter. See also *Reeves v Sprecher* [2007] EWHC 117 (Ch), [2007] 2 BCLC
614, in which it was said that, save in exceptional circumstances, the courts of the place of incorporation would be the appropriate forum to hear a derivative action.

[30] This exception is repeated in the EC Regulation on the law applicable to contractual relations
('Rome I'). Rome I is discussed later in this chapter.

4.3.2 Transactions that are unknown to the foreign law

A question which arises concerning the basic rule as just described is whether a corporation can engage in transactions outside its country of incorporation that are unknown to the law of its place of incorporation. An example would be the case of a foreign company, incorporated in a civil law country, which wishes to grant a floating charge over its English assets. Generally speaking, civil law does not comprehend the concept of a floating charge. It might be argued that as the corporation only has power to engage in activities if it is authorised to do so in accordance with the law of its place of incorporation, it cannot be authorised to do something unknown to that law.

4.3.2.1 The starting point in addressing this issue is to determine whether, upon a proper interpretation, the foreign law of incorporation by its silence does intend to prohibit corporations from engaging in the relevant activity or, by contrast, would permit them within some wider concept of acceptable dealings. It may, for instance, permit corporations to give security over their assets but not be concerned by the form that the security might take. On the other hand, if it transpires that the foreign law would take the view that transactions were only permitted if they fell within concepts that were understood under its law, or that the particular type of transaction offended against that law's concept of acceptable dealings, then the conclusion should be that the corporation does not have the requisite power to enter into the relevant transaction.

4.3.3 Illegality under the foreign law

A further issue concerns the effect of a provision of the law of the place of incorporation which may prohibit a corporation from undertaking an otherwise lawful activity or which may impose conditions upon its doing so. An example would be the effect of a provision in the law of a corporation's home country which prohibited its corporations from giving financial assistance to acquire their own shares even though, in a different context, the activity may be perfectly lawful. A different example might concern the exchange control laws of the country which may prohibit its entities from making payments abroad in a foreign currency. An English court may view such questions as relating to a corporation's capacity but it might, in the alternative, treat them as involving the effect of illegality.

4.3.3.1 It is again submitted that the question that must first be addressed is whether the relevant foreign law would consider the issue as concerning a matter of corporate capacity, so that the corporation lacks the capacity to engage in the activity, or as some form of limitation upon an otherwise lawful activity. If it is the latter then it is submitted that an English court would treat the corporation as having the inherent capacity to enter into the transaction. The court would then have to consider the effect of the foreign law as one concerning foreign illegality, in accordance with the rules on that subject that are addressed later in this chapter.

4.3.4 The role of local law

In addition to the basic rule, issues concerning a company's ability to enter into a transaction, to conduct business, and to hold assets may also be subject to the law of the place where a corporation is proposing to enter into the transaction, conduct its business, or where it may hold assets,[31] if that place is different from the place of its incorporation. For instance, there may be local law limitations upon the power of any corporation or of a foreign corporation to hold land in that place. It may be necessary for a foreign corporation to be registered in a jurisdiction before it can hold assets or carry on business there. There may also be other requirements before it can conduct its business as, for instance, in the United Kingdom pursuant to the Financial Services and Markets Act 2000 (FSMA). It is important to understand that such local law requirements are additional to the need for a corporation to have the capacity to engage in the relevant activities under the law of its place of incorporation. Hence, if it does not have the power or capacity to be a bank and to carry on banking activities under the law of the place where it is incorporated then the fact that it may hold a licence to be a bank in a foreign place will not cure the essential lack of power or capacity.

4.4 Principal and Agent

4.4.1 The relationship between principal and agent

It is stated by *Dicey, Morris & Collins* that where the relationship between a principal and its agent arises by virtue of a contract between them then the rights and obligations as between a principal and its agent will be governed by the law that governs that contract, as ascertained in accordance with the Rome Convention.[32] Whilst that may be the general position, it is submitted that this should not be the case in those instances where the agency is derived from and thus arises in the context of a corporation and those that may lawfully act on its behalf in pursuance of their functions as its officers or its formal organs. In that case, the issue should be characterised as one relating to a corporate matter. The relationship and the rights

---

[31] See Nourse LJ in *Janred Properties Ltd v Ente Nazionale Per Il Turismo* [1989] 2 All ER 444, at 452.

[32] See *Dicey, Morris & Collins*, at paras 33R-404 to 33-427, which says (at 33-409) that the position is less clear if the agency comes about through an instrument such as a power of attorney.

and duties arising under it will be governed by the law of the place of incorporation or establishment of the corporation, which law would also determine the right of the parties by contract to amplify or subtract from those rights and duties.

4.4.2 The agent's authority to bind the principal

A question may arise as to whether a person acting or purporting to act as the agent of another (its principal) had the authority (or the ability) to act on behalf of its principal, particularly in entering into transactions on behalf of the principal, so as to bind the principal to the transaction. This issue is excluded from the ambit of the Rome Convention by Article 1(2)(f) of the Convention. As a corporation can only act through the agency of its organs and its officers having the right to act on its behalf, this question will often be an issue that will arise when considering a corporation's involvement in a transaction. To that extent, it is submitted that in the same way as the relationship between the corporation and such organs and persons will depend upon the law of the place of incorporation as suggested above, the authority of such an agent will also depend upon that law. Third parties should be entitled to rely on the ability of the organs of the corporation, such as it board of directors and its officers, to act on its behalf as laid down by the law that governs the corporation. In other situations, including where an agent who is not an officer or organ of a company purports to act on its behalf, the rules will be as described below.

4.4.2.1 English law classifies the authority of an agent to act on behalf of its principal as being a matter of either actual authority or of apparent or ostensible authority. *Dicey, Morris & Collins*, whilst acknowledging that the position is uncertain, suggests that whether an agent has actual authority, and the scope of that authority, should be determined by the law that governs the contract between them.[33] In *Marubeni Hong Kong & South China Ltd v The Mongolian Government*[34] Cresswell J held that the question of an agent's apparent or ostensible authority to bind its principal to a contract is governed by the putative governing law of the contract allegedly entered into by the agent.[35] His Lordship held that this applies in the case of both private entities and governmental or public entities. To make any distinction in the application of the principle between the two types of entity would lead to inconsistencies of approach and would defeat the need for certainty in international commerce.

4.4.2.2 Provided that the agent had authority to bind its principal, the rights and liabilities as between the principal and the other contracting party will be governed by

---

[33] See *Dicey, Morris & Collins*, at paras 33R-428 to 33-445.

[34] [2004] EWHC 472 (Comm), [2004] 2 Lloyd's Rep 198 (the case was the subject of an appeal to the Court of Appeal but the appeal did not concern this issue. The appeal is reported at [2005] EWCA Civ 395, [2005] 1 WLR 2497). A similar approach was suggested by Andrew Smith J in *Donegal International Ltd v Republic of Zambia* [2007] EWHC 197 (Comm), [2007] 1 Lloyd's Rep 397.

[35] See the summary of the case law provided by Cresswell J in *Merrill Lynch Capital Services Inc v Municipality of Piraeus* [1997] 6 Bank LR 241, at 252.

the law that governs the contract that was concluded on the principal's behalf by the agent with that other party.[36]

In relation to the formal validity of a contract that is entered into by an agent on behalf of its principal, Article 9(3) of the Rome Convention, when taken with Articles 9 (1) and (2), provides that where the agent and the other party to the contract are in the same place, the contract will be formally valid if it complies with the requirements of that place or the law which governs the contract. If the agent and that other person are in different countries, the contract will be formally valid if it meets the requirements of the law of either country or the law which governs the contract.

4.4.2.3

4.4.3 Rome I

It was originally proposed that the law in this area would be governed by the EC Regulation on the law applicable to contractual obligations (Rome I). That proposal was dropped in the later stages of the formulation of Rome I and so the position under English law as stated above will remain unchanged.

4.5 Contractual Matters

4.5.1 Introduction

Under this heading fall most issues that relate to a contract, such as the rules to determine the governing or applicable law of a contract, and, largely in consequence of that determination (but with some exceptions), the law or laws that govern its material validity, its interpretation and construction, the requirements for performance under the contract and if those requirements have been met, if the contract has been breached and, to some extent, the consequences of breach, and if the contract has been determined or extinguished.

4.5.1.1 *The approach at common law*

The traditional conflicts approach at common law was to find the 'proper law' of the contract, being the law which the parties intended to govern the contract, as expressed or presumed from the terms of the contract and the surrounding circumstances. Such an expressed choice of the proper law would be respected, provided it was 'bona fide and legal' and was not avoided on the ground of public policy.[37] Where it was not possible to find an agreed choice by the parties, the contract would be governed by the law of the country with which the transaction had

---

[36] *Maspons v Mildred* (1883) 8 App Cas 874.
[37] See Lord Wright in *Vita Food Products Inc v Unus Shipping Co Ltd* [1939] AC 277, at 290.

its closest and most real connection.[38] It was not always easy to distinguish situations where there had been a presumed, or implied, choice of the proper law from situations where that was not the case and the test of the closest and most real connection would be applied.

4.5.1.2 *The introduction of the Rome Convention*

The application of the common law's contractual conflicts rules in England was replaced[39] by the Rome Convention of 1980 on the law applicable to contractual obligations, which applies by virtue of the Contracts (Applicable Law) Act 1990 (the Act).[40] The Convention applies in each Member State of the EU. For the purposes of the application of the Convention, each part of the United Kingdom is treated as a separate country.[41] Article 2 of the Convention provides that the law that governs a contract (hereinafter referred to as the 'applicable law' or the 'governing law' of the contract), as determined under the rules of the Convention, will apply even if it is the law of a non-EU country. Section 3 of the Act provides that, for the purpose of interpreting the Convention, regard may be had to the *Giuliano-Lagarde Report*.[42] Although the Convention is not a community instrument, it is now possible for referrals to be made to the European Court of Justice for guidance as to its interpretation, pursuant to the Brussels Protocol that was signed in 1988 and which came into force in 2004.[43] Pursuant to section 3(2) of the Act, a decision or opinion of the European Court of Justice would have binding effect. Article 18 of the Convention states that the rules of the Convention should be interpreted with a view to their international character and also states a general wish for uniform interpretation and application, which has the effect of making decisions in other Member States relevant to the interpretation of the rules in the Convention.

4.5.1.3 *Rome I*

At the time of writing, the EC Regulation on the law applicable to contractual obligations (Rome I)[44] was about to be adopted, with the intention that it would come into force towards the end of 2009. The Regulation would supplant the Rome Convention. The Regulation is based on the Convention but in certain

---

[38] *Bonython v Commonwealth of Australia* [1951] AC 201, at 219 (PC).

[39] Except in situations where the Convention does not apply.

[40] The Convention applies as from 1 April 1991. See the Contracts (Applicable Law) Act 1990 (Commencement No 1) Order 1991 (SI 1991/707).

[41] S 2(3) of the Act.

[42] *The Report on the Rome Convention* by Professor Mario Giuliano and Professor Paul Lagarde (OJ C282 31/10/80).

[43] Implemented in the UK by the Contracts (Applicable Law) Act 1990 (Commencement No. 2) Order 2004 (SI 2004/3448).

[44] At the time of writing, the final and official text of the Regulation had not been published. Further details are provided later in this chapter.

respects it changes and expands upon the rules contained in the Convention. The UK has the right to refuse to participate in the adoption of the proposed Regulation. At the time of writing, it was not certain if the UK would refuse to participate, although the UK Government had given a tentative indication that it was minded to proceed with the adoption of the Regulation, subject to the outcome of a consultation exercise which it was then launching. If the UK does refuse to participate then the Rome Convention would continue to apply as a matter of English law in accordance with the Contracts (Applicable Law) Act 1990. As it is uncertain if the proposed Regulation will have effect as a matter of English law, the changes that it would bring about will be discussed separately later in this chapter. What now follows will address the existing position under the Rome Convention. Much of the discussion would remain relevant if Rome I is adopted.

4.5.2 The Rome Convention: introductory comments

The application of the Rome Convention is mandatory, in the sense that the parties to a contract cannot contract out of its provisions. Section 2(1) states in unequivocal terms that, subject to the exceptions set out in the Act, the Convention 'shall have the force of law in the United Kingdom'. Article 1(1) of the Convention says in mandatory terms that 'The rules of the Convention shall apply to contractual obligations in any situation involving a choice between the laws of different countries'.[45] This is reinforced by the language of Article 17, which states that the rules of the 'Convention shall apply to contracts made after the date on which the Convention entered into force with respect to that State'.[46] In practice, this means that an English court is bound to apply the rules of the Convention in the matters it covers pursuant to the Act, notwithstanding an attempt by the parties to contract out of its provisions.

4.5.2.1 Exclusions

There are a number of exclusions from the ambit of the Convention, where resort must be had to the relevant common law conflicts rules. Most of the exclusions are set out in Article 1 of the Convention, but there are two other exclusions that arise by specific derogations made by the UK as set out in the Act.[47] The Convention also provides for situations where mandatory provisions of the law of the forum (the *lex fori*) and the public policy of the forum may override the contradictory requirements of the applicable law of the contract.[48] Article 21 also recognises the primacy of the application of other treaties or conventions to which a

---

[45] If no such choice arises, that is, in an entirely domestic situation, the Convention will have no application and the domestic law will apply.

[46] In the case of the UK, 1 April 1991.

[47] I.e. to Arts 7(1) and 10(1)(e). See s 2(2) of the Act.

[48] See Arts 7(2) and 16.

State is, or may become, a party.[49] Amongst the exclusions contained in Article 1 are the following: the obligations that arise under bills of exchange, cheques and promissory notes, and obligations under other negotiable instruments which arise out of their negotiable character;[50] agreements as to jurisdiction and arbitration for the resolution of disputes;[51] corporate matters;[52] the authority of an agent to bind its principal and of an organ to bind its corporate body;[53] matters relating to trusts;[54] contracts of insurance (other than of re-insurance[55]) which cover risks situated in EU Member States.[56]

4.5.2.2 *The law of a State*

Article 1(1) of the Convention provides that the rules of the Convention shall apply to determine the applicable law that will govern contractual obligations in any situation involving a choice between the laws of different States. Article 19(1) provides that where a State consists of several territorial units, each having its own contract laws, each unit shall be treated as a separate State for the purposes of identifying the applicable law. Accordingly, New York and Texas, being separate territorial units of the USA with their own State laws of contract, would be treated by an English court as separate States for the purposes of determining the applicable law of a contract. The same would apply to each of the States in Australia and the provinces in Canada.

4.5.2.3   A different issue arises where the parties wish to nominate a system or set of principles that does not amount to the law of a State. In *Beximco Pharmaceuticals Ltd v Shamil Bank of Bahrain EC*[57] the Court of Appeal held that the consequence of Article 1(1) was that there had to be a choice between the laws of legal jurisdictions and not some wider and less defined concept that the parties might have nominated such as, in that case, the principles of Sharia law, or the law mercantile, or general principles of commercial or international law. Hence, the parties cannot under Article 3(1) purport to choose such vague concepts to govern their contract. On the other hand, and subject to meeting the requirements of certainty as to content and the rules for incorporation under the applicable law, it might be

---

[49] For instance, the International Monetary Fund Agreement (the 'Bretton Woods Agreement') to which the UK is a party. See para 4.11.3 below.

[50] Art 1(2)(c).

[51] Art 1(2)(d). See the commentary on this by Morrison J in *Horn Linie GmbH v Panamericana Formas E Impresos SA* [2006] EWHC 373, [2006] 2 Lloyd's Rep 44.

[52] Art 1(2)(e).

[53] Art 1(2)(f).

[54] Art 1(2)(g).

[55] Art 1(4).

[56] Art 1(3).

[57] [2004] EWCA Civ 19, [2004] 1 WLR 1784. The decision was followed in *Halpern v Halpern* [2007] EWCA Civ 291, [2007] 2 Lloyd's Rep 56.

possible for the parties to incorporate as terms of the contract codes such as those laid down in the Hague-Visby Rules. In such a case, the incorporated terms would be relevant to ascertaining the contents of the agreement and their interpretation, but matters affecting the contract as a whole and its validity (such as the consequences of mistake, duress, and repudiation or termination of the agreement) would be dealt with in accordance with the governing law of the contract.[58]

4.5.2.4 Disapplication of renvoi

The applicable law of the contract as determined under the Convention, will be the domestic law of the relevant country, excluding its conflict of laws rules. This is provided for by Article 15 of the Convention, which thereby excludes the application of the doctrine of 'renvoi'.[59]

4.5.2.5 Contractual obligations

The concept of 'contractual obligations' is not defined in the Convention, nor is there much guidance given in the *Giuliano-Lagarde Report*, except that the Report states that the Convention is only concerned with contractual obligations, so that it does not extend to property rights nor to intellectual property rights.[60] It is submitted that, in the broad spirit of characterisation to which Mance LJ referred in *Raiffeisen Zentralbank Osterreich AG v Five Star General Trading LLC*,[61] an English court would give the concept of contractual obligations as used in the Convention a fairly wide interpretation, to mean any consensual agreement between the parties under which they intended to agree their mutual rights and obligations, even if it were not supported by consideration or some other requirement for material validity which applied under purely English domestic law.[62]

---

[58] *Halpern v Halpern* [2007] EWCA Civ 291, [2007] 2 Lloyd's Rep 56, in which it was also pointed out that by virtue of s 46 of the Arbitration Act 1996, the parties may agree that disputes should be determined by arbitration and that the arbitral tribunal should apply principles that are outside the laws of a chosen jurisdiction. An English court would then be empowered to enforce an arbitral award that was made on that basis, pursuant to the enforcement provisions of the Act: see *Musawi v RE International (UK) Ltd* [2007] EWHC 2981 (Ch).

[59] Which was also the position under the common law: *Amin Rasheed Shipping Corp v Kuwait Ins Co, the Al Wahab* [1984] AC 50, at 61–62. A similar outcome could be achieved by stating that the governing law should be the 'internal law' of the relevant jurisdiction: see *C v D* [2007] EWHC 1541, [2007] 2 All ER (Comm) 557 (the case was the subject of an appeal, where this point did not arise: [2007] EWCA Civ 1282).

[60] At p 10. This means that the contractual aspects of a transaction may fall within the ambit of the Convention, but not the purely proprietary aspects. Nonetheless, if the applicable law governing the proprietary aspects refers back to the contract then the Convention would be relevant in establishing the applicable law to determine those contractual matters.

[61] [2001] EWCA Civ 68; [2001] QB 825, at [26]–[33]. See also Auld LJ in *Macmillan Inc v Bishopsgate Investment Trust PLC (No 3)* [1996] 1 WLR 387, at 407.

[62] See *Dicey, Morris & Collins* at paras 32-023 to 32-024. This is supported by the approach that is taken by the Convention, which provides in Art 8(1) that questions of material validity should be determined by the putative governing law of the contract.

However, where a case involves several concurrent claims involving the same facts, in addition to a claim in contract, each claim should be dealt with separately and not assimilated with the contractual claim.[63] It would be a matter for the English court hearing the claim to determine in such a case where the boundaries of each claim lay.

4.5.3 The applicable law of a contract

Articles 3 and 4 of the Rome Convention lay down the fundamental rules for determining the applicable or governing law of a contract.[64] Article 3 provides for the parties to choose that law. Article 4 provides for the rules in the absence of such a choice. Both articles recognise the possibility that different parts of a contract may be governed by different laws[65] ('dépeçage'). By Article 3(2) the parties may agree to change the governing law that previously applied, but that is to be without prejudice to the contract's formal validity under Article 9 and such a change cannot adversely affect the rights of third parties. Each of Article 3 and 4 will now be examined.

4.5.3.1 Article 3: choice of law

Article 3(1) provides that the parties may choose the governing law of their contract. There is no requirement that the law which is chosen must have any connection with either the parties or the facts of the contract. Subject to Article 3(3), they are entitled to choose, if they wish, a law that is 'neutral' to the parties and the facts. For instance, English law is often chosen because of its expertise and the experience it has in the subject matter of the contract. The choice may be an express choice or it may be implied if 'demonstrated with reasonable certainty by the terms of the contract or the circumstances of the case'.[66] An express choice is obviously preferable and any well drawn contract should contain a choice of law clause.

4.5.3.1.1   In the absence of such an express clause, it will be necessary to determine if a choice may be implied in accordance with the foregoing rubric. In *Egon Oldendorff v Liberia Corp*[67] it was held by Clarke J that there had been an implied choice of English law because the contract was an English language standard form of contract that provided for disputes to be determined by arbitration in London, and English law, not being associated with either party, was a neutral law between

---

[63] *Base Metal Trading Ltd v Shamurin* [2004] EWCA Civ 1316, [2005] 1 WLR 1157.

[64] This is subject to the provisions of Art 5 with respect to certain consumer contracts and Art 6 with respect to individual employment contracts.

[65] See Arts 3(1) and 4(1).

[66] It has been held that the test requires both the terms of the contract and the circumstances of the case to be considered: see Aikens J in *Marubeni Hong Kong & South China Ltd v Mongolian Government* [2002] 2 All ER (Comm) 873, at [42].

[67] [1996] 1 Lloyd's Rep 380.

them. The court was of the view that the parties must have intended arbitrators sitting in London and dealing with an English language document to apply English law to it. They had a 'clear intention' to make a 'real choice' of English law to govern the contract.[68] In *Turkiye Is Bankasi AS v Bank of China*[69] it was held by Phillips J that a counter-guarantee for the obligations of an issuer of a guarantee, where the guarantee contained an express choice of law, would also be governed by the same law. This was because the counter-guarantee was in the form as circulated by the issuer of the guarantee, and the implication to be drawn from that circular was that both the guarantee and the counter-guarantee would be governed by the same law. In *Samcrete Egypt Engineers & Contractors SAE v Land Rover Exports Ltd*[70] it was held that where a draft of the contract had contained a choice of law and jurisdiction clause, but that clause was deleted and did not appear in the final version of the contract, there could have been no implied choice of the governing law. On the other hand, it was held by Aikens J in *Marubeni Hong Kong & South China Ltd v Mongolian Government*[71] that where an English jurisdiction clause had been retained in the final version of a guarantee, but the choice of English law in an earlier draft had been deleted, there was still a good arguable case that the parties impliedly intended the guarantee to be governed by English law. The parties had chosen a neutral jurisdiction to hear any dispute that arose and they had not wished the guarantee to be governed by the law of the guarantor's country. A choice of jurisdiction would imply that the parties expected the chosen court to apply its own law in settling any dispute. There was no specific evidence why the governing law clause had been deleted, so that could not be taken as evidencing an intention against the presumption in favour of the choice of law following the choice of jurisdiction.

It is submitted, in addition, that where there is a principal contract which contains an express choice of law and a related subsidiary contract, between the same parties or between one of them and a third party, the inference that may normally be drawn is that (in the absence of an express choice of law to govern the subsidiary contract) the parties to the subsidiary contract intended that it should be governed by the same law as the principal contract.[72] This would be the case, for instance, with respect to the law that governed a guarantee of the obligations of a party under a principal contract, where there was an express choice of the law that governed the principal contract. This would have been the case under the previous common

4.5.3.1.2

---

[68] The test of a clear intention to make a real choice, as formulated by Clarke J in *Egon Oldendorff v Liberia Corp* [1996] 1 Lloyd's Rep 380, at 387, was approved by Potter LJ in *Samcrete Egypt Engineers & Contractors SAE v Land Rover Exports Ltd* [2001] EWCA Civ 2019, at [26]–[27].

[69] [1993] 1 Lloyd's Rep 132.

[70] [2001] EWCA Civ 2019.

[71] [2002] 2 All ER (Comm) 873.

[72] The *Giuliano-Lagarde Report*, at p 17, mentions specifically the case of two related contracts between the same parties. It also refers to the relevance of a previous course of dealing between the same parties where there was an express choice.

law rules.[73] It should be noted, however, that the Court of Appeal rejected this solution in *Samcrete Egypt Engineers & Contractors SAE v Land Rover Exports Ltd*,[74] which was a case where a choice and law and jurisdiction clause had deliberately been removed from an earlier draft of the document, before the contract was finalised.

4.5.3.1.3   It should be noted that Article 3(4) provides that the validity and consent of a party to the choice of the applicable law of a contract should be determined in accordance with Article 8 (material validity), Article 9 (formal validity), and Article 12 (incapacity of natural persons).

4.5.3.2 *Article 3(3): a limitation upon choice*

Article 3(3) imposes a limitation upon the effectiveness of a choice of law by the parties. It provides as follows:

> The fact that the parties have chosen a foreign law, whether or not accompanied by the choice of a foreign tribunal, shall not, where all the other elements relevant to the situation at the time of the choice are connected with one country only, prejudice the application of rules of the law of that country which cannot be derogated from by contract, hereinafter called 'mandatory rules'.

Article 3(3) could apply where English law has been chosen by the parties as the governing law of their contract, but all the relevant elements are connected with another country. In the alternative, it could apply where the law of one foreign country has been chosen, but all the relevant elements are connected with yet another foreign country. Whilst in theory Article 3(3) could also apply in the case of a chosen foreign law where all the relevant elements are connected with England, that situation is more likely to be dealt with by an English court under Article 7(2), to which reference is made below.

4.5.3.2.1   Four issues arise in considering Article 3(3). The first issue concerns the matters that are to be taken into account in determining if the relevant elements are solely concerned with such another country (the 'third country'). The second issue concerns the date as at which that determination should be made. The third issue relates to the concept of the mandatory rules of the third country from which there can be no derogation. The fourth issue concerns the date as at which the inconsistency must exist as between the governing law and the mandatory rules of the law of the third country.

4.5.3.2.2   As to the first and second issues, Article 3(3) refers to the 'elements relevant to the situation at the time of the choice'. It is only the relevant elements at the time of the choice of law which fall to be considered. Elements that arise subsequent

---

[73] See *Wahda Bank v Arab Bank plc* [1996] 1 Lloyd's Rep 470 and *Broken Hill Pty Co Ltd v Xenakis* [1982] 2 Lloyd's Rep 304.

[74] [2001] EWCA Civ 2019, at [23]–[29].

to that date should not be taken into account. However, the consideration of the relevant elements will involve a wider set of facts than simply the elements which arise under the contract itself.[75] In the case of a loan agreement, the elements could include the purpose for which the agreement was entered into, the destination of the proceeds of drawings, the language of the agreement, the identity of the lender, and the places to which the borrower should make repayment.[76] A relevant element would also be the location of the parties to the contract, so that if they were in different countries then it could not be said that all of the elements were solely connected with one country.[77]

As to the third issue, it should be a matter for the law of the third country to determine if the relevant rules of its law are mandatory in the sense that they cannot be derogated from by the contract; the court hearing the case must determine the matter by the application of the law of the third country. It may be the case, for instance, that under the law of the third country, rules which might in other situations be obligatory may not apply in the particular circumstances of the contract and so would not be mandatory in their application in the sense that is required by Article 3(3). The types of mandatory rules that are likely to arise will concern matters such as consumer protection, employment, anti-competitive practices, and insolvency.   **4.5.3.2.3**

On the fourth issue, it is arguable that the validity of the contract and its effectiveness should not be detrimentally affected by changes in the law of the relevant third country that have come about subsequently to the time of their choice of law. On the other hand, it would also seem unreasonable to say that the contract could not be saved by beneficial changes to the law of the third country which were intended to lift the restrictions that might previously have been applicable to the contract. There is no guidance provided by the *Giuliano-Lagarde Report* on this point. It is submitted that, prima facie, it would be a matter for the law of the third country to determine the effect on the contract of changes in its law that come into effect after the time of the parties' choice of the governing law. However, if a court before which the matter came felt that it would be repugnant to its principles of public policy to permit a law of the third country to have retrospective effect, it could fall back on Article 16 and refuse to give effect to the relevant provision.   **4.5.3.2.4**

4.5.3.3 Article 4: absence of choice

To the extent[78] that there is no express or implied choice of the governing law under Article 3 then the applicable law will fall to be determined in accordance

---

[75] *Caterpillar Financial Services Corp v SNC Passion* [2004] EWHC 569 (Comm), [2004] 2 Lloyd's Rep 99.

[76] Ibid.

[77] *NM Rothschild Ltd v Equitable Life Assurance Society* [2002] EWHC 1021 (QB).

[78] This means that the parties may have made a partial choice of the governing law, so that Art 4 will apply to the extent they have not made a choice.

with Article 4 of the Convention.[79] Article 4(1) provides that the applicable law will be that of the country with which it is most closely connected. Article 4(2) provides a set of presumptions that should be used to find that country, but these are subject to the exceptions contained in Articles 4(3), 4(4), and 4(5), to which further reference will be made below.

4.5.3.3.1 Article 4(2)   The starting point under Article 4(2) is that the contract is presumed to be most closely connected with the country of the party whose performance is 'characteristic of the contract'. The *Giuliano-Lagarde Report*[80] says that this should be the party that is supplying the relevant goods or services under the contract and not the party that is receiving or paying for them. In a contract that involves a reciprocal supply of goods or services, there will not be a single party that can be identified as having the essential role that is characteristic of the contract. In such a case, it might be possible to split the contract into severable parts and deal with each separately under Article 4(2). It is submitted, however, that the better approach, particularly where there is an inter-dependence of each party's rights and obligations, would be to apply Article 4(5) instead of attempting to apply the presumptions under Article 4(2).

4.5.3.3.1.1   Once the party whose performance is characteristic has been identified, it is then necessary to determine the country with which that party was associated, which should be ascertained as at the time of contracting. It will be the law of that place which will be the governing law of the contract. Article 4(2) lays down a series of steps to make that determination, which are as follows:

(i)   in a case where the party is an individual, it will be the law of the place of his habitual residence, but this is subject to (iii) below;

(ii)   in a case where the party is a corporate or unincorporated body, it will be the law of the place of its central administration, but this is also subject to (iii) below;

(iii)   if the party has contracted in the course of a trade or profession, it will be the law of his or its principal place of business, unless the terms of the contract provide for it to effect performance through another of its places of business,[81] in which case it will be the law of that place.

4.5.3.3.1.2   Putting Article 4(2) into the context of banking transactions, the *Giuliano-Lagarde Report* says[82] that the party that is supplying banking services should be regarded

---

[79] Art 4(1) contemplates the possibility that, by way of exception, severable parts of the contract may be governed by different laws if those parts are closely connected with separate countries.

[80] At p 20.

[81] See *Iran Continental Shelf Oil Co v IRI International Corp* [2002] EWCA Civ 1024 and *Ennstone Building Products Ltd v Stanger Ltd* [2002] EWCA Civ 916, [2002] 1 WLR 3059.

[82] At p 20.

as the party whose performance is characteristic of the contract. Thus, in a contract between a banker and its customer, the characteristic performance will be that of the bank. As the bank will supply those services in the course of its business and usually it will do so from the branch where the account is maintained, it will be the law of that place of business (i.e. the branch) which will be the governing law of the contract.[83] It follows that in a commercial loan (not being a consumer loan, to which the provisions of Article 5 may apply), the characteristic performance will be that of the lender. Under a guarantee, the characteristic performance will be that of the guarantor[84] and, similarly, in a contract of indemnity, the characteristic performance is that of the indemnifier.[85]

The position under a letter of credit is more complicated, as there are several different contracts that may arise under it, rather than one single contract. Each of the contracts has a separate characteristic performance and, potentially, a different governing law.[86] In any event, as discussed below, it may be more appropriate to apply Article 4(5) in displacement of Article 4(2).[87] If Article 4(2) is to be applied, then the characteristic performance of the contract between the issuer and the beneficiary will be that of the issuer; as between the issuer and the confirming bank, the characteristic performance will be that of the confirming bank; and as between the confirming bank and the beneficiary, it will also be that of the confirming bank.[88]

4.5.3.3.2 Articles 4(3) and 4(4)   Articles 4(3) and 4(4) provide for different presumptions to those given in Article 4(2). Article 4(3) provides that to the extent that the subject matter of a contract concerns a right in or to use immovable property, it shall be presumed that the contract is most closely connected with the situs of the property. Otherwise, the presumptions in Article 4(2) should apply. Article 4(4) deals with a contract for the carriage of goods, including single voyage charter parties. It states that Article 4(2) does not apply at all to contracts for the carriage of goods. Instead, it provides a presumption that the contract is most closely connected with the country of the principal place of business of the carrier at the time the contract is entered into, if that is also the place of loading or discharge or the principal place of business of the consignor. There is no statement as to the

---

[83] *Sierra Leone Telecommunications Co Ltd v Barclays Bank plc* [1998] 2 All ER 821, at 826–827. Much the same result would have been achieved under the common law rules: see *Libyan Arab Foreign Bank v Bankers Trust Co* [1989] QB 728, at 746.

[84] *Samcrete Egypt Engineers & Contractors SAE v Land Rover Exports Ltd* [2001] EWCA Civ 2019, at [38]. See also the *Giuliano-Lagarde Report*, at p 21.

[85] *Opthalmic Innovations International (United Kingdom) Ltd v Opthalmic Innovations International Inc* [2004] EWHC 2948 (Ch).

[86] *PT Indonesia Bank Ltd TRK v Marconi Communications International Ltd* [2005] EWCA Civ 422; [2005] 2 All ER (Comm) 325, at [61].

[87] As was done in *PT Pan Indonesia Bank Ltd TBK v Marconi Communications International Ltd*.

[88] *Bank of Baroda v Vysya Bank Ltd* [1994] 2 Lloyd's Rep 87, at 92.

position if it falls outside those parameters, but presumably Article 4(5) should apply.

4.5.3.3.3 Article 4(5) Article 4(5) is capable of overriding each of Articles 4(2), 4(3), and 4(4). It is as follows:

> [Article 4(2)] shall not apply if the characteristic performance cannot be determined, and the presumptions in [Articles 4(2), 4(3), and 4(4)] shall be disregarded if it appears from the circumstances as a whole that the contract is more closely connected with another country.

4.5.3.3.3.1 It will be seen that Article 4(5) addresses two situations. The first is where it is impossible to determine the party whose performance is characteristic of the contract. This would include situations where each party has reciprocal obligations for the supply of goods or services under the contract, as would be the case in a barter transaction or a contract for the exchange of obligations as, for instance, under a commodity or interest swap. It might also cover a syndicated loan agreement, where there are several lenders operating from different countries, although it might be argued that the matter should be determined under the second part of Article 5(2) on the basis that the contract is most closely connected with the location of the facility agent, which has the responsibility for administering the facility on behalf of the banks.

4.5.3.3.3.2 The second situation that is dealt with in Article 4(5) is where it would be inappropriate to apply the law found by the operation of the presumptions because it appears from the circumstances as a whole that the contract is more closely connected with a different country from that found by the application of the presumptions. As the Court of Appeal commented in *PT Pan Indonesia Bank Ltd TBK v Marconi Communications International Ltd*,[89] if Articles 4(1) and 4(5) were taken together without the interposition of Article 4(2), the position would be much the same as used to apply under the common law rules. The effect of the common law rules was that in the absence of a choice of law, the contract would be governed by the system of law with which the contract had its closest and most real connection.

4.5.3.3.3.3 The question arises as to the weight that should be given to the presumptions in Articles 4(2), 4(3), and 4(4) and what is required for them to be displaced under Article 4(5). The *Giuliano-Lagarde Report* states that they are only presumptions and that each case should be considered on its merits.[90] In *Samcrete Egypt Engineers and Contractors SAE v Land Rover Exports Ltd*[91] and in *Ennstone Building Products*

---

[89] [2005] EWCA Civ 422; [2005] 2 All ER (Comm) 325, at [41]. The court's judgment was delivered by Potter LJ.
[90] At pp 21–22.
[91] [2001] EWCA Civ 2019, at [41] and [45].

Ltd v Stanger Ltd[92] the Court of Appeal held that the presumption in Article 4(2) could be displaced if there was a preponderance of contrary factors which clearly demonstrated the existence of connecting factors which justified such a course.[93] The Court of Appeal in *PT Pan Indonesia Bank Ltd TBK v Marconi Communications International Ltd*[94] followed that approach. It declined to adopt the stricter approach taken in the Netherlands, where the Hoge Raad in *Societe Nouvelle des Papeteries de L'Aa SA v BV Machinefabriek BOA*[95] had said that the presumption in Article 4(2) should only be disregarded if the locality of the party which is to effect the characteristic performance of the contract had no real significance as a connecting factor. In *PT Pan Indonesia Bank Ltd TBK v Marconi Communications International Ltd*[96] it was accepted that the correct approach was to look at how the contract was intended by its terms to operate at the time it was made, rather than to look at what in fact occurred.

The burden of proof lies on the party which asserts that Article 4(5) should apply and that the presumptions should be disregarded.[97]   **4.5.3.3.3.4**

In *Definitely Maybe (Touring) Ltd v Marek Lieberberg Konzertagentur GmbH*[98] it   **4.5.3.3.3.5** was accepted that Article 4(5) applied to displace Article 4(2). Although the party providing its services had its place of business in England for the purposes of Article 4(2), the place of performance by both parties was in Germany, the centre of gravity of the dispute was in Germany, and Germany was more closely connected with the contract than England. Hence, the contract should be regarded as governed by German law pursuant to Article 4(5). In *Kenburn Waste Management Ltd v Bergmann*[99] Article 4(5) was applied to displace the presumption under Article 4(2) (which was the place of the habitual residence of the relevant party, which was German) where the contract, which was an agreement in settlement of litigation with undertakings being given, was otherwise entirely related to England, to which the undertaking related.

On the other hand, in *Samcrete Egypt Engineers and Contractors SAE v Land Rover*   **4.5.3.3.3.6** *Exports Ltd*[100] it was held that Article 4(2) should apply and that it was not displaced by Article 4(5). The connecting factors with the relevant party's principal

---

[92] [2002] EWCA Civ 916, [2002] 1 WLR 3059, at [41].

[93] See also the Lord President and Lord Cameron in the Scottish case of *Caledonia Subsea Ltd v Microperi SRL* [2003] SC 70.

[94] [2005] EWCA Civ 422, [2005] 2 All ER (Comm) 325.

[95] 25/9/2002. The case is referred to in the *PT Pan Indonesia* case

[96] [2005] EWCA Civ 422; [2005] 2 All ER (Comm) 325, at [55].

[97] *Samcrete Egypt Engineers and Contractors SAE v Land Rover Exports Ltd* [2001] EWCA Civ 2019, at [37].

[98] [2001] 1 WLR 1745.

[99] [2002] EWCA Civ 98, [2002] CLC 644.

[100] [2001] EWCA Civ 2019.

place of business were such that it could not be said that there was a sufficient linkage to another country. In *Iran Continental Shelf Oil Co v IRI International Corp*[101] it was held that there were insufficient factors connecting the contract with another country to displace the presumption under Article 4(2). The linkage under that presumption was to one of the specified places of the relevant party's business, which was nominated in the contract as the place from which it would perform the contract.

4.5.3.3.3.7   The approach to be taken under the second part of Article 4(5) is also illustrated by the decision of the Court of Appeal in *PT Pan Indonesia Bank Ltd TBK v Marconi Communications International Ltd*.[102] The case was concerned with a letter of credit that had been issued by one bank in Indonesia and confirmed by another bank in Indonesia in favour of an English company in England as the beneficiary. The letter of credit provided for it to be advised to the beneficiary by an English bank in London. The English advising bank was authorised in the letter of credit to negotiate it. In fact, the English bank, acting as the collecting bank on behalf of the beneficiary (rather than as a negotiating bank), presented the documents and the drafts drawn by the beneficiary to the confirming bank. The confirming bank, having referred the documents to the issuing bank, refused to pay, claiming discrepancies. The beneficiary sought leave to commence proceedings before the High Court in England and to serve the proceedings on the confirming bank. To do so, the beneficiary had to show that there was a good arguable case that the relevant contract was governed by English law or that the contract was made within the jurisdiction or that there was a breach of a contract within the jurisdiction of the court.[103] The confirming bank argued that the contract was governed by Indonesian law, in accordance with the presumption provided by Article 4(2) of the Rome Convention, because it (and perhaps the issuing bank as well) was the party whose performance was characteristic of the contract and each of them was in Indonesia. It also argued that the contract was made in Indonesia and that any breach of the contract occasioned by its failure to pay occurred in Indonesia.

4.5.3.3.3.8   The court held that there was a good arguable case that Article 4(5) applied in displacement of Article 4(2), because the contract was more closely connected with England than with Indonesia. The preponderance of factors at the time the contract was made connected the letter of credit with England. For this purpose, the relevant contract was that between the confirming bank and the beneficiary. Whilst it was desirable[104] that each of the contracts under the letter of credit

---

[101] [2002] EWCA Civ 1024.

[102] [2005] EWCA Civ 422, [2005] 2 All ER (Comm) 325.

[103] See CPR 6.20, paras 5 and 6.

[104] See *Bank of Credit and Commerce Hong Kong Ltd v Sonali Bank* [1995] 1 Lloyd's Rep 227 and *Bank of Baroda v Vysya Bank Ltd* [1994] 2 Lloyd's Rep 87.

should be governed by the same governing law (i.e. the contracts between the issuer and the confirming bank, between the issuer and the beneficiary, between the confirming bank and the beneficiary, and, if applicable, between the bank which negotiates the credit and the confirming bank), that was not essential. Looking at the circumstances concerning the contract as between the beneficiary and the confirming bank, the overall purpose of the letter of credit was to provide the beneficiary with the right to receive payment in England against compliant documents. The letter of credit was to be communicated by the advising bank to the beneficiary in England, the documents to be presented under it were to be presented to the advising and negotiating bank in England, where they would be checked, and the letter of credit contemplated that payment under the letter of credit would be made in England. It was of less importance to regard the place where the contract was made as being of a close connection with the contract, given electronic communication. In any event, England would have been the place where the contract was made, as the advising bank would be regarded as having been the agent of the confirming bank for the purpose of communicating the opening of the credit to the beneficiary.[105] The fact that the advising bank was not also a confirming bank was immaterial to the outcome.[106] As the court noted, the outcome reached in this case was the same as would have been reached under the common law rules. At common law it had been held that the contract with the beneficiary under a letter of credit was most closely connected with the place at which the documents were to be presented and at which authority was given to make payment of sums due under the credit or to accept drafts drawn under it.[107]

4.5.4 Qualifications to the application of the governing law

Having described the conflict of laws rules that apply to determine the applicable, or governing, law of a contract, it will be relevant to discuss the matters that will be determined by the governing law. Before doing so, however, it is sensible to discuss some of the qualifications to those rules and the relevance that other laws may have. In this regard, Articles 3(3), 5, 6, 7(2), 8, 9, and 16 of the Convention contain qualifications to the application of the governing law. It should be noted, however, that the UK has elected not to apply Articles 7(1) and 10(1)(e)

---

[105] See *Bank Melli Iran v Barclays Bank* [1951] 2 Lloyd's Rep 362, at 376.

[106] It should be noted that this is consistent with the view taken by Mance J in *Bank of Baroda v Vysya Bank* [1994] 2 Lloyd's Rep 87 where it was held that a letter of credit that was confirmed by a bank in London, being the place where it was payable and had been advised, was governed by English law, so that the confirming bank was entitled to treat English law as governing its right of reimbursement from the foreign issuing bank. Mance J had been of the view that the same would have applied if the letter of credit had only been advised in London and had not been confirmed in London.

[107] See *Offshore International SA v Banco Central SA* [1977] 1 WLR 399 and *Power Curber International Ltd v The National Bank of Kuwait SAK* [1981] 1 WLR 1233.

of the Convention.[108] As previously noted, Article 3(3) contains an exception to a choice of the applicable law in respect of the mandatory rules of a country with which the contract is otherwise connected. Articles 5 and 6 contain special rules with respect to certain consumer contracts and with respect to individual employment contracts. Articles 8 and 9 will be examined later.

4.5.4.1 Mandatory rules of the forum

Article 7(2) of the Convention provides for the application of the mandatory rules of the forum in preference to the rules of the law that might otherwise apply to the contract. It provides as follows:

> Nothing in this Convention shall restrict the application of the rules of the law of the forum in a situation where they are mandatory irrespective of the law otherwise applicable to the contract.

4.5.4.1.1 The exception under Article 7(2) only applies where the rules of the forum are mandatory in the particular situation and they must be mandatory irrespective of the law that would otherwise be applicable to the contract. Hence, if the rule of the forum is intended only to apply in a domestic context and the contract has nothing to do with that context, the exception will not apply.[109] Nor would a contradictory rule of the law of the forum be applied under Article 7(2) where that law permits the contract to disapply the relevant rule. On the other hand, if the rule is intended to apply notwithstanding a choice of a foreign law as the applicable law, Article 7(2) would be engaged.[110] Although it is not expressly stated, it would appear that the foreign law should be applied except to the extent that it was incompatible with the law of the forum, so that questions of interpretation of the contract would probably continue to be governed by the chosen law pursuant to Article 10(1)(a). It is not clear if Article 7(2) would apply in a case where the law of the forum was inconsistent, not with the chosen applicable law of the contract but, instead, with the mandatory rules of a third country that were to be applied pursuant to Article 3(3). Article 7(2) refers to 'the law otherwise applicable to the contract', which appears to mean the applicable law of the contract, rather than the mandatory rules of the law of a third country that might apply irrespective of the chosen applicable law, particularly if those rules only relate to some specific aspect of the contract. In this regard, it may be significant that the language that is used in Article 7(2) is narrower than that which is used in Article 16, where the wording refers to 'a rule of the law of any country specified by this Convention'.

---

[108] See s 2(2) of the Contracts (Applicable Law) Act 1990.
[109] See, for instance, the provisions of s 26 of the Unfair Contract Terms Act 1977 in relation to international supply contracts.
[110] See, for instance, s 27(2) of the Unfair Contract Terms Act 1977.

An example of where an English court would apply Article 7(2) would be where   **4.5.4.1.2**
the contract that was governed by a foreign law called for the commission of an act
which would be unlawful as a matter of English law because it constituted an illegal criminal act under an English law that was intended to have extra-territorial
application.[111]

The question arises as to whether Article 7(2) would be applied by an English   **4.5.4.1.3**
court in relation to a contract that was governed by a foreign law of country A,
where the contract validly required under its governing law performance in
another foreign country B and such performance was rendered unlawful by the
law of country B (the *lex loci solutionis*). There is no doubt, at least in the case of
supervening illegality arising after the contract was made, that an English court
would not enforce such a contract if it were governed by English law.[112] Equally, if
the foreign governing law excused performance, an English court, in the application of that law, would not enforce performance. It is not clear if, as a matter of the
principles of English conflict of laws, English law would take the same view where
the contract is governed by a foreign law that did not excuse performance in such
a situation. If English law would excuse performance in the latter situation, then
it would do so under Article 7(2). If, on the other hand, English law would only
excuse performance in consequence of the application of the governing law of the
contract (whether English or some other law)[113] then Article 7(2) would not apply,
because there would be no rule of the forum that was mandatory irrespective of
the governing law of the contract.

4.5.4.2 *Mandatory rules of a closely connected country*

It should be noted that the type of situation just discussed, where the governing
law would not excuse performance even though it was unlawful by the law of the
place of performance (the *lex loci solutionis*), would have been dealt with under
Article 7(1) of the Convention, but that provision does not have effect under
English law.[114] Article 7(1) provides as follows:

> When applying under this Convention the law of a country, effect may be given to
> the mandatory rules of the law of another country with which the situation has a
> close connection, if and in so far as, under the law of the latter country, those rules
> must be applied whatever the law applicable to the contract. In considering whether

---

[111] *Boissevain v Weil* [1950] AC 327, *Shanshal v Al-Kishtaini* [2001] EWCA Civ 264, [2001] 2
All ER (Comm) 601.

[112] *Ralli Bros v Compania Naviera Sota y Aznar* [1920] 2 KB 287. This case is discussed further
below.

[113] This question is also examined further below in the discussion relating to the *Ralli Bros* case.

[114] See s 2(2) of the Contracts (Applicable Law) Act 1990. This power of reservation was exercised by the UK pursuant to Art 22 of the Convention. Nor does it have effect in Germany, Ireland,
Luxembourg, Portugal, Latvia, and Slovenia.

to give effect to these mandatory rules, regard shall be had to their nature and purpose and to the consequences of their application or non-application.

4.5.4.2.1 There can be little doubt that the *lex loci solutionis* has the necessary connection with the situation and, subject to the consideration that is required to be given to the nature and purpose of the relevant rules of that law and the consequences of applying or not applying them, Article 7(1) could be engaged in the type of situation referred to above.

4.5.4.2.2 The principal problems with Article 7(1) are in determining the types of situation where a mandatory rule of a foreign law might be said to have a sufficiently close connection, and then in taking into account both the nature and purpose of such a rule and the consequences if it were to be applied or not applied, in determining if it should be given effect by the court. These are vague and uncertain concepts and would no doubt cause difficulties to the courts if they had to try and make sense of them. By way of example, one might consider the facts of *Libyan Arab Foreign Bank v Bankers Trust Co.*[115] In that case, which was decided before the Rome Convention came into force in England, a US law was promulgated for political reasons which purported to prevent branches of US banks, including those in England, from making repayment of deposits held with them by Libyan entities. The London branch of a US bank held a deposit for such an entity, which had demanded repayment of the deposit. By the application of common law rules, Staughton J refused to take account of the US law and ordered the bank to repay the deposit. If Article 7(1) had applied under English law, it would have been necessary for the judge to consider whether the US law had a sufficiently close connection with the situation concerning the customer's deposit and its demand for repayment of its deposit. He would then have been required to consider the nature and purpose of the US law including, perhaps, its political purpose. Finally, he would have been forced to take account of the consequences were he to decide either to apply or not to apply the US law. Such consequences might extend beyond the immediate consequences to the parties and might, again, enter into the political arena. It is possible that the types of foreign laws that could fall within the compass of Article 7(1) might include foreign sanctions laws, anti-trust, usury, and 'fair dealing' laws intended to give protection to one or other contracting party.

4.5.4.3 *Public policy of the forum*

Article 16 of the Convention provides that a rule of the law of any country specified by the Convention that might otherwise apply may be overridden if its application would be, 'manifestly incompatible with the public policy ('ordre public')

---

[115] [1989] QB 728. The case is discussed further below.

of the forum'. It should be noted that this is not confined merely to a rule of the applicable law of the contract, and it could apply, for instance, to a mandatory rule of a third country which might otherwise be given effect under Article 3(3). In the *Giuliano-Lagarde Report*[116] it is said that the use of 'manifestly' in Article 16 indicates that there must be something special about the impugned rule, being of an exceptional nature which was offensive to the public policy of the forum, before the exception will apply. Jacob J in *In the Matter of Colt Telecom Group plc*[117] said that Article 16 was concerned with matters of sufficient manifest importance so as to fall within the status of an *ordre public* and not minor technicalities.

4.5.5 Matters governed by the applicable law

It is now relevant to outline the matters that are governed by the applicable law, in accordance with the Rome Convention.

4.5.5.1 Material validity

Article 8 of the Convention concerns the material validity of a contract and its terms, that is, the existence and validity of the contract and its terms. Material validity goes to matters such as the formation of the contract, including intention to contract, offer and acceptance, and the provision of consideration to support the contract. It also covers issues such as whether the contract was invalidated by mistake, misrepresentation, duress, and undue influence,[118] and whether the contract, or a term of the contract, is unenforceable by reason of its being illegal under its applicable law.[119]

Article 8(1) provides that such matters shall be determined by the governing law of the contract or by the putative governing law if the contract or term were assumed to be valid.

4.5.5.1.1

By way of exception, Article 8(2) provides that a party may rely upon the law of the place of his habitual residence to establish that he did not consent to entering into the contract, if it appears from the circumstances that it would not be reasonable to determine the effect of his conduct in accordance with the governing law of the contract. Conduct could include both action and inaction, such as silence. It has been held, in cases involving corporate bodies, that the question of reasonableness in the determination of the effect of a party's conduct under Article 8(2)

4.5.5.1.2

---

[116] At p 38.

[117] [2002] EWHC 2815 (Ch), at [75]–[76].

[118] See *The Epsilon Rosa* [2002] EWHC 2033 (Comm), [2002] 2 Lloyd's Rep 701 (affd on other grounds, [2002] EWCA Civ 938, [2002] 2 Lloyd's Rep 701) and *Morin v Bonhams & Brooks Ltd* [2003] EWHC 467 (Comm); [2003] 2 All ER (Comm) 36, at [23] (affd, without reference on this point: [2003] EWCA Civ 1802, [2004] 1 Lloyd's Rep 702).

[119] See *Egon Oldendorff v Liberia Corp* [1995] 2 Lloyd's Rep 64; *Surzur Overseas Ltd v Ocean Reliance Shipping Co Ltd* [1997] CLY 906.

was to be assessed by the adoption of a dispassionate and internationally minded approach, rather than by the application of either the putative governing law of the contract or the law of the place of the habitual residence of the person challenging the validity of the contract. The mere fact that the choice of the contractually expressed governing law might be contrary to, or even offend, the public policy of the law of the place of that party's habitual residence would not be sufficient to displace the chosen law.[120]

4.5.5.1.3 The phrase 'habitual residence' remains undefined in the Rome Convention,[121] although it is used in several places, including Articles 4(2), 5, 8(2), and 9(5). Although the concept of habitual residence is usually associated with natural persons, it appears that its use in the context of the Rome Convention also includes corporate bodies. In English law, the location of a person's habitual residence is a question of fact, which depends upon the circumstances of the particular case,[122] but the meaning of the phrase will vary from its use in one piece of legislation to another.[123] It implies more than merely temporary or subsidiary residence; duration and some sense of settlement should be relevant factors.[124] Evidence of an intention to settle permanently may be relevant but not essential, as habitual residence may arise by the effluxion of time without a deliberate intention at any particular point to settle permanently.[125] It should be noted that Rome I will contain a definition of the phrase.

4.5.5.2 *Formal validity*

Article 9 of the Convention concerns the formal validity of a contract and of acts relating to a proposed or existing contract. There is no definition in the Convention of what is meant by the concept of formal validity. The *Giuliano-Lagarde Report*[126] says that the concept of 'form' includes 'every external manifestation required on the part of a person expressing the will to be legally bound, and in the absence of which such expression of will would not be regarded as fully effective.' It goes on to say that this would not include special requirements to protect those under a disability, and it specifically states that it would not include the requirement under English law for the giving of a notice of a statutory assignment. It would, presumably, cover the necessity of a document being notarised if that were required

---

[120] Per Morison J in *Horn Linie GmbH v Panamericana Formas E Impresos SA* [2006] EWHC 373 (Comm), [2006] 2 Lloyd's Rep 44, following the approach taken by Mance J in *Egon Oldendorff v Liberia Corp* [1995] 2 Lloyd's Rep 64.

[121] There is a useful review of the concept of habitual residence in *Dicey, Morris & Collins*, at paras 6-125 to 6-131.

[122] *Re M (Minors) (Residence Order: Jurisdiction)* [1993] 1 FLR 495.

[123] *Mark v Mark* [2005] UKHL 42; [2006] 1 AC 98, at [15].

[124] See, for instance, *Stojevic v Komercni Banka AS* [2006] EWHC 3447 (Ch), [2007] BPIR 141.

[125] *Al Habtoor v Fotheringham* [2001] EWCA Civ 186, [2001] 1 FLR 951.

[126] At p 29.

as a matter of validity, as opposed to being merely an evidentiary matter.[127] By virtue of Article 1(2)(h), matters that relate to evidence and procedure are not within the ambit of the Convention, although that provision is stated to be without prejudice to Article 14, which concerns matters such as the burden and mode of proof. It may be that the requirements under English law for the execution of a deed could be considered as being matters of formal validity, although it is also arguable that they go to material validity or that they are evidentiary. A query also arises in relation to section 4 of the Statute of Frauds 1677, which requires that a guarantee, or a note or memorandum thereof, should be in writing, signed by the guarantor or his lawfully authorised agent. The requirement could be seen as an evidentiary matter or as a matter going to formal validity or, perhaps, as a matter going to proof within Article 14(4).

The rules for determining formal validity are as follows. The basic rule is that the governing law of a contract will determine if it is formally valid.[128] The *Giuliano-Lagarde Report* suggests[129] that if separate parts of the contract are subject to differing governing laws, 'it would seem reasonable to apply the law applicable to the part of the contract most closely connected with the disputed condition on which its formal validity depends'. Article 3(2) also provides that a decision by the parties to change the governing law of a contract, after it has been entered into, will not prejudice the existing formal validity of the contract. The change of law might, in fact, save the contract if it was not valid under the old governing law but would be valid under the new governing law. Where the contract is concluded between parties (or by an agent for a party) in the same country, it will also be formally valid if it satisfies the formal requirements of the law of that country.[130] If one or more of the parties (or their agent) are in different countries when the contract is concluded, it will also be formally valid if it satisfies the formal requirements of any of those countries.[131] Unilateral acts relating to a concluded or contemplated contract will be formally valid if done in accordance with the governing law of the contract or the law of the country where the act was done.[132] This covers acts such as a notice of termination, the remission of a debt, and a declaration of rescission or repudiation.[133] It has also been suggested that a unilateral offer, capable of acceptance, would fall within the concept of such a unilateral act.[134]

4.5.5.2.1

---

127 The *Giuliano-Lagarde Report* says, at p 29, that Art 9 does apply to such 'public acts'.
128 Art 9(1) and (2).
129 At p 30.
130 Art 9(1) and (3).
131 Art 9(2) and (3).
132 Art 9(4). See also the *Giuliano-Lagarde Report* at p 29.
133 Ibid.
134 See *Chitty on Contracts* (29th edn, 2004), at para 30-134.

4.5.5.2.2 There are special rules concerning the formal validity of consumer contracts to which Article 5[135] applies and contracts relating to a right in or to use immovable property.[136] With respect to a contract concerning the latter, the contract will be subject to the mandatory requirements as to form of the *lex situs*, if those requirements apply irrespective of the country where the contract was concluded and of the governing law of the contract.

4.5.5.3 Article 10: the scope of the applicable law

Article 10 of the Convention provides as follows:

1. The law applicable to a contract by virtue of Articles 3 to 6 and 12 of this Convention shall govern in particular—
   (a) interpretation;
   (b) performance;
   (c) within the limits of the powers conferred on the court by its procedural law, the consequences of breach, including the assessment of damages in so far as it is governed by rules of law;
   (d) the various ways of extinguishing obligations, and prescription and limitation of actions;
   (e) the consequences of nullity of the contract.[137]
2. In relation to the manner of performance and the steps to be taken in the event of defective performance regard shall be had to the law of the country in which performance takes place.

4.5.5.3.1 It would appear that the list in Article 10(1) was not intended to be exhaustive, because of the use of the words 'in particular'. It has been suggested, for instance, that as a general matter of English law the governing law of a contract would determine the effect of a novation of a contract,[138] whether a person had become a party to a contract,[139] the effect of a contract on third parties,[140] and whether a defence of contributory negligence would be available to a contractual claim.[141]

4.5.5.3.2 Under Article 10(1)(a), the interpretation of a contract, including the meaning of its words, falls to be determined by the applicable or governing law. This is only

---

[135] See Art 9(5).

[136] See Art 9(6).

[137] Para (e) does not apply in the UK: see s 2(2) of the Contracts (Applicable Law) Act 1990 (this power having been exercised by the UK pursuant to Art 22 of the Convention). Under English law, the consequence of a purported contract being a nullity would be a matter for the law of restitution.

[138] See Mance LJ in *Raiffeisen Zentralbank Osterreich AG v Five Star General Trading LLC* [2001] EWCA Civ 68; [2001] QB 825, at [34]. In so far as a party was discharged by the novation, that would be a matter for the governing law of the contract in consequence of Art 10(1)(d).

[139] *Laemthong International Lines Co Ltd v ARTIS* [2005] EWHC 1595 (Comm).

[140] *Raiffeisen Zentralbank Osterreich AG v Five Star General Trading LLC* [2001] EWCA Civ 68; [2001] QB 825, at [34].

[141] *Meridien Biao Bank GmbH v Bank of New York* [1997] 1 Lloyd's Rep 437.

to be expected and is consistent with the approach that was taken at common law.[142]

Under Article 10(1)(b), the applicable law will govern the performance of the obligations arising under the contract. The *Giuliano-Lagarde Report*[143] states that, 'this appears to embrace the totality of the conditions . . . in accordance with which the act that is essential for the fulfilment of an obligation must be performed, but not the manner of its performance'. It then gives examples of those conditions, as follows:

4.5.5.3.3

> the diligence with which the obligation must be performed; conditions relating to the place and time of performance; the extent to which the obligation can be performed by a person other than the party liable; the conditions as to performance of the obligation both in general and in relation to certain categories of obligation (joint and several obligations, alternative obligations, divisible and indivisible obligations, pecuniary obligations); where performance consists of the payment of a sum of money, the conditions relating to the discharge of the debtor who has made the payment, the appropriation of the payment, the receipt, etc.

This should include the liability to pay interest and the rate of interest. It is submitted that whether a party's obligations have been discharged by performance, or modified or discharged by the operation of the civil law concept of *force majeure*, or discharged in consequence of the common law doctrine of frustration, will fall to be determined by the applicable law of the contract, partly as a result of Article 10(1)(b) and partly by virtue of Article 10(1)(d).

The conditions for performance as governed by the applicable law pursuant to Article 10(1)(b) must be distinguished from issues relating to the manner of performance and the steps to be taken if there has been defective performance. In the latter case, Article 10(2) requires that regard shall be had to the law of the place where performance should take place. The difference is between the substance of the obligation that is to be performed and the mode (or the manner and method) of its performance.[144] It is not easy to judge where the line of the distinction should be drawn. This is acknowledged by the *Giuliano-Lagarde Report*[145] which says that this will be a matter to be determined by the *lex fori*, but it does give the following examples of matters that would fall within the ambit of Article 10(2): the rules governing the effect of public holidays, the manner in which goods should be examined, and the steps to be taken if they are refused. A distinction has been drawn between a requirement (or an invariable custom) of the place of

4.5.5.3.3.1

---

[142] *St Pierre v South American Stores (Gath & Chaves) Ltd* [1937] 3 All ER 349.
[143] At pp 32–33.
[144] Per Thomas J in *East West Corp v DKBS 1912* [2002] EWHC 83 (Comm); [2002] 1 All ER (Comm) 676, at [34] (the point was not dealt with in the appeal: [2003] EWCA Civ 83, [2003] QB 1509).
[145] At p 33.

performance, to which Article 10(2) would be relevant, and a mere practice, to which Article 10(2) would not be relevant.[146] It should also be noted that Article 10(2) is not drafted in mandatory language. It merely requires that 'regard shall be had' to the law of the place of performance. The *Giuliano-Lagarde Report*[147] says that this confers a discretion on a court in determining the extent to which the law of the place of performance should be applied. *Dicey, Morris & Collins*[148] says that the law of the place of performance would govern whether an interest payment must be made in cash or may be made by cheque, but that the obligation to pay interest and the rate of interest will be governed by the applicable law of the contract.[149]

4.5.5.3.4 Article 10(1)(c) provides that the applicable law of the contract will govern the consequences of breach of the contract, including the assessment of damages. To this there are stated to be two qualifications. First, there is a recognition of the limits of the powers of the court under its procedural law. Secondly, the assessment of damages is only to the extent it is governed by rules of law. The *Giuliano-Lagarde Report*[150] says that the expression 'consequence of breach' refers to 'the consequences which the law or the contract attaches to the breach of a contractual obligation, whether it is a matter of the liability of the party to whom the breach is attributable or of a claim to terminate the contract for breach. Any requirement of service of notice on the party to assume his liability also comes within this context.' This appears to include rights to treat the contract as rescinded or repudiated.

4.5.5.3.4.1 At common law, there was a distinction between the right to damages, the heads of damage, and matters of remoteness, which were governed by the governing law of the contract, and the quantification or measure of damages, which was governed by the *lex fori* as matters of procedure and remedies.[151] One would expect that distinction to continue under the Convention, as Article 1(2)(h) provides that matters of procedure do not fall within the ambit of the Convention. Article 10(1)(c) certainly continues the common law rule in relation to matters concerning the right to damages, heads of damage, and remoteness, but it appears that the governing law of the contract may now also be relevant, at least in part, to issues concerning the quantification or measure of damages, because it talks of the

---

[146] See Clarke J in *SA Sucre Export v Northern River Shipping Ltd, The Sormovskiy 3068* [1994] 2 Lloyd's Rep 266, at 275.

[147] At p 33.

[148] At para 32-200.

[149] For which proposition a case at common law is cited: *Mount Albert Borough Council v Australasian Temperance & General Mutual Life Assurance Society Ltd* [1938] AC 224 (PC).

[150] At p 33.

[151] See, in relation to claims in tort, the discussion by Lord Hoffmann in *Harding v Wealands* [2006] UKHL 32.

'assessment of damages in so far as it is governed by rules of law'. The *Giuliano-Lagarde Report*[152] says that this means that questions of fact relating to the assessment of damages would not be governed by the applicable law of the contract, for example, mathematical calculations, but it follows that substantive questions, such as whether the governing law or the contract imposed a limit on compensation or a rule for assessment of compensation, would fall within the ambit of Article 10(1)(c). Presumably, the effectiveness of a penalty or liquidated damages clause or a clause imposing a contractual limitation on damages would be determined by the governing law of the contract.[153] The right to interest in consequence of default would be governed by the applicable law.[154] It has been suggested that the assessment of such interest, including the rate of interest, would fall within the province of the *lex fori* as a procedural matter,[155] but it is difficult to square this with the approach taken in the *Giuliano-Lagarde Report*, that only questions of fact, such as the simple matter of arithmetic, would fall for determination by the *lex fori*. It is also submitted that the liability for exchange losses consequent upon a late payment would be a substantive matter to be governed by the applicable law of the contract,[156] but the same uncertainty arises, as in the case of interest, as to whether the relevant exchange rate should be determined as a substantive or a procedural matter.

A question arises as to whether equitable relief for a breach of contract, such as by way of an injunction or an order for specific performance, should be considered as a substantive matter under Article 10(1)(c) or as a procedural matter to be determined by the *lex fori*.[157] Prima facie, it would appear that the availability of such relief would be a matter concerning a consequence of a breach of contract and thus a substantive matter to be governed by the applicable law of the contract pursuant to Article 10(1)(c). If the availability of equitable relief is primarily a matter for the law governing the contract, it would appear to follow that an English court may find itself being requested to grant equitable relief in a situation where it might not do so purely as a matter of domestic English law, as, for instance, where it would say in domestic law that damages were an adequate remedy. However, the court may be entitled to rely upon the opening words of Article 10(1)(c), 'within the limits of the powers conferred on the court by its procedural law' in denying such equitable relief where it concerned a foreign defendant and the

4.5.5.3.4.2

---

[152] At p 33.

[153] See *Dicey, Morris & Collins*, at para 32-201.

[154] See Brooke LJ in *Lesotho Highlands Development Authority v Impregilo SpA* [2003] EWCA Civ 1159; [2003] 2 Lloyd's Rep 497, at [45] (the result in the case was overturned by the House of Lords [2005] UKHL 43, [2006] 1 AC 221, but this point did not arise for review).

[155] Ibid, at [50].

[156] As was the position at common law: *President of India v Lips Maritime Corp* [1988] AC 395.

[157] Traditionally, English law would have regarded this as a procedural matter.

203

court felt unable to supervise any order it might make. English courts, acting *in personam*, have been prepared to grant equitable relief concerning foreign assets where the defendant has been within the jurisdiction, so that the order could be enforced against it,[158] but if the court cannot enforce the order, it will decline to make it.[159]

4.5.5.3.5 Article 10(1)(d) provides that the applicable law of the contract will govern, 'the various ways of extinguishing obligations, and prescription and limitation of actions'. As previously stated, the subject matter of this provision will, to some extent, overlap with Article 10(1)(b), because if a contract has been fully performed then it will be discharged by performance, and if the obligation to perform has been abrogated, such as by the operation of the concepts of *force majeure* or frustration, then the contractual obligation will also have discharged. In similar spirit to Article 10(1)(d) it has been held, at common law, that the governing law of the contract will determine if a party's obligations have been discharged, such as in consequence of the intervention of legislation giving rise to a novation of the contract.[160]

4.5.5.3.5.1 In relation to a contractual claim, the treatment of a purported set-off or counterclaim against the claim will depend upon whether the set-off or counterclaim is substantive or procedural. English domestic law distinguishes between a right to set-off which has the effect of operating as a substantive defence to a claim, such as would be the case in English law in relation to a claim for a contractual set-off and for an equitable or transaction set-off, and a procedural claim to a set-off or counterclaim, such as in English law would be the case with legal set-off, which arises where two unrelated claims may conveniently be tried together, and the amount due under one claim can be set off against the amount due under the other claim.[161] In conflict of laws terms, it will be a matter for the governing law of the contract to determine if a set-off or cross claim is substantive and available

---

[158] See, for instance, *Penn v Lord Baltimore* (1750) 1 Ves Sen 444, 27 ER 1132 and *British South Africa Co v De Beers Consolidated Mines Ltd* [1910] 2 Ch 502.

[159] *'Morocco Bound' Syndicate v Harris* [1895] 1 Ch 534.

[160] *Wight v Eckhardt Marine GmbH* [2003] UKPC 37, [2004] 1 AC 147. Curiously, the House of Lords in a case decided shortly afterwards failed to refer to either the *Eckhardt Marine* case or to the Rome Convention in determining if a third party debt order would have the effect of discharging the third party's obligation to make payment to its original creditor: *Societe Eram Shipping Co Ltd v Hong Kong & Shanghai Banking Corp Ltd* [2003] UKHL 30, [2004] 1 AC 260. It arrived at the conclusion that the issue would be governed by the *lex situs* of the debt. See also the House's decision (decided on the same day as the *Societe Eram* case) in *Kuwait Oil Tanker Co SAK v UBS AG* [2003] UKHL 31, [2004] 1 AC 300.

[161] As to the distinction in English law between legal and equitable or transaction set-off, see Lord Hoffmann in *Stein v Blake* [1996] AC 243, at 251; Hoffmann LJ in *Aectra Refining & Marketing Inc v Exmar NV* [1994] 1 WLR 1643, at 1649–1653; Clarke LJ in *Glencore Grain Ltd v Agros Trading Co Ltd* [1999] 2 Lloyd's Rep 410, at 415–417; and Buxton LJ in *Smith v Muscat* [2003] EWCA Civ 962; [2003] 1 WLR 2853, at [37]–[45].

to operate as a defence to the claim under Article 10(1)(d).[162] On the other hand, the effectiveness of a procedural set-off or counterclaim would be a matter to be determined by the *lex fori*.

It should be noted, however, that different considerations may arise when a set-off **4.5.5.3.5.2** is claimed by the respondent in an arbitration. It has been held that the availability of a counterclaim to set-off will depend upon the scope of the arbitrator's jurisdiction, as laid down by the terms of the agreement to arbitrate and, by incorporation therein, any relevant rules that apply to the arbitrators, such as under the UNCITRAL Arbitration Rules. The availability of set-off may be precluded or limited as a procedural matter by that agreement or such rules, which will be binding upon the arbitrators. As a matter of English law, there is no rule that the governing law of the contract, which may permit such a set-off, should prevail over any conflicting procedural rules that governed the arbitration.[163]

In relation to prescription and limitation of actions, Article 10(1)(d) provides **4.5.5.3.5.3** that they are to be assessed by reference to the governing law of the contract and so are not procedural matters to be determined by the *lex fori*.[164] It has been suggested that the operation of equitable doctrines, such as the equitable doctrines of laches and acquiescence, would also fall to be determined as substantive matters governed by the applicable law of the contract under either Article 10(1)(c) or Article 10(1)(d), rather than as being purely procedural and governed by the *lex fori*.[165]

4.5.5.4 Voluntary assignments

Article 12 provides rules in relation to voluntary assignments, which are examined in detail in Chapter 12. Article 12(1) provides that the governing law of the contract between the assignor and assignee will apply to their mutual obligations. Article 12(2) provides that the governing law of the right that has been assigned will determine the assignability of the debt, the relationship between the debtor and the assignee, the conditions under which the assignment can be invoked against the debtor, and whether the debtor's obligations have been discharged.

---

[162] See Tomlinson J in *Prekons Insaat Sanayi AS v Rowlands Castle Contracting Group Ltd* [2006] EWHC 1367 (QB), at [12].

[163] See Field J in *Econet Satellite Services Ltd v Vee Networks Ltd* [2006] EWHC 1664 (Comm) who preferred to follow the analysis of Cresswell J in *Metal Distributors (UK) Ltd v ZCCM Investment Holdings PLC* [2005] EWHC 156 (Comm); [2005] 2 Lloyd's Rep 37, at [18], to that (which was obiter) of Gross J in *Ronly Holdings Ltd v JSC Zestafoni G Nikoladze Ferroalloy Plant* [2004] EWHC 1354 (Comm), at [33].

[164] See, similarly, the Foreign Limitation Periods Act 1984.

[165] See *Chitty on Contracts* (29th edn, 2004) at para 30-160. This matter would fall within Art 19 of Rome II, which is discussed later in this chapter.

4.5.5.5 Subrogation

Article 13 is headed 'subrogation' but it only relates to subrogation of contractual claims, not of other claims like tortious claims, such as where an insurer may wish to succeed to the claim of the insured against a torfeasor.[166] Article 13(1) provides that where a third party has a duty to satisfy a claim against another person (the 'debtor') or has done so in discharge of such a duty, the law which governs the third party's duty to satisfy the claim shall determine if, and the extent to which, the third party will be subrogated to the rights of the original claimant (the 'creditor') against the debtor under the law governing the relationship between the debtor and the creditor. The *Giuliano-Lagarde Report*[167] says that the duty may arise under a contract, such as a guarantee or by law. It also suggests that it may arise in consequence of 'an economic interest recognised by law', although it says this would be at the discretion of the court, without any indication of the considerations that the court should take into account. Article 13(2) goes on to deal with what would, in English law, fall within rights of contribution, which one debtor might have against its fellow obligors for the same debt, where that first debtor has satisfied the debt. The right of the paying debtor that satisfied the underlying claim of the creditor to assert a right of contribution from the other debtors will be governed by the law which obliged the paying debtor to satisfy the creditor.

4.5.6 Foreign currency obligations

Because of its importance in the field of international finance, this topic has been selected for separate treatment at this point, although most of the issues that arise will concern questions of interpretation and the performance of contracts, so the discussion in a more truncated form could be included as part of the coverage of Article 10 of the Rome Convention. The following issues will be discussed. The first will be the difference between the currency of account and the currency of payment for monetary obligations. Secondly, each of those concepts will be explored. Thirdly, it will be necessary to address the method of ascertaining the legal tender of a currency and the nominal value of a currency.

4.5.6.1 The currency of account v the currency of payment

The currency of account of a contractual monetary obligation is the currency in which a party's monetary obligation will be calculated and measured. It will also usually be the currency in which a party's liability in damages may be measured. The currency of payment (which is not necessarily the same as the currency of account[168]) is the currency in which the payment of the obligation or damages

---

[166] See the *Giuliano-Lagarde Report*, at p 35.
[167] Ibid.
[168] See, for instance, *Woodhouse AC Israel Cocoa Ltd SA v Nigerian Produce Marketing Co Ltd* [1972] AC 741.

should be paid or discharged and, if necessary, converted from the currency of account into the currency of payment.

4.5.6.2 *The currency of account*

The currency of account of a payment obligation should be ascertained as a matter of the interpretation and performance of the contract, in accordance with Articles 10(1)(a) and (b) of the Rome Convention and so would fall to be determined by the governing law of the contract. At common law it had been held that, in a contract governed by English law, the currency of account would be the currency either expressly or impliedly specified in the contract as the currency of account. In the absence of such a choice, it would be presumed that the currency of account was the currency of the country with which the contract was most closely connected, which may not necessarily be the country of the governing law of the contract.[169] The currency of account in a claim for damages for breach of contract would be determined by the governing law of the contract, pursuant to Article 10(1)(c), as it would go to the consequences of breach and the assessment of damages. It has been held that in a claim for unliquidated damages for breach of a contract governed by English law, the damages should primarily be calculated in the contractual currency of account, but that, in the absence of a strong contrary indication in the contract, damages might also be awarded in another currency if that was the currency in which the loss was suffered, being that which most truly expressed the loss that had been suffered.[170]

4.5.6.3 *The currency of payment*

The currency of payment will be the currency in which a contractual monetary obligation or damages will be payable, to be converted, if necessary, from the currency of account into the currency of payment. Whilst it is not without doubt, it is submitted that ascertaining the rate of conversion should be regarded as a substantive matter to be determined by the governing law of the contract, by analogy with the view taken above that the contractual rate of interest payable on a debt would be determined by the governing law of the contract.[171] At common law, the currency of payment was identified in accordance with any stipulation to that effect in the contract but, in the absence thereof, it would be determined by the law of the place where the payment was to be made.[172]

---

[169] See *Bonython v Commonwealth of Australia* [1951] AC 201(PC).

[170] *Services Europe Atlantique Sud v Stockholms Rederaktiebolag Svea* [1979] AC 685 and *Virani v Manuel Revert Y Cia SA* [2003] EWCA Civ 1651, [2004] 2 Lloyd's Rep 14.

[171] See also *Dicey, Morris & Collins*, at para 36-053. It had been held at common law that under an English law contract, an amount payable in England would be converted at a prevailing London market rate: *Barclays Bank International Ltd v Levin Bros (Bradford) Ltd* [1977] QB 270.

[172] *Adelaide Electric Supply Co Ltd v Prudential Assurance Co Ltd* [1934] AC 122.

4.5.6.3.1 It is not certain how this matter is now to be determined under the Rome Convention. It is arguable that it is a matter relating to substantive performance within Article 10(1)(b) of the Convention and so would be determined by the governing law of the contract. It is also arguable, however, that it might be a matter relating to the manner of performance under Article 10(2), in which case regard should be had to the law of the place of performance. In this context, it may be that the concept of the manner of performance should be confined to technical matters, such as the mechanics as to how the payment should be transmitted through the banking system, whether the receipt could be treated as being in immediately available funds (or whatever other stipulation there was as to the availability and immediacy of the funds in the hands of the recipient), and the time for effecting transfers between accounts, rather than the more substantive matter of the currency in which the payment should be made. In any case, Article 10(2) only requires the court to have 'regard' to the law of the place of performance, which presumably means that it could still apply the governing law of the contract if it felt it more appropriate to do so.

4.5.6.3.2 The *Giuliano-Lagarde Report* does not directly address the issue. It does say,[173] however, that 'where performance consists of the payment of a sum of money, the conditions relating to the discharge of the debtor who has made the payment, the appropriation of the payment [and] the receipt', are matters that fall within the ambit of Article 10(1)(b). It is arguable that where there is a contractual stipulation as to the currency of payment, that might be considered as a condition relating to the discharge of the debtor and the receipt of the payment.

4.5.6.3.3 It has been held in relation to a contract governed by English law where England was also the place of payment, that the debtor may pay in the currency of account or, if it is different, in sterling, converted at the prevailing market rate at the date of payment, unless the contract requires payment to be made in a stipulated currency.[174] If the debtor has such an option but is precluded from making payment in the foreign currency, it must pay in sterling.[175]

4.5.6.4 *Legal tender*

What constitutes legal tender in a country should be determined by the law of that country.[176] If English law is the governing law of the contract, the nominal value of a currency which is the currency of account would be unaffected by internal or external changes in such currency.[177] It is submitted that in a contract governed by

---

[173] At p 33.
[174] *Marachen v Ashton* [1943] AC 311.
[175] *Libyan Arab Foreign Bank v Bankers Trust Co* [1989] QB 728.
[176] See *Chitty on Contracts* (29th edn, 2004), at para 30-178.
[177] *Re Chesterman's Trusts* [1923] 2 Ch 466.

any other law, it would be for the governing law to decide if the same principle applied, because that issue relates to a substantive matter of the interpretation and performance of the contract. As to changes in the value of the currency of payment, it is submitted that whether that should be a factor to be taken into account will depend upon the view one takes of the interplay between Article 10(1)(b) and Article 10(2) of the Rome Convention, as discussed above. If the correct view is that the determination of the currency of payment falls to be made in accordance with the governing law of the contract, then it would follow that the amount of the payment and its value would also be determined by the governing law. On the other hand, if the law of the place of payment should determine the currency of payment then that law should determine if changes in the value of the currency should be taken into account in determining the amount of the payment.

4.5.7 Foreign money judgments in the English courts

Until 1975, the general rule was that an English court could only award a judgment for payment of a debt or for damages in sterling, whether the contract was governed by English or a foreign law. An amount due to a foreign creditor had to be converted into sterling at the exchange rate prevailing at the date when the cause of action arose, for instance, when the breach of contract occurred. That meant that a creditor was at risk of a decline in the value of sterling after that date.

In 1975, the House of Lords in *Miliangos v George Frank (Textiles) Ltd*[178] decided that an English court could give judgment in the same currency as that in which a debt was payable under the contract. This has been extended to cases involving claims for breach of contract involving both liquidated and unliquidated damages and whether the contract was governed by English[179] or a foreign law[180] to claims in tort,[181] and to arbitration awards.[182] For the purposes of enforcement in England, the judgment may be converted into sterling at the date when the court authorises enforcement.[183]
    4.5.7.1

The Insolvency Rules 1986[184] provide that for the purpose of proving in an English liquidation, a claim in a foreign currency should be converted into sterling at 'the official exchange rate'[185] prevailing on the date the company went
    4.5.7.2

---

[178] [1976] AC 443.
[179] *Services Europe Atlantique Sud v Stockholms Rederaktiebolag Svea* [1979] AC 685.
[180] *The Despina R* [1979] AC 685.
[181] Ibid.
[182] *Jugoslavenska Oceanska Plovidba v Castle Investment Co Inc* [1974] QB 292.
[183] *Miliangos v George Frank (Textiles) Ltd* [1976] AC 443.
[184] Rule 4.91(1). See also *Re Lines Bros Ltd* [1983] Ch 1.
[185] Defined in Rule 4.91(2) of the Insolvency Rules 1986.

into liquidation[186] or, if that was preceded by its administration, the date it entered administration.[187]

4.5.7.3 The ability of the court to give judgment in a foreign currency is a matter of English procedure governed by English law, irrespective of the governing law of the contract,[188] and, as such, it should be unaffected by the Rome Convention, by virtue of Article 1(2)(h) of the Convention.

4.5.7.4 Currency exchange losses due to late payment

In passing, it is worth noting that an English court may also be willing to award damages for currency exchange losses that have arisen in consequence of the late payment of a debt or other liquidated sum.[189]

4.5.8 The EC Regulation (Rome I)

As mentioned earlier, there is to be an EC Regulation on the law applicable to contractual obligations (Rome I)[190] which it is intended will supplant the Rome Convention.[191] The Regulation would come into force 18 months after the date it was formally adopted. At the time of writing, it was anticipated that the Regulation would come into force towards the end of 2009. The Regulation would apply to contracts that were entered into after it came into force.[192]

4.5.8.1 The UK has the right to refuse to participate in the adoption of the proposed Regulation. At the time of writing, it was uncertain if the UK would participate, although it appeared that the UK Government was minded to proceed with participation, subject to a consultation exercise which it had launched.[193] Unlike the position under the Rome Convention, where the UK has exercised its right to refuse to apply two of the provisions contained in the Convention,[194] the Regulation will apply in whole if it is adopted. It will not be possible for the UK to participate in part.

---

[186] I.e. the date of the resolution for winding up in a voluntary winding up or the date of the winding-up order for a compulsory winding up: s 247(2) of the Insolvency Act 1986.

[187] I.e. the date when the appointment of the administrator took effect: para 1(2)(b) of Sch B1 to the Insolvency Act 1986.

[188] *The Despina R* [1979] AC 685, at 704.

[189] *President of India v Lips Maritime Corp* [1988] 1 AC 395.

[190] At the time of writing, the final and official text of the Regulation had not been published. A copy of the Regulation will be found at Annex B to the Consultation Paper dated 2/4/2008 that was issued by the Ministry of Justice, as referred to below.

[191] Art 24 of the Regulation.

[192] Art 28 of the Regulation.

[193] See the Consultation Paper CP05/08 dated 2/4/2008, issued by the Ministry of Justice. The text of the Consultation Paper is available at <http://www.justice.gov.UK/publications/consultations.htm>. It is understood that Ireland, which enjoyed a similar right to decline to participate, has decided to participate. Denmark will not participate in the adoption of the Regulation and it will not be binding in that State: see Recital (46) to the Regulation.

[194] I.e. Arts 7(1) and (10)(1)(e) of the Convention.

The Regulation is based on the Rome Convention but in a number of respects it **4.5.8.2** changes and expands upon the application of and the rules contained in the Convention. As a Community instrument, the Regulation would be subject to interpretation by the European Court of Justice.

What now follows will address the important changes that would be effected to **4.5.8.3** English law as described above, were the Regulation to come into force in its present form in the UK. There appears to be no role contemplated for the *Giuliano-Lagarde Report* in the interpretation of the Regulation (except, perhaps, by implication), so the guidance that it provided concerning the Convention may become obsolete. For convenience, in the discussion that follows an article of the Convention will be described as 'old Article' and an article of the Regulation will be described as 'new Article'.

4.5.8.4 *Scope of application*

New Article 1(1) states that the Regulation is to 'apply, in situations involving a conflict of laws, to contractual obligations in civil and commercial matters'. It goes on to state that it will not apply to revenue, customs, or administrative matters.[195] New Article 1(2) provides for the situations where the rules in the Regulation will not apply, which are broadly similar to the position under the Convention, with the following changes that are relevant in the present context. The Regulation will not apply to obligations arising from a pre-contractual relationship.[196] The former exclusion relating to insurance contracts[197] has been largely removed,[198] and so the previous saving for re-insurance contracts[199] has been deleted. With respect to the exclusion concerning the negotiable character of negotiable instruments, it has been made clear that bills of lading fall within the scope of the exclusion.[200]

The position relating to the effect of other international treaties or conventions to **4.5.8.4.1** which a Member State is a party is more circumscribed than was the case in relation to the Rome Convention. New Article 25 provides that only certain existing treaties or conventions will take precedence over the Regulation.

---

[195] Recital (7) to the Regulation requires it to be read consistently with the EC Regulation on jurisdiction and recognition of judgments (EC 44/2001 OJ L 12/1 16/1/20), so authority on that Regulation will be relevant in determining the scope of civil and commercial matters. Art 1 of the 2001 Regulation states that it applies only to civil and commercial matters and, in particular, that it will not apply to revenue, customs, or administrative matters. The same will be the case with the Rome I Regulation (and, for that matter, the Rome II Regulation, which contains the same principle of only being applicable to civil and commercial matters).

[196] New Art 1(2)(i) and Recital (10) to the Regulation.

[197] Old Art 1(3).

[198] See new Art 1(2)(j). Old Art 1(3) has been deleted.

[199] Old Art 1(4).

[200] See Recital (9) to the Regulation and new Art 1(2)(d).

4.5.8.5 Choice of law

New Article 3 deals with the right of the parties to choose, expressly or impliedly, the governing law of their contract, as did old Article 3. As to an implied choice, the wording of new Article 3(1) now requires that the implied choice should be 'clearly demonstrated' by the terms of the contract or the circumstances of the case, in place of the old wording which required the demonstration 'with reasonable certainty'. Recital (12) to the Regulation states that if the parties have agreed to confer exclusive jurisdiction in favour of the courts or tribunals of an EU Member State, that should be one of the factors that might demonstrate an implied choice of the same law as that of the jurisdiction. This begs the question as to what inference should be drawn where the parties have chosen an arbitral tribunal sitting in a Member State, or the courts of (or an arbitral tribunal sitting in) a non-Member State.

4.5.8.5.1 Recital (13) to the Regulation effectively states that the parties might choose to incorporate 'by reference into their contract a non-State body of law or an international convention'. In addition, new Article 1(1) does not refer to the conflict of laws being between the laws of different countries, as did the old Article 1(1). It remains to be seen if those two provisions will have the effect of reversing the decision of the Court of Appeal in *Beximco Pharmaceuticals Ltd v Shamil Bank of Bahrain EC*,[201] which was based upon the wording of old Article 1(1). The court held that the parties could not validly choose a non-State law to govern the whole of their contract. However, the court did admit the possibility that such a body of law might be incorporated by reference as part of the contract, which may be what Recital (13) is now saying. Accordingly, it remains unclear if the new provisions have really advanced the position beyond where it was left by that case.

4.5.8.5.2 New Article 3(3) deals with the exception that was previously found in old Article 3(3), which provided for the application of the mandatory rules of a country with which the relevant elements at the time of contracting were wholly connected, apart from the choice of law. Recital (15) to the Regulation provides that the wording of new Article 3(3) is not intended to effect any substantial change to the position as it applied under old Article 3(3). It should be noted, however, that new Article 3(3) speaks of the laws 'which cannot be derogated from by agreement', and that Recital (37) to the Regulation draws a distinction between such laws and those that should be construed more restrictively. The latter apply in exceptional circumstances of public interest and qualify as 'overriding mandatory provisions'.

4.5.8.5.3 New Article 3(4) provides that the application of the chosen law, if that is the law of a non-EU Member State, should be without prejudice to the rules of EU law

---

[201] [2004] EWCA Civ 19, [2004] 1 WLR 1784.

which cannot be derogated from by contract, if all other elements of the situation at the time of contracting are connected to one or more EU Member States.

There are special rules that apply for consumer contracts (new Article 6), insurance contracts (new Article 7), and employment contracts (new Article 8). **4.5.8.5.4**

4.5.8.6 *Absence of choice*

New Article 4, which replaces old Article 4, contains the rules that should be applied in the absence of a choice of law under new Article 3. In some respects, new Article 4 is in different terms to the provisions of old Article 4. The principal difference is that the concept of the presumptions contained in old Articles 4(2), 4(3), and 4(4) have gone. Instead, new Article 4(1) provides a set of rules for a number of different contractual situations. They provide for the governing law to be that of the country of the 'habitual residence' of one of the parties to the contract, being the seller of goods, the supplier of services, the franchisee under a franchise, and the distributor under a distribution contract. There are also special rules relating to immovable property and leases thereof, sales by auction, and contracts under multilateral systems for buying and selling financial instruments.

For contracts that are not specified in new Article 4(1) or which would fall under **4.5.8.6.1** more than one of its rules, the fall back is to be found in new Article 4(2). New Article 4(2) provides that the contract shall be governed by the law of the country which is the habitual residence of the party who is required to effect the characteristic performance of the contract. Recital (19) to the Regulation provides that: 'In the case of a contract consisting of a bundle of rights and obligations capable of being categorised as falling within more than one of the [types of contract specified in new Article 4(1)], the characteristic performance of the contract should be determined having regard to its centre of gravity.'

New Article 4(3) is to similar effect (with one difference) as the second part of old **4.5.8.6.2** Article 4(5). It applies as an alternative to the rules in new Articles 4(1) and 4(2). It provides that 'where it is clear from all the circumstances of the case the contract is manifestly more closely connected with a country other than that indicated in' those other rules, the law of that more closely connected country should apply. The difference is that new Article 4(3) requires there to be a manifestly closer connection, whereas old Article 5(2) simply referred to a closer connection. Recital (20) to the Regulation states that in determining the relevant country, account should be taken (inter alia) of whether the contract has a very close relationship with one or more other contracts.

New Article 4(4) applies where it is not possible to make a determination at all **4.5.8.6.3** under the rules contained in new Articles 4(1) and 4(2). In such a case, the contract will be governed by the law of the country with which the contract is most closely connected. Recital (21) to the Regulation (like Recital (20)) provides that, in such a case, account should be taken (inter alia) of whether the contract has a very close relationship with another contract or contracts.

4.5.8.6.4 There is also a special rule that applies to contracts of carriage, in the absence of an express choice. It is contained in new Article 5.

4.5.8.7 *Habitual residence*

The 'habitual residence' of a party will be determined in accordance with new Article 19. The phrase was left undefined in the Rome Convention. Recital (39) to the Regulation states that, for the sake of certainty, 'there should be a clear definition of habitual residence, in particular for companies and other bodies, corporate or unincorporated. Unlike Article 60(1) of Regulation EC 44/2001, which establishes three criteria, the conflict of laws rule should proceed on a single criterion; otherwise the parties would be unable to foresee the law applicable to their situation'.[202] Article 60(1) of that Regulation provides three criteria to determine the 'domicile' of a corporate or unincorporated body for the purpose of locating the primary place where proceedings could be brought against it, being the place of its (a) statutory seat, (b) central administration, or (c) principal place of business. They may not necessarily all be in one place.

4.5.8.7.1 The basic rule under new Article 19(1) is that for corporate and unincorporated bodies, their 'place of central administration' should be considered to be their habitual residence. The principal place of business of a natural person who concludes a contract in the course of his business will be considered as being his habitual residence. Under new Article 19(2), if a corporate or unincorporated body concludes the contract in the course of the operation of a 'branch, agency or establishment' or 'if under the contract performance is the responsibility of such a branch, agency or establishment', the place where the branch etc. is located will be considered to be the place of habitual residence. The Regulation gives no guidance as to the meaning of an 'establishment'. In the EC Insolvency Regulation[203] the expression 'establishment' is defined to mean, 'any place where the [relevant person or entity] carries out a non-transitory economic activity with human means and goods.' One can only speculate if the same definition would be adopted in interpreting new Article 19(2).

4.5.8.8 *Overriding mandatory provisions*

New Article 9 provides for the effect of the overriding mandatory provisions of the laws of (i) the forum or (ii) another country where the contract is to be performed. It will be recalled that the UK opted out of old Article 7(1), which related to contracts that had a 'close connection' with a third country. As mentioned above,

---

[202] Regulation EC 44/2001 on jurisdiction and recognition of judgments (OJ L12/1 16/1/2001).
[203] 1346/2000/EC OJ L160/1 30/6/2000.

if the UK decides to adopt the Regulation, it will be unable to opt out of any of its individual provisions, so the courts in the UK would have to apply the whole of new Article 9.

New Article 9(1) provides a definition of what is meant by the phrase 'overriding mandatory provisions'. It is as follows:

4.5.8.8.1

> Overriding mandatory provisions are provisions the respect for which is regarded as crucial by a country for safeguarding its public interests, such as its political, social or economic organisation, to such an extent that they are applicable to any situation falling within their scope, irrespective of the law otherwise applicable to the contract under this Regulation.

In this regard, it should also be noted that Recital (37) to the Regulation makes a distinction between the 'overriding mandatory provisions' of a country's laws and provisions of those laws which cannot be derogated from by agreement, the latter applying in the case of new Articles 3(3) and 3(4) and being construed less restrictively than the former. The Recital states that:

> Considerations of public interest justify giving the courts of Member States the possibility, in exceptional circumstances, of applying exceptions based on public policy and overriding mandatory provisions. The concept of 'overriding mandatory provisions' should be distinguished from the expression 'provisions which cannot be derogated from by agreement' and should be construed more restrictively.

It is apparent that the position should be assessed from the perspective of the country whose rules are under consideration. Just how an English court is to make that assessment with respect to the laws of another country is far from clear, as it involves an enquiry into policy matters which is often a difficult task for a court when considering the laws of its own country, let alone the laws of another country. Generally speaking, English courts have shied away from delving into policy matters in another country.

New Article 9(2) replaces the wording that was used in old Article 7(2). It concerns the overriding mandatory provisions of the forum. However, the nature of those rules must now be assessed in light of the definition set out in new Article 9(1). Instead of simply deciding whether the application of a particular rule of its law is mandatory in the situation before the court (as used to be the case under old Article 7(2)), the court must now ascertain if the rule should be considered as being crucial to the public interests of its country, including its political, social, or economic organisation.

4.5.8.8.2

New Article 9(3) replaces the provisions of old Article 7(1). It relates to the laws of the place of performance of a contractual obligation. From an English perspective, it is more satisfactory than the old provision, as it does not use the 'close connection' concept which was objectionable to the application of the old provision. However, as noted above, the new provision may involve an English court in

4.5.8.8.3

making enquiries which it may prefer not to make. New Article 9(3) provides as follows:

> Effect may be given to the overriding mandatory provisions of the law of the country where the obligations arising out of the contract have to be or have been performed, in so far as those overriding provisions render the performance of the contract unlawful. In considering whether to give effect to those provisions, regard shall be had to their nature and purpose and to the consequences of their application or non-application.

The article should allow an English court to take account of the situations in both *Ralli Bros v Compania Naviera Sota y Aznar*[204] and *Foster v Driscoll*[205] but without having to bother whether the rules in those cases only applied to contracts governed by English law or applied more generally.

4.5.8.9 *Consent and material validity*

New Article 10 is in much the same form as old Article 8, apart from the heading, which has been amended to read 'Consent and material validity', rather than just 'Material validity'.

4.5.8.10 *Formal validity*

New Article 11 replaces old Article 9. Whilst there are various changes in the wording of the article and in the way in which its paragraphs are ordered, they mostly do not achieve much difference in substance, but the following changes should be noted. New Article 11(1) (which replaces old Articles 9(1) and, in part, 9(3)) refers, as one of the alternatives, to the law which governs the contract in substance, to allow for the possibility that other laws might also be relevant to the contract. The same concept occurs in other parts of new Article 11. New Article 11(2) (which replaces old Articles 9(2) and, in part, 9(3)) adds the law of the habitual residence of a party as an alternative.

4.5.8.10.1   There are also some amendments to what was formerly old Article 9(4) and is now new Article 11(3) which are worth noting. First, it is made clear that the provision is only intended to apply to unilateral acts, which was not explicitly stated in the former provision but was generally taken to be the case. Secondly, the formal validity of such acts under the governing law of the contract is now stated to be the substantive governing law of the contract. Thirdly, the provision also now permits the formal validity of a unilateral act to be judged by the law of the country in which the person who did the act had his habitual residence at the time the act was done.

---

204 [1920] 2 KB 287.
205 [1929] 1 KB 470.

4.5.8.11 Scope of the applicable law

New Article 12 repeats old Article 10, with one small addition. By way of clarification, in new Article 12(1)(c), the wording has been changed from, 'the consequences of breach', as used in old Article 10(1)(c), to read, 'the consequences of the total or partial breach of obligations'. If the UK decides to apply the new Regulation then new Article 12(1)(e), which provides for the consequences of nullity of the contract, will apply as a matter of English law for the first time.[206]

4.5.8.12 Voluntary assignments and contractual subrogation

New Article 14 replaces old Article 12 (which dealt with voluntary assignments) and part of old Article 13(1) (which dealt with subrogation). Old Article 12 is the subject of detailed comments in Chapter 12. The new article has been expanded to cover both voluntary assignments and contractual subrogation,[207] and they are now dealt with in the same way.

In new Article 14(3) (which did not appear in the Rome Convention), it is provided that, 'The concept of assignment in this Article includes outright transfers of claims, transfers of claims by way of security and pledges or other security rights over claims.' In consequence of this, it might be argued that the various forms of security that are known to English law should all be encompassed within the concept of an 'assignment', including charges (which do not involve any concept of a transfer of title) and equitable mortgages by way of equitable assignments where notice is not given to the underlying debtor. It remains to be seen if such an argument will succeed, as charges and unnotified equitable mortgages are not really assignments as commonly understood in civil law terms. They do not involve a transfer which would have the effect of putting the debtor into a direct relationship with the security taker. **4.5.8.12.1**

In new Article 14(1) (which replaces old Article 12(1)) the wording now refers to the 'relationship' between the assignor and the assignee, and provides that the relationship is to be governed by the law of the contract between them. In this regard, Recital (38) to the Regulation provides that: **4.5.8.12.2**

> In the context of voluntary assignment, the term 'relationship' should make it clear that Article 14(1) also applies to the property aspects of an assignment, as between assignor

---

[206] That provision of the Convention, to be found in old Art 10(1)(e), does not apply in the UK by virtue of s 2(2) of the Contracts (Applicable Law) Act 1990.

[207] The latter being used in some jurisdictions in place of assignment, which is more difficult to achieve. For a description of the use of contractual subrogation in France as, in effect, a method of factoring receivables, see Warren J in *Cofacredit SA v Morris* [2006] EWHC 353 (Ch), [2007] 2 BCLC 99 particularly at [64]–[69] and [79]. Obviously, the new provisions would also apply to the right to a contractual subrogation under English law (assuming that the UK applies the Regulation), but the right to subrogation (and, indeed contribution from other co-sureties) would also fall within new Art 15, which deals with subrogation arising by law, as to which see further below.

and assignee, in legal orders where such aspects are treated separately from the aspects under the law of obligations. However, the term 'relationship' should not be understood as relating to any relationship that may exist between assignor and assignee. In particular, it should not cover preliminary questions as regards a voluntary assignment or a contractual subrogation. The term should be strictly limited to the aspects which are directly relevant to the voluntary assignment or contractual subrogation in question.

It would appear to follow from this that, under English law, the proprietary effect of an assignment, as between the assignor and the assignee, should be governed by the law of the contract between them and not, for instance, by the *lex situs* of the underlying debt or by the governing law of that debt.

4.5.8.12.3   With some small differences, new Article 14(2) is to the same effect as old Article 12(2). The differences are (i) that new Article 14(2) refers to both assignments and contractual subrogation, and (ii) for the purposes of clarity, new Article 14(2) refers to the law governing 'the assigned or subrogated claim', instead of the law governing 'the right to which the assignment relates'.

4.5.8.12.4   Whereas an early draft of the Regulation contained a provision to deal explicitly with priority issues as they related to competing assignments, that provision was deleted in the negotiations which led to the final form of the Regulation. It should be noted, however, that new Article 27(2) provides that this issue should be re-visited within a specific period after the adoption of the Regulation, so the issue may be revived and an amendment might be introduced into the Regulation at a later date.

4.5.8.13 *Legal subrogation*

New Article 15 deals with the part of old Article 13(1) that covered subrogation as a matter of law. It is concerned with subrogation in favour of a third party who has satisfied a contractual claim as between the original parties to the contract. This might arise under English law, for instance, pursuant to section 5 of the Mercantile Law Amendment Act 1856. It provides that the law which governs the duty of the third party to satisfy the claim shall determine the right of the third party to proceed against the original obligor.

4.5.8.14 *Contribution*

New Article 16 (headed 'multiple liability') replaces the somewhat more truncated provision that used to appear as old Article 13(2). It provides for the law that should determine the rights to contribution as between joint or several obligors. Somewhat curiously, there is no explicit requirement in the provision that the relevant claim must arise under a contract, but that would probably be implied by the general wording in new Article 1(1), which states that the Regulation applies to contractual obligations. It also provides that the defendants to a claim for contribution may raise defences based on defences they had against the original creditor.

4.5.8.15 Set-off

New Article 17 deals with rights of set-off to the extent that they are not agreed in the contract. It is an entirely new provision. New Article 17 provides that rights of 'set-off shall be governed by the law applicable to the claim against which the right to offset is asserted'. The concept of set-off is not defined and it is not clear what the position would be with respect to a contractual provision which precluded a party from exercising a right of set-off. The concept of set-off could, conceivably, extend to matters such as rights of procedural set-off, netting and counterclaim, equitable set-off, and insolvency set-off. It might also include the statutory reduction in damages arising from a claim akin to one for contributory negligence. Hitherto, a number of those matters might have been considered as being procedural, to be determined by the *lex fori*. If they were matters of substance, they would have fallen to be determined by the governing law of the contract pursuant to old Article 10(1), now new Article 12(1). It is also uncertain how this fits with new Article 1(3), which provides that procedural matters are outside the scope of the Regulation.

4.6 Unlawfulness in the Intended Place for Performance of a Contract: the English Perspective

4.6.1 Unlawfulness in the place of performance

The issue for discussion at this point concerns the situations in which an English court will decline to enforce performance of a contract where the performance would be unlawful in the intended place of performance under the contract. Subject to the application of the rules of public policy,[208] if the governing law of the contract would excuse performance where such performance was unlawful in the intended place of performance, then an English court would apply the governing law and excuse performance.[209] In *Ralli Bros v Compania Naviera Sota y Aznar*[210] the Court of Appeal held in relation to a contract that was governed by English law that a party would be excused from performance if the relevant obligation under the contract had become unlawful in the place of performance after the date the contract was entered into (a 'supervening illegality'). The same rule probably applies in the case of an illegality that had existed from the time of contracting.[211]

---

208 See Upjohn J in *Re Helbert Wagg & Co Ltd's Claim* [1956] Ch 345–346 and 351–352, approved by the Court of Appeal in *Empresa Exportadora De Azucar v Industria Azucarera Nacional SA, The Playa Larga* [1983] 2 Lloyd's Rep 171, at 189–190.

209 This was the position at common law: *Kahler v Midland Bank Ltd* [1950] AC 24 and *Zivnostenska Banka v Frankman* [1950] AC 57.

210 [1920] 2 KB 287.

211 *Toprak v Finagrain* [1979] 2 Lloyd's Rep 98, at 107 (Robert Goff J) and 117 (CA) and *Ispahani v Bank Melli Iran* [1998] Lloyd's Rep Bank 133, at 136.

4.6.1.1 The principle will only apply if the contract necessarily requires performance to be effected in the place where it would be unlawful. If the contract permits lawful performance in another place then performance will not be excused.[212] Accordingly, a party will not be excused performance in one country simply because it would be unlawful by the laws of another country being its place of incorporation or where it carries on business.[213]

4.6.1.2 It is not settled whether the principle in the *Ralli Bros* case might apply to contracts that are governed by a foreign law which is different from that of the place of performance, if the governing law would require performance notwithstanding the unlawfulness in the place of performance. Lord Reid indicated in one case that the principle only applied to contracts that were governed by English law.[214] He said almost immediately afterwards, in another case, that the principle applied irrespective of the governing law of the contract.[215] If it does so apply then it might be possible to argue that it is a mandatory rule of English law and so an English court should apply it pursuant to Article 7(2) of the Rome Convention.[216]

4.6.2 Public policy: unlawful acts in another country

There is a separate ground,[217] based upon public policy, under which an English court may refuse to enforce a contract that involves an unlawful act in another country. On this ground, an English court will refuse to enforce a contract if the object or intention of the parties when they entered into it was the commission of an act that would be unlawful in a foreign and friendly country.[218] The intention need not be explicitly stated in the contract if, on a 'realistic view of the practicalities', that was its intention.[219] The intention must be to commit the unlawful act in that foreign and friendly country,[220] albeit that there may also have been consequences

---

[212] *Toprak v Finagrain* [1979] 2 Lloyd's Rep 98 and *Libyan Arab Foreign Bank v Bankers Trust Co* [1989] QB 728.

[213] *Kleinwort, Sons & Co v Ungarische Baumwolle Industrie AG* [1939] 2 KB 678; *Toprak v Finagrain* [1979] 2 Lloyd's Rep 98; and *Libyan Arab Foreign Bank v Bankers Trust Co* [1989] QB 728.

[214] *Kahler v Midland Bank Ltd* [1950] AC 24, at 48.

[215] *Zivnostenska Banks v Frankman* [1950] AC 57, at 78. See also *Mackender v Feldia AG* [1967] 2 QB 590, at 601.

[216] *Dicey, Morris & Collins*, at paras 32-149 to 32-150 suggests that Art 7(2) would not cover such a situation. It also suggests that it would not fall to be considered to be a rule of public policy that fell within the exception addressed in Art 16 of the Rome Convention. See also the discussion earlier in this chapter as to the effect of Art 9(3) of Rome I.

[217] See Robert Goff J in *Toprak v Finagrain* [1979] 2 Lloyd's Rep 98, at 107 and Staughton J in *Libyan Arab Foreign Bank v Bankers Trust Co* [1989] QB 728, at 745.

[218] *Foster v Driscoll* [1929] 1 KB 470; *Regazzoni v KC Sethia Ltd* [1958] AC 301.

[219] See Scrutton LJ and Lawrence LJ in *Foster v Driscoll* [1929] 1 KB 470, at 497 and 514 respectively; Viscount Simonds in *Regazzoni v KC Sethia Ltd* [1958] AC 301, at 317; and *Ispahani v Bank Melli Iran* [1998] Lloyd's Rep Bank 133, at 140.

[220] Ibid, at 139–140.

in other countries as well.[221] It is not clear if the principle also applies to a case of supervening illegality, as well as original illegality.[222] The rule applies both to contracts governed by English law and to contracts governed by a foreign law, irrespective of whether that is also the law of the place of performance.[223]

4.7 The Conflict of Laws Rules for Tortious and Similar Issues

4.7.1 Introduction

Tortious claims, such as claims in negligence, for misrepresentation, for inducing a breach of contract, or for some other non-contractual civil wrong, may arise in relation to financing transactions, particularly where a claimant may not have a direct contractual claim that it can assert against the defendant, or where, probably for procedural reasons or because of remoteness rules, it wishes to assert the claim additionally to any contractual claim that it may have. It is possible that a tortious claim may have cross-border elements to it. In the case of a claim in negligence or for a misrepresentation, for instance, the statement or advice may have been delivered in one country, received in another, acted upon in a third country, and the damage may have been suffered in any one of those countries or in yet another country. It is necessary, therefore, to consider the conflict of laws rules that apply concerning the issues that may arise for a claim in tort.

4.7.2 The common law rule

The common law conflicts principles for tortious claims depended upon the 'double actionability' rule, as originally propounded by Willes J in *Phillips v Eyre*,[224] and as subsequently developed by the House of Lords in *Boys v Chaplin*[225] and by the Privy Council in *Red Sea Insurance Ltd v Bouygues SA*.[226] The two limbs of the rule are as follows. An act done in a foreign country will be regarded as an actionable tort in England if (a) it would be regarded as a tort if it had occurred in

---

[221] In *Regazzoni v KC Sethia Ltd* [1958] AC 301, the relevant aspect under Indian law was the unlawful export of the jute bags with the intention that they would ultimately be shipped on to South Africa.

[222] See Staughton J in *Libyan Arab Foreign Bank v Bankers Trust Co* [1989] QB 728, at 745.

[223] *Royal Boskalis Westminster NV v Mountain* [1999] QB 674, at 692, 703, and 734–736. In *Far Eastern Shipping Co Public Ltd v Scales Trading Ltd* [2001] 1 All ER (Comm) 319, at 328 (PC), Lord Scott appeared to put the proposition generally, without reference to the governing law of the contract.

[224] (1870) LR 6 QB 1.

[225] [1971] AC 356.

[226] [1995] 1 AC 190. In the *Red Sea* case it was held that an English court could dispense with the application of one or other of the two limbs of the common law rule. In *In the Matter of T&N Ltd* [2005] EWHC 2990 (Ch) David Richards J held that the *Red Sea* case was authoritative in English law.

England, and (b) it would be an actionable wrong in the country where it occurred. It is understood that the old common law double actionability rule still applies, with appropriate territorial modification, in some common law countries. It is interesting to note that the High Court of Australia has decided that it should no longer have application in Australia[227] and has thus removed the requirement that the first limb of the rule (i.e. that there must be an actionable tort in the relevant Australian state or territory) must be satisfied.

4.7.3 The statutory rule

For nearly all purposes, the common law rule has ceased to apply in England. This is because Part III of the Private International Law (Miscellaneous Provisions) Act 1995 abolished the previous common law conflicts rules for determining liability for tortious claims[228] (except concerning claims in defamation and two other cases[229]). Instead, it sets out the English conflicts rules that apply to acts or omissions giving rise to a tortious claim, if they occurred after 1 May 1996, which was the date upon which the legislation came into force. Claims for acts or omissions giving rise to a tortious claim that occurred before that date remain subject to the old common law conflicts rules.[230]

4.7.3.1 The rules under Part III of the 1995 Act will themselves be replaced by EU legislation. An EC Regulation (Rome II) will provide a uniform set of conflict of laws rules throughout the EU to determine the applicable law relating to non-contractual obligations in civil and commercial matters. The Regulation will be addressed after the provisions of Part III of the 1995 Act have been discussed.

4.7.4 Part III of the 1995 Act

The following provisions of Part III of the 1995 Act are relevant to the discussion that follows:

> 9 *Purpose of Part III*
>   (1) The rules in this Part apply for choosing the law (in this Part referred to as 'the applicable law') to be used for determining issues relating to tort . . .
>   (2) The characterisation for the purposes of private international law of issues arising in a claim as issues relating to tort . . . is a matter for the courts of the forum.

---

[227] *Regie National des Usines Renault SA v Zhang* (2002) 210 CLR 491.
[228] See s 10.
[229] See ss 9(3) and 13. *Dicey, Morris & Collins*, at para 35-017, states that, by virtue of ss 10 and 14(2), Part III also does not apply to torts committed on the high seas, nor to aerial torts, as those were not matters that would previously have fallen within the common law rules abolished by s 10.
[230] S 14(1). In *In the Matter of T&N Ltd* [2005] EWHC 2990 (Ch) David Richards J held that the Act would not apply if the acts or omissions giving rise to the claim had occurred before that date, even though the resulting damage manifested itself afterwards.

(3) ...

(4) The applicable law shall be used for determining the issues arising in a claim, including in particular the question whether an actionable tort . . . has occurred.

(5) The applicable law to be used for determining the issues arising in a claim shall exclude any choice of law rules forming part of the law of the country or countries concerned.

(6) For the avoidance of doubt (and without prejudice to the operation of section 14 below) this Part applies in relation to events occurring in the forum as it applies in relation to events occurring in any other country.

(7) ...

(8) ...

10 *Abolition of certain common law rules*

The rules of the common law, in so far as they—

    (a) require actionability under both the law of the forum and the law of another country for the purpose of determining whether a tort . . . is actionable; or

    (b) allow (as an exception for the rules falling within paragraph (a) above) for the law of a single country to be applied for the purpose of determining the issues, or any of the issues, arising in the case in question,

are hereby abolished so far as they apply to any claim in tort . . . which is not excluded for the operation of this Part by S. 13 below.

11 *Choice of applicable law: the general rule*

(1) The general rule is that the applicable law is the law of the country in which the events constituting the tort . . . in question occur.

(2) Where elements of those events occur in different countries, the applicable law under the general rule is to be taken as being—

    (a) [claims for death or personal injury];

    (b) for a cause of action in respect of damage to property, the law of the country where the property was when it was damaged; and

    (c) in any other case, the law of the country in which the most significant element or elements of those events occurred.

(3) ...

12 *Choice of applicable law: displacement of general rule*

(1) If it appears, in all the circumstances, from a comparison of—

    (a) the significance of the factors which connect a tort . . . with the country whose law would be the applicable law under the general rule; and

    (b) the significance of any factors connecting the tort . . . with another country,

that it is substantially more appropriate for the applicable law for determining the issues arising in the case, or any of those issues, to be the law of the other country, the general rule is displaced and the applicable law for determining those issues or that issue (as the case may be) is the law of that other country.

(2) The factors that may be taken into account as connecting a tort . . . with a country for the purposes of this section include, in particular, factors relating to the parties, to any of the events which constitute the tort . . . in question or to any of the circumstances or consequences of those events.

13 *Exclusion of defamation claims from Part III* . . .

14 *Transitional provisions and savings*

(1) Nothing in this Part applies to acts or omissions giving rise to a claim which occurs before the commencement of this Part.

(2) Nothing in this Part affects any rules of law (including rules of private international law) except those abolished by section 10 above.

(3) Without prejudice to the generality of subsection (2) above, nothing in this Part—

(a) authorises the application of the law of a country outside the forum as the applicable law for determining issues arising in any claim in so far as to do so—

(i) would conflict with principles of pubic policy; or

(ii) would give effect to such a penal, revenue or other public law as would not otherwise be enforceable under the law of the forum; or

(b) affects any rules of evidence, pleading or practice or authorises questions of procedure in any proceedings to be determined otherwise than in accordance with the law of the forum.

4.7.5 The concept of tortious issues

In *Trafigura Beheer BV v Kookmin Bank Co*[231] Aikens J held that a 'tort' for the purposes of section 9(1), and thus for the purposes of Part III, should be given a broad construction, 'so as to embrace non-contractual civil wrongs that give rise to a remedy'. Having determined what was meant by the word 'tort', Aikens J then said that, 'the phrase "issues in tort" as used in section 9(1) must mean all those relevant factual issues which relate to the civil wrong in dispute between the parties.' As pointed out earlier in this chapter, when discussing the way in which English law characterises the issues that are involved in a situation involving conflict of laws, the interpretation that his Lordship provided is very wide and could include any non-proprietary claim for a restitutionary remedy. It might cover, for instance, a claim for compensation for breach of an alleged fiduciary duty in which there was not a demand for the return of misapplied or misappropriated assets, as could be the case in claims relating to a conflict of interests, a breach of a duty of confidence, or for a failure by the fiduciary to exercise proper care and skill.

4.7.5.1 Such an approach would be inconsistent with that taken in other cases, although they have not themselves produced a consistent approach. In *A-G for England & Wales v R*[232] the New Zealand Court of Appeal said that where the claim arose from a contractual relationship, the claim would be characterised as one relating to a contract. On the other hand, in *Base Metal Trading Ltd v Shamurin*,[233] the Court of Appeal in England was concerned with a case involving a claim that a director

---

[231] [2006] EWHC 1450 (Comm); [2006] 2 Lloyd's Rep 455, at [68].
[232] [2002] 2 NZLR 91 (affd by the Privy Council on other grounds [2003] UKPC 22, [2003] EMLR 24).
[233] [2004] EWCA Civ 1316, [2005] 1 WLR 1157.

of a foreign company had breached his fiduciary duty towards the company. It would appear from that case that an English court would determine the underlying basis of the relationship on which it was alleged that the duty arose, and then it would apply the law that governed that relationship to determine the nature and extent of any duty that might arise from it, as well as the consequences of any breach of that duty. In the *Base Metal Trading* case it was held that the claim against a director of a company for an alleged breach of his fiduciary duty as a director to exercise proper care and skill was a claim concerning issues relating to a corporate matter and so was governed by the law of the place of incorporation of the company. That law governed the relationship between a company and its directors, being inherently a matter of company law. Even though the alleged facts raised the possibility of concurrent claims for breach of the director's contract of employment or in tort, neither the law which governed the contract nor the law of the tort was applicable in determining the law which governed the claim for breach of the fiduciary duty. It was also held that it would be a matter for the law of the place of incorporation, being that which governed the fiduciary duty, to determine if the nature or scope of that duty could be modified by the contract of employment.

4.7.6 The statutory rules

It will be seen that the scheme laid down in Part III for finding the applicable law for the determination of tortious issues is that a general rule is laid down in section 11, which has within itself different rules depending upon where the element or elements that constituted the tort took place. The putative applicable law as determined under section 11 may be displaced, either wholly or for particular issues, by the application of the rule in section 12. Those sections will now be considered.

4.7.7 The general rule

Section 11 provides the general rule for ascertaining the applicable law that will govern the tortious issues in a claim and it uses geographical tests. If all of the relevant events constituting the tort occurred in one country then the law of that country will be the applicable law. If those events occurred in different countries then section 11(2) will apply. In a case not involving a claim for damage to property, it will be necessary under section 11(2)(c) to find the country in which the most significant element or elements of those events occurred. That will involve identifying all of the factual elements of the tort and making a value judgment regarding the significance of those different elements.[234] Under the previous

---

[234] See Moore-Bick J in *Protea Leasing Ltd v Royal Air Cambodge Co Ltd* [2002] EWHC 2731 (Comm), at [76]–[80]; Mance LJ in *Morin v Bonhams & Brooks Ltd* [2003] EWCA Civ 1802; [2004] 1 Lloyd's Rep 702, at [16]; Aikens J in *Dornoch Ltd v Mauritius Union Assurance Co Ltd*

common law rules, the place where the loss was sustained was regarded as crucial in identifying the law that governed the tort. Under Part III, however, whilst the place where the loss that was suffered is a relevant factor, it probably will not be the most significant element.[235] In one case it was held that the most significant element of the events in a claim for procuring a breach of contract was where the acts of procuration had taken place, not where the resultant damage had been suffered.[236] In a different case it was held that where a misrepresentation or negligent misstatement was made in one country prior to the recipient travelling to another country and, on the strength of it, bidding in an auction in that other country, there was a continuum of reliance and that the most significant element of the relevant events took place where the bid was made in reliance upon the information that had been provided.[237]

4.7.8 Displacement of the general rule

Section 12 involves a consideration of whether there were any factors that connected the tort constituting the claim with a country other than found under the general rule in section 11. If so, it is necessary to determine whether the significance of those factors is such that it is substantially more appropriate for the law of that other country to be applied as the applicable law relating to the one or more of the issues that arise. Section 12 was considered by Aikens J in *Trafigura Beheer BV v Kookmin Bank Co*,[238] and what follows is a summary of his conclusions as to its meaning and effect. There is no precondition to the court considering the relevance of section 12 and the section was broadly stated. Although there were some specific factors identified in section 12(2), they were not exclusive. Mance LJ in *Morin v Bonhams & Brooks Ltd*[239] had said that the factors that might be considered under section 12 could be wider than those that might be relevant to section 11(2)(c). The relevance of section 12 would depend on the facts of the individual case; in some cases there may only be a limited scope to consider the

---

[2005] EWHC 1887 (Comm), at [104]; and Aikens J in *Trafigura Beheer BV v Kookmin Bank Co* [2006] EWHC 1450 (Comm); [2006] 2 Lloyd's Rep 455, at [77]–[79]. In the last of those cases, Aikens J also said (at [87]) that cases concerning Art 5(3) of the EC Regulation on jurisdiction and judgments (EC 44/2001 OJ L12/1 16/1/2001) and its predecessor in the Brussels Convention were of no help in relation to s 11.

[235] See Moore-Bick J in *Protea Leasing Ltd v Royal Air Cambodge Co Ltd* [2002] EWHC 2731 (Comm) and Aikens J in *Trafigura Beheer BV v Kookmin Bank Co* [2006] EWHC 1450 (Comm), [2006] 2 Lloyd's Rep 455.

[236] *Protea Leasing Ltd v Royal Air Cambodge Co Ltd* [2002] EWHC 2731 (Comm).

[237] *Morin v Bonhams & Brooks Ltd* [2003] EWCA Civ 1802; [2004] 1 Lloyd's Rep 702, at [19]. It was also acknowledged that had the recipient stayed in the original place where the information had been received and bid by telephone, the significance of the geographical elements would have been different and a different applicable law may have applied (see at [21]).

[238] [2006] EWHC 1450 (Comm), [2006] 2 Lloyd's Rep 455.

[239] [2003] EWCA Civ 1802; [2004] 1 Lloyd's Rep 702, at [21].

application of section 12, whilst in others there may be more scope. Aikens J also said that the decision to apply section 12 involved a value judgment as to the significance of the factors that pointed to an applicable law other than that identified by the application of the general rule under section 11. It was for the party seeking to rely on section 12 to demonstrate that the factors relevant to section 12 clearly led to the result that it was substantially more appropriate to apply the law found by section 12 to determine the issues than the law found under section 11.[240]

His Lordship also considered that the concept of the 'factors which connect a tort' with a country might include the parties' expressed or implied choice of the law to govern a relevant pre-existing contractual relationship, which was connected with the events that gave rise to the tortious claim. Mance LJ had mentioned this possibility, without determining the point, in *Morin v Bonhams & Brooks Ltd*.[241] Aikens J said that the phrase in section 12(2), 'factor relating to the parties', was broad enough to include the fact of a pre-existing relationship between the parties, whether contractual or otherwise. It also included the law that the parties had expressly or impliedly chosen to govern that relationship. If that relationship gave rise to the events which constituted the alleged tort, then the factual and contractual context in which the events took place and the governing law of the related contracts were factors within section 12(2). He also mentioned that a chosen jurisdiction provision within such a contract could be a relevant factor.

        4.7.8.1

A question that was not addressed by Aikens J is whether the parties can conclusively agree that any claim in tort should be governed by a chosen law, where there is no other contractual relationship between them. A different question, which could be very relevant to a person providing an opinion, advice, information, or services to a recipient outside a contractual relationship, would be whether that person could effectively stipulate that any duty it might have, and any consequent liability, was to be determined in accordance with a stated law. It is submitted that in both circumstances the choosing or specifying of the relevant law could be considered to be a significant factor under section 12. However, it cannot be presumed that it would always be treated as a conclusive factor that outweighed all the other relevant factors. As Aikens J made clear, each case will depend upon its own facts, and a decision under section 12 involves a value judgment which has to be arrived at by weighing up all of the relevant factors of the case.

        4.7.8.2

---

240 It is worth noting, however, that Waller LJ said in *Roerig v Valiant Trawlers Ltd* [2002] EWCA Civ 21; [2002] 1 WLR 2304, at [21(v)], that the general rule under s 11 'is not to be dislodged easily' by s 12.

241 [2003] EWCA Civ 1802; [2004] 1 Lloyd's Rep 702, at [23].

4.7.9 Exclusion of liability

It is suggested by *Dicey, Morris & Collins*[242] that where a defence to a tortious claim is based on a contractual provision, such as a clause that purports to exclude or restrict liability, the availability of the provision as a defence would first have to be determined by the applicable law of the tort.[243] If under that law it was possible to affect liability in that manner then the interpretation of the provision and its intended effect would fall to be governed by the applicable law of the contract. The view that the availability of such a defence must first be assessed by the applicable law of the tort appears to be supported by *Morin v Bonhams & Brooks Ltd*,[244] where Mance LJ made a passing reference to such an approach, but he did not address the issue in any depth.

4.7.10 Substantive v procedural matters

At common law, as exemplified by the decision of the House of Lords in *Boys v Chaplin*,[245] a distinction was drawn between the kind of damage which constituted an actionable injury which, being substantive, was determined by the law of the tort (the '*lex causae*'), as opposed to the assessment of compensation (damages) for the injury, which was procedural and was determined in accordance with the law of the forum (the '*lex fori*'). Thus rules which excluded damage from the scope of liability on the grounds that it did not fall within the ambit of liability, or that there was no causal connection of the damage to the liability, or that the damage was not foreseeable, were substantive matters going to the existence of liability. By contrast, whether the award to be made should be money damages and the amount of damages or whether there should be restitution in kind were questions of remedy and so were procedural. In *Boys v Chaplin* the majority of the House of Lords had held that the relevant foreign law which denied liability for non-economic damage was a substantive requirement of the *lex causae*. All of the Law Lords who heard that case, however, had agreed that the quantification of damages for actionable heads of damage under the *lex causae* was a question of remedy or procedure and should be determined by the *lex fori*.

4.7.10.1 In *Harding v Wealands*[246] the House of Lords held that the common law distinction between questions of liability and questions of remedy or procedure had not been affected by Part III of the 1995 Act and continued to apply. Although section 14(3)(b) only used the word 'procedure', it was clearly intended to refer as well to 'remedies', as the words had been used interchangeably in the case law before the

---

242 At para 35-049.
243 This would be the position under Art 15(1) of Rome II.
244 [2003] EWCA Civ 1802; [2004] 1 Lloyd's Rep 702, see at [24].
245 [1971] AC 356.
246 [2006] UKHL 32, [2007] 2 AC 1. Lord Hoffmann delivered the leading judgment.

Act was passed. In addition, section 14(3) was expressed to be without prejudice to the generality of section 14(2), which in turn provides that Part III should not affect any rules of law except those abolished by section 10. That section was only concerned with the rules that determined, 'whether a tort . . . is actionable'. It did not purport to abolish the rules that were concerned with the remedies that were available for an actionable injury.

It had been suggested that a statutory limit or cap on the damages that were recoverable in a claim should be regarded as substantive rather than procedural, based on the decisions at first instance and in the Court of Appeal in *Cope v Doherty*.[247] The House of Lords held in *Harding v Wealands*[248] that those decisions had been misconstrued. The correct proposition to be drawn from them was that a contractual term which limits the obligation to pay damages for a breach of contract or a tort, and a statutory provision which is deemed to operate as such a term of a contract, qualifies the substantive obligation, and its effect will fall to be determined by the *lex causae*. It will not fall within the province of the *lex fori* as a procedural matter. Difficulties might still arise, however, in cases which do not fall within the confines of the principle that was to be derived from *Cope v Doherty*, in determining if a statutory limitation was intended to have substantive effect. In some cases it may be difficult, if not impossible, to discover the distinction between the concept of actionable damage and the concept of a remedy for that damage.

4.7.10.2

4.7.11 The EC Regulation on the law applicable to non-contractual obligations (Rome II)

The EC Regulation on the law applicable to non-contractual obligations[249] will provide a uniform set of conflict of laws rules throughout the EU to determine the applicable law relating to non-contractual obligations in civil and commercial matters. It will not apply to revenue, customs, or administrative matters.[250] The Regulation applies from 11 January 2009 with respect to events giving rise to damage which occur after that date.[251]

The applicable law as found by the rules laid down in the Regulation will apply even if that is the law of a country outside the EU.[252] The Regulation will apply in a case involving a non-contractual claim, such as one in tort, brought before a

4.7.11.1

---

[247] (1858) 4 K&J 367 and (1858) 2 DeG&J 614.
[248] [2006] UKHL 32, [2007] 2 AC 1.
[249] EC/864/2007 OJ L199/40 31/7/2007.
[250] Art 1(1).
[251] Arts 31 and 32. See however n 21 above, as to the possibility that the Regulation may apply to events giving rise to damage which occurred after 20 August 2007.
[252] See Art 3.

court in a Member State of the EU, with the exception of Denmark.[253] It will lead to a different set of rules from those which currently apply under English law, which have been discussed above. As a Community instrument, the Regulation will be subject to interpretation by the European Court of Justice.

4.7.11.2 Scope of application

Save for specific exceptions which the Regulation provides will not fall within its compass, the Regulation will apply to a much wider variety of claims than would be understood in English law as being purely tortious. Essentially, it will apply to most types of non-contractual obligations (and to damage[254] which is suffered relating to a tort) which arise or are likely to arise under civil law (i.e. not criminal law). In English terms, the Regulation will cover tortious claims, claims for unjust enrichment and other types of restitutionary claims, equitable claims based on a breach of fiduciary duties, claims asserting constructive trusts and resulting trusts, claims for infringement of intellectual property rights, claims for unfair commercial practices, claims for environmental damage, claims for a breach of a warranty of authority, and claims based on rules of strict liability.[255] There are grey areas where it is uncertain whether, and if so the extent to which, the Regulation will apply, for instance, as to the assertion of property rights (other than the assertion of intellectual property rights, which are covered) and tracing rights and the consequences of the infringement or dispossession of such property rights.

4.7.11.3 There are various specific exclusions from the scope of the Regulation, that are set out in Article 1(2), some of which are similar to those to be found in the proposed EC Regulation concerning contractual obligations (Rome I), as addressed above. These include exceptions with respect to family relationships, succession, negotiable instruments, and evidence and procedure. Like Rome I, there is also an exception for company law (and other corporate and unincorporated bodies) matters, but the exception extends to the liability of auditors to the company and its members. Similarly, there is an exception for 'non-contractual obligations arising from relationships between the settlors, trustees and beneficiaries of a trust created voluntarily', which may not cover certain types of constructive trusts or resulting trusts. There is an exclusion for claims in privacy and for defamation. There is also an exclusion for acts of the State done in the exercise of public authority.[256] Unlike Rome I, there is no exclusion concerning agreements as to court jurisdiction and arbitration. The position relating to the effect of international treaties or

---

[253] Art 1(4). The UK has decided to 'opt in' to the Regulation. As an EC Regulation it will be directly applicable and so it will apply as a matter of English law.

[254] 'Damage' includes any consequence arising from the commission of a tort: Art 2(1).

[255] As to strict liability, see Recital (11) to the Regulation.

[256] See Recital (9) and Art 1(1).

conventions to which a Member State is a party at the time the Regulation is adopted is dealt with in Article 28.

4.7.11.4 Specific and general rules

The Regulation lays down various rules for ascertaining the applicable law. For some types of claim there are specific rules, such as claims concerning defective products,[257] unfair commercial practices,[258] environmental damage,[259] infringement of intellectual property rights,[260] unjust enrichment relating to an existing relationship,[261] dealings prior to entry into a contract,[262] and breach of a warranty of authority.[263] Some of those rules will be examined separately, later. For the remaining general body of tortious claims, there are general rules. There are also rules based on a choice of law, which will be examined first. It should also be noted that the Regulation excludes the operation of the doctrine of renvoi.[264]

4.7.11.5 Choice of law

Article 14 of the Regulation allows the parties a freedom of choice in choosing the applicable law of a tort, although the choice may not prejudice the rights of third parties. Like the Rome Convention, a choice may be express or it may be implied 'if demonstrated with reasonable certainty by the circumstances of the case'.[265] The parties to a dispute that has already arisen may choose the applicable law to resolve the dispute that has arisen. Where all the parties exercise commercial activities, they may 'by an agreement freely negotiated' agree before the event giving rise to the damage has occurred on their choice of the applicable law. It is debatable if this will cover standard form contracts or agreements where there was a disparity in the bargaining power of the parties. There are two further limitations on the effect of a choice of the applicable law. The first, which is like that to be found in Article 3(3) of the Rome Convention and Article 3(4) of Rome I, is that the choice should be without prejudice to the mandatory provisions of the law of the country in which all the elements concerning the situation were located when the relevant event giving rise to the damage occurred. The second preserves the relevance of Community law if all the elements concerning the situation were located in one or more EU Member States when the relevant event etc. occurred.

---

[257] Art 5.
[258] Art 6.
[259] Art 7.
[260] Arts 8 and 13.
[261] Art 10
[262] Art 12.
[263] Art 11.
[264] Art 24.
[265] Unlike Rome I which also includes reference to 'the behaviour of the parties'.

4.7.11.6 *General fall-back rule*

In the absence of such a choice, Article 4 of the Regulation sets out a general rule, which applies unless there is a specific rule. The general rule is in three parts, which operate as a hierarchy. The first, which is subject to being overridden by the application of the second or the third part, is that the applicable law should be the law of the country in which the damage occurred, irrespective of the place or places in which the event or events giving rise to the damage occurred or the country or countries in which the indirect consequences of that event or those events might arise. Secondly, where at the time the damage occurred both the claimant and the defendant have their 'habitual residence'[266] in the same country, the law of that country will apply. That would be irrespective of any connection between that country and the place where the damage occurred or any other causal element. Thirdly, by way of overriding qualification to both the first and the second parts, where it was clear from all the circumstances, such as under a pre-existing relationship arising from a contract, that the tort was manifestly more closely connected with another country than that ascertained under either of the other parts, the law of that other country would apply.

4.7.11.6.1 These rules should operate tolerably well in cases concerning death, personal injury, and physical damage to property. It is not at all clear how well they would work in purely financial claims, such as in negligence giving rise to economic loss, or for a financial restitutionary claim. Nor is it clear how they would work in the case of an equitable claim.

4.7.11.7 *Special rules*

As previously mentioned, there are special rules to deal with particular types of obligation. The following might be relevant in a financial context.

4.7.11.7.1 Unjust enrichment Article 10 provides a special rule for an obligation arising from unjust enrichment, including for wrongfully received monetary payments. The relevant non-contractual obligation must concern an existing relationship between the parties, such as one which arises under a contract or in tort. The primary rule is that the obligation will be governed by the law that governs that relationship. If that law cannot be determined and the parties each have an habitual residence in the same country as that in which the event occurs which gave rise to the unjust enrichment, the claim will be governed by the law of that country. Failing that, the claim will be governed by the law of the country in which the event occurred that gave rise to the unjust enrichment. All of the foregoing is subject to a proviso, which is as follows. Where it is clear from all the circumstances that the relevant obligation is manifestly more closely connected to

---

[266] Which is defined in Art 23, in a manner similar to that contained in Rome I.

another country than indicated by the earlier tests, the law of that country will apply.

4.7.11.7.2 Pre-contractual dealings Article 11 concerns obligations that arise from dealings prior to the entry into of an intended contract, whether or not the contract was actually entered into. An example might be a claim for a misrepresentation which induced the claimant to enter into the contract. The primary rule is that such an obligation will be governed by the law that governs the contract, or which would have done so had the contract been entered into. There are various fall-back rules if it is not possible to determine what that law should have been, being (1) the law of the place where the damage occurred, irrespective of the places where the event or events occurred that give rise to the damage or where any indirect consequences of those events occurred, and (2) if each of the parties have a common country in which their habitual residence is situated, the law of that country. The fall-back rules will be overridden where, from all the circumstances of the case, the obligation is manifestly more closely connected with some other country, in which case the law of that country will apply.

4.7.11.7.3 Subrogation Article 19 concerns rights of subrogation in non-contractual claims. It relates to a situation where a person (the 'creditor') has a non-contractual claim against a defendant and also has a right to be reimbursed or otherwise satisfied by a third party. The third party may then claim to be subrogated to the creditor's claim against the defendant. The right to subrogation will be governed by the law which governs the obligation of the third party towards the creditor.

4.7.11.7.4 Direct claims against a defendant's insurer Article 18 relates to the position where a person who has suffered damage wishes to claim directly against the defendant's insurer.

4.7.11.7.5 Contribution Article 20 deals with rights of contribution as between joint tortfeasors.

4.7.11.8 Mandatory rules

Article 16 provides for the effect of overriding mandatory rules of the forum, notwithstanding what may otherwise be provided in the Regulation (whether as to determining the applicable law or as to the effect of that law). In such a case, the court may also apply those rules if they are mandatory irrespective of the law that would otherwise govern the situation.

4.7.11.9 Public policy

There is also a public policy exception in Article 26, to the effect that the rule of any law otherwise determined in pursuance of the Regulation may be disregarded if it is manifestly incompatible with the public policy of the forum. It should be noted that Recital (32) to the Regulation provides that such incompatibility could include a foreign law 'causing non-compensatory, exemplary or punitive damages'.[267]

4.7.11.10 The scope of the applicable law

The Regulation provides that the law to be applied as determined under the Regulation would govern most of the matters that would arise in a claim in tort. This is covered by Article 15, which provides that such law would govern the following:

(a) the basis and extent of liability, including the determination of persons who are liable for acts performed by them;

(b) the grounds for exemption from liability, any limitation of liability and any division of liability;

(c) the existence, the nature and the assessment of damages or the remedy claimed;

(d) within the limits of powers conferred on the court by its procedural law, the measures which a court may take to prevent or terminate injury or damage or to ensure the provision of compensation;

(e) the question whether a right to claim damages or a remedy may be transferred, including by inheritance;

(f) the persons entitled to compensation for damage sustained personally;

(g) liability for the acts of another person;

(h) the manner in which an obligation may be extinguished and the rules of prescription and limitation, including rules relating to the commencement, interruption and suspension of a period of prescription or limitation.

4.7.11.10.1   Quite clearly, substantive matters will be governed by the applicable law including, for instance, the determination of liability and the kinds of loss for which compensation may be provided. It would also appear that matters that might previously have been considered as being procedural at common law,[268] such as remedies and the rules for assessment of compensation, would also fall to be determined under the applicable law. One would expect that the Regulation would preserve the distinction rather than remove it, as Article 1(3) of the Regulation provides that matters of evidence and procedure do not fall within the ambit of the Regulation. Nonetheless, Article 15(c) provides for the assessment of damages and other remedies to be a matter to be governed by the applicable law. As was discussed above in relation to Article 10(1)(c) of the Rome Convention, the *Giuliano-Lagarde Report*[269] states that the use of phrase the 'assessment of damages in so far as it is governed by rules of law', as used in Article 10(1)(c) of the Convention,

---

[267] As to the position under English law, see s 5 of the Protection of Trading Interests Act 1980.
[268] See the discussion by Lord Hoffmann in *Harding v Wealands* [2006] UKHL 32, [2007] 2 AC 1.
[269] At p 33.

means that pure questions of fact relating to the assessment of damages would not be governed by the applicable law, for example, mathematical calculations, but it implies that the basis of making an assessment and questions such as whether the governing law imposed a limit on compensation or a rule for assessment of compensation, would fall within the ambit of Article 10(1)(c). The right to interest in consequence of default would probably be governed by the applicable law.[270] It has been suggested that the assessment of such interest, including the rate of interest, would fall within the province of the *lex fori* as a procedural matter,[271] but it is difficult to square this with the approach taken in the *Giuliano-Lagarde Report*, that only questions of fact, such as the simple matter of arithmetic, would fall for determination by the *lex fori*.

4.8 The Conflicts Rules for Proprietary Transactions

4.8.1 Introduction

The conflicts issues that typically may arise in transactions which are intended to have proprietary consequences will concern the ownership of an asset, the transfer of title in the asset, the relationship between the transferor and the transferee, the creation and effectiveness of security over an asset (including matters of attachment and perfection of the security), the obligations that may be secured under such security, and priorities where there are rival claimants to an asset, be they claimants asserting an outright interest in the asset or a security interest in the asset. These issues should be distinguished from purely contractual issues that may also arise in connection with a proprietary transaction.[272] The purely contractual issues, such as the payment of the price and the interpretation of warranties that are given in the contract and whether they have been breached, will fall to be considered in accordance with the conflicts rules for contractual matters. Furthermore, questions regarding the formal and material validity of the contract would be determined in accordance with the rules set out in the Rome Convention. The proprietary aspects of the transaction will be dealt with in accordance with the rules that are set out below. It may be, nonetheless, that the rules for the determination of the proprietary issues may themselves refer to the contract, such as would be the case under English law in a sale of goods transaction to determine if property had passed to the buyer under the contract.

---

270 By analogy with the view of Brooke LJ in *Lesotho Highlands Development Authority v Impregilo SpA* [2003] EWCA Civ 1159; [2003] 2 Lloyd's Rep 497, at [45] (the result in the case was overturned by the House of Lords [2005] UKHL 43, [2006] 1 AC 221, but this point did not arise for review).

271 Ibid, at [50].

272 See the distinction that is drawn in this regard by the *Giuliano-Lagarde Report*, at p 10.

4.8.2 By way of general qualification to the discussion that follows, the effect of the insolvency of the owner of an asset upon its and other persons' rights in the asset may well be subject to considerations relating to insolvency.[273] The rules of English public policy may also intervene when considering proprietary matters, such as in cases where an English court may refuse to give effect to the law of the situs of an asset because it considers the law to be repugnant to principles of justice and fairness.[274]

4.8.3 Classification of assets

It is important as a first step to classify the asset that is involved in a particular situation, as the classification that it is given will determine the conflict of laws rule that should be applied in finding the relevant law that governs the matters that might arise concerning it. In the field of conflict of laws, English law follows an international pattern in the classification of assets, by dividing them between immovable and movable property (or assets), and in further dividing movable property between tangible and intangible movables. Under English law, immovable property is land and an interest in land, and everything else will be movable property. Whilst the distinction between immovable and movable property has a rough equivalence in the English domestic concepts of real and personal property, it is only a rough equivalence, and care should be taken not to fall into the trap of believing that the approach that is taken in the field of conflict of laws will always be the same as that which is used in domestic law. For instance, under English conflicts principles, a mortgagee's interest in land[275] and the right of a tenant under a lease[276] are treated as immovable property, although in domestic law they are treated as a personality.

4.8.3.1 The English classification of an asset will not be determinative if the asset is located elsewhere. The classification of an asset that is situated outside England will depend upon the classification given to it by its *lex situs*, i.e. the law of the place where it is situated at the relevant time at which the determination has to be made. It thus becomes necessary to determine the situation of the different types of asset. To some extent, this could be a rather circular exercise, as the *lex situs* of an asset determines the type of asset concerned, but the rules for determining situs depend upon ascribing a description to an asset in the first place. The only way out of this dilemma is for English law to ascribe a provisional description to an asset on which its situs can be located and, once that has been done, the rules of the situs

---

[273] See, for instance, the position under Art 5 of the EC Insolvency Regulation (1346/2000/EC OJ L160/1 30/6/2000).

[274] See para 4.10.4 below.

[275] *Re Hoyles* [1911] 1 Ch 179. In Australia, on the other hand, such an interest is treated as movable property: see *Haque v Haque* (1965) 114 CLR 411.

[276] *Freke v Carbery* (1873) LR 16 Eq 461.

can make any correction that may be necessary. In most cases, common sense should result in the provisional description that has been given by English law matching the label that is accorded to an asset by the *lex situs*, particularly if English law takes into account the rules of the likely situs.

4.8.4 The situs of an asset

What follows describes the English rules in finding the situs of an asset.

4.8.4.1 Immovable property and tangible movable property

There should be no difficulty in recognising the location of an immovable asset and, in general, in determining the location at the relevant time of a tangible movable asset. It has been suggested, however, that ships and aircraft may for some purposes be situated in their port or country of registration, particularly when they are outside the territorial borders of a State.[277]

4.8.4.2 Intangible movables

Of their very nature, intangible movables do not have a physical presence and so a conceptual approximation as to their location has to be made. The English approach is based broadly on finding the place where they are recoverable or enforceable against the relevant debtor or obligor.[278] Probably the most important type of intangible asset is a debt. The rules for determining the situs of a debt are discussed in Chapter 12.

A claim under a letter of credit is situated where the letter of credit is payable against presentation of documents.[279] **4.8.4.2.1**

Negotiable instruments and securities transferable by delivery with or without endorsement are situated where the security happens to be for the time being, although it may be possible to separate the situs of the instrument from the debt due under it, which would be located in accordance with the rules relating to the situs of a debt. Thus, in determining issues relating to title to the instrument, **4.8.4.2.2**

---

277 See *Dicey, Morris & Collins*, at paras 22-E057 to 22-061. Gross J, commenting upon the view put forward by *Dicey, Morris & Collins*, said in *Air Foyle Ltd v Center Capital Ltd* [2002] EWHC 2535 (Comm); [2003] 2 Lloyd's Rep 753, at [40] that 'there are overwhelming reasons for treating an aircraft as situate in the State where it physically is for the time being, at least unless it is either over the high seas or over or on territory which is not under the sovereignty of any State'. For aircraft (including airframes and engines), helicopters, and other types of high value mobile equipment, such as rolling stock and space property, see also the Cape Town Convention (the UNIDROIT Convention of 2001 on international interests in mobile equipment), as to the effect of the registration of security and quasi-security interests in an internationally recognised register. The concept of an asset being situated at its place of registry is supported, in the context of an insolvency, by Art 2(g) of the EC Insolvency Regulation (EC 1346/2000 OJ L160/1 30/6/2000).

278 *Kwok Chi Leung Karl v Commissioner of Estate Duty* [1988] 1 WLR 1035.

279 *Power Curber International Ltd v National Bank of Kuwait* [1981] 1 WLR 1233.

the situs of the instrument at the relevant time would be the relevant issue. In enforcing the instrument against an obligor, his location would be important.[280] Whether an instrument is negotiable and, if so, whether it has been successfully negotiated would appear to depend on a combination of the rules of the situs of the instrument at the relevant time and the *lex fori*.[281]

4.8.4.2.3 Shares in companies will primarily be treated as located in the place of incorporation but, if there are one or more registers located in different places to the place of incorporation, they might be treated as located at the place where the register is kept on which they are registered.[282]

4.8.4.2.4 The position concerning interests in immobilised and dematerialised securities is discussed in Chapter 10.

4.8.4.2.5 A 'specialty' (an obligation due under a deed or a State or government obligation[283]) is treated as located where the deed, State, or government is situated. This gives rise to particular difficulties where there is a mortgage deed. As previously seen, the interest of a mortgagee of land is characterised by English rules of conflict of laws as being an interest in an immovable asset and so it is situated where the mortgaged land is located. The position becomes more confused if the mortgage is registered in a land registry. For most purposes, English law will ascribe the situation of the mortgagee's rights as being that of the land.[284]

4.8.4.2.6 A right in intellectual property will be located at the place whose law governs its existence and protection.[285]

4.8.4.2.7 If a beneficiary under a trust has a right in the trust property, the right will be located at the place of the relevant property.[286] Otherwise, the right of the beneficiary will be located where the trust is enforceable against the trustee.[287]

---

[280] *Dicey, Morris & Collins*, at para 22-041, suggests that the location of the debtor may also be important in expropriation cases for determining the holder's entitlement and whether that has been expropriated.

[281] See Staughton and Auld LJJ in *Macmillan Inc v Bishopsgate Investment Trust PLC (No 3)* [1996] 1 WLR 387, at 400 and 411. See also s 72 of the Bills of Exchange Act 1882. In *Re Harvard Securities Ltd* [1988] BCC 567, at 571, Neuberger J proceeded on the basis that the *lex fori* should determine if an instrument was negotiable.

[282] This reflects the different approaches that were taken in the Court of Appeal in *Macmillan Inc v Bishopsgate Investment Trust PLC (No 3)* [1996] 1 WLR 387, by Staughton LJ at 405, by Auld LJ at 411, and by Aldous LJ at 424–425.

[283] *Royal Trust Co v A-G for Alberta* [1930] AC 144.

[284] *Re Hoyles* [1911] 1 Ch 179.

[285] Per Neuberger J in *Peer International Corp v Termidor Music Publishers Ltd* [2002] EWHC 2675 (Ch). The judgment was upheld on appeal by the Court of Appeal at [2003] EWCA Civ 1156, [2004] Ch 212, but the appeal did not concern this point. Difficult questions may arise in determining the situs of an EC community trade mark.

[286] *Re Berchtold* [1923] 1 Ch 192.

[287] *Re Smythe* [1898] 1 Ch 89.

4.8.5 The rules for proprietary issues

It is now possible to move to a consideration of the rules that an English court would apply to determine the law that governs the proprietary issues that relate to an asset. The application of these rules would, however, be subject to some general reservations. The first relates to situations where an English court would refuse to recognise the effect of a foreign law on public policy grounds.[288] The second is where the effect of a foreign law would be contradictory to a mandatory provision of English law that was applicable irrespective of the possible relevance of a foreign law.[289] The third concerns the effect of insolvency, where a party's rights may be subject to the application of insolvency rules as, for instance, in the application of the EU Insolvency Regulation. The fourth concerns situations where an English court may act *in personam* against a party within the jurisdiction with respect to a promise that party has made relating to assets abroad. For instance, if a party agrees to give security over foreign assets and subsequently brings the proceeds of sale of the assets into England, the court may treat the proceeds as being subject to the agreement to give the security, even though the security itself may have been invalid under the *lex situs* of the assets over which the security was purportedly granted.[290]

4.8.5.1 Determination by a foreign court

Before examining the English rules, it is interesting to note the attitude that the English courts will take to the determination by a foreign court of proprietary issues concerning a foreign asset. The position was addressed by Lord Mance in giving the advice of the Privy Council in *Ali v Pattni*.[291] His Lordship said that a foreign judgment would be treated as a judgment *in rem* which would be capable of recognition and enforcement in England if it was a judgment by a court where the relevant property was situated which adjudicated upon the title or disposition of the property and was intended to be binding upon the whole world and not just the parties to the litigation which had led to the judgment. A judgment *in personam*, on the other hand, only binds the parties to the proceedings. The distinction is based on *Cammell v Sewell*[292] and *Castrique v Imrie*.[293] This reflected a more general principle that the transfer or disposition of property was a matter for the courts and the legal authorities in the jurisdiction where the property was situated. Such authority should be recognised by the courts in other States.

---

[288] To which further reference is made below.
[289] See the fourth exception mentioned by Slade J in *Winkworth v Christie, Manson and Woods Ltd* [1980] Ch 496, at 501 and his obiter acceptance of that exception, at 514.
[290] See *Re Anchor Line (Henderson Brothers) Ltd* [1937] 1 Ch 483.
[291] [2006] UKPC 51, [2007] 2 AC 85.
[292] (1860) 5 H&N 728.
[293] (1870) LR 7 HL 414.

4.8.5.1.1 By way of guidance in determining if a judgment had such an *in rem* effect, Lord Mance said that the nature and terms of the foreign court's jurisdiction to make such a determination should be considered, and a judgment would not be considered as having an *in rem* effect if it had been made by consent of the parties before the court. In addition, a judgment would not be considered to be *in rem* if it determined or related to the existence of property rights merely as between the parties, but was not intended to be binding as against the whole world.

4.8.5.1.2 The position concerning an *in rem* judgment should be distinguished from that relating to a judgment *in personam* which purported to determine the contractual rights of parties in property, particularly in relation to tangible movable property and intangible property, wherever it was situated. An English court should be prepared to recognise and give effect, as between the parties, to a judgment of a foreign court relating to such property, subject to any particular rules under English law concerning such property (e.g. that the disponee was a person suffering from a legal restriction and thus not entitled to be vested with the property) and the usual requirements concerning matters, such as that the foreign court properly had jurisdiction to hear the case (e.g. by submission of the parties), the effect of fraud, and the requirements of natural justice and public policy. His Lordship said that the position may be different in relation to a foreign judgment concerning immovable property situated in England. As discussed below, whilst an English court may be prepared to give an *in personam* judgment to enforce contractual or equitable rights relating to foreign land it was uncertain if the same considerations would apply in reverse.

4.8.5.2 Immovable property

For immovable property, proprietary matters should be determined in accordance with the *lex situs* of the property,[294] including the conflict of laws rules of the *lex situs*.[295]

4.8.5.2.1 There is an important qualification to that statement. At common law, an English court does not have jurisdiction to determine questions relating to the title in, or a right to possession of, foreign land; nor may it entertain an action for trespass to such an immovable.[296] There are, in turn, three exceptions to this principle. The first arises under section 30(1) of the Civil Jurisdiction and Judgments Act 1982, which permits an action for trespass or another tort concerning foreign land unless the action is 'principally concerned with a question of title to, or the right to possession of' the land, that is, that the real issue in the action concerns the title to

---

[294] *Nelson v Bridport* (1846) 8 Beav 547; *Norton v Florence Land and Public Works Co* (1877) 7 ChD 332; and Staughton and Auld LJJ in *Macmillan Inc v Bishopsgate Investment Trust PLC (No 3)* [1996] 1 WLR 387, at 399 and 410.

[295] *Re Duke of Wellington* [1947] Ch 506 (approved on appeal at [1948] Ch 118).

[296] *British South Africa Co v Companhia de Mozambique* [1893] AC 602; *Hesperides Hotels Ltd v Aegean Turkish Holidays Ltd* [1979] AC 508.

the land.[297] The second exception arises under the rule in *Penn v Lord Baltimore*[298] which permits an English court, acting *in personam*,[299] to enforce a pre-existing relationship between the parties which arises under a contract or a fiduciary or other equitable obligation with respect to foreign land.[300] For instance, the court may enforce the following, that is to say, a contract to convey title to land,[301] a contract to create a mortgage,[302] the right of a mortgagor under the rule against clogging the equity of redemption,[303] and an obligation of a trustee or other fiduciary[304] to convey title to a beneficiary.[305] Thirdly, an English court may be prepared to determine a matter concerning the title to foreign land where it arises incidentally or collaterally to some other issue[306] or where it is capable of determination as a matter of fact.[307]

4.8.5.3 *Tangible movable property*

For tangible movable property, proprietary questions, including the effect of a purported transfer of title, will be determined by the *lex situs* of the object at the time of the relevant transaction.[308] For this purpose, the *lex situs* includes only the domestic rules of the relevant jurisdiction; it does not include its conflict of

---

[297] *Re Polly Peck International plc (No 2)* [1998] 3 All ER 812, in which the Court of Appeal also dismissed the concept of a remedial constructive trust being accepted in English law. It is submitted that the same approach to a claim in trespass would be taken in light of the wording in Art 22(1) of the EC Regulation on jurisdiction and judgments (EC 44/2001 OJ L12/1 16/1/2001).

[298] (1750) 1 Ves Sen 444, 27 ER 1132.

[299] Per Lord Selborne LC in *Ewing v Orr Ewing* (1883) 9 App Cas 34, at 40.

[300] It is doubtful if an English court would recognise the reverse, that is, an order of a foreign court concerning English land: see Lord Mance giving the advice of the Privy Council in *Ali v Pattni* [2006] UKPC 51; [2007] 2 AC 85, at [26].

[301] *Richard West and Partners (Inverness) Ltd v Dick* [1969] 2 Ch 424. In *Penn v Lord Baltimore*, specific performance was ordered to effect an agreement as to the boundaries to foreign land.

[302] *Re Smith; Lawrence v Kitson* [1916] 2 Ch 206.

[303] *British South Africa Co v De Beers Consolidated Mines Ltd* [1910] 2 Ch 502.

[304] Provided the obligation was proved: *Cook Industries Inc v Galliher* [1979] Ch 439.

[305] *Re Duke of Wellington* [1947] Ch 506 (approved on appeal at [1948] Ch 118).

[306] Per Lord Herschell LC in *British South Africa Co v Companhia de Mozambique* [1893] AC 602, at 626. See also Sir Robert Megarry V-C in *Tito v Waddell (No 2), Tito v Attorney General* [1977] Ch 106, at 262, 271, and 311.

[307] *Duff Development Co. Ltd v Kelantan Government* [1924] AC 797.

[308] See Pollock CB in *Cammell v Sewell* (1858) 3 H&N 617, at 638 (affd by Crompton J at (1860) 5 H&N 728, at 744–745); Maugham J in *Re Anziani* [1930] 1 Ch 407, at 420; Devlin J in *Bank voor Handel en Scheepvaart v Slatford* [1953] 1 QB 248, at 257; and Diplock LJ in *Hardwick Game Farm v Suffolk Agricultural Poultry Producers Assoc* [1966] 1 WLR 287, at 330 (affd at [1969] 2 AC 31). In *Air Foyle Ltd v Center Capital Ltd* [2002] EWHC 2535 (Comm), [2003] 2 Lloyd's Rep 753 Gross J applied this rule to hold that a judicial sale of an aircraft in the Netherlands was effective as the aircraft was there at the time of the sale. The House of Lords applied the *lex situs* rule as a matter of Scots law in *Inglis v Robertson* [1898] AC 616 in the case of a purported grant of security over goods in Scotland and held that the security had not been validly granted under Scots law. It may be that the determination of the effectiveness of a maritime lien falls to be decided by the *lex fori*: see *Bankers Trust International Ltd v Todd Shipyard Corp, The Halcyon Isle* [1981] AC 221. It is submitted that the Privy Council in that case did not decide that there was a different rule generally

laws rules.[309] An entitlement as so determined will continue until, or to the extent that, it is displaced by a later transaction having a proprietary effect in accordance with the *lex situs* at the time of the later transaction.[310] A transfer of title in accordance with the *lex situs* will be effective as between the immediate parties to it, just as much as it will also be effective with respect to other persons.[311] The effect of a lack of bona fides on the part of a party to a transaction should also be a matter for the *lex situs*.[312] The *lex situs* will also govern questions of title in new goods.[313] There is a possible exception to the application of a rule based on the *lex situs*, which concerns the position where the location of the asset was unknown at the time of a purported dealing with it, or if its location was purely 'casual' at that time. *Dicey, Morris & Collins*[314] suggests that in such a case, the validity of the dealing would be governed by the applicable law of the transaction concerned.

4.8.5.3.1 The resolution of the proprietary entitlement in tangible movables should be distinguished from the issue as to an entitlement to the possession or an immediate right to the possession of them, where the goods have been bailed to another person. In such a case, it would appear that the entitlement will be ascertained in accordance with the contract of bailment and so will be determined by the governing law of the contract.[315]

4.8.5.3.2 The Cape Town Convention There is a qualification to the rule based on situs that will arise in the case of certain types of mobile equipment, pursuant to the Cape Town Convention,[316] when it comes into force by adoption in the UK. The Convention was adopted at a diplomatic conference held in Cape Town on 16 November 2001. A Protocol to the Convention dealing with Matters Specific to Aircraft Equipment (i.e. airframes, aircraft engines, and helicopters)

---

for determining priorities between competing security interests and that its advice was confined to determining the effectiveness of maritime liens.

[309] *Islamic Republic of Iran v Berend* [2007] EWHC 132 (QB), [2007] 2 All ER (Comm) 132. It should be noted, however, that Slade J reached a tentative view to the contrary in *Winkworth v Christie, Manson and Woods Ltd* [1980] Ch 496, at 514.

[310] *Winkworth v Christie, Manson and Woods Ltd* [1980] Ch 496.

[311] Per Moore-Bick J in *Glencore International AG v Metro Trading Inc* [2001] 1 All ER (Comm) 103, at [28]–[32].

[312] See Moore-Bick J in ibid, at [33].

[313] *Glencore International AG v Metro Trading Inc* [2001] 1 All ER (Comm) 103, at [35].

[314] At paras 24E-016 to 24-017. This was accepted, obiter, by Slade J in *Winkworth v Christie, Manson and Woods Ltd* [1980] Ch 496, at 501 and 514.

[315] See *Kahler v Midland Bank Ltd* [1950] AC 24 and *Zivnostenska Banks v Frankman* [1950] AC 57 and the explanation of those decisions by Upjohn J in *Re Helbert Wagg & Co Ltd* [1956] Ch 323, at 352 and by Moore-Bick J in *Glencore International AG v Metro Trading Inc* [2001] 1 All ER (Comm) 103, at [27].

[316] The UNIDROIT Convention of 2001 on international interests in mobile equipment, which was signed on 16 November 2001 and entered into force on 1 April 2004. It has not yet been ratified by the UK.

was also signed on that occasion.[317] In 2007, another protocol was signed, dealing with railway rolling stock.[318] The scheme of the Convention is to lay down a set of rules for various types of mobile equipment having an international character of usage, which can be adopted or varied in a modified form to suit the specific circumstances of different types of equipment by the relevant protocols. The Convention provides for the recognition in the signatory States of security interests and quasi-security interests (i.e. title retention through conditional sale and leasing) in equipment which is capable of moving from one State to another. It will thus be of benefit to equipment financiers who provide secured finance or title finance through the mechanisms of conditional sale or lease. The Convention also allows for a protocol to extend its application to sales of equipment and the consequences of such sales. Central to the Convention is the concept of an international interest in mobile equipment. The Convention will apply where the relevant debtor is situated in a contracting State (the Aircraft Equipment Protocol extends this to situations where an airframe or helicopter is registered in a contracting State). The owner or security holder will be able to protect its interest through registration in an international register established under the relevant protocol. Registration will give notice of an interest to third parties and thus provide for priority, although a contracting State will be able to provide for derogations from the priority rules. The Convention also deals with the assignment of associated rights to the international interest (e.g. to payment by the debtor) and priority matters relevant thereto, the consequences of default by the debtor, and the enforcement of a financier's rights, as well as the effect of a registered interest in an insolvency of the debtor.

4.8.5.4 *Intangible movable property*

The position concerning intangible movable property is more complex, particularly in relation to dealings in debts, which is examined in detail in Chapter 12 and in dematerialised and immobilised securities, which is examined in Chapter 10. Apart from those items, the determination of proprietary rights in other types of monetary obligation and intangible movables will generally be governed by the *lex situs* of the relevant intangible.[319] It has been held that such a rule will apply to

---

[317] Protocol to the Convention on international interests in mobile equipment on matters specific to aircraft equipment, signed on 16 November 2001 and entered into force on 1 March 2006. It has not yet been ratified by the UK.

[318] The Luxembourg Protocol to the Convention on international interests in mobile equipment on matters specific to railway rolling stock, signed in Luxembourg on 23 February 2007. It has not yet been ratified by the UK.

[319] See Staughton and Auld LJJ in *Macmillan Inc v Bishopsgate Investment Trust PLC (No 3)* [1996] 1 WLR 387, at 401–402, and 410.

shares in a corporation,[320] negotiable instruments[321] (which are assimilated to tangible movables, because of the physical piece of paper which encapsulates them), letters of credit,[322] and intellectual property rights.[323] With respect to intellectual property rights, however, the English courts do not have jurisdiction at common law to determine the validity of foreign rights, but, so long as it is unnecessary to determine if those rights are valid, they may determine an action for infringement of those rights in the country where they subsist.[324]

4.8.6 Enforcement by attachment against assets

As a matter of general principle, an English court will not seek to attach assets that are located outside the jurisdiction,[325] and it follows that it would not recognise an attempt by a foreign court to do so outside its own jurisdiction. The House of Lords has held, accordingly, that an English court will not order the attachment of a foreign debt by way of garnishee (or third party debt) order,[326] although it has been suggested that it might be prepared to make such an order if the order would be recognised in the situs of the debt as being effective to discharge the debt.[327] It is submitted that such a qualification is not warranted because it is contrary to the basic principle against making such an order at all.[328]

---

[320] *Macmillan Inc v Bishopsgate Investment Trust PLC (No 3)* [1996] 1 WLR 387.

[321] Ibid. See however s 72 of the Bills of Exchange Act 1882.

[322] *Power Curber International Ltd v National Bank of Kuwait* [1981] 1 WLR 1233.

[323] *Peer International Corp v Termidor Music Publishers Ltd* [2002] EWHC 2675 (Ch).

[324] *Pearce v Ove Arup Partnership Ltd* [2000] Ch 403, which also discusses the decision of the High Court of Australia in *Potter v Broken Hill Proprietary Co Ltd* (1906) 3 CLR 479. Note also that in *Pearce's* case it was said that the same conclusion could be drawn from Art 16(4) of the Brussels Convention of 1968 (Art 16(4) of the Lugano Convention of 1988). By analogy, the same would apply to Art 22(4) of the EC Regulation on jurisdiction and judgments (EC 44/2001 OJ L12/1 16/1/2001).

[325] See Vaughan Williams LJ in *Martin v Nadel (Dresdner Bank, Garnishees)* [1906] 2 KB 26, at 29 and Lord Hoffmann in *Société Eram Shipping Co Ltd v Compagnie Internationale de Navigation* [2003] UKHL 465; [2004] 1 AC 260, at [54]. The court may, however, make an order *in personam* that relates to enforcement of a contract concerning foreign assets, where the defendant is before the court: *British South Africa Co v De Beers Consolidated Mines Ltd* [1912] AC 52.

[326] See Hill J in *Richardson v Richardson* [1927] P 228, at 235–236, approved by the House of Lords in *Société Eram Shipping Co Ltd v Compagnie Internationale de Navigation* [2003] UKHL 465, [2004] 1 AC 260. This was immediately followed by the House of Lords in *Kuwait Oil Tanker Co SAK v UBS AG* [2003] UKHL 31; [2004] 1 AC 300.

[327] See Lords Bingham and Millett in *Société Eram Shipping Co Ltd v Compagnie Internationale de Navigation* [2003] UKHL 465; [2004] 1 AC 260, at [26] and [111].

[328] As the principle was explained by Lord Hoffmann in ibid, at [54]–[59].

4.9 Trusts

4.9.1 Introduction

The Recognition of Trusts Act 1987[329] gives effect in the UK, and thus in English law, to the Hague Convention on the law applicable to trusts and on their recognition.[330] The Act applies the Convention to trusts whenever they were created but without affecting anything done or omitted before 1 August 1987. The concept of a 'trust' is given a wide definition by Article 2 of the Convention, which would cover trusts as understood under English law and certain types of concept that apply in civil law systems. Article 2 also states that the Convention applies to trusts that are created *inter vivos* or on death when the trust assets have been placed under the control of a trustee for the benefit of a beneficiary or for a specified purpose where such trusts are created voluntarily and are evidenced in writing.[331] Section 1(2) of the Act extends this to cover other trusts of property arising under the law of any part of the UK or which arise by virtue of a judicial decision in the UK or elsewhere, such as constructive trusts, which might also arise orally or not be evidenced in writing, and statutory trusts. Matters concerning 'the constitution of trusts and the relationship between settlors, trustees and beneficiaries' are excluded from the ambit of the Rome Convention and Rome I.[332] The position is a little different under Article 1(2)(e) of Rome II, where the exclusion is expressed as concerning 'non-contractual obligations arising from relationships between the settlors, trustees and beneficiaries of a trust created voluntarily'. This could mean that Rome II will be inconsistent with the extension that the 1987 Act gave to the Hague Convention and, to that extent, the Act would have to be repealed,[333] unless the position is dealt with under Article 28 of Rome II.

4.9.2 Scope of application

The Convention draws a distinction between preliminary issues concerning the transactions or instruments under which assets are transferred to the trust, to which the Convention does not apply[334] (and which would therefore fall to be

---

[329] Which came into force on 1 August 1987: Recognition of Trusts Act 1987 (Commencement) Order 1987 (SI 1987/1177).

[330] Concluded on 1 July 1985, which entered into force on 1 January 1992. It was signed by the UK on 10 January 1986 and ratified on 17 November 1989. It has also been ratified (with reservations in some cases) by Australia, Canada, Italy, Luxembourg, Malta, the Netherlands, Liechtenstein, and San Marino.

[331] See also Art 3.

[332] By Art 1(2)(g) in each case.

[333] To the extent that the Act goes beyond the provisions of the Convention, it would not be saved by Art 28 of Rome II.

[334] Art 4.

dealt with in accordance with the applicable law that would normally govern such issues) and matters concerning the validity and administration of a trust, and the rights of beneficiaries, to which the Convention does apply. It is also provided by Article 5 that the Convention does not apply to the extent that the applicable law that would be specified under the Convention does not recognise the trusts or the category of trusts that are involved.

4.9.2.1 Article 13, which does not apply in the UK, provides that a trust does not have to be recognised if it is mainly connected with a State which does not have the institution of trusts or the category of trusts involved. Articles 15 and 16, which apply in the UK, provide for the application of the mandatory provisions of the *lex fori* to the extent they are inconsistent with the provisions of the Convention. Article 18, which also applies in the UK, provides for the provisions of the Convention to be disregarded if their application would be manifestly incompatible with public policy.

4.9.3 The governing law

Articles 6 and 7 lay down the rules to ascertain the governing or applicable law of a trust. Article 6 allows the settlor to choose the governing law, such choice being either express or to be implied from the terms of the trust instrument, interpreted (if necessary) in the light of the circumstances of the case. Article 6 further provides that if the chosen law does not provide for trusts or the category of trusts involved, the choice shall be ignored and the governing law shall be that found by the application of Article 7. In default of a valid choice, Article 7 provides that the governing law of a trust will be that with which it is most closely connected by reference, in particular, to the place of administration of the trust designated by the settlor, the situs of the trust assets, the place of residence or business of the trustee, and the objects of the trust and the places where the objects are to be fulfilled.

4.9.4 Application of the governing law

Article 8 provides that the governing law will govern matters concerning the validity of the trust, its interpretation, its effect, and its administration. It then sets out a number of matters that in particular would be governed by that law, including the rights, powers, and duties of trustees, their appointment and capacity to act, their powers of administration, investment, disposal, and acquisition of assets, giving security over the assets, distribution of assets, the duration of the trust and the right to accumulate income, the variation or termination of the trust, and the relationship to (and the liability of) the trustees to the beneficiaries.

4.9.5 Recognition of foreign trusts

Article 11 provides for the recognition of foreign trusts that have been validly created in accordance with their governing law, including the recognition of the trust property as a separate fund and the right of the trustee to act as such. It goes on to provide that such recognition shall imply, in particular, that the trust assets will not be considered to be part of the trustee's estate and will not be available to the personal creditors of the trustee, including in the trustee's insolvency. It should also be noted that Article 14 preserves the forum's trust law to the extent that it provides rules that are more favourable to the recognition of trusts.

4.10 The Public Policy Grounds on which an English Court may Refuse to Give Effect to a Foreign Law

4.10.1 Introduction

From the earlier discussion in this chapter, it will be seen that there are circumstances in which an English court is entitled to refuse to give effect to a foreign law which it would otherwise have been obliged to apply with respect to a matter concerning a contract or, when the Rome II Regulation comes into force, a matter concerning a non-contractual civil obligation, such as a tortious or restitutionary claim. That will include situations where the putative applicable law is trumped by the application of the mandatory rules of the forum or by the application of the mandatory rules of the law of a country to which all the circumstances of the case apply except the law that has been chosen by the parties. English law also recognises a further ground on which a court may refuse to give effect to a foreign law, namely, where the foreign law is incompatible with English public policy. Indeed, the UK legislation concerning conflict of laws in tortious matters permits an English court as the forum hearing a claim to refuse to apply a foreign law if it would be manifestly incompatible with the public policy of the forum.[335] It is therefore relevant to examine the grounds on which an English court will refuse to entertain a claim or, in some cases, a defence, because the foreign law on which a claim or defence is based offends against public policy as it is understood by English law.

4.10.2 Recognition v enforcement

It is necessary in this context to distinguish between the concepts of recognition and enforcement, as there may be circumstances where an English court may be prepared to recognise the consequences of a foreign law as it may affect a party to

---

[335] See also s 14(3)(a) of the Private International Law (Miscellaneous Provisions) Act 1995.

proceedings when it would not be prepared to enforce the foreign law in England.[336] By way of example, it will be seen from the discussion below that an English court will not enforce a foreign revenue, penal, or public law. Accordingly, at common law a foreign State cannot sue in England in an action in debt for collection of a foreign tax[337] or fine. Nonetheless, if a trustee has to pay taxes in a foreign country, the trustee should be able to recover the payment out of the trust assets.[338] Similarly, whilst an English court will not enforce a fine payable for breaching the law of a foreign country, neither will it enforce a contract which involves the doing of an unlawful act in a friendly foreign country, such as through the implementation of a scheme for tax evasion[339] or as an evasion of its customs and export regulations,[340] its exchange controls,[341] or its laws on the sale or consumption of certain types of beverages.[342] In *Re Helbert Wagg & Co Ltd*[343] Upjohn J was prepared to recognise the effect of a foreign public law, which was part of the governing law of the contract, by way of exchange and economic control which had the effect of varying the payment obligations on a debt.

4.10.3 Foreign revenue, penal, and other public laws

At common law, an English court will not enforce a foreign revenue,[344] penal,[345] or other public law.[346] It will not do so directly, nor will it do so indirectly.[347] The characterisation of the foreign law will be a matter for the forum, although regard

---

[336] See Robert Walker LJ in *Ispahani v Bank Melli Iran* [1998] Lloyd's Rep Bank 133, at 139.

[337] This is now subject to Art 39 of the EC Regulation on insolvency (EC 1346/2000 OJ L160/1 30/6/2000) and the UNCITRAL Model Law on cross-border insolvency, adopted in Great Britain by the Cross-Border Insolvency Regulations 2006 (SI 2006/1030): see Art 13(3) of the Regulations.

[338] *Re Lord Cable* [1977] 1 WLR 7.

[339] *Re Emery's Investment Trusts* [1959] Ch 410.

[340] *Regazzoni v KC Sethia Ltd* [1958] AC 301.

[341] See Lord Scott in *Far Eastern Shipping Co Public Ltd v Scales Trading Ltd* [2001] 1 All ER (Comm) 319, at 328.

[342] *Foster v Driscoll* [1929] 1 KB 470.

[343] [1956] Ch 323, at 351–352.

[344] *Government of India v Taylor* [1955] AC 491. See however the qualification stated at n 337 above.

[345] *Huntington v Attrill* [1893] AC 150, but held on the facts not to be a claim to enforce a penal law.

[346] See Lord Denning MR in *A-G of New Zealand v Ortiz* [1984] AC 1 (affd on different grounds) and *A-G (UK) v Heinemann Publishers Australia Pty Ltd* (1988) 165 CLR 30 (High Ct of Aust).

[347] *Rossano v Manufacturers' Life Insurance Co Ltd* [1963] 2 QB 352 (a foreign tax law); *QRS 1 Aps v Fransden* [1999] 3 All ER 289 (a foreign tax law); *Banco de Vizcaya v Don Alfonso de Bourbon y Austria* [1935] 1 KB 140 (a foreign penal law); *A-G of New Zealand v Ortiz* [1984] AC 1 (affd on different grounds) (a foreign penal or public law); *United States of America v Inkley* [1989] QB 255 (a foreign penal or public law).

will be had to the perceived character of the law in that foreign country.[348] The general policy which underlies this approach is that such laws are of a sovereign character and involve the exercise by the State of its sovereign authority, which is not justiciable before the English courts. On the other hand, if the foreign State is bringing a claim that could be brought by an ordinary citizen and which does not involve the assertion of a sovereign right then the claim should be justiciable.[349]

A penal law has been defined in this context to mean a fine or other exaction, having a criminal complexion, imposed by a State for a violation of the public order.[350] It is not easy to define the class of foreign laws that might be considered as 'other public laws', where they are not also of a revenue or penal nature. Whilst there is an overlap in the concepts of a revenue or penal law and a public law[351] as, by definition, laws that are of a revenue or penal character must also be public in their nature, the reverse may not necessarily be the case. The Court of Appeal has said that in assessing whether a claim was based upon a foreign revenue, penal, or other public law, the court should consider the party in whose favour the claim was created, the purpose of the foreign law, and the general context of the claim.[352] In essence, the court is seeking to determine if the claim which is based on such laws is a claim which asserts sovereign authority.[353] The types of foreign laws that fall within the description of 'other public laws' will include such matters as exchange controls,[354] currency, economic and price controls,[355] export controls,[356] and foreign defence and security matters.[357] A foreign law imposing exemplary or multiple damages would probably not be considered at common law as falling within the category of an objectionable foreign public law[358] but it has effectively been made such by statute,[359] as has the enforcement of certain foreign anti-trust laws.[360]

4.10.3.1

---

348 *Huntington v Attrill* [1893] AC 150, at 155.

349 *Mbasogo v Logo Ltd* [2006] EWCA Civ 1370, [2007] QB 846, applied in *Tasarrif Murduati Sigorta Fonu v Demirel* [2006] EWHC 3354 (Ch) (appealed on other grounds: [2007] EWCA Civ 799).

350 *Huntington v Attrill* [1893] AC 150, at 155.

351 See, for instance, the difference between Lord Denning MR and Ackner and O'Connor LJJ in *A-G of New Zealand v Ortiz* [1984] AC 1 (affd on different grounds).

352 *United States of America v Inkley* [1989] QB 255, at 265–266.

353 *Mbasogo v Logo Ltd* [2006] EWCA Civ 1370, [2007] QB 846.

354 *Camdex International Ltd v Bank of Zambia* [1997] 6 Bank LR 44; *Isphani v Bank Melli Iran* [1998] Lloyd's Rep Bank 133, at 139.

355 See *Dicey, Morris & Collins* at para 5-033.

356 Lord Denning MR in *A-G of New Zealand v Ortiz* [1984] AC 1.

357 *A-G (UK) v Heinemann Publishers Australia Pty Ltd* (1988) 165 CLR 30 (High Ct of Aust).

358 Lord Denning MR in *SA Consortium General Textiles v Sun and Sand Agencies Ltd* [1978] QB 279, at 299–300 said it would not be considered as offending against English public policy.

359 S 5 of the Protection of Trading Interests Act 1980, and see the interpretation thereof by the Court of Appeal in *Lewis v Eliades* [2003] EWCA Civ 1758, [2004] 1 WLR 692.

360 S 1 of the Protection of Trading Interests Act 1980, implemented by the Protection of Trading Interests (US Antitrust Measures) Order 1983 (SI 1983/900).

4.10.3.2 It may sometimes be questionable whether what appears in the guise of a private right is really of a public nature so that it might be considered to be a foreign revenue, penal, or other public law, rather than a private right.[361] For instance, in some States public utilities are part of the government and an attempt by the utility to recover charges and levies may be viewed as relating to a foreign revenue or penal law.[362] In other States, the same functions may now rest in the hands of non-governmental corporate bodies, and it is questionable if the same view would be taken; it might, rather, be viewed as the recovery of a debt for the supply of goods or services. However, the position may be further complicated if such a body, whilst itself being a private entity, was exercising powers that were conferred on it by statute, and it might be argued that it was really performing a public function on behalf of the State. Once again, the clue in seeking to resolve this dilemma may be to ask whether the claim is, essentially, based upon an exercise of sovereign authority and thus is of a sovereign character, or whether, by contrast, it is a private law nature even if it is asserted by, or on behalf of, a foreign State or governmental entity.

4.10.4 Foreign laws that offend against English principles

An English court will not recognise,[363] nor will it enforce, a foreign law or a transaction with a foreign State that is repugnant to English principles of public policy, in the sense that the foreign law or transaction outrages its sense of justice, fairness, and decency.[364] Public policy for these purposes is to be judged by contemporary standards[365] and in an international rather than a purely domestic sense, so that considerations that may be relevant in a domestic setting may not necessarily be applied at the transnational level.[366] Where public policy intervenes, it will cut across the act of State doctrine[367] under which the acts of a foreign State within its own territory are considered to be 'non-justiciable' before the national courts of another State.[368]

---

[361] See the discussion in *United States of America v Inkley* [1989] QB 255, but at least in that case it was a foreign State which had brought the proceedings to recover the penalty. See also the outcome in *Huntington v Attrill* [1893] AC 150.

[362] See, for instance, *Municipal Council of Sydney v Bull* [1909] 1 KB 7.

[363] For instance, in *Kuwait Airways Corp v Iraqi Airways Co* [2002] UKHL 19, [2002] 2 AC 883, the House of Lords refused to give any recognition to the domestic effect in the relevant foreign country of a law of the country that infringed this principle.

[364] Per Scarman J in *Re Fuld's Estate (No 3)* [1968] P 675, at 698. See also Lord Nicholls in *Kuwait Airways Corp v Iraqi Airways Co* [2002] UKHL 19; [2002] 2 AC 883, at [18].

[365] Per Lord Nicholls in ibid, at [28].

[366] See Lord Steyn in ibid, at [114].

[367] For that doctrine, see Lord Wilberforce in *Buttes Gas and Oil Co v Hammer (Nos 2 & 3)* [1982] AC 888, at 932.

[368] See Lord Nicholls and Lord Hope in *Kuwait Airways Corp v Iraqi Airways Co* [2002] UKHL 19; [2002] 2 AC 883, at, respectively, [26] and [135]–[138].

It has been held that the following are repugnant to such principles of public policy: foreign laws that are racially discriminatory and confiscatory,[369] foreign laws that are in breach of human rights,[370] foreign laws where English concepts of morality have been infringed,[371] where the observance or enforcement of a foreign law would be contrary to English principles of justice,[372] a contract with an enemy alien,[373] and a foreign law that represents a flagrant violation of the rules of international law that are of fundamental importance, especially those exemplified by the Charter of the United Nations or as laid down by a resolution of the UN Security Council.[374] In a related area, it has also been held that an English court will not enforce a contract to perform an act in a foreign friendly country that is contrary to the laws of that country.[375]

4.10.4.1

4.10.5 Foreign expropriation of assets

Public policy may also intervene, but to a more limited extent, in cases which involve assets that have been the subject of an expropriation under a foreign law.[376] There are a three preliminary matters that may need to be taken into account in considering an allegation that there has been such an expropriation. The first is the need to determine whether the foreign State did purport to expropriate the particular asset concerned or if it falls outside the category of the assets that were intended to be expropriated.[377] Secondly, it may be necessary to determine if the act of the foreign State might fall within the categories of acts that transgress the principles of English public policy in the manner outlined above, so that an English court would refuse to give any effect to the purported act of expropriation.[378] Thirdly, it may be necessary to consider if the entity that purported to expropriate the asset would be considered by an English court as having had the authority to

---

[369] See Upjohn J in *Re Helbert Wagg & Co Ltd* [1957] Ch 323, at 334 and Lord Cross of Chelsea in *Oppenheimer v Cattermole (Inspector of Taxes)* [1976] AC 249, at 277–278.

[370] See Lord Steyn in *Kuwait Airways Corp v Iraqi Airways Co* [2002] UKHL 19; [2002] 2 AC 883, at [115].

[371] *Robinson v Bland* (1760) 2 Burr 1077, at 1084; *Mitsubishi Corp v Aristidis I Alafouzos* [1988] 1 Lloyd's Rep 191.

[372] E.g. a contract obtained by duress or undue influence: *Royal Boskalis Westminster NV v Mountain* [1999] QB 674; *Israel Discount Bank of New York v Hadjipateras* [1984] 1 WLR 137.

[373] *Robson v Premier Oil and Pipe Line Co* [1915] 2 Ch 124; *Dynamit AG v Rio Tinto Co Ltd* [1918] AC 260.

[374] This was the decision in *Kuwait Airways Corp v Iraqi Airways Co* [2002] UKHL 19, [2002] 2 AC 883.

[375] *Foster v Driscoll* [1929] 1 KB 470; *Regazzoni v KC Sethia Ltd* [1958] AC 301.

[376] The expression 'expropriation' is used here to describe the process by which a State purports compulsorily to deprive a person of its ownership of an asset, whether by way of confiscation or requisition without payment or acquisition in return for payment, and whether the consequence is to vest the asset in the State or some other entity.

[377] *Lecouturier v Rey* [1910] AC 262.

[378] As, for instance, was the case in *Kuwait Airways Corp v Iraqi Airways Co* [2002] UKHL 19, [2002] 2 AC 883.

act in that fashion, particularly in circumstances where there had been a change of regime and the new regime had effected the expropriation.

4.10.5.1 In relation to the third of those matters, the policy of the UK since 1980 has been to recognise foreign States rather than governments, so there will be no official guidance available from the Crown in deciding if recognition should be accorded to foreign governments or other executive bodies and the acts they carry out. However, the question as to the authority and legitimacy of a foreign regime to act as the government of a foreign State has been considered by the English courts in the context of action taken by a new regime, and certain guidelines have been laid down. The guidelines were set out by Hobhouse J in *Republic of Somalia v Woodhouse Drake & Carey (Suisse) SA, The Mary*.[379] They were followed and applied by Cresswell J in *Sierra Leone Telecommunications Co Ltd v Barclays Bank PLC*.[380] Before setting out the guidelines, Hobhouse J had said that if Her Majesty's Government was already dealing with the foreign government or regime on a regular and normal basis then it would be likely that the English courts would treat such a foreign government or regime as the legitimate authority of the foreign State.[381] The guidelines are as follows:

(a) whether the foreign body is the constitutional government of the State;

(b) the degree, nature, and stability of administrative control, if any, that it exercises over the territory of the State;

(c) whether Her Majesty's Government has any dealings with it and if so what is the nature of those dealings; and

(d) in marginal cases, the extent of international recognition that it has as the government of the State.

4.10.5.2 Subject to what has already been said, the basic principle that will apply in considering an act of expropriation is that, in pursuance of the act of State doctrine, a foreign State has sovereign authority within its own territory. Accordingly, assets that are within that State at the time of the expropriation will normally be considered by an English court to have been effectively subject to the expropriation. In consequence, title in those assets will vest in accordance with the act of expropriation, and such title will be acknowledged even if the assets subsequently leave that State[382] until, of course, title passes again in accordance with the relevant rules previously discussed in this chapter.

---

[379] [1993] QB 54, at 68.
[380] [1998] 2 All ER 821, at 829.
[381] [1993] QB 54, at 65–66.
[382] *Luther v Sagor* [1921] 3 KB 532; *Princess Olga Paley v Weisz* [1929] 1 KB 718; *Williams and Humbert Ltd v W and H Trade Marks (Jersey) Ltd* [1986] AC 368.

However, if the assets are not in the foreign State at the time of its purported expropriation of them, an English court will not recognise the intended effect of the foreign law,[383] even if the assets are requisitioned by a foreign State which is in friendly relations with the UK, it is for a limited period and in return for compensation.[384] Neither the nationality of the owner of the assets nor the fact that compensation may be paid is relevant to the foregoing considerations.[385] **4.10.5.3**

It should follow from the foregoing that if assets that originally were not within the foreign country are taken into it and by its terms are then subject to the act of expropriation under the law of that country, that act will be recognised as being effective. **4.10.5.4**

The principles outlined above are subject to a qualification concerning an entitlement to the possession, or an immediate right to the possession, of tangible movables, where the relevant goods have been bailed to another person. In such a case, the entitlement will be ascertained in accordance with the contract of bailment and will be determined by the governing law of the contract, so that if under the governing law they may not be returned to the bailor's possession, it would appear that an English court would refuse to restore possession to the bailor.[386] This would appear to be the case even if the bailor's right to possession had, effectively, been expropriated by virtue of a change in the law governing the contract of bailment. The effect of this qualification can amount to a shameful lapse in the public policy concerns in English law for justice, fairness, and decency. **4.10.5.5**

4.11 Investment and Foreign Exchange Controls and Similar Legislation

4.11.1 Introduction

Foreign countries not infrequently impose restrictions on commercial activities, such as in requiring official consents and the like to be obtained before a contract may be entered into or performed. In similar vein, a State may impose restrictions

---

[383] *Bank Voor Handel en Scheepvaart NV v Slatford* [1953] QB 248 and *Peer International Corp v Termidor Music Publishers Ltd* [2002] EWHC 2675 (Ch) (Neuberger J 11/12/2002) and [2003] EWCA Civ 1156, [2004] Ch 212 (Court of Appeal).

[384] See the Court of Appeal in *Peer International Corp v Termidor Music Publishers Ltd* [2003] EWCA Civ 1156, [2004] Ch 212 overruling the decision of Atkinson J in *Lorentzen v Lydden & Co Ltd* [1942] 2 KB 202.

[385] Ibid, and Upjohn J in *Re Helbert Wagg & Co Ltd* [1956] Ch 323.

[386] See *Kahler v Midland Bank Ltd* [1950] AC 24 and *Zivnostenska Banks v Frankman* [1950] AC 57 and the explanation of those decisions by Upjohn J in *Re Helbert Wagg & Co Ltd* [1956] Ch 323, at 352 and by Moore-Bick J in *Glencore International AG v Metro Trading Inc* [2001] 1 All ER (Comm) 103, at [27].

on the acquisition and use of assets within its territory, such as by limiting the ability of externally situated investors to invest in or to hold assets in the country. For most practical purposes, the effect of such restrictions is likely to be determined by the courts within the State concerned. Sometimes, however, the issue may be pertinent to proceedings before an English court and so it is relevant to discuss the extent to which an English court would be willing to recognise or enforce such a restriction. The discussion will examine the general position at common law and then look at the particular position concerning exchange control legislation.

4.11.2 Common law

The position at common law is an application of matters that have been addressed above. In relation to the performance of contractual obligations, if the governing law of the contract would refuse to give effect to the contract because the performance of the relevant obligation was unlawful then an English court would not require performance of the contract. That may be the case, for instance, because the governing law was the same as the law of the place of performance. Similarly, a contract that was governed by English law would excuse performance if it was unlawful to perform the contractual obligation in the place in which performance was required to be undertaken by the contract. However, if the contract, interpreted in accordance with its governing law, permitted performance of the obligation in another country where it could validly be performed then an English court would not excuse the obligation. The court would require such performance to take place, notwithstanding that it may be unlawful to do so by the law of the place of residence or nationality of the party that was required to perform the obligation or that such law might have excused the requirement to perform.[387] An English court would not require performance of an act that was unlawful in a foreign friendly country, nor will it recognise or enforce a foreign law that offended against English public policy, such as by being racially oppressive or discriminatory. An English court will not enforce a foreign public law, such as a foreign exchange control law, but it may recognise the effect of such a law, if it forms part of the governing law of the contract, in determining if a party's contractual obligations have been discharged.

4.11.2.1   If the law of a foreign State restricts or imposes conditions upon the entitlement of a national or any other person or entity to invest in or own assets within the State,

---

[387] See *Kleinwort Sons & Co v Ungarische Baumwolle Industrie AG* [1939] 2 KB 678; *Toprak v Finagrain* [1979] 2 Lloyd's Rep 98; *Libyan Arab Foreign Bank v Bankers Trust Co* [1989] QB 728; and Aikens J in *The Argo Fund Ltd v Essar Steel Ltd* [2005] EWHC 600 (Comm), [2005] 2 Lloyd's Rep 203 (affd *Essar Steel Ltd v The Argo Fund Ltd* [2006] EWCA Civ 241, [2006] 2 Lloyd's Rep 134). See, however, the earlier discussion at para 4.5.8.8, concerning the effect of Rome I, should it come into force in the UK.

that should be a matter for its sovereign competence, with which the English courts will not interfere, except to the extent that the court may refuse to recognise the consequences of a foreign law that offended against English public policy. As discussed earlier, in so far as a restriction under a foreign law purports to have an effect on the proprietary entitlement to assets that are located outside the territory of the relevant foreign State, an English court would not be prepared to give effect to it, as it would be considered to be beyond the legislative competence of the relevant country.[388]

4.11.3 Foreign exchange control regulations

The UK presently does not have any exchange control regulations of its own, the previous legislation having been suspended and then repealed.[389] However, the UK is a signatory to the International Monetary Fund Agreement (the 'Bretton Woods Agreement'). Article VIII(2)(b) of the Agreement, which has the force of law in the UK,[390] has the effect of requiring the courts in the UK to refuse enforcement of exchange contracts that are in breach of another country's exchange control laws. By virtue of Articles 7(2) and 21 of the Rome Convention,[391] an English court would be obliged to apply the article in precedence to the conflicting effect of a foreign law of a third country that might otherwise be applicable to the relevant contractual obligations. Article VII(2)(b) provides as follows:

> Exchange contracts which involve the currency of any member [of the International Monetary Fund] and which are contrary to the exchange control regulations of any member maintained or imposed consistently with [the Bretton Woods Agreement] shall be unenforceable in the territories of any member.

The article applies to 'exchange contracts', which has been given a rather limited interpretation. In *Wilson, Smithett and Cope Ltd v Terruzzi*[392] Lord Denning MR said[393] that an exchange contract was a transaction to exchange the currency of one country for the currency of another. This was upheld by Lord Diplock in the House of Lords in *United City Merchants (Investments) Ltd v Royal Bank of Canada*[394] who said that the expression should be 'confined to contracts to exchange the currency

4.11.3.1

---

[388] See the discussion above, at para 4.10.5.3.

[389] The UK used to have exchange controls under The Exchange Control Act 1947. The operation of that Act was suspended by the Exchange Control (General Exemption) Order 1979 (SI 1979/1660) and the Act was finally repealed by s 72(7) of the Finance Act 1987.

[390] Pursuant to the Bretton Woods Agreement Order in Council (SR&O 1946 No 36, Art 3) made under the Bretton Woods Agreements Act 1945 and continued under s 6(2) of the International Monetary Fund Act 1979.

[391] And, if it comes into force, Arts 9 and (assuming due notification to the European Commission by the UK) 25 of the Rome I Regulation.

[392] [1976] QB 683.

[393] At 714.

[394] [1983] 1 AC 168, at 188.

of one country for the currency of another; it does not include contracts entered into in connection with sales of goods which require the conversion by the buyer of one currency into another in order to enable him to pay the purchase price'. This view may be contrasted with a wider interpretation that Lord Denning had previously given in *Sharif v Azad*[395] where his Lordship had said that an exchange contract included a contract that 'in any way affects the country's exchange resources'.

4.11.3.2 On the other hand, it has also been held that the court must look at the substance of the transaction and not its form. Hence, a disguised transaction will be caught.[396] Accordingly, the court can look behind the apparent independent nature of an instrument, such as a negotiable instrument[397] or a letter of credit[398] to discern the true guise of the transaction. Nonetheless, in light of the narrow scope of the definition of an exchange contract, it is possible that an obligation to repay a genuine loan, and to pay interest thereon, in the currency in which the loan was advanced would not be an obligation under an exchange contract and so, if otherwise valid, would be enforceable before the English courts.

4.11.3.3 Various other points have also been dealt with by the courts in considering Article VIII(2)(b). The effect of a breach of the article is to make the transaction unenforceable but not illegal,[399] so that, for instance, if there has been a total failure of consideration, any money paid under the transaction should be recoverable.[400] If part of the transaction is affected and another part is genuinely not part of it, only the tainted part of the transaction will be unenforceable,[401] assuming that the contract can be severed. The court is obliged to take notice that a transaction involves an exchange contract, even if it is not raised by the parties and irrespective of the governing law of the transaction or the place for its performance.[402] However, the court will require to be satisfied that the relevant country is a member of the IMF and that its exchange control regulations were maintained in accordance with the Bretton Woods Agreement.[403]

4.11.3.4 It is not clear if the relevant exchange control regulations of the country concerned must have been in force and applied to the transaction at both the date of contracting and at the time for performance of the transaction, or whether the only

---

[395] [1967] 1 QB 605, at 613–614.
[396] *Wilson, Smithett and Cope Ltd v Terruzzi* [1976] QB 683; *United City Merchants (Investments) Ltd v Royal Bank of Canada* [1983] 1 AC 168.
[397] *Mansouri v Singh* [1986] 1 WLR 1393.
[398] *United City Merchants (Investments) Ltd v Royal Bank of Canada* [1983] 1 AC 168.
[399] *Singh Batra v Ebrahim* [1982] 2 Lloyd's Rep 11; *United City Merchants (Investments) Ltd v Royal Bank of Canada* [1983] 1 AC 168.
[400] See Lord Denning MR in *Singh Batra v Ebrahim* [1982] 2 Lloyd's Rep 11, at 13.
[401] Ibid.
[402] *Singh Batra v Ebrahim* [1982] 2 Lloyd's Rep 11; *United City Merchants (Investments) Ltd v Royal Bank of Canada* [1983] 1 AC 168.
[403] *Mansouri v Singh* [1986] 1 WLR 1393.

relevant date is the date of performance. It seems sensible to take the view that regulations which had ceased to apply to the transaction at the time for its performance would not be considered to be relevant. The position is more difficult where the regulations (or their application to a transaction) had come into force after the date of contracting but before the date for performance of the transaction. By analogy with the effect of the supervening illegality in *Ralli Bros v Compania Naviera Sota y Aznar*[404] it might be possible to say that the court should apply the regulation and refuse to give effect to the transaction. On the other hand, it appears that Article VIII was aimed at denying assistance to 'Parties entering into exchange contracts',[405] from which it might be thought that the intention was to strike only at transactions which infringed the regulations at the time of contracting.[406]

In view of the limited interpretation that the courts have given to the expression 'exchange contracts', it is relevant to consider if the common law principles that are outlined above may still remain relevant to the extent that a transaction falls outside the compass of Article VIII of the Bretton Woods Agreement. That will depend upon whether the intention in implementing the article as part of the law of the UK was to legislate entirely with respect to the consequences of foreign exchange controls, or if the intention was only to legislate for the specific matter of exchange contracts. The article is expressly confined to the effect of exchange contracts, and it is difficult to envisage that, in its implementation as part of the law in the UK, it was intended to change the law in relation to matters that were not specifically addressed by the article.[407]

4.11.3.5

---

[404] [1920] 2 KB 287.

[405] See para 1 of the *Interpretation* that was issued by the Executive Directors of the IMF, which is quoted in *Dicey, Morris & Collins* at para 36-070.

[406] This is the view that is taken by Procter in *Mann on the Legal Aspect of Money* (6th edn, 2005) at para 15.28.

[407] This was the view which was taken by Robert Walker LJ in his discussion of the point in *Isphani v Bank Melli Iran* [1998] Lloyd's Rep Bank 133, at 137–139.

5

CROSS-BORDER INSOLVENCIES

5.1 Introduction

5.1.1 An initial point to make in a discussion about cross-border insolvency is that a distinction must be drawn between States on the one hand and other types of legal entities and persons on the other hand. Whilst a State may demonstrate the economic characteristics of being insolvent, a State cannot be made the subject of insolvency proceedings, unlike the position for everyone else. What follows in this chapter will therefore concern the types of entity and persons that can be the subject of insolvency proceedings. The position concerning States will be reviewed in Chapter 7.

5.1.2 A cross-border insolvency is likely to involve an individual or a corporate entity (for convenience, hereunder referred to as the 'debtor') which has become insolvent and which has a presence and assets that are located (using that term rather loosely) in more than one jurisdiction. The debtor is also likely to have creditors in different jurisdictions. This will probably mean that the debtor, its assets, and its creditors may, in addition to, or to the exclusion of, England, be subject to the jurisdiction of courts and insolvency proceedings in one or more different countries.

5.1.3 An English court may have to determine the effect in England of those various factors, including if England is an appropriate place for insolvency proceedings to be commenced or maintained, the domestic, foreign law, and jurisdictional issues that may arise, and the possibility of concurrent insolvency proceedings in the other jurisdictions (including the fact that other jurisdictions may apply different insolvency rules to those which apply in England). The court will also have to consider the theoretical and practical hurdles that must be overcome if the various jurisdictions and their insolvency practitioners are to recognise each other's proceedings and achieve some consensus for the benefit of all the creditors of the debtor. Similarly, a court in a foreign jurisdiction may have to consider similar issues, but it may not come to the same conclusions as an English court. It is not possible in this work to say what courts in other jurisdictions would make of such a situation, although the discussion may highlight the issues that would need to be considered. Nonetheless, in light of EC legislation, in cross-border insolvency proceedings that are within the confines of the EU (except Denmark[1]), a common

---

[1] For the purposes of the discussion that follows, Denmark will be treated as if it were not an EU country.

approach to jurisdictional matters should be taken by courts in other EU countries to that which would be taken by the English courts.

What follows will examine the attitude that an English court would take in 5.1.4 addressing such a situation. As the issues are more likely to arise in a commercial and corporate context than in an entirely private situation, the analysis will concentrate on the insolvency of corporate entities rather than individual debtors.

The approach to insolvency that is taken by English law is made up of a mixture 5.1.5 of English statutory and common law, and the modifications to that law that have been brought about by EC law and the UNCITRAL (the United Nations Commission On International Trade Law) Model law on cross-border insolvency. To set the scene, the discussion will begin with a brief review of domestic insolvency proceedings and other matters that arise in an English context. It will then move to an examination of the cross-border issues.

5.2 Domestic Insolvency Proceedings

5.2.1 Insolvency and insolvency proceedings

Under English law, a corporate debtor is judged to be insolvent if it is unable to pay its debts[2] which, essentially, comes down to being unable to pay its debts as they fall due for payment,[3] or if its assets are less than its liabilities (taking into account its contingent and prospective liabilities).[4] As a matter of domestic law concerning local debtors, if a corporate debtor is insolvent it may find itself subject to winding up (or liquidation) proceedings[5] (bankruptcy if the debtor is an individual), an administration (which, with the exception of insolvent partnerships, does not concern individuals), a scheme of arrangement under section 895 of the Companies Act 2006[6] if it is a company, a voluntary arrangement, or a receivership of its business or assets. It may also come to entirely private arrangements with some or all of its creditors. Sometimes there may be a combination or succession of more than one insolvency procedure as, for instance, where a voluntary arrangement or a scheme of arrangement is put in place for a company that is in administration and a receivership may continue during a liquidation.

---

2 S 122 (1)(e) of the Insolvency Act 1986.

3 Which arises under s 123(1) of the Insolvency Act 1986 and may be based on the failure to pay a specific creditor which has taken action to enforce or establish its debt or on the basis of a deficiency in present and anticipated cash flows: see *Re Cheyne Finance plc* [2007] EWHC 2402 (Ch).

4 See s 123(2) of the Insolvency Act 1986.

5 Insolvency is the principal reason for a company to be wound up but there are other grounds as well, such as the court is of the opinion that it is just and equitable for it to be wound up or on grounds of public interest. See ss 122 and 124A of the Insolvency Act 1986 (as amended).

6 Formerly s 425 of the Companies Act 1985.

5.2.1.1 An English company may be wound up compulsorily by the court pursuant to section 117 of the Insolvency Act 1986, or it may be wound up voluntarily under section 84 of that Act. A company that is incorporated under one of the Companies Acts may go into administration or a voluntary arrangement.[7] These various possibilities are subject to the operation of the EC Regulation on insolvency proceedings[8] (hereinafter referred to as the EC Insolvency Regulation), as will be explained further below.

5.2.1.2 *Winding up and bankruptcy*

The winding up (also called liquidation) of a company will lead to the cessation of its activities, the distribution of its assets to its creditors, and its dissolution. Bankruptcy of an individual places his affairs and assets in the hands of his trustee, who distributes the assets to his creditors, and, eventually, the bankrupt receives his discharge and returns to normal life.

5.2.1.3 *Administration*

An administration of a company will confer immediate protection from enforcement and similar action by its creditors, including secured creditors and title financiers, and will usually be intended to achieve, in whole or in part, the restructuring of its affairs, if that is possible, which could include a compromise or arrangement with its creditors. An insolvency practitioner (sometimes there may be more than one), called the administrator, is appointed and he takes charge of the company, its business, and its assets. Whilst there are certain similarities between administration and the US procedure of Chapter 11 bankruptcy proceedings, such as in relation to the protection that is given against enforcement action, there are a number of differences as well, particularly in the way that the affairs of the debtor are conducted. Under administration, the directors and management cease to have authority to run the company and the administrator takes charge. The administrator then prepares a plan for the way forward and puts it to the creditors for them to vote upon it. Under US Chapter 11 proceedings, the existing management are usually not dispossessed in the same fashion and it can be seen as a form of debtor in possession proceedings. The management will put forward a plan to the creditors and stockholders as to restructuring and the way forward on which they will vote. The plan must also be submitted to the court for its approval. In addition, there are procedures available within Chapter 11 proceedings for new debt to be raised which by law is given a right of repayment in priority to existing indebtedness.[9] No such advantage exists within an administration and any new

---

7 See the Insolvency Act 1986 (Amendment) Regs (SI 2005/879).
8 EC 1346/2000 OJ L160/1 30/6/2000.
9 See § 364 of the US Bankruptcy Code.

finance has to be negotiated on its own merits, although sometimes it might be provided within an existing secured facility.

5.2.1.4 *Voluntary arrangement*

A voluntary arrangement is a procedure under which, with the approval of specified majorities of its shareholders and creditors, a company (or an individual) may arrive at a compromise with its creditors. If the necessary votes are achieved, the arrangement will be binding upon all of its creditors (although it cannot affect the right of a secured creditor to enforce its security, without that creditor's consent). For certain corporate debtors, a moratorium is imposed on the creditors so as to prevent them from taking action against the company and its assets whilst proposals for the arrangement are being put forward and considered.

5.2.1.5 *Receivership*

Unlike the other procedures, which are collective insolvency procedures concerning the debtor and all of its creditors, receivership is really an enforcement procedure for the protection and realisation of an individual secured creditor's security, which is initiated by that creditor for its own benefit.[10] Administrative receivership[11] is a form of comprehensive enforcement procedure under which a receiver and manager is appointed to the whole or substantially the whole of a company's assets and undertaking.[12]

5.2.2 Foreign debtors

The position in England with respect to foreign debtors is as follows. The court has jurisdiction to wind up a foreign company pursuant to section 221 of the Insolvency Act 1986, if the company is insolvent.[13] The position concerning the bankruptcy of individuals with a foreign connection is provided for by section 265 of that Act. However, if the centre of main interests of the debtor (whether a corporate or an individual debtor) is located within another EC country, the power to institute insolvency proceedings in England is limited by the EC Insolvency Regulation.[14] A foreign company may go into administration or

---

[10] With the exception of the rare occasions where the court may appoint a receiver pursuant to s 37(1) of the Supreme Court Act 1981.

[11] S 72A of the Insolvency Act 1986 takes away the right to appoint an administrative receiver in many cases, where the security was taken after 15/9/2003.

[12] See the definition of 'administrative receiver' in s 29(2) of the Insolvency Act 1986. It encapsulates more neatly and precisely the concept that lies behind the definition of a 'holder of a qualifying floating charge' in para 14 of Sched B1 to that Act.

[13] A foreign company cannot be wound up voluntarily. See s 221(4) of the Insolvency Act 1986.

[14] As well as by the Credit Institutions (Reorganisation and Winding Up) Regs (SI 2004/1045) and the Insurers (Reorganisation and Winding Up) Regs (SI 2004/353), which are derived from EC Directives.

voluntary arrangement if it is incorporated in another EEA Member State or has its centre of main interests in an EC State,[15] including the UK.[16] Once again, this is limited by or in consequence of EC legislation.

5.2.2.1   The apparently wide power that the court is given to wind up foreign companies under section 221 of the Insolvency Act 1986 is limited by EC legislation, by the fact that it is a discretionary power,[17] and by three limits that the courts have imposed upon their own powers. Those limits were spelt out by Lloyd J in *Re Latreefers Inc, Stocznia Gdanska v Latreefers Inc*[18] as follows:

(1)   There must be a sufficient connection with England and Wales which may, but does not necessarily have to, consist of assets within the jurisdiction.

(2)   There must be a reasonable possibility, if a winding-up order is made, of benefit to those applying for the winding-up order.

(3)   One or more persons interested in the distribution of assets of the company must be persons over whom the court can exercise a jurisdiction.

In that case, it was held that the possibility of a liquidator bringing claims for misfeasance or wrongful or fraudulent trading might be sufficient within the first of the grounds. However, in another case,[19] the Court of Appeal held that the second ground had not been fulfilled where claims that the liquidator might wish to bring against a third party, upon which it was said the first ground was met, could not be pursued or enforced effectively.

5.2.3 Secured creditors in an insolvency

At common law, secured creditors have traditionally been given a large degree of protection, so that their security has been unaffected by the insolvency of the debtor which has given the security. Generally speaking, and subject to the requisite grounds for enforcement having occurred, secured creditors have been entitled to have recourse to their security as and when they felt like it, without having to pay much regard to the interests of the debtor, its liquidator, or the general body of its unsecured creditors.[20]

---

15   See the Insolvency Act 1986 (Amendment) Regs (SI 2005/879).

16   Although it pre-dates the relevant statutory instrument, such an order was made in relation to a corporation established in Delaware, which had its centre of main interests in England: *Re BRAC Rent-A-Car International Inc* [2003] EWHC 128 (Ch), [2003] 1 WLR 1421.

17   See Morritt LJ in *Re Latreefers Inc, Stocznia Gdanska v Latreefers Inc* [2001] 2 BCLC 116, at 140.

18   [2001] 2 BCLC 116, at 120. It was expressly approved by the Court of Appeal in the same case, at [2001] 2 BCLC 116, at 137–141.

19   *Banco Nacional de Cuba v Cosmos Trading Corp* [2000] 1 BCLC 813.

20   See, for instance, the explanation of the position of secured creditors provided by Lord Millett in *Re Leyland DAF, Buchler v Talbot* [2004] UKHL 9, [2004] 2 AC 298 and the description of the considerations concerning the exercise of their rights in *China & South Sea Bank v Tan* [1990] AC 536. Of course, the defaulting debtor can pay off the outstanding amount and resume control

Over the years, the rather sanctified position of secured creditors has been eroded
by statute. Most of the relevant statutory provisions are now to be found in the
Insolvency Act 1986 (as amended),[21] but some relevant provisions will be found
in other legislation. The principal provisions are to the following effect. The net
recoveries under floating charges (that is, charges that were originally created as
floating charges, irrespective of their subsequent crystallisation) have to be made
available to meet the unsatisfied claims of the liquidator for liquidation expenses
and of preferential creditors,[22] and a proportion of such recoveries has to be set
aside for the benefit of unsecured creditors.[23] Any disposition, which includes the
giving of security as well as outright transfers of assets, by a company that is made
after the commencement of its winding up by the court is void, unless validated
by the court.[24] There is a moratorium upon enforcement action by holders of
security and quasi-security from the time that a company begins to go into administration,[25] which continues during the administration.[26] A similar moratorium is
imposed whilst certain types of company are seeking a voluntary arrangement.[27]
The right to appoint an administrative receiver has also been restricted.[28]

5.2.4 Upsetting transactions

The liquidator or administrator of a company is given the power to challenge
transactions, including the giving of security, that have occurred within defined
periods prior to the onset of the liquidation or administration of the company[29]
(sometimes referred to as the process of 'clawback'), and the insolvency practitioner or a 'victim' of a transaction to defraud creditors may also mount such a
challenge.[30] It has been held that the right of the insolvency practitioner or such a
victim to challenge such transactions applies with respect to the beneficiaries of

---

of the asset. It may also apply to the court for an order for sale of the secured property under s 91(2)
of the Law of Property Act 1925. See *Palk v Mortgage Services Funding plc* [1993] Ch 330.

21 References hereinafter to that Act will be to it as amended, including by the Enterprise Act 2002.
22 Respectively, s 176ZA and ss 40 and 175(2)(b) of the Insolvency Act 1986 and s 196 of the
Companies Act 1985.
23 S 176A of the Insolvency Act 1986.
24 S 127(1) of the Insolvency Act 1986. A similar provision concerning individuals is contained
in s 284(1) of the Insolvency Act 1986. For a discussion of the considerations under which the court
would be prepared to validate a disposition and the basis on which a liquidator can reclaim the assets
wrongly disposed of, see *Re Tain Construction Ltd; Rose v AIB Group (UK) PLC* [2003] EWHC 1737
(Ch), [2003] 1 WLR 2791.
25 Para 44 of Sched B1 to the Insolvency Act 1986.
26 Para 43 of Sched B1 to the Insolvency Act 1986.
27 Para 12 of Sched A1 to the Insolvency Act 1986.
28 S 72A of the Insolvency Act 1986.
29 Ss 238 (transactions at an undervalue), 239 (preferences), and 245 (floating charges) of the
Insolvency Act 1986. For the position in the bankruptcy of individuals, see ss 339 (transactions at
an undervalue) and 340 (preferences) of that Act.
30 S 423 of the Insolvency Act 1986.

such transactions wherever they may be, both within and outside the jurisdiction.[31] Although there is no authority expressly on the point, it is reasonable to assume that such a right exists in the case of foreign insolvent debtors just as it applies to cases involving domestic debtors.[32] However, there are various grounds that must be made out if such a challenge is to be made and, even if that is done, the court still has a discretion as to whether it should make an order and as to what it should order. Where the person against whom an order is sought is outside the jurisdiction, it may be necessary to obtain the court's leave to serve the defendant abroad. Sir Donald Nicholls V-C said in *Re Paramount Airways (No 2)*[33] that in deciding if the court should exercise its discretion to make an order against a foreign defendant,

> the court will need to be satisfied that . . . the defendant is sufficiently connected with England for it to be just and proper to make the order against him despite the foreign element . . . the court will look at all the circumstances, including the residence and place of the business of the defendant, his connection with the insolvent [company], the nature and purpose of the transaction being impugned, the nature and locality of the property involved, the circumstances in which the defendant became involved in the transaction or received a benefit from it or acquired the property in question, whether the defendant acted in good faith, and whether under any relevant foreign law the defendant acquired an unimpeachable title free from any claims even if the insolvent had been adjudged bankrupt or wound up locally. The importance to be attached to these factors will vary from case to case. By taking into account and weighing these and any other relevant circumstances, the court will ensure that it does not seek to exercise oppressively or unreasonably the very wide jurisdiction conferred by the sections.[34]

5.2.4.1 In addition to the various statutory grounds for cutting down transactions and the effect of security that have just been mentioned, there is also a compulsory registration requirement relating to the giving of most types of security by companies. A failure to meet those requirements will result in the security being avoided as against the liquidator, administrator, and other 'creditors'[35] of the company.[36]

---

[31] *Re Paramount Airways (No 2)* [1993] Ch 223.

[32] It has been held that the provisions of English insolvency law apply as much to foreign companies as they do to domestic companies. See *Re International Tin Council* [1987] Ch 419, at 446 and *In the matter of HIH Casualty and General Insurance Ltd* [2006] EWCA Civ 732; [2007] 1 All ER 177, at [38].

[33] [1993] Ch 223, at 239.

[34] See also *Re Unigreg Ltd* (unreported 12/2/2004, HHJ Weeks sitting in the Chancery Division of the High Court).

[35] I.e. secured creditors. See Romer LJ in *Re Ehrmann Bros Ltd* [1906] 2 Ch 697 and Lord Brightman in *Victoria Housing Estates Ltd v Ashpurton Estates Ltd* [1983] Ch 110.

[36] Ss 860 and 874 of the Companies Act 2006, formerly s 395 of the Companies Act 1986 (which, in the case of financial collateral, is subject to the ameliorations provided for by the Financial Collateral Arrangements (No 2) Regs 2003 (SI 2003/3226)).

There are more limited registration requirements concerning transactions that are entered into by individuals.[37]

5.3 The Effect of Foreign Insolvency Proceedings in England

It is now relevant to consider the effect of foreign insolvency proceedings in England, both at general law and by virtue of statute. It will then be relevant to discuss the changes that have been introduced by EC legislation and by virtue of the adoption of the UNCITRAL Model Law on cross-border insolvency.

5.3.1

5.3.2 The position at general law

Once a winding-up order has been made by an English court (whether of an English or a foreign company) it is, at least in theory, of universal and equal application. Thus, all of its unsecured creditors, wherever they may be, have the right to prove in the liquidation and to receive a distribution of its assets on a *pari passu* basis[38] (realistically, such assets are translated into the cash collections upon realisation by the liquidator of the assets it had). Under the principle of hotchpot, however, a creditor who has proved and received a dividend in foreign proceedings will have to bring the benefit of that into account in the English winding up.[39] The company remains the owner of its assets,[40] albeit that it effectively holds them for the benefit of its creditors and the liquidator takes control of them for that purpose.[41] In practical terms, an English liquidator will be constrained in his ability to get in foreign assets by the recognition and assistance that will be given to him in the relevant foreign jurisdictions.[42]

---

[37] Under the Bills of Sale Act 1878, the Bills of Sale Act (1878) Amendment Act 1882 and s 344 of the Insolvency Act 1986.

[38] See Pearson J in *Re Kloebe* (1884) 28 ChD 175, at 180; Sir Nicholas Browne-Wilkinson V-C in *Re Bank of Credit and Commerce International SA* [1992] BCC 83, at 89, Sir Richard Scott V-C in *Re Bank of Credit and Commerce International SA (No 10)* [1997] Ch 213, at 241–242, and Lord Hoffmann in *Cambridge Gas Transport Corp v Official Committee of Unsecured Creditors of Navigator Holdings plc* [2006] UKPC 26; [2007] 1 AC 508, at [16]–[17].

[39] See Lord Scott in *Cleaver v Delta American Reinsurance Co* [2001] UKPC 6; [2001] 2 AC 328, at [18]; David Richards J in *McMahon v McGrath, Re HIH Casualty and General Insurance Ltd* [2005] EWHC 2125 (Ch); [2006] 2 All ER 671, at [156]–[158] (appealed on different grounds [2006] EWCA Civ 732, [2007] 1 All ER 177).

[40] Subject, in exceptional cases, to an order vesting assets in the liquidator pursuant to s 145(1) of the Insolvency Act 1986.

[41] See Lord Hoffmann in *Cambridge Gas Transport Corp v Official Committee of Unsecured Creditors of Navigator Holdings plc* [2006] UKPC 26; [2007] 1 AC 508, at [14] and [20]. The position in an English bankruptcy is different, as the assets vest automatically in the trustee: see Lord Hoffmann, ibid, at [14].

[42] *Re Bank of Credit and Commerce International SA (No 10)* [1997] Ch 213, at 242.

5.3.2.1 In the situation where a debtor is subject to a foreign winding up and there is no English liquidation, the English courts will assist the foreign liquidator by recognising that he is entitled to act on behalf of the debtor in the realisation of its assets in England. This is subject to such safeguards as the court may feel appropriate,[43] particularly for the protection of English creditors who might be prejudiced by the removal of assets from England.[44] Much the same will apply if the debtor is an individual and is the subject of foreign bankruptcy proceedings, but movable property in England will vest in the foreign trustee in bankruptcy if the trustee was appointed in the country where the debtor was domiciled.[45]

5.3.3 Co-operation at common law with foreign principal proceedings

At common law, where a foreign company is the subject of winding-up proceedings in both England and in its jurisdiction of incorporation, the English courts are willing to achieve a measure of practical co-operation with the foreign proceedings by regarding the English proceedings as being ancillary to those other proceedings, which would be regarded as the principal proceedings. The English proceedings, essentially, are confined to admitting proofs from creditors, wherever they may be, getting in and realising assets in England, and assisting the liquidator in the principal proceedings, by transmitting the realised assets to him so that there can be a pooling on a worldwide basis of all the realisations and a *pari passu* distribution by that liquidator to all the creditors.[46]

5.3.3.1 Nonetheless, the English court is bound to apply the substantive rules of English insolvency law in its proceedings and cannot make an order which would have the effect of disapplying the substantive rules, although it may be prepared to dispense with mere procedural rules in giving assistance to the principal proceedings. The rules of mandatory set-off in insolvency are part of the substantive rules and cannot be disapplied.[47] In *Felixstowe Dock & Railway Co v United States Lines Inc*[48] the court said that assets should not be removed for the benefit of foreign creditors and to the detriment of English creditors. Similarly, in *McMahon v McGrath, Re HIH Casualty and General Insurance Ltd*[49] it was held by David Richards J that the rules for a *pari passu* distribution amongst all of the creditors proving in a liquidation are part of the substantive rules of an English winding up. Accordingly,

---

[43] See Lord Hoffmann in *Cambridge Gas Transport Corp v Official Committee of Unsecured Creditors of Navigator Holdings plc* [2006] UKPC 26; [2007] 1 AC 508, at [20].

[44] See *Felixstowe Dock & Railway Co v United States Lines Inc* [1989] QB 360.

[45] See Lord Hoffmann in the *Cambridge Gas Transport* case, at [19].

[46] *Re Bank of Credit and Commerce International SA (No 10)* [1997] Ch 213, at 246.

[47] *Re Bank of Credit and Commerce International SA (No 10)* [1997] Ch 213.

[48] [1989] QB 360.

[49] [2005] EWHC 2125 (Ch), [2006] 2 All ER 671 (appealed on different grounds [2006] EWCA Civ 732, [2007] 1 All ER 177).

an English court would not permit the transfer of funds to the foreign liquidators if substantially the same requirements for a *pari passu* distribution amongst all of the creditors, including the creditors who had proved in the English proceedings, did not apply in the foreign proceedings. His Lordship explained that the statutory scheme of an English liquidation conferred enforceable personal rights upon the creditors to require distribution of the assets of the insolvent company in accordance with the statutory scheme so that each creditor's claim should be treated in accordance with its statutory entitlement. That right would not be compromised where the distribution by a foreign liquidator was along the same lines as would apply in an English liquidation, but it would be wrongly prejudiced if a distribution failed to meet such a requirement.[50] In addition, where there are preferential creditors in the English liquidation, the court will not order the transfer of funds to the foreign liquidator without requiring a retention to be made to meet the claims of the preferential creditors. The court had no power to discharge an English liquidator from the statutory duty towards preferential creditors.

5.3.4 Section 426(4) of the Insolvency Act 1986

Section 426(4) of the Insolvency Act 1986, as supplemented by section 426(5) of the Act, provides a further basis, this time a statutory basis, on which an English court may provide assistance in certain foreign proceedings emanating from other Commonwealth countries and countries whose systems are derived from English law. In pursuance of section 426(4), the English courts have made orders for the administration of a foreign company[51] and an order for the examination of a witness for the purposes of a foreign liquidation.[52]

Sections 426(4) and (5) are as follows: 5.3.4.1

> (4) The courts having jurisdiction in relation to insolvency law in any part of the United Kingdom shall assist the courts having the corresponding jurisdiction in . . . any relevant country or territory.
> (5) For the purposes of subsection (4) a request made to a court in any part of the United Kingdom by a court in . . . a relevant country or territory is authority for the court to which the request is made to apply, in relation to any matters specified in the request, the insolvency law which is applicable by either court in relation to comparable matters falling within its jurisdiction.

---

[50] The case ultimately went on appeal to the House of Lords ([2008] UKHL 21. The House was evenly divided as to whether the position at common law, as explained by David Richards J, should be changed, so as to remove the constraints to which he had referred. Lord Hoffmann (with whom Lord Walker agreed) would have removed the constraints in favour of a broad principle of unity which led to comity and co-operation with foreign insolvency proceedings. Lords Scott and Neuberger upheld the approach that had been taken by David Richards J and refused to adopt the broad principle favoured by Lord Hoffmann. Lord Phillips refused to be drawn on the issue.

[51] *Re Dallhold Estates (UK) Pty Ltd* [1992] BCC 394.

[52] *Re Southern Equities Corp Ltd, England v Smith* [2001] Ch 419.

In exercising its discretion under this subsection, a court shall have regard in particular to the rules of private international law.

5.3.4.2 In *Hughes v Hannover Ruckversicherungs AG*[53] Morritt LJ said that section 426(5) extended the general jurisdiction and powers that an English court would have in insolvency proceedings. In consequence, an English court to which a request for assistance was made under section 426(4) had available to it, in addition to its own general jurisdiction and powers, either the powers conferred on it by English insolvency law or so much of the law of the relevant foreign country as 'corresponds' to English insolvency law. However, it was implicit in the fact that the powers were conferred on a court that the exercise of those powers was qualified by what the court may properly do as a court, that is, to do justice in accordance with the law. That qualification was not confined simply to matters relating to the observance of public policy. The court had to consider, within its discretion, if the assistance that had been requested could properly be granted. The fact that the request had been made was a weighty factor to be taken into account but it was not conclusive. If it could not accede to the request in the form in which it had been made, the court should consider whether assistance in some other way might be given.

5.3.4.3 In the later case of *In the matter of HIH Casualty and General Insurance Ltd*[54] his Lordship, in his role as the Chancellor sitting as a member of the Court of Appeal, held that the court would have jurisdiction to entertain a request under section 426 to order a transfer of assets to the foreign liquidator in the principal proceedings, even though the result of the transfer would be to interfere with the English statutory scheme for distribution amongst creditors as imposed by the Insolvency Act 1986. It was not relevant whether or not this would be a matter of disturbing a substantive or a procedural rule of the statutory scheme. The Chancellor said that it would be a matter for the English court, in the exercise of its discretion, to decide if it should make such an order. This would involve a consideration of all of the circumstances, including whether the transfer would prejudice the English creditors or any particular class of them and whether there might be other advantages or considerations that would be sufficient to counteract such prejudice. Such countervailing considerations would include matters such as whether the relevant creditors had consented, whether there were sufficient savings in costs by avoiding duplication so as to overcome any financial prejudice that might otherwise have arisen, and whether there would be an increase in the overall pool of distributable assets to offset any loss in priority that the English creditors would otherwise have enjoyed under an English liquidation.[55]

---

[53] [1997] BCC 921, at 937–939.
[54] [2006] EWCA Civ 732, [2007] 1 All ER 177.
[55] On appeal to the House of Lords ([2008] UKHL 21), the decision of the Court of Appeal as to the application of s 426 on the facts was reversed. The Court of Appeal had refused to accede

The Chancellor also said in *In the matter of HIH Casualty and General Insurance Ltd*[56] that he gained no assistance in considering the question of the court's jurisdiction and the exercise of its discretion by the concluding sentence in section 426(5). That sentence states that: 'In exercising its discretion under this subsection, a court shall have regard in particular to the rules of private international law.' He agreed with Lawrence Collins J in *Re Television Rentals Ltd*[57] that the words were obscure and ill-thought. No account should be taken of them in construing the intention of sections 426(4) and (5).

5.3.4.4

5.4 The EC Insolvency Regulation

5.4.1 Introduction

The EC Insolvency Regulation[58] came into force on 31 May 2002. Being an EC Regulation, it is directly applicable in each EU Member State except Denmark, to which it has no application[59] (for the purposes of what follows, Denmark should be treated as if it were not an EU Member State). It concerns collective insolvency proceedings which involve the partial or total divestment of the debtor for the benefit of its creditors and the appointment of a 'liquidator'.[60] The overall scheme of the Regulation is to provide the rules which determine the courts of EU Member States that should have jurisdiction in insolvency proceedings concerning an insolvent debtor, the extent of their jurisdiction, the mutual recognition of such proceedings throughout the EU, the law or laws which will govern the various issues that might arise in an insolvency, and the procedures for lodgement and admission of claims. The Regulation recognises that the insolvency laws of the EU Member States differ widely. It does not purport to harmonise those laws but to determine which State's law should be applied to the matters that will arise in an insolvency. The Regulation goes to international jurisdiction and not domestic territorial jurisdiction, so that it will still be necessary to establish that a particular court has power under its own rules to assume jurisdiction in any particular case

---

to the request of the foreign court because the order of distribution in that jurisdiction would have the effect of preferring creditors who would not have a preferential position under an English insolvency. The House said that where the foreign jurisdiction was a relevant country or territory for the purposes of s 426 then, in principle, the English court should accede to the request even though the order of distribution in the foreign jurisdiction may not be the same as in an English insolvency.

[56] [2006] EWCA Civ 732; [2007] 1 All ER 177, at [55].
[57] [2002] EWHC 211 (Ch); [2002] BCC 807, at [17].
[58] EC 1346/2000 OJ L160/1 30/6/2000.
[59] Recital (33) to the Regulation.
[60] Hence it does not encompass 'debtor in possession' proceedings, such as Chap 11 bankruptcy proceedings in the USA. Nor does it apply to receiverships, as there is no 'liquidator' appointed, nor is there a divestiture for the collective benefit of the debtor's creditors.

to which the Regulation may allocate it authority to open proceedings.[61] The Regulation does not apply to debtors that are insurance undertakings,[62] credit institutions,[63] or certain types of investment undertakings.

5.4.1.1 Although it is not expressly stated in the Regulation, it should be legitimate to have regard to the Report of Virgos and Schmit (hereinafter the *Virgos & Schmit Report*) which was written as a commentary to the proposed European Convention on Insolvency Proceedings of 1995, which was the forerunner of the Regulation. The Convention never came into force.[64]

5.4.1.2 It should be noted that Article 44(2)(b) of the Regulation preserves the effect of section 426(4) of the Insolvency Act as it relates to other Commonwealth countries. Article 44(2)(b) provides that the Regulation is not to apply in the UK, to the extent that it is irreconcilable with any obligations under arrangements existing with Commonwealth countries when the Regulation came into force, concerning bankruptcy and the winding up of insolvent companies.

5.4.2 Jurisdiction and the concept of the debtor's 'centre of main interests'

With certain exceptions, the Regulation applies to individual and incorporated insolvent debtors[65] whose 'centre of main interests' (hereunder a debtor's 'COMI') is located in an EU Member State. As will be seen, the concept of COMI is not synonymous with a corporate debtor's place of incorporation, so if an insolvency involves a debtor that is incorporated in an EU country but whose COMI is

---

61 See Recital (15).

62 For an insurance undertaking with its head office in an EEA Member State, the EC Directive on the reorganisation and winding up of insurance undertakings (EC 2001/17 OJ L110/28 20/4/2001) applies. The Directive has been implemented in the UK by the Insurers (Reorganisation and Winding Up) Regs 2004 (SI 2004/353, as amended by SI 2004/546).

63 For a credit institution established in an EEA Member State, the EC Directive on the reorganisation and winding up of credit institutions (EC 2001/24 OJ L125/15 5/5/2001) applies. The Directive has been implemented in the UK by the Credit Institutions (Reorganisation and Winding Up) Regs 2004 (SI 2004/1045).

64 A copy of the *Virgos & Schmit Report*, with restricted circulation, was produced as EU Council Document 6500/96, DRS 8 (CFC) dated 3/5/1996. It is set out in Appendix 2 to Moss Fletcher & Isaacs, *The EC Regulation on Insolvency Proceedings, A Commentary* (OUP, 2002). The *Report* does not have any authoritative status but it gives a valuable insight into the matters that were considered relevant in drafting the text of the Convention and, thus, the Regulation. In *Eurofood IFSC Ltd* Case C-341/04, [2006] ECR I-3813, [2005] BCC 1021 the Advocate General (Sir Francis Jacobs) said in his Opinion that the *Virgos & Schmit Report* provided 'useful guidance' in the interpretation of the Regulation.

65 As the Regulation is concerned with insolvent debtors, it will not be relevant to a solvent winding up of a company by the court. In such cases where there is a cross-jurisdictional issue involving another EU or EEA Member State, the respective provisions of Art 22(2) of the Regulation on jurisdiction and judgments (EC 44/2001 OJ L12/1 16/1/2001) and Art 16(2) of the Lugano and Brussels Conventions will apply: see Lawrence Collins J in *Re Drax Holdings Ltd* [2003] EWHC 2743 (Ch); [2004] 1 WLR 1049, at [28].

located outside the EU (such as might be the case for an English incorporated company whose COMI is located in a country outside the EU, even if it has a branch or branches in one or more EU countries), the Regulation will not apply and the insolvency jurisdiction of the courts in an EU Member State concerning such a debtor will be entirely dependent upon the law of that State. Similarly, the Regulation will not apply in the case of a debtor which is incorporated and whose COMI is located outside the EU, even though it has a branch or branches in one or more EU countries. On the other hand, a company that is incorporated outside the EU may still have its COMI within an EU State, in which case the Regulation will apply to it.[66]

As will be apparent from what has just been said, at the heart of the Regulation is the concept of a debtor's COMI being within an EU Member State. The application of the Regulation is founded on that concept. Similarly, the Regulation confers principal insolvency jurisdiction upon the courts of the EU State in which the debtor's COMI is located, as Article 3(1) of the Regulation provides that the courts in the Member State in which a debtor's COMI is located shall have the jurisdiction to open the main insolvency proceedings concerning the debtor. It is important to understand what is involved in the concept of a debtor's COMI. In the case of a company or other legal person, a debtor's COMI is presumed by Article 3(1) to be the place where its registered office is located unless the contrary is proved. Recital (13) to the Regulation[67] adds that the debtor's COMI should be the place where the debtor conducts the administration of its interests on a regular basis and which is ascertainable by third parties.

5.4.2.1

The European Court of Justice considered the concept of a debtor's COMI, as it is used in the Regulation, in the case of *Eurofood IFSC Ltd*,[68] which was a case concerning a corporate debtor. The simple presumption laid down by Article 3(1) would normally apply and could only be rebutted by the application of the criteria laid down by Recital (13). In light of that Recital, the court said that a debtor's COMI, if different from the place of its registered office, must be identified by

5.4.2.2

---

[66] *Re BRAC Rent-A-Car International Inc* [2003] EWHC 128 (Ch), [2003] 1 WLR 1421.

[67] In *Schweizerische Lactina Panchaud AG v Germany* Case C-346/88 [1991] 2 CMLR 283 the European Court of Justice said that where a regulation was unclear or imprecise, regard may be had to the recitals to determine the aims of the legislation and its meaning.

[68] Case C-341/04, [2006] ECR I-3813, [2006] Ch 508. The Advocate General's opinion was delivered on 27/9/2005 and the Court's decision was given on 2/5/2006. The concept of a debtor's COMI has also been considered by the English courts on various occasions. See *Re BRAC Rent-A-Car International Inc* [2003] EWHC 128 (Ch), [2003] 1 WLR 1421 (in which a Delaware incorporated company was found to have its COMI in England), *Re Daisytek-ISA Ltd* [2003] BCC 562 (where the presumption relating to the registered offices of two subsidiary companies was rebutted in favour of the place of the groups' headquarters. Query if the same result would now occur in light of the *Eurofoods IFSC* case) and the Court of Appeal in *Shierson v Vlieland-Boddy* [2005] EWCA Civ 974, [2005] 1 WLR 3966.

reference to criteria that were both objective and ascertainable by third parties. This required that a third party would be able to establish an actual situation that was different from that provided by the presumption. That might be the case for a 'letterbox' company which did not carry on any business in the State of its registered office. However, where a company carried on business in the State of its registered office, the mere fact that its economic choices were controlled by its foreign parent was not sufficient to rebut the presumption.

5.4.2.3 The approach to be taken concerning the COMI of an individual, non-corporate, debtor is different, as there is no presumption of the type specified by Article 3(1) for corporate debtors. An individual's COMI must therefore be established using the criteria that are mentioned in Recital (13). An English court has reviewed the position.[69] It said that Recital (13) provides a 'description' rather than a definition of the concept of a debtor's COMI. It concluded that the debtor's COMI would be where the focal point of his economic interests was located. If the debtor was a professional, that would be at the place of his professional domicile. Where the debtor was otherwise carrying on a business in his own right, it would be his main place of business. For any other debtor, his COMI should be his habitual place of residence, namely, his settled, permanent home, rather than any other more temporary place where he may reside from time to time (which might be described as an 'ordinary' place of residence). The court also said that an individual who was involved in the running of a company should not thereby be considered as carrying on his own business, and so his COMI may be different from that of the company or indeed the place where he worked on behalf of the company.

5.4.2.4 It is interesting to observe that in *Shierson v Vlieland-Boddy*[70] the Court of Appeal recognised the possibility that the debtor might change its COMI, which it might do deliberately so as to avail itself of a more sympathetic jurisdiction should it become insolvent. In the light of this, it is difficult to understand why the Regulation says that it is important that the location of the COMI should have been readily apparent to and ascertainable by the debtor's creditors, given that their debts may have come into existence some time before the date on which a determination has to be made for the purposes of the Regulation. It is perfectly possible that the COMI might have been moved in the meantime to a different country. It is worth noting that various instances have occurred where debtors have deliberately moved their COMIs at a time of impending insolvency, to jurisdictions that have insolvency procedures that are more to their liking than those in the countries of their original COMI. England has become popular for this purpose, with its procedures that might facilitate rescue and reorganisation of businesses.

---

[69] *Stojevic v Komercni Banka AS* [2006] EWHC 3447 (Ch), [2007] BPIR 141.
[70] [2005] EWCA Civ 974, [2005] 1 WLR 3966.

In addition, there is the possibility under English law of using the UNCITRAL Model Law on cross-border insolvency where the debtor might also find itself subject to insolvency proceedings in countries outside the EU.

In the *Eurofood IFSC* case the court did not address the time as at which a debtor's COMI should be established. However, in an earlier case[71] the ECJ held, in relation to proceedings that had been commenced by the debtor, that the relevant time was the date when the debtor applied to open the proceedings. By contrast, in *Shierson v Vlieland-Boddy*[72] Chadwick LJ said that the time as at which this issue should be assessed was when the court was first called upon to consider whether proceedings should be opened, whether that be in hearing the petition for winding up or bankruptcy or when an earlier application in the proceedings was before the court. It is respectfully suggested that the approach taken by the ECJ is to be preferred and that the relevant time to determine a debtor's COMI in the case of all proceedings should be when they are formally commenced.

5.4.2.5

5.4.3 The date of opening of proceedings

The date as at which proceedings should be treated as having been opened is relevant to a number of the provisions in the Regulation, such as Articles 3(3), 3(4), 5, and 7, and Chapter II of the Regulation. In the *Eurofood IFSC* case, the court said that the appointment by the Irish courts of a provisional liquidator of the relevant debtor company,[73] following upon the presentation of the petition for its winding up, was to be regarded as a judgment opening insolvency proceedings for the purposes of the Regulation. It declined to decide upon an obiter view that had been expressed by the Advocate General (Sir Francis Jacobs) in the case. He had said that where, under national law, the effect of a winding-up order is effectively backdated to the date on which the petition is presented,[74] the order would be treated for the purposes of the Regulation as having been effective as from the date of the presentation of the petition, so that the proceedings would be treated as having been opened at that earlier date.

5.4.4 The main proceedings

Article 3(1) of the Regulation provides that the main or principal insolvency proceedings should be opened before the courts of the EU Member State in which a debtor's COMI is situated. So far as England and Wales are concerned, such proceedings may be by way of bankruptcy, compulsory winding up by the court

---

[71] *Susanne Staubitz-Schreiber* Case C-1/04, [2006] ECR I-701, [2006] BCC 639.

[72] [2005] EWCA Civ 974; [2005] 1 WLR 3966, at [39].

[73] In circumstances similar to those provided for under English law by s 135 of the Insolvency Act 1986.

[74] As would be the case pursuant to s 129(2) of the Insolvency Act 1986.

or a winding up supervised or confirmed by the court (such as a creditors' voluntary winding up so supervised), administration, and company voluntary arrangement.[75] Receivership is not a relevant insolvency proceeding because it is not a collective insolvency procedure. Main proceedings have all of the attributes of normal insolvency proceedings and extend to all of the debtor's affairs, including all of its assets, subject to the effect of any secondary proceedings that may have been opened in another EU Member State.

5.4.5 Territorial and secondary proceedings

Under Article 3(2) of the Regulation, insolvency proceedings (which are usually referred to as 'territorial proceedings') may also be opened before the courts of another EU Member State which is not that of the debtor's COMI, if the debtor has an 'establishment' in that State. An establishment is defined in Article 2(h) to mean 'any place of operations where the debtor carries out a non-transitory economic activity with human means and goods'.[76] This is a two-fold requirement, in that there must be both a place of business and the carrying-on of that business with human means and goods. Such proceedings are territorially limited in that they are confined to the assets situated[77] within that jurisdiction. If such proceedings are opened after the main proceedings, then they are 'secondary proceedings' and are confined to 'winding-up' proceedings, which in England would be compulsory winding up, bankruptcy, and voluntary winding up supervised or confirmed by the court.[78]

5.4.5.1   By Article 3(4), such territorial proceedings may only be opened before the main proceedings if either the main proceedings cannot then be opened because conditions under the law of the State of the debtor's COMI prevent them from being opened or if the opening of the territorial proceedings is requested by a creditor who meets either (or both) of the following two requirements. First, the creditor is connected by its domicile, habitual residence, or registered office to the State of the location of the 'establishment' or, secondly, if the creditor's claim arises from the operation of that establishment. Territorial proceedings in such a case are not limited to winding-up proceedings, but under Article 37 the insolvency practitioner in subsequently opened main proceedings may request that the territorial proceedings should be converted into secondary or 'winding-up' proceedings.

---

[75]   See Art 2(a) and Annex A.

[76]   Which inevitably raises a question as to whether there can be an 'establishment' for a debtor that is only carrying on a services business, even if it owns assets in the relevant country. In *Telia AB v Hilcourt (Docklands) Ltd* [2002] EWHC 2377 (Ch), [2003] BCC 856 Park J held that a company did not have an establishment in the UK simply because it had a subsidiary incorporated in the UK with a place of business in the UK.

[77]   The situation of an asset is to be determined in accordance with Art 2(g).

[78]   See Art 2(c) and Annex B.

The insolvency practitioner in the main proceedings may request the opening of secondary proceedings.[79] He may also request that secondary proceedings should be stayed for one or more limited periods.[80]

Chapter III of the Regulation (Articles 27 to 38) contains further provisions concerning secondary proceedings.

5.4.6 Recognition of proceedings

Chapter II of the Regulation (Articles 16 to 26) provides for the recognition throughout the EU of insolvency proceedings, whether main or secondary, that have been opened under Article 3 and of the functions and powers of the insolvency practitioner appointed in such proceedings. For instance, under Article 18 the insolvency practitioner is entitled within certain limits to seize and remove assets in any Member State, although he cannot do so in a State where there is another such practitioner in place under secondary proceedings. There is a public policy exception to the principle of recognition in Article 26, which permits a Member State and its courts to refuse recognition on the grounds of public policy.[81]

5.4.7 Lodgement of claims and information

Chapter IV of the Regulation (Articles 39 to 42) deals with the right of creditors to lodge claims in insolvency proceedings[82] and for the provision of information to creditors. It should be noted that Article 39 permits the tax and social security authorities in an EU Member State, other than that in which insolvency proceedings have been opened, to lodge their claims in such proceedings. This effects a reversal of the traditional public policy position under English law, under which an English court will not enforce, directly or indirectly, the revenue or tax claims of another State.[83]

5.4.8 Governing law

Having described the scheme and general effect of the Regulation, as well as the rules to determine where insolvency proceedings should be opened, it is now relevant to consider the provisions of the Regulation which specify the rules that will determine the laws that should govern insolvency proceedings. It is also relevant

---

[79] Art 29.

[80] Art 33.

[81] Which was considered by the ECJ in the *Eurofood IFSC Ltd* case.

[82] Which is slightly at variance with Art 32.

[83] *Government of India v Taylor* [1955] AC 491 and *QRS 1 Aps v Fransden* [1999] 3 All ER 289. See the discussion on this point at Chap 4.

to consider the provisions of the Regulation that concern proprietary and similar rights and rights of set-off.

5.4.9 The law governing the insolvency proceedings

Article 4(1) of the Regulation contains the general provision which determines the law that governs insolvency proceedings and their effect.[84] That law is the law of the State in which the proceedings were opened. Article 4(2) then provides that such law shall govern the conditions for opening the proceedings, their conduct, and their closure. It then specifically provides for a number of matters to which the governing law should apply, as follows (using the same paragraph numbering as in Article 4(2)):

(a) against which debtors' insolvency proceedings may be brought on account of their capacity;

(b) the assets which form part of the estate and the treatment of assets acquired by or devolving on the debtor after the opening of the insolvency proceedings;

(c) the respective powers of the debtor and the liquidator;

(d) the conditions under which set-offs may be invoked;

(e) the effects of insolvency proceedings on current contracts to which the debtor is a party;

(f) the effect of the insolvency proceedings on proceedings brought by individual creditors, with the exception of lawsuits pending;

(g) the claims which are to be lodged against the debtor's estate and the treatment of claims arising after the opening of insolvency proceedings;

(h) the rules governing the lodging, verification and admission of claims;

(i) the rules governing the distribution of proceeds from the realisation of assets, the ranking of claims and the rights of creditors who have obtained partial satisfaction after the opening of insolvency proceedings by virtue of a right *in rem* or through a set-off;

(j) the conditions for and the effects of closure of insolvency proceedings, in particular by composition;

(k) creditors' rights after the closure of insolvency proceedings;

(l) who is to bear the costs and expenses incurred in the insolvency proceedings;

(m) the rules relating to the voidness, voidability or unenforceability of legal acts detrimental to all the creditors.

5.4.9.1 The effect of the foregoing in relation to English insolvency proceedings (subject to a number of exceptions to which reference will be made below) is that such proceedings and the various issues that arise in consequence of the proceedings will be governed by English law. Three examples will now be given concerning the effect of Article 4(2).

---

[84] Which is effectively repeated by Art 28 with reference to secondary proceedings.

278

Paragraph (d) refers to the invocation of rights of set-off. As a matter of English **5.4.9.1.1**
law, and subject to the further discussion below as to the effect of Article 6 of the
Regulation, this means that the English rules of mandatory set-off in insolvency[85]
would apply in English insolvency proceedings by way of winding up, bankruptcy,
and, possibly, administration.

Paragraph (e) refers to the effect of the insolvency proceedings on current con- **5.4.9.1.2**
tracts, irrespective of their governing law. Under English law, the insolvency of a
contracting party does not mean that the contract is automatically terminated.[86]
Nonetheless, the liquidator of a company is entitled to disclaim 'onerous property' which includes unprofitable contracts.[87] The rules as to disclaimer would
apply in English insolvency proceedings.

Paragraph (m) relates to the grounds upon which transactions that the insolvent **5.4.9.1.3**
debtor entered into may be challenged, because they are detrimental to the interests of its whole body of creditors. Such grounds would include, for instance,
where the debtor wrongly disposed of assets, or where the liquidator or administrator wished to pursue rights of claw back relating to transactions into which the
debtor had entered to the detriment of its creditors. Under English law, this would
include challenges that might be mounted by the relevant insolvency practitioner
relating to transactions at an undervalue,[88] transactions to defraud creditors,[89]
preferences,[90] floating charges,[91] and dispositions of assets after the commencement of a compulsory winding up[92] or bankruptcy[93] of the debtor. As will be seen
below, paragraph (m) provides for an important limitation upon the separate rules
that apply with respect to proprietary rights, the passing of title in assets, and the
rights of set-off.

It should be noted, however, that the effect of paragraph (m) is made subject to the **5.4.9.1.4**
provisions of Article 13 of the Regulation. Article 13 gives the beneficiary of a
transaction that might be subject to a challenge in pursuance of paragraph (m) a
defence if the beneficiary can demonstrate two things. First, that the transaction

---

[85] S 323 of the Insolvency Act 1986 and Rules 2.85 and 4.90 of the Insolvency Rules 1986 (as amended).

[86] See, *Ex p Chalmers* (1873) LR 8 Ch App 289; *Jennings's Trustee v King* [1952] Ch 899; *The British Wagon Company v Lea & Co* (1879–80) LR 5 QBD 149; *Tolhurst v Associated Portland Cement Manufacturers Ltd* [1902] 2 KB 660, affd [1903] AC 414. In a contract for the sale of goods, the seller can refuse to deliver until it has been paid in cash: *Ex p Chalmers*.

[87] S 178 of the Insolvency Act 1986. A trustee in bankruptcy is given a similar power by s 315 of that Act.

[88] Ss 238 and 339 of the Insolvency Act 1986.

[89] S 423 of the Insolvency Act 1986.

[90] Ss 239 and 340 of the Insolvency Act 1986.

[91] S 245 of the Insolvency Act 1986.

[92] S 127(1) of the Insolvency Act 1986.

[93] S 284 of the Insolvency Act 1986.

between it and the debtor was subject to the law of a different EU Member State to that in which the insolvency proceedings were opened, and, secondly, that the law of that other Member State does not allow any means of challenging the transaction on the facts of the case.

5.4.9.2 Article 4(2) is reinforced by Article 20(1) of the Regulation. It provides that, subject to the provisions of Articles 5 and 7,[94] a creditor who obtains payment of his claim after the opening of the main proceedings by taking enforcement action against assets in another EU Member State, must turn the payment over to the insolvency practitioner in the main proceedings. In addition, Article 20(2) in effect requires account to be taken of any dividend obtained by a creditor in one set of insolvency proceedings in determining what is payable to him as a creditor in another set of insolvency proceedings.

5.4.9.3 Although it contains no express reference to Article 4, Article 14 of the Regulation also provides an exception to the general effect of Article 4, including paragraph (m). It relates to immovable assets, to ships and aircraft that are registered in a public register, and to 'securities whose existence presupposes registration in a register laid down by law', which the debtor has disposed of for consideration after the opening of the insolvency proceedings. It allows for a defence based upon the validity of the disposition under the law of the State within which the immovable property is situated or under the authority of which the register is kept. As the article is headed 'Protection of third party purchasers', it is arguable that it intends only to provide protection to purchasers (in the colloquial sense) rather than others who might have acquired different types of proprietary interests in such assets, but this is not clear. Article 14 does not say that the relevant State must be an EU Member State. The obverse situation, where it is the debtor who has rights in such assets, is dealt with in Article 11, to which further reference is made below.

5.4.9.4 The rules provided by Article 4 of the Regulation are subject to a number of other specific rules provided in Articles 5 to 15, which will now be examined.

5.4.10 Rights *in rem*

Article 5(1) of the Regulation provides that rights *in rem* [95] in the debtor's assets which are held by creditors or other third parties (including rights held by way of security) where, at the time the insolvency proceedings are opened, such assets[96] are situated in a different EU Member State to that of the law of the insolvency

---

[94] Curiously, there is no cross-reference in Art 20(1) to Art 6 but surely it was not intended to require a creditor to turn over the benefit of a set-off that the creditor was enabled to assert in consequence of the operation of Art 6.

[95] Which are more particularly described in Arts 5(2) and 5(3).

[96] Para 96 of the *Virgos & Schmit Report* says that Art 5(1) is directed at and applies to rights *in rem* that have been created prior to the opening of the insolvency proceedings. That begs the question

proceedings, shall not be affected by the opening of such proceedings. Article 5(1) applies to rights in specific assets and in collections of indefinite assets, such as would arise under a floating charge. Article 5(1) says that the opening of the insolvency proceedings is not to 'affect' rights *in rem*. Although it is not free from doubt, it is submitted that it is both the opening of the insolvency proceedings and the action that may be taken in consequence of such proceedings that are not to affect the rights *in rem*. Otherwise, a secured creditor may find that its rights to take possession and sell the assets could be affected, for instance, by a stay of enforcement action under the proceedings. Similarly, it is suggested that it is not just the right itself that is protected, but the application of that right to the debt it secures, in the sense that the insolvency proceedings should not be able to neutralise or diminish the effectiveness of the right by eliminating or reducing the debt it secures, such as might otherwise occur under a compromise or arrangement that was forced upon the debtor's creditors by a scheme of arrangement or something similar.

5.4.10.1 Article 5(1) depends upon the relevant asset being situated in an EU Member State other than that where the insolvency proceedings are taking place. Article 2(g) provides rules to determine if certain assets are situated in an EU Member State. Not unexpectedly, tangible movables are to be taken as situated where they are physically located. Property and other rights and entitlements which must be registered in a public register are treated as situated in the Member State under whose authority the register is kept. 'Claims', such as choses in action, are taken to be situated in the EU Member State where the relevant obligor has its COMI, which is different from the rules that would apply under English law to determine their situs.[97] Thus, for the purposes of Article 5(1), the right of a depositor in a bank account would be situated at the COMI of the bank and not at the branch of the bank where the deposit was maintained. Hence, an account maintained at a branch of a bank which had its COMI outside the EU would not be an asset that was situated in an EU Member State and, similarly, an account that was maintained at a branch in one EU Member State of a bank whose COMI was in another such State would be situated at the place of the bank's COMI and not where the account was kept. It is not clear what is meant by the word 'claims', but it is suggested that the expression would be given a wide meaning to encompass nearly every type of intangible asset, except where the right depends upon registration, as such assets inherently depend upon the assertion of a right against some other person.

---

as to whether or not the right *in rem* can exist for this purpose (e.g. under security over future assets) if the assets have not yet come into existence at that time.

[97] Essentially, the situs of a debt or other chose in action at common law is where the debtor or obligor resides.

5.4.10.2 It should be noted, however, that Article 5(4) provides that the application of the rule stated in Article 5(1) is to be without prejudice to the operation of Article 4(2)(m). In consequence, the insolvency practitioner (subject to Articles 13 and 14) may seek to challenge the validity of a right *in rem* in accordance with the law governing the insolvency proceedings, notwithstanding that the right *in rem* may be effective under the law which would otherwise govern that right.

5.4.10.3 Article 5(1) does not specify which law should be applied to determine the existence, extent, and effectiveness of rights *in rem* in assets of the debtor which are situated in another EU Member State if that matter should arise in the insolvency of the debtor. The issue is addressed, however, by Recital (25) to the Regulation which states that: 'The basis, validity and extent of such a right in rem should . . . normally be determined according to the lex situs and not be affected by the opening of insolvency proceedings.' For most types of asset, English law already follows a *lex situs* approach to such matters.

5.4.10.4 There could be difficulties, however, in relation to choses in action and similar claims. As already explained, Article 2(g) of the Regulation provides a different rule to determine the situs of a claim than that which would apply under normal English conflicts rules. Furthermore, Article 12 of the Rome Convention provides its own rule for ascertaining the law that should govern matters concerning an assignment of a claim, which is that the governing law of the claim should determine matters of effectiveness and the like concerning the assignment. It is also uncertain what rule should govern priority disputes as between competing rights *in rem* in the same asset. In addition to those difficulties, it is not made clear in Recital (25) if the application of the *lex situs* in determining the basis, validity, and extent of the right *in rem* should include the insolvency law of the *lex situs*.

5.4.10.5 It would appear that Article 5(1), when taken with Recital (25), was intended to oust altogether the application of the law of the insolvency proceedings to the rights *in rem* of creditors and third parties (subject, of course, to the possible application of Article 4(2)(m), as previously discussed). On occasions, this could work to the disadvantage of a secured creditor or other person asserting a proprietary interest in cases where the secured creditor or such a person may actually be better off by the application of the law of the insolvency proceedings than if all of its rights were determined in accordance with the *lex situs* of the relevant asset (or some other test). The position is not completely clear as Article 5(1) says that the opening of insolvency proceedings 'shall not affect' the rights *in rem*, which might be taken to imply that it only addresses a situation where the right *in rem* would be adversely affected by the law of the insolvency proceedings and was not intending to go any further. This may be contrasted with the wording of Article 8 of the Regulation, which says that the effect of insolvency proceedings on a contract concerning immovable property 'shall be governed solely by' the *lex situs* of the property.

Article 5(1) also says nothing about the position where assets of the debtor are situ- **5.4.10.6**
ated outside the territorial boundaries of the EU, nor does it provide any guidance
in determining where such assets may be situated, although the rules under Article
2(g) would have to be applied initially to confirm that the assets were not situated
in an EU Member State. It is submitted that the conflict of laws rules of the law
governing the insolvency proceedings would determine the approach that should
be taken in dealing with this matter. After all, the EU cannot expect that its writ
should run outside the confines of its own boundaries. Accordingly, if English law
was the law governing the insolvency proceedings, it would apply its own conflict
of laws rules concerning proprietary matters to find the situs of the assets (having
already applied Article 2(g) to confirm that they were not situated within an EU
Member State) and then to determine the law applicable to issues concerning the
effectiveness and extent of the relevant rights *in rem*.

5.4.11 Rights of set-off

Another limitation to the general principle of Article 4 is that contained in Article
6(1) of the Regulation, concerning rights of set-off. Subject again to the operation
of Article 4(2)(m),[98] as itself limited by Article 13, Article 6(1) provides that the
insolvency proceedings will not affect the rights of the insolvent debtor's creditors
to demand the set-off of their claims against the claims of the debtor, where such
a set-off is permitted by the law which governs the debtor's claim.

There is an apparent inconsistency between Article 6(1) and Article 4(2)(d) of the **5.4.11.1**
Regulation, which provides that the law of the insolvency proceedings will govern
'the conditions under which set-offs may be invoked'. It might be possible, for
instance, to find a situation where the law governing the insolvency proceedings
precluded set-off but the law governing the debtor's claim permitted the set-off.
This was addressed by the *Virgos & Schmit Report*. The *Report* states[99] that Article
6(1) constitutes an exception to the effect of Article 4, where the law governing
the insolvency proceedings would not permit a set-off to take place within the
proceedings. This view is supported by Recital (26) to the Regulation which states
that: 'If set-off is not permitted under the law of the opening state, a creditor
should nevertheless be entitled to set-off if it is possible under the law applicable
to the claim of the insolvent debtor. In this way, set-off will acquire a kind of guarantee function based on legal provisions on which the creditor concerned can rely
at the time when the claim arises.'

Accordingly, Article 6(1) would allow set-off where the law which governs a **5.4.11.2**
contract under which the insolvent debtor's claim against the creditor arose, as

---

[98] See Art 6(2).
[99] At paras 107–111 of the *Report*.

ascertained in accordance with the rules contained in the Rome Convention 1980, would permit the set-off to take place. It should be noted that the governing law of the debtor's claim, as so ascertained, need not be the law of an EC Member State. It should also be noted that the relevant law for the purposes of Article 6(1) is that which governs the insolvent debtor's claim, rather than the law which governs the creditor's claim.

5.4.11.3 The *Virgos & Schmit Report* goes on to say that Article 6(1) only applies to set-off rights that have accrued prior to the commencement of the insolvency proceedings. Potential claims that accrue after that time will be subject to the law of the insolvency proceedings in accordance with Article 4(2) of the Regulation. On the other hand, it also appears from the *Report* that a claim would be considered as having accrued, and so capable of giving rise to a claim to set-off, even if it has not become liquidated, matured, and payable by the date of the commencement of the insolvency proceedings, provided that the law governing the debtor's claim against which the set-off is to be applied would regard it as capable of giving rise to the set-off. By reference to English concepts of set-off, under a contract governed by English law it would be possible to assert a right of set-off if it is a form of transaction or equitable set-off, or, indeed, where the contract provided for the set-off. However, legal or statutory set-off is really a procedural matter and so it is not a contractual matter governed by the law which governs the contract. Accordingly, it would not qualify within the requirements of Article 6(1).[100]

5.4.11.4 It is not clear if Article 6(1) contemplates rights of set-off that might arise in favour of the debtor outside a contractual situation, for instance, where the debtor's claim arises in tort. In such a case, the right of the debtor to set off its claim would probably be a procedural matter arising in litigation rather than being inherent in the claim itself and the law which governs it.

5.4.12 Passing of title

Article 7 of the Regulation relates to the passing of title in an asset where either the seller or the purchaser becomes subject to insolvency proceedings, but its provisions are also made subject to Article 4(2)(m).

5.4.12.1 Article 7(1) concerns the situation where insolvency proceedings have been opened against the purchaser. It provides that this will not affect the rights of the seller based on a reservation of title where, at the time the proceedings were

---

[100] For the distinction between transaction or equitable set-off and legal or independent set-off see Hoffmann LJ in *Aectra Refining & Marketing Inc v Exmar NV* [1994] 1 WLR 1634, at 1649–1653; Lord Hoffmann in *Stein v Blake* [1996] AC 243, at 251; Clarke LJ in *Glencore Grain Ltd v Agros Trading Co Ltd* [1999] 2 Lloyd's Rep 410, at 415–417; Clarke LJ in *Bim Kemi AB v Blackburn Chemicals Ltd* [2001] EWCA Civ 457, [2001] 2 Lloyd's Rep 93; and Buxton LJ in *Smith v Muscat* [2003] EWCA 962, [2003] 1 WLR 2853.

opened, the relevant asset was in a different EU Member State to that in which the proceedings have been opened.

Article 7(2) deals with the position where insolvency proceedings have been opened against the seller after the asset was delivered, if the asset was in a different EU Member State to that in which the proceedings were opened. The opening of the proceedings will not constitute grounds to rescind or terminate the sale nor prevent the purchaser from acquiring good title.

It is interesting to note that Articles 7(1) and 7(2) are drafted without reference to the effect of the law of the place where the relevant asset happens to be situated when the insolvency proceedings are opened. They are drafted in absolute terms, in the sense that the opening of the insolvency proceedings, taken on its own, is not to affect the seller's rights under reservation of title in one case nor the buyer's title in the other case. There is no specific reference to the effect of the law of the place where the asset happens to be when the proceedings are opened.

It should also be noted that Article 7 says nothing about the position where the relevant asset is in a country outside the EU when the insolvency proceedings were opened. In such a case, presumably, the conflict of laws rules of the forum would be applied.

5.4.13 Immovable property

Article 8 of the Regulation concerns contracts relating to the acquisition or use of immovable property. The effect of the opening of insolvency proceedings upon the contract is to be governed by the *lex situs* of the asset.

5.4.14 Payment and settlement systems and financial markets

A further limitation on the effect of Article 4 is to be found in Article 9(1) of the Regulation, which preserves the integrity of the obligations of the parties to a payment or settlement system or to a financial market. Their rights are to be governed solely by the law of the Member State which is applicable to the relevant system or market.

Article 9(2) reinforces the generality of Article 9(1). It states that Article 9(1) shall not preclude any action which may be taken under the law applicable to the relevant payment system or financial market, to set aside payments or transactions on the grounds of voidness, voidability, or unenforceability.[101] This is a departure from the other provisions discussed above, where such matters are expressed to be subject to the law of the insolvency proceedings, by virtue of Article 4(2)(m). It should also be noted that Article 9(1) is expressed to be without prejudice to Article 5(1) which, it will be recalled, provides the rule relating to rights *in rem*.

---

[101] Curiously, Art 9(2) omits to mention settlement systems.

5.4.14.2 The purpose and intended effect of Article 9 is addressed by Recital (27) to the Regulation, which is as follows:

> There is also a need for special protection in the case of payment systems and financial markets. This applies for example to the position-closing agreements and netting agreements to be found in such systems as well as to the sale of securities and to the guarantees provided for such transactions as governed in particular by [the Settlement Finality Directive[102]]. For such transactions, the only law which is material should thus be that applicable to the system or market concerned. This provision is intended to prevent the possibility of mechanisms for the payment and settlement of transactions provided for in the payment and set-off systems or on the regulated financial markets of Member States being altered in the case of insolvency of a business partner. [The Settlement Finality Directive] contains special provisions which should take precedence over the general rules in this Regulation.

5.4.15 Rights subject to registration

Article 11 of the Regulation deals with the rights of the debtor in immovable property, a ship, or aircraft which is subject to registration in a public register. The effect of insolvency proceedings on such rights is to be determined in accordance with the law of the EU Member State under whose authority the register is kept.

5.4.16 Protection of third party purchasers

Article 14 of the Regulation relates to the rights of purchasers of an immovable asset, a ship, or aircraft that is registered on a public register and securities that are registered in a register laid down by law. If the debtor disposes of such assets after the opening of insolvency proceedings, the validity of the disposition will be governed by the law in which the immovable asset is situated or by the authority of which the register is kept. As noted above, the article refers to a disposition for consideration. In light of the reference in the title to the article merely to 'purchasers', it is not clear if the only dispositions to which the article relates are sales, rather than other types of transaction, such as by way of mortgage.

5.4.17 Community intellectual property rights

Article 12 of the Regulation provides that the rights of the debtor in an EU Community patent, trade mark, or similar right may only be the subject of main proceedings under Article 3(1).

5.4.18 Pending lawsuits in divested assets and rights

Article 15 operates as an exception to the effect of Article 4(2)(f). Article 4(2)(f) provides that the law governing the insolvency proceedings is to determine the

---

[102] 98/26/EC OJ L166/45 11/6/98.

effect of the insolvency proceedings on proceedings brought by individual creditors. Article 15 provides that, where proceedings have been brought in an EU Member State and concern an asset or a right of which the debtor has been divested (and which would otherwise fall into the insolvent estate), the effect on such proceedings of the opening of the insolvency proceedings is to be governed by the law of that State.

5.5 Insolvent Credit Institutions

5.5.1 Introduction

As previously stated, the EC Insolvency Regulation does not apply to credit institutions nor to insurance undertakings. The position concerning the insolvency of a credit institution that is set up within a Member State of the EU or the European Economic Area and of its branches within other Member States is dealt with by the EC Directive on the reorganisation and winding up of credit institutions[103] (the CID), which has been implemented in the UK by the Credit Institutions (Reorganisation and Winding Up) Regulations 2004[104] (the UK Regulations). As a matter of English law, an insolvent non-EEA/EU credit institution will be subject to the application of the common law and, if relevant, section 426(4) of the Insolvency Act, as previously described. For convenience, the relevant provisions of the CID will be referred to in the discussion that follows.

For the purposes of the CID, a credit institution is an institution that has been established in an EU or EEA Member State and which either receives deposits or other repayable funds from the public and grants credits for its own account or is an electronic money institution, unless in either case it is within a specified list.[105] Under the CID, such a credit institution may only be reorganised (that is, in accordance with measures that are intended to preserve or restore its financial position, which may include suspension of payments, suspension of enforcement measures, or reduction of claims[106]) in accordance with the laws of its home Member State and under the control of the authorities in that State. Similarly, such a credit institution may only be wound up in its home Member State, that is, the State in which it has its head office and by which it is authorised to act as a

5.5.1.1

---

[103] EC 2001/24 OJ L125 5/5/2001.

[104] SI 2004/1045.

[105] See Art 1(1) of Directive EC 2001/24, which in turn refers to the definition of a credit institution in Art 1 of the EC Directive relating to the taking up and pursuit of the business of a credit institution (EC 2000/12 OJ L126 26/5/2000). The exclusions will be found in Art 2(3) of Directive EC 2000/12.

[106] See Art 2.

credit institution. It is not possible for secondary or separate insolvency measures or proceedings to be commenced in other EU or EEA Member States.[107]

5.5.2 Governing law in general

The law of the home Member State shall govern the reorganisation measures or winding-up proceedings.[108] In many respects, the provisions of the CID concerning matters arising in a reorganisation or a winding up are the same as will be found in the EC Insolvency Regulation,[109] and there are also similar provisions concerning rights *in rem*,[110] passing of title in a sale of an asset,[111] and set-off,[112] and reference should be made to the comments on those matters that have been made above.

5.5.3 Proprietary rights in 'instruments'

Article 24 of the CID relates to proprietary rights in 'instruments'[113] whose existence or transfer is recorded in a register, account or centralised deposit system held or located in an EEA Member State. It provides that the enforcement of such rights shall be governed by the law of that Member State.

5.5.4 Repurchase agreements

Article 26 of the CID refers to repurchase agreements, without defining what such agreements cover. They are to be governed solely by their contractual governing law.

5.5.5 Transactions on regulated markets

Article 27 of the CID refers to transactions carried out in the context of a regulated market,[114] in contrast to the subject matter of Article 9 of the EC Insolvency Regulation, namely rights and obligations under payment and settlement systems and financial markets. It provides that such transactions are to be governed solely by their contractual governing law.

5.5.6 Third party purchasers

Article 31 of the CID is similar to Article 14 of the EC Insolvency Regulation and provides protection for third party purchasers. However, it differs in that instead

---

[107] Arts 3 and 9.

[108] Arts 3(2) and 10(1).

[109] See, as to winding up, Art 10(2) of the Directive and note Art 30, which concerns 'detrimental acts' and is similar to Art 13 of the EU Regulation.

[110] Art 21.

[111] Art 22.

[112] Art 23.

[113] Art 2 defines 'instruments' to mean all the instruments referred to in Section B of the Annex to the Investment Services Directive (93/22/EC OJ L141/27 11/6/93).

[114] As defined in Art 2.

of referring to 'securities' (as in Article 14 of the Regulation), it refers to 'instruments' and rights in instruments which are recorded in a register, an account, or a centralised deposit system that is held or located in an EEA Member State.

5.5.7 Information

Article 19 of the CID makes brief provision for information to be given where winding-up proceedings are taken in a host Member State of a branch of a credit institution whose head office is outside the EU or the EEA and which also has a branch in another Member State.

5.5.8 Netting

There is one particular provision in the CID for which an equivalent provision will not be found in the EC Insolvency Regulation. Article 25 of the CID provides that: 'Netting agreements shall be governed solely by the law of the contract which governs such instruments.' There is no definition of netting agreements in the CID, nor is any guidance given as to the intended scope of this provision in the recitals to the CID. Regulation 34 of the UK Regulations provides no further guidance. There is a definition of 'close-out netting provision' in the EC Directive on financial collateral arrangements[115] which would cover the concept of termination and close-out netting mentioned above. Presumably, Article 25 of the CID would also cover netting in other contexts, such as transaction netting during the course of a transaction.

5.6 Insolvent Insurance Undertakings

Brief mention will be made concerning the position of insurance undertakings which have their head office in an EU or EEA Member State. Reorganisation and winding-up proceedings concerning such an undertaking are the subject of the EC Directive on the reorganisation and winding up of insurance undertakings,[116] which has been implemented in the UK by the Insurers (Reorganisation and Winding Up) Regulations.[117] It contains a number of provisions in similar vein to the CID concerning credit institutions, but notably without the provision dealing with netting. **5.6.1**

So far as may otherwise be relevant, an insolvent non-EU/EEA insurance undertaking will be subject to the application of the common law and, if available, section 426(4) of the Insolvency Act, as previously described. **5.6.2**

---

[115] EC 2002/47 OJ L168 27/6/2002.
[116] EC 2001/17 OJ L110 20/4/2001.
[117] SI 2004/353, as amended by SI 2004/546.

5.7 Adoption in Great Britain of the UNCITRAL Model Law on Cross-border Insolvency

5.7.1 Introduction

Section 14 of the Insolvency Act 2000 makes provision for the adoption in Great Britain (i.e. England and Wales and Scotland) of the UNCITRAL Model Law on cross-border insolvency. The power under that section was exercised by the Cross-Border Insolvency Regulations 2006,[118] which came into force on 4 April 2006. This followed upon a Consultation Paper published by the Insolvency Service on 22 August 2005 and a Paper issued by the Insolvency Service on 2 March 2006, containing a summary of responses to the Consultation Paper and the Government Reply to those responses. The Regulations give effect to the Model Law in Great Britain, but not in Northern Ireland, which is now dealt with by separate but virtually identical legislation[119] (for convenience, the following explanation will be confined to the position in Great Britain, where the Model Law was first applied, but it should also be relevant to the position in Northern Ireland). UNCITRAL put forward the Model Law in 1997.[120] Essentially, the Model Law applies within Great Britain where there is a cross-border element to an insolvency. It will not be relevant to a purely domestic insolvency.[121]

5.7.1.1 The Model Law was designed to assist States in amending their insolvency laws by providing a model of legislation that they could use but without attempting to achieve a substantive unification of insolvency laws, thereby respecting the differences in national procedural laws. The basic aim was to address the circumstances of cross-border insolvencies, by allowing for the recognition of foreign insolvency proceedings, co-operation between different jurisdictions in dealing with cross-border insolvencies, and local court access for foreign insolvency practitioners and creditors in a cross-border insolvency. In many respects, the provisions of the Model Law follow along the similar lines to the EC Insolvency Regulation, which has been outlined above. As at the end of 2007, UNCITRAL reported that the Model Law had been adopted by the USA (through a new Chapter 15 of the Bankruptcy Code), the British Dependent Territories, the British Virgin Islands, Colombia, Eritrea, Japan, Mexico, Montenegro, New Zealand, Poland, South Africa, Romania, and Serbia. There were also proposals for its adoption in Australia and Canada. A country which adopts the Model Law, called an 'Enacting State' may do so in whole or in part.

---

[118] SI 2006/1030.

[119] The Cross-Border Insolvency Regulations (Northern Ireland) 2007 (SR 2007/115, which came into force on 12/4/2007).

[120] UNCITRAL 30th Session 12–30 May 1997: Official Records of The General Assembly 52nd Session, Supplement No 17 (A/52/17) Pt II paras 12–225, Annex 1.

[121] See Art 1(1) of Sched 1 to SI 2006/1030.

The approach taken in adopting the Model Law in Great Britain has been to follow the drafting used in the Model Law so far as practicable, with some modification so that it is adapted for application in Great Britain. Guidance to the interpretation of the Model Law may be obtained from the UNCITRAL Guide to Enactment[122] as well as from UNCITRAL working papers.[123] It is also provided that the Model Law should be interpreted with an internationalist approach, to promote uniformity in its application and the observance of good faith.[124]   **5.7.1.2**

In structural terms, the Cross-Border Insolvency Regulations 2006 provide for the adoption of the Model Law in the form set forth in Schedule 1 to the Regulations, with procedural matters in England and Wales being dealt with in Schedule 2 and procedural matters for Scotland being contained in Schedule 3. Schedule 4 concerns notices that have to be given to the registrar of companies, and Schedule 5 contains prescribed forms for use in relevant proceedings. For convenience, references hereunder to the version of the Model Law adopted in Great Britain will be referred to as the 'GB Model Law'.   **5.7.1.3**

The GB Model Law complements the application of section 426(4) of the Insolvency Act 1986 and the co-operative approach taken by the English courts at common law where there are principal insolvency proceedings in the jurisdiction of the debtor's place of incorporation, as described above, to which recourse may be had in addition to the GB Model Law,[125] but not in contradiction of the GB Model Law.[126] To the extent, however, that the EC Insolvency Regulation applies in the insolvency of a debtor then the GB Model Law provides that the EC Insolvency Regulation will prevail in any conflict with the application of the provisions of the Model Law.[127]   **5.7.1.4**

There are a number of other instances where the Model Law will not apply,[128] such as in relation to building societies, credit institutions, insurers, and certain regulated utility companies (the position regarding credit institutions and insurers may be re-visited at a later date). There are also exceptions for matters covered by Part VII of the Companies Act 1989 (financial markets insolvencies), Part III of the Financial Markets and Insolvency (Settlement Finality) Regulations 1999[129] (transfer orders through a designated system and collateral security), and Part 3 of   **5.7.1.5**

---

122 UNCITRAL document A/CN.9/442, UN Publication ISBN 92-1-133608.
123 See Reg 2(2) of SI 2006/1030.
124 Art 8 of Sched 1 to SI 2006/1030.
125 Art 7 of Sched 1 to SI 2006/1030.
126 Reg 3 of SI 2006/1030.
127 Art 3 of Sched 1 to SI 2006/1030.
128 As set out in Arts 1(2)–1(7) of Sched 1 to SI 2006/1030.
129 SI 1999/2979.

the Financial Collateral Arrangements (No 2) Regulations 2003[130] (modification of insolvency law for financial collateral arrangements).

5.7.1.6 It is interesting to note that the adoption of the GB Model Law and its application in the case of foreign insolvency proceedings is not based, nor dependent, upon the principle of reciprocity. That is, there is nothing which limits the application of the Model Law to foreign proceedings (and insolvency practitioners appointed in such proceedings) in countries that have also adopted the Model Law. It will be interesting to see if, nonetheless, the British courts might take a lack of reciprocity into account in situations where they have a discretion in determining a matter arising under the Model Law.

5.7.1.7 There now follows a summary of the principal features of the GB Model Law.

5.7.2 Application

The GB Model Law will apply to an individual or corporate debtor that has a place of business, a place of residence, or assets in Great Britain, where there is also a connection of the debtor with a foreign jurisdiction. The Model Law will be relevant to action that a British insolvency practitioner wishes to take in such a foreign jurisdiction, to the co-operation between British and foreign proceedings, and to the recognition and assistance in Great Britain of creditors' rights, of foreign proceedings, or action that the foreign insolvency practitioner may wish to take in Great Britain.

5.7.3 Foreign proceedings

'Foreign proceedings' are proceedings of a collective judicial or administrative nature, including interim proceedings, under which the affairs and assets of a debtor are subject to the control or supervision of the foreign court for the purpose of reorganisation or liquidation.[131] On that basis they would not include a receivership but, unlike the position under the EC Insolvency Regulation, they may include debtor in possession proceedings if they are subject to the supervision of a foreign court. Foreign proceedings will be categorised as being either 'main' or 'non-main' proceedings.

5.7.3.1 Foreign main proceedings

Foreign main proceedings will be in the State where the debtor has its 'centre of main interests', which is a phrase that is also used in the EC Insolvency Regulation. The phrase is not given a definition in the Model Law although there is a rebuttable presumption that it will be located in the place of a debtor's registered office (if a corporation) or habitual residence (if an individual).[132] It should be

---

[130] SI 2003/3226.
[131] Art 2(i) of Sched 1 to SI 2006/1030.
[132] Art 16(3) of Sched 1 to SI 2006/1030.

noted that the similar presumption in the EC Insolvency Regulation does not refer to a debtor's habitual residence. It should also be noted that, unlike the relevant recital in the EC Insolvency Regulation,[133] there is no reference in the GB Model Law to the place where the debtor conducts the administration of its interests as being a determinant in locating the debtor's centre of main interests. As discussed above, the phrase is gradually being defined by judicial proceedings for the purposes of the EC Insolvency Regulation. It remains to be seen whether a similar or different approach will be taken to the use of the expression in Britain and on the international stage. Presumably, the courts in Britain will strive to use the same interpretation as will apply to the EC Insolvency Regulation. It is possible, however, that a different approach to interpretation may arise elsewhere, bearing in mind that, unlike the EC Insolvency Regulation, the Model Law does not refer to the place of administration of a debtor's interests as being of essential significance in locating the centre of main interests. It is also conceivable that courts in different jurisdictions that are involved in the same insolvency might take divergent views as to the location of a debtor's centre of main interests.

5.7.3.2 *Foreign non-main proceedings*

Foreign non-main proceedings will take place in a State where a debtor has an 'establishment' which is defined to mean 'any place where the debtor carries out a non-transitory economic activity with human means and assets or services'.[134] That definition is wider than the definition of 'establishment' as used in the EC Insolvency Regulation.[135] The latter refers only to '. . . human means and goods'. As with the EC Insolvency Regulation, there must, in any event, be a place of business of the debtor in the place of establishment.

5.7.4 Co-operation

The GB Model Law provides for co-operation between British and foreign insolvency proceedings[136] and the co-ordination of those proceedings,[137] as well as the co-operation of insolvency practitioners in those proceedings. It encourages the British courts and insolvency practitioners to co-operate as much as possible with foreign courts and foreign practitioners,[138] but only (in the case of a British insolvency practitioner) if that would be consistent with his duties under the law in Britain.[139]

---

133 Recital (13).
134 Art 2(e) of Sched 1 to SI 2006/1030.
135 Art 2(h).
136 See Chap IV of Sched 1 to SI 2006/1030.
137 See Chap V of Sched 1 to SI 2006/1030.
138 Chap IV of Sched 1 to SI 2006/1030.
139 Art 26(1) of Sched 1 to SI 2006/1030.

5.7.4.1 It also provides for foreign creditors to commence and prove in British insolvency proceedings.[140] It should be noted that this may include claims by foreign tax and social security authorities,[141] which would not have been permitted under previous common law rules. A similar provision will be found in Article 39 of the EC Insolvency Regulation.

5.7.5 Conflict of laws

Notwithstanding the desire for co-operation and co-ordination of proceedings, there is an issue that may arise in relation to the matters that should be governed by the law of the foreign proceedings or, indeed, by British proceedings. The GB Model Law does not provide for a conflict of laws rule to determine the law that should govern such matters. By contrast, the EC Insolvency Regulation prescribes that, for the most part, the consequences of insolvency proceedings will be governed by the law of those proceedings.[142] It provides, for instance, that the governing law of the proceedings will determine matters such as the effect of the debtor's insolvency on current contracts to which the debtor is a party and the rules relating to the setting aside or adjustment of prior transactions that had been entered into or performed by the debtor prior to the commencement of the insolvency. It is not clear if the same approach would be followed under the GB Model Law, although there is provision (as indicated below) for a foreign insolvency practitioner to bring proceedings before a British court in relation to such prior transactions.

5.7.6 Recognition of foreign proceedings and assistance to foreign representatives

Chapter III of the GB Model Law provides for the recognition of foreign proceedings upon the application of a foreign insolvency practitioner (the 'foreign representative') and the relief that will be available to the foreign representative in Great Britain. Upon recognition of foreign main proceedings, any British proceedings would be restricted to assets located or that should be administered in Great Britain[143] and to co-operating with any relevant foreign proceedings. Relief in British proceedings may include a stay of actions by individual creditors or of enforcement proceedings against the debtor and its assets, as well as a suspension of the debtor's right to dispose of or encumber its assets.[144] Similar relief would be automatic upon recognition of the foreign main proceedings.[145] A foreign representative will have access to the British courts to seek temporary relief and to

---

140 Art 13 of Sched 1 to SI 2006/1030.
141 Art 13(3) of Sched 1 to SI 2006/1030.
142 See para 5.4.9 above.
143 Art 28 of Sched 1 to SI 2006/1030.
144 Art 21 of Sched 1 to SI 2006/1030.
145 Art 20 of Sched 1 to SI 2006/1030.

enable the courts to determine what co-ordination with the foreign proceedings may be needed and if more substantive relief should be granted. The foreign representative may initiate insolvency proceedings in Britain or participate in British proceedings concerning the debtor.

There are protections for security rights and insolvency set-off rights may continue to be exercised.[146]   **5.7.6.1**

The foreign representative, whether appointed in foreign main or non-main proceedings, may request the court to be given power to administer and realise assets in Britain[147] and for the assets to be entrusted to him for distribution by him, subject to the court being satisfied that the interests of British creditors have been 'adequately protected'.[148] The foreign representative may bring proceedings for the setting aside or adjustment of prior transactions along the lines provided for in provisions such as sections 238, 239, 244, 245, 339, 340, 343, and 423 of the Insolvency Act 1986 (e.g. transactions at an undervalue, preferences, extortionate credit transactions, and transactions defrauding creditors).[149]   **5.7.6.2**

The court may grant discretionary relief for the benefit of both main and non-main foreign proceedings, including access to information concerning the debtor's assets (e.g. as to bank accounts),[150] appointment of a person to administer the assets, and a stay to protect the assets from third party action against them. This could include urgent interim relief.   **5.7.6.3**

There are some safeguards provided to local creditors in Britain, including secured creditors, as well as protections for debtors and third parties. The court may not grant discretionary relief that may affect such persons unless they are given adequate protection, and the court may also modify or terminate any relief if it adversely affects their interests.[151] In addition, recognition of foreign main proceedings will not prevent local creditors from initiating or continuing British proceedings.[152] There is a public policy exception which provides that a British court may refuse to take any action that is manifestly contrary to public policy.[153]   **5.7.6.4**

---

[146] Art 20(3) of Sched 1 to SI 2006/1030.
[147] Art 21(1)(2) of Sched 1 to SI 2006/1030.
[148] Art 21(2) of Sched 1 to SI 2006/1030. See the discussion on this point by Sir Andrew Morritt C in *In the matter of HIH Casualty and General Insurance Ltd* [2006] EWCA Civ 732; [2007] 1 All ER 177, at [18]–[21].
[149] Art 23 of Sched 1 to SI 2006/1030.
[150] Art 21(1)(d) of Sched 1 to SI 2006/1030.
[151] Art 22 of Sched 1 to SI 2006/1030.
[152] Arts 20(4) and 20(5) of Sched 1 to SI 2006/1030.
[153] Art 6 of Sched 1 to SI 2006/1030.

6

JURISDICTION AND THE RESOLUTION OF DISPUTES

6.1 Introduction

6.1.1 It is an unfortunate fact of life that the parties to a transaction may fall out and find themselves in dispute or, indeed, that a dispute may arise outside the ambit of a transaction, such as one which relates to a non-contractual claim. Unless the opponents can resolve their differences in an informal and amicable way or through a process of alternative dispute resolution (ADR), it is likely that they will have to resort to a court or another tribunal to enforce or defend their respective positions. If the dispute has cross-border elements, that is, where the dispute is not entirely confined within the domestic boundaries of one jurisdiction, it will be necessary to consider which court or other tribunal has the jurisdiction or author-ity to hear and determine the dispute. It may also be the case that a dispute comes before more than one court or tribunal in different jurisdictions, and so it will be relevant, in addition, to consider how the conflict between the rival or competing proceedings should be resolved.

6.1.2 The discussion that follows will begin by considering the resolution of disputes by the courts and then it will look at arbitration as an alternative mechanism to adju-dicate upon disputes.

6.2 Court Jurisdiction

6.2.1 There are various theoretical bases on which courts in different countries might be willing to assume jurisdiction in a dispute which has cross-border elements. Which ground or grounds are available will depend upon the *lex fori*, that is, the law that applies in the country concerned (which may itself have been modified by the application of an international treaty or convention or, in the case of an EU Member State, by EC legislation).

The principal grounds on which jurisdiction may be assumed are usually selected **6.2.2** from amongst the following. First, jurisdiction may be taken by a court in the country of the defendant's domicile, which is the basic rule of jurisdiction under the principal EC legislation on the subject. Secondly, jurisdiction may be founded on a geographical or territorial connection between the dispute and the country in which the court is situated, such as where a breach of contract is committed within the country, the contract is governed by the law of that country, or the event comprising a tortious claim takes place there or the loss or damage that flows from such a claim is suffered there. Thirdly, a court may take jurisdiction because the claimant is a national of or is domiciled within that country, which is the basic rule in France. Fourthly, jurisdiction may be founded on some territorial connection between the defendant and the relevant country, such as the defendant's presence in the country when the proceedings are served on him. Finally, the jurisdiction of the court may be based upon an agreement between the parties that the court should be empowered to determine the dispute which has arisen.

The jurisdiction of the High Court in England is derived in part from EC legisla- **6.2.3** tion and international conventions that are to much the same effect. To the extent that it is not inconsistent with such legislation or conventions, the court also derives its authority to hear a case from the English rules of jurisdiction founded on service upon the defendant, either with or, in some cases, without the court's leave. Those bases of jurisdiction will be addressed in turn.

6.3 The EC Regulation on Jurisdiction and Judgments and the Brussels and Lugano Conventions

6.3.1 Introduction

The relevant EC legislation and international conventions are:

(1) the EC Regulation on jurisdiction and the recognition and enforcement of judgments in civil and commercial matters (in the discussion that follows, called the 'EC Regulation on jurisdiction and judgments' or the 'Regulation'),[1] which came into force on 1 March 2002;

(2) the Brussels Convention of 1968 on jurisdiction and the enforcement of judgments in civil and commercial matters;[2] and

(3) the Lugano Convention of 1988 on jurisdiction and the enforcement of judgments in civil and commercial matters.[3]

---

[1] EC 44/2001 OJ L12/1 16/1/2001.

[2] As amended by conventions relating to the accession of new Member States to the European Community.

[3] On 30 October 2007 a new Convention was signed between the EC and the EFTA States which, on ratification, is intended to replace the existing Convention of 1988. The provisions of the

6.3.1.1 The Brussels Convention regulated the position as between the Member States of the European Community and the European Union and, save with respect to Denmark (to which the Convention remains relevant),[4] was replaced by the Regulation. The Lugano Convention was entered into between certain of the Member States of the European Community and the EFTA countries. The States that are currently party to the Lugano Convention are Belgium, Denmark, France, Germany, Greece, Ireland, Italy, Luxembourg, the Netherlands, Poland, Spain, Sweden, and the UK (being EU Member States), and Switzerland, Iceland, and Norway (being the remaining EFTA countries). The two Conventions run in parallel and contain much the same provisions. With some modifications, the Regulation is in similar terms to the Conventions and so the case law that was decided concerning the Conventions will remain relevant in considering the Regulation. For convenience, the discussion that follows will concentrate upon the provisions in the Regulation.

6.3.2 Scope of application

The Regulation and the two Conventions apply to disputes which are of a civil or commercial nature[5] and that are not purely domestic. Amongst other exclusions, it is expressly stated in Article 1 that the Regulation does not apply to revenue,[6] customs, or administrative[7] matters, and matters concerning the legal capacity of corporations, insolvency proceedings,[8] and arbitration.[9] It has also been held that the Regulation does not apply so as to override the application of the doctrine of sovereign immunity, but was to be read as being subject to it. Sovereign immunity

---

new Convention are intended to be more closely aligned to the EC Regulation on jurisdiction and judgments than are the provisions of the old Convention. For the purposes of this chapter, references to the Lugano Convention will be to the Convention of 1988 rather than to the new Convention.

[4] Recitals (21) and (22) of the Regulation. The position with Denmark will be regularised by an Agreement between the European Community and Denmark (OJ L299/62 16/11/2005).

[5] Art 1(1).

[6] See *QRS 1 Aps v Fransden* [1999] 1 WLR 2169.

[7] See *Sonntag v Waidmann* Case C-172/91 [1993] ECR 1-1963 and *Grovit v De Nederlandsche Bank* [2005] EWHC 2944 (QB), [2006] 1 Lloyd's Rep 636 (upheld on appeal: [2007] EWCA Civ 953).

[8] In *UBS AG v Omni Holding AG* [2000] 1 WLR 916 it was held that the exclusion only applied if the proceedings derived directly from the insolvency, not simply that they related to an insolvent company. The claim in that case was held to be a commercial dispute which fell within the ambit of the Lugano Convention.

[9] *Through Transport Mutual Insurance Assoc (Eurasia) Ltd v New India Assurance Co Ltd* [2004] EWCA Civ 1598, [2005] 1 Lloyd's Rep 67, in which it was held that a dispute as to whether a contested insurance claim was subject to an agreement to arbitrate, was a matter relating to arbitration within the exception to the application of the Regulation. The Court of Appeal arrived at this conclusion in reliance upon *Marc Rich & Co AG v Società Italiana Impianti PA, The Atlantic Emperor* Case C-190/89, [1991] ECR I-3855 and *Navigation Maritime Bulgare v Rustal Trading Ltd, The Ivan Zagubanski* [2002] 1 Lloyd's Rep 106.

is based upon the principles of international law, to which the Regulation is subject. EC legislation must respect the principles of international law.[10]

Under the Regulation, the general rule is that jurisdiction should be founded upon the place of domicile of the defendant, where the defendant is domiciled in an EC country (irrespective of the defendant's nationality). Articles 5, 22, and 23 of the Regulation (amongst other articles) provide for exceptions to the general rule of jurisdiction under the Regulation. Article 5 provides for an additional ground of jurisdiction in cases such as claims based in tort or in breach of contract. Article 22 provides for exclusive jurisdiction in certain cases relating to immovable property, corporate issues, entries in public registers, intellectual property (IP) rights, and enforcement actions. Article 23 provides for jurisdiction by agreement between the parties.

6.3.3 Mandatory effect

Subject to the effect of Article 27 of the Regulation, a court on which jurisdiction is conferred by the Regulation cannot decline jurisdiction in favour of a court in another Member State which does not have jurisdiction.[11] Indeed, the European Court of Justice held in *Owusu v Jackson*[12] that a court which has jurisdiction under the Regulation based upon the defendant's domicile may not decline to exercise it in favour of a court in a non-Member State on the basis of the doctrine of *forum non conveniens*. The same principle probably applies where another basis of jurisdiction applies under the Regulation as against the defendant. However, there is some doubt about the position where an English court is faced with a question relating to subject matter of a type that would fall within Article 22 of the Regulation (were it located in another EU Member State) when it is located in a non-EU Member State (e.g. a question relating to land in such a State or intellectual property registered in that State). The ECJ refused to answer that question. An English court has decided, however, that it may stay proceedings before it against a defendant domiciled in England if there was an exclusive jurisdiction clause in favour of proceedings taking place before a court in a non-Member State.[13]

---

[10] *Grovit v De Nederlandsche Bank* [2005] EWHC 2944 (QB), [2006] 1 Lloyd's Rep 636 (upheld on appeal: [2007] EWCA Civ 953), applying principles drawn from the decision of the European Court of Justice in the *Poulsen and Diva* case C-286/90, [1992] ECR 1-06019, at para 9 and the decision of the House of Lords in *A (FC) v Sec of State for the Home Dept* [2005] UKHL 71, at [29].

[11] *Re Harrods (Buenos Aires) Ltd* [1992] Ch 72.

[12] Case C-281/02, [2005] ECR I-1383, [2005] QB 801.

[13] *Konkola Copper Mines plc v Coromin* [2005] EWHC 898 (Comm), [2005] 2 Lloyd's Rep 555 (an appeal to the Court of Appeal did not deal with this issue: [2006] EWCA Civ 5, [2006] 1 Lloyd's Rep 410). The decision drew upon the *Schlosser Report on the Brussels Convention*, at [1979] OJ C59, paras 174–176 and a view expressed in *Corek Maritime GmbH v Handelsveem BV* Case C-387/98, [2000] ECR 1-9337.

6.3.4 The standard of proof

The question arises as to the standard of proof that should be applied in determining whether a claimant has made out a sufficient case that an English court has jurisdiction on one basis or another under the Regulation. In an application before an English court to determine jurisdiction, this is a matter to be determined in accordance with the *lex fori*.[14] Toulson LJ said in *Benatti v WPP Holdings Italy SRL*[15] that 'definitive guidance' on the point had been given by the Privy Council in *Bols Distilleries BV v Superior Yacht Services Ltd*.[16] The court must be as satisfied as it can be that there is a 'good arguable case' that it has jurisdiction, bearing in mind the interlocutory nature of the process of determining jurisdiction. Where the issue is contested, so that one party asserts that a different court has jurisdiction under the Regulation, the test is to the effect that one party or the other has the better side of the argument. Taking the point further, although he did not wish finally to decide the point in this case, his Lordship said it might even be possible for the court to take jurisdiction where the court could not decide which party had the better of the argument and felt that the competing arguments as to jurisdiction were finely balanced. He noted that the point had also been discussed in *Konkola Copper Mines plc v Coromin Ltd*,[17] but no final conclusion had been reached.

6.3.5 Jurisdiction founded on the defendant's domicile

The basic rule in the Regulation, contained in Article 2, is that jurisdiction is founded on the domicile of the defendant, if the place of domicile is within a Member State, whether or not the defendant is a national of that State.[18] On that basis, the court of the place of domicile has jurisdiction in a claim against the defendant. Those rules are subject to Article 22, under which jurisdiction in certain matters is exclusively conferred on particular courts, regardless of domicile. Article 23 also provides for jurisdiction by agreement, for which domicile is not an essential element. Subject to Articles 22 and 23, if the defendant is not domiciled in an EU Member State, the ordinary domestic rules applicable to a court's jurisdiction will apply.[19]

---

[14] *Bols Distilleries BV v Superior Yacht Services Ltd* [2006] UKPC 45, [2007] 1 WLR 12, applying *Sjevill v Presse Alliance SA* Case C-68/93, [1995] ECR I-415.

[15] [2007] EWCA Civ 263; [2007] 1 WLR 2316, at [37].

[16] [2006] UKPC 45, [2007] 1 WLR 12.

[17] [2006] EWCA Civ 5, [2006] 1 Lloyd's Rep 410.

[18] Art 2(1). Art 2(2) then provides that persons who are not nationals of the Member State in which they are domiciled shall be subject to the same rules of jurisdiction as apply to the nationals of that State.

[19] Art 4(1). Art 4(2) then provides that such a defendant may be sued in the courts of a Member State by a person who is domiciled in that State, but not a national of that State, to the same extent as a national of that State may sue such a defendant.

Articles 59 and 60 lay down some common rules relating to the ascertainment **6.3.5.1** of a person's domicile. Article 59 provides that a person's domicile should be determined in accordance with the law of the alleged place of domicile. Article 60 provides a rule to determine the domicile of a corporation or other similar entity. It provides as follows:

1. For the purposes of this Regulation, a company or other legal person or association of natural or legal persons is domiciled at the place where it has its:
   (a) statutory seat, or
   (b) central administration, or
   (c) principal place of business.
2. For the purposes of the United Kingdom and Ireland 'statutory seat' means the registered office or, where there is no such office anywhere, the place of incorporation or, where there is no such place anywhere, the place under the law of which the formation took place.
3. In order to determine whether a trust is domiciled in the Member State whose courts are seised of the matter, the court shall apply its rules of private international law.

It is not clear what the position would be if a corporation (or other body) had **6.3.5.2** its statutory seat (e.g. its registered office) in a different country to the place of its central administration or its principal place of business. Presumably, it was not intended that it might have more than one place of domicile at one and the same time.

6.3.6 Alternative bases of jurisdiction

The Regulation contains alternative bases of jurisdiction to that provided for by Article 2. Those that might be relevant in the context of commercial financing transactions will be found in Articles 5, 6, 22, 23, and 24.[20] It will also be relevant at a later stage to examine the rules in the Regulation that deal with cases where proceedings concerning the same dispute may be on foot in more than one Member State.

6.3.7 Article 5: jurisdiction based on a close connection with the dispute

Article 5 of the Regulation (and Article 5 in each of the Brussels and Lugano Conventions) provides for various instances where a defendant who is domiciled in a Member State may be sued before the courts in another Member State, where

---

[20] The Regulation also contains other bases of jurisdiction that are not of immediate relevance to the present subject matter. Briefly, they are as follows. Art 5(2) (maintenance), Art 5(7) (salvage of cargo or freight), Art 7 (limitation of liability concerning the use or operation of a ship), Arts 8–14 (matters relating to insurance, including marine insurance), Arts 15–17 (consumer contracts), and Arts 18–21 (individual contracts of employment).

that other Member State has a close connection with the case. It is important to note the overriding condition that Article 5 only applies where a defendant is domiciled in a Member State. The situations where Article 5 can apply include the following.

6.3.7.1 *Place of performance of a contractual obligation*

Under Article 5(1), the defendant may be sued in matters relating to a contractual obligation in the courts of the place of performance of the contract.[21] Article 5(1)(b) (which does not appear in either the Brussels or Lugano Conventions) provides rules to determine the place of performance in sale of goods contracts and supply of services contracts, unless otherwise agreed. In the case of a contract for the sale of goods,[22] the place of performance should be where the goods were to be delivered under the contract rather than, for instance, the place where payment for the goods was to be made or title was to pass.[23] In the case of a contract for the provision of services,[24] the place of performance will be where the contract provided for the services to be provided. In other situations, it will be necessary to determine the relevant place of performance of the obligation on which the claim is founded, rather than by searching for what might be thought to be an overall characteristic obligation of the contract.[25]

6.3.7.1.1 It has been made clear by the European Court of Justice that the interpretation of Article 5(1) is to be achieved in an autonomous fashion as a jurisdictional matter, without recourse to concepts of national law which might confine its application.[26]

---

[21] It should be noted that Art 63 imposed an additional requirement in the case of a defendant who was domiciled in Luxembourg, which requirement fell away at the end of February 2008.

[22] As opposed to a bailment of goods or another type of supply of goods not being a sale of the goods (e.g. a lease or, perhaps, a hire purchase agreement).

[23] As to the difficulty in ascertaining the place where delivery was to take place, see *Scottish & Newcastle International Ltd v Othon Ghalanos Ltd* [2006] EWCA Civ 1750, [2007] 2 Lloyd's Rep 341, in which it was held that the proper law of the contract of sale would determine where delivery was to take place. In a contract for the carriage of goods by sea governed by English law, it was the legal concept of delivery under the Sale of Goods Act 1979 that was relevant, rather than, if different, the ultimate destination of the goods once shipped. Query the position under a letter of credit which relates to an underlying contract for the sale of goods. For the purposes of Art 5(1), it is not clear if the obligations under the letter of credit would be considered as relating to the underlying contract, or if they would be considered as arising under an entirely separate contract and, if so, if they would be considered as relating to the provision of a service.

[24] There is no definition of 'services'. Query if the lending of money under a loan facility would be considered a service. Lord Goff of Chieveley in *R v Preddy* [1996] AC 815, at 840, thought that the lending of money was not a service.

[25] Art 5(1)(c), taken with Art 5(1)(a). See also *Ets A de Bloos SPRL v Société en commandite par actions Bouyer* Case 14/76, [1976] ECR 1497; *Custom Made Commercial Ltd v Stawa Metallbau GmbH* Case C-288/92, [1994] ECR I-2913; Rix LJ in *Royal & Sun Alliance Insurance plc v MK Digital FZE (Cyprus) Ltd* [2006] EWCA Civ 629; [2006] 2 Lloyd's Rep 110, at [90]–[100].

[26] *Fonderie Officine Meccaniche Tacconi SpA v Heinrich Wagner Sinto Maschinenfabrik GmbH* Case C-334/00, [2002] ECR I-7357, at para 19. This would appear to be at odds with the approach

The same approach should be taken to Article 5(3),[27] which concerns non-contractual claims for civil wrongs. Accordingly, a court must first determine the question of its jurisdiction in accordance with Article 5 before it chooses and then applies the law that would determine the substance of the claim.

A number of issues arise in relation to Article 5(1). For instance, it would appear that a claim does not come within Article 5(1) if it relates to an admittedly void contract[28] or an obligation that never came into existence,[29] but the position may be different if there is a dispute as to the validity of the contract or the relevant obligation on which the claim is based.[30] The claim must relate to a contractual obligation that has been freely entered into by the defendant.[31] It appears that the claim may be brought by a third party which relies upon the Contracts (Rights of Third Parties) Act 1999.[32] Whilst it is not free from doubt, the same should apply to the right of an assignee to bring a claim, at least where a legal assignment has occurred, so as to put the defendant in a direct relationship with the claimant assignee. It is unclear if a restitutionary claim that relates to an actual or alleged contract would come within Article 5(1). In a case that does not fall within Article 5(1)(b), there is a risk that the contract may call for performance of separate obligations in different places or for performance of an obligation in several places. It is not clear which courts would have jurisdiction or, indeed, if several courts may be given jurisdiction in such cases.[33]

6.3.7.2 Non-contractual claims for civil liability

Article 5(3) provides that in matters relating to 'tort, delict or quasi-delict', the courts in the place where the harmful event occurred should have jurisdiction.

6.3.7.1.2

6.3.7.2.1

---

taken by Rix LJ in *Scottish & Newcastle International Ltd v Othon Ghalanos Ltd* [2006] EWCA Civ 1750, at [39].

[27] Ibid.

[28] *Kleinwort Benson Ltd v Glasgow City Council* [1999] 1 AC 153.

[29] *Fonderie Officine Mecchaniche Tacconi SpA v Heinrich Wagner Sinto Maschinenfabrik GmbH* Case C-334/00, [2002] ECR I-7357.

[30] *Boss Group Ltd v Boss France SA* [1997] 1 WLR 351; *Agnew v Länsförsäkringsbolagens AB* [2001] 1 AC 223. At least the court should be entitled, as a preliminary matter, to determine if the contract existed: *Effer SpA v Kantner* Case 38/81, [1982] ECR 825.

[31] *Jakob Handte & Co GmbH v Soc Traitements Mécano-Chemiques des Surfaces* Case C-26/91, [1992] ECR I-3967, at para 18.

[32] Per Toulson LJ in *Benatti v WPP Holdings Italy SRL* [2007] EWCA Civ 263; [2007] 1 WLR 2316, at [53]–[55].

[33] See the divergent approaches taken in *Shenavai v Kreischer* Case 266/85, [1987] ECR 239, *Leathertex Divisione Sintetici SpA v Bodetex BVBA* Case C-420/97, [1999] ECR I-6747, and *De Bloos Sprl v Bouyer SA* Case 14/76, [1976] ECR 1497. Nonetheless, in *Royal & Sun Alliance Insurance plc v MK Digital FZE (Cyprus) Ltd* [2006] EWCA Civ 629; [2006] 2 Lloyd's Rep 110, at [93], Rix LJ said that where a claim involved a number of obligations, the court would be guided by the principle, 'accessorium sequitur principle', so that the principal obligation of those obligations would determine jurisdiction.

It has been held that Article 5(3) covers any case which seeks to establish a defendant's liability which is not related to a contract.[34] This appears to recognise a fairly clear demarcation between a dispute which involves or is derived from a contractual obligation, to which Article 5(1) would apply, and a dispute involving a non-contractual liability, to which Article 5(3) would apply. In cases which may be pleaded in both contract and tort, it will be necessary to determine if the substance of the claim is based on a contractual relationship, in which case Article 5(1) will apply, as for instance would be the case of a claim based upon a contractual obligation to exercise due care and skill. It will be more difficult to determine the correct approach where a claim is pleaded exclusively in tort, but is met by a defence based upon a contractual limitation of liability. Subject to those distinctions, the concept of a non-contractual liability would appear to be very broad, although it is still necessary that the claim should be based on an alleged liability of the defendant.[35] It might cover non-contractual claims not just in tort but also claims to enforce certain types of equitable obligations and restitutionary claims.[36] It has been held that a claim for dishonest assistance in a breach of trust would fall within Article 5(3).[37] However, if such claims arise in consequence of, or perhaps in relation to acts and statements made in anticipation of, a contract into which the defendant has entered, they are likely to fall within the ambit of Article 5(1) rather than Article 5(3).

Article 5(3) confers jurisdiction upon the courts in the place where the harmful event occurred. In *Handelswekerij GJ Bier BV v Mines de Potasse d'Alsace SA*[38] the European Court of Justice held that such a place could be either the place where the damage occurred or the place of the event giving rise to and being the origin of that damage. If they are different, the claimant has the option to choose between them. As there are two alternate limbs, it is necessary to examine each of the limbs separately to discuss their ingredients.

6.3.7.2.2 The first limb is based upon a determination of the place where the damage occurred. This may give rise to a difficulty in a case that involves a claim for consequential damage in addition to any immediate damage that might have been suffered by either the claimant or someone else. It has been held that the relevant

---

[34] *Kalfelis v Bankhaus Schröder Münchmeyer Hengst & Co* Case 189/87, [1988] ECR 5565.

[35] *Reichert v Dresdner Bank (No 2)* Case C-261/90, [1992] ECR I-2149; *Fonderie Officine Meccaniche Tacconi SpA v Heinrich Wagner Sinto Mashinenfabrik GmbH* Case C-334/00, [2002] ECR I-7357; and *Verein Für Konsumenteninformation v Henkel* Case C-167/00, [2002] ECR I-8111.

[36] Although the House of Lords in *Kleinwort Benson Ltd v Glasgow City Council* [1999] 1 AC 153 rejected the possibility that a restitutionary claim would fall within Art 5(3), it is submitted that this is inconsistent with the approach that has been taken by the European Court of Justice.

[37] *Casio Computers Co Ltd v Sayo* [2002] EWCA Civ 661, [2001] ILPr 694.

[38] Case 21/76, [1976] ECR 1735; [1978] QB 708, at paras 19 and 25.

damage should be the initial, direct, immediate, or physical damage that first occurred.[39] Hence, a holding company's derivative claim for financial loss will not be for the relevant damage where the claim is derived from harm suffered by its subsidiary company as a result of action taken by the defendant against the subsidiary.[40] A claim for consequential financial loss following upon initial damage suffered by the claimant cannot be founded, for jurisdictional purposes, upon the place where the consequential loss was suffered; it must be based upon the place where the initial damage was suffered.[41] It has been held in England that in a case for negligent misstatement, the relevant damage is likely to have occurred in the place where the misstatement was received and acted upon, rather than the place where the statement was originally made.[42]

The second limb is based upon the place of the event which gave rise to, and was the origin of, the relevant damage. Difficulties may arise if there was a chain of events which took place in more than one country. For instance, this may be the case in a claim in defamation or for misrepresentation, where a false statement was made in one place and received and acted upon in another. It has been held that in such cases, the relevant event will have occurred where the statement was made rather than in the place where it was received.[43]

6.3.7.2.3

6.3.7.3 Claims involving a branch

In a dispute concerning the operations of a branch, agency, or other establishment of a defendant, Article 5(5) confers jurisdiction upon the courts of the place in which the branch, agency or other establishment is situated. In a sense, a form of quasi-domicile is conferred upon the place of the branch with respect to the operations conducted from that place. The relevant body must be a true agency of the defendant in the sense that it should have a fixed and reasonably permanent (as opposed to a transitory) place of business, it should be under the direction and

---

[39] *Dumez France v Hessische Landesbank (Helaba)* Case C-220/88, [1990] ECR I-49; *Marinari v Lloyds Bank plc* Case C-364/93, [1995] ECR I-2719, [1996] QB 217; *London Helicopters Ltd v Heliportugal LDA-INAC* [2006] EWHC 108 (QB), at [17]–[20].

[40] *Dumez France v Hessische Landesbank (Helaba)* Case C-220/88, [1990] ECR I-49.

[41] *Marinari v Lloyds Bank plc* Case C-364/93, [1995] ECR I-2719, [1996] QB 217.

[42] *Domicrest Ltd v Swiss Bank Corp* [1999] QB 548; *Alfred Dunhill Ltd v Diffusion Internationale de Maroquinerie de Prestige SARL* [2002] 1 All ER (Comm) 950; *London Helicopters Ltd v Heliportugal LDA-INAC* [2006] EWHC 108 (QB), at [22]–[25].

[43] *Shevill v Presse Alliance SA* Case C-68/93, [1995] ECR I-415 (defamation); *Domicrest Ltd v Swiss Bank Corp* [1999] QB 548 (negligent misstatement); *Alfred Dunhill Ltd v Diffusion Internationale de Maroquinerie de Prestige SARL* [2002] 1 All ER (Comm) 950 (negligent misstatement); *ABCI v Banque Franco-Tunisienne* [2003] EWCA Civ 205, [2003] 2 Lloyd's Rep 146 (fraudulent misrepresentation); *Newsat Holdings Ltd v Zani* [2006] EWHC 342 (Comm), [2006] 1 All ER (Comm) 607. The contrary approach taken by Steyn J in *Minster Investment Ltd v Hyundai Precision & Industry Co Ltd* [1988] 2 Lloyd's Rep 621, which emphasised the place where the statement was received and acted upon, was disapproved in *Domicrest, Alfred Dunhill, ABCI* and *Newsat*.

control of the defendant, and it should be able to act on behalf of the defendant and bind it.[44] The dispute must arise out of the operations of the branch, although the activity may take place elsewhere.[45]

6.3.7.4 Trusts

Article 5(6) provides that a settlor, trustee, or beneficiary of a trust (if such trust arises by operation of statute or by a written instrument or, if created orally, it is evidenced in writing) may be sued in the courts of the Member State where the trust is domiciled. The domicile of the trust should be ascertained in accordance with the conflict of laws rules of the court before whom the claim is brought.[46] Jurisdiction under Article 5(6) may be displaced by a conferral of jurisdiction within the trust instrument pursuant to Article 23(4).

6.3.8 Related claims

Articles 6(1) to 6(3) of the Regulation provide for jurisdiction to be taken against a person who is domiciled in another Member State by the court in which proceedings in related claims have been brought. It is confined, essentially, to claims against co-defendants, third party proceedings, and counterclaims that are connected with such proceedings.

6.3.8.1 Article 6(4) provides for a contractual claim against a defendant who is domiciled in a Member State to be brought in the courts of another Member State if the contractual claim relates to a claim against the same defendant concerning immovable property in that other State.

6.3.9 Exclusive jurisdiction under Article 22

Article 22 of the Regulation[47] confers exclusive jurisdiction in relation to certain types of claim, regardless of the domicile of the defendant, along the following lines.

6.3.9.1 By Article 22(1), proceedings which have as their object rights *in rem* in immovable property or certain tenancies in immovable property should be brought in the Member State where the property is situated.[48]

---

[44] *De Bloos Sprl v Bouyer SA* Case 14/76, [1976] ECR 1497; *Somafer SA v Saar-Ferngas AG* Case 33/78, [1978] ECR 2183; *Blanckaert & Willems PVBA v Trost* Case 139/80, [1981] ECR 819; *SAR Schotte GmbH v Parfums Rothschild Sàrl* Case 218/86, [1987] ECR 4905.

[45] *Lloyd's Register of Shipping v Societe Campenon Bernard* Case C-439/93, [1995] ECR I-961; *Anton Durbeck GmbH v Den Norske Bank ASA* [2003] EWCA Civ 147, [2003] QB 1160.

[46] Art 60(3). For the position under English law, see para 12 of Sched 1 to the Civil Jurisdiction and Judgments Order 2001(SI 2001/3929).

[47] Which takes the place of Art 16 of the Brussels and Lugano Conventions.

[48] The European Court of Justice has held that a claim in nuisance was not within Art 16(1)(a) of the Brussels Convention (the equivalent of Art 22(1) of the Regulation), as it did not have as its

Article 22(2) provides that certain matters relating to companies and other types of body, such as partnerships and unincorporated associations, should be determined in the Member State where the relevant company or body has its 'seat'. The proceedings must have as their object matters relating to the validity of the company's or body's constitution, or the nullity or dissolution of the company or body, or the validity of the decisions of its organs.[49] By contrast with Article 60, the seat for this purpose should be determined in accordance with the conflict of laws rules of the court before which the claim is brought.[50]   **6.3.9.2**

Article 22(3) concerns proceedings about the validity of entries in a public register maintained in a Member State.   **6.3.9.3**

Article 22(4) deals with intellectual property rights.   **6.3.9.4**

Article 22(5) relates to the enforcement of judgments.   **6.3.9.5**

The Court of Appeal has held that, despite Article 27(1) of the Regulation and the ruling of the European Court of Justice in *Erich Gasser GmbH v MISAT srl*,[51] a court which has exclusive jurisdiction pursuant to Article 22 may proceed to entertain a case, notwithstanding that earlier proceedings had already been commenced before the courts of another Member State.[52] The exclusive character of proceedings under Article 22 is reinforced by Article 25 which provides that any other court which is seised of such proceedings must declare of its own motion that it has no jurisdiction, even if the point is not raised by one of the parties. Similarly, a voluntary submission under Article 24 has no effect if another court has exclusive jurisdiction under Article 22.   **6.3.9.6**

6.3.10 Jurisdiction by agreement

Articles 23(1) to 23(3) of the Regulation, which take the place of Article 17 of the Brussels and Lugano Conventions, provide for the parties to a dispute to agree, either in an agreement entered into before the dispute arose (e.g. in a commercial   **6.3.10.1**

---

object a claim *in rem*. The latter related to claims to determine the extent, content, ownership, or possession of immovable property, or the existence of other rights *in rem* therein and the protection of the powers attached to their interests: *Land Oberösterreich v CEZ as* Case C-343/04, [2006] 2 All ER (Comm) 665.

[49] A challenge to the composition of the board of a company's board of directors would be a matter going to the validity of the decisions of the board: *Bambino Holdings Ltd v Speed Investments Ltd* [2004] EWCA Civ 1512, [2005] 1 WLR 1936. In light of the decision in *Grupo Torras SA v Sheikh Fahad Mohammed Al-Sabah* [1996] 1 Lloyd's Rep 7, proceedings against validly appointed directors for misfeasance, where the validity of their decision is not challenged, would probably not fall within Art 22(2).

[50] In the UK, to be determined pursuant to para 10 of Sched 1 to the Civil Jurisdiction and Judgments Order 2001(SI 2001/3929).

[51] Case C-116/02, [2003] ECR I-14693, [2005] QB 1.

[52] *Bambino Holdings Ltd v Speed Investments Ltd* [2004] EWCA Civ 1512, [2005] 1 WLR 1936.

contract by which they agree to submit any disputes that may arise to a nominated court) or once it has arisen, that the courts of a Member State should have jurisdiction to hear the dispute.[53] The jurisdiction conferred upon a court under Article 23 will prevail over the jurisdiction that would otherwise apply under Articles 2, 5, and 6 of the Regulation.[54] It should be noted, however, that by virtue of Article 23(5) such an agreement cannot oust the jurisdiction that would apply in consequence of Articles 13 (insurance matters), 17 (consumer contracts), 21 (employment contracts), or 22. A party may also waive its right to insist upon the jurisdiction of the agreed court by submitting to the jurisdiction of the court of another Member State, pursuant to Article 24.[55] An agreement as to jurisdiction under Article 23 will bind an assignee or successor of rights under a contract to which the agreement relates,[56] and it is submitted that the same would apply to a third party to the contract relying upon rights in its favour under the contract pursuant to the Contracts (Rights of Third Parties) Act 1999.

Articles 23(1) to 23(3) provide as follows:

1. If the parties, one or more of whom is domiciled in a Member State, have agreed that a court or the courts of a Member State are to have jurisdiction to settle any disputes which have arisen or which may arise in connection with a particular legal relationship, that court or those courts shall have jurisdiction. Such jurisdiction shall be exclusive unless the parties have agreed otherwise. Such an agreement conferring jurisdiction shall be either:
   (a) in writing or evidenced in writing; or
   (b) in a form which accords with practices which the parties have established between themselves; or
   (c) in international trade or commerce, in a form which accords with a usage of which the parties are or ought to have been aware and which in such trade or commerce is widely known to, and regularly observed by, parties to contracts of the type involved in the particular trade or commerce concerned.
2. Any communication by electronic means which provides a durable record of the agreement shall be equivalent to 'writing'.
3. Where such an agreement is concluded by parties, none of whom is domiciled in a Member State, the courts of other Member States shall have no jurisdiction over their disputes unless the court or courts chosen have declined jurisdiction.

---

[53] It should be noted that until the end of February 2008, Art 63 restricted the agreement to one that fell within Art 2(1)(a) and effectively imposed additional formal requirements in the case of a defendant who was domiciled in Luxembourg. See *Porta-Leasing GmbH v Prestige International* Case 784/79, [1980] ECR 1517.

[54] As to Art 23 prevailing over Art 6, see *Hough v P&O Containers Ltd* [1999] QB 834.

[55] Which would have the effect of amounting to an agreed variation of the contract: *Elefanten Schuh GmbH v Jacqmain* Case 150/80, [1981] ECR 1671.

[56] *Corek Maritime GmbH v Handelsveem BV* Case 387/98, [2000] ECR I-9337; *Glencore International AG v Metro Trading International Inc* [2001] 1 All ER (Comm) 103, [2001] 1 Lloyd's Rep 284.

Although Article 23(1) contemplates that the agreed court may have exclusive jurisdiction, it has been held that, pursuant to Article 27,[57] such a court must stay its proceedings if the court of another Member State is first seised of the claim, so that the other court can determine which court should have jurisdiction under the Regulation to hear the case.[58] It follows that an English court cannot issue an anti-suit injunction to restrain a party from proceeding before the court that was first seised, even if that party is doing so in breach of the agreement as to jurisdiction.[59]

6.3.10.2

Unless the parties are agreed that the chosen court does have jurisdiction in accordance with the alleged agreement as to jurisdiction, it will be necessary for the party which asserts that a court has jurisdiction based upon Article 23 to show that there was such an agreement and that the dispute falls within the subject matter of the agreement for jurisdiction, which would be a matter for determination by the court that was first seised.[60] Such a court would have to determine the existence of the alleged agreement (including the fulfilment of the formal requirements that are required to demonstrate the existence of the agreement, such requirements being as referred to in paragraphs (a), (b), or (c) of Article 23(1)[61]) and matters going to its scope, including its construction and interpretation. The European Court of Justice has held that the formal requirements of Article 23 (and its predecessor in the Conventions) must be strictly construed, so that an alleged agreement as to jurisdiction must be 'clearly and precisely demonstrated'[62] and that the requirements stated in Article 23 are directed to achieving that end.[63] It has also been said that it is necessary to show that there was a consensus between the parties as to the agreement as to jurisdiction, so that it would not be sufficient merely to show that it was a clause in a standard form contract, where there is a danger

6.3.10.3

---

[57] Art 21 of the Brussels and Lugano Conventions.

[58] *Erich Gasser GmbH v MISAT srl* Case C-116/02, [2003] ECR I-14693, [2005] QB 1, which was applied in *JP Morgan Europe Ltd v Primacom AG* [2005] EWHC 508 (Comm), [2005] 2 Lloyd's Rep 665.

[59] *Turner v Grovit* Case C-159/02, [2004] ECR I-3565, [2005] 1 AC 101. There may be a claim for damages for breach of contract: *Union Discount Co v Zoller* [2001] EWCA Civ 1755, [2002] 1 WLR 1517.

[60] *Powell Duffryn PLC v Petereit* Case C-214/89, [1992] ECR I-1745.

[61] As to the formalities required in para (a), see the conflicting approaches taken by the European Court of Justice in *Estasis Salotti di Colzani Aimo et Gianmario Colzani v RÜWA Polstereimaschinen GmbH* Case 24/76, [1976] ECR 1831 and *Galeries Segoura sprl v Bonakdarian* Case 25/76, [1976] ECR 1851, with the approach in *The Tilly Russ* Case 71/83, [1984] ECR 2417 and *Powell Duffryn plc v Petereit* Case C-214/89, [1992] ECR I-1745.

[62] *Estasis Salotti di Colzani Aimo et Gianmario Colzani v RÜWA Polstereimaschinen GmbH* Case C-24/76, [1976] ECR 1831.

[63] In *Bols Distilleries BV v Superior Yacht Services Ltd* [2006] UKPC 45, [2007] 1 WLR 12 it was held that there was neither a written agreement nor an oral agreement evidenced in writing by which the parties agree to the jurisdiction of a particular court.

that the jurisdiction clause might have been overlooked by one of the parties.[64] However, if the contract that is signed by both parties (or the documents that contain their signatures) expressly refers to the general conditions of one of them, which included a jurisdiction clause, that might be sufficient to satisfy the requirements of Article 23. In such a case, it would not be necessary that the agreement as to jurisdiction should be set out in the signed documents.[65] It has been held, nonetheless, that there must be an agreement under which the parties intended to create legal relations, which were to be legally enforceable.[66]

6.3.10.4   It seems to be clear that purely formal matters should fall to be determined by a simple application of the article itself, so that a language requirement under the *lex fori* would not be relevant.[67] It has also been accepted that Article 23 would still apply where the applicant for jurisdiction is asserting that a contract containing an agreement as to jurisdiction had come to an end, for instance, because of an accepted repudiatory breach.[68] However, a party to a dispute cannot rely on such a provision in a contract to which it denies that it was a party and by which it denies that it was bound, so as to obtain a negative declaration concerning the contract from the court nominated in the contract.[69]

6.3.10.5   The position is more difficult where there is a dispute as to a substantive issue concerning the validity of the agreement for submission, such as where there is an allegation of fraud, *non est factum*, or common mistake, or as to whether the particular dispute falls within the scope of the agreement, which would go to its interpretation. The European Court of Justice has favoured the view that such matters should be determined under Community law in an autonomous manner as a matter of fact to see if there was consensus and without reference to the substantive law that might govern the agreement in which the alleged submission is contained.[70] Nonetheless, a court which had to determine the matter may feel that it should use some reference point in determining such matters of substance. One possibility is that the court should refer to the law that governs the agreement for submission or, where its validity is challenged, the law which would govern it if it were found to be valid. As such matters are excluded from the ambit of the

---

[64]   *The Tilly Russ* Case 71/83, [1984] ECR 2417 and *Corek Maritime GmbH v Handelsveem BV* Case C-387/98, [2000] ECR 1-9337.

[65]   *7E Communications Ltd v Vertex Antennentechnik GmbH* [2007] EWCA Civ 140, [2007] 1 WLR 2175.

[66]   *Implants International Ltd v Stratec Medical* [1999] 2 All ER (Comm) 933.

[67]   *Elefanten Schuh GmbH v Jacqmain* Case 150/80, [1981] ECR 1671

[68]   *Francesco Benincasa v Dentalkit Srl* Case C-269/95, [1997] ECR I-3767.

[69]   *Andromeda Marine SA v OW Bunker & Trading A/S* [2006] EWHC 777 (Comm)

[70]   *Corek Maritime GmbH v Handelsveem BV* Case C-387/98, [2000] ECR 1-9337, *Trasporti Castelletti Spedizioni Internazionali SpA* Case C-157/97, [1997] ECR I-1597. See also the approach taken by the Court of Appeal in *IP Metal Ltd v Ruote OZ SpA* [1994] 2 Lloyd's Rep 560.

Rome Convention[71] they would fall to be determined, if they came before an English court, in accordance with the proper law of the contract, to be ascertained under common law conflict of laws principles.[72]

An English court would apply the *lex fori* in establishing, under its standard of proof, that it had jurisdiction by agreement to hear a claim.[73] As previously indicated, it would be necessary for the applicant to demonstrate its case that the court had jurisdiction based on Article 23 to the standard of a good arguable case, that is, the better argument on the available material.[74] It has also been suggested that an English court would adopt the same approach if it had to decide whether it should decline to hear a case, where otherwise it would have jurisdiction, because of an alleged agreement between the parties that another court should have jurisdiction.[75]

6.3.10.6

Subject as already stated, Article 23(1) provides that if one or more of the parties is domiciled in a Member State (not necessarily the State upon which jurisdiction is conferred by the agreement), the agreement as to jurisdiction will be exclusive of a court in another Member State having jurisdiction, unless the parties have agreed that the jurisdiction of the nominated court is only to be non-exclusive.[76] If it is agreed that the jurisdiction of the nominated court is only to be non-exclusive, then that court would have jurisdiction in addition to the jurisdiction that another court may have under the Regulation.[77] If the parties choose more than one court

6.3.10.7

---

[71] By Art 1(2)(d) of the Rome Convention.

[72] These matters should now be read in light of the decision of Flaux J in *Deutsche Bank AG v Asia Pacific Broadband Wireless Communications Inc* [2008] EWHC 918 (Comm) who said that the existence and validity of an agreement as to jurisdiction must be judged in accordance with autonomous European law and the clear requirements that had been laid down by the European Court of Justice, as summarised in *Bols Distilleries v Superior Yacht Services Ltd* [2006] UKPC 45, [2007] 1 WLR 12, which had also addressed the standard of proof that an English court should adopt in deciding if the relevant requirements had been met. The scope of the agreement as to jurisdiction, which was a matter of construction of the agreement, should be decided in accordance with the national law which governed the agreement.

[73] *Bols Distilleries BV v Superior Yacht Services Ltd* [2006] UKPC 45, [2007] 1 WLR 12, applying *Shevill v Presse Alliance SA* Case C-68/93, [1995] ECR I-415.

[74] *Canada Trust Co v Stolzenberg (No 2)* [1998] 1 WLR 547, aff'd [2002] 1 AC 1 and approved by the Privy Council in *Bols Distilleries BV v Superior Yacht Services Ltd* [2006] UKPC 45, [2007] 1 WLR 12.

[75] *Konkola Copper Mines plc v Coromin* [2006] EWCA Civ 5, [2006] 1 Lloyd's Rep 410.

[76] This differs from the wording of Art 17 of the Brussels and Lugano Conventions, which provides that, 'If an agreement conferring jurisdiction was concluded for the benefit of only one of the parties, that party shall retain the right to bring proceedings in any other court which has jurisdiction by virtue of this Convention'. Although that wording does not appear in Art 23 of the Regulation, it is submitted that the parties could agree that, as against one or some of them, the agreement to jurisdiction should be regarded as an exclusive choice, whilst reserving to another party the right to treat it as a non-exclusive choice.

[77] *Kurz v Stella Musical Veranstaltungs GmbH* [1992] Ch 196; *Insured Financial Structures Ltd v Elektrocieplownia Tychy SA* [2003] EWCA Civ 110, [2003] QB 1260.

to have jurisdiction then, as against courts that have not been nominated, the nominated courts should each be entitled to assume jurisdiction under Article 23. As between them, the first that is seised will prevail in accordance with Article 29 if they are each stated to have exclusive jurisdiction.[78]

6.3.10.8 By virtue of Article 23(3), if none of the parties is domiciled in a Member State, the chosen court will have exclusive jurisdiction, unless it declines to accept jurisdiction. Whilst it is not explicitly stated in Article 23(3), presumably the parties also could agree, in a case where none of the parties is domiciled in a Member State, that the chosen court is only to have non-exclusive jurisdiction.

6.3.10.9 It is not clear as at which date the question of domicile of the parties is to be determined for the purposes of Articles 23(1) and 23(3). One possibility is that their domicile should be determined at the date that they enter into the agreement as to jurisdiction. Another possibility is that the date should be determined at the time a court is seised of jurisdiction.

6.3.11 Jurisdiction by agreement in a trust instrument

6.3.11.1 Article 23(4) concerns the conferral of jurisdiction in a trust instrument. It provides as follows:

> The court or courts of a Member State on which a trust instrument has conferred jurisdiction shall have exclusive jurisdiction in any proceedings brought against a settlor, trustee or beneficiary, if relations between those persons or their rights or obligations under the trust are involved.

Article 23(4) contains no requirement as to the form of the instrument, nor is there any requirement that any of the relevant persons should be domiciled in a Member State. It does not make provision for a purported conferral of non-exclusive jurisdiction.

6.3.11.2 As is the case with Article 23(1), it should be noted that by virtue of Article 23(5) such a purported conferral of jurisdiction cannot oust the jurisdiction that would apply in consequence of Articles 13 (insurance matters), 17 (consumer contracts), 21 (employment contracts), or 22.

6.3.12 Jurisdiction by appearance

Article 24 of the Regulation provides for a court to have jurisdiction where a defendant enters an appearance, provided it was not just to contest jurisdiction or a matter for which exclusive jurisdiction is conferred by Article 22.

---

[78] *Kurz v Stella Musical Veranstaltungs GmbH* [1992] Ch 196, which concerned the equivalent provision in Art 23 of the Brussels and Lugano Conventions.

By Article 26(1), if a defendant fails to enter an appearance, the court must stay its   **6.3.12.1**
proceedings if the defendant is domiciled in another EU Member State and jurisdiction is not derived on some other basis under the Regulation.

6.3.13 Concurrent proceedings

It is possible that the same or related proceedings might be brought concurrently
before courts in different EU Member States. Articles 27 to 30 provide rules to
deal with such a situation.

6.3.13.1 *The same cause of action between the same parties*

Article 27 of the Regulation[79] provides as follows:

1. Where proceedings involving the same cause of action and between the same
   parties are brought in the courts of different Member States, any court other than
   the first seised shall of its own motion stay its proceedings until such time as the
   jurisdiction of the court first seised is established.
2. Where the jurisdiction of the court first seised is established, any court other than
   the court first seised shall decline jurisdiction in favour of that court.

A number of issues are raised in considering Article 27. The first of them concerns   **6.3.13.1.1**
the date upon which a court could be said to be seised of a case. It had been held
that for the purposes of the Brussels and Lugano Conventions, the *lex fori* of the
national court before which a claim was brought would determine the date that
the court was seised of the claim.[80] Under English law, that would be the date on
which the claim form or other commencing process was served on the defendant.[81] The position is different under the Regulation. Article 30 of the Regulation
provides a rule for determining when a national court should be considered as
seised of a case, which depends upon the method by which proceedings may be
commenced in the relevant court. If the proceedings are commenced by lodging
the papers with the court and then serving them, as is the case in England, the
court will be seised at the time of lodgement, provided that the claimant does not
fail to take the requisite steps to effect service on the defendant. If the proceedings
are commenced by serving the papers before they are lodged at the court, the court
will be seised at the time the papers are delivered to the authority that is responsible for service, provided that the claimant does not fail to take the requisite steps
to lodge the papers with the court. The foregoing is consistent with the decision
of the Court of Appeal in *Benatti v WPP Holdings Italy SRL*.[82]

---

[79] Art 21 of the Brussels and Lugano Conventions.
[80] *Zelger v Salinitri (No. 2)* Case 129/83, [1984] ECR 2397.
[81] *Neste Chemicals SA v DK Line SA, The Sargasso* [1994] 2 Lloyd's Rep 6.
[82] [2007] EWCA Civ 263, [2007] 1 WLR 2316.

6.3.13.1.2 The second issue concerns a determination that the competing proceedings concern the same parties. A problem may arise where the rival proceedings do not involve a precise identity in one of the parties, on one side or the other (or on both sides). It has been held in England that in determining if two persons should really be treated as one for the purposes of the proceedings (which is a substantive matter, rather than a procedural issue) the essential question is whether the interests of the two persons are 'identical and indissociable from' each other, which involves a consideration of the issues and the nature of the interests that were involved.[83] In admiralty proceedings, where there are claims *in rem* and *in personam*, the determination should be based on who are the real parties to the different proceedings.[84] In claims involving the insurers of cargo, the owners of the cargo, the insurers of the vessel, the owners of the vessel, and of the cargo, it was held that the parties would be the same if their interests were identical and could not be dissociated from each other.[85] A company and its liquidator may be treated as the same person,[86] as may an assignor and an assignee of a claim that is the subject of the proceedings.[87]

6.3.13.1.3 A third issue concerns whether the rival proceedings involve the same cause of action. The phrase 'the same cause of action' as used in Article 27(1) involves two concepts, derived from the text of the Article in French. One ('la même cause') comprises the facts and the rule of law relied on as the basis of the action. The other ('la même objet') means the end that the action had in view, that is, the essential issue raised in the action. Both concepts have to be fulfilled for the rival proceedings to involve the same cause of action.[88] The matter should be assessed by reference to the claims that had been lodged, ignoring any defences that might have been filed. This is because Article 27 is concerned with the causes of action on initiation of the claims.[89]

---

[83] *Kolden Holdings Ltd v Rodette Commerce Ltd* [2007] EWHC 1597 (Comm), [2007] 4 All ER 62.

[84] *The Indian Grace (No 2)* [1998] AC 878; *The Tatry* Case C-406/92, [1994] ECR I-5439.

[85] *Drout Assurances SA v Consolidated Metallurgical Industries* Case C-351/96, [1998] ECR I-3075.

[86] *Re Cover Europe Ltd* [2002] EWHC 861 (Ch), [2002] 2 BCLC 61.

[87] *Kolden Holdings Ltd v Rodette Commerce Ltd* [2007] EWHC 1597 (Comm), [2007] 4 All ER 62.

[88] *The Tatry* Case C-406/92, [1994] ECR I-05439; *Glencore International AG v Shell International Trading & Shipping Co Ltd* [1999] 2 Lloyd's Rep 692; *Haji-Ioannou v Frangos* [1999] 2 Lloyd's Rep 337; and *JP Morgan Europe Ltd v Primacom AG* [2005] EWHC 508 (Comm), [2005] 2 Lloyd's Rep 665. In the *Primacom* case, it was held that a claim that an obligation to pay interest under a loan agreement should be unenforceable, based upon alleged 'immoral' covenants (covenants to provide information and not to dispose of assets), did not involve the same 'objet' as an action to enforce those covenants in their own right. The action to enforce those covenants was not stayed. On the other hand, claims to enforce the obligation to pay interest and to accelerate the loan for non-payment of the interest did involve the same cause of action and were stayed.

[89] *Gantner Electronic GmbH v Basch Exploitatie Maatschappij BV* Case C-111/01, [2003] ECR I-402; *Kolden Holdings Ltd v Rodette Commerce Ltd* [2007] EWHC 1597 (Comm), [2007] 4 All ER 62.

In accordance with Article 27, it is a matter for the court that is first seised to **6.3.13.1.4**
determine which court properly has jurisdiction under the Regulation to hear the
case.[90] Any other court must stay its proceedings pending that determination,
even if that court believes it properly has exclusive jurisdiction by agreement
between the parties pursuant to Article 23 of the Regulation.[91] If the court that is
first seised decides that it does have jurisdiction to hear the case, the other court
must decline to assert jurisdiction altogether. A stay of a claim pursuant to Article
27(1) does not mean that the claim before the later seised court must be dismissed.
It is merely stayed pending a determination by the court that is first seised of
which court has jurisdiction to hear the claim; the court is only deprived finally of
jurisdiction to hear the claim if the court that is first seised determines under
Article 27(2) that it has jurisdiction.[92]

Notwithstanding Article 27, a court which is not the first seised of a claim is **6.3.13.1.5**
empowered to grant interim protective measures under Article 31 of the
Regulation.

6.3.13.2 Anti-suit injunctions

A court in one EU Member State cannot issue an anti-suit injunction to restrain
a party from continuing with a case before a court in another EU Member State
in a matter that falls within the Regulation; it may not do so even if it believes that
it has the primary claim to assert jurisdiction.[93] The Court of Appeal has held,
however, that an English court has the power to determine whether a dispute was
covered by an agreement to submit to arbitration, notwithstanding that proceedings were already on foot before a court in another EU Member State, because the
Regulation had no application to matters relating to arbitration. It also held that
an English court could issue an anti-suit injunction to restrain a party from continuing with proceedings in another Member State if such proceedings would be
in breach of the agreement to submit the dispute to arbitration and even though

---

[90] Which Art 25 explicitly requires it should do of its own motion if another court has exclusive jurisdiction under Art 22.

[91] This is based upon the principle of mutual trust and comity: *Erich Gasser GmbH v MISAT srl* Case C-116/02, [2003] ECR I-14693, [2005] QB 1, as observed by an English court in *JP Morgan Europe Ltd v Primacom AG* [2005] EWHC 508 (Comm), [2005] 2 Lloyd's Rep 665. The Court of Appeal has decided, by way of exception to this principle, that the court that is secondly seised may continue to hear a case if it has exclusive jurisdiction under Art 22 of the Regulation (Art 16 of the Brussels and Lugano Conventions): *Bambino Holdings Ltd v Speed Investments Ltd* [2004] EWCA Civ 1512, [2005] 1 WLR 1936. It is submitted that this is incorrect, as it is inconsistent with the express wording of Art 27 and the principle of mutual trust and comity as between the courts of the EU Member States as explained by the European Court of Justice in *Erich Gasser GmbH v MISAT srl*.

[92] *JP Morgan Europe Ltd v Primacom AG* [2005] EWHC 508 (Comm), [2005] 2 Lloyd's Rep 665.

[93] *Turner v Grovit* Case C-159/02, [2004] ECR I-3565, [2005] 1 AC 101.

the other court had not yet determined if it had jurisdiction.[94] The House of Lords has now submitted those matters to the European Court of Justice, seeking an authoritative determination as to whether an English court (or, indeed, a court in another EU Member State) is able to restrain a party in such circumstances from maintaining proceedings in another EU Member State.[95]

6.3.13.3 *Related actions before different courts*

Article 28 of the Regulation[96] concerns related actions that may be pending before courts in more than one EU Member State. Related actions are defined by Article 28(3) to be those which, whilst not involving the same cause of action, are so closely connected that it is expedient that they should be heard and determined together, so as to avoid conflicting judgments. Article 28(1) provides that where related actions are pending before courts in different Member States, a court which is not first seised may stay its proceedings. Article 28(2) further provides that a first instance court which is not the first seised in the related actions may decline jurisdiction if the court which is first seised in one of those actions has jurisdiction and it can consolidate the actions. The language of Article 28 is permissive rather than mandatory. There is no obligation for the proceedings to be stayed or for jurisdiction to be declined. The court has a discretion to decide if it will grant the stay or decline jurisdiction. An English court has held that it would not be expedient for related actions to be tried together where they involved the application of different laws, in one case English contract law and the other matters of German public policy.[97] In the same case, it was held that the court should, in any event, refuse to exercise its discretion to grant a stay because the German proceedings had been brought in breach of an exclusive jurisdiction clause in the relevant contract.

6.3.13.4 *Two courts with exclusive jurisdiction*

Article 29 of the Regulation[98] provides that where competing actions fall within the exclusive jurisdiction of more than one court, any court other than the first seised should decline jurisdiction.

---

[94] *Through Transport Mutual Insurance Assoc (Eurasia) Ltd v New India Assurance Co Ltd* [2004] EWCA Civ 1598, [2005] 1 Lloyd's Rep 67. Once again, it is submitted that the approach taken by the Court of Appeal on this issue is inconsistent with the principle in *Erich Gasser GmbH v MISAT srl* Case I-116/02, [2003] ECR I-14693, [2005] QB 1. The matter has now been referred to the European Court of Justice: *West Tankers Inc v RAS Riunione Adriatica di Sicurta SpA* [2007] UKHL 4, [2007] 1 Lloyd's Rep 391. In the event and based upon factual considerations, the Court of Appeal declined to issue an injunction in the exercise of its discretion.

[95] *West Tankers Inc v RAS Riunione Adriatica di Sicurta SpA* [2007] UKHL 4, [2007] 1 Lloyd's Rep 391.

[96] Art 22 of the Brussels and Lugano Conventions.

[97] *JP Morgan Europe Ltd v Primacom AG* [2005] EWHC 508 (Comm), [2005] 2 Lloyd's Rep 665.

[98] Art 23 of the Brussels and Lugano Conventions.

6.3.13.5 Provisional orders

By way of supplementary jurisdiction, Article 31 of the Regulation[99] permits a court of an EU Member State that would not have substantive jurisdiction in a claim to grant provisional orders, including protective orders, such as by way of an injunction or a freezing order affecting the defendant's assets, pending the determination of the claim by the court that has substantive jurisdiction. An English court might be prepared to grant an interim injunction to restrain an alleged breach of contract pending a determination by another court under Article 27 as to which court should hear the claim concerning the breach.[100]

6.4 The Residual Jurisdiction of the High Court under English Law

6.4.1 Introduction

To the extent that it is not inconsistent with the position that obtains under the EC Regulation on jurisdiction and judgments or the Brussels and Lugano Conventions, the High Court may have jurisdiction in accordance with the Civil Procedure Rules (the CPR)[101] to hear a claim.[102] The three pre-conditions to such jurisdiction are:

(1) that the claim does not concern a matter over which the English courts will refuse to take jurisdiction;[103]
(2) that the court is not precluded from hearing a case because there is a valid and binding agreement to submit the dispute to arbitration;[104] and
(3) that the process which initiates the claim has been served on the defendant.

---

[99] Art 24 of the Brussels and Lugano Conventions.

[100] *JP Morgan Europe Ltd v Primacom AG* [2005] EWHC 508 (Comm), [2005] 2 Lloyd's Rep 665.

[101] Which replace the Rules of the Supreme Court (the RSC) and the Orders and rules made thereunder.

[102] The English courts may also have jurisdiction pursuant to the adoption in the UK of certain international conventions dealing with specialist subject matter in the areas of carriage by air, road, or sea, navigation, and pollution.

[103] E.g. a dispute as to the title to foreign land or as to the validity of a foreign intellectual property right or a claim where the defendant is entitled to assert the benefit of sovereign or diplomatic immunity or an immunity under an Order made pursuant to the International Organisations Act 1968 or a similar statutory provision.

[104] Under s 9 of the Arbitration Act 1996, on the application of a party to the arbitration agreement, the court must stay its proceedings in that event, irrespective of whether the arbitration agreement is governed by English or a foreign law and of whether the seat of the arbitration would be in England or elsewhere.

6.4.1.1 Such service may take place on a defendant (or its duly appointed agent to accept service[105]) that is within the jurisdiction or by service upon the defendant outside the jurisdiction. The latter requires the leave or permission of the court in most cases,[106] whereas the former arises as of right, although the court has a discretion to grant a stay of the proceedings, or to strike out or dismiss them, so as to prevent injustice. The presence of the defendant within the jurisdiction at the time of service may be transitory, but that is sufficient.[107]

6.4.1.2 There are special rules that relate to the manner in which service may be effected, for instance, on defendants within the jurisdiction by service through the post to the registered office[108] or at the principal office or any place of business in England[109] of a corporation that is incorporated in England. There are also provisions for service upon a foreign company with a branch or an established place of business in the jurisdiction.[110]

6.4.2 Leave to serve out of the jurisdiction

CPR rule 6.20 contains a list of the heads of claims for which leave to serve out of the jurisdiction may be sought from the court. The claimant must show, to the standard of a reasonable prospect of success, that it has a cause of action against the defendant, on the basis of a serious issue to be tried on the merits of the claim, that falls within one or more of the heads.[111] It may not pursue any additional claim that does not fall within one of the heads.[112]

6.4.2.1 The discretionary principles

The granting of leave is discretionary and will depend upon the court deciding that the claim should be heard by it. This is additional to and separate from the need to establish that the claim comes within one of the heads in CPR rule 6.20.[113] The principles which underlie the decision as to whether the discretion should be exercised in favour of the claimant are, first, that the case is a fit and proper one for

---

[105] Pursuant to CPR r 6.15(1).

[106] Permission will not be required where the court has jurisdiction under Art 23 of the EC Regulation on jurisdiction and judgments or under Art 17 of the Brussels or Lugano Conventions. See further CPR r 6.19.

[107] *Colt Industries Inc v Sarlie* [1966] 1 WLR 440.

[108] S 1139(1) of the Companies Act 2006 (formerly s 725 of the Companies Act 1985).

[109] CPR r 6.6.

[110] S 1139(2) of the Companies Act 2006 (formerly s 695 of the Companies Act 1985).

[111] CPR r 6.21(1)(b), *Seaconsar Far East Ltd v Bank Markazi Iran* [1994] 1 AC 438; *Carivll America Inc v Camperdown UK Ltd* [2005] EWCA 645, [2005] 2 Lloyd's Rep 457. The *Seaconsar* case was decided under the previous rules that applied pursuant to RSC Ord 11 rule 4(2). The decision in that case has also been applied to CRR r 6.21(1)(b): *Opthalmic Innovations International UK Ltd v Opthalmic Innovations International Inc* [2004] EWHC 2948 (Ch). See also *The Islamic Republic of Pakistan v Zardari* [2006] EWHC 2411 (Comm), [2006] 2 CLC 667.

[112] *Donohue v Armco Inc.* [2001] UKHL 64, [2002] 1 Lloyd's Rep 425.

[113] *Seaconsar Far East Ltd v Bank Markazi Iran* [1994] 1 AC 438.

service out of the jurisdiction, and, secondly, that the English court is the appropriate or proper place in which the claim should be tried,[114] that is, where it could most suitably be tried in the interests of the parties and for the ends of justice.[115] The principles are essentially the same as those that should be considered in an application by the defendant for a stay of proceedings on the basis of *forum non conveniens*, although the burden of proof in an application for leave is on the claimant, whereas it falls on the defendant in an application for a stay.[116] The standard of proof in both stay and leave applications is that of a 'good arguable case', bearing in mind that the issue has to be decided at an early stage and before all the evidence can be heard in a full hearing.[117]

In a leave case, the claimant must convince the court that it is proper to exercise its **6.4.2.2** discretion to grant leave to serve out and the court must be mindful that the granting of leave is in the exercise of an 'exorbitant' jurisdiction, in the sense that an English court may not be happy to recognise the reverse situation where a foreign court assumed jurisdiction over an English defendant.[118] The relevant considerations in granting leave will vary from one case to another and different emphasis will be placed upon them, depending upon the facts and circumstances of the case. The factors that are relevant are discussed later in relation to applications for a stay, but include the following:

(a) the efficiency, expedition, and economy of bringing the claim;

(b) the presence and availability of witness and other evidence;

(c) the desire to avoid a multiplicity of proceedings involving the same or similar parties or factual evidence;

(d) the availability of legal aid;

(e) the level of damages that might be recovered in other jurisdictions and the availability in another jurisdiction of the remedy that is sought;[119]

(f) the availability and likely level of interest on the damages; and

(g) if the claim may be statute-barred in England or in another jurisdiction.

---

[114] CPR r 6.21 (2A).

[115] Per Lord Goff in *Spiliada Maritime Corp v Cansulex Ltd, The Spiliada* [1987] AC 460; *The Islamic Republic of Pakistan v Zardari* [2006] EWHC 2411 (Comm), [2006] 2 CLC 667.

[116] This matter is discussed, obiter, in *Konkola Copper Mines plc v Coromin Ltd* [2006] EWCA Civ 5, [2006] 1 Lloyd's Rep 410.

[117] *Seaconsar Far East Ltd v Bank Markazi Iran* [1994] 1 AC 438. In *Canada Trust Co v Stolzenberg (No 2)* [1998] 1 WLR 547, Waller LJ also mentioned a further refinement of the 'good arguable case' requirement, namely, that one side had 'a much better argument'. This was discussed by Rix LJ in *Konkola Copper Mines plc v Coromin Ltd* [2006] EWCA Civ 5; [2006] 1 Lloyd's Rep 410, at [80] and [81] and in *Ashton Investments Ltd v OJSC Russian Aluminium* [2006] EWHC 2545 (Comm), at [45]–[48].

[118] Ibid.

[119] *Petroleo Brasiliero SA v Mellitus Shipping Inc* [2001] EWCA Civ 418, [2001] 2 Lloyd's Rep 203.

6.4.2.3 Heads of claim

The following are paragraphs of CPR rule 6.20 which contain the likely types of claim that would be relevant to disputes concerning financing transactions.

6.4.2.3.1 Paragraph 1 covers a claim against a defendant who is domiciled within the jurisdiction.[120]

6.4.2.3.2 Paragraph 5 covers a claim in respect of a contract, being (a) a contract that is made within the jurisdiction, (b) a contract that was made by or through an agent trading or residing within the jurisdiction, (c) a contract that is governed by English law, or (d) a contract which contains a provision conferring jurisdiction upon the court. The existence of the contract, its governing law, and its terms should be determined in accordance with the principles of English conflict of laws,[121] generally by the application of the Rome Convention, although an agreement as to jurisdiction is outside the remit of the Convention,[122] so the common law conflicts rules would apply to that type of agreement.

6.4.2.3.3 Paragraph 6 covers a claim that is made in respect of a breach of contract committed within the jurisdiction, whether or not it is a contract falling within the list of contracts referred to in paragraph 5. It may not be entirely clear where the breach took place if the contract called for performance in one place but no performance was made. It may also be arguable that a claim for inducing a breach of contract or for the breach of a fiduciary duty arising from a contract might fall within this paragraph. A similar argument might also apply in considering paragraph 5.

6.4.2.3.4 Paragraph 7 covers a claim for a declaration that no contract exists which, if it did exist, would come within paragraph 5.

6.4.2.3.5 Paragraph 8 concerns a claim made in tort where (a) the damage was sustained within the jurisdiction, or (b) the damage which was sustained resulted from an act that was committed within the jurisdiction. It is uncertain if this paragraph requires that there has to be a completed cause of action in tort, as understood under English law[123] or if it is sufficient for the claim to be characterised as a tortious claim for conflict of laws purposes.[124] Paragraphs (a) and (b) reflect the

---

[120] For this purpose, domicile is determined in accordance with Sched 1 to the Civil Jurisdiction and Judgments Order 2001 (SI 2001/3929).

[121] *Amin Rasheed Shipping Corp v Kuwait Insurance Co* [1984] AC 50.

[122] Art 1(2)(d) of the Convention.

[123] *Metall & Rohstoff AG v Donaldson Lufkin & Jenrette Inc* [1990] 1 QB 391, which concerned the predecessor provision in RSC Ord 11, r 1(1)(f), which required a claim 'founded on a tort'.

[124] Which gains support by reference to the approach taken by Part III of the Private International Law (Miscellaneous Provisions) Act 1995.

jurisprudence that has developed in the interpretation of Article 5(3) of the EC Regulation on jurisdiction and judgments.[125]

Paragraph 10 concerns a claim where the whole subject matter of the claim relates to property located within the jurisdiction. The claim may concern any type of property, whether real or personal. It applies to any claim for relief concerning such property. It also applies to claims concerning the proceeds of sale of such property, although the grant of leave is still discretionary.[126]

6.4.2.3.6

Paragraph 11 applies to a claim to execute the trusts of a written instrument if they ought to be executed in accordance with English law[127] and the defendant is the trustee. It is not necessary that the trust property should be located within the jurisdiction.

6.4.2.3.7

Paragraph 14 concerns a claim that is made against a defendant for a remedy as a constructive trustee where the defendant's liability arises from acts committed within the jurisdiction. It is not clear if it must be the defendant's acts which give rise to the liability or if a third party's acts might suffice,[128] and there is also uncertainty as to whether all the relevant acts giving rise to the alleged liability, or just a substantial proportion of them, must have occurred within the jurisdiction.[129]

6.4.2.3.8

Paragraph 15 covers a claim that is made for restitution where the defendant's liability arises out of acts committed within the jurisdiction.

6.4.2.3.9

6.5 Situations where the High Court may Decline to Hear a Case or may Grant an Anti-suit Injunction to Restrain a Party from Continuing Foreign Proceedings

6.5.1 Introduction

There are various circumstances where the High Court may decline to hear a case. One such circumstance has already been examined, namely, where it may refuse to grant leave for service of proceedings on a foreign defendant. The other circumstances concern situations where service has been effected on the defendant but

---

125 And applied in *Newsat Holdings Ltd v Zani* [2006] EWHC 342 (Comm), [2006] 1 All ER (Comm) 607.

126 *Banca Carige SpA Cassa di Risparmio de Genova e Imperia v Banco Nacional de Cuba* [2001] 1 WLR 2039; *The Islamic Republic of Pakistan v Zardari* [2006] EWHC 2411 (Comm), [2006] 2 CLC 667.

127 *Chellaram v Chellaram* [2002] EWHC 632 (Ch).

128 RSC Ord 11 r 1(1)(t) covered both possibilities.

129 *The Islamic Republic of Pakistan v Zardari* [2006] EWHC 2411 (Comm), [2006] 2 CLC 667.

the defendant requests the court to stay or dismiss the proceedings. It is also relevant to consider a related topic, namely, the circumstances in which the High Court may grant an injunction (an 'anti-suit injunction') to restrain a party from bringing foreign proceedings, with the intention that the case should be heard in the English court.

6.5.1.1 In deciding these various matters, the court is usually dealing with a situation where a case might be heard by two or more courts, of which it is one. It is seeking to determine which court is the natural or clearly the more appropriate forum to hear the case for the interests of all the parties and the ends of justice.[130] However, if the court is asked to restrain a party from bringing proceedings, either in England or abroad, in breach of an agreed choice of jurisdiction, the court will generally approach the matter as one of holding a party to its agreement.

6.5.1.2 There are some important caveats to bear in mind when considering these matters. For the reasons that have already been explained, pursuant to the EC Regulation on jurisdiction and judgments and the Brussels and Lugano Conventions, an English court may have no discretion and may be obliged either to hear a case or to stay or decline to hear a case. In addition, it may not issue an anti-suit injunction to prevent a party maintaining or continuing proceedings before a court in another EU Member State in a matter covered by those instruments. The Court of Appeal has held, however, that an English court is entitled to issue an anti-suit injunction to restrain a party from maintaining proceedings before a court in another EU country in a matter that falls outside the scope of the Regulation or the Conventions.[131] This matter is now subject to adjudication by the European Court of Justice, pursuant to a reference made by the House of Lords.[132] The remaining caveat concerns proceedings that have been brought in breach of a valid and binding arbitration agreement. An English court is obliged to stay its proceedings at the request of a party to the arbitration agreement.[133]

---

[130] *Spiliada Maritime Corp v Cansulex Ltd* [1987] AC 460. The position is different in Australia, where the test is based on the concept that it would be vexatious and oppressive for the impugned proceedings to be continued: *BHP Billiton Ltd v Schulz* [2004] HCA 61, (2004) 211 ALR 523. That used to be the approach in England as propounded by the Court of Appeal in *St Pierre v South American Stores (Gath and Chaves) Ltd* [1936] 1 KB 382. The English position began to change with the decision of the House of Lords in *The Atlantic Star* [1974] AC 436 and is now represented by *Spiliada Maritime Corp v Cansulex Ltd* [1987] AC 460.

[131] *Through Transport Mutual Insurance Assoc (Eurasia) Ltd v New India Assurance Co Ltd* [2004] EWCA Civ 1598, [2005] 1 Lloyd's Rep 67.

[132] *West Tankers Inc v RAS Riunione Adriatica di Sicurta SpA* [2007] UKHL 4, [2007] 1 Lloyd's Rep 391.

[133] S 9 of the Arbitration Act 1996.

6.5.2 Stays of English proceedings and refusals to grant leave to serve out of the jurisdiction

Some of the factors that may be relevant in considering if a stay should be granted have been referred to above. In more detail, factors that arise in consequence of *Spiliada Maritime Corp v Cansulex Ltd*[134] and which would be relevant to a determination of whether the court should, on the application of the defendant, stay its proceedings in favour of proceedings in a foreign court that is preferred by the defendant, are as follows. First, that England is not the natural or appropriate forum,[135] that it is clearly more appropriate that the case should be heard in the foreign court,[136] and that the case can be heard in the foreign court.[137] Secondly, the existence of concurrent proceedings between the parties in the foreign court is a relevant, but not conclusive, factor.[138] Thirdly, that there may be reasons of justice which preclude the granting of a stay, such as that justice will not be done in the foreign jurisdiction. However, a stay will not be refused merely because the claimant will be deprived of some personal advantage if substantial justice will be done in the foreign court.

6.5.3 Jurisdiction agreements

One particular matter that may be relevant to the grant of a stay or to an application for leave to serve out of the jurisdiction is the presence of an agreement by which the parties have agreed to confer jurisdiction on either the English or a foreign court. The existence of such an agreement will not be conclusive as to whether a stay or leave should be granted, as it will still be a matter for the court to determine in the exercise of its discretion.[139]

The validity and interpretation of, and the scope of the types of claim covered by, such an agreement will fall to be ascertained in accordance with the law which governs it. The rules for determining the governing law of such an agreement are excluded from the ambit of the Rome Convention,[140] so such matters would fall to be determined in accordance with the proper law of the agreement, to be

6.5.3.1

---

134 [1987] AC 460.

135 If there is an agreement between the parties that the English court is to have jurisdiction, then it would be difficult to argue that the English court is not a natural or appropriate forum: *Mercury Communications Ltd v Communications Telesystems International* [1999] 2 All ER (Comm) 33.

136 That is, that the claim has the most real and substantial connection with the foreign court.

137 So that the claimant can institute proceedings before the foreign court: *Lubbe v Cape plc* [2001] 1 WLR 1545; for instance, because the defendant has undertaken to submit to the jurisdiction of the foreign court.

138 *Konkola Copper Mines plc v Coromin Ltd* [2006] EWCA Civ 5, [2006] 1 Lloyd's Rep 410.

139 *The Eleftheria* [1970] P 94; *The El Amria* [1981] 2 Lloyd's Rep 119; and *Donohue v Armco Inc* [2001] UKHL 64, [2002] 1 Lloyd's Rep 425.

140 By Art 1(2)(d) of the Rome Convention.

ascertained under common law conflict of laws principles. In many cases, the agreement as to jurisdiction will be contained within a larger contract, the applicable or governing law of which will be found by the application of the rules of the Rome Convention. In theory, there is a risk that the enquiry under the rules at common law, to find the proper law that governs the agreement as to jurisdiction, may not be the same as that to be applied under the Convention in relation to the wider contract. In practice, it is likely that much the same result will be reached where there has been the same identity of choice in each instance between the governing law of the contract and the jurisdiction of the court to resolve disputes concerning the contract. Indeed, the existence of an express choice of jurisdiction may be influential in determining if there was an implied choice of law to govern the wider contract.[141] It might also be said that, in a practical sense, the parties may have wished that the same law should govern the agreement concerning jurisdiction as governs the wider contract.

6.5.3.2 Difficulties may arise, however, where there has been a conflicting choice of the governing law of the wider contract from the choice of the court to determine disputes. It should also be remembered that there are various circumstances that are provided for in the Convention in which the court may refuse to apply the chosen law of the contract and, instead, apply its own mandatory rules. In addition, if there has been no express choice of law to govern the wider contract and it is not possible to imply a choice, the rules of Article 4 of the Convention will have to be applied to find the governing law of the contract, which could lead to a different approach in finding the law that governs the wider contract from that to be used at common law in ascertaining the law that governs the agreement as to jurisdiction.

6.5.3.3 A further difficulty could arise in a situation where it is claimed that the wider contract is invalid or unenforceable. It might then be argued that the matters causing the wider contract to be invalid or unenforceable also taint the agreement as to jurisdiction contained within it. It might, for instance, be argued that the wider agreement is void or unenforceable on such grounds as illegality, duress, or mistake. In one case, it was held that the validity of the jurisdiction agreement would not be affected by the fact that the wider contract was merely unenforceable, although the position may have been different had it been void or of no effect altogether.[142] Whilst it does not provide a precise parallel (because of the relevance of section 7 of the Arbitration Act 1996 to an agreement for arbitration) it has been held that an arbitration clause in an alleged contract will survive the failure of the contract and be considered to be valid and binding so that arbitrators could

---

[141] *Marubeni Hong Kong & South China Ltd v Mongolian Government* [2002] 2 All ER (Comm) 873.

[142] *Mackender v Feldia AG* [1967] 2 QB 590.

be appointed to determine the validity of the contract and the consequences of its failure.[143] The Supreme Court of New South Wales has applied that principle in the case of a jurisdiction agreement.[144]

The court will apply the governing law of the jurisdiction agreement to ascertain, as a matter of construction and interpretation of the agreement, whether the parties intended to confer jurisdiction exclusively upon a chosen court or whether they only intended it to have non-exclusive jurisdiction; perhaps even intending to nominate more than one court to have the right to assume jurisdiction. In the absence of explicit wording indicating that the parties intended a single court to have exclusive jurisdiction, an English court would construe the agreement to determine if the agreement operated 'transitively', in the sense of imposing on the parties an obligation to refer their disputes exclusively to the nominated court, or 'intransitively', in the non-exclusive sense that the parties intended to consent to the jurisdiction of the nominated court should it be invoked by one of the parties.[145] It will also be a matter of construction and interpretation of the agreement to ascertain the types of claim which are covered by it; for instance, as to whether equitable or tortious claims that are based upon or connected with the agreement are within the scope of the claims covered by the submission to jurisdiction. It has been said that the practice of the English courts is to give such an agreement a generous interpretation in determining the scope of its application.[146]

6.5.3.4

In considering the effect of a jurisdiction agreement and the exercise of its discretion, the attitude that the court takes towards an agreement that confers exclusive

6.5.3.5

---

[143] *Harbour Assurance Co (UK) Ltd v Kansa General International Insurance Co Ltd* [1993] QB 701. See also, more recently, the approach taken by the House of Lords in *Fiona Trust & Holding Corp v Privalov* [2007] UKHL 40, [2007] 4 All ER 951.

[144] *FAI General Insurance Co Ltd v Ocean Marine Mutual Protection and Indemnity Association* (1997) 41 NSW LR 559. See now, however, the discussion of this point by Flaux J in *Deutsche Bank AG v Asia Pacific Broadband Wireless Communications Inc* [2008] EWHC 918 (Comm).

[145] *Austrian Lloyd Steamship Co v Gresham Life Assurance Society Ltd* [1903] 1 KB 249; *Konkola Copper Mines plc v Coromin* [2005] EWHC 898 (Comm), [2005] 2 Lloyd's Rep 555 (an appeal to the Court of Appeal did not deal with this issue: [2006] EWCA Civ 5, [2006] 1 Lloyd's Rep 410). See also *Sinochem International Oil (London) Co Ltd v Mobil Sales and Supply Corp (No 2)* [2000] 1 Lloyd's Rep 670 and the decision of Hobhouse J in *Pathe Screen Entertainment Ltd v Handmade Films (Distributors) Ltd* (11/7/1989, set out as an attachment to the judgment of Morison J in *Tonicstar Ltd v American Assurance Co* [2004] EWHC 1234 (Comm)). The relevant portion of Hobhouse J's judgment is quoted by Langley J in *Sea Trade Maritime Corp v Hellenic Mutual War Risks Assoc (Bermuda) Ltd, The Athena* [2006] EWHC 2530 (Comm); [2007] 1 Lloyd's Rep 280, at [100].

[146] Lord Bingham in *Donohue v Armco Inc* [2001] UKHL 64, [2002] 1 Lloyd's Rep 425, at [14]. This is supported by the approach that is taken to the construction of the scope of arbitration agreements, in which it has been held that they should be construed liberally, in an inclusive manner, and without engaging in overly fine distinctions as to the scope of what they cover: *Fiona Trust & Holding Corp v Privalov* [2007] UKHL 40, [2007] 4 All ER 951. See also the discussion of this point by Flaux J in *Deutsche Bank AG v Asia Pacific Broadband Wireless Communications Inc* [2008] EWHC 918 (Comm).

jurisdiction upon a chosen court is bound to be more robust than its approach towards a non-exclusive choice of jurisdiction. Nonetheless, a chosen court that falls within the latter type of agreement will, at least, be regarded, as an available and a suitable forum in which the case may be heard[147] within the tests in *Spiliada Maritime Corp v Cansulex Ltd*.[148] An agreement as to non-exclusive jurisdiction may also be taken as an indication that neither party would object to proceedings being taken before the nominated court and that neither of them would attempt to frustrate or prevent the bringing of such proceedings by, for instance, instituting proceedings elsewhere.[149] Sometimes the parties may expressly contemplate that proceedings might be commenced in courts other than that upon which jurisdiction has been agreed, and even that proceedings might be brought in two or more jurisdictions at the same time. In such a situation, an English court may permit proceedings to take place concurrently in more than one jurisdiction.[150]

6.5.4 Stays of English proceedings when an agreement confers exclusive jurisdiction upon a foreign court

The basis on which an English court will grant a stay of its own proceedings in favour of a dispute being heard in a foreign court, to which exclusive jurisdiction had been granted by agreement between the parties, was set out by Brandon LJ in *The 'El Amria'*,[151] in which his Lordship adopted what he had said earlier at first instance in *The 'Eleftheria'*.[152] The approach taken by Brandon J in *The 'Eleftheria'* was approved by Lord Bingham of Cornhill in *Donohue v Armco Inc*[153] (which was a case where the reverse situation applied, that is, where the English court in whose favour there was an exclusive jurisdiction clause was requested to issue an anti-suit injunction directed against the continuance of proceedings in a foreign court). Brandon LJ said that the court had a discretion which it was not bound to exercise, but it should do so unless strong cause (or to use Lord Bingham's phrase 'strong reasons'[154]) was shown against its doing so. The burden was upon the party resisting the application for the stay. The court should take into account all the circumstances of the case, although little weight would be given in favour of the

---

147 *Mercury Communications Ltd v Communications Telesystems International* [1999] 2 All ER (Comm) 33.
148 [1987] AC 460.
149 *Sabah Shipyard (Pakistan) Ltd v Islamic Republic of Pakistan* [2002] EWCA Civ 1643, [2003] 2 Lloyd's Rep 571.
150 *Royal Bank of Canada v Cooperatieve Centrale Raiffeisen-Boerenleenbank RA* [2004] EWCA Civ 7, [2004] 1 Lloyd's Rep 471.
151 [1981] 2 Lloyd's Rep 119, at 123–124.
152 [1970] P 94, at 99.
153 [2002] 1 Lloyd's Rep 425, at 432–433.
154 *Donohue v Armco Inc* [2001] UKHL 64; [2002] 1 Lloyd's Rep 425, at 433.

continuance of the foreign proceedings to mere matters of the convenience of witnesses or mere procedural advantages.

Brandon LJ then set forth a number of matters to which the court might have   **6.5.4.1**
regard (which is not a mandatory or comprehensive list[155]), which may be summarised as follows:

(a) whether the evidence was situated in the place of, or more readily available to, the foreign court and the effect of that on the relative convenience and cost of a trial in, respectively, the foreign or English court;

(b) whether the law of the foreign court would apply to determine the issues in dispute and the extent to which that law differed from English law;

(c) the country to which either party was connected and how closely;

(d) whether the party promoting the trial in the foreign court was genuinely desirous of a trial in that jurisdiction or only seeking procedural advantages; and

(e) whether the party desiring a trial in England would be prejudiced by having to proceed in the foreign court because of (i) being deprived of security for its claim, (ii) being unable to enforce any judgment it might obtain, (iii) being faced with a time bar that was inapplicable in England, or (iv) being unlikely to obtain a fair trial in the foreign country because of political, racial, religious, or other reasons. Mere matters of convenience as to one forum or the other were largely, if not entirely, irrelevant.[156]

Nonetheless, the court may decline to grant a stay (or to grant an anti-suit injunc-   **6.5.4.2**
tion) where the interests of other parties (i.e. parties other than those bound by the jurisdiction agreement) were involved or the dispute before the foreign court involved matters that were not covered by the jurisdiction agreement.[157]

6.5.5 Anti-suit injunctions directed against the continuance of foreign proceedings

A party that wishes to promote its case before an English court may seek to obtain an injunction from that court to restrain another party from maintaining proceedings before a foreign court (usually referred to as an 'anti-suit injunction'). In theoretical terms, the injunction is directed to the other party rather than directly at the foreign court. In reality, it amounts, in an indirect way, to an attempt at interference with the rights and process of the foreign court. Accordingly, it has

---

[155] Lord Bingham in *Donohue v Armco Inc* [2001] UKHL 64; [2002] 1 Lloyd's Rep 425, at 433.
[156] *Sinochem International Oil (London) Co Ltd v Mobil Sales and Supply Corp (No 2)* [2000] 1 Lloyd's Rep 670.
[157] *Donohue v Armco Inc* [2001] UKHL 64, [2002] 1 Lloyd's Rep 425.

been said that caution should be taken in granting such an injunction,[158] especially if the injunction is aimed at preventing a party from conducting proceedings in its own jurisdiction.[159] As previously mentioned, such an injunction may not be granted in relation to proceedings in the court of another EU or EEA Member State,[160] at least in relation to matters that fall within the EC Regulation on jurisdiction and judgments, the Brussels Convention, or the Lugano Convention, although it has been held by the Court of Appeal that the same constraint does not operate in matters to which those instruments do not apply.[161] The injunction must be necessary to protect the English proceedings and the applicant's legitimate interest in those proceedings.[162] The issuing of such an injunction is discretionary and it also depends upon the *in personam* jurisdiction of the court, which means that the respondent must be amenable to that jurisdiction.[163] The respondent might be so amenable (1) by service upon the respondent within the jurisdiction, (2) by service outside the jurisdiction where it is available as of right,[164] (3) if the foreign respondent is already an actively participating party to proceedings before the court,[165] or (4) with the leave of the court, by service upon the respondent outside the jurisdiction. In the latter case, it will be necessary to find a ground within the paragraphs of CPR rule 6.20.[166] There is no such ground based simply upon the wish to obtain an anti-suit injunction.

6.5.5.1   In a general sense, the discretion to grant an anti-suit injunction is exercised so as to avoid injustice[167] because the foreign proceedings are contrary to equity and

---

[158]   *British Airways Board v Laker Airways Ltd* [1985] AC 58; *SNI Aérospatiale v Lee Kui Jak* [1987] AC 871; *Airbus Industrie GIE v Patel* [1999] 1 AC 119.

[159]   *Metall und Rohstoff AG v ACLI Metals Ltd* [1984] 1 Lloyd's Rep 598.

[160]   *Turner v Grovit* Case C-159/02, [2005] 1 AC 101.

[161]   *Through Transport Mutual Insurance Assoc (Eurasia) Ltd v New India Assurance Co Ltd* [2004] EWCA Civ 1598, [2005] 1 Lloyd's Rep 67. As previously noted, the issue has now been referred to the European Court of Justice.

[162]   *Airbus Industrie GIE v Patel* [1999] 1 AC 119; *Turner v Grovit* [2001] UKHL 65, [2002] 1 WLR 107.

[163]   *The Siskina* [1979] AC 210; *SNI Aérospatialle v Lee Kui Jak* [1987] AC 871; *Donohue v Armco Inc.* [2001] UKHL 64, [2002] 1 Lloyd's Rep 425.

[164]   I.e. in consequence of Art 23 of the EC Regulation on jurisdiction and judgments or pursuant to Art 17 of the Brussels or Lugano Conventions.

[165]   For instance, where the respondent had launched related proceedings in the jurisdiction or had submitted to the proceedings and made a counterclaim within those proceedings. On the other hand, if the party was merely a defendant that had been served pursuant to CPR r 6.20 and had simply entered an appearance to contest the particular claim served upon it, it would not be actively participating: *Airbus Industrie GIE v Patel* [1999] 1 AC 119; *Donohue v Armco Inc* [2001] UKHL 64, [2002] 1 Lloyd's Rep 425; *Glencore International AG v Exeter Shipping Ltd* [2002] EWCA Civ 528, [2002] 2 All ER (Comm) 1.

[166]   Which might arise, for instance, under CPR r 6.20(5)(d) (an agreement conferring jurisdiction upon the English courts).

[167]   *Castanho v Brown & Root (UK) Ltd* [1981] AC 557.

good conscience,[168] such as by being vexatious and oppressive, an interference with the due process of the court, or in breach of a jurisdiction agreement. Except where the injunction is based upon an agreement between the parties in favour of English jurisdiction,[169] it is also necessary for the applicant to show that the English court is the natural forum to hear the case,[170] so as to provide an efficient and, if possible, an economic resolution of the dispute, and to avoid a multiplicity of proceedings in different countries. Even if the applicant can make out a case for the injunction to be granted, the respondent is entitled to resist it by showing that it had a legitimate substantive or procedural interest in pursuing the foreign proceedings and that it would be prejudiced in pursuing that interest by the injunction,[171] provided that those proceedings were being pursued in a natural forum to hear the case.[172] This may be supplemented by the giving of an undertaking by the respondent that it will not pursue any remedy in the foreign proceedings that would cause an injustice to the other party.[173] Nonetheless, the court may still grant the injunction if the bringing of the foreign proceedings might be considered to be unconscionable in the sense of being an infringement upon the applicant's equitable rights. It might do this, for instance, where the claim in the foreign proceedings was based upon a cause of action under the law of that forum which was unknown to English law and which involved circumstances that it was alleged had not taken place within the territory of that forum.[174]

One area in which a court may exercise its discretion to grant an anti-suit injunction is where the pursuit of the foreign proceedings would be 'vexatious and oppressive' or an interference with the due process of the court. Those are rather nebulous concepts which remain undefined and have been left to be worked out on a case-by-case basis.[175] They do not involve the same considerations as those that the court must consider in determining whether to grant a stay or leave to

6.5.5.2

---

[168] *Carron Iron Co v Maclaren* (1855) 5 HLC 416.

[169] *SNI Aérospatiale v Lee Kui Jak* [1987] AC 871.

[170] Ibid; *Airbus Industrie GIE v Patel* [1999] 1 AC 119.

[171] *SNI Aérospatiale v Lee Kui Jak* [1987] AC 871.

[172] *Smith Kline & French Laboratories Ltd v Bloch* [1983] 1 WLR 91.

[173] As was done in *Donohue v Armco Inc* [2001] UKHL 64, [2002] 1 Lloyd's Rep 425, where the respondents undertook not to pursue multiple or punitive damages in their American proceedings.

[174] *British Airways Board v Laker Airways Ltd* [1985] AC 58; *Midland Bank plc v Laker Airways Ltd* [1986] 1 QB 689. In those cases, the foreign proceedings involved US anti-trust proceedings. In the former, the injunction was refused, because the applicant had carried on a business in the USA which related to the foreign claim. In the latter, the injunction was granted as the claim, which was brought by an English plaintiff, was based upon alleged activities of the applicants in England.

[175] Per Lewison J in *Law Debenture Trust Corp PLC v Concord Trust* [2007] EWHC 2255 (Ch), at [27(ii)]. The position in Australia is rather more certain, where foreign proceedings will be considered to be vexatious and oppressive if nothing further can be gained above what is possible in the local court, or if they were instituted after the local proceedings with the predominant purpose of preventing the continuance of the local proceedings: *CSR Ltd v Cigna Insurance Australia Ltd* [1997] HCA 33, (1997) 189 CLR 345.

serve out of the jurisdiction on the basis of *forum non conveniens*, and the court must take account of the injustice to each party of the pursuit of the proceedings in one or other court.[176] The following are examples of the types of consideration that would be relevant in determining if the maintenance of foreign proceedings would be considered as being vexatious and oppressive or an interference with the due process of the court: bad faith on the part of the respondent in bringing the foreign proceedings;[177] the bringing of foreign proceedings that are bound to fail;[178] where the applicant might be subjected to oppressive procedures or circumstances in the foreign jurisdiction;[179] extreme inconvenience to the applicant caused by the foreign proceedings;[180] where the foreign proceedings were part of a campaign to wear down the applicant through the difficulty and expense of fighting on several fronts;[181] the risk of a multiplicity of proceedings which may conflict with each other[182] or which may undermine the management and efficiency of the English proceedings,[183] especially where the foreign proceedings had been brought to secure a tactical advantage when England provided the appropriate forum to determine the issues;[184] and cases which could and should have formed part of an earlier English action and which seek to challenge a matter that has already been decided in that action.[185]

6.5.5.3 Whilst it is still a discretionary matter,[186] the court will more readily grant an anti-suit injunction to restrain the maintenance of foreign proceedings, where such proceedings have been brought in breach of an agreement conferring jurisdiction on the English courts or an agreement not to be sued in that jurisdiction.[187] As previously discussed, it may be necessary to establish the validity and scope of the jurisdiction agreement. Assuming that the agreement is valid, it is not necessary

---

176 Ibid.

177 *Midland Bank plc v Laker Airways Ltd* [1986] 1 QB 689.

178 *British Airways Board v Laker Airways Ltd* [1985] AC 58; *Shell International Petroleum Co Ltd v Coral Oil Co Ltd* [1999] 2 Lloyd's Rep 606.

179 *A/S D/S Svendborg v Wansa* [1997] 2 Lloyd's Rep 183.

180 *Logan v Bank of Scotland (No 2)* [1906] 1 KB 141.

181 *Glencore International AG v Exeter Shipping Ltd* [2002] EWCA Civ 528, [2002] 2 All ER (Comm) 1.

182 *SNI Aérospatiale v Lee Kui Jak* [1987] AC 871, although the court will be less willing to interfere if the parties permitted the possibility of different proceedings in their agreement as to jurisdiction: *Royal Bank of Canada v Cooperatieve Centrale Raiffeisen-Boerenleenbank RA* [2004] EWCA Civ 7, [2004] 1 Lloyd's Rep 471.

183 *Glencore International AG v Exeter Shipping Ltd* [2002] EWCA Civ 528, [2002] 2 All ER (Comm) 1.

184 *Tonicstar Ltd v American Assurance Co* [2004] EWHC 1234 (Comm).

185 *Law Debenture Trust Corp PLC v Concord Trust* [2007] EWHC 2255 (Ch).

186 Even where there is an agreement conferring exclusive jurisdiction upon the English courts: *Donohue v Armco Inc* [2001] UKHL 64, [2002] 1 Lloyd's Rep 425.

187 Ibid.

to demonstrate that England is the natural forum, nor that the foreign proceedings are vexatious and oppressive.[188]

The factors that are relevant to the exercise of the court's discretion in granting the injunction to uphold the jurisdiction agreement include those described above concerning the grant of a stay of proceedings based upon an agreement conferring jurisdiction on a foreign court. They were set out by Brandon LJ in *The 'El Amria'*,[189] in which Brandon LJ had adopted what he had said at first instance in *The 'Eleftheria'*.[190] Lord Bingham of Cornhill approved Brandon LJ's approach in *Donohue v Armco Inc*,[191] which was a case where the English court in whose favour there was an exclusive jurisdiction clause was requested to issue an anti-suit injunction directed against the continuance of proceedings in a foreign court. In that case, the House of Lords refused to grant an anti-suit injunction against the continuance of proceedings in the USA. This was because the interests of parties other than those bound by the jurisdiction agreement were involved, and the dispute before the foreign court involved matters that were not covered by the jurisdiction agreement.

6.5.6 Arbitration agreements

A related area to that just discussed is where an English court would be prepared to grant an injunction to restrain a party from maintaining foreign proceedings in breach of an agreement to refer the dispute to arbitration. In essence, the court is recognising and protecting the applicant's contractual right to have the dispute settled by arbitration. This was recognised by Millett LJ in *The Angelic Grace*,[192] who said that the court should not be diffident in granting the injunction. Nonetheless, in *Bankers Trust Company v PT Jakarta International Hotels*[193] Cresswell J said that the applicant for an injunction to restrain foreign proceedings in favour of arbitration in England pursuant to an arbitration agreement governed by English law had to demonstrate a high degree of probability that its case against the respondent was right and that the matter was covered by a valid agreement to arbitrate in England. This went further than the ordinary test for interlocutory relief based upon the test laid down in *American Cyanamid Company v Ethicon Ltd*,[194] which would preserve the status quo pending a trial, because the

---

[188] *SNI Aérospatiale v Lee Kui Jak* [1987] AC 871; *Airbus Industrie GIE v Patel* [1999] 1 AC 119.

[189] [1981] 2 Lloyd's Rep 119, at 123–124.

[190] [1970] P 94, at 99.

[191] [2002] 1 Lloyd's Rep 425, at 432–433.

[192] [1995] 1 Lloyd's Rep 87, at 96. His Lordship followed the test laid down by Colman J in *Bankers Trust Company v PT Mayora Indah* (unreported, 20/1/1999).

[193] [1999] 1 Lloyd's Rep 910.

[194] [1975] AC 396.

injunction, if granted, would be intended to continue for the duration of the arbitral process and the making of an arbitral award.

6.5.6.1 The Court of Appeal said in *Through Transport Mutual Insurance Assoc (Eurasia) Ltd v New India Assurance Co Ltd*[195] that an injunction could be granted to prevent a party maintaining proceedings in another EU Member State in alleged breach of an agreement to submit disputes to arbitration, because the English proceedings seeking the injunction fell within the exception concerning arbitration in Article 1(2)(d) of the EC Regulation on jurisdiction and judgments. As indicated earlier, the approach taken by the Court of Appeal might be considered to offend against the principle of comity and mutual respect as between the courts of the EU Member States, as enshrined in the judgments of the European Court of Justice in *Erich Gasser GmbH v MISAT*[196] and in *Turner v Grovit*.[197] The House of Lords has now referred the matter to the European Court of Justice for a definitive determination.[198]

6.6 Arbitration

6.6.1 Introduction

In former times it was unusual for a dispute concerning a finance transaction to be submitted to arbitration for adjudication. The practice has become more common recently. There are a number of reasons for this change of approach, which include the following:

(1) arbitral proceedings may be conducted privately, without the publicity and open hearings that may be involved in court proceedings;
(2) where transactions involve States and State entities or international organisations, it may be more palatable for the State and its entity or such an organisation to submit itself to an independent arbitral tribunal than to the courts of another State;
(3) in some instances, an aggrieved private claimant may be able to institute an arbitration against a State pursuant to a bilateral investment treaty when it would have difficulty commencing proceedings in a neutral forum against the State;[199]

---

[195] [2004] EWCA Civ 1598, [2005] 1 Lloyd's Rep 67.
[196] Case C-116/02, [2003] ECR I-14693, [2005] QB 1.
[197] Case C-159/02, [2004] ECR I-3565, [2005] 1 AC 101.
[198] *West Tankers Inc v RAS Riunione Adriatica di Sicurta SpA* [2007] UKHL 4, [2007] 1 Lloyd's Rep 391.
[199] As for instance had occurred in *Occidental Exploration & Production Company v Republic of Equador* [2005] EWCA Civ 1116, [2005] 2 Lloyd's Rep 707 and in *AIG Capital Partners Inc v ABN Amro Mellon Global Securities Services BV* [2005] EWHC 2239 (Comm).

(4) particularly in disputes involving technical matters, it is possible to have arbitrators who are experts in the field with adequate technical knowledge to understand the matters in dispute;

(5) arbitration may be more flexible and quicker than court proceedings and it may involve less pre-trial skirmishing and procedures. It may also be easier to arrive at a compromise than full-blown court proceedings;

(6) under section 46(1)(b) of the Arbitration Act 1996, the parties can agree that the arbitral tribunal should make its decision concerning the transaction between them by taking into account considerations other than those dictated by the governing law of a particular State, whereas under the Rome Convention, a court can only take account of the law of State as the governing law of their transaction;[200]

(7) there are international treaties that permit action to be taken for the cross-border enforcement of arbitral awards as, for instance, pursuant to the New York Convention 1958, the Convention on the Settlement of Investment Disputes Between States and Nationals of Other States 1965, and the Geneva Convention 1927. As a result, it may be possible to enforce such a foreign arbitral award in a country in circumstances where it may not be possible to enforce a foreign judgment in that country.

Generally speaking, a dispute can only be submitted to arbitration pursuant to an arbitration agreement between the parties to the dispute and it cannot bind a third party who is not a party to the arbitration agreement. There is no inherent jurisdiction for arbitration. Such an agreement may be entered into at the beginning of a commercial transaction and thus relate to any future dispute that may arise under it, or the parties may agree to submit a matter to arbitration after the dispute has arisen. The exception to the need for an agreement between the parties to the dispute arises where a party can invoke the benefit of a bilateral investment treaty between two States, under which the nationals of one of the States are entitled to refer disputes involving the other State to arbitration. In effect, the State has bound itself by the treaty to agree to the submission of such disputes to arbitration. **6.6.1.1**

An arbitral tribunal may consist of one or more arbitrators. It is not uncommon to have three arbitrators, one selected by each party and the third chosen by the two who have been so selected. The third will usually act as the chairman and have a casting vote. It is also possible, usually where there is an even number of arbitrators, to provide for the appointment of an umpire, who is empowered to make the final decision where there is an even split between the views of the arbitrators. **6.6.1.2**

---

[200] Pursuant to the Arbitration Act 1996, an English court could enforce an arbitral award that had been made on that basis: see Waller LJ in *Halpern v Halpern* [2007] EWCA Civ 291; [2007] 2 Lloyd's Rep 56, at [37]–[38].

These matters, as well as other matters concerning the arbitrators and the various procedural matters involved in an arbitration, may be dealt with in the arbitration agreement or, more probably, under the rules of one of the international arbitral bodies whose rules are incorporated by reference in the arbitration agreement.[201] Part I of the Arbitration Act 1996 contains certain fall-back rules concerning the composition of arbitral tribunals and the practice and procedure of arbitral proceedings. It also contains provisions for the court to assist arbitral proceedings and provisions relating to the making of arbitral awards.

6.6.2 The Arbitration Act 1996

The Arbitration Act 1996 provides most of the legal framework under English law concerning the law of arbitrations.[202] The Act came into force on 31 January 1997. It is in four parts, the two material parts for the purposes of this chapter being Part I and Part III.[203] Part I deals with the English law concerning arbitrations, particularly those whose seat is in England. Part III concerns the recognition and enforcement of foreign arbitral awards pursuant to the New York Convention. It is also possible for foreign awards to be recognised and enforced at common law and under section 66 of the Act. The enforcement of certain foreign awards may also be dealt with under other legislation, such as under the Administration of Justice Act 1920, the Foreign Judgments (Reciprocal Enforcement) Act 1933, Part II of the Arbitration Act 1950, and the Arbitration (International Investment Disputes) Act 1966.

6.6.3 Part I of the Arbitration Act 1996

Part I relates to the application of English law to arbitrations that arise pursuant to an 'arbitration agreement' and concerns, in the main but with some additional cases, arbitrations whose seat is in England. It deals with the law of arbitration pursuant to such an agreement, the powers and duties of arbitrators and the courts, matters relating to the appointment of arbitrators, matters of practice and procedure relating to arbitration proceedings, the situations where the court may exercise

---

201 For instance, the rules of the International Chamber of Commerce, the rules of the London Court of International Arbitration, and the UNCITRAL Arbitration Rules.

202 The Act applies in England and Wales and in Northern Ireland. For convenience, references in this chapter to the application of the Act in England will include the position for Wales and for Northern Ireland as well. Unlike the position in Scotland and a number of other countries that have adopted it, the Act does not incorporate the UNCITRAL Model Law for International Commercial Arbitration, which was approved by resolution of the UN's General Assembly in 1976.

203 Part II concerns consumer arbitration agreements, small claims arbitration, the appointment of judges as arbitrators, and statutory arbitrations. Part IV concerns some consequential general provisions.

powers in support of arbitral proceedings, and provisions relating to the making and enforcement of arbitral awards.

Section 1 of the Act provides three principles that govern Part I, which are as follows: **6.6.3.1**

   (a) the object of arbitration is to obtain the fair resolution of disputes by an impartial tribunal without unnecessary delay or expense;

   (b) the parties should be free to agree how their disputes are resolved, subject only to such safeguards as are necessary in the public interest;

   (c) in matters governed by this Part the court should not intervene except as provided by this Part.

Overall, the effect of section 1 is to honour the agreement that the parties have reached as to the submission of their disputes to arbitration, subject to matters concerning the public interest,[204] and to prevent the courts from interfering with that agreement and an arbitration commenced under it, except as specifically provided by the Act. This most probably has the effect of removing any inherent jurisdiction to interfere that the courts might otherwise have been able to assert.[205] **6.6.3.1.1**

There are two concepts that are central to Part I. They are, first, the concept of the 'seat' of an arbitration and, secondly, the necessity for an agreement between the parties, called an 'arbitration agreement', that a dispute should be submitted to arbitration. **6.6.3.2**

6.6.3.2.1 The seat of an arbitration

The seat of an arbitration is the place where it is juridically grounded, rather than the geographic place where hearings may occur, evidence may be taken, or, indeed, where the arbitral award may be signed, despatched, or delivered.[206] The law of the seat of the arbitration will govern the arbitral procedure. Furthermore, by choosing England as the seat of an arbitration, the parties are taken to have agreed that proceedings on an award issued by the arbitral tribunal, and any challenge to it, should governed by, and subject to, the provisions of English law.[207]

Section 3 of the Act is central to the concept of the seat of an arbitration and provides as follows: **6.6.3.2.1.2**

> In this Part 'the seat of the arbitration' means the juridical seat of the arbitration designated:
>
> (a) by the parties to the arbitration agreement, or

---

[204] See also s 81(1)(c).
[205] See also s 81(2).
[206] S 53.
[207] *C v D* [2007] EWCA Civ 1282.

(b) by any arbitral or other institution or person vested by the parties with powers in that regard, or

(c) by the arbitral tribunal if so authorised by the parties,

or determined, in the absence of any such designation, having regard to the parties' agreement and all the relevant circumstances.

Such a determination should only take into account the circumstances up to the point where the arbitration was commenced.[208] It should be noted that the same definition of 'seat of the arbitration' also applies for the purposes of Part III of the Act.[209]

6.6.3.2.1.3 Section 2(1) of the Act provides that the provisions of Part I of the Act apply where the seat of an arbitration is located in England and Wales or in Northern Ireland (for convenience, this will be abbreviated to 'England'). There are some additional situations where provisions in Part I will apply in other situations, as outlined in the remainder of section 2. For example, sections 9 to 11 (stay of legal proceedings) and 66 (enforcement of arbitral awards) apply irrespective of the seat of the arbitration.[210] In addition, the court is entitled to exercise any power conferred upon it by Part I where no seat of an arbitration has been designated or ascertained, but there is a sufficient connection with England to justify the exercise of the power.[211] Section 7, which lays down the principle of separability, applies where the arbitration agreement is governed by English law, irrespective of the seat of the arbitration.[212]

6.6.3.2.2 An arbitration agreement

Section 6(1) of the Act provides that for the purposes of Part I an 'arbitration agreement' means an agreement to submit present or future disputes (whether contractual or otherwise) to arbitration. However, section 5(1) of the Act states that Part I only applies where the arbitration agreement is in writing, which includes being recorded by any means.[213] The remainder of section 5 amplifies the requirement as to writing.[214] It has been held that an agreement in writing by a State to submit to arbitration may be constituted by the terms of a bilateral investment treaty to which the State is one of the signatory parties.[215] It is possible to incorporate an arbitration agreement by reference to an arbitration clause or a

---

[208] *Dubai Islamic Bank PJSC v Paymentech Merchant Services Inc* [2001] 1 Lloyd's Rep 65.
[209] S 100(2).
[210] S 2(2).
[211] S 2(4).
[212] S 2(5).
[213] S 5(6).
[214] It should be noted that the expression 'agreement in writing' as it is used in Part III of the Act has the same meaning as it does in Part I of the Act: s 100(2).
[215] *Republic of Ecuador v Occidental Exploration and Production Co* [2005] EWCA Civ 1116, [2005] 2 Lloyd's Rep 707.

provision contained in a separate document,[216] such as in the rules of an association. The normal contractual principles apply under English law to determine if an arbitration clause or other provisions relating to arbitration that are contained in another document have been so incorporated, such as by the use of general words of incorporation, except in so-called 'two contract' cases.[217] In the latter type of case, a stricter test will be applied, so that some express reference to arbitration or perhaps to the actual clause will be needed.[218] The position may, of course, be different if some law other than English law should be applied to determine if the relevant provisions have been incorporated to form the arbitration agreement or some part of it.

A contract can validly provide for a dispute to be referred to arbitration as an alternative to the commencement of proceedings before the courts. It may also give one of the parties the right to pre-empt the commencement or continuation of court proceedings concerning a dispute by insisting upon the matter being referred to arbitration.[219] English law does not require that there should be a mutuality of entitlements upon the parties to have a matter referred to arbitration.[220] It has also been held that a party could validly be given a superior right to have a dispute heard by the courts in place of it being otherwise submitted to arbitration.[221]   **6.6.3.2.2.1**

It is appropriate, now, to examine matters concerning arbitration agreements in more detail.   **6.6.3.2.2.2**

6.6.4 The governing law of an arbitration agreement

It will be necessary to determine the governing law of the arbitration agreement, as the governing law will be applied to determine matters such as the scope and interpretation of the agreement.[222] In this quest, the rules of the Rome Convention will not apply, as arbitration agreements are excluded from the ambit of the

---

[216] S 6(2).

[217] I.e. situations where there is a difference of parties between the two contracts and one contract purports to incorporate the arbitration clause in the other contract, such as the situation in charterparty/bill of lading contracts.

[218] Per Bingham LJ in *The Federal Bulker* [1989] 1 Lloyd's Rep 103, at 105 and Langley J in *Sea Trade Maritime Corp v Hellenic Mutual War Risks Assoc (Bermuda) Ltd, The Athena* [2006] EWHC 2530 (Comm).

[219] *NB Three Shipping Ltd v Harebell Shipping Ltd* [2004] EWHC 2001 (Comm), [2005] 1 Lloyd's Rep 509.

[220] Per Fox LJ in *Pittalis v Sherefettin* [1986] QB 868, at 875.

[221] *Law Debenture Trust Corp plc v Elektrim Finance BV* [2005] EWHC 1412, [2005] 2 Lloyd's Rep 755, approved in *Fiona Trust & Holding Corp v Privalov* [2007] EWCA Civ 20, [2007] Bus LR 686 (this aspect was not subject to the appeal before the House of Lords).

[222] It has been held that arbitration agreements governed by English law should be construed liberally, in an inclusive manner, and without engaging in overly fine distinctions that would restrict their intended scope. It will be assumed (unless the contrary is expressed) that the parties wished an arbitral tribunal to have the power to determine all matters that might arise in a dispute, including

Convention.[223] It is not certain which rule or rules should be applied to find the governing law of an arbitration agreement. There is a word of caution that must be expressed before the possibilities are examined. It relates to the position where there is a clause or provision that constitutes an arbitration agreement, which is contained within an overall contract (the 'matrix contract') between the parties. As a result of the 'principle of separability' which applies as a matter of English law (to which further reference is made below), the arbitration agreement may fall to be treated separately from the matrix contract in which it is purportedly contained. One consequence of the principle is that the existence and validity of an arbitration agreement may be assessed independently from any similar question relating to the matrix contract. It also follows from the principle that an agreement to arbitrate which is contained in a matrix contract may have a separate governing law from the law that governs the matrix contract or which would govern it if the matrix contract were valid.[224]

6.6.4.1   Some indication of the approach that might be used in finding the governing law of an arbitration agreement is provided by section 4(5) of the Act. Section 4 (by reference to Schedule 1 to the Act) states the provisions of Part I that are mandatory, notwithstanding any agreement by the parties to the contrary and irrespective of the law that governs the arbitration agreement. The remaining provisions of Part I are not mandatory and may be excluded by the parties.[225] Section 4(5) provides that a choice of a foreign governing law to govern a non-mandatory provision is equivalent to an option to exclude the application of Part I to it. Section 4(5) goes on to recognise that the parties may choose a governing law either by an express or implied choice, in the absence of which it says that the applicable law of their agreement should be determined objectively. At least the section recognises the effectiveness of an express choice of the governing law.

6.6.4.2   In the absence of an express choice, it is not clear what tests should be used to find an implied choice, nor is it clear what objective criteria should be used where neither an express or implied choice can be found. An implied choice might be presumed from the terms of the contract and the surrounding circumstances. For instance, a choice of English law might be implied where the contract was

---

the validity of the agreement for arbitration: *Fiona Trust & Holding Corp v Privalov* [2007] UKHL 40, [2007] 4 All ER 951.

223   Art 1(2)(d) of the Rome Convention. The same applies under Art 1(2)(e) of Rome I.

224   In *Deutsche Schachtbau- und Tiefbohrgesellschaft mbH v Ras al Khaimah National Oil Co* [1987] 3 WLR 1023 (reversed on other grounds at [1990] 1 AC 295), the Court of Appeal recognised that an arbitration agreement could have a different governing law from the law that governed the matrix contract. See also *Hamlyn & Co v Talisker Distillery* [1894] AC 202 and *Black Clawson International Ltd v Papierwerke Waldhof-Aschaffenburg AG* [1981] 2 Lloyd's Rep 446.

225   Where relevant to the discussion of a provision of Part I in this chapter, it will be stated whether the provision is mandatory or non-mandatory.

written in English and provided for the arbitration to take place in London.[226] If it was not possible to find an implied choice then the common law approach would be to say that an agreement was governed by the law with which the contract had its closest and most real connection. It has been held at common law that in the absence of a choice of law to govern an arbitration agreement, it will be governed by the law of the place where the seat of the arbitration is located, because of the strength of that connection.[227]

There is something to be said for the proposition that, in the absence of an express **6.6.4.3** choice, the parties should generally be taken to have intended that the same law would govern both the matrix contract and the arbitration agreement, particularly where there was no question concerning the validity of the matrix contract. Thus, in a case where there has been an express choice of law to govern the matrix contract but no separately expressed choice of law to govern the arbitration agreement, it would make practical sense that parties should be treated as having chosen the same governing law for the arbitration agreement as they have chosen for the matrix contract. Alternatively, it might be said that the arbitration agreement had its closest and most real connection with the matrix contract and the law that governed the latter. However, it would not be possible to use this approach where the matrix contract is treated as being of no effect from the outset or in a situation where there is uncertainty as to the governing law of the matrix contract.[228]

6.6.5 The existence and validity of an arbitration agreement

A separate question concerns the law that should be applied to ascertain the existence and essential validity of an arbitration agreement, that is, whether there is a valid arbitration agreement in existence. It is here that the 'principle of separability' comes into play, as the existence and validity of the arbitration agreement must be determined separately from the existence and validity of the matrix contract. It may, for instance, be argued that the supposed matrix contract was a nullity or has been rescinded, and it will then be necessary to decide if the alleged arbitration agreement remains binding or if it is similarly ineffective.

As a matter of English law, the possibility that the arbitration agreement may exist **6.6.5.1** independently of the matrix contract is reflected in section 7 of the Arbitration Act 1996, which applies where the applicable law of an arbitration agreement is English law (see section 2(5) of the Act). Section 7 provides that an arbitration agreement shall be treated as distinct from the matrix contract to which it relates,

---

226 *Egon Oldendorff v Liberia Corp* [1996] 1 Lloyd's Rep 380.
227 *Deutsche Schachtbau- und Tiefbohrgesellschaft mbH v Ras al Khaimah National Oil Co* [1987] 3 WLR 1023 (reversed on other grounds at [1990] 1 AC 295).
228 Ibid.

so that the arbitration agreement is not to be regarded as invalid and of no effect simply because the matrix contract is invalid, of no effect, or never came into existence. If the arbitration agreement can be treated as valid in its own right then an arbitral tribunal appointed under it could, provided it fell within the scope of its adjudicative powers under the arbitration agreement, proceed to determine if the matrix contract were void or voidable, and it could also determine the consequences of such a finding.

6.6.5.2 Section 7 of the Act reflects the position at common law, as reflected in the decision of the Court of Appeal in *Harbour Assurance Co (UK) Ltd v Kansa General International Insurance Co Ltd*.[229] It was held in that case that, in consequence of the principle of separability as it relates to an arbitration agreement governed by English law, an arbitration agreement should be considered as separate from the matrix contract, so that the arbitration agreement would not be rendered void or invalid solely because the matrix contract was void or invalid or had been avoided, so long as the arbitration agreement was not, when considered on its own, independently void or invalid.

6.6.5.3 The principle of separability, and its consequences, were examined by the House of Lords in *Fiona Trust & Holding Corp. v Privalov*.[230] In particular, the decision looked at the circumstances in which the validity of an arbitration agreement might be impeached on the same grounds as the matrix contract. This might arise, for instance, because neither the matrix agreement, nor the arbitration agreement that is contained physically within the matrix agreement, exists at all because of a successful plea of *non est factum* or forgery. Similarly, both the matrix agreement and the arbitration agreement may be impeached because an alleged agent lacked any authority to enter into either agreement on behalf of a party. On the other hand, the fact that the matrix agreement may be set aside (e.g. because of fraud, duress, initial illegality, or, as in this case, as a result of bribery (and the ensuing lack of or excess of authority of the bribed agent), was not enough to impeach the agreement to arbitrate. It would have to be shown on the facts that such matters also impeached the arbitration agreement.[231] Thus, an attack on the validity of the matrix agreement is not necessarily to be taken as an attack on the arbitration agreement. If there is an arbitration agreement, it will be presumed that the parties

---

[229] [1993] QB 701. See also *Credit Suisse First Boston (Europe) Ltd v Seagate Trading Co Ltd* [1999] 1 Lloyd's Rep 784 and *Vee Networks Ltd v Econet Wireless International Ltd* [2004] EWHC 2909 (Comm), [2005] 1 Lloyd's Rep 192.

[230] [2007] UKHL 40, [2007] 4 All ER 951.

[231] In *El Nasharty v J Sainsbury PLC* [2007] EWHC 2618 (Comm) it was held, following the decision in the *Fiona Trust* case, that the fact that the matrix agreement may have been entered under duress did not serve to impeach the arbitration agreement which was contained within the matrix agreement.

intended such matters concerning the matrix agreement to be determined by arbitration.

Various possibilities have been advanced as to which law should be applied to determine the existence and essential validity of an arbitration agreement when it has purportedly been contained within a matrix contract. One approach has been to apply the putative proper or governing law of the matrix agreement as a whole, that is, the law which would govern it were it to be valid.[232] An alternative test is to apply the 'objective proper law' of the matrix contract, that is, the law of the place with which the matrix contract had its closest and most real connection.[233] It might well be objected, however, that neither of those approaches makes proper allowance for the principle of separability. Taking that principle into account, it is submitted that the relevant putative or objective proper law should be that of the arbitration agreement itself, looked at separately from any question as to the putative or objective proper law of the matrix contract, although it is quite likely that they may often amount to the same thing. A final possibility, when other avenues are unavailable, is to decide the matter in accordance with the rules of the *lex fori*.[234]

6.6.6 Stays of proceedings and challenges to the validity of an arbitration agreement

Section 9 of the Arbitration Act 1996, which is mandatory[235] and applies wherever the seat of the arbitration may be[236] and whatever the governing law of the arbitration agreement, provides that, at the request of a party to an arbitration agreement against whom court proceedings have been brought, the court should stay its proceedings in respect of a matter which should be referred to arbitration under the arbitration agreement unless the court decides that the arbitration agreement is 'null and void, inoperative, or incapable of being performed'. Subject to that exception, which is contained in section 9(4), the court has no discretion in the matter. It is obliged to grant the stay of its proceedings. The party requesting the stay may only do so if it has not taken any step in the court proceedings to answer the substantive claim in the proceedings.[237] As previously noted, an English court may also be prepared to grant an anti-suit injunction to restrain a party from bringing or continuing foreign proceedings in breach of an arbitration agreement.

---

[232] *The Parouth* [1982] 2 Lloyd's Rep 351; *The Atlantic Emperor (No 1)* [1989] 1 Lloyd's Rep 548.

[233] See the discussion on this in *The Heidberg* [1994] 2 Lloyd's Rep 287.

[234] Ibid.

[235] I.e. it cannot be excluded by agreement between the parties: s 4(1) and Sched 1.

[236] S 2(2).

[237] S 9(3).

6.6.6.1 Where there is a challenge to the validity of the arbitration agreement in proceedings before an English court under section 9(4), the court must decide if it should determine the issue or permit the arbitral tribunal to do so under other provisions of the Act, such as section 30 or section 72. The factors that the court should consider under section 9 in deciding if it or the arbitral tribunal should decide such an issue were addressed at first instance by HHJ Humphrey Lloyd QC in *Birse Construction Ltd v St David Ltd*.[238] They were approved by Waller LJ in the Court of Appeal in *Ahmed Al-Naimi v Islamic Press Agency Inc*.[239] In summary, they are as follows. The court is not required in all cases to remit to the arbitral tribunal the question of the arbitrators' jurisdiction, including the validity and scope of the arbitration agreement. If the position is clear on the evidence, the court should decide the matter. If there is a genuine dispute as to the existence of a valid arbitration agreement, the court should decide the issue. If the court is virtually certain that there is an arbitration agreement or if there is only a dispute as to the ambit or scope of such an agreement, it would be appropriate to leave the matter to the arbitral tribunal. The court should also take into account the likelihood of a challenge under sections 67 or 69 to any arbitral award by the arbitrators concerning their jurisdiction, because that would mean that unnecessary delay or expense might be incurred in having, essentially, two hearings to determine the issue.[240] Waller LJ added that if the court decides that it should try the issue then, unless the parties otherwise agree, there should be a trial of the issue with full evidence, rather than a decision being made on the basis of affidavits.

6.6.6.2 By way of explanation, there are other sections of the Act which also concern the respective entitlements of the court and an arbitral tribunal to decide on the validity and scope of an arbitration agreement, but (except for section 66) they only apply where the seat of the arbitration is in England, or, if no seat has been designated or otherwise determined in accordance with section 3, where there is an appropriate connection with England (see sections 2(1) and 2(4) of the Act). There are various limitations on the right of a party to mount a challenge under those provisions as, for instance, where a party has lost its right to object pursuant to section 73.

6.6.6.2.1 Section 30 permits the arbitral tribunal, if the parties agree, to determine matters of its substantive jurisdiction, including the validity and scope of the arbitration agreement and if the arbitral tribunal is properly constituted.[241] Section 32[242]

---

238 [1999] BLR 194.

239 [2000] 1 Lloyd's Rep 522. See also Longmore LJ in *Fiona Trust & Holding Corp v Privalov* [2007] EWCA Civ 20, [2007] Bus LR 686 (this aspect was not subject to the appeal before the House of Lords).

240 See also *Azov Shipping Co v Baltic Shipping Co* [1999] 1 Lloyd's Rep 68.

241 The meaning of 'substantive jurisdiction' is contained in s 30(1).

242 Which is mandatory and cannot be excluded by the parties: s 4(1) and Sched 1.

provides that, with the agreement of the parties or the permission of the arbitral tribunal, the court may determine any question as to the substantive jurisdiction of the arbitrators if the court decides it is appropriate for it to decide the matter and it will save costs. Section 66, to which further reference is made below and which applies whatever the seat of the arbitration, relates to the enforcement of an arbitral award but preserves the right of a person against whom the award is to be enforced to challenge the substantive jurisdiction to make the award. Section 67[243] permits a party to an arbitration to apply to the court challenging the arbitral award on the basis that the arbitral tribunal lacked substantive jurisdiction. Section 69[244] provides for a party to an arbitration, with the agreement of the other parties or with the leave of the court, to appeal to the court on a point of law. Such an appeal could include a challenge to a decision by an arbitral tribunal under section 30. Under section 72,[245] a party who has taken no part in the arbitration may challenge the validity of the arbitration agreement or its scope before the court.[246]

6.6.7 The arbitral tribunal: determinations, powers, remedies and challenges

Sections 46 to 49[247] of the Act lay down the rules for determination of a dispute and the remedies that may be awarded. The parties may also make provision by agreement for the powers and remedies of the arbitral tribunal. It is worth noting that in the absence of such agreement, section 48 gives an arbitral tribunal the power to order the payment of a sum of money in any currency[248] and to grant declaratory and other equitable relief, including by way of injunction, specific performance, and rectification.

Section 68[249] permits a party to challenge an award on the ground of a serious irregularity affecting the tribunal, the proceedings, or the award, which has caused

6.6.7.1

---

[243] Which is mandatory and cannot be excluded by the parties: s 4(1) and Sched 1.

[244] Which is not mandatory and may be excluded by the parties, as it is not included in the list in Sched 1: s 4(2).

[245] Which is mandatory and cannot be excluded by the parties: s 4(1) and Sched 1.

[246] As to the relationship between s 72 and s 9 of the Act, see Longmore LJ in *Fiona Trust & Holding Corp v Privalov* [2007] EWCA Civ 20, [2007] Bus LR 686 (this aspect was not subject to the appeal before the House of Lords).

[247] None of which is mandatory and so may be excluded or modified by the parties: s 4(2). The sections only apply where the seat of the arbitration is in England and Wales or Northern Ireland or, if no seat has been designated or otherwise determined in accordance with s 3, where there is an appropriate connection with England (see ss 2(1) and 2(4) of the Act).

[248] As to the power to award pre-interest under s 49 and the currency in which an award was made, see *Lesotho Highlands Development Authority v Impregilo SpA* [2005] UKHL 43, [2006] 1 AC 221.

[249] Which is mandatory and cannot be excluded by the parties: s 4(1) and Sched 1. It only applies, however, where the seat of the arbitration is in England and Wales or Northern Ireland, or, if no seat has been designated or otherwise determined in accordance with s 3, where there is an appropriate connection with England (see ss 2(1) and 2(4) of the Act).

or will cause substantial injustice to that party. Section 68(2) sets out what is meant by a 'serious irregularity', which includes (in paragraph (b)) that the tribunal exceeded its powers, otherwise than by exceeding its substantive jurisdiction.[250] Section 68 only applies, however, where the seat of the arbitration is in England and Wales or Northern Ireland, or, if no seat has been designated or otherwise determined in accordance with section 3, where there is an appropriate connection with England.[251]

6.6.8 Enforcement of awards

Section 66 concerns the enforcement of arbitral awards made pursuant to an arbitration agreement, regardless of the seat of the arbitration.[252] It is a mandatory provision which cannot be excluded by the parties.[253] By leave of the court, but subject to a right to refuse recognition and enforcement of an arbitral award on the grounds of public policy,[254] an award may be enforced as if it were a judgment or order of the court. As previously mentioned, the party against whom an award is made may challenge the giving of leave for its enforcement under section 66(3) on the basis that the arbitral tribunal lacked substantive jurisdiction to make the award. As the section applies to arbitral awards wherever the seat of the arbitration, provided they have been made pursuant to an arbitration agreement, it is possible to enforce a foreign award pursuant to section 66.[255] Where they apply, however, it is more likely that recognition and enforcement of such an award would be sought under the provisions of Part III of the Act or under Part II of the Arbitration Act 1950, and that possibility is specifically preserved by section 66(4). As noted below, it may be possible under section 66 to enforce an arbitral award against a State where the reference to arbitration occurred pursuant to a bilateral investment treaty to which the State was a signatory.

6.7 The Recognition and Enforcement of Foreign Arbitral Awards

6.7.1 Introduction

There are various possible means by which a foreign arbitral award may be recognised and enforced in England. As previously mentioned, the award may be

---

[250] As to the approach to be taken to a challenge under s 68 and, in particular, one based upon s 68(2)(b) see *Lesotho Highlands Development Authority v Impregilo SpA* [2005] UKHL 43, [2006] 1 AC 221.

[251] Ss 2(1) and 2(4).

[252] S 2(2).

[253] S 4(1) and Sched 1.

[254] S 81(1)(c).

[255] S 104 expressly recognises that a New York Convention award may be enforced under s 66.

enforced pursuant to section 66 of the Arbitration Act 1996. It may also be possible for an award to be enforced at common law. In addition to those two methods, a New York Convention award (the meaning of which is explained below) may be recognised and enforced under Part III of the Act, which is the usual course that is taken. An award to which the Geneva Convention 1927 applies may be enforced under Part II of the Arbitration Act 1950, unless it is also a New York Convention award.²⁵⁶ Awards made pursuant to the Convention on the Settlement of Investment Disputes Between States and Nationals of Other States 1965²⁵⁷ (the Washington Convention) are enforceable under the Arbitration (International Investment Disputes) Act 1966. It is also possible to enforce certain awards under the Administration of Justice Act 1920 and the Foreign Judgments (Reciprocal Enforcement) Act 1933. There is a specific provision in the State Immunity Act 1978 dealing with the enforcement of arbitral awards against States, to which further reference is made in Chapter 7.

What follows will discuss, briefly, the position at common law and then move on to examining the position, first, pursuant to Part III of the Arbitration Act 1996 in relation to the recognition and enforcement of New York Convention Awards, secondly, under the Arbitration (International Investment Disputes) Act 1966 in relation to arbitral awards made pursuant to the Washington Convention, and, finally, in relation to awards that that are made by arbitral tribunals appointed pursuant to bilateral investment treaties.

6.7.1.1

6.7.2 Enforcement at common law

At common law, it is possible to enforce a foreign arbitral award, provided that there is an arbitration agreement which is valid in accordance with its governing law and by which the parties had submitted their dispute to the arbitration and that the award was valid and final.²⁵⁸ It is not certain if the enforcement in England is of the arbitration agreement or just the award.²⁵⁹ However, recognition and enforcement might be refused on grounds of a lack of jurisdiction in the arbitrators to make the award, that the award was obtained by fraud or in breach of the rules of natural justice, or on public policy grounds.²⁶⁰

---

²⁵⁶ S 99.

²⁵⁷ 575 UNTS. A copy of the Convention is set out as a schedule to the Arbitration (International Investment Disputes) Act 1966.

²⁵⁸ *Norske Atals Insurance Co Ltd v London General Insurance Co Ltd* (1927) 28 Ll LR 104. It is not material at common law that a confirmatory court judgment might be required under the law that governed the arbitration: *Union Nationale des Cooperatives Agricoles v Catterall* [1959] 2 QB 44. If such a judgment were obtained then the action in England may be to enforce the judgment, rather than the award.

²⁵⁹ *Norske Atals Insurance Co Ltd v London General Insurance Co Ltd* (1927) 28 Ll LR 104; *Bremer Oeltransport v Drewry* [1933] 1 KB 753; *Agromet Motimport Ltd v Maulden Engineering Co (Beds) Ltd* [1985] 1 WLR 762.

²⁶⁰ *Dicey, Morris & Collins on the Conflict of Laws* (14th edn, 2006), Rule 60.

6.7.3 Enforcement of New York Convention awards

Under the New York Convention on the Recognition and Enforcement of Foreign Arbitral Awards 1958,[261] the signatory States agreed to the principles under which they would recognise and enforce arbitral awards made in other contracting States[262] (the New York Convention awards). The concept of recognition relates to the issues decided in a case, in that they are treated as finally determined and do not have to be re-determined so that, for instance, they can be pleaded by way of a defence, counterclaim, or set-off, as provided for in section 101(1) of the Arbitration Act 1996. Enforcement goes to obtaining a judgment so as to enforce an award or a judgment, usually for a monetary amount. Enforcement is provided for by section 101(2) of the Arbitration Act 1996. The procedures laid down by the Convention may be particularly useful in situations where it would be difficult to enforce or obtain recognition of a court judgment obtained in one State against a defendant and its assets in another State. This may, for instance, be because of the absence of recognition and enforcement procedures for foreign judgments in the State where it was wished to enforce the judgment or have its effect recognised.

6.7.3.1 The provisions for the recognition and enforcement in England of New York Convention awards made in another State are contained in Part III of the Arbitration Act 1996,[263] the material provisions of which provide in outline as follows:

100. *New York Convention awards*

(1) ... a 'New York Convention award' means an award made, in pursuance of an arbitration agreement, in the territory of a state (other than the United Kingdom) which is a party to the New York Convention.
(2) For the purposes of ... this Part relating to such awards—
    (a) 'arbitration agreement' means an arbitration agreement in writing, and
    (b) an award shall be treated as made at the seat of the arbitration, regardless of where it was signed, despatched or delivered to any of the parties.

In this subsection 'agreement in writing' and 'seat of the arbitration' have the same meanings as in Part I ...

101. *Recognition and enforcement of awards*

(1) A New York Convention award shall be recognised as binding on the persons as between whom it was made, and may accordingly be relied on by those persons

---

[261] New York 10 July 1958; TS 20 (1976); Cmnd 6419.
[262] But not if made in the same contracting State as that in which enforcement is sought. Hence, an award made by an arbitral tribunal whose seat was in England would fall to be enforced under s 66 of the Act, rather than under Part III of the Act.
[263] As previously stated, such an award may also be capable of enforcement under s 66 of the Act.

by way of defence, set-off or otherwise in any legal proceedings in England and Wales or Northern Ireland.

(2) A New York Convention award may, by leave of the court, be enforced in the same manner as a judgment or order of the court to the same effect.

102. *Evidence to be produced by party seeking recognition or enforcement . . .*

103. *Refusal of recognition or enforcement*

(1) Recognition or enforcement of a New York Convention award shall not be refused except in the following cases.

(2) Recognition or enforcement of an award may be refused if the person against whom it is invoked proves—(a) [incapacity of a party]; (b) [invalidity of the arbitration agreement under its governing law or, if there is no indication of such a law, where the award was made]; (c) [no proper notice of the arbitration and inability to present case]; (d) [award deals with a difference beyond the terms of the submission or is otherwise outside the scope of submission]; (e) [invalid composition of the tribunal. Note: this is subject to section 103(4)]; (f) [award not yet binding or set aside or suspended under the law where it was made].

(3) Recognition or enforcement of the award may also be refused if the award is in respect of a matter which is not capable of settlement by arbitration, or if it would be contrary to public policy . . .

(4) [separation of relevant from irrelevant matters in the decision contained in the award].

(5) [discretion to adjourn proceedings if there is an application to set aside or suspend the award under the law where it was made].

104. *Saving of other bases of recognition or enforcement*

Nothing in the preceding provisions of this Part affects any right to rely upon or enforce a New York Convention award at common law or under S. 66.

In *Svenska Petroleum Exploration AB v Government of the Republic of Lithuania*[264]   **6.7.3.2**
the Court of Appeal held that section 103 is a mandatory provision which must be applied in accordance with its terms. The party against whom the award has been made is entitled to challenge its recognition and enforcement under Part III of the Act on any of the grounds set out in that section. On that basis, it is always open to such a party to oppose the recognition and enforcement of the award under Part III of the Act.[265] The fact that the arbitral tribunal had decided the matter under challenge or that the award could no longer be contested before the courts in the country of the seat of the arbitration proceedings would not give rise to an issue estoppel. In light of the approach taken by the Court of Appeal, the position concerning the effect of an allegation of illegality in the underlying transaction to which an award relates is not entirely clear. In one case,

---

[264] [2006] EWCA Civ 1529, [2007] QB 886.
[265] In *Gater Assets Ltd v Nak Naftogaz Ukrainiy* [2007] EWCA Civ 988, it was decided that an English court should not order security for costs against an applicant for enforcement of an award.

the court refused to enforce an award on public policy grounds where the illegality concerned smuggling in the place of performance,[266] but in another case, the court was prepared to enforce the award where the arbitral tribunal had investigated and rejected the allegation.[267] Perhaps the decision in the latter case would now need to be re-considered, if enforcement might be considered to fall foul of English public policy.

6.7.4 Enforcement of ICSID awards

The Washington Convention established the International Centre for the Settlement of Disputes (ICSID), which is an arbitral institution with its own autonomous set of rules and procedures, particularly as set out in the ICSID Arbitration Rules. Arbitration before ICSID relates to investment disputes between a contracting State to the Convention and the national of another contracting State. The Convention provides that an arbitration can only take place where both parties have consented in writing to the exercise of ICSID jurisdiction.[268] Various ICSID arbitral tribunals have been prepared to hold that such an agreement in writing can be given by a State in a Bilateral Investment Treaty to which it is a signatory.[269] Article 42 of the Convention contains specific provisions for finding the law that governs the subject matter of the dispute, primarily in accordance with any law chosen by the parties. In the absence of such a choice, the tribunal may apply the law of the contracting State (including by reference to its rules on the conflict of laws), moderated by the rules of international law. With the consent of the parties, the tribunal may also decide a dispute in justice and good faith. The law which governs the arbitral proceedings is exclusively that of the Convention and the ICSID Arbitration Rules.[270] That law includes all available appellate procedures,[271] to the exclusion of any right of recourse to any domestic court.[272] The Convention further states that an ICSID pecuniary award should be enforced in the contracting States to the Convention as if the award were a final judgment of the courts of the relevant State.[273]

6.7.4.1   The Arbitration (International Investment Disputes) Act 1966 provides the procedures for the enforcement in England of ICSID awards. Unlike the position concerning New York Convention awards, there is no right to challenge the validity of the award or of the jurisdiction of the tribunal to make the award. In *AIG*

---

266 *Soleimany v Soleimany* [1999] QB 785.
267 *Westacre Investments Inc v Jugoimport-SPDR Holding Co Ltd* [2000] QB 288.
268 Art 25 of the Convention.
269 For instance, in *Olguin v Paraguay* (2000) 6 ICSID Rep 154, at 161–162.
270 Arts 26, 44, and 53 of the Convention.
271 Art 52 of the Convention.
272 Art 53 of the Convention.
273 Art 54 of the Convention.

Capital Partners Inc v Republic of Kazakhstan[274] it was held, however, that the rules in the State Immunity Act 1978 as to the enforcement of a judgment by execution against the property of a State are unaffected by the 1966 Act. This was in conformity with an express acknowledgement in the Washington Convention of the primacy of the immunities under the laws of any contracting State protecting that State or any foreign State from execution of judgment.[275]

Bilateral investment treaties are treaties between two States which, amongst other 　6.7.4.2
things, provide a right of recourse by a national of one of the States against the other State where there is an investment dispute. The treaties often confer such a right of recourse by way of arbitral proceedings, although sometimes there may also be a right of recourse to the courts of the State against which the claim is to be brought. Sometimes, the treaty may provide for such arbitral proceedings to be brought before ICSID or under UNCITRAL rules if the seat of the arbitration is located in a contracting State to the New York Convention[276] alone and sometimes a choice of arbitral proceedings may be permitted. If the arbitration is before ICSID then the position, including as to enforcement in England of the award, will be as outlined above in relation to such awards. If the award qualifies as a New York Convention Award, the position as to enforcement in England will fall to be dealt with under the Arbitration Act 1996, also as outlined above. By being a signatory to the bilateral investment agreement, a State will be treated as having agreed in writing to the arbitration for the purposes of meeting that requirement under the 1996 Act.[277]

---

[274] [2005] EWHC 2239; [2006] 1 All ER 284, at [5]–[6].

[275] Art 55 of the Convention.

[276] As was the case in *Republic of Ecuador v Occidental Exploration and Production Co* [2005] EWCA Civ 1116, [2005] 2 Lloyd's Rep 707. It should be noted that the award in that case did not qualify to be enforced as a New York Convention award, as the seat of the arbitration was in England. Accordingly, enforcement proceedings were brought under s 66 of the Arbitration Act 1996.

[277] *Republic of Ecuador v Occidental Exploration and Production Co* [2005] EWCA Civ 1116, [2005] 2 Lloyd's Rep 707.

7

SOVEREIGN IMMUNITY, INTERNATIONAL ORGANISATIONS, AND STATE INSOLVENCY

7.1 Introduction

This chapter begins by examining the concept of sovereign (or State) immunity, **7.1.1**
under which a State may enjoy the right not to be the subject of proceedings
before the English courts. It then moves to discussing the extent to which international organisations may enjoy a similar immunity. The chapter will conclude
with a discussion concerning the consequences where a State becomes unable
to meet its financial commitments to its creditors, particularly its external
creditors.

7.2 Sovereign Immunity

7.2.1 Introduction

The historical position at common law was that the English courts would not entertain proceedings against a foreign State.[1] That was in accordance with the absolute theory of sovereign (or State) immunity which was said to be observed by all nations. During the course of the 20th century, the theory of sovereign immunity began to change to a restrictive theory. Under the restrictive theory, a distinction was drawn between the activities of a State which were undertaken in the exercise of its sovereign authority, which were labelled '*acta jure imperii*', and activities or transactions that a State undertook in a particular case which were of a kind that might otherwise appropriately have been undertaken by private individuals, labelled '*acta jure gestionis*'. The protection of sovereign immunity remained for claims against States in relation to the former type of activity. It would not be available with respect to claims that fell into the latter category provided, of course, that the courts would otherwise have jurisdiction to hear the case.

7.2.1.1 The distinction founded upon the doctrine of restricted immunity was recognised by the courts in a series of cases, beginning with the decision of the Privy Council in *Philippine Admiral (owners) v Wallem Shipping (Hong Kong) Ltd, The Philippine Admiral*[2] and was advanced by Lord Denning MR in *Trendtex Trading Corp v Central Bank of Nigeria*.[3] It was approved by the House of Lords in *I Congreso del Partido*.[4] The change in the approach of the common law was in turn largely overshadowed and replaced by the State Immunity Act 1978, which came into force on 22 November 1978.

7.2.1.2 In *Grovit v De Nederlandsche Bank*[5] it was held that the EC Regulation on jurisdiction and judgments[6] did not override the application of the doctrine of sovereign immunity as it was understood under English law, but was to be read as being subject to it. Sovereign immunity was based upon the principles of international law, to which the Regulation was subject. EC legislation must respect the principles of international law.[7]

---

[1] See, for instance, Lord Atkin in *Compania Naviera Vascongado v Steamship Cristina* [1938] AC 485, at 490.

[2] [1977] AC 373.

[3] [1977] 1 QB 529.

[4] [1983] 1 AC 244. See also the review by Lord Diplock in *Alcom Ltd v Republic of Colombia* [1984] AC 580.

[5] [2005] EWHC 2944 (QB), [2006] 1 Lloyd's Rep 636 (Upheld: [2007] EWCA Civ 953).

[6] EC 44/2001 OJ L12/1 16/1/2001.

[7] See the decision of the European Court of Justice in the *Poulsen and Diva* Case C-286/90, [1992] ECR 1-06019, at para 9, the decision of the House of Lords in *A (FC) v Sec of State for the Home Dept*

7.2.2 Judicial restraint

Separately from the theories of sovereign immunity is the concept of 'judicial restraint'. Under that concept, the courts exercise restraint in the exercise of their jurisdiction where it might involve making enquiries into the activities and decision-making processes of a foreign State and its representative bodies, by virtue of the subject matter of a claim. This is so that embarrassment will not be caused to the domestic State or to the foreign State. The concept may be applied whether or not the foreign State is a party to the proceedings, if the proceedings might involve an unacceptable enquiry concerning the foreign State. For example, the courts will be unwilling to conduct an enquiry into the following matters: the decision-making processes of a foreign government;[8] matters involving diplomatic relations between States; political decisions; and matters that concern sensitive international disputes.

In *Buttes Gas and Oil Co v Hammer (Nos 2 & 3)*,[9] which was a case involving issues concerning the outcome of relations and transactions between States, Lord Wilberforce said:[10]

7.2.2.1

> the important inter-state issues and/or issues of international law which would face the court . . . have only to be stated to compel the conclusion that these are not issues upon which a municipal court can pass . . .[T]here are . . . no judicial or manageable standards by which to judge these issues, or to adopt another phrase . . . the court would be in a judicial no-man's land: the court would be asked to review transactions in which four sovereign states were involved, which they had brought to a precarious settlement, after diplomacy and the use of force, and to say that at least part of these were 'unlawful' under international law. I would just add . . . that it is not to be assumed that these matters have now passed into history, so that they now can be examined with safe detachment.

In litigation that involves a State, the concept of judicial restraint 'seeks to distinguish disputes involving sovereign authority which can only be resolved on a State to State level from disputes which can be resolved by judicial means'.[11] The concept of judicial restraint is a distinct concept which continues and is unaffected by the State Immunity Act 1978.[12] Its application, however, is sensitive to the issues in a given case, so that it is not of universal application.[13] For instance, it has been held that whilst in general the courts will refrain from seeking to interpret

---

[2005] UKHL 71, at [29], as well as the approach taken in relation to the Brussels Convention by s 31 of the Civil Jurisdiction and Judgments Act 1982.

  8 Per Lightman J in *Banca Carige SpA v Banco Nacional de Cuba* [2001] 1 WLR 2039, at [30]. See also the Court of Appeal in *Mbasogo v Logo Ltd* [2006] EWCA Civ 1370; [2007] QB 846, at [64]–[66].
  9 [1982] AC 888.
  10 Ibid, at 938.
  11 Per Brooke LJ in *Kuwait Airways Corp v Iraqi Airways Co* [2001] 1 Lloyd's Rep 161, at 214.
  12 Per Lightman J in *Banca Carige SpA v Banco Nacional de Cuba* [2001] 1 WLR 2039, at [29].
  13 Per Brooke LJ in *Kuwait Airways Corp v Iraqi Airways Co* [2001] 1 Lloyd's Rep 161, at 214.

international treaties, they will be prepared to do so in circumstances where it might be necessary for an English court to interpret a treaty for the purpose of determining private rights and obligations under domestic law.[14] It has also been held that in the context of a bilateral investment treaty, the States that were party to that treaty might confer private rights to seek arbitration in the determination of a dispute and the court was entitled to consider the treaty and its purpose to ascertain if that was intended to be the case.[15]

7.2.3 The State Immunity Act 1978

The Act is in three parts but it is Part I of the Act which is relevant to the subject matter of this book and that will be the principal focus in the discussion that follows. With minor exceptions[16] that are not relevant to financial transactions, the right of the English courts to adjudicate upon claims involving foreign States and State entities and the enforcement of such claims against their assets is now dealt with by Part I of the Act. In reviewing the overall scheme of Part I of the Act, Lord Diplock in *Alcom Ltd v Republic of Columbia*[17] drew a distinction that he saw in the Act between the 'adjudicative' jurisdiction of the courts, which concerned sections 1 to 12, and the 'enforcement' jurisdiction which principally concerned section 13 and a part of section 14. That distinction will be followed below. The Act applies throughout the UK but the discussion will focus on the position in England.

7.2.3.1 Whilst the Act deals with the issue of the immunity of States from proceedings before the English courts, and the exceptions to such immunity, it does not have the consequence that the courts will automatically have jurisdiction in any matter where a State would lack immunity. It will still be necessary to found the court's jurisdiction to hear the claim in the same way as in any other case, and the identity of the defendant as a State, or as a separate entity of a State, will not be relevant to that consideration.

7.2.3.2 The Act does not precisely follow the distinction at common law between acts that are *jure imperii* and acts that are *jure gestionis*, although something of that distinction does appear in sections 3 and 13. Instead, the Act begins in section 1(1) by laying down a general statement of immunity for foreign States,[18] but it then

---

[14] *R v Prime Minister of the UK, ex parte Campaign for Nuclear Disarmament* [2002] EWHC 2777 (QB).

[15] In *Republic of Ecuador v Occidental Exploration and Production Co* [2005] EWCA Civ 1116, [2005] 2 Lloyd's Rep 707.

[16] As set out in s 16 of the State Immunity Act 1978. With respect to the exception contained in s 16(2), see *Holland v Lampen-Wolfe* [2000] 1 WLR 1573, in which it was held that the common law doctrines concerning sovereign immunity continued to apply.

[17] [1984] AC 580, at 600.

[18] Which includes proceedings to register and enforce a foreign judgment under the Administration of Justice Act 1920 or the Foreign Judgments (Reciprocal Enforcement) Act 1933:

contains a wide-ranging number of exceptions to that principle. Section 1(2) provides that the courts must honour a State's immunity if it does not appear in the proceedings.

7.2.3.3 States and State entities

Before considering the adjudicative and enforcement jurisdictions of the courts, it is necessary to refer to the concept of a State that is employed in the Act, as well as the distinction that is drawn in the Act between a State and a 'State entity'. This is dealt with in the first two subsections of section 14, which is in Part I of the Act. There are further parts of section 14 that will need to be considered later when the discussion moves to examining the enforcement jurisdiction of the courts under Part I of the Act.

Sections 14(1) and 14(2) provide as follows: **7.2.3.3.1**

(1) The immunities and privileges conferred by this Part of this Act apply to any foreign or commonwealth State other than the United Kingdom; and references to a State include references to—
   (a) the sovereign or other head of that State in his public capacity;
   (b) the government of that State; and
   (c) any department of that government,

   but not to any entity (hereafter referred to as a 'separate entity') which is distinct from the executive organs of the government of the State and capable of suing or being sued.

(2) A separate entity is immune from the jurisdiction of the courts of the United Kingdom if, and only if—
   (a) the proceedings relate to anything done by it in the exercise of sovereign authority; and
   (b) the circumstances are such that a State . . . would have been so immune.

Section 21 of the Act says that a certificate provided by the Secretary of State shall   **7.2.3.3.2**
be conclusive evidence as to the existence of a State and as to the persons who should be regarded as the head of the State or its government.

7.2.3.3.3 State officials   It has been held that the employees and officials of a State were entitled to benefit from a claim to sovereign immunity if they were acting in an official capacity. This covers their actions undertaken in pursuance of that capacity, even if their actions might be characterised as being malicious or amounting to torture or some other serious national or international crime.[19]

AIC Ltd v The Federal Government of Nigeria [2003] EWHC 1357 (QB). See also s 31 of the Civil Jurisdiction and Judgments Act 1982.

[19] *Jones v Ministry of the Interior* [2006] UKHL 26, [2007] 1 AC 270; *Grovit v De Nederlandsche Bank* [2005] EWHC 2944 (QB), [2006] 1 Lloyd's Rep 636 (Upheld: [2007] EWCA Civ 953). The possible exception referred to in the latter case for torture and other serious international crimes

By way of example, officials have been permitted to claim immunity in cases involving allegations against them for malicious publication in a libel case,[20] contempt of court,[21] and negligence or corruption.[22] An English case[23] has also cited with approval certain US cases where officials were able to assert immunity, such as cases concerning illegality and malicious conduct[24] and a convergence between a personal interest and a regulatory function, giving rise to a malicious intention and causing a wrongful dishonour of a letter of credit.[25]

7.2.3.3.4 Agents of a State Where a foreign State (or, indeed, a foreign central bank or monetary authority) would be entitled to assert immunity from suit under the State Immunity Act 1978, the same immunity would extend to the agents or representatives acting on its behalf in a broad sense. This would be the case even where those agents or representatives were not strictly acting as an agent but more on a principal to principal basis with the State (or central bank or monetary authority).[26]

7.2.3.3.5 Separate entities The Act does not indicate which law should be applied in determining whether an entity is a separate entity. It is submitted that this should be the law of the relevant foreign State in which the entity is established. The constitutional law of that State should determine matters of the existence and components of the State, its government, and the executive organs of the State. The law of that State, being the law of the entity's place of establishment, should also determine corporate matters relating to any separate existence and legal personality of the entity. As a matter of conflict of laws, it is the law of the place of establishment of the entity that determines if it has a separate legal personality and is capable of suing and being sued as a separate entity. Nonetheless, it was said in the Court of Appeal in *Trendtex Trading Corp Ltd v Central Bank of Nigeria*[27] that this matter has an element of international law, so that the functions and status of the entity should be assessed both in accordance with the perceived intention behind the establishment of the entity under its domestic law as

---

(i.e. to which immunity would not apply) was based on the decision of the Court of Appeal in the former case, which was overruled by the House of Lords in that case.

[20] *Holland v Lampen-Wolfe* [2001] 1 WLR 1573.
[21] *Propend Finance Pty Ltd v Sing* (The Times 2/5/1997).
[22] *Zoernsch v Waldock* [1964] 1 WLR 675.
[23] *Grovit v De Nederlandsche Bank* [2005] EWHC 2944 (QB), [2006] 1 Lloyd's Rep 636 (Upheld: [2007] EWCA Civ 953).
[24] *Herbage v Meese* (1990) F Supp 60.
[25] *Chuidian v Philippine National Bank* (1990) 912 F.2d 1695.
[26] *Koo Golden East Mongolia v Bank of Nova Scotia* [2007] EWCA Civ 1443, citing Sir George Jessell MR and James LJ in *Twycross v Drefus* (1877) 5 ChD 605, at 618 and 618–619, respectively, and Lord Bingham in *Jones v The Ministry of the Interior of Saudi Arabia* [2006] UKHL 26; [2007] 1 AC 270, at [10].
[27] [1977] 1 QB 529, at 559–561 (Lord Denning MR), 564 (Stephenson LJ), and 575 (Shaw LJ).

well as in accordance with commonly accepted standards in international law. That case, however, dealt with the position at common law before the passing of the State Immunity Act 1978. Thus, it did not have the benefit of the statutory recognition, which is contained in section 14(2) of the Act, that even a separate entity may be performing sovereign tasks. For that reason, the *Trendtex* case should not now be considered as authoritative on this point.

Although it is not expressly stated in section 14(1), it has been suggested that an entity will only qualify as a 'separate entity' for the purposes of section 14(2) if it is owned or controlled by the State.[28]   **7.2.3.3.5.1**

The effect of section 14(2) is that there is a presumption that a separate entity does **7.2.3.3.5.2** not have immunity from suit for the consequences of its actions. It then throws the onus on to the separate entity to show that it is entitled to claim immunity. Furthermore, in *Kuwait Airways Corp v Iraqi Airways Co*[29] the House of Lords held that a separate entity could not claim immunity simply because it acted on the instructions of the State, since such an act might be of a commercial rather than a sovereign nature. To qualify for immunity, the act had to be something done at the behest of the State that also possessed the character of sovereign authority and which would have attracted immunity under the Act had it been done by the State itself. Accordingly, the actions of the defendant (the separate entity) in that case in seizing and removing commercial aircraft on the instructions of the Iraqi State as part of an act of war were protected by the claim to immunity. The subsequent holding and use of the aircraft by the defendant for its own purposes as a commercial airline were not protected, even though they were authorised by State legislation.

7.2.3.4 The adjudicative jurisdiction under the State Immunity Act 1978

As previously mentioned, section 1(1) of the Act lays down a general statement of immunity for foreign States.[30] Sections 2 to 11 then contain a number of wide-ranging exceptions to that principle. Sections 2, 3, and 9 contain the exceptions that are relevant in the context of financing transactions and they will be mentioned below, after which a reference will be made to section 12, which deals with service of proceedings.

7.2.3.4.1 Submission to proceedings   Section 2 of the Act provides for an exception from immunity in proceedings before the courts where a State has submitted to the proceedings. Such a submission may be contained in a prior written

---

[28] Per Lord Goff in *Kuwait Airways Corp v Iraqi Airways Co* [1995] 1 WLR 1147, at 1158.

[29] [1995] 1 WLR 1147.

[30] Which includes proceedings to register and enforce a foreign judgment under the Administration of Justice Act 1920 or the Foreign Judgments (Reciprocal Enforcement) Act 1933: *AIC Ltd v The Federal Government of Nigeria* [2003] EWHC 1357 (QB).

agreement or may be made after the dispute has arisen,[31] such as by instituting the proceedings or taking a substantive step in the proceedings.[32] The head of the State's diplomatic mission in the UK is deemed to have authority to agree to such a submission, and any person who has entered into a contract on behalf of the State with its authority is deemed to have authority to agree to such a submission with respect to proceedings arising out of the contract.[33] A choice of English law to govern a contract is not to be taken as a submission to jurisdiction.[34] It has been held that a general waiver of rights to sovereign immunity in relation to an arbitration agreement was not specific enough to constitute a waiver from immunity for the purposes of section 2.[35]

7.2.3.4.2 Commercial transactions and contracts to be performed in the UK
Section 3 of the Act (along with section 13, to which further reference is made later) comes closest in Part I to incorporating the distinction between sovereign and commercial acts. Section 3 contains an exception from immunity in relation to proceedings concerning a 'commercial transaction' (as defined) or a contractual obligation to be performed (in whole or in part) within the UK. Immunity is preserved if the parties to the dispute have so agreed.[36] Immunity is also preserved where the dispute is between States and, in cases relating to a contractual obligation to be performed in the UK, where the obligation arises under a non-commercial contract which was made in the State and the obligation is governed by the State's administrative law.[37]

7.2.3.4.2.1   Section 3 provides as follows:

(1) A State is not immune as respects proceedings relating to—
   (a) a commercial transaction entered into by that State; or
   (b) an obligation of the State which by virtue of a contract (whether a commercial transaction or not) falls to be performed wholly or partly in the United Kingdom.
(2) This section does not apply if the parties to the dispute are States or have otherwise agreed in writing; and subsection (1)(b) above does not apply if the contract (not being a commercial transaction) was made in the territory of the State concerned and the obligation in question is governed by its administrative law.
(3) In this section, 'commercial transaction' means—
   (a) any contract for the supply of goods or services;
   (b) any loan or other transaction for the provision of finance and any guarantee or indemnity in respect of any such transaction or of any other financial obligation, and

---

[31] S 2(2).
[32] S 2(3), but note the qualifications to this in ss 2(4)–2(6).
[33] S 2(7).
[34] S 2(2).
[35] *Svenska Petroleum Exploration AB v Government of the Republic of Lithuania* [2006] EWCA Civ 1529, [2007] QB 886.
[36] S 3(2).
[37] Ibid.

(c) any other transaction or activity (whether of a commercial, industrial, financial, professional or other similar character) into which a State enters or in
which it engages otherwise than in the exercise of sovereign authority;

but neither paragraph of subsection (1) above applies to a contract of employment
between a State and an individual.

7.2.3.4.2.2 Enforcement of foreign judgments or awards Section 3(1) does not
apply to proceedings to enforce a foreign judgment, even if the underlying dispute on which that judgment is founded related to a commercial transaction.[38]
This is because the proceedings in England are directed at the enforcement of the
foreign judgment, rather than being proceedings relating to the underlying
transaction which was the source of the legal relationship which gave rise to the
foreign judgment.[39] Similarly, proceedings for the enforcement of a foreign
arbitral award will not fall within section 3.[40] It has also been said that section
3(1) was not intended to apply to a dispute that relates to a purely domestic
transaction within the relevant State. There must be some international element
to the transaction.[41]

7.2.3.4.2.3 Disputes between States Section 3(2) preserves immunity with
respect to disputes between States. It has been held, however, that although the
underlying transaction might have been between two States, a dispute concerning
a promissory note that had been issued as a means of payment for the transaction
and which was held by a third party, did not concern a dispute between the two
States. The promissory note was an independent negotiable instrument and was
enforceable in its own right.[42] It has also been pointed out that the literal wording
of section 3(2) would not cover the position where one of the two States had
assigned its rights to a private entity and the assignee was suing to enforce those
rights, as the dispute would not then be between States.[43] It was suggested, however, that the State obligor might still be able to assert immunity from suit because,
on basic principles relating to assignments, an assignment is subject to equities
and one such equity could be the right to claim immunity from enforcement of
the right.

7.2.3.4.2.4 Commercial transactions Section 3(3) contains a definition of a 'commercial transaction' which, by virtue of section 17(1), also applies with reference
to the expression 'commercial purposes' when it is used in Part I of the Act as, for

---

[38] *AIC Ltd v The Federal Government of Nigeria* [2003] EWHC 1357 (QB).
[39] See also s 31 of the Civil Jurisdiction and Judgments Act 1982.
[40] *Svenska Petroleum Exploration AB v Government of the Republic of Lithuania* [2006] EWCA
Civ 1529, [2007] QB 886.
[41] *AIC Ltd v The Federal Government of Nigeria* [2003] EWHC 1357 (QB).
[42] *Cardinal Financial Investments Corp v Central Bank of Yemen* [2001] Lloyd's Rep Bank 1.
[43] *Donegal International Ltd v Republic of Zambia* [2007] EWHC 197 (Comm), [2007] 1 Lloyd's
Rep 397.

instance, in Section 13(4). Paragraph (a) of section 3(3) provides that any contract for the supply of goods or services is to be regarded as a commercial transaction.[44] Similarly, paragraph (b) provides that any loan or other transaction for the provision of finance and any guarantee or indemnity in respect of any such transaction or of any other financial obligation, should be regarded as a commercial transaction. It is important to note that there is no requirement that any such contract, loan, financial transaction, guarantee, or indemnity should relate to an underlying commercial transaction. To put it another way, the fact that the ultimate intention of the State in entering into the transaction was for a sovereign purpose will not affect the treatment of the transaction under section 3, which will be treated as being for a commercial purpose.

7.2.3.4.2.5 Paragraph (c) of section 3(3) has the effect of including within the concept of a commercial transaction virtually every other type of transaction or activity into which a State enters or in which it engages, unless it does so in the exercise of its sovereign authority.[45] In *Svenska Petroleum Exploration AB v Government of the Republic of Lithuania*[46] the Court of Appeal gave guidance as to the interpretation of paragraph (c). It said that paragraph (c) mirrored the distinction drawn at general law and in the new UN Convention on Jurisdictional Immunities of States and Their Property[47] between commercial transactions and transactions entered into in the exercise of sovereign authority.[48] This is similar to the distinction that has been drawn at common law between acts of a public law character and acts of a private law character, being acts that any private person could perform. Article 2.2 of the Convention says that in applying the distinction, reference should be made primarily to the nature of the contract or transaction itself. In the *Svenska Petroleum* case, the transaction concerned the exploitation of the State's oil reserves. The transaction was between the State and a separate State entity on the one hand, and a commercial third party on the other hand. The court said that the transaction had characteristics that could be either public or private and, because it did not have to do so, it declined to express a view as to which way the transaction should be characterised.

---

[44] A joint venture between a State and a third party, to exploit oil reserves of the State as a commercial opportunity on a profit-sharing basis, would not be considered as a supply of goods or services by the third party to the State within para (a): *Svenska Petroleum Exploration AB v Government of the Republic of Lithuania* [2006] EWCA Civ 1529, [2007] QB 886.

[45] Per Lord Diplock in *Alcom Ltd v Republic of Colombia* [1984] AC 580, at 600.

[46] [2006] EWCA Civ 1529, [2007] QB 886.

[47] General Assembly Resolution 59/38 of 16/12/2004.

[48] See also the reference to the Convention by Lord Bingham in *Jones v Ministry of the Interior* [2006] UKHL 26; [2007] 1 AC 270, at [8], in which his Lordship approved the citation of the Convention on this point by Aikens J in *AIG Capital Partners Inc. v Republic of Kazakhstan* [2005] EWHC 2239; [2006] 1 All ER 284, at [80].

The following activities have been held to be in the nature of commercial activities **7.2.3.4.2.6** which should, accordingly, fall within the concept of a commercial transaction: the transfer of shares in a corporation;[49] the issuance of, and the obligations falling due under, a promissory note;[50] the issuance of a letter of credit;[51] and the making of payment from an embassy's bank account to settle liabilities incurred in commercial transactions such as in payment of the price of goods sold to the State.[52]

The following activities have been held to be of a sovereign nature and so they **7.2.3.4.2.7** would not be considered as constituting commercial transactions within paragraph (c): the regulation and use of a country's foreign exchange reserves[53] or its gold reserves;[54] the acquisition and issuance of bank notes;[55] the investment in the international financial markets of a State's national fund for the good of the State and its people;[56] and the payment of expenses incurred for sovereign purposes.[57]

7.2.3.4.3 Proceedings relating to arbitration
Section 9 of the Act provides an exception from immunity in relation to arbitration matters. It provides as follows:

(1) Where a State has agreed in writing to submit a dispute which has arisen, or may arise, to arbitration, the State is not immune as respects proceedings in the courts of the United Kingdom which relate to the arbitration.

(2) This section has effect subject to any contrary provision in the arbitration agreement and does not apply to any arbitration agreement between States.

The Court of Appeal has held that an application before the English courts for **7.2.3.4.3.1** enforcement of a New York Convention award under Part III of the Arbitration Act 1996 fell within the expression 'proceedings . . . which relate to the arbitration' within section 9(1). Accordingly, the State did not enjoy immunity from the proceedings for recognition and enforcement of the award, including proceedings to have judgment entered on the award[58] (but not for enforcement against assets, which is addressed in section 13 of the Act). At first instance in the same case, it was also said that there was no reason why section 9(1) should be limited to awards

---

[49] *Banca Carige SpA v Banco Nacional de Cuba* [2001] 1 WLR 2039.
[50] *Cardinal Financial Investments Corp v Central Bank of Yemen* [2001] Lloyd's Rep Bank 1.
[51] *Trendtex Trading Corp Ltd v Central Bank of Nigeria* [1977] 1 QB 529.
[52] *Alcom Ltd v Republic of Colombia* [1984] AC 580.
[53] *Crescent Oil & Shipping Services v Banco Nacional De Angola* (unreported, 28/5/99 (QB)); *Camdex International Ltd v Bank of Zambia (No 3)* [1997] 6 Bank LR 44.
[54] *Koo Golden East Mongolia v Bank of Nova Scotia* [2007] EWCA Civ 1443.
[55] *Camdex International v Bank of Zambia (No 2)* [1997] 1 All ER 728.
[56] *AIG Capital Partners Inc v Republic of Kazakhstan* [2005] EWHC 2239, [2006] 1 All ER 284.
[57] *Alcom Ltd v Republic of Colombia* [1984] AC 580.
[58] *Svenska Petroleum Exploration AB v Government of the Republic of Lithuania* [2006] EWCA Civ 1529, [2006] QB 886.

made in commercial disputes.[59] There was no reference to that point in the decision of the Court of Appeal.

7.2.3.4.4 Other exceptions to immunity   By way of completing the picture, the other sections of the Act containing exceptions to immunity from proceedings before the English courts are as follows: sections 4 (contracts of employment), 5 (personal injury and damage to property), 6 (ownership, use and possession of property), 7 (intellectual property), 8 (membership of corporate and other bodies), 10 (ships used for commercial purposes and cargo), and 11 (customs and similar duties and rates for commercial premises).

7.2.3.4.5 Service of process on a State   Section 12 of the Act provides for service of process on a foreign State. The principal method for effecting service is via the Foreign and Commonwealth Office for transmission by it to the State's foreign ministry, with service being effected when the process is received at that ministry, as set forth in section 12(1).[60] It should be noted that, in addition to the formal methods for service laid down in section 12, section 12(6) permits service to be effected in any manner to which the State has agreed. In *ABCI v Banque Franco-Tunisienne*[61] it was accepted by the judge at first instance and apparently also accepted on appeal by the Court of Appeal, that a State could proclaim generally to the world that it might be served in a particular way and that this would constitute an agreement for the purposes of section 12(6). To be effective, however, it would have to be shown that such a general agreement was clearly intended by the State concerned to include proceedings in the courts of other States. Normally, a provision in a State's legislation as to service on the State would be understood to be limited to service in domestic proceedings within that State.

7.2.3.5 The enforcement jurisdiction under the State Immunity Act 1978

As previously mentioned, a distinction may be drawn in the way that Part I of the Act is regarded, between the adjudicative powers of the courts (to which reference has been made above) and the court's enforcement powers (which will now be addressed). The fact that the court may have jurisdiction to entertain a claim against a State and to give judgment against it does not mean that the judgment, or the relevant arbitration award, can be enforced against the property of the State.[62] The same point can be made concerning the power of the courts to make

---

[59] Per Gloster J in *Svenska Petroleum Exploration AB v Government of the Republic of Lithuania* [2005] EWHC 2437 (Comm), at [65]–[73].

[60] The necessity of complying strictly with the requirements of s 12(1) is demonstrated by *Kuwait Airways Corp v Iraqi Airways Co* [1995] 1 WLR 1147.

[61] [2002] 1 Lloyd's Rep 511, at [177]–[185] (HHJ Chambers QC) and [2003] 2 Lloyd's Rep 146, at [29]–[34] (Court of Appeal).

[62] See, for instance, in relation to the enforcement of arbitral awards, *AIG Capital Partners Inc v Republic of Kazakhstan* [2005] EWHC 2239; [2006] 1 All ER 284, at [5]–[6] and *Svenska Petroleum*

mandatory orders against a State. This is illustrated by section 13(3) which provides that a submission by a State to the jurisdiction of the court does not automatically carry with it a consent by the State to the exercise of the enforcement powers of the court.

The powers of the court to impose penalties or to make mandatory orders **7.2.3.5.1** against a State or to order enforcement against a State's property, and the limits on those powers, fall to be determined within the separate enforcement powers of the court which are addressed in section 13 of the Act.[63] There are also restrictions on the exercise of the enforcement powers of the court in relation to a State's separate entities and, whether or not they are such entities, a State's central bank or other monetary authority. Section 14 contains provisions that relate to that issue.

The relevant provisions in section 13 concerning States will be addressed first and **7.2.3.5.2** then the position concerning separate entities, central banks, and other monetary authorities will be addressed.

7.2.3.5.3 Enforcement action against States   Section 13 of the Act, in so far as it applies in England,[64] provides as follows:

(1) No penalty by way of committal or fine shall be imposed in respect of any failure or refusal by or on behalf of a State to disclose or produce any document or other information for the purposes of proceedings to which it is a party.

(2) Subject to subsections (3) and (4) below—
  (a) relief shall not be given against a State by way of injunction or order for specific performance or for the recovery of land or other property;
  (b) the property of a State shall not be subject to any process for the enforcement of a judgment or arbitration award or, in an action in rem, for its arrest, detention or sale.

(3) Subsection (2) above does not prevent the giving of any relief or the issue of any process with the written consent of the State concerned; and any such consent (which may be contained in a prior agreement) may be expressed so as to apply to a limited extent or generally; but a provision merely submitting to the jurisdiction of the courts is not to be regarded as a consent for the purposes of this subsection.

(4) Subsection 2(b) above does not prevent the issue of any process in respect of property which is for the time being in use or intended for use for commercial purposes; but [there follows a qualification concerning States which are a party to the European Convention on State Immunity].

(5) The head of a State's diplomatic mission in the United Kingdom, or the person for the time being performing his functions, shall be deemed to have authority

---

Exploration AB v Government of the Republic of Lithuania [2006] EWCA Civ 1529; [2007] QB 886, at [117].

[63] See also s 31(4) of the Civil Jurisdiction and Judgments Act 1982.
[64] S 13(6) only applies to Scotland.

to give on behalf of the State any such consent as is mentioned in subsection (3) above and, for the purposes of subsection (4) above, his certificate to the effect that any property is not in use or intended for use by or on behalf of the State for commercial purposes shall be accepted as sufficient evidence of that fact unless the contrary is proved.

7.2.3.5.3.1 The scheme of section 13   Section 13 addresses three types of enforcement or similar order that the courts may be invited or feel tempted to make with respect to a State and its assets. The first type of order, having a disciplinary nature, would be for a penalty by way of committal or fine relating to misbehaviour in litigation to which the State is a party. Section 13(1), which is absolute in its terms, forbids the courts from making any such order against a State and there is no exception to the prohibition provided in section 13 or elsewhere. Secondly, a court may be invited to grant relief by way of an injunction,[65] an order for specific performance or for the recovery of land or other property. Thirdly, the court may be requested to grant an enforcement order, by way of execution against the property of a State or for an order for the arrest, detention or sale of such property (e.g. a vessel) in an action *in rem*. The second and third types of order, to which reference is made in, respectively, sections 13(2)(a) and 13(2)(b), may only be made if in the particular circumstances they fall within the permitted exceptions contained in sections 13(3) or 13(4).

7.2.3.5.3.2 Consent to relief or enforcement   Section 13(3) permits the court to grant relief (as described in section 13(2)(a)) or to order enforcement against a State's property (as described in section 13(2)(b)) within the terms of any written consent given by the State. Such consent may be expressed in a general or a limited manner. Section 13(3) specifically provides that consent is not to be inferred from a mere submission to the jurisdiction of the English courts. The consent may be contained in a prior agreement, such as in a credit agreement or in a guarantee given by the State. It has been held that a consent clause in a commercial agreement should be construed in accordance with the normal rules of construction for commercial agreements, and it should not be construed restrictively or in a highly legalistic way simply because it involved a State's waiver of its immunities pursuant to section 13(3).[66] It has also been held that if a State had consented to enforcement

---

[65] As for instance in the granting of an anti-suit injunction against the maintenance of proceedings in a foreign jurisdiction: *Sabah Shipyard (Pakistan) Ltd v Islamic Republic of Pakistan* [2002] EWCA Civ 1643, [2003] 2 Lloyd's Rep 571.

[66] Per Waller LJ in *Sabah Shipyard (Pakistan) Ltd v Islamic Republic of Pakistan* [2002] EWCA Civ 1643, [2003] 2 Lloyd's Rep 571, at [25]–[26], Saville J in *A Co Ltd v Republic of X* [1990] 2 Lloyd's Rep 521, at 523, and Lord Diplock in *Alcom Ltd v Republic of Colombia* [1984] AC 580, at 600.

action against its property, that would allow a freezing order (formerly called a Mareva injunction) to be made against that property.[67]

By virtue of section 13(5), the head of a State's diplomatic mission in the UK, or the person for the time being performing his functions, shall be deemed to have authority to give consent under section 13(3) on behalf of the State. Whilst it is not specifically stated, it should be possible for the consent to be given on behalf of a State by any other person who is duly authorised to do so, as section 13(5) is couched in permissive rather than exclusive language.

7.2.3.5.3.3

A reservation which must be made to that view, however, arises from the fact that the wording that is used in section 13(5) is different to that used in section 2(7), which relates to the giving of consent on behalf of a State to the adjudicative jurisdiction of the courts. In section 2(7) it is made clear that, in addition to the deeming of authority in favour of the relevant diplomat, a person who has authority to contract on behalf of a State shall also be deemed to have authority to give consent on its behalf to proceedings arising out of the contract. That additional wording is not present in section 13(5). Nonetheless, it is submitted that the discrepancy in the wording should not affect the conclusion that has been drawn above concerning persons other than the relevant diplomat who may give a consent on behalf of a State for the purposes of section 13(3), provided that it can be shown that they have been duly authorised to give the consent. It would be sensible to ensure that there is an express authorisation which refers explicitly to the right to give consent for the purposes of section 13(5).

7.2.3.5.3.4

7.2.3.5.3.5 Commercial assets Even without any such consent, section 13(4) permits the court to order enforcement against a State's property, if such property is 'for the time being in use or intended for use for commercial purposes'. By virtue of section 17(1), the phrase 'commercial purposes' is to be read synonymously with the wide concept of a 'commercial transaction' in section 3(3), and reference should be made to the discussion on that issue, above. Nonetheless, it has been held that property which appears to be commercial in its nature but which is held for a sovereign purpose will fall outside the scope of section 13(4).[68] In the case of a bank account, which is indivisible, unless the whole of the balance on the account (save for de minimis transactions) is being used or is intended for use for commercial purposes, it will not be possible to take enforcement proceedings against it.[69] The time as at which the matter is to be tested is when the enforcement action is taken. Hence, an account which may previously have been used for commercial

---

[67] *A Co Ltd v Republic of X* [1990] 2 Lloyd's Rep 521.
[68] *AIG Capital Partners Inc. v Republic of Kazakhstan* [2005] EWHC 2239, [2006] 1 All ER 284.
[69] *Alcom Ltd v Republic of Colombia* [1984] AC 580.

purposes but which had become dormant and for which there was no present intention that it should be used again for such a purpose, could not be said to be in use or intended for use for commercial purposes.[70] The onus of proof lies on the judgment creditor to prove the requisite use or intention.[71] It is further provided by section 13(5) that a certificate provided by the head of a State's diplomatic mission in the UK, or the person for the time being performing his functions, to the effect that property does not have the requisite commercial connection shall be prima facie evidence unless the contrary is proved.[72]

7.2.3.5.3.6 Property The concept of 'property' as it is used in sections 13 and 14 should be given a wide construction. It has been held that it will 'include all real and personal property and will embrace any right or interest, legal or equitable or contractual in assets that might be held by a state or an emanation of the state . . .'.[73] It has thus been held to include the credit balance on a bank account,[74] no matter whether it was held beneficially or only legally by the named account holder,[75] and securities held in an investment account.[76]

7.2.3.5.4 Enforcement against a separate entity, central bank, or monetary authority There are separate provisions relating to enforcement action concerning a State's 'separate entities' (which expression is defined in section 14(1), as referred to above) and, whether or not they are separate entities, its central bank or other monetary authority. The provision concerning separate entities is to be found in section 14(3). Section 14(4) deals with a State's central bank or other monetary authority.

7.2.3.5.4.1 Sections 14(3) and 14(4) provide as follows:

> (3) If a separate entity (not being a State's central bank or other monetary authority) submits to the jurisdiction in respect of proceedings in the case of which it is entitled to immunity by virtue of [section 14(2)], subsections (1) to (4) of [section 13] shall apply to it in respect of those proceedings as if references to a State were references to that entity.
>
> (4) Property of a State's central bank or other monetary authority shall not be regarded for the purposes of [section 13(4)] as in use or intended for use for

---

[70] *AIC Ltd v The Federal Government of Nigeria* [2003] EWHC 1357 (QB).

[71] *Alcom Ltd v Republic of Colombia* [1984] AC 580.

[72] As to the use of such certificates, see *Alcom Ltd v Republic of Colombia* [1984] AC 580, *AIC Ltd v The Federal Government of Nigeria* [2003] EWHC 1357 (QB), and *AIG Capital Partners Inc v Republic of Kazakhstan* [2005] EWHC 2239, [2006] 1 All ER 284.

[73] Per Aikens J in *AIG Capital Partners Inc. v Republic of Kazakhstan* [2005] EWHC 2239, [2006] 1 All ER 284, at [45].

[74] *Alcom Ltd v Republic of Colombia* [1984] AC 580.

[75] *AIC Ltd v The Federal Government of Nigeria* [2003] EWHC 1357 (QB); *AIG Capital Partners Inc v Republic of Kazakhstan* [2005] EWHC 2239, [2006] 1 All ER 284.

[76] *AIG Capital Partners Inc v Republic of Kazakhstan* [2005] EWHC 2239, [2006] 1 All ER 284.

commercial purposes; and where such bank or authority is a separate entity subsections (1) to (3) of [section 13] shall apply to it as if references to a State were references to the bank or authority.

7.2.3.5.4.2 Separate entities   It is not a straightforward exercise to unravel the position concerning a State's separate entity (other than a State's central bank or other monetary authority). In summary, it is as follows. Generally speaking, as it has its own personality distinct from the State, a separate entity will not enjoy immunity from suit or from the disciplinary or enforcement powers of the court. In a particular case, however, the entity may be able to assert immunity from the jurisdiction of the court for proceedings against it, in reliance upon section 14(2) (i.e. it was acting on behalf of the State in circumstances in which the State would have been entitled to immunity). In such a case, it and its property will be immune from the disciplinary and enforcement powers of the court to the same extent as if it were the State that was subject to such proceedings. In such a particular case, the immunity of the entity from the disciplinary and enforcement powers of the court will not be lost if the separate entity submits to the jurisdiction of the court in respect of the proceedings against it. By virtue of section 14(3), the position will then be governed by the provisions relating to the enforcement powers of the court, as contained in sections 13(1) to 13(4), as if references in those sections were to the separate entity rather than to a State. For instance, the entity could consent expressly to the exercise of such powers. Its commercial assets will not be immune from enforcement action in any event.

7.2.3.5.4.3 Central banks and monetary authorities   The position relating to a State's central bank or other monetary authority is as follows. By virtue of section 14(4), whether or not it is a separate entity, its property will be immune from the enforcement powers of the courts for all purposes, unless it specifically consents to the exercise of such powers. This is because its property is deemed, for all purposes, to have the benefit of immunity and (irrespective of any normal commercial nature) is treated as not being held for commercial purposes. If it is not a separate entity and so is part of the State, it will (except for the wider immunity of its property) enjoy the immunities that are given to a State under section 13. If it is a separate entity then by virtue of section 14(4) it is put in the same position (except for the wider immunity of its property) as a State would be in under section 13.

7.2.3.5.4.4 A central bank's property   The concept of 'property' for the purposes of sections 13 and 14 has been referred to above. There are two additional points to be made in this regard in relation to a central bank's property. First, it has been held that an asset will be 'property' of a central bank whether it holds the asset legally or beneficially. Thus, the benefit of an account held in the name of a central bank with another bank will be the central bank's 'property' and immune from the enforcement powers of the court under section 14(4). This will be the case even if the central bank holds the account for another party, such as its State, and despite the fact that the account might have been intended to be used for a commercial purpose of the central bank or of that other party.[77]

7.2.3.5.4.4.1   Secondly, the position concerning the exercise of rights of set-off raises different issues. By way of example, a central bank may have placed a deposit with a commercial bank in London and it may also owe money to that commercial bank. The latter may wish to exercise its banker's right of set-off, so that it can apply the deposit against the debt due to it. The exercise of a banker's right of set-off (or, indeed, an enhanced right of contractual set-off, if the contract so provides) in such circumstances is, essentially, a self-help remedy. It is not a court process of enforcement, so it does not fall within the purview of section 13(2)(b). Accordingly, there is no reason why the bank should not exercise the right of set-off, provided that it would otherwise be entitled to do so as a matter of general law. One reason why the banker may not be entitled to do so at general law would be if it was aware that, despite the deposit being held in the name of the central bank, the beneficial ownership of the deposit was vested in someone other than the central bank, so that the essential requirement of mutuality was lacking.[78]

7.3   The Immunities of International Organisations

7.3.1   Background

An international organisation is generally established under the auspices of a treaty between States or the governments of States. Such treaties usually contain provisions along the following lines:[79]

(1) that the international organisation should be established for the purposes outlined in the treaty;

(2) that the organisation should have separate legal and juridical personality;

(3) that it should be given wide ranging powers and capacities, such as to contract, to acquire, hold, and dispose of property, to establish and maintain a

---

[77] *AIC Ltd v The Federal Government of Nigeria* [2003] EWHC 1357 (QB); *AIG Capital Partners Inc v Republic of Kazakhstan* [2005] EWHC 2239, [2006] 1 All ER 284.

[78] The position at general law is illustrated by the facts of *Barclays Bank Ltd v Quistclose Investments Ltd* [1970] AC 567, where the bank was prevented from exercising its rights of set-off because it was aware that the beneficial interest in the deposit was vested in a third party. An example of the opposite situation, where a bank wished to set-off a liability to it on loan account of one customer (C) against a credit balance in the name of another customer (D) because it thought that, beneficially, the credit balance was held for C, is to be found in *Saudi Arabian Monetary Authority v Dresdner Bank* [2004] EWCA Civ 1074, [2005] 1 Lloyd's Rep 12. It was held that it could not do so as it was unable to prove that the beneficial entitlement in the deposit was vested in C.

[79] This is taken from the review conducted by Kerr LJ in *JH Rayner (Mincing Lane) Ltd v The Department of Trade and Industry* [1989] Ch 72, at 143–146.

head and other offices, to institute and conduct legal proceedings, to employ staff and carry out its administrative and other functions;

(4) that it (and its officers, representatives, and bodies) should have certain immunities, exemptions, and privileges in the signatory States, particularly in the territory of a host State where it has a presence; and

(5) that these various matters should be recognised and given effect in the domestic laws of the signatory States. Sometimes it is also stated that the signatory States should not be liable for the acts of the organisation.

7.3.2 The effect of treaties in the UK

International treaties to which the UK is a party do not have direct effect in the domestic law of the UK, so it is necessary for legislation to be put in place to implement such treaties for the purposes of the law in the UK. Occasionally, the UK has done this by an Act of Parliament which simply provides that the relevant treaty is to have the force of law in the UK, but that is now rare. The more usual pattern is for an Act of Parliament to make provision for Orders in Council to deal with the implementation in the UK of matters concerning international organisations. For instance, under the International Monetary Fund Act 1979 and the Overseas Development and Co-Operation Act 1980, Orders in Council have been made concerning the International Monetary Fund, the International Bank For Reconstruction and Development (the World Bank), and the International Finance Corporation.[80]

In most cases, however, the matter has been dealt with by an Order in Council made in pursuance of the Diplomatic Privileges (Extension) Acts of 1944, 1946, and 1950, which were consolidated into the International Organisations (Immunities and Privileges) Act 1950 (the 1950 Act), and under the International Organisations Act 1968 (the 1968 Act). The 1968 Act repealed and replaced the 1950 Act but the validity of Orders in Council made under the 1950 Act was preserved and continued by the 1968 Act.[81] The 1968 Act provides that Orders made under it may confer immunities from suit and legal process upon an international organisation of which the UK is a member and upon members of its various bodies, its officers, staff, and representatives.

7.3.2.1

7.3.3 The effect of Orders in Council

The pattern of such Orders in Council is that they confer on the relevant organisation 'the legal capacities of a body corporate'. They also confer privileges and immunities on the organisation and its officers and representatives. However,

---

[80] For the position concerning agencies of the UN, see the discussion in *Entico Corp Ltd v UNESCO* [2008] EWHC 531 (Comm).

[81] S 12(5) of the 1968 Act.

whilst they may refer to the separate status of the organisation as intended to be conferred in the treaty, they usually do not provide explicitly that the organisation should have separate legal or juridical personality of a company incorporated in the UK or that it should have the status in domestic law of a body corporate. They also refrain from repeating any statement in the treaty that the signatory States were to be free from any responsibility for the acts and omissions of the organisation.

7.3.3.1   An example of the width of the immunities that an organisation may nonetheless enjoy under such Orders in Council is given by the various litigation involving the International Tin Council.[82] On the other hand, it was also held in part of that litigation that in one instance there had been an effective contractual waiver by the Council of its right to immunity.[83]

7.3.4 Common law

The position concerning the immunities of international organisations at common law, in the absence of legislative provision, is uncertain. In one case it was said that such an organisation would not enjoy any immunity at common law.[84] In another case it was held that the relevant organisation would have such immunity and its director-general would be in a similar position for acts done by him in his official capacity.[85]

7.4 State Insolvency

7.4.1 Introduction

The position concerning States which become unable to meet their debts and other financial commitments is rather different from that for other legal entities and natural persons. By way of example of the difficulties in which States can find themselves,[86] Argentina has defaulted in the payment of its external debt (i.e. debt due to foreign creditors) five times in the last 115 or so years, and over that period a number of countries have defaulted more frequently, including France, Germany, Brazil, and Mexico. It was reported in 2004 that Turkey's external debt was equal to 55 times its gross domestic product and Brazil's ratio was 24 times its GDP. A ratio of 15 times would be considered to be more satisfactory.

---

82 *Re International Tin Council* [1987] Ch 419 (affd at [1989] Ch 309); *Shearson Lehman Brothers Inc. v Maclaine Watson & Co Ltd (No 2)* [1988] 1 WLR 16; and *Maclaine Watson & Co Ltd v International Tin Council (No 2)* [1989] Ch 286.
83 *Standard Chartered Bank v International Tin Council* [1987] 1 WLR 641.
84 Ibid, at 647–648.
85 *Arab Monetary Fund v Hashim* [1993] 1 Lloyd's Rep 543, at 573–574 (reversed by the Court of Appeal on other grounds: [1996] 1 Lloyd's Rep 589).
86 The figures quoted in this paragraph are taken from an article in the *Financial Times* of 21/4/2004.

A State may display either or both of the two attributes of insolvency that are com-   **7.4.1.1**
monly understood, that is, an inability to pay its debts as they fall due or an excess
of liabilities over the country's assets and other potential resources, but there are
no formal insolvency procedures of a collective nature that can then be instituted
to wind it up, to bind it and all of its creditors to a collective procedure, or to
appoint an insolvency practitioner to administer its affairs. If such procedures
were possible, they would have to be available on an international basis, as States
commonly have both domestic creditors and a large number of foreign external
creditors. They would all need to be bound by the procedures to make them effective. Such compromises and other arrangements as have been achieved have been
by agreement between the relevant State and various types of its external creditors.
For instance, under the Paris Club arrangements,[87] a number of debtor States have
come to compromise and debt restructuring agreements with other States that
have been their creditors. Other compromise and restructuring agreements have
been put in place with non-State creditors, but that has become increasingly difficult as the number and variety of such creditors have greatly increased in recent
years.

In former years, the external creditors of a State (apart from other States) tended   **7.4.1.2**
to be the international agencies and the larger international banks, which had
provided funds under credit and drawing facilities. The creditors were limited in
number and could usually be persuaded to come to agreements with their debtors.
More recently, States have tended to raise much more of their debt on the international capital markets and where the debt has been raised by loans, the loan participations have been divided into smaller portions and then sold. These factors
have resulted in a much wider spread of creditors, with disparate groups holding
parcels of the debt. It has been difficult to achieve a consensus amongst the creditors, with differing views being held on the action that should be taken if a State
debtor has defaulted.

7.4.2 Purchase and enforcement of 'distressed debt'

It has not been uncommon for sovereign debt that is hovering on the edge of
default, or which is actually in default, to be acquired at a considerable discount
to its face value by entities, such as hedge or vulture funds, which specialise in the
acquisition of such debt (which is sometimes referred to as 'distressed debt'). Such
creditors (sometimes referred to as 'holdout creditors') have been prepared to
refuse to agree to compromise and restructuring arrangements, even if the majority of the creditors have been sympathetic towards the debtor. They then engage

---

[87] There is a useful description of these arrangements in *Donegal International Ltd v Republic of
Zambia* [2007] EWHC 197 (Comm), [2007] 1 Lloyd's Rep 397.

in the rigorous pursuit of the debtor so as to achieve payment, which has not infrequently been accomplished at a considerable profit over the original cost of acquisition. There have been a number of instances where such entities have pursued the debtor in the courts, particularly in the USA[88] but also in England,[89] which sometimes have been prepared to entertain such suits.[90] In the USA, the courts have even allowed attachment of assets by way of enforcement of a judgment.[91]

7.4.3 The SDRM proposal

In 2002, the International Monetary Fund (IMF) proposed that an international insolvency procedure should be established to enable States to obtain protection from their external creditors in the context of implementing a restructuring of their external debt, on lines that would be similar to a US-style Chapter 9 bankruptcy proceeding for municipalities and local government bodies. The proposed procedure was called the 'Sovereign Debt Restructuring Mechanism' (SDRM), to which the members of the IMF would be bound by international treaty and an amendment of the IMF's Articles of Agreement.[92] The IMF's member States would then make the SDRM mechanism binding through adoption of it in their own laws.

7.4.3.1 Briefly summarised, the SDRM would involve the State putting a restructuring plan to its external creditors, which would be voted upon by such creditors and agreed or not depending upon whether the requisite majority was in favour. There would be a suspension of legal proceedings against the State whilst the plan was being formulated and put to the external creditors. The debtor State would be obliged to formulate the plan and enter into negotiations on it in good faith. The plan could include some new finance with priority over the rights of existing creditors. There would be a forum, called the Sovereign Debt Dispute Resolution Forum, to adjudicate upon disputed claims of external creditors. Unlike a domestic insolvency, however, there would be no court supervision, nor the appointment of an insolvency practitioner to take charge of the restructuring.

---

[88] For instance, *Allied Bank International v Banco Credito Agricola de Cartago* 757 F. 2d 516 (2d Cir 1985), *Elliot Associates v Republic of Panama* 975 F. Supp 332 (1977); *Pravin Banker Associates Ltd v Banco Popular de Peru* 109 F. 3d 850 (2d Cir 1997); *Elliot Associates LLP v Banco de la Nacion and the Republic of Peru* 194 F. 3d 363 (1999 US App).

[89] For instance, *Camdex International Ltd v Bank of Zambia* [1998] QB 22.

[90] Which would not be protected by the doctrine of sovereign immunity because of the commercial nature of the transactions, which are an exception to the operation of the doctrine.

[91] As for instance occurred in *Elliot Associates LLP v Republic of Panama* 975 F. Supp 332 (1997). Action has also been taken to freeze payments in clearing and settlement systems in other countries, as occurred in Belgium in *Elliott Associates LLP v Peru* (Court of Appeals, Brussels 26/9/2000).

[92] The proposals were described by Anne Krueger, first deputy director of the IMF, in an IMF publication *A New Approach to Sovereign Debt Restructuring* (April 2002), ISBN 1-58906-121-7.

Not entirely unexpectedly, the proposal proved to be controversial and did not **7.4.3.2** prosper. It was shelved in 2003.

7.4.4 Collective action clauses

An alternative suggestion, which has been more popular, was for the adoption of 'Collective Action Clauses' in capital markets issues of bonds which have been issued by State issuers, under which amendments in the terms and conditions of a bond issue could be made upon a majority vote of the holders of the bonds, which would bind all of the holders of the bonds. Such amendments might affect the financial terms and the dates for payment of the bonds, so that a temporary moratorium and a longer term restructuring could be put into place. Clauses permitting a majority of the bond holders to approve such amendments have traditionally been the case in bond issues that take place under English law, but they had not customarily been present in bond issues that took place under New York law.

A further refinement has been to extend the effect of such clauses, by the use of **7.4.4.1** 'Aggregation Clauses'. Such clauses permit creditors' committees to negotiate on behalf of creditors holding debt in different issues. The result is that amendments can be proposed that would take effect across more than one of a State's bond issues. The clause provides that amendments will be binding if they are approved by a majority vote of the holders of the bonds in all of the issues.

The use of Collective Actions Clauses has not been an entirely satisfactory solu- **7.4.4.2** tion, however, because they may not prevent precipitate action being taken at an early stage, before a majority vote can be obtained. In addition, they cannot bind creditors who may not be a party to an agreement or set of bond conditions containing such clauses.

8

LEGAL OPINIONS

8.1 Introduction

It is a fairly common requirement in financing transactions, usually specified as **8.1.1**
one of the conditions precedent to the obligation for the granting of credit or the
advancement or provision of the funds or other relevant matter, that one or more
legal opinions should be delivered for the benefit of those who are to advance the
funds or provide credit and such like under the transaction. This is particularly the
case in cross-border transactions, although it is also a relatively common requirement in commercial transactions that are confined to a domestic jurisdiction, if
they are of any significant amount.[1] In the context of cross-border transactions,

---

[1] For instance, a financial institution may require a legal opinion concerning a transaction so
that it can be shown to its auditors as part of their review in conducting an audit. In this sense, the

legal opinions are intended to address, amongst other things, the conflict of law issues that arise because of the nature of the transaction. It is likely that several opinions may have to be delivered, respectively addressing the position in each relevant jurisdiction.

8.1.2 A legal opinion is written by a lawyer or a law firm and it addresses various legal issues that relate to a transaction and the obligors which are involved in the transaction.[2] The legal opinion is intended to provide a measure of assurance to those who are providing the funds, credit, or other benefit under it that the transaction is valid, that it gives rise to enforceable obligations and rights as against the obligors, and, if assets are to be transferred or security is to be given, that the transaction will result in the transfer of the assets or the creation of the security.

8.1.3 Limitations upon an opinion

There are a number of limitations, however, that concern the scope and contents of such opinions and the consequences in receiving them.

8.1.3.1 In the first place, they are (as their title indicates) opinions concerning the law and not cast iron guarantees of the legal position. It follows that an opinion may have been expressed in good faith and on reasonable grounds but it may turn out to be incorrect. This may particularly be the case in situations where there is no (or only limited) available legislation or authority or other reliable guidance on a point that is in issue,[3] or where a change may have occurred since a search or other investigation was carried out on which the opinion is based. It also follows that the mere fact that an opinion sets out a conclusion as to the legal position on an issue does not mean that the law must inevitably be as it was so stated. If the lawyers who gave the opinion made a mistake then the consequence may be that those who suffered loss may have a claim against them which, of course, will be subject to establishing liability and the recoverable loss, as well as in then attempting to enforce any judgment that may be given against the defendants. Whilst many lawyers have insurance cover against such claims, there are limits on the cover, and the value of transactions often exceeds the available insurance cover.

8.1.3.2 Secondly, a legal opinion should only address matters of law, not commercial matters going to the economic viability of a transaction, the creditworthiness of the obligors in such a transaction, or the commercial value of the assets that may be involved in the transaction. Such matters should be investigated by the

---

opinion is used in the process of verifying the existence and value of the bank's investment in the transaction.

[2] It is unusual for legal opinions to address personal issues that relate only to the providers of the funds, such as their own existence and powers to enter into the transaction.

[3] In some jurisdictions the particular issue may remain uncertain or may not be addressed at all by the legal system and the laws of the jurisdiction or it may not be possible to obtain up-to-date copies of recent legislation. In other jurisdictions the law may not be publicly available.

commercial parties and they may properly be addressed, as well, in the representations and covenants that are expressed as being given or undertaken by the relevant obligors in the contractual documentation, but they are not matters for which the lawyer should be expected to take responsibility.

Thirdly, an opinion will address the position as at a particular time, being the time it is written; it should not predict the future, as the law may change in ways that cannot be predicted. A well drawn opinion will also make it clear that the writer accepts no responsibility to advise of any changes in the law.[4]

8.1.3.3

Fourthly, an opinion will usually be given on the basis of certain assumptions, being matters of fact which the writer cannot be expected to know[5] or matters of law, including foreign law, which cannot be verified or in which the writer does not profess any expertise.[6] The assumptions will vary depending upon the facts and circumstances and the nature of the particular transaction.

8.1.3.4

Fifthly, the opinion will address the transaction as represented by the documentation into which the parties have entered which, in turn, reflects the outcome of the negotiations that took place before the documentation was finalised. The opinion should not be regarded as an assessment of the advantages of the negotiated position, nor as confirmation that every conceivable negotiating or commercial point has been covered.[7] Nor can the opinion address matters that fall outside the scope of the documentation as, for instance, may arise under side letters or other undisclosed agreements or arrangements.

8.1.3.5

Sixthly, the opinion is likely to be given subject to a number of qualifications relating to matters of law which may adversely affect or qualify the legal rights and obligations that might be expected to arise under the transaction. Such qualifications need to be relevant to the particular transaction in hand but reflect the fact that it is simply impossible to have a perfect world (or a world that leans entirely in favour of one type of party in a transaction), whichever system of law may be involved and notwithstanding the respective viewpoints of the parties.[8] It may be

8.1.3.6

---

[4] Of course, if the writer of an opinion is aware of a definite change that is about to be implemented and which is relevant to the transaction, that matter should be referred to in the opinion.

[5] Once again, such matters could be the subject of representations and covenants in the contractual documentation.

[6] Matters of foreign law should be addressed in a separate legal opinion provided by a lawyer who practises in the relevant jurisdiction.

[7] This is particularly important where a party to a transaction may not have been involved in the negotiations that were conducted before the documentation was concluded as, for instance, would be the case concerning a syndicate member which enters into a syndicated loan agreement.

[8] Nonetheless, it may be desirable that an obligor should confirm that the grounds upon which a qualification may be based will not arise in practice. For instance, an English opinion will usually contain a qualification relating to the rule against penalties, particularly as it may affect a default interest provision, which applies during the period in which a borrower under a credit facility is in default in making a payment. Despite such a qualification in the legal opinion, it is not unreasonable that a borrower should be required to confirm that, from its perspective, such a default interest

a consequence of this that the writer of the opinion has the opportunity, through the mechanism of the legal opinion, to consider and set out such qualifications in a more formal and systematic manner than might otherwise have been available to him, given the exigencies of time and the speed with which many modern transactions have to be undertaken and completed.

8.1.3.6.1 Nonetheless, the lawyer who is giving an opinion should consider the qualifications that are relevant and appropriate to the transaction. If necessary, the writer should be prepared to explain why the qualifications are needed. It may be the case that a qualification that is relevant in one situation may be inappropriate in a different type of transaction. For instance, most opinions on English law contain a qualification relating to the effect of the insolvency of a party to the transaction. If, however, the transaction involves a party in giving security then a blanket qualification excepting the effect of such an insolvency from the validity and enforceability of the transaction would have the result that the opinion failed to address the essential purpose in taking the security. A similar point can be made in relation to an opinion which addresses rights of netting and set-off. Such rights are most likely to be relevant when a party to a transaction becomes insolvent.

8.1.3.7 Finally, where a particular difficulty is raised by a legal opinion (for instance, because of one or more qualifications contained in the opinion) or a point of law needs further clarification, it may be necessary for those receiving the opinion to take further advice before deciding if they wish to proceed with the transaction.

8.1.4 Reviewing an opinion

Quite often it will fall to a lawyer who is advising the banks (or other providers of credit) to review the opinions that are to be provided by other lawyers who are involved in the transaction. It is a reasonable rule of thumb for a lawyer when conducting such a review, taking into account the assumptions on which the opinions are based and the qualifications to which they are expressed as being subject, that the reviewer should not expect the lawyers who are giving the opinions to go beyond what the reviewer would himself be prepared to say if he was the person giving the opinion.[9] In other words, 'do unto others as you would have them do unto you'.

---

provision represents a reasonable pre-estimate of the loss or additional risk that a lender may be expected to suffer in consequence of a default by the borrower in making a payment on the due date. In similar vein, an obligor might be expected to confirm that a certain provision reflects a reasonable allocation of risk as a matter of fact, even though a legal opinion may be unable to confirm such an outcome as a matter of law (e.g. as to the effect of a clause that excludes or limits liability within the context of the Unfair Contract Terms Act 1977).

[9] In his professional practice, the author has witnessed situations where another lawyer, usually educated in the UK or the USA, has aggressively pursued the writer of a draft legal opinion, requiring that the latter should remove an assumption or qualification in the opinion or that the latter should confirm a point when it was unreasonable to expect such action to be taken. Such conduct is deeply regrettable.

8.1.5 Types of opinion

The concept of a legal opinion as referred to in this chapter relates to an opinion that addresses the legal consequences of a transaction. It is intended to be for the benefit of those who are involved in the transaction, as parties or in some other related manner. It should also be mentioned that the expression 'legal opinion' is sometimes used in a different context where it is not intended to be for the benefit of those involved in a transaction. An example of this is the situation where a regulatory body may require that an opinion should be furnished addressing matters concerning a particular entity or the effect of one or more transactions on that entity. In such a context, the opinion may be required as part of the process of licensing or granting an authorisation to such an entity as a regulated person, or so as to enable it to gain the benefit of a certain type of regulatory treatment, as for instance for capital adequacy purposes.[10]

8.2 The Beneficiaries of a Legal Opinion

There may be a number of persons who may wish to rely upon and receive the **8.2.1** benefit of a legal opinion relating to a transaction. They will include those who provide the funding, credit, or some other benefit in the transaction, be they lenders or providers of finance through the capital markets, a counterparty in a derivatives or similar transaction, or a bank which may be taking a counter-indemnity from an obligor in connection with the issuance of a bank guarantee, a bond, a letter of credit, or a similar instrument. In addition, various other persons may also have an involvement in a transaction and wish to have the benefit of a legal opinion, such as a credit rating agency which is to ascribe a credit rating to debt instruments in a capital markets transaction.[11] The trustee of security or, in a bond issue, the trustee for the bondholders, may also wish to receive an opinion, at least confirming for its own personal benefit that the trust has been properly constituted, and addressing its own rights and obligations as trustee.[12] In a syndicated

---

[10] E.g. an opinion that is given in connection with a financial institution's legal risk in a securitisation or as to the availability to it of netting and set-off in a derivatives or other transaction.

[11] The rating agency will base its rating on the legal position as described in the opinion. For that reason, rating agencies will usually subject a proposed opinion to a critical examination so as to ensure that the legal issues that arise are properly addressed in the opinion.

[12] The issuance of an opinion for the benefit of the trustee can cause difficulties in distinguishing between the personal position of the trustee and, in that regard, its need to know that the documentation that it has entered into is effective and binding, on the one hand, and its representative capacity on behalf of the bondholders or other subsequent parties on the other hand. As to the latter, the writers of an opinion may be unwilling to incur responsibilities, via the trustee, towards bondholders or such other subsequent parties who acquire their investments or participations in the secondary market, for the reasons given below.

facility, the opinion will usually be addressed to the facility agent but be expressed to be for the benefit of the agent and the syndicate of banks.

8.2.2 Subsequent parties

A question that may arise concerns the extent to which an opinion should be made available for the benefit of subsequent parties to a transaction, such as transferees of a loan participation, sub-participants in a loan participation, or bondholders who acquire their investments in the secondary market. In the first instance, this question will depend upon the responsibilities that the givers of the opinion might undertake to such persons as a matter of law, which is examined below. Most legal opinions, however, seek to limit any such responsibility by stating that it has been given for the benefit of the original parties to the transaction, who may be named or otherwise identified, and may not be relied upon by such subsequent parties.[13] One common exception to this restrictive approach concerns facilities where it is intended that the transaction should be syndicated a short time after the initial provision of funds by a selling-down exercise. In such a case, the writers of the opinion may agree either that the opinion can be relied upon by the banks when they join the syndicate or that a fresh opinion will be issued at the time of the syndication.[14]

8.3 The Legal Opinions that should be Given in a Transaction

8.3.1 Introduction

It is desirable that legal opinions should be obtained in relation to each of the jurisdictions that is significant in the context of the transaction and the obligors involved in the transaction. An opinion should address the legal issues that relate to the transaction and those involved in it as they arise under the laws of the jurisdiction concerned. No one opinion will be able to address comprehensively the legal issues that arise in all of the jurisdictions but, taken together, the opinions should cover substantially all of those issues. The writers of the opinions may be unable to give positive confirmations on all of the various matters referred to

---

[13] It is argued, in terms of issues concerning foreseeability and remoteness of liability, that the writers of an opinion should only be expected to assume responsibility to those with whom they have an immediate and proximate relationship when the opinion is given, whose commercial and factual interest can be known to those writing the opinion, rather than to other persons who are not so easily identified, whose interests may not be consonant with the interests of those involved at the outset of the transaction, and whose numbers cannot be known.

[14] If a fresh opinion is to be issued, it will be necessary to determine the date as at which the opinion should speak, in other words, if the new opinion should address matters that may have arisen in the period since the original opinion was issued.

below (thus, legal opinions are likely to contain various assumptions and qualifications), so it may be necessary for those who wish to receive the opinions to take further advice and then decide if they are willing to proceed with the transaction.

To illustrate the matters that are usually covered by legal opinions and for ease of explanation, an example of a transaction will be used, as is set out below. The example would have to be adapted to suit other circumstances and types of transaction. For instance, it might be the case that only two jurisdictions may be involved, instead of the three jurisdictions mentioned in the example.[15] Alternatively, the transaction may involve other types of obligor than just a borrower. In addition, the transaction may not involve a loan facility, as is the case in the example, but some other type of transaction, such as one that involved the acquisition and transfer of title in an asset or the grant of a right to possession and use of an asset, as under an equipment financing transaction.

8.3.2

The sample transaction involves a loan facility, where the borrower is incorporated in the State of Ruritania. The borrower has its principal asset in the form of immovable property in the State of Absurdia. The property is to be given as security for the borrower's obligations to the lender. The lender is based in London and the loan agreement is to be governed by English law.

8.3.2.1

8.3.3 The borrower's home jurisdiction

One opinion would address the legal issues that are pertinent under the law of Ruritania, being the place of the borrower's incorporation or establishment and, in addition, a place where it is possible that enforcement action might be taken if the borrower should default in the performance of its obligations. The opinion should be given by lawyers who are qualified to practise in matters of Ruritanian law. It would relate to the borrower's due incorporation, continuing existence,[16] and status under the law of Ruritania.[17] It would also cover the borrower's right and entitlement, both under its own constitutional documentation and any other relevant matters of private or public law in Ruritania, to carry on its business, own its assets wherever they may be located, enter into the transaction, perform the obligations that it undertakes under the transaction, and give the security. The opinion should confirm that no part of the transaction offends or is contrary

---

[15] By way of example, the borrower's home jurisdiction and the place where the security is located may be the same, in which case one legal opinion would cover all of the matters that, in the example, would be covered in the Ruritanian and the Absurdian legal opinions.

[16] The opinion should also confirm that the borrower is not subject to any insolvency proceedings, which would not necessarily be included within the concept of its continuing existence.

[17] In US opinions, this is usually accompanied by a statement that the borrower is 'in good standing' under the law of the relevant State in which it is organised. That expression has a particular meaning in the USA which is usually not replicated in other jurisdictions, where its use should be avoided.

to the law of Ruritania and that there will be no adverse tax consequences arising from the transaction, such as may arise in consequence of the imposition of with-holding taxes on payments to be made by the borrower or which may make the lender resident or otherwise subject to taxation under Ruritanian law.[18]

8.3.3.1 The opinion should also confirm that the correct internal and external decision-making processes[19] and consents[20] have been undertaken and obtained for the borrower to enter into the transaction, execute the documentation, and give the security. It should confirm that the relevant documentation has been duly exe-cuted by or on behalf of the borrower, and, if necessary, that any notarial, filing, registration, or similar processes have been undertaken, and any documentary taxes paid, so that the documentation would be regarded as valid and binding and of evidential worth as a matter of Ruritanian law.

8.3.3.2 As it is possible that enforcement proceedings may have to be taken against the borrower in Ruritania, the opinion should confirm that the borrower would be subject to suit before the courts in Ruritania, and it should also address matters relating to the recognition by Ruritanian law and the courts of Ruritania of the choice of law and jurisdiction provisions in the documentation, and confirm that such courts would be prepared to apply the chosen law and recognise and enforce a judgment of the chosen courts or, if relevant, an award of a prescribed arbitral tribunal. The opinion should also confirm that Ruritanian law, particularly its insolvency law, would recognise the effectiveness of the security that is to be given, to the extent that the same is effective as a matter of Absurdian law. The opinion should confirm that neither the borrower nor its assets enjoys any right of immun-ity from suit or enforcement of a judgment in Ruritania.

8.3.3.3 The lender should also require confirmation that it will not have to be registered or otherwise licensed or authorised in Ruritania if it is to participate in the transac-tion or take enforcement action in Ruritania against the borrower and its assets.[21]

8.3.4 The location of secured assets

A second opinion would relate to Absurdian law, being the place (under the example) where the immovable property is located over which the security is to

---

[18] The lender may have to accept that the legal opinion can only address the tax consequences of the particular transaction taken in isolation from any other activities and transactions in which the lender may be involved and of which the writers of the opinion may be unaware.

[19] For instance, by resolutions of its board or boards of directors and its shareholders.

[20] Which might include consents from third parties who may exercise control in relation to the borrower and its activities, and governmental and administrative consents including, for instance, consents relating to inward investment, exchange control requirements, and the making of payments abroad.

[21] A similar qualification may apply in this regard as is mentioned at n 18 above.

be taken.[22] The opinion should be given by an Absurdian lawyer and should include matters relating to the borrower's title in and its right to possession and occupation of the property,[23] that the security has been properly executed, and that the necessary formalities have been observed.[24] The opinion should confirm the validity, effectiveness, and priority ranking[25] of the security under Absurdian law as the law that governs such matters.

The Absurdian opinion should also address matters concerning the borrower that are relevant to its activities in Absurdia and its giving of the security. Such matters would include its recognition in Absurdia as a legal entity and its entitlement to carry on business in that State, to own, possess, and occupy the property, and to give the security, including as to any necessary licences and consents that may be required.[26]   **8.3.4.1**

As the whole point in taking security is so that the creditor may have recourse to the security as a method of enforcement and recovery should the borrower default in the performance of its obligations under the loan facility, the opinion should address the effectiveness and enforceability of the security. It should therefore confirm that the borrower could be sued in Absurdia and that neither the borrower nor its assets enjoyed any right of immunity from suit or enforcement of judgment in Absurdia. It should confirm that the law and the courts of Absurdia would recognise and enforce the secured obligations as they arise under the loan facility, including recognition of the chosen law that governs such facility and of any judgment or award handed down by the courts or arbitral tribunal as chosen in the facility agreement. It should then go on to confirm that the security would be effective if insolvency proceedings were pursued against the borrower in Absurdia and that the security could be enforced in Absurdia for all of the obligations expressed to be secured under it (as well as describing any procedures that would be involved in enforcement). It should also address priority issues, by confirming that the rights of the creditor under the security would rank ahead of any third party that might wish to assert an interest in the assets that were the subject of the security.   **8.3.4.2**

---

[22] As the example concerns security that is to be taken over immovable property that is situated in Absurdia, matters concerning the security will essentially fall to be dealt with as a matter of Absurdian law (unless, of course, that law defers to some other law). Where security is to be taken over other types of asset, it may be relevant to consider if other opinions may be required relating to jurisdictions other than that of the situs of the asset at the time of the transaction. For instance, if the relevant asset is a debt, it may be relevant to obtain opinions addressing the matters that arise under the governing law of the agreement to give the security and the governing law of the debt.

[23] Including, for instance, that the borrower has the necessary permits and consents to own and occupy the property.

[24] Such as notarial, filing, registration, and fees requirements.

[25] An English lawyer would be reluctant to confirm the priority of security as a matter of English law, because of the difficulties that priority issues raise in English law.

[26] Including as to any licences or consents that may be necessary to enforce the security and repatriate any proceeds of enforcement in application against amounts outstanding by the borrower.

8.3.4.3 The opinion should confirm that no part of the overall transaction offends or is contrary to the laws of Absurdia and that there will be no adverse tax or regulatory consequences arising from the transaction, such as may arise in consequence of the enforcement of the security and the remittance of the proceeds of enforcement to the creditor outside Absurdia. The opinion should confirm that such procedures will not make the lender resident or otherwise subject to taxation under Absurdian law. The lender should also require confirmation that it will not have to be registered or otherwise licensed or authorised in Absurdia if it is to take the benefit of the security or pursue enforcement action in Absurdia against the borrower and the secured property.

8.3.5 The Facility Agreement

A third opinion under the example would relate to the Facility Agreement under its governing law, bearing in mind that the Facility Agreement will be the effective principal agreement in the transaction. This opinion should usually be given by the lawyers who advised the creditor providing the finance (or, in the case of a syndicated facility, their representative), such lawyers being qualified to practise in the jurisdiction of the governing law of the agreement.

8.3.5.1 The opinion should address matters along the following lines:

- that the Facility Agreement is valid, binding, and enforceable against the borrower under its governing law,[27] and that the transaction does not contravene such law;
- that the choice of the governing law of the agreement is a valid choice under the conflict of laws rules of the jurisdiction;
- that the agreement has been duly executed in accordance with the requirements of its governing law and that all other necessary steps and requirements have been taken and observed for its validity and enforceability, including as to the payment of any relevant taxes and duties and the notarisation and registration of any relevant documentation;
- that neither the borrower nor its assets would enjoy immunity from suit or enforcement of judgment;
- that the borrower would be amenable to suit before the chosen courts or arbitral tribunal (most probably in consequence of an agreed submission to jurisdiction and the appointment of an agent to accept service of process on behalf of the borrower); and

---

[27] In US opinions, this is often accompanied by a statement that the facility agreement is 'enforceable in accordance with its terms'. Such language is inappropriate in an English opinion because it implies that the courts would grant a mandatory order, such as by way of an order for specific performance, to enforce strict compliance with each and every provision in the agreement. Generally speaking, that would not be the case under English law. The usual remedy for breach of an agreement is an award of damages to be assessed by the court and, in any event, there are numerous qualifications to the concept of an enforceable obligation.

- that the obligations of the borrower under the agreement would be enforceable before such courts or tribunal, which would apply the chosen governing law in relation to the agreement.

Whilst the opinion should address the governing law of the Facility Agreement, and so it will be focused in the main on the domestic principles of that law, it could also include a reference to the application of the conflict of laws principles of that law, particularly with respect to the recognition of the foreign laws that will govern the matters dealt with in the other opinions as mentioned above.   **8.3.5.2**

The opinion should also address the freedom to make payments as required under the Facility Agreement without restriction, including the absence of any withholding taxes or other regulatory requirements (or that the necessary clearances have been obtained).   **8.3.5.3**

8.4 Who Should Give the Opinions?

As mentioned above, the legal opinions should be given by lawyers who are qualified to practise in relation to the laws of the jurisdiction which are the subject of the opinion. In an ideal world, the party which is to receive the benefit of the legal opinions might prefer that the opinions should be given by its own lawyers. In that way, it could be sure that the opinions were given by lawyers who had their own client's interests at heart and thereby any possibility of a conflict of interests would be avoided.[28] Practically speaking, such an expectation may not be realistic. For instance, such a party may not have instructed the lawyers who are involved in a transaction. Thus, it may only be a participating bank in a syndicated transaction in which a number of banks are involved, it may be a security trustee that is to hold security on behalf of a number of creditors as part of an overall transaction, or it may be a credit rating agency that is to give a rating for a bond issue. Such entities would have to rely on an opinion that has been obtained at the behest of a party that is more closely involved at the heart of the transaction. It is also not uncommon for the lawyers who are advising an obligor in a finance transaction to give an opinion to the bank or banks providing the finance in relation to matters arising under the law of the obligor's place of incorporation or in relation to security   **8.4.1**

---

[28] In relation to the giving of legal opinions, the issue as to possible conflicts of interest deserves more attention than is commonly given to it. As mentioned below, it is not unusual in a finance transaction for an obligor's lawyers to give an opinion to the party that is providing the finance. The same lawyers may find themselves subsequently advising the obligor on whether there are any legal grounds on which the transaction may be avoided or unenforceable. That exercise may involve them in reconsidering the same issues that were the subject of their legal opinion. The lawyers may, however, be saved from possible embarrassment if the relevant issues were covered by one or more qualifications that were set out in the legal opinion.

that it is to give. In securitisation transactions, the lawyers advising the originator will usually give an opinion concerning the effectiveness of the transaction, for the benefit of the other parties to the transaction.

8.4.2   Where an opinion is to be given by one or more lawyers advising an obligor, it is preferable that those lawyers should not be employees of the obligor, although such persons do sometimes give opinions. The reason why it is best that an opinion should not be given by a person who is so closely related to the obligor is that an employee may be perceived as having an insufficient degree of independence in assessing the relevant issues that may have to be addressed in the opinion. He may also be subject to pressure from his employer to ignore any difficulties and deliver a 'clean' opinion.[29] There is also a more mercenary consideration that arises, as an employee is unlikely to have very much by way of available assets and other resources, such as insurance cover, to satisfy a judgment should he be sued because the opinion was incorrect.

8.5   The Form of a Legal Opinion

8.5.1   A legal opinion will usually take the form of a letter written by the lawyers who are giving the opinion. The contents of the letter are usually set out in the order that follows below.

8.5.1.1   Specimen forms of legal opinion

For illustrative purposes, three sample forms of legal opinion are set out at the end of this chapter. They are not intended to be definitive in their form or content but are provided as examples of the types of opinion that might be given. The three forms of opinion are as follows: first, an opinion on English law concerning an unsecured syndicated loan agreement, with a non-English corporate borrower; secondly, an opinion on foreign law, given with respect to a borrower incorporated in the jurisdiction of that foreign law; and thirdly, an opinion on foreign law, given with respect to security created over immovable property in the jurisdiction of that foreign law, where the security is created by a borrower incorporated in yet another jurisdiction.

8.5.2   Preliminary matters

The opinion will be addressed to one or more of the parties that it is intended should receive the benefit of the opinion. It should also state (or describe) who else

---

[29] On the other hand, because of his connection with his employer and his knowledge of its affairs, an in-house lawyer may be able to refer in his opinion to certain factual matters relating to his employer which an external lawyer would be unable to cover.

may rely upon the opinion and it should exclude reliance by any other person. Sometimes the statement concerning reliance is placed at the very end of the opinion.

The opinion should describe the documentation to which it relates. Sometimes that documentation will be the original documents as executed by the parties, and on other occasions the writers will say that they have only seen copies or drafts of the documents.[30] The opinion should state what specific searches and investigations have been made in giving the opinion.[31] It should state the law and legal jurisdiction that it addresses. It should also contain a statement that the writers are duly qualified to practise in that jurisdiction and advise on its laws. The opinion should make it clear that it only addresses the law as at a particular date and that the writers accept no responsibility as to any subsequent changes in the law.

8.5.2.1

The writers of the opinion may also wish to make it clear that they have only been retained for the purpose of giving an opinion in relation to the specific transaction. In consequence they should state that they do not purport to comment upon the adequacy of the documentation from a commercial or negotiated perspective, nor of any general policy or similar considerations that may apply to the decision-making processes within the recipients. They should go on to state that they do not hold instructions to advise the recipients generally and so they do not purport to comment upon any other transactions that may be affected by the transaction upon which they are opining, nor of the effect of that transaction on any other transactions.

8.5.2.2

Where the lawyers giving the opinion were instructed in a representative fashion on behalf of those whom it is contemplated may rely upon the opinion, the opinion may state that the lawyers have participated in discussions with those who instructed them and that they are delivering their opinion on that basis. This is to make it clear that the lawyers may have raised points with those who instructed them which may not be apparent in either the contractual documentation or in the opinion.

8.5.2.3

8.5.3 Assumptions

The opinion will then set forth the assumptions on which it is given, being matters of fact or law, including foreign law, which the writers have been unable to investigate or as to which they are unable to give an opinion. For instance, in an

---

[30] In which case, the opinion will include an assumption as to the accuracy and conformity of the copies or drafts to the originals.

[31] From the point of view of the recipients of an opinion, it is desirable that the writers of the opinion should also confirm that they have made such other enquiries as they have considered necessary to render their opinion.

English opinion concerning an English company, the writers will normally state that they have assumed that board meetings were duly convened and held, that resolutions were duly passed at such meetings, and that the relevant persons who were reported as being at the meetings and who executed the documentation were duly appointed and were not fictitious. If the opinion concerns a foreign company, the writers of the opinion will usually state that they have assumed the correctness of the various matters that are to be covered in a separate opinion from lawyers in its jurisdiction of incorporation. The writers of an English opinion may also have to assume that the transaction cannot be challenged on grounds such as that there was an undervalue in the consideration received by a relevant party or because of duress, mistake, or undue influence operating upon the will of a party to the transaction. They may also wish to assume that each of the parties to the transaction entered into it for its own benefit and not as the agent of a third party.

8.5.4 The opinion

There then follows the actual opinion addressing the relevant legal issues that arise under the law of the jurisdiction concerned and which relate to the transaction, along the lines referred to above.

8.5.5 Qualifications

Finally, the writers of the opinion will set out the various qualifications concerning matters of law, to which their opinion is subject. Such qualifications can be quite extensive in an English opinion.

8.5.5.1 By way of example, which is not intended to be exhaustive, an English opinion will commonly contain qualifications on matters such as the following:

- the insolvency of a party as it may affect the effectiveness and enforceability of that party's obligations and the transactions into which it may have entered;[32]
- in relation to a choice of law clause in a contract, the Contracts (Applicable Law) Act 1990 and the Rome Convention contain exceptions to the principle that the chosen law will govern all matters arising in connection with the contract;
- where a contract or other transactional document purports to specify a chosen law to govern matters that arise under it, such a chosen law may not apply to govern matters that might be characterised as being of a non-contractual nature,

---

[32] This qualification will have to be modified where the legal opinion addresses the validity of security that has been given, so that it does not have the effect of wholly negating the statement in the opinion which confirms the validity and effectiveness of the security in an insolvency of the borrower. Nonetheless, the writers of the opinion may still have to qualify their opinion in relation to aspects of insolvency law which may affect the giving of the security in the first place, such as may arise under ss 127, 238, 239 or 245 of the Insolvency Act 1986. The qualification may also remain relevant to other aspects of the transaction.

such as corporate matters (e.g. the status of the company and its powers and objects, the issuance and transference of shares, the relationship between the company and its shareholders, the rights and obligations of the shareholders *inter se*, and the relationship between the company and its directors and other officers), tortious matters, or proprietary matters;

- the construction and interpretation of a contract will follow the rules for construction as developed by the courts,[33] so that a contract may not be given a literal interpretation and the courts may imply or refuse to imply a term, depending upon the particular circumstances of the case;

- a statement as to the validity and binding nature of a party's obligations does not mean that mandatory orders or other equitable relief will be granted to enforce those obligations, as such remedies are discretionary and the normal remedy for breach of a contract is damages which, if unliquidated, will have to be assessed by the court;

- a contract may be terminated by the operation of the doctrine of frustration, so that the obligations of the parties under it may cease, although a restitutionary remedy may be available under the Law Reform (Frustrated Contracts) Act 1943 with respect to matters that have taken place prior to the time of the frustration;

- a claim may be subject to set-off, abatement or counter-claim;

- there are limits on the availability of restitutionary remedies and such remedies may be subject to defences, such as in consequence of a change of position;

- there are limits on a third party's rights to enforce a contract, although these have been ameliorated by the Contracts (Rights of Third Parties) Act 1999 in the circumstances where it may apply;

- there are limits on the extent to which contractual and other rights may be assignable or enforced for the benefit of the assignee;[34]

- an English court may excuse performance of a contractual obligation if it would be unlawful to perform the obligation in the place where the contract requires it to be performed and public policy considerations may also apply so as to relieve a party from the performance of its stated obligations;

---

[33] Particularly as laid down in a number of speeches in the House of Lords, such as those of Lord Wilberforce in *Prenn v Simmonds* [1971] 1 WLR 1381, at 1384–1386; Lord Hoffmann in *Investors Compensation Scheme Ltd v West Bromwich Building Society* [1998] 1 WLR 896, at 912–913; Lord Hoffmann in *Bank of Credit and Commerce International SA v Ali* [2001] UKHL 8; [2002] 1 AC 251, at [39]; Lord Steyn in *Mannai Investment Co Ltd v Eagle Star Life Assurance Co Ltd* [1997] AC 749, at 771; and Lord Steyn in *Sirius International Insurance Co (Publ) v FAI General Insurance Ltd* [2004] UKHL 54; [2004] 1 WLR 3251, at [18]–[19]. As to the approach to the construction of an expression that is used in a contract that does not have a natural or an obvious meaning, see *Proforce Recruit Ltd v The Rugby Group Ltd* [2006] EWCA Civ 69.

[34] See, for instance, *Dawson v Great Northern & City Railway Co* [1905] 1 KB 260.

- the application of the equitable doctrine against penalties may result in an English court refusing to enforce a provision which has the effect that an additional payment should be made in consequence of a default, such as under a default interest clause[35] or under a clause in an equipment financing transaction by way of lease or hire purchase, which requires (by one amount or otherwise) the remaining instalments to be paid notwithstanding an earlier termination of the transaction;[36]

- the effectiveness of clauses which purport to exclude or limit liability, excuse an obligation to make performance, or which limit or exclude the availability of a remedy may be subject to review under relevant legislation;[37]

- there are limits on the ways in which a party may exercise discretionary powers under a contract;[38]

- an English court may decline to accept or maintain jurisdiction, notwithstanding a jurisdiction clause in its favour contained within the relevant contractual documentation;

- an English court may refuse to adjudicate upon the title to an asset that is situated abroad or as to proprietary claims concerning such an asset;

- by its conduct, a party may be found to have waived its rights or be estopped from asserting such rights; and

- the enforcement of rights will be subject to the need to commence proceedings within the relevant periods under the Limitation Act 1980.

8.6 The Responsibilities that may Arise in Giving a Legal Opinion

8.6.1 The issue for examination at this point concerns the duties in law that lawyers accept in giving an opinion and the liabilities that they may incur in giving the opinion if the opinion should be wrong. Such duties and liabilities may be framed in contract or in tort. Conflict of laws issues may also be relevant in determining the nature and extent of such duties and liabilities, particularly where the person who relies upon an opinion is located in a different jurisdiction to that in which the opinion was written or delivered, or brings its claim in another jurisdiction to that where the lawyers are located.

---

[35] In the context of a finance transaction, see *Lordsvale Finance plc v Bank of Zambia* [1996] QB 752.

[36] See, for instance, *Lombard North Central PLC v Butterworth* [1987] QB 527.

[37] In particular, under the Misrepresentation Act 1967 and the Unfair Contract Terms Act 1977.

[38] See *Paragon Finance plc v Nash & Staunton* [2001] EWCA Civ 1466, [2002] 1 WLR 685; *Paragon Finance plc v Pender* [2005] EWCA Civ 760, [2005] 1 WLR 3412; and *Lymington Marina Ltd v Macnamara* [2007] EWCA Civ 151, [2007] 2 All ER (Comm) 825.

8.6.2 Under English domestic law

As a matter of English domestic law,[39] where the opinion was given by the lawyers who were retained by the person bringing the claim, the duties and consequential liabilities may be framed in either contract or in tort and are likely to be based on an allegation that the lawyers were negligent in failing to exercise due care and skill in giving their opinion. If the person bringing the claim did not have such a contractual relationship with the lawyers who wrote the opinion, then it is unlikely that the claim could be framed in contract, unless the claimant could argue that it was entitled to the benefit of the contract (that is, the contract between the lawyers and those who instructed them) as a third party pursuant to the Contracts (Rights of Third Parties) Act 1999. It is more likely that such a person would bring its claim in tort.

A claim based on an allegation of negligence will depend upon questions such as whether a duty of care existed and if it had been breached, whether the breach gave rise to the loss that has been suffered, and if that loss was reasonably foreseeable when the opinion was written, in the case of a claim in tort, or at the time of the contract, in the case of a claim in contract. A claim in tort would also have to establish that the person bringing the claim fell within the class of persons who were reasonably envisaged, at the time the opinion was written, as being likely to rely upon it. In passing, it is worth mentioning that an English solicitor who instructs a foreign lawyer on behalf of his client may have a duty of care in the supervision of the foreign lawyer, such as to check that the foreign lawyer has carried out his tasks; it cannot just be assumed that the tasks have been properly carried out.[40]

8.6.2.1

8.6.3 Conflict of laws issues

As indicated above, conflict of laws issues may also be relevant in considering the duties and liabilities of the lawyers who wrote a legal opinion. For instance, the claimant may be based in a different jurisdiction to that of the lawyers who wrote the opinion or it may bring its claim in another jurisdiction to that in which the lawyers are located. It would thus be necessary to determine the law that would govern the claim. The analysis that follows is based upon English principles of conflict of laws. However, if a claim was brought in another jurisdiction then different principles would apply, as a court in that jurisdiction would apply its own rules.

---

[39] See further the discussion in Chap 9 as to claims for a breach of a duty of care arising in either contract or tort.

[40] *Gregory v Shepherds* [2000] PNLR 769, (2001) 81 P&CR 113.

8.6.3.1 *Contractual claims*

Under English conflict of laws rules, if the claim was based in contract then the rules under the Rome Convention would be applied to determine the applicable law of the contract, which (subject to the various exceptions contained in the Contracts (Applicable Law) Act 1990 and the Convention itself) would be used to assess the nature and extent of such duties and liabilities and, within the limitations contained in Articles 1(2)(h) and 10 of the Rome Convention, the consequences of a breach by the lawyers of their contractual duty.[41]

8.6.3.2 *Tortious claims*

If the claim was based in tort, the applicable or governing law of the tort would be determined in accordance with either the rules under Part III of the Private International Law (Miscellaneous Provisions) Act 1995 (the 1995 Act) or, after it has come into effect, the EC Regulation on the law applicable to non-contractual obligations (Rome II).[42] Each of those alternatives will be examined in turn.[43]

8.6.3.2.1 The 1995 Act Under the general rule in section 11 of the 1995 Act, the applicable law of the tort would be the law of the country where the events which constituted the alleged tort took place and, if they occurred in different countries, where the most significant of those events occurred. In the context of a legal opinion, it is likely that there may be a number of relevant places where the events constituting the alleged tort occurred, such as: the place where the writers issued their opinion; the place where the claimant suffered its loss, but the suffering of loss may not be regarded as the most significant of the events;[44] the place where the claimant received the opinion; the place where the claimant decided to proceed with the transaction in reliance upon the opinion; and the place where the claimant contracted or made the funds available, having decided to proceed.[45] As there may be a number of different places involved, it may be difficult to determine the applicable law under the general rule in section 11.

8.6.3.2.1.1 An alternative approach may be to find the applicable law of the tort under section 12 of the 1995 Act, which can displace the application of section 11. This would be on the basis that it was substantially more appropriate for the applicable law to be determined under section 12 because of the significance of the factors

---

[41] If Rome I comes into force in the UK then these matters will fall to be dealt with in accordance with that EC Regulation, in place of the Rome Convention.

[42] EC/864/2007 OJ L199/40 31/7/2007.

[43] See further the discussion in Chap 4 concerning Part III of the 1995 Act and Rome II.

[44] See Moore-Bick J in *Protea Leasing Ltd v Royal Air Cambodge Co Ltd* [2002] EWHC 2731 (Comm) and Aikens J in *Trafigura Beheer BV v Kookmin Bank Co* [2006] EWHC 1450 (Comm), [2006] 2 Lloyd's Rep 455.

[45] By analogy with *Morin v Bonhams & Brooks Ltd* [2003] EWCA Civ 1802, [2004] 1 Lloyd's Rep 702.

connecting the tort with one particular country, which outweighed the matters that would lead to an applicable law being determined under section 11. In particular, the writers of the opinion may argue that the law that they have addressed in their opinion should also be the applicable law that governs their duties and liabilities with respect to the opinion that they have issued. They may even have inserted a provision in their opinion specifying that this should be the case. Whilst there is no conclusive guidance on the point, it is submitted that such matters should be regarded as significant factors for the purposes of section 12. Nonetheless, it cannot be presumed that they would always be conclusive factors that would outweigh other factors and displace the operation of the general rule under section 11. Each case will depend upon its own facts and a decision relating to sections 11 and 12 of the Act involves a value judgment which has to be arrived at by weighing up all of the relevant factors of the case.[46]

In a claim in tort brought before an English court, which was governed by the law of another country, the assessment of damages (as opposed to the actionable heads of damage) would fall to be determined by the application of English law as the *lex fori.*[47]

8.6.3.2.1.2

8.6.3.2.2 Rome II
Rome II will come into force on 11 January 2009 and will apply to tortious claims where the relevant events giving rise to tortious damage occurred after that date. In the context of the present discussion, it allows for the parties to a tortious claim to choose the law that should govern the tort on which the claim is founded. In the absence of such a choice, there is a general fall-back rule to determine the law that should govern the tort.

Under Article 14 of Rome II, the claimant and defendant may agree upon the law (the governing or applicable law) that should govern a claim in tort. Such a choice may not prejudice the rights of third parties and the choice cannot have the effect of excluding the operation of the mandatory rules of a country with which all the relevant elements of the events giving rise to the tortious damage were connected. The choice may be agreed after the dispute has arisen or, in the context of commercial activities, before the relevant events occurred which gave rise to the damage upon which the claim is based. The issuance of a legal opinion, and the tortious duties that arise in consequence of it, would be within a commercial context, so the choice could be made when the opinion was issued. The choice may be either express or implied 'if demonstrated with reasonable certainty by the circumstances of the case'. It is submitted that a choice could be implied where the legal opinion contained a stipulation that the duties and liabilities of the writers were to be

8.6.3.2.2.1

---

[46] *Trafigura Beheer BV v Kookmin Bank Co* [2006] EWHC 1450 (Comm), [2006] 2 Lloyd's Rep 455.

[47] *Harding v Wealands* [2006] UKHL 32, [2007] 1 AC 1.

governed by a particular law and that reliance on the opinion was subject to such a stipulation.

8.6.3.2.2.2 In the absence of a choice of the law to govern a claim in tort, the applicable law of the tort would be found in accordance with the general rule that is laid down in Article 4 of Rome II. The general rule is in three parts, which operate as a hierarchy. The first, which is subject to being overridden by the application of the second or the third part, is that the applicable law should be the law of the country in which the tortious damage occurred, irrespective of the place or places in which the event or events giving rise to the damage occurred or the country or countries in which the indirect consequences of that event or those events might arise. Secondly, where at the time the damage occurred both the claimant and the defendant have their 'habitual residence'[48] in the same country, the law of that country will apply. That would be irrespective of any connection (or a lack of connection) between that country and the place where the damage or any other causal element occurred. Thirdly, by way of an overriding qualification on both the first and the second parts, where it was clear from all the circumstances, such as under a pre-existing relationship arising from a contract between the parties, that the tort was manifestly more closely connected with another country than that ascertained under either of the other parts, the law of that other country would apply.

8.6.3.2.2.3 Under the first part of the general rule, it may not be clear where the damage was suffered when one is considering a negligence claim relating to a legal opinion that has been given in the context of a financing transaction. One possibility would be to locate the place where an obligation under the financing transaction should have been performed had it been enforceable against the relevant obligor and then to say that was the place where the damage was suffered. It might, in the alternative, be the place where the obligor would have been sued to enforce the obligation. In a proprietary transaction, the place of damage would probably be where the proprietary interest would have been situated, had it been created, although it may also be arguable that the relevant place would be where the loss was suffered in consequence of not having the proceeds of enforcement of the security. Under the second part of the general rule, if both the lawyers and the claimant have their habitual residence in the same country, that will provide a prima facie governing law of the tort, but there may be cases where it would be inappropriate to apply that law as the governing law of the tort (e.g. where English lawyers based in an office outside England issued a legal opinion on a transaction governed by English law to a local bank). Given the potential difficulties that may arise under both the first and the second parts of the rule, it is submitted that the third part of the

---

[48] The concept of habitual residence under Rome II follows the same concept as is found in Rome I, which is discussed at Chap 4.

general rule should usually be applied. Under that part, it could be said that the governing law of the tort should be the law addressed by the legal opinion, because an error in the opinion would lead to the claim in tort and so it could be said that the tort was most closely connected with the country or jurisdiction of that law.

By virtue of Article 15 of Rome II, the governing law of the tort will govern the substantive issues that may arise when considering the duties and liabilities of the lawyers who wrote a legal opinion. This would include, for instance, the determination of liability and the kinds of loss for which compensation may be provided. It would also appear that matters that might previously have been considered as being procedural at common law,[49] such as remedies and the rules for assessment of compensation, would also fall to be determined under the governing law. One would expect that Rome II should have preserved the distinction between those matters, rather than remove it, as Article 1(3) of the Regulation provides that matters of evidence and procedure do not fall within the ambit of the Regulation. Nonetheless, Article 15(c) provides for the assessment of damages and other remedies to be a matter to be governed by the applicable or governing law of the tort.[50]

8.6.3.2.2.4

---

[49] See the discussion by Lord Hoffmann in *Harding v Wealands* [2006] UKHL 32, [2007] 2 AC 1.
[50] See further the discussion at Chap 4.

APPENDIX 1

English Law Legal Opinion

(English law unsecured syndicated loan agreement with foreign corporate borrower)

To: [

]

(the 'Agent' for itself and as agent

for the Banks, as defined below).   [date]

Dear Sirs,

We refer to the Facility Agreement (the 'Agreement') dated [ ] between [ ] (the 'Borrower'), the banks and financial institutions set forth in the First Schedule thereto (the 'Banks'), [ ](the 'Arranger') and [ ](the 'Agent');

We have received instructions from and participated in discussions with [   ] concerning the Agreement and the provisions therein and on that basis we are delivering this opinion pursuant to Clause [   ] of the Agreement.

Terms which are defined in the Agreement and which are used herein shall, unless the context otherwise requires, have the same meaning herein as therein. When used herein and unless the context otherwise requires,

A. the expressions 'person' and 'party' shall include an individual, corporation, company, partnership, unincorporated association, state or government and any agency or political, administrative or other sub-division thereof and any other entity;

B. the masculine shall include the feminine and neuter genders and vice versa; and

C. references to legislation shall be to legislation (as the same may have been amended up to the date hereof) as is in force in England at the date hereof.

For the purposes of rendering this opinion, we have examined [an executed original] [a copy] of the Agreement.

[If relevant, insert wording which relates to the conduct of Companies Registry searches and winding up enquiries by telephone]

Except as stated above we have not, for the purposes of giving this opinion, examined any contracts, instruments or other documents entered into by or affecting the parties to the Agreement or any other person and nor have we made any other factual enquiries or searches.

The opinion set forth herein relates only to English law as the same is in force at the date hereof. We do not purport to give any opinion herein as to the effect of the laws of any other jurisdiction or as to the effect of English law or proceedings or any matter purporting to be governed by English law, in any other jurisdiction.

This opinion is to be governed by and construed in accordance with English law as the same is in force at the date hereof and any person who seeks to rely on this opinion may only do so on the basis that he or it has agreed thereto. [Only the English courts shall have jurisdiction in relation to proceedings against us concerning this opinion and matters dealt with in it.]

This opinion is also based upon certain assumptions, namely:

(i) that all seals and signatures on any documents submitted to us as originals are genuine and that such documents are authentic and complete;

(ii) that all copies or drafts submitted to us of original documents conform in all respects to such original documents, that such original documents are authentic and complete and that any such original document is the same as any such draft;

(iii) that each of the parties to the Agreement duly exists as a fully competent, independent and separate legal entity, without limit as to time, being duly incorporated or established under the laws of its respective jurisdiction of incorporation or establishment and that, in accordance with the laws of each jurisdiction which may be relevant (other than, with respect to the Borrower as a party to the Agreement, such requirements as may be imposed by English domestic law), each such party has the full power, capacity and authority to enter into, enjoy the benefits expressed to be conferred upon it under and to perform in accordance with the provisions of the Agreement;

(iv) that each such party and their respective officers and signatories has duly executed, delivered and complied with all other applicable requirements with respect to the Agreement and any other relevant document in accordance with the requirements of applicable law and their own internal requirements (other than, with respect to the Borrower as a party to the Agreement, such requirements as may be imposed by English domestic law) and that its so doing will not breach or infringe the rights of any third party under any contract or arrangement or otherwise breach or infringe any restriction binding upon it, its officers or signatories or its assets;

(v) that, save with respect to English law, there is no rule of any jurisdiction, including any rule of public policy, which would affect any matter relevant to this opinion;

(vi) that no party to the Agreement or any transaction relevant thereto entered into the same for any unlawful purpose or at a time when it was insolvent, subject to insolvency proceedings or otherwise unable to pay its debts, that no such party was induced by fraud, duress, misrepresentation or mistake to enter into the same, that each such party so entered in full knowledge of the meaning and effect of the same and deliberately and on its own behalf and not as the agent or trustee of any other person, that it did so in good faith and for the legitimate purposes of its authorised business without intending to prefer or prejudice any of its present or future creditors, that it also did so for full and sufficient consideration and not at an undervalue and for its own real and substantial benefit commensurate with the risks it was thereby undertaking and that it will not become insolvent or otherwise unable to pay its debts in consequence thereof;

(vii) that the Agreement does not concern or relate to any transaction which is 'extortionate' within the meaning of section 244(3) of the Insolvency Act 1986;

(viii) that there are no other arrangements concerning the Agreement or any other relevant transaction or document which might modify, replace or supersede the whole or any of the provisions of the Agreement or such transaction or document;

(ix) that all relevant persons have complied and will comply with the Financial Services and Markets Act 2000 concerning the Agreement and any other relevant transaction, document, action or arrangement;

(x) that the Borrower is not a company incorporated within, nor does it have (nor will it have) any assets or a place of business or branch within, any part of the United Kingdom;

(xi) [assumption as to accuracy of searches and winding up enquiries and no subsequent matters having arisen since the date they were conducted].

On the basis of the foregoing and subject to the qualifications hereinafter appearing, we are of the opinion that:

1. the execution, delivery and performance of the Agreement by the Borrower will not exceed or contravene the laws of England;

2. the Agreement constitutes the valid and binding obligations of the Borrower under English law;
3. it is not necessary to file, register or record the Agreement in any public office in England so as to ensure the legality, validity or enforceability thereof under English law;
4. no authorisations, approvals, consents or other permissions of any governmental or regulatory authority or body in England are required for the execution, delivery and performance of the Agreement by the Borrower or for the enforcement of the Agreement against the Borrower or for the making of any payments under the Agreement;
5. no stamp duty or other documentary tax is payable under English law on the execution or delivery of the Agreement by the Borrower;
6. the choice of English law to govern the Agreement will be recognised as a valid choice of law under English law in accordance with the provisions of the Rome Convention as applied in pursuance of the Contracts (Applicable Law) Act 1990, subject to the restrictions, qualifications and exclusions therein contained;
7. subject to the due commencement and service of process upon the Borrower in accordance with the requirements of English law and provided that it was made for bona fide reasons, the submission of the Borrower under the Agreement to the jurisdiction of the courts of England is a valid submission to such jurisdiction for the purpose of determining disputes that may arise under the Agreement and, accordingly, the English courts would assume jurisdiction in accordance therewith. [The Borrower is not entitled to claim immunity from such jurisdiction in proceedings brought against it under the Agreement.]

The qualifications to which this opinion is subject are as follows:

(a) the obligations and rights of the parties to the Agreement will take effect subject to any limitations resulting from bankruptcy, insolvency, moratorium, liquidation, re-organisation, re-construction or similar laws generally affecting creditors or third party rights and to any execution, attachment or distraint;
(b) under English law, the obligations of a party to a contract, whilst being valid and binding, may not be enforced in accordance with their terms. For instance, enforcement may be limited by considerations of public policy and by general principles of equity, the granting of mandatory orders, such as an order for specific performance or an injunction, is discretionary and are not granted in the usual course but only in particular instances, bearing in mind that damages is the ordinary remedy in civil cases, in general, only a person who is a party to a contract can enforce it (save to the extent that the Contracts (Rights of Third Parties) Act 1999 applies for the benefit of a non-contracting third party), terms may or may not be implied into a contract, the strict literal wording of a contract may not be enforced if the court or tribunal feels that it would not be appropriate to do so, damages will be assessed in accordance with general principles and damages may only be computed for a nominal sum where a contractual obligation is intended to be for the benefit of a person who is not the party to the contract seeking to enforce it. English law may also require that both the assignor and the assignee are parties to any enforcement of a right or a claim that has been assigned and the assignee cannot be in a better position than the assignor would have been but for the assignment. It is not possible under English law for a party to a contract which has an obligation thereunder to assign that obligation of its own volition;
(c) we express no opinion as to the availability of restitutionary remedies or of any defence thereto, whether at common law or in equity, including (but without limitation) as to tracing, an obligation to account, subrogation or an action for money had and received;
(d) an English court may refuse to determine proprietary entitlements in certain types of foreign assets, including immovable property and intellectual property;
(e) where a contract or other document purports to specify a chosen law to govern matters contemplated by it, such a chosen law may not apply to govern matters that might be characterised for the purposes of the English rules as to conflict of laws as being of a non-contractual nature, such as corporate matters (eg. the status of a corporate entity and its powers and objects, the

issuance and transference of shares in its capital, the relationship between the entity and its shareholders, the rights and obligations of the shareholders inter se, the relationship between the entity and its directors and other officers and the authority of such directors and officers to act or enter into obligations on its behalf), matters concerning non-contractual civil rights and claims or proprietary matters;

(f) any proceedings brought before a court in England would be subject to the need to comply with the rules for the commencement and maintenance of such proceedings [and the intended defendant or respondent and its assets may also have the protection of sovereign immunity]. Without limitation upon the foregoing, if it was wished to serve a person via an agent within the jurisdiction then it would be necessary to show that such agent was and remained duly appointed for that purpose at the time of service;

(g) claims and proceedings may become statute barred or be subject to a defence of set-off or abatement and to counterclaims;

(h) the question whether or not provisions which may be invalid can be severed from other provisions and the effect of such severance would be determined by a court in its discretion;

(i) where a person is vested with a discretion or may determine a matter in its opinion, English law may require that such discretion is exercised objectively and reasonably, not arbitrarily or in a discriminatory way, and that such an opinion is based on reasonable and objective grounds;

(j) any provision providing that certain calculations, determinations or certificates will be conclusive and binding or will be of evidentiary value will not necessarily be binding or prevent enquiry by a court into the merits;

(k) obligations may not be enforceable under English law if the same are unenforceable on account of illegality, fraud, duress or mistake or are overridden by considerations of public policy;

(l) where an obligation is to be performed or is intended to be performed in a jurisdiction outside England then it may not be enforced under English law or by a court in England if it would be illegal or otherwise unlawful or unenforceable, contrary to public policy or impossible of performance in such first mentioned jurisdiction;

(m) a provision which has the effect of imposing an additional burden consequent upon a default or a burden that would not arise at general law should a default occur, such as by requiring the payment of additional interest or an additional amount on overdue sums, or which requires an amount to be paid representing interest or income that would have been received had a default not occurred, may be construed as a penalty and would be unenforceable;

(n) an obligation on a person to pay the costs of another person in respect of an unsuccessful claim or proceedings brought by such second mentioned person, may not be enforceable and an obligation on a person to pay all of the costs and expenditure of a successful other person who has brought a claim or proceedings, may not be enforceable;

(o) a judgment or award on a contractual obligation may supersede the obligation. For instance, an obligation to pay a contractual rate of interest after judgment may not be enforced but, instead, might be superseded by the judgment. Further, the court may vary an obligation to pay interest and it may determine that any such obligation shall be at a rate of interest, by a method of calculation and in a currency determined by it in place of any other agreed or determined currency, rate or method of calculation;

(p) notwithstanding that the parties to the Agreement may have chosen the English courts to have jurisdiction (whether exclusive or non-exclusive) concerning any disputes that may arise in relation to the Agreement and that such a party or parties may have submitted to such jurisdiction for that purpose, the English courts may still decline to accept jurisdiction or may stay a claim or proceedings brought before them if a similar claim or proceedings have been brought elsewhere or if applicable legislation or a treaty or convention to which the UK is a party provides to the contrary. The English courts may also refuse to restrain the bringing or maintenance of a claim or proceedings in another jurisdiction even where a similar claim or proceedings have been commenced before the English courts;

(q) [we express no opinion as to whether the English courts would recognise or enforce the judgment of a foreign court or any arbitral award][, save that recognition and enforcement in England of a judgment of a court of another EU member state would be subject to the provisions of the EC Regulation on jurisdiction and judgments (EC 44/2001 OJ L12/1 16/1/2001)] [insert other wording, as relevant, to deal with the Lugano Convention, the Administration of Justice Act 1920, the Foreign Judgments (Reciprocal Enforcement) Act 1933 and enforcement of arbitral awards];

(r) the obligations of a party to a contract may be limited, terminated or expunged by the provisions of English law applicable to contracts which have been frustrated;

(s) a court in England would be prepared to give judgment for a monetary amount in a currency other than sterling but the amount may have to be converted into sterling for the purposes of enforcement of a judgment or award or for proving or asserting rights in insolvency proceedings. Foreign currency amounts for which a creditor proves or claims in an English winding up or other insolvency proceedings may have to be converted into sterling at the rate prevailing as at the date prescribed as being relevant to the winding up or proceedings. No opinion is given as to any provision providing for the conversion at or in a particular manner or time of one currency for another or as to any currency indemnity;

(t) the effectiveness of terms excusing or limiting (or, as in the case of an indemnity, having the effect of excusing or limiting) a person from liabilities or duties otherwise owed or which otherwise have the effect of preventing or imposing conditions or requirements upon the exercise of a person's rights or remedies, is limited by English law and in particular, but without limitation, by the Unfair Contract Terms Act 1977, the Misrepresentation Act 1967 and the Unfair Terms in Consumer Contracts Regulations 1999 (SI 1999/2083);

(u) no opinion is expressed as to the correctness of any provisions (howsoever expressed) in the Agreement containing representations or warranties;

(v) insofar as any provision imposes an obligation on a person either to pay stamp duty which may be payable by another person or to reimburse such second mentioned person for stamp duty which it may have paid, such obligation may be invalid;

(w) we express no opinion as to taxation, save as stated in paragraph 5, above;

(x) a person who brings a claim or proceedings may be ordered to provide security for costs;

(y) notwithstanding any provision to the contrary, the provisions of a contract may be varied or waived expressly or impliedly or by course of conduct. We express no opinion as to the effect thereof on the Agreement;

(z) a failure or delay in exercising a right may constitute a waiver of that right despite any provision to the contrary;

(aa) we have no knowledge of the financial position of the Borrower or as to its entitlement to any assets or rights therein.

This opinion is limited to the matters stated herein and is not to be read as extending, by implication or otherwise, to any matters not specifically stated herein. It is rendered solely in relation to the Agreement and only for the benefit of the Agent and the Banks who are original parties to the Agreement. It is not to be delivered or disclosed to, acted upon or filed with any other person without our express prior written consent.

The views expressed herein are based upon English law as of the date hereof. Any change to English law may affect such views. We assume no obligation to give notice of or to advise upon any such change, whether or not material.

Yours faithfully,

APPENDIX 2

Foreign Law Opinion As To Foreign Borrower

(English law bilateral loan agreement with foreign corporate borrower and foreign security in a third country)

To: [

]

For the attention of [   ]   [date]

Dear Sirs,

Loan Agreement (the 'Agreement') dated [   ] between [   ] (the 'Borrower') and [   ] (the 'Bank').

We have been requested to render this opinion to you, pursuant to Clause [   ] of the Agreement.

Terms which are defined in the Agreement and which are used herein shall, unless the context otherwise requires, have the same meaning herein as therein. When used herein and unless the context otherwise requires,

A. the expressions 'person' and 'party' shall include an individual, corporation, company, partnership, unincorporated association, state or government and any agency or political, administrative or other sub-division thereof and any other entity;

B. the masculine shall include the feminine and neuter genders and vice versa and the singular shall include the plural and vice versa;

C. references to legislation shall be to legislation in the form as is [known by us to be] in force in [the Republic of Ruritania] at the date hereof;

D. the expression 'Appendix' shall mean the Appendix hereto; and

E. the expression 'Security Documents' shall mean the documents specified as such in the Appendix and the other expressions which are given a defined meaning in the Appendix shall have the same respective meanings herein.

For the purpose of rendering this opinion, we have examined:

I. [Executed originals] [Photocopies] of the Agreement and the Security Documents; and

II. The other documents [and copy documents] specified in Part I of the Appendix.

For that purpose, we have also conducted the searches and enquiries specified in Part II of the Appendix on the date therein specified.

Except as stated above we have not, for the purpose of giving this opinion, examined any contracts, instruments or other documents entered into or affecting the Borrower, the Bank or any other person and nor have we made any other factual enquiries or searches.

We [are licensed to] practise law as [avocats] in [the Republic of Ruritania]. The opinion set forth herein relates only to the laws of [the Republic of Ruritania] as the same are in force at the date hereof[, in so far as such laws are accessible to us]. [Any matters of law which may have been dealt with by any secret, unpublished or generally unavailable decree, legislation, instrument or other decision or normative materials or matters may affect or contradict our opinion which is, therefore, subject thereto.] We do not purport to give any opinion herein as to the effect of the laws of [the Republic of Ruritania] in any other jurisdiction. This opinion is to be governed by and construed in accordance with the laws of [the Republic of Ruritania].

This opinion is also based upon certain assumptions, namely:

   (i) that all seals and signatures on any documents submitted to us as originals are genuine and that such documents are authentic and complete;

  (ii) that all copies or drafts submitted to us of original documents conform in all respects to such original documents, that such original documents are authentic and complete and that any such original document is the same as any such draft;

 (iii) that the documents specified in Part I of the Appendix are true, accurate, complete, fully operative, up to date and remaining fully in force as at the date hereof, without amendment, withdrawal or revocation;

 (iv) that, save for the Borrower, each of the other parties to the Agreement and the Security Documents has at all relevant times existed as a fully competent natural person or as an independent and separate legal entity and, if not a natural person, has at such times been duly incorporated or established as a separate and independent legal entity under the laws of its respective jurisdiction of incorporation or establishment and that, in accordance with such laws, each such other party has at such times had the full power, capacity and authority to enter into, enjoy the benefits expressed to be conferred upon it under and to perform in accordance with the provisions of the Agreement and the Security Documents;

  (v) that, save with respect to the requirements of the laws of [the Republic of Ruritania], each of the parties to the Agreement and the Security Documents has duly executed, delivered and complied with all the requirements of applicable law with respect to the Agreement, the Security Documents and any other relevant document;

 (vi) that, save with respect to the laws of [the Republic of Ruritania], there is no rule of any jurisdiction, including any rule of public policy, which would affect any matter relevant to this opinion;

 (vii) that the choice of English law by the parties to govern the Agreement and of the law of [the Republic of Absurdia] to govern the Security Documents was a choice freely made, for bona fide reasons and not so as to evade the laws of any other relevant jurisdiction;

(viii) that the Agreement is enforceable under the laws of England in accordance with its terms and that the Security Documents are enforceable under the laws of [the Republic of Absurdia] in accordance with their terms;

 (ix) that there are no other arrangements concerning the Agreement, the Security Documents or any other relevant document which might modify, replace or supersede the whole or any of the provisions of the Agreement, the Security Documents or such document;

  (x) that the information revealed by the searches and enquiries specified in Part II of the Appendix is accurate and up to date.

On the basis of the foregoing and subject to the qualifications hereinafter appearing, we are of the opinion that:

1. the Borrower is an [open joint stock company] duly incorporated in [the Republic of Ruritania] with limited liability[, with indefinite duration,] as [a commercial institution] under the laws of [the Republic of Ruritania] and its [Charter] fully complies with such law. It has duly adopted its [Charter].

2. the Borrower is duly authorised under its Charter and is duly licensed and authorised under the laws of [the Republic of Ruritania] to carry on business as [a commercial institution] in [the Republic of Ruritania] and to own and use the assets that are the subject of the Security Documents and there is no limitation or restriction thereon;

3. No [petitions for winding up, liquidation or administration] of the Borrower have been presented [and are outstanding] before any relevant court, tribunal or other authority in [the Republic of Ruritania] and the Borrower is not [currently] subject to any other insolvency or dissolution proceedings or action in [the Republic of Ruritania];

4. the Borrower has the corporate power and authority to enter into the Agreement and the Security Documents, to enjoy its rights and perform its obligations thereunder and to give the security

expressed to be given under the Security Documents and all necessary corporate action has been taken to authorise its entry into and its execution and performance of the Agreement and the Security Documents and the giving of the security under the Security Documents [in accordance with their respective terms]. The Agreement and the Security Documents have been duly executed and delivered on behalf of the Borrower;

5. the execution, delivery and performance of the Agreement and the Security Documents by the Borrower and the Bank is in conformity with and does not exceed or contravene the laws of [the Republic of Ruritania] or the Borrower's [Charter];

6. under the laws of [the Republic of Ruritania], the obligations of the Borrower under the Agreement and the Security Documents constitute its direct and unconditional obligations. The security that is given under the Security Documents in favour of the Bank will rank ahead of the claims of its other creditors, save for other obligations which are mandatorily preferred by law. To the extent that the security might be insufficient in value to secure the Borrower's remaining obligations under the Agreement, the Borrower's obligations under the Agreement will rank at least pari passu with the claims of its other creditors, save for such mandatorily preferred obligations;

7. [save for [   ] (which has been done as reflected by the document[s] specified at [   ] in the Appendix,] it is not [otherwise] necessary to notarise, file, register or record the Agreement or the Security Documents before or with a notary or any other person in [the Republic of Ruritania] so as to ensure the legality, validity or enforceability thereof against the Borrower and its assets under the laws of [the Republic of Ruritania]. The Agreement and the Security Documents are in proper form for enforcement before the courts in [the Republic of Ruritania];

8. save for those which [have been obtained as reflected by the document[s] specified at [   ] in the Appendix or those which] are of a routine or minor nature and which are customarily granted in due course after due and straightforward application, no authorisations, approvals, consents or other permissions of any governmental or regulatory authority or other body or person in [the Republic of Ruritania] are required for [the provision of finance to the Borrower by the Bank under the Agreement, for] the execution, delivery and performance by the Borrower and the Bank of the Agreement and the Security Documents and for the creation of security under the Security Documents, for the remittance by the Borrower of moneys payable by it under the Agreement in [currency] or for the enforcement of the Agreement and the Security Documents against the Borrower and its assets;

9. [save for [   ],] no stamp duty or other taxes, fees or duties are payable to any office or other person in [the Republic of Ruritania] with respect to the Borrower's or the Bank's execution or delivery of the Agreement and the Security Documents or the performance or observance respectively by each of them of their provisions, the creation of security under the Security Documents or for the enforcement of the Agreement and the Security Documents against the Borrower;

10. the choice of the laws of England to govern the Agreement will be recognised as a valid choice of law under the laws of [the Republic of Ruritania]. If the Agreement came before a court in the [Republic of Ruritania], that court would apply English law as the governing law of the Agreement, including (without limitation) in construing the Agreement;

11. the choice of the laws of [the Republic of Absurdia] to govern the Security Documents will be recognised as a valid choice of law under the laws of [the Republic of Ruritania]. If the Security Documents came before a court in the [Republic of Ruritania], that court would apply the law of [the Republic of Absurdia] as the governing law of the Security Documents, including (without limitation) in construing the Security Documents;

12. the submissions by the Borrower in the Agreement to the respective jurisdictions of the courts of [the Republic of Ruritania] and the courts of England in accordance with Clause [   ] of the Agreement, are valid and binding upon the Borrower under the laws of [the Republic of Ruritania];

13. the submissions by the Borrower in the Security Documents to the respective jurisdictions of the courts of [the Republic of Ruritania], the courts of [the Republic of Absurdia] and the courts of England in accordance with [   ] of the Security Documents, are valid and binding upon the Borrower under the laws of [the Republic of Ruritania];

14. a judgment of an English court obtained against the Borrower with respect to its obligations under the Agreement would be recognised and enforced against the Borrower by the courts of [the Republic of Ruritania] [without any further formality or the payment of any fees or taxes provided that the following matters are satisfied:];

15. the obligations of the Borrower under the Agreement and the creation of the security under the Security Documents would be considered under the laws of [the Republic of Ruritania] to be commercial in nature and subject to civil law. The execution, delivery and performance by the Borrower of the Agreement and the Security Documents constitutes its private and commercial acts and not governmental or public acts and neither the Borrower nor its assets has any right of immunity from any claim or proceedings that may be brought against it by the Bank under the Agreement or the Security Documents;

16. the appointment of [   ] under Clause [   ] of the Agreement as the agent for service of process upon the Borrower of proceedings commenced under the Agreement before the courts of England, is valid under the laws of [the Republic of Ruritania];

17. the appointment of [   ] under [   ] of the Security Documents as the agent for service of process upon the Borrower of proceedings commenced under the Security Documents before the courts of [the Republic of Absurdia], is valid under the laws of [the Republic of Ruritania];

18. on the additional assumptions that the Bank is not operating through an office or branch for the purposes of the Agreement or the Security Documents in [the Republic of Ruritania] and that (save for being a party to the Agreement and the Security Documents, performing its obligations and enforcing its rights thereunder and receiving and enforcing the benefit of the security under the Security Documents) the Bank has no other connection with [the Republic of Ruritania], then under the laws of [the Republic of Ruritania]:

    (i) it is not necessary for the Bank to be licensed, registered or otherwise qualified to carry on business in [the Republic of Ruritania] in order for it to enter into, perform under or enforce the Agreement or the Security Documents or to receive the benefit of the security under the Security Documents; and

    (ii) the Bank will not be, nor be deemed to be, resident, domiciled or carrying on business in [the Republic of Ruritania] solely by reason of its entering into, performance or enforcement of the Agreement or the Security Documents or its receipt of the benefit of the security under the Security Documents.

The qualifications to which this opinion is subject are as follows:

[insert specific qualifications as to the laws of the Republic of Ruritania].

This opinion is limited to the matters stated herein and is not to be read as extending, by implication or otherwise, to any matters not specifically stated herein. It is rendered solely to and for the benefit of the Bank for the purpose of the Agreement and the Security Documents. Save for the Bank and its advisers, it is not to be delivered or disclosed to, acted upon or filed with any other person without our express prior written consent.

The views expressed herein are based upon the laws of [the Republic of Ruritania] as of the date hereof. Any change to those laws may affect such views. We assume no obligation to advise you or your advisers of any such change, whether or not material.

Yours faithfully,

[Appendix]

APPENDIX 3

Foreign Law Opinion As To Foreign Security

(English law bilateral loan agreement with foreign borrower and foreign security in a third country)

To: [

]

For the attention of [   ]   [date]

Dear Sirs,

Loan Agreement (the 'Agreement') dated [   ] between [   ] (the 'Borrower') and [   ] (the 'Bank').

We have been requested to render this opinion to you, pursuant to Clause [] of the Agreement.

Terms which are defined in the Agreement and which are used herein shall, unless the context otherwise requires, have the same meaning herein as therein. When used herein and unless the context otherwise requires,

A. the expressions 'person' and 'party' shall include an individual, corporation, company, partnership, unincorporated association, state or government and any agency or political, administrative or other sub-division thereof and any other entity;

B. the masculine shall include the feminine and neuter genders and vice versa and the singular shall include the plural and vice versa;

C. references to legislation shall be to legislation in the form as is [known by us to be] in force in [the Republic of Absurdia] at the date hereof;

D. the expression 'Appendix' shall mean the Appendix hereto; and

E. the expression 'Security Documents' shall mean the documents specified as such in the Appendix and other expressions which are given a defined meaning in the Appendix shall have the same respective meanings herein.

For the purpose of rendering this opinion, we have examined:

I. [Executed originals] [Photocopies] of the Agreement and the Security Documents; and

II. The other documents [and copy documents] specified in Part I of the Appendix.

For that purpose, we have also conducted the searches and enquiries specified in Part II of the Appendix on the date therein specified.

Except as stated above we have not, for the purpose of giving this opinion, examined any contracts, instruments or other documents entered into or affecting the Borrower, the Bank or any other person and nor have we made any other factual enquiries or searches.

We [are licensed to] practise law as [avocats] in [the Republic of Absurdia]. The opinion set forth herein relates only to the laws of [the Republic of Absurdia] as the same are in force at the date hereof[, in so far as such laws are accessible to us]. [Any matters of law which may have been dealt with by any secret, unpublished or generally unavailable decree, legislation, instrument or other decision or normative materials or matters may affect or contradict our opinion which is, therefore, subject thereto.] We do not purport to give any opinion herein as to the effect of the laws of [the Republic of Absurdia] in any other jurisdiction. This opinion is to be governed and construed in accordance with the laws of [the Republic of Absurdia].

This opinion is also based upon certain assumptions, namely:

(i) that all seals and signatures on any documents submitted to us as originals are genuine and that such documents are authentic and complete;

(ii) that all copies or drafts submitted to us of original documents conform in all respects to such original documents, that such original documents are authentic and complete and that any such original document is the same as any such draft;

(iii) that the documents specified in Part I of the Appendix (other than the Security Documents) are true, accurate, complete, fully operative, up to date and remaining fully in force as at the date hereof, without amendment, withdrawal or revocation;

(iv) that, save where incorporated or established under the laws of [the Republic of Absurdia], the Borrower and each of the other parties to, respectively, the Agreement and the Security Documents has at all relevant times been duly incorporated or established as a separate and independent legal entity under the laws of its respective jurisdiction of incorporation or establishment and that, in accordance with such laws, the Borrower and each such other party has at such times had the full power, capacity and authority to enter into, to give or receive the security expressed to be given or received by it in, to enjoy the benefits expressed to be conferred upon it under and to perform its obligations in accordance with the provisions of, as the case may be, the Agreement and the Security Documents;

(v) that, save with respect to the requirements of the laws of [the Republic of Absurdia], each of the parties to the Agreement and the Security Documents has duly executed, delivered and complied with all the requirements of applicable law with respect thereto and any other relevant document;

(vi) that, save with respect to the law of [the Republic of Absurdia], there is no rule of any jurisdiction, including any rule of public policy, which would affect any matter relevant to this opinion;

(vii) that the choice of English law by the parties to govern the Agreement was a choice freely made, for bona fide reasons and not so as to evade the laws of any other relevant jurisdiction;

(viii) that the Agreement is enforceable under the laws of England in accordance with its terms;

(ix) that there are no other arrangements concerning the Agreement, the Security Documents or any other relevant document which might modify, replace or supersede the whole or any of the provisions of the Agreement, the Security Documents or such document;

(x) that the information revealed by the searches and enquiries specified in Part II of the Appendix is accurate and up to date.

On the basis of the foregoing and subject to the qualifications hereinafter appearing, we are of the opinion that:

1. the Borrower is duly authorised and has the power and authority under the laws of [the Republic of Absurdia] to carry on business and to own the assets which are stated to be the subject of the Security Documents and there is no limitation or restriction thereon. [The Borrower is duly recorded as the full and unencumbered owner of [those assets] in [name of register];

2. no [petitions for winding up, liquidation or administration] of the Borrower have been presented [and are outstanding] before any relevant court, tribunal or other authority in [the Republic of Absurdia] and the Borrower is not [currently] subject to any other insolvency or dissolution proceedings or action in [the Republic of Absurdia];

3. under the laws of [the Republic of Absurdia], the Borrower has the power and authority to enter into the Agreement and the Security Documents, to give the security expressed to be given by it under the Security Documents and to enjoy its rights and perform its obligations under the Agreement and the Security Documents and all necessary action has been taken to authorise its entry into and its execution and performance of the Agreement and the Security Documents and to give the security expressed to be given under the Security Documents [in accordance with the respective terms thereof]. The Agreement and the Security Documents have been duly executed on behalf of the Borrower and the Bank;

4. the execution, delivery and performance of the Agreement and the Security Documents by the Borrower and the Bank and the giving of the security expressed to be given under the Security Documents is in conformity with and does not exceed or contravene the laws of [the Republic of Absurdia];

5. the Security Documents and the security created thereunder are subject to and governed by the laws of [the Republic of Absurdia];

6. under the laws of [the Republic of Absurdia], the obligations of the Borrower under the Agreement and the Security Documents constitute its direct and unconditional obligations and the security which is expressed to be given under the Security Documents is effective to secure the obligations expressed to be secured thereby, will be effective in an insolvency of the Borrower and will rank with first priority ahead of the claims or entitlements of all other persons[, save for other obligations which are mandatorily preferred by law];

7. [save for [ ] (which has been done as reflected by the document[s] specified at [ ] in the Appendix,] it is not [otherwise] necessary to notarise, file, register or record the Agreement or the Security Documents before a notary or any other person or in any registry or office in [the Republic of Absurdia] so as to ensure the legality, validity, effectiveness, perfection, priority or enforceability thereof or of the security thereunder under the laws of [the Republic of Absurdia]. The Agreement and the Security Documents are in proper form for enforcement in [the Republic of Absurdia];

8. save for those which [have been obtained as reflected by the document[s] specified at [ ] in the Appendix or those which] are of a routine or minor nature and which are customarily granted in due course after due and straightforward application, no authorisations, approvals, consents or other permissions of any governmental or regulatory authority or other body or person in [the Republic of Absurdia] are required for the ownership and use of the assets which are intended to be the subject of the Security Documents or for the execution, delivery and performance by the Borrower and the Bank of the Agreement and the Security Documents, for the holding, perfection or enforcement by the Bank of the security given under the Security Documents or for the making or remittance of any payments connected therewith (whether before, after or in consequence of the enforcement of security under the Security Documents);

9. [save for [ ],] no stamp duty or other taxes, fees or duties are payable to any office, registry or other person in [the Republic of Absurdia] with respect to the Borrower's or the Bank's execution or delivery of the Agreement and the Security Documents or the performance or observance respectively by each of them of their provisions or for the perfection or enforcement of the Agreement or the Security Documents against the Borrower or the assets or security the subject thereof;

10. the choice of the laws of England to govern the Agreement will be recognised as a valid choice of law under the laws of [the Republic of Absurdia]. If the Agreement came before a court in the [Republic of Absurdia], that court would apply English law as the governing law of the Agreement, including (without limitation) in construing the Agreement;

11. the submission by the Borrower in the Agreement to the jurisdiction of the courts of England is valid and binding upon the Borrower under the laws of [the Republic of Absurdia];

12. the submission by the Borrower in the Agreement and in the Security Documents to the jurisdiction of the courts of [the Republic of Absurdia] is valid and binding upon the Borrower under the laws of the [Republic of Absurdia];

13. a judgment of an English court obtained against the Borrower with respect to its obligations under the Agreement would be recognised and enforced against the Borrower by the courts of [the Republic of Absurdia] [without any further formality or the payment of any fees or taxes provided that the following matters are satisfied:]];

14. the obligations of the Borrower under the Agreement and the Security Documents and the giving of the security expressed to be given under the Security Documents would be considered under the laws of [the Republic of Absurdia] to be commercial in nature and subject to civil law.

The execution, delivery and performance by the Borrower of the Agreement and the Security Documents and its giving of such security constitutes its private and commercial acts and not governmental or public acts and neither the Borrower nor its assets has any right of immunity in [the Republic of Absurdia] from any claim or proceedings or enforcement action that may be brought against it or them by the Bank under the Agreement or the Security Documents;

15. the appointment of [   ] under Clause [   ] of the Agreement and Clause [   ] of the Security Documents as the agent for service of process upon the Borrower of proceedings commenced before the courts in [the Republic of Absurdia], is valid under the laws of [the Republic of Absurdia];

16. on the additional assumptions that the Bank is not operating through an office or branch in [the Republic of Absurdia] for the purposes of the Agreement and the Security Documents and that (save for being a party to the Agreement and the Security Documents, performing and enforcing its rights under them and holding and enforcing the security given to it under the Security Documents) the Bank has no other connection with [the Republic of Absurdia], then under the laws of [the Republic of Absurdia]:

   (i) it is not necessary for the Bank to be licensed, registered or otherwise qualified to carry on business or hold assets or rights in assets in [the Republic of Absurdia] in order for it to enter into, perform under, enjoy its rights (including the holding and enforcement of such security) under and enforce the Agreement and the Security Documents; and

   (ii) the Bank will not be, nor be deemed to be, resident, domiciled or carrying on business in [the Republic of Absurdia] solely by reason of its entering into, performance or enforcement of the Agreement or the Security Documents or its holding or enforcement of such security.

The qualifications to which this opinion is subject are as follows:

[insert specific qualifications as to the laws of the Republic of Absurdia].

This opinion is limited to the matters stated herein and is not to be read as extending, by implication or otherwise, to any matters not specifically stated herein. It is rendered solely to and for the benefit of the Bank for the purposes of the Agreement and the Security Documents and is not to be delivered or disclosed to, acted upon or filed with any other person without our express prior written consent.

The views expressed herein are based upon the laws of [the Republic of Absurdia] as of the date hereof. Any change to those laws may affect such views. We assume no obligation to advise you of any such change, whether or not material.

Yours faithfully,

[Appendix]

PART C

COMPOSITE AND SPECIALISED FINANCING TRANSACTIONS

Chapter 9 discusses syndicated lending.

Chapter 10 discusses bond issues.

Chapter 11 discusses derivatives transactions.

Chapter 12 discusses loan transfers, securitisation, and structured finance.

Chapter 13 discusses project finance.

COMPOSITE AND SPECIALISED FINANCING TRANSACTIONS

9

SYNDICATED LENDING

9.1 Introduction

9.1.1 Syndicated lending was developed to enable loan finance to be provided for large amounts that could not readily be made available by a single bank acting on its own, due to factors affecting such a bank, including its assessment of the risk and exposure to a single borrower (and its group), capital adequacy considerations, and the limits on the bank's own resources and sources of funding. Syndicated lending evolved as economic conditions in the period after the Second World War led to a requirement for ever larger amounts of finance to fund the activities of borrowers, with the borrowers ranging from corporate entities to public authorities and States and their instrumentalities. The rather ad hoc alternative involved a borrower obtaining a series of individual bilateral loans from various different banks, which was a cumbersome procedure that was not really to the advantage of either the banks or the borrower. From the borrower's perspective, it meant finding the banks and attracting them to enter into discussions with the borrower, and, thereafter, negotiating with each bank separately, with the possibility of different terms and conditions applying to each loan, in both a commercial and a documentary sense. Thus the borrower might find that the period, interest rate, and the contractual provisions concerning undertakings, events of default and the like for each loan differed, dependent upon the outcome of its negotiations with the separate banks. From the perspective of the banks, they would not necessarily be aware of the position concerning the other banks, and each of them would have to undertake its own preliminary credit and other investigations, and then negotiate separately with the borrower. Syndicated lending obviated a great deal of the unnecessary duplication associated with separate bilateral lending by each bank. It provided a mechanism by which a group of banks could be found that were prepared to advance funds to the borrower in a co-ordinated fashion on the same terms and through the mechanism of the same facility.

9.1.2 Although those requiring large amounts of debt finance may now often prefer to raise funds through an issuance of debt instruments in the capital markets, syndicated lending is still used in many large financing transactions. For instance, it remains a common mechanism for project financing. There are also occasions where it might not be possible or convenient for a capital markets transaction to take place, as might be the case if it is desired to keep the matter confidential (e.g. to finance a hostile takeover bid, where the facility must be arranged before the bid is made), where the flexibility under a multicurrency facility is required, where a borrower desires to have a revolving facility for short-term advances, or where the borrower does not have a sufficient reputation to make it an attractive proposition to investors in the capital markets. Another benefit of a syndicated facility is that it is possible to structure the facility so that the borrower is given a range of different options that it may utilise under the facility, and thus, for example, the facility arrangements may comprise not just a loan facility but also an acceptance credit facility and a bonding and guarantee issuance facility. Such a facility is normally referred to as a multi-option facility.

In basic outline, a syndicated facility involves a group of banks being brought **9.1.3** together to form a syndicate, which will provide funds to the borrower within the compass of a single facility. In a relatively straightforward syndication, which will provide the basis for the discussion in this chapter, the syndicate of banks will be present from the outset when the transaction is signed and entered into. In other situations, the facility documentation may contemplate the mechanics of a syndicated loan, but the wider syndicate will be brought together at a later stage, by virtue of a 'selling down' exercise, under which the bank or small group of banks that initially entered into the transaction with the borrower (often referred to as 'underwriters' or 'co-arrangers') will transfer participations of their commitments and exposures to the larger syndicate at some time after the facility agreement has been entered into between the borrower and the initial bank or banks.[1] In the latter case, the method of effecting the syndication will involve a transference of the participations, using the techniques for transferring loan and facility participations, most probably by the use of transfer certificates to effect novations, as discussed in Chapter 12. Nonetheless, many of the issues that are discussed in this chapter will also be relevant in relation to that situation and the position that follows during the remaining life of the transaction.

The cast list of entities involved in a syndicated transaction will include the **9.1.4** following.

(1) The borrower needs no particular introduction, but in some cases there may be more than one borrower and other entities that are linked to it may also be involved, such as in acting as guarantors. The guarantee could be given as a separate document or it may be included within the provisions of the facility agreement, in which case the guarantor would be a party to that agreement. There may even be mechanisms so that borrowers and guarantors can be added in or removed from the cast list.

(2) The arranger is the financial institution that is commissioned by the borrower to arrange or put the transaction together, which will include finding the syndicate and taking the transaction through to the stage where the facility documentation is signed or, in a 'selling down' exercise, the later date when the syndicate is brought in to the contractual arrangements. There will usually be one principal arranger, which may be called the lead manager, but other

---

[1] When there is an initial group of banks which formally agree to provide the facility and a later syndication to a wider group, this two-stage process is sometimes referred to as the 'primary syndication' and 'secondary syndication'.

entities may be accorded a similar sounding status, such as co-arranger, co-lead manager, underwriter, manager, or book runner, which may reflect their assistance in finding syndicate members or the relative proportions of the facility that they have taken or were prepared to take onto their own books (i.e. to underwrite) if other syndicate members could not be found.

(3) The agent bank, sometimes called the facility agent, is the co-ordinator of the facility once it has been formalised by the signing of the documentation. Its role begins upon execution of the facility agreement and will continue, unless it is replaced by another agent, until the conclusion of the transaction. Its role is crucial to the management and effective co-ordination of the arrangements between the banks and as between them and the borrower. The facility agent may be assisted in a complicated facility by other entities which perform specific roles. If security is to be taken, there may be a separate security agent, failing which, the facility agent will also hold the security, usually as trustee on behalf of the banks.

(4) The syndicate of banks will provide the lending to the borrower, with each of them having a specified commitment to provide a set proportion of the overall facility amount.

9.2 The Obligations and Rights of the Banks and the Relationship Between Them

9.2.1 The dichotomy

The concept of a syndicated transaction involves certain dichotomies. On the one hand, the banks agree to provide their participations in the facility in a co-ordinated fashion under the umbrella of a single facility agreement, they agree to majority voting on many (although not all) of the matters that might arise for their decision, and they agree that they should be treated on a *pari passu* basis with respect to repayment. If security is taken, it is usually taken in a composite manner on behalf of all the banks. Each of those matters tends to emphasise the collective nature of a syndicated transaction. On the other hand, the facility agreement usually provides that each bank's respective obligations are limited to its specified participation, so that no bank accepts responsibility for the liabilities of any other members of the syndicate to provide their share of the facility. It also provides that their rights, as against the borrower, should be separate and not joint. Thus, the facility agreement makes it clear that if one bank defaults in making its participation available, the other banks should not be obliged to make up the shortfall;[2]

---

[2] This should be contrasted with the usual position under a subscription agreement in a bond issue, under which the managers who agree to subscribe for the issue contractually undertake a joint and several liability to subscribe for the whole of the issue.

each of them is owed separately a debt for the money it has advanced to the borrower and the banks do not wish to share the profits that they earn from the transaction.

What follows will begin by addressing the provisions in a facility agreement that tend to emphasise the collective nature of a syndicated transaction, namely the provisions that provide for the *pari passu* distribution of receipts as between the banks and the provisions relating to the making of decisions. It will then be necessary to examine the possible legal consequences that might arise from the nature of a syndicated transaction and the relevant provisions in a facility agreement that address them.

9.2.1.1

9.2.2 *Pari passu* distribution and the sharing clause

It is a standard principle of syndicated facilities that payments which are to be made by the borrower (or another person, such as a guarantor) and the recoveries from enforcement action should be paid to and received by the agent, which will then distribute them on a pro rata basis amongst the banks (except in the unusual case where only one bank is entitled to receive the payment). This is reflected in the payment clauses in the facility agreement.

A sharing clause deals with the situation where that procedure is bypassed, so that a particular bank receives or recovers payment directly when the other banks have not been paid or, alternatively, where it receives or recovers more than its fair share with respect to a payment that is due by the borrower. The clause requires such a bank to pay to the agent the amount in excess of its pro rata share, so that the agent can then distribute the excess amongst the other banks. The effect of the clause is to achieve the *pari passu* position as to the distribution of payments amongst the syndicate of banks as originally laid down by the contract, which would have been by-passed by the direct payment or recovery received by the individual bank. The clause usually applies both to payments made to the relevant individual bank and to other means of recovery by that bank, such as by the exercise of set-off rights or the enforcement of security. It is usually expressed, however, not to apply to recoveries obtained through litigation or arbitration proceedings where the recipient bank has invited the other banks to join those proceedings and they have declined to do so.

9.2.2.1

If the sharing clause simply provided for the receiving bank to pay over the excess amount to the agent then that bank might be at a disadvantage, as the borrower could claim that it had paid, or should be treated as having paid, the full amount (including the excess) to that bank, so that the state of the account as between them had been reduced by the full amount rather than by the lesser amount that the bank has been able to retain in consequence of the operation of the sharing clause. To overcome such an argument, the clause will provide for one or more mechanisms that are intended to restore to the bank the right to claim from the

9.2.2.2

borrower an amount equivalent to the excess that it has paid over to the agent. One such mechanism is to provide that the receiving bank will be subrogated to the rights of the other banks against the borrower to the extent that they have participated in a distribution by the agent of the excess.[3] Another mechanism is for the clause to state that the receiving bank is to be treated as if it had never received the amount of the excess, so that the outstanding account as between it and the borrower will only be reduced by the amount the bank has been able to retain. The agreement will go on to provide that, in consequence, the accounts as between the borrower and the other banks will be treated as reduced by the amount of the excess that they have received via the agent. A third mechanism is for the other banks, to the extent that they have received a payment out of the excess, to assign their rights against the borrower to the original receiving bank.[4]

9.2.2.3   The sharing clause will also contain other safeguards for the bank that originally received or recovered the payment. If the mechanisms referred to above are not effective as a matter of law or if the bank is under an obligation to return the excess to the borrower then the obligation of the bank under the clause to pay over the excess to the agent will not apply or the sharing will be unwound, as the case may be.

9.2.3 Voting and decision making by the banks

The facility agreement is likely to state that in some circumstances the consent of all of the banks is required before a decision can be made, such as in making amendments to the basic economic elements of the facility, including as to the rate of interest, the amount or date of any payment that should be made by the borrower, any change in the financial obligations of the banks, as well as in making any change in the method of ascertaining the requisite majority of the banks that can make decisions where the agreement provides for decisions being made by the majority. Otherwise, the facility agreement is likely to provide that decisions may be taken by a majority vote of the banks.[5] The method of ascertaining what

---

[3] This would be a form of contractual subrogation, as distinguished from subrogation to prevent unjust enrichment which can operate outside a contractual agreement: see Lord Hoffmann in *Banque Financière de la Cité v Parc (Battersea) Ltd* [1999] 1 AC 221. If there is the possibility that a bank may wish to be subrogated to any security held by or for the benefit of the other banks, it would be sensible to provide for that in the relevant clause, as it has been held that the mere fact that money is provided to discharge a secured debt does not, of itself, entitle the provider to be subrogated to the security: see Oliver J in *Paul v Speirway Ltd* [1976] Ch 220, at 230 and Lord Diplock in *Orakpo v Manson Investments Ltd* [1978] AC 95, at 105.

[4] This last mechanism was used in the original forms of syndicated facility agreements but is rarely used nowadays. It was thought that it might give rise to a liability to pay stamp duty or other documentary taxes, potentially on the whole amount of the facility, and there might also be conflict of laws difficulties in achieving recognition of the assignment, for instance, in the borrower's jurisdiction.

[5] As explained below in relation to the role of the facility agent, in the absence of a decision by the majority, the agent will be able to exercise its own discretion in determining matters that relate

constitutes a majority of the banks will be specified in the facility agreement. It is normally determined as amounting to a two-thirds majority of the banks, judged by the amount (by value) of their participations in the facility.

There are some constraints at general law on the ability of a majority to bind a dissenting minority through a vote of those concerned.[6] They are as follows.

9.2.3.1

There must be a power conferred by the relevant contractual documentation for a decision to be made by the relevant majority and the vote must concern a matter upon which a decision may be made.[7] If the matter is outside the subject matter on which a vote may be taken and a majority decision made, then the vote will be ineffective.[8] It is necessary for the vote to be passed by the requisite majority as laid down in the facility documentation.

9.2.3.1.1

As a general matter (but subject as already stated), the majority can bind the minority and those forming the majority may vote in their own interests.[9] This is particularly the case where, from the outset of the transaction, there is an obvious potential for a conflict in the interests of those who may be called upon to vote and where the identity of those who could be involved is likely to change from time to time.[10]

9.2.3.1.2

If there is a special or secret advantage that is to be given to or conferred upon a voting participant to secure its vote within the majority, that must be disclosed. If it is not disclosed, the vote will be invalid.[11] However, if the advantage is fully disclosed, the participant may vote in favour of the decision and the vote will be valid.[12]

9.2.3.1.3

---

to the facility, except for those matters that are reserved for a unanimous decision of all of the banks.

[6] The propositions that are stated below are largely derived from the judgment of Rimmer J in *Redwood Master Fund Ltd v TD Bank Europe Ltd* [2002] EWHC 2703 (Ch), [2006] 1 BCLC 149 and, to some extent, from cases concerning bond issues.

[7] *Hay v Swedish & Norwegian Ry Co* (1889) TLR 460; *Mercantile Investment & General Trust Co v International Co of Mexico* [1893] 1 Ch 484.

[8] E.g. where the facility agreement provides that a matter may only be decided by a unanimous vote of all of the banks.

[9] *British America Nickel Corp Ltd v MJ O'Brien Ltd* [1927] AC 369. See also *Law Debenture Trust Corp PLC v Concord Trust* [2007] EWHC 1380 (Ch). Rimmer J in *Redwood Master Fund Ltd v TD Bank Europe Ltd* [2002] EWHC 2703 (Ch) said that a borrower should be entitled to rely on this principle unless it was on notice that the vote of the majority was tainted by one of the matters that will shortly be mentioned, where the vote by the majority may be upset.

[10] See Rimmer J in ibid, who followed the approach taken by the High Court of Australia in *Peters American Delicacy Co v Heath* (1938–39) 61 CLR 457 and the Privy Council in *Howard Smith Ltd v Ampol Petroleum Ltd* [1974] AC 821.

[11] *British America Nickel Corp Ltd v MJ O'Brien Ltd* [1927] AC 369.

[12] *North-West Transportation Co v Beatty* (1887) 12 App Cas 589; *Goodfellow v Nelson Line* [1912] 2 Ch 324.

9.2.3.1.4 The court may intervene if there has been some other unfairness or oppression, in the sense of some deliberate intention on the part of the majority to damage or oppress the interests of the minority. Evidence of this may be difficult to obtain, but the court may be prepared to conclude that there was a lack of good faith along those lines if the outcome of the vote is so manifestly disadvantageous, discriminatory, or oppressive towards the minority that the only reasonable conclusion which the court could draw is that the majority must have been motivated by dishonest considerations that were inconsistent with a proper exercise of its powers.[13] However, in a case where negotiations between the borrower and a committee of the banks had been openly conducted and involved proposals put forward by the borrower, it was held that allegations of unfairness and oppression could not be substantiated.[14]

9.2.3.1.5 Possibly, by analogy with case law concerning bonds, if the facility agreement provides that a separate vote is required of a special class or section of the banks, the vote must be exercised for the benefit of the class as a whole and not merely so as to benefit individual members of that class.[15] It is not entirely clear, in such a situation, how the benefit of the class as a whole should be identified. It would appear that if the minority's interests (i.e. a minority within the class) are being interfered with then that would not be to the benefit of the class as a whole.[16] It has also been suggested that the test might be assessed by reference to what would be in the interests of an individual hypothetical member of the class,[17] but it may be rather difficult to identify such a mythical person amongst a divergent body of banks.

9.2.4 Partnership

In light of the collective provisions as described above, it is relevant to discuss if the banks, by joining in a syndicated facility, may be considered as constituting a partnership. The primary consequence, should they be a partnership, is that they would have joint and several liability for the defaults of any of their members. Section 1(1) of the Partnership Act 1890 defines a partnership as the 'relation which subsists between persons carrying on a business in common with a view to profit'. The elements of the definition are, first, that the persons should be carrying on a business in common, and, secondly, that they should be doing so with a view to profit. Those elements will be examined in turn, following which mention will be made of the provisions that are commonly to be found in the syndicated

---

13 See Rimmer J in *Redwood Master Fund Ltd v TD Bank Europe Ltd* [2002] EWHC 2703 (Ch).
14 *Redwood Master Fund Ltd v TD Bank Europe Ltd* [2002] EWHC 2703 (Ch).
15 *British America Nickel Corp Ltd v MJ O'Brien Ltd* [1927] AC 369.
16 Ibid.
17 See Sir Raymond Evershed MR in *Greenhalgh v Arderne Cinemas Ltd* [1951] Ch 286, at 291.

facility documentation aimed at displacing any risk that the banks may be responsible for each other's obligations.

By joining in the facility, the banks undoubtedly are acting in common. In addition, they agree to act on many matters through their collective agent and to be bound by a majority vote on many of the matters on which a decision is required. The question then turns to whether by doing so they are carrying on a business in common. Section 45 of the Partnership Act 1890 defines 'business' to include 'every trade, occupation or profession' which, in effect, means that any commercial activity or venture could be considered as a business. At first sight, the concept of carrying on a business in common might be thought to imply the necessity of there being some element of continuity in carrying on the business. A syndicated loan is an isolated transaction entered into for that transaction alone, rather than with a view to establishing an on-going business intended to grant loans and facilities under several different transactions. The banks which join the syndicate do so simply for that transaction. Hence it might be argued that the banks are not carrying on a business so as to constitute a partnership. The need for some element of continuity was mentioned by Brett LJ in *Smith v Anderson*[18] in relation to the prohibition that then existed under the Companies Act 1862, which prevented more than 20 persons from carrying on a business for gain. Support for this view might also be drawn from cases relating to the Moneylenders Act 1900 (now repealed), in which it was said that the concept of 'carrying on business as a moneylender' required a 'repetition of acts, the sum of which constitutes the "business"'.[19] Similarly, Slade J said in *Skelton Finance Co Ltd v Lawrence*[20] that two isolated loan transactions by a lender 'did not import the necessary element of system, repetition and continuity necessary to constitute a moneylending business'. That was doubted, however, by the Court of Appeal in *Conroy v Kenny*[21] in which Kennedy LJ said[22] that a lender who sets himself up as a licensed moneylender may still be regarded as having a moneylending business even if he only makes one loan. Furthermore, Lord Keith said in *Davies v Sumner*[23] that a 'one-off adventure in the nature of trade, carried through with a view to profit' could constitute a course of trade or business within the Trade Descriptions Act 1968. Perhaps the distinction between these various approaches lies in gauging whether the relevant person or persons has set himself or themselves up with the intention of carrying on a business, even if he or they only enters into one transaction, as opposed to intending from the outset only to enter into an isolated transaction. This is consistent with

---

[18] (1879) 15 ChD 247.
[19] Per Lord Atkinson in *Kirkwood v Gadd* [1910] AC 422, at 431.
[20] (1976) 120 SJ 147.
[21] [1999] 1 WLR 1340.
[22] At 1346–1347.
[23] [1984] 1 WLR 1301, at 1305.

the approach that was taken by Moore-Bick LJ in *GE Capital Bank Ltd v Rushton*[24] when considering the provisions of Part III of the Hire Purchase Act 1964.

9.2.4.2 In relation to the Partnership Act, however, it has been held that a single trading venture entered into by two or more persons may constitute a partnership.[25] This is reinforced by section 32(b) of the Act which provides that a partnership which is entered into for a single adventure or undertaking will be dissolved upon the termination of that adventure or undertaking, so quite clearly the Act itself contemplates the possibility that a partnership may be constituted by a single venture. In addition, a syndicated transaction is intended to continue for the period of the facility, so it will be carried on over a period of time, rather than being merely an entirely isolated incident. There must, therefore, be a risk that the banks may be held to be carrying on a business in common by virtue of them joining in the syndicate.

9.2.4.3 It is next relevant to consider if what the banks are doing is with a view to profit or, to put it more fully, with a view to sharing the profits.[26] By profit is meant the net amount received from the receipts of the business after deducting the expenses and outgoings incurred in the business.[27] This should be contrasted with the concept of merely agreeing to share the 'gross returns' of a venture, under which each party bears its own expenses and losses connected with its participation in the transaction and receives its own share of the receipts generated by the transaction. In this connection, section 2 of the Partnership Act 1890 provides that, in determining if a partnership exists, regard shall be had to various rules, including the following:

> (2) The sharing of gross returns does not of itself create a partnership, whether the persons sharing such returns have or have not a joint or common right or interest in any property from which or from the use of which the returns are derived.

9.2.4.4 A syndicated loan looks very much like a transaction under which the banks intend that they will each separately bear their own expenses and losses of the transaction and that they will only share the gross returns, that is, the receipts from the borrower that are passed on by the facility agent to the banks.[28] Each bank has

---

24 [2005] EWCA Civ 1556; [2006] 3 All ER 865, at [39]–[40].

25 *Mann v D'Arcy* [1968] 1 WLR 893.

26 See Lord Lindley in *Mollwo, March & Co v Court of Wards* (1872) LR 2 PC 419.

27 Lord Herschell in *Gresham Life Assurance Soc v Styles* [1892] AC 309, at 322–323, expressed it as follows, 'When we speak of the profits or gains of a trader we mean that which he has made by his trading. Whether there be such a thing as profit or gain can only be ascertained by setting against the receipts the expenditure or obligations to which they have given rise'. The approach taken by Lord Herschell was referred to with approval by Lord Templeman in *Beauchamp v JW Woolworth PLC* [1990] 1 AC 478, at 489.

28 It is submitted that the sharing clause (which is described above) does not destroy this concept. The banks will still individually suffer the loss, if any, on their ultimate recoveries.

to find the amount of its own contribution to the facility and, if the borrower defaults in making repayment of the amount advanced by that bank, it will suffer on its own the loss attendant upon that default. Further, the profit that a bank makes on the amount it has lent, that is, the yield that it receives by way of interest, fees, and commission, will depend upon its own cost base and, in particular, the cost to it of providing the money it has lent. Thus the profit of each bank depends on its own individual circumstances, as contrasted with the position in a partnership where the partners share the profits remaining after taking into account any losses and net of the expenses incurred in earning the profits.

It might also be added that a scheme which permits any bank to transfer its rights and obligations to a new entity, as is commonly the case in consequence of the transfer provisions in syndicated facility documentation, is rather inconsistent with the concept of a partnership. In partnership terms, if such provisions operated then they would have the effect of causing a dissolution of the existing partnership and the commencement of a new partnership. It is inconceivable that this could be the case, especially as such provisions often operate without the necessity of any approval being given by the other banks. The lack of any requirement for such approval would stretch to breaking point the concepts of good faith and fair dealing that underlies the concept of partnership and the duties of good faith that are owed as between prospective partners.[29] **9.2.4.5**

It is submitted that the position as just described is not weakened by the fact that the banks may find themselves having to bear some of the expenses of the facility agent connected with the operation and management of the facility. The facility documentation will usually provide that the borrower should bear the expenses incurred by the facility agent but that if the borrower fails to do so, the banks will indemnify the facility agent for its outstanding expenses. It has been held that the parties to a venture may agree that they will share the gross receipts and the running expenses of the venture without thereby constituting themselves as a partnership.[30] **9.2.4.6**

To resolve any residual doubt, the facility documentation will usually provide that the obligations of the banks are several and that no bank will be responsible for the failure of any other bank to perform its obligations. It is further provided that the amount advanced by each bank shall be regarded as a separate and independent debt due to that bank by the borrower and that the rights attached to that debt are **9.2.4.7**

---

[29] As to such duties, see Lawrence Collins J in *Conlon v Simms* [2006] EWHC 401 (Ch), [2006] 2 All ER 1024, approved on appeal at [2006] EWCA Civ 1749, [2007] 3 All ER 802.

[30] *French v Styring* (1857) 2 CBNS 357, which involved the two joint owners of a racehorse, who agreed to share their winnings and the expenses of keeping, feeding, and training the horse.

separately vested in the bank. As a party to the agreement, the borrower will be bound by such provisions.[31]

9.2.4.8 A further issue has arisen in the USA that does not arise under English law. In *Credit Français International SA v Sociedad Financiera de Comercio CA*[32] the Supreme Court of New York held that the participation of the banks in the syndicate constituted a joint venture, with the consequence that under the law of New York enforcement action against the borrower had to be taken by the banks acting collectively; a single bank was unable to take enforcement action on its own. It should be noted that there was no severability clause in the documentation in that case, whereas now such a clause will almost invariably appear, as noted above. Furthermore, a joint venture has no special significance under English law.

9.2.5 Collective investment schemes

It is arguable that syndicated lending might come within the definition of a 'collective investment scheme' within sections 235(1) to (4) of the Financial Services and Markets Act 2000 (FSMA) unless it falls into one of the exemptions to the definition that is provided, through delegated legislation, by virtue of section 235(5) of FSMA. If the definition does catch syndicated lending then the consequence would be that those involved in 'establishing' or 'operating' the transaction would have to be authorised under FSMA to do so.[33] That would be apt to catch the activities of the arranger and others in arranging the transaction and the activities of the facility agent during the lifetime of the transaction.[34] Furthermore, banks which intended to transfer their participations would have to consider if

---

[31] It is an interesting question whether the borrower could pray in aid the provisions of s 3 of the Unfair Contract Terms Act 1977 (described further below, at 9.5.5.6), to challenge the effect of such provisions, by seeking to argue that they have the effect of excusing the banks from the obligations that they would otherwise have as partners. The borrower will not be dealing as a consumer but query if it could be argued that the banks were dealing on their standard terms of business. The use of standard forms for syndicated lending has become widespread in the London financial market. Even though there will usually be some variation of the forms in consequence of the negotiations for each transaction, that does not destroy the possibility that the documentation might still be considered as constituting standard terms of business: see *St Albans City & District Council v International Computers Ltd* [1996] 4 All ER 491. However, the further question will then arise as to whose terms are represented by the contract, given that the documentation will have been propounded in the first instance by the arranger rather than by the banks and will have been sent to the banks in draft form at the request of the borrower. See further below as to the role of the arranger and as to s 3.

[32] 490 NYS 2d 670 (1985).

[33] See Arts 4 and 51 of the Financial Services and Markets Act 2000 (Regulated Activities) Order 2001 (SI 2001/544), as amended (the Regulated Activities Order).

[34] There is also a restriction on promoting a collective investment scheme by virtue of s 19 of FSMA, which itself is subject to exemptions contained in the Financial Services and Markets Act 2000 (Promotion of Collective Investment Schemes) (Exemptions) Order 2001 (SI 2001/1060), as amended.

they might be dealing in a security,[35] which would also need to be authorised under FSMA.[36]

Section 235 of FSMA provides as follows:

9.2.5.1

(1) ...'collective investment scheme' means any arrangements with respect to property of any description, including money, the purpose or effect of which is to enable persons taking part in the arrangements (whether by becoming owners of the property or any part of it or otherwise) to participate in or receive profits or income arising from the acquisition, holding, management or disposal of the property or sums paid out of such profits or income.

(2) The arrangements must be such that the persons who are to participate ('participants') do not have day-to-day control over the management of the property, whether or not they have the right to be consulted or to give directions.

(3) The arrangements must also have either or both of the following characteristics—
  (a) the contributions of the participants and the profits or income out of which payments are to be made to them are pooled;
  (b) the property is managed as a whole by or on behalf of the operator of the scheme.

(4) If arrangements provide for such pooling as is mentioned in subsection 3(a) in relation to separate parts of the property, the arrangements are not to be regarded as constituting a single collective investment scheme unless the participants are entitled to exchange rights in one part for rights in another.

(5) The Treasury may by order provide that arrangements do not amount to a collective investment scheme—
  (a) in specified circumstances; or
  (b) if the arrangements fall within a specified category of arrangement.

Arden LJ (with whom Ward LJ and Collins J agreed) provided some guidance as to the definition of 'collective investment scheme' in *Financial Services Authority v Fradley & Woodward*.[37] Her Ladyship said that the wording used in section 235, including 'arrangement' and 'property of any description', should be given a wide interpretation and that the application of the section depended upon the specific facts of each case. She said that there was no formality required for there to be an 'arrangement', although she did not decide if it had to be a legally binding arrangement. There was no requirement for a participant's contributions to be invested in some investment. It was also immaterial that the scheme involved bets which were null and void by virtue of section 18 of the Gaming Act 1845. She also said that 'profits' could include winnings on such bets. However, she did qualify her comments by saying that, with its criminal context if there should be a breach of

9.2.5.2

---

[35] A unit (which is defined by s 237(2) of FSMA) in a collective investment scheme is a 'security' within Art 81 of the Regulated Activities Order and so would fall within Art 14 of the Regulated Activities Order (which concerns dealing in such a security), subject to any applicable exemptions, such as under Art 15 of the Regulated Activities Order.

[36] See Art 14 of the Regulated Activities Order.

[37] [2005] EWCA Civ 1183. See, in particular, at [32]–[33].

the requirements of the FSMA, the section should not be interpreted to include matters that were not fairly within it. Arden LJ went on to say that[38] there could be more than one operator of a scheme but if two or more services were offered together, it did not necessarily follow that they formed only one set of arrangements. There can still be a collective investment scheme even if only some of the participants have transferred day-to-day control to the operator of the scheme, whilst others may have not done so,[39] and there can be a pooling of the participants' moneys despite the fact that there might be a trust of such moneys in their favour, with each participant's entitlement being separately identified, thus giving each of them a proprietary right in the pooled fund.[40] It would follow from the last point that the case would be even stronger if such an entitlement did not exist.

9.2.5.3 It will be seen that section 235(1) provides a basic definition of a collective investment scheme, which is further refined by the requirements of sections 235(2) to (4). Looked at from the perspective of the banks which participate in a syndicated loan, the transaction appears to fall within the definition. When the banks make an advance under the facility, they do so by paying their respective contributions to the facility agent which, having received the contributions into its account, then disburses the combined amount as one sum to the borrower. When the borrower makes a payment of interest or principal under the facility, it pays the relevant amount as one sum to the facility agent which, having received the amount in its account, then distributes the proceeds amongst the banks. The banks are thus participating in the amount lent under the pooled facility and they are receiving income from the facility, which is payable by the borrower on the amount that has been lent to it through the facility agent. The facility agent deals on behalf of the banks with the borrower and has the management of the facility. Whilst the banks may be consulted by the agent and have the right to give it directions, the facility agent remains in effective day-to-day control of the facility.

9.2.5.4 As previously mentioned, syndicated lending will not come within the definition of a collective investment scheme if it falls within one or more of the exemptions that are specified by virtue of section 235(5) of FSMA. The exemptions are to be found in the Financial Services and Markets Act 2000 (Collective Investment Schemes) Order 2001.[41] Article 3 of the Order specifies that the kinds of arrangements, as set out in the Schedule to the Order, will not amount to a collective investment scheme. There are two relevant exemptions that arise by virtue of the Schedule.

---

[38] Ibid, at [37].
[39] Ibid, at [46].
[40] Ibid, at [47].
[41] SI 2001/1062, as amended.

The first exemption is contained in paragraph 6 of the Order, which provides as follows:

> Arrangements do not amount to a collective investment scheme if—
> (a) they are arrangements under which the rights or interests of participants are rights to or interests in money held in a common account; and
> (b) that money is held in the account on the understanding that an amount representing the contribution of each participant is to be applied—
>   (i) in making payments to him;
>   (ii) in satisfaction of sums owed by him; or
>   (iii) in the acquisition of property for him or the provision of services to him.

It is submitted that paragraph 6 is apt to describe the position with respect to the money (i.e. the credit balance) from time to time held by the facility agent in its account, which is to be applied either in making payments to the borrower or in making payments to the banks.

The second exemption is contained in paragraph 9 of the Order, which provides as follows—

> (1) Subject to sub-paragraph (2), arrangements do not amount to a collective investment scheme if each of the participants—
>   (a) carries on a business other than the business of engaging in any regulated activity of the kind specified by any of articles 14, 21, 25, 37, 40, 45, 51 to 53 or, so far as relevant to any of those articles, article 64 of the Regulated Activities Order;[42]
>   (b) enters into the arrangements for commercial purposes related to that business.
> (2) Sub-paragraph (1) does not apply where the person will carry on the business in question by virtue of being a participant in the arrangements.

The relevant business of each of the banks is that of taking money on deposit (an activity that is regulated by Article 5 of the Regulated Activities Order), or borrowing money in the inter-bank market or from other sources and lending that money to borrowers (the activity of lending, per se, is not a regulated activity within the FSMA). Each of the banks enters into the syndicated facility for the purpose of that business, that is, as a method of lending money that it has taken through deposits or by borrowing from other banks or sources. Except for banks whose only activity or, perhaps, principal activity is entering into syndicate lending transactions, the qualification in sub-paragraph (2) should not be relevant.

---

[42] I.e. the Regulated Activities Order as defined above.

9.3 Arrangement of the Facility by the Arranger

9.3.1 The arranger is the financial institution that is commissioned by the borrower to arrange the transaction, that is, put the transaction together. This will include finding the syndicate (and the underwriters, if required) and taking the negotiations for the transaction through to the stage where the facility documentation is signed or, in a 'selling down' exercise, the later date when the wider syndicate is brought in to the contractual arrangements. There will usually be one principal arranger, which may be called the lead manager, but other entities may be accorded a similar sounding status, such as co-arranger, co-lead manager, underwriter, manager, or book runner, which may reflect their assistance in finding syndicate members or the relative proportions of the facility that they have taken or were prepared to take onto their own books if other syndicate members could not be found. For the purposes of this chapter, it will be assumed that there is only one arranger, but the issues that are discussed will be just as relevant if there is more than one entity involved in fulfilling that role.

9.3.2 The mandate

After negotiations between the arranger and the borrower, the arranger is awarded a mandate by the borrower to assemble and bring the transaction to fruition. The documentation that forms the mandate or which accompanies it will describe the proposed transaction (and its principal economic and other terms) in outline, probably in the form of a term sheet. It will specify, possibly in a separate letter, the fees or commission that will be paid to the arranger and the others involved in the arrangement, underwriting, and syndication exercises. The arranger will undertake to use its reasonable, or (very infrequently) its best, endeavours[43] to achieve the transaction.[44] Nonetheless, there is likely to be a provision which will permit the arranger to withdraw[45] or to amend the terms,[46] particularly those relating to the financial return that the banks will receive and the more significant other terms, in the event of the occurrence (after the date of the mandate) of an adverse change in general economic and other conditions affecting the financial markets and the availability of finance for the transaction or if an adverse change should occur in the circumstances of the borrower and its affiliate group

---

[43] See the discussion at Chap 1.

[44] See the discussion at Chap 1 as to whether the arrangements as agreed between the arranger and the borrower would be considered sufficient to constitute a binding contractual agreement between them.

[45] Usually referred to as a 'material adverse change' provision.

[46] Usually referred to as a 'market flex' provision.

of companies.[47] The underwriters (if any) will also wish to see that the arranger has such rights and they may be keen to reach an understanding with the arranger that it will take their interests into account in deciding if it will exercise the rights.

9.3.2.1 *Market flex provisions*

It is worth considering in a little more detail the provision in the mandate which permits the arranger to amend the basic terms of the transaction (as originally set out in the mandate and the term sheet) in the event that there is an adverse change in general economic conditions affecting the financial markets and the availability of finance for the transaction. This is usually referred to as a 'market flex' provision. The intention behind such a provision is that the arranger should be able to 'sweeten' the terms, so as to make them more attractive to the banking community, if the arranger considers that it would not be possible to conclude the transaction on the original terms because of the occurrence of such an adverse change. The most likely amendment would be to the financial terms of the transaction, such as in relation to the interest rate, fees, the overall facility amount, or the period of the facility. The arranger may also consider that other amendments may be required, such as in relation to guarantees and security cover or to financial and other covenants.

The provision is usually worded (at least in the form as initially presented by the arranger in its first draft of the mandate) so as to invest the arranger with a considerable amount of discretion in determining if the relevant conditions have arisen and as to the nature and extent of the amendments that will be required. It also normally provides that the discretion may be exercised at any time up to the date when the banks (or at least the initial syndicate) have entered into the formal legal documentation representing the facility agreement and so have become legally obliged to provide the facility. Quite obviously, a borrower should be concerned as to the apparent width of the discretion that the arranger wishes to reserve to itself, and the borrower may wish to limit the discretion. The borrower may, for instance, wish to stipulate that it may terminate the mandate if it is unhappy with the way in which the discretion has been exercised. It may also wish to have the right to be consulted before the discretion is exercised. Neither of those stipulations will be of much value if the borrower is in the position where it has no real option but to accept what the arranger proposes. The borrower may wish, therefore, to insert some more precise definition of the circumstances in which the discretion may arise, as well as placing restrictions upon the extent to which the arranger may amend the terms. On the other hand, the arranger will resist

9.3.2.2

---

[47] As to a provision that relates to material adverse change which affects the circumstances of the borrower, see the further discussion on such provisions in Chap 3.

limits being placed upon its discretion, arguing that it must be a matter for the exercise of its own judgment in deciding if the discretion should be exercised and what amendments should be made so that the transaction will proceed. As with many aspects of commercial life, the parties will have to resolve the debate by negotiation.

9.3.3 The role of the arranger

The role that the arranger undertakes in consequence of having been awarded the mandate is usually threefold, although it does depend upon the co-operation of the borrower.

9.3.3.1 First, the arranger agrees to assist the borrower in compiling the information that will be required to enable the banks to assess the proposed transaction and decide if they wish to take part in it. Most of the information will have to be provided by the borrower and the arranger's task will mainly involve it in advising the borrower on what has to be provided and in assembling the information in a readable and acceptable form of presentation. That information will include financial and commercial material concerning the borrower and its affiliated entities, such as copies of accounts (both audited and, if available, more up-to-date unaudited accounts) together with earnings and cash flow statements, information about immediate and long-term liabilities, information about the business and assets of the relevant entities, the markets and conditions in which they operate, and projections of future prospects and activities. A copy of the term sheet summarising the transaction will also be included. The package of information will usually be assembled in an information memorandum, which the arranger will then distribute to the banks.

9.3.3.2 Secondly, the arranger agrees to use its reasonable (or, very exceptionally, its best) endeavours to approach the banks (including, if required, underwriters) that it believes would be interested in the transaction and to obtain their agreement in principle to participate in the syndicate. This will depend, to a large extent, on the attractiveness of the proposal that is put to them, not just in the profitability of the proposed transaction but also in terms of the risk that they will undertake as it is disclosed in the information memorandum and any other information that is sent to the banks. The arranger may be assisted in this task by other banks who have agreed to act as underwriters, that is, that they undertake to provide up to a certain proportion of the total facility in the event that other banks cannot be found to complete a wide syndication of the risk.

9.3.3.3 Thirdly, the arranger will prepare the facility documentation, having appointed lawyers to assist it in that task. The documentation will reflect the outline represented by the term sheet. The procedure that is usually followed is that the lawyers appointed by the arranger will prepare a draft of the documentation for review by the arranger, following which it will be sent to the borrower and reviewed by the borrower and its lawyers, and then discussed between the arranger, the borrower, and their respective lawyers. Once they have agreed to the form of the documentation, the arranger will send copies to the banks for their review. The arranger will receive any comments that the banks may wish to make, discuss them with the borrower, and, perhaps after further negotiation, the documentation will be settled in an agreed final form for signature by all concerned.

In a straightforward syndication, where the full complement of the banks is present from the date of signing the facility agreement, the arranger's role comes to an end once the facility documentation has been finalised and entered into by the parties. Where syndication to a wider syndicate is to take place through a 'selling down' process after the documentation has been signed, the arranger's role will be completed once the full syndicate has been brought into the transaction by accession to the documentation. Although the arranger will usually be named as a party to the principal facility agreement and will enter into it as such,[48] that is done so that it can gain various contractual protections, as will be discussed further below, rather than to cater for any further role of a contractual nature.

9.3.4

9.4 Areas of Risk to the Arranger

9.4.1 A claim by the borrower

One possible area of risk to the arranger would be where the borrower is unhappy with the performance of the tasks undertaken by the arranger in attempting to put the transaction together, in particular, where the arranger fails to bring about the syndicated facility. This will depend upon the terms of the mandate that was agreed between the borrower and the arranger and whether the arranger has complied with the obligations that it undertook in the mandate. If the borrower wishes to bring a claim against the arranger, it is likely that the claim would be framed against the arranger for breach of contract in failing to meet the obligations imposed upon the arranger by the contract. There may also be a claim framed in the tort of negligence. For present purposes, it will be assumed that the contract and any tortious claim would be governed by English law, so that law would apply to the contractual and any tortious claim, including as to whether it had been performed or breached its obligations and, in broad terms, the consequences of

---

[48] Additionally, it will probably be a party to the facility agreement as a bank within the syndicate, as it would be difficult for it to sell the transaction to other banks if it did not intend to take a participation in the facility for itself. It may also fulfil the role of being the facility agent.

the breach. So long as the arranger has approached its task competently and exercised reasonable care and skill, it is unlikely that the borrower would be able to pursue a successful claim against the arranger.

9.4.2 Claims by the syndicate members

Of greater concern to the arranger will be its possible exposure to claims that the members of the banking syndicate may bring against it in the event that the facility had been entered into and the borrower had made drawings under it but then defaulted in meeting its obligations. If it turns out that the transaction was more risky than the banks had thought when they agreed to join the syndicate and that they were not fully appraised of all of the factors that were relevant in deciding to join the transaction, they may wish to visit their discontent by claiming against the arranger for the loss they have suffered.[49] They may well, of course, have a claim against the borrower, but that may be worth little if the borrower is insolvent and unable to satisfy its obligations. In such a case, it is not inconceivable that the banks may wish to consider the possibility of bringing a claim against the arranger, bearing in mind its involvement from the outset in arranging the transaction and the likelihood that it will have the financial resources to meet any claim that was successfully brought against it. It is unlikely that any such claim could be founded in contract as, at the time the arranger was performing its role, there would have been no contractual relationship between the arranger and the banks that it approached to join the syndicate. The claim will have to be based on some other ground. It may be conceived on the basis that the arranger had a general duty towards the banks to ensure that the transaction was a good credit risk or, at least, as a duty to point out to the banks any deficiencies which they should have taken into account in deciding to proceed. In the alternative, it may be put more narrowly and concentrate on a failure to perform a specific task or on the inaccuracy in some particular information that was supplied to the banks, for instance in the information memorandum, on which the banks relied in deciding to enter into the transaction.

9.4.2.1 Before proceeding to examine the bases of the possible claims against the arranger under English law, it is relevant to refer, briefly, to the conflict of laws issues that may arise[50] concerning those claims. This is because of the jurisdictional and

---

[49] In *NatWest Australia Bank Ltd v Tricontinental Corp Ltd* (Supreme Ct of Victoria 26/7/1993). Unreported on this issue but noted and reported, on a different point, at (1993) ATPR (Digest) 46–109), a bank successfully obtained judgment against the arranger for damages amounting to the whole of the bank's participation in the syndicated facility, based upon a claim against the arranger for a negligent misstatement.

[50] See further, Chap 4.

conflict of laws issues that might arise when considering a claim, namely, the possibility that a claimant might commence proceedings in a foreign jurisdiction, and, in addition to that matter or separately, the need to identify the applicable law that a court (whether an English or a foreign court) would apply as the law governing the issue or issues in dispute. This could well be relevant where there is a cross-border element in the situation; for instance, where one or more of the banks was dealing from an office situated outside England and received the relevant information on which its claim is based in that office. The English rules relating to conflict of laws are discussed in Chapter 4 and the reader is referred to that chapter for further consideration of the conflicts issues that may arise.

Assuming that the issues will be determined in accordance with English law, it is **9.4.2.2** now necessary to state more precisely the possible causes of action on which the claims of the banks may be based. The claims might be framed as follows: first, as a claim in the tort of negligence, based either upon an alleged general duty of care owed by the arranger to the banks or, more narrowly, for a negligent misstatement that it made in relation to the information that it provided to them (as this is the most likely basis of a claim against the arranger and because it is also relevant in the context of various other relationships that may be found in financing transactions, it will be given a greater degree of examination than the other possible bases of claim); secondly, as a claim in the tort of deceit with respect to a misstatement that was made by the arranger; thirdly, as a claim for misrepresentation within sections 2(1) or 2(2) of the Misrepresentation Act 1967 (as amended), concerning an incorrect (albeit not deliberate) representation that was made by the arranger; fourthly, as a claim that the arranger was in the position of a fiduciary towards the banks and that it breached its fiduciary duties towards them in failing to act in their best interests, which would be a fairly broad basis of claim. Each of those bases of claim will now be examined. After that, it will be relevant to see if the arranger can successfully avoid or limit any duty or responsibility that it may have by the use of appropriately worded disclaimers of responsibility, whether set out in a contractual form or by another means.

9.4.3 A claim in the tort of negligence

A claim by the banks against an arranger in the tort of negligence will almost certainly be one to recover for pure economic loss, rather than being dependent upon physical injury or damage. The decision of the House of Lords in *Hedley Byrne & Co Ltd v Heller & Partners Ltd*[51] established the possibility that a claimant could bring a claim in the tort of negligence for pure economic loss that was not dependent upon the claimant suffering physical injury or damage to its property.

---

[51] [1964] AC 465.

That possibility had been rejected by the majority of the Court of Appeal a few years earlier in *Candler v Crane Christmas & Co*[52] but the House of Lords in *Hedley Byrne* decided to adopt the minority view of Denning LJ in *Candler v Crane Christmas* that it should be possible to recover for pure economic loss. Such a claim may relate to the negligent giving of advice or information or the negligent performance of other services,[53] and it may cover negligent acts and omissions. The relationship giving rise to the duty may arise by express words or by implication from the circumstances, such as where the defendant had some special expertise or knowledge which he should have appreciated would be relied upon by the claimant.[54]

9.4.3.1   In outline, the matters which must be established if a claimant is to succeed in a claim in negligence are set out below. Whilst they are set out as distinct steps, in practice they will usually be inter-dependent, in that they cannot be taken in pure isolation and the same issue may transcend several of the steps. The matters are first, that the defendant owed the claimant a duty of care; secondly, that the scope of the duty must be shown; thirdly, that the defendant failed to act reasonably within the scope of its duty of care to the claimant; fourthly, that the claimant reasonably relied upon the defendant in the exercise of that duty towards it; fifthly, that the loss which was suffered arose in consequence of the breach of the duty, that is, that it was caused by the breach; finally, to the extent that it has not already fallen to be considered in establishing the existence of a duty of care, that at the time the breach occurred, the loss was a reasonably foreseeable consequence of the breach of the defendant's duty of care. As this is still a developing area, those matters will now be examined in more detail by looking at their constituent elements in theory and, once that has been done, by then applying the theory to the position of an arranger to see whether a case could be made out against it.

9.4.3.2 *The existence of a duty of care*

The tests for establishing in any particular situation the existence of a duty of care or, more accurately, a duty to exercise reasonable care, hark back to a passage in the famous speech of Lord Atkin in *Donoghue v Stevenson*,[55] in which his Lordship said:

> The rule that you are to love your neighbour becomes in law, you must not injure your neighbour; and the lawyer's question, Who is my neighbour? receives a restricted reply. You must take reasonable care to avoid acts or omissions which you can reasonably foresee would be likely to injure your neighbour. Who, then, in law is my neighbour?

---

[52] [1951] 2 KB 164.
[53] See Lord Goff of Chieveley in *Henderson v Merrett Syndicates Ltd* [1995] 2 AC 145, at 180.
[54] See Lord Morris of Borth-y-Gest in *Hedley Byrne & Co Ltd v Heller & Partners Ltd* [1964] AC 465, at 502–503 and Lord Goff in *Henderson v Merrett Syndicates Ltd* [1995] 2 AC 145, at 180.
[55] [1932] AC 562, at 580.

The answer seems to be—persons who are so closely and directly affected by my act that I ought reasonably to have them in contemplation as being so affected when I am directing my mind to the acts or omissions which are called into question.

Despite such an auspicious beginning, there have been divergent approaches in the case law over the years, particularly in the House of Lords, in determining the circumstances under which a duty of care may arise in cases involving a new situation where the claim has been for pure economic loss. The divergence of approach is reflected in the review of the case law that was conducted by the House of Lords in *HM Commissioners of Customs and Excise v Barclays Bank plc.*[56] Three possible tests, as outlined below, have been put forward in the case law to determine if a duty of care exists in a situation that is not covered by existing authority, although no one of those tests will be determinative in every situation.[57] To a large extent, the House of Lords signalled in the *Barclays Bank* case that the tests should be applied on a pragmatic, rather than a theoretical, basis and that the concepts that are used in the tests are not precise but should be seen as guides rather than definitive tests. What is important is to discover what could reasonably be inferred from the defendant's conduct against the background of all of the circumstances of the case, and that this was not just a question of fact, as questions of fairness and policy would also enter into the decision.[58] In the *Barclays Bank* case the decision was largely based upon whether, as a matter of policy, it was fair, just, and reasonable to impose a duty of care upon the defendant. None of this makes it easy to say how the courts will deal with any particular set of new circumstances when they arise.

9.4.3.2.1 The first test is that of an 'assumption of responsibility', that is, whether the defendant voluntarily assumed responsibility for what he said and did vis-à-vis the claimant, or is to be treated by the law as having done so. This test was championed by Lord Goff of Chieveley in three cases: *Spring v Guardian Assurance plc,*[59] *Henderson v Merrett Syndicates Ltd,*[60] and *White v Jones.*[61] Lord Goff based the test, in particular, on Lord Devlin's speech in *Hedley Byrne & Co Ltd v Heller & Partners Ltd.*[62] Lord Walker said in the *Barclays Bank* case[63] that the concept of a 'voluntary' assumption meant a conscious, considered, or deliberate decision on the part of the defendant. Lord Bingham said in the *Barclays Bank* case[64] that in some cases a party can be said to have assumed responsibility and that can be seen

---

56 [2006] UKHL 28.
57 See, for instance, the review conducted by Lord Mance in the *Barclays Bank* case and his summary at the end of his review, at [93].
58 See Lord Hoffmann in the *Barclays Bank* case, at [35].
59 [1995] 2 AC 296.
60 [1995] 2 AC 145, at 178.
61 [1995] 2 AC 207, at 268.
62 [1964] AC 465, at 528–529.
63 [2006] UKHL 28, at [73].
64 At [4].

as a sufficient condition of liability, but such an assumption should never be regarded as a necessary condition of liability. The paradigm situation where such an assumption may exist is where there is a relationship having an equivalence to the characteristics of a contract, save for the presence of consideration. Lord Bingham said that this was the position in *Hedley Byrne & Co Ltd v Heller & Partners Ltd*,[65] in *White v Jones*,[66] and in *Henderson v Merrett Syndicates Ltd*.[67] Presumably the same could be said in cases where a claim in tort is brought as an alternative to a claim in contract.[68] The reference to an equivalence to the characteristics of a contract should not be taken too literally, as an assumption of responsibility has also been found in situations that were some way removed from any equivalence to a contract between the claimant and defendant, as in *Smith v Eric S Bush*,[69] *White v Jones*,[70] and *Phelps v Hillingdon London Borough Council*.[71]

9.4.3.2.2 Lord Bingham also said in the *Barclays Bank* case[72] that the assumption of responsibility test is to be applied objectively and not just by a consideration of the defendant's subjective thoughts or intentions.[73] The concept of a subjective assumption of responsibility might still be relevant in cases where it could be demonstrated that a defendant had intended to accept responsibility or had expressly disavowed an acceptance of responsibility.[74] Lord Bingham also said that the further the assumption test is removed from subjective considerations, so that the more it becomes a notional assumption of responsibility, the less of a distinction will exist between this test and the threefold test, which is the second test as outlined below.

9.4.3.2.3 Lord Mance said in the *Barclays Bank* case[75] that the concept of an assumption of responsibility may be particularly useful in two situations concerning special relationships that had been identified by Lord Browne-Wilkinson in *White v Jones*[76]

---

[65] [1964] AC 465.
[66] [1995] 2 AC 207.
[67] [1995] 2 AC 145.
[68] See Lord Goff in *Henderson v Merrett Syndicates Ltd*, [1995] 2 AC 145, at 184–194.
[69] [1990] 1 AC 83.
[70] [1995] 2 AC 207.
[71] [2001] 2 AC 619.
[72] [2006] UKHL 28, at [5].
[73] See Lord Griffiths in *Smith v Eric S Bush* [1990] 1 AC 831, at 862; Lord Oliver in *Caparo Industries plc v Dickman* [1990] 2 AC 605, at 637; and Lord Slynn in *Phelps v Hillingdon LBC* [2001] 2 AC 619, at 654. See also Lord Goff in *Henderson v Merrett Syndicates Ltd* [1995] 2 AC 145, at 181.
[74] Although such a disavowal should be considered as an attempt to exclude or restrict liability for negligence and so should be subject to the need to satisfy the requirement of reasonableness in s 11 of the Unfair Contract Terms Act 1977. See Lord Jauncey in *Smith v Eric S Bush* [1990] 1 AC 831, at 873.
[75] [2006] UKHL 28, at [92]–[93].
[76] [1995] 2 AC 207, at 273–274.

namely, where the defendant had a fiduciary duty towards the claimant and where the defendant had voluntarily assumed responsibility when it knew or ought to have known that the claimant would rely upon the defendant. In that situation, the test of voluntary assumption may effectively subsume all of the aspects of the threefold test.

9.4.3.2.4 The second test is the 'threefold' test, which was outlined by Lord Bridge of Harwich in *Caparo Industries plc v Dickman*.[77] The three elements of the test are (a) whether the loss to the claimant was a reasonably foreseeable consequence of what the defendant did or failed to do; (b) whether the relationship between the defendant and the claimant was one of sufficient proximity; and (c) whether in all the circumstances it was fair, just, and reasonable to impose a duty of care on the defendant towards the claimant.[78] Although Lord Bingham in the *Barclays Bank* case said[79] that this test may not provide a straightforward answer in a novel situation to whether a duty exists, Lord Hoffmann said in *Sutradhar v Natural Environment Research Council*[80] that the threefold test provides the 'standard framework' within which the question of whether a duty of care exists will usually be examined. He went on to say in that case (albeit in the context of a case which involved physical injury alleged to have arisen in consequence of a negligent statement) that the concept of proximity involved the defendant in having 'a measure of control over and responsibility for' the situation giving rise to the loss, in distinction to the loss merely being foreseeable but outside that element of control and responsibility.[81]

Lord Goff said in *Henderson v Merrett Syndicates Ltd*[82] that in a situation where there has been a voluntary assumption of responsibility by the defendant towards the claimant, it is unnecessary to show that it would be 'fair, just and reasonable' to impose liability. See also Lord Steyn in *Williams v Natural Life Health Foods Ltd*.[83] Lord Hoffmann made a similar point in the *Barclays Bank* case.[84]

9.4.3.2.5

In *Caparo Industries plc v Dickman*[85] it was held that the auditors of a public company did not owe a duty of care in the conduct of their audit towards potential

9.4.3.2.6

---

[77] [1990] 2 AC 605, at 617–618.

[78] Which, Lord Bingham noted with approval in the *Barclays Bank* case [2006] UKHL 28, at [4], Kirby J had labelled as 'policy' in *Perre v Apand Pty Ltd* [1999] HCA 26; (1999) 198 CLR 180, at para 259.

[79] At [6].

[80] [2006] UKHL 33, at [32].

[81] *Sutradhar v Natural Environment Research Council* [2006] UKHL 33; [2006] 4 All ER 490, at [38]. See also Lord Brown of Eaton-under-Heywood in the same case, at [48].

[82] [1995] 2 AC 145, at 180–181.

[83] [1998] 1 WLR 830, at 834.

[84] [2006] UKHL 28, at [35]–[36].

[85] [1990] 2 AC 605.

investors in the company, whether such investors were shareholders who were considering making a further investment on the strength of the audited accounts of the company, or members of the public at large who might invest on the strength of such accounts. The relationship was not sufficiently proximate between such investors and the auditors. The auditors performed their functions pursuant to a statutory duty, for the more limited purpose of enabling the body of the shareholders to exercise informed control of their company rather than enabling potential investors, whether they might already be shareholders or not, to decide if they wished to make an investment by acquiring shares in the company.[86] It was similarly held in *Al Saudi Banque v Clark Pixley*[87] that the auditors of a company did not owe a duty of care to banks which were contemplating the provision or continuance of facilities to a company. Even if it was foreseeable that a copy of the audited accounts might be provided to the banks which might rely on them in deciding to provide or continue facilities, there was not a sufficiently close or direct relationship to establish the necessary degree of proximity to give rise to a duty of care. That case was distinguished, however, in the later Scottish case of *Royal Bank of Scotland plc v Bannerman Johnstone Maclay*[88] where the auditors were aware that a copy of the audited accounts would be made available to a bank as a condition to the making available or continuance of a facility, the auditors had requested sight of the facility documentation to confirm that the facility would be available to the company, subject to the satisfaction of that condition, and so were specifically aware of the fact that the bank would place reliance upon the audited accounts in making the facility available to the company. It was not necessary also to prove, additionally, an intention on the part of the auditors that the accounts would be relied upon by the bank for that purpose.

9.4.3.2.7 The third test is the 'incremental' test and is based upon the observation of Brennan J in *Sutherland Shire Council v Heyman*,[89] which was approved by Lord Bridge in *Caparo Industries plc v Dickman*,[90] to the effect that the law should develop new categories of negligence incrementally and by analogy with established categories and not by extending the categories in a massive manner with only limited and ill-defined restraints. Lord Bingham said in the *Barclays Bank* case[91] that the incremental test is of little value in itself and will only be of use when combined with one of the other tests. The closer the case is to the facts of a

---

[86] For a different approach to the problem, where it was said that in certain specific circumstances, an auditor might be held to owe a duty of care to shareholders and potential investors, see *Man Nutzfahrzeuge AG v Freightliner Ltd* [2007] EWCA Civ 910.

[87] [1990] 1 Ch 313.

[88] [2003] SLT 181, [2003] PNLR 6 (Lord MacFadyen in the Outer House of the Court of Session).

[89] (1985) 157 CLR 424, at 481.

[90] [1990] 2 AC 605, at 618.

[91] [2006] UKHL 28, at [7].

previous case where a duty of care has been found to exist, the more willing the court will be, by use of the incremental test, to find a duty of care based on one of the other two tests. The converse will also be true.

9.4.3.2.8 Tripartite situations involving an agent It is important to note, however, that in *Williams v Natural Life Health Foods Ltd*[92] the House of Lords held that in a tripartite situation where an agent acted on behalf of a principal in dealing with the claimant, then whilst the principal may have a duty of care towards the claimant, the agent will not be liable unless it can be shown, on an objective basis, that the agent had undertaken its own personal duty of care by an assumption of responsibility towards the claimant and, in addition, that it was reasonable for the claimants to place reliance upon the agent.[93] That case involved an allegation that a director of a company, who was its moving force, should be made liable for the financial loss that the claimants had suffered through the negligence of the company. Whilst the case involved a company director, Lord Steyn, who gave the leading speech in the House of Lords, said that the same principle would apply generally in situations involving an agent acting on behalf of or representing a natural or corporate principal.[94] A similar approach has been taken in cases where claims have been brought against sub-contractors who supplied services or gave advice to the claimant pursuant to a contract with a head contractor who had contracted with the claimant for the provision of such services or advice.[95] In the *Williams* case the House declined to hold the director liable, as there was no objective basis on which it could be said that he had assumed responsibility towards the claimants; nor was there any evidence that the claimants had relied upon the director or that it would have been reasonable for them to have done so.[96] Lord Hoffmann made the additional point in the *Barclays Bank* case[97] that in determining if a relationship has arisen in cases of loss caused by the provision of information (and also, presumably, advice), it was critical to determine if it was the defendant, as opposed to someone else, who had assumed the responsibility

---

[92] [1998] 1 WLR 830.

[93] See Lord Steyn, at 835–836.

[94] [1998] 1 WLR 830, at 835. See also Lord Hoffmann in *Standard Chartered Bank v Pakistan National Shipping Corp (No 2)* [2003] 1 AC 959, at 969.

[95] For instance, in *Henderson v Merrett Syndicates Ltd* [1995] 2 AC145, *Riyad Bank v Ahli United Bank (UK) plc* [2006] EWCA Civ 780, [2006] 2 Lloyd's Rep 292, and *BP plc v AON Ltd* [2006] EWHC 424 (Comm), [2006] 1 All ER (Comm) 789, in each of which the sub-contractor was found to be liable to the claimant because it had assumed responsibility.

[96] See Lord Steyn's comment that even if there was reliance, it had to be reasonable to place reliance on the agent or employee, at [1998] 1 WLR 830, at 837. See also Lord Steyn's reference to the decision of La Forest J in Supreme Court of Canada in *Edgeworth Construction Ltd v ND Lea & Associates Ltd* [1993] 3 SCR 206, at 212.

[97] [2006] UKHL 28, at [35].

from which the alleged relationship arose,[98] to whom the obligation had been assumed,[99] and for what purpose the information had been provided.[100]

9.4.3.3 The scope of the duty

Assuming that it can be shown that the defendant owed a duty of care towards the claimant, it is then necessary to establish the scope or the extent of that duty, because a defendant cannot be made liable for loss which was suffered by the claimant if it arose from a matter that was outside the ambit of the defendant's duty of care. In relation to an arranger, this issue will be important in distinguishing between (a) whether the arranger owed the banks a general duty of care, essentially to use reasonable care so as to ensure that the transaction was suitable for them or, alternatively, so as to ensure that the banks were correctly appraised of all the risks associated with the transaction that could reasonably have been investigated by the arranger, and (b) a more limited duty to use reasonable care to ensure that the information that was supplied to them by the arranger was accurate and not misleading or that any specific task which it undertook was performed to the appropriate standard of care and skill. If the duty is limited to the second category then the arranger will not be liable for a loss that might have been suffered despite the accuracy of the information that it supplied to the banks or the satisfactory performance of the task it undertook.

9.4.3.3.1 The importance of the distinction is illustrated by the decision of the House of Lords in *Aneco Reinsurance Underwriting Ltd v Johnson & Higgins Ltd*[101] which was a case concerned with the liability of insurance brokers in placing excess of loss cover on behalf of the claimant reinsurance company. If the duty of the brokers had been limited to placing cover for the claimant, their liability would have been limited to some US$11m, which was the amount of cover that they were asked to place and which they failed to do. However, it was held that the duty of the brokers extended more widely to advising the reinsurance company on what course it should adopt in entering into its commitments, and they had failed to advise that reinsurance cover was generally unavailable in the market. Had the brokers properly advised the claimant, it would not have proceeded with the transaction. Accordingly, the claimant was awarded damages for a loss of US$35m, being the amount of loss that if suffered in consequence of entering into the transaction.

---

[98] Cf *Williams v Natural Life Health Foods Ltd* [1998] AC 830 and the discussion concerning liability in a case where there are 'chains' of contractual relationships in the Court of Appeal in *Riyad Bank v Ahli United Bank (UK) Ltd* [2006] EWCA Civ 780, [2006] 2 Lloyd's Rep 292.

[99] Cf *Smith v Eric S Bush* [1990] 1 AC 831; *Henderson v Merrett Syndicates Ltd* [1995] 2 AC 145; and *White v Jones* [1995] 2 AC 207.

[100] Cf *Caparo Industries plc v Dickman* [1990] 2 AC 605.

[101] [2001] UKHL 51, [2002] 1 Lloyd's Rep 157.

9.4.3.4 Reasonable care

The fact that a person or entity has a duty of care does not mean that it will be obliged to prevent any and all loss that may be suffered for matters that may fall within the scope of that duty. The duty is to exercise reasonable care, not to provide absolute protection, and loss may still be suffered even where reasonable care has been exercised.[102] The reasonableness test is normally to be judged by the standard of the ordinary man in the street or on the famous Clapham omnibus, that is, whether the ordinary man or woman, faced at the same time with the same circumstances, would have acted in the way in which the defendant acted. It has been held, however, that a professional person or entity which purports to have specialist skill and knowledge will have a higher duty than might be expected of the ordinary man in the street. In such a case, the test is the standard of the ordinary skilled person exercising and professing to have that special skill.[103] This does not require that the defendant should exercise the highest level of expertise and skill of a person in his position, just that of an ordinary competent person in that position or, to put it another way, consistently with the reasonable average.[104] However, it has also been held that acting in accordance with a common practice in a profession or trade is not necessarily sufficient to discharge the duty of care if that practice is inherently negligent, in that there was a foreseeable risk that could have been avoided.[105]

9.4.3.5 Reasonable reliance

The claimant must show that it reasonably relied upon the defendant in the exercise of the duty of care towards it.[106] There are two facets to this issue.[107] First, the claimant must show that it did in fact rely upon the defendant to exercise reasonable care towards the claimant. If, for instance, the claimant placed no store in the

---

[102] See, for instance, Mocatta J in *Stafford v Conti Commodity Services Ltd* [1981] 1 Lloyd's Rep 466, at 474–475 with respect to the provision of advice concerning investments in volatile markets. His Lordship pointed out that advice may have been given with the exercise of reasonable care concerning the making of such investments which, with the benefit of hindsight, may turn out to have been incorrect as the markets may not have performed in the manner that was expected when the advice was given.

[103] *Bolam v Friern Hospital Management Committee* [1957] 1 WLR 582. A similar approach has been taken in the case of professional trustees: Brightman J in *Bartlett v Barclays Bank Trust Co Ltd* [1980] Ch 515, at 534.

[104] *Eckersley v Binnie* [1988] 18 Con LR 1.

[105] *Edward Wong Finance Co Ltd v Johnson Stokes & Master* [1984] AC 296 (PC).

[106] See, for instance, the references to reliance made by Lord Morris and by Lord Hodson in *Hedley Byrne & Co Ltd v Heller & Partners Ltd* [1964] AC 465, at 503 and 514.

[107] See Lord Steyn in *Williams v Natural Life Health Foods Ltd* [1998] 1 WLR 830 and his discussion of two Canadian cases that are relevant to this issue: *London Drugs Ltd v Kuehne & Nagel International Ltd* (1992) 97 DLR (4th) 261 and *Edgeworth Construction Ltd v MD Lea & Associates Ltd* [1993] SCR 206.

competence of the defendant or on what it was told by the defendant, then it will not have relied upon the defendant. Secondly, even if it asserts that it did rely upon the defendant, a claimant can only recover if, in the circumstances, it was reasonable for it to place such reliance upon the defendant.

9.4.3.5.1   Situations may arise, however, in which it may be held that a defendant had a duty of care towards the claimant where, at the time the duty was breached, the claimant was unaware of the defendant and of the task undertaken by it. In such a situation, it will be difficult, if not impossible, to demonstrate reliance as a matter of fact by the claimant upon the defendant. This is demonstrated by the decision of the House of Lords in *White v Jones*[108] in which a solicitor, who was negligent through inexcusable delay in failing to prepare a will before the testator died, was held liable to intended beneficiaries who did not receive bequests that the testator had intended to confer upon them. In many such cases, an intended beneficiary may be unaware of the proposed bequest and, perhaps, even of the existence of the testator, so the claimant can hardly claim any deliberate or overt reliance on its part. Nonetheless, Lord Browne-Wilkinson was prepared to allow such claimants to recover.[109] In such cases, the reliance may be said to arise by implication from the claimant's ignorance of the existence of the relevant relationship and its total dependence upon the claimant in the absence of being in a position to make any judgment of its own.

9.4.3.6 Causation

The claimant must show that the loss which it has suffered was caused by the defendant's breach of duty. Lord Hoffmann explored this issue in *South Australia Asset Management Corp v York Montague Ltd*[110] (the *SAAMCO* case), in which he gave the graphic example of the mountaineer who goes to his doctor about his knee before embarking upon a mountaineering expedition. The doctor negligently pronounces his knee to be fit. Had the doctor correctly diagnosed the faulty knee, the claimant would not have gone on the expedition. He suffers injury whilst on the expedition but it has nothing to do with his knee. He has not suffered a loss which can be recovered against the doctor. The *SAAMCO* case involved a case against a valuer which negligently valued a property for a lender that was proposing to take a mortgage of the property, which it duly did in reliance upon the valuation. The borrower subsequently defaulted and the lender enforced the mortgage, but recovered substantially less upon enforcement than the amount of the valuation. However, this was partly due to a general fall in the market value

---

108   [1995] 2 AC 207.

109   See Lord Browne-Wilkinson, at 275–277. It is arguable, on the facts of the case, that there was reliance as a matter of fact, as the intended beneficiaries had been informed of the testator's intentions and that the solicitor had been instructed to prepare the will.

110   [1997] AC 191.

of property. The lender argued that it would not have entered into the transaction at all if it had received a correct valuation. The House of Lords held that the scope of the defendant's duty had been to report on the true value of the property and so the lender could only recover the amount of its loss that was attributable to the negligent valuation, that is, the loss attributable to the information provided by the valuer being incorrect (i.e. the difference between the proper market value and the reported value at the date of the valuation), not for the loss which would have been suffered in any event, even if the valuation had been correct (i.e. the loss attributable to the fall in the property market).

As can be seen from the *SAAMCO* case, the question of causation is inter-mixed with the issue as to the scope of the defendant's duty, as is also apparent from the *Aneco Reinsurance* case. In that case, the defendants were held liable for the whole loss suffered because of the breach of their duty to give the claimant general advice as to the transaction, rather than merely to carry out the more limited task of arranging specific excess of loss cover. Hence, in that case, the loss that the claimant was able to recover reflected the wider scope of the duty owed by the defendants to the claimant.

9.4.3.6.1

9.4.3.7 Foreseeable loss

The defendant can only be made liable for the loss that was reasonably foreseeable by the defendant at the time the breach of duty occurred. This requirement is mentioned by Lord Atkin in the passage of his speech in *Donoghue v Stevenson* quoted above. The relevance of a test based upon foreseeability was laid down by the Privy Council in *Overseas Tankship (UK) Ltd v Morts Docks Engineering Co Ltd*,[111] which is usually referred to as *Wagon Mound (No 1)*. The requirement as to foreseeability is referred to in most of the cases dealing with recovery for economic loss, such as in *Hedley Byrne* and in *Caparo*. In fact, it comprises the first part of the three criteria for establishing a duty of care as formulated in *Caparo*. Foreseeability is also closely linked with causation and with the scope of the defendant's duty of care, as the defendant can only be liable for the loss that was reasonably foreseeable and which arose from the breach of duty. Thus, if the scope of the defendant's duty was limited then loss will not be recoverable, even if it was foreseeable, where the loss falls outside the matters for which the defendant was responsible. Similarly, if the loss which occurred was not reasonably foreseeable by the defendant, it will not be recoverable, despite the fact, if such it be, that the loss might otherwise have arisen in consequence of the breach of duty.[112]

---

[111] [1961] AC 388.

[112] The Privy Council in *Wagon Mound (No 1)* said that the decision of the Court of Appeal in *Re Polemis and Furness, Withy & Co Ltd* [1921] 3 KB 560 had been wrongly decided. In *Re Polemis* it had been held that the defendant would be liable for all of the direct consequences of its negligence, no matter how remote.

9.4.4 The position of the arranger in an action in negligence

A useful starting point in examining the position of the arranger in a claim in negligence is to determine the scope of any possible duty of care that it might be alleged to owe to the banks. It will be recalled that this could be framed either as a general duty to take care of the interests of the banks or as a more limited duty with respect to particular information that it supplies to the banks or other tasks that it might undertake on their behalf. It is then relevant to consider if the banks placed reliance upon the arranger with respect to the exercise of that duty and, if so, if it was reasonable for them to do so. It must also be remembered that the duty is to take reasonable care; it is not an absolute obligation to prevent any and all loss from being suffered. It may be that, despite exercising reasonable care, a loss may still be suffered. For instance, the arranger may have made reasonable efforts to check the information that was provided, yet the information may turn out to be incorrect. Similarly, the arranger may have done its best to assess projections as to the future prospects of the borrower's business, which cannot guard against unforeseen hazards that may arise in the future. Further, the loss that was suffered may not (either in part or in whole) be attributable to any breach of the duty on the part of the arranger, or it may not have been foreseeable as at the time the alleged breach of the duty occurred.

9.4.4.1 A general duty of care

In examining the question whether an arranger owes a general duty of care to the banks and if the necessary elements of reliance can be made out, it is convenient to examine its role in two stages. The first stage covers the period up until the banks commit in principle to participate in the transaction, during which the arranger invites the banks to participate and is involved in supplying them with information relevant to their decision, in principle, to join the syndicate. The second stage relates to the period in which the arranger is involved in the preparation and negotiation of the formal facility documentation.

9.4.4.1.1 The first stage   It is submitted that in respect of its role in the first stage, an arranger of a syndicated loan, which is acting in pursuance of a mandate granted to it by the borrower, should usually be in the position as addressed by *Williams v Natural Life Health Foods Ltd*, in that it is acting on behalf of the borrower rather than purporting to accept its own independent responsibility towards the banks. On that basis, it will not have a duty of care towards the banks unless it can be shown, judged objectively on the basis of what it said and the actions that it took, that it had accepted responsibility towards the banks and the consequential duty of care to them. In the normal case, the arranger would clearly have been acting on behalf of the borrower, rather than on behalf of the banks. This should be fairly obvious, not least because it is usually stated in communications between the arranger and the banks that the arranger acts on behalf of the borrower, pursuant to a mandate granted by the borrower, and that any information that it distributes is sent to the banks at the borrower's request, was prepared from material supplied by the borrower, and had not been verified by the arranger.[113] In those circumstances, it is submitted that a general duty of care should not arise and, even if it did, it is unlikely that the banks would have placed reliance upon the arranger, nor would it have been reasonable for them to do so. It is also submitted that this view is in line with accepted practice in the financial markets that operate in London.

9.4.4.1.2 The second stage   The position as to the second stage may appear to be less clear but, in the end, it is unlikely that the arranger will be found liable to the banks in negligence. It must, however, be conceded that it is very unlikely that the arranger could be said, in any practical sense, to be acting on behalf of the borrower once it has reached the stage of preparing and negotiating the facility documentation. Accordingly, an argument in favour of the arranger based upon *Williams v Natural Life Health Foods Ltd* is unlikely to succeed. By this stage, the arranger will have appointed lawyers to advise it in the preparation of the documentation and the borrower will have appointed its own lawyers to give it advice (the practice in the London markets is that the facility agreement itself is based on standard forms of precedent, amended to take account of factors that are pertinent to the relevant transaction). There will often be fairly extensive, and sometimes vigorous, negotiation between the two sides (particularly of the commercial matters and security dealt with in the documentation) before a mutually acceptable draft of the documentation is settled between them. During that negotiation, the stance that the arranger usually takes is to put forward the likely views of the banks and what they would find acceptable, because it knows that the banks will not proceed on the basis of unacceptable documentation. These factors indicate that the arranger is no longer acting as the agent and the mouthpiece of the borrower, but has moved away from that role and towards a position that reflects its perception of the interests of the banks, including possibly its own position as a potential syndicate member.[114] However, just because it is not acting as the agent of the borrower does not lead automatically to the conclusion that the arranger has accepted a duty of care towards the banks, but it does mean that the argument is not as clear-cut as it would have been in considering its role in the first stage. Looked at objectively, the first two of the three criteria for a duty of care as outlined in *Caparo* appear to be present in examining the arranger's role in the second stage, namely, foreseeability of possible harm and proximity, as quite clearly the

---

[113] See, for instance, the statements that accompanied the syndicate information memorandum in *IFE Fund SA v Goldman Sachs International* [2007] EWCA Civ 8. It was accepted that this was fairly typical of the position in arranging syndicated facilities.

[114] See, for instance, Lehane, 'The role of managing and agent banks: duties, liabilities, disclaimer clauses' [1982] International Law Review 235.

arranger must have the banks in its contemplation when it is involved in the task of preparing and negotiating the documentation.

9.4.4.1.3 The question remains whether, in terms of the third of the criteria in *Caparo*, it would be fair, just, and reasonable to impose a duty of care upon the arranger acting in the second stage and, linked to that question, are the issues as to the scope of any duty that the arranger might owe to the banks, and if it was reasonable for the banks to place reliance upon the arranger in the role it undertook. It is convenient to take those various matters together, as they demonstrate collectively why it is unlikely that the arranger would be found liable in negligence. Almost invariably, the arranger distributes the documentation to the banks in the form as negotiated with the borrower. The arranger asks the banks for their comments on the documentation. The banks will thus have been afforded the opportunity to review the documentation for themselves and to raise any queries or doubts that they may have following upon their own review. In relation to any commercial matters arising in the transaction, they will have been alerted to them by the term sheet and the other information distributed to the banks and they should have been able to appreciate their significance when reading the documentation. In terms of the contents and legal enforceability of the documentation, the arranger will argue that the documentation (particularly the facility agreement itself) was largely based upon precedents commonly accepted in the London markets and that it instructed lawyers to prepare the documentation. So long as it instructed lawyers who were generally seen as being competent to fulfil their role in such transactions, the arranger had done all that reasonably could be expected of it within the scope of any duty it might have undertaken. In so far as the lawyers failed to perform their tasks, the banks may have a claim against them. Otherwise, the banks made their own decisions in deciding if they wished to proceed. Taking all these matters together, it can be seen that such duty as the arranger might have would be narrow in its scope and, in any event, it would be difficult for the banks to establish that it was reasonable for them to place reliance upon the arranger. Once again, it is submitted that this view is consistent with accepted practice in the financial markets that operate in London.

9.4.4.2 A limited duty of care

Turning now to a claim based upon a more limited duty of care, the argument that might be raised is that even though the arranger may not have undertaken a general duty of care towards the banks, nonetheless in a more limited way the arranger had a duty of care, to one or more of the banks, with respect to some specific task that it undertook or concerning some particular information that it supplied. In essence, the argument would be that the arranger accepted or assumed responsibility in that more limited manner. Such an argument is illustrated by two cases involving an arranger in which it was held that, in the circumstances, the arranger had assumed responsibility, in one case for particular information it provided to a bank and, in the other, for action that it took to protect the banks' interests.

In the Australian case of *NatWest Australia Bank Ltd v Tricontinental Corp Ltd*[115] **9.4.4.2.1** it was held that the arranger of a syndicated loan, in responding to a specific query raised by a bank that was to join the syndicate, had assumed a duty of care in the response that it gave to that bank, to ensure the accuracy of its reply. Prior to the query being made, the arranger had distributed an information memorandum which contained accounting and financial information concerning the borrower. The query that was raised by the bank concerned whether there were any contingent liabilities of the borrower, as there was no reference to any such liabilities in the information memorandum. The arranger responded that there were no such liabilities in existence, despite the fact that the arranger itself enjoyed the benefit of guarantees given by the borrower for the liabilities of another company connected to the borrower. In those circumstances, the court held that in giving its response to the bank, the arranger had assumed a duty of care towards the enquirer. It is interesting to note that the court said that, in the absence of such a specific request, a different conclusion might have been reached with respect to the possibility of a duty of care in relation to the contents of the information memorandum. Some care needs to be taken in relation to the outcome of the case, as the facts are rather extraordinary and are unlikely to arise very often, given that the arranger actually had information in its own possession which contradicted the response that it gave, and its response had the effect of denying something which already existed in its own favour. It would appear that the arranger purported to answer the specific query entirely of its own volition, without making any effort to check the accuracy of its response, without any apparent reference to the borrower for a response, and by giving the impression that it was providing the answer on its own account. In addition, it was held that the disclaimer of responsibility by the arranger contained in the information memorandum only related to the contents of that document, and it appears that there was no other attempt by the arranger to convey to the banks any limit on the role it had undertaken.

In the English case of *Sumitomo Bank Ltd v Banque Bruxelles Lambert SA*[116] the **9.4.4.2.2** arranger put in place a mortgage indemnity insurance policy for the benefit of the syndicate of banks, under which the insurer was meant to cover a certain amount of the deficiency that might arise after enforcement of security that was to be taken on behalf of the banks. When a claim was made under the policy, the insurer

---

[115] McDonald J in the Supreme Ct of Victoria, 26/7/1993. Unreported on this issue but noted and reported on a different point at (1993) ATPR (Digest) 46–109. The relevant passages of the judgment on the matter under discussion are contained at pp 109–117 of the transcript.
[116] [1997] 1 Lloyd's Rep 487.

alleged that the policy had been avoided for the non-disclosure of a material fact by the arranger when the policy was incepted. The claim under the policy had to be compromised. The banks successfully claimed against the arranger for the loss they had suffered, in failing to receive full cover under the policy. Langley J held that the arranger had accepted or assumed a responsibility towards the syndicate with respect to the policy, when it had taken action in their interests in putting the policy in place for their benefit.

9.4.5 A claim in the tort of deceit

Given the seriousness of such a claim it is to be hoped that the circumstances where it may be alleged against an arranger will be very rare. For present purposes, a claim in deceit relates to a dishonestly untruthful statement that is made, usually in the context of the negotiations leading to a contract, so as induce the recipient of the statement to enter into the contract, provided that the recipient does rely upon it in deciding to enter into the contract.

9.4.5.1 The grounds for dishonesty as a constituent of the claim were set out by Lord Herschell in *Derry v Peek*[117] and can be advanced on any of three bases: first, that the maker of the false statement told a deliberate lie; secondly, that the maker of the false statement had no belief in the truth of the statement;[118] and thirdly that the maker of the false statement was reckless, that is, careless as to its truth or falsity.[119] The fact that the maker of the statement felt that he had some commercial justification in making the statement or that it was unlikely that any harm would result, is no defence.[120] However, dishonesty lies at the heart of the tort of deceit and mere carelessness is not sufficient in itself to make out the claim.[121] Dishonesty in the tort of deceit is judged subjectively, whereas in the criminal law

---

[117] (1889) 14 App Cas 337.

[118] It is difficult to know at what point it could be said that the maker of the statement might meet this test; for instance, whether a mere feeling of unease would be sufficient to say that there was a lack of belief, particularly in the case where the claim involved a statement made by a relatively junior person in an organisation who might be judged differently, in terms of knowledge and intention, from a more senior person under whose instructions he was acting: see the discussion on this point by Tugendhat J in *GE Commercial Finance Ltd v Gee* [2005] EWHC 2056 (QB); [2006] 1 Lloyd's Rep 337, at [100]–[111]. This second ground was not mentioned by the Court of Appeal when it formulated a description of the tort in *Society of Lloyd's v Jaffray* [2002] EWCA Civ 1101, at [49] and [62], nor was it mentioned by Potter LJ in *Twinsectra v Yardley* [1999] EWCA Civ 1290; [1999] 1 Lloyd's Rep Bank 438, at [38].

[119] Bowen LJ in *Angus v Clifford* [1891] 2 Ch 449, at 471 said that carelessness in this context did not mean simply failing to take care. It meant 'indifference to the truth, the moral obliquity which consists in a wilful disregard of the importance of the truth'.

[120] Evans LJ in *Standard Chartered Bank v Pakistan National Shipping Corp* [2000] 1 Lloyd's Rep 218, at [2] and [3].

[121] See Lord Hershell in *Derry v Peek* (1889) 14 App Cas 337, at 369 and 373, and Jacob J in *Thomas Witter Ltd v TBP Industries Ltd* [1996] 2 All ER 573, at 587.

there is a combined objective and subjective test.[122] In contrast to the position for a claim in negligence,[123] in *Standard Chartered Bank v Pakistan National Shipping Corp (No 2)*[124] the House of Lords held that an agent who makes a fraudulent or deceitful statement cannot hide behind his agency in a claim in deceit against him. He can be sued directly, even if he made the statement within the apparent course of his employment or retainer by the principal.

9.4.5.2
There is a heavy burden on the claimant in alleging a claim in deceit, as the claimant must prove a lack of honest belief on the part of the defendant, although the standard of proof is the same as in other civil claims.[125] In addition, under the relevant code of conduct, counsel may not plead fraud unless he has clear instructions to do so and has before him reasonably credible material to establish a prima facie case.[126] Furthermore, section 6 of the Statute of Frauds Amendment Act 1828 effectively provides that in a claim in fraudulent misrepresentation[127] relating to a representation as to the 'character, conduct, credit, ability, trade or dealings' of another person, which is intended to lead to the granting to that person (or his obtaining) credit, money, or goods, the representation must have been in writing signed by the maker of the statement.

9.4.5.3
The remedies for deceit are recission of the contract which was induced by the misrepresentation and a claim for tortious damages.[128] However, the right to rescind can be lost, for instance because of delay, or because it is not possible to restore the parties to the position they were in before the contract, and/or because of the adverse effect of a recission upon third parties.[129] Damages are at large and will be awarded for the whole loss suffered by the claimant in consequence of entering into the contract, whether the loss was foreseeable or unforeseeable.[130] A claimant has even been awarded damages to reflect the lesser profit it made after

---

122 *R v Ghosh* [1982] QB 1053. See also *Society of Lloyd's v Jaffray* [2002] EWCA Civ 1101, at [66].

123 As to which see *Williams v Natural Life Health Foods Ltd* [1998] 1 WLR 830.

124 [2002] UKHL 43, [2003] 1 AC 959.

125 *Hornal v Neuberger Products Ltd* [1957] 1 QB 247.

126 Para 704(c) of the *Code of Conduct* of the Bar in England and Wales. See further *Medcalf v Mardell* [2002] UKHL 27, [2003] AC 120.

127 In *Banbury v Bank of Montreal* [1918] AC 626 it was held that the section was restricted to claims in fraudulent misrepresentation only. See, however, the Court of Appeal in *UBAF Ltd v European American Banking Corp* [1984] QB 713, where it was said that the section extended to claims for innocent misrepresentation under s 2(1) of the Misrepresentation Act 1967, because of the reference in s 2(1) to the circumstances in which a claim could be brought, had it been a claim for fraudulent misrepresentation.

128 The claimant can recover damages in tort as well as rescind the contract: *Newbiggin v Adam* (1886) 34 ChD 582, at 592. Although the recission for deceit is *ab initio* (*Johnson v Agnew* [1980] AC 367), so that a claim for damages cannot be brought under the contract, the claim for damages is in tort which is independent of the contract.

129 See Jacob J in *Thomas Witter Ltd v TBP Industries Ltd* [1996] 2 All ER 573, at 588.

130 *Smith New Court Securities Ltd v Scrimgeour Vickers (Asset Management) Ltd* [1997] AC 254.

entering into a contract, as compared with the profit it would have made if the representation had been true.[131]

9.4.6 A claim under section 2(1) of the Misrepresentation Act 1967

Section 2(1) of the Misrepresentation Act 1967 provides as follows:

> Where a person has entered into a contract after a misrepresentation has been made to him by another party thereto and as a result thereof he has suffered loss, then, if the person making the misrepresentation would be liable to damages in respect thereof had the misrepresentation been made fraudulently, that person shall be so liable notwithstanding that the misrepresentation was not made fraudulently, unless he proves that he had reasonable ground to believe and did believe up to the time the contract was made that the facts represented were true.

9.4.6.1 The section was introduced to overcome the problem that at common law it was not possible to claim damages for an innocent misrepresentation.[132] Unless the representation had become a term of the contract, in which case a claim for damages would lie for breach,[133] the only remedy that was available at common law was recission,[134] and the right to rescind could be easily lost, for instance, due to delay,[135] acquiescence, or affirmation,[136] that it was not possible to restore the parties to their pre-contractual position[137] or where the representation had been incorporated into and become a term of the contract or the contract had been performed.[138] It is still necessary, however, to show that the representation was as to a matter of fact, as opposed to a statement of opinion, although the courts have been prepared in some instances to imply into a statement of opinion,

---

[131] *Clef Aquitaine SARL v Laporte Materials (Barrow) Ltd* [2001] QB 488.

[132] *Heilbut, Symonds & Co v Buckleton* [1913] AC 30.

[133] *Dick Bentley Productions Ltd v Harold Smith (Motors) Ltd* [1965] 1 WLR 623.

[134] It is very unlikely that recission would be appropriate in any situation now under consideration as the claim of the banks is based upon the fact that they have already lent their money and they are unable to recover it from the borrower. They are looking for a claim in damages against the arranger to recover the loss they have suffered having performed their part of the contract with the borrower.

[135] *Leaf v International Galleries* [1950] 2 KB 86. In that case, the delay prevented recission even though the representee only discovered the true position shortly before it commenced proceedings.

[136] See *Peyman v Lanjani* [1985] Ch 457.

[137] At least in a substantial sense, if not precisely: see Lord Blackburn in *Erlanger v New Sombrero Phosphate Co* (1878) 3 App Cas 1218, at 1278–1279. It has also been held that it is not possible to have a partial recission: see the extensive review conducted by Colman J in *De Molestina v Ponton* [2002] 1 All ER (Comm) 587, at [6.1]–[6.7], including his discussion, at [6.5]–[6.6], of the contrary decision of the High Court of Australia in *Vadasz v Pioneer Concrete (SA) Pty Ltd* (1995) 184 CLR 102 and the reference made to that case by the Privy Council in *Far Eastern Shipping Co Public Ltd v Scales Trading Ltd* [2001] 1 All ER (Comm) 319.

[138] S 1 of the Misrepresentation Act 1967 now provides for a right of recission where the representation has become a term of the contract or the contract has been performed.

for instance, as to a future intention, another statement that the opinion was genuinely held.[139]

It is fundamental to a claim for misrepresentation to show that a representation **9.4.6.2** was made by the defendant, which was incorrect and upon which the claimant relied in deciding if it wished to enter into the contract. If no such representation was made, there can be no success in claiming for misrepresentation. This basic proposition is demonstrated by the decision of the Court of Appeal in *IPE Fund SA v Goldman Sachs International*,[140] which concerned the arrangement of a syndicated facility.[141] In the information memorandum that was distributed by the arranger to the potential syndicate members, the arranger specifically stated that it made no representations concerning the truth or accuracy of the information contained in the information memorandum and disclaimed any responsibility to check such information or to correct it. It was held that this had the effect that what was stated in the information memorandum could not be treated or relied upon by the banks as being represented to them by the arranger.[142]

A claim under section 2(1) can only be brought by a claimant which became a **9.4.6.3** party to the contract in circumstances where the misrepresentation was made to it by another person who also became a party to the contract. If the representor never became a party to the contract, the section will be unavailable unless it can be argued that the claimant and the defendant were parties to a collateral contract upon the strength of which the claimant entered into the principal contract, in which case there may be a claim in relation to the collateral contract.[143] Otherwise, the claimant will be thrown back on its remedies, such as they may be, in some other area, such as for a negligent misstatement. The claimant will also be in difficulties if the representation was made by a person that was acting as an agent for another person, provided the agent was acting within the scope of its authority on behalf of the principal. In such case, the statement should be treated as having been made by the principal, and the claimant will have to pursue its remedies

---

139 *Edgington v Fitzmaurice* [(1885) 29 ChD 459.

140 [2007] EWCA Civ 811.

141 In fact, the syndication was of debt instruments, but that fact is not material to the point under discussion.

142 The arranger did, however, concede that it had impliedly represented that it was acting in good faith in distributing the information memorandum to the potential syndicate members. The court said that it followed from such a representation that the arranger would be obliged to correct any information which had been distributed which it actually discovered (prior to syndication taking place) to be incorrect or misleading. However, it had no duty to inform the banks if it merely became aware of the possibility that the information might be misleading or incorrect, as opposed to knowing that it was actually incorrect or misleading.

143 See *Shanklin Pier Ltd v Detel Products Ltd* [1951] 2 KB 854.

against the principal,[144] rather than the agent,[145] which will be of little comfort if the principal is not worth pursuing. This is obviously important in relation to the role of the arranger acting on behalf of the borrower in distributing information to the banks.

9.4.6.4 The claimant must show that it was induced by the representation to enter into the contract and that it was incorrect. Those aspects were explored by Rix J in *Avon Insurance PLC v Swire Fraser Ltd*.[146] The inducement must have played a 'real and substantial' part of the decision of the claimant to enter into the contract, as opposed to something that was merely observed, considered, supported, or encouraged the decision. However, it need not be the sole or decisive inducement, so long as it materially contributed to the decision. A statement will be correct for these purposes if it is substantially correct, even though it may not be entirely correct.

9.4.6.5 The defendant may argue that, although it had misrepresented the position, the misrepresentation had been corrected before the contract had been entered into by the parties. In such cases it is not enough for the representor to show that the recipient of the misrepresentation could have discovered the truth if it had made its own enquiries. The representor must show that the representee did discover the truth, either in consequence of a correction actually made by the representor which it had brought to the attention of the representee before contracting, or through enquiries made by the representee itself which revealed the true state of affairs before that date.[147]

9.4.6.6 It has also been said that a claim under section 2(1), in so far as it relates to a representation as to the 'character, conduct, credit, ability, trade or dealings' of a person must be in writing, as would be required for a claim in deceit, by virtue of section 6 of the Statute of Frauds Amendment Act 1828.[148]

9.4.6.7 If the claimant is able to make out its case that the representation was incorrect and that it induced the claimant to enter into the contract, the burden then shifts under section 2(1) to the defendant which, if it is to escape liability, has to prove, first, that when it made the statement it had reasonable grounds to believe in the truth of the statement, and, secondly, that it continued in that belief up to the time the contract was entered into. It is important to note that the defendant's

---

[144] *Gosling v Anderson* (1972) 223 EG 1743.

[145] *The Skopas* [1983] 1 WLR 857.

[146] [2000] 1 All ER (Comm) 573, at [14]–[18].

[147] *Redgrave v Hurd* (1881) 20 ChD 1; *Assicurazioni Generali v Arab Insurance Group* [2002] EWCA Civ 1642; [2003] 1 All ER (Comm) 140; *Flack v Pattinson* [2002] EWCA Civ 1762; *Peekay Intermark Ltd v Australia & New Zealand Banking Group Ltd* [2006] EWCA Civ 386, [2006] 2 Lloyd's Rep 511.

[148] *UBAF Ltd v European American Banking Corp* [1984] QB 713.

belief must be based on reasonable grounds, which imports an element of objectivity and that a claim may lie under the section even though the representor may not have owed a duty of care to the representee with respect to the statement that was made,[149] although, practically speaking, the two may often coincide.

It was held by the Court of Appeal in *Royscott Trust Ltd v Rogerson*[150] that the meas- **9.4.6.8** ure of damages for a claim under section 2(1) should be on the same basis as for a claim in the tort of deceit, namely, that the claimant should be put back in the financial position it would have been if the contract had not been made.[151] If this is correct, the claimant will usually be better off claiming damages under section 2(1) than in undertaking the more onerous burden of suing in either the tort of deceit or in the tort of negligence, which causes one to wonder if the *Royscott Trust* case was correctly decided.

9.4.7 A claim under section 2(2) of the Misrepresentation Act 1967

Sections 2(2) and 2(3) of the Misrepresentation Act 1967 provide as follows:

> (2) Where a person has entered into a contract after a misrepresentation has been made to him otherwise than fraudulently, and he would be entitled, by reason of the misrepresentation, to rescind the contract, then, if it is claimed, in any proceedings arising out of the contract, that the contract ought to be or has been rescinded, the court or arbitrator may declare the contract subsisting and award damages in lieu of recision, if of opinion that it would be equitable to do so, having regard to the nature of the misrepresentation and the loss that would be caused by it if the contract were upheld, as well as to the loss that recision would cause to the other party.
>
> (3) Damages may be awarded against a person under subsection (2) of this section whether or not he is liable to damages under subsection (1) thereof, but where he is so liable any award under the said subsection (2) shall be taken into account in assessing his liability under the said subsection (1).

As with section 2(1) of the Act, section 2(2) is concerned with a misrepresentation **9.4.7.1** made by one person to another to induce that other to enter into the contract to which they both became parties. It will be of no avail if the necessary elements of representation, reliance, and falsity are not present, as previously discussed. Nor will the section be available as against an agent which made the misrepresentation within the scope of its agency. Section 2(2) gives the relevant tribunal a discretion to award damages but it does not give the representee a right to damages. The section also permits the representor to request the award of damages, within

---

[149] *Howard Marine and Dredging Co Ltd v A Ogden & Sons (Excavations) Ltd* [1978] QB 574.

[150] [1991] 2 QB 297.

[151] As to the measure of damages in a claim in deceit, see the decision of the House of Lords in *Smith New Court Securities Ltd v Citibank NA* [1997] AC 254. It should be noted that both Lord Browne-Wilkinson, at 267, and Lord Steyn, at 283, in the *Smith New Court* case declined to say if the *Royscott* case was correct on the issue of the measure of damages under s 2(1) of the Act.

the discretion of the tribunal, in lieu of recision of the contract. It is unclear if the section only applies if the right to rescind continues to exist at the time of the proceedings, or if it is merely necessary to show that at some time there was a right to rescind even if it is no longer in existence.[152] There is no defence of 'innocence' under section 2(2), so a claim under section 2(2) would be valuable to a representee which could not achieve an award of damages under section 2(1) in a case where the defence would apply under section 2(1). The tribunal has a discretion in making an award of damages under section 2(2), although it should take into account the relative difference between the loss that would be suffered to the representee if the contract were upheld as compared with the loss to the representor if the contract were rescinded.[153] It is also clear from section 2(3) that it is possible for the court to entertain claims under both section 2(1) and 2(2), although, by virtue of section 2(3), an allowance must be made in an award of damages under section 2(2) for any damages awarded under section 2(1). It has been suggested that the measure of damages under section 2(2) should normally be less than under section 2(1).[154]

9.4.8 A claim for breach of fiduciary duty[155]

The final basis of claim that may be alleged against the arranger is that it was in the position of a fiduciary towards the banks and that it breached its equitable fiduciary duties towards them in failing to act in their best interests, which would be a fairly broad basis of claim. It is unlikely that such a claim would succeed as it is difficult to envisage how an arranger could be in such a position. Millett LJ defined a fiduciary as: 'Someone who has undertaken to act for or on behalf of another in a particular matter in circumstances which give rise to a relationship of trust and confidence. The distinguishing obligation of a fiduciary is the obligation of loyalty.'[156] His Lordship later expanded upon this when he said that: 'Confidence is the very essence of the relationship. Unless a relationship is one of trust and confidence, it is not fiduciary. There are many commercial situations in which one man undertakes to act for the benefit of another without any trust or confidence being reposed in him. In such a case there is no fiduciary relationship.'[157]

---

[152] Mustill J in *Atlantic Lines & Navigation Co Inc v Hallam Ltd; The Lucy* [1983] 1 Lloyd's Rep 188, HHJ Humphrey Lloyd QC in *Floods of Queensferry Ltd v Shand Construction Ltd* [2000] BLR 81, and HHJ Jack QC in *Zanzibar v British Aerospace (Lancaster House) Ltd* [2000] 1 WLR 2333 thought that the right to rescind had to continue in existence, whereas Jacob J in *Thomas Witter Ltd v TBP Industries Ltd* [1996] 2 All ER 573, at 590–591, was of the view that it did not matter if the right to rescind had been lost.

[153] See Jacob J in the *Thomas Witter* case, at 591.

[154] Ibid.

[155] See further the discussion at para 9.6.2.1 below.

[156] *Bristol & West Building Society v Mothew* [1998] Ch 1, at 18.

[157] *R v Chester and North Wales Legal Aid Area Office, ex p Floods of Queensferry Ltd* [1998] 1 WLR 1496, at 1500.

From those passages it can be seen that there must be an obligation of loyalty owed **9.4.8.1** by the fiduciary to its beneficiaries and that the latter must invest the fiduciary with their trust and confidence. In a commercial setting a mere obligation, if undertaken at all, by one person to act for the benefit of another or others will not be sufficient. As can be seen from the earlier discussion relating to a possible claim against an arranger in negligence, the elements of trust and confidence will be lacking. For most of what it does, the arranger is acting as the agent of the borrower, which can hardly be said to give rise to any obligation of loyalty towards the banks. Even in the documentation stage of the arranger's functions, it is very unlikely that the arranger could be said to owe the banks a duty of care, and, if it does, it is a very limited duty and there will still be a substantial question as to whether the banks can reasonably place reliance upon the arranger. Taking those matters into account, it is submitted that an arranger should not be considered as being in the even more onerous position of a fiduciary towards the banks.

It is submitted that the decision of the Court of Appeal in *UBAF Ltd v European* **9.4.8.2** *American Banking Corp*[158] does not alter the view expressed above. That case concerned interlocutory proceedings for leave to serve out of the jurisdiction, in a claim brought against an entity which had been the arranger of two syndicated loans and which became the agent bank (and the security trustee) for the syndicates of the banks. The proceedings had been brought by a bank in the syndicates for damages for fraudulent misrepresentation, for misrepresentation within section 2(1) of the Misrepresentation Act 1967, and for negligent misrepresentation. In considering the case, it is important to bear in mind that the defendant, which had acted as the arranger of the facilities, upon signature of the facility documentation was appointed by the banks as their facility and security agent, under which it took and then held security on behalf of the syndicates of banks. It was alleged that the defendant, when it had been the arranger, had misrepresented certain facts concerning the security, by concealment, so as to induce the claimant bank to enter into the facilities. In response, it was said by the defendant that the claim had been brought out of time so that it was barred by the Limitation Act 1980. It was held by the court that the limitation period had not begun to run until the claimant bank had discovered the concealment because the defendant, as the facility agent and trustee of the security on behalf of the banks, had been under a continuing fiduciary duty towards the claimant bank to divulge the relevant information during the lifetime of the facilities.

That finding, however, related to the defendant's alleged fiduciary position as the **9.4.8.3** facility and security agent, which position it undertook once the facility documentation had been signed and under which it held security on behalf of the syndicates. If the defendant had never become the facility agent and security trustee,

---

[158] [1984] QB 713.

and its role had been confined to being merely the arranger of the facilities, then it would not have been in that position. Furthermore, even if it had been held that the arranger, as such, was in a fiduciary position in that case towards the banks that it invited to become members of the syndicates, that would not mean that the case should be taken as a general authority for the proposition that all arrangers of syndicated facilities should be considered to be in a fiduciary position towards the banks that they invite to become members of a syndicate. The facts of the case were unusual, in that the syndicated facility effected a re-financing of bilateral lending that the arranger had previously extended in its personal capacity to the borrowers. The arranger directly benefited from the re-financing arrangements, there was an allegation of fraud, and the arranger appears to have played the role of a principal rather than merely acting as the mouthpiece of the borrowers in arranging the new facilities.

9.4.9 Contributory negligence

A defence of contributory negligence, when it is available, may result in an award of damages against a defendant being reduced to take account of the claimant's own share of responsibility for the loss that arose. The defence would be raised under section 1(1) of the Law Reform (Contributory Negligence) Act 1945 which, so far as material, provides as follows:

> Where any person suffers damage as the result partly of his own fault and partly of the fault of any other person or persons, a claim in respect of that damage shall not be defeated by reason of the fault of the person suffering the damage, but the damages recoverable in respect thereof shall be reduced to such extent as the court thinks just and equitable having regard to the claimant's share in the responsibility for the damage.

Section 4 of the Act provides that:

> 'Fault' means negligence, breach of statutory duty or other act or omission which gives rise to a liability in tort or would, apart from this Act, give rise to the defence of contributory negligence.

9.4.9.1 Section 1(1) applies to claims in tort, such as in negligence. It has been held, however, that it will not apply to a fraud claim or a claim for deceit.[159] The defence will apply to claims in contract where there would be a concurrent claim in tort,[160] and to claims under section 2(1) of the Misrepresentation Act 1967 where there is a concurrent claim in tort.[161] It is not clear if a defence of contributory negligence

---

[159] *Standard Chartered Bank v Pakistan National Shipping Corp (No 2)* [2003] 1 AC 959. See also *Alliance & Leicester Building Soc v Edgestop Ltd* [1993] 1 WLR 1462.

[160] *Forsikringsaktieselskapet Vesta v Butcher* [1989] AC 852 and *UCB Bank plc v Hepherd Winstanley & Pugh* [1999] Lloyd's Rep PN 963, although a contrary view was taken in Australia in relation to similar legislation: *Astley v Austrust Ltd* [1999] Lloyd's Rep PN 758.

[161] *Gran Gelato Ltd v Richcliff (Group) Ltd* [1992] Ch 560. Presumably the same would apply to the award of damages under s 2(2) of the Misrepresentation Act 1967.

can be raised to a claim under section 2(1) of the Misrepresentation Act 1967 if there is not a concurrent claim available for a negligent misrepresentation.

Where the defence is available, the court has a wide discretion to determine how much of a reduction should be made to the award of damages. The reduction should be to such an extent as the court believes to be 'just and equitable' in light of the responsibility of the claimant for the damage or loss that was suffered. In *Platform Home Loans Ltd v Oyston Shipways Ltd*[162] the House of Lords held that where the scope of a claim in negligence was for the more limited duty to use reasonable care so as to ensure that the information that was supplied was accurate and not misleading, rather than the more general duty to give advice, the reduction in damages should be calculated on the loss actually suffered (as would be the case if the scope of the duty was to advise), rather than on the lesser amount of damages for the negligent advice. Otherwise the claimant would suffer a double deduction from the loss it had suffered.

9.4.9.2

9.5 Protecting the Arranger

It is now appropriate to consider the protective steps that an arranger might consider taking, just in case there remains any risk that it may be held to have responsibilities towards the syndicate of banks for the role it undertakes as the arranger. Having done that, it will then be relevant to consider how effective such steps will be as a matter of law, particularly in light of legislative restrictions upon exclusions or limitations of certain types of liability.

9.5.1

9.5.2 The means of protection

There are two levels of protection that an arranger will seek.

The first will be conveyed in written communications that it has with the banks,[163] in which it will explain that it is acting at the request of the borrower in pursuance of a mandate granted to it by the borrower. The arranger will go on to explain that any information that it supplies has been prepared at the borrower's request and is based on information supplied by the borrower. There is likely to be a statement that the arranger has not checked or verified any information supplied by the borrower, nor does it undertake to do so.[164] There is also likely to be an express

9.5.2.1

---

[162] [2000] 2 AC 190.

[163] A good example of this will be found in *IPE Fund SA v Goldman Sachs International* [2007] EWCA Civ 811.

[164] In *NatWest Australia Bank Ltd v Tricontinental Corp Ltd* (McDonald J in the Supreme Ct of Victoria, 26/7/1993. Unreported on this issue but noted and reported on a different point at (1993) ATPR (Digest) 46–109. The relevant passage of the judgment on the matter under discussion is at

statement that the arranger does not purport to act on behalf of the banks or represent their interests, and a disclaimer of any responsibility on the part of the arranger towards the banks.[165] This first level of intended protection will be extra-contractual,[166] but, it is submitted, it will fall within the description of a 'notice' for the purposes of the Unfair Contract Terms Act 1977.[167]

9.5.2.2 The second level of protection will be contained in the syndicated facility agreement,[168] to which the arranger will be made a party for the purpose of gaining the protection expressed to be given in its favour.[169] The wording of the relevant provisions in that document is likely to contain an explicit agreement or acknowledgement on the part of the banks that the arranger owed no fiduciary or other types of duties or responsibilities towards them, as well as an exclusion of any liability that might otherwise attach to the arranger. There is also likely to be a clause, which is usually called a 'non-reliance clause', by which the banks confirm that, in deciding to enter into the agreement, they made their own enquiries and investigations, both as to factual matters and as to the meaning, scope, and contents of the facility documentation, that they did not receive, nor rely upon, any representations made by the arranger, and that they did not otherwise rely upon the arranger in making their decision to proceed with the transaction.

---

p 114 of the transcript) it was said that the disclaimer of responsibility in the information memorandum that the arranger distributed to the banks did not extend to cover the subsequent statement made by the arranger to the bank which raised a specific query with that arranger.

165 An example of the effectiveness of such a provision in precluding the possible existence of a duty of care at common law for a negligent misstatement is to be found in *Hedley Byrne & Co Ltd v Heller & Partners Ltd* [1964] AC 465, in which it was held, on the facts, that there was an effective disclaimer of liability. Such a provision would now be subject to s 2(2) of the Unfair Contract Terms Act 1977.

166 As it is extra-contractual, the effect of such a notice is that the reader is taken voluntarily to have assumed or assented to the risk of the loss and damage that might occur if it elects to proceed with the matter to which the notice relates or, to put the matter according to its traditional maxim, *Volenti non fit injuria*. The notice can only serve to protect a defendant if it can be shown that the claimant was aware of its contents and had a choice whether to proceed. If the claimant was obliged to proceed in any event, it could not be said voluntarily to have assumed or assented to the risk. See *McCawley v Furness Ry Co* (1872) LR 8 QB 57; *Buckpitt v Oates* [1968] 1 All ER 1145; *Bennett v Tugwell* [1971] 2 QB 267; *Birch v Thomas* [1972] 1 WLR 294; and *Burnett v British Waterways Board Ltd* [1973] 1 WLR 700. See also now the effect of s 2(3) of the Unfair Contract Terms Act 1977.

167 S 14 of the Act defines a notice to include: 'An announcement, whether or not in writing, and any other communication or pretended communication.' The Court of Appeal appears to have overlooked this point in the approach it took in *IPE Fund SA v Goldman Sachs International* [2007] EWCA Civ 811.

168 Usually within the agency clause, which is expressed in the relevant parts to be for the benefit of the arranger as well as the facility agent.

169 The importance of ensuring that these provisions are expressed to cover the arranger is demonstrated by *Sumitomo Bank Ltd v Banque Bruxelles Lambert SA* [1997] 1 Lloyd's Rep 487, in which it was held, at 493, that the protective provisions in the facility agreement were only intended to protect the agent in performing its role as the agent, rather than in also covering the role of the arranger prior to the establishment of the facility. This was despite the fact that the agent and the arranger were one and the same entity.

9.5.3 Construction of the provisions

In considering the effect of such provisions, which are commonly referred to as exemption provisions or clauses, the first task is to determine their intended scope and meaning, as a matter of construction, to see if they cover the events as they have occurred. It is then necessary to consider if they are subject to any statutory qualifications as to their effectiveness, particularly under section 3 of the Misrepresentation Act 1967 and under the Unfair Contract Terms Act 1977.[170]

An exemption provision, by which a person seeks to avoid or restrict a liability or the consequences of such a liability, will be construed strictly, and the person relying upon the provision will have the burden of proving that the event which has happened falls within the provision;[171] but if the provision is expressed clearly and unambiguously, it will be read in accordance with its terms, and there is no reason why the wording should be given a strained or artificial meaning to avoid the exclusion or restriction of liability that it expresses.[172] If there is an ambiguity, the provision will be construed more stringently against the party who drafted the clause and who then seeks to rely upon it.[173] In cases where there is an exception to the exemption, such as a provision which states that a party will not be liable for loss or damage arising from negligence 'except for wilful neglect or default', it is for the party which seeks to argue that the facts fall within the exception to prove that is the case.[174] The so-called doctrine of 'fundamental breach', by which it had been said that if a contract was terminated for a repudiatory breach of contract then an exemption clause in the contract would also fall away and thus could not operate to relieve the party in breach from liability, has been held no longer to apply.[175]

9.5.3.1

---

[170] Whilst it would not be relevant to the subject matter of this work, in contracts with consumers, it would also be relevant to consider the relevant provisions in light of the Unfair Terms in Consumer Contracts Regs (SI 1999/2083).

[171] *Ailsa Craig Fishing Co Ltd v Malvern Fishing Co Ltd* [1983] 1 WLR 964, at 969 and 970.

[172] See Lord Diplock in *Photo Production Ltd v Securicor Transport Ltd* [1980] AC 827, at 850–851. In the light of this, there must be doubt about cases where it had been held that exemption clauses should be read down if they would otherwise be inconsistent with the main purpose of the contract (e.g. *Glynn v Margetson & Co* [1893] AC 351, at 357), or if they absolved a party from all duties and liabilities. See *Swiss Bank Corp v Brink's Mat Ltd* [1986] 2 Lloyd's Rep 79, at 93. Similarly, it is submitted that the so-called 'four corners' rule, by which an exemption clause in a contract will only apply to liability falling within the four corners of the contract and not outside it (e.g. *Alderslade v Hendon Laundry Ltd* [1945] KB 189, at 192), should really be confined to dealing with cases where, on a proper construction of the exemption provision, it was not intended to cover non-contractual liability.

[173] *Pera Shipping Corp v Petroship SA* [1984] 2 Lloyd's Rep 363, at 366.

[174] *Kenyon Sons & Craven Ltd v Baxter Hoare Ltd* [1971] 1 WLR 232.

[175] See *Photo Production Ltd v Securicor Transport Ltd* [1980] AC 827; *Ailsa Craig Fishing Co Ltd v Malvern Fishing Co Ltd* [1983] 1 WLR 964; and *George Mitchell (Chesterhall) Ltd v Finney Lock Seeds Ltd* [1983] 2 AC 803.

9.5.3.2 It is possible for a provision to exclude or restrict liability for negligence if the wording that is used does so sufficiently clearly.[176] A clause that seeks to exclude liability for negligence altogether will be construed more strictly than one which only seeks to limit the damages that will be payable.[177] The approach to be taken in construing such provisions, so as to ascertain if the provision was intended to cover negligence, was summarised by Lord Morton in *Canada Steamship Lines Ltd v The King*[178] in which his Lordship set out three guidelines or tests. First, if the provision clearly exempts the defendant from negligence then effect must be given to it in accordance with its terms.[179] Secondly, if there is no express reference to negligence, the court must consider if the wording is wide enough, in its ordinary meaning, to cover negligence, with any doubt being resolved against the defendant. Thirdly, if the words are wide enough within the second guideline, the court must consider if the wording might be intended to cover some other head of damage or ground of liability apart from negligence,[180] but not if that would be so fanciful or remote as to fall outside the area of desired protection.[181] On the other hand, the courts will not permit a defendant to rely on an exclusion clause to protect it from its own fraud, as 'fraud unravels all'.[182]

9.5.3.3 A similar approach has been taken towards clauses which seek to give a claimant an indemnity against the consequences of its own negligence, for instance if it becomes liable to a third party. Whilst there is a general inclination against construing such a provision as extending the indemnity to cover the consequences of negligence,[183] such an indemnity can be given if clear words are used and the three tests laid down by Lord Morton in *Canada Steamship Lines Ltd v The King*[184] will usually be applied.[185]

---

[176] An exclusion clause can cover both negligence and other matters: see Lord Wilberforce in *Photo Production Ltd v Securicor Transport Ltd* [1980] AC 827, at 846.

[177] See, for instance, *Ailsa Craig Fishing Co Ltd v Malvern Fishing Co Ltd* [1983] 1 WLR 964, at 970 and *George Mitchell (Chesterhall) Ltd v Finney Lock Seeds Ltd* [1983] 2 AC 803, at 814.

[178] [1952] AC 192, at 208.

[179] For instance, 'At sole risk': *Rutter v Palmer* [1922] 2 KB 87; 'No liability of any nature': *HIH Casualty and General Insurance Ltd v Chase Manhattan Bank* [2003] UKHL 6; [2003] 2 Lloyd's Rep 61, at [12]–[13]; 'Loss howsoever caused or arising': *Rutter v Palmer* [1922] 2 KB 87, at 94, *White v Blackmore* [1972] 2 QB 651. However, it is still necessary to construe the wording in its context, and even wording which is superficially clear if taken on its own might, in context, not be as definite as appears at first sight.

[180] This was taken from Lord Greene MR in *Alderslade v Hendon Laundry Ltd* [1945] 1 KB 189, at 192.

[181] See May LJ in *Lamport & Holt Lines Ltd v Coubro & Scrutton (M&I) Ltd* [1982] 2 Lloyd's Rep 42, at 50.

[182] See Lord Bingham of Cornhill in *HIH Casualty and General Insurance Ltd v Chase Manhattan Bank* [2003] UKHL 6; [2003] 2 Lloyd's Rep 61, at [15]–[16]. His Lordship declined to determine if the same principle applied where the fraud was that of a party's agent, but he did say that, at the very least, clear wording would have to be used (see at [16]).

[183] See *Smith v South Wales Switchgear Co Ltd* [1978] 1 WLR 165, at 168.

[184] [1952] AC 192, at 208.

[185] *Smith v South Wales Switchgear Co Ltd* [1978] 1 WLR 165.

Contracts sometimes purport to extend the benefit of an exclusion clause to third **9.5.3.4**
parties, such as the servants or agents of a contracting party. There was previously
a real difficulty at general law in achieving this as the doctrine of privity of contract
would intervene to prevent the third party, which was not a party to the contract,
from relying upon the provision or being able to enforce it.[186] There were, however, certain circumstances in which the protection of an exclusion clause might
be enforced for the benefit of a third party, as, for instance, where an agent or trustee had contracted for the benefit of the third party.[187] A contract may also contain
a promise by a party not to sue the servants or agents of the other party, and the
latter should be able to prevent the promisor from breaching the contract if it sues
the servants or agents.[188] It should be noted that at common law, two parties to a
contract cannot impose the burden of an exclusion or limitation clause upon a
third party that is a stranger to the contract.

The position at general law regarding privity of contract has been substantially **9.5.3.4.1**
affected by the Contracts (Rights of Third Parties) Act 1999,[189] although the Act
does not detract from any right that a third party may have at general law[190] so that
if, for some reason, the third party cannot avail itself of the Act, it might still be
able to fall back on one of the limited exceptions that applied at general law to the
doctrine of privity of contract.[191] The Act provides that a third party which is
intended to benefit from a provision of a contract[192] will be able to enforce the
contract in its own right, unless on a proper construction it is apparent that the
third party is precluded by the contract from doing so.[193] The Act makes it clear
that the third party has the right to enforce an exclusion or limitation clause that

---

[186] See, for instance, *Scruttons Ltd v Midland Silicones Ltd* [1962] AC 446; *Cosgrove v Horsfall* (1945) 62 TLR 140; and *Genys v Matthews* [1966] 1 WLR 758. See generally the discussion of this issue in Chap 1.

[187] See *New Zealand Shipping Co Ltd v AM Satterthwaite & Co Ltd (The Eurymedon)* [1975] AC 154 and *Port Jackson Stevedoring Pty Ltd v Salmond and Spraggon (Australia) Pty Ltd (The New York Star)* [1981] 1 WLR 138. Clauses under which a party to a contract has acted as an agent in obtaining protection for a third party, when used in a contract for the carriage of goods by sea, are often referred to as 'Himalaya clauses' after the name of the ship that was involved in *Adler v Dickson* [1955] 1 QB 158.

[188] *Snelling v John G Snelling Ltd* [1973] QB 87.

[189] Which applies to contracts made after 11 May 2000 (s 10(2) of the Act). As to the operation of the Act see, generally, Chap 1.

[190] S 7(1).

[191] In addition, in *Nisshin Shipping Co Ltd v Cleaves & Co Ltd* [2003] EWHC 2602 (Comm) it was held that a third party could avail itself of the Act even though at general law the contract might have been enforceable for its benefit under a trust in its favour of the contractual benefit.

[192] I.e. it is expressly named as being entitled to enforce the provision, it is a member of an identified class of intended beneficiaries or if it answers a particular description, even if it was not in existence at the time of the contract: s 1(3).

[193] S 1(2). In *Nisshin Shipping Co Ltd v Cleaves & Co Ltd* [2003] EWHC 2602 (Comm), it was held that the third party will be entitled to enforce the term for its own benefit unless the right to do so was contrary to the intention of the parties in the contract. Thus, if the contract is neutral on the point, s 1(2) will not operate against the third party.

was intended for its benefit,[194] but that right is itself subject to any restriction on the operation of such a clause that might arise by virtue of other legislation, such as the Unfair Contract Terms Act 1977.[195] However, if a third party wishes under the Act to enforce a positive obligation in its favour in the contract, its right to do so will be subject to any limitations on that right that are imposed by the contract, such as a limitation or exclusion of liability for breach of the contract that is contained in the contract for the benefit of the promisor.[196]

9.5.4 Legislative limitations upon exclusions or restrictions of liability or for damages

It is now relevant to turn to the statutory provisions that limit the effectiveness of purported attempts to exclude or restrict liability (or the damages which flow from liability) for a tortious act, including for misrepresentation, or for a breach of contract. The two relevant pieces of legislation that will be examined are the Unfair Contract Terms Act 1977 and section 3 of the Misrepresentation Act 1967 (as amended).[197]

9.5.5 The Unfair Contract Terms Act 1977

Despite its rather general sounding name, the Unfair Contract Terms Act 1977 has a more limited scope of application, as it does not really purport to deal with contractual unfairness in a general sense. On the other hand, it is wider in another aspect, in that it also applies to non-contractual notices in so far as they relate to negligence. It applies to attempts to exclude or restrict liability for loss or damage arising in the tort of negligence or for breach of an occupier's duty of care or in consequence of a breach of contract, and it also applies to attempts in a contract to excuse or modify performance of a party's obligations under that contract. The scheme of the Act is as follows. Part I of the Act deals with matters arising under English law and some of the provisions in Part I will be relevant in a consideration of the position of an arranger. Part II of the Act concerns matters of Scottish law, which will not be addressed in this work. Part III of the Act, together with the Schedules to the Act, are relevant to Part I and will also be mentioned. The matters that are covered in Part I concern liability in negligence, attempts to exclude or modify contractual obligations, unreasonable indemnity clauses concerning consumers and guarantees of consumer goods, and contracts relating to the sale or supply of goods. Of those matters, the provisions concerning liability in negligence will

---

194 S 1(6).

195 S 3(6).

196 Ss 3(1)–3(5). It would also appear that the provisions of the Unfair Contract Terms Act 1977 (except for s 2(1)) would not affect the rights of the promisor under ss 3(1)–3(5).

197 It is not intended here to deal with the Unfair Terms in Consumer Contracts Regulations 1999 (SI 1999/2083) for, as the name implies, the provisions of the regulations will not be relevant to the types of situation that are the subject of this chapter.

be relevant to a consideration of the position of an arranger and will be dealt with below. It will also be relevant at a later stage in this chapter to revert to the provisions of Part I when considering the position of a facility agent. The provisions of Part I are also relevant in a consideration of equipment finance.[198]

With one limited exception,[199] Part I of the Act applies only to a 'business liability', that is, a liability arising in the course of a business.[200] There are a number of exceptions to the operation of Part I, as provided for in section 1(2) and set out in Schedule 1 (for example, with respect to contracts concerning insurance, interests in land, intellectual property rights, corporate matters, the creation or transfer of securities, employment contracts, and maritime and aircraft matters). There is also an exception for international supply contracts for the supply of goods.[201] It is further provided that Part I of the Act will not apply to a contract that is governed by English law if, but for the choice of law, the contract would be governed by the law of some place outside the UK.[202] On the other hand, it is also provided that if a contract is expressed to be governed by some other law and it appears that the choice of the foreign law has been chosen to evade the operation of the Act, nonetheless the Act will apply.[203]   **9.5.5.1**

In considering whether a contractual provision or a notice has the effect of excluding or restricting a liability or a contractual obligation, the court will be concerned with its substance and not just its mere form.[204] This approach is also consistent with section 13(1) of the Act which provides that to the extent that Part I of the Act prevents the exclusion or restriction of any liability it also prevents: **9.5.5.2**

    (a) making the liability or its enforcement subject to restrictive or onerous conditions;[205]

    (b) excluding or restricting any right or remedy in respect of the liability, or subjecting a person to any prejudice in consequence of his pursuing any such right or remedy;[206]

    (c) excluding or restricting rules of evidence or procedure.

---

[198] See Chap 15.

[199] Under s 6(4), the provisions of s 6 (which applies to implied undertakings as to title in contracts for the sale of goods or in hire-purchase agreements), apply with respect to any liability under the relevant contracts or agreements, irrespective of whether or not the liability is a business liability.

[200] S 1(3). A 'business' is defined in s 14 to include: 'A profession and the activities of any government department or local or public authority.'

[201] S 26. See further *Amiri Flight Authority v BAE Systems PLC* [2003] EWCA Civ 1447, [2003] 2 Lloyd's Rep 767.

[202] S 27(1).

[203] S 27(2).

[204] See Stuart-Smith LJ in *Johnstone v Bloomsbury Health Authority* [1992] QB 333, at 346.

[205] For instance, subjecting the making of a claim to a time-limit.

[206] For instance, by precluding the exercise of a right of set-off in an equipment supply and installation transaction: *Stewart Gill Ltd v Horatio Myer & Co Ltd* [1992] QB 600, but see also *Governor & Co of the Bank of Scotland v Singh* (Unreported. HHJ Kershaw QC, sitting in the High Court in Manchester, 17/6/2005). Note, however, that s 13(3) provides that a written submission to arbitration is not to be treated as an exclusion or restriction of any liability.

Section 13(1) goes on to provide that, to the same extent, Part I of the Act also prevents an exclusion or restriction of liability by reference to terms and notices which exclude or restrict the relevant obligation or duty from arising in the first place. This would be relevant to a provision which purports to preclude a duty or obligation (as opposed to a liability for a breach of duty or an obligation) from arising at all as, for instance, by the insertion of a provision which contains a disavowal of responsibility or liability of the type that was used in *Hedley Byrne & Co Ltd v Heller & Partners Ltd*.[207]

9.5.5.3 *Liability in negligence*

Section 2 of the Act deals with attempts by a contractual term or a notice to exclude or restrict a liability for negligence. A 'notice' includes 'an announcement, whether or not in writing, and any other communication or pretended communication'.[208] It would include a disclaimer of liability by an arranger in communications if sent to the potential syndicate members.

9.5.5.3.1 'Negligence' is defined by section 1(1) to mean the breach:

    (a) of any obligation, arising from the express or implied[209] terms of a contract, to take reasonable care or exercise reasonable skill in the performance of a contract;

    (b) of any common law duty to take reasonable care or exercise reasonable skill (but not any stricter duty);

    (c) [the statutory duty of care imposed upon occupiers of land].

9.5.5.3.2 It is doubtful if the definition of negligence includes the duty of care and skill that is imposed upon fiduciaries,[210] even though it is of much the same standard as that which arises in tort[211] or under section 13 of the Supply of Goods and Services Act 1982. The duty of care and skill of a fiduciary arises in equity, in consequence of the relationship of trust and confidence between the fiduciary and its beneficiary,

---

    207 [1964] AC 465. See further Lord Griffiths and Lord Jauncey in *Smith v Eric S Bush* [1990] 1 AC 831, at 857 and 873, respectively. Lord Griffiths referred to a 'but for' test, i.e. that, but for the exclusion, a liability would have arisen. It is submitted that the approach taken by the Court of Appeal on this aspect in *IPE Fund SA v Goldman Sachs International* [2007] EWCA Civ 811 was incorrect. In that case, the court said that an express disclaimer of liability had the same effect as in the *Hedley Byrne* case, that is, it meant that no liability could arise in the first place, because the defendant had disclaimed any acceptance of responsibility from arising. The *Hedley Byrne* case, of course, was decided long before the 1977 Act was passed. There was no reference in the *IPE* case to s 13 of the Act.

    208 S 14.

    209 E.g. by virtue of s 13 of the Supply of Goods and Services Act 1982.

    210 See the discussion on the point by Tuckey LJ in *Baker v JR Clark & Co (Transport) Ltd* [2006] EWCA Civ 464, at [18]–[21].

    211 See Lord Browne-Wilkinson in *Henderson v Merrett Syndicates Ltd* [1995] 2 AC 145, at 204–205 and Millett LJ in *Bristol & West Building Society v Mothew* [1998] Ch 1, at 16–17.

independently of the common law or any contract.[212] This will be relevant in considering the position of the agent, which is discussed later in this chapter.

Section 2(3) provides that a person's knowledge or awareness of a contract term or notice which purports to exclude or restrict liability for negligence is not of itself to be taken as an indication of that person's voluntary acceptance of any risk.

9.5.5.3.3

Section 2(1) deals with the liability that would arise for death or personal injury resulting from negligence, which cannot be excluded or restricted in any circumstances. It is very unlikely that an arranger would be involved in a situation giving rise to such a liability and nothing further will be said here about section 2(1).

9.5.5.4

Section 2(2) deals with attempts by a contract term or notice to exclude or restrict liability for any other type of loss or damage resulting from negligence and would be relevant to an attempt by an arranger to protect itself from the consequences of its negligence. Section 2(2) provides that a person cannot exclude or restrict his liability for negligence except in so far as the contractual term or notice satisfies 'the requirement of reasonableness', as set forth in section 11. It should be noticed that it is the term or notice which has to satisfy the requirement of reasonableness, not the application of the term to the particular facts of a case. Section 2 will not, however, apply to a term by which one party agrees to indemnify another party for loss suffered by third parties in consequence of the indemnified party's negligence.[213]

9.5.5.5

9.5.5.6 Liability arising in contract

Section 3 of the Act provides that, where a contracting party is dealing as a consumer or on the other party's standard terms of business, that other party cannot by a contractual term exclude or restrict his own liability for breach of the contract, nor purport in pursuance of such a term to render no performance at all or to render a substantially different performance from what was reasonably to be expected under the contract,[214] except in so far as the term satisfies the requirement of reasonableness in section 11.

It is difficult to see how section 3 could apply with respect to any possible liability of the arranger to the banks, as such a liability would not arise from a breach of contract between them but from the arranger's pre-contractual activities. However, as the question must later be discussed concerning the possible liability of the facility agent to the banks, it is convenient to consider section 3 within the present

9.5.5.6.1

---

212 See further below.
213 *Thompson v T Lohan (Plant Hire) Ltd* [1987] 1 WLR 649.
214 See, for instance, *Purnell Secretarial Services Ltd v Lease Management Services Ltd* [1994] Tr LR 337.

discussion relating to the Act.[215] There are, for instance, provisions in a syndicated facility agreement (particularly in the agency clause) which have the effect of limiting or excluding the possible liability of the agent for defective performance of its obligations and other provisions which either excuse it from having to perform and observe the obligations that might otherwise be expected of it or which modify those obligations. In that sense, the spirit of section 3 might be engaged.

9.5.5.6.2   The section only applies if either the party (or parties) against whom the relevant provisions are relied upon (that is, the banks) was dealing as a consumer in entering into the contract, or if the party relying upon those provisions (that is, the agent) is dealing on its written standard terms of business. It could not sensibly be argued that any of the parties to a syndicated facility was dealing as a consumer, so the question becomes whether the agent is relying upon its standard terms of business. At one stage, syndicated facility documentation was individually prepared and negotiated. There were no standard forms. More recently, however, standard forms of syndicated facility documentation have become common in the London market, particularly those put forward by the Loan Market Association. It has been held that the use of a standard form put forward by a trade association or a similar body can be treated as being a party's standard terms of business if that party 'invariably or at least usually' contracts on those terms.[216] It has also been held that there could still be standard terms of business where there had been some negotiation of the provisions of a contract, if the terms remained effectively the same, which is a question of fact.[217] Whilst there will often be negotiation of the provisions of a facility agreement dealing with commercial matters, it is unusual for the provisions of the agency clause in a syndicated facility agreement to be negotiated and they are usually accepted without dissent. Accordingly, there must be some risk that the provisions on which the agent relies might be held to be its written standard terms of business if the document is based upon the commonly used standard forms. It then falls to be considered whether the relevant provisions satisfy the requirement of reasonableness.

9.5.5.7 The requirement of reasonableness

Section 11 of the Act provides for the 'reasonableness test', that is, the test for meeting the requirement of reasonableness as referable to various provisions of the Act, such as sections 2(2) and 3, and also as referable to section 3 of the

---

[215] S 3 will also be relevant when considering attempts by financiers to escape liability under claims relating to equipment financing transactions, as in the *Purnell* case.

[216] *British Fermentation Products Ltd v Compair Reavell Ltd* [1999] 2 All ER (Comm) 389, at [46].

[217] Nourse LJ held in *St Albans City and District Council v International Computers Ltd* [1996] 4 All ER 481, at 491 that it was a question of fact whether there had been a dealing, i.e. a contracting, on one of the party's standard terms and that there could still be standard terms even if there had been prior negotiations, so long as the terms remained effectively untouched by the negotiations.

Misrepresentation Act 1967, to which further reference is made below. The party relying upon the contract term or notice has the onus of showing that the requirement of reasonableness has been met.[218]

With respect to a contract term, section 11(1) provides that the test is whether:

> The term shall have been a fair and reasonable one to be included having regard to the circumstances which were, or ought reasonably to have been, known to or in the contemplation of the parties when the contract was made.

It is the incorporation of the term in the contract that must satisfy the requirement of reasonableness. The relevant time to assess if that requirement has been met is the time of contracting, so it is not relevant to judge the matter at the time of a later breach of duty or by reference to the way the term has operated in relation to the specific facts of the case[219] except, perhaps, if those facts should have been in the parties' contemplation when the contract was made. The relevant circumstances must have been known to or in the contemplation of both of the parties, not just the party seeking to rely upon the clause. Section 11(2) provides certain guidelines, which are set out in Schedule 2 to the Act, to which regard may be had in assessing the reasonableness of a term. Whilst the guidelines, strictly speaking, are expressed only to apply to sections 6 and 7 of the Act,[220] they are generally taken as being relevant in providing guidance as to the application of the reasonableness test in relation to other provisions of the Act as well.[221] Not all of the guidelines would be relevant in considering the position of an arranger and the syndicate members, but the following two might be relevant: (a) the strength of the relative bargaining positions of the parties, taking into account alternate means by which a claimant's requirements could have been met; and (b) whether a party knew or should have known of the relevant provision, taking into account market practice and previous dealings between the parties.

For a notice that is not part of a contract, the test of reasonableness is contained in section 11(3), namely:

> That it should be fair and reasonable to allow reliance on [the notice], having regard to all the circumstances obtaining when liability arose or (but for the notice) would have arisen.

The relevant time in this instance is when the liability arose and, in contrast to section 11(1), the test is judged with respect to all of the circumstances at the time

---

[218] S 11(5).

[219] See Stuart-Smith LJ in *Stewart Gill Ltd v Horatio Myer & Co Ltd* [1992] QB 600, at 608.

[220] And they are not an exhaustive list: see for instance the further tests outlined by Potter LJ in *Overseas Medical Supplies Ltd v Orient Transport Services Ltd* [1999] 2 Lloyd's Rep 273, at 276–277.

[221] See Stuart-Smith LJ in *Stewart Gill Ltd v Horatio Myer & Co Ltd* [1992] QB 600, at 608.

rather than by reference to the circumstances which were or should have been known to the parties, as would be the case under section 11(1). Thus, under section 11(3), the court may take into account the defendant's conduct as a relevant circumstance, whereas under section 11(1), such conduct would only be relevant as a possible example of something that might have been contemplated by the parties at the time of contracting.

9.5.5.7.3 Section 11(4) makes provision for contractual terms or notices which seek to restrict the liability of a person to a specified sum of money, in which case regard should be had to the resources that the person could have expected to be available to him to meet the liability if it arose and how far it was open to him to obtain insurance cover.[222]

9.5.5.7.4 The position as to reasonableness will vary from one set of circumstances to another, so the decisions in the cases which depend on factual matters must be regarded with caution. However, in general the courts have been reluctant to intervene and hold unreasonable a provision which excludes or restricts the liability of a person in situations involving experienced commercial parties of equal bargaining power and adequate resources. They have regarded such provisions as representing an agreed allocation of risk in which the courts should not interfere. Chadwick LJ said in *Watford Electronics Ltd v Sanderson CFL Ltd*:[223]

> Where experienced businessmen representing substantial companies of equal bargaining power negotiated an agreement, they may be taken to have had regard to the matters known to them. They should, in my view, be taken to be the best judges of the commercial fairness of the agreement which they have made; including the fairness of each of the terms of that agreement.[224]

In the light of statements such as that of Chadwick LJ, it is submitted that it would be unlikely that a court would hold to be unreasonable protective provisions aimed at protecting the arranger from liability towards the syndicate members for negligence arising from a general duty of care, whether in notices contained in materials sent out by the arranger to the banks prior to the execution of the facility agreement or in contractual provisions in such an agreement. Such an approach would also be consistent with market practice in the syndicated loan market in which it is generally accepted that the arranger should not be expected to accept responsibility towards the syndicate. The position may be different, however,

---

[222] The availability of insurance cover would be a relevant factor under s 11(1) as well: Lord Griffiths in *Smith v Eric S Bush* [1990] 1 AC 831, at 858. But the actual existence or otherwise of insurance cover is irrelevant: *Flamar Interocean Ltd v Denmac Ltd* [1990] 1 Lloyd's Rep 434.

[223] [2001] EWCA Civ 317; [2001] 1 All ER (Comm) 696, at [63].

[224] See also Clarke LJ in *National Westminster Bank PLC v Utrecht-America Finance Co* [2001] EWCA Civ 658; [2001] 3 All ER 733, at [57]–[62] and Tucker LJ in *Granville Oil and Chemicals Ltd v Davies Turner & Co Ltd* [2003] EWCA Civ 570; [2003] 2 Lloyd's Rep 356, at [31].

where it is proved that an arranger accepted responsibility for a specific matter. In such a case, the reasonableness of the protection that was sought by the arranger would have to be examined.

As each case will depend upon its own facts, it is of interest to note the outcome of some of the cases in various different areas in the context of commercial transactions, financing arrangements, and the granting of credit, as follows. In *Walker v Boyle*[225] a vendor of land was held not to be protected in relation to a misstatement in an answer to preliminary enquiries. In *Smith v Eric S Bush*[226] a provision under which a surveyor commissioned by a putative mortgagee purported to disclaim liability towards a purchaser, the putative mortgagor, for a negligent survey of a dwelling house (the survey having been commissioned by the mortgagee at the expense of the mortgagor), was held to be unreasonable. Lord Griffiths[227] referred to a number of matters that were relevant, including the relative bargaining positions of the parties, if it would have been feasible, taking into account factors such as cost and time, to obtain alternative advice, the difficulty of the task that was undertaken for which liability was excluded, the practical consequences for the parties, bearing in mind the amounts of money involved, the availability of insurance, and the relative ability of the different parties to bear the loss. By contrast, in *Omega Trust Co Ltd v Wright Son and Pepper*[228] it was held that in a commercial context, as opposed to the domestic context in *Smith v Eric S Bush*, it was reasonable for valuers to exclude liability towards a third party for a negligent valuation of leasehold properties, especially as the existence of the third party was unknown to them. The third party was a commercial entity which could easily have obtained its own valuation, those involved were of equal bargaining power, and the third party could have approached the valuers directly if it wished them to accept responsibility towards it. In *St Alban's City and District Council v International Computers Ltd*[229] and in *Salvage Association v Cap Financial Services*[230] provisions in relation to the supply of computer software which limited liability to an aggregate amount were held not to be reasonable. In *Stewart Gill Ltd v Horatio Myer & Co Ltd*[231] a clause which precluded a purchaser from setting off a claim for damages against the payment of the price for the supply and installation of equipment was held to be unreasonable, within the context of section 13(1)(b) of the Act. However, clauses precluding the exercise of a right of set-off have also

---

[225] [1982] 1 WLR 495.
[226] [1990] 1 AC 831.
[227] At 858–859.
[228] [1997] PNLR 424.
[229] [1996] 4 All ER 481.
[230] [1995] FSR 654.
[231] [1992] QB 600.

been upheld: *Schenkers Ltd v Overland Shoes Ltd*,[232] *Surzur Overseas Ltd v Ocean Reliance Shipping Co Ltd*,[233] *Skipskredittforeningen v Emperor Navigation*,[234] *WRM Group Ltd v Wood*,[235] and *Governor & Co of the Bank of Scotland v Singh*.[236]

9.5.6 Section 3 of the Misrepresentation Act 1967[237]

Section 3 will be relevant in relation to an attempt in a contract, such as a facility agreement, to exclude or restrict any liability of an arranger that may arise in relation to a misrepresentation claim against the arranger relating to that contract.

9.5.6.1 The section provides as follows:

> If a contract contains a term which would exclude or restrict—
> (a) any liability to which a party to a contract may be subject by reason of any misrepresentation made by him before the contract was made; or
> (b) any remedy available to another party to the contract by reason of such a misrepresentation,
> that term shall be of no effect except in so far as it satisfies the requirement of reasonableness as stated in S. 11(1) of the Unfair Contract Terms Act 1977; and it is for those claiming that the term satisfies that requirement to show that it does.

It should be noted that the onus of proof is upon the person, the misrepresentor, who relies upon the relevant term. It is the term as a whole that must satisfy the requirement of reasonableness and not the application of the term to the particular facts.[238] Thus, a term which purports to exclude or restrict liability for any misrepresentation, including a fraudulent misrepresentation, would not be considered to be reasonable.

9.5.6.2 It has been held, however, that a clause in a contract (which is usually called a 'non-reliance clause') by which a party in the position of a possible representee confirms that it made its own enquiries and investigations, both as to factual and other matters, in deciding to enter into the agreement, and that it did not receive or rely upon any representations from the putative representator in deciding to proceed with the transaction, will act as an evidential estoppel, which will preclude the putative representee from claiming that it had relied upon any representation in deciding to enter into the contract.[239] In effect, the putative representee is itself

---

232 [1998] 1 Lloyd's Rep 498.
233 [1997] CLY 906.
234 [1998] 1 Lloyd's Rep 66.
235 [1998] CLC 189.
236 Unreported. HHJ Kershaw QC, sitting in the High Court in Manchester, 17/6/2005.
237 As amended by s 8(1) of the Unfair Contract Terms Act 1977.
238 Jacobs J in *Thomas Witter Ltd v TBP Industries Ltd* [1996] 2 All ER 573, at 598.
239 See Chadwick LJ in *Watford Electronics Ltd v Sanderson CFL Ltd* [2001] EWCA Civ 317; [2001] 1 All ER (Comm) 696, at [38]–[41]. Note, however, that Jacob J in *Thomas Witter Ltd v TBP Industries Ltd* [1996] 2 All ER 573, at 596–597, expressed the view that such a provision should be

confirming or representing that no representation was made to it or that it has not placed reliance upon anything that was said. On that basis, section 3 will not be engaged at all, as it will not be possible to claim the essential element of reliance in bringing a claim based upon misrepresentation. It has been held, however, that such a provision will only be effective to operate as an estoppel if its meaning and intention is clear and unambiguous, it was reasonably intended to be relied upon and that it was so relied upon.[240]

9.6 The Agent

9.6.1 The appointment, role, duties, and powers of the agent

The agent bank, sometimes called the facility agent, is the co-ordinator of the facility once it has been formalised by the signing of the documentation. Its role begins upon execution of the facility agreement and will continue, unless it resigns and is replaced by another agent, until the conclusion of the transaction.[241] Its role is crucial to the management and effective co-ordination of the arrangements between the banks and as between them and the borrower. The facility agent may be assisted in a complicated facility by other entities which perform specific roles and, if security is to be taken, there may be a separate security agent, failing which, the facility agent will also hold the security, in either case as trustee on behalf of the banks.[242] Quite often, the same entity that acted as the arranger will be appointed as the facility agent, but it is important to distinguish between the two roles and to understand that the facility agent takes up its role when it is appointed by the banks to act as their agent. The appointment is normally contained in the facility agreement. Most of the provisions concerning the agent will be found in a

---

viewed as an attempt to exclude or restrict liability for a misrepresentation, rather than as precluding the claim for misrepresentation from arising.

[240] See Diplock J (sitting as an additional member of the Court of Appeal) in *Lowe v Lombark Ltd* [1960] 1 All ER 611, at 616. Chadwick LJ referred to this refinement in *Watford Electronics Ltd v Sanderson CFL Ltd* [2001] EWCA Civ 317; [2001] 1 All ER (Comm) 696, at [40]. In *Quest 4 Finance Ltd v Maxfield* [2007] EWHC 2313 (QB) it was held that the recipient of the confirmation or acknowledgement had not relied upon it, so the putative representee was not estopped from pleading the misrepresentation by that recipient.

[241] The facility agreement should contain provisions dealing with the resignation and replacement of the agent. Such provisions should ensure that the protective provisions in the agreement relating to the agent will continue to protect a retired agent in relating to matters concerning the period whilst it was the agent.

[242] The representative capacity of a facility agent and a security trustee to act and hold security on behalf of the banks, as well as the right of the agent to bind the banks, was examined in *British Power & Energy Trading Ltd v Credit Suisse* [2008] EWCA Civ 53. That case concerned a syndicated facility. This is subject, of course, to the terms of the facility agreement or other documentation under which the agent and the trustee are appointed to act and to hold the security on behalf of the syndicate members, which may place restrictions upon their functions and powers.

specific clause in the facility agreement, which is usually referred to as the 'agency clause'. For convenience, the facility agent will be referred to in the discussion that follows simply as the 'agent'.

9.6.1.1 The agent is appointed by the banks to act as their agent. It is usually provided expressly that the agent does not act on behalf of the borrower or any other person. The agent performs various roles in acting as the agent of the banks, which may be summarised as acting as a representative of the banks, acting as a co-ordinator of the banks and of the facility, and acting in an administrative and mechanical capacity. It acts as the representative of the banks in dealings with the borrower. In that sense, it is the interface between the banks and the borrower, and the facility agreement will usually provide that the borrower should deal with the agent rather than directly with the banks. Information and other materials that have to be transmitted by the borrower to the banks will be given to the agent to be distributed to the banks. Similarly, requests that the borrower wishes to make and notices that it wishes to give will be given to the agent, which will then inform the banks of what has been received from the borrower. Where a notice or some other matter, such as a consent, is to be given to the borrower, it will be given on behalf of the banks by the agent. With respect to payments that are to be made under the facility, the banks will send their respective contributions to the agent and then an amount equivalent to the total of such contributions will be transmitted by the agent to the borrower. If the borrower is to make a payment under the facility, such as a payment of interest or principal, it will make the payment in an aggregate amount to the agent, which will then divide up the payment and transmit the relevant proportionate amounts to the banks. The agent will make the calculations that are required during the facility, such as concerning the respective amounts of each bank's contribution to an advance that is to be made, each bank's entitlement in any payment that the agent receives from the borrower, and in the determination of the amounts of interest and other amounts that are payable and related matters such as concerning interest periods. In a multicurrency facility, the agent will make the currency conversion and other calculations for the administration of the facility.

9.6.1.2 On its face, the agent would appear to be invested with a large and wide amount of discretion in acting on behalf of the banks. There are limitations, however, on the apparent width of the agent's authority, which will be stated in the facility agreement. As previously mentioned, in some circumstances the consent of all of the banks is required to certain matters. In other situations, the facility agreement will usually permit the majority of the banks to intervene by making decisions and giving instructions to the agent. The agent will also be given the right to seek instructions from the majority of the banks and to act as instructed by the majority. The agreement will provide that the agent may require security or an indemnity

from the banks if it is to carry out the instructions of the majority.[243] In the absence
of a decision by the majority, the agent will be entitled to act as it thinks fit unless
the facility agreement provides to the contrary, as, for instance, in relation to a situation where it prescribes that the consent of all the banks is required. A good
example of the interplay between the capacity of the agent to make decisions on
its own and to act as instructed by the majority of the banks will usually be found
in the events of default clause in the facility agreement. The clause will normally
provide that if an event of default occurs, the agent may take action of its own
volition, such as by demanding repayment or suspending the facility, but that the
agent will take such action if it is so instructed by the majority of the banks.

9.6.2 Areas of risk to the agent

The agent may be at risk if the banks are unhappy about the agent's performance
of its tasks. They may wish to claim against the agent for breach of its obligations
towards them. The discussion that follows proceeds on the assumption that
English law would be the applicable law to determine each of the issues that are
involved in a dispute. However, it is always relevant to consider if there might be
conflict of laws issues that may arise in a particular case. The reader is referred to
Chapter 4 for a discussion of those matters. As a matter of English law, the possible
areas of claim against the agent will lie in contract, tort, and for breach of fiduciary
duty.

9.6.2.1 Fiduciary duty[244]

The duties of a fiduciary arise in equity from the relationship between it and its
principal. At the heart of the relationship is the trust and confidence that the principal reposes in the fiduciary and which, accordingly, is due by the fiduciary to the
principal.[245] It follows that the principal feature of a fiduciary's duties is the obligation of loyalty, from which other equitable obligations will arise. This was explained
by Millett LJ in *Bristol & West Building Society v Mothew*[246] as follows:

> The distinguishing obligation of a fiduciary is the obligation of loyalty. The principal
> is entitled to the single-minded loyalty of his fiduciary. This core liability has several
> facets. A fiduciary must act in good faith; he must not make a profit out of his trust;

---

[243] The right of the agent to such protection will fall to be considered in much the same way as
that of a trustee under a bond issue when it seeks an indemnity or security from the bond holders
before taking action on their behalf. The position of such a trustee was examined by the House of
Lords in *Concord Trust v Law Debenture Trust Corporation PLC* [2005] UKHL 27, [2005] 1 WLR
1591.

[244] See the helpful summary in *Australian Securities and Investment Commission v Citigroup
Global Markets Australia Pty Ltd* [2007] FCA 963, at [256]–[307].

[245] See Millett LJ in *R v Chester and North Wales Legal Aid Area Office, ex p Floods of Queensferry
Ltd* [1998] 1 WLR 1496, at 1500.

[246] [1998] Ch 1, at 18.

he must not place himself in a position where his duty and his interest may conflict; he may not act for his own benefit or the benefit of a third person without the informed consent of his principal. This is not intended to be an exhaustive list, but it is sufficient to indicate the nature of fiduciary obligations.

His Lordship went on to say[247] that if the fiduciary is acting for two (or more) principals:

he must act in good faith in the interests of each and must not act with the intention of furthering the interests of one principal to the prejudice of the other.

9.6.2.1.1 As to the duty to act in good faith, see *Re Second East Dulwich etc Building Society*.[248] For the duty not to make an unauthorised profit, see *Bray v Ford*.[249] For the duty to avoid a conflict of interest, see *Keech v Sandford*.[250] For the duty not to act for its own or a third party's benefit, see *Boardman v Phipps*.[251] To that list may be added a further duty, to act with care and skill, but although the duty may arise in consequence of the fiduciary relationship, because of the relationship that arises between them, it is more akin to the duty of care in negligence that arises at common law. Whilst the remedy will be for equitable compensation, it will be assessed in a similar way to damages at common law. The rules which apply at common law as to causation and remoteness of damage may also apply to such a claim against the fiduciary.[252]

9.6.2.1.2 Despite the apparent severity of the position as it was outlined by Millett LJ, the nature and extent of the duties of a fiduciary to its principal will depend upon the context in which it is acting, particularly the contractual context in a situation where the fiduciary is acting pursuant to an appointment arising from the contract.[253] The fiduciary duties that are owed by an express trustee will not be the same as the less extensive duties owed by some other types of fiduciary, such as an agent.[254] It is also possible (especially in a commercial context) for the nature and scope of the duties of a fiduciary that might otherwise arise to be restrictively defined and modified or even excluded by contract,[255] except with respect to

---

[247] [1998] Ch 1, at 19.

[248] (1889) 68 LJ Ch 196.

[249] [1896] AC 44. Lord Browne-Wilkinson said in *Henderson v Merrett Syndicates Ltd* [1995] 2 AC 145, at 206 that, so far as he was aware, this was a common duty to every fiduciary, subject to any authorisation of the profit.

[250] (1726) Sel Cas Ch 61.

[251] [1967] 2 AC 46.

[252] See Lord Browne-Wilkinson in *Henderson v Merrett Syndicates Ltd* [1995] 2 AC 145, at 205–206 and Millett LJ in *Bristol & West Building Society v Mothew* [1998] Ch 1, at 16–17.

[253] See Lord Wilberforce in *New Zealand Netherlands Society 'Oranje' Inc v Kuys* [1973] 1 WLR 1126, at 1129–1130 (PC); Mason J in *Hospital Products Ltd v United States Surgical Corp* (1984) CLR 41, at 97 (High Ct of Aust); and Lord Browne-Wilkinson in *Henderson v Merrett Syndicates Ltd* [1995] 2 AC 145, at 206.

[254] See Lord Browne-Wilkinson in *Henderson v Merrett Syndicates Ltd* [1995] 2 AC 145, at 206.

[255] Ibid.

situations involving dishonesty or lack of good faith on the part of the fiduciary.[256] For instance, in *Kelly v Cooper*[257] Lord Browne-Wilkinson, who delivered the advice of the Privy Council, said that it was inherent in the nature of the role played by an estate agent, a stockbroker, and others selling property, shares, or goods on behalf of their principals that they will probably act for several different principals at the same time. Conflicts of interest may arise concerning the interests of their principals, yet they must be free to act for several competing principals as, otherwise, they would be unable to perform their functions. They might, for instance, hold confidential information concerning one principal that may be relevant to the interests of another principal, yet they would not be compelled to divulge such information to the other principal.

Generally speaking, whilst it is usual (in the absence of appropriate contractual limitations) that an agent may be considered to be in the position of a fiduciary towards its principal,[258] it is also important to note that not every agent will be considered to be in that position. In *Henry v Hammond*[259] Channell J held that a shipping agent who was instructed to sell the cargo of a vessel in distress was not in a fiduciary position. The agent was not obliged to keep the sale moneys separate from its own funds, but was entitled to mix those moneys with its own funds, with the consequence that it was merely a debtor for those moneys to its principal. Lord Upjohn in *Boardman v Phipps*[260] said that: 'The facts and circumstances must be carefully examined to see whether in fact a purported agent and even a confidential agent is in a fiduciary relationship to his principal. It does not necessarily follow that he is in such a position' (see *Re Coomber, Coomber v Coomber*[261]).

9.6.2.1.3

It is important to keep the background mentioned above in mind when considering the statement that was made by Ackner LJ, on behalf of himself and Oliver LJ,[262] in *UBAF Ltd v European American Banking Corp*.[263] His Lordship said that as the agent of two syndicated loan facilities had received the funds from the banks which were to be lent to the borrowers and it was holding security from the borrowers as trustee on behalf of the banks, the agent was acting in a fiduciary

9.6.2.1.4

---

[256] See Millett LJ in *Armitage v Nurse* [1998] Ch 241, at 251–256.

[257] [1993] AC 205 (PC).

[258] See for instance the references to an agent as a fiduciary by Lord Browne-Wilkinson in *Henderson v Merrett Syndicates Ltd* [1995] 2 AC 145, at 205–206.

[259] [1913] 2 KB 515.

[260] [1967] 2 AC 46, at 127.

[261] [1911] 1 Ch 723.

[262] There was no third member of the court.

[263] [1984] QB 713, at 728. The facts are noted at para 9.4.8.2 above. The decision of the Court of Appeal was given in an interlocutory appeal and, as noted above, the appeal was only heard by a panel of two judges, so it may be open to review. However, the point under discussion concerning the fiduciary capacity of the agent was directly relevant to the finding of the court on s 32(1)(b) of the Limitation Act 1980, so it cannot be regarded as merely being *obiter dicta*.

capacity towards the banks. As such, it had a fiduciary duty to pass on any information that it might have received which related to the facility and such security. In so far as it was acting as the trustee of the security on behalf of the syndicate, that view might be correct (unless the relevant documentation provided otherwise).

9.6.2.1.5 It is doubtful, however, if the same would be the true position had the agent merely been acting as the agent under the facility agreement, at least if the facts and the documentation were consistent with what has been the practice in the syndicated loan markets for quite a number of years. For many years the almost invariable practice has been that the syndicated facility agreement will provide expressly that the agent does not act in a fiduciary capacity towards the banks or, indeed, anyone else, and there are a number of other provisions that are intended to overcome any fiduciary duties that might otherwise arise or be implied from the role that the agent plays. Further, there is commonly no obligation in such documentation for the agent to hold any funds that it receives from or for the banks in a separate account pending their disbursement. The funds will usually be paid into the agent's own general accounts and will thus be mixed with any other funds it may have. Accordingly, any payment it makes with respect to what it has received will not be of the precise same funds it has received but of an equivalent amount. On the basis of what was said in *Henry v Hammond* and by Lord Upjohn in *Boardman v Phipps*, this fact, when taken with the express provisions in the facility agreement to which reference has just been made, should mean that no fiduciary relationship will exist as between the agent and the banks.

9.6.2.2 Contractual duties

As the agent is appointed in the facility agreement by the banks to be their agent then quite clearly there is a contractual relationship between the agent and the banks. The facility agreement contains a number of provisions concerning the functions that the agent undertakes, particularly as to administrative and mechanical matters. The agency clause in the usual form of facility agreement will also set out the duties and responsibilities of the agent. For instance, the agent is expressed to have a qualified duty to pass on information and the contents of any notices that it receives from the borrower, and if the agent becomes aware that there has been a default, it must tell the banks.

9.6.2.2.1 In addition to the matters dealt with expressly by the agreement, there could also be various duties and obligations on the part of the agent that might be implied into the contract. Under section 13 of the Supply of Goods and Services Act 1982, there is an implied contractual duty to exercise reasonable care and skill in the supply of services that is imposed upon a person which, under a contract, is supplying services in the course of a business.[264] It may also be argued (if rather faintly) that something similar to some of the duties that might apply to a fiduciary may also be implied into the contract as between the agent and the banks, such as the duty on the part of the agent to act in good faith, not to have a conflict of interests, and to pass on to the banks any relevant information that may come into its possession.

As will be seen, the various duties and functions of the agent are expressed in the **9.6.2.2.2** facility agreement to be of a rather limited nature, and will be subject to a number of qualifications and limitations that are contained in the agreement.

9.6.2.3 *Tortious duties*

In addition to any contractual duty of care and skill that is owed by the agent to the banks, the agent may also have a duty of care in tort towards the banks which may arise at general law from the relationship between them.

At one time it was considered that it was not possible to have concurrent duties of **9.6.2.3.1** care in both contract and tort. For instance, Lord Scarman, when delivering the advice of the Privy Council in *Tai Hing Cotton Mill Ltd v Liu Chong Hing Bank Ltd*,[265] expressed the view that in commercial relationships, and particularly in the relationship between a banker and its customer, such a relationship should be governed solely by the terms of the contract, so that on the facts of that case it was not possible for the customer to owe a separate duty of care in tort to the banker. That view, however, was rejected by Lord Goff of Chieveley, who gave the leading speech in the House of Lords in *Henderson v Merrett Syndicates Ltd*.[266] After conducting an extensive review of the case law, including the judgment of Oliver J in *Midland Bank Trust Co Ltd v Hett Stubbs & Kemp*,[267] Lord Goff arrived at the conclusion, in express agreement with that reached by Oliver J in the *Midland Bank Trust* case, that it was perfectly possible for a contracting party to owe the other party a duty of care in tort concurrently with the duties that might arise under the contract. Lord Goff said that, subject to the effect of an exclusion clause, a party to the contract was entitled to assert whichever cause of action was most

---

264 By s 12 of the Act, a contract for the supply of a service means a contract under which a person, the supplier, agrees to carry out a service, whether or not goods are to be transferred or bailed under the contract. S 16(1) of the Act provides that, subject to the Unfair Contract Terms Act 1977, the implied duty may be negatived. S 16(2) provides that an express term in a contract will not negative the implied term unless it is inconsistent with it.

265 [1986] AC 80, at 107.

266 [1995] 2 AC 145, at 184–194, which included a reference to *Tai Hing*, at 186.

267 [1979] Ch 384.

advantageous in its legal consequences to him, be it in contract or in tort. Lord Goff summarised his conclusions [268] on the point as follows:

> My own belief is that, in the present context, the common law is not antipathetic to concurrent liability, and that there is no sound basis for a rule which automatically restricts the claimant to either a tortious or a contractual remedy. The result may be untidy; but, given that the tortious duty is imposed by the general law, and the contractual duty is attributable to the will of the parties, I do not find it objectionable that the claimant may be entitled to take advantage of the remedy which is most advantageous to him, subject only to ascertaining whether the tortious duty is so inconsistent with the applicable contract that, in accordance with ordinary principles, the parties must be taken to have agreed that the tortious remedy is to be limited or excluded.

9.6.2.3.2   It is arguable whether the starting point should be to determine if a duty of care might arise and then to decide if the parties have agreed in their contract to limit or abrogate the duty [269] or whether the two issues should somehow be interwoven. [270] What is clear, however, is that the contract must evince something stronger than mere silence if it is to demonstrate an intention by the parties to preclude or limit the possibility of a tortious duty from arising. The general approach is that the intention of the parties to exclude or limit liability in negligence must be clear, and that it is for the party asserting that the liability has been excluded or limited to prove the point. [271]

9.6.2.3.3   In deciding whether to pursue its remedies in contract or in tort, a claimant will have in mind that there are certain differences that may be relevant in deciding between the two heads of claim, particularly as to the rules concerning damages and limitation periods. Putting it rather simply, and therefore at the risk of an over-simplification, [272] the principal differences may be summarised as follows. In contract, the requirements as to foreseeability and remoteness are judged as at the date of contracting, whereas in tort they are judged as at the time of breach. In contract, damages are assessed on the basis of putting the claimant in the position it would have been in if the contract had been performed. In tort, it is to put the

---

[268] [1995] 2 AC 145, at 193–194.

[269] See Lord Goff and Lord Browne-Wilkinson in *Henderson v Merrett Syndicates Ltd* [1995] 2 AC 145, at 194 and 206, respectively. See also Colman J in *BP PLC v AON Ltd* [2006] EWHC 424 (Comm); [2006] 1 All ER (Comm) 789, at [66-point vi].

[270] See the discussion in *Riyad Bank v Ahli United Bank (UK) PLC* [2006] EWCA Civ 780; [2006] 2 Lloyd's Rep 292 per Longmore LJ, at [21] and per Neuberger LJ, at [45]–[48].

[271] See, for instance, Scrutton LJ in *Rutter v Palmer* [1922] 2 KB 87, at 92 and Buckley LJ in *Gillespie Bros Ltd v Roy Bowles Transport Ltd* [1973] QB 400, at 419.

[272] For instance, the rules as to the assessment of damages in tort for negligence will differ between a claim for breach of a duty in providing information and a claim for breach of a duty in providing advice: see para 9.4.3.3 above and *South Australia Asset Management Corp v York Montague Ltd* [1997] AC 191 and *Aneco Reinsurance Underwriting Ltd v Johnson & Higgins Ltd* [2001] UKHL 51, [2002] 1 Lloyd's Rep 157.

claimant in the position it would have been in if the tort had not been committed. In contract, the limitation period will run from the date of breach, whereas in tort it will begin to run from the date the damage is suffered.

9.6.3 Protecting the agent

It is now appropriate to consider the protection that the facility agreement might seek to confer upon the agent, in terms of excluding, limiting, or qualifying the duties and the liabilities that it might otherwise owe to the banks as a matter of general law. The protective provisions will be found in the agency clause of the facility agreement. Having referred to those provisions, it will then be relevant to consider how effective such steps will be as a matter of law, particularly in light of legislative restrictions upon exclusions or limitations of certain types of liability.

As already mentioned, it is usually the case that the agency clause will contain a **9.6.3.1** provision which provides that the agent is not to be considered as acting in a fiduciary capacity towards the banks or any other person. For reasons of caution (for instance, in case it might be argued that the relevant matters should be implied as part of the contract of agency) the agency clause will probably also contain provisions addressing each of the types of duty that a fiduciary may theoretically have, such as in relation to conflicts of interest, having a personal interest in the facility, and the payment of remuneration to the agent by the borrower. For example, the clause may provide that the agent may engage in other business and transactions involving the borrower and its group, including other banking and advisory business, as well as providing that the agent may also be a bank under the facility, and may vote in its own interests and otherwise derive the benefit of being a bank. There will be provisions which deal with the payment by the borrower to the agent for its own account of fees, as well as provisions by which the borrower is obliged to reimburse the agent for expenditure that the agent may incur. Various rules have been developed as to the construction of such provisions. The relevant provision will be construed restrictively but fairly, according to the natural meaning of the words that have been used. Liability can only be limited or excluded by clear, unequivocal, and unambiguous terms, but it would appear that a strict *contra proferentum* rule will not be applied.[273]

There is also likely to be a provision which provides that the division or section of **9.6.3.2** the entity which is the agent should be treated as if it were separate from the remainder of that entity, so that information which is held at any time by any other part of that entity will not be treated as being known by the agent for the purposes of its functions as the agent under the facility agreement, such as in relation

---

[273] See Millett LJ in *Armitage v Nurse* [1998] Ch 241, at 255–256; *Bogg v Raper* (1998/99) 1 ITELR 267, at 280–285; *Wight v Olswang (No 2)* (1999/2000) 2 ITELR 689.

to its obligation to pass on relevant information to the banks. Such a provision on its own may not give all of the protection that the entity needs, because of the risk that information may seep from one part of the entity to the agency division or section. To be sure that this will not be a problem in practice, the entity should have adequate 'Chinese walls' in place to ensure that the information will not pass into the hands of those who work in the agency section, although there is always a risk that the barrier so erected may be found to be porous and inadequate.[274]

9.6.3.3 The agency clause will also contain various provisions designed to negative any responsibility that it might otherwise be alleged that the agent has, within a duty of care and skill, to look out for and protect the interests of the banks.[275] This will include a provision stating that the agent has no responsibility for the adequacy or effectiveness of any relevant documentation or of any information that may be provided, that it may rely on what it is told by the borrower or in a certificate provided by the borrower, that it has no obligation to monitor or investigate the borrower's affairs, that it may instruct and rely upon the advice of experts, and a provision by which any liability that might arise for any omission or wrongful act is excluded,[276] save where the same arises in consequence of the agent's deliberate or wilful misconduct or gross negligence. There is also likely to be a separate acknowledgement by the banks that they made their own investigations before deciding to enter into the facility, and that they did not rely on the agent in making that decision.

9.6.3.4 As the expression 'gross negligence' is often used when qualifying the protection afforded under an exemption clause, it is relevant to consider how the courts might construe the phrase. It would be a matter of construction of the contract in accordance with established principles,[277] but it is submitted that the following considerations should be relevant.

9.6.3.4.1 The concept of gross negligence is not easily understood in English civil law, but the case law has recently given some helpful guidance as to how the courts would

---

[274] As to the adequacy and effectiveness of Chinese walls see *Prince Jefri Bolkiah v KPMG* [1999] 2 AC 222 and *Young v Robson Rhodes* [1999] 3 All ER 524. See also the summary provided in *Australian Securities and Investment Commission v Citigroup Global Markets Australian Pty Ltd* [2007] FCA 963, at [308]–[321].

[275] As to the construction of such provisions, see para 9.5.3 above.

[276] This is likely to be extended to cover the directors, employees, and agents of the agent and the arranger, and such persons will be given the benefit of the Contracts (Rights of Third Parties) Act 1999 to enforce the provision for their own benefit. See further para 9.5.5 above.

[277] See Lord Wilberforce in *Prenn v Simmonds* [1971] 1 WLR 1381, at 1384–1386 and in *Reardon Smith Line Ltd v Yngvar Hansen-Tangen* [1976] 1 WLR 989, at 995–997, Lord Hoffmann in *Investors Compensation Scheme Ltd v West Bromwich Building Society* [1998] 1 WLR 896, at 912–913 and in *Bank of Credit and Commerce International SA v Ali* [2002] 1 AC 251, at [39], and Lord Steyn in *Sirius International Insurance Co (Publ) v FAI General Insurance Ltd* [2004] UKHL 54; [2004] 1 WLR 3251, at [18] and [19].

view it. In criminal law, it is one of the constituent elements of a charge of involuntary manslaughter (see the discussion by Lord Mackay of Clashfern LC in *R v Adomako*[278]), but it would be dangerous and may be inappropriate to transfer criminal concepts into the civil law. Millett LJ said in *Armitage v Nourse*[279] that English lawyers had a 'healthy disrespect' for distinguishing negligence from gross negligence. Lynskey J said in *Pentecost v London District Auditor*[280] that there was no distinction between the two.

Nonetheless, other civil cases have sought to draw a distinction between the concepts of negligence and gross negligence. In cases concerning the liability of a gratuitous bailee, the concept has been likened to 'culpable default', as opposed to some mere want of foresight or mistake of judgment: see Lord Chelmsford in *Giblin v McMullen*.[281] Sitting in the Jersey Court of Appeal, Sir Godfrey Le Quesne QC said in *Midland Bank Trustee (Jersey) Ltd v Federated Pension Services Ltd*,[282] when considering a trustee exemption clause, that the concept of gross negligence did not import a requirement for an intentional disregard of danger or recklessness, but rather meant 'a serious or flagrant degree of negligence'. In Scotland, in the context of professional negligence, the Lord President (Clyde) said in *Hunter v Hanley*[283] that 'the phrase "gross negligence" [indicated] so marked a departure from the normal standard of conduct of a professional man as to infer a lack of that ordinary care which a man of ordinary skill would display'. In *Tradigrain SA v Intertrek Testing Services (ITS) Canada Ltd*[284] Colman J had to consider the expression as a matter of German law.

9.6.3.4.2

Perhaps the most useful guidance as to the approach to construing the phrase 'gross negligence' is to be found in the decision of Mance J in *Red Sea Tankers Ltd v Papachristidis (The Hellespont Ardent)*.[285] In the course of a review of both American jurisprudence, particularly the position under New York law, and some English cases, Mance J said (in relation to the construction of provisions in a commercial agreement under which an exemption for liability was qualified by reference, inter alia, to acts and the consequences of gross negligence) that:

9.6.3.4.3

> the concept of 'gross negligence' [under New York law] appears to me to embrace serious negligence amounting to reckless disregard, without any necessary implication of consciousness of the high degree of risk or the likely consequences of the conduct on the part of the person acting or omitting to act. If the matter is viewed

278 [1995] 1 AC 171.
279 [1998] Ch 241, at 254.
280 [1951] 2 All ER 330, at 332.
281 (1868) 5 Moo NS 434, at 461.
282 [1996] PLR 179, at 206.
283 [1955] SLT 213, at 217.
284 [2006] EWHC 778 (Comm).
285 [1997] 2 Lloyd's Rep 547, at 586–588.

according to purely English principles of construction, I would reach the same conclusion. 'Gross negligence' is clearly intended to represent something more fundamental than failure to exercise skill and/or care constituting negligence. But, as a
matter or ordinary language and general impression, the concept of gross negligence
seems to me capable of embracing not only conduct undertaken with actual appreciation of the risks involved, but also serious disregard of or indifference to an obvious
risk . . . the question whether any negligence in the present case was 'gross' appears to
me ultimately still very much a matter of degree and judgment[286] . . . The conclusion
which I reach is that the concept of gross negligence in [the clauses under review in
that case] does not involve, necessarily, any subjective mental element of appreciation of risk. It may therefore include, taking the language of the American
Restatement,[287] conduct which a reasonable person would perceive to entail a high
degree of risk of injury to others coupled with heedlessness or indifference to or disregard of the consequences. The heedlessness, indifference or disregard need not be
conscious . . .[Although rigid restrictions were not justified in limiting the concept
of gross negligence to occasions where there was a high degree of serious risk of injury
or there were probable consequences of serious injury with a complete absence of any
attempt to avoid or minimise the serious risk of injury] I see no difficulty in accepting
that (a) the seriousness or otherwise of any injury that might arise, (b) the degree of
likelihood of its arising and (c) the extent to which someone takes any care at all are
all potentially material when considering whether particular conduct should be
regarded as so aberrant as to attract the epithet of 'gross' negligence . . . No single factor must be determinative. All the circumstances must be weighed and balanced
when considering whether acts or omissions causing damage resulted from negligence meriting the description 'gross' and forfeiting the contractual immunity prima
facie afforded by [the exemption provisions].

9.6.4 The Unfair Contract Terms Act

Finally, it would be relevant to turn to the Unfair Contract Terms Act 1977 to see
if any of the provisions in the agency clause which have the effect of acting as limitations or exclusions of duty or liability might be struck down by the Act and, in
particular, by section 2(2) of the Act, which concerns attempts by contract to limit
or exclude liability for negligence, or by section 3 of the Act, which concerns
attempts to limit or restrict contractual liability. The Act is examined at paragraph
9.5.5 above and the reader is referred to what is said there in relation to sections
2(2) and 3, as well as in relation to the requirement of reasonableness under
section 11. It is submitted that the protective provisions in the facility agreement
would not be struck down by the Act.[288] This is principally because they will be
regarded as meeting the requirement of reasonableness, in that they represent an

---

[286] This last point was made after his Lordship had referred to the speech of Lord Mackay of
Clashfern LC in *R v Adomako* [1995] 1 AC 171.
[287] Para 500 of the Second Restatement of Contracts.
[288] This assumes that the provisions do not go too far by seeking to protect the agent from the
consequences of its deliberate or wilful misconduct or, perhaps, gross negligence.

agreed allocation of risk as between experienced commercial parties on a basis that is commonly accepted in the London syndicated loan market. In addition, for the technical reasons outlined in the discussion of the Act earlier in this chapter, it is doubtful if the provisions of section 2(2) would apply to attempts to limit or exclude any duty of care and skill that the agent may have arising from a fiduciary relationship between it and the banks.

10

BOND ISSUES

10.1 Introduction

10.1.1 Bond issues are one of the principal types of transaction that take place in the capital markets, and bonds are one type of capital market instrument. Bond issues represent a significant part of the way in which finance is raised in the world's financial markets. It was estimated that the aggregate global issuance of investment grade bonds in June 2007 alone amounted to US$289.4 billion and that the aggregate global issuance high yield bonds (sometimes referred to as 'junk bonds') in that month came to a further US$22.5 billion. That month, however, immediately preceded the turmoil that occurred in the financial markets in the second half of 2007. In the following month of July, after the crisis had arisen, the respective aggregate figures had declined to US$98.4 billion and US$2.4 billion, which were the same figures as had been achieved, respectively, in August 2004 and October 2002.[1] It is interesting to note both the rapid increases in the issuance of bonds in the years preceding the onset of the crisis and then the comparatively higher decline in the issuance of high yield bonds as against the position for investment grade bonds, reflecting the nervousness in the markets towards the more risky types of instruments represented by high yield bonds.[2]

Bond issues come in various shapes and sizes. An issue may, for instance, be a straightforward means by which a State, an institution, or a commercial enterprise raises finance. Alternatively, a bond issue may form a component of a structured finance transaction, under which a special purpose vehicle issues bonds to raise finance to acquire a portfolio of debt or debt instruments. It is also relevant to mention the issuance of 'Sukuk' bonds, which are instruments similar to bonds that comply with Islamic principles. It has been estimated that in the first half of 2007, an aggregate of US$24.5 billion of such instruments were issued,[3] reflecting the growing interest all over the world in obtaining finance raised from them and the increasing willingness of those with Islamic beliefs to invest in such instruments.

10.1.2

The expression 'eurobond' has been used traditionally to describe the instrument, or security, that is issued in an international bond issue. That name developed initially to describe bonds denominated in US dollars which were subscribed for and held by investors using dollar funds they held in accounts outside the USA. The range of currencies in which bonds were issued was then broadened to attract subscribers who had funds in other currencies that were also held in off-shore accounts. With the advent of the euro as a separate currency in its own right there is a tendency now, so as to avoid confusion, to refer to such issues either as international bond issues or simply as bond issues. As with many things in this area, the nomenclature that is used, often rather nonchalantly, is usually not of great importance, so long as the true nature of the transaction and the ensuing instrument is properly understood.

10.1.3

For convenience, the discussion in this chapter will refer in general to 'bonds'. In theory there are a number of different types of instrument that may be issued, although some of the distinctions have been blurred over time. Strictly speaking, 'bonds' are debt instruments that have a life from issuance to maturity in excess of about five years and which either bear interest at a fixed rate or do not bear interest

10.1.4

---

[1] Figures quoted in the *Financial Times* 30/9/2007.
[2] In fact, the *Financial Times* was reporting that by the middle of October 2007, corporate issuances of investment grade bonds had been largely unaffected by the turmoil in the financial markets (*Financial Times* 22/10/2007).
[3] Figures quoted in the *Financial Times* 3/9/2007.

at all. The interest on a bond is usually called the 'Coupon' (which expression was derived from the coupons on the side of the bond which were torn off and presented for payment of interest on the interest payment days). 'Deep Discount Bonds' are bonds that are issued at a substantial discount to their par (or nominal face) value. 'Notes' are instruments which either bear interest at a floating rate (sometimes called 'Floating Rate Notes' or 'FRNs') or which are issued at a fixed rate of interest for a period of less than about five years. 'Medium Term Notes' are notes that are usually issued in a programme of several issues. 'Commercial Paper' concerns debt instruments that are issued for a year or less, usually as part of a pro-gramme of issuances of the paper.[4] The markets for the issuance of commercial paper were particularly hard hit by the financial turmoil that occurred in the sec-ond half of 2007, especially in relation to vehicles that were raising finance to fund or maintain structured finance transactions.

10.2 A Comparative Analysis by Reference to Loans and Other Transactions

10.2.1 A bond issue is a means by which the issuer raises funds usually for fairly large aggregate amounts. In some respects the issuance of bonds resembles borrowing money by way of loan, and in other respects it has its own characteristics. In either case, a debt will arise. In the case of a loan, the terms and conditions relating to it will probably, but not necessarily, be documented in some form of loan or facility agreement which will govern matters such as the right to borrow, the obligation to pay interest, and the obligation to repay the loan. It is possible as a matter of English law, however, to have a loan without any documentation, and the obliga-tions as to repayment and other matters will then depend upon the evidence of the oral transaction that was agreed, or which it is assumed was agreed, between the debtor and the creditor. In the case of a bond, the debt is represented by and encapsulated in the bond instrument itself, which is expressed as being payable to bearer. The person that holds the instrument for the time being (usually referred to as the 'bond holder') is the person entitled, as against the issuer, to payment of the debt at its maturity, being its due date for payment. The terms and conditions of the issue, to the extent not appearing on the face of the instrument, will be found in the terms and conditions on and subject to which the instrument was issued, which are usually to be found printed on the reverse side of each definitive instrument and set out, as well, in schedules to the documentation under which the issue took place and in the prospectus. As will be seen, one of the attractions to an investor of holding bonds is the ability to buy and sell them. This means that

---

[4] See the definition contained in Art 9(3) of the Financial Markets and Services Act 2000 (Regulated Activities) Order 2001 (SI 2001/544) as amended by SI 2002/682.

the identity of the bond holders may be changing frequently and that, at least in its traditional form, the legal relationship at any particular time will be between the issuer and whoever is the bond holder at that time.

10.2.2 The private nature of a loan transaction

A loan transaction will involve a single or a limited number of lenders, using funding in the main obtained from deposits held by the lender, wholesale funds borrowed in the interbank market, and, perhaps, funds raised in the capital markets. Essentially, the loan transaction is a private matter between the borrower and the lender or lenders who enter into the transaction with the borrower, although the modern practice in syndicated facilities allows for transference of loan participations to new creditors. Nonetheless, the group of creditors is likely to remain fairly restricted and the provisions of the documentation can control the circumstances in which transfers may take place and the disclosure of information that will be permitted.[5] Being private, a loan facility is well suited as a method of financing transactions of a confidential nature, such as a takeover bid (and strict obligations of confidence would be imposed so as to preserve the secrecy of the purpose for which the funds are to be used, at least until the matter has become known publicly), and the borrower can insist upon controls as to the transference by the lenders of their participations in the facility. Indeed, controlling the identity of the lenders may be important more generally to the borrower for relationship and other reasons, although the transfer mechanisms that are now commonly found in syndicated facility documents do tend to undermine that aspect.

10.2.3 The public nature of a bond issue

A bond issue, on the other hand, is usually a public transaction and contemplates that the bond holders will be drawn from a wide group of investors. There will be a distribution of information as part of the process of the issue (unless it is an issue by way of a private placement, in which case there will only be a small group of subscribers and a limited opportunity for transference of the subscribers' investments thereafter). On the other hand, a bond issue also implies anonymity as to the holders of the bonds, which will be bearer instruments, payable to the bearer, so the identity of the bond holders who hold the instruments will not be known. It is inherent in the nature of bonds that they are transferable, and so the composition of the investor group is liable to change from time to time. Initially the funds will be subscribed by a small syndicate of specialists who operate in the primary

---

[5] In fact, it is inherent in the relationship between a banker and its customer that the banker has an obligation not to disclose its customer's affairs except in limited circumstances, one of which is disclosure with the customer's consent. See Bankes LJ in *Tournier v National Provincial & Union Bank of England* [1924] 1 KB 461. For this reason, it is common for the borrower in the contract to permit disclosure to potential transferees.

market. After a relatively short period the bonds will be sold on to the much wider secondary market which is the true market of investors at which the issue will be aimed.

10.2.3.1 As a bond issue is public and aimed at a wide group of investors, which may change in their identity during the life of the issue because of trading in the bonds, it is likely to be considered as being an offer of debentures[6] to the public[7] and, perhaps, as involving a regulated market on which the bonds may be traded. It is also possible that the bonds may be listed. This will mean in the UK that private companies, that is, those which are not public companies, will be unable to issue bonds because of the limitations imposed by section 755 of the Companies Act 2006[8] and section 75(3) of the Financial Services and Markets Act 2000 (FSMA).[9] Other issuers, who are not affected by those restrictions, could be States and their central banks, international bodies such as the World Bank, and other types of public and local authorities. Various other regulatory matters will also need to be considered, such as whether a prospectus will be required (see further below).

10.2.4 The financial attractions to investors and their profile

One of the attractions of a bond issue to the issuer is that, as already mentioned, it is a method of raising funds from a wider base of investors than the traditional sources in raising funds from banks. It should therefore be possible to raise the funds more cheaply than by borrowing them from the banks. From the perspective of the bond-holding investors, by subscribing for and holding the bonds they should be able to obtain a higher rate of return than would be available by depositing their funds with a bank. It is also possible to tailor issues so that they will appeal to investors with different inclinations for their investment strategies. For instance, some investors may be looking for long-term investments that bear a yield, or a rate of return, at or equivalent to a fixed rate of interest, whilst others may be looking for something shorter that bears a floating rate of interest. Some investors may prefer, perhaps for tax reasons, to earn a return that is not reflected by bonds that bear interest but rather by bonds that are issued at a discount to their ultimate redemption amount, so that the return or yield will be represented by the difference between the issue price and the redemption or par value. Some investors will be interested in bonds issued in one currency rather than another. In terms of the yield that will be earned, some investors may prefer to invest in an

---

6 'Debenture' is defined in s 738 of the Companies Act 2006 (formerly s 744 of the Companies Act 1985) to include bonds.

7 See s 756 of the Companies Act 2006 (formerly s 742A of the Companies Act 1985) as to the meaning of the expression 'offer to the public'.

8 Formerly s 81(1) of the Companies Act 1985.

9 See also Reg 3(a) of the Financial Services and Markets Act 2000 (Official Listing of Securities) Regs 2001 (SI 2001/2956) and para 3.2 of the Listing Rules.

issue that is perceived as having a relatively low risk of default and which, in consequence, bears a low rate of return, whilst other investors will be content to invest in an issue that bears a higher yield in return for the greater perceived risk of default. Some investors may prefer to invest in 'payment in kind' (PIK) bonds, by which they will receive further issuances of bonds in place of interest or a yield paid in cash. 'Toggle' bonds allow an issuer to choose between paying interest in cash or issuing further bonds in cover of the interest. All of these matters will be relevant to an issuer and its advisers in deciding upon the type and characteristics of the issue that it should make and to an investor in deciding if it is prepared to invest in an issue.

10.2.5 Flexibility and rigidity

On the other hand, a loan facility can be structured to give flexibility in ways that might not be possible with a bond issue. A loan facility might be a multicurrency facility, allowing borrowings to be maintained in a number of different currencies at the same time, and it might also be a revolving facility which allows the borrower to utilise the facility when it needs funds and repay them temporarily when the funds are not required. It is likely that the facility will permit the borrower to repay early and to terminate the facility if it is not needed. In contrast, a bond issue will be denominated in one currency, it will involve an initial subscription for the whole amount of the issue,[10] and the borrower usually does not have a right of early redemption except in specific circumstances (for instance, because of a change in taxation which has an adverse effect on the issuer in relation to its obligations concerning the bonds).

10.2.6 Terms and conditions

There are also benefits from the perspective of the lenders in making funds available through a loan facility. By and large, provisions such as those relating to continuing covenants and undertakings, representations and warranties, and events of default are more extensive and favourable to the lenders in a loan facility than will be found in the terms and conditions that are attached to a bond issue. The equivalent provisions in the terms and conditions of a bond issue are, generally speaking, not as favourable to the bond holders and, indeed, representations and warranties usually will not be found at all in the terms and conditions that attach to a bond (although, as mentioned below, the initial subscribers in the primary market do usually receive the benefit of representations and warranties in the separate documentation by which they agree to take up their subscriptions). By way of

---

[10] However, with short- and medium-term issues, it is possible to have a programme for further issues after the first issue and for new issues to replace issues that are redeemed on maturity.

further example, the events of default in a loan agreement are usually fairly wide ranging, whereas they tend to be more limited in a bond issue; limited in the sense that they are not nearly as extensive in their subject matter and because they tend to contain generous grace periods and other qualifications to their operation. These various differences are justified by the difficulties and the attendant formalities in obtaining consents and waivers from a large body of bond holders, when compared with the more tightly knit body of lenders under a loan facility, and the relative ease and informality with which they can be approached and their decisions obtained.

10.2.6.1 The position is a little different where a bond issue is structured initially as a high risk or 'junk bond' issue. In such a case, the terms and conditions that are attached to the bonds, dealing with the covenants and undertakings, and the events of default, might be more extensive and stricter than would be found in an investment grade issue, although they are still likely to be more favourable to an issuer than would be found in the equivalent provisions of a loan facility.

10.2.6.2 Whilst the terms and conditions attached to bonds are unlikely to contain representations and warranties, the general body of bond holders might be able to gain some more limited form of comfort from the prospectus. As will be also be seen below, there are representations and warranties in the primary subscription documentation which are given for the benefit of the syndicate of the initial subscribers to the issue at the time of their subscription, but they do not endure for the benefit of the subsequent body of bond holders.

10.2.7 Credit checks

Potential investors in a bond issue, particularly those who operate in the secondary market, are unlikely to have conducted the level of investigations and enquiries that a bank will typically undertake before it commits to lend money to a borrower. This gap is filled to some extent by the information that will be contained in a prospectus, and in the supplementary information that has to be supplied annually to update its contents. The gap is also partly addressed by the credit ratings that will be ascribed to an issuer and its securities by the credit rating agencies such as Moody's Investor Services, Standard & Poor's, Duff & Phelp's, and Fitch Ratings. The ratings give a general view of the risk of non-performance that a ratings agency considers is appropriate to an investment and its issuer. By way of example, the highest or best rating that Standard & Poor's will ascribe is AAA and its lowest is D. The lowest investment grade rating that Standard & Poor's will give is BBB, below which it considers an investment to be speculative or, in common parlance, 'junk'. A rating will be given at the outset of an issue but it may change over time, either upwards or downwards. Apart from giving a general view of the risk associated with an investment, the ratings can be important because some investors, such as pension funds, are precluded from investing in or holding investments with less than an investment grade rating. A decline in the ratings during the life of an issue may result in a number of investors declining to buy the securities or having to sell their holdings in an issue, with an almost inevitable adverse effect on the market value of the securities. Although it is not common, some bond issues provide that a decline in the ratings of an issue will lead to an increase in the interest rate on the bonds, and it has sometimes even appeared as an event of default. It may also have the consequence that the issuer may be required to post security (margin), or additional security, for the benefit of the bond holders.

10.2.8 Issuing equity capital

A comparison has already been made between bond issues and loan facilities, as different means of raising finance. Another comparison that can be made is between a bond issue and an equity issue by way of shares. Historically, both involved the concept of an issuance of securities in return for subscriptions made by investors with the possibility, where there had been a public issuance, of subsequent trading in the securities. However, there are a number of differences between the two types of securities. Bonds are a form of debt and must be repaid by redemption at their maturity,[11] irrespective of whether the issuer has the requisite profits or reserves to fund the repayment. In fact, it is possible for the payment obligation on a bond to be accelerated if, for instance, an event of default has occurred. It is possible for a company to issue redeemable shares, but the obligation for redemption is subject to the company having the requisite reserves at the time redemption is to take place. Otherwise, share capital cannot be redeemed and is only repayable at the conclusion of a winding up or by a capital reduction in the limited circumstances permitted by legislation. Similarly, interest will be payable on bonds that bear interest without suffering from the limitations that apply to the declaration and payment of dividends on shares. Bonds may be issued at a discount, whereas shares historically could not be issued at a discount to their par value.[12] It is possible for bonds to be secured. Otherwise, they will rank *pari passu* with the other ordinary creditors of the issuer in its winding up, unless the bonds have been subordinated, as occurred in *Re British & Commonwealth Holdings plc (No 3)*.[13] In any event, they will rank ahead of the claims of the shareholders.

---

[11] Except for perpetual debentures which it is possible for a company to issue by virtue of s 739 of the Companies Act 2006 (formerly s 193 of the Companies Act 1985). They are usually issued by financial institutions as a method of raising regulatory capital.

[12] But see the reforms, originally advocated in *The White Paper on Company Law Reform* (Cm 6456 March 2005), as reflected in s 1295 of and Sched 16 to the Companies Act 2006.

[13] [1992] 1 WLR 672.

10.3 Trading in Bonds

10.3.1 There is a further matter that is important to an investor which is a bond holder. It concerns the ability of the bond holder to realise its investment at some time before the maturity date of the bonds. It may wish to do this because it needs the funds for some other purpose, if it feels that the risk attached to the bonds has deteriorated or if it wishes to realise a profit ahead of the redemption date, due to an increase in the value of the bonds since they were acquired. If the investor, instead of investing in bonds, had deposited its funds with a bank, it would have done so in the fairly confident belief as to the safety of its investment, but without hoping to realise any profit by a gain in the underlying value of the deposit. It could have made the deposit on the basis that it could withdraw the funds when it wished, or it might have made a term deposit. Unless the bonds in which it wishes to invest have a relatively short term to maturity, it is unlikely that the investor will have a similar opportunity of redemption or repayment by the issuer as it would in making a deposit with a bank, because the bonds will only have to be redeemed by the issuer at their maturity, unless an event of default has occurred giving rise to an acceleration of the issuer's payment obligations. Subject to such an acceleration, the issuer has the certainty of the funds it has raised for the life of the issue.

10.3.2 Such a conundrum for the investing bond holder may be resolved if the bond holder is able to sell the bonds, although it cannot do much about the risk of a deterioration in the value of its investment if there is a change in the assessment of the risk of default on the bonds (except, perhaps, by buying protection through the use of a credit derivative). Apart from the commercial issues concerning the price of the sale, the answer will depend largely upon whether the bonds can be easily and safely transferred, so that the seller can be divested of its interest and the transaction will be safe for the purchaser. In particular the purchaser will wish to be sure that it will obtain a good title to the bonds that it has bought and that, in consequence, it will be treated as the unencumbered owner of the bonds.

10.3.3 Historically, such an outcome could be achieved if it was possible to treat the bonds as being negotiable instruments and if the circumstances of the transfer of the instrument fulfilled the necessary requirements to confer on the transferee the protection of becoming a holder of a negotiable instrument, particularly as a holder in due course. For the reasons that will be examined further below, it was possible to meet those requirements as a matter of English law. Modern developments, however, have meant that the historical position has been overtaken by the computerised forms of trading and recording of interests that now obtains in the capital markets. The concept of holding and transferring bonds as physical instruments has largely disappeared and, with it, the certainty that was associated with the concept of negotiable instruments. It will also be necessary in the examination below to consider the legal consequences of the new regime.

10.4 Bonds as Negotiable Instruments

As previously mentioned, it was an important feature in the development of bonds **10.4.1** that they were transferable in the sense that the transferee could be certain of receiving a good title in the instrument that it purchased. That involved two matters. First, that the instrument would be treated as a negotiable instrument, which involved the requirements that (i) the instrument was transferable by delivery, whether or not accompanied by an endorsement, and (ii) that a transferee upon delivery was able to acquire a full legal title in the instrument, free of any equities and defects in title that may have affected prior holders of the instrument and the immediate parties to it.[14] In this respect, a transferee could acquire a better title than its transferor, which was an exception to the general rule that it is not possible to transfer a better title than that enjoyed by the transferor. In considering this issue, it is also important to understand that the concept of negotiability is additional to the concept of transferability. Not all instruments (or, indeed, other types of rights) that may be transferable, such as by assignment or endorsement, are negotiable. The second matter was that the transferee in a particular transaction should obtain a good title in consequence of the negotiation of the instrument to it, which depended upon the circumstances of the transaction in which the instrument was delivered to it and its own state of knowledge.

10.4.2 Conflict of laws

Conflict of laws issues may also arise in looking at each of those matters. Subject to section 72 of the Bills of Exchange Act 1882,[15] under the English principles of conflict of laws, the question of whether an instrument qualifies to be treated as a negotiable instrument is to be determined by the law of the place where the instrument was when the purported negotiation of it took place,[16] or by either that law or the law of the forum.[17] Whether it has been successfully negotiated will depend upon the law of the place where the purported negotiation took place.[18] Under section 72 of the Bills of Exchange Act 1882, the relevant conflict of laws questions will be determined by the law of the place where the relevant act under consideration took place, with special rules permitting the instrument to be treated as negotiable if it meets the relevant requirements of the law in the UK.

---

[14] See Blackburn J in *Crouch v Credit Foncier of England Ltd* (1873) 8 QB 374, at 381.

[15] Which concerns bills of exchange, promissory notes, and cheques.

[16] See Auld LJ in *Macmillan v Bishopsgate Investment Trust (No 3)* [1996] 1 WLR 387, at 412–413.

[17] See Staughton LJ in *Macmillan v Bishopsgate Investment Trust (No 3)* [1996] 1 WLR 387, at 401, who declined to choose between the two tests.

[18] See Staughton LJ and Auld LJ in *Macmillan v Bishopsgate Investment Trust (No 3)* [1996] 1 WLR 387, at 401 and 412–413.

10.4.3 The tests for negotiability

Assuming that these matters are to be resolved under English law, as the applicable law determined in accordance with the conflict of laws rules, an instrument will qualify to be treated as negotiable if it fulfils the requirements laid down in the Bills of Exchange Act 1882 or, if it fails to meet those requirements, if it is otherwise treated as being a negotiable instrument by the law merchant, as ascertained by mercantile custom. A bearer bond will not qualify to be treated as a negotiable instrument under the Act because it is too hedged about with conditions and uncertainties on its face to meet the definitions contained in sections 3, 73, and 83 of the Act, which require that the relevant instruments should be unconditional orders or promises to pay a sum certain on demand or at a fixed or future determinable time.[19] It is therefore necessary to consider if a bearer bond might qualify to be treated as a negotiable instrument in accordance with mercantile custom and usage. The list of instruments which may so qualify is not fixed or closed and it is possible for new types of instrument to acquire the status of negotiable instruments by mercantile usage, even if the practice is of recent origin.[20] It should be noted, however, that a particular instrument can only qualify to be treated as being negotiable if there is nothing contained within it to negative the intention that it should be negotiable.[21]

10.4.3.1 In *Edelstein v Schuler & Co*[22] Bigham J held that a bearer bond that had been issued by an English company, which was expressed to be freely negotiable and transferable, would be treated as a negotiable instrument in accordance with mercantile custom.[23] It had previously been held that bearer bonds issued by a foreign government[24] or by a foreign corporation[25] were negotiable instruments. It does not matter that there is security for the bonds nor that there are provisions for their early redemption or for the calculation or payment of interest by reference to an index or other factor that cannot be immediately determined on their face.[26] Bonds that are expressed to be payable to bearer have been held to be negotiable

---

[19] For an example of the application of those requirements, see *Claydon v Bradley* [1987] 1 WLR 521.

[20] See Lord Wright in *Bank of Baroda Ltd v Punjab National Bank* [1944] AC 176, at 183; *Bechuanaland Exploration Co v London Trading Bank* [1898] 1 QB 658, at 674–678; and *Edelstein v Schuler & Co* [1902] 2 KB 144.

[21] See, for instance, *London and County Banking Co Ltd v London and River Plate Bank Ltd* (1889) 20 QBD 232.

[22] [1902] 2 KB 144.

[23] See also *Bechuanaland Exploration Co v London Trading Bank* [1898] 1 QB 658.

[24] *Gorgier v Mieville* (1824) 3 B&C 45.

[25] *Venables v Baring Bros & Co* [1892] 3 Ch 527.

[26] *Re Olathe Silver Mining Co* (1884) 27 ChD 278; *Venables v Baring Bros & Co* [1892] 3 Ch 527; *Bechuanaland Exploration Co v London Trading Bank* [1898] 1 QB 658; and *Edelstein v Schuler & Co* [1902] 2 KB 144.

even though (as is common practice) there is a separate trust deed which contains a covenant by the issuer to pay the amounts due on the bonds to the trustee, so long as the intention is that the bonds should create obligations payable to the bearer and not to the trustee, even though there may be limitations on the holder's right to sue the issuer, provided that in the circumstances where the holder is entitled to sue it may do so independently in its own name.[27] It follows that bonds which are subordinated may still be regarded as being negotiable, as they transfer such rights as are represented by the bonds. It is worth noting that Megaw LJ in *Customs & Excise Cmrs v Guy Butler (International) Ltd*[28] said that certificates of deposit issued by banks were accepted in the market as being negotiable instruments.[29]

10.4.4 The rights of the transferee

The next issue to be determined, assuming that a particular bond is treated as a negotiable instrument, is whether the transferee of that bond is able to enjoy the full benefits of the negotiability of the instrument, so as to be free of any defects in the title of its predecessors. To be in that position, the transferee needs to be classified as a 'holder in due course', which expression is defined in section 29 of the Bills of Exchange Act 1882.[30] Essentially, a holder in due course is a person who, bona fide and for value, takes a negotiable instrument that is complete and regular on its face, before it has become overdue, and without notice of previous dishonour or of any defect in the title of a previous holder. To preserve the value of the instrument to a person who has the status of a holder in due course, section 29(3) provides that another person who, other than by fraud or illegality, derives his title from a holder in due course may assert the same rights as the holder in due course.

If the transferee is able to meet these various requirements, then it will enjoy the benefits of being a holder in due course of a negotiable instrument and the associated protections that arise in consequence of its enjoyment of that status.   **10.4.5**

10.4.6 Global bonds and the lack of definitive individual bonds

The foregoing applies in the case of definitive instruments that are intended to be held by individual investors. As will be seen below, the modern practice is that individual definitive instruments are rarely issued and, hence, investors in a bond

---

27 *Re Olathe Silver Mining Co* (1884) 27 ChD 278; *Venables v Baring Bros & Co* [1892] 3 Ch 527.
28 [1976] 2 All ER 700, at 702.
29 See also Slade J in *Libyan Arab Foreign Bank v Bankers Trust Co* [1989] QB 728, at 754–755, but contrast *Claydon v Bradley* [1987] 1 WLR 521.
30 Although the Act contains its own definition of the requirements for the recognition of bills, promissory notes, and cheques as negotiable instruments under the Act, it was regarded as codifying much of the common law as it related to negotiable instruments. This is why s 97(2) preserves the common law except where the Act is expressly inconsistent with it.

issue cannot claim to be the physical holders of negotiable instruments and able to assert the benefits of being holders in due course of such instruments. Their investments, not being represented by and encapsulated within physical instruments, will depend on the legal consequences of the trading and settlement systems in which such investments are traded, and in the recording of their interests in book entry accounting systems. Instead, there is usually one such global instrument in existence at any time. It is very doubtful, however, if the status of being a negotiable instrument would be accorded to global instruments which represent the whole of an issue.

10.4.6.1 The temporary global bond that is issued at the outset of the issue is only in existence for a short time, with the intention that it will be exchanged, usually after 40 days, by the permanent global bond (sometimes labelled, instead, as the semi-permanent global bond, to acknowledge the faint possibility that definitive bonds might be issued at a future date). In its form, the permanent global bond is expressed to be an instrument payable to bearer, but in practice the intention is that the instrument will never be traded or negotiated. Instead, it will be held by a custodian which holds it as a depository for the computerised trading and settlement systems on which the real trading in the issue will take place. It is unlikely that the global instrument will see the light of day except if it has to be produced in enforcement action or for its cancellation upon redemption or if definitive bonds are to be issued in replacement for the global instrument. Anyone who tried to deal in such an instrument would be regarded with a great deal of suspicion. It is inconceivable that a bona fide purchaser would accept such an instrument. On that basis, it must be very doubtful that the global bond would be regarded, in accordance with mercantile custom, as being a negotiable instrument.

10.5 The Modern System of Recording and Dealing in Securities

10.5.1 The problems with the old paper based system

There are a number of practical problems in the traditional system of issuing definitive instruments which represent and encapsulate an investor's entitlement in the securities in which it has invested. There is the risk of theft and loss of the instrument. There is the risk of fraud and forgery and the consequential cost of security printing and authentication of the instruments. To achieve a transfer, there has to be physical delivery of the instrument to the transferee. To obtain payment of the principal on the bond, it has to be surrendered at the relevant place of payment and to achieve the payment of interest, the relevant coupon has to be delivered for payment, with the consequential loss to the holder if there is delay in delivery of the bond or the coupon.

10.5.2 Centralised systems

It was to overcome those difficulties that the use of physical instruments has largely been phased out and replaced by centralised and computerised systems for holding and recording interests, and dealings therein, of investments in securities issued by a wide range of issuers, be they debt or equity securities. For instance, the systems provided by Euroclear in Brussels, Clearstream in Luxembourg, and CREST in London.[31] There may be either no physical securities held in such systems at all or, alternatively, there might be one global instrument that represents the whole of an issue of securities. In the case of securities dealt with in the CREST system, individual securities may be represented by electronic means or, alternatively, physical securities may exist outside the system. If there is no underlying physical instrument in existence then the securities are said to be 'dematerialised'. In the alternative, as with international bond issues dealt with in the Euroclear and Clearstream systems, there might be one global instrument for the whole issue of the securities. Such instrument will have been deposited with a custodian or common depository which holds it for the centralised system or systems. Such a security is said to be 'immobilised'. In effect, an entire issue of securities will be represented by interests recorded in the system against the accounts of the participant members of the relevant system.

10.5.3 Recording and tiering of interests

Such participants in the system might have their own direct commercial interest in the securities recorded against their names in such accounts or they might be holding such interests, in whole or in part, for third parties who do not participate directly in the system. Such third parties (e.g. an investment manager or a stockbroker) may, in turn, be holding their entitlements on behalf of others, who might be the ultimate investors or there might be even more intermediate holdings and levels or tiers going further down the line. Thus, there can be a tiering of holdings represented by computerised or book entries in accounts at the various levels, each of which could represent an amalgamation of various clients' interests. For instance, the stockbroker may be holding an entitlement in an investment, which is recorded in its name in the accounts maintained by a participating member in the clearing and settlement system. The stockbroker, in its turn, may hold its entitlement on behalf of several of its clients. The holding recorded in the relevant participating member's accounts in the centralised system might represent an amalgamation of its own investments in that security and other investments in that security which are being held by it for several different persons (including

---

[31] The systems in Brussels and Luxembourg are sometimes referred to as 'Central Securities Depository' (CSD) or as an 'International Central Securities Depository' (ICSD).

that of the stockbroker). Thus, the ultimate investor's recorded interest in a security could be some way removed from the issuer of the security and, if it exists, the underlying physical instrument.

10.5.3.1 A person who maintains a holding with respect to a security on behalf of others at any one of the tierings mentioned above is usually referred to as an 'intermediary' with respect of those others and the allocation of that holding as between those others will usually be recorded as entries (usually in a computerised form) in the accounts and records that the intermediary maintains. The entitlement represented by such entries is often referred to as an 'intermediated security'.

10.5.3.2 It is necessary to determine the nature of the entitlements of the parties as recorded respectively at the various levels in the tiering and the effect on those entitlements of any unauthorised dealings or the insolvency of an intermediary (or the effect of any proprietary enforcement action against an intermediary) whose records show that it is holding its entitlement, in whole or in part, on behalf of other parties. It must be borne in mind that the entitlement of a party at a step in the tiering is represented by an entry in the records of the intermediary immediately above him (perhaps accompanied by some documentation which sets forth the intended relationship between them). The recorded interest has no physical aspect; at best, when taken with any accompanying documentation, it will probably only represent some type of intangible claim or right against the intermediary, being the next person up in the chain. In other words, the recorded interest will depend upon the robustness of the intermediary's own entitlement as recorded in the records of the next intermediary and so on.

10.5.3.3 Being realistic, a person's individual recorded interest in the records of his own intermediary, being the person immediately above him in the chain, is likely not to be recognised or discernible further up in the chain of tierings, as each of the intermediaries at higher levels is only likely to record in its own records the entitlements of each of the people immediately under it, on whose behalf (perhaps as well as itself) it holds its own entitlement. An alternative, but less plausible, analysis is to say that, via the ascending and descending chain of recorded entitlements as recorded at the different tiers, the entitlement of the ultimate holder of an individual investment at the bottom of the pile can be traced up to the ultimate source at the highest level. It is submitted that this cannot be correct, given the fact that at each level there will simply be a recording by the relevant intermediary of gross entitlements as allocated to the persons next down in the chain, without differentiating between claimants of sub-intermediaries in each of those gross entitlements. The position might be different if some type of recording or identification could be made from the highest level downwards of the individual entitlements of the ultimate holders of investments, but that is an unlikely scenario, except where there are only one or two levels of interest, so that such a system might be feasible.

The discussion that follows will examine the issues that arise from the above under **10.5.4**
English law, then in other jurisdictions. It will be necessary, as well, to consider the
conflict of laws issues that may arise. Finally, it will be relevant to mention the
proposals that have been put forward for a UNIDROIT convention to deal with
both the domestic and cross-border legal issues. Given the vast amounts (both in
absolute terms and by way of value) of intermediated securities that are dealt with
on a global basis and referable to recorded interests in centralised systems, it is
astonishing that so many issues remain unresolved and that substantial harmonisation has not yet been achieved in the approaches that are taken, both within and
as between different jurisdictions.

10.5.5 The English domestic position

In a purely English law setting, it should be possible to construct a series of trusts
to protect separately the various interests at each level in the tiers of holdings, as
against their respective intermediaries, provided that there is sufficient evidence of
an intention for such trusts to be created, the relevant trust property can be identified when it is necessary to do so, and it is certain who are the intended beneficiaries of the trust. In effect, at each level the intermediary holding an entitlement in
a fund on behalf of others would be regarded as a trustee of that entitlement on
behalf of those others as its beneficiaries. Where such a beneficiary is in fact acting
as an intermediary on behalf of its own beneficiaries then it would hold its rights
in the fund held by the first mentioned trustee on behalf of those beneficiaries. In
effect, there would be a trust at each level in the tierings.

That could most easily be achieved if it was possible to separate out each benefi- **10.5.5.1**
ciary's interest from the overall allocation held by its trustee (e.g. by the use of separate security numbers that can identify a specific allocation for each beneficiary).
This is unlikely to be a practical solution, as the trustee is more likely to be holding
its entitlement in the form of an overall fungible quantity, or bulk, without any
separate identification of specific securities of identifiable parts or units for each of
its beneficiaries. It has been held that this does not present an insuperable difficulty as it is possible to have a valid trust in an intangible asset held in a bulk or
fungible form (a true mixed fund) for the benefit of beneficiaries for whom there
is only a proportionate allocation of interests in that bulk.[32] An example would be
where a trustee holds a quantity of identical investments in a bond issue or a parcel

---

[32] See *Hunter v Moss* [1994] 1 WLR 452; *Re Harvard Securities, Holland v Newbury* [1997]
2 BCLC 369; and *Re CA Pacific Finance Ltd* [2000] 1 BCLC 494. This should be contrasted with
the position at common law concerning ill-fated attempts to establish an entitlement in a bulk of
goods. See *Re Wait* [1927] 1 Ch 606, *Re London Wine Co (Shippers) Ltd* [1986] PCC 121 and *Re
Goldcorp Exchange Ltd* [1995] 1 AC 74. The position relating to goods was partially alleviated by the
introduction of ss 20A and 20B, Rules 5(3) and (4) of s 18, and a definition of 'bulk' in s 61(1) into
the Sale of Goods Act 1979, which were introduced by the Sale of Goods (Amendment) Act 1995.

of shares. It is not clear if the beneficiaries in such a situation would hold their entitlements in the pooled trust property as tenants in common or on some other basis, bearing in mind that the pool or bulk is likely to be an ever changing quantity as interests are bought and sold on behalf of individual beneficiaries.

10.5.5.2   Such an approach will only work, however, if it is clear that a beneficiary's entitlement is in a bulk held by the trustee in a particular issue of a security rather than in a mixture of different issues of securities without an indication of the beneficiary's intended interests in each of the issues (unless they are entirely of the same nature and interchangeable). It is also important to bear in mind that the entitlement of the beneficiary is in what is held by the trustee. The beneficiary's entitlement can be no better or more extensive than the trustee's own entitlement. If for some reason the trustee's apparent entitlement is defective or non-existent then the beneficiary will suffer accordingly, although it may be that the beneficiary might have some personal claim against its trustee if there has been misfeasance or incompetence on the part of the trustee.

10.5.5.3   A difficulty will also arise under English law if there is a discrepancy at any level between the quantities of entitlements that are recorded in the intermediary's (acting as the trustee) records for the relevant beneficiaries with respect to an issue of a security and the aggregate quantity of interests in that issue that are actually held by the intermediary for them, particularly in the context of an insolvency of the intermediary (where a personal claim to make up the shortfall would not be of much use). It is not clear how that difficulty would be resolved, bearing in mind again the fact that the overall quantity within each bulk of a security is likely to change from time to time as sales and purchases are made for the beneficiaries. In addition, over the period new beneficiaries will be allocated an entitlement in the fund and the entitlement of some beneficiaries will be extinguished.

10.5.5.4   One possible answer is to apply the rule in *Clayton*'s case [33] which provides a presumption as to the appropriation of payments into and out of an account or a fund in situations where there has not been an express agreement as to the way in which the appropriation is to be made. The rule is to the effect that the earliest payments or withdrawals out of an account or fund are to be treated as having been drawn against the earliest payments or contributions into the account or fund.[34] The operation of the rule may have the effect, however, of working an injustice, particularly with respect to those persons who were the earliest contributors to the fund. As the rule is really more in the nature of a presumption to be applied where there has not been an express agreement as to appropriation, it is

---

[33]   *Devaynes v Noble: Clayton's case* (1816) 1 Mer 572.

[34]   For the benefit of law students, the rule is often characterised by the letters 'FIFO'—first in against first out.

possible for the rule to be displaced where it would not be suitable for it to be applied, such as where it would cause an injustice or if it would be impractical to apply the rule in unravelling what had happened. In any event, the rule does not apply where a trustee holds an account with contains his own money and the funds of others. If the trustee makes a withdrawal from the account for his own benefit, the withdrawal is allocated first against the trustee's own entitlement in to the account.[35] Doubt has also been expressed as to whether the rule in *Clayton's* case applies, in any event, in tracing claims or to claims not involving a banking account.[36]

An alternative to the application of the rule in *Clayton's* case is to allocate un-authorised withdrawals or an unauthorised deficiency arising in the trust property on a rateable basis against the beneficiaries in the fund at the time each withdrawal was made. This is also likely to be an onerous and impractical exercise. A third possibility, which has gained approval in various recent English cases, is to allocate the total amount of the fund on a *pari passu* basis, so that it is applied rateably amongst all of the claimants. Even this method is far from perfect and it may discriminate against those who were the last to make contributions, in favour of those who managed to exit from the fund before the intervention of the trustee's breach of trust or insolvency.[37] This is also the approach taken under Article 8 (Revised) of the American Law Institute's Uniform Commercial Code (UCC).[38]

10.5.5.5

10.5.6 Other approaches to entitlements

In the USA, under Article 8 (Revised) of the UCC, a person is given a 'security entitlement' in the rights in a securities account held by an intermediary, so that those rights are treated as not belonging to the intermediary and so do not fall into its estate in its insolvency.[39] The rights are treated as shared on a pro rata basis by the entitlement holders.[40] A similar position applies in relation to the recorded entitlements in securities in the systems and recorded entitlements operated and maintained by Euroclear and Clearstream and their participants in Belgium and Luxembourg.[41]

---

[35] *Re Hallett's Estate, Knatchbull v Hallett* (1880) 13 Ch D 696.
[36] See Leggatt LJ in *Barlow Clowes International Ltd v Vaughan* [1992] 4 All ER 22, at 43–44.
[37] See *Barlow Clowes International Ltd v Vaughan* [1992] 4 All ER 22; *El Ajou v Dollar Land Holdings plc (No 2)* [1995] 2 All ER 213; *Russell-Cooke Trust Co v Prentis* [2003] 2 All ER 478; and *Commerzbank AG v IMB Morgan plc* [2004] EWHC 2771 (Ch), [2005] 1 Lloyd's Rep 298.
[38] UCC § 8-503(b).
[39] UCC § 8-503(a).
[40] UCC § 8-503(b).
[41] Under Belgium Royal Decree No 62 of 10/11/1967 (as amended) and under Luxembourg Grand-Ducal Decree of Feb 1971 (as amended).

10.5.7 Conflict of laws issues

So far the discussion has assumed that the issues may be looked at under the domestic rules of one jurisdiction. A consideration of the issues, however, will often involve a conflict of laws problem, because it is quite possible that there will be different locations for the issuer, the common depository, the centralised system or systems, the various intermediaries that might be involved, and the ulti-mate investor. The conflicts position up until now in English law has been rather confused.

10.5.7.1 One possible answer has been to follow the 'look through' approach, by which the entitlements and relevant issues would be governed by the law governing the underlying instrument from which the various tiers of rights might have been derived. The difficulty with this approach is that it fails to recognise that a person's rights might be some way removed from the underlying instrument, and it may be difficult to ascribe proprietary entitlements flowing through each of the tier-ings in the chain, despite the approach that might be taken at the level of the underlying security. Furthermore, this approach fails to take into account the position where there is no underlying instrument as, for instance, if the securities are dematerialised.

10.5.7.2 An alternative approach is to look separately at each level in the tier of holdings and to apply the law of the place where the account or register in which a holding at the relevant level is recorded so as to determine the nature of the rights and obli-gations associated with the entitlements represented by the entries in that account or register. This is the PRIMA approach (the 'place of the relevant intermediary approach'). There was an attempt to introduce a PRIMA approach into English law on a general basis by the Financial Markets and Insolvency (Settlement Finality) Regulations 2001[42] but they never came into force.[43]

10.5.7.3 *The PRIMA approach at the EU level*

At the EU level, PRIMA was adopted by Article 9 of the Settlement Finality Directive[44] and by Article 9 of the Directive on Financial Collateral Arrange-ments.[45] The former Directive applies to transactions involving designated securi-ties settlement or payment systems, the participants therein, and the European Central Bank and the European System of Central Banks. The latter Directive,

---

[42] SI 2001/997.

[43] See SI 2001/1349.

[44] EC 1998/26 OJ L166 11/6/98, which was implemented in the UK by the Financial Markets and Insolvency (Settlement Finality) Regs 1999 (SI 1999/2979), as amended. See, in particular, Reg 23.

[45] EC 2002/47 OJ L168 17/6/2002, which was implemented in the UK by the Financial Collateral Arrangements (No 2) Regs 2003 (SI 2003/3226). See, in particular, Reg 19.

although wider in its scope, is nonetheless limited in its application to transactions by way of collateral (in the form of secured transactions or title transfer transactions) involving securities or cash (i.e. money credited to an account or similar claims for repayment of money, such as money market deposits). The PRIMA approach is also recognised in Article 24 of the Directive on the reorganisation and winding up of credit institutions[46] in relation to the enforcement of proprietary and other rights in 'instruments'. An instrument is defined[47] by reference to those instruments that are referred to in Schedule B to the EC Directive on investment services,[48] such as transferable securities. Unfortunately, it is not clear if the concept of transferable securities is only meant to refer to negotiable instruments.[49]

10.5.8 The Hague Convention

The Hague Convention on the law applicable to certain rights in respect of securities held with an intermediary, was signed on 13 December 2002 by 53 States and it remains open for ratification. In December 2003 the European Commission put forward a proposal that the Convention should be ratified by the EU on behalf of all of the EU Member States, which would have entailed some modifications to the Settlement Finality Directive and the Financial Collateral Directive.[50] It has not yet been ratified in that manner. The rules of the Convention will apply in cross-border situations to matters concerning debt or equity securities represented by book entries in accounts (whether physical or computerised), where such securities are held for an account holder in an account with an intermediary whose business involves it in acting in that manner, but it will not apply to cash as such. Subject to national law, it will also apply to central securities depositories and the operators of centralised systems. It will not apply to purely contractual matters between the intermediary and the account holder. It will cover issues such as the entitlement of the account holder as represented by the entries on the securities account, the effect of an acquisition or disposition of such an entitlement (whether by way of an outright disposition or by way of security), requirements for perfection, and priority matters. The Convention provides for a modified form of PRIMA in ascertaining the governing law concerning those matters. It expressly disavows the 'look-through' approach (see Article 6).

---

[46] EC 2001/24 OJ L125 5/5/2001.
[47] In Art 2.
[48] EC 93/22 OJ L141 11/6/93.
[49] See the definition in Art 1, but contrast that with the statement in the Recital to the Directive that the concept of transferable securities is only meant to cover negotiable instruments.
[50] See the European Commission's Proposal dated 15/12/2003 (COM (2003) 783).

10.5.8.1 *The primary rule*

The primary conflicts rule provided by Article 4 of the Convention is that the applicable law concerning the matters dealt with by the Convention will be the law of the State specified in the account agreement between the intermediary and the account holder as the governing law of the agreement or, if so specified, the law stated in the agreement which is intended specifically to govern such matters provided, in either case, that the intermediary has an office which maintains securities accounts in that State for such purposes. The Convention provides for a State to include the separate territorial units of a State.

10.5.8.2 *Fall back rules*

There are fall back rules in Article 5 in case there is not an effective express choice of law stated in the account agreement in accordance with Article 4. The first is that if the account agreement unambiguously provides that the intermediary entered into the agreement in a State where it has an office relevant to maintaining securities accounts as an intermediary then the applicable law will be the law of that State.[51] Failing that, the second fall back is that the applicable law will be the law of the place of incorporation or organisation of the intermediary at the time the agreement is entered into or the account is opened.[52] The third fall back is that the applicable law will be that of the State where the intermediary has its principal place of business at the time of the agreement or when the account is opened.[53]

10.5.8.3 There are also provisions dealing with the effect of an amendment in the account agreement which is intended to change the relevant applicable law.[54]

10.5.8.4 *The applicable law*

The applicable law will apply to govern the matters dealt with in the Convention which have occurred before the opening of insolvency proceedings, but not so as to prejudice the effect of insolvency laws concerning the ranking of claims, preferences, transactions at an undervalue, or the enforcement of rights after the opening of the insolvency proceedings.[55] The relevant applicable law determined in accordance with the Convention will apply irrespective of whether or not the State whose law is to be applied is a signatory to the Convention.[56] The application of the applicable law determined by the rules in the Convention may be

---

[51] Art 5(1).
[52] Art 5(2)(a).
[53] Art 5(2)(b).
[54] Art 7.
[55] Art 8.
[56] Art 9.

overridden by the public policy of the forum hearing a dispute or the mandatory rules of the forum, except as to priorities and perfection requirements.[57]

10.5.9 The UNIDROIT Convention

It is relevant at this stage to mention the work that has been done in this area by UNIDROIT (the International Institute for the Unification of Private Law). Following an earlier draft, UNIDROIT put forward a proposed international convention, to be called the Convention on Substantive Rules Regarding Intermediated Securities,[58] with a view to its adoption in 2008. The objective of the Convention is to achieve a harmonisation of the domestic laws of the States that will be signatories to the Convention. It seeks to do this by advancing the overall aims of (i) enhancing the internal soundness of the laws relating to the holding and transfer of intermediated securities (i.e. entitlements in securities as recorded or credited to an intermediary's accounts and records), and (ii) ensuring the cross-border compatibility of such laws.

10.5.9.1 The Convention will provide a set of rules that should govern the following matters: the effectiveness of entries in securities accounts held by intermediaries (including, for instance, proprietary entitlements and priority rights), the methods by which transactions should take place (including the creation and realisation of security and other limited interests), the integrity of the entries in an intermediary's accounts and the effectiveness of those entries in favour of account holders as against third parties claiming against the intermediary or the claims of creditors of the intermediary, the exercise of rights related to intermediated securities, such as voting rights and rights to income, the effect of set-off rights, and the effect of rules of law which might reverse or challenge the integrity of a transaction in intermediated securities.

10.5.9.2 It is likely that the Convention will be adopted by the EU, as it follows many of the recommendations that were made by the EU's Legal Certainty Group.[59] The Group published a report [60] which concluded that there was a need for a common legal framework across the EU for the treatment of interests in securities. It said that the framework should include procedures for the creation, perfection, and enforcement of such interests. It also said that the absence of a common framework was an important source of legal risk in cross-border transactions.

10.5.9.3 In 2007, the Law Commission published a valuable review of the position under English law and of the Legal Certainty Group's study, as well as a review of a

---

[57] Art 11.
[58] Fourth Session, Rome, 21–25 May 2007, Study LXXVII, published on 9 August 2007.
[59] Sometimes referred to as the 'Giovannini Group'.
[60] *Cross-Border Clearing and Settlement Arrangements within the European Union*, November 2001.

preliminary draft of the proposed UNIDROIT Convention.[61] In broad terms, the Commission favoured the approach put forward in the Convention.[62]

10.6 The Process of a Bond Issue

10.6.1 The lead manager and the mandate

Before looking at the detailed matters concerning the documentation that is involved in a bond issue and the relevant regulatory matters, it is pertinent at this stage to give an overview of the process under which a bond issue takes place. There are various stages leading to the conclusion, or 'closing', of a bond issue. The process usually begins with the awarding of a mandate by the issuer to a lead manager. The lead manager plays a pivotal role in the process, in that it arranges the issue and is likely to act in a number of roles in the documentation that is entered into. The mandate will reflect a number of issues including the following:

- whether the issuer should be the holding or parent company in a group or a finance subsidiary (in which case a guarantee might be required from the holding or parent company);
- if the issue should be secured (as would be the case in a securitisation) or unsecured;
- if there should be a listing on an exchange such as in London, Luxembourg, or Dublin;
- if there should be a trustee (as would be required if the issue is to be secured) or a fiscal agent;
- the likely syndicate in the primary market who would make the initial subscription for the issue and the nature of the participants in the secondary market to whom the issue should be aimed;
- matters concerning the pricing of the issue and whether it should bear interest or be issued at a discount; and
- taxation matters (such as the likely incidence of a withholding tax. This may be relevant in determining the identity of the issuer) and the fees and costs that will be incurred.

---

[61] *Updated Advice to the Treasury*, May 2007.
[62] The Law Commission's review was further updated in the form of a *Further Updated Advice* in May 2008.

10.6.2 Due diligence

The due diligence exercise will begin, which is particularly relevant to the preparation of the prospectus and its contents. This will involve the issuer and its directors, and the lead manager and their respective lawyers and other advisers.

10.6.3 Launch of the issue

The lead manager will 'launch' the issue by announcing it in the markets and, at the same time, it will invite members of the primary market to join the syndicate of initial subscribers for the issue. Having received responses from them, the lead manager will allocate to them their respective allotments.

10.6.4 Listing

If the issue is to be listed then the procedures to obtain a listing will commence in accordance with the listing rules of the relevant exchange. The lead manager will play an important role in obtaining the listing. A benefit of obtaining a listing is that pursuant to sections 874(3) and 882 of the Income Tax Act 2007 the bonds will qualify for UK tax purposes as 'quoted eurobonds', provided that the bonds have been issued by a company, that they carry interest, and that the listing is on a recognised stock exchange.[63] If those conditions are met then interest on the bonds will be free of the obligation under the law in the UK to make a deduction from interest that would otherwise apply under sections 874(1) and (2) of the Act. Another benefit of obtaining a listing is that it makes for a wider investor base which might invest in the securities, as some institutional investors and funds are restricted to holding only listed securities. A listing on a European exchange may also assist in meeting the requirements under Regulation S to gain an exemption from the registration requirements of the US Securities Act 1933 (see below). It used to be the case that if a listing was obtained before the offering in the secondary market, then it was unnecessary to have a prospectus that complied with the requirements of the Public Offer of Securities Regulations 1995 because listing particulars would be in force. That meant that the offerors in the secondary market did not need to accept responsibility for the contents of a prospectus. That is no longer the case, in light of the implementation of the Prospectus Directive and the repeal of the 1995 Regulations (see further below).

10.6.5 The signing

A few weeks after the mandate was awarded, the 'signing' will take place. At or shortly before the signing, the issuer (and any guarantor) will have passed the

---

[63] Defined in s 987 of the Income Tax Act 2007.

necessary corporate resolutions to approve the transaction, the documentation to be entered into, the prospectus, the application for listing, and other matters. At the signing, the Subscription Agreement is entered into between the issuer, the lead manager, and the managers, being the members of the syndicate which has agreed to make the initial subscription for the issue (as to the Subscription Agreement see further below). As between themselves, the managers and the lead manager will also enter into the Agreement Among Managers (as to the Agreement Among Managers see further below).

10.6.6 The closing

About a week later, the 'closing' will take place when the bond issue comes into effect and the issuer receives the proceeds of the subscriptions from the managers. The remaining documentation will be executed and delivered by the issuer, the guarantor, the trustee or the fiscal agent, and the paying agents (see further below). In return for the issuance by the issuer of the Temporary Global Bond (see further below), which is authenticated by the lead manager and delivered to the common depository on behalf of the clearing systems (the depository will have executed an acknowledgement that it holds the Temporary Global Bond and its successor, the Permanent Global Bond, for safe custody on behalf of the clearing systems), the lead manager will receive the subscription moneys from the syndicate and pay them over to the issuer, and the securities accounts of the syndicate members in Euroclear and Clearstream will be credited with their allocations in the issue.

10.7 Regulatory Matters

10.7.1 The principal regulatory matter that needs to be considered concerns the requirement for a prospectus and matters that relate to the prospectus, which will be dealt with first. Other matters to which reference will be made concern compliance with the requirements introduced under the EC Directive on markets in financial instruments, the use of stabilisation techniques relating to the pricing of the bonds, listing requirements, and the restriction on taking deposits under FSMA. Reference will also be made to certain US regulatory matters.

10.7.2 Prospectus requirements

The EC Prospectus Directive[64] aims to facilitate access to financial markets across the EEA. It had to be implemented by 1 July 2005. It was implemented in the UK

---

[64] EC 2003/71 OJ L345 31/12/2003.

pursuant to the Prospectus Regulations 2005.[65] The regulations made substantial amendments to Part VI of FSMA and to the Financial Services and Markets Act 2000 (Official Listing of Securities) Regulations 2001.[66] In addition, the Public Offer of Securities Regulations 1995[67] and the Financial Services and Markets Act 2000 (Offers of Securities) Order 2001[68] were revoked. The Financial Promotion Order 2001 was replaced by a new Financial Promotion Order 2005 (SI 2005/1529). At the same time the Financial Services Authority introduced a new three-part block in its *Handbook* containing new Listing Rules, Disclosure Rules (required to implement the Market Abuse Directive[69]) which were introduced pursuant to the Financial Services and Markets Act 2000 (Market Abuse) Regulations 2005,[70] and the Prospectus Rules.

10.7.2.1 Summary

By way of a short preliminary summary, the Prospectus Directive, with limited exceptions, requires the production of a prospectus (in the bond markets sometimes called an 'offering circular') when there is an offer of securities to the public within the EEA or where there is an admission of securities to trading on a regulated market in the EEA. It provides for the production of a single prospectus approved in the relevant home Member State. All prospectuses must meet specified content and disclosure standards. Once approved, a prospectus may be used throughout the EEA. The required content of prospectuses is governed by the EU Regulation on Prospectuses,[71] which imposes different levels of requirements depending on the types of securities that are involved. The EU Regulation should be read in conjunction with the Committee of European Securities Regulators (CESR) Guidelines[72] that were issued in February 2005. There is also a continuing updating obligation under the Directive to provide information on an annual basis.

10.7.2.2 The relevant securities

The 'securities' to which the Prospectus Directive relates (in the UK Prospectus Rules, the expression 'transferable security' is used to mean the same thing) are defined in Article 2(1)(a) initially by reference to the definition of 'securities' in Article 1(4) of the Investment Services Directive[73] with the exception of money

---

65 SI 2005/1433.
66 SI 2001/2956.
67 SI 1995/1537.
68 2001/2958.
69 EC 2003/6 OJ L096 12/4/2003.
70 SI 2005/381.
71 EC 809/2004 OJ L149/1 30/4/2004.
72 05-054b.
73 EC 93/22 OJ L141 11/6/93.

market instruments having a maturity of less than 12 months. Essentially, the definition catches shares, bonds, and securitised debt 'negotiable on the capital markets'. However, Article 1(2) of the Prospectus Directive provides a list of instruments to which the Directive has no application which include the following (although it is possible in some of those cases voluntarily to draw up a prospectus (Article 1(3)):

- securities issued or guaranteed by a Member State of the EEA or one of its local authorities, or by the European Central Bank or a central bank of a Member State, or by an international body of which a Member State is a member (paragraphs (b) to (d));
- certain types of securities issued in a continuous or repeated manner by a credit institution (paragraph (f));
- securities in an offer where the total consideration in a 12-month period is less than EUR2.5 million (paragraph (h));
- certain types of non-equity securities issued in a continuous or repeated manner by a credit institution where the total consideration in a 12-month period is less than EUR50 million (paragraph (j)).

It should be noted that if it is desired to obtain a listing in the UK on the Professional Securities Market (see below) or otherwise on the Official List, it will be necessary to prepare listing particulars for debt securities within paragraphs (f) and (j) above.[74] As to listing particulars, see below.

10.7.2.3 *The need for a prospectus*

Article 3 of the Directive sets out the two situations where there is an obligation to publish a prospectus, but there are exceptions to that obligation contained in Article 4. The two situations are, first, where there is an offer of securities to the public within one or more Member States, and, secondly, if there is an admission of securities to trading on a regulated market operating within a Member State. A prospectus may be required under either or both of those situations, so the fact, for instance, that it might not be intended to apply for admission to trading on a regulated market will not avoid the requirement for a prospectus if there is to be an offer to the public. However, provided that a prospectus remains current pursuant to Article 9, only one prospectus will be needed even if the prospectus is required under both situations.

10.7.2.3.1 An offer of securities to the public   Subject to certain exceptions, Article 3(1) of the Directive provides that an offer of securities to the public within one or more Member States shall not be made unless there has been a prior

---

[74] See LRs 2.2.11, 4.1.1, 4.1.2, and 17.2.1.

publication of a prospectus. An 'offer of securities to the public' is defined in Article 2(1)(d) to mean as follows:

> a communication to persons in any form and by any means, presenting sufficient information on the terms of the offer and the securities to be offered, so as to enable an investor to decide to purchase or subscribe to these securities. This definition shall be applicable to the placing of securities through financial intermediaries.

It would appear that this definition will not be met if the communication fails to include information about the price, but this is subject to Article 8(1), which relates to providing information about a final offer price and the final amount of securities to be offered. It should be noted that the requirement for a prospectus may be placed on an offeror who might not be the issuer. It may be appropriate to obtain undertakings from the issuer to assist in the preparation of a prospectus if that situation might arise.

10.7.2.3.1.1 Excepted offers   The exceptions to the requirement in Article 3(1) of the Prospectus Directive are contained in Article 3(2) and they are as follows:

(a) an offer only to 'qualified investors'. That expression is defined in Article 2(1)(e) to cover the following:

 (i) legal entities which are authorised or regulated to operate in the financial markets (e.g. credit institutions, investments firms, other financial institutions, insurance companies, pension funds) and unregulated or unauthorised entities whose corporate purpose is solely to invest in securities;

 (ii) national and regional governments, central banks, international and supranational bodies;

 (iii) legal entities that are not small and medium-sized enterprises (SMEs);

 (iv) natural persons who qualify as qualified investors;

 (v) SMEs which qualify as qualified investors;[75]

(b) an offer addressed to fewer than 100 natural or legal persons per Member State, excepting qualified investors;

(c) an offer addressed to investors who acquire securities of a total consideration of at least EUR50,000 per investor for each separate offer;

(d) an offer whose denomination per unit amounts to at least EUR50,000;

(e) an offer whose total consideration is less than EUR100,000 over any period of 12 months.

---

[75] Note: there is a UK register of natural persons and SMEs that qualify as qualified investors. See s 87R of FSMA (as amended by SI 2005/1433).

It should be noted that any subsequent resale by any of the foregoing is to be regarded as a separate offer, which will require a prospectus unless it falls within one of the above exceptions in its own right (Article 3(2)).

10.7.2.3.2 *Admission of securities to trading*

Article 3(3) of the Prospectus Directive provides that a prospectus must be published if there is an admission of securities to trading on a regulated market operating within a Member State. A 'regulated market' is defined in Article 2(1)(j) of the Directive by reference to Article 1(13) of the Directive on investment services.[76] The regulated markets in the UK are the markets operated by the London Stock Exchange for securities listed on the Official List, LIFFE, and Virt-x. It should be noted that on 1 July 2005 the London Stock Exchange established a new recognised trading platform called the Professional Securities Market. It is designed for issues of specialist securities, such as bonds. It will have the status of a recognised stock exchange (which is important in determining if a debt security qualifies as a 'quoted eurobond' for the purposes of sections 874(3), 882, and 978 of the Income Tax Act 2007). Although it will be a listed market, it will not be a regulated market for the purposes of the Prospectus Directive so that the requirement for publication of a prospectus under Article 3(3) will not apply to specialist debt securities listed on that market. However, Chapter LR 4 of the Listing Rules deals with the requirements for approval by the UK Listing Authority and publication of listing particulars for securities listed on the Professional Securities Market.[77]

10.7.2.4 *Exemptions*

Article 4 of the Prospectus Directive contains exemptions from the requirements for publication of a prospectus in Article 3. Article 4(1) sets out the exemptions relevant to an offer of securities to the public, and Article 4(2) sets out the exemptions relevant to an admission to trading on a regulated market. The exemptions concern matters such as the substitution, conversion, and exchange of securities, takeovers and mergers, bonus and rights issues, admission on a second regulated market, shares for directors and employees, and a *de minimis* level for securities of the same class already admitted to trading.

10.7.2.5 *Form and content*

Article 5 of the Prospectus Directive deals with the requirements for the form and content of a prospectus. Article 5(3) provides that the prospectus may be in three documents, being a registration document about the issuer, a securities note giving details of the securities, and a summary note, or in a single document

---

[76] EC 93/22 OJ L141 11/6/93.
[77] See also Chap LR 17 of the Listing Rules for listed debt securities.

comprising those elements. For non-equity securities issued under an offering programme by any issuer or in a continuous or repeated manner by a credit institution, Article 4(4) provides the option of having a base prospectus which can be supplemented. Article 5(1) contains a general statement of what is required to be contained in a prospectus, but this is subject to the exception in Article 8(2), dealing with matters such as confidential information and information which should not be disclosed in the public interest. Article 5(1) states as follows:

> The prospectus shall contain all information which, according to the particular nature of the issuer and of the securities to be offered to the public or admitted to trading on a regulated market, is necessary to enable investors to make an informed assessment of the assets and liabilities, financial position, profit and losses, and prospects of the issuer and of any guarantor, and of the rights attaching to such securities. This information shall be presented in an easily analysable and comprehensible form.

Article 5(2) requires that the prospectus should contain information concerning **10.7.2.5.1** the issuer and the relevant securities and that it must contain a summary conveying the essential characteristics and risks associated with the issuer, any guarantor, and the securities. It must also contain warnings as set forth in Article 5(2). The detailed requirements for the contents of prospectuses is contained in the EC Regulation on prospectuses[78] which lays down different requirements, by the use of a set of scheduled annexes and 'building blocks' which will depend upon matters such as the types of issuer and securities, whether there is a third party involved, such as a guarantor, and whether the securities are to be listed. Note should also be taken of Article 16 of the Prospectus Directive which requires the prospectus to be supplemented for any new factor, material mistake, or inaccuracy relating to the information in a prospectus which is capable of affecting the assessment of the securities and which arises or is noted between the time when the prospectus is approved and the final closing of the offer or when trading on a regulated market begins. Investors may withdraw their acceptances in consequence of any such supplementing of information under Article 16. In addition, Article 10 requires that issuers whose securities have been admitted to trading on a regulated market, except with respect to non-equity securities whose denomination amounts to at least EUR50,000, should provide at least annually an update of information that they have published or made available during the previous 12 months, including corporate and accounting information.

10.7.2.6 Approval

Article 15 provides that a prospectus may not be published unless it has been approved. Approval is a matter for the competent authority of the 'home Member

---

[78] EC 809/2004 OJ L149 30/4/2004.

State', which is defined in Article 2(1)(m). At the risk of oversimplification, the following is a summarised guide to that definition:

(i) for an EEA issuer of equity securities or other securities not within (ii): where the issuer's registered office is situated;

(ii) for issues of non-equity securities where the per unit denomination is at least EUR1,000 (or equivalent) or certain convertible or exchangeable issues:
   • the Member State where the issuer has its registered office, or
   • the Member State where the securities are admitted to trading on a regulated market, or
   • the Member State where the securities are offered to the public

   (at the choice of the issuer, the person asking for admission or the offeror, as the case may be);

(iii) for non-EU issuers (except where falling within (ii)):
   • the Member State in which the securities are first offered to the public, or
   • the Member State where the securities are first admitted to trading on a regulated market

   (at the choice of the issuer, the person asking for admission or the offeror, as the case may be).

10.7.2.6.1 Once a prospectus has been approved in the relevant home Member State, it has validity throughout the EEA under Article 17, following notification to other Member States under Article 18. The provisions dealing with the application for approval of a prospectus in the UK are dealt with in PR 3.1 of the Prospectus Rules, and the provisions for filing and publication are dealt with in PR 3.2 of the Prospectus Rules. Under Article 9 a prospectus remains valid for 12 months from the date of its publication, subject to its being updated, if required, under Article 16 and the other matters specified in Article 9.

10.7.2.7 *Responsibility for the contents of a prospectus*

Article 6 makes provision for those who must accept responsibility for a prospectus. Article 6(1) requires the Member States to ensure that responsibility for the information given in a prospectus attaches at least to the issuer or its administrative, management, or supervisory bodies, the offeror, the person asking for admission to trading on a regulated market, or the guarantor, as the case may be. There must also be a clear identification of those responsible, such as by names, functions, or registered offices in the prospectus. There must also be declarations by them that, to the best of their knowledge, the information contained in the prospectus is in accordance with the facts and that the prospectus makes no omission likely to affect its import. It appears that an 'offeror' and the person requesting admission may have responsibility for the information contained in a prospectus, even if they did not prepare it and are relying upon a prospectus issued within the previous 12 months (but see below). The UK rules for responsibility will be found in PR 5 of the Prospectus Rules. PR 5.5.4 R and PR 5.5.8 R of the Rules deal with the responsibility concerning debt securities, and PR 5.5.5 R and PR 5.5.6 R of the Rules contain some exemptions. There are two further important exemptions. Under PR 5.5.7 R of the Rules the offeror will not have responsibility if the issuer has responsibility, the issuer was primarily responsible for the preparation of the prospectus, and the offeror is making the offer in association with the issuer. Under PR 5.5.9 R of the Rules there is an exemption for a person giving advice in a professional capacity.

Article 6(2) provides that the Member States shall ensure that their laws on civil liability apply to those persons responsible for the information given in a prospectus. However, no civil liability is to attach to any person solely on the basis of the summary document in a prospectus, unless it is misleading, inaccurate, or inconsistent when read together with the other parts of the prospectus.[79] It should be noted that Article 5(2)(d) requires that the summary in a prospectus must contain a warning that civil liability attaches to those persons who have tabled the summary but only if the summary is misleading etc. when taken together with the other parts of the prospectus.

10.7.2.7.1

In the UK, section 91 of FSMA[80] provides for penalties for breach of rules relating to prospectuses or listing particulars. Section 90 of the Act[81] provides for compensation to be payable by any person who is responsible for a prospectus or listing particulars if it contains any untrue or misleading statement or omits any matter that should have been included therein. The compensation is payable to any person who has acquired securities to which the prospectus or particulars relates and who has suffered loss in respect of the securities as a result of the error. That person could be an initial subscriber or a later purchaser in the secondary market. For these purposes, if the prospectus or particulars should have confirmed the absence of any matter and are silent about it, that is treated as a statement that there was no such matter. It is not necessary for the claimant to prove that he relied on the erroneous matter in deciding to proceed with the acquisition of the securities. He merely has to show that he has suffered loss as a result of the error; for instance, that upon the error coming to light after he acquired the securities there was a fall in the value of the securities.

10.7.2.7.2

---

[79] See also s 90(12) of FSMA (as amended).
[80] As amended by Reg 7 of the Prospectus Regs 2005 (SI 2005/1433) and s 1272 of and Sched 15 to the Companies Act 2006.
[81] As amended by Reg 6 of SI 2005/1433.

10.7.2.7.3 There are defences to a claim under section 90 which are contained in Schedule 10 to the Act, covering matters such as having had a reasonable belief in the truth of a statement, reliance upon statements by experts that are included in the prospectus, that the error had been corrected before the securities were acquired, reliance upon official statements, and that the claimant knew of the error when the securities were acquired. Section 90(12) also expressly incorporates the exception from civil liability provided for in Article 6(2) of the Prospectus Directive (this applies with respect to any civil liability, not just to claims that would otherwise arise under section 90). The Act does not provide for how the compensation should be assessed.[82] The likely possibilities are either that the claimant should be compensated for all the loss it has suffered in buying the securities (i.e. the difference between what was paid and the value on re-sale, which is what would be ordered in a claim in deceit: see *Smith New Court Securities Ltd v Scrimgeour Vickers (Asset Management) Ltd*[83]) or the difference on the date of purchase between what was paid and the true value on that date.

10.7.2.7.4 In addition to the statutory right to compensation, there might also be the possibility under English law of a claim at general law for any loss that the investor might have suffered in consequence of an error in the prospectus. Section 90(6) preserves the right to bring a claim at general law, but this will be subject to the exemption from civil liability that is provided for by section 90(12). Such a claim at general law might be founded in areas such as deceit, misrepresentation, negligent misstatement, or breach of contract, but will, of course, depend on the facts and circumstances and the need to make out the case on the normal grounds, such as the need to show causation and reliance to bring a claim in negligent misrepresentation and the rules as to foreseeability, remoteness, and the assessment of damages.

10.7.3 MiFID

The EC Markets in Financial Instruments Directive[84] (MiFID) had to be implemented throughout the EC and the wider EEA by 1 November 2007 (it is understood that quite a number of States failed to respect that deadline). It replaced the Investment Services Directive[85] (ISD), upon which it expanded in large measure. Under the Lamfalussy process, MiFID was supported by some further

---

[82] S 90B of FSMA (inserted in consequence of s 1270 of the Companies Act 2006) provides that the Treasury may make regulations concerning the liability of issuers of securities and other persons with respect to incorrect information given to holders of the securities, to the market, or to the public generally. At the time of writing, no such regulations had been made.

[83] [1997] AC 254.

[84] 2004/39/EC OJ L145/1 30/4/2004.

[85] 93/22/EEC OJ L141/27 11/6/93.

EC level 2 legislation.[86] At level 3, the CESR published various guidance for adoption by regulators at the fourth or national level, including the Financial Services Authority (the FSA) in the UK. It was hoped that this process would lead to conformity in the interpretation and implementation of MiFID across the EC and EEA. The UK claims that it implemented MiFID in an 'intelligent copy-out' form, as reflected in amendments that were made to the Financial Services and Markets Act 2000 (Regulated Activities) Order 2001[87] (the Regulated Activities Order) and to the FSA's Rule Book, for instance by new Conduct of Business rules (COBS) and changes to the Market Conduct (MAR) rules to incorporate the new transparency requirements for securities markets. The subject matter dealt with by MiFID is enormous and complicated. What follows is intended to provide a brief overview of the effect of MiFID.

MiFID applies to firms whose regular occupation is to provide specified services or to perform specified activities on a 'professional basis'.[88] The services and activities must relate to specified financial instruments (including 'transferable securities', such as company securities, bonds and other forms of securitised debt,[89] money market instruments, units in collective investment schemes, and derivatives instruments) and ancilliary services, as respectively listed in Schedules A, B, and C in Annex 1 to MiFID. It should be noted, in particular, that MiFID extended upon the scope of the ISD so as to include the giving of investment advice (which was already covered in the UK in any event), and it included commodity derivatives within the concept of financial instruments. The concept of commodity derivatives is far from easy to comprehend. It has led to extensive additions to the definitions of options, futures, and contracts for differences in Articles 83, 84, and 85 of the Regulated Activities Order.[90]   **10.7.3.1**

Firms to whom MiFID applies must be authorised for their specified services or activities by their home State regulator, that is, in the EC or EEA State in which they are established.[91] Such authorisation will give them a 'passport', which enables them to supply those services and conduct those activities in other EC or EEA States.[92] It should be noted, however, that if they do so through a branch in   **10.7.3.2**

---

[86] EC Regulation implementing Directive 2004/39/EC (1287/2006/EC OJ L241/1 2/9/2006) and EC Directive implementing EC Directive 2004/39/EC (OJ L241/26 2/9/2006).

[87] SI 2001/544, as amended (particularly by SI 2006/3384).

[88] A concept which remains undefined. The FSA's view is that the relevant factors in understanding the concept 'will include the existence or otherwise of a commercial element and the scale of the activity' (*Perimeter Guidance relating to MiFID—Feedback on CP 06/9 & CP 06/14* PS 07/5, Q. 7).

[89] The definition of 'transferable securities' is contained in Art 4(1)(18) of MiFID.

[90] See Chap 11.

[91] This is dealt with in Title II of MiFID.

[92] See Chapter III of Title II of MiFID.

another such State (the host State), they must comply with the conduct of business rules of the host State.[93]

10.7.3.3   There are certain exceptions from those to whom MiFID applies.[94] These include: authorised credit institutions (but they will have to comply with MiFID's organisational and operational requirements[95]); firms established outside the EC/EEA (but host regulators in the EC or the EEA will be expected to require that such firms comply with MiFID's organisational and operational requirements); firms engaged entirely in relevant intra-group activities; insurance, assurance, or re-insurance undertakings; collective investment undertakings and their managers (but managers of UCITS who provide discretionary management or advice to non-fund clients will be subject to most of the organisational and operational requirements); some high street financial advisers and other distributors of retail investment products;[96] persons who provide an investment service which is incidental to a regulated professional activity; and persons (other than market makers) who only deal on their own account (subject to certain criteria).

10.7.3.4   MiFID also provides for the regulation of various financial markets in a more extensive manner than applied under the ISD. This extends to off-market trading. In effect, the requirements of MiFID will apply to the traditional regulated markets, as well as to Multilateral Trading Facilities (MTFs), Systematic Internalisers, and market makers.[97] Such entities, for instance, are subject to MiFID's transparency requirements.

10.7.3.4.1   MTFs are alternative trading systems, usually operating through trading platforms, which bring together multiple third party buying and selling of financial instruments and operate in accordance with non-discretionary rules.[98] They may be operated by an investment firm or by a separate operator. They are regulated on the basis of being investment firms, with regulatory obligations that are analogous to those which apply to a regulated market. For instance, they are required to undertake regular monitoring (e.g. of transactions) so as to ensure compliance with their rules by users of their systems and to detect breaches of the rules, disorderly trading conditions, or market abuse. They must also report breaches of their rules to the authorities and assist in investigations and prosecutions.[99]

---

[93] Art 32(7) of MiFID.
[94] See, generally, Art 2 of MiFID.
[95] See Art 1(2) of MiFID.
[96] See Art 3 of MiFID and the Financial Services and Markets Act 2000 (Markets in Financial Instruments) Regs 2007 SI 2007/126, as amended.
[97] See Title III of MiFID (as to regulated markets) and Arts 26–30 of MiFID as to the others.
[98] The definition is contained in Art 4(1)(15) of MiFID.
[99] Art 26 of MiFID.

Systematic Internalisers[100] are investment firms which deal on their own account by executing client orders outside a regulated market or an MTF on an organised, regular, and systematic basis. **10.7.3.4.2**

Title II of MiFID obliges investment firms to comply with various organisational (i.e. prudential) and operational (i.e. conduct of business) rules. In the UK, the conduct of business rules are contained in a new COBS Rulebook in the FSA's Handbook, which contains principles and high-level rules, in place of the more detailed rules in the old COB section of the Handbook, which have ceased to apply. These rules require firms to categorise clients into the categories of retail clients, professional clients, and eligible counterparties. Different levels of obligation by the firm apply to each category, with the least obligations applying with respect to eligible counterparties. The rules also provide for: information and documentation that should be provided to clients; requirements that must be met as to suitability of a transaction for professional and retail clients (except with respect to execution-only transactions in certain types of non-complex financial instruments); requirements concerning the appropriateness of recommendations that are provided to retail and professional clients; obligations as to best execution (i.e. to obtain the best result for the client after taking into account the price and various other factors); and conflicts of interest.[101] **10.7.3.5**

With respect to transparency requirements[102] (in the UK, these will be found under the MAR rules in the FSA's Handbook), investment firms must make post-trade disclosure to market participants and report off-market trades. Any transaction which is traded on a regulated market must be reported to the home State regulator (or the host State regulator in the case of a branch). There are also pre-trade transparency requirements that are imposed upon MTFs and Systematic Internalisers with respect to shares. At the time of writing, the EC Commission had deferred a decision as to whether the transparency requirements of MiFID should apply to the bond markets. A decision was expected to be made by November 2008. **10.7.3.6**

10.7.4 Stabilisation

Stabilisation is the process by which the price of securities is supported or dampened through an under-allotment or an over-allotment ('ancillary stabilisation') of the securities at or about the time of issuance. There is usually an authority given to the lead manager, in its discretion, to engage in stabilisation activities in the Subscription Agreement and the Agreement Among Managers. This activity is

---

[100] Defined in Art 4(1)(7) of MiFID.
[101] Art 18 of MiFID.
[102] See Title III, Chapter 2, Section 3 of MiFID.

permitted by Chapter III of an EC Regulation,[103] if it is within certain parameters concerning the time in which it may be done, the requirement for disclosure that it may be done (for instance, in the prospectus), limits to the price at which stabilisation may be executed, and further requirements as to over-allotment.

10.7.5 UK Listing Rules and Listing Particulars

In July 2005 the Financial Services Authority promulgated new Listing Rules, which replaced the listing rules that were current up until then. The rules will be found as part of a new three-part block in the FSA's Handbook. The FSA took the opportunity to re-order and re-word the rules for listing securities. The rules cover eligibility for listing, continuing obligations for listed issuers, and the role of sponsors. The rules contain separate provisions that apply to debt securities. The rules that relate to debt securities for which a prospectus is not required will be found in Chapter LR 4 of the Listing Rules. They require that listing particulars must be prepared, approved by the FSA, and published for any debt securities that are to be listed on either the Official List or the Professional Securities Market.[104] The requirements for the content and format of listing particulars are specified (see LR 4.2), which are a cut-down version of the requirements for a prospectus. There is a requirement for supplementary listing particulars with respect to significant changes and new matters arising in the period between the submission of the original particulars and the commencement of dealings in the securities.[105]

10.7.5.1 Part 3 of the Financial Services and Markets Act (Official Listing of Securities) Regulations 2001[106] specifies those who are to be responsible for listing particulars,[107] but there is an exemption with respect to issuers that are non-EEA States or non-EEA local or regional authorities.[108]

10.7.5.2 Chapter LR 17 applies to debt and other specialist securities. It deals with the requirements for listing of the securities and listing applications, requirements with continuing application, and disclosure requirements. However, the requirements are lessened for issuers that are States, regional and local authorities, and international bodies.[109]

---

[103] The Regulation regarding exemptions for buy-back programmes and stabilisation of financial instruments (EC 2273/2003 OJ L 336/33 23/12/2003).

[104] See LR 4.1 and LR 2.2.11, taken with LR 17.2.1.

[105] LR 4.4.

[106] SI 2001/2956 (as amended).

[107] See also LR 4.2.12.

[108] LR 4.2.13(2).

[109] LR 17.5.

10.7.6 Deposit taking

Technically, it is arguable that an offering of debt securities for subscription might constitute accepting deposits as a specified kind of activity within the meaning of Article 5 of the Financial Services and Markets Act 2000 (Regulated Activities) Order 2001.[110] To overcome that problem, Article 9(1) of the Order exempts a subscription for debt securities from being considered as a deposit within Article 5, if the securities are of a kind specified in Articles 77 (instruments creating or acknowledging indebtedness, such as bonds) or 78 (government and public securities). However, with respect to commercial paper,[111] the exemption only applies to commercial paper having a redemption value of not less than £100,000 (or equivalent) that is issued to persons falling within specified categories and which is only transferable in parcels of not less than £100,000.

10.7.7 Sterling issues

The controls that formerly applied under the Control of Borrowing Order 1958[112] no longer apply, following their repeal pursuant to the Government Trading Act 1990.[113] Those controls had required approval from the Bank of England for issues of sterling securities in excess of £3 million. They were replaced by a requirement to notify the Bank of England of any new sterling issue for more than £20 million, with a maturity of one year or more.[114]

10.7.8 US restrictions

There are substantial US legislative requirements and restrictions relating to securities, which are beyond the scope of this work, so what follows is of only a general descriptive nature. The legislation, which includes securities legislation and tax legislation, covers matters concerning the issuance, subscription, offering, sale, and re-sale of securities. These various matters are the reason for the fairly substantial US selling restrictions that will usually be found in bond documentation, for instance, in the Subscription Agreement and in the Permanent (or Semi-permanent) Global Bond.

Registration of securities is required under section 5 of the Securities Act 1933.[115]   **10.7.8.1**
There are various exemptions to the requirement for registration, some of which may be relevant to a bond issue. In the case of 'off-shore' transactions, it is possible

---

[110] SI 2001/544, as amended.

[111] Defined in Art 9(3) to be debt securities having a maturity of less than one year.

[112] SI 1958/1208, as amended.

[113] See s 4 and Sched 2, by which the Borrowing (Control and Guarantees) Act 1946 was repealed. The Order had been made under that Act.

[114] Bank of England Notices dated 1/3/1996 and 18/3/1997.

[115] 15 USC § 77e.

to avoid the requirements for registration under the 1933 Act by compliance with the 'safe harbour' exemptions that are contained in Regulation S.[116] There are two such exemptions under Regulation S. The first relates to the initial subscription and issuance of securities and the distribution process by securities professionals pursuant to contract; and the second concerns re-sales of securities by other persons. There are a number of requirements that must be met so as to satisfy these exemptions. Any offer or sale of securities must be an 'offshore transaction', that is, that no offer should be made to persons in the USA, and the buyer and the transaction should be consummated offshore. There must be no 'directed selling efforts' in the USA. There are limits as to the connection between the issuer and the USA, which depend upon the relevant category of the issuer and may include a restricted period for 'distribution compliance' of 40 days in which the securities may not be sold to US persons, a requirement that the offer documents contain certain selling restrictions and warnings, and the receipt of confirmations of those restrictions. There is also a requirement that the managers should only sell their 'allotment securities' into a market rather than by private transactions.

10.7.8.2 There is an exemption from the registration requirements under the Securities Act 1933 for private placements, which applies under section 4(2) of the Act.[117] There is also an exemption for downstream private placements under Rule 144A,[118] which is a rule promulgated by the Securities and Exchange Commission. It applies to private placements of eligible securities with large institutional investors in the USA, who qualify as 'qualified institutional buyers'.

10.7.8.3 Under section 4(3) of the Securities Act 1933,[119] dealers may sell certain securities into the USA after a period of 40 days from the closing date of the offering of the securities. This also applies to secondary market transactions with US persons.

10.7.8.4 There are also restrictions that may be relevant under the US law and, in particular, under the Tax Equity and Fiscal Responsibility Act 1982 (TEFRA), which aims to discourage the offering and distribution of bearer debt securities as tax avoidance mechanisms. There is an exemption covering commercial paper issues and genuine secondary market sales to US persons. There are also exemptions under the 'C Rules' and the 'D Rules'.[120] The former are only relevant to securities that are issued outside the USA and its possessions by an issuer that does not engage in 'interstate commerce' with respect to the issue. The latter, which is used more frequently in connection with bonds, is relevant if there are 'reasonable arrangements'

---

116 Vol 17 Code of Federal Regulations (CFR) § 240.901 et seq.
117 15 USC § 77d(2).
118 17 CFR § 230.144A.
119 15 USC § 77d(3).
120 US Treas Reg §1.163–5.

in place to prevent the securities being sold to US persons in connection with the primary offering, the securities carry a specified legend, and there is no payment of interest in the USA. The reasonable arrangements involve requirements along the lines that in a restricted period of 40 days the bonds may not be offered or sold to a person within the USA or its possessions or to a US person (with certain exceptions), the bonds may not be delivered in definitive form within the USA or its possessions in connection with a sale within the restricted period, and a certificate of ownership must be provided to the issuer concerning the purchaser or subscriber of the bond.

10.8 The Documentation

A bond issue involves a vast amount of documentation and paperwork, which **10.8.1** includes the prospectus or, if relevant, listing particulars, the documentation relating to the subscription and initial issuance of the securities, the alternative forms of documentation that will govern the nature of the issue, the rights and obligations of the issuer, the guarantor (if there is one), the bond holders, any security that may be given, and mechanical matters such as payment of interest and principal. Not least in the list will be the bonds themselves. It is now appropriate to describe the documentation in more detail, including the considerations that are relevant in deciding on certain aspects of the structure of an issue which will affect the documentation and its contents.

10.8.2 Governing law and jurisdiction clauses

As a preliminary point which will be relevant to all of the contractual documentation, there should be provisions containing an express choice of law and a choice of jurisdiction in the case of disputes. For the purposes of the following discussion, it will be assumed that each of the documents will have an express choice of English law as its governing law and a submission by the parties to the jurisdiction of the English courts.

10.8.3 The bonds

As indicated above, it is no longer the practice for definitive bonds to be issued as a matter of course and held by the investors in an issue, although the investors are usually still referred to as the bond holders. It remains theoretically possible that definitive bonds might be issued at some point during the life of an issue, but the circumstances where this might arise are limited to particular situations (usually as stipulated in the Permanent Global Bond) such as where it is necessary for tax purposes to overcome an unfortunate imposition of some adverse tax consequence, where the clearing and settlement systems have ceased to operate for a period of time, and where there has been default by the issuer. Save in such particular situations, the bond holders will never physically hold bonds and will have to rely upon the intermediaries and the clearing and settlement systems to which reference has already been made.

10.8.3.1 There are usually two successive global instruments that are issued. They represent the whole of the issue. The first is called the Temporary Global Bond which is issued at the Closing, as previously described. It is normally current for the first 40 days of the issue (that period corresponding with the requirements of US securities and tax laws), upon the expiry of which it is exchanged for the Permanent Global Bond (sometimes called the Semi-Permanent Global Bond to meet US tax restrictions) which, barring the circumstances described above, will remain current in whole for the remainder of the life of the issue. The forms of these two instruments will be scheduled to the Trust Deed or the Fiscal Agency Agreement, as will the terms and conditions to which they are subject. The global bonds, like definitive bonds, are in the form of bearer instruments, and so, in theory, the person who has the possession of them is the person entitled to payment under them. As previously mentioned, they will be held by a common depository, or custodian, for the clearing and settlement systems.

10.8.3.1.1 *The Temporary Global Bond*

The face of the Temporary Global Bond will state the name of the issuer and of the guarantor, if any, and it will certify that an amount, being the total amount of the issue, will be payable to the bearer on the specified maturity date. If the issue is secured or subordinated, that status will be stated. It will also state that it is subject to the trust deed, if there is one, and to the terms and conditions of the bonds as set forth in a schedule to the trust deed or the Fiscal Agency Agreement. It will provide that it may be exchanged for the Permanent Global Bond on the specified exchange date. There is also likely to be a requirement for a certificate to be presented at the time of the exchange confirming various matters relating to US regulatory and tax rules. The bond will be executed on behalf of the issuer and any guarantor, and authenticated by the Fiscal Agent or the Principal Paying Agent.

10.8.3.1.2 *The Permanent Global Bond*

The form of the Permanent Global Bond (sometimes referred to as the Semi-Permanent Global Bond) will begin in much the same way as the Temporary Global Bond, but it will then go on to deal with the following matters. It will provide for the circumstances when it may be exchanged for definitive bonds to be held by investors. It will provide for the payment of principal and interest and for the giving of notices to investors through the mechanisms of the clearing systems and a few other mechanical matters. It will be executed and authenticated.

10.8.3.2 *Definitive Bonds*

The definitive bonds, if ever issued, will be for a specified denomination for each individual bond and will be security printed. Each bond will specify the name of the issuer and of any guarantor and the principal amount of the bond, the interest it bears (if it carries interest), the date of its maturity, that it is part of a series or issue, and its status if it is secured or subordinated. It will carry numbers to identify the international securities identification number for the issue and the serial number of the particular bond. It will certify that the principal amount of the bond is payable to bearer at maturity upon its delivery to a paying agent. It will also state that it is subject to the terms and conditions printed on its reverse side and to the trust deed, if there is one. If the bond bears interest, there will be coupons at the side of it which are detachable, with one coupon for each interest payment date. Each coupon is stated to be payable to the bearer upon presentation to a paying agent, and is signed on behalf of the issuer and authenticated. There may also be a talon, which can be presented to obtain further coupons if the bond has a long period to maturity. The bond will be executed on behalf of the issuer and the guarantor and will be authenticated by the Fiscal Agent or the Principal Paying Agent.

10.8.3.3 The global bonds and the definitive bonds are expressed as being subject to detailed terms and conditions, which will now be described.

10.8.4 The terms and conditions of the bonds

The terms and conditions of the bonds are the detailed contractual provisions by which the issuer and the bond holders are bound. They deal with matters such as the form, denomination, title, and status of the bonds, the covenants and undertakings that the issuer agrees to abide by during the life of the issue, the redemption and purchase of bonds by the issuer, payment provisions and taxation, prescription, the calculation of interest, events of default, meetings of bond holders, quorum requirements, voting, and the passing of resolutions and the giving of notices. These matters will be examined in further detail below. The terms and conditions are printed on the reverse side of the definitive bonds if they are issued. Copies of them will also be found as schedules to the fiscal agency agreement or the trust deed and in the prospectus or listing particulars.

10.8.4.1 *Title, status, and ranking*

The provision concerning the title of the bonds will confirm that the bonds will be payable to the bearer and that the holder will be treated as the owner and absolutely entitled to them. The status of the bonds concerns matters such as whether they are secured or unsecured and if, as between themselves, they rank *pari passu* or in a stated order or ranking of payment; if they are unsecured, whether they will rank *pari passu* with other creditors, or if they will be subordinated behind the payment rights of the other creditors of the issuer, particularly on the insolvency of the issuer. The subordination provisions will be contained in the terms and conditions or in some other document, such as a schedule to the Fiscal Agency Agreement or the Trust Deed, to which reference will be made in the terms and conditions. If a guarantee is to be given and the guarantor joins in executing the bonds, rather than executing a deed poll or in giving the guarantee in the trust deed, the terms and conditions will contain the relevant provisions dealing with the guarantee.

10.8.4.2 *Covenants and undertakings and events of default*

The covenants and undertakings of the issuer (and the guarantor) and the events of default will be contained in the terms and conditions. They are likely to be softer, or more lenient, than the comparable provisions in a loan agreement except, perhaps, in the case of a high yield or 'junk' issue. For example, if there is a negative pledge then it is likely to contain a number of exceptions and perhaps only relate to its obligations under other bond issues (there has been some disquiet about this as bond holders have sometimes found that if the issuer gets into financial difficulties, it may give security to its bankers and other creditors to gain their support of its continuing existence. If the issuer does subsequently become insolvent or default on the bonds, those secured creditors will rank ahead of the bond holders). The events of default will usually be limited to a few events and may contain generous grace periods. For instance, it is not unusual to find a lengthy grace period for non-payment of interest, and, if there is a trustee, for discretion to be given to the trustee in determining if the event which has occurred is of sufficient seriousness to be considered as constituting an event of default, and if enforcement action should be taken following the occurrence of an event of default (see further on this aspect below). If there is a trustee then there will be a 'no action clause', which limits the right of the individual bond holders to take action against the issuer, as further described below.

10.8.4.3 *Interest*

The provisions concerning interest (if the bonds are to carry interest) will deal with mechanical matters concerning the calculation and payment of interest and the payment of default interest if payment is in arrears. If interest is payable at a floating rate or if there are to be circumstances where a fixed rate of interest is to be stepped up or down, then relevant mechanisms for calculating and dealing with those matters will be found in the terms and conditions.

10.8.4.4 *Redemption, purchase, and payments by the issuer*

There will be provisions dealing with the redemption and purchase of the bonds by the issuer and their consequential cancellation, including whether the issuer is to have a right of early redemption, either generally or in limited circumstances, such as for tax reasons. There will also be provisions concerning the method and making of payments on the bonds and taxation matters, including the consequences of an imposition of a withholding tax on the payment of interest on the bonds and whether the issuer will be required to gross-up the payments so as to make up any consequential shortfall in the amount received by the bond holders. There will be a clause dealing with prescription which provides that if a claim for payment is not made within the relevant specified period of the due date, the claim will become void. The usual periods are five years for interest and ten years for principal.

10.8.4.5 *Meetings of the bond holders and voting*

The terms and conditions will also make reference to voting matters, including the calling of meetings, the quorum that is required for holding a meeting, and the requisite majorities that are required for the passing of resolutions. These matters may be set out explicitly in the terms and conditions, or there may be a cross-reference in them to a schedule of the trust deed or the fiscal agency agreement where they are set out more fully. Meetings will usually be convened by the trustee or, if there is no trust deed, by the issuer, either of their own volition or at the request of a specified proportion of the bond holders, by the giving of notice to the bond holders. The reasons for calling meetings are many and various. For instance, a meeting may be convened if there has been a default by the issuer or if there has been a request by the issuer for a waiver, variation, or consent relating to the terms and conditions of the bonds or of the other documentation relevant to the issue. If there is a trustee, a meeting may be called because it involves a matter that the trustee cannot or is not prepared to deal with within its discretion, or if the trustee wishes to obtain instructions from the bond holders or they wish to give the trustee instructions. The trustee may also decide to call a meeting to obtain exoneration from a liability it may have incurred or in connection with its retirement and replacement by a new trustee. If there has been a default on the bonds a meeting may decide to appoint a committee of the bond holders to represent the interests of the bond holders in negotiations with the issuer.

10.8.4.5.1 There will be provisions in the documentation as to how the notice convening the meeting should be given and the period of notice that is required. The Permanent Global Bond will often provide for notices to be given through the clearing and settlement systems. Otherwise, it is likely that notices will be given through the newspapers. If definitive bonds have been issued then voting certificates will be issued to bond holders who wish to vote, during which time their bonds will have to be deposited with the paying agents. If definitive bonds are not in issue then the provisions dealing with voting will provide for voting instructions to be given via the clearing and settlement systems or, alternatively, for voting certificates to be issued to those who wish to attend a meeting.

10.8.4.5.2   There are usually special voting requirements concerning certain matters that are considered to be vital to the interests of the bond holders, which require a vote (usually by 75 per cent by value) to amend or change matters, for instance, concerning the amount of principal or interest that is payable or the dates for maturity or payment, to change the currency of the bonds, to amend or release security or a guarantee, to approve the appointment of a new trustee, or to change such special voting requirements. It should be noted that in the USA unanimity is required on such matters by virtue of section 316(b) of the Trustee Indenture Act 1939 and that certain civil law jurisdictions prescribe the voting requirements.

10.8.4.6 Binding the minority

Having described the procedural matters relating to voting, it is now relevant to consider if, as a matter of law, there are any constraints on the ability of a majority to bind a dissenting minority through the vote on a resolution that is put to the bond holders. The answer can best be described in a number of propositions.

10.8.4.6.1   The first point is straightforward. There must be a power conferred by the documentation for a resolution to be passed by the relevant majority and the vote must concern a matter upon which a resolution may be passed.[121] If the matter is outside the subject matter on which a vote may be taken then the vote will be invalid. There is no general right to hold a vote on any matter under the sun and thereby to exclude or override the rights of the minority.

10.8.4.6.2   Secondly, it is necessary that the procedures laid down in the documentation should be observed for calling the meeting, for giving notice, and for a quorum to be present. It is also necessary for the vote to be passed by the requisite majority as laid down in the documentation.

10.8.4.6.3   Thirdly, as a general matter, the majority can bind the minority and those forming the majority may vote in their own interests.[122] This is particularly the case where, from the outset of the transaction, there is an obvious potential conflict in the interests of those who may be called upon to vote and where the identity of those who could be involved is likely to change from time to time.[123]

---

121 *Hay v Swedish & Norwegian Ry Co* (1889) TLR 460; *Mercantile Investment & General Trust Co v International Co of Mexico* [1893] 1 Ch 484.

122 *British America Nickel Corp Ltd v MJ O'Brien Ltd* [1927] AC 369. The issuer should be able to rely upon this principle unless it has notice that the vote of the majority was tainted by one of the matters referred to in the following propositions: *Redwood Master Fund Ltd v TD Bank Europe Ltd* [2002] EWHC 2703 (Ch), [2006] 1 BCLC 149.

123 See Rimmer J in ibid (which was a case concerning majority voting in a syndicated loan facility). His Lordship followed the approach taken by the High Court of Australia in *Peters American Delicacy Co v Heath* (1938–39) 61 CLR 457 and the Privy Council in *Howard Smith Ltd v Ampol Petroleum Ltd* [1974] AC 821.

Fourthly, if there is a special or secret advantage that is to be given to or conferred **10.8.4.6.4** upon a bond holder to secure its vote within the majority, that must be disclosed. If it is not disclosed, the vote will be invalid.[124] However, if the advantage is fully disclosed, the bond holder may vote in favour of the resolution and the vote will be valid.[125]

Fifthly, the court may intervene if there has been some other unfairness or oppres- **10.8.4.6.5** sion, in the sense of some deliberate intention on the part of the majority to dam-age or oppress the interests of the minority. Evidence of this may be difficult to obtain, but the court may be prepared to conclude that there was a lack of good faith along those lines if the outcome of the vote is so manifestly disadvantageous, discriminatory, or oppressive towards the minority that the only reasonable con-clusion which the court could draw is that the majority must have been motivated by dishonest considerations that were inconsistent with a proper exercise of its powers.[126] In a case where negotiations between the issuer and the trustee or a committee of bond holders have been conducted openly and involved proposals put forward by the issuer, it would be difficult (if well nigh impossible) to substan-tiate an allegation of unfairness or prejudice.[127]

Sixthly, if a vote is required of a special class of the bond holders, the vote must be **10.8.4.6.6** exercised for the benefit of the class as a whole and not merely so as to benefit indi-vidual members of that class.[128] It is not entirely clear how the benefit of the class as a whole should be identified. It would appear that if the minority's interests are being interfered with then that would not be to the benefit of the class as a whole.[129] It has also been suggested that the test might be assessed by reference to what would be in the interests of an individual hypothetical member of the class[130] but it may be rather difficult to identify such a mythical person amongst a rather divergent body of bond holders.

10.8.5 The initial subscription

There are two important documents dealing with the process by which the syndi-cate of managers agrees to subscribe for the issue at the outset. The first document

---

[124] *British America Nickel Corp Ltd v MJ O'Brien Ltd* [1927] AC 369.

[125] *North-West Transportation Co v Beatty* (1887) 12 App Cas 589; *Goodfellow v Nelson Line* [1912] 2 Ch 324.

[126] See Rimmer J in *Redwood Master Fund Ltd v TD Bank Europe Ltd* [2002] EWHC 2703 (Ch), [2006] 1 BCLC 149.

[127] Ibid. A similar attitude was taken in *Law Debenture Trust Corp PLC v Concord Trust* [2007] EWHC 1380 (Ch) in relation to allegations that the trustee and the issuer had failed to keep a bond holder informed of material matters, when the relevant information had been passed on to a com-mittee of the bond holders and they were advised by their own legal advisers.

[128] *British America Nickel Corp Ltd v MJ O'Brien Ltd* [1927] AC 369.

[129] Ibid.

[130] See Sir Raymond Evershed MR in *Greenhalgh v Arderne Cinemas Ltd* [1951] Ch 286, at 291.

is the Subscription Agreement and the other document is the Agreement Among Managers.

10.8.5.1 The Subscription Agreement

The parties to the Subscription Agreement are the issuer, the guarantor (if there is one), the lead manager, and the syndicate of managers. It is entered into at the Signing. It records the basis upon which the managers agree to subscribe for the issue. Their agreement is expressed to be on a joint and several basis, so that each of them is liable to the issuer for the whole amount of the issue (the position as between the managers is dealt with in the Agreement Among Managers). This should be contrasted with the position that normally obtains in a syndicated loan facility where the liability of the banks is expressed to be several, so that each bank is only responsible to lend its own proportion of the total commitment of the banks.

10.8.5.1.1 There is another important difference between the two methods of raising finance. If a lender defaults in its contractual obligation to lend money to a borrower (assuming that there truly has been a default by the lender and that the lender is not entitled to refuse to lend, for instance, on the ground that a condition precedent remains unfulfilled) the borrower will be confined to seeking damages for the breach of the contract, and, in that respect, it may run into difficulties in proving its loss because of the rule as to remoteness under *Hadley v Baxendale*.[131] It is also unlikely that a borrower could obtain a mandatory order against the lender for performance of the contract, such as by way of an order for specific performance.[132] On the other hand, a company which is a bond issuer will have the benefit of section 740 of the Companies Act 2006[133] which provides that a contract to subscribe for debentures may be enforced by an order for specific performance. The expression 'debenture' is defined to include bonds.[134] However, the ambit of the section is probably confined to an issuer which is a company formed and registered under the Companies Act 2006 and its predecessor legislation.[135]

10.8.5.1.2 The Subscription Agreement, either expressly or by reference to another document, will deal with the pricing of the issue (e.g. the issue price, including any discount or premium to the par value of the bonds and the interest, if any, that the

---

[131] (1854) 9 Exch 341. But see now the decision of the House of Lords in *Sempra Metals Ltd v HM Commissioners of Inland Revenue* [2007] UKHL 34 and the commentary at Chap 3.

[132] See *South African Territories Ltd v Wallington* [1898] AC 309.

[133] Formerly s 195 of the Companies Act 1985.

[134] See s 738 of the Companies Act 2006 (formerly s 744 of the Companies Act 1985).

[135] See s 1(1) of the Companies Act 2006 (formerly s 735(1) of the Companies Act 1985). Despite the qualifying wording in s 1(1), it is unlikely that the context of s 740 of the Companies Act 2006 could justify a wider interpretation.

bonds will bear) and the fees and commissions that will be payable by the issuer to the managers. It will set out various conditions precedent that the issuer must satisfy before the managers will be obliged to subscribe for the issue, including matters such as the following: a satisfactory rating of the issue by the rating agencies; the furnishing of legal opinions and accountants' reports and associated documents; the approval, publication, and filing of the prospectus or listing particulars; the admission to listing; and the execution of the other documentation for the issue to proceed, including the furnishing of the Temporary Global Bond. The document will most probably contain a provision giving the managers the right to terminate their obligations to subscribe for the issue if a *force majeure* event, relating to economic or market events, should occur before the Closing which may impede the successful offering and distribution of the issue to the secondary market.[136]

The agreement will also contain representations and warranties that are given by the issuer and the guarantor, which will be repeated as at the Closing. In this respect, the managers are in a preferable position to the ordinary body of bondholders who will not have the benefit of such representations and warranties from the issuer when they decide to invest in the issue. Nor will they have the benefit of matters such as the legal opinions that will be delivered for the benefit of the managers as conditions precedent under the Subscription Agreement. **10.8.5.1.3**

The issuer and the guarantor will give various covenants in favour of the managers relating to the steps required to fulfil the matters required for the issue to proceed, including, for instance, an obligation to update the prospectus if that is necessary. They will also give an indemnity to the managers in respect of claims that might be made against them for errors in the prospectus. **10.8.5.1.4**

Finally, the agreement will contain undertakings by the managers to observe various selling restrictions in offering and distributing the issue, such restrictions arising out of the need to observe the regulatory requirements of various jurisdictions including the UK and the USA. **10.8.5.1.5**

10.8.5.2 The Agreement Among Managers

The Agreement Among Managers is an agreement to which the managers and the lead manager are the parties. It is usually in an industry standard form (for instance, as promulgated for use by the International Primary Markets Association). It allocates, as between the managers, their responsibility to take up the issue. It delegates certain powers and authorities in favour of the lead manager. It also, expressly

---

[136] For a similar provision relating to syndication of a syndicated facility, see the commentary at Chap 9.

or by reference to another document, provides for the division of the fees and commission received from the issuer.

10.8.6 The difference between an issue with a fiscal agent and an issue with a trustee

Before proceeding to describe the relevant documentation, it is relevant to discuss the difference between an issue where there is to be a trustee and an issue where there is to be a fiscal agent. A bond issue will have either a fiscal agent or a trustee. If there is to be a fiscal agent then there will be a Fiscal Agency Agreement. If there is to be a trustee then there will be a Trust Deed, under which the trust will be constituted and the trustee appointed, and a Paying Agency Agreement. It is important to understand the difference between the two alternatives and the considerations that are relevant in deciding which should be followed in structuring an issue. A decision must be made at an early stage as to which alternative is to be pursued and the decision will be reflected in the mandate.[137]

10.8.6.1 A fiscal agent is appointed by the issuer and acts as the issuer's agent, to whom it owes its duties and responsibilities. A trustee is appointed as the trustee for the bond holders and owes it duties, as a fiduciary, to them. The following are the considerations that will be relevant in making a decision (a number of these points will receive further consideration later in this chapter), commencing with the arguments in favour of having a trustee and then turning to the arguments in favour of having a fiscal agent.

10.8.6.2 If security is to be taken, as for instance in a securitisation, then the most convenient and practical way of doing so is through the use of a trust, by which the security is given to the trustee acting on behalf of the bond holders for the time being.[138] It is not feasible for security to be taken individually by each bond holder and, in any event, there would be difficulty in the investors asserting their rights in the security unless they held definitive instruments. There would be further difficulties presented by transfers of the entitlements to new investors. These considerations

---

[137] In the USA, a trustee is required to be appointed because of the requirements of the Trust Indenture Act 1939, although there are some exemptions to the requirement. There was formerly a requirement that to obtain a listing of debt securities on the London Stock Exchange a trustee was required (per pre-2005 Listing Rules, para 13.12) but there was an exemption for 'specialist debt securities', including eurobonds (per pre-2005 Listing Rules Chap 23). The 2005 version of the Listing Rules has removed altogether the requirement for a trustee (see LR 17.2.1 and LR 2).

[138] The representative capacity of a security trustee in holding security on behalf of its beneficiaries, as well as the right of an agent to bind its principals, was examined in *British Power & Energy Trading Ltd v Credit Suisse* [2008] EWCA Civ 53. That case concerned a syndicated facility but the same principles would be relevant to the position of a security trustee under a bond issue. This is subject, of course, to the terms of the trust deed, which may place restrictions upon the powers of the trustee.

assume, however, that the trustee's position would be recognised in the relevant jurisdictions where the secured assets are located and where the security would be enforced. Not all jurisdictions (and in fact very few civil law jurisdictions) recognise the concept of a trust and, so far, the Hague Convention on the law applicable to trusts and their recognition of 1985[139] has only had a limited acceptance by ratification.[140] However, the trustee may still be able to gain some recognition in countries that do not acknowledge the trust, by arguing that it is acting as the agent or fiduciary of the bond holders, or, if it can obtain the global bond, by presenting itself as the bond holder which is seeking to enforce its security for the debt due to it as the bearer of the bond. It is also possible for a guarantee to be taken in a similar manner, although a guarantee can also be given by the guarantor joining in and being a party to the bonds or by the execution of a deed poll by the guarantor in favour of the bond holders for the time being.[141] If the bonds are to be subordinated, that can also be achieved conveniently through the use of a trust, as was the case in *Re British & Commonwealth Holdings plc (No 3)*[142] where in an insolvent liquidation the trustee was required to hold the benefit of any payment that was received first for the senior creditors and thereafter for the subordinated bond holders.[143]

10.8.6.3 By having a trustee, the issuer is enabled to deal with one representative of all of the bond holders, rather than the bond holders individually. The trustee can call and chair meetings of the bond holders and pursue action that should be taken in consequence of the meeting. Technically, the debt that is owing on the bonds is expressed by the trust deed to be due to the trustee and that goes in parallel with the trustee's powers of enforcement on default. Unless the trust deed provides otherwise (as it may do if there is a ranking of bond holders into different classes), in acting on behalf of the bond holders the trustee, being a fiduciary, must do so by treating the bond holders equally, as one class, without favouring any one or any group of them over the other bond holders,[144] which is a benefit to smaller bond holders who may lack the means to protect themselves or may not be able to

---

[139] Which was given effect under English law by the Recognition of Trusts Act 1987 and came into force on 1 January 1992.

[140] The countries that have ratified the Convention are Australia, Canada, Italy, Luxembourg, Malta, the Netherlands, and the UK.

[141] For a discussion of the relevant factors concerning a guarantee given by deed poll, see *Moody v Condor Insurance* [2006] EWHC 100 (Ch), [2006] 1 WLR 1847.

[142] [1992] 1 WLR 672.

[143] However, a trust structure was not available in *Re Maxwell Communications Corporation plc* [1993] 1 WLR 1402 because the issuer was a Swiss corporation and the trust would not be recognised by Swiss civil law.

[144] See Millett LJ in *Bristol & West Building Soc v Mothew* [1998] Ch 1, at 19. This is usually reinforced by a provision to that effect in the trust deed or in the terms and conditions of the bonds.

do so as effectively as the larger bond holders.[145] In this connection, an English style of trust deed will usually contain a 'no action clause', by which the bond holders are precluded from taking their own enforcement action against the issuer. The trustee is usually given certain powers to give consents and waivers for matters that are not material, it can decide whether a matter is material and requires further action to be taken, or that it is immaterial and does not need to be pursued at all or in the same manner as it would be if it was material. The trustee is often given powers to agree to a substitution of the issuer or the guarantor by another person so long as it is satisfied that the bond holders will not be prejudiced.

10.8.6.4 The arguments in favour of having a fiscal agent are mainly on the issuer's side rather than that of the bond holders. For a straightforward unsecured issue, particularly where the issuer enjoys a good credit rating, the issue should proceed perfectly well without a trustee. If the issuer has no connection with a jurisdiction that recognises trusts then there may not be much point in having a trustee. Generally speaking, it is cheaper not to have a trustee, as the fees, costs, and expenses of the trustee will be avoided, although, in the scale of things, those items are unlikely to be significant. The issuer may prefer not to have the unifying influence of a trustee acting for all of the bond holders, in the belief that it may be able to pursue a policy of divide and rule. However, the issuer will lose the benefit of the 'no action' clause when things go wrong, and, in any event, it is likely that a committee of the bond holders would be formed to conduct negotiations and to co-ordinate action by the bond holders.

10.8.6.5 Having examined the competing arguments in support of the alternative structures, it is now convenient to examine the documentation that reflects those alternatives.

10.8.7 The Fiscal Agency Agreement

The parties to this agreement are the issuer, the guarantor (if any), the fiscal agent (acting as fiscal agent and as a paying agent), and the other paying agents, who will be needed if payments may be made in several jurisdictions.[146] It is likely that the lead manager or a company in its group will be appointed as the fiscal agent, and one or more of the other paying agents will also be linked to the lead manager. The fiscal agent and the paying agents are appointed to be the agents of the issuer. The agreement provides for the issuance of the bonds. The forms of the bonds (temporary global, permanent global, and definitive) are set forth in a schedule to the agreement, as are the terms and conditions attached to the bonds.

---

[145] This may not be as strongly in favour of the smaller bond holders as it sounds because the smaller bond holders may be out-voted on a resolution supported by the larger bond holders.

[146] It should be noted that LR 17.3.7 of the UK Listing Rules requires that there should be a paying agent in the UK.

The agreement provides for the mechanisms by which the paying agents, on behalf of the issuer, will make the payments that will fall due on the bonds, and for the issuer to put them in funds to make such payments. The agreement also makes provision for various other matters such as the issuance and authentication of bonds and the replacement of lost or destroyed bonds, the procedures for the calling of meetings of the bond holders, and for the fiscal agent to receive and hold information from the issuer for inspection by the bond holders (but it is stated that the fiscal agent has no obligation to review or assess that information). There will also be provision for payment by the issuer of the fees and expenses of the fiscal agent and the paying agents.

10.8.8 The Paying Agency Agreement

In passing, it should be noted that if there is to be a trust deed with a trustee then there will be a Paying Agency Agreement instead of the Fiscal Agency Agreement. The parties will be the issuer, the guarantor, the paying agents, and the trustee. Under this agreement, there will be similar provisions as those in the Fiscal Agency Agreement dealing with payments on behalf of the issuer and the issuance, authentication, and replacement of bonds. The paying agents explicitly covenant with the trustee to act on its instructions if there is a default by the issuer on the bonds and to make all payments thereafter to the trustee.

10.8.9 The Trust Deed

The parties to this document are the issuer, the trustee, and, if there is one, the guarantor. It provides for the appointment of the trustee (as well as the resignation or retirement of the trustee and the appointment of a replacement trustee), the establishment of the trust, and the constitution and creation of the bond issue. The trustee is appointed to be the trustee for the bond holders, and the bonds are stated to be subject to the trust and the provisions of the trust deed. The forms of the bonds (temporary global, permanent global, and definitive) are set forth in a schedule to the trust deed, as are the terms and conditions attached to the bonds, and the procedures for the calling of meetings of the bond holders and the passing of resolutions. If security is to be given then it will be given in favour of the trustee, or its nominee, and the security will be constituted by the trust deed or in a subsidiary document to it. The same will apply to any guarantee that is to be given, unless the guarantor is to give its guarantee by joining in to the bonds themselves. The following are important matters that are covered in the trust deed.

10.8.9.1 Covenant to pay

The trust deed contains a covenant by the issuer in favour of the trustee to pay the principal and interest on the bonds to the trustee. It goes on to provide that this obligation will be treated as satisfied if payment is made in the normal course by the issuer's paying agents under the mechanisms provided for in the Paying Agency Agreement. However, upon default the trustee has the right to require that all further payments should be made directly to it which goes with the trustee's ability to take enforcement action in consequence of a default.

10.8.9.2 *The trustee's discretions*

There are discretions that are conferred on the trustee in the trust deed and in the terms and conditions of the bonds (the considerations that are relevant to the exercise of the trustee's discretion will be examined later). For instance, it may receive an application from the issuer for a waiver from the need to comply with a covenant set forth in the terms and conditions of the bonds or with respect to a potential event of default or for a consent to a variation of the requirements concerning such a matter. The trustee is usually given power to consent to such an application if it determines that the matter is of a formal, minor, or technical nature, or that the outcome will not be materially prejudicial to the interests of the bond holders. Alternatively, the trustee may have to decide if an event which has occurred is materially prejudicial to the interests of the bond holders so that it should be treated as an event of default and declared to be an event of default. In addition, the trustee may have to decide if an event of default is capable of remedy by the issuer or if the trustee should take enforcement action following the occurrence of an event of default.

10.8.9.3 *Information and advice*

The trust deed will contain provisions for information to be supplied to the trustee by the issuer and the guarantor. For the protection of the trustee, however, the deed normally provides that the trustee is entitled to assume that no event of default has occurred unless it has express notice of the same. The trust deed commonly provides that the trustee may rely upon certificates provided by the issuer as to due compliance by the issuer with its obligations under the trust deed and the terms and conditions of the bonds. It is also common for the deed to provide that the trustee may seek professional advice, for instance, from lawyers and accountants, and that it may rely on any such advice that it receives.

10.8.9.4 *The 'no action' clause*

Brief mention has already been made of the 'no action' clause which will be found in either (or both) the terms and conditions of the bonds or the trust deed, and it is appropriate to mention it here in more detail. Such a provision will be found when there is a trustee. It is not appropriate to have the provision if there is no trustee, as there is no unifying force acting on behalf of the bond holders in whom their rights are vested.

The clause is usually to the effect that the bond holders may not take their own individual enforcement action against the issuer unless the trustee, having become bound to act, fails to do so within a requisite period. The no action clause fits into an overall scheme which is intended to prevent individual bond holders from taking enforcement action against the issuer, when the rights of the bond holders are meant to be protected and pursued on a collective basis by the trustee in whom their rights are vested. Each bond holder, no matter how large or small, stands to benefit from, and is bound by, the consequences of action that is taken on their behalf by the trustee, without discrimination as between the bond holders. The issuer thereby is relieved from the difficulty of negotiating with individual bond holders in circumstances where it is under financial and other pressures. The issuer is also relieved from direct action or influence being exerted by an individual bond holder taking its own independent enforcement action (or a number of individual holders pursuing their own actions) in circumstances where collective action is being pursued by the trustee or where the trustee and the other bond holders are content not to take action.[147] The restriction in the no action clause will usually cease to bind individual holders where the trustee has become obliged by a vote of the holders to take action but fails to do so within a given period. **10.8.9.4.1**

The construction of 'no action' clauses and effect that should be given to them have come before the courts at first instance in three recent cases. It is worth looking at them in some detail, although it is regrettable that the judgment in the first of the three cases was not referred to in the two later cases. **10.8.9.4.2**

The first case was a decision by Jacob J in *In the Matter of Colt Telecom Group plc*.[148] The relevant clause provided that a bond holder could not 'pursue any remedy with respect to' the trust deed or the bonds if there had been an event of default unless the trustee, having become obliged to pursue such a remedy by a vote of the bond holders, had failed to do so. Although the trust deed in that case was expressed to be governed by the laws of the State of New York, his Lordship proceeded on the basis that the principles to be applied would be the same as those under English law. He held that there was no principle of public policy that was infringed by such a contractual restriction upon a creditor from bringing insolvency proceedings and so a bond holder could be prevented by such a provision from bringing insolvency proceedings against the issuer.[149] In the case under consideration, the **10.8.9.4.2.1**

---

147 See the explanation provided in *Law Debenture Trust Corp PLC v Concord Trust; Elektrim SA v Vivendi Holdings 1 Corp* [2007] EWHC 2255 (Ch), at [54].

148 [2002] EWHC 2815 (Ch), [2003] BPIR 324.

149 His Lordship said that the principle in *Re Peverill* [1898] 1 Ch 122, which held that a shareholder could not be prevented from bringing winding-up proceedings against his company, should be confined to striking down provisions in the articles of association of a company which sought to prevent the shareholder from pursuing such proceedings. Jacob J said that such a principle did not

bond holder had sought to present a petition for the administration of the issuer under the then provisions of Part II of the Insolvency Act 1986.[150] Jacob J held that the clause was effective to prevent action being taken by a bond holder before an event of default had occurred, despite the fact that in its literal wording it only referred to the pursuit of a remedy if an event of default had occurred. He also held that the concept of a remedy as referred to in the clause would extend to the bringing of insolvency proceedings and was not confined to proceedings for private relief.

10.8.9.4.2.2　His Lordship reached those conclusions by taking a purposive approach to the construction of the clause. It was part of the overall commercial deal agreed between the issuer and the bond holders by which the issuer was left to get on with its affairs without interference by the bond holders so long as it was not in default. If it was in default then the procedures that could be taken were as laid down in the documentation. It would be illogical if the bond holders could interfere before there had been a default but not afterwards. It would also be inconsistent with the intention of the clause if the bond holders could commence insolvency proceedings when they were precluded from suing for recovery of their debts.

10.8.9.4.2.3　A similar approach to that taken in the *Colt Telecom* case was taken by Lewison J in *Law Debenture Trust Corp PLC v Concord Trust; Elektrim SA v Vivendi Holdings 1 Corp*.[151] The relevant provision in the trust deed in this case was effectively repeated in the conditions attached to the bonds. The provision in the trust deed was as follows:

> Only the Trustee may enforce (i) [against the security provided by the issuer/guarantor] or (ii) the provisions of these presents. No bondholder shall be entitled to proceed directly against [the issuer or the guarantor] to enforce the performance of any of the provisions of these presents unless the Trustee having become bound [to do so in accordance with the provisions of the Trust Deed] to take proceedings fails to do so within a reasonable time and such failure is continuing.

In construing the phrase 'enforce performance of', his Lordship said that it went beyond claims for specific performance and extended, at least, to claims for damages, whether in contract or in tort, for non-performance. He said that the clause

extend to similar provisions in a separate contract between the company and a shareholder or to any other contract between the company and a creditor by which, in any such case, such a shareholder or creditor agreed not to present a winding-up or other type of insolvency petition, as evidenced by the common practice in the Companies Court under which creditors undertook not to present such petitions.

---

[150] Since, in effect, replaced by the provisions of Schedule B1 to the Act, as the Act was amended by the Enterprise Act 2002. Nonetheless, it is submitted that the same considerations would apply with respect to an application to the court for the appointment of an administrator under paras 10–13 of Schedule B1.

[151] [2007] EWHC 2255 (Ch)

should be given a purposive and substantial meaning and should not just be confined to procedural matters or be confined strictly within the literal wording of the phrase. In light of the reasons for having a 'no action' clause, it was apt to include any action taken by a bondholder which had the effect of enforcing or laying claim to its rights as a bondholder. His Lordship went on to hold that the loss claimed by the bond holder was one that would be suffered by the bondholder in its capacity as a bondholder, and, if substantiated, would be one which was suffered by the bondholders as a class, rather than by this particular bondholder individually. The action of the bondholder in bringing its own proceedings against the issuer in another jurisdiction fell within the scope of the prohibition upon it that arose from the 'no action' clause. It therefore amounted to a breach of contract and an anti-suit injunction lay to prevent the bondholder from continuing the foreign proceedings.

By contrast to those two cases, the approach taken by Warren J in *Elliott International LP v Law Debenture Trustees Ltd*[152] (which is a case that was heard in the period between the other two cases) towards the construction of the 'no action' clause in that case was more restricted. His Lordship took a narrower approach based upon a stricter construction of the relevant provision. He held that the clause only related to proceedings that would be contradictory to proceedings that could be taken by the trustee for enforcement of the bond holder's rights and analogous insolvency proceedings. It left an individual bond holder free to pursue other action which, in that case, involved it in opposing the making of a certain type of French insolvency order against the issuer. It is interesting to note, however, that there was no challenge in the case to the underlying validity of the clause; the case was determined simply by reference to the wording of the relevant provision.

10.8.9.4.2.4

To avoid the risk that a court might take a strict view of the circumstances that were covered by a 'no action' clause, it would be advisable for an issuer to ensure that the wording of the clause makes it clear that the restraints on the bond holders from pursuing their own actions and proceedings were intended to apply both before and after the occurrence of an event of default, and related to any type of claim or procedure that a bond holder might wish to assert against the issuer relating to the bond issue or the bonds it held. It should also be made clear that the clause was intended to cover both individual causes of action for recovery, causes of action that related to the rights or the bond holders collectively, and joining in proceedings commenced by any other person, as well as proceedings to obtain a declaratory or mandatory order. It should also cover taking, joining in, or intervening in insolvency proceedings of any type (save for proving as a creditor).

10.8.9.4.2.5

---

[152] [2006] EWHC 3063 (Ch).

10.9 The Duties and Discretions of the Trustee and the Protections Afforded to it

10.9.1 As has already been seen, the trustee is appointed to act as the trustee for the bond holders, to whom it owes its duties. It has various powers and discretions vested in it, and it has duties and obligations to the bond holders. It is now relevant to examine the nature of those powers, discretions, duties and obligations, the requirements that are placed upon the trustee by the general law, and the extent to which those requirements may be modified in the trust deed. The issues involved in this subject will be examined in the following order:

(1) the duty of care and skill that arises at general law and by statute;

(2) the nature of the equitable fiduciary duty that arises at general law;

(3) the ability at general law to define, limit or exclude a trustee's duties by the use of relevant provisions in the trust deed and associated documentation;

(4) the statutory restrictions on such provisions;

(5) the considerations that are relevant to the exercise by the trustee of its powers and discretions; and

(6) the circumstances in which the court will interfere in the exercise by the trustee of its powers and discretions.

10.9.1.1 Before moving to examine those matters, it should always be remembered that, almost invariably, the trust deed in a bond issue will contain provisions which entitle the trustee to seek and rely upon instructions that are given to it by a duly qualified majority of the bond holders; indeed the bond holders may give it instructions without a request from the trustee. Provided that the vote which has led to the giving of those instructions has been properly taken (e.g. that the meeting of the bond holders was properly convened and quorate, and that the vote cannot be impugned on the grounds as previously discussed) and, if the trustee is seeking instructions, that there has been full disclosure of the facts and other matters that are relevant to the decision that has to be made, then the trustee may rely on the instructions so given to it.

10.9.1.2 It is also worth noting that in *Citibank NA v MBIA Assurance SA*[153] the Court of Appeal held that the trust deed in a bond issue may provide, quite validly, that the trustee should act in accordance with instructions that are given to it from time to time by a particular person, including a person who was not a bond holder. It had been argued, in reliance upon the decision of Millett LJ *Armitage v Nourse*,[154] that it was incompatible with the concept of a trust that the trustee could be placed in

---

[153] *Citibank NA v MBIA Assurance SA* [2007] EWCA Civ 11, [2007] 1 All ER (Comm) 475.
[154] [1998] Ch 241, at 253.

a position where the trustee was not obliged, nor entitled, to consider the interests of the bond holders, who were its beneficiaries, when it acted in accordance with instructions given to it by the relevant person. Nonetheless, the Court of Appeal held that, despite the fact that such person was given very wide powers over the subject matter of the trust and the exercise of the powers and discretions of the trustee, the trust remained in place and the trust property was held on identifiable trusts. The trustee still had functions to perform. If it was not given directions or if the right of the relevant person to give directions ceased, then the normal position as to the exercise by a trustee of its powers and discretions would apply. Whilst various of the trustee's powers and discretions had been surrendered, that was done as a commercial arrangement when the trust was constituted. The bond holders took their interests on that basis and had to accept it.

10.9.2 The duty of care and skill

At general law a trustee, as a fiduciary, has a duty to its beneficiary or principal to act with care and skill in the performance of its functions. It also has an equitable duty of loyalty to its beneficiary from which other subsidiary obligations arise. The two sets of duties are not of the same nature. The duty of care and skill, although it arises in equity because the trustee is a fiduciary, is essentially the same as the duty of care that would arise at common law in negligence, and the rules that apply at common law as to causation, remoteness of damage, and measure of damages will also apply in a claim against the fiduciary.[155] The basic standard of this duty for an individual trustee is to exercise such care and skill in the performance of its duties as an ordinary prudent businessman would exercise in managing his own affairs.[156] However, with respect to the exercise of a trustee's power of investment, the standard of care that is required is to take such care as an ordinary prudent man would take if he were minded to make an investment for the benefit of other people for whom he felt morally bound to provide.[157] A higher general standard of care will apply to a professional trustee, which will be required to exercise the special care and skill which it professes to have, as evidenced by statements that it has made, such as in its promotional literature.[158] It has been held that where the bond holders were advised by their own legal advisers, the trustee had no obligation (even assuming that it might have been under some relevant duty in the first place) to provide legal advice to them in relation to the consequences of various legal issues that had arisen concerning the issuer and concerning insolvency

---

[155] See Lord Browne-Wilkinson in *Henderson v Merrett Syndicates Ltd* [1995] 2 AC 145, at 204–205 and Millett LJ in *Bristol & West Building Society v Mothew* [1998] Ch 1, at 16–17.
[156] Per Lord Blackburn in *Speight v Gaunt* (1883) 9 App Cas 1, at 19.
[157] Per Lindley LJ in *Re Whiteley* (1886) 33 ChD 347, at 355.
[158] Per Brightman J in *Bartlett v Barclays Bank Trust Co Ltd* [1980] Ch 515, at 534.

proceedings that affected the issuer.[159] As will be seen, there are statutory constraints upon attempts in the trust deed or elsewhere to limit or exclude the trustee's liability for breach of the general law duty to exercise care and skill.

10.9.2.1 There is also a statutory duty of care that is imposed by section 1 of the Trustee Act 2000, to 'exercise such care and skill as is reasonable in the circumstances', which applies in relation to the matters set out in Schedule 1 to the Act, such as in making investments, acquiring land, appointing agents, nominees, and custodians, compounding liabilities, insuring property, and in matters concerning reversionary interests. It should be noted that the list does not include the performance by the trustee of its functions in other areas, for instance in exercising its discretions under the trust deed in deciding if it should agree to waivers, modifications, or consents as requested by the issuer. The statutory duty of care under section 1 can be excluded by appropriate wording in the trust deed.[160]

10.9.2.2 In addition to the statutory duty under section 1 of the Act, there are certain specific duties that the Act imposes on a trustee in the exercise of its powers, not all of which can be excluded. Of those specific duties, the following might be of relevance to a trustee of a bond issue. If the trustee is exercising a power of investment, it must have regard to the 'standard investment criteria',[161] review the investments periodically,[162] and obtain and consider 'proper advice'.[163] It is uncertain if it is possible to exclude or restrict these obligations.[164] It is also uncertain if the restrictions on appointment of agents and the ability to delegate asset management[165] only apply to the exercise of corresponding powers under the Act[166] or also apply to similar powers in the trust deed. There is an obligation to review appointments of agents, nominees, and custodians,[167] but this may be excluded or restricted by the trust deed.[168] As will be seen, however, there are other statutory constraints upon attempts by contract to limit or exclude the trustee's liability for breach of the general law duty to exercise care and skill.

---

[159] *Law Debenture Trust Corp PLC v Concord Trust; Elektrim SA v Vivendi Holdings 1 Corp* [2007] EWHC 2255 (Ch), at [35].
[160] Sched 1 para 7.
[161] Ss 4(1) and (3) of the Act.
[162] S 4(2).
[163] S 5.
[164] See the uncertain wording of s 6.
[165] Contained in ss 14 and 15.
[166] S 11.
[167] S 22(1).
[168] Ss 21(3) and 26.

10.9.3 The equitable fiduciary duty of a trustee

The principal feature of a fiduciary's purely equitable duty is the obligation of loyalty, from which other subsidiary equitable obligations will arise. This was explained by Millett LJ in *Bristol & West Building Society v Mothew*[169] as follows:

> The distinguishing obligation of a fiduciary is the obligation of loyalty. The principal is entitled to the single-minded loyalty of his fiduciary. This core liability has several facets. A fiduciary must act in good faith; he must not make a profit out of his trust; he must not place himself in a position where his duty and his interest may conflict; he may not act for his own benefit or the benefit of a third person without the informed consent of his principal. This is not intended to be an exhaustive list, but it is sufficient to indicate the nature of fiduciary obligations.

His Lordship later said[170] that if the fiduciary is acting for two principals:

> he must act in good faith in the interests of each and must not act with the intention of furthering the interests of one principal to the prejudice of the other.

As to the duty to act in good faith, see *Re Second East Dulwich etc Building Society*.[171] For the duty not to make an unauthorised profit from the trust, see *Bray v Ford*.[172] For the duty to avoid a conflict of interest, see *Keech v Sandford*.[173] For the duty not to act for his own or a third party's benefit, see *Boardman v Phipps*.[174] **10.9.3.1**

If there has been a breach of trust giving rise to a loss to the trust fund, the trustee is liable to restore the lost property or to pay compensation for the loss, which is to be assessed at the date of judgment ordering the trustee to pay the compensation.[175] Because the liability of the trustee is to restore the property or to pay compensation if it cannot be restored, it will be liable even if the loss is immediately attributable to the dishonesty or failure of a third party (for instance, where the trustee unintentionally but wrongly put the trust property into the hands of a rogue) if the loss would have been avoided but for the breach of trust. There is no scope in this area to apply the common law concepts of causation, foreseeability, or remoteness in assessing liability.[176] On the other hand, if the loss would have been suffered whether or not the breach of trust had occurred, the trustee will not be liable to make it good.[177] **10.9.3.2**

---

169 [1998] Ch 1, at 18.
170 Ibid, at 19.
171 (1889) 68 LJ Ch 196.
172 [1896] AC 44.
173 (1726) Sel Cas Ch 61. See also the valuable summary provided in *Australian Securities and Investment Commission v Citigroup Global Markets Australia Pty Ltd* [2007] FCA 963, at [256]–[307].
174 [1967] 2 AC 46.
175 *Caffrey v Darby* (1801) 6 Ves 488; *Target Holdings Ltd v Redferns* [1996] AC 421.
176 Per Lord Browne-Wilkinson in ibid, at 434.
177 Ibid.

10.9.4 Modification or exclusion of a trustee's duties

A study of the attributes of a fiduciary's duties mentioned by Millett LJ in the *Mothew* case, as quoted above, will draw attention to a number of matters that could cause both theoretical and practical difficulties for a trustee of a bond issue if it had to comply with them to the letter. For instance, the trustee commonly charges fees and earns a commercial reward for its services; it may act as trustee for different issues by the same issuer and for different classes of bond holders who do not rank on a *pari passu* basis (for instance, some may have priority in a distribution of security, some may be secured and others unsecured, and some unsecured bond holders may be subordinated in right of payment behind the entitlement of other bond holders); it may act as trustee for other persons who hold investments in the issuer through the trustee; and, if it is a bank or a member of a banking group, it may engage in various commercial activities with the issuer and it may provide advisory services to the issuer. Clearly, these potential problems would mean that the trustee could not act as a trustee unless it was possible for them to be overcome by some modification, limitation or exclusion of the strict position as it arises at general law.

10.9.4.1 Subject to the effect of statutory limitations, it is possible for the nature and scope of the duties of a fiduciary, such as a trustee, that would otherwise arise and its liability for a breach of trust to be restrictively defined, modified, limited, or excluded by the use of appropriate clauses in the trust deed or associated documentation[178] except with respect to situations involving the dishonesty or lack of good faith on the part of the fiduciary.[179] Various rules have been developed as to the construction of such clauses. The relevant provision will be construed restrictively but fairly, according to the natural meaning of the words that have been used. Liability can only be limited or excluded by clear, unequivocal, and unambiguous terms, but it would appear that a strict *contra proferentum* rule will not be applied.[180] Accordingly, it is common for wording to be used in the trust deed with the intention of limiting or modifying the duties of a trustee in a bond issue, with the intention of overcoming the problems referred to above, and so as to permit the trustee to act notwithstanding the potential conflicts of interest that might arise. Careful attention will need to be paid to the drafting of such provisions to ensure that they will meet that objective.

10.9.4.2 Whilst in any event the potential problems concerning a possible conflict of interests may never arise in practice, if they do arise the trustee may find itself in an

---

[178] See Lord Browne-Wilkinson in *Henderson v Merrett Syndicates Ltd* [1995] 2 AC 145, at 206.
[179] See Millett LJ in *Armitage v Nurse* [1998] Ch 241, at 251–256.
[180] See Millett LJ in ibid, at 255–256; *Bogg v Raper* (1998/99) 1 ITELR 267, at 280–285; *Wight v Olswang (No 2)* (1999/2000) 2 ITELR 689.

invidious position, as it may be difficult for it to show that it has acted impartially,[181] and the beneficiaries may argue that they were forced to accept the position as presented by the trust deed,[182] although that particular argument might not carry very much weight, given that the trust deed is referred to in the prospectus/offering circular, is available for inspection during the life of the issue, and the provisions of trust deeds in bond issues are in a fairly standard form and in common use. If the trustee finds itself in a position of conflict, such as where there might be diverging interest between different classes or categories of bond holders, it may be well advised to appoint a further trustee or to delegate its powers to another person (provided that such a course of action is permitted by the trust deed) so that the divergent interests will have separate representation.[183] It would also be sensible for the trustee to have proper 'Chinese walls' in place in any situation where there is a risk that it may come by information concerning the issuer from some source unconnected with the particular bond issue for which the trust has been constituted.[184]

10.9.5 Statutory restrictions on limitations or exclusions of liability

It is now relevant to turn to the statutory limitations that might apply to clauses in the trust deed or elsewhere which seek to exclude or restrict the liability of the trustee.

10.9.5.1 Section 750 of the Companies Act 2006

The first such statutory provision to be considered is that contained in section 750(1) of the Companies Act 2006,[185] which provides as follows:

Any provision contained:-

(a) in a trust deed for securing an issue of debentures; or
(b) in any contract with the holders of debentures secured by a trust deed,

is void in so far as it would have the effect of exempting a trustee of the deed from, or indemnifying him against, liability for breach of trust where he fails to show the degree of care and diligence required of him as trustee, having regard to the provisions of the trust deed conferring on him any powers, authorities or discretions.

---

181 See, for instance, *Re Dorman Long & Co Ltd* [1934] 1 Ch 635 where a scheme that was put forward favoured the commercial interests of the trustee.

182 Ibid.

183 As, for instance, was done in *Re British & Commonwealth Holdings plc (No 3)* [1992] 1 WLR 672.

184 As to the use of Chinese walls and their effectiveness, see *Prince Jefri Bolkiah v KPMG* [1999] 2 AC 222; *Young v Robson Rhodes* [1999] 3 All ER 524; *Australian Securities and Investment Commission v Citigroup Global Markets Australia Pty Ltd* [2007] FCA 963, at [308]–[321].

185 Formerly s 192(1) of the Companies Act 1985.

10.9.5.1.1 This section probably only applies with respect to an issue by a company incorporated in Great Britain, because the definition of 'debenture'[186] (which includes bonds) refers to a 'company' which, in turn, is presumed (unless the contrary intention appears from the context) to mean a company incorporated under the Companies Act 2006 and its predecessors.[187] Nonetheless, it is common in the drafting of clauses which seek to give protection to trustees in international bond issues to use wording which reflects the restrictions imposed by the section.

10.9.5.1.2 The import of section 750(1) is not entirely clear, because of the obscurity behind the following words which will be found at the conclusion of the section: 'having regard to the provisions of the trust deed conferring on him any powers, authorities or discretions'. Those words cannot have been intended to allow for an exemption to have effect if the trust deed or such a contract seeks to provide that the trustee can be as negligent as it likes and has a discretion to sit back and do nothing in the performance of its functions as a trustee. That would be to defeat the object of the section. The better view[188] is that the words were intended to protect a trustee if, pursuant to provisions of the trust deed, it obtains and acts on advice it has received from experts, if it delegates functions to someone else, or if it relies on information or certificates provided to it in circumstances contemplated by the trust deed. Even if that view is adopted, it is submitted that it would not entirely relieve the trustee in those circumstances, because the trustee would still have to use reasonable care in appointing and supervising its advisers and delegates and in reviewing what it receives, particularly if it is a professional trustee and therefore subject to the higher duty of care described in *Bartlett v Barclays Bank Trust Co Ltd*.[189] It cannot blindly rely on others and on what it receives and abrogate all responsibility to check their work and the accuracy and correctness of what it has been given. It should also make further enquiry if its review reveals something untoward.

10.9.5.1.3 Section 750(2) of the Companies Act 2006[190] goes on to permit a release to be given by the debenture holders for past defalcations and omissions by the trustee and for the trust deed to contain provisions which provide for such a release to be given on a 75 per cent vote of the debenture holders. This, however, is subject to the requirement at general law that a trustee may only be relieved if the beneficiaries were properly informed as to the relevant facts and circumstances.[191] It is also

---

[186] Which is contained in s 738 of the Companies Act 2006 (formerly s 744 of the Companies Act 1985).

[187] S 1(1) of the Companies Act 2006 (formerly s 735 of the Companies Act 1985).

[188] This view is consistent with that which was put forward by the *Cohen Committee on Company Law Amendment* (Cmnd 6659, particularly para 64).

[189] [1980] Ch 515, at 534.

[190] Formerly s 192(2) of the Companies Act 1985.

[191] *Ryder v Bickerton* (1743) 3 Swan 80n, at 83n; *Walker v Symonds* (1818) 3 Swan 1, at 69 and 73.

possible for a trustee to apply to the court under section 61 of the Trustee Act 1925 for relief if it 'has acted honestly and reasonably, and ought fairly to be excused'.[192]

10.9.5.2 The Unfair Contract Terms Act 1977

The two sections of the Act that require consideration for present purposes are section 2(2) and section 3, which will be addressed in turn.

For quite some time, it was not clear if a clause which purported to exempt or exclude liability on the part of the trustee for negligence might also be subject to the application of section 2(2) of the Unfair Contract Terms Act 1977. That section provides that (in a case other than one concerning death or personal injury[193]) a person cannot by reference to a term of a contract or a non-contractual notice given to persons generally or to a particular person[194] exclude or restrict his liability for loss or damage arising from negligence except in so far as the term or notice satisfies the requirement of reasonableness in section 11 of the Act.[195]

10.9.5.2.1

The reason for the doubt as to the application of the Act in cases concerning a trustee's negligence was because of the definition of 'negligence' in section 1(1) of the Act. So far as relevant, it defined negligence to mean the breach of (a) any obligation, arising from the express or implied terms of a contract, to take reasonable care or to exercise reasonable skill in the performance of the contract, or (b) any common law duty to take reasonable care or to exercise reasonable skill. It was argued that a trustee could not fall within that definition for two reasons. First, because a trust deed, especially one such as used in a bond issue, should not be regarded as a 'contract' within (a). The trust deed is entered into between the issuer as the settlor and the trustee. The obligations of the trustee and the rights that are conferred under the trust deed on the bond holders as the intended beneficiaries of the trust, and the restriction on those rights, arise and are enforceable in equity and not in contract at common law.[196] Secondly, it was also argued, so

10.9.5.2.1.1

---

[192] This will be a more difficult hurdle for a professional trustee than for an ordinary trustee. See *National Trustees of Australasia Ltd v General Finance Company of Australasia Ltd* [1905] AC 373, at 381 and *Re Windsor Steam Coal Co (1901) Ltd* [1929] 1 Ch 51, at 164–165.

[193] Which is dealt with under s 2(1) of the Act.

[194] A 'notice' is defined in s 14 of the Act to include an announcement, whether or not in writing, and any other communication or pretended communication.

[195] The types of consideration that are relevant to s 11 are set out in s 11(4) and in Schedule 2 to the Act. Strictly speaking, that schedule applies to contractual terms concerning the supply of goods, but it has been held that the schedule provides general guidance as to the factors that are relevant to s 11. See *Singer (UK) Ltd v Tees & Hartlepool Port Authority* [1988] 2 Lloyd's Rep 164, at 169.

[196] It is worth noting that if a beneficiary sought to argue that it was a third party with respect to a contract entered into between the settlor of the trust and the trustee, and so was relying upon its right to enforce the contract under the Contracts (Rights of Third Parties Act) 1999 (assuming that its right to do so had not been excluded under s 1(2) of the 1999 Act), s 2(2) of the 1977 Act would

far as (b) is concerned, that a trustee's duty does not arise at common law. It arises in equity, albeit that it is substantially the same as the common law duty.[197] The position has now been clarified, as those arguments were accepted by Tuckey LJ in *Baker v JR Clarke & Co (Transport) Ltd.*[198]

10.9.5.2.2 For much the same reasons, it is submitted that section 3 of the Unfair Contract Terms Act 1977 would not apply with respect to the position of a trustee of a bond issue. That section relates to attempts to exclude or restrict liability for breach of contract and matters concerning contractual performance. To begin with, there is no contract between the trustee and the bond holders. In addition, such duties as a trustee might have towards the bond holders arise in equity and cannot be described as arising under a contract between the trustee and the bond holders.

10.9.6 The considerations that are relevant to the exercise by the trustee of its powers and discretions

It is now appropriate to consider the powers and discretions that will commonly be conferred upon a trustee of a bond issue and the factors that are relevant to the exercise of those powers and discretions by the trustee. It is also relevant, in that regard, to consider the trustee's right to indemnification if it takes action on behalf of the bond holders.

10.9.6.1 The trust deed and the terms and conditions of the bonds will usually contain a number of provisions which confer powers and discretions on the trustee, and which provide that the trustee's determination of a matter shall be conclusive and binding. Some of these provisions have already been mentioned, including those concerning applications by the issuer to the trustee for waivers, consents, and variations concerning the provisions of the terms and conditions of the bonds. The trustee is normally given a power to approve any such application made by the issuer if the trustee is of the opinion that the matter is of a minor or technical nature or that its effect will not be of material prejudice to the interests of the bond holders. Another area where the trustee is given discretion in making decisions is in relation to the possible occurrence of events of default and the action to be taken against the issuer.

10.9.6.2 It is also worth noting, in particular, four provisions that will usually be found in the events of default and enforcement clauses within the terms and conditions of the bonds.[199] The first of them is to the effect that certain of the listed events in the

---

not apply to the exclusion clause because the application of s 2(2) is barred in such a situation by virtue of s 7(2) of the 1999 Act.

[197] See further the Law Commission's Consultation Paper, *Trustee Exemption Clauses* No 171, paras 2.57–2.64.

[198] [2006] EWCA Civ 464, at [18]–[21].

[199] See also the earlier discussion at 10.8.9.2.

events of default clause (such as those relating to a breach of the issuer's covenants, the occurrence of a cross-default, the bringing of enforcement proceedings by other creditors, and certain insolvency events) should only constitute an event of default if the trustee certifies that in its opinion the occurrence of such an event is materially prejudicial to the interests of the bond holders. The second concerns the discretion that is given to the trustee to determine whether an event of default that has occurred is capable of remedy so that enforcement action should not be taken if, in the opinion of the trustee, adequate steps can be and are taken by the issuer to remedy the default. The third is to the effect that, unless it is instructed by a certain percentage of the bond holders to do so, the trustee is given a discretion as to whether to accelerate the issuer's obligation to make payment of the principal on the bonds following the occurrence of an event of default. The fourth type of provision provides that the trustee may demand that it should receive an indemnity to its satisfaction before it embarks on enforcement action against the issuer and any guarantor.

Valuable guidance has been given by the courts in relation to the exercise of such **10.9.6.3** powers and discretions by a trustee for bond holders, as well as in relation to its rights to indemnification. In *Law Debenture Trust Corp PLC v Acciona SA*[200] Peter Smith J (one of the first decisions in a long line of cases relating to the same bond issue) considered a provision of the first type mentioned above, which was contained in the events of default clause. It was to the effect that enforcement action could only be taken where a relevant event had occurred if the trustee had determined that the occurrence of the event was 'materially prejudicial to the interests of the bondholders'. His Lordship held that in making such a determination, the trustee had first to conclude that the event was a present event, and, secondly, that it was prejudicial to the interests of the bond holders in a material way.[201] By way of further amplification, his Lordship said[202] that the interests of the bond holders related to their interests in the bonds, that is, their contractual entitlement to the payment of interest and capital, and, as well, any ancillary rights which the bond holders might have to protect their entitlement to the payment of interest and principal, such as security rights and significant rights having a commercial protective interest, including the right of the bond holders in that case to appoint a director to the board of the issuer. Material prejudice did not necessarily mean the same thing as material breach, as such prejudice might exist even without such a breach and the existence of a material breach might not, on the facts, mean that the interests of the bond holders had been materially prejudiced.[203]

---

[200] [2004] EWHC 270 (Ch).
[201] See [41].
[202] At [42].
[203] See [44]–[45].

10.9.6.3.1 In most cases, the trustee would need to investigate the circumstances and their consequences to determine if the relevant element of material prejudice existed.[204] However, the facts on their face might be sufficient to establish the relevant degree of material prejudice without the need for further investigation, as was the position with respect to the assumed facts in the case before his Lordship.[205] In the case before him, the relevant terms and conditions of the bond issue had required the issuer to appoint a director to its board nominated by the bond holders and the issuer had agreed that it would not take certain decisions unless the nominated director consented to them. It was alleged that the issuer had subsequently excluded the nominated director from the board without good grounds for doing so and had entered into transactions without the nominated director's consent. That was sufficient on its own to constitute material prejudice, without the need for further investigation.

10.9.6.4 It should be noted that the proceedings before Peter Smith J had been between the trustee and certain of the bond holders. In consequence of the decision of Peter Smith J, the trustee served a notice of default upon the issuer and the bond holders, by the requisite majority, instructed the trustee to demand repayment by the issuer and take enforcement action against the issuer. The issuer, however, had not been a party to the proceedings, so the judgment did not bind it. The issuer subsequently disputed that it had been in breach, which was relevant in relation to a second set of proceedings between the trustee and the bond holders, which eventually reached the House of Lords as *Concord Trust v Law Debenture Trust Corp PLC*.[206] The leading judgment in the House of Lords was given by Lord Scott of Foscote.

10.9.6.4.1 So far as is relevant in the present context the second set of proceedings concerned two issues.[207] The first issue concerned whether, on the wording of the relevant clause in the terms and conditions, the trustee retained any discretion to determine if enforcement action should be taken, after it had been instructed to do so by the bond holders (assuming that the trustee was given an acceptable indemnity by the bond holders). The second issue concerned the trustee's right under the documentation to seek indemnification from the bond holders for any enforcement action it was required to take against the issuer and the guarantor.

---

[204] See [46]–[56].

[205] See [50]–[54] and [56].

[206] [2005] UKHL 27, [2005] 1 WLR 1591.

[207] In fact, the second set of proceedings also explored the important issue, which is examined elsewhere in this work (see Chap 3), of the extent to which a trustee of a bond issue, and indeed an agent in a syndicated loan facility or a lender in a bilateral loan facility, might be exposed to a claim against it for damages for loss that the issuer or a borrower might suffer in consequence of a wrongful purported acceleration of the issuer's or borrower's payment obligations.

The trustee raised the first issue because the issuer had disputed that an event of default had occurred. The clause in the terms and conditions of the bonds provided as follows:

> The Bond Trustee at its discretion may, and if so requested [or directed] by [the relevant proportion of bondholders] shall (subject . . . to being indemnified to its satisfaction), give notice to the Issuer and the Guarantor that the Bonds are, and they shall immediately become, due and repayable at their relevant redemption value, together with the accrued Interest Amount as provided in the Bond Trust Deed, upon the occurrence of any of the following events ('Events of Default').

Lord Scott held[208] that, subject to resolution of the second issue in the proceedings concerning the trustee's right to an indemnity, the trustee was obliged to take enforcement action on behalf of the bond holders, having been instructed to do so by the requisite proportion of the bond holders. As between the trustee and the bondholders, the fact that an event of default had occurred had been conclusively settled by the proceedings before Peter Smith J. There was nothing further for the trustee to determine; nor did the trustee have a remaining discretion to decide if it should take enforcement action.

The second matter concerned the right of the trustee to seek indemnification, to its satisfaction, against the liabilities it might incur in taking enforcement action against the issuer, by demanding repayment of the outstanding amount of the bonds and interest thereon, following instructions to do so by the bondholders given in accordance with the terms and conditions of the bonds.[209] The trustee argued that the quantification of its right to an indemnity should include any possible exposure (however remote) that it might have to damages in a suit brought against it by the issuer, should it turn out that (as against the issuer) the trustee was not entitled to take enforcement action because the declaration of default was invalid. Lord Scott accepted that the trustee was entitled to be indemnified if the issuer's claim might (rather than would) succeed, that is, that it was reasonably arguable that the issuer's claim could succeed,[210] or, to put it in another way, unless the issuer's claim was certain to fail and was merely fanciful.[211] It was also accepted that, at the least, the trustee was entitled to be indemnified against its liability for legal costs in any proceedings that might be taken.[212] The critical issue was whether the trustee was also at risk of incurring a liability to the issuer in damages for loss caused by giving an invalid notice. His Lordship went on to hold that the trustee

---

208 See [22]–[29].

209 The right of a trustee at general law to be indemnified out of the trust assets for its expenses and liabilities (including contingent liabilities) and its lien on the trust assets for that purpose, was explored in *Law Debenture Trust Corp PLC v Concord Trust* [2007] EWHC 1380 (Ch).

210 See [35].

211 See [34].

212 Ibid.

was not at risk of incurring such a liability and so the trustee was not entitled to demand indemnification against the possibility of such a liability.[213]

10.9.6.5 The remaining questions that require discussion concern the extent to which the courts may intervene by directing a trustee as to how it should exercise its discretion and how it should act, especially in situations where a trustee may have an apparently unfettered discretion to decide whether and how it might act. Linked to that question is the further issue of the extent to which the court would be prepared to overturn the consequences of an exercise of a trustee's discretion.

10.9.6.5.1 The Trustee Act 2000 may require the trustee to take certain action (see above), in which case it must comply with the law. If the trust deed requires it to take certain action then it must comply with that requirement.[214] Otherwise, it must make its decision for bona fide reasons[215] and it must consider if it should act.[216] In general terms, and save where the trust deed requires the trustee to consult the bond holders or to seek their instructions and accede to their wishes, the trustee is free to make its own decisions until such time as the bonds have been redeemed in full and all other liabilities of the issuer have been discharged.[217] Subject again to the specific requirements of the trust deed, the trustee is not obliged to give reasons for its decisions,[218] although the trustee will often do so as a practical matter. Nonetheless, in making a decision and in the action it takes, the trustee will have to meet the level of care and skill that is required of it as a professional trustee,[219] although it may be entitled to obtain and rely upon professional advice, if that is permitted by the trust deed. It has also been held that in making a decision as to whether it should exercise a power or discretion, a trustee should inform itself of the matters that are relevant to its decision,[220] and the court can interfere if the

---

[213] See [36]–[45].

[214] See, for instance, the action that the trustee was obliged to take following a resolution of the bond holders in *Concord Trust v Law Debenture Trust Corporation PLC* [2005] UKHL 27; [2005] 1 WLR 1591, per Lord Scott, at [22]–[29].

[215] *Gisborne v Gisborne* (1877) 2 App Cas 300.

[216] Per James LJ in *Re Gresham Life Assurance Society* (1872) LR 8 Ch App 446, at 450.

[217] This is stated by application of the rule in *Saunders v Vautier* [1841] Cr & Ph 240, in which it was held that until such time as the trust should be wound up and the trust assets distributed to the beneficiaries (being fully entitled to all such assets), the trustee has the right to make its own decisions and not take instructions from the beneficiaries. See also Lightman J in *Don King Productions Inc v Warren* [2000] 1 WLR 291, at 321, who relied upon *Re Brockbank* [1948] Ch 206, although query if that case may be confined to the exercise by the trustee of a statutory discretion and, in any event, the beneficiaries could have called for a transfer of the trust assets to them and a winding up of the trust, so they hardly needed the assistance of the court.

[218] *Re Gresham Life Assurance Society* (1872) LR 8 Ch App 446. If it does give reasons, the court is entitled to examine them: *Klug v Klug* [1918] 2 Ch 67, Harman LJ in *Re Londonderry's Settlement* [1965] Ch 918, at 928–929.

[219] *Bartlett v Barclays Bank Trust Co Ltd* [1980] Ch 515, at 534.

[220] *Scott v National Trust for Places of Historic Interest or Natural Beauty* [1998] 2 All ER 705, at 717.

trustee has failed to do so responsibly[221] or if it has approached its task perversely or irrationally.[222]

Finally, there is the rule concerning the circumstances in which the court will overturn the outcome of an exercise of a trustee's discretion, which was laid down by the Court of Appeal in *In re Hastings-Bass, decd.*[223] It is not entirely clear how the rule fits with the propositions that have been stated above. It may depend upon the acquiescence of the trustee in a challenge to any decision that it has made. The rule was explained by Lloyd LJ (sitting as a judge of the Chancery Division), after an extensive review of the case law, in *Sieff v Fox.*[224] Paraphrasing the explanation of Lloyd LJ, the rule and its consequences as relevant for present purposes may be stated in the following terms. First, where a trustee has acted in pursuance of a discretion given to it by the terms of the trust, in circumstances in which it was free to decide whether or not to exercise that discretion, but the effect of the exercise of that discretion is different from that which was intended, the court will interfere if it is clear that the trustee would not have acted as it did had it taken into account considerations which it ought, but failed, to take into account (including the fiscal consequences of its actions), or if it took into account considerations which it ought not to have taken into account. Secondly, the court will also interfere if the trustee was obliged to act but had a discretion as to the action it should take, in a situation where the trustee might (rather than would) have acted differently, and the court considers that the trustee took the wrong course of action. It is not necessary to show that that the trustee was at fault in arriving at its decision.[225] It is not clear from the rule if the effect of the court's interference should mean that the trustee's decision is treated as void or merely voidable. The difference may be relevant to the effect upon third parties and to defences based upon pleas such as laches and acquiescence.[226]

10.9.6.5.2

---

[221] Ibid.

[222] *Edge v Pensions Ombudsman* [2000] Ch 602, at 627–630.

[223] [1975] Ch 25.

[224] [2005] EWHC 1312 (Ch), [2005] 3 All ER 693.

[225] Contra Lightman J in *Re Barr's Settlement Trusts, Abacus Trust Co (Isle of Man) v Barr* [2003] EWHC 114 (Ch); [2003] Ch 409, at [22]–[24].

[226] See the discussion on this point by Lightman J in *Re Barr's Settlement Trusts*, at [28]–[33].

11

DERIVATIVES TRANSACTIONS

11.1 Introduction

11.1.1 Derivatives transactions have been amongst the fastest growing transactions in the financial world. It was reported that at the end of the second quarter of 2006, the aggregate notional value of outstanding derivatives held globally came to US$370,000 billion or, in net value, US$10,000 billion. It was also estimated that the global notional outstanding amount of interest rate swaps came to US$262,000 billion and that there was US$38,000 billion in the notional amount of outstanding foreign exchange derivatives.[1] In light of the turmoil in the financial markets in the second part of 2007, it appeared that the volume of transactions had diminished.

11.1.2 Whilst derivative transactions have the capability of spreading risk and thus making it easier for the international banking system to absorb financial shocks, there

---

[1] Figures as published by the Bank for International Settlements, as quoted in the *Financial Times* 18/11/2006.

have been a number of concerns raised in relation to such transactions and the effect they may have.[2] One concern is that through the use of derivatives banks have shifted the risk of financial transactions to other sectors, including the insurance sector (operating through subsidiary companies), which has been an active participant in the derivatives market. Another concern, particularly in relation to equity derivatives, is that banks which sell such products may have a conflict of interests resulting from knowledge they may hold as bankers and advisers to the company or other entity to which the product relates. There has also been a concern that through the use of equity derivatives, such as options, persons may be able clandestinely to build up stakes in companies which would not come to light through the traditional disclosure rules to be found in legislation and other disclosure requirements, such as those relating to stake building under takeover rules.[3] Concerns have also been expressed as to the effect of the rules introduced by the international accounting standards (IAS). IAS 39 will require movements in the market price of holdings in derivatives held by an entity to be reflected in its profit and loss account, even where the derivatives are held as hedging instruments against an underlying transaction. That could also lead to adverse consequences for financial covenants in funding documentation and unfortunate tax consequences for such an entity. A final concern is that the speed at which new products are being devised and the complexity of the transactions in which derivatives are used may result in a failure to appreciate their commercial and legal consequences. This concern is reflected in some of the criticism that was levelled at structured finance products in which derivatives were a constituent element, such criticism arising in consequence of the turmoil in the financial markets in the second part of 2007.

The expression 'derivative' when applied in the context of these transactions imports   **11.1.3**
the concept that they are derived from some underlying transaction, instrument, or even an index of transactions or instruments. As will be seen, the underlying transaction or instrument may actually exist or it may be purely notional. In one sense, a derivative reflects the financial consequences of movements in the price or the risk associated with the underlying transaction. This can be illustrated by an example taken from a forerunner of the derivatives transaction, the commodity futures transaction. Such a transaction is based upon a notional transaction involving a specified quantity of a particular commodity (e.g. copper) to be settled on a specified date in the future, under which one party is the seller and the other the buyer. The price is agreed in the contract. On the settlement date, the contract price is compared against the prevailing market price, which may be higher, lower, or the same as the

---

[2] For a more detailed review of the types of concern that may arise, see the Report of the Counterparty Risk Management Policy Group II, dated 27/7/2005, *Toward Greater Financial Stability: A Private Sector Perspective* (available at <http://www.crmpolicygroup.org>).

[3] The Takeover Panel in the UK now requires that holdings of derivatives, including options, should be disclosed if (when added to other holdings) a person's holdings amount to more than 1% of a company which is the subject of a bid (*Response Statement* No 2005/2, dated 5/8/2005).

contract price. Assuming there is a difference then depending upon in whose favour the difference lies, the amount of the difference will be paid by one party to the other. Thus, if the market price is higher than the contract price, the seller will pay the difference to the buyer. If the difference lies the other way then the buyer will pay the difference to the seller. What the buyer has managed to do through such a transaction is to protect itself against an adverse upwards movement in the market price against the contract price that it negotiated when the contract was entered into. If the buyer uses or deals in the underlying commodity in its business then it has managed effectively to hedge itself against the consequences of an adverse upwards move in the market price by the end of the life of the contract. Alternatively, if it is a speculator then it has made a profit. Of course, if the market price has fallen against the contract price then the buyer will have to pay out the difference, but it can hardly complain as it was always willing to accept the contract price.

11.1.4 Derivatives transactions may be based upon a wide variety of underlying transactions, instruments, or, indeed, indices of transactions and instruments. They may relate to the notional principal sum of a loan or a debt security, to equity securities or the issuer of such securities, or even to the prices of utilities, such as gas or electricity. The reasons for entering into such transactions may also vary. In some cases, a party may wish to hedge itself against the adverse consequences to it of movements in the pricing of a transaction in which it is actually engaged. Thus, a borrower or a lender under a loan agreement may enter into a swap transaction to hedge against adverse movements in the market in interest rates or currencies which could have a direct effect on its financial position arising from the loan agreement. More generally, a party to a derivatives transaction may wish to gain protection for a whole book of business; for example, a lender which has a book of fixed rate loans to borrowers and which is funding itself in the interbank market may wish to hedge against an adverse movement of market rates of interest against the fixed rate of interest it is receiving under the loans it has made to its borrowers. Another alternative is that a party to a derivatives transaction may have entered into it for speculative purposes, having spotted what it believes is an opportunity to make a profit against movements of the underlying price. Finally, whatever the reason for initially entering into a derivatives transaction, a party may wish to lay off some of the risk it has undertaken by entering into subsidiary or consequential derivatives transactions, of an opposite character to that under the principal transaction, for some part of the risk it has undertaken in the principal transaction.

11.2 Types of Transaction

11.2.1 What follows provides a description of derivatives transactions looked at largely as individual transactions. Often, however, they are included in and form part of a larger overall transaction. For instance, a derivatives contract might be used in conjunction with an underlying pool of debt securities so that the currency in which the securities are denominated is converted into a cash flow in another currency (an example of which, that did not turn out very satisfactorily, will be seen in *Peekay Intermark Ltd v Australia and New Zealand Banking Group Ltd*[4]). By use of a derivatives contract, fixed interest that is payable on a bond issue may be exchanged for floating rate interest or vice versa. Another example concerns securitisation transactions. Derivatives contracts may be used as either an interest rate matching mechanism or a currency conversion mechanism to ensure that receipts from the underlying portfolio of receivables in the securitisation are sufficient to match obligations on the funds that were raised to purchase the portfolio. Alternatively, in a synthetic securitisation, one or more credit derivatives may stand as a proxy for the pool of underlying receivables or debt instruments so that the pool remains in the hands of the originator, at least until default in payment of a receivable.

Although it is now a little dated (for instance, it does not refer to credit derivatives, which did not exist at the time), there is a useful introductory description of various types of derivatives transaction contained in an appendix to the judgment of the Divisional Court in *Hazel v Hammersmith and Fulham LBC*.[5] What follows below is an explanation of the more common types of transaction that will be found in the London markets. **11.2.2**

11.2.3 Swaps

Under a swap transaction, the parties to the transaction agree that each of them will pay to the other, at regular intervals during the life of the transaction, set amounts or variable amounts that are calculated by reference to a notional principal sum, amount, or quantity. An illustration of the potential benefits of swap transactions was provided by Lord Templeman in *Hazell v Hammersmith and Fulham LBC*.[6]

11.2.3.1 Currency swaps

A currency swap involves one party agreeing to pay an amount in a stipulated currency to the second party on the payment dates and the second party agreeing to pay the first-mentioned party an amount on those dates in another stipulated currency. Such a transaction is a useful device for a bank which has funded itself in one currency, exchanged the amount raised into a different currency, and then lent the resulting currency amount to its borrower. Without the benefit of the swap, the bank is at risk that the currency in which it has lent the funds to the

---

4 [2006] EWCA Civ 286, [2006] 2 Lloyd's Rep 511.
5 [1990] 2 QB 697, at 739–741.
6 [1992] 2 AC 1, at 23–24.

borrower will depreciate against the value of the currency in which it originally raised the funds. The swap effectively converts the payments that the bank receives from the borrower, which will be in the currency of the loan to the borrower, into funds in the currency needed by the bank to service its own funding obligations. An example of such a transaction is set out in Figure 11.1.

11.2.3.2 Interest rate swaps

An interest rate swap is based on the calculation of interest on a notional principal amount. One party will agree to pay to the second party, at set intervals during the life of the agreement, a sum equivalent to interest calculated at a floating rate on the nominal principal sum, whilst the second party will agree to pay to the first party a sum equivalent to interest at a fixed rate on that principal sum. This would be a useful transaction for a bank which has funded itself in the inter-bank market at a floating rate of interest and agreed to lend the funds to the borrower at a fixed rate of interest. The swap effectively converts the fixed rate receipts of interest from the borrower into a floating rate of interest which the bank can use to meet its floating rate obligations on the funds it has raised in the inter-bank market (an example of this type of transaction will be found in the Scottish case of *Bank of Scotland v Dunedin Property Investment Co*[7]). Alternatively, the bank may have funded itself by issuing bonds at a fixed rate, the amount of which it has lent to its borrowers at a floating rate of interest. The swap will have the effect of converting the floating rate interest receipts from the borrowers into amounts calculated at a fixed rate, which can then be used to service the fixed rate interest payments due under the bonds. An example of such a transaction is set out in Figure 11.2.

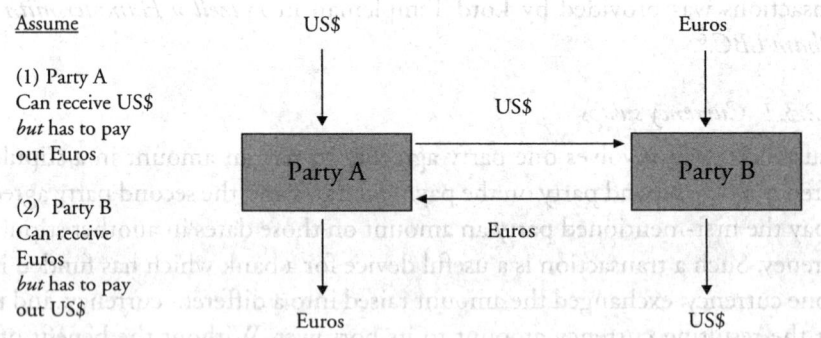

Figure 11.1 Hedging—Currency Swap

---

7 [1999] SLT 470.

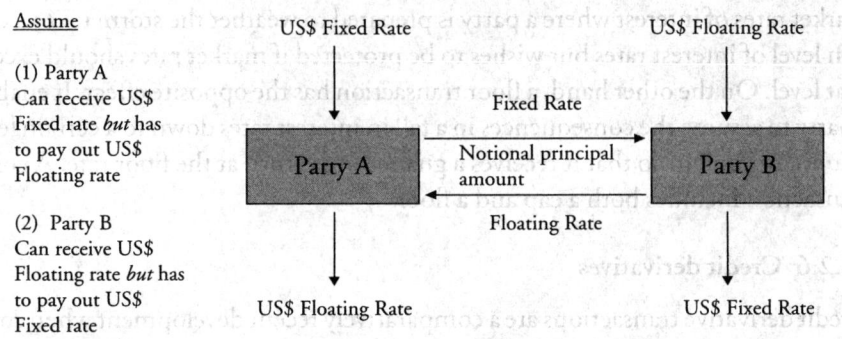

Figure 11.2 Hedging—Interest Rate Swap

11.2.3.3 Other swaps

Various other types of swap transaction have been devised. An example is pro-vided by the Australian case of *Enron Australia Finance Pty Ltd v TXU Electricity Ltd*.[8] In that case, the swap involved prices for electricity to be paid for successive periods over the length of the swap agreement. One party agreed to pay to the sec-ond party an amount equivalent to a price calculated at a fixed rate on a notional usage of electricity for each period. The second party agreed to pay to the first party an amount equivalent to the prevailing market price on the notional usage for the period.

11.2.4 Forward transactions

Forward or futures transactions involve a contract under which the parties agree to make an exchange, often of amounts in different currencies, at a future date or dates, at a rate of exchange or price agreed at the time the contract is entered into. For instance, the contract may provide for the exchange of a set amount of euros into a set amount of US dollars at a date in two years' time. A forward rate agree-ment is an agreement which has similar characteristics to an interest rate swap except that the period to which it relates will commence at a future date rather than the date of the agreement.

11.2.5 Caps, floors, and collars

A cap transaction has the effect of capping the interest rate on a principal amount. The party granting the cap, in return for a fee, agrees that if the rate rises above the agreed level, it will pay the difference. It is useful in the context of fluctuating

---

8 [2003] NSWSC 1169.

market rates of interest where a party is prepared to weather the storm up to a certain level of interest rates but wishes to be protected if market rates should exceed that level. On the other hand, a floor transaction has the opposite effect. It enables a party to assume the consequences in a fall in interest rates down to a certain level but not beyond it, so that it receives a guaranteed return at the floor rate. A collar transaction includes both a cap and a floor.

11.2.6 Credit derivatives

Credit derivative transactions are a comparatively recent development when compared to interest and currency swaps. They involve a mechanism for the transference of risk, particularly default risk, associated with a specified entity, transaction, or instrument (or groups or portfolios thereof).[9] The market in such transactions is growing rapidly, as is their variety and complexity. In consequence, it is difficult to be definite about the characteristics of these types of transaction. Nonetheless, the credit default swap is a fairly common type of transaction and its characteristics will now be described.[10] In following this description, it might be helpful to have in mind the following factual situation, although it must be borne in mind that a transaction may be entered into for entirely speculative reasons that are not connected with any particular underlying interest of either party.

11.2.6.1   The example involves a financial institution which holds or intends to hold bonds or other securities that have been issued by an entity such as a corporation or, in the case of certain types of debt securities, a bank. The financial institution is concerned as to the risk of default by the issuer but wishes to retain its investments. It would like to obtain protection against that risk. On the other hand, another institution, which is more sanguine about the risk, is looking to make a profit from covering such a risk without having to make an initial capital outlay in purchasing the securities. The two institutions would be the parties to the credit default swap, the principal features of which will now be described. The transaction would be for a defined period, which might be a number of years. The parties are often described as the buyer of protection or the seller of risk on the one part (the financial institution which holds or intends to hold the investments in the example) and, on the other, the seller of protection or buyer of risk (the other

---

[9] In addition to credit default swaps as mentioned below, examples of other types of transaction include those structured by reference to an index of securities and those which are in the form of an option or a credit linked note. They may also involve obligations which are calculated by reference to the notional return or payment stream that would be received on an assumed underlying security or portfolio of securities.

[10] It was estimated that at the end of 2006, there was globally some US$34,000bn in notional outstanding amount of credit default swaps, representing about ten times more than the aggregate outstanding amount of the underlying transactions to which they were referenced (figures quoted by the *Financial Times* on 8/8/2007).

institution in the example). The first named party will make payment to the second named party for taking on the risk under the transaction. It is likely that this payment obligation will involve the payment of periodic sums during the life of the transaction. The transaction will identify the specified or reference entity to which or to whose securities or obligations the transaction relates.[11] The specified or reference obligations, if relevant, will be the particular securities or obligations of the specified or reference entity to the performance of which the credit derivatives transaction relates (e.g. particular securities issued by the issuer or securities issued by it having defined characteristics).[12] It may be that particular securities or obligations will not be so specified, in which case the transaction will relate more generally to the specified entity as, for instance, where the financial institution in the example does not wish to be tied down to holding particular securities of that entity. The transaction will provide that on the occurrence of a relevant event (e.g. an insolvency event or a general default relating to the specified or reference entity) and perhaps the satisfaction of certain other conditions (e.g. public notice that the event has occurred and service of a notice that a credit event has occurred) the seller of protection/buyer of risk will make a payment to the buyer of protection/seller of risk, against the delivery by the latter to the former of 'deliverable obligations' which conform to a description provided for in the contract (e.g. securities of the specified or reference entity[13]). In the alternative, there may be a cash settlement without the necessity for delivery of deliverable obligations.

---

[11] Consideration may need to be given to events that may affect the identity of that entity, such as a merger or other form of amalgamation, a de-merger or hiving off of a part of the enterprise, and a transfer of obligations that may occur under a scheme of arrangement or pursuant to legislation, such as under Part VII of the Financial Services and Markets Act 2000 or a specific Act of Parliament. Under English conflict of laws rules, these matters would be governed primarily by the law of the place of incorporation. See, for instance, *Eurosteel v Stinnes* [2000] 1 All ER (Comm) 964. However, there may also be local law issues in a place of business or where assets or liabilities are located. For instance, the effect of an English Act of Parliament may not hold much sway in another jurisdiction, which may continue to treat the relevant initial entity as still continuing or as if the merger had not occurred.

[12] There could be a problem if it is argued that the issuer or debtor has been discharged, for instance by operation of law, rather than that it has defaulted in its obligations. Under Art 10(1)(b) and (d) of the Rome Convention 1980 (which applies in English law by virtue of the Contracts (Applicable Law) Act 1990), the applicable/governing law of a contract should determine if the debt has been discharged. However, the House of Lords in *Société Eram Shipping Co Ltd v Hong Kong and Shanghai Banking Corp Ltd* [2003] UKHL 30, [2004] 1 AC 260 ignored the Rome Convention and held that the issue should be determined either by the *lex situs* of the debt or by a combination of its *lex situs* and its governing law. The Privy Council, shortly before, had decided that at common law (i.e. outside the ambit of the Rome Convention) the issue was governed by the governing law of the debt: *Wight v Eckhardt Marine* [2003] UKPC 37, [2004] 1 AC 147.

[13] For an example, see *Nomura International PLC v Credit Suisse First Boston International* [2003] EWHC 160, [2003] 2 All ER (Comm) 56.

11.2.6.2 Experience has taught that precision is needed in identifying the requirements of the various matters to which these types of transaction relate. As already mentioned, difficulties have arisen in relation to the identification of the specified or reference entity where a merger or de-merger has occurred during the life of the transaction. In addition, the effect of debt and corporate re-schedulings and reconstructions have made it difficult to determine if a relevant event has occurred and, as *Nomura International PLC v Credit Suisse First Boston International*[14] demonstrates, it may be difficult to identify the requirements as to deliverable obligations. A number of these matters have been clarified by further refinement of the contractual provisions.[15]

11.2.7 Equity derivatives

These are derivatives transactions that relate to equity securities rather than credit instruments. In many senses, their characteristics are similar to credit derivatives, in that they provide real or assumed protection against a failure of an issuer of equity securities or a decline in the value of such securities. Unlike credit derivatives, however, they are mainly dealt with by exchange traded transactions rather than through direct dealings between the parties in the 'over the counter' market.

11.2.8 Options

In the context of derivatives transactions, an option, as the name implies, is an agreement under which one party grants the other an option, which may be exercised within an agreed period or on a particular date, to enter into a further transaction, such as a swap (a 'swaption') or a forward transaction or a transaction relating to an asset, on the terms agreed in the option. The party in whose favour the option is granted (the 'grantee' or 'optionee') is free to choose whether or not it wishes to exercise the option. The party granting the option (the 'grantor' or 'optionor') will normally receive a fee in payment for the grant. A further amount will usually be payable if the option is exercised. Under a put option, the grantee has the right to require the grantor in effect to take over its position in a transaction or an asset. A call option gives the grantee the right to require the grantor to transfer to it the benefit of a transaction or an asset. A simple example would concern an option relating to an equity security. A put option would allow the grantee the right to require the grantor to buy the security at the price determined in the option.

---

[14] Ibid.

[15] See, for instance, the definitions contained in the 2003 version of the Credit Derivatives Definitions promulgated by the International Swaps and Derivatives Association (ISDA) which, as will be seen further below, are now used for nearly all derivatives transactions entered into using the ISDA Master Agreement. Further reference is made to the Master Agreement below.

It can be used by the grantee as a method of hedging against the risk of a decline in the value of the security during the period of the option. A call option, on the other hand, would have the reverse effect. It can be used by the grantee as a method of realising any profit to be gained from an increase in the value of the security over the option period without in the first place having to lay out the capital cost of acquiring the security. Rather than having a physical delivery when the option is exercised, the parties may agree a cash settlement, under which the grantor will pay to the grantee the difference between the market price or value of the underlying transaction or asset and the price agreed in the option.

11.2.9 Cash settled transactions

It is not just the outcome of option arrangements that are cash settled. Whilst the explanation of a number of the transactions provided above has assumed that a party to the relevant transaction will pay to the other party, on each payment date, the absolute amount that is calculated as the amount payable by it under the agreement or, alternatively, transfer the relevant securities or other asset, in practice that will often not to be the case. For transactions involving a single outcome, it is likely that a balance amount will be calculated, representing the financial result that the transaction has produced as, for instance, in relation to the financial outcome of the exercise of an option. Where the transaction is continuing and involves amounts payable by each of the parties in the same currency at periodic intervals (e.g. under an interest rate swap) the contract will usually provide that their obligations on each payment date will be netted off so that only the difference or the balance will be payable by one party to the other.[16] In this sense, many derivatives transactions might be thought of as being for the payment of differences, which has implications when considering if the transactions might be characterised as gaming or wagering contracts, as to which see further below. In any event, a 'contract for differences' is a specified kind of investment for the purposes of section 22 of the Financial Services and Markets Act 2000 (FSMA) (see below).

11.2.10 Credit enhancement and credit support

One matter that deserves attention when a party is considering a derivatives transaction is the risk of default by the counterparty, particularly in consequence of the insolvency of the counterparty. It is all very well to enter into a derivatives transaction in the belief that it will alleviate or hedge against risk, but the transaction will not be of much use if the counterparty cannot honour or refuses to honour its obligations. This will be the subject of further discussion below. In the meantime,

---

[16] This is a form of transaction netting. For an example, see s 2(c) in the standard form of ISDA Master Agreement (2002 edition).

it is relevant here to mention some of the additional protection by way of credit enhancement and credit support that might be used to guard against the consequences of default by the counterparty. One possibility is to take a guarantee from another person which may be considered more creditworthy than the counterparty, or least able to bear some of the load should the counterparty default. It might also be possible to take security over assets of the counterparty or of such a guarantor.

11.2.10.1 Margin

A security mechanism that is well suited to derivatives transactions is the use of margin.[17] A simple form of margin involves cash payments but it is also possible that margin might include other assets such as marketable securities. A party may be required to lodge and maintain margin with the other party, calculated on either a daily basis or at intervals during the life of the transaction. The value of margin that is required at any particular time will fluctuate and reflects the potential loss that the party providing the margin might make on the transaction, measured by comparing the amount it has to pay under the contract at the settlement date against the market value of its position under the transaction at the time of calculation. It may be required to maintain margin to the value of the whole amount of that discrepancy or for a proportion of it. It should also be entitled to a return of margin to the extent that its position improves during the course of the transaction.

11.3 The Markets on which Derivatives Transactions Take Place

11.3.1 There are, essentially, two types of market on which derivatives transactions take place. They are the market on which exchange based transactions take place and the 'over the counter' private market in which individually negotiated transactions take place directly between the parties.

11.3.2 Exchange based transactions

Exchange based transactions take place through the medium of an exchange, between the members of the exchange. An example is transactions traded on Eurnonext.liffe. A member may be acting on its own behalf or on behalf of its customer. When acting for a customer, it is likely that the rules of the exchange or of the relevant clearing house will require that the member should contract as principal vis-à-vis the clearing house and the other party to the transaction. The characteristic of such transactions is that they are in a standard form, covering

---

17 An example of the use of margin will be found in *SCF Finance Co. Ltd v Masri (No 2)* [1987] QB 1002.

fixed amounts, periods, and terms and conditions, with the price for the transaction being the matter that is negotiated between the parties.

Such transactions may involve a clearing house which is interposed into the transaction so that, strictly speaking, each party (i.e. each exchange member) contracts with the clearing house rather than with the other negotiating counterparty. This is a risk mitigation mechanism as each party, by contracting with the clearing house, is only taking the risk of a failure by the clearing house rather than the other counterparty. The robustness of the clearing house itself will depend upon the capital resources requirements that it imposes on its members and the backing it has by way of a right to call on the members to contribute to its resources in the event of financial difficulty. Further, it is likely that margin payments may have to be made by a contracting party to the clearing house. The requirement for margin, which is likely to be calculated on a daily basis, will be measured against the extent to which the party's financial interest in the transaction moves adversely during the term of the transaction against the market price on the exchange. One further measure of protection that is enjoyed by the clearing house that operates in the Euronext.liffe market, London Clearing House, is that it is a recognised clearing house for the purposes of Part VII of the Companies Act 1989, which modifies insolvency law so that the default procedures of the clearing house and security interests held by it prevail over the general laws of insolvency.

11.3.2.1

11.3.3 The OTC market

By far the wider market, however, is the private market, usually referred to as 'over the counter' (OTC) market, of transactions entered into directly between parties outside the confines of an exchange. This encompasses transactions that reflect the commercial terms agreed between the parties on whatever basis they wish and so it is not confined to the more regularised commercial terms and characteristics that apply to transactions conducted through the medium of an exchange. A good deal of the trading in the OTC market now takes place through the use of electronic trading platforms, which match parties to intended transactions. Whilst the parties are free to negotiate whatever commercial terms they feel appropriate for the transaction they wish to undertake, most of the transactions in this market these days are recorded using standard forms of contract that will be entered into between the parties and which are modified to include the consequences of the relevant commercial terms that have been agreed. Indeed, the standard forms make provision for inserting the commercial terms and provide for some alternatives on other matters to be included or discarded as the parties have negotiated between them.

By far the most common of the standard forms of contract that are in use are those promulgated by the International Swaps and Derivatives Association (ISDA), which first put forward a standard form of master agreement in 1987. The scheme

11.3.3.1

contemplated by the master agreement is that each set of potential counterparties will enter into a master agreement between them which will govern all the transactions that will at any time exist between them. The master agreement contains a schedule in which the choice of the parties as to the various alternatives contemplated by the master agreement and other amendments to the text of the document can be recorded. The commercial terms that apply to any particular such transaction will be identified in a form of Confirmation, which has the effect of bringing the transaction within the ambit of the master agreement. There have been two revisions of the master agreement since 1987, being the 1992 version and the 2002 version.[18] The form of master agreement is accompanied by a number of other common form documents, such as credit support documents and documents containing definitions relevant to the particular type of transaction that the parties may enter into (e.g. the 2003 version of the ISDA Credit Derivatives Definitions). There will be further study of the 2002 version of the master agreement below.

11.4 UK Regulatory Matters

11.4.1 An outline of the regime

Regulation of derivatives transactions in the UK arises pursuant to the Financial Services and Markets Act 2000 (FSMA) and subordinate legislation. A detailed review of the requirements that are imposed by the legislation is beyond the scope of this chapter. What follows is intended to give an overview of the requirements of the Act as it relates to derivatives transactions. It supplements the commentary that will be found in Chapter 2.

11.4.1.1 Section 19 of FSMA provides that no person may carry on a regulated activity in the UK (which is given an extended meaning by virtue of section 418 of FSMA) unless he has been authorised under the Act or is exempted from the need to be authorised. By section 22 a regulated activity is an activity of a specified kind which is carried on by way of business and which relates to an investment of a specified kind. The specified kinds of activity and the specified kinds of investment will be found in the FSMA (Regulated Activities) Order 2001,[19] as amended (the Regulated Activities Order). A breach of section 19 is an offence. There is also a restriction on financial promotion by an unauthorised person (section 21).

---

[18] ISDA has published protocols which allow the parties to existing forms of master agreement to update them to bring them into line with the latest version if they so wish.
[19] SI 2001/544.

By section 26 of FSMA, an agreement made by a person in breach of the prohibi-   **11.4.1.2**
tion upon him under section 19 (except if the breach concerns taking deposits[20])
is unenforceable by him against the other party, and the latter is entitled to the
return of any money paid or transferred by him under the agreement. He is also
entitled to compensation (assessed under section 28(2)), but this is subject to an
obligation, which is imposed by section 28(7), to return any money or property
that he received. Section 27 imposes similar consequences where an authorised
person enters into an agreement in consequence of something said or done by an
unauthorised person. Section 28(3) provides, however, that the court may allow
the agreement affected by sections 26 or 27 to be enforced, or that money or
property received in breach of the Act may be retained if the court is satisfied that
it is just and equitable to so allow.[21] Sections 28(4) to (6) make provision for the
matters to be taken into account under section 28(3). Section 28(9) limits the
further civil consequences of a breach of the requirement for authorisation. In
consequence of the foregoing, the innocent counterparty to an unauthorised
transaction can elect to perform it and enforce it against the defaulting unauthorised party.

11.4.2 Derivatives transactions

In terms of sections 19 and 22 of FSMA, entering into derivatives transactions in
the UK as a business activity will be a specified kind of activity for which authorisation is required under FSMA, unless an exception applies. This is because derivatives contracts are likely to be classified as specified kinds of investment under
Articles 83 to 85 and, as relevant thereto, Article 89 of the Regulated Activities
Order. Entering into such a contract, as principal or agent, or arranging such a
transaction is likely to constitute the specified activity of dealing in such investments as a principal or agent or as arranging investments under, respectively,
Articles 14, 21, and 25 of that Order. Each of those matters will now be discussed,
beginning with the relevant definitions of specified kinds of investment and then
turning, more briefly, to the concept of a specified kind of activity.

11.4.3 Specified kinds of investment

The relevant definitions are to be found in Articles 83, 84, 85, and 89 of the
Regulated Activities Order. Each of them will be discussed separately. In so doing,
it will be necessary to divide the discussion of the definitions in Articles 83, 84,

---

[20] S 26 does not apply to the unauthorised taking of deposits, which is dealt with separately
under s 29.
[21] In *CR China Trading Ltd v China National Sugar and Alcohol Group Corp* [2003] EWHC
79 (Comm), [2003] 1 Lloyd's Rep 279, David Steel J noted the point, but did not decide it, as to
whether the reference in s 29(3) to the 'court' included an arbitrator before whom an issue of invalidity under ss 26 or 27 had arisen.

and 85 into two parts. The first part will deal with the definitions as they applied originally under the Regulated Activities Order. In practice, given the apparent width of the second of the definitions, the first part will often appear to be superfluous.

11.4.3.1   The second part will deal with the additional definitions (the 'MiFID definitions') that have been inserted in consequence of the EC Markets in Financial Instruments Directive[22] and related EC subordinate legislation[23] (collectively referred to here as 'MiFID'). The MiFID definitions relate to various of the financial instruments as listed in Section C of Annex 1 to the main Directive, as amplified by Chapter V1 of a Commission Regulation,[24] which are set out as Schedule 2 to the Regulated Activities Order. In essence, the additional matters covered by the MiFID definitions fall within the following:

(a) They are derivatives within the following (using the same number scheme as applies under MiFID[25]):

(5) Derivatives that relate to commodities that may or must be settled in cash.

(6) Derivatives that relate to commodities that can be physically settled if they are traded on a regulated market or a Multilateral Trading Facility (an MTF).

(7) Derivatives not falling within (6) that relate to commodities that can be physically settled and which are not intended for commercial purposes and have the characteristics of other financial instruments (commercial purposes would include a derivative entered into with or by an operator or administrator of an energy transmission grid, energy balancing mechanism, or pipeline network, where it is necessary to keep in balance the supplies and uses of energy at a given time).[26]

(8) With respect to Article 85 of the Regulated Activities Order, credit derivatives that are not options within Article 83 of that Order.

(10) Derivatives that relate to climatic variables, freight rates, emission allowances, inflation rates, or other official economic statistics that may or must be settled in cash and derivatives relating to other assets, rights, obligations, indices, and measures which, having regard to certain criteria (e.g. whether they are traded on a regulated market or an MTF, are cleared and settled through a recognised clearing house, or are subject to regular margin calls), have the characteristics of derivative financial instruments

---

[22] 2004/39/EC OJ L145 30/4/2004/1.

[23] EC Regulation implementing Directive 2004/39/EC (1287/2006/EC OJ L241 2/9/2006/1) and EC Directive implementing EC Directive 2004/39/EC (OJ L241 2/9/2006/26).

[24] EC Regulation implementing Directive 2004/39/EC (1287/2006/EC OJ L241 2/9/2006/1).

[25] Section B of Annex A to Directive 2004/39/EC.

[26] See further Part 2 of Sched 2 to the Regulated Activities Order.

(e.g. which relate to telecoms bandwith, commodity storage capacity, transmission or transportation capacity, permits relating to energy derived from renewable sources, geological, environmental variables, fungible assets or rights that are capable or being transferred, and price or value indexes).[27]

(b) They must relate to a transaction to which one of the following applies:

- An investment firm or a credit institution is providing or performing investment services or activities[28] on a professional basis.[29]
- A UCITS management company is providing an investment service or an ancillary service of a specified type.[30]
- A market operator is providing an investment service of a specified type.[31]

11.4.3.2 *Futures*

Article 84 concerns 'futures'.

The first part of the definition falls under Article 84(1) and means rights under a contract for the sale of a commodity or property of any other description (which is defined in Article 3(1) to include sterling or any other currency) under which delivery is to be made at a future date and at a price agreed when the contract is made.[32] However, Article 84(2) provides an exclusion for rights under a contract which is made for commercial and not investment purposes, the difference being amplified by Articles 84(3) to (7), as follows.

11.4.3.2.1

- Under Article 84(3), a contract is to be regarded, without exception, as made for investment purposes if it was made or traded on a recognised investment exchange (such as Euronext.liffe) or is otherwise expressed to be traded on such an exchange or on the same terms as an equivalent contract would be made on such an exchange.
- Under Article 84(4), a contract not falling within Article 84(3) is to be regarded as made for commercial purposes if it provides that delivery under it is to be made within seven days, unless the parties had a different understanding.
- Under Article 84(5), it is an indication that a contract not falling within either Article 84(3) or Article 84(4) is made for commercial purposes if one or more

---

[27] Ibid.

[28] See Parts 3 and 4 of Sched 2 to the Regulated Activities Order.

[29] The concept of a 'professional basis' is undefined by MiFID but the FSA's view is that the relevant factors 'will include the existence or otherwise of a commercial element and the scale of the activity' (*Perimeter Guidance relating to MiFID—Feedback on CP 06/9 and CP 06/14* PS 07/5, Q. 7).

[30] See Arts 83(4) (b), 84(1D)(b),and 85(4)(b) of the Regulated Activities Order.

[31] See Arts 83(4)(c), 84(1D)(c), and 85(4)(c) of the Regulated Activities Order.

[32] The concept of an agreed price is amplified by Art 84(8) which provides for a determination of the price by reference to a market or exchange price.

of the parties produces the commodity or uses it in his business, or if the seller intends to deliver the property or the purchaser intends to take delivery of the property.[33] If those matters are lacking, it is an indication that the contract is made for investment purposes.

- Under Article 84(6), it is an indication that the contract is made for commercial purposes if the price, lot, delivery date, or other terms have been individually negotiated rather than determined by reference to published prices or standard lots, dates or terms.

- By Article 84(7), it is an indication that a contract is made for investment purposes if it is expressed to be traded on an investment exchange (as opposed to a recognised investment exchange as referred to in Article 84(3)), if performance of the contract is ensured by such an exchange or by a clearing house or if there are arrangements for the payment or provision of margin.

11.4.3.2.2 The second part of the definition, which applies in the case where the first part of the definition does not apply, covers futures within the MiFID definitions that may be settled physically. This is by virtue of Articles 84(1A) to 84(1E).

11.4.3.3 Contracts for differences

Article 85 concerns 'contracts for differences'.

11.4.3.3.1 The first part of the definition falls under Article 85(1) and means (a) rights under a contract for differences, or (b) rights under a contract the actual or pretended purpose of which is to secure a profit or avoid a loss by reference to fluctuations in the value or price of any type of property or in an index or other contractually designated factor. In that regard, the following factors will be relevant:

- In relation to (a), in *Universal Stock Exchange Ltd v Strachan*,[34] the House of Lords held that a contract for differences was a contract under which the parties agreed that on the settlement day one would pay the other the difference between the contract price for the relevant securities with which that case was concerned and a market price or some other externally assessed price or value for them, even though the contract provided that one of the parties could, if it wished, insist on actual delivery of the securities.

---

[33] See the guidance provided in *CR China Trading Ltd v China National Sugar and Alcohol Group Corp* [2003] EWHC 79 (Comm), [2003] 1 Lloyd's Rep 279 as to the interpretation of the predecessor to Art 84(5) contained in the para 8(4) of Sched 1 to the Financial Services Act 1986 (which, so far is material, was in the same terms). It should be noted from that case that the intention to take delivery is to be gauged as at the time the parties enter into the contract, unless they do so pursuant to an option, when the relevant time will be the time the option was granted.

[34] [1896] AC 166.

- In *City Index Ltd v Leslie*[35] Lord Donaldson MR[36] said that the meaning of a contract for differences was confined to contracts relating to the sale or purchase of shares or commodities, so the spread betting transactions with which that case was concerned would now fall within (b) rather than being considered as contracts for differences within (a). Leggatt LJ[37] said that the concept was wider and would include contracts relating to the published prices of a stock, commodity, or other property, or, alternatively, of an index. In accordance with his view, the spread betting activities could fall within (a) or (b) as set out above.

- The views taken by those two judges in the *City Index* case may have been influenced by the fact that the legislation under consideration in that case[38] did not distinguish, to the same extent as does Article 85(1) of the present legislation, between (a) and (b). Nonetheless, in relation to the words 'securing a profit' as used in (b), the guidance provided by the Court of Appeal in the *City Index* case should still be relevant. It held that those words included the concept of making a profit under the derivatives transaction, rather than simply referring to securing or preserving a profit on some other transaction.

- Article 85(2) contains a number of exclusions from Article 85(1). One exclusion is for contracts of the type that would fall within (b) where the parties collectively intend that the profit is to be made or the loss avoided by one or more of them taking delivery of the relevant property to which the contract relates. By analogy with the guidance provided in *CR China Trading Ltd v China National Sugar and Alcohol Group Corp*,[39] the time to gauge the parties' intention should be at the time they entered into the contract, unless they do so pursuant to the exercise of an option. Another exclusion concerns a contract under which a deposit of money bears interest or another return calculated by reference to an index or other factor. Rights under a qualifying contract of insurance are also excluded.[40]

The second part of the definition, which applies in the case where neither the first part of the definition nor Article 83 applies, covers credit derivatives futures that fall within category (a)(8) of the MiFID definitions. This is by virtue of Articles 84(3) and 84(4).

11.4.3.3.2

11.4.3.4 Options
Article 83 concerns options.

---

35 [1992] 1 QB 98.
36 At 107.
37 At 111.
38 Para 9 of Pt 1 to Sched 1 of the Financial Services Act 1986.
39 [2003] EWHC 79 (Comm), [2003] 1 Lloyd's Rep 279.
40 See the definition in Art 3(1), which relates to long-term insurance contracts.

11.4.3.4.1   The first part of the definition falls under Articles 83(1)(a) to (d) and concerns options to acquire or dispose of a 'security' or a 'contractually based investment', or sterling or any other currency, or a precious metal, or an option over any such option.

- Subject to exceptions relating to the definitions of the particular types of security concerned, a security is defined in Article 3(1) (by reference to various investments specified in the Regulated Activities Order) to mean shares or stock in corporate and unincorporated bodies, debentures and other instruments creating or acknowledging indebtedness, government, supra-national and public securities, warrants and other instruments giving an entitlement to securities, depository receipts and other certificates conferring contractual or proprietary rights in securities, units in collective investment schemes, rights under stakeholder pension schemes, and rights or interests in any of the foregoing.

- Subject again to exceptions within their own respective definitions, a contractually based investment is defined in Article 3(1) (by reference to other provisions in the Order) to mean rights under a qualifying contract of long-term insurance, a futures contract, a contract for differences, a funeral plan, and rights or interests in any of the foregoing.

11.4.3.4.2   The second part of the definition covers options that (1) may be settled physically, (2) which do not fall within the first part of the definition, and (3) which fall within the MiFID definitions. It also covers an option relating to such an option, except an option relating to an option that would come within category (a)(8) of the MiFID definitions. This is by virtue of Articles 83(1)(e), 83(2), 83(3), and 83(4).

11.4.3.5 Other rights or interests

Article 89 is a sweep-up provision and covers rights or interests in most things that might in itself qualify as a specified investment in Part III of the Regulated Activities Order, such as securities and contractually based investments.

11.4.4 Specified kinds of activity

Of the numerous types of specified kinds of activity in the Regulated Activities Order, the most likely to apply in the context of those involved in a derivatives transaction will be Article 14 (dealing in investments as a principal, by buying, selling, subscribing for, or underwriting investments[41]), Article 21 (dealing in investments as an agent), and Article 64 (agreeing to carry on certain types of specified activity).

---

[41] Note that 'buying' and 'selling' are given expanded meanings by virtue of Art 3(1).

Each of those provisions has its own set of exceptions.[42] For instance, Article 16 **11.4.4.1**
provides, in effect, that Article 14 will not apply to a person who enters into a
derivatives transaction with or through an authorised person. Article 19 exempts
certain derivatives transactions from Article 14 if they have been entered into by
an entity for risk management purposes relating to a business (which can be its
own or a related company's business or a business of another with whom it is
engaged in a joint enterprise) that is not mainly involved in regulated activities.
Neither party to the transaction may be an individual. There are also exemptions
relating to transactions involving trustees, nominees, and personal representatives
(Article 66), activities carried on in connection with the sale of goods or the supply
of services (Article 68), and transactions between members of the same group and
between participators in a joint enterprise (Article 69).

11.5 Legal Issues

It is only to be expected that a number of legal issues might arise in considering the **11.5.1**
effectiveness and consequences of derivatives transactions. The remainder of this
chapter will be devoted to those issues, as they arise under English law. After mentioning the local authority swaps cases, the following other legal issues and their
consequences will also be examined:

(1) if a derivatives transaction might be classified as a gambling contract;
(2) if a derivatives transaction might amount to an insurance contract;
(3) the possible exposure of a party to a claim for mis-selling or non-disclosure
     concerning a derivatives product; and
(4) the effect of the insolvency and default of a party to a derivatives contract.

11.6 The Local Authority Swaps Cases

There were many cases, beginning in 1989 and going on into the 1990s, which **11.6.1**
were the result of challenges made to the binding effect of derivatives transactions
that had been entered into in the 1980s by UK local authorities. The cases were
brought on the basis that the local authorities lacked the power to enter into
derivatives transactions, because of restrictions placed on the scope of their permitted activities by the Local Government Act 1972 (as amended). The first case,
which came before the Divisional Court, was *Hazell v Hammersmith and Fulham*

---

[42] The exceptions do not apply (and so must be disregarded) in the case of an investment firm or
a credit institution: Art 4(4).

London Borough Council.[43] The Divisional Court held that the local authority had no power to enter into derivatives transactions which, in that case, involved interest rate swaps, swap options, caps, floors and collars, forward rate agreements, and gilts and cash options. The decision of the Divisional Court was ultimately upheld by the House of Lords.[44] Most of those cases are not of peculiar relevance to derivatives transactions as such, but some are worthy of mention because they highlight important issues that are relevant to many types of commercial transaction, including derivatives transactions.

11.6.2 Money paid under mistake of law

As just mentioned, various legal issues of general importance in the development of English law were settled by the series of litigation involving local authorities. For instance, in *Kleinwort Benson Ltd v Lincoln City Council*[45] the House of Lords held that money paid as a result of a mistake of law, as well as under a mistake of fact, could be recovered under the law of restitution, subject to defences such as that based on a change of position. Previously, it had only been possible to make a restitutionary claim based on a mistake of fact rather than a mistake of law. A mistake of law might include a mistake based on a settled understanding of the law before it was overturned by a subsequent decision of the courts. It was also held that it was no defence to such a restitutionary claim that the defendant had honestly believed at the time it received the money or property being reclaimed that it was entitled to retain the money or property. Nor was it a sufficient defence on its own that the void contract had been fully performed. In addition, it was held that the claimant in an action based on mistake could assert the benefit of section 32(1)(c) of the Limitation Act 1980, which provided that the limitation period did not begin to run in respect of such a claim until the mistake had been discovered or could have been discovered with reasonable diligence.

11.6.2.1 In *Westdeutsche Landesbank Girozentrale v Islington London Borough Council*[46] the House of Lords held that the recipient of funds which had been paid under a contract that was set aside for mistake did not hold them under a resulting trust; nor did it owe any fiduciary duties to the claimant in relation to the funds. Accordingly, as the claim for the refund of the funds was a restitutionary claim at common law for money had and received, the principal sum involved in such a claim could only carry simple interest rather than compound interest. Compound interest could only be awarded in a claim for fraud or against a trustee or other person owing fiduciary duties. The point concerning the availability of compound interest was

---

[43] [1990] 2 QB 697.
[44] At [1992] 2 AC 1.
[45] [1999] 2 AC 349.
[46] [1996] AC 669.

reversed by the House of Lords in *Sempra Metals Ltd v HM Commissioners of Inland Revenue*.[47]

11.6.3 Power and capacity to contract

The local authority cases also highlight an important issue that must be addressed in any commercial transaction involving parties other than natural persons, namely, as to whether each of the parties has the power and capacity to enter into the transaction. At its heart, that was the issue on which the derivatives transactions in the local authority swaps cases foundered. It was held by the courts that the powers of the local authorities were circumscribed by the legislation under which they operated so that they were not entitled to enter into the transactions.

It should also be interposed at this point that a corporate entity should follow the correct internal procedures when a decision is made that the entity should enter into the transaction. It is also necessary that whoever signs and executes the documentation on its behalf was duly authorised to do so. Whilst these matters are now made somewhat easier under English law when one is dealing with a company incorporated under the Companies Act 2006, or its predecessor legislation, because of sections 39 and 40 of the Companies Act 2006,[48] those provisions do not apply with respect to other types of entity, such as statutory bodies (e.g. local authorities) and foreign corporations. Under English conflict of laws rules, issues concerning an entity's corporate powers and its internal processes will fall to be determined by reference to the law of the entity's place of incorporation or establishment.[49] Of course, there may be other constraints which add an additional level of complexity as, for instance, where local legislation requires the satisfaction of various requirements before an entity is entitled to enter into the relevant transactions (e.g. a requirement for local registration of a foreign entity or authorisation of the transaction by the authorities in the place where the transaction takes place).

11.6.3.1

11.7 Gambling

11.7.1 The Gambling Act 2005

The law as to the effect of gaming and wagering contracts was changed radically by the Gambling Act 2005. By virtue of section 334 of that Act, the prohibitions

---

[47] [2007] UKHL 34.

[48] Previously ss 35 and 35A of the Companies Act 1985.

[49] See Millett J in *Arab Bank plc v Mercantile Holdings Ltd* [1994] 2 Ch 71, at 82–83 (point (5)) and Cresswell J in *Merrill Lynch Capital Services Inc v The Municipality of Piraeus* (1997) 6 Bank LR 241, at 250–251 and in *Sierra Leone Telecommunications Co Ltd v Barclays Bank plc* [1998] 2 All ER 821, at 827.

on the enforcement of gaming and wagering contracts (and contracts associated therewith) that had previously applied under section 18 of the Gaming Act 1845 and section 1 of the Gaming Act 1892 were repealed. For good measure, section 335 of the 2005 Act provides that the fact that a contract relates to gambling[50] shall not prevent it from being enforceable simply because of that connection. The repeal, however, only applied with respect to contracts that were entered into after sections 334 and 335 of the 2005 Act came into force.[51] A good many derivatives transactions that were entered into before that date will remain current for some considerable time thereafter. This means that it is still relevant to consider the previous law with respect to contracts that were entered into before that date. The previous law may also be relevant in other parts of the Commonwealth which inherited the 1845 and 1892 Acts. Accordingly, the previous law will be examined below.

11.7.1.1 Before leaving the Gambling Act 2005, it is relevant to mention that the Act requires a gambling business to be licensed. The question which arises for present purposes is whether entering into derivatives transactions might be gambling which might mean that a licence was required. 'Gambling' is defined by section 3 of the Act to mean (inter alia) the activities of gaming or betting. It is convenient to take those two activities in reverse order.

11.7.1.1.1 'Betting' is defined by section 9(1) of the Act to mean:

> making or accepting a bet on—
>
> (a) the outcome of a race, competition or other event or process, or
> (b) the likelihood of anything occurring or not occurring, or
> (c) whether anything is or is not true.

Sections 9(2) and (3) of the Act make it clear that it is irrelevant for these purposes whether or not the relevant thing has already occurred or failed to occur or that one of the parties knows the outcome. Quite clearly, derivatives transactions could fall within this definition. However, section 10 of the Act provides that a regulated activity for the purposes of section 22 of FSMA will not constitute a bet under the Gambling Act 2005.

11.7.1.1.2 It should be noted, however, that the Gambling Act 2005 clearly contemplates that an activity might be both betting and gaming. This is because section 16(3) of the Act provides that an activity which might amount to both betting and gaming will fall to be considered, for the purposes of the Act, as gaming rather than betting. It is thus relevant to consider the definition of gaming and whether a derivatives transaction might fall within that definition.

---

[50] The definition of which is contained in s 3 of the Act.
[51] The sections came into force on 1 September 2007 (see Art 2(4) of the Gambling Act 2005 (Commencement No 6 and Transitional Provisions) Order 2006 (SI 2006/3272).

'Gaming' is defined by section 6 of the Gambling Act 2005 as follows:

(1) In this Act 'gaming' means playing a game of chance for a prize.

(2) In this Act 'game of chance'—
  (a) includes—
    (i) a game that involves both an element of chance and an element of skill,
    (ii) a game that involves an element of chance that can be eliminated by superlative skill, and
    (iii) a game that is presented as involving an element of chance, but
  (b) does not include a sport.

(3) For the purposes of this Act a person plays a game of chance if he participates in a game of chance—
  (a) whether or not there are other participants in the game, and
  (b) whether or not a computer generates images or data taken to represent the actions of other participants in the game.

(4) For the purposes of this Act a person plays a game of chance for a prize—
  (a) if he plays a game of chance and thereby acquires a chance of winning a prize, and
  (b) whether or not he risks losing anything at the game.

(5) In this Act 'prize' in relation to gaming . . .
  (a) means money or money's worth, and
  (b) includes both a prize provided by a person organising gaming and winnings of money staked.

(6) The Secretary of State may by regulations provide that a specified activity, or an activity carried on in specified circumstances, is or is not to be treated for the purposes of this Act as—
  (a) a game;
  (b) a game of chance;
  (c) a sport.

At the time of writing, no relevant order had been made under section 6(6).

Quite a number of the elements of the above definition might be present in a **11.7.1.1.4** derivatives transaction, including the element of chance (whether or not skill is also involved), participation by one or more persons, and the opportunity of obtaining a prize in the sense of a payment of money or money's worth dependent upon the outcome of the transaction and the fact that participating for such an opportunity does not necessarily involve the risk of losing if the outcome is unfavourable. Notwithstanding those matters, the definition still requires that there must be a game of chance if an activity that is pursued by a participant is to fall within the definition. Previous authority has suggested that the participant must be actively involved in playing the game, such as by exercising some degree of skill, making a choice, or doing some physical act;[52] mere passivity is not sufficient as,

---

[52] See *DPP v Regional Pool Promotions Ltd* [1964] 2 QB 244 and *Armstrong v DPP* [1965] AC 1262.

for instance, where numbers are drawn in a bingo game. The word 'game' also tends to suggest that the activity should be carried on by a participant as a recreational contest or for competitive amusement, rather than for business purposes (except, of course, in the case of an enterprise that operates a gambling facility). On that basis, it is submitted (albeit rather tentatively) that entering into a derivatives transaction would not normally be considered as being 'gaming' within the Act. Nonetheless, it would be preferable that the matter was resolved in an authoritative manner by using the mechanism in section 6(6) of the Act, so as to make provision, in a similar way as for betting under section 10, that a regulated activity under section 22 of FSMA would not constitute gaming under the Gambling Act 2005.

11.7.2 In considering the law as it applied historically, attention will first be directed to the general position under which transactions might be invalidated as gaming or wagering contracts. The commentary will then turn to the savings that were provided by section 412 of FSMA.[53]

11.7.3 The Gaming Acts 1845 and 1892

Section 18 of the Gaming Act 1845 provided that a contract or agreement by way of gaming or wagering was null and void and unenforceable before the courts. This was bolstered by section 1 of the Gaming Act 1892 which provided that any contract, whether express or implied, 'to pay any person any sum of money paid by him under or in respect of any [gaming or wagering contract made invalid by section 18 of the 1845 Act] or to pay any sum of money by way of commission, fee, reward, or otherwise in respect of such contract or of any services in relation thereto or in connection therewith, shall be null and void, and no action shall be brought or maintained to recover any such sum of money.' It had been held that this prevented a person who had paid out a bet on behalf of the loser from recovering the payment from the loser.[54] It had also been held that a loan knowingly made for the purpose of funding a bet or a wager or to provide the funds lost under a bet or wager would be a loan for an unlawful purpose and would be irrecoverable.[55] However, if the lender had not known that the borrower intended to use the proceeds of the loan to fund or pay off a bet or if the lender had not stipulated that the loan should be so applied, the lender was not affected by the use of the funds for the unlawful purpose and the loan remained enforceable against the borrower.[56]

---

[53] S 412 was also repealed by s 344 of the Gambling Act 2005 with respect to contracts that were entered into after s 344 came into force.
[54] *CHT Ltd v Ward* [1965] 2 QB 63.
[55] *MacDonald v Green* [1951] 1 KB 594.
[56] Ibid.

The question as to whether a party to an unlawful wagering contract could recover cash or securities deposited as margin or security with the other party was not straightforward. In *Universal Stock Exchange Ltd v Strachan*[57] the House of Lords held that securities which had been deposited by one of the parties to secure its payment obligations under the void contract could be recovered. However, in separate proceedings between the same parties, the Court of Appeal held in *Strachan v Universal Stock Exchange Ltd (No 2)*[58] that money that had been deposited by the same party could not be recovered. It would appear that the reason for the distinction is that in the second case the money had been applied under the contract in reduction of the depositor's negative balance on the contract prior to the date that he demanded its return, whereas in the first case the securities had not been dealt with in the same way prior to the demand for their return.

Generally speaking, the case law concerning the Acts had held that gaming contracts involved playing a game (e.g. a card game) for money or money's worth, with the game involving some form of contest between the participants to the gaming contract.[59] A wagering contract was more difficult to define but was also likely to be more relevant in considering derivatives transactions. A useful starting point in examining the meaning of the concept of wagering is the decision of Hawkins J in *Carlill v The Carbolic Smoke Ball Company*.[60] In summary, his Lordship said that a wagering contract involved the following elements. First, it was a contract between two persons professing to hold opposite views on the outcome of a future uncertain event. Secondly, they agreed in the contract that upon the outcome, one should win from the other a sum of money or other stake. Thirdly, neither of the parties had any real interest in the contract other than the sum or stake he would win or lose. Fourthly, each party had to be in the position where he might win or lose. If either party might win but could not lose or might lose but could not win, that was not a wagering contract. Fifthly, which party would win and which would lose was dependent upon and unknown before the outcome of the relevant event. Sixthly, the parties must have entered into the contract for the mutual purpose of wagering. If one party had some other intention under the contract, it would not be a wagering contract. However, it would still be a wagering contract if a party had an additional separate interest quite apart from his interest in the bet. For instance, a wager on a horse race would still be a bet even though one of the parties owned the horse. Finally, in determining the nature of

---

57 [1896] AC 166.
58 [1895] 2 QB 697.
59 *Ellesmere (Earl) v Wallace* [1929] 2 Ch 1, at 55. See also the discussion at 11.7.1.1.4 above.
60 [1892] 2 QB 484, at 490–493. The decision of the Court of Appeal in this case (at [1893] 1 QB 256) is famous, not least to undergraduate law students, for determining the issue of whether there had been a valid offer and acceptance of the alleged contract. The Court of Appeal simply affirmed the decision of Hawkins J on the wagering point.

the transaction, it was necessary to examine the substance of the transaction rather than judging it simply by its form, as 'a wagering contract may be sometimes concealed under the guise of language which, on the face of it, if words were only to be considered, might constitute a legally enforceable contract'.[61]

11.7.3.3　As previously noted, in *Universal Stock Exchange Ltd v Strachan*[62] the House of Lords held that a contract for differences, under which the parties agreed that on the settlement day one would pay the other the difference between the contract price for the relevant securities and a market price or some other externally assessed price or value for them, could be considered as a wagering contract, even though the contract provided that one of the parties could, if it wished, insist on actual delivery of the securities. The evidence in that case showed that in none of the transactions had delivery been demanded and that the parties did not really intend that delivery should be made. Very many derivatives and commodities futures contracts might be considered on this basis to fall within the definition of being contracts for differences, as in reality they contemplate cash settlement of the difference between the contract price and the prevailing external market price or value on the settlement date. Which party will have to pay will depend upon whether the contract price is greater or less than the external price. It is interesting to note, however, that Staughton J in *Libyan Arab Foreign Bank v Bankers Trust Co*[63] appeared to accept that contracts relating to commodities futures were valid where cash settlement was invariably undertaken because they provided, as a fall back, for actual delivery of the commodity if cash settlement did not take place.

11.7.3.4　On the basis of the *Carbolic Smoke Ball* case and the decision of the House of Lords in the *Strachan* case, it might be thought at first sight that many types of derivatives transactions would fall to be considered as wagering contracts. If, however, a party entered into a derivatives transaction for a genuine commercial purpose, such as hedging, then it would not be a wagering contract even if it was intended that the transaction should be cash settled and the other party had entered into it for purely speculative purposes.[64] In *Morgan Grenfell and Co Ltd v Welwyn Hatfield DC*[65] Hobhouse J, when considering interest rate swaps as contracts for differences, said that they had the potential to be viewed as wagering contracts but that it depended upon the other features of the transaction to ascertain

---

[61] At 493.

[62] [1896] AC 166.

[63] [1989] QB 728, at 764.

[64] See the third and sixth elements extracted above from the judgment of Hawkins J in the *Carbolic Smoke Ball* case, Leggatt LJ in *City Index Ltd v Leslie* [1992] 1 QB 98, at 112, and Hobhouse J in *Morgan Grenfell and Co Ltd v Welwyn Hatfield DC* [1995] 1 All ER 1, at 9–10.

[65] Ibid.

if there was a justifiable purpose behind them. He went on to say[66] that, 'In the context of interest rate swap contracts entered into by parties or institutions involved in the capital market and the making or receiving of loans, the normal inference will be that the contracts are not gaming or wagering but are commercial or financial transactions to which the law will, in the absence of some other consideration, give full recognition and effect.' Although that case specifically concerned an interest rate swap, the context in which his Lordship's remarks were made shows that his comments should be taken more widely and could be applied to derivatives transactions generally. For instance, he had said a little earlier[67] that, 'Provisions for the payment of differences are commonplace in certain types of commercial or financial contract. The mere fact that there is a provision for the payment of differences does not mean that the contract must be a wagering contract.'

11.7.4 Statutory saving of transactions

Nonetheless, as there remained some doubt as to whether derivatives and other types of transaction might fall within the prohibitions in the Gaming Acts of 1845 and 1892, it was thought fit to provide protection by statute.

Section 412 of FSMA[68] provided for the saving of certain transactions that would otherwise have fallen foul of section 18 of the Gaming Act 1845 and section 1 of the Gaming Act 1892 (as well as the relevant law in Northern Ireland and Scotland). Section 412 should be read in conjunction with the Financial Services and Markets Act 2000 (Gaming Contracts) Order 2001[69] (the Gaming Contracts Order). Those provisions replaced section 63 of the Financial Services Act 1986 but the case law on section 63 remained relevant to the interpretation of section 412 and the Gaming Contracts Order. Section 412(1) provided that no contract which met certain requirements would be void or unenforceable under section 18 of the 1845 Act or section 1 of the 1892 Act. The requirements may be summarised as follows (although the steps as outlined below are not in the same order as the provisions in the legislation).

11.7.4.1

First, by virtue of section 412(2)(a), the contract had to be entered into by either party or each party 'by way of business'. In the *City Index* case, Lord Donaldson MR pointed out[70] that it was sufficient if only one of the parties contracted in the course of its business, even if the other party did so for private purposes. In the

11.7.4.1.1

---

[66] At 10.
[67] Ibid.
[68] Repealed, as noted at n 53 above.
[69] SI 2001/2510.
[70] At 106.

Welwyn Hatfield case, Hobhouse J[71] held that 'by way of business' should be given a broad, rather than a narrow, construction, conforming to what in ordinary parlance would be described as a business transaction, in contrast to something that was personal or casual. The frequency with which transactions were entered into would not be a reliable guide, as a transaction might still be entered into by way of business even though it was the first time the relevant person had entered into such a transaction, so long as it had done so as part of its overall business activities. Nor was it necessary that the party should be engaged in trading or commercial activities as its main business or undertaking. It was sufficient that the relevant contracts were entered into in what might commonly be thought of as being for commercial purposes. In the *Welwyn Hatfield* case, the parties were local authorities which had entered into the contracts either as part of their debt management activities or simply to make a profit. Nonetheless, that would be considered in ordinary parlance as being by way of business. His Lordship also said that it did not matter that the transactions were *ultra vires* the local authorities, as it was the factual existence and characteristics of the transactions that were relevant in assessing if they had been entered into by way of business.

11.7.4.1.2 Secondly, by virtue of section 412 (2)(c) and Article 2(2) of the Gaming Contracts Order, the contract had to relate to a 'security' or a 'contractually based investment', as defined by Article 3(1) of the Financial Services and Markets Act 2000 (Regulated Activities) Order 2001[72] (the Regulated Activities Order). A 'security' meant an investment of a kind specified by Articles 76 to 82 (e.g. equity and debt securities, depository receipts, units in collective investment schemes, and rights under a stakeholder pension scheme) or, so far as relevant thereto, by Article 89 of the Regulated Activities Order. A 'contractually based investment' meant rights under a qualifying (long-term) contract of insurance, any investment of a kind specified by Articles 83, 84, or 85 (e.g. options, futures, and contracts for differences) or, so far as relevant thereto, by Article 89 of the Regulated Activities Order. Spread betting activities, although quite obviously gambling, fell within the definition of a contractually based investment and so they could be treated as giving rise to enforceable obligations, subject to meeting the other requirements to obtain the benefit of section 412.[73] It should be noted that a contract would not relate to a security or a contractually based investment if it fell within an exception or exclusion to the relevant definition (e.g. a futures contract that had been made for commercial rather than investment purposes as outlined by Article 84 of the Regulated Activities Order, or a contract that would have fallen within Article 85 of that Order but for the intention of the parties that delivery should be taken by

---

[71] At 11–14.
[72] SI 2001/544.
[73] See the *City Index* case and Rix LJ in *Spreadex Ltd v Battu* [2005] EWCA Civ 855, at [14].

one or more of the parties). It is unlikely that such a contract would fall to be considered as a wagering contract in any case, but it is regrettable that, for the avoidance of doubt, such contracts were not included so that they were covered explicitly by the Gaming Contracts Order.

Thirdly, by virtue of section 412(2)(b) and Article 2(1) of the Gaming Contracts Order, the entry into or performance of the contract by either party had to constitute an activity specified by Articles 14 (dealing in investments as principal), 21 (dealing in investments as agent), or, so far relevant thereto, 64 (agreeing to carry on those activities) of the Regulated Activities Order, or would have done so but for the activity falling within an exclusion to one of those provisions. It should be noted that there was no requirement that either party was authorised to carry on the relevant activity or was exempted from that requirement.

11.7.4.1.3

11.8 Insurance Contracts

This subject is of relevance in the present context because of the consequences at general law if a derivatives contract might constitute a contract of insurance, which will now be considered. In addition, under Article 10 of the Regulated Activities Order, effecting or carrying out an insurance contract as principal is a specified kind of activity for which authorisation is required by section 19 of FSMA. A 'contract of insurance' is defined for that purpose by Article 3(1) of that Order and includes a contract of long-term insurance or a contract of general insurance (each as defined).

11.8.1

11.8.2 The nature of insurance

By way of summary of a vast field of law in its own right, a contract of insurance, usually called a policy, is a contract under which the insurer undertakes with the insured, in return for the payment of a premium (or some other consideration), to make a payment or sometimes to provide some other consideration or benefit, arising from the risk of a future event which is uncertain, either as to its occurrence at all or as to the date of its occurrence. The premium may be payable in one lump sum or by instalments, and may be variable depending on the amount of risk undertaken. In most cases, but not all, an insurance policy will be an indemnity policy to pay out against the loss that is suffered on the happening of an insured casualty.[74] However, in the case of a contingency policy, such as a life policy or an accident policy, the contract may provide for payment of a fixed sum without further proof of loss. Some indemnity policies are 'valued', that is, that a specified

---

[74] *Castellain v Preston* (1883) 11 QBD 380; *Firma C-Trade SA v Newcastle Protection and Indemnity Association* [1991] 2 AC 1.

sum is agreed to be the loss that will be suffered.[75] Because of the nature of an indemnity policy, the insured cannot recover beyond the extent of the insured loss so that if the insured has more than one policy and fully recovers his loss under one policy, he cannot claim further recovery under the other policy or policies.[76]

11.8.2.1 Insurable interest

In general, the insured who takes out the policy must have what is called an 'insurable interest' in the subject matter of the insurance. Of its very nature this is required under indemnity insurance and probably applies in most other cases.[77] Such an interest may arise because the insured has a legal, beneficial, or possessory entitlement in the asset covered by the insurance (as in property insurance), because the insured will suffer some legal liability associated with the subject matter of the insurance (as in liability insurance), because the insured will suffer some loss directly associated with the damage or destruction of an asset,[78] or, in the case of a life policy, because it is the life of the assured that is covered. The time when the interest must exist will depend upon the type of insurance that is involved. Under an indemnity policy, the interest must exist when the loss is suffered.[79] Under a life policy, the interest must exist when the policy is taken out.

11.8.2.2 The obligation of good faith and disclosure

An insurance policy is considered by the general law to be a contract '*uberrimae fidei*', that is, it is a contract of the utmost good faith on the part of the parties and if that requirement is not honoured by either party then the other may avoid the policy.[80] The duty is most readily apparent in the obligation of each of the parties to disclose to the other all material facts known to it or which ought to be known to it, and which are not known to the other party, at or before the making of the policy.[81] Except in the case of fraud, it is possible to limit the duty by contract. Save where the duty has been modified, the insured must disclose to the insurer all facts which a prudent insurer would take into account in assessing the risk, the

---

[75] *Goole Steam Towing Co v Ocean Marine* [1928] 1 KB 589; *Elcock v Thomson* [1949] 2 KB 755.

[76] *Burnand v Rodocanachi* (1882) 7 App Cas 333, at 339.

[77] See, for instance, under the Life Assurance Act 1774 and the Marine Insurance Act 1906. Without an insurable interest, there was a risk that the policy might have been characterised as a void gaming or wagering contract under s 18 of the Gaming Act 1845.

[78] But not if the loss would only be indirect, as would be the case of a shareholder in respect of losses suffered by his company: *Macaura v Northern Assurance Co Ltd* [1925] AC 619.

[79] *Anderson v Morice* (1876) 1 App Cas 713.

[80] *HIH Casualty and General Insurance Ltd v Chase Manhattan Bank* [2003] UKHL 6; [2003] 2 Lloyd's Rep 61, at [5] and [42].

[81] The Law Commission, in a wide ranging review of insurance contracts, has proposed that the duty of disclosure should be modified (Consultation Paper No 182, *Insurance Contract Law* 17/7/2007).

premium, and any conditions to the policy if, as a matter of fact, the absence of disclosure induced the insurer to write the policy on the basis on which it was written.[82] There is also an obligation of disclosure on the insurer if it has knowledge of facts that are material to the risk, such as facts which show that the risk is less than that which has been covered and thus would be relevant in determining the need for or the extent of the cover, or which would be relevant in determining the premium.[83] The remedy for non-disclosure of a material fact is that the other party may avoid the policy.[84]

11.8.2.3 *The insurer's rights upon payment*

Under an indemnity policy, the insurer has certain rights once it has paid a claim. These include a right of subrogation to payments or benefits received by the insured from other sources in respect of the loss and in respect of any causes of action that the insured may have in respect of the loss.[85] The insurer also has an equitable right of contribution from other insurers who are liable to the insured for the same loss.[86]

11.8.3 Relevance to derivatives transactions

Notwithstanding the attributes of an insurance policy as outlined above, it is submitted that the nature and characteristics of derivatives contracts are such that they should not be considered as constituting insurance contracts except, perhaps, in unusual circumstances. The reasons for saying this may vary according to the type of transaction that is under examination.

11.8.3.1 *The general position*

Many derivatives transactions are predicated on the basis of an exchange of mutual, but actual, obligations, which may be settled by making delivery or by one party paying the other the balance representing the difference between their respective positions, determined on the relevant payment date or dates. For instance, in a swap or in a forward or futures transaction, each party's obligation is calculated on the basis of an underlying gross amount payable by it, which is then settled by netting off the difference between them, resulting in a balance amount payable by one to the other. Which party will have to pay the net amount will depend on the

---

[82] *Pan Atlantic Insurance Co Ltd v Pine Top Insurance Co. Ltd* [1995] 1 AC 501.

[83] See Lord Templeman in *Banque Financière de la Cité SA v Westgate Insurance Co Ltd* [1991] 2 AC 249, at 280 and Mummery LJ in *Norwich Union Life Insurance Co Ltd v Qureshi* [1999] 2 All ER (Comm) 707, at 714.

[84] See Mummery LJ in *Qureshi*, at 716. However, in *HIH Casualty and General Insurance Ltd v Chase Manhattan Bank* [2001] 2 Lloyd's Rep 483 Rix LJ, at [70], did suggest that damages might be available in an exceptional case.

[85] *Castellain v Preston* (1883) 11 QBD 380.

[86] *American Surety Co v Wrightson* (1910) 27 TLR 91.

outcome of the settlement process. They cannot each be considered as insurers of the other's risk. Under an insurance policy, on the other hand, one party is the insurer who undertakes to pay the other, the insured, only on the occurrence of the stipulated contingency, which at the time they enter into the policy must be in the nature of an uncertain event. It is not based on the concept of each party having a gross position which is then settled, either by delivery or by calculation and netting off of the gross positions.

11.8.3.2 Where a derivatives transaction is entered into by a party for purely speculative purposes, the transaction will not bear any relationship to some underlying insurable interest of that party to which an insurance policy could relate; nor could any amount payable to such a party on settlement of the transaction be considered as compensation for a loss suffered by that party on some underlying proprietary or other interest. The position must be even clearer where both parties have entered into the transaction for speculative purposes. The situation in such cases is more akin to that of gaming or wagering contracts which, of course, is an entirely different area of the law; the validity of such contracts being a matter for various legislative provisions, as discussed above.

11.8.3.3 Credit derivatives

In relation to a credit derivatives transaction, the position is more difficult but the same conclusions should be drawn in most situations. Taking a credit default swap as an example, the argument that it might be seen as a form of insurance is based on the contingent nature of the obligations of the buyer of risk/seller of protection. In return for payment of the premium, the seller of risk/buyer of protection is buying protection so that if a relevant event occurs, the buyer of risk will pay out under the contract, thereby compensating the seller of risk for the loss it has suffered in connection with the occurrence of the relevant event. In return, the buyer of risk is sometimes 'subrogated' (using that expression loosely) to the seller of risk's rights in the deliverable obligations, which must be transferred in return for payment made by the buyer of risk.

11.8.3.3.1 That gives only a superficial impression, however, of the nature and consequences of the transaction. To begin with, in the circumstances in which such transactions take place, there is no requirement, or even an understanding, that the seller of risk should have any interest, either at the time of contracting or at any time thereafter, connected with the relevant event, the specified entity, or the specified obligations. The transaction may be entirely speculative for its whole period, or the seller of risk may have disposed of any connected interest, perhaps even for a profit, before the relevant event occurs. Nonetheless, the clear intention behind the contract is that the other party will pay out on the occurrence of the relevant event, even though the recipient may have suffered no loss at all or may even have made a profit by having sold out at an earlier date. Unless its transfer obligation has been cash settled, the seller of risk may have to acquire the deliverable obligations so that they can be transferred which, in the context of insurance, would be rather like the insured acquiring an insurable interest after the casualty event occurred on which the insured loss has been based. It follows that the seller of risk may be a party to separate contracts with more than one counterparty, each having the same subject matter and economic consequences. As there is no indemnity principle involved and it is implicit that there is no need to establish a loss based on an insurable interest, the seller of risk is entitled to be paid under each contract without reference to any payment it may have received under any of the other contracts. It is submitted that a better way of viewing such transactions is that they are really either an entirely speculative transaction or a form of notional conditional purchase transaction, under which the seller of risk has the right to sell the relevant deliverable obligations to the other party if a relevant event occurs, or perhaps to cash settle, at the price agreed in the contract at the time the contract was entered into.

11.8.3.3.2 The position is less certain, however, where the seller of risk/buyer of protection enters into the credit derivatives contract so as to purchase protection against the risk of loss relating to an underlying position or transaction which it intends to, or must, hold for the whole period covered by the credit derivatives contract. In such a case, there is a risk that the credit derivatives contract might be characterised as being more akin to insurance than anything else.

11.8.3.3.3 The position is also uncertain in some complicated structures in which an insurance company, acting through a dedicated vehicle, effectively provides cover against the risk of loss on financial transactions (such transactions are sometimes labelled as 'transformers'). In such situations, the vehicle might be named as the buyer of risk/seller of protection under a credit derivative contract that the vehicle enters into with a third party. In turn, the vehicle covers itself by entering into a reciprocal contract with the insurance company, which is likely to be in the form of an insurance policy, because of restrictions on the business in which insurance companies may engage. The risk is that the role of the vehicle might be seen as being entirely nominal, or that of an agent, and that the transaction, taken as a whole, is really one in which the insurance company issues an insurance policy in favour of the third party, through the medium of the vehicle.[87]

11.9 Mis-selling and Non-disclosure concerning Derivatives Products

11.9.1 On some occasions, derivatives transactions may be 'sold' by a financial institution to its customer, rather than being a transaction between two experienced parties. The institution enters into the transaction with the customer or, alternatively,

---

[87] See the Financial Services Authority's paper, *Cross Sector Risk Transfers*, issued in May 2002.

the institution arranges for the customer to enter into the transaction with some-one else. In addition to the payments to be made within the transaction itself, the institution might charge the customer a fee. Questions may arise as to whether the institution has any responsibility to advise the customer about the transaction and its consequences, to disclose material relevant to the transaction, and to ensure that the transaction is a suitable or appropriate transaction for the customer. In addition, the customer may claim that it relied upon a representation that was made to it by the institution, which induced the customer to enter into the contract and which turned out to be incorrect. It might also be argued that a seller of risk/buyer of protection may have certain obligations of disclosure towards its counterparty when entering into a credit derivatives transaction. These various issues will be approached by considering first the statutory position under English law and then moving to an examination of the position under English common law.

11.9.2 Under statute

Section 150 of FSMA (which replaced section 62 of the Financial Services Act 1986) provides a civil liability in damages for loss suffered in consequence of a breach by an authorised person of certain of the rules made by the Financial Services Authority. However, the liability only accrues in favour of a 'private per-son' who has suffered such a loss.[88] Cases concerning claims brought under sec-tion 62 of the 1986 Act have included *Morgan Stanley UK Group v Alfio Puglisi Cosentino*[89] and *Diamantides v JP Morgan Chase Bank*.[90] In *Gorham v British Telecommunications plc*[91] the Court of Appeal held that the predecessor provision to section 150 (i.e. section 62 of the Financial Services Act 1986) did not displace the general law, so that any right of action that might exist at common law was not displaced or cut down by the statute. In addition, a customer may complain directly to the Financial Services Authority and seek compensation under the procedures provided for in Part XXV of FSMA.

11.9.2.1 It is also worth bearing in mind that private customers and small businesses may have the right to bring disputes against an authorised person before the Ombudsman under the scheme established pursuant to Part XVI of FSMA. Presently, the Ombudsman can make awards up to £100,000. The Ombudsman has a wide basis on which decisions can be made if he feels that an authorised

---

[88] Compare 'private person' as used in s 150 of FSMA with 'private investor' under s 62 of the Financial Services Act 1986. See *Gorham v British Telecommunications PLC* [2000] 1 WLR 2129. See also the expanded definition of 'private person' provided by the Financial Services and Markets Act 2000 (Rights of Action) Regs (SI 2001/2256).

[89] [1998] CLC 481.

[90] [2005] EWHC 263 (Comm).

[91] [2000] 1 WLR 2129.

person has failed in its obligation to its customer and that it is fair and reasonable for him to make a finding against the authorised person.[92]

11.9.3 A claim at general law

At general law, a claim is likely to be in tort or in contract. If there is any cross-border element involved, the first step will be to decide upon the applicable law governing the claim, to be ascertained by the application of the appropriate conflict of laws rule. The principles concerning conflict of laws are discussed in Chapter 4. In the discussion that follows, it will be assumed that the court has determined that English law will apply both to claims in contract and to claims in tort.

11.9.3.1 A general obligation to disclose

In the absence of an express provision imposing an obligation of good faith, it is very unlikely that a party could successfully argue that a derivatives contract was a contract *uberrimae fidei* (of the utmost good faith) which imported an obligation of disclosure by the other party of all material facts within that other party's knowledge that were relevant to the risk being undertaken in entering into the contract. For the reasons already expressed, the contract would not be treated as an insurance contract, and it is improbable, unless the contract otherwise provides, that it would be considered as a contract *uberrimae fidei* for any other reason. Except if the facts demonstrate otherwise (e.g. because a party was acting as a trustee in relation to the other party and its affairs) it is also unlikely that a party to a derivatives contract would be considered to be a fiduciary owing fiduciary duties to the other party, given that the transaction is entered into within a commercial relationship between them.

11.9.3.2 A limited obligation of disclosure

Although it is improbable that a claim could be based on a breach of a fiduciary duty or that the contract was one that was *uberrimae fidei*, it has been held in relation to contracts of guarantee, that there is a more limited duty of disclosure that is due by the beneficiary to the guarantor. By analogy, it might be argued that a similar duty of disclosure might arise in relation to a derivatives transaction where the customer was, in effect, providing hedging to the seller (i.e. the seller would have recourse under the derivatives transaction against the customer if the seller's position in the underlying transaction moved adversely to the seller). The duty concerning a contract of guarantee is that the beneficiary should disclose to the guarantor any unusual features that have been agreed between the beneficiary and the principal debtor which concern the transaction under which the guaranteed liabilities will arise and which may make that transaction materially different in a

---

[92] See *R (on the application of IFG Financial Services Ltd) v Financial Ombudsman Services Ltd* [2005] EWHC 1153 (Admin).

potentially disadvantageous way from what the guarantor might naturally expect.[93] It may be that the obligation of disclosure can be explained as arising from an implied representation based on the conduct of the beneficiary, if a reasonable potential guarantor would have assumed by that conduct that the true state of affairs did not exist and that it should have been informed of the true facts.[94] The obligation of disclosure relates only to unusual features of the guaranteed contract and not to other unusual features relating to the risk. The beneficiary does not have to disclose matters of which it was unaware, even if it was aware of matters that could have led to further enquiry revealing the unusual features.[95] Of course, if the guarantor is aware of the unusual features then it has no cause for complaint.[96] Furthermore, it is always possible to provide for disclosure obligations in the contract by way of express terms of the contract, and that would be the best course if a party was concerned that there may be relevant matters that might not otherwise be disclosed. In the alternative, it is possible to provide that no representations are given by the seller and that it undertakes no obligations of disclosure[97] and to obtain an acknowledgement from the customer to that effect.[98]

11.9.3.3 *Misrepresentation*

A claiming party may argue that a misrepresentation was made to it by the other party which induced the claimant to enter into the contract. Assuming that the claim is not one based in deceit, which would be improbable, the claim may be for either a negligent misrepresentation or a claim based on sections 1 and 2 of the Misrepresentation Act 1967. The claim will depend on the facts, including whether such a misrepresentation was made. In the discussion that follows, it will be assumed that the claim will be brought under the 1967 Act. The issues concerning a claim in negligent misrepresentation will fall within the later discussion concerning negligence.

11.9.3.3.1   With regard to a claim for misrepresentation under the 1967 Act, it may be alleged that the misrepresentation was made explicitly or (as discussed above) that it should be implied from the conduct of the alleged representor.[99] The claimant must show that the representation was as to a factual matter, that it was false, and that it was induced by the representation to enter into the contract. If the claim is brought under section 2(1) of the Misrepresentation Act 1967, the alleged

---

[93] *Levett v Barclays Bank plc* [1995] 1 WLR 1260. See the commentary at Chap 16.

[94] See *Geest plc v Fyffes plc* [1999] 1 All ER (Comm) 672.

[95] *Credit Lyonnais Bank Nederland NV v Export Credits Guarantee Department* [1996] 1 Lloyd's Rep 200 (appealed on other grounds, see [2000] 1 AC 486).

[96] *London General Omnibus Co v Holloway* [1912] 2 KB 72.

[97] *IFE Fund SA v Goldman Sachs International* [2007] EWCA Civ 811.

[98] *Peekay Intermark Ltd v Australia and New Zealand Banking Group Ltd* [2006] EWCA Civ 386, [2006] 2 Lloyd's Rep 511.

[99] See *Geest plc v Fyffes plc* [1999] 1 All ER (Comm) 672, noted above.

representor may have a defence as set forth in that section (i.e. it had reasonable grounds to believe in the truth of what it said and that it continued in that belief up to the time the contract was made).[100] Assuming that the claimant can establish that an actionable misrepresentation was made, either expressly or by implication, its remedies will be to assert a right to rescind the contract (which would be subject to the court or arbitral tribunal, as an alternative, awarding damages under section (2) of the Misrepresentation Act 1967) or it may claim damages under section 2(1) of the Act.

It is not easy to succeed in a claim based upon misrepresentation in relation to these types of transaction, especially if the claimant is an experienced investor. This is demonstrated by the approach that was taken by the Court of Appeal in *Peekay Intermark Ltd v Australia and New Zealand Banking Group Ltd*.[101] In that case, it was held that a serious misdescription of the nature of a proposed derivatives transaction, which was communicated by the seller to its customer prior to signature of the contractual documentation, should be regarded as no more than a rough and ready preliminary indication of what was proposed. As the true nature and incidents of the transaction were contained in the contract which the parties signed, there had been no actionable misrepresentation. It had not, for instance, been represented that the contract failed to contain an accurate account of the transaction into which the parties were to enter. The customer was an experienced investor and should have appreciated that the contract would contain the real transaction as agreed between the parties. It behoved the customer to check the contract, which the customer had failed to do. In that sense, the customer was the author of its own fate. Perhaps the court might have taken a different attitude if the customer had been inexperienced in such transactions, as an inexperienced investor might not be in a position to understand the contract and the significance of what it contained. Whilst it was not part of the decision, the court also indicated that if the customer signs an acknowledgement, to the effect that only sophisticated investors should enter into such transactions, that it fully understood the transaction as represented by the contract, and that it had made its own assessment of the risks, that would operate as an estoppel which would prevent the customer from alleging that it had been misled.

11.9.3.3.2

11.9.3.4 Negligence

A claim for breach of a duty of care might be brought by a customer against the seller in contract or in tort.[102] It may be based on an allegation that advice was

---

[100] These matters are discussed in further detail at Chap 9.

[101] [2006] EWCA Civ 386, [2006] 2 Lloyd's Rep 511.

[102] The possibility of claiming concurrently in both tort and contract was established by Lord Goff of Chieveley in *Henderson v Merrett Syndicates Ltd* [1995] 2 AC 145, at 184–194.

given which was negligent or that a negligent misstatement had been made.[103] It should be borne in mind, however, that it must be shown that the advice or statement was relied upon (as opposed to the customer making up its own mind), that it caused the loss which is claimed, and that such loss was reasonably foreseeable. It must also be remembered that advice or a statement may be given or made which turns out with the benefit of hindsight to have been incorrect (in the sense that a loss was suffered in consequence of acting in accordance with the advice or the statement) but which, nonetheless, may have been given or made with all due care, especially concerning dealings in volatile markets.[104]

11.9.3.4.1 In the alternative, the customer may allege that the seller had a duty of care to advise the customer about the transaction and its consequences, and to ensure that the transaction was a suitable or appropriate transaction for the customer. The allegation would go on to say that the seller had failed in that duty and that the customer had suffered loss in consequence of that failure. Once again, the customer would need to show that it relied upon the seller, that the loss that had been suffered arose from a breach of the duty, and that the loss was reasonably foreseeable. In the absence of some actual express term of the contract by which the institution undertook the duty to its customer, the customer would have to show that the term was implied in the contract[105] or that the duty arose in tort.

11.9.3.4.2 It is submitted that, in the absence of proving that the duty arose as an express term of the contract or that there was some specific assumption of responsibility by the seller towards the customer, the customer is unlikely to succeed in substantiating its claim, especially where the customer is experienced and capable of understanding the nature of the transactions involved. This view is based on the attitude that the courts have taken when considering the relationship between a bank and its customer, and by reference to a case that specifically concerned a derivatives transaction. In the context of the relationship between a bank and its customer, in general the courts have been reluctant to find that a bank has any duty to advise its customer on the suitability of a transaction or to protect the customer from entering into imprudent transactions.[106] Of course, if the bank holds

---

[103] As, for instance, was alleged in *Gorham v British Telecommunications plc* [2000] 1 WLR 2129. See also *Woods v Martins Bank Ltd* [1959] 1 QB 55.

[104] See Mocatta J in *Stafford v Conti Commodity Services Ltd* [1981] 1 Lloyd's Rep 466, at 474–475.

[105] For instance, in consequence of rules made by the Financial Services Authority (e.g. because the customer had been classified as a private customer).

[106] See the summary provided by HHJ Taylor (sitting in the High Court) in *Verity v Lloyds Bank plc* [1995] CLC 1557, at 1570–1572. See also Hart J (at 1st Instance) in *Frost v James Finlay Bank Ltd* [2001] Lloyd's Rep Bank 302, at [27]–[32] (the decision of Hart J was reversed on appeal but not on this point of law).

itself out as competent to give advice and encourages its customer to rely on its advice then it must do so without being negligent.[107]

In a case concerning interest rate swap transactions, Mance J in *Bankers Trust* **11.9.3.4.3** *International plc v PT Dharmala Sakti Sejahtera*[108] followed a similar line, in relation to transactions under which a bank 'sold' the transactions to its customer. He said that there was no general duty on the bank to explain the nature or effect of the proposed transactions to the customer, especially as the customer was experienced and competent to understand the nature of the transactions and the risks inherent in them. If the bank did, however, provide an explanation or give advice, then it had a duty to do so 'fully, accurately and properly' but that, in turn, would depend on the precise nature of the circumstances and of the explanation or advice which was given.[109] He later said[110] that if the bank had made representations about the nature or the risks of a transaction, its duty of care would oblige it to present the financial implications of the proposal including, in a balanced fashion, the downside and the upside of the proposal.[111] It is submitted that the courts would take the same approach to transactions where the financial institution was not a bank.

11.9.4 Exclusions or limitations of liability

As there may, at least in theory, be some risk of a claim in contract or tort being brought against a seller by a disgruntled customer or other counterparty, it would be sensible for the seller to seek protection. It might attempt to do this by the use of provisions in its contractual documentation (and in other materials that it distributes) by which it expressly sought to avoid, disclaim, or limit its responsibility towards the customer. Such provisions might include wording intended to exclude or limit any responsibility towards the customer, as well as limiting or excluding its liability for financial loss arising from its negligence, wording designed to protect it against a claim being successfully brought for misrepresentation, and provisions aimed at negating any obligation to make disclosure of any relevant facts

---

107 *Woods v Martins Bank Ltd* [1959] 1 QB 55 and *Verity v Lloyds Bank plc* [1995] CLC 1557.
108 (1995) 4 Bank LR 381.
109 At 394.
110 At 419
111 See also the Australian case law concerning foreign currency lending. In *Lloyd v Citicorp Australia Ltd* (1986) 11 NSWLR 286 it was conceded that the bank had a duty of care to monitor the customer's position and give him advice. On the facts, it was found that the bank had discharged its duty and that the customer had ignored the advice that had been given to him. In *McEvoy v ANZ Banking Group Ltd* [1990] Aust Torts Rep 81,014 it was held that the customer had sufficient experience to make his own decisions and could not be held to have placed reliance on the bank, which had not, in any event, held itself out as experienced to give advice. However, in *Foti v Banque Nationale de Paris* [1990] Aust Torts Rep 81,025 the bank was held liable, on the basis of the bank's assurances towards the customers and their comparative lack of experience.

or other material. As a general point of construction, clauses which seek to limit or exclude liability are strictly construed, and the party relying on such provisions has the burden of demonstrating that the relevant clause covers what has occurred.[112]

11.9.4.1 There are statutory limits on the effectiveness of such provisions.[113] If the party against whom the protective provision is asserted is a 'consumer', that is, a natural person acting for purposes outside his trade, business, or profession, then any such provision which is a standard provision in the institution's documentation may fail in light of the Unfair Terms in Consumer Contract Regulations 1999.[114] In other situations, the provision may be subjected to the hurdles presented by section 3 of the Misrepresentation Act 1967 and by the Unfair Contract Terms Act 1977 (strictly speaking, section 3 of the 1967 Act and the provisions of the 1977 Act also apply for the benefit of those dealing as consumers, but such persons are more likely to rely directly on the 1999 Regulations).

11.9.4.1.1 Section 3 of the 1967 Act provides that a term in a contract which purports to exclude or restrict liability for a pre-contractual misrepresentation or to exclude or restrict any remedy for such a misrepresentation, shall be of no effect unless the term satisfies the requirement of reasonableness in section 11(1) of the 1977 Act.[115] It is the whole term considered on its own that must satisfy the requirement of reasonableness and not just the term in its application to the particular facts. Thus, a term which included an exclusion covering fraudulent misrepresentation would not be considered to be reasonable, even though the particular facts of the case only concerned an innocent misrepresentation.[116] However, it has been held that a provision by which a party acknowledges that it has not relied on any statement or other representation by the other in deciding to enter into the contract will be effective, subject to its terms, to operate as an evidential estoppel. It will thereby preclude a claim for misrepresentation from arising and will not fall within the purview of section 3.[117]

---

[112] See, for instance, the approach to the interpretation of such clauses as set forth by Lord Diplock in *Photo Production Ltd v Securicor Transport Ltd* [1980] AC 827, at 850–851. In relation to clauses purporting to exclude a liability in negligence, see Scrutton LJ in *Rutter v Palmer* [1922] 2 KB 87, at 92 and Buckley LJ in *Gillespie Bros Ltd v Roy Bowles Transport Ltd* [1973] QB 400, at 419. See also the discussion in Chap 9.

[113] In addition to those mentioned, see s 150(3) of FSMA and Regs 6(2) and 6(3) of the Financial Services and Markets Act 2000 (Rights of Action) Regs 2001 (SI 2001/2256).

[114] SI 1999/2083.

[115] See generally the discussion in Chap 9.

[116] See Jacob J in *Thomas Witter Ltd v TBP Industries Ltd* [1996] 2 All ER 573, at 598.

[117] Per Chadwick LJ in *Watford Electronics Ltd v Sanderson CFL Ltd* [2001] 1 All ER (Comm) 696, at [38]–[40]. This is subject to the provision meeting the three requirements set forth by Diplock J in *Lowe v Lombank Ltd* [1960] 1 WLR 196, including that the original putative representor (i.e. the recipient of the acknowledgement) believed it to be true and relied upon it. In *Quest 4*

[118]Under section 2(2) of the 1977 Act, an attempt to exclude or restrict liability for **11.9.4.1.2**
loss or damage arising from negligence (other than for death or personal injury) is
only effective if the relevant contractual term or extra-contractual 'notice' satisfies
the requirement of reasonableness in section 11 of the Act.[119] Under section 3 of
the Act, an attempt by a party through a contractual term to exclude or restrict liability for breach of contract or for defective or sub-standard performance of the
contract, where the contract is on that party's written standard terms of business[120]
or if the other party is 'dealing as consumer',[121] is only effective in so far as the term
satisfies the requirement of reasonableness in section 11.

Schedule 1(1)(e) to the 1977 Act[122] provides, however, that neither section 2 nor **11.9.4.1.3**
section 3 of that Act applies to 'any contract in so far as it relates to the creation or
transfer of securities or of any right or interest in securities'. There is no definition
of 'securities' for the purposes of that provision but presumably both debt and
equity securities would be included. In *Micklefield v SAC Technology Ltd*[123] it
was held that the benefit of Schedule 1(1)(e) applied in the case of a share option
agreement. It is doubtful, however, if the wording of Schedule 1(1)(e) would
cover a derivatives contract that related by reference to but did not actually
concern the creation or transfer of either securities or a right or interest in them
(e.g. a contract that merely related to fluctuations in an index of securities). It is
also difficult to envisage that agreements relating to interest rates or currencies
would be within the provision, as they could not be said to be 'securities'.[124] It
should also be noted that Schedule 1(1)(e) is not relevant when considering if the
requirement of reasonableness has been met for the purposes of section 3 of the
Misrepresentation Act 1967.

In situations where Schedule 1(1)(e) of the 1977 Act is not available to save a clause **11.9.4.1.4**
which seeks to exclude or restrict liability, the party relying on protection under
the clause must show that the provision meets the requirement of reasonableness

---

Finance Ltd v Maxfield [2007] EWHC 2313 (QB) it was held that those requirements had not been
met on the facts of the case.

118 Which includes a written or unwritten announcement and any other form of actual or pretended communication: see s 14. This could include a leaflet accompanying other documentation.

119 See generally the discussion in Chap 9.

120 See *St Albans City and District Council v International Computers Ltd* [1996] 4 All ER 481.

121 See s 12, *R&B Customs Brokers Co Ltd v United Dominions Trust Ltd* [1988] 1 WLR 321,
Feldaroll Foundry plc v Hermes Leasing (London) Ltd [2004] EWCA Civ 747, (2004) 101 (24)
LSG 32.

122 Which applies by virtue of s 1(2).

123 [1990] 1 WLR 1002.

124 For instance, they are not treated as such by the Financial Services and Markets Act 2000
(Regulated Activities) Order 2001 (SI 2001/544) which instead treats them as 'contractually based
investments'.

under section 11.[125] Section 11(4) provides two guidelines for determining the reasonableness of provisions which limit a party's liability to a specific sum. Although they are not directly applicable in the case of contractual terms within sections 2 and 3 of the 1977 Act and section 3 of the 1967 Act, the guidelines given in Schedule 2 of the 1977 Act provide useful guidance of the considerations that will be relevant generally in considering the reasonableness of a provision.[126] Included amongst the considerations contained in the guidelines are: (i) the strength of the relative bargaining positions of each party, taking into account (inter alia) alternative means by which the customer's requirements might have been satisfied; (ii) whether the customer received any inducement to accept the provision or had the opportunity to enter into a similar transaction with a third party without having to accept the provision; and (iii) whether the customer knew or should reasonably have known of the provision.

11.9.4.1.5 It will be more difficult to justify standard form provisions than where there has been a genuine negotiation of the terms and provisions of the contract and agreement as to allocation of risk. It has been held, as well, that in deciding if the requirement of reasonableness has been met, where commercial parties freely negotiate the terms of a contract, are of equal bargaining power, understand what they are doing, and choose through an exemption clause to allocate the risk of loss arising from a breach or other failure by a party to a contract, the court will recognise the wish of the parties to achieve certainty and it will be more ready to uphold their allocation of risk rather than to interfere under the Act.[127]

11.10 The Effect of the Default and Insolvency of a Party to a Derivatives Contract

11.10.1 The risk of default by a counterparty, particularly if it is insolvent, should be a major area of concern to a party that enters into a derivatives transaction. For instance, if a party has entered into a derivatives transaction as a means to hedge its exposure elsewhere, the hedging will be of little value if the counterparty is insolvent and unable to perform. The position can be even more difficult where there is more than one outstanding derivatives transaction between the same parties.

---

[125] Under s 11(6) of the 1977 Act and s 3 of the 1967 Act, the onus is upon that party to show that the requirement has been met.

[126] *Singer (UK) Ltd v Tees and Hartlepool Port Authority* [1988] 2 Lloyd's Rep 164, at 169. See also Stuart-Smith LJ in *Stewart Gill Ltd v Horatio Myer and Co Ltd* [1992] QB 600, at 608.

[127] See Clarke LJ in *National Westminster Bank plc v Utrecht-America Finance Co.* [2001] 3 All ER 733, at [58]–[61]; Chadwick LJ in *Watford Electronics v Sanderson* [2001] 1 All ER (Comm) 696, at [55]; Tuckey LJ in *Granville Oil and Chemicals Ltd v Davies Turner and Co Ltd* [2003] 1 All ER (Comm) 819, at [31].

This aspect of risk will be examined by looking, first, at the position generally under English law and the measures that might be taken under English law to overcome or alleviate the risk. Secondly, it will be relevant to consider the additional issues that might arise if there is a cross-border element to the transaction, such as where the counterparty is a foreign entity. As it is the most drastic in its effect, for the purposes of this examination it will be assumed that the insolvent counterparty is a company which has gone into insolvent winding up, either by compulsory winding-up proceedings before the court or by a voluntary resolution for winding up. There are also other insolvency proceedings under English law, namely administration, voluntary arrangement, receivership and, in conjunction with insolvency proceedings, a scheme of arrangement (for instance, where debt is to be exchanged for equity), which relate to the insolvency of companies. For individuals, there is the possibility of bankruptcy or a voluntary arrangement. In practical effect, a great deal of the analysis that follows would also be relevant to such other proceedings.

11.10.2 The effect of insolvency on current contracts

Under English law, an order or resolution for the bankruptcy or insolvent winding up of a party to a contract does not, of itself, lead automatically to the termination of the contract, in the absence of a contractual provision to that effect.[128] On the other hand, the liquidator or trustee in bankruptcy has no obligation to ensure that the insolvent debtor continues to perform contracts that were current at the commencement of the insolvency proceedings. As will be seen below, the solvent party is rather unfairly treated in this respect when its position is compared against the statutory right of the liquidator of the insolvent party to terminate 'unprofitable contracts'. Of course, that statutory right would not be needed if such contracts were automatically determined by the entry into winding up.

11.10.3 Termination for default[129]

As far as the solvent party is concerned, the right to terminate the contract and claim damages for loss of bargain will depend upon the usual requirement of demonstrating that its counterparty has breached the contract in such a manner that the breach can be treated as being of a repudiatory nature or that the counterparty has manifested an intention no longer to perform the contract. It might be

---

[128] See, *Ex p Chalmers* (1873) LR 8 Ch App 289; *Jennings's Trustee v King* [1952] Ch 899; *The British Wagon Company v Lea and Co* (1879–80) LR 5 QBD 149; *Tolhurst v Associated Portland Cement Manufacturers Ltd* [1902] 2 KB 660, affd [1903] AC 414. See also Branson J in *Shipton Anderson and Co (1927) Ltd v Micks Lambert and Co* (1936) 55 Lloyd's Law Rep 384, at 389. In a contract for the sale of goods, the seller can refuse to deliver until it has been paid in cash: *Ex p Chalmers*.
[129] See generally Chap 1.

possible to draw such a conclusion, on the facts of the particular case, if the insolvent party is hopelessly insolvent and does not have the resources for its liquidator to continue with performance of the contract. As mentioned below, the consequence of drawing the wrong conclusion, should the liquidator decide to continue with performance, could be drastically adverse to the interests of the solvent party. If the grounds to terminate the contract for repudiatory breach are established, the non-defaulting party can then elect to bring the remaining primary obligations of both of the parties under the contract to an end.[130] Even so, not all of the provisions of the contract will come to an end. Ancillary obligations and provisions of the contract may continue, and the primary obligations of the party in default are replaced by a secondary obligation to pay damages arising in consequence of the breach and termination of the contract.[131]

11.10.3.1 The election by the innocent party to terminate the contract does not have the effect of discharging the rights, and the corresponding obligations, of either party which have accrued or been 'unconditionally acquired' prior to the date of termination.[132] This means, for instance, that amounts that have fallen due for payment under the contract prior to its termination remain payable, as would amounts which have been earned but where the contract provides for postponement of their payment.[133]

11.10.3.2 A further risk to the solvent party is that if it purports to terminate the contract when it is not entitled to do so then it will itself have committed a repudiatory breach of contract and the tables will be turned upon it. It has been held, for instance, that the failure to pay an instalment or two of hire or rental due under a hire purchase or equipment lease agreement does not, of itself, amount to a repudiatory breach of contract.[134] The creditor's only remedy for recovery is to sue for the outstanding amounts that have fallen due and remain unpaid.

11.10.3.3 In general,[135] it is open to the parties when they contract to identify in the contract those terms of the contract that are considered sufficiently important, usually referred to as conditions, that a breach of them will amount to a repudiatory

---

[130] See Lord Diplock in *Moschi v Lep Air Services Ltd* [1973] AC 331, at 350.

[131] See Lord Diplock in *Moschi*, ibid.

[132] See Sir Owen Dixon in the High Court of Australia in *McDonald v Dennys Lascelles Ltd* (1933) 48 CLR 457, at 476–477; Lord Wilberforce in *Johnson v Agnew* [1980] AC 367, at 396; Lord Brandon in *Bank of Boston Connecticut v European Grain and Shipping Ltd* [1989] AC 1056, at 1098–1099; and Rix LJ in *Explora Group plc v Hesco Bastion Ltd* [2005] EWCA Civ 646, at [82]–[90].

[133] See Lord Brandon in *Bank of Boston Connecticut v European Grain and Shipping Ltd* [1989] AC 1056, at 1098–1099 and Rix LJ in *Explora Group plc v Hesco Bastion Ltd* [2005] EWCA Civ 646, at [82]–[90].

[134] See *Financings Ltd v Baldock* [1963] QB 104.

[135] But see Lord Reid in *L Schuler AG v Wickman Machine Tool Sales Ltd* [1974] AC 235, at 251–252.

breach of the contract. For instance, the contract may provide that prompt payment of each amount falling due under the contract is to be of the essence of the contract (a 'time of the essence' provision), the effect of which is to turn the relevant payment obligations into conditions of the contract so that a failure to pay can be treated as a repudiatory breach of the contract.[136] If the contract does not identify the provisions that should be considered as having the status of conditions then it may be difficult in practice to determine if a repudiatory breach has occurred. Ultimately, it will involve a mixture of determining on the facts which provisions of the contract should be treated as conditions, so that a breach of them will be treated as being repudiatory in its nature and, otherwise whether there has been a continuing pattern of breaches which evince an intention by the defaulting party to repudiate the contract.

It should be noted, however, that a provision which merely permits a contract to be terminated for a failure to make a payment under it, without also specifying that such an obligation is of the essence of the contract, will not have the effect that any non-payment will be treated as a repudiatory breach. Whilst such a provision would allow the contract to be terminated, it would not give rise to a claim for damages for repudiatory breach of the contract unless it could be proved, on the facts, that such a breach had occurred.[137]

11.10.4 Damages

Assuming that the non-defaulting party has successfully terminated the contract in consequence of a repudiatory breach by the other party, it may then wish to claim damages for the loss it has suffered in consequence of the breach and termination of the contract. It will need to prove its loss, which will not simply be assumed to be the aggregate of the remaining amounts payable under the contract. This is consistent with the approach taken by the courts in cases concerning the consequences of the termination upon breach of foreign exchange contracts where the courts treated the contracts as if they related to the purchase and sale of commodities.[138] Although the House of Lords held in *Miliangos v George Frank (Textiles) Ltd*[139] that foreign currencies should no longer be regarded under English law as mere commodities, the outcome in those cases should still hold good. For instance, in the cases concerned with instalment payment obligations under hire

---

[136] See Mustill LJ in *Lombard North Central PLC v Butterworth* [1987] QB 527, at 271–272.

[137] *Financings Ltd v Baldock* [1963] QB 104; *Capital Finance Co Ltd v Donati* (1977) 121 SJ 270.

[138] See *Re British American Continental Bank (Goldzieher and Penso's Claim)* [1922] 2 Ch 575; *Re British American Continental Bank (Lisser and Rosenkranz's Claim)* [1923] 1 Ch 976; *Bank of India v Patel* [1982] 1 Lloyd's Rep 506 (upheld [1983] 2 Lloyd's Rep 298).

[139] [1976] AC 443.

purchase and finance leases[140] the courts have held that the damages to be awarded against the defaulting hirer or lessee on termination will not be simply the outstanding balance amount that would have been paid had the contract run its course.[141] Accordingly, account will have to be taken of the various consequences of the termination of the contract.[142] This will include the benefit gained by the claimant in not having to perform its own continuing obligations and there will be a duty to mitigate its loss, such as by finding another person with whom a replacement contract could be entered into.

11.10.5 Set-off

Because the claim of the innocent party is for unliquidated damages, which have to be proved and assessed, it is not possible for that party simply to assert a right to set-off amounts that may be due by it, for instance under other contracts, against amounts that would have been payable by the defaulting party under the contract had it not been terminated. Before the set-off can be put into effect and completed, the value of the relevant claims, including those for damages, must be ascertained and quantified. This is relevant when considering the position concerning insolvency set-off under Rules 2.85 and 4.90 of the Insolvency Rules,[143] which relate, respectively, to set-off in the administration and winding up of companies, and under section 323 of the Insolvency Act 1986, which relates to bankruptcy.

11.10.6 Liquidated damages

It would be tempting to try and circumvent the cumbersome procedure of having to prove the loss that has been suffered in consequence of a default and termination, by providing in the contract for a pre-determined stipulated sum that was to be paid by the defaulting party as compensation for the loss suffered by the other party (sometimes referred to as a 'liquidated damages' clause). Such a provision, however, runs the risk that it may be struck down by the courts as being an unenforceable penalty.[144]

---

[140] Such as *Lombard North Central PLC v Butterworth* [1987] QB 527.

[141] This should be contrasted with the position where the repayment of a loan is accelerated in consequence of the operation of an events of default clause. In that situation, the creditor is entitled to demand repayment of the debt, although it will not be able to enforce a provision that provides for it to receive, as well, the whole of the future interest that it would have been entitled to receive had the loan run its full course. See *The Angelic Star* [1988] 1 Lloyd's Rep 122.

[142] See the reference to the 'balance sheet' approach in calculating the benefits and losses arising on termination of a contract, as outlined in *Chitty on Contracts*, 29th edn, Vol 1, para 26-001, a similar version of which in the 28th edn of that work was referred to with approval by Mance LJ in *Cine Bes Filmcilik Ve Yapimcilik v United International Pictures* [2003] EWCA Civ 1669, at [21].

[143] SI 1986/1925, as amended by the Insolvency (Amendment) Rules 2005 (SI 2005/527).

[144] Most commentaries on this subject begin with the speech of Lord Dunedin in *Dunlop Pneumatic Tyre Co Ltd v New Garage and Motor Co Ltd* [1915] AC 79, particularly at 87–88. See also more recently *Export Credits Guarantee Department v Universal Oil Products Co* [1983] 1 WLR 399;

For further discussion of this issue, the reader is referred to the section on penalties that is contained in Chapter 3.[145]

11.10.7 Disclaimer of onerous property

Under section 178 of the Insolvency Act 1986, a liquidator in an English liquidation has the right to 'disclaim onerous property'. The meaning of that phrase will be discussed below. Under section 178(4) the disclaimer operates to determine the rights, interests, and liabilities of the insolvent company under the disclaimed contract, although that does not affect the rights or liabilities of third parties, such as guarantors.[146] Subject to its ascertainment and quantification, the loss or damage sustained by the other party to the contract in consequence of the disclaimer is provable in the liquidation (section 178(6)). A person who is faced with a contractual counterparty that has gone into liquidation can force the liquidator's hand by requiring him, by notice, to decide if he wishes to disclaim the contract. If, following the giving of such a notice, the liquidator fails to disclaim within the requisite period then he cannot do so later (section 178(5)). Similar provisions will be found in section 315 of the Insolvency Act 1986 concerning the powers of a trustee in bankruptcy to disclaim onerous property, including unprofitable contracts. It should be noted that the powers to disclaim are confined to winding up and bankruptcy and will not be found in relation to other insolvency proceedings.

The power to disclaim does not apply to market contracts or to contracts effected **11.10.7.1** by an exchange or clearing house to realise margin under a market contract;[147] nor does it apply to a transfer order or a contract to realise security within the Financial Markets and Insolvency (Settlement Finality) Regulations 1999;[148] nor with respect to financial collateral arrangements within the Financial Collateral Arrangements (No 2) Regulations 2003.[149] These are important limitations on the power of disclaimer with respect to derivatives transactions. Essentially, the power is only exercisable with respect to OTC contracts that are not part of a financial collateral arrangement or within the 1999 Regulations.

The Angelic Star [1988] 1 Lloyd's Rep 122; *Workers Trust and Merchant Bank Ltd v Dojap Investments Ltd* [1993] AC 573; *Philips Hong Kong Ltd v The Attorney General of Hong Kong* (1993) 61 BLR 49; *Lordsvale Finance Ltd v Bank of Zambia* [1996] QB 752; *Jeancharm v Barnet Football Club* [2003] EWCA Civ 58, (2003) 92 Con LR 26; Mance LJ in *Cine Bes Filmcilik Ve Yapimcilik v United International Pictures* [2003] EWCA Civ 1669 at [9]–[21]; and *Murray v Leisureplay* [2005] EWCA Civ 963.

145 In particular, at para 3.12.
146 See *Hindcastle Ltd v Barbara Attenborough Associates Ltd* [1997] AC 70.
147 S 164(1) of the Companies Act 1989.
148 SI 1999/2979 (Reg 16(1)).
149 SI 2003/3226 (Reg 10(4)).

11.10.7.2   The definition of 'onerous property' is contained in section 178(3) of the Insolvency Act 1986, as follows:

> The following is onerous property for the purposes of [section 178]:
>
> (a) any unprofitable contract, and
>
> (b) any other property of the company which is unsaleable or not readily saleable or is such that it may give rise to a liability to pay money or perform any other onerous act.

It has been said that the purposes for which the power to disclaim is conferred on a liquidator are, first, to enable the liquidator to bring the liquidation to an end without being held up by continuing obligations under unprofitable contracts or continued ownership and possession of assets that are of no value to the insolvent estate of the company and, secondly, in an insolvent liquidation to avoid the continuance of liabilities which would be payable as expenses of the liquidation to the detriment of unsecured creditors.[150]

11.10.7.3   It is conceivable that a derivatives contract could fall within either of the two paragraphs in the definition, although it is more likely that such a contract would fall to be considered within paragraph (a). The concept of an unprofitable contract is addressed further below. Paragraph (b) addresses worthless property ('property' is given a wide definition in section 426 of the Act and includes both tangible and intangible assets, including things in action and whether involving a present or future, actual or contingent right, and a right that arises out of or which is incidental to property) and assets to which there is attached some continuing onerous obligation. A good example would be a lease of land to which there is attached the burden of paying rent. It has been said that for something to be 'property' it must involve some element of benefit or entitlement for the person who holds it.[151] If there is nothing left under a contract for the benefit of the debtor at the time of the liquidation then it could not be considered to be property. Hence, a derivatives contract under which all that remains at the time of the liquidation (from the perspective of the insolvent party) are obligations which it must perform would not fall within paragraph (b).

---

[150] Professor Sir Roy Goode, *Principles of Corporate Insolvency Law* (3rd edn, 2005), at para 6-20, referred to with approval by Chadwick LJ in *Manning and Squires (Liquidators of SSSL Realisations (2002) Ltd) v AIG Europe (UK) Ltd* [2006] EWCA Civ 7; [2006] Ch 610, at [43]. See also Lord Millett in *In re Park Air Services PLC* [2002] 2 AC 172, at 184.

[151] See Lloyd J in *Re SSSL Realisations (2002) Ltd* [2004] EWHC 1760 (Ch); [2005] 1 BCLC 1, at [60], which was approved by Chadwick LJ in the appeal in that case, reported as *Manning and Squires (Liquidators of SSSL Realisations (2002) Ltd) v AIG Europe (UK) Ltd* [2006] EWCA Civ 7; [2006] Ch 610, at [35].

It has been held[152] that an 'unprofitable contract' is one which imposes on the **11.10.7.4** company continuing financial obligations without sufficient reciprocal benefits. It must give rise to prospective liabilities. A contract is not unprofitable merely because it is financially disadvantageous or because the company could have made a better bargain. Contracts that will delay the winding up, which will have to be performed over a substantial period of time, and which will involve irrecoverable expenditure, to the detriment of the unsecured creditors, are unprofitable. If the insolvent party was obliged under a derivatives contract to pay out more during the period of the liquidation than it was due to receive in that period then that would be an unprofitable contract. On the other hand, if the contract was potentially profitable to the insolvent company, albeit that it was disadvantaged in being unable to compel performance by the solvent party because, under provisions of the contract, the insolvency had suspended the solvent party's payment obligations, that would not amount to an unprofitable contract within section 178.[153]

11.10.7.5 'Cherry picking'

The definition of an unprofitable contract in section 178(3)(a) refers, in the singular, to any contract. Similarly, the definition in section 178(3)(b) contemplates an item of property in the singular. In consequence, there is no requirement for the liquidator to take into account the position under other contracts or property relationships between the same parties, where the balance may lie in the opposite direction. This entitles the liquidator to decide, on a contract by contract and property by property basis, which particular contracts or items of property he wishes to disclaim (and thereby bring to an end) and which he wishes to keep going. This will be so even if the consequence is that the liquidator may decide to disclaim one or more contracts or items of property with a party but continue with one or more other contracts or items of property with the same party because they might be profitable to the insolvent party or because he may wish to continue them for some other reason. This is sometimes referred to as 'cherry picking'. In the context of several derivatives contracts between the same parties, where one of them has gone into liquidation, the risk to the solvent party is that the liquidator

---

[152] See Lloyd J in *Re SSSL Realisations (2002) Ltd* [2004] EWHC 1760 (Ch), [2005] 1 BCLC 1; Chadwick LJ in the appeal in that case, reported as *Manning and Squires (Liquidators of SSSL Realisations (2002) Ltd) v AIG Europe (UK) Ltd* [2006] EWCA Civ 7, [2006] Ch 610; and the Australian cases of *Transmetro Corporation Ltd v Real Investments Pty Ltd* (1999) 17 ACLC 1314, *Global Television Pty Ltd v Sportsview Australia Pty Ltd* (2000) 35 ACSR 484, *Rothwells Ltd v Spedley Securities Ltd* (1990) 8 ACLR 783, *Dekala Pty Ltd v Perth Land and Leisure Ltd* (1989) 12 ACLR 585, which were referred to with approval by Chadwick LJ.

[153] See the facts of the Australian case of *Enron Australia Finance Pty Ltd v TXU Electricity Ltd* [2003] NSWSC 1169 (which is described further below), which was decided with reference to specific additional Australian legislative provisions that are not matched under English law. Nonetheless, it is submitted that the same result would have been reached in England. The case concerned a swap contract that was subject to the 1992 version of the ISDA Master Agreement.

may cherry pick between the contracts, keeping going those which are profitable to the insolvent company, whilst terminating those which are unprofitable to it. The solvent party will find itself in the uncomfortable position of continuing to perform under the remaining contracts whilst being left with its right to prove in the insolvency for the loss it has suffered in consequence of the termination of the disclaimed contracts.

11.10.8 It is relevant in a discussion concerning the consequences of the insolvency of a party to a contract to mention the *British Eagle* principle. The name comes from the decision of the House of Lords in *British Eagle International Airlines Ltd v Cie Nationale Air France*[154] and reflects the legislative provisions which are now to be found in sections 107 and 328(3) of the Insolvency Act 1986 and Rule 4.181 of the Insolvency Rules 1986. The *British Eagle* principle requires that the available assets of the insolvent debtor, such as they might be, should be used to meet the claims of its unsecured creditors on a *pari passu*, rateable basis. Accordingly, arrangements agreed between a debtor and certain of its ordinary creditors will be struck down if they have the effect in the insolvent winding up of the debtor of putting the claims of those creditors ahead of the debtor's other unsecured creditors without their consent. The debtor cannot contract out of the rules as to *pari passu* distribution. The House of Lords held, by majority, that the debtor had attempted to contract out of those rules in the *British Eagle* case itself. Under the agreement between the insolvent airline company and other airlines, the debts and credits of all of the participants in the agreement were netted off on a composite basis, through a clearing arrangement, into a pool, so that each individual airline ended up as either a net creditor or a net debtor and either paid or received the relevant balance amount to or from the pooled arrangement. In so far as concerned the insolvent airline, that arrangement had the effect of depriving its other creditors of participating on a *pari passu* basis in the distribution of its assets.

11.10.8.1 It has been held, however, that the *British Eagle* principle does not apply to subordination arrangements, where an unsecured creditor effectively agrees to put its claims behind those of other unsecured creditors;[155] nor is it relevant to arrangements by which assets of the company are impaired so that they will not be immediately and wholly made available to meet the claims of the unsecured creditors.[156]

---

[154] [1975] 1 WLR 758. Reference should also now be made to the decision of the High Court of Australia in *International Air Transport Association v Ansett Australia Holdings Ltd* [2008] HCA 3, in which the outcome in the *British Eagle* case was distinguished because the scheme that was considered by the House of Lords had been subsequently amended, so that the High Court was able to find that the amended scheme did not infringe the *pari passu* rule.

[155] See *Re British and Commonwealth Holdings (No 3)* [1992] 1 WLR 672; *Re Maxwell Communications Corporation plc* [1993] 1 WLR 1402; *Re SSSL Realisations (2002) Ltd* [2004] EWHC 1760 (Ch), [2005] 1 BCLC 1.

[156] See *Carreras Rothman Ltd v Freeman Mathews Treasure Ltd* [1985] Ch 207; *Re SSSL Realisations (2002) Ltd* [2004] EWHC 1760 (Ch), [2005] 1 BCLC 1.

There are also statutory exceptions to the operation of the principle, such as those to be found in Part VII of the Companies Act 1989, Part III of the Financial Markets and Insolvency (Settlement Finality) Regulations 1999,[157] Article 9 of the EC Regulation on insolvency proceedings,[158] and Article 27 of the EC Directive on the reorganisation and winding up of credit institutions.[159]

11.11 Protective Measures

Given the various difficulties that the solvent party to a derivatives contract will face at general law if its counterparty becomes insolvent, as described above, it is now relevant to consider if it is possible to construct, by contract, protective devices which will assist it in overcoming those difficulties or, at least, assist it in alleviating their consequences. In discussing the techniques that might be used, reference will be made to the provisions of the 2002 version of the Master Agreement produced by the International Swaps and Derivatives Association (ISDA) as an example of the deployment of those techniques.   **11.11.1**

It is appropriate, at this stage, to give a brief description of the contractual scheme employed by the Master Agreement. The 2002 version of the Master Agreement follows earlier versions in 1987 and 1992. The scheme that it envisages is that there should be a separate Master Agreement concluded bilaterally between parties who may wish to enter into derivatives and other similar types of transaction between themselves. Thus, any particular entity may have entered into several, if not tens or hundreds, of separate Master Agreements, with one separate agreement for each counterparty with whom it does business. The Master Agreement provides for the terms and conditions on which the parties to it will enter into transactions between them. There is a schedule to the Master Agreement which allows the parties to make modifications to the terms and conditions to suit what they have agreed between them and by which they may also choose between various options that are provided for in the Master Agreement (e.g. the schedule provides for the parties to choose the governing law of the Master Agreement). The commercial terms of each particular transaction (or deal) that is entered into between the parties will be recorded in a confirmation, which will also incorporate, by reference, the relevant definitions promulgated by ISDA for that type of transaction.[160]   **11.11.2**

---

157 SI 1999/2979.
158 EC 1346/2000 OJ L160 30/6/2000.
159 EC 2001/24 OJ L125 5/5/2001.
160 E.g. the 2003 Credit Derivatives Definitions for credit derivatives transactions.

11.11.3 Credit support and security

Before looking at the techniques contained within the Master Agreement, it is worth mentioning, in passing, the role that can be played by security, including margin, and by guarantees, which may themselves be secured or unsecured. The Master Agreement makes mention of these instruments as Credit Support Documents, and a guarantor will be a Credit Support Provider. Such security and guarantees can provide a level of protection so that the non-defaulting party will not suffer as merely an unsecured creditor in the insolvency of its counterparty, at least to the extent of the true value of the protection that it holds.

11.11.4 One overall contract

The first technique that is furnished by the Master Agreement is to provide that all transactions that are entered into between the parties will be treated as forming part of one overall contract, rather than each of them being a separate contract.[161] The confirmation for each transaction is intended to support this by making reference to the Master Agreement as covering the transaction (this intention might be defeated on the facts if the confirmation fails to refer to the Master Agreement and if it can be shown that the parties did not have the Master Agreement in mind as being applicable to the transaction when they agreed to enter into the transaction[162]). This technique is intended to operate as part of the mechanism to defeat the ability of a liquidator to cherry pick between the transactions because they will not be constituted by separate contracts. It will also be of assistance with respect to the operation of the conditions precedent and in implementing the close out and netting arrangements that will be described below.

11.11.5 Conditions precedent to performance

Conditions precedent may be imposed on the payment obligations of each of the parties, in particular, that no actual or potential event of default, such as a payment default or an insolvency event, has occurred and is continuing with respect to the other party, and that nothing has occurred which has led to action being taken to achieve an early termination of the outstanding transactions under the agreement.[163] In effect, the payment obligations of the non-defaulting party are suspended where the condition concerns an event of default relating to the other party and the payment obligations of both parties are suspended if the termination procedures have been commenced. An example of the operation of such a provision will be seen in the Australian case of *Enron Australia Finance Pty Ltd v*

---

[161] See s 1(c) of the Master Agreement.
[162] See further the discussion relating to the contractual necessity for a mutual intention to contract and certainty of subject matter in terms, in Chap 1.
[163] See s 2(a)(iii) of the Master Agreement.

TXU Electricity Ltd.[164] An insolvency event of default had occurred with respect to one party. In reliance upon the condition precedent in the Master Agreement that no event of default should have occurred relating to that party, the other party refused to make payments that would otherwise have fallen due to be made by it. The court held that the other party was entitled to rely on the provision, even though on a net basis it owed money to the insolvent party and despite the fact that it had not exercised its right to terminate the transaction following the occurrence of the insolvency event in relation to the insolvent party. Once again this is a useful device to prevent a liquidator of the insolvent party from benefiting by cherry picking because it denies the insolvent party the payment stream that would come from transactions where the solvent party would otherwise have to make payments to the insolvent party.

11.11.6 Transaction netting

The Master Agreement provides for transaction netting during the life of transactions. The basic provision[165] is that amounts falling due between the parties on the same day, in the same currency, and under the same transaction will be netted out, so that only a balance amount will be payable by one party to the other. The parties are given the choice to extend this to netting across transactions if they wish to do so.

11.11.7 Termination and close-out netting

Perhaps the most important risk reduction mechanisms concern what happens when a party becomes insolvent or otherwise defaults. A part of those mechanisms has already been mentioned, namely, the right of a party to refuse to make payments if an actual or potential event of default (including an insolvency event) has occurred concerning the other party, or, if different, that the procedures for an early termination of outstanding transactions have been commenced. The remainder of those mechanisms are usually referred to as 'termination and close-out netting'. They concern, first, the right of the party that is not in default to bring the outstanding transactions to an end where an event of default,[166] such as an insolvency event,[167] has occurred relating to the other party,[168] and, secondly, the

---

164 [2003] NSWSC 1169. It is an interesting question whether what occurred in this case in consequence of the condition precedent provision in the contract might have amounted, in effect, to a deprivation of the insolvent party's rights under the contract and its overall benefit of the contract, and, if so, whether it might have fallen within the ambit of the 'deprivation principle' which is referred to below.

165 To be found in s 2(c).

166 The events of default are contained in s 5(a) of the Master Agreement.

167 The insolvency events, called 'bankruptcy', will be found in s 5(a)(vii) of the Master Agreement.

168 In fact, Part 1(e) of the Schedule to the Master Agreement allows the parties to choose if they wish for automatic termination on the occurrence of an insolvency event of a party. If they do not so

consequences of the termination of the transactions.[169] In effect, upon the non-defaulting party serving the termination notice, the obligations of the parties under each terminated transaction cease[170] and the non-defaulting party calculates, by reference to one 'Termination Currency',[171] first, the net balance (which could be a positive or a negative figure) which results from calculating the losses, costs, or gains to it in consequence of replacing each of the terminated transactions or in providing for their economic equivalent, and, secondly, the net balance of the unpaid amounts that were owing by each of the parties to the other under the transactions as at the time of termination.[172] The two balance amounts are then combined to give an overall net sum payable by one party to the other.[173] It should be noted that the Master Agreement provides that in making the first mentioned set of calculations, the non-defaulting party must 'act in good faith and use commercially reasonable procedures in order to produce a commercially reasonable result'. Those procedures may include obtaining quotations for replacement transactions or using relevant market data or information from its own internal sources.[174] Further, the non-defaulting party may take into account losses or gains from terminating, liquidating, or re-establishing hedge transactions that it had entered into relating to the terminated transactions.[175]

11.11.7.1 In consequence of the operation of the termination and close-out netting provisions, the non-defaulting party, assuming it is unsecured, will be put into a more

---

choose then, as is the case with respect to the other events of default, the non-defaulting party will have the right, by notice, to institute the termination provisions if it decides to do so (see s 6(a) of the Master Agreement). In *Enron Australia Finance Pty Ltd v TXU Electricity Ltd* the non-defaulting party had that right but declined to exercise it, which put it in a favourable position, as already explained. It is understood that in some jurisdictions, such as the USA, it is desirable to stipulate for automatic termination on the insolvency of a party, but that would not be necessary under English law.

[169] It should be noted, in this respect, that the 2002 version of the Master Agreement differs from that employed in the 1992 version. The changes were introduced to overcome the type of difficulties that were encountered in cases such as *Australia and New Zealand Banking Group Ltd v Société Generale* [2000] 1 All ER (Comm) 682 and *Peregrine Fixed Income Ltd v Robinson Department Store Public Co Ltd* [2000] Lloyd's Rep Bank 304.

[170] See s 6(c) of the Master Agreement.

[171] As specified in Part 1(f) of the Schedule to the Master Agreement or, failing that, as ascertained pursuant to the definition in s 14. The process for converting amounts into the Termination Currency is outlined in the definition of 'Termination Currency Equivalent'.

[172] See s 6(e)(i) and(ii) and the definitions of 'Close-out Amount' and 'Unpaid Amounts' in s 14 of the Master Agreement.

[173] Under s 6(d).

[174] In *Socimer International Bank Ltd v Standard Bank London Ltd* [2008] EWCA Civ 116 the Court of Appeal considered the approach that should be taken where the non-defaulting party used its own internal valuation exercise in ascribing value to a terminated transaction. It examined the fetters that might apply in the way in which the non-defaulting party exercised its discretion in conducting that exercise.

[175] This is provided to overcome the consequences of the decision in *Australia and New Zealand Banking Group Ltd v Société Generale*.

straightforward and, perhaps, an economically better position than it would otherwise have to accept in the insolvent winding up of its counterparty, unless the insolvent party was making an overall loss on the transactions which were terminated. A net single position will be achieved promptly which will result in a single amount which is due either to or by the insolvent estate.

11.12 Legal Issues Concerning Termination and Close-out Netting

There are various legal issues that need to be considered concerning the effectiveness of such termination and close-out netting provisions.[176] They are: **11.12.1**

(1) whether the termination of transactions might infringe the public policy principle against contracts which have the effect of depriving an insolvent of its assets in consequence of its insolvency (which will be referred to as the 'deprivation principle'). In this regard, the rights of the insolvent party under a transaction, such as to receive payments, could be considered as being assets of the insolvent;

(2) if the effect of the provisions might be that assets of the insolvent are distributed to the non-defaulting party ahead of the claims of its other unsecured creditors, thereby infringing the *British Eagle* principle;

(3) if the effect of the provisions might give rise to a preference that could be challenged in the insolvency of the insolvent party; and

(4) if the provisions might be construed as an unenforceable penalty which arises in consequence of the default of the insolvent party.

Those issues will now be addressed in turn.

11.12.2 The deprivation principle[177]

The first of the issues concerns the operation of the deprivation principle. In *Money Markets International Stockbrokers Ltd v London Stock Exchange Ltd*[178] Neuberger J, after a review of the case law, provided a useful summary of his conclusions concerning the deprivation principle.[179] He confirmed that the principle is based on the common law rule of English public policy, that the assets of an

---

[176] It should be noted, however, that if the termination and close-out netting provisions are part of a financial collateral arrangement or are part of another arrangement of which a financial collateral arrangement forms a part then they will normally survive the insolvency of the entity that has given the collateral, pursuant to Reg 12 of the Financial Collateral Arrangements (No 2) Regs 2003 (SI 2003/3226).

[177] This principle is also discussed in Chap 15.

[178] [2002] 1 WLR 1150.

[179] At [116]–[118].

insolvent should be available to meet the claims of its creditors on a *pari passu* basis, which also underlay the basis of the decision of the House of Lords in the *British Eagle* case. The principle has been applied where the effect of a contract has been that, upon its insolvency, the insolvent has been deprived of an asset, either by it passing to another[180] or by its being confiscated. His Lordship acknowledged, however, that there are circumstances in which the principle does not apply (for instance, in relation to forfeiture provisions in leases of land), but that there are no very coherent criteria which determine when the principle does apply and when it does not apply. He set out ten propositions that could be derived from the case law on the subject.[181]

11.12.2.1 It is not intended here to go through each of the propositions, but the following, which are propositions numbered by his Lordship as 5, 6, and 7, may be relevant in the present context:

> (5) In deciding whether a deprivation provision exercisable other than on insolvency offends against the principle, one is primarily concerned with the effect of the provision and not with the intention of the parties, but it may be that, if the deprivation provision is exercisable for reasons which are not concerned with the owner's insolvency, default or breach, then its operation will not be within the principle.
> (6) However, if the intention of the parties when agreeing the deprivation provision was to evade the insolvency rules, then that may invalidate a provision which would otherwise have been valid, and if the intention of the parties was not to evade the insolvency laws, the court will be more ready to uphold the deprivation provision if it provides for compensation for the deprivation.
> (7) The court will scrutinise with particular care a deprivation provision which would have the effect of preferring the person to whom the asset reverts or passes, as against other unsecured creditors of the insolvent person whose estate is deprived of the asset pursuant to the provision.

From those propositions, it is possible to draw a couple of themes which would be relevant in assessing if a provision might fall foul of the principle. First, the intention of the parties is not conclusive but if their intention was to evade the insolvency laws that will be relevant, particularly if the consequence of the operation of the provision was to put the person who benefits from it in a better position than other unsecured creditors. Secondly, compensation for the deprivation will be a relevant factor in upholding the provision if the parties did not intend to evade the insolvency laws.

---

[180] For example, in *Fraser v Oystertec plc* [2003] EWHC 2787 (Ch), [2004] BCC 233 the transferee of a patent was required by the contract to re-transfer it to the transferor upon the transferee's insolvency.

[181] At [118].

It has to be admitted that the effect of the operation of the termination and close-out provisions may be to the advantage of the non-defaulting party, as it will circumvent some of the difficulties that it would otherwise face as an unsecured creditor in the insolvency of its counterparty. Quite clearly, it is intended that the termination and close-out netting provisions will be triggered by the insolvency of a party to the contract, so they cannot be justified within the second part of the fifth proposition. Nonetheless, it is submitted that the operation of the termination and close-out netting provisions do not infringe the deprivation principle, for the following reasons.[182]

11.12.2.2

First, the principle appears to be aimed at situations where the insolvent may be deprived of its ownership of an asset or the possession or use of the asset, where the asset can be identified separately from the deprivation provision. It does not appear to strike at situations where the asset is a contractual right which is flawed in the sense that the definition of the right includes the fact that it is dependent, and may be terminated, upon the occurrence of prescribed events, including insolvency events. That is the position concerning the insolvent party's rights under the Master Agreement. They are purely contractual rights whose continuance is subject to the right of the other party to bring the termination and close-out netting provisions into effect upon the occurrence of specified events.

11.12.2.3

Secondly, on broader grounds, it can be said that the operation of the provisions does not offend against the public policy behind the deprivation principle. The rights of the insolvent party are not taken away and vested in the solvent party. Although they cease to accrue, they are replaced, in effect, by the valuation ascribed to them as part of the closing out procedure. If the rights have any value then that value will be acknowledged in the calculations that have to be made by the non-defaulting party. Thus, if a transaction would have been profitable to the insolvent party at the time of the termination, that would mean that the solvent party would have been making net payments to the insolvent party. The replacement cost of that transaction to the non-defaulting party would be a negative amount (that is, a credit in favour of the insolvent party) as, in effect, the non-defaulting party would be offering to the market, actually or notionally, a transaction under which it would be making payments.

11.12.2.4

Thirdly, it may also be relevant in justifying the provisions that at the time the parties enter into transactions, the termination and close-out provisions are neutral. Depending upon events, they will operate on the insolvency of either party.

11.12.2.5

---

[182] In *Shipton Anderson and Co (1927) Ltd v Micks Lambert and Co* (1936) 55 Lloyd's Law Rep 384, at 389, such a provision was held to be valid and binding in a transaction concerning commodities.

So they are not deliberately designed to protect the position of only one party; they could operate for the benefit of either party.

11.12.3 The *British Eagle* principle

The second of the issues outlined above concerns whether the operation of the termination and close-out netting provisions might be taken to infringe the *British Eagle* principle,[183] as it might be said that they enable the non-defaulting party to be paid ahead of the insolvent party's other unsecured creditors. This is because they appear to go further than would be permitted by the rules of insolvency set-off, where essentially the real value of outstanding claims has to be determined before the set-off can be effected, and they permit the non-defaulting party to have recourse to the netting arrangements so as to recoup the losses that it might suffer in consequence of the insolvent party's default.

11.12.3.1 The answer to that argument is that the provisions achieve the same result as would be achieved by the operation of insolvency set-off. They take into account the outstanding liquidated amounts that were payable up to the time of termination, and they operate to determine the commercial values of the rights that have been terminated. This is strengthened by considering that they apply within the compass of one whole contract, so it is really a case of striking a balance of the respective positions of the parties within that contract, rather than setting-off claims under separate contracts.

11.12.4 Preferences

Section 239 of the Insolvency Act 1986 provides that a liquidator or administrator of a company in liquidation or administration may challenge a transaction that took place within a defined period[184] prior to the onset of the insolvency proceedings, if it amounted to a preference of a person who had previously been a creditor (or a guarantor or surety for the company). To amount to a preference, the following three conditions must be met:

(1) the transaction must be one in which the company did something, or suffered it to be done, which had the result of putting the other party in a better position than it would have been in as an unsecured creditor in a winding up of the company;

(2) the company must have been influenced by a desire to achieve that result; and

(3) at the time the transaction occurred, the company must then have been insolvent or it must have become insolvent in consequence of the preference.[185]

---

183 Which is described at para 11.10.8 above.
184 The possible period is set out in s 240(1) of the Act.
185 The requirement for insolvency is contained in s 240(2) of the Act.

It is submitted that, for much the same reasons as advanced above in relation to dismissing the relevance of the 'deprivation principle', it would be unlikely that the effect of termination and close-out netting would amount to a preference of the non-defaulting party. In entering into the contract which contained the provisions entitling the termination and close-out netting to take place, each of the parties did so for its business purposes, rather than with a view to preferring the other party to the transaction. At that time, the provisions were neutral, in that they could apply whichever party might subsequently become the defaulting party, and the application might result in the defaulting party being the overall beneficiary of the netting.

11.12.5 Penalties

The final issue is whether the termination and close-out netting provisions might constitute a penalty and so be unenforceable.[186] It is difficult to see how they could amount to a penalty. The right to terminate a party's rights in a transaction in consequence of the occurrence of an event of default is not, in itself, a penalty.[187] It is also submitted that the provisions for calculating the economic consequences of the termination and netting out those consequences would not amount to a penalty, as they should instead be considered as a genuine attempt by the parties to legislate in the contract for determining those consequences. They provide a mechanism for determining the commercial consequences of the termination, they make provision for the defaulting party to receive credit for transactions that were beneficial to it at the time of termination, and they provide for an account to be taken of outstanding amounts that were payable to the defaulting party up to the time of termination of the transactions.[188]

11.13 Insolvency and the Cross-border Element of Transactions[189]

It is now relevant to consider the consequences if the insolvent party (the 'debtor') **11.13.1** is incorporated or has its centre of main interests in a foreign jurisdiction. That jurisdiction might be another EU or European Economic Area Member State or

---

[186] See the discussion at para 11.10.6 above and in Chap 3.

[187] See, in the context of a loan transaction, *The Angelic Star* [1988] 1 Lloyd's Rep 122. In the context of a hire purchase transaction, see *Transag Haulage Ltd v Leyland Daf Finance PLC* [1994] 2 BCLC 88.

[188] S 6(e)(v) of the Master Agreement contains wording intended to reflect that argument. It would not be binding but it would give an indication of the parties' intention.

[189] For a fuller discussion of cross-border insolvency, see Chap 5. What follows here is a summary.

it might lie outside the boundaries of the EU or the EEA. The debtor might be a credit institution or some other type of entity. Each of those factors must be taken into consideration. In the discussion that follows, it will be assumed that the issues are to be addressed in accordance with insolvency law as it applies in England. Of course, a court in another jurisdiction might take a different approach, particularly if it is outside the boundaries of the EU or the EEA.

11.13.2 EC Insolvency Regulation

If the debtor has its centre of main interests (COMI) in an EU Member State, other than Denmark, then the EC Regulation on insolvency proceedings[190] will apply (being an EC Regulation, it is directly applicable in each of the Member States, except for Denmark), unless the debtor is a credit institution, an insurance undertaking, a collective investment undertaking, or within certain other categories of investment undertaking.[191] The Regulation provides (in Article 3(1)) that the main or principal insolvency proceedings (as listed in Annex A to the Regulation) must take place in the Member State where the COMI is situated.[192] Secondary proceedings may be opened in a Member State where the entity has an 'establishment'.[193] The secondary proceedings should be restricted to the assets of the debtor within the State where the proceedings are commenced.[194] The general rule under the Regulation is that the applicable law of the insolvency proceedings will be the law of the Member State where the proceedings take place.[195] That law is expressed to govern, in particular, the assets which form part of the insolvent estate,[196] the conditions under which set-offs may be invoked,[197] the effect of insolvency proceedings on the debtor's current contracts,[198] the claims which are to be lodged against the debtor's estate,[199] the rules governing the distribution of proceeds from the realisation of assets, the ranking of claims and the rights of

---

190 EC 1346/2000 OJ L160 30/6/2000.

191 See Art 1(2) of the Regulation. There is specific legislation dealing with the insolvency of credit institutions and insurance undertakings, as referred to below. There is no specific EC legislation dealing with the insolvency of investment undertakings or collective investment undertakings.

192 Which is presumed to be where a company or legal person has its registered office. However, that can be rebutted by the facts. See, for instance, *Re BRAC Rent-A-Car International Inc* [2003] EWHC 128 (Ch), [2003] 1 WLR 1421, which involved a Delaware corporation, and *Re Daisytek-ISA Ltd* [2003] BCC 562, which involved German and French companies.

193 That is, a place of operations where the debtor carries out non-transitory activity with human means and goods. See Art 3(2) and Art 2(h). The operations must be conducted by the debtor itself and not by one of its subsidiaries: see *Re a Company No 6394/2002* (unreported but noted at [2003] JIBLR 110 at 112).

194 Art 3(2).

195 Art 4(1). See also Art 28 as to the law of secondary proceedings.

196 Art 4(2)(b).

197 Art 4(2)(d).

198 Art 4(2)(e).

199 Art 4(2)(g).

creditors who have obtained partial satisfaction after the opening of insolvency proceedings by virtue of a right *in rem* or through a set-off,[200] and the rules relating to the voidness, voidability, or unenforceability of legal acts detrimental to all of the creditors.[201] It should be noted that the operation of the last mentioned rules is subject to a limitation as provided for in Article 13. From this it will be seen that the general intention of the Regulation is that a good many issues that will often arise in an insolvency should be governed by the law of the insolvency proceedings.

11.13.2.1 *Rights* in rem

There are, however, certain limitations to that general principle. Subject to one important exception, Article 5 of the Regulation provides that the rights *in rem* of creditors and third parties in the debtor's assets that are situated in another Member State will not be affected by the insolvency proceedings. The exception is that issues concerning the voidness, violability, or unenforceability of a right *in rem*, such as the rules concerning preferences, transactions at an undervalue, transactions defrauding creditors, and avoidance of certain types of security for lack of value (e.g. under sections 239, 238, 423, and 245 of the Insolvency Act 1986), will be subject to the overriding operation of Article 4(2)(m), so that they will be governed by the law of the insolvency proceedings. This, however, is itself subject to Article 13.

11.13.2.2 *Set-off*

Another limitation to the general principle is that contained in Article 6 of the Regulation, concerning rights of set-off. Subject again to the operation of Article 4(2)(m), as itself limited by Article 13, Article 6(1) provides that the insolvency proceedings will not affect the rights of the insolvent debtor's creditors to demand the set-off of their claims against the claims of the debtor, where such a set-off is permitted by the law which governs the debtor's claim. There is an apparent inconsistency between this provision and Article 4(2)(d) of the Regulation, which provides that the law of the insolvency proceedings will govern 'the conditions under which set-offs may be invoked'. It could be possible to find a situation where the law governing the insolvency proceedings precluded set-off but the law governing the debtor's claim permitted the set-off. This was addressed by Miguel Virgos and Etienne Schmit in their *Report on the Convention on Insolvency Proceedings*.[202]

---

[200] Art 4(2)(i).

[201] Art 4(2)(m).

[202] The EC Regulation was modelled on the 1995 text of the Convention, which never came into effect, because the UK (for political reasons unconnected with the Convention) refused to ratify it. A copy of the text of the Convention was set out in the 7th Report of the House of Lords Select Committee on the European Communities, dated 26/3/1996 (HL Paper 59). A copy of the Virgos and Schmit *Report*, with restricted circulation, was produced as EU Council Document 6500/96,

The *Report* states[203] that Article 6 constitutes an exception to the effect of Article 4, where the law governing the insolvency proceedings would not permit a set-off to take place within the proceedings. Article 6 would allow set-off to take place where the law which governs a contract under which the insolvent debtor's claim against the creditor arose (as ascertained in accordance with the rules contained in the Rome Convention 1980[204]) would permit the set-off to take place. In this regard, it is at least arguable that the close-out netting provisions in a derivatives contract might amount to a form of contractual set-off which would fall within the compass of Article 6. It should be noted that the governing law of the debtor's claim, as so ascertained, need not be the law of an EC Member State.[205] It should also be noted that the relevant law is that which governs the insolvent debtor's claim, rather than the law which governs the creditor's claim. The *Report* goes on to say that Article 6 should only apply to set-off rights that have accrued prior to the commencement of the insolvency proceedings. Potential claims that accrue after that time should be subject to the law of the insolvency proceedings in accordance with Article 4(2) of the Regulation. It appears from the *Report* that a claim would be considered as having accrued and so be capable of giving rise to a claim to set-off even if it has not become liquidated, matured, and payable by the date of the commencement of the insolvency proceedings, provided that the law governing the debtor's claim against which the set-off is to be applied would regard it as capable of giving rise to the set-off.

11.13.2.2.1 By reference to English concepts of set-off, under a contract governed by English law it should be possible to assert a right of set-off if it is a form of transaction or equitable set-off, or, indeed, where the contract provided for the set-off. However, legal or statutory set-off is really a procedural matter and so it is not a contractual matter governed by the law which governs the contract. Accordingly, it would not qualify within the requirements of Article 6.[206] It is possible that Article 6 also contemplates rights of set-off that might arise outside a contractual situation, for instance, where the debtor's claim arises in tort. On the other hand, it might

---

DRS 8 (CFC) dated 3/5/1996. It is set out in Appendix 2 to Moss, Fletcher, and Isaacs, *The EC Regulation on Insolvency Proceedings, A Commentary* (OUP, 2002). The *Report* does not have any authoritative status but it gives a valuable insight into the matters that were considered relevant in drafting the text of the Convention and, thus, the Regulation.

203 At paras 107–111 of the *Report*.
204 Which is set forth in Sched 1 to the Contracts (Applicable Law) Act 1990.
205 See Art 2 of the Rome Convention.
206 For the distinction between transaction or equitable set-off and legal or independent set-off see Hoffmann LJ in *Aectra Refining and Marketing Inc v Exmar NV* [1994] 1 WLR 1634, at 1649–1653; Lord Hoffmann in *Stein v Blake* [1996] AC 243, at 251; Clarke LJ in *Glencore Grain Ltd v Agros Trading Co Ltd* [1999] 2 Lloyd's Rep 410, at 415–417; Clarke LJ in *Bim Kemi v Blackburn Chemicals* [2001] EWCA Civ 457, [2001] 2 Lloyd's Rep 93; Buxton LJ in *Smith v Muscat* [2003] EWCA 962, [2003] 1 WLR 2853.

be argued that the right of the debtor to set off its claim was a procedural matter arising in litigation rather than being inherent in the claim itself and the law which governs it.

11.13.2.3 Payment and settlement systems and financial markets

A further limitation on the effect of Article 4 is to be found in Article 9 of the Regulation. Subject to Article 4(2)(m), as limited by Article 13, Article 9 preserves the integrity of the obligations of the parties to a payment and settlement system or to a financial market. Their rights are to be governed by the law of the Member State which is applicable to the relevant system or market.

11.13.3 Insolvent credit institutions

The position concerning the insolvency of a credit institution that is set up within a Member State of the EEA and of its branches within other Member States is governed by the EC Directive on the reorganisation and winding up of credit institutions,[207] which has been implemented in the UK by the Credit Institutions (Reorganisation and Winding Up) Regulations 2004.[208] For convenience, the relevant provisions of the Directive will be referred to in the discussion that follows. A credit institution is an institution that has been established in an EC or an EEA Member State, and which either receives deposits or other repayable funds from the public and grants credits for its own account, or is an electronic money institution, unless in either case it is within a specified list.[209]

Under the Directive, a credit institution may only be reorganised (that is, in accordance with measures that are intended to preserve or restore its financial position, which may include suspension of payments or of enforcement measures or reduction of claims[210]) in accordance with the laws of its home Member State and under the control of the authorities in that State. A credit institution may only be wound up in its home Member State, that is, the State in which it has its head office and by which it is authorised to act as a credit institution. It is not possible for secondary or separate insolvency measures or proceedings to be commenced in other EC or EEA Member States.[211] The law of the home Member State governs the reorganisation measures or winding-up proceedings.[212]

11.13.3.1

---

[207] EC 2001/24 OJ L125 5/5/2001.

[208] SI 2004/1045.

[209] See Art 1(1) of Directive EC 2001/24, which in turn refers to the definition of a credit institution in Art 1 of the EC Directive relating to the taking up and pursuit of the business of a credit institution (EC 2000/12 OJ L126 26/5/2000). The exclusions will be found in Art 2(3) of Directive EC 2000/12.

[210] See Art 2.

[211] Arts 3 and 9.

[212] Arts 3(2) and 10(1).

11.13.3.2 In many respects, the provisions of the Directive concerning matters arising in a reorganisation or a winding up are the same as will be found in the EC Regulation,[213] and there are also similar provisions concerning rights *in rem*[214] and set-off[215] and reference should be made to the comments on those matters that have been made above.[216] In addition, Article 26 refers to repurchase agreements, without defining what such agreements cover. Article 27 refers to transactions carried out in the context of a regulated market,[217] instead of the reference in Article 9 of the EC Regulation to payment and settlement systems and financial markets. Article 19 also makes brief provision for information to be given where winding-up proceedings are taken in a host Member State of a branch of a credit institution whose head office is outside the EEA and which also has a branch in another Member State.

11.13.3.3 Netting provisions

There is one particular provision in the Directive that is particularly relevant to the present discussion and which will not be found in the EC Regulation. Article 25 of the Directive provides that: 'Netting agreements shall be governed solely by the law of the contract which governs such instruments.' There is no definition of netting agreements in the Directive, nor is any guidance given as to the intended scope of this provision in the recitals to the Directive. Regulation 34 of the UK Regulations provides no further guidance. There is a definition of 'close-out netting provision' in the Directive on financial collateral arrangements[218] which would cover the concept of termination and close-out netting mentioned above. Presumably, Article 25 would also cover netting in other contexts, such as transaction netting during the course of a transaction.

11.13.4 Insurance undertakings

Brief mention should be made concerning the position of insurance undertakings which have their head office in an EEA Member State. Reorganisation and winding-up proceedings concerning such an undertaking are the subject of the EC Directive on the reorganisation and winding up of insurance undertakings,[219] which has been implemented in the UK by the Insurers (Reorganisation and

---

213 See, as to winding up, Art 10(2) of the Directive and note Art 30.

214 Art 21.

215 Art 23.

216 In passing, attention is drawn to Art 24, which relates to proprietary rights in instruments whose existence or transfer is recorded in a register, account, or centralised deposit system held or located in an EEA Member State. It provides that the enforcement of such rights shall be governed by the law of that Member State.

217 As defined in Art 2.

218 EC 2002/47 OJ L168 27/6/2002.

219 EC 2001/17 OJ L110 20/4/2001.

Winding Up) Regulations.[220] It contains a number of provisions in similar vein to the Directive concerning credit institutions, but notably without the provision dealing with netting.

11.13.5 The residual English jurisdiction

Save in the situations already referred to, the High Court has jurisdiction under section 221 of the Insolvency Act 1986 to wind up any 'unregistered company' which, by virtue of section 220, includes a foreign corporation. The courts have recognised that there should be some limitation to the apparently wide scope of this power. In *Re Latreefers Inc; Stocznia Gdanska v Latreefers Inc,*[221] Lloyd J said that there were three requirements that should be satisfied before the court should entertain an application for the winding up of a foreign company. First, there must be a sufficient connection between the company and the jurisdiction, such as (but not necessarily confined to) the presence of assets in the jurisdiction. Secondly, there must be a potential benefit to the company's creditors.[222] Thirdly, the petitioning creditor must be subject to the jurisdiction.

If the principal insolvency proceedings regarding an insolvent debtor are taking place in a foreign jurisdiction, then the English court will regard its role as being to assist, or as ancillary to, the foreign proceedings, and the English proceedings essentially will be confined to getting in and realising the English assets and admitting proofs, as well as providing such assistance to the foreign proceedings and the insolvency official appointed under them as may be convenient.[223] In that spirit, the English liquidator should co-operate with the foreign liquidator. However, the English proceedings will be bound by English insolvency law in the conduct of the English insolvency and the resolution of issues that arise in that insolvency. So, for instance, the English rules of insolvency set-off, being mandatory, must be observed, notwithstanding that they would be inconsistent with the insolvency law of the foreign jurisdiction, and, it is submitted, the *British Eagle* principle and the 'deprivation principle' would also apply.[224] Mention should also be made of section 426 of the Insolvency Act 1926, which provides a statutory basis for the English courts to assist certain foreign courts in insolvency proceedings.

11.13.5.1

---

[220] SI 2004/353, as amended by SI 2004/546.

[221] [2001] BCC 174, which was confirmed on appeal at [2001] BCC 174, at 189.

[222] See, for instance, *Banco Nacional de Cuba v Cosmos Trading Corp* [2001] 1 BCLC 813, where there was no benefit because the company's assets would be immune from attachment.

[223] *Cambridge Gas Transport Corp v The Official Committee of Unsecured Creditors of Navigator Holdings PLC* [2006] UKPC 26, [2007] 1 AC 508.

[224] See Hirst J in *Felixstowe Dock and Railway Co v US Lines Inc* [1989] QB 360 and Sir Richard Scott V-C in *Re Bank of Credit and Commerce International SA (No 10)* [1997] Ch 213.

11.13.6 The UNCITRAL Model Law

Finally, it is relevant to make mention of the Model Law. It has been adopted in the UK.[225] The Model Law was designed to assist States in amending their insolvency laws by providing a model of legislation that they could use but without attempting to achieve a substantive unification of insolvency laws, thereby respecting the differences in national procedural laws. The basic aim was to address the circumstances of cross-border insolvencies, by allowing for the recognition of foreign insolvency proceedings, co-operation between different jurisdictions in dealing with cross-border insolvencies, and local court access for foreign insolvency practitioners and creditors in a cross-border insolvency. In a general sense, the provisions of the Model Law follow along the same lines as the EC Regulation on Insolvency Proceedings. In addition to the UK, the Model Law has been adopted by the USA (through a new Chapter 15 of the Bankruptcy Code), the British Virgin Islands, Japan, Mexico, Poland, South Africa, Romania, Serbia and Montenegro, and Eritrea. There are also proposals for its adoption in Australia, Canada, and New Zealand. A country which adopts the Model Law, called an 'Enacting State', may do so in whole or in part. The reader is referred to Chapter 5 for a discussion of the Model Law, as adopted in Great Britain.

---

225 In Great Britain by the Cross-Border Insolvency Regulations 2006 (SI 2006/1030), as from 4 April 2006, and in Northern Ireland by the Cross-Border Insolvency Regulations (Northern Ireland) 2007 (SR 2007/115), as from 12 April 2007.

12

LOAN TRANSFERS, SECURITISATION, AND STRUCTURED FINANCE

12.1 Introduction

12.1.1 In colloquial terms, the concept of a 'loan transfer' is broader than might first appear, as it may have to address a number of different underlying factors. A transfer may concern a loan that has already been made or a transfer of a facility under which advances have yet to be made or in which some advances have already been made with further advances that may fall to be made in the future. As will be seen, it is relatively straightforward to contemplate the transfer by an assignment of the lender's rights in a debt that is already owing to it. Under English law, it is also possible for a potential creditor to assign the right to debts that may arise in the future. It is a different matter to attempt a transfer by assignment of the lender's obligation under a facility to make advances to a borrower.

Whilst the transfer may be intended, if viewed from an economic perspective, to **12.1.1.1**
pass on the risks and rewards of the facility from the transferor to the transferee,
the mechanism that is used to achieve the transaction may, as a matter of law,
amount to something other than a simple transfer by assignment of the transferor's rights or a declaration of a trust of those rights. It may, for instance, be
structured as a novation or, entirely differently, it might amount merely to a contractual arrangement between the transferor and the transferee by way of a sub-
participation, under which the transferee acquires no direct rights in the facility.

A facility that is to be transferred may comprise a bilateral facility between a single **12.1.1.2**
bank and a borrower, or the transfer might involve the transferor's participation in
a syndicated facility. The facility may be secured or unsecured, and there may be
one or more guarantees that have been given by parties other than the borrower,
which may themselves also be secured. The transfer will need to take account of
those factors in addition to the transfer of the underlying debt.

The transfer may concern a single debt or a pool or portfolio of debts. It may relate **12.1.1.3**
to indebtedness arising under loan facilities, commercial debt, or indebtedness where
credit has been extended in other situations, such as in relation to the financing of
equipment or consumer durables, as well as other types of consumer credit. It may
also involve rights under financial instruments, such as bonds and other types of
securities. The transfer may be a private transaction between a transferor and transferee, such as between banks, or it may be more public and involve a transfer that is
funded by investors in the financial markets, such as through a securitisation.

12.1.2 Securitisation

In its most straightforward and simplest sense, a securitisation builds upon the
concept of an assignment of debts by the transferor, which is usually referred to as
the 'originator'. Such debts may have arisen from loans made by the originator,
but they may also have arisen in consequence of other types of credit that had been
extended to the debtors, such as under credit cards issued by the originator or
amounts owing under various types of asset finance. It may also involve debts or
debt instruments that the transferor has itself acquired from other sources. The
transfer will involve a portfolio of such debts (and, if relevant, instruments).

The transferee which acquires the portfolio will be a dedicated vehicle without **12.1.2.1**
much initially in the way of its own resources which it could use to fund the purchase. Instead, the acquisition will be funded by a capital markets transaction
under which the vehicle raises the funds to purchase the portfolio by the issuance
of capital markets debt instruments.

In the nature of such a transaction, it will also be necessary to convince the markets in **12.1.2.2**
which the debt instruments are to be issued and subsequently traded or, more practically, the credit rating agencies, that the purchasing vehicle will be able to service its

payment obligations on the instruments that it has issued. That will involve an assessment of the purchaser's ownership rights in the portfolio it has purchased, the likelihood of satisfactory performance in the underlying portfolio, and the adequacy of credit enhancement, credit insurance, and liquidity facilities that may have been put in place as back-ups to support the economic position of the purchasing vehicle.

12.1.3 The economic effect of a securitisation in the form just outlined is that the originating creditor's payment rights in the portfolio that has been transferred (and the risk of non-payment) are devolved, via the purchasing vehicle and the trustee which holds security over all of the vehicle's assets, upon the investors who hold the securities that have been issued by the purchasing vehicle (such securities are sometimes called 'Asset Backed' or 'Mortgage Backed' securities). In return, the transferor receives a capital sum and is relieved of the risks and rewards of its original ownership of what has been transferred. Synthetic securitisations and other transactions, which will be examined later in this chapter, take matters even further, and may also include the use of derivatives in the overall structure of the transaction. It is also common for the securities that are issued in a securitisation transaction to become part of another portfolio of debt and debt instruments which are themselves sold into a structure that is funded by the issuance of further securities (called 'Collateralised Debt Obligations'). The various techniques by which underlying portfolios of debts and debt instruments become the subject matter of investments in securities that are issued and traded in the capital markets falls with the overall description of 'structured finance'.

12.1.4 Reasons for a transfer

There are a number of possible reasons as to why a bank or other financial institution may wish to dispose of its rights, and perhaps its obligations, in debt facilities and other credit or debt instruments that it has granted or which it may hold. One or more may be relevant in any particular situation.

12.1.4.1 In the first place, it may wish to control its risk of loss arising from a default or a possible default of the debtors. The default may not yet have occurred, but the seller may be unwilling to maintain the risk. In this sense, it wishes to get out whilst the going is good. If default has already occurred or is imminent, the seller may feel that it does not wish to expend the time and effort to continue with its exposure, but would prefer to suffer the loss immediately and expend its energies elsewhere. There are institutions which specialise in purchasing such 'distressed' debt, usually at some substantial discount to the face value of the debt; the size of the discount reflecting the level of the anticipated loss in recovery. The purchaser can make a profit from recovering more than it paid in the first place, perhaps by taking a more hard-headed attitude in bringing enforcement proceedings or by engaging in activities designed to achieve a 'turn-around' in the business and fortunes of the debtor. Thus, debt purchased for 20 pence in the pound, where there is a recovery of 25 or 30 pence in the pound, will result in a substantial profit to the purchaser.

Secondly, the transfer may be used to achieve a more balanced overall portfolio, by reducing exposure in one segment of the market and, perhaps, increasing commensurately an exposure in one or more other segments of the market. This was the case in the 1970s and 1980s when banks found that they had uneven exposures to various geographic sectors of sovereign debt. There was an active market in which such debt was traded.   **12.1.4.2**

Thirdly, the sale and transfer of a debt will raise funds which can be used to fund new business, which may yield a higher return than the seller was able to obtain from the debt (and its associated facility, if there is one) that it has transferred. This may be especially true if account is taken of the burden which the transferor would otherwise sustain if it had to maintain a commitment to provide undrawn funds. The new business may be in a different area or line of business, it may involve a different type of risk, and it may be more profitable than what had gone before.   **12.1.4.3**

Fourthly, a bank may have been involved in establishing a facility and have earned fees and other returns at the outset. Thereafter, the level of continuing reward may not be as great (and the carrying costs may be too much), so it does not have the same incentive to remain tied-in to the facility, at least to the same extent as previously. It will look to transfer its position to one or more banks or into some form of structured finance.   **12.1.4.4**

There are, however, problems that may arise in consequence of this type of situation. In the first place, the originating bank is reliant upon finding other banks to take over its position or it must be able to effect a transfer of its debt via a securitisation. Both of those avenues of escape became scarce as a consequence of the crisis in the financial markets in the second part of 2007. Secondly, there is the temptation that, in incepting the facility, the transferor bank may only have regard to its own short term interests, without paying proper attention to the situation of the debtor and its ability to observe its obligations under the facility, leaving any ensuing difficulties to be suffered by the banks or other entities that take over its position. This second problem became evident as a result of the financial crisis that arose in the second part of 2007 concerning US sub-prime mortgage lending. Much of the sub-prime lending had been done on lax and insufficiently rigorous lending policies, and a great deal of it went into default when economic conditions worsened in the US housing market. The debt had been sold and was widely dispersed through various forms of structured finance, so that the consequences of the defaults were felt widely in the financial markets. That was one of the prime causes of the financial crisis that followed.   **12.1.4.4.1**

Fifthly, the transfer may be designed to free-up regulatory capital by the reduction of the transferor's risk exposures, particularly in enabling a bank to meet its capital   **12.1.4.5** adequacy and large exposure requirements for regulatory purposes (see further Chapter 2).

12.1.4.6 Sixthly, the transfer may have beneficial consequences in an accounting sense for the seller's balance sheet. Subject to meeting the relevant requirements, it can use the funds it has received on the sale to reflect a cash asset or to repay the liabilities it incurred in funding the debt that it has sold. It can also remove any commitment to lend funds and any associated provisions for moneys advanced that may be reflected in its accounts.

12.1.5 Benefits to the transferee

It stands to reason that if a transfer is to proceed, there should also be perceived advantages for the purchaser of the debt or for investors in securities that have been issued by the purchasing vehicle. Some banks which have relatively little presence in a particular sector may see an opportunity, via the debt transfer, to acquire knowledge and contacts with debtors which can be used by them to improve their experience and their involvement in that sector. As already mentioned, a purchaser of debt that has fallen into default (distressed debt) may feel that it can make a profit by acquiring the debt relatively cheaply and recovering, by one means or another, a greater amount than it paid. For debt that is considered to be a good credit risk, the holding of the debt (or of an investment derived from it) should provide a relatively safe and dependable use of funds, as well as a steady income or yield. The acquisition may also provide a quick profit, if the debt or investment is sold on for more than the cost of the acquisition. On the other hand, of course, anticipated profits may turn to dust if the actual or ascribed value of the debt (or the securities that are held) declines or market conditions deteriorate, as occurred in the second half of 2007 with the chaos in the world's financial markets, particularly in relation to securities that were dealt with in the capital markets.

12.1.6 Effectiveness of the transfer

There is another important factor that such a purchaser or investor should bear in mind. It concerns the effectiveness of the transfer of the underlying debt from the transferor and whether the transfer will be robust enough to survive a challenge, particularly in a subsequent insolvency of the transferor. It is essential that the transfer should stand as an outright and unimpeachable sale, so that it cannot be upset and recast or re-categorised as some form of secured financing which might be susceptible to challenge in the insolvency.

12.1.7 Chapter plan

This chapter will proceed by examining two important preliminary issues that need to be considered before the transaction can commence, namely, matters concerned with conflict of laws issues, and matters relating to a banker's duty of confidence concerning its customer's affairs. The chapter will then move on to discuss the methods that are available under English law for a debt to be transferred and the consequences of those methods. After that, it will address securitisations of portfolios of debts and the related topic of structured finance. It will conclude with a brief summary of the accounting aspects that may arise in debt transfers, the banking regulatory issues having been discussed in Chapter 2 on banking regulation.

12.2 Conflict of Laws Issues

12.2.1 Introduction

There are a number of possible conflict of laws issues that may arise when considering a loan or credit transfer. This is relevant if there are cross-border elements in the transaction, such as where the transferor and the transferee are in different jurisdictions, or the debtor, the guarantor, or any relevant assets that have stood as security are located in more than one place. It is essential that these issues should be explored at an early stage before a transaction is agreed, as they will have an important bearing in considering what can be achieved by the proposed transaction, how it may be achieved, and the overall consequences of the transaction.

12.2.1.1 The issues that may arise will concern matters along the following lines: the relationship between the transferor and the transferee; the proprietary consequences of the transaction, if any; the effect of the transaction on the debtor; the ensuing relationship between the debtor and the transferee; and the priority that the transferee will enjoy against rival claimants in the debt, both in terms of other transfers generated by the transferor and in consequence of involuntary enforcement proceedings taken against the debtor or the transferor and the insolvency of the debtor or the transferor.[1]

12.2.1.2 The discussion that follows will proceed on the assumption that the issues will be resolved by the application of the English principles of conflict of laws as applied by an English court as the forum for determining those issues. Of course, a court in another country might take a different approach, and it is always necessary when considering a transaction with cross-border elements to take advice in each relevant jurisdiction.

12.2.2 Novation v assignment

The most likely difficulties that may arise will be where the transaction representing the transfer of the underlying debt or portfolio of debts is intended to take

---

[1] The analysis that follows should also apply to a transaction by way of security, in addition to one by way of transfer by sale.

effect as an assignment by the transferor to the transferee of the transferor's rights in the debt or debts. What follows will concentrate on that aspect. On the other hand, if the transaction is intended to be effected by a novation of the contractual rights and obligations of the respective parties then the conflict of laws issues will be mainly concerned with a determination of how the novation should be put in place so as to achieve a mutual release of the debtor and the transferor and the establishment of a new contract as between the debtor and the transferee. The novation of the credit facility (and any accompanying guarantee) will be characterised as a contractual matter and will be determined in accordance with the governing law of the contract to be terminated and the governing law that will apply to the new contract. Those respective governing laws will be ascertained by applying the rules under the Rome Convention on the Law Applicable to Contractual Obligations, which was incorporated into English law by the Contracts (Applicable Law) Act 1990.[2] If, in pursuance of the novation, existing security is to be released and new security taken, it will be necessary to consider the law that will apply to achieve the release and the new security. The relevant conflicts principles are discussed in Chapter 4.

12.2.3 Characterisation

At the outset, it is necessary to characterise the relevant issue or issues that may need to be considered. The English approach to characterisation was described by Mance LJ in *Raiffeisen Zentralbank Osterreich AG v Five Star General Trading LLC*.[3] English concepts will be used in determining how an issue should be characterised so that a conflicts rule can be allocated to it, although, as his Lordship pointed out, this should be done with reference to the substance of the issue rather than by applying a purely mechanistic formula that might apply in a purely domestic setting, bearing in mind that the court should strive to identify the most appropriate law to govern the relevant issue. For the purposes of the discussion that follows, it will be assumed that the issues should be characterised as relating to the voluntary assignment of a debt.

12.2.4 Article 12 of the Rome Convention

A useful starting point in an examination of the conflicts rules relating to assignments is Article 12 of the Rome Convention, which is in two parts.[4] Its subject is

---

[2] This is consistent with the *obiter* view expressed on this point by Mance LJ in *Raiffeisen Zentralbank Osterreich AG v Five Star General Trading LLC* [2001] EWCA Civ 68; [2001] QB 825, at [34].

[3] Ibid, at [26]–[33].

[4] The Rome Convention is due to be replaced towards the end of 2009 by the EC Regulation on the law applicable to contractual relations (Rome I). Rome I is discussed in Chap 4. As noted in that chapter, it was not certain at the time of writing if Rome I would be adopted in the UK. Art 14 of Rome I is broadly similar to Art 12 of the Rome Convention, but there are some differences as mentioned in that chapter. Further reference is made to Rome I below. The text of Rome I is set out

the voluntary assignment of rights.[5] The word 'voluntary' in Article 12 is used in the sense of something freely undertaken between the assignor and the assignee, as opposed to an involuntary assignment, such as would occur under a compulsory seizure or transfer of rights or assets (e.g. by garnishee or attachment proceedings). The first part of Article 12 concerns the mutual obligations that arise as between the assignor and the assignee. The second part concerns matters such as the assignability of the underlying debt, the effect of the assignment upon the debtor and if the assignment can be invoked against it, if the debtor will be discharged by making payment to the assignee, and the procedures to make the assignment effective against the debtor.

Article 12 provides as follows: **12.2.4.1**

1. The mutual obligations of assignor and assignee under a voluntary assignment of a right against another person ('the debtor') shall be governed by the law which under this Convention applies to the contract between the assignor and the assignee.
2. The law governing the right to which the assignment relates shall determine its assignability, the relationship between the assignee and the debtor, the conditions under which the assignment can be invoked against the debtor and any question whether the debtor's obligations have been discharged.

12.2.5 The effect of Article 12

On its face, Article 12 appears to cover most of the matters that might be relevant in considering the effect of a voluntary assignment. Quite clearly, the contractual relationship as between the assignor and the assignee will come within the scope of Article 12(1) and be governed by the relevant applicable law of the contract between them. Nothing much turns on that issue, as the same rule would apply in consequence of the application of Articles 3 and 4 of the Rome Convention.

Before the decision of the Court of Appeal in the *Raiffeisen Zentralbank* case,   **12.2.5.1**
however, there had been doubt as to whether, under English principles as to the conflict of laws, the comprehensive approach that appeared to be contemplated by Article 12 was applicable to the other matters that arise in an assignment of debts and other contractual rights. It had been suggested that some other rule might not be more appropriate, at least in so far as the proprietary issues relating to the effect of an assignment were concerned. Possible candidates were a rule based upon the *lex situs* of the debt, or, in cases of assignments of a portfolio of debts, the residence of the assignor. The doubts reflected the traditional approach

---

in Annex B to a Consultation Paper issued by the Ministry of Justice on 2/4/2008, No CP05/08, entitled 'Rome I—Should the UK opt in?'

[5] See the *Report on the Rome Convention* by Professors Giuliano and Lagarde at OJ 1980 C 282/34. Reference may be made to the *Report* in ascertaining the meaning or effect of the Convention: see s 3(3) of the Contracts (Applicable Law) Act.

in English domestic law to assignments of debts and other choses in action. The English approach proceeds on the basis that an assignment should be seen primarily as a proprietary transaction rather than as a contractual matter (although it may also have consequences relating to the performance of the debtor's obligations). An assignment involves an alienation of the transferor's property through a transfer of the rights of the assignor in the debt to the assignee. It is a subsidiary question as to the consequential effect of an assignment upon the debtor, which will mainly depend on the debtor receiving notice of the assignment.[6] The English approach gained support from the statement in the Giuliano-Lagarde *Report*[7] that the Rome Convention was concerned only with the law applicable to contractual obligations and not with property rights.

12.2.5.2   In the *Raiffeisen Zentralbank* case, Mance LJ (with whom Aldous LJ and Charles J agreed) held that the relevant English conflicts rule in relation to issues concerning the voluntary assignments of debts was that provided by Article 12 of the Rome Convention. His Lordship reached that conclusion on the basis that, in the context of Article 12 as part of the Rome Convention, the effect of an assignment was essentially contractual, in that it put the assignee into the position by which the debtor's contractual obligations thereafter fell to be performed in favour of the assignee.[8] It had been argued in the case that a distinction should be drawn between the proprietary matters that were involved in an assignment, which would fall to be considered under the relevant common law conflicts principles, and the ensuing consequences of a successful assignment upon the debtor, which would be considered under Article 12(2). If there had not been a successful assignment in a proprietary sense as judged under common law principles, then there would be nothing to which Article 12(2) could be relevant. That argument was rejected by Mance LJ. He said:[9]

> Article 12(1) concentrates on its face on the contractual relationship between assignor and assignee. In contrast, there is no hint in Art. 12(2) of any intention to distinguish between contractual and proprietary aspects of assignment. The wording appears to embrace all aspects of assignment. If the draftsmen [of the Rome Convention] had conceived that the basic issue, whether and under what conditions an assignee acquires the right to sue the obligor, could involve reference to a quite different law to either of the two mentioned in Art. 12(1) and (2), one would have expected them to say so, if only to avoid confusion. Further, on [the contrary case as it had been

---

[6] See, for instance, the famous commentary provided by Lord Macnaghten in *William Brandt's Sons & Co v Dunlop Rubber Co Ltd* [1905] AC 454, at 462. As to the proprietary effect in English law of the assignment between the assignor and the assignee, even without notice being given to the debtor, see Cotton LJ and Bowen LJ in *Gorringe v Irwell India Rubber & Gutta Percha Works* (1887) 34 ChD 128, at 132 and 135, respectively.

[7] Giuliano-Lagarde *Report*, n 5 above, at OJ 1980 C 282/10.

[8] See [2001] QB 825, at [34]–[57]. His Lordship left undecided the appropriate conflicts rule where the issue concerns the effect of an involuntary assignment, such as where there have been garnishee proceedings: see Mance LJ's discussion of the point at [2001] QB 825, at [57].

[9] Ibid, at [45].

argued], it is unclear why the draftsmen troubled to refer so explicitly in Art. 12(2) to the relationship of the parties and the conditions under which the assignment could be invoked against the debtor. It seems self-evident that an assignee could not succeed to any other relationship with the debtor than that established by the contract assigned, and that he could not avoid any conditions prescribed by the contract.

The facts of the *Raiffeisen Zentralbank* case involved a purported equitable assignment of claims under a marine insurance policy, of which notice had been given to the French insurers, who were the 'debtors' for the purposes of Article 12.[10] There had also been an attempt to attach the policy and the proceeds of a claim in France following procedures under French law. Those involved in the attachment had challenged the effectiveness of the assignment. The policy was stated to be governed by English law. In pursuance of Article 12(2), Mance LJ applied English law, as the governing law of the policy under which a claim would arise, to determine if the benefit of any claims under the policy had been assigned and, in consequence, if such assignment bound the insurers to pay the assignee. He held that there had been a successful assignment in favour of the assignee.

12.2.5.3

12.2.6 Article 12(2)

Mance LJ in the *Raiffeisen Zentralbank* case indicated that the reference in Article 12(2) to 'the law governing the right' assigned was a reference to the governing law of the contract under which the relevant obligation arose which gave rise to the right.[11] He also said that when Article 12(2) refers to the 'conditions' under which an assignment will bind the debtor, it was referring to matters such as the necessity (or otherwise) of giving notice to the debtor.[12] As English law was the governing law of the insurance policy and notice had been given to the insurers of the assignment, sufficient steps had been taken to make the assignment effective against the insurers and to require them to pay the assignee,[13] notwithstanding that the insurers were located in France. The alternative argument that had been put to the court, which was rejected, was that the effectiveness of the assignment should be determined by the application of French law which was the *lex situs* of the policy and of any claims payable under it.

Article 12(2) of the Rome Convention refers to the 'assignability' of the debt or other right which is the subject of a purported assignment. A clause in the underlying

12.2.6.1

---

[10] Although the point was not referred to in the judgment, it was presumably felt that the contract of insurance under which the assigned debt arose was not excluded from the operation of the Rome Convention by virtue of Art 1(3) of the Convention, on the basis that the risk insured (collision on the high seas) was situated outside the territories of the EU Member States.

[11] See [2001] QB 825, at [43]. See also Staughton LJ in *Macmillan Inc v Bishopsgate Investment Trust PLC (No 3)* [1996] 1 WLR 387, at 400–401.

[12] Ibid.

[13] *William Brandt's Sons & Co v Dunlop Rubber Co Ltd* [1905] AC 454.

debt contract which was intended to preclude or restrict an assignment would be a matter relevant to the assignability of the debt[14] and so, on the face of Article 12(2), the interpretation and effect of such a clause would be a matter to be determined in accordance with the governing law of that contract.[15] Under that governing law, if the assignment is effective as against the debtor then it follows that the transaction should also be considered, as to the assignability of the debt, as being effective as between the assignor and the assignee. Although it is not free from doubt, if the transaction is intended by the assignor and the assignee to be effective as against the debtor but fails to achieve that result because it is unassignable, as determined in pursuance of Article 12(2), then it would seem to follow that it should also be treated, as between the assignor and the assignee, as having failed to achieve a transfer to the assignee of the assignor's rights against the debtor, at least in the sense of putting the assignee in a direct relationship with the debtor as would be the case under an English form of legal assignment. The consequences as between the assignor and the assignee would then fall to be resolved in accordance with Article 12(1), through the application of the governing law of their transaction.[16]

12.2.6.2 The stipulation in Article 12(2), that the governing law of the debt should determine if the debtor will be discharged, for instance if the debtor pays the assignee, is consistent with Article 10(1) of the Rome Convention. Article 10(1) provides that the governing law of a contract will determine matters concerning its performance and if the obligations under the contract have been extinguished. The same approach would be reached by the application of the common law conflicts principles, under which it has been held that the governing law of a contract will determine if the obligations under it have been discharged.[17] An interesting question arises as to the application of rights of set-off that the debtor may wish to assert against its obligation to pay the assigned debt. It is submitted that if the

---

[14] See further below as to the effect of such provisions under English domestic law.

[15] Under Art 9 of the UNCITRAL Convention, such a clause does not affect the validity of an assignment, in so far as it relates to assignments of receivables arising from the supply or lease of goods or services, construction contracts, contracts for the sale or lease of real property, the sale or use of IP, the payment obligation under credit cards, and the net settlement of netting agreements between two or more parties. This, however, is inconsistent with Art 29 of the Convention, which is in very similar terms to Art 12(2) of the Rome Convention.

[16] If the contract between them is a nullity, the consequences under English law would not fall to be dealt with in accordance with Article 10(1)(e) of the Rome Convention, as the UK did not adopt that paragraph of the Convention: see s 2(2) of the Contracts (Applicable Law) Act 1990.

[17] See Lord Hoffmann, giving the advice of the Privy Council, in *Wight v Eckhardt Marine* [2003] UKPC 37; [2004] 1 AC 147 (PC), at [13]–[15]. It is submitted that the approach taken in that case is preferable to that taken shortly afterwards by the House of Lords in *Société Eram Shipping Co Ltd v Hong Kong & Shanghai Banking Corp Ltd* [2003] UKHL 30, [2004] 1 AC 260, where there was a dichotomy of approaches, alternating between a rule based upon the governing law of the debt and a rule based upon the *lex situs* of the debt. It is regrettable that the House overlooked the Rome Convention, which should have been relevant to the issues before it.

governing law of the debt would treat the proposed set-off as affecting the substance of the debtor's contractual obligation and would permit the debtor to assert a
right of set-off then the debtor should be permitted to do so.[18] However, if the right
of set-off is procedural and so arises as a form of procedural defence or counterclaim then the right to assert the set-off would be determined by the laws of the
forum rather than the governing law of the debt.

12.2.7 Priorities

It would also appear that matters of priorities as between competing assignees, in
so far as might concern the debtor (because, for instance, the debtor may be in a
dilemma as to who to pay if it has received notice of competing assignments),
would also be resolved by applying the governing law of the debt in pursuance of
the rule under Article 12(2).[19] As will be seen below, it is probable that the position at common law, ignoring the Rome Convention, is that questions of priority
between different claimants should be governed by the *lex situs* of a debt. A rule
based upon either the governing law of the debt or the *lex situs* of the debt does
mean that in so far as the debtor might be affected, he should be able to ascertain
the position by reference to a law that is directly related to him or the contract to
which he is a party. By contrast, the UNCITRAL Convention on the Assignment
of Receivables in International Trade[20] provides for a basic rule, to which there are
exceptions, that priorities should be determined by the law of the place where the
assignor is located.[21] That rule is designed to cover the situation where there is a

---

[18] For instance, under English law if the right of set-off that is asserted is that of a transaction or
equitable set-off that impugns the entitlement of the creditor under the contract (see the discussion
by Buxton LJ in *Smith v Muscat* [2003] EWCA 962, [2003] 1 WLR 2853; see also s 53(1)(a) of the
Sale of Goods Act 1979), then it would be a substantive right governed by the governing law of the
contract. On the other hand, if the set-off that is asserted is a legal set-off then that is a procedural
right that would arise if English law was the *lex fori* of the proceedings.

[19] See the discussion by Mance LJ in the *Raiffeisen Zentralbank* case at [2001] QB 825, at [49]–
[52] in which his Lordship appeared to prefer the position that had been reached by the courts in
Germany, in preference to that expressed by the Dutch courts, which had held that the question
should be resolved by applying the law that governed the relationship between the assignor and the
assignee as determined pursuant to Art 12(1). See also Staughton LJ in the *Macmillan* case at [1996]
1 WLR 387, at 400–401. As Mance LJ noted, however, it was unnecessary for him to express a final
view because English law would have applied as both the governing law of the debt and as the governing law of the contract of assignment in the case before him.

[20] Adopted by Resolution 56/81 of the General Assembly of the United Nations in its 56th
Session in 2001.

[21] Art 22. By Art 5, a person is located where it has its place of business or, if it does not have a
place of business, the location of its habitual residence. If a person has more than one such place in
a country, it will be located where it exercises its central administration. If it has a place of business
in more than one country, the place of business will be that which has the closest connection with
the original contract, that is, the contract under which the subject debt arose. A similar approach
to Art 22 is taken by Art 6(1) of the UNIDROIT Convention on International Factoring (Ottawa,
28/5/1988).

portfolio or a large number of debts that is or are the subject of an assignment and the practical difficulty of treating the issue differently for each of the debts depending upon its individual *lex situs* or governing law.

12.2.7.1 Whilst a rule for determining priorities based upon the location of the assignor has an apparent simplicity, it is not free from difficulties. One immediate point is the problem in determining when it will apply. If it is only to apply where there is an assignment of a portfolio or a large number of debts, then the question arises as to when that numerical situation will have arisen; in other words, when will it be considered that the assignment concerns a sufficient number of debts to invoke the rule? It also removes the focus from a situation that is associated with a debtor to one solely connected with the original creditor. If the debtor is faced with a number of competing claims he may find himself in some difficulty if the priority between them is to be determined under a system of law that is unconnected with the debtor or the governing law of the contract under which the debt has arisen. Furthermore, such a rule will create obvious difficulties where there is a competition involving successive assignments and sub-assignments with the respective assignees and sub-assignees located in different jurisdictions.

12.2.7.2 It should be noted that Article 27(2) of the EC Regulation on the law applicable to contractual relations (Rome 1), contains a reference to priorities between competing assignments. Rome I is intended to replace the Rome Convention.[22] Article 14 of Rome I will replace Article 12 of the Convention. Article 27(2) contemplates that a priorities rule might be incorporated into Rome I in the future. The EC Commission is charged by Article 27(2) to investigate the matter and recommend if such a change should be made. This follows a provision in an early draft of the Regulation which contained a specific rule dealing with priorities. That provision was not carried through to the final version of the Regulation when it was finally adopted. It would have provided that priorities should be determined by the law of the place of the habitual residence of the assignor.

12.2.8 Disposition other than by way of notified assignment

Notwithstanding what was said in the *Raiffeisen Zentralbank* case, it is unclear if Article 12 applies at all where the transaction between the disponor and the disponee is not one contemplated by Article 12(2). Such would be the situation where the transaction was not intended to have any legal effect upon the debtor because there was to be no change in the person to whom the contractual obligation of the debtor is due, as for instance under the English forms of unnotified equitable assignment or declaration of trust.[23] It is submitted that Article 12(2)

---

[22] Rome 1 is referred to earlier in this chapter and is discussed in Chap 4.

[23] An example of a declaration of trust as a method of disposing of a contractual right will be found in the judgment of Lightman J in *Don King Productions Inc v Warren* [2000] Ch 291

should have no role in such a situation. Both the Giuliano-Lagarde *Report* and the approach taken by Mance LJ in the *Raiffeisen Zentralbank* case indicate that Article 12(2) is to be viewed in the context of the contractual obligations of the debtor and the effect that an assignment would have on those obligations. If the transaction is not intended to affect the debtor's obligations and will leave the debtor contractually obliged to its original creditor then Article 12(2) should not be relevant at all.

Assuming that Article 12(2) would have no relevance in such a situation, it now falls to be considered whether Article 12(1) has any role to play in finding: **12.2.8.1**

(1) a governing law to determine the obligations of the disponor to the disponee;
(2) the consequential relationship between them (including, for instance, if there are any proprietary consequences of that relationship, which may be a crucial issue if the assignor becomes insolvent and the assignee is faced with a claim that the debt falls into the estate of the insolvent assignor); and
(3) the effect upon the relationship of a restrictive clause in the underlying debt contract which purports to prohibit or restrict assignments.

In the overall context of Article 12, it appears that the concept of a voluntary assignment, as mentioned in Article 12(1), is that contemplated by Article 12(2) and not other forms of transaction which are intended to have an effect as between the disponor and the disponee but to leave the debtor's relationship with its original creditor unaffected. Further, in the overall scheme of Article 12, the issue as to assignability is placed in Article 12(2), which implies that it is not a matter to be considered under Article 12(1) or as a consequence of the mutual obligations of the assignor and the assignee to which that article makes reference.

In a purely contractual sense, nothing very much will turn on whether the contractual relationship between the assignor and the assignee is determined by reference to Article 12(1) or by the application of the general rules in the Rome Convention, particularly those in Articles 3 and 4.[24] In so far, however, as it might be relevant to determine the proprietary consequences of a purported assignment   **12.2.8.2**

(approved by the Court of Appeal at the same citation). His Lordship emphasised that the effect of the declaration of trust in such a situation would be to leave the underlying relationship between the debtor and its original creditor (which would become the trustee) unaffected by the declaration of trust. It is not clear, however, where that would leave the beneficiary if the trustee refused to act on its behalf and the beneficiary wished to invoke the right to enforce the debt against the debtor using the procedure outlined by the Privy Council in *Vandepitte v Preferred Accident Ins Corp of New York* [1933] AC 70. See further the discussion at paras 12.6 and 12.9.4.3.1 below and the *obiter* views of the majority in *Barbados Trust Co Ltd v Bank of Zambia* [2007] EWCA Civ 148. It is arguable that the *Vandepitte* procedure (as that description implies) is merely a matter of procedure, so the issue would fall to be resolved by the *lex fori* rather than by the governing law of the assignment.

24 As Mance LJ noted in the *Raiffeisen Zentralbank* case, [2001] QB 825 at [52], Art 12(1) restates the contractual position that would flow from the other provisions of the Rome Convention.

or a similar dealing, such as might arise under a declaration of trust or a charge, the Convention should not apply, bearing in mind the statement in the Giuliano-Lagarde *Report*, to which reference has already been made, that the Rome Convention was concerned only with the law applicable to contractual obligations and not with property rights.

12.2.9 The common law approach and the *lex situs*

If that view is correct then it is necessary to fall back on the conflicts approach that would be taken at common law, without taking account of Article 12.[25] Jenkins LJ in *Re United Railways of the Havana and Regla Warehouses Ltd*[26] said that the validity and effect of an assignment of a debt was governed by the *lex situs* of the debt rather than by the proper, or governing, law of the debt. This view was approved by Lord Hoffmann in the Privy Council in *Wight v Eckhardt Marine GmbH*.[27] The problem with an approach based upon the *lex situs*, however, lies in determining the location of the situs.[28] Unlike the position with physical assets, the concept of a situs (or location) of a debt is rather artificial. The situs of a debt is said to be where the debtor resides, on the basis that the place of residence would be where enforcement action would be taken against the debtor.[29]

12.2.9.1   Difficulties will arise if the debtor has more than one place of residence or moves. If one of several places of residence of the debtor is also specified in the contract as the place where the debt should be paid, it will be regarded as being the situs of the debt.[30] In the absence of such specificity, Lord Hobhouse in *Société Eram Shipping*

---

[25] It is submitted that the analysis that follows would apply to both an unnotified equitable assignment and to a declaration of trust. Under English conflicts rules, the law governing matters such as the administration of the trust would depend upon the application of the Hague Convention on the Law Applicable to Trusts and their Recognition of 1985, which applies under English law by virtue of The Recognition of Trusts Act 1987. However, Art 4 of the Convention provides that the Convention does not apply to preliminary issues concerning the validity of the establishment of the trust and the transfer of the assets to the trust. Thus, the Convention would not be relevant in considering if a restrictive clause in the contract under which the debt arises might prevent the effective establishment of the trust over the contractual rights affected by the clause.

[26] [1960] Ch 52, at 84–88. A similar approach was taken in *Re Maudsley Sons & Field, Maudsley v Maudsley* [1900] 1 Ch 602, but the majority of the Court of Appeal rejected this approach in *Republica de Guatamala v Nunez* [1927] 1 KB 669.

[27] [2003] UKPC 37; [2004] 1 AC 147, at [13]–[15].

[28] Interestingly, Art 2(a) of the EC Insolvency Regulation (EC 1346/2000 OJ L160/1) specifies that intangible assets will be treated as situated at the place of the debtor's centre of main interests.

[29] See, for instance, *Jabbour (F & K) v Custodian of Israeli Absentee Property* [1954] 1 WLR 139 and *Alloway v Phillips* [1980] 1 WLR 888. With respect to the obligations of a bank under a letter of credit, see *Power Curber International Ltd v National Bank of Kuwait SAK* [1981] 1 WLR 1233.

[30] *Re Helbert Wagg & Co Ltd* [1956] Ch 323. This would be the case with respect to the payment obligations of a bank on an account in credit which is maintained for its customer: see Lord Hobhouse in *Société Eram Shipping Co Ltd v Hong Kong & Shanghai Banking Corp Ltd* [2003] UKHL 30; [2004] 1 AC 260, at [73].

Co Ltd v Hong Kong & Shanghai Banking Corp Ltd[31] speculated that in the case where the debtor was an ordinary trading company and the debt was an ordinary commercial debt, the debtor might be sued wherever it had a place of residence and, consequently, there might be more than one situs for the debt. In any event, enforcement action may be taken in places other than where the debtor has a residence such as, for instance, where the debtor has assets (including assets which have been given as security for payment of the debt) or where it has submitted to jurisdiction, as it might do expressly in a loan agreement. All of this goes to demonstrating the artificial nature of a concept of the situs of a debt, as well as the problems that might arise in determining the situs in particular cases. These difficulties were referred to by Mance LJ in the *Raiffeisen Zentralbank* case.[32]

It is tentatively submitted that under English common law conflicts principles **12.2.9.2** (in cases where Article 12(2) of the Rome Convention did not apply) the *lex situs* of a debt would also determine matters of priority as between rival dispositions of the debt. This follows from *Re Queensland Mercantile and Agency Co, ex p Australasian Investment Co, ex p Union Bank of Australia*[33] and from *Re Maudsley Sons & Field, Maudsley v Maudsley*.[34] This is said with some hesitancy because it may be that the authority of the first of those cases should be confined to an issue involving the determination of the priority of an involuntary assignment over an earlier voluntary assignment. Furthermore, the same result would have been achieved in *Re Maudsley Sons & Field*, on the facts of the case, if the proper law of the debt had been applied rather than the *lex situs*.[35]

In relation to the effect of a clause in the contract under which the debt arises, **12.2.9.3** which purports to prohibit or restrict the ability of the creditor to deal with the debt or its rights in relation thereto, it is submitted that English common law conflicts principles would apply the governing law of the debt to determine the effect of such a clause. The interpretation of the clause must be ascertained in accordance with contractual principles, by the application of the governing law of the contract, to be found by the application of the Rome Convention.[36] It is reasonable for the debtor to expect that the consequences of such a clause should also be determined by the governing law of the contract.[37]

---

[31] Ibid.
[32] At [2001] QB 825, at [36] and [37].
[33] [1892] 1 Ch 219.
[34] [1900] 1 Ch 602.
[35] See Mance LJ in the *Raiffeisen Zentralbank* case at [2001] QB 825, at [53]–[56].
[36] See Art 10(1)(a).
[37] Art 10(1)(c) of the Rome Convention provides that the consequences of a breach of the contract should be determined by the governing law of the contract.

12.2.9.4 Notwithstanding the views expressed above, in *Dicey, Morris & Collins*[38] it is suggested that the common law, ignoring the Rome Convention, would take an approach similar to that taken under Article 12. Thus, the view is advanced in that work that the effect of an intended assignment as between the assignor and the assignee should be determined by the governing law of their transaction, whilst the question as to the right to alienate a debt would be governed by the governing law of the debt.[39] The examination in that work on this point is based upon an assignment of contractual rights and appears to assume that the assignment is intended to have an effect upon the debtor. Where the transaction between the disponor and disponee is not intended to have that effect, the view that they put forward might not apply. The Court of Appeal made some general *obiter* comments on the conflicts rules relating to assignment of debts in *Macmillan Inc v Bishopsgate Investment Trust PLC (No 3)*.[40] The comments were made in the context of a battle over competing priorities in shares in a corporation, and none of the comments was addressed to the specific issue of the right to alienate a debt in a situation where Article 12(2) may not be applicable. Staughton, Auld, and Aldous LJJ generally appeared to favour the approach taken by *Dicey, Morris & Collins* in relation to matters concerning the assignment of debts, but not other intangible rights. Their views as to the assignment of debts, however, were influenced by Article 12.[41] For the reasons stated above, it is submitted that those views should not apply to a situation that is outside the scope of Article 12.

12.3 The Banker's Obligation of Confidence

12.3.1 In *Tournier v National Provincial and Union Bank of England*[42] the Court of Appeal held that a banker has a duty to maintain the confidence of information concerning its customer's affairs which becomes known to the banker during the course of the banking relationship between them.[43] This includes information from other sources of which the bank becomes aware in the course of that relationship.[44] In the absence of an express term, the duty arises from an implied term of the contract between the bank and its customer.[45] One of the four exceptions to

---

[38] *The Conflict of Laws* (14th edn, 2006).

[39] Ibid at para 24-054.

[40] [1996] 1 WLR 387.

[41] Ibid, at 400–401 (Staughton LJ), 410 (Auld LJ), and 419 (Aldous LJ).

[42] [1924] 1 KB 461.

[43] See, in particular, Bankes LJ in ibid.

[44] Ibid.

[45] It should be noted that both the Banking Code and the Business Banking Code (the latest editions of which, at the time of writing, were published in March 2005) expressly incorporate the duty (and the four exceptions to it) in similar terms, although the codes go further in at least one respect, namely, that the duty is stated to apply to 'all your personal information', not just to information

the duty, where disclosure is permitted within the compass of the implied term of the contract, is disclosure with the customer's consent. Such consent may be given prospectively by a customer in the facility agreement between it and the bank, or it may be given at the time that the bank intends to make the disclosure to a potential purchaser.[46] In passing, it should be noted that another one of the exceptions, disclosure in the bank's own interests, will not permit disclosure for the purposes of a loan transfer. That exception, whilst appearing on its face to be fairly wide, has generally been construed narrowly and covers action which a bank has to take in its own self-defence, such as in legal proceedings. It may also extend to action that a bank takes to protect its commercial reputation.[47]

In addition to the duty arising under *Tournier*'s case, a similar (although less easily comprehended) duty may arise under the Data Protection Act 1998, concerning information that might be held by a bank, as a data controller, in its computer and manual systems, about its customers and others who might be individuals. For instance, any 'processing' of data (which includes the disclosure of information) may only be done if it complies with the eight data protection principles set out in Part 1 of Schedule 1 to the Act. This includes the principles that personal data must be used fairly and lawfully, be obtained and used only for specified purposes, and that measures are taken to protect against unauthorized or unlawful use. The principle as to processing that is a fair and lawful use involves satisfying further conditions laid down in Schedule 2. The further conditions include a requirement that data should only be processed with the customer's consent or in conformity with the requirements for entry into or performance under the contract or to comply with a legal obligation or for a public purpose. There is a further, and rather nebulous, alternative that fair and lawful use includes necessary use for the 'legitimate interests' of the data controller or third parties to whom the data has

12.3.2

---

gained in the course of the banking relationship. Whilst the duty under *Tournier*'s case does not extend to information gained after the relationship terminates, it does continue with respect to information gained during the relationship, even after it has terminated. It should also be noted that information of a confidential nature which is imparted in circumstances of confidence may be protected under the more general law as to confidential information (see Lord Goff of Chieveley in *Attorney-General v Guardian Newspapers Ltd (No 2)* [1990] 1 AC 109, at 281–282). Examples of the difficulties that a bank may find itself in if it breaches the obligation of confidence will be seen in *United Pan-Europe Communications NV v Deutsche Bank AG* [2000] 2 BCLC 461 and in *Jackson v Royal Bank of Scotland plc* [2005] UKHL 3, [2005] 1 WLR 377.

46 Whilst *Tournier*'s case contemplates that the customer's consent may be given impliedly (see, for instance, Atkin LJ at [1924] 1 KB 461, at 484), *Turner v Royal Bank of Scotland plc* [1999] 2 All ER (Comm) 664 indicates that it may be difficult in practice to establish circumstances from which the consent could be implied. Nonetheless, it might be argued that if the facility agreement specifically contemplates a disposal by the bank of its rights then the customer could be taken impliedly to have consented to disclosure of information in connection with such a disposal. It is unlikely that such an argument would succeed in a case covered by one of the Codes, which provide for disclosure with the customer's 'permission'.

47 See Chadwick LJ in *Christofi v Barclays Bank PLC* [1999] 2 All ER (Comm) 417, at 425.

been disclosed, except for unwarranted processing which prejudices the rights and freedoms and legitimate interests of the relevant individual.

12.3.3 In summary, in the context of a transaction under which a bank proposes to transfer (using the expression in a broad sense) facilities involving individual customers or loans owing to it by such customers, the bank must bear in mind that, in pursuance of its duty of confidentiality, it should not make disclosure to the proposed purchaser or others of any details concerning the identity of its customers and the loans it has made to them without their consent. If such disclosure is not possible then it is unlikely that the transaction could proceed, as the purchaser and others will wish to investigate what is to be bought, which cannot be done without the relevant information.[48]

12.4 The Methods of Transfer under English Law

12.4.1 There are various possible methods of structuring a transaction under English law so as to achieve a transfer of a debt or a credit facility. The nature and characteristics of the underlying facility and the rights vested in the transferor, as well as its continuing obligations under the facility, will be important matters that should be taken into account in deciding upon the method to be chosen, as well as the relationship that it is desired to achieve between the transferee and the debtor. The methods are as follows:

(1) an assignment of the transferor's rights, either by way of an absolute, or legal, assignment under section 136 of the Law of Property Act 1925 or as an equitable assignment of those rights;

(2) a declaration of trust of the benefit of the transferor's rights;

(3) a novation of the transferor's rights and obligations under the underlying facility between it and the borrower; and

(4) a contractual sub-participation granted by the transferor to the transferee.

12.4.2 Each of those methods of structuring a transaction will be outlined in turn. Because of the size and complexity of the issues involved, there will then follow an examination of a number of legal issues that might affect an assignment (nearly all of these issues will also be relevant to a declaration of trust). After that, there will be a discussion concerning the structures that might be used for transfers of

---

[48] In this regard, it is interesting to note the Financial Services Authority's former requirement, as set out in s 6.2(a) of Chapter SE in the Interim Prudential Sourcebook for Banks, contained in its *Handbook of Rules and Guidance* that 'the transfer should not contravene the terms and conditions of the underlying asset agreement and all the necessary consents [must] have been obtained'. The Interim Prudential Sourcebook was replaced by the GENPRU and BIPRU sections of the FSA's *Handbook*, in implementation of the EC Banking Consolidation Directive (2006/48/EC OJ L177/1 30/6/2006), as explained in Chap 2.

portfolios of debts, debt instruments, and credit facilities under securitisations and other forms of structured finance.

12.5 Assignment

There are two forms of assignment of debts and other choses in action that are recognised by English law. In historical order of development they are an equitable assignment and an absolute (or legal) assignment under section 136 of the Law of Property Act 1925. As between the assignor and the assignee, each of them will achieve a transfer of the assignor's rights, so that in the assignor's insolvency, the transferred rights will be treated as belonging to the assignee and will thus fall outside the ambit of the insolvent's estate.[49] However, there may still be a practical difficulty, particularly in the case of an unnotified equitable assignment, if the assignor has collected the proceeds and dissipated them in such a way as to defeat an attempt to trace the funds. The principal benefit of an assignment within section 136 is a procedural benefit, as the legal right in the assigned debt is vested in the assignee, so that the assignee can sue in its own name at law to recover the debt and the debtor is obliged to pay the assignee.

12.5.1

The discussion that follows will begin by looking at the particular characteristics of each of these methods of assignment. It will then examine a number of issues that are common to both of them. In the background to many of those issues are the basic principles that the debtor should not be put in a worse position in consequence of an assignment than that in which the debtor would have been placed without the assignment, and that an assignee cannot inherit a better position or a wider set of rights than was possessed by the assignor.[50]

12.5.1.1

12.5.2 Absolute or legal assignment

Section 136 of the Law of Property Act 1925[51] provides that a debt or other legal thing in action may be assigned at law. The section substantially re-enacts the

---

[49] As to the proprietary effect in English law of the assignment between the assignor and the assignee, even without notice being given to the debtor, see Cotton LJ and Bowen LJ in *Gorringe v Irwell India Rubber & Gutta Percha Works* (1887) 34 ChD 128, at 132 and 135, respectively. This assumes, however, that the assignment is intended to be an outright assignment by way of sale, rather than by way of security. If the assignment is a form of security then other considerations will also apply, particularly concerning the need to register the assignment under s 860 et seq of the Companies Act 2006 (formerly s 395 et seq of the Companies Act 1985).

[50] See *Dawson v Great Northern & City Railway Co* [1905] 1 KB 260. However, it may be possible for a party to a contract to assign an accrued right that arises from a breach of contract by the other party, even though the loss or damage that follows from the breach had not manifested itself before the assignor had disposed of the subject matter of the contract, so that the assignor had not personally suffered any loss: see *Technotrade Ltd v Larkstore Ltd* [2006] EWCA Civ 1079, [2006] 1 WLR 2926.

[51] Similar provisions will be found in s 1 of the Policies of Assurance Act 1867 and s 1 of the Policies of Marine Insurance Act 1868 (now s 50 of the Marine Insurance Act 1906).

provisions of section 25(6) of the Judicature Act 1873, which introduced the concept of an assignment which would be effective at law, rather than merely in equity. Before that time, it was not possible to have an assignment that would be recognised at law.

12.5.2.1   Such an assignment at law will only be effective if the following requirements are met. The assignment must be in writing and signed by the assignor;[52] the assignment must be absolute and not merely conditional nor by way of charge;[53] as the assignment must be of a debt or other legal thing in action, it must be in existence at the time of the assignment, although it need not then be due for payment, and it must be an assignment of the whole debt and not merely a part of it; and written notice of the assignment must be given to the debtor.[54] There is no requirement that the assignment must be for valuable consideration.[55]

12.5.2.2   If the requirements of section 136 are met then the effect of the assignment is that, from the time the notice is given, the assignment will be recognised at common law, so that the legal right in the debt will be transferred to the assignee, who will acquire the right to give a good discharge to the debtor and to sue the debtor in the assignee's own name, without having to join the assignor in the suit. The corollary of this is that the debtor will not obtain a good discharge of the debt if it pays the assignor. If the debtor is in doubt, section 136 provides that it can gain protection by interpleading and paying the debt into court. It should be noted that the right of the assignee is expressly made subject by section 136 to any equities which have priority over the assignee, such as rights of set-off that the debtor may wish to assert and the rights of third parties who assert competing priorities.[56]

---

[52] The requirement for the assignor's signature is dispensed with in relation to a financial collateral arrangement by virtue of Reg 4(3) of the Financial Collateral Arrangements (No 2) Regs (SI 2003/3226).

[53] As to which see *Tancred v Delagoa Bay & East Africa Ry Co* (1889) 23 QBD 239, 58 LJQB 459.

[54] Curiously, the section does not specify who should give the notice. Common sense might dictate that the notice should be given by the assignor, being the person to whom the debtor was obliged before the assignment, rather than by the assignee, of whom the debtor would be unaware. Nonetheless, a notice which was given by the assignee's solicitors was held to be an effective notice for the purposes of s 25(6) of the Judicature Act 1873, which was the predecessor of s 136: see *Denney, Gasquet & Metcalfe v Conklin* [1913] 3 KB 177.

[55] *Harding v Harding* (1886) 17 QBD 442; *Re Westerton* [1919] 2 Ch 104. However, a lack of proper value received by the assignor may be relevant to a challenge mounted in the context of insolvency proceedings concerning the assignor: see the following sections of the Insolvency Act 1986: ss 238 and 339 (transactions at an undervalue), s 423 (transactions defrauding creditors), ss 239 and 340 (preferences), and s 245 (avoidance of floating charges).

[56] See *E Pfeiffer Weinkellerei-Weineinkauf GmbH v Arbuthnot Factors Ltd* [1988] 1 WLR 150, at 161–163 and *Compaq Computer Ltd v Abercorn Group Ltd* [1991] BCC 484, at 497–502 where it was said that the rules of priority as between competing interests, be they legal or equitable interests, will be the same as those that apply as between competing equitable assignments. Those rules and the rules concerning the debtor's rights of set-off, are discussed further below.

It will be apparent that section 136 will not apply, and so it will not be possible to **12.5.2.3** have an assignment under that section, if any of the requirements mentioned above are missing. For instance, if the proposed assignment is to be for part only of the debt, if notice is not to be given to the debtor, or if the assignment is to be of a future debt, then a different method of achieving the transfer will have to be found, such as by using the form of an equitable assignment.

12.5.3 Equitable assignment

Historically, equity was willing to recognise assignments of choses in action, whether by way of outright transfer or by way of security, thereby supplying proprietary effect to transactions which the common law was unable to comprehend. Indeed, equity even recognised assignments of parts of choses in action and assignments of future property. In effect, equity directed the assignor to act on behalf of the assignee, such as by directing the assignor to sue the debtor and to hold the benefit of the chose, including the proceeds of payment, on trust for the assignee. Despite the passing of the Judicature Act 1873, it remained possible to have an equitable assignment of legal or equitable property and to have an equitable assignment in situations where the requirements of section 25(6) of that Act or of section 136 of the Law of Property Act 1925 may not have been met (e.g. an assignment of part of a debt, an assignment of future property, or where notice had not been given to the debtor).[57]

An equitable assignment does not require any particular form or procedure.[58] **12.5.3.1** Indeed, except in cases where section 53(1)(c) of the Law of Property Act 1925 requires it, an equitable assignment does not even have to be in writing.[59]

There remains the question, however, as to whether an equitable assignment must **12.5.3.2** be supported by valuable consideration.[60] In this, there are two of the famous equitable maxims in play. One is that equity recognises as done that which ought to be done. The other is that equity will not assist a volunteer. In his speech in

---

[57] See Lord Macnaghten in *William Brandt's Sons & Co v Dunlop Rubber Co Ltd* [1905] AC 454, at 461.

[58] Lord Macnaghten in *William Brandt's*, at 462. However, there must be a sufficient externally observable indication of an intention to assign: see *Finlan v Eyton Morris Winfield* [2007] EWHC 914 (Ch); [2007] 4 All ER 143, at [33]. In *The Argo Fund Ltd v Essar Steel Ltd* [2005] EWHC 600 (Comm), [2005] 2 Lloyd's Rep 203, it was held that it was incompatible with such an intention that the parties had structured the transaction as a novation. They could not, if the novation failed, then assert that they really intended an assignment.

[59] A point that was of some significance when a written assignment might have attracted stamp duty. Duty on such transactions was abolished by the Finance Act 2003.

[60] The concept of consideration in equity requires real value or detriment (for instance, *Glegg v Bromley* [1912] 3 KB 474) and is different from the simple consideration or agreement by way of deed that is required at law to support a contract.

William Brandt's Sons & Co v Dunlop Rubber Co Ltd[61] in which he described equitable assignments, Lord Macnaghten did refer to the presence of value in support of an equitable assignment. Nonetheless, value is not always required in equity to support an assignment of either legal or equitable property,[62] as evidenced by the discussion of the Court of Appeal in *Milroy v Lord*,[63] in which the court acknowledged the possibility of a voluntary assignment but said that the court would not perfect an imperfect gift. Thus, it would not enforce an imperfect voluntary assignment by imposing a trust and vice versa. This left for subsequent generations the question as to what steps must have been taken, by the donor in particular, to establish the validity of the gift.[64] A voluntary conditional agreement[65] to assign property will be regarded as an imperfect gift, and so as not binding on the purported assignor where the fulfilment of the condition is within the discretion of that person. There are instances, however, where value will undoubtedly be required. One is where there is an agreement to assign future property.[66] Another concerns the granting of an equitable charge.[67]

12.5.4 Future property

Future property means property that is not in the hands of the purported assignor at the time it agrees to assign the property. The property may not exist at all (e.g. next year's apple crop) or, whilst in existence, it may not yet have vested in the hands of the assignor (e.g. the apple in the shop that the assignor is about to purchase). Particularly in the case of debts and other contractual rights, future property should be distinguished from presently existing property, such as where there is an accrued right to performance at a future date. Thus, a debt that has been incurred but which is payable at a future date is presently existing property of the creditor.

12.5.4.1 The common law is unable to recognise, in a proprietary sense, transactions in future property. At best, it may conclude that there was a binding contract to

---

[61] [1905] AC 454, at 462.

[62] However, a lack of proper value received by the assignor may be relevant to a challenge mounted in the context of insolvency proceedings concerning the assignor: see the following sections of the Insolvency Act 1986: ss 238 and 339 (transactions at an undervalue), s 423 (transactions defrauding creditors), ss 239 and 340 (preferences), and s 245 (avoidance of floating charges).

[63] (1862) 4 De G F & J 264.

[64] In *Kekewich v Manning* (1851) 1 De GM&G 176, it was held that there had been a binding voluntary settlement of an equitable interest in property as sufficient had been done to effect a transfer of the property so as to bind the settlor. In *Fortescue v Barnett* (1834) 3 My&K 36, it was held that a voluntary deed of assignment of a life policy was binding upon the assignor. Two recent cases which have examined the subject are *T Choithram International SA v Pagarani* [2001] 1 WLR 1 (Privy Council) and *Pennington v Waine* [2002] EWCA Civ 227, [2002] 1 WLR 2075.

[65] Including where there is only past consideration.

[66] See Lord Macnaghten in *Tailby v The Official Receiver* (1888) 13 App Cas 523, at 543.

[67] See *Re Earl of Lucan, Hardinge v Cobden* (1890) 45 ChD 470.

assign the property when it came into the hands of the purported assignee. All it can do in relation to such a contract is to award damages if the contract is breached. Such an award of damages is not of much use if the defendant is insolvent.

In *Holroyd v Marshall*[68] the House of Lords held that equity, however, was able to give proprietary recognition to such transactions,[69] so that an equitable interest may vest in the transferee as soon as the asset comes into existence in the hands of the transferor. This was developed further by the House of Lords in *Tailby v The Official Receiver*,[70] where it was held that such recognition will be given so long as the transaction is supported by valuable consideration, there is sufficient identity of the relevant assets so that when they come into existence they were clearly intended to be caught by the agreement, and the intention between the parties is that immediately the assets come into existence in the hands of the putative transferor (and without further condition) the intended proprietary interest should vest in the transferee. Such a transferee could be either an absolute purchaser or someone taking security. In *Re Lind*[71] it was said that the principle will apply notwithstanding an intervening insolvency of the intended transferor which occurs after the date of contracting but before the asset comes into existence.[72]

12.5.4.2

12.6 Declaration of Trust

The decision of the Court of Appeal in *Milroy v Lord*[73] is authority for the basic proposition that it is possible in equity to alienate a right under a contract, such as a debt or other chose in action, by the means of an equitable assignment or by a

12.6.1

---

68 (1862) 10 HLC 191, 11 ER 999.

69 Except in the case of sale of goods: see *Re Wait* [1927] Ch 606.

70 (1888) 13 App Cas 523. See, in particular, the speech of Lord Macnaghten where the requirements are clearly set out. His Lordship also dispelled the red-herring linking the recognition of assignments of future property to a requirement that the transaction should be one that was capable of being the subject of a decree for specific performance, which had arisen from what had been said by Lord Westbury in *Holroyd v Marshall* (1862) 10 HLC 191, at 209 and 211.

71 [1915] 2 Ch 345. In *Peer International Corp and ors v Termidor Music Publishers Ltd & ors* [2002] EWHC 2675 (Ch) Neuberger J said, at [74]–[82], that he preferred the analysis in *Re Lind* to that of the Court of Appeal in *Collyer v Isaacs* (1881) 19 ChD 342. See further the discussion by Meagher, Gummow & Lehane, *Equity: Doctrines and Principles* (4th edn, 2002), at paras 6-275 to 6-330.

72 Where, however, the purported assignor subsequently becomes bankrupt and an asset arises in the course of the trustee in bankruptcy running the business, such an asset will vest in the trustee, despite an earlier purported assignment executed before the assignor became bankrupt: *Re Jones, ex p Nichols* (1882) 22 ChD 782. This is consistent with s 306 of the Insolvency Act 1986, by virtue of which property comprised in the bankrupt's estate vests in the trustee. The position may be different in a winding up, as the assets of the insolvent company do not vest in the liquidator unless the court, at his request, makes an order vesting the property in the liquidator pursuant to s 145(1) of the Insolvency Act 1986.

73 (1862) 4 De G F & J 264.

declaration of trust. In *Don King Productions Inc v Warren*[74] it was held that it may be possible to construe a restrictive clause in a contract which prohibited an assignment by a party of its contractual rights as not being applicable to a transaction by way of a declaration of trust.[75] Apart from that point, which depends for its validity on a technical distinction in the construction of the relevant restriction, it is difficult to envisage circumstances where it would be better to structure a transaction as a declaration of trust rather than an equitable assignment. The issues discussed below in relation to assignments are also of relevance in relation to declarations of trust.

12.7 Novation

12.7.1 In structural terms, a novation of a loan facility involves an agreement between the old lender and the borrower that they should each be discharged, either in whole or in part, from their rights and obligations towards each other under the existing contract and an agreement between the new lender and the borrower that, to the same extent as the discharged rights and obligations, they will enter into an agreement under a new contract that was of similar effect to the old contract that was terminated by the novation.

12.7.2 There are a number of points that can be made to illustrate a novation in contrast to an assignment.[76]

12.7.2.1 First, a novation requires the agreement, and thus the consent, of all the parties that are involved.[77] In the absence of restrictions on assignment in the contract,[78] an assignment of contractual rights does not require the consent of the debtor.

12.7.2.2 Secondly, a novation effects a termination, in whole or in part, of one contract and its replacement, to that extent, by a new one. An assignment effects a transfer of the assignor's contractual rights but the contract remains in place, the assignor remains a party to it and is obliged to perform its remaining obligations under it.

12.7.2.3 Thirdly, a novation may involve the transfer of both rights and obligations, whereas an assignment can only concern a transfer of rights,[79] although the assigned rights

---

74 [2000] Ch 291.

75 See further para 12.9.4.3.1 below.

76 See Aikens J in *The Argo Fund Ltd v Essar Steel Ltd* [2005] EWHC 600 (Comm), [2005] 2 Lloyd's Rep 203. The case was the subject of an appeal (reported at [2006] EWCA Civ 241, [2006] 2 Lloyd's Rep 134) which did not touch on this aspect.

77 Albeit that in a syndicated facility document the borrower's agreement is often contained within the mechanisms provided by the facility agreement, as to which see further below.

78 And, it might be added, except for those limited categories of contractual rights that may not be assigned, such as under a contract for personal services.

79 See Sir Richard Henn Collins MR in *Tolhurst v Associated Portland Cement Manufacturers (1900) Ltd* [1902] 2 KB 660

are 'subject to equities', such as the debtor's rights of set-off and the priorities of third parties.

Fourthly, both the termination of the old contract and the creation of a new contract under a novation must be supported by consideration, whereas at least absolute assignments under section 136 of the Law of Property Act 1936 and, it might be added, some types of equitable assignment, do not need to be supported by consideration.   **12.7.2.4**

Fifthly, whereas a novation can achieve a transfer of all of the transferor's stated rights and obligations, an assignment may not achieve a transfer of those rights which are entirely connected with and personal to the old lender, such as rights under indemnity clauses and rights to levy a charge for increased costs associated with the lender's capital adequacy position and, perhaps, grossing up for the imposition of withholding tax on interest payments to the old lender.[80]   **12.7.2.5**

Sixthly, if the old lender enjoyed the benefit of guarantees or security, they will expire with the release of the borrower from its obligations to the old lender. It will be necessary for the new lender to take new guarantees and security for its own benefit.[81] In an assignment,[82] it should be possible to include an assignment of such guarantees and security in so far as they relate to the rights of the old lender against the borrower that are included in the assignment.[83]   **12.7.2.6**

12.7.3 Syndicated facilities

It is common in syndicated facilities to find a mechanism providing for the syndicate members to be able to transfer their participations in the facility, that is their rights and obligations, by way of a novation through use of transfer certificates in a form scheduled to the facility agreement. Aikens J in *The Argo Fund Ltd v Essar Steel Ltd*[84] looked at the mechanics by which a novation came about in consequence of the use of such a transfer certificate, in view of the fact that the borrower

---

[80] This could be covered by specifying an assignee as an intended beneficiary of such provisions within the contemplation of s 1 of the Contracts (Rights of Third Parties) Act 1999.

[81] However, it is possible when taking the guarantees or security to construct a trust, under which the guarantees or security are given or constituted in favour of a security trustee, which will hold the same for the benefit of the lenders for the time being. This is commonly done in the context of syndicated lending (see, for instance, *British Energy Power & Energy Trading Ltd v Credit Suisse* [2008] EWCA Civ 53). A similar structure is used in relation to bond issues, where there can be a trustee which holds such security for the bond holders for the time being.

[82] Subject to any restrictions that might apply.

[83] As noted above, if there is any risk that new security which is taken with respect to novated debt might be vulnerable (for instance, because of hardening periods under relevant insolvency law or because of the risk of third parties gaining priority in the secured assets) then it may be advantageous to assign the existing debt and the security which secures that debt.

[84] [2005] EWHC 600 (Comm), [2005] 2 Lloyd's Rep 203. The case was the subject of an appeal, as noted at n 76 above.

was not physically involved in the process of the novation at the time it took place.[85] His Lordship's analysis may be summarised as follows.

12.7.3.1 The novation is achieved through the provisions of the syndicated facility agreement on the basis of there being unilateral contracts, under which there is a standing offer by the borrower to accept the discharge of the old contract and a standing offer by the borrower to accept the agreement with the new lender constituted by the new contract.[86] The standing offer by the borrower to terminate the old contract is made to each member of the syndicate for the time being, which can be accepted by the delivery by the transferring lender of a transfer certificate to the Facility Agent, as specified in the facility agreement. The consideration to support the agreement to terminate is provided by the mutual agreement of the borrower and the old lender to give up their respective rights and obligations. The standing offer by the borrower to enter into a new contract on the terms of the facility agreement is made to those who were eligible to be a transferee. The act of acceptance of that offer by the new lender was not spelt out in the relevant agreement in that case, but his Lordship said it would arise by the new lender's agreement to the transfer on the terms set out in the facility agreement and its agreement to the transferor sending the Transfer Certificate to the Facility Agent. Although there was no provision in the facility agreement for the transfer to be notified to the borrower, it is not a requirement for the conclusion of a contract that the person accepting an offer in the manner specified in the offer must also notify the offeror of that acceptance.

12.7.3.2 Whilst it was not mentioned in the judgment, a similar analysis would apply to the novation that is usually provided for in such facility documentation concerning the respective rights and obligations as exist between the old lender, the other members of the syndicate, the Facility Agent, the Arranger, and the new lender. That is important in relation to matters such as those which arise under the

---

[85] A preliminary point, which is illustrated by that case, is the necessity of ensuring that the intended transferee falls within the category of persons which the documentation states will be acceptable as a transferee. Aikens J held that the requirement was met on the facts although David Steel J had arrived at a contrary conclusion at an earlier stage in proceedings in the same case, *The Argo Fund Ltd v Essar Steel Ltd* [2004] EWHC 128 (Comm). Except for a brief note that the earlier proceedings had taken place, there is no further reference made by Aikens J to the earlier proceedings or to David Steel J's judgment, which is unfortunate. The Court of Appeal construed the relevant wording more generously, but otherwise upheld the decision of Aikens J (*Essar Steel Ltd v The Argo Fund Ltd* [2006] EWCA Civ 241, [2006] 2 Lloyd's Rep 134; for related proceedings, see *Argo Capital Investors Fund SPC v Essar Steel Ltd* [2005] EWHC 2587 (Comm)). See also the approach taken by the Court of Appeal in *Barbados Trust Co Ltd v Bank of Zambia* [2007] EWCA Civ 148, [2007] Lloyd's Rep 495, which concerned the description of permitted assignees under a loan agreement.

[86] See *Carlill v Carbolic Smoke Ball Co* [1892] 2 QB 484 and *New Zealand Shipping Co Ltd v AM Satterthwaite & Co Ltd; The Eurymedon* [1975] AC 154.

sharing clause, the agency clause, and the provisions relating to the effect of a majority vote (see further, Chapter 9).

12.8 Sub-participation

Sub-participation arrangements are usually documented as a contract entered **12.8.1** into between two banks (or similar institutions) in relation to a loan or a similar facility made available by one of the banks to a borrower. The sub-participation arrangement will normally take a form by which the lending bank, the grantor, grants a sub-participation to the other bank, the grantee, concerning the receipt by the grantor of payments of principal and interest under the loan facility. The grantor agrees to pay to the grantee amounts equivalent to the principal payments that it receives from the borrower. The grantor will also agree to pay to the grantee amounts referable, in whole or in part, to interest payments and the like that are received from the borrower.[87] In return the grantee will make a payment to the grantor at the outset of an amount equivalent to the outstanding amount of the facility. In effect, the grantee takes on the risk of failure by the borrower and the reward of future performance by the borrower. From the commercial perspective of the grantor, it has parted with the risks and rewards of the facility, and, if properly structured, should therefore obtain a regulatory benefit for its own capital adequacy and large exposures positions. Indeed, obtaining that benefit is often an important reason for the grantor entering into a sub-participation.

A less common arrangement[88] is a risk participation. It has a similarity with a **12.8.2** guarantee or a credit default derivative contract. It arises where the grantee agrees to make a payment to the grantor of the outstanding principal amount under the facility if and when the borrower defaults. In return, the grantor agrees to pay to the grantee all or some portion of the interest it receives until default, whereafter it will pay over any amounts of principal and interest received from the borrower.

Unlike an assignment, where the lending bank transfers a proprietary right in the **12.8.3** facility, the intention (which, for the sake of prudence, should be stated explicitly) under a properly drawn contract of sub-participation is that the grantor should remain as the beneficial owner of its rights against the borrower. The grantee is merely given a contractual right by the grantor to be paid equivalent amounts by

---

[87] It is likely that the grantor will agree to pay over all of the interest it receives as, otherwise, it will have a continuing economic interest in the underlying facility which will cause it accounting and regulatory difficulties.

[88] Because its regulatory treatment will not be as favourable to the grantor, as it will be assessed as having a continuing risk in the facility, albeit referable to the risk of default by the grantee.

the grantor if and when it receives payments by the borrower. An important consequence of this is that if the grantor becomes insolvent and goes into liquidation, the grantee merely has an unsecured claim against the grantor and cannot claim any proprietary entitlement in the underlying facility, even with respect to payments made by the borrower after the commencement of the insolvency of the grantor. It has often been said that the grantee has therefore assumed a 'double credit risk'; namely, the risk of default by either (or both) the borrower and the grantor.

12.8.4 In *Lloyds TSB Bank PLC v Clarke (Liquidator of Socimer International Bank Ltd) and Chase Manhattan Bank Luxembourg SA*,[89] which concerned the more usual form of sub-participation arrangements and not a risk participation, the Privy Council confirmed that under a sub-participation the grantee will receive no proprietary rights in the facility. Hence, on the facts of the case before it, the sub-participant was found to have no claim in the underlying facility and was just an ordinary unsecured creditor in the grantor's insolvency.[90] Of course, as the arrangement between the grantor and the grantee depends upon the terms of the contract between them, it might always be possible for the contract to depart from the usual form and be fashioned, perhaps unwittingly, as an assignment of the grantor's rights under the facility or it might include a charge over those rights, but that would be unusual.

12.8.5 On a practical level,[91] it will be necessary for the contract to provide for the making of decisions in relation to the conduct of the facility and the exercise of the lender's rights, as well as for the carrying out of enforcement action should the borrower default. The grantee would normally wish to be able to determine such matters, but the grantor may be reluctant to concede the point if it has a continuing exposure to, or other commercial connection with, the borrower. In any event, the grantor would wish the grantee to accept the responsibility for any costs and expenses that might be incurred by the grantor in taking action against the borrower for the benefit of the grantee. Difficulties may also be encountered where the grantor has other exposures to the borrower in addition to the participated facility. There could then be a problem in determining if a payment, or its equivalent, had been received by the grantor which was referable to the participation, particularly if the grantor had received a benefit through the operation of set-off rights, either before or in consequence of the insolvency of the borrower, or through the realisation of security or a guarantee that was held by the grantor. If the grantor is to be treated as having received a payment from the borrower, it will

---

89 [2002] UKPC 27, [2002] 2 All ER (Comm) 992.

90 The decision of the Privy Council was referred to by Andrew Smith J in *Adolfo Altman v Australia and New Zealand Banking Group Ltd* [2002] EWHC 2488 (Comm).

91 Many of these points will also be relevant in the case of an equitable assignment, particularly if it is only a partial assignment of the original lender's exposure to the borrower.

then be a question of determining the extent to which that payment should be allocated towards the participation, as opposed to the other exposures that the grantor has towards the borrower. If there is any likelihood of those circumstances arising, they should be addressed in the contract between the grantor and the grantee.

12.9 Common Issues Concerning Assignments

It is now convenient to examine a number of issues that relate to assignments and are common to whichever form of assignment is undertaken. A great many of them should also apply in the case of a declaration of trust. As previously mentioned, in the background to many of those issues is the basic principle that the debtor should not be put in a worse position in consequence of an assignment than that in which the debtor would have been placed without the assignment, and that the assignee cannot acquire greater rights against the debtor than were possessed by the assignor.

12.9.1

12.9.2 Rights v obligations

One difficulty with assignments is that it is only possible for the assignor to assign its rights. It cannot assign its obligations.[92] Thus, if at the time of the assignment the assignor remains obligated to make further performance under the relevant contract, such as would be the case under a loan agreement if the borrower has the right to request further drawings, the assignor cannot transfer that obligation, at least without the consent of the borrower, in which case there would be a novation of the contractual obligations rather than an assignment of such obligations.[93] This problem may have regulatory and accounting consequences for the transferor, as (in the absence of such consent) it will not have divested itself of its responsibilities and so it cannot say that it has transferred all of the risks and rewards associated with the facility.

12.9.3 Rights that are personal to the assignor

It is a principle of the law of assignments that the rights of the assignee are subject to equities, which includes the proposition that the debtor/obligor whose obligation

---

[92] See, for instance, Sir Richard Henn Collins MR in *Tolhurst v Associated Portland Cement Manufacturers (1900) Ltd* [1902] 2 KB 660, at 668.

[93] There may be an advantage in structuring a transaction as an assignment of the assignor's accrued rights to payment and a novation of its obligations as to future performance, particularly if security was given for the original debt. If there is any risk that the new security which is taken with respect to the novated debt might be vulnerable, for instance because of hardening periods under relevant insolvency law or because of the risk of third parties gaining priority in the secured assets, then an assignment of the existing debt with the security for it may be advantageous.

has been assigned should not be put in a worse position in consequence of the assignment than he would have been if the assignment had not taken place. One example of this is to the effect that the assignee cannot recover from the debtor or other obligor more than the assignee could have recovered if there had been no assignment. Thus, the assignee cannot recover from the debtor/obligor for loss that would not have been suffered by the assignor if the claim had not been assigned. In *Dawson v Great Northern & City Railway Co*,[94] an assignee was refused recovery of extra loss it had suffered which was referable to the assignee's circumstances and which the assignor would not have suffered. Another example relates to the debtor's rights of set-off which it could have asserted against the assignor and which it is permitted to assert against the amount payable to the assignee.[95] As with most principles in the law, the devil is in the detail.

12.9.3.1 From the principle stated above, it follows that not all of the rights that are granted to the lender in a facility agreement may be capable of assignment in the sense of conferring the same advantages upon the transferee as were applicable to the transferor. This is because some of the rights may be characterised as being personal to the transferor and its own circumstances and so not capable, through assignment, of conferring protection upon the transferee for its personal position. For instance, the protection that is commonly given to a lender under a change in circumstances or an increased costs clause in a loan facility agreement relates to the consequences of a diminution in the lender's rate of return arising from matters such as an increase in the costs of complying with capital adequacy requirements. If the lender has transferred the loan then it should not suffer from those consequences.[96] A similar problem might arise under an indemnity clause designed to give the lender, as a contracting party under the agreement, protections against the outcome of various adverse matters affecting the lender. It is debateable if at common law such clauses can be effective in conferring the protection upon a transferee that was originally intended to be given to the transferor, because of the rules as to privity of contract and the inability of a contracting party to recover damages for a breach of contract with respect to a loss suffered by someone other than itself.[97]

---

[94] [1905] 1 KB 260.

[95] See Lord Hobhouse in *Government of Newfoundland v Newfoundland Railway Co* (1888) 13 App Cas 199, at 212–213; Templeman J in *Business Computers Ltd v Anglo-African Leasing Ltd* [1977] 1 WLR 578; and Buxton LJ in *Smith v Muscat* [2003] EWCA Civ 962, [2003] 1 WLR 2853.

[96] The original creditor may be entitled to assign an accrued right to claim compensation under such a provision if, for instance, the claim, although accrued due, is not payable until some later date.

[97] See the discussions in Chap 1 and Chap 3.

It is now possible, however, to overcome such problems by the use of the provi- **12.9.3.2**
sions of the Contracts (Rights of Third Parties) Act 1999 which, of course, can
only be the case if the Act has not been disapplied.[98] In consequence of section
1(1) of the Act, if it is clear that the relevant provisions are intended to be for the
benefit of the transferee or, indeed, another person such as an affiliate of the lender,
such a transferee or other person may enforce the provisions for its own benefit
and in its own name.[99]

12.9.4 Contractual restrictions upon dealing

The lender may be precluded by the contract from assigning or otherwise dealing
with its rights if the contract contains a provision to that effect.[100] Most contractual rights are assignable in the absence of some particular restriction upon assignment.[101] Such a restriction may be imposed in the contract under which the
relevant right arises.

Before examining the effectiveness of such provisions, it is pertinent to consider **12.9.4.1**
the various reasons why a debtor may wish to impose them upon its creditor.

First, the debtor may wish to keep available its rights of set-off against its original **12.9.4.1.1**
creditor, not just in relation to claims arising out of the same or a closely related
transaction to that under which the debt arose, but also in relation to present and
future claims of a more general nature. Once a debtor has received notice of an
assignment of a debt, the availability to it of set-off in the latter type of general situation becomes limited, essentially, to claims which have accrued due prior to its
receipt of a notice of the assignment.[102]

Secondly, in a winding up of the creditor or the debtor, the debtor may wish to be **12.9.4.1.2**
able to bring into account the debt it owes the creditor against amounts due to it

---

[98] Under s 1(2) of the Act. See further, as to the requirement for disapplication, as opposed to
opting in to the Act, *Nisshin Shipping Co Ltd v Cleaves & Co Ltd* [2003] EWHC 2602 (Comm);
[2004] 1 Lloyd's Rep 38, at [23]. See the discussion in Chap 3.

[99] It may also be possible to construct protection for the third party by the use of the concept
of agency or trust: see *New Zealand Shipping Co Ltd v AM Satterthwaite & Co Ltd, The Eurymedon*
[1975] AC 154, which alternative remains unaffected by the Act.

[100] For a more detailed treatment of this subject, see the author's article, in two parts, 'Contractual
Restrictions on a Creditor's Right to Alienate Debts' at [2003] JIBL 1 and [2003] JIBLR 43.

[101] However, the benefit of a contract for personal skill and confidence is not assignable without
the servant's or employee's consent but such a person can assign his right to be paid: see Lightman
J in *Don King Productions Inc v Warren* [2000] Ch 291, at 319; *Devefi Pty Ltd v Mateffy Pearl Nagy
Pty Ltd* [1993] RPC 493, at 503 (Fed Ct of Aust); and *Akai Holdings Ltd v RSM Robson Rhodes LLP*
[2007] EWHC 1641 (Ch). It is also arguable that certain rights conferred by statute, such as a right
to levy fees or duties in return for the supply of a statutory service, may not be assignable in the
absence of a statutory permission, especially where the grantee of the rights is performing a quasi-
administrative or quasi-official role.

[102] See *Business Computers Ltd v Anglo-African Leasing Ltd* [1977] 1 WLR 578.

from the creditor for the purposes of section 323 of the Insolvency Act 1986 and Rules 2.85 and 4.90 of the Insolvency Rules 1986,[103] which it can only do if the person beneficially entitled to the debt is the same creditor.[104]

12.9.4.1.3 Thirdly, the debtor will be at risk if, having received a notice of assignment, it overlooks the notice and pays the original creditor rather than the assignee. In such a case, the debtor will not obtain a good discharge for payment of the debt and will remain liable to pay the financier, being left to seek a refund from the creditor, for what that is worth.[105]

12.9.4.1.4 Fourthly, the debtor will be at risk if, having received a notice of the assignment, the debtor pays the assignee and thereafter wishes to claim a refund, for instance due to a total failure of consideration concerning the underlying contract, as it must seek its refund from the original creditor and not the assignee whom it paid, despite the fact that the assignee has the money and the original creditor may by then be insolvent.[106]

12.9.4.1.5 Fifthly, and subject to the question as to whether such provisions can be effective in favour of an assignee, the debtor may be exposed to higher costs if the identity of its creditor changes. This would be due to the effect of certain provisions in loan agreements such as increased costs and tax clauses, although it is not uncommon for such agreements to contain provisions designed in part to protect the debtor against such adverse effects if they arise in consequence of a change of its creditor.

12.9.4.1.6 Sixthly, on a more general and commercial basis, the debtor may be concerned to ensure that its creditor remains the same. Indeed, the assignee may be a person with whom the debtor would not wish to have a commercial relationship, and it may even at some time have rejected that possibility. The debtor may wish that the creditor should remain in place not just on a superficial or nominal basis but also substantively, because of the working relationship that exists between them. The debtor may feel that the original creditor would be more amenable to requests for

---

[103] As amended by SI 2005/527.

[104] See *In re City Life Assurance Co Ltd; Stephenson's case* [1926] Ch 191, at 214.

[105] See, in relation to an absolute assignment at law, s 136 of the Law of Property Act 1925. In *William Brandt's Sons & Co v Dunlop Rubber Co Ltd* [1905] AC 454 the House of Lords held that the same consequences would arise under an equitable assignment of a legal chose in action where notice had been given to the debtor. See also the majority of the Court of Appeal in *Three Rivers District Council v Bank of England* [1996] QB 292. With respect to the latter case, it is submitted that the minority view expressed by Staughton LJ, who queried the approach taken on this point by the House of Lords, is much to be preferred to that of Waite and Peter Gibson LJJ who comprised the majority. The importance of giving notice of the assignment to the relevant obligor is illustrated by the Court of Appeal's decision in *Warner Bros Records Inc v Rollgreen Ltd* [1976] QB 430 (a case which concerned the popular music artiste Rod Stewart).

[106] *Pan Ocean Shipping Co Ltd v Creditcorp Ltd* [1994] 1 WLR 161.

consents and assistance when times become hard than would an assignee which has a more limited concern simply to be paid. Even if the assignee only has an equitable interest whilst the original creditor remains nominally as the legal owner of the debt, the assignee is likely to be in the driving seat behind the scenes and thus, realistically, the person dictating the attitude to be taken towards the debtor.

There are counter-arguments in support of the original creditor being able to transfer its rights without the impediments placed upon it by such restrictions. **12.9.4.2**

First, it may become unlawful for such a creditor to maintain a loan, which difficulty might be overcome by the creditor transferring its rights to a third party which is not affected by the illegality. **12.9.4.2.1**

Secondly, an original creditor may be exposed to an increase in its regulatory costs of maintaining the loan, or there might be a tax imposition upon the creditor or the debtor which could perhaps be mitigated by a transfer. **12.9.4.2.2**

Thirdly, the original creditor might have extended its credit to the debtor on the basis of the debtor's then existing creditworthiness. That may have subsequently declined, thereby exposing the creditor to a greater degree of risk than it had originally been prepared to accept or which may no longer justify a favourable rate of interest enjoyed by the debtor. **12.9.4.2.3**

Fourthly, if the debtor is in default, the original creditor may wish to crystallise its losses by disposing of the debt. **12.9.4.2.4**

Fifthly, on a more positive note, it may be the case that the original creditor funds its business by selling its debts, thereby generating new finance to make further loans or to provide its working capital. If it did not do so then it would not be able to extend credit to people or entities like the debtor in the first place. **12.9.4.2.5**

Finally, where the transfer is of a whole portfolio of debts, it might be thought to be an unreasonable imposition upon the transferee if it has to check each contract under which a debt arises to see if there might be some restriction which could prevent the debt from being assigned. **12.9.4.2.6**

12.9.4.3 *The effect of a contractual restriction*

Having considered the arguments for and against restrictive provisions, it is now possible to examine their effectiveness as a matter of English law. The starting point is to discern the nature and extent of the restriction, which will depend upon its proper construction.[107] The rules for the construction of contracts and their provisions were summarised by Lord Hoffmann in *Investors Compensation*

---

[107] See generally the approach taken by Lord Browne-Wilkinson in *Linden Gardens Trust Ltd v Lenesta Sludge Disposals Ltd* [1994] AC 85.

Scheme Ltd v West Bromwich Building Society[108] and have been addressed in several cases subsequently.[109] The process of construction will involve a determination of the rights under the contract to which the restriction relates and the extent to which dealings with those rights are intended to be restricted. As to the rights to which the restriction relates, it will generally be assumed that a restriction upon a party's right to deal with and assign its benefit of a contract is intended to cover both the party's underlying rights to demand performance by the other party and the fruits of those rights manifested in the right to be paid.[110] It is possible, however, for the restriction to be aimed at preventing a dealing by a party with its underlying right to future performance whilst leaving it free to assign or otherwise deal with the fruits thereof.[111]

12.9.4.3.1 Subject to an argument based upon public policy, which will be examined below, it will also be a matter of the proper construction of a contract to determine the types of dealings which the restriction is intended to prevent.[112] It has been held that a prohibition upon assignment will generally be taken as being intended to prevent both legal and equitable assignments.[113] It has also been held that it is a matter of construction of the relevant restriction to determine if other types of dealings might fall within its compass, such as by way of a declaration of trust[114]

---

108 [1998] 1 WLR 896, at 913.

109 For instance, by Lord Hoffmann again in *Bank of Credit and Commerce International SA v Ali* [2001] UKHL 8, [2002] 1 AC 251. See also Lord Steyn in *Sirius International Insurance Co (Publ) v FAI General Insurance Ltd* [2004] UKHL 54; [2004] 1 WLR 3251, at [18]–[19], who emphasised the need to take a commercially sensible, rather than a strictly literal, approach. Arden LJ in *Static Control Components (Europe) Ltd v Egan* [2004] EWCA Civ 392; [2004] 2 Lloyd's Rep 429, at [27], said that a court is obliged to construe a contract in the light of the factual background within which it was concluded, notwithstanding that the document may appear to have a clear meaning on its face. See generally the discussion at Chap 1.

110 See Lord Browne-Wilkinson in *Linden Gardens Trust Ltd v Lenesta Sludge Disposals Ltd* [1994] AC 85.

111 As, for instance, occurred in *R v Chester and North Wales Legal Aid Area Office (No 12), ex p Floods of Queensferry Ltd* [1998] 1 WLR 1496.

112 A point originally made by Professor Sir Roy Goode in a *Note* at (1979) 42 MLR 553 and subsequently developed by Lord Browne-Wilkinson in the *Linden Gardens* case at [1994] 1 AC 85, at 104. See also *Bawejem Ltd v MC Fabrications Ltd* [1999] BCC 157. In addition to the possibility that the restriction might be intended to prevent a legal assignment, an equitable assignment, or both, Sir Roy also suggested that the restriction might, alternatively, be construed as either a mere personal undertaking which was not intended to prevent a dealing with the relevant rights or as being a provision of such importance that a breach would amount to repudiatory conduct which would entitle the innocent party to terminate the contract for repudiatory breach. Lord Browne-Wilkinson in the *Linden Gardens* case said (at 104) that he thought neither additional interpretation was likely to arise in practice.

113 The *Floods of Queensferry Ltd* case, [1998] 1 WLR 1496. The same view appears to have been taken by Croom-Johnson J in *Helston Securities Ltd v Hertfordshire County Council* [1978] 3 All ER 262, at 263–266.

114 *Don King Productions Inc v Warren* [2000] Ch 291; *Devefi Pty Ltd v Mateffy Pearl Nagy Pty Ltd* [1993] RPC 493 at 505 (Fed Ct of Aust); and *Barbados Trust Co Ltd v Bank of Zambia* [2007] EWCA Civ 148, [2007] 1 Lloyd's Rep 495.

or by the grant of a security interest over the relevant right. An indication of the difficulties that might be presented in going through the process of construction is provided by the outcome of *Don King Productions Inc v Warren*[115] in which it was held that a restriction that prevented a contracting party from assigning, either at law or in equity, the benefit of its rights under a contract would not prevent it from declaring a trust of that benefit. From the perspective of the debtor, if it wishes to ensure that such a view would not be taken in another case, the practical advice must be to make sure that the wording of the relevant restriction clearly covers all of the possible dealings by the creditor that it wishes to prevent.

The public policy argument was initially raised by Professor Sir Roy Goode[116] and was referred to, without deciding the point, by Lord Browne-Wilkinson in *Linden Gardens Trust Ltd v Lenesta Sludge Disposals Ltd.*[117] The point concerns a principle of public policy which is against making property inalienable, as the right of alienation is an incident of ownership.[118] It is submitted, however, that the principle does not have application in this area. From a practical perspective, a debtor does have a legitimate interest in asserting the restriction for the various reasons advanced earlier, which would continue whilst it remains indebted. The legitimacy of the debtor's interest in the restriction (to which the creditor has, presumably, freely consented) should be more than a counterweight to the operation of the public policy seeking to protect the creditor's property rights. In any event, it

12.9.4.3.2

---

[115] [2000] Ch 291. The author criticised that finding in his article at [2003] JIBL 1 and [2003] JIBLR 43. The approach to the construction of the restrictive clause that was taken in the case contrasts with the approach taken in the same case to the construction of the arrangements under which it was said that the declaration of trust arose and does not fit well with the commercially sensible and not strictly literal approach advocated by Lord Steyn in *Sirius International Insurance Co (Publ) v FAI General Insurance Ltd* [2004] UKHL 54; [2004] 1 WLR 3251, at [18]–[19]. Nonetheless, in *obiter* comments, it was suggested by Rix and Waller LJJ in *Barbados Trust Co Ltd v Bank of Zambia* [2007] EWCA Civ 148, [2007] 1 Lloyd's Rep 495 that a distinction could be made, on similar lines to that in the *Don King* case, so that a bar upon legal and equitable assignment might not prevent a declaration of trust. Their Lordships even suggested that a beneficiary under a declaration of trust may be able to enforce the debt directly against the debtor (in a case where the trustee was reluctant to act) by employing the procedure laid down in *Vandepitte v Preferred Accident Ins Corp of New York* [1933] AC 70, even though the obvious reason for the prohibition upon assignment was to prevent the debtor from being sued by such a person. With respect, it is submitted that such reasoning flies in the face of commercial reality and the application of the rules of construction to achieve a commercially sensible result. For that reason, its correctness must be questioned. If the prohibition upon assignment reflected an agreement between the original creditor and the debtor that the debtor should not be placed in a position where it might be sued by someone other than the original creditor, then surely they should be taken also to have intended that the debtor should not be at risk of being sued by a third party via the combined mechanism of a declaration of trust by the original creditor of its rights and the use by the beneficiary under that trust of the *Vanderpitte* procedure. It is a very strange use of the rules of construction that could lead to such an odd result as the judgments contemplated.

[116] In his *Note* at (1979) 42 MLR 553.

[117] [1994] AC 85.

[118] The principle is discussed in *Halsbury's Laws of England* (4th edn reissue), Vol 35, paras 1268–1270.

is submitted that the restriction should not be viewed as something separate from the creditor's property, acting as an impediment preventing the creditor from alienating that property. It is not a matter of the creditor receiving an item of property and then agreeing to a restriction upon the alienation of that property. The restriction actually forms an integral part of the definition of that property. In other words, the nature and character of the creditor's property is the benefit or rights, the chose in action, that it has under the contract and the restriction goes to defining and limiting the scope of the chose. Thus, the restriction is not preventing an alienation of property but forms part of the make-up of the property.

12.9.4.3.3 If that analysis is incorrect, it may still be possible to have a partial restriction upon alienation by the creditor. The operation of the rule of public policy does allow for a partial restriction upon alienation provided that the restriction does not prevent the restricted party from enjoying the substantial right to dispose of its property.[119] Thus, a restriction upon entering into a legal assignment of the party's rights should be permissible if it could assign them equitably or dispose of them by way of a declaration of trust.

12.9.4.3.4 In *Foamcrete (UK) Ltd v Thrust Engineering Ltd*[120] it was suggested in *obiter* comments that a restrictive clause could not be relevant if there was, in order of time, first an assignment of future property which would encompass the relevant contractual rights when they came into existence, and, secondly, the contract containing the rights which was entered into after the date of the assignment. With respect, it is submitted that this is incorrect. An agreement supported by valuable consideration to assign future property, under the principles established in *Tailby v The Official Receiver*,[121] operates so as to bind onto the property when it comes into existence, but to treat that as having been effective from the date of the earlier agreement to assign.[122] It is, however, the property of the assignor/chargor which is bound, and, as previously discussed, the property in this situation is a chose in action whose nature and character is defined and circumscribed by the restriction. Thus, the asset that would fall into the apparent compass of the assignment or charge is not a right free of the restriction but a right defined and circumscribed by the restriction. Put simply, the inherent nature of the asset is that it cannot be assigned or charged and so it cannot fall within the ambit of the assignment or charge. Further, the argument advanced in *Foamcrete* ignores the legitimate expectation of the debtor, for whose protection the restriction exists. The debtor will have contracted on the basis that the debt may not be assigned or charged. At its

---

[119] See, for instance, *Re Rosher, Rosher v Rosher* (1884) 26 ChD 801 in which it was said that a restriction upon alienation to a particular person or class of persons may be permitted.

[120] [2002] BCC 221, at [22]–[33], per Mummery LJ (with whom Keene LJ agreed).

[121] (1888) 13 App Cas 523.

[122] *Re Lind; Industrials Finance Syndicate Ltd v Lind* [1915] 2 Ch 345.

most extreme, the debtor could be faced by an assignment of which it has subsequently been given notice, thereby forcing it to deal with and pay the assignee when it contracted on the basis that its only relationship would be with the original creditor.

12.9.4.4 *Where the debtor's consent may not be unreasonably withheld*

Sometimes the restrictive provision will be qualified by stating that the creditor may not assign etc. its rights without the debtor's consent, such consent not to be unreasonably withheld. A provision along those lines was considered by the Court of Appeal in *Hendry v Chartsearch Ltd*[123] where, in disregard of the clause, there was a purported legal assignment without a request for consent. Evans LJ thought that the assignment might have been effective if, notwithstanding the lack of any request for consent, it would have been unreasonable on the facts for consent to be refused. However, Henry and Millett LJJ held[124] that there could not have been a valid assignment where consent had not been requested at all. Henry LJ said that an assignment could only be valid if either the consent had been granted or, if it had been refused, the court had declared that the consent had been 'unnecessarily' refused.[125] Millett LJ said that the assignment could not proceed unless consent had been given or, following a request, the consent had been unreasonably refused.[126]

The approach that was taken by Henry LJ is supported by the outcome of the later majority decision of the Court of Appeal in *Barbados Trust Co Ltd v Bank of Zambia*.[127] The relevant clause in that case required that the debtor's consent should be sought before an assignment took place, but it went on to provide that the consent should not be unreasonably withheld and would be deemed to have been given if the borrower failed to respond within a stipulated period after the consent was sought. It was held that the failure to receive the debtor's consent or to wait for the period to elapse before proceeding with the purported assignment meant that the purported assignment was entirely ineffective.

12.9.4.4.1

The safest course, when faced with such a provision like that in *Hendry v Chartsearch*, would be to request consent from the debtor. If consent is refused and it is thought that the refusal is unreasonable (and there is no deeming provision similar to that in the *Barbados Trust* case), an application should be made to the court for a declaration that the refusal was unreasonable, before proceeding with the assignment.

12.9.4.4.2

---

[123] [1998] CLC 1382.
[124] At [1998] CLC 1382, at 1393, and 1393–1394, respectively.
[125] [1998] CLC 1382, at 1393.
[126] [1998] CLC 1382, at 1394.
[127] [2007] EWCA Civ 148, [2007] 1 Lloyd's Rep 495.

12.9.5 Negative pledges and anti-disposal provisions in third party contracts[128]

For the purpose of the discussion that follows, the putative assignor is the original creditor and the debt that is to be assigned may fall within the subject matter of an agreement between the original creditor and a third party, such as a financier that has provided funding to the original creditor. It may also fall within the covenants given by the original creditor in a security instrument, such as a mortgage or a charge. Pursuant to the agreement or covenant, the original creditor may have agreed with the third party that the original creditor will not to dispose of, nor give security over, its assets or, at least, the debt or debts that it wishes to assign or over which it wishes to create security. The compass of such a provision will depend upon its drafting and interpretation. For instance, it is not uncommon to find in a loan agreement that the provision permits disposals of business assets at a fair or market value.

12.9.5.1 If the original creditor chooses to ignore the provision when it would be applicable to what the creditor proposes to do and proceeds to assign a debt in breach of it then, obviously, that will amount to a breach of contract on the part of the original creditor. That may, in turn, amount to an event of default under the original creditor's funding arrangements, with the additional risk of triggering cross-default provisions in other agreements. There may also be a claim by the third party against the original creditor in damages for breach of contract. If the third party discovers in time that the original creditor intends to breach its contract, it may be able to obtain an injunction to restrain the threatened breach of the negative stipulation, provided it acts expeditiously and has not condoned the proposed breach, relying upon the principle propounded by Lord Cairns LC in *Doherty v Allman*.[129] It is unusual, however, for a third party to be given advance warning by a person in the position of the original creditor, that the latter intends to breach its contract.

12.9.5.2 The aggrieved third party may also wish to visit its anger upon the assignee. It will not have a contractual claim against the assignee. Instead, it will have to ground its claim in the economic tort of inducing or procuring a breach of contract. If it succeeds, it should be able to claim tortious damages which, however, may be difficult to establish in a substantial amount. More importantly, the third party may be able to obtain an injunction against the assignee, to prevent the assignee from relying upon or benefiting from the assignment.[130] To succeed in establishing that

---

[128] This matter is discussed in Chap 3. For a more detailed treatment of this subject, see the author's article, *Restrictions on Dealing with Assets in Financing Documents: Their Role, Meaning and Effect* [2002] JIBL 193. See also the review by Lord Hoffmann of the torts of inducing a breach of contract and causing loss by unlawful means, which is contained in his speech in *OBG Ltd v Allan; Douglas v Hello! Ltd; Mainstream Properties v Young* [2007] UKHL 21.

[129] (1878) 3 App Cas 709.

[130] As was contemplated by Browne-Wilkinson J in *Swiss Bank Corpn v Lloyds Bank Ltd* [1979] Ch 548.

the tort has been committed, however, the third party must prove that the assignee acted with sufficient knowledge of the relevant contractual provision[131] and that it intended, in the sense of having a specific subjective intention, to cause the claimant harm.[132] If the assignee was unaware of the restriction then it cannot be responsible for the consequences of the original creditor's wrongful acts. Furthermore, if the assignee was aware of the relevant contractual stipulation but, before taking the assignment, obtained confirmation from the original creditor that it had obtained the third party's consent to the transaction, it will not have the relevant intention to cause harm to the third party and, once again, it will not be responsible for the consequences.[133]

12.9.6 The debtor's rights of set-off

This issue concerns the effect of an assignment upon rights of set-off that the debtor may have wished to assert against the assignor, had the assignment not occurred. Without the assignment, the effect of such a set-off, where available, would be to reduce the amount of the debt that would be payable by the debtor when the debt fell due for payment, to the extent of the set-off. Thus, if the debt was for an amount of £100 and the debtor had a counter-claim back against its creditor for £25, the debtor's liability would be reduced to a sum of £75. Such a right of set-off may relate to a counter-claim that had accrued either before the date of the assignment or at a later date. It is also relevant to note that, in addition to rights of set-off, the debtor may also wish to raise substantive defences and rights of abatement that were available against the title of the original creditor to sue the debtor. Such a right of abatement, for instance, would arise under section 53(1)(a) of the Sale of Goods Act 1979[134] and the debtor could also raise against the assignee, in a claim for the price of the goods, a defence based upon the debtor's rejection of the goods.

In the context of an assignment of the debt, the question that must be addressed is the extent to which the debtor can assert those rights against the assignee or whether the assignee takes free of them, leaving the debtor in the position that it must make a separate claim against the assignor for rights which it might, but for the assignment, have been entitled to claim a right of set-off or abatement.

12.9.6.1

---

[131] Ibid. Sir John Donaldson MR in *Merkur Island Shipping Corpn v Laughton* [1983] 2 AC 570, at 591, suggested that 'almost certain knowledge' would suffice, which gains some support by the approach that was taken by Lord Hoffmann in *OBG Ltd v Allan; Douglas v Hello; Mainstream Properties Ltd v Young* [2007] UKHL 21; [2007] 4 All ER 545, at [39]–[44].

[132] *OBG Ltd v Allan; Douglas v Hello; Mainstream Properties Ltd v Young* [2007] UKHL 21, [2007] 4 All ER 545.

[133] Ibid.

[134] Although Hoffmann LJ in *Aectra Refining & Marketing Inc v Exmar NV* [1994] 1 WLR 1643, at 1648–1649, included a common law abatement of the price of goods or services for breach of warranty as a form of transaction or equitable set-off.

12.9.6.2 The underlying position as to the availability to the debtor of rights of set-off or abatement that it can assert against an assignee was set out by James LJ in *Roxburghe v Cox*,[135] who said as follows:

> Now an assignee of a chose in action . . . takes subject to all rights of set-off and other defences which were available against the assignor.[136]

In practice, the two particular rights of set-off to which this principle applies are rights of legal set-off and rights of transaction or equitable set-off to which the debtor may be entitled. For this purpose, rights of abatement are treated as if they were rights of transaction set-off. In an historic sense, the principle was originally applied in the context of equitable assignments but it has been held that the principle applies as much to an assignment at law under section 136 of the Law of Property Act 1925 as it does to an equitable assignment. This is because section 136 makes express provision that the assignment is 'subject to equities having priority over the right of the assignee' and such equities include the same rights of set-off as would be available to the debtor in the context of an equitable assignment.[137]

12.9.6.3 The debtor may be precluded, however, from asserting rights of set-off against its original creditor by a clause in the contract to that effect,[138] and if the debtor cannot assert the set-off against the original creditor then, similarly, it will be unable to do so against the assignee. The effectiveness of such a clause is dependent upon its interpretation.[139] It may also be subject to the operation of the Unfair Contract Terms Act 1977[140] and the Unfair Terms in Consumer Contracts Regulations 1999.[141]

---

[135] (1881) 17 ChD 520, at 526.

[136] See also Lord Hobhouse in *Government of Newfoundland v Newfoundland Railway Co* (1888) 13 App Cas 199, at 212–213.

[137] *Lawrence v Hayes* [1927] 2 KB 111, at 120–121 and *E Pfeiffer Weinkellerei-Weineinkauf GmbH v Arbuthnot Factors Ltd* [1988] 1 WLR 150. See also Buxton LJ in *Smith v Muscat* [2003] EWCA Civ 962; [2003] 1 WLR 2853, at [47].

[138] See *Coca-Cola Financial Corp v Finsat International Ltd* [1998] QB 43; *John Dee Group v WMH (21) Ltd* [1998] BCC 972; *International Lease Finance Corp v Buzz Stansted Ltd* [2004] EWHC 292 (Comm).

[139] See *Connaught Restaurants v Indoor Leisure* [1994] 1 WLR 501; *The Teno* [1997] 2 Lloyd's Rep 289; *BOC Group v Centeon* [1999] 1 All ER (Comm) 970.

[140] See *Stewart Gill Ltd v Horatio Meyer & Co Ltd* [1992] QB 600, in which it was held by the Court of Appeal that a clause in an equipment lease which purported to prevent the lessee from asserting a right to set off its claims against the lessor, for defects in the leased goods, against the lessee's obligation to pay rent, had the effect under s 13(1)(b) of the Act of unreasonably excluding or restricting a party from pursuing a right or remedy in respect of a liability of the other party, which would itself have been subject to the provisions of s 3 of the Act. Not all anti-set-off provisions will fall within the compass of the Act, as demonstrated by *Governor & Co of the Bank of Scotland v Singh* (unreported, HHJ Kershaw QC, sitting in the High Court in Manchester, 17/6/2005).

[141] SI 1999/2083. In particular, see para (b) of Sched 2 to the Regulations. Not all anti-set-off provisions in consumer contracts will be caught by the Regulations: See *Governor & Co of the Bank of Scotland v Singh*.

12.9.6.4 Legal rights of set-off

The rights of legal set-off[142] which the debtor can assert against the assignee were summarised by Templeman J in *Business Computers Ltd v Anglo-African Leasing Ltd*.[143] A separate and unconnected debt or other liquidated sum which has accrued due by the assignor to the debtor before the date on which notice of the assignment is received by the debtor, whether or not it is payable before that date, may be set-off by the debtor against the assignee. If such a debt or sum has not accrued due, even though it arises under a contract made before such date, it may not be set-off.[144] The latter would be the position, for instance, where rent falls due by a tenant after the date the notice of an assignment was received, even though the lease of the property was entered into before that date.[145] It would also be the case in relation to a cross-claim by the debtor that relates to a wrongful repudiation by its creditor of a separate hire purchase agreement which was entered into before notice of assignment was received by the debtor but where the repudiation was not accepted until after that date.[146]

12.9.6.5 Equitable transaction set-off

The rights of equitable or transaction set-off which the debtor can assert against the assignee were summarised by Buxton LJ in *Smith v Muscat*,[147] who took the position as laid down by Lord Hobhouse in *Government of Newfoundland v Newfoundland Railway Co*.[148] In essence, there must be an inseparable connection between the dealings and transactions which give rise to the assigned debt and the claim of the debtor which it seeks to set-off.[149] Usually, the assigned right will be a

---

[142] As to a legal right of set-off and the distinction between that and equitable or transaction set-off, see Lord Hoffmann in *Stein v Blake* [1996] AC 243, at 251, Hoffmann LJ in *Aectra Refining & Marketing Inc v Exmar NV* [1994] 1 WLR 1643, at 1649–1653 and Clarke LJ in *Glencore Grain Ltd v Agros Trading Co Ltd* [1999] 2 Lloyd's Rep 410, at 415–417.

[143] [1977] 1 WLR 578.

[144] See also *Christie v Taunton, Delmard, Lane & Co* [1893] 2 Ch 175 and Clauson J in *In re Pinto Leite and Nephews, ex p Visconde des Olivaes* [1929] 1 Ch 221, at 233 and 236.

[145] *Watson v Mid Wales Railway Co* (1867) LR 2 CP 593.

[146] The *Business Computers* case itself. By contrast, hire which had fallen due in that case before the notice of assignment of the separate debt was received could be set-off.

[147] [2003] EWCA Civ 962; [2003] 1 WLR 2853, at [47]–[50]. Buxton LJ also provided a summary of the nature of equitable or transaction set-off, at [37]–[45]. Further guidance is provided in the cases mentioned at n 142 above and by Potter LJ in *Bim Kemi AB v Blackburn Chemicals Ltd* [2001] EWCA Civ 457, [2001] 2 Lloyd's Rep 93.

[148] (1888) 13 App Cas 199, at 212–213.

[149] It is respectfully submitted that the test was mis-stated by Templeman J in the *Business Computers* case, where his Lordship said, at 585, that the two claims should arise out of the same contract or that the claim to be set-off should be closely connected with that contract. In the *Government of Newfoundland* case, Lord Hobhouse said, at 212–213, that there was 'no universal rule that claims arising out of the same contract may be set against one another in all circumstances'. As was made clear by Potter LJ in *Bim Kemi AB v Blackburn Chemicals Ltd* [2001] EWCA Civ 457, [2001] 2 Lloyd's Rep 93, what is important is that the claims should have an 'inseparable connection'

liquidated sum and the set-off will be in respect of an unliquidated claim for damages, but the right to equitable set-off can also be asserted where both the claims are for unliquidated damages.[150]

12.9.6.6 Successive assignments

The position is complicated if there have been successive assignments of the original debt owed by the debtor to the original creditor.[151] The debtor should be able to assert rights of set-off that arise as between the debtor and the original creditor, on the basis and to the extent outlined above. The debtor should also be able to assert a legal set-off as between the debtor and the ultimate assignee, where notice has been given of that assignment, for the reasons outlined below. The question then arises as to whether the debtor should be entitled to assert, as against the ultimate assignee, a set-off with respect to a claim of the debtor against an intermediate assignee, particularly a claim to legal set-off. The position would appear to be that if the intermediate assignment was merely equitable and no notice of the assignment was given to the debtor, the ultimate assignee should not be affected by the claim of the debtor against the intermediate assignee, because the ultimate assignee is asserting the rights, and suing in the name, of the original creditor, not those of the intermediate assignee.[152] However, if the intermediate assignment was effective at law under section 136 of the Law of Property Act 1925 or, perhaps, if it was an equitable assignment that was notified to the debtor,[153] the debt would be enforceable by the assignee in its own right and the ultimate assignee would be suing upon an assignment of that right and so would be subject to the equities available against the intermediate assignee.[154] This should be the case whether the assignment to the ultimate assignee was equitable or statutory.

12.9.6.7 Direct counter-claims against the assignee

Where the assignee, in its own name, sues the debtor then the debtor should also be able to assert any legal right of set-off for a separate liquidated claim that may have accrued due to it by the assignee. This is a simple application of the

---

even if they come about under different, but closely related, contracts arising out of a long-standing trading relationship.

[150] See Potter LJ in the *Bim Kemi* case, at [21]–[23].

[151] See the discussion on this point in Derham, *The Law of Set-off* (3rd edn, 2003), at paras 17.47–17.50.

[152] See Parker J in *Banco Central SA v Lingoss and Falce Ltd, The Raven* [1980] 2 Lloyd's Rep 266, at 273.

[153] By application of the decision of the House of Lords in *William Brandt's Sons & Co v Dunlop Rubber Co Ltd* [1905] AC 454, in which it was held that the equitable assignee could sue in its own name. This was followed by the Court of Appeal in *Three Rivers District Council v Bank of England* [1996] QB 292, in which it was held that the proper person to sue on the assigned claim was the assignee if notice of the equitable assignment had been given to the obligor under the claim.

[154] See Lord Esher MR in *Read v Brown* (1888) 22 QBD 128, at 132.

procedural rights of legal set-off that are available as between the parties to an action at law.

12.9.6.8 *Claims that arise against the assignor after the payment of the debt*

Such claims cannot be the subject of a set-off, for the simple reason that they arose after the payment of the debt. Accordingly, the debtor will be at risk if the debtor pays the assignee and thereafter a claim arises against the assignor, even if the claim is closely connected with the transaction that gave rise to the debt. An example would be a claim based upon a total failure of consideration concerning the underlying transaction between the debtor and the assignor. In such a case, the debtor must seek its refund from the original creditor and not the assignee whom it paid, despite the fact that the assignee has the money and the original creditor may by then be insolvent.[155]

12.9.7 Priorities

In English law it is possible for one, two, or several people to claim proprietary interests in the same asset, whether by way of ownership or security, particularly if the asset is a chose in action such as a debt. Such an extravagance of interests arises from the recognition that is given to the possible existence of legal and equitable interests in assets,[156] to transactions taking place at law or in equity and the willingness of equity to contemplate the possibility of several different equitable interests existing at the same time in an asset.

A dichotomy of interests may be perfectly acceptable on the facts of the particular   12.9.7.1
case and the claims will then be ranked in the order that those involved will understand and expect. An example is the case of a single creditor which has taken security from a borrower. Each of them has an interest in the same asset, but the secured creditor's interest should prevail to the extent of its legitimate interest. Another example is where two creditors have taken forms of fixed security over the same asset.[157] If the second in time has done this with its eyes wide open and in knowledge of the earlier security, then it will expect to rank behind the first

---

[155] *Pan Ocean Shipping Co Ltd v Creditcorp Ltd* [1994] 1 WLR 161.

[156] Note, however, that if there is only one person with an interest in an asset, that interest can only be the full comprehensive legal title, as it is not possible to have a separate legal and equitable title vested in one person if there is no other person with an interest in the asset: see Viscount Radcliffe in *Commissioner of Stamp Duties (Qld) v Livingstone* [1965] AC 694, at 712; Slade J in *Re Bond Worth Ltd* [1980] Ch 228; and Lord Browne-Wilkinson in *Westdeutsche Landesbank Girozentrale v Islington LBC* [1996] AC 669, at 706.

[157] The position will be different if one of the securities is by way of floating charge, as the granting of a subsequent fixed security is likely to fall within the ordinary course of the chargor's business and will thus be given priority over the earlier floating charge: *Re Benjamin Cope & Sons Ltd* [1914] 1 Ch 800. Similarly, a purchaser will usually take free of the floating charge: *Re Florence Land and Public Works Co, ex p Moor* (1878) 10 ChD 530; *Hamer v London, City & Midland Bank Ltd* (1918) 87 LJKB 973, even if the floating charge instrument contains provisions restricting the chargor's

creditor,[158] at least, in so far as the first creditor has made advances before it learns of the second security.[159] Nonetheless, they will each have a proprietary interest in that asset, but the second creditor's interest will be subject to the prior rights of the first secured creditor. Alternatively, the two secured creditors may agree between themselves as to the ranking of their respective interests, under a priority agreement which should be determinative of their respective positions.[160]

12.9.7.2 Unfortunately, situations may arise where there is not such harmony and there will then be a battle for supremacy, or, to give it the correct terminology, there will be a competition for priority between the competing interests. This might arise because of fraud on the part of a party granting an interest in an asset, or through a mistake or administrative oversight. There are rules to resolve the conflict which are of a somewhat piecemeal nature and which tend to depend upon the nature of the particular asset concerned. Nonetheless, the effect of notice looms large in this. It should also be noted that the priority conflict may exist between different types of interest (e.g. legal v equitable, equitable v equitable, security v security, purchaser v security, and purchaser v purchaser), and the resolution of the conflict may have to cross over between the different interests.

12.9.7.3 The basic rule

The basic rule of priorities as between competing interests in a chose in action, such as a debt, is that, where the equities are equal, the first in time prevails.[161]

12.9.7.4 The rule in Dearle v Hall

That basic rule, however, is subject to the operation of the rule in *Dearle v Hall*,[162] which is to the effect that the holder of the second interest in time[163] may displace

---

right to deal with the charged property: see Slade J in *Siebe Gorman & Co Ltd v Barclays Bank Ltd* [1979] 2 Lloyd's Rep 142, at 160.

[158] Save in the case where the second security is a purchase money security interest taken to secure an advance to fund the purchase price of the asset. See *Abbey National Building Soc v Cann* [1991] 1 AC 56.

[159] See s 94 of the Law of Property Act 1925 (which applies with respect to assets other than registered land). Once the earlier security holder receives notice of the later security, it is in danger of losing its priority for any further advances it makes. Much the same will apply if the earlier security holder receives notice of a purchaser's interest and continues to make advances: *Siebe Gorman & Co Ltd v Barclays Bank Ltd* [1979] 2 Lloyd's Rep 142.

[160] *Cheah v Equiticorp Finance Group Ltd* [1992] AC 472 and see, also, s 94(1)(a) of the Law of Property Act 1925. It is also possible by agreement to regulate the priorities between a purchase interest and a security interest.

[161] See Phillips J in *E Pfeiffer Weinkellerei-Weineinkauf GmbH v Arbuthnot Factors Ltd* [1988] 1 WLR 150, at 161–163 and Mummery J in *Compaq Computer Ltd v Abercorn Group Ltd* [1991] BCC 484, at 497–502.

[162] *Dearle v Hall, Loveridge v Cooper* (1828) 3 Russ 1, 38 ER 475. A comprehensive exposition of the rule is to be found in Meagher, Gummow and Lehane, *Equity: Doctrines and Remedies* (4th edn, 2002), at paras 8-095 to 8-215.

[163] Other than an interest acquired through an involuntary assignment. However, the holder of such an interest may preserve its priority as against subsequent interests by giving notice to the debtor. See Meagher, Gummow and Lehane, at para 8-175.

the priority of the first interest in time if it meets two conditions. First, that at the time that value was given for the second interest,[164] its holder had no notice of the first interest. Secondly, that notice of the second interest in time was given to the debtor before notice was given to the debtor of the first interest in time.[165] The same approach applies if there is a multiplicity of competing interests, so that the holder of a later interest will prevail over an earlier interest of which it was unaware when it gave value, provided that notice is given to the debtor of the later interest before notice of the earlier interest is given to the debtor.

The rule in *Dearle v Hall* applies to competitions resulting from assignments of equitable interests and equitable assignments of legal interests.[166] It has also been held to apply where the competition involves a legal assignment under section 136 of the Law of Property Act 1925,[167] thereby displacing the possible operation of a rule in favour of the bona fide purchaser of the legal estate taking without notice of an earlier equitable interest. This was explained by Phillips J in *E Pfeiffer Weinkellerei-Weineinkauf GmbH v Arbuthnot Factors Ltd*.[168] Section 136 provides that the effectiveness of an assignment under that section is to be 'subject to equities having priority over the right of the assignee'. Section 136 replaced section 25(6) of the Judicature Act 1873 but intended to re-enact the earlier provision. Section 25(6) had used slightly different wording when it said that an assignment under section 25(6) was 'subject to all equities which would have been entitled to priority over the right of the assignee if this Act had not been passed'. As it was not possible to have assignments at law of choses in action before section 25(6) was enacted, the intention was that whilst conferring the procedural advantages upon an assignee of being able to sue the debtor at law, the priority rules that applied beforehand should continue and be equally applicable to legal assignments as they were to equitable assignments.

12.9.7.4.1

---

164 The rule does not apply for the benefit of a volunteer who seeks to assert priority over an earlier interest: see Chadwick J in *United Bank of Kuwait plc v Sahib* [1997] Ch 107, at 119–120. However, an earlier volunteer who has given notice to the debtor will gain priority over a subsequent purchaser: *Mutual Life Assurance Soc v Langley* (1886) 32 ChD 460.

165 As notice must be given to the debtor, it is not possible for the purpose of gaining priority under the rule to give notice before the debt has come into existence (as opposed to giving notice where the debt exists but is payable in the future). Hence, where there is an assignment of future property, it is not effective to give notice to someone who may become a debtor in the future. The notice can only be given once the debt has come into existence. See the discussion on this point in Meagher, Gummow and Lehane, at para 8-165.

166 *Marchant v Morton Down & Co* [1901] 2 KB 829; Phillips J in *E Pfeiffer Weinkellerei-Weineinkauf GmbH v Arbuthnot Factors Ltd* [1988] 1 WLR 150, at 163; Mummery J in *Compaq Computer Ltd v Abercorn Group Ltd* [1991] BCC 484, at 498–499.

167 See Phillips J in *E Pfeiffer Weinkellerei-Weineinkauf GmbH v Arbuthnot Factors Ltd* [1988] 1 WLR 150, at 161–163 and Mummery J in *Compaq Computer Ltd v Abercorn Group Ltd* [1991] BCC 484, at 497–502.

168 [1988] 1 WLR 150, at 161.

12.9.7.4.2 There are two circumstances in which the rule in *Dearle v Hall* may not apply, although the position is not entirely clear. The first is where the holder of the postponed interest manages to get in payment of the debt in a situation where it does not have notice, at the time of receipt of the payment, of the other interest that had priority in the debt. In such a case it has been argued that by getting in the payment, the recipient establishes a legal entitlement in that payment which overreaches the claim of the other party in the debt.[169] Secondly, doubt has been expressed as to whether the rule can apply where the assignor had assigned its beneficial interest under a trust or where such rights as it purportedly acquired were already subject to comprehensive trusts with their own beneficial interests that were inconsistent with the alleged interest of the assignor, so that the assignor really had no beneficial interest that it was capable of assigning.[170]

12.9.7.4.3 It is essential that the party which is attempting to gain priority in reliance upon the rule in *Dearle v Hall* should not have had notice[171] of the earlier interest over which it is claiming priority under the rule. The relevant time for considering if it had notice is the point at which that party gave value for its interest[172] not, if it were earlier, the date it took its interest.

12.9.7.5 Notice

Section 199(1)(ii) of the Law of Property Act 1925[173] provides for the circumstances in which a 'purchaser', which includes a person taking a security interest,[174] is affected by notice of 'any other instrument or matter or any fact or thing', although section 199(3) makes it clear that section 199 is not intended to expand upon the circumstances where, before the statute, a purchaser would have been taken to have knowledge. The circumstances provided for by section 199(1)(ii) are as follows.

---

[169] This point was discussed but left unresolved by Phillips J in *E Pfeiffer Weinkellerei-Weineinkauf GmbH v Arbuthnot Factors Ltd* [1988] 1 WLR 150, at 163 and it was conceded in *Compaq Computer Ltd v Abercorn Group Ltd* [1991] BCC 484 (see at 500).

[170] See Eve J in *Hill v Peters* [1918] 2 Ch 273, at 297; the House of Lords in *BS Lyle Ltd v Rosher* [1959] 1 WLR 8; and the discussion in *Compaq Computer Ltd v Abercorn Group Ltd* [1991] BCC 484, at 499–500. The approaches taken in *Hill v Peters* and in *BS Lyle Ltd v Rosher* have been trenchantly criticised by Meagher, Gummow and Lehane, at paras 8-180 to 8-215. It is clear, at least, from *BS Lyle Ltd v Rosher* that the rule in *Dearle v Hall* will apply to successive assignments of the same interest, where the assignor did have an interest capable of assignment at the time of the first of those assignments, albeit that the assignor had thereby evinced an intention to deprive itself of anything that it could further assign under the subsequent assignment.

[171] Including constructive notice: *Spencer v Clarke* (1878) 9 ChD 137.

[172] *Mutual Life Assurance Society v Langley* (1886) 32 ChD 460.

[173] S 199(1)(i) concerns transactions to which the Land Charges Act 1925 might apply.

[174] See s 205(1)(xxi) of the Law of Property Act 1925.

First, if the relevant matter is within the purchaser's own knowledge,[175] that is, it **12.9.7.5.1**
has actual notice of the matter. This would probably include reasonably explicit
information, even if it has come from a disinterested person.[176]

Secondly, a purchaser will have notice of any matter imputed to it by virtue of the **12.9.7.5.2**
actual or constructive knowledge of the purchaser's agent, including its legal representative, provided that the agent has come by that knowledge whilst acting in
the same transaction.[177] It has been held that this will only apply if the knowledge
came to the agent whilst acting on behalf of the principal.[178]

Thirdly, a purchaser will be affected by constructive notice, which will be relevant **12.9.7.5.3**
in cases where the purchaser has made no enquiries or where the enquiries that
were made were insufficient. Because of its importance, it is relevant to examine
the doctrine of constructive notice in further detail.

12.9.7.6 Constructive notice

A purchaser (which, as noted above, includes a person taking a security interest)
will have constructive notice of those matters that would have come to the purchaser's knowledge if it had conducted such enquiries and inspections as ought
reasonably to have been made.[179] What is reasonable will be judged by the standard of what would usually be done as a matter of prudence in the protection of
their interests by men of business in similar circumstances.[180] Nonetheless, Lindley
LJ said in *Manchester Trust v Furness*[181] that the doctrine of constructive notice
generally does not apply to commercial transactions. It is doubtful, however, if
this goes much further than giving a purchaser protection in cases concerning the
sale of goods in the ordinary course of business, as it would not be practical to
require such a person to undertake extensive investigations, in contrast to what

---

175 S 199(1)(ii)(a).
176 *Lloyd v Banks* (1868) LR 3 Ch App 488.
177 S 199(1)(ii)(b).
178 *Société Generale de Paris v Tramways Union Co Ltd* (1884) 14 QBD 424; *Halifax Mortgage Services Ltd v Stepsky* [1996] Ch 207.
179 S 199(1)(ii)(a).
180 *Bailey v Barnes* [1894] 1 Ch 25, at 35; *Abigail v Lapin* [1934] AC 491, at 505–506. See also the approach taken by Millett J at first instance in *Macmillan Inc v Bishopsgate Investment Trust (No 3)* [1995] 1 WLR 978, at 1000 and 1014. This particular aspect did not arise in the judgments in the Court of Appeal, which affirmed the result at first instance on other grounds (at [1996] 1 WLR 387).
181 [1895] 2 QB 539, at 545–546. See also Neill J in *Feuer Leather Corp v Frank Johnstone & Sons* [1981] Comm LR 251 (a sale of goods case).

would be undertaken in a conveyancing transaction.[182] As Millett J said in *Macmillan Inc v Bishopsgate Investment Trust (No 3)*:[183]

> It is true that many distinguished judges in the past have warned against the extension of the equitable doctrine of constructive notice to commercial transactions (see *Manchester Trust v Furness* . . . per Lindley LJ), but they were obviously referring to the doctrine in its strict conveyancing sense with its many refinements and its insistence on a proper investigation of title in every case. The relevance of constructive notice in its wider meaning cannot depend on whether the transaction is 'commercial': the provision of secured overdraft facilities to a corporate customer is equally 'commercial' whether the security consists of the managing director's house or his private investments. The difference is that in one case there is, and in the other case there is not, a recognised procedure for investigating the mortgator's title which the creditor ignores at his peril.

12.9.7.6.1   In an analogous area of liability for knowing receipt of trust property, the courts have sometimes been prepared to admit liability based upon constructive knowledge, rather than actual knowledge.[184] Furthermore, in *Spencer v Clarke*[185] it was held that a purchaser of a life policy by way of equitable assignment, who gave notice to the relevant life company, was affected by constructive notice of an earlier equitable mortgage of the policy because the earlier equitable mortgagee had possession of the policy documents. That should have put the subsequent purchaser on enquiry, which enquiry the purchaser failed to make, relying upon a deceitful excuse proffered by the assignor as to why the documents were unavailable.

12.9.7.6.2   Of particular relevance, in the context of constructive notice, is the question of whether it would be reasonable to expect a person taking an interest in a debt from a company, whether the interest to be taken is to be by way of security or purchase, to search the register of company charges maintained under section 860 et seq of the Companies Act 2006[186] before the interest is taken, so as to ascertain if any security over the debt was already registered against the person from whom the interest was to be taken.[187] It would appear from the passage in *Macmillan Inc v Bishopsgate Investment Trust (No 3)* which is quoted above that Millett J would expect a person taking security to make the usual enquiries, such as by conducting searches which, it is submitted, should include a search of the register of charges where the person giving the security is a company. By similar reasoning, where the

---

[182] See Goode, *Commercial Law* (3rd edn, 2004), at p 666.

[183] [1995] 1 WLR 978, at 1000, but see n 180 above.

[184] See, for instance, Millett J in *Agip (Africa) Ltd v Jackson* [1990] 1 Ch 265, at 291–292; Richardson J in *Westpac Banking Corp v Savin* [1985] NZLR 41, at 53; and Nourse LJ in *Bank of Credit and Commerce International (Overseas) Ltd v Akindele* [2001] Ch 437, at 450 and 455.

[185] (1878) LR 9 ChD 137.

[186] Formerly s 395 et seq of the Companies Act 1985.

[187] S 860(7)(f) of the Companies Act 2006 (formerly s 396(1)(e) of the Companies Act 1985) requires that a charge given by a company over its book debts should be registered. See n 157 above as to the effect of an earlier floating charge.

seller of a debt is a company and the purchaser is a financial institution, it would be reasonable to expect the purchaser to make such a search.

12.9.7.7 Further advances

Where the interest which has priority[188] is a security interest, the holder of that security is in danger of losing its priority for any advances that it makes after it receives notice of a subsequent security or purchase interest. Under section 94 of the Law of Property Act 1925, which applies with respect to assets other than registered land,[189] a prior mortgagee[190] which makes advances after it receives notice[191] of a subsequent mortgage or charge will lose priority under its security for those advances unless the second security holder agreed that the priority would be preserved or the prior security holder was obliged by the terms of its security instrument to make the advances. Whilst the receipt of notice will not affect its priority for advances made before the notice was received, the prior security holder will be in danger of effectively losing that priority if it is lending upon a revolving account, with advances made by withdrawals from the account and repayments being credited to the account, by virtue of the operation of the rule in *Clayton's* case.[192] This can be overcome by ruling off the account and opening a new account from which further advances are made and into which repayments are credited, thereby preserving the protected position for advances that were outstanding when the notice was received.

Section 94 does not apply where the subsequent interest is a purchase interest **12.9.7.7.1** rather than a security interest but much the same consequences will follow. In *Siebe Gorman & Co Ltd v Barclays Bank Ltd*[193] Slade J held that a prior security holder, whose fixed security encompassed certain specific debts[194] due to the chargor and which continued in its discretion to make advances after receiving notice of a purchaser's interest in those debts which the purchaser had acquired by assignment, should have its security for those further advances postponed behind the interest of the purchaser of those debts. His Lordship held that it would be

---

188 Either under the first in time rule or under the rule in *Dearle v Hall*, n 162 above.

189 To which there are separate provisions that apply under s 49 of the Land Registration Act 2002.

190 Which expression includes a chargee, by virtue of s 205.

191 It is submitted that such notice would have to be actual notice and that constructive notice, such as by virtue of the registration of the second security under s 860 of the Companies Act 2006 (formerly s 395 of the Companies Act 1985), would be insufficient notice for the purposes of s 94. It would not be reasonable to expect the prior security holder to conduct a search before each occasion on which it makes a further advance. It might, however, be reasonable to expect it to search before making its first advance, if there was a gap in time between the date it took its security and the date it made the advance.

192 *Devaynes v Noble, Clayton's Case* (1816) LJ Ch 256, 35 ER 767. This was the position under the general law before s 94 was introduced: *Deeley v Lloyds Bank Ltd* [1912] AC 756.

193 [1979] 2 Lloyd's Rep 142.

194 In fact, they were rights in negotiable instruments.

inequitable to allow the security holder to assert its priority for advances it made with notice of the purchaser's interest, to the detriment of the purchaser, when it had not been obliged to make those advances. It follows that if the security holder had been under a committed obligation to make the further advances, it would have been able to assert its priority for those further advances.

12.9.8 The risk of re-characterisation

Re-characterisation is the process by which a transaction that has the appearance of, or is labelled as being, one type of transaction is held by the courts to be another type of transaction. Different considerations and consequences may apply in such a case to those that would have been relevant to the transaction in its originally intended form. In the context of financing transactions,[195] this issue may arise where finance has been provided to a person on the strength of a supposed acquisition by the provider of the finance of an outright proprietary interest in assets that were previously owned by that person or which are in that person's use. In relation to the purchase, through an assignment, of debts that are or may become owing to the seller,[196] the argument may be advanced that the transaction, when taken as a whole, really represents an extension of finance to the seller on the strength of security that it has given over the debts, rather than through an outright purchase of the debts. In other words, that a proprietary transaction that has the superficial appearance of a sale is more truly a transaction under which credit was extended to the transferor in return for the transferor creating a proprietary interest in the debts in favour of the supplier of the credit, such interest being by way of security rather than an outright sale.

12.9.8.1 The argument is most likely to arise in the context of a liquidation or administration of the transferor, because it is unlikely that the assignment would have been registered as a 'charge' under section 860 of the Companies Act 2006.[197] If it really was a charge, it should have been lodged for registration with the Companies Registry within the prescribed period.[198] Failure to do so has the result that the security is avoided[199] as against the relevant insolvency practitioner or another

---

[195] The issue may arise in other areas, such as in the fields of landlord and tenant (see *Street v Mountford* [1985] AC 809 and *Bruton v London & Quadrant Housing Trust* [2001] 1 AC 406) and taxation (see *Furniss v Dawson* [1984] AC 474).

[196] The point has also been raised, in the context of financing transactions, in relation to requirements under the Bills of Sale Act (1878) Amendment Act 1882 and legislation that is now repealed, such as the Moneylenders Acts 1900–1927 and the Hire Purchase Acts 1938–1965.

[197] Formerly s 395(1) of the Companies Act 1985.

[198] Either as a charge over book debts under s 860(7)(f) of the Companies Act 2006 (formerly s 396(1)(e) of the Companies Act 1985) or as a floating charge under s 860(7)(g) of the Companies Act 2006 (formerly s 396(1)(f) of the Companies Act 1985).

[199] Under s 874(1) of the Companies Act 2006 (formerly s 395(1) of the Companies Act 1985). Under s 874(3) of the Companies Act 2006 (formerly s 395(2) of the Companies Act 1985), the

secured creditor.[200] A further risk that could then follow is that the nature of the security would be characterised as a floating charge[201] with the disadvantages that are suffered by such a security.[202]

It is also possible that other persons might raise an argument as to the true nature of the transaction. For instance, the point has been raised in relation to a negative pledge provision in a security document which prevented a company from creating other security over its assets. The question then turned upon whether a subsequent proprietary transaction, which the parties intended to be by way of sale, had been entered into in breach of that provision, which would have been the case if it were to be re-characterised as a form of security.[203]

12.9.8.2

12.9.8.3 *The bases for challenge*

There are two bases in English law for challenging the nature of a transaction.[204] The first is that the outward form of the transaction is a sham, deliberately designed

---

amount secured by the security becomes immediately payable, which is not of very much practical use if the chargor is insolvent.

200 The liquidator or administrator would be acting in a representative capacity on behalf of the chargor and its unsecured creditors: *Smith (Administrator of Cosslett (Contractors) Ltd) v Bridgend CBC* [2002] 1 AC 336. A third party with competing security, if registered, may also rely on s 874 (1) of the Companies Act 2006 (formerly s 395(1) of the Companies Act 1985) to claim that the unregistered security is void against the third party: see Lord Brightman (sitting in the Court of Appeal) in *Victoria Housing Estates Ltd v Asphurton Estates Ltd* [1983] 1 Ch 110. In *Orion Finance Ltd v Crown Financial Management Ltd* [1996] BCC 621, the Court of Appeal held that the debtor whose debt had been assigned, with notice, could also take the point that the security was void against it where the assignor was in liquidation or administration, so as to avoid the double jeopardy of being liable to the insolvent assignor and being also subject to the risk of a demand by the assignee.

201 In accordance with the approach taken by the Privy Council in *Agnew v Inland Revenue Cmr* [2001] UKPC 28, [2001] 2 AC 710 and by the House of Lords in *National Westminster Bank PLC v Spectrum Plus Ltd* [2005] UKHL 41, [2005] 2 AC 680.

202 E.g. that it has to defer to the claims of the preferential creditors of the chargor under ss 40 and 175(2)(b) of the Insolvency Act 1986 and s 754 of the Companies Act 2006 (formerly s 196 of the Companies Act 1985), and that there will be depredations from recoveries in the hands of an insolvency practitioner on enforcement, to be placed into a fund for the unsecured creditors of the chargor pursuant to s 176A of the Insolvency Act 1986 (as amended). It is also possible that third party purchasers with a rival claim in the assets may claim that they have priority over the security if they have taken their interests in consequence of disposals by the chargor in the ordinary course of business.

203 *Welsh Development Agency v Export Finance Co Limited* [1991] BCLC 936 and [1992] BCLC 148.

204 See the review provided by Millett LJ in *Orion Finance Ltd v Crown Financial Management Ltd* [1996] BCC 621, at 625–627. The facts in that case did not involve an assignment of debts or receivables in the usual types of debt financing transactions. Instead, the case involved a situation where the rental stream payable to the assignor under an equipment lease had been assigned with reference to the obligations of the assignor under an associated hire purchase agreement, under which the assignor had financed its acquisition of the equipment. It was argued that the assignment was the consideration provided in satisfaction of the obligations of the assignor under the hire purchase agreement. The Court of Appeal held, however, that the assignor retained an interest in the assigned rental stream and that the assignment was by way of security for the assignor's obligations under the hire purchase agreement. Such security was in the nature of a form of non-recourse security (as to the

to cloak its true nature.[205] Challenges on this basis are now rare in the field of financing transactions, as they are tantamount to an allegation of a deliberate attempt to mislead.[206] Secondly, and more probably, the challenge may be mounted on the basis that, despite the descriptive form used by the parties and their expressed intention, when the true legal effect of the transaction as documented is examined, what the parties actually achieved was really a form of security in support of the provision of finance. There is often a fine dividing line in coming to a conclusion on this subject. The discussion that follows will concentrate on the second basis for challenging a transaction.

12.9.8.4 The equity of redemption

If the transaction is one by way of security for finance that has been provided then the person granting the security will have an equity of redemption, that is, the right to regain the unencumbered title in the asset once the secured obligation has been discharged. If the transaction is by way of outright sale, the seller does not retain any interest in the asset it has sold.[207] Unfortunately, the quest does not simply end at this point, as the difficulty is in determining if there is an equity of redemption. The essential question is to discern whether the interest that was conferred upon the transferee is defeasible upon satisfaction of the relevant liability. If so, then, in consequence, the transferor is taken to have retained a proprietary interest in the asset, which is protected by its equity of redemption. The right to the unencumbered title in the asset will revert to it when the liability has been satisfied.[208] It also follows that the transferee will not have acquired an outright interest when it entered into the transaction, but merely an interest by way of security.

---

efficacy of such a form of non-recourse security, see the decision of the House of Lords in *Mathew v Blackmore* (1857) 1 H&N 762, which was followed in *De Vigier v IRC* [1964] 1 WLR 1073.

[205] See, for instance, *North Central Wagon Finance Co Ltd v Brailsford* [1962] 1 WLR 1288.

[206] In *Kensington International Ltd v Republic of the Congo* [2005] EWHC 2684 (Comm) Cooke J explored the basis for the court to look through a sham, and thereby to pierce a corporate veil, in a case involving an allegation that a series of transactions were a sham or a façade to conceal the true nature of the real underlying ownership of assets.

[207] Per Romer LJ in *Re George Inglefield Ltd* [1933] 1 Ch 1 at 28. See also Lord Hoffmann in *Re Bank of Credit & Commerce International SA (No 8)* [1998] AC 214. Romer LJ was attempting to explain the difference between a transaction by way of sale as opposed to one by way of security. He said that a sale conferred an outright title on the purchaser, whereas under a security the obligor had the right to redeem the property. In addition, if the transaction was a sale, the purchaser would be entitled to any profit on re-sale and would suffer the loss if the re-sale was for less than the original price. If the transaction was by way of security, the profit would have to be handed over to the chargor/mortgagor, but if there was an insufficiency, the chargor/mortgagor would have to make up the loss. As Millett LJ pointed out in *Orion Finance Ltd v Crown Financial Management Ltd* [1996] BCC 621, at 625, the additional tests put forward by Romer LJ are not determinative, as it is possible in a sale for the parties to agree how any future profit should be allocated between them, and it is also possible for a secured transaction to be without recourse to the borrower: see *Mathew v Blackmore* (1857) 1 H&N 762 and *De Vigier v IRC* [1964] 1 WLR 1073.

[208] See Slade J in *Re Bond Worth Ltd* [1980] Ch 228, at 248–256 and Millett LJ in *Orion Finance Ltd v Crown Financial Management Ltd* [1996] BCC 621, at 625–627.

12.9.8.5 *The commercial characteristics of the transaction*

The question as to the true nature of a transaction has arisen in a number of cases concerning the purported purchase of portfolios of debts or receivables (such as block discounting transactions), where the debtors had not been notified of the purchase and had continued to treat the seller as their creditor. In those transactions, the seller had often been given a right to re-purchase the debts it had sold and it had undertaken a recourse obligation by way of guaranteeing the payment by the debtors of their debts. In some cases the seller had continued to collect payment from the debtors without having to account for the collections to the purchaser or to hold them on trust pending payment over to the seller. The reason why the seller had been allowed to collect the payments from the debtors, effectively for itself, was because the seller had undertaken its own payment obligation to the purchaser, under which the seller undertook to pay to the purchaser the amount it expected to receive by way of repayment of the financing, irrespective of what, if anything, was collected from the debtors. In other situations, the seller had only been required to account to the seller for a proportion of the collections, equivalent to the finance that had been provided, with the seller retaining any excess that was recovered by it from the debtors. Alternatively, where it was contemplated that payment by the debtor would be collected and so received by the purchaser (e.g. where notice of the assignment had been given to the debtors), the purchaser had undertaken to pay over to the seller the balance remaining once the purchaser had deducted sufficient to be reimbursed for its charges and the finance it had provided.

When such transactions are considered from a purely commercial or economic **12.9.8.5.1** perspective, the overall impression is that they were really no more than a form of secured financing. It appeared that the purchaser was really looking to the seller for the recoupment of the finance provided by the purchaser to the seller, that the seller retained an interest in the debts it had assigned by way of its right to repurchase the debts (and its right to retain or to be paid any balance over the finance it had received), and that the purchaser was only interested in the underlying portfolio of debts as a security backstop. The seller would only intervene for its own account if it decided to enforce its security. Those factors might be taken to indicate that the seller had retained a real connection with the debts it had purported to sell and that it continued to bear the risks and rewards attached to the assets. Seen in that light, it might be difficult to escape the conclusion that such transactions should really be seen as a form of secured lending.

12.9.8.6 *The traditional approach of the courts*

Generally speaking, however, the traditional attitude taken by the English courts in the context of such purported debt or receivables purchase transactions has been against re-characterising them as forms of secured finance. The courts have taken a fairly lenient attitude, in honouring the intention of the parties as expressed in the documentation and giving precedence to legal form over the economic and commercial substance of a transaction. This can particularly be seen from decisions such as those of the Court of Appeal in *Re George Inglefield*[209] and of the House of Lords in *Lloyds & Scottish Finance Ltd v Cyril Lord Carpet Sales Ltd*.[210] It may also be seen, in the context of an apparent sale of chattels, but in reality a financing based on receivables, in the decision of the Court of Appeal in *Welsh Development Agency v Export Finance Co. Ltd*.[211] The following propositions can be drawn from such cases.

12.9.8.6.1 First, that the intention of the parties, as expressed in the documentation, is important in determining the true nature of the transaction. If the parties expressed their intention that the transaction should be by way of sale rather than by way of loan, then the courts will be loath to intervene. Instead, the courts will be prepared to uphold the transaction in the form as so expressed, save in exceptional circumstances.[212]

12.9.8.6.2 Secondly, the mere fact that the transaction concerned the provision of finance should not be determinative, as the real question is whether the finance has been extended by way of loan rather than by some other means.[213] Nor is it relevant that the financier had obtained a proprietary interest, as a form of quasi-security, for its protection.[214]

12.9.8.6.3 Thirdly, the fact that the purchaser had a right of recourse against the seller, should a debtor default in making payment, is not determinative of the position, even if it meant that the seller continued to bear the economic risk associated with the assets that it had sold.[215]

12.9.8.6.4 Fourthly, the seller might legitimately have an option to repurchase the debts it had sold. That is not be taken to represent an equity of redemption, such as would arise if security had been created.[216]

---

[209] [1933] Ch 1.

[210] [1992] BCLC 609 (despite the date of the report, the case was decided in 1979).

[211] [1992] BCLC 148.

[212] The high water mark of such an approach is reflected in the judgments of the Court of Appeal in *Welsh Development Agency v Export Finance Co Ltd* [1992] BCLC 148, but it is also reflected in earlier cases, such as in the opinion of Lord Herschell LC in *McEntire v Crossley Bros Ltd* [1895] AC 457, at 463–466 and in the opinion of Lord Wilberforce in *Lloyds & Scottish Finance Ltd v Cyril Lord Carpet Sales Ltd* [1992] BCLC 609, at 614–619.

[213] See Romer LJ in *Re George Inglefield Ltd* [1933] Ch 1, at 27 and Lord Devlin in *Chow Yoong Hong v Choong Fah Rubber Manufactory* [1962] AC 209, at 216–217.

[214] See Lord Herschell LC in *McEntire v Crossley Bros Ltd* [1895] AC 457, at 465–466 (which was a case concerning equipment financing).

[215] See *Re George Inglefield Ltd* [1933] Ch 1; *Olds Discount Co Ltd v John Playfair Ltd* [1938] 3 All ER 275; and *Lloyds & Scottish Finance Ltd v Cyril Lord Carpet Sales Ltd* [1992] BCLC 609.

[216] See Lord Macnaghten in *Manchester, Sheffield & Lincolnshire Ry Co v North Central Wagon Co* (1888) 13 App Cas 554, at 567–568.

Fifthly, the seller might continue to collect the debts and it was not necessary that it should hold the proceeds of collection separately from its other moneys, nor account for and pay over to the purchaser what it had received from the debtors. Instead, it would be acceptable that the seller should make payments from its own resources to the seller of amounts that were sufficient to recoup to the seller the amount of finance that it had extended.[217]

12.9.8.6.5

Sixthly, the parties might stray in the practical operation of their transaction from the strict requirements as laid down in the documentation without imperilling its nature as a sale.[218]

12.9.8.6.6

Seventhly, the language used in a debt purchase transaction may bear similarities with the language used in a loan, such as by using words like 'repayment' and 'facility'. This would not mean that the transaction should be construed as a loan rather than a sale.[219]

12.9.8.6.7

Eighthly, in *Lloyds & Scottish Finance Ltd v Cyril Lord Carpet Sales Ltd*[220] the House of Lords thought that it was material that in a debt purchase transaction, the purchaser would calculate the consideration for the purchase of a debt by deducting a discount from the face value of the debt, determined at the time of purchase. The discount would be charged without taking into account any factor relating to the time it took for that debt to be paid or the average time that it took for the purchased portfolio of debts to be paid. This was because a factor of the latter type would more closely resemble a calculation of interest on the outstanding amount of loan finance, rather than for a purchase of an asset, to which a discount was more appropriate. Nonetheless, the Court of Appeal in *Welsh Development Agency v Export Finance Co Ltd*[221] came to the conclusion that such a distinction was not material and that there could still be a valid purchase of assets where the purchase price reflected a variable interest calculation which depended on the daily balance of the outstanding amount of finance that had been provided and not recouped.

12.9.8.6.8

12.9.8.7 A change in judicial approach

There may now, however, be a change in judicial attitudes as to the approach that will be taken in the future in characterising transactions, particularly as to the

---

[217] *Re George Inglefield Ltd* [1933] Ch 1; *Olds Discount Co Ltd v Cohen* [1938] 3 All ER 281n; *Olds Discount Co Ltd v John Playfair Ltd* [1938] 3 All ER 275; and *Lloyds & Scottish Finance Ltd v Cyril Lord Carpet Sales Ltd* [1992] BCLC 609.

[218] *Olds Discount Co Ltd v Cohen* [[1938] 3 All ER 281n; *Olds Discount Co Ltd v John Playfair Ltd* [1938] 3 All ER 275; and *Lloyds & Scottish Finance Ltd v Cyril Lord Carpet Sales Ltd* [1992] BCLC 609.

[219] Ibid.

[220] [1992] BCLC 609.

[221] [1992] BCLC 148.

weight that is to be given to the expressed intention of the parties. Lord Millett, in giving the advice of the Privy Council in *Agnew v Inland Revenue Commissioner*[222] (*'Brumark'*) in relation to determining if a charge was fixed or floating, said that the parties' expressed intention was not determinative of the character of the transaction. Their intention was relevant as a matter of construction of the contract, so as to determine what rights and obligations they had wished to confer under the contract. However, the characterisation of the consequences of the transaction was a matter of law.[223] That approach was approved by the House of Lords in *Smith (Administrator of Cosslett (Contractors) Ltd) v Bridgend CBC*,[224] which was a case involving the question of whether the transaction was in the nature of security or something else and, if it was by way of security, if it was a fixed or a floating charge. Lord Millett's approach in *Brumark* was again approved by the House of Lords in *National Westminster Bank PLC v Spectrum Plus Ltd*.[225] The approach taken by Lord Millett in *Brumark* has echoes of what was said by Hoffmann J (as he then was) in *Re Brightlife Ltd*[226] and the approach taken in land law cases concerning the difference between a lease of land and a licence to occupy the land.[227]

12.9.8.7.1 It remains to be seen just how far this new line of judicial approach will, in the future, affect transactions purporting to be by way of an assignment of debts.[228]

---

222 [2001] UKPC 28, [2001] AC 710.

223 The approach that his Lordship took in the *Brumark* case should be compared with the approach that he had taken earlier in the Court of Appeal in *Orion Finance Ltd v Crown Financial Management Ltd* [1996] BCC 621, at 625–627. In the *Orion Finance* case, he said that the court should consider the transaction as represented by the documents and, unless taken as a whole they compelled a different conclusion, the categorisation of the transaction should be done in conformity with the intention of the parties as expressed in the documentation.

224 [2001] UKHL 58, [2002] AC 336. See, in particular, Lord Hoffmann, at [40]–[42] and Lord Scott, at [53].

225 [2005] UKHL 41, [2005] 2 AC 680. See, for instance, Lord Walker, at [141]. It is interesting to note that Lord Walker put this as a matter of public policy rather than simply a matter of the consequence of a transaction as between the parties to it. This contrasts with the approach taken in earlier cases, where the courts discounted the policy argument in favour of the freedom of the parties to so arrange their transactions that they could escape the net of the relevant legislation. See, for instance, Lord Hanworth MR and Romer LJ in *Re George Inglefield Ltd* [1933] Ch 1, at 22–23 and 26–27, respectively.

226 [1987] Ch 200, at 209.

227 See, for instance, Lord Templeman in *Street v Mountford* [1985] AC 809, at 819 and 826; and Lord Hoffmann in *Bruton v London & Quadrant Housing Trust* [2001] 1 AC 406, at 411–412.

228 In its Report, *Company Security Interests* (Law Com No 296, August 2005) the Law Commission recommended that, as part of the new regime for company security interests that it suggested should be adopted in England and Wales, sales of debts ('receivables') by way of factoring or discounting transactions should be treated as the equivalent of a secured transaction and therefore would be registrable transactions by way of 'filing' of a financing statement against the assignor. However, this would only apply to debts or receivables generated under a transaction concerning the supply of goods or services or for energy supplied or generated or as brokerage fees and not the broader type of receivables that feature in some types of securitisation. See Part 4 of the Report (paras 4.1–4.46). It appears very unlikely that the Law Commission's recommendations will be adopted

Given the authority provided by the decision of the House of Lords in *Lloyds & Scottish Finance Ltd v Cyril Lord Carpet Sales Ltd*[229] in relation to the efficacy of debt purchase transactions by way of invoice discounting, it is unlikely that the lower courts would be willing, or indeed able, to upset transactions which followed the pattern of the transaction in that case. In light of the approach taken by the Court of Appeal in *Welsh Development Agency v Export Finance Co Ltd*,[230] it is unlikely that any court under the House of Lords would upset a purported debt purchase transaction, except in a very unusual case.[231] It would need a re-assessment of the position by the House of Lords.[232]

Assuming that such a review were to take place and that the House decided to depart from the liberal view taken in its earlier decision, it is submitted that the likely approach that the courts would then take would be to look at an accumulation of factors in deciding if a transaction was a genuine sale or a form of secured financing. They would not place much reliance upon the label that was given to a transaction by the parties, nor upon the expressed intention of the parties. However, a right of recourse against the seller, an element of the purchase price being deferred or the seller retaining an option for repurchase of the debts (particularly at a market or other realistic value) should not necessarily mean that a transaction would be vulnerable to an attack, as those elements can often be found in a genuine sale transaction.[233] The most vulnerable transactions would be those where the seller continued to collect in the debts effectively for its own account, without having to separate out the proceeds and hold them on trust, pending payment over to the assignee,[234] particularly if the assignor was making payments to the financier of pre-ordained amounts irrespective of the actual amounts received from the debtors.

12.9.8.7.2

---

so, if the matter is to be reviewed and the law changed, the review will have to be undertaken by the courts.

[229] [1992] BCLC 609.

[230] [1992] BCLC 148.

[231] As occurred in the unusual circumstances of *Orion Finance Ltd v Crown Financial Management Ltd* [1996] BCC 621.

[232] In light of the decision by the Court of Appeal in *National Westminster Bank PLC v Spectrum Plus Ltd* [2004] EWCA Civ 670, [2004] Ch 337 (reversed on other grounds: [2005] UKHL 41, [2002] 2 AC 680) as to the binding effect of one of its judgments on future cases before that court, the *Welsh Development Agency* case could only be overruled by a decision of the House of Lords. Of course, in other jurisdictions which follow broadly the English system, such constraints may not be relevant and the courts there might decide to make their own determinations, rather than waiting for a re-consideration by the House of Lords.

[233] As was pointed out by Millett LJ in *Orion Finance Ltd v Crown Financial Management Ltd* [1996] BCC 621.

[234] See, for instance, the approach taken by Jonathan Parker J in *Re ILG Travel Ltd* [1996] BCC 21, at 44–45.

12.10 Securitisation and Structured Finance

12.10.1 Introduction

Structured finance involves an underlying portfolio or pool of debts or debt instruments, which is used as the basis on which finance is raised through an issuance of securities in the capital markets. It combines the techniques relating to the transfer of debts and similar intangible rights with the structures for raising finance through an issuance of debt securities in the capital markets. In effect, the rights of the creditor in the underlying portfolio or pool are devolved, in a commercial sense, upon the investors who hold the securities that are held by investors in the capital markets. A securitisation is the most common method of achieving a structured finance transaction.

12.10.1.1 In its simplest form, a securitisation will involve the sale by the seller which owns a portfolio of debts (commonly called the 'originator') to a purchaser (the 'SPV'), which is a special purpose vehicle set up for the transaction. The SPV raises most of the funds for the purchase by issuing bonds or notes (for simplicity, hereinafter referred to as bonds) to investors. The bonds are secured upon the portfolio of debts and any other assets of the SPV. That portfolio will be assembled on the basis of a perceived track record of quality and low levels of default. The bonds and other securities that are issued in the capital markets are sometimes referred to as 'mortgaged backed', or 'asset backed', securities. Having that backing, the securities have traditionally been awarded a high credit rating by the credit rating agencies and investors were attracted by investments with a low level of risk. The crisis in the financial markets in the second half of 2007 served to challenge those conclusions.

12.10.1.2 It is also possible that such securities may themselves form part of yet another portfolio of debt instruments that are packaged together to form the basis of further issues of debt in the capital markets. Such further issues may take a variety of forms, from commercial paper issued on a revolving basis to medium term notes or longer dated securities. The transactions may, in addition, use derivatives as part of the structure that is employed. The securities that are issued in these transactions are sometimes referred to as 'collateralised debt obligations' or 'CDOs'. They may be issued in single tranches with common rights as between themselves, or in several tranches bearing different levels of risk and commensurate rights to payment.

12.10.1.3 Securitisation is perceived to be an economically efficient method by which an originator may raise funds, as the amount that is raised is based upon the quality, and thus the value, of the underlying pool of debts and debt instruments. It is thought to be more economically efficient than other methods of raising finance because the calculation of risk in relation to the finance that is to be raised is based on the quality of the underlying portfolio, rather than the overall business, including all of the liabilities and assets, of the originator, which is to be the final recipient of the funds that have been raised.

It is crucial to the assessment of the risk that will be undertaken that the whole   **12.10.1.4**
structure of the securitisation is seen as robust, so that it will be unaffected by an insolvency of the originator, that the SPV will acquire high quality assets for a proper value and as their full beneficial owner. It is also crucial that the SPV will be remote from the risk of its own insolvency, that is, that it is unlikely the SPV could become insolvent and that there is adequate support to ensure, from a practical perspective, that it does not become insolvent. Finally, the investors should be protected by a comprehensive security package in case the worst occurs and there is an insolvency of the SPV. Each of these matters will be examined further below.

In addition to the fairly straightforward form of securitisation that has already   **12.10.1.5**
been described, there are other types of structure that are also used. These include securitisations of revolving credits, 'synthetic' securitisations, 'whole business' securitisations, 'covered bonds', and transactions that are secured or protected by insurance cover, referred to as 'monoline' insurance. Those different forms of structured finance transactions, which have commonly been in use, will also be described. It must be remembered, however, that this is a field that has been subject to a great deal of innovation, generated partly by economic and commercial considerations and partly by the need to accommodate issues that arise in consequence of conflict of laws and other jurisdictional considerations.[235] Another important factor that arose in the second part of 2007 was the widespread doubt in the financial markets as to the safety of a number of these types of transaction, so it may be that the future may not see as much activity and innovation as has been experienced heretofore. After providing descriptions of the transactions, most of the remaining discussion will concentrate on matters of immediate concern under English law in a straightforward 'true sale' transaction, but many of the issues discussed will also be relevant in other types of transaction as well.

To complete these introductory comments, it is appropriate to give some idea of   **12.10.1.6**
the volume of transactions that have taken place. In 2005, structured finance transactions amounted to some 43 per cent of the global amount of debt instruments in issue in the capital markets, an increase of some 26 per cent from the previous year. In absolute figures, that amounted to approx. US$2,524 billion in volume.[236]

---

[235] For instance, the use of structures that use 'Fonds Commun de Créances' under French law.
[236] Figures reported in the *Financial Times* 30/12/2005.

In 2006, US$1,000 billion of CDOs were in issue globally.[237] In the first quarter of 2007, the global figure for CDO issuances was US$ 251 billion.[238] However, the market for further issuances was hit hard by the crisis in the financial markets in the second half of 2007, with a severe lack of confidence by investors in asset backed instruments and in CDOs.

12.10.2 Securitisation through a 'true sale' of term debt

A fairly straightforward form of securitisation involves a 'true sale' transference of a portfolio of debts by the originator to the SPV, with the SPV issuing bonds to raise the funds to pay for its purchase of the portfolio. Figure 12.1 contains a diagram of such a transaction.

12.10.2.1 The form of the sale under English law will be by an equitable assignment of the portfolio and its constituent elements, including any security and guarantees that are held by the originator, to the SPV. Notice of the assignment will not be given to the debtors unless subsequent events intervene which necessitate or make it desirable that notice should be given, such as the insolvency of the originator or its default in its administration of the portfolio. The bonds may be issued on an

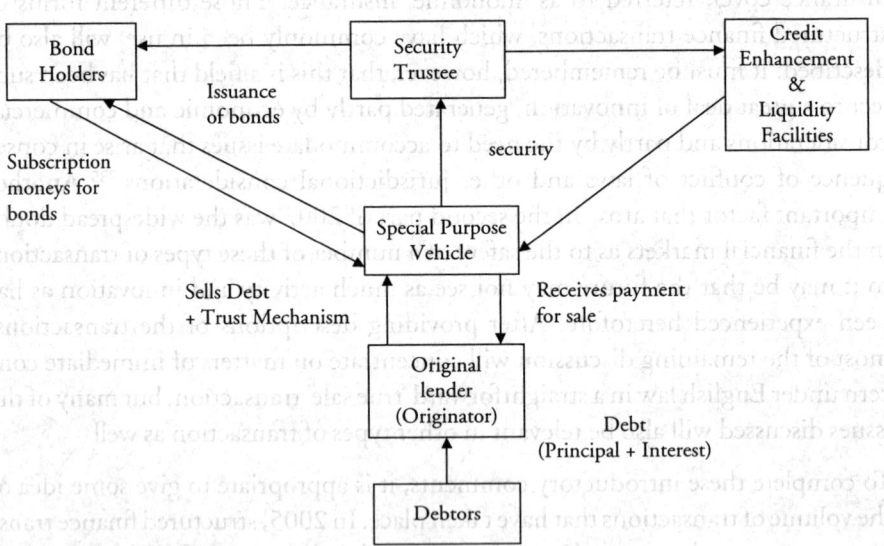

Figure 12.1 True Sale Debt Securitisation

237 Figures reported in the *Financial Times* 27/6/2006.
238 Figures reported in the *Financial Times* 12/6/2007.

entirely *pari passu* basis or there may be rankings of the bonds, with the lower rankings receiving a higher coupon (rate of interest) to reflect the additional risk of being postponed or subordinated behind the higher ranked bonds in right of payment. The portfolio might comprise a pool of mortgages, other shorter term debts, or even various types of debt securities. The debts comprised in the portfolio might have been incepted by the originator itself, or it may have assembled the portfolio ('packaged' it) by buying in its constituent elements from elsewhere.

12.10.2.2 As it takes the form, under English law, of an equitable assignment, the various issues that have been discussed above concerning such assignments must be taken into account, including issues relating to priorities, the debtor's rights of set-off, and the effect of negative pledges and contractual restrictions upon assignment.

12.10.2.3 The SPV will use the income which arises from the portfolio to pay its own interest obligations on the bonds it has issued. It will use the capital accruing on redemption of the underlying obligations comprised in the portfolio to repay the bonds. To overcome any short-term cash flow difficulties that it may encounter, such as by reason of a mismatch in the time of receipts of income from the portfolio against its own obligations on the bonds, the SPV may have been granted, at the outset, a liquidity facility by a bank, which can be drawn for short periods during the life of the bonds.

12.10.2.4 It is possible that the SPV might also encounter other financial difficulties. Those problems can be met by the use of credit enhancement facilities that are granted to it, again at the outset, for use on a longer term basis than for drawings under a liquidity facility. Such credit enhancement facilities are designed to overcome longer-term difficulties, including matters like interest and currency mismatches and the risk of an inadequate return on surplus funds. The mechanisms used would include hedging arrangements and the investment of such surplus funds at a guaranteed rate of return.[239] As security for its own obligations on the bonds it has issued, the SPV will give security over all of its assets to a trustee, which takes such security primarily on behalf of the bond holders and, secondarily, on behalf of the providers of the liquidity facility and the credit enhancement facilities.[240]

12.10.2.5 This form of transaction serves to demonstrate the point made above, that through the transaction, the originator has managed to raise funds through the sale of the portfolio, which funds were themselves raised by an issuance of bonds. Provided that the sale of the portfolio by the originator to the SPV was genuine and cannot be upset (i.e. that it is a 'true sale'), the risk associated with the bonds will be based

---

[239] Such surplus funds may arise because the income that is being received by the SPV exceeds its outgoings or because of early redemptions in the underlying portfolio, which means that the funds received upon redemption have to be held until the maturity of the bonds that the SPV has issued.

[240] Sometimes the provider of the liquidity facility will rank equally with the bond holders.

upon an assessment of the assets of the SPV, mainly the portfolio it has purchased, without having to take account of the overall financial position of the originator, which will be the ultimate beneficiary of the fund raising exercise. It should follow that the cost of the funds which have been raised, as reflected in the 'coupon' (the interest rate) on the bonds, will be less than the cost that the originator would have to bear if it had raised the funds directly, by borrowing in its own name.

12.10.2.6 Although the originator, through the sale to the SPV, may have transferred the risk associated with its ownership of the portfolio, it is likely to continue an association with the portfolio and it may derive some further economic benefit in consequence of that association. This, in turn, may give rise to accounting and regulatory concerns relating to the originator. The accounting issues are referred to below. The regulatory issues are discussed in Chapter 2. Two of the ways in which the originator is likely to continue its association with the portfolio relate, first, to its role as the administrator of the portfolio and, secondly, to that part of the price for the sale of the portfolio which is not funded by the bond issue and remains outstanding during the life of the securitisation.

12.10.2.7 The originator will remain as the administrator of the portfolio, which follows from the nature of the assignment as an unnotified equitable assignment, with the consequence that the debtors will continue to treat the originator as their creditor. The originator will be required to hold the benefit of the portfolio, and any payments it receives from the debtors, expressly on trust for the SPV as the purchaser, as provided for in the sale agreement. There will also be an administration agreement between the originator and the SPV which governs the way in which the originator performs its role as administrator and under which it will be paid a fee for doing so.[241] By this means, the originator will earn an income from the portfolio.

12.10.2.8 It is likely that some relatively small part of the sale price will remain outstanding after the sale and will not be funded by the moneys received by the SPV through the bond issue. This is sometimes referred to as 'over-collateralisation', as the SPV

---

[241] The administration agreement will make provision for the manner in which the portfolio will be administered, for collections from the debtors and payment of receipts into bank accounts, for setting and variation of interest rates (with reference to ensuring that the rate keeps pace with that payable by the SPV on the bonds), and for default procedures. There will also be provision for the dismissal of the current administrator and its replacement by another administrator in the event of the insolvency or default of the administrator, and, in anticipation that this may occur, a substitute administrator will have been provisionally nominated (and agreed to act) at the outset of the transaction. One purpose of the administration agreement is to ensure that the originator performs its tasks as administrator on an objective basis and is not overly lenient in its treatment of the debtors, which might be a temptation, bearing in mind its previous relationship with them, its desire to maintain a favourable reputation in the market place, and the fact that it will remain as the lender of record until the assignment is notified to the debtors.

has purchased, in terms of face-value, a greater amount of the underlying portfolio than that for which it has paid at the outset.[242] In effect, the SPV has been given a cushion. The remaining amount of the purchase price will be left outstanding and paid to the originator at a later date, probably when the securitisation is finally brought to an end and the liability of the SPV to the bond holders has been paid off. The amount payable to the originator will reflect the value of the rump of the portfolio that remains, together with interest that has been received upon it. This is likely to be off-set by the exercise by the originator of an option to buy back that rump.

12.10.3 Securitisation of revolving credits

It is also possible to devise a securitisation for a portfolio of revolving credit receivables, such as credit card receivables. Figure 12.2 contains a diagram of such a transaction.

In a securitisation of term debts, the underlying portfolio does not revolve. If debts comprised in the portfolio are paid off then the capital receipt will be held until maturity of the bonds and will be used finally in redemption of the bonds.[243] Different considerations will apply where the underlying portfolio

12.10.3.1

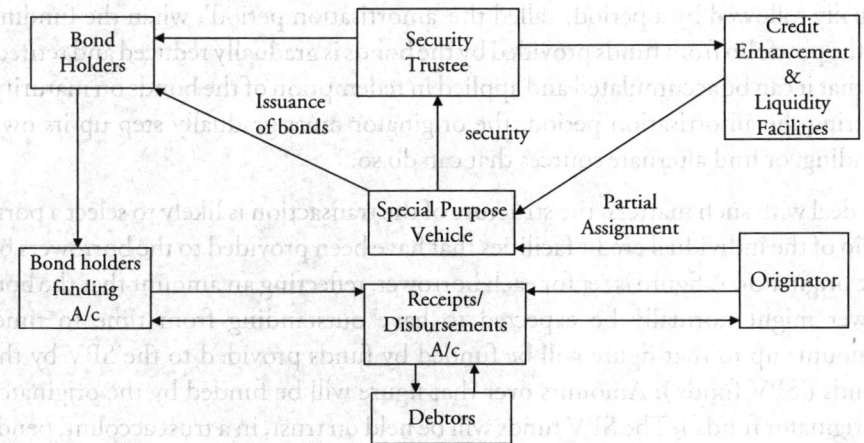

Figure 12.2 Revolving Securitisation

---

[242] Over-collateralisation is one of the techniques that makes up the credit enhancement provided to the SPV, as referred to below.

[243] There may be limited circumstances where the receipts can be re-used, perhaps in purchasing further debts to add in to the portfolio. Otherwise, the funds will be invested and held pending redemption.

involves revolving credit. Unless the greater part of the portfolio is seriously in default, the funds raised by the SPV through the bonds it has issued are unlikely to be fully deployed for the whole period of the securitisation until redemption of the bonds. Indeed, even at the outset, they may not be fully deployed. Furthermore, the pattern of usage of revolving credit will vary from one borrower to another and it is likely to vary between different times of the year. Thus, some borrowers may normally maintain small amounts utilised on their accounts, sometimes borrow more, and usually repay in full on a timely basis, whilst others may remain fully drawn, or almost so, for most of the time. Other borrowers will be somewhere in between. This means that the structure must reflect the likelihood of variations in the balances on the debtors' accounts, the deployment of the funds that have been raised from time to time, and their temporary repayment, all in uncertain amounts.

12.10.3.2 A further factor that must be taken into account is that the period of the securitisation, that is, the date to the maturity of the bonds, will come to an end but the revolving credit facility offered to the borrowers by the originator is likely to continue beyond that date. The structure will thus have to accommodate, as well, the retirement of the funding provided by the bonds through the securitisation and its replacement by other resources of the originator or through a further securitisation. The period when the funds provided by the bonds can be utilised in full by the SPV for funding the portfolio is often called the 'revolving period'. That is usually followed by a period, called the 'amortisation period', when the funding of the portfolio from funds provided by the bonds is gradually reduced and retired, so that it can be accumulated and applied in redemption of the bonds on maturity. During the amortisation period, the originator must gradually step up its own funding, or find alternate sources that can do so.

12.10.3.3 To deal with such matters, the structure of the transaction is likely to select a portfolio of the individual credit facilities that have been provided to the borrowers by the originator. A figure is set for each borrower, reflecting an amount that the borrower might normally be expected to have outstanding from time to time. Amounts up to that figure will be funded by funds provided to the SPV by the bonds ('SPV funds'). Amounts over that figure will be funded by the originator ('originator funds'). The SPV funds will be held on trust, in a trust account, pending their initial deployment, their temporary repayment, and their final accumulation for redemption of the bonds. There will be a second account, which will probably also be a trust account, which will be operated by the originator. The second account will receive the SPV funds and the originator funds when they are required from time to time and disburse the same to (or for the account of) the borrowers. It will also receive amounts repaid by the borrowers from time to time and pay the relevant proportions to the trust account for the SPV funds and to the originator. Once the amortisation period has commenced, the funds paid into the trust account for the SPV funds will gradually be accumulated and not re-deployed.

At the same time, the originator will gradually have to assume responsibility for funding the whole portfolio or make other arrangements.

12.10.4 Synthetic securitisation

A synthetic securitisation is intended to replicate much of the economic effect of a true sale securitisation but through the use of derivatives, such as credit default swaps. A fairly simple form of a synthetic securitisation will now be described. Figure 12.3 contains a diagram of such a transaction.

Instead of the originator transferring the underlying portfolio to the SPV at the outset of the transaction, the originator remains the owner of the portfolio but transfers the risk of default for some part of the portfolio to the SPV. This is done by the originator and the SPV entering into a credit default swap, under which the SPV assumes the risk of default in the relevant part of the portfolio.[244] The fee payable to the SPV by the originator for assuming the risk is payable from the income earned by the originator on the portfolio. If a default is suffered that is covered by the arrangement, the debt (or the relevant part thereof) is then transferred to the SPV in return for the originator receiving from the SPV the outstanding

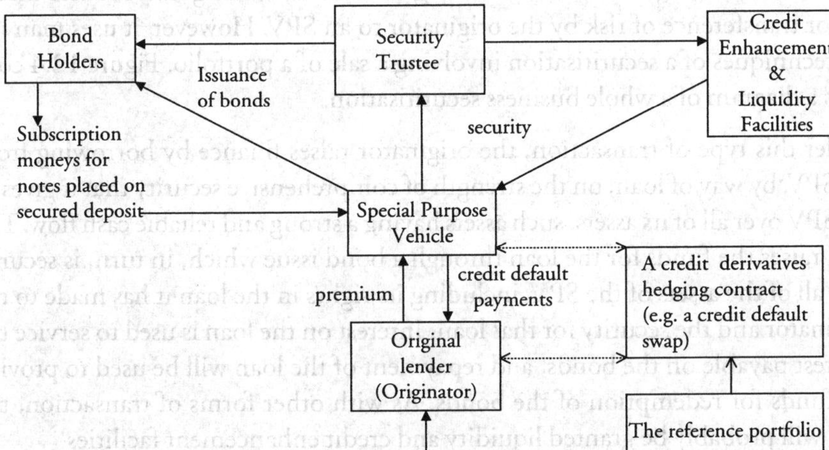

12.10.4.1

Figure 12.3 Synthetic Securitisation

---

[244] A description of a credit default swap will be found in Chap 11.

amount due for that debt or part.[245] Alternatively (and more conveniently), the matter may be cash settled without a transfer. The SPV may itself lay off some or most of the risk it has undertaken by entering into reciprocal credit default swaps with third parties.

12.10.4.2 The SPV issues bonds in the capital markets, the principal of which is placed on deposit at a rate of interest which matches, or exceeds, the rate payable by the SPV on the bonds. The principal amount so deposited will be available to meet any obligations of the SPV under the credit default swap with the originator, to the extent that such obligations have not been laid-off by the SPV under reciprocal swaps. The amount of the principal that remains held on deposit at the conclusion of the securitisation will be used in redemption of the bonds. In addition to any credit default swaps that the SPV enters into with third parties, there may also be liquidity and credit enhancement facilities that will be granted in its favour. Once again, the SPV will give comprehensive security over all of its assets, including the capital amount held on deposit, to a trustee for the bond holders and the providers of liquidity and credit enhancement facilities.

12.10.5 Whole business securitisation

This is really a form of secured financing received by an originator rather than a sale or transference of risk by the originator to an SPV. However, it uses many of the techniques of a securitisation involving a sale of a portfolio. Figure 12.4 contains a diagram of a whole business securitisation.

12.10.5.1 Under this type of transaction, the originator raises finance by borrowing from the SPV, by way of loan, on the strength of comprehensive security that it gives to the SPV over all of its assets, such assets having a strong and reliable cash flow. The SPV raises the funds for the loan through a bond issue which, in turn, is secured over all of the assets of the SPV, including its rights in the loan it has made to the originator and the security for that loan. Interest on the loan is used to service the interest payable on the bonds, and repayment of the loan will be used to provide the funds for redemption of the bonds. As with other forms of transaction, the SPV will probably be granted liquidity and credit enhancement facilities.

12.10.6 Covered bonds

In essence, covered bonds are bonds that are secured against a defined package or portfolio of an originating bank's loan assets, such that the bond holders will have a primary claim against those assets, ahead of any other creditors, in the event of a

---

[245] Subject to the SPV receiving good title from the originator of the originator's rights in the debt and any associated security, and the debt originally meeting the requirements for its inclusion in the portfolio.

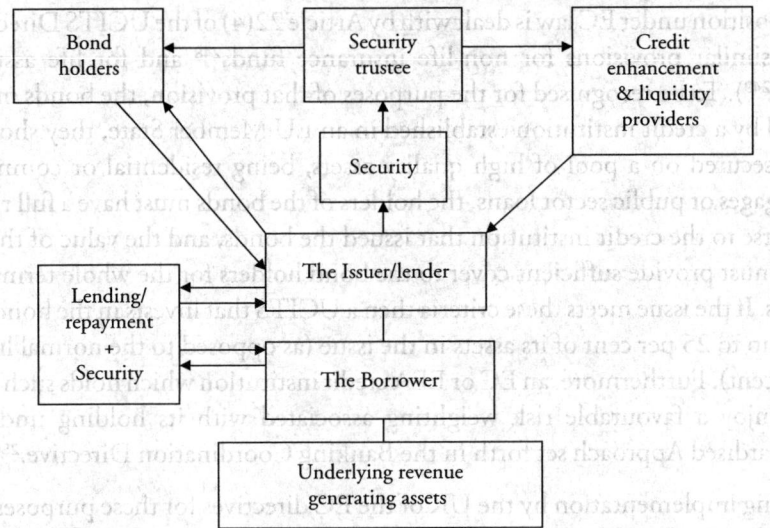

Figure 12.4 Whole Business Securitisation

default on the bonds or in an insolvency. The transaction is structured so that the value of the portfolio should at all times be sufficient to cover the bond holders' claims. The bond holders also have a claim against the issuer (being the originator or its wholly-owned subsidiary). In that respect, the transaction differs markedly from a true sale securitisation, where the originator would normally have no liability with respect to the bonds that are issued and held by the investors.

Under EC law, covered bonds that meet prescribed requirements receive special treatment for regulatory purposes. In the first place, there is a favourable treatment of covered bonds in terms of the percentage of assets that may be invested by an undertaking for collective investment in transferable securities (a UCITS). Secondly, there is a favourable risk weighting that is ascribed to the bonds, in terms of capital adequacy treatment, where the bonds are held by an EC or EEA bank. At the time of writing, the UK had yet to establish the necessary legislation to enable advantage to be taken of the EC rules, but it was expected that legislation would be introduced by March 2008.[246] Pending that development, UK banks and building societies have sought to achieve a similar structure to that which is envisaged under EC rules, but without obtaining the regulatory benefits. Interestingly enough, banks in some EU countries have also issued covered bonds using the UK model.

12.10.6.1

---

[246] Introduced by the Regulated Covered Bonds Regs 2008 (SI 2008/346), in force 6/3/2008.

12.10.6.1.1 The position under EC law is dealt with by Article 22(4) of the UCITS Directive[247] (and similar provisions for non-life insurance funds[248] and for life assurance funds[249]). To be recognised for the purposes of that provision, the bonds must be issued by a credit institution established in an EU Member State, they should be fully secured on a pool of high quality assets, being residential or commercial mortgages or public sector loans, the holders of the bonds must have a full right of recourse to the credit institution that issued the bonds, and the value of the asset pool must provide sufficient cover to the bond holders for the whole term of the bonds. If the issue meets these criteria then a UCITS that invests in the bonds may hold up to 25 per cent of its assets in the issue (as opposed to the normal limit of 5 per cent). Furthermore, an EC or EEA credit institution which holds such bonds will enjoy a favourable risk weighting associated with its holding under the Standardised Approach set forth in the Banking Coordination Directive.[250]

12.10.6.2 Pending implementation by the UK of the EC directives for these purposes, issuers in the UK (being UK banks and building societies or their finance subsidiaries) have taken to issuing so-called 'structured covered bonds'. Such instruments are designed to resemble what might be achieved under EC law, but without obtaining the relevant regulatory benefits. In essence, the structure of the transaction has been as follows.

12.10.6.2.1 Bonds are issued by the relevant bank, building society, or finance subsidiary (the issuer) which are guaranteed by a special purpose vehicle (the guarantor) that is owned and controlled by the bank or building society (the originator). The guarantor has tended to be a limited liability partnership (an LLP). The issuer lends the proceeds of the issue to the guarantor, which uses those proceeds to acquire a pool of mortgage assets from the originator. The guarantor gives comprehensive security over all its assets, including the pool, to a security trustee for the bond holders. Provided the issuer meets all its obligations and pays off the bonds, the guarantor will be obliged to repay the issuer. The transaction provides, however, that should the issuer default under the bonds, the usual consequences will follow as against the issuer. On the other hand, the guarantor will become obliged to service the bonds as if a default had not occurred. Should the guarantor default in meeting its own obligations, the security trustee may then enforce the security against the guarantor's assets on an accelerated basis. The guarantor is required to ensure that the value of the pool is sufficient to cover the principal amount of the

---

247 Directive on the co-ordination of laws, regulations and administrative provisions relating to undertakings for collective investment in transferable securities (UCITS) 85/611/EEC OJ L375/3 31/12/1985 (as amended).

248 Art 22(4) of the Third Non-Life Directive 92/49/EC OJ L228/1 11/8/92.

249 Art 22(4) of the Consolidated Life Directive 2002/83/EC OJ L345/1 19/12/2002.

250 See Annex VI (Part 12, para 12) of EC Directive 2006/48/EC (OJ L177/1 30/6/2006). For a description of the Standardised Approach see Chap 2.

bonds. The pool continues to be administered and serviced by the originator. The FSA has required that banks and building societies that are involved in such a covered bond issue should observe certain parameters, in terms of an initial monitoring requirement and, at a higher level, the possibility of having to meet increased capital requirements.

12.10.7 Monoline insurance

Traditionally, this type of insurance (sometimes called wrap around insurance) was issued to provide cover against the risk of default in payment of bonds issued in the USA by local municipalities. The insurer will usually be licensed and regulated under New York state insurance law and it is likely that any policy that it writes will be expressed as being subject to New York law. It is called monoline insurance because the insurer only issues one type of policy, being 'financial guaranty insurance', as opposed to a 'multiline' insurer which issues several different types of policy. In more recent times, monoline insurance has expanded to include coverage of structured products on a wider scale, such as securitised bonds, collateralised debt obligations (CDOs), and bonds that have been issued to finance Private Finance Initiative (PFI) and similar projects.[251] Its value has been seen in the enhancement that the insurance cover provided to the credit ratings ascribed to the relevant bonds and CDOs, because the investors had the benefit of an extra layer of protection against default under the insurance cover. To achieve and maintain that enhancement, the insurer that issued the insurance policy had to enjoy a high credit rating itself, which became doubtful as a consequence of the turmoil in the financial markets in the second part of 2007.

The insurance cover is written on the basis that if there is a default by the issuer of the relevant securities, the insurer will pay out in accordance with the pre-default payment obligations under the securities and not in accordance with the issuer's accelerated obligations that might have arisen in consequence of the default.   **12.10.7.1**

12.11 A True Sale Securitisation

It is intended in this section to examine in further detail the matters that are relevant to achieving a successful 'true sale' securitisation. Under such a transaction, an originator transfers to an SPV, by sale, a portfolio of debts. The acquisition by the SPV is funded by an issuance of bonds in the capital markets. The success of   **12.11.1**

---

[251] It was estimated that in the period between 1992 and 2007, some 700 PFI projects (with an aggregate value of £50bn) had been covered by monoline insurance. During that period, one insurer alone had written more than £11bn cover for bond issues in the European infrastructure and regulated securities markets. These figures were quoted in the *Financial Times* of 16/11/2007.

such a transaction depends upon the robustness of the SPV's position, in terms of its ownership of the assets (i.e. the portfolio of debts and any security for such debts) that it has purported to acquire, that the utility and value of such assets is real and not susceptible to a substantial diminution from their face value, that the SPV's own solvency and financial position will not be at risk, and, consequently, that the investors who hold bonds that the SPV has issued will have a safe and dependable investment and that they will be adequately protected. It is also important that the originator should achieve its objectives in embarking upon the transaction.

12.11.2 The originator's objectives in a true sale securitisation

One of the objectives of the originator has already been mentioned, namely, its wish to raise finance through the sale of the portfolio at a favourable price, especially when compared with the alternative of raising the funds itself based upon its own balance sheet. A further objective, especially for a bank or a similar financial institution, is to achieve a positive recognition of the transaction for the purposes of its balance sheet and for regulatory capital adequacy purposes, so that the portfolio is treated as having been removed from the balance sheet of the originator and it is also removed in the calculation of the originator's risk weightings for capital adequacy purposes. In general terms, this will depend upon whether the originator has sufficiently divested itself of the risks and rewards that are associated with the portfolio. However, as a part of this, it is essential that the SPV is seen as being unconnected, in a corporate sense, with the originator, so that the affairs of the SPV will not be linked into those of the originator for accounting or regulatory purposes.[252]

12.11.2.1 That objective (concerning the independence of the SPV) will be achieved if it can be demonstrated that the originator has no interest in the capital of the SPV and that the originator does not control it nor influence it. Accordingly, the SPV should be established as an independent entity, whose share capital is held directly by, or indirectly through a trustee for, someone that has no connection with the originator or the transaction, such as one or more charities. The financial calculations that are made at the outset of the transaction should show that there is an expectation that a small amount of residual cash will be left in the SPV once the securitisation has come to an end, which can be distributed to its ultimate shareholders. It is also likely that the originator will have no representation on the board of directors of the SPV, or, if it does, that it will have only a single director nominated by it.

12.11.2.2 The originator will also be unwilling to accept any responsibility for the future creditworthiness of the debtors or for the due and punctual performance of

---

[252] E.g. that the SPV will not be considered as a subsidiary undertaking of the originator, nor that the originator will have a participating interest in the SPV.

their obligations. Accordingly, it will not undertake any obligation by way of recourse or to repurchase the portfolio or any part of it.[253] On the other hand, it may stipulate for an option, exercisable within its discretion, to repurchase the residual rump of the portfolio at the conclusion of the securitisation, once the bond holders have been paid out. It may also have to give warranties as to matters of fact as at the date of the sale to the SPV, covering such issues as the past history of the debts included in the portfolio, their compliance with various specified criteria at the time of inception and at the time of sale, its unencumbered full title in the portfolio (including that no third party has a relevant interest), and that there are no rights of set-off or counterclaim that the debtors could assert.

12.11.3 The safety of the transaction

It is important that the transaction should represent a low level of risk to the SPV and, through it, the investors who will take up and hold the bonds that the SPV is to issue. To achieve such an outcome, it is necessary that a number of matters should be addressed. In the first place, that the quality and real value of the portfolio that the SPV is to purchase should be assured, so far as is reasonably practicable. Secondly, that the SPV should acquire a full beneficial interest in the portfolio which will be enforceable for its own benefit and that such an interest cannot be upset, particularly in consequence of an insolvency of the originator. Thirdly, that the SPV will have sufficient resources to remain solvent and able to meet its obligations as they fall due and that its activities will be limited so as to reduce the risk of it incurring liabilities that it cannot satisfy. Finally, that the position of the investors who hold the SPV's bonds will be adequately protected against any possibility of a default by the SPV, through a comprehensive security package that is held on their behalf by a trustee. Those various matters will be examined below.

To enable the transaction to proceed, it is necessary that an assessment should be made to determine that those matters, and their attendant risks, will be dealt with in a satisfactory manner. Such an assessment is undertaken by the credit ratings agencies which will then issue a credit rating for the bonds that the SPV is to issue. The transaction will only succeed if a favourably high rating is forthcoming from the agencies, at least with respect to the senior ranking bonds that the SPV will issue. It is worth noting, however, the scepticism that arose in the financial markets in the wake of the turmoil in the second half of 2007, concerning the real value of securitised assets and the reliability of the ratings that had been ascribed to securities by the rating agencies. Amongst other things, the Committee of European Securities Regulators (CESR) announced in November 2007 that its

12.11.3.1

---

[253] With the exception of an obligation to repurchase if the originator is in default of a factual warranty given at the time of purchase.

work would include a review of the rating of securities that were involved in structured finance transactions.[254]

12.11.4 The portfolio

An investigation of the portfolio of debts that is to be purchased by the SPV will be concerned with both practical and legal issues. To some extent, there will be a sampling taken from particular debtors' files to assess these matters, where it would not be feasible to consider every file separately.

12.11.4.1   The practical matters will involve the likely incidence of default by the debtors and the adequacy of any security cover that might exist. Figures for default and recovery rates will be examined, as will the adequacy and sufficiency of the lending criteria employed by the originator when it incepted the loans to the debtors. The originator should be required to demonstrate that it honoured such criteria when it made the loans. It became apparent in the sub-prime lending crisis in the USA in the second part of 2007 that these matters may not have been given the attention they deserved when loans were made to less than creditworthy borrowers.

12.11.4.2   The legal investigation will be concerned with the title of the originator in the portfolio and its constituent elements, that the portfolio exists, and that the originator had the right to make the loans and enforce recovery, including compliance with matters concerned with consumer credit licences and the requirements and procedures laid down by statute.[255] A failure to observe such requirements might result in the debts being unenforceable and irrecoverable, or, alternatively, that more onerous procedures may need to be followed to recover the debts and to enforce security. The investigation will also consider if the debts, security, and related rights are assignable, which will include an examination of the standard forms of documentation used by the originator to determine, so far as practicable, that there were no restrictions on assignment by the originator of its rights and title in the assets transferred.

12.11.5 The SPV's acquisition of the portfolio

This mainly concerns the method by which the SPV is to acquire ownership of the portfolio and its constituent elements. Under English law, this will normally be achieved by an equitable assignment. It is important that the SPV should have the right to turn the equitable assignment into an absolute assignment by giving

---

[254] See the CESR's Press Release of 5/11/2007, ref CESR/07-728, available at <http://www.cesr.eu>.
[255] E.g. under the Consumer Credit Acts 1974 and 2006 and subsidiary statutory instruments, under the Financial Services and Markets Act 2000 (as amended) and orders made thereunder (e.g. in relation to entering into and administering 'regulated mortgage contracts', as specified by Art 61 of the FSMA (Regulated Activities) Order 2001 (SI 2001/544), as amended) and under the Unfair Terms in Consumer Contracts Regs 1999 (SI 1999/2083).

notice to the relevant debtors and other obligors,[256] particularly in a situation where the originator had become insolvent or otherwise was in breach of its continuing obligations, such as in its administration of the portfolio. There should also be express trusts created in favour of the SPV by the originator over any moneys payable to and received by the originator, with a requirement to hold such moneys in a separate bank account until paid over to the SPV.

As previously mentioned, the SPV may not acquire a good title if the originator is prevented from assigning its rights by a restriction in the contract under which the rights arise. In a large portfolio, it is impractical that every contract should be examined to ensure that this will not be a difficulty. The matter is usually dealt with by a warranty given by the originator that no such restriction exists.

12.11.5.1

There are other matters that might affect the SPV's entitlement which will also be dealt with by warranties given by the originator. The first concerns the possibility of rival third party claimants in the subject matter of the sale. The originator will warrant that it is solely entitled to the subject matter at the time of the sale and that it has not created any rights therein in favour of third parties. The second matter relates to possible rights of set-off and counterclaim that the obligors may wish to assert against the originator and, after the assignment, against the entitlement of the SPV. This might be a particular issue in the case of the assignment of debts arising under equipment finance transactions because of the terms as to condition, quality, and fitness for purpose that are implied by statute.[257] The originator will warrant that no such rights will exist or perhaps give an undertaking to reimburse the SPV if they are asserted against it.

12.11.5.2

There might also be statutory requirements that the SPV may be required to meet, in relation to its business, its holding of the portfolio, and the enforcement of the debtors' obligations and any security that is held with respect to those obligations. Accordingly, it may need to hold various licences and authorisations and observe any requirements imposed by statute in enforcing its rights.[258]

12.11.5.3

12.11.6 Upsetting the transfer

The robustness of the SPV's title in the portfolio that is has acquired from the originator will depend upon whether the transfer might be upset, particularly in the event that the originator becomes subject to insolvency proceedings.

---

[256] In the case of a mortgage of registered land, also by registering the transfer at the Land Registry: see *Paragon Finance PLC v Pender* [2005] EWCA Civ 760, [2005] 1 WLR 3412.

[257] As to entitlement to sell and supply, see s 12 of the Sale of Goods Act 1979 (sales), s 8 Supply of Goods (Implied Terms) Act 1973 (hp), and s 7 Supply of Goods and Services Act 1982 (leases). As to quality and fitness for purposes, see s 14 of the SGA 1979, s 10 of the SG(IT)A 1973, and s 9 of the SG&SA 1982.

[258] The types of provisions are noted at n 255 above.

Of primary concern is that the portfolio (or some part of it) may have to be re-vested in the originator or that some element of restitution or compensation may have to paid to the originator or its liquidator or other representative in its insolvency.[259] Under English law, the areas of risk cover, first, the possibility of a re-characterisation of the transfer of the portfolio as amounting to a form of secured finance which might be avoided for lack of registration, and, secondly, an argument that the disposal of the portfolio by the originator amounted to a transaction at an undervalue within the compass of section 238 of the Insolvency Act 1986.

12.11.6.1 The issue concerning the re-characterisation of debt purchases has already been examined above. For the reasons there given, it is submitted that it would be unlikely that the English courts would upset a true sale transaction by re-characterising it as a form of secured finance. This is despite the possibilities that an element of the purchase price might remain outstanding and that the originator may have an option to buy back the rump of the portfolio that remains at the end of the securitisation, after the bonds have been redeemed by the SPV. Those elements are not inconsistent with the circumstances in which a genuine sale might take place. The position is strengthened in a true sale transaction by the fact that it would be highly unlikely that the originator would agree to accept an obligation, by way of a recourse or repurchase obligation, to make good any losses suffered by the SPV by reason of a default by any of the debtors which arises after the transfer has taken place.[260]

12.11.6.2 It might also be alleged that, to the extent of over-collateralisation provided by the originator, there had been a transaction at an undervalue, within section 238 of the Insolvency Act 1986.[261] This would be on the basis that the originator, to that extent, did not receive the full consideration for the sale of the portfolio at the time the sale took place. In summary, a liquidator or administrator of a company is entitled to challenge before the court a transaction as being one at an undervalue if it occurred within a relevant time (essentially, within a period of two years before the onset of the insolvency proceedings, if the company was insolvent at the time of the transaction or became insolvent in consequence of the transaction[262]). The transaction will be at an undervalue if either the transaction was a gift by the company[263] or if the value, in money or money's worth, of the consideration that it was

---

[259] Such as an administrator. For convenience, all such persons will be included in the expression 'liquidator'.

[260] If for no other reason, because of regulatory constraints against the originator, if it is a bank, undertaking such an obligation. See Chap 2.

[261] As to transactions at an undervalue, see Chaps 14 and 16.

[262] See s 240 of the Act.

[263] Quite clearly, the transaction would not be classified as a gift.

to receive for the transaction was significantly less than that which it provided.[264] The court may make such order as it thinks fit to restore the position to the pre-transaction position.[265] Under section 238(5), however, the transaction will be saved if the court is satisfied, first, that the company entered into the transaction in good faith and for the purpose of carrying on its business, and, secondly, that at the time it entered into the transaction, there were reasonable grounds for believing that the transaction would benefit the company.

It is unlikely that a true sale transaction would be liable to successful attack under section 238 on the basis outlined above. In the first place, whilst the originator may not have received the whole of the consideration at the outset, the arrangement would provide for it to receive the deferred element of the consideration in the future, when the securitisation came to an end. What would then be payable to it (after taking into account any offset referable to its re-purchase of the rump of the portfolio that remained outstanding), when added to what it had received at the outset, would reflect the actual adjusted value of the whole of the portfolio that was sold to the SPV. Secondly, it should be possible to demonstrate that the saving requirements of section 238(5) were met at the time of the transaction, so that the court would not make an order under section 238 if there had, technically, been a transaction at an undervalue. In that regard, it should be possible to show that the subjective elements of good faith and business purpose were met and, also, that the objective element of benefit to the originator was present.

12.11.6.2.1

12.11.7 The risk of the SPV's insolvency

Taken in isolation, there are various theoretical reasons why the SPV might become insolvent and be unable to meet its obligations. Those reasons include the risk that the SPV may engage in extraneous activities under which it incurs liabilities that it cannot satisfy, that it may not have enough cash flow at any particular time to pay its debts as they fall due, or that, at such a time, its liabilities (being the aggregate of its short- and long-term liabilities) exceed its assets.[266] Various mechanisms

---

[264] As to the relevant tests for assessing the value of the consideration provided and received, including the application of the hindsight principle, see *Re MC Bacon Ltd* [1991] Ch 127; *Phillips v Brewin Dolphin Bell Lawrie Ltd* [2001] 1 WLR 143; *Re Thoars; Reid v Ramlort* [2002] EWHC 2416 (Ch), [2003] 1 BCLC 499; *Re Thoars (Decd)* [2004] EWCA Civ 800, [2004] BPIR 985; and *Hill (as Trustee in Bankruptcy of Nurkowski) v Spread Trustee Co Ltd* [2006] EWCA Civ 542, [2006] BCC 646.

[265] The range of the orders that the court may make is illustrated by s 241 of the Act, but there are safeguards provided for in that section to protect certain innocent third parties who acquired a derivative interest (i.e. an interest not immediately acquired from the insolvent company) without notice.

[266] A useful definition of insolvency is that employed by ss 123(1)(e) and 123(2) of the Insolvency Act 1986, which respectively provide two alternative tests of insolvency, namely, the inability of a company to pay its debts as they fall due ('cash flow insolvency') or that its liabilities exceed its assets, taking into account contingent and prospective liabilities ('balance sheet insolvency').

are employed in a true sale securitisation which are designed to overcome, so far as practicable, the possibility that such an insolvency might occur, as well as the consequences should it occur, which will now be examined.

12.11.7.1 *The SPV's activities*

To limit the liabilities that the SPV might incur, restrictions will be imposed upon the activities that it may undertake. Such restrictions are likely to be found in its Memorandum of Association and may also be covered as undertakings in the conditions attached to the bond issue documentation. In essence, the SPV will be limited to performing its role in the securitisation transaction and, perhaps, any other securitisations linked to it. It will not be permitted to undertake other activities or incur other types of liability. For instance, it will not be permitted to employ any staff. The economics of the transaction will also be devised to ensure that the affairs of the SPV will be tax neutral, so that it does not generate a liability to pay or account for taxation or similar levies or duties. By these means, it is likely that such liabilities as the SPV might incur will be limited to the creditors that arise in consequence of the securitisation transaction and that there will not be any outside creditors, such as legal and other advisers, who will not be paid in the ordinary course. This factor is also important when considering the effectiveness of the security that the SPV will grant, as some element of that security may be comprised in a floating charge which would have to defer to the rights of preferential creditors[267] and the rights of unsecured creditors to a share of the recoveries from a floating charge.[268]

12.11.7.2 *Liquidity support*

To give support to the SPV against short-term cash flow difficulties, a liquidity facility may be provided to the SPV by one or more banks, which will enable the SPV to make short-term drawings if cash is required, for instance, to meet an interest payment on the bonds. The most likely reasons for the SPV not having sufficient immediately available cash at any particular time would be that the dates for interest receipts from the underlying portfolio do not coincide with the dates on which interest is payable on the bonds, or where an increase in the market rate payable on the bonds cannot immediately be passed on by a matching increase in interest payable by the underlying debtors. Bearing in mind that liquidity support is one of the factors that will be taken into account by the credit rating agencies in making their assessment of the transaction, it is essential that the banks

---

[267] Under ss 40, 175(2)(b) of the Insolvency Act 1986 and s 754 of the Companies Act 2006 (formerly s 196 of the Companies Act 1985). For these purposes, the definition of a 'floating charge' is that given in s 251 of the Insolvency Act 1986, which is similar to that used in s 754 of the Companies Act 2006 (and its predecessor section) and in s 176A of the Insolvency Act 1986 (as amended).

[268] Under s 176A of the Insolvency Act 1986 (as amended).

which grant such facilities are themselves seen to be of an acceptable standing, usually judged in terms of their own credit ratings. The same applies to the financial institutions that provide credit enhancement to the SPV.

12.11.7.3 Credit enhancement

Credit enhancement is concerned with the longer-term financial viability of the SPV. It is likely to include a number of the following techniques.

The first method is that of over-collateralisation, which has already been described. It provides the SPV with a cushion of additional assets in excess of its liabilities on the bonds. This will probably be accompanied by the grant of an option to the originator to buy back the remainder, or the rump, of the portfolio at the termination of the securitisation. If the option is exercised, the amount payable by the originator to repurchase the rump will be off-set against the SPV's residual liability to pay for the over-collateralised portion of the portfolio it originally purchased. This will also enable an orderly winding up of the SPV's affairs to take place.

12.11.7.3.1

A second method is the provision to the SPV of a term loan facility which will rank, in right of repayment, behind the bonds (or, at least, the bonds that enjoy a senior ranking in right of payment). An alternative, or sometimes additional, mechanism is that the bonds are ranked, so that the rights attached to some of the bonds will be subordinated behind the rights attached to the first ranking bonds. There may even be several tiers of bonds, ranking in their order in the tiering.

12.11.7.3.2

A third method is the use of 'spread' accounts, by which the amount received by the SPV from the underlying portfolio is greater than the amount of its expenditure so that, gradually, a cash pool can be built up as a reserve held by the SPV.

12.11.7.3.3

A fourth method is the use of a guaranteed investment contract, under which a financial institution, probably a bank, undertakes to pay a rate of return on any spare cash held by the SPV from time to time that is at least equal to the rate of interest payable by it on the bonds.

12.11.7.3.4

A fifth method is provided by interest rate or currency swaps and other types of derivatives contracts that the SPV may enter into with one or more financial institutions. The intention is to provide hedging to the SPV to protect it against adverse movements in interest or currency rates. These transactions will only be required if the SPV is at risk; for instance, if some part of the underlying portfolio of loans carries interest at a fixed rate, whilst the bonds carry interest at a floating rate, or if some part of the underlying portfolio of debts is denominated in one or more currencies that differ from the currency of the bonds.

12.11.7.3.5

12.11.7.4 Security given by the SPV

The final area of protection that is available, this time against the consequences of the insolvency of the SPV, is the comprehensive package of security that the SPV gives to the security trustee. The trustee holds the security and acts on behalf of the bond holders and the providers of the liquidity facility and credit enhancement, often in that order. The security follows the liberal pattern that English law allows, in that it will secure all of the SPV's obligations, actual and contingent, and the security will extend to all of its present and future assets. The principal element of its assets will be the portfolio of debts and other rights that it purchased from the originator. In so far as is legally possible,[269] the security that is taken will be fixed security but some element of the security will be subject to a floating charge.[270]

12.11.7.5 *Administrative receivers*

One traditional feature of such a comprehensive package of security has been the ability of the security holder (the 'chargee') to appoint a receiver and manager (defined by section 29(2) of the Insolvency Act 1986 as an 'administrative receiver') of the business and all (or substantially all) of the assets of the company (the 'chargor') which has given the security. Notwithstanding the legal fiction that the administrative receiver acts as the agent of the chargor until it goes into liquidation,[271] the administrative receiver is appointed by the chargee (in the present case, the security trustee) and owes its primary responsibility to the chargee.[272] As the administrative receiver acts, in a technical sense, as the agent of the chargor, the chargee is not responsible for his actions unless the chargee intervenes in the receivership, for instance, by giving the administrative receiver instructions as to how he should pursue his functions.[273]

12.11.7.5.1   A further benefit that flows from the appointment of an administrative receiver is that it effectively blocks the subsequent appointment of an administrator[274] and the right of the directors of an eligible company to obtain a moratorium within the context of making a proposal for a company voluntary arrangement.[275] If an administrator has been appointed, or such a moratorium is in place, that will act

---

[269] As to which, see the decision of the House of Lords in *National Westminster Bank PLC v Spectrum Plus Ltd* [2005] UKHL 41, [2005] 2 AC 680 and that of the Privy Council in *Agnew v Inland Revenue Commissioner* [2001] UKPC 28, [2001] AC 710.

[270] Which, in any event, is desirable for the purposes of satisfying the definitional requirements presented by s 29(2) of and para 14 of Sched B1 to the Insolvency Act 1986 (as amended). The floating charge element of the security package can be nominal. See *Re Croftbell Ltd* [1990] BCLC 844.

[271] See s 44(1)(a) of the Insolvency Act 1986.

[272] As to the duties and obligations of an administrative receiver, see the comprehensive treatment of the subject by Lightman J (sitting as an additional judge of the Court of Appeal) in *Silven Properties Ltd v Royal Bank of Scotland PLC* [2003] EWCA Civ 1409, [2004] 1 WLR 997.

[273] *American Express v Hurley* [1985] 3 All ER 564, [1986] BCLC 52.

[274] As to the position before 15/9/2003, see s 9(3) of the Insolvency Act 1986 (now repealed). The position after that date is governed by paras 17(b), 25(c), and 39 of Sched B1 to the Insolvency Act 1986 (as amended).

[275] See para 4(1)(c) of Sched A1 to the Insolvency Act 1986 (as amended).

as a serious impediment to the rights of the chargee to enforce its security.[276] There are also provisions, which might be prejudicial to the interests of a secured creditor, as to the disposal of charged property by an administrator or by the company within a moratorium.[277]

The appointment of an administrative receiver is thus a very convenient tool for the protection and enforcement of security, when looked at from the perspective of the chargee and those it represents.

12.11.7.5.2

That happy state of affairs, in being able to appoint an administrative receiver, is now subject to two important statutory limitations which are themselves, however, subject to exceptions under which it will remain possible to appoint an administrative receiver if the circumstances fall within an applicable exception. It is necessary now to discuss the limitations and the exceptions to them.

12.11.7.5.3

12.11.7.5.4 Sections 72A and 72B of the Insolvency Act 1986 (as amended)

One limitation on the power to appoint an administrative receiver was introduced by section 72A of the Insolvency Act 1986 (as amended),[278] which essentially provides that it is not possible to appoint an administrative receiver of a company.[279] This restriction only applies, however, with respect to security taken after the section came into force[280] and is subject to a number of exceptions, as outlined in sections 72B to 72H of the Act. The most relevant of those exceptions in relation to securitisation transaction is that contained in section 72B.[281] The section is woven with a number of intricate technicalities, which need to be studied carefully.

Section 72B provides for the right to appoint an administrative receiver under 'an agreement which is or forms part of a "capital market arrangement"'. The following matters, which will be examined in turn, must be satisfied if section 72B is to

12.11.7.5.4.1

---

[276] As to the effect of an administration, see paras 43 and 44 of Sched B1 to the Insolvency Act 1986 (as amended). As to the effect of a moratorium, see paras 12–14 of Sched A1 to the Act.

[277] As to administration, see paras 70–73 of Sched B1 to the Act. As to a company within a moratorium, see paras 18–22 of Sched A1 to the Act.

[278] The relevant amendments to the Insolvency Act 1986 were made by the Enterprise Act 2002.

[279] A 'company' for these purposes (by virtue of s 251 of the Insolvency Act 1986, as amended) having the meaning given by s 1(1) of the Companies Act 2006 (formerly s 735 of the Companies Act 1985), i.e. a company formed and registered under that Act or its predecessor Acts.

[280] 15 September 2003 (see the Insolvency Act 1986, Section 72A (Appointed Date) Order 2003 (SI 2003/2095)).

[281] There are a number of other exceptions to s 72A of the Act which are not relevant for present purposes, but include exceptions for public–private partnerships (s 72C), utility projects (s 72D), urban regeneration projects (s 72DA), project finance (s 72E), security given within the context of the financial markets systems (s 72F), registered social landlords (s 72G), and railway companies (s 72GA). It should be noted that s 72H contains provisions by which amendments may be made to the scope of the exceptions, additional exceptions may be created, and existing exceptions may cease to have effect.

apply. First, there must be an 'agreement' which is or forms part of a capital market arrangement. Secondly, there must be a 'capital market arrangement'. Thirdly, the arrangement must involve the issuance of a 'capital market investment'. Fourthly, a 'party'[282] must incur or, when the agreement was entered into was expected to incur, a debt of at least £50 million under the arrangement.

12.11.7.5.4.2 An 'agreement' is defined to include a contract, deed, or any other instrument that is intended to have legal effect in any relevant jurisdiction.[283] It would include the trust deed or other instrument under which security is created or constituted in favour of the security trustee.

12.11.7.5.4.3 A 'capital market arrangement' is an arrangement[284] that falls within one of the various alternatives contained in paragraph 1(1) of Schedule 2A to the Insolvency Act 1986 (as amended).[285] The different types of securitisation transaction described earlier in this chapter should fall within at least one of the alternatives. The alternative types of arrangement specified in paragraph 1(1) are as follows:

(a) it involves a grant of security to a person holding it as trustee for a person who holds a capital market investment issued by a party to the arrangement, or

(aa) it involves a grant of security to:
  (i) a party to the arrangement who issues a capital market investment, or
  (ii) a person who holds the security as trustee for a party to the arrangement in connection with the issue of a capital market investment, or

(ab) it involves a grant of security to a person who holds the security as trustee for a party to the arrangement who agrees to provide finance to another party, or

(b) at least one party guarantees the performance of obligations of another party, or

(c) at least one party provides security in respect of the performance of obligations of another party, or

(d) the arrangement involves an investment of a kind described in articles 83 to 85 of the Financial Services and Markets Act 2000 (Regulated Activities) Order 2001 (SI 2001/544) (options, futures and contracts for differences).

12.11.7.5.4.4 A 'capital market investment' is an investment that falls within paragraph 2 or paragraph 3 of Schedule 2A to the Act. Essentially, paragraph 2 applies to capital markets debt instruments that are, or are designed to be, rated by an internationally recognised rating agency, listed on the official list maintained by the Financial

---

282 A 'party' to an arrangement is defined in para 1(3) of Sched 2A to the Act to include a party to an agreement which forms part of the arrangement, which provides for the raising of finance as part of the arrangement, or which is necessary for the purposes of implementing the arrangement.

283 See para 4 of Sched 2A to the Act, which has effect in relation to s 72B by virtue of s 72H(1), as well by specific reference in some cases.

284 The word 'arrangement' is not defined but clearly it is intended to have a wide compass in the context of para 1 of Sched 2A to the Act. The word is one of the alternative components of the definition of 'transaction' in s 436 of the Act.

285 See also the further amplification provided in paras 1(2) and 1(3).

Services Authority, or traded under the rules of a recognised investment exchange or on a foreign market.[286] Paragraph 3 applies to bonds or commercial paper issued to specified types of person, such as investment professionals, high net worth individuals, or companies, sophisticated investors, and certain foreign persons.

The final requirement is that under section 72B(1)(a) of the Act, 'a party incurs or, when the agreement was entered into was expected to incur, a debt of at least £50 million under the arrangement'. The party which incurs or is expected to incur the debt need not be the same person as creates the security. Accordingly, the debt need not arise under the agreement under which the receiver is appointed so long as it is or will be incurred under the overall capital market arrangement, of which the agreement forms a part.[287] The figure of £50 million may be incurred in sterling or the equivalent in other currencies.[288] The debt may be incurred at any time during the life of the arrangement[289] and the whole amount need not remain outstanding at the time the receiver is appointed.

12.11.7.5.4.5

Guidance as to the phrase 'expected to incur' was provided by Lewison J in *Feetum v Levy*,[290] which was a case that concerned similar wording to be found in section 72E of the Act. His Lordship distinguished between hope and the more objective concept of an expectation, the latter being what was required if there were to be an expectation of incurring a debt of at least £50 million under the relevant agreement. An expectation depends on the likelihood of meeting the conditions to its fulfilment. His Lordship also noted that the section requires an expectation that 'at least' £50 million will be borrowed, rather than 'up to' a figure, even if higher. In the Court of Appeal, in the same case, Jonathan Parker LJ, in agreeing with the approach taken by Lewison J, said that the wording should be taken to require that at the date the relevant agreement is entered into the indebtedness that is to be incurred is expected to amount to at least £50 million, and he expressly approved the statement by Lewison J that 'at least' does not mean 'up to'.[291]

12.11.7.5.4.6

12.11.7.5.5 The moratorium concerning a proposed company voluntary arrangement The other important restriction upon the power to enforce security by the appointment of an administrative receiver arises under this type of moratorium. Section 1A of the Insolvency Act 1986 (as amended)[292] provides for

---

286 See further paras 2(2) and 2(3).
287 See *Feetum v Levy* [2005] EWHC 349 (Ch); [2005] 1 WLR 2576, at [35] (the decision at first instance was affirmed by the Court of Appeal: *Cabvision Ltd v Feetum* [2005] EWCA Civ 1601).
288 See para 5 of Sched 2A to the Act.
289 See para 5(a) of Sched 2A to the Act.
290 [2005] EWHC 349 (Ch); [2005] 1 WLR 2576, at [41]–[45] (affd *Cabvision Ltd v Feetum* [2005] EWCA Civ 1601).
291 *Cabvision Ltd v Feetum* [2005] EWCA Civ 1601, at [86]–[89].
292 In particular, by the Insolvency Act 2000.

the directors of a company to take steps to obtain a moratorium in the context of making a proposal for a company voluntary arrangement. Schedule A1 to the Act makes provision for the companies that would be eligible for a moratorium ('eligible companies'), the procedure for obtaining such a moratorium, and the effects of the moratorium. What follows will describe briefly the procedures for obtaining a moratorium and the effect of the moratorium. It will then look at the definition of eligible companies and the exclusion which prevents a moratorium in the case of a company that is involved in a capital market arrangement.

12.11.7.5.5.1 The directors of an eligible company may obtain a moratorium by filing with the court various statements relating to the proposed voluntary arrangement, including as to the terms of the proposed voluntary arrangement, a statement of the company's affairs, the consent of the nominee to act, and his opinion as to the viability of the proposals.[293] The moratorium begins (i.e. becomes effective) upon the filing of the statements with the court. Its potential duration is for an initial period of up to 28 days,[294] which may be extended for up to a further period of two months.[295] The effect of the moratorium is similar to the freeze upon enforcement action that applies under an administration, including as to the enforcement of security, the right to appoint an administrative receiver and the enforcement of rights under equipment finance arrangements.[296] There are also provisions as to the disposal of charged property by the company during a moratorium.[297] It should also be noted that if an eligible company has given a floating charge, a provision in the charging instrument is void if it provides for the obtaining of a moratorium, or the doing of anything with a view to obtaining a moratorium, to be grounds for crystallising the charge or for appointing a receiver, or if it causes restrictions to come into force as to the right of the company to dispose of its property.[298]

12.11.7.5.5.2 Subject to a number of exceptions,[299] an eligible company is one which meets two or more of the requirements for being a small company within section 382 of the Companies Act 2006[300] in the year ending with the date upon which the moratorium will begin or in its last financial year ended before that date.[301] In other

---

[293] The requirements and procedures for obtaining a moratorium are set out in paras 6–8 of Sched A1 to the Act.

[294] See para 8 of Sched A1 to the Act.

[295] See para 32 of Sched A1 to the Act.

[296] See paras 12–14 of Sched A1 to the Act.

[297] See paras 18–22 of Sched A1 to the Act.

[298] See para 43 of Sched A1 to the Act.

[299] As set out in paras 2(2), 4, or 4A–4K of Sched A1 to the Act.

[300] Formerly s 247(3) of the Companies Act 1985, as amended by Reg 2 of the Companies Act 1985 (Accounts of Small and Medium-Sized Enterprises and Audit Exemption) (Amendment) Regs 2004 (SI 2004/16).

[301] See para 3 of Sched A1 to the Act.

words, if it meets for the relevant period any two of the following requirements: turnover (defined in section 474(1) of the Companies Act 2006[302]) not exceeding £5.6 million; balance sheet total (i.e. total assets as shown in the balance sheet) not exceeding £2.8 million; and employees (taken as an average over the year) not exceeding 50.

Paragraph 4A of Schedule A1 to the Insolvency 1986 Act[303] sets out the exclusion from the right to a moratorium, which relates to a company concerned in a capital market arrangement. It is similar to that which applies under section 72B of the Act, as outlined above. There are certain differences, however, the principal of which are as follows. First, the minimum amount of indebtedness that is incurred or that was expected to be incurred under the arrangement is the much lower sum of £10 million. Secondly, the list of arrangements that qualify as a capital market arrangement is reduced but this is partly compensated for by a separate exclusion, under paragraph 4C of Schedule A1, that applies in the case of a company that has, on the date of the filing with the court, incurred a debt under an agreement of £10 million or more. Such a liability includes a liability under a guarantee, indemnity or security.

12.11.7.5.5.3

12.12 Accounting Considerations

The transferor of a loan or a portfolio will usually wish to achieve recognition of the transfer for accounting purposes, particularly so that its balance sheet will reflect the fact that the transfer has taken place. Instead of the loan or portfolio appearing as an asset, the transferor will wish to show an entry reflecting the consideration received for the transfer (with appropriate additional changes to reflect any repayment of funding associated with its holding of the loan or portfolio).

12.12.1

The approach taken to the accounting treatment of a transaction differs from the more formal legal approach in analysing the transaction. The accounting treatment is concerned with ascertaining and recognising the financial and economic substance of a transaction, rather than just its strict legal characteristics. Essentially, this involves ascertaining where the economic risks and rewards associated with the relevant assets lie following the transaction. Much of the commentary below will concentrate upon the position under the International Accounting Standards, as it is likely that most entities which enter into loan transfers and securitisation

12.12.1.1

---

[302] Formerly s 262 (1) of the Companies Act 1985.
[303] Which is supplemented by the following paras of Sched A1 to the Act: para 4D (interpretation of 'capital market arrangement'); paras 4E and 4F (the definitions of 'capital market investment'); para 4G (which relates to the debt of £10 million); and para 4K ('person').

transactions will be subject to those standards. By way of comparison, there will first be a brief description of the historic UK standard.

12.12.2 FRS 5

The historic position in the UK under Financial Reporting Standard (FRS) No 5[304] and Application Notes D and E thereto ('Securitised Assets' and 'Loan Transfers') was to provide for three possible treatments of a transaction, depending upon the analysis of the transaction.

12.12.2.1 First, there was the possibility of 'Derecognition', which treated the transaction for the purposes of the balance sheet as having achieved an outright sale of the relevant assets, so that they were removed from the seller's balance sheet. This was only available where the seller had been paid all of the consideration for the sale and retained no material risks or rewards in the assets. This treatment was not available if the seller had given any assurance as to the future performance of the assets, such as by way of a guarantee or a recourse obligation for default by the debtors, although it was permissible for the seller to give warranties as to factual matters as at the time of the transfer. In addition, the treatment was not available if the seller continued to receive an economic reward from the assets, such as by way of a margin of the interest payable on the assets.

12.12.2.2 The second method of treatment was 'Linked presentation', which showed the amount of the finance raised by the transaction as a deduction from the value of the assets on the seller's balance sheet. This treatment was appropriate where the seller retained some risks or rewards associated with the assets that had been sold (e.g. there was some element of deferred consideration), but the continuing risks to the seller associated with the assets were capped and the seller had no obligation to repurchase the assets.

12.12.2.3 The third method of treatment, which applied if neither of the other two treatments was appropriate, was 'Separate presentation'. In this case, the assets remained shown on the seller's balance sheet and the finance that had been raised was shown as a corresponding liability within creditors.

12.12.3 IAS 39

International Accounting Standard (IAS) No 39 provides for only two possible treatments of a transaction on a seller's balance sheet.[305] The transaction will lead either to derecognition of the asset (called a 'financial asset') from the seller's

---

[304] Published by the Accounting Standards Board in April 1994 (as amended).
[305] The relevant provisions will be found at paras 17–37 of IAS 39.

balance sheet following the sale or the asset will continue to be recognised, to some extent, on the balance sheet.

For the purposes of the standard, an entity (e.g. the seller) transfers an asset if either (a) it transfers the contractual right to receive the cash flows derived from the asset, or (b) whilst retaining the right to receive the cash flows, it assumes a contractual obligation to pay them over to the buyer, such as under a loan sub-participation. In the case of (b), the transaction may be treated as a transfer if (i) the seller only has to pay over to the buyer once it has received the relevant amounts (but short-term advances, prior to receipt, with a right of recapture plus interest, will be acceptable), (ii) the seller is prohibited by the terms of the contract with the buyer from selling or giving security over the assets, except in favour of the buyer, and (iii) it is obliged to remit receipts to the buyer without material delay (and there are further limitations as to investment of the cash flows in the meantime). **12.12.3.1**

The next issue to be addressed is to determine if there has been a substantial transfer of all of the risks and rewards of ownership. If the seller has so transferred the asset, derecognition would be appropriate. If it has retained substantially all of the risks and rewards, then the asset should remain on its balance sheet. This is assessed by comparing its exposure to the variability of the cash flows generated by the asset before and after the transfer. It will only have achieved an effective transfer if after the transfer its exposure to such variability is not significant. For instance, if it has an option to buy back the asset at its fair value at the time of the repurchase, that will be an effective transfer. On the other hand, if it has a buy-back obligation at a fixed price or at the sale price plus a lender's return, that will not be an effective transfer. **12.12.3.2**

If the seller has neither retained nor transferred substantially all of the risks and rewards associated with an asset, the next question is to determine if it has relinquished 'control' of the asset. The concept of control depends upon the buyer's ability to sell the asset. If the buyer has the practical ability to sell the asset in its entirety to an unrelated third party and is able to do so entirely of its own volition without needing to impose additional restrictions upon the transfer, then control has been surrendered to the buyer and the seller has not retained control. If it has relinquished control, then derecognition is appropriate. Otherwise, the asset should continue to be recognised on the seller's balance sheet to the extent of its continuing involvement. The extent of its continuing involvement is the extent to which the seller is exposed to changes in the value of the asset, such as by virtue of its liability under a guarantee or put option. **12.12.3.3**

When the seller has to recognise a continuing involvement in an asset, it must also recognise the carrying amount of an associated liability, and this cannot be offset against the carrying amount of the asset. Nor can it offset any income arising from the asset against any expense incurred on the associated liability. **12.12.3.4**

12.12.3.5 If the relevant transfer relates to only part of an asset (e.g. part of a loan), it is necessary to determine if derecognition can be applied to the part that has been transferred. This will only be possible if the relevant part comprises a specifically identified cash flow or a fully proportionate share of a cash flow from an asset. However, if the seller agrees to transfer something that is less distinct, such as the first or last 90 per cent of cash collections, that cannot be treated as a transfer of a distinct part of the asset and the transaction will fall to be assessed in relation to the seller's connection with the whole of the relevant asset.

12.13 Regulatory Matters

These matters are dealt with in Chapter 2.

13

PROJECT FINANCE

13.1 Introduction

13.1.1 The purpose of this chapter

In many senses, project finance amounts to a practical application of the legal principles that arise in the rest of this book, as it concerns lending money and extending credit on a secured basis, usually in conjunction with the principles of the conflict of laws for cross-border transactions. The purpose of this chapter, therefore, is to provide an overview of project finance by outlining the structures that are used, the identity of those involved and the relationships between them, the practical issues that arise, and the risks that are involved in project finance (especially from the perspective of those who finance such projects), rather than to repeat what is said in the other chapters of the book. For that reason, the reader is referred to the more technical discussion of the associated legal principles that are to be found elsewhere in the book, to which cross-references will be made as appropriate.

13.1.2 Basic definition

Project financing involves the provision of finance to fund the development and exploitation of asset-based projects or concessions that are associated with the use of the assets, where the servicing and repayment of the finance is linked to and, in the main, dependent upon the assets concerned and the revenues generated by the project or concession. Save for risks that are specifically allocated to them, there is likely to be a large element of limited recourse or no recourse at all for repayment and servicing of the debt to the commercial parties or other entities (such as governments or States) which are associated with the project. Because of that factor and the consequential dependency for payment upon the project itself, financiers who are considering the financing of a project must address their minds to the viability and creditworthiness of the underlying project, which will include an assessment of where the possible commercial and legal risks may be which could affect a successful and profitable outcome. To a large extent, the structure of the project and its financing has to be tailored to meet the practical requirements of the project and the allocation of risks amongst those concerned with the project, including the risks of failure that the financiers are prepared to accept.

13.1.3 Types of project

There are no boundaries to the types of project that may be involved but, typically, they are likely to be of a large scale and involve engineering, infrastructure, natural resources, IT, or construction projects. Examples include projects for the extraction and exploitation of oil, gas, and minerals; the design, construction, and operation of roads, bridges, tunnels, airports, seaports, dams, stadiums and sports facilities, refineries, pipelines, power stations, utilities distribution networks, and telecoms networks, and the building, launch, and operation of satellites. Sometimes this will involve an entirely new scheme and on other occasions it may involve the enhancement or renewal of an existing facility or set of assets. The project may comprise a single whole or it may be multi-faceted with discrete elements, as may be the financing (e.g. separate financing packages may be arranged for different aspects of the project), with the consequent need for co-ordination as between the different elements.

13.1.4 PPP

An area that overlaps with such projects is that of the public–private partnership (PPP), in which a private contractor is given a concession by a governmental or other public authority to operate a service facility for the benefit of the public, usually to a set of standards or performance requirements that must be met over the life of the arrangement. The relevant public authority pays a periodic fee to the operator in return for the provision of the services to the public under the facility. Quite often it will involve an initial element of capital works by the contractor in constructing the facility which will then be operated by it during the lifetime of the concession that has been granted by the public authority. In the UK, this type of arrangement falls under the private finance initiative (PFI). Typical examples in the UK include the building, or repair and upgrading, and then the operation and maintenance of hospitals, prisons, and public transport facilities.

13.1.5 A typical model

Given the variety of projects that take place around the world, it is impossible to be prescriptive as to their foundation and the methods by which they are structured and constituted. Nonetheless, a fairly typical model for a project will involve the grant of a licence or concession by a governmental authority for the construction or development and subsequent exploitation of an asset over a period of time or sometimes for the whole of the useful life of the asset. The grantee will be a 'vehicle' (using that term rather loosely for the moment) formed by or comprising the commercial parties that are interested in the project, who are often referred to as the 'sponsors'. It or the sponsors will have bid or tendered for the grant, usually through a competitive bid or tendering process, having undertaken preliminary investigations and feasibility studies before deciding if they wished to proceed. The vehicle will then enter into contractual arrangements for the construction work and for the subsequent operation and maintenance of the completed project asset, as well as for the exploitation of that asset or what it produces. There may, in addition, be contracts for the supply of raw materials that are required in the production of end products. Insurance protection will also be an important factor. In the case of concession arrangements concerning infrastructure projects, the transaction may involve the project vehicle in building the relevant facility (e.g. a toll road, bridge, or tunnel) and then operating the facility for a period of time, sufficient to recoup the cost of building and the return of a profit, after which it will be transferred to the relevant public authority. Such projects are labelled as 'Build, Operate, Transfer' (or 'BOT') projects.

13.1.6 The model that has been outlined above is one that is commonplace. As already mentioned, however, not all projects will conform to that model. For instance, some projects may not involve the necessity of obtaining a licence or concession from a governmental authority, as the owner of an asset may simply be seeking to develop and exploit it for its own commercial purposes. In other cases there may be only one sponsor that undertakes the project, employing contractors under its supervision, whilst in yet other cases one sponsor may undertake the project on behalf of itself and the other sponsors. For convenience of explanation, the model that has been outlined above will be that which is addressed in this chapter.

13.1.7 Sources of finance

There are various sources of finance, or for assurance of repayment, that may be available for a project, and it is possible that more than one source may be used in relation to a project. Multilateral development banks and similar international organisations and agencies, such as the International Finance Corporation (IFC) and the European Bank for Reconstruction and Development (EBRD), are frequently involved in providing finance for projects in developing countries, quite often in conjunction with finance provided by commercial banks. The latter may be provided under the umbrella of the arrangements entered into by the international agency, through the commercial bank providing part of the funding that is advanced by the agency. Export credit agencies in developed countries, including the Export Credits Guarantee Department in the UK (ECGD),[1] may provide funding or guarantees or insurance cover, including cover for political risks, for finance associated with the supply of goods and services to foreign customers in less prosperous countries. Commercial banks may combine to provide a syndicated facility, which is a fairly common method of financing projects. Less common is finance that is initially raised through a bond issue, but sometimes a bond issue may be used as the method of re-financing a successful project. Similar considerations would apply to a securitisation of the receipts generated by a project. It is also common that some part of the finance that is required for the project, albeit a comparatively small part in the context of the total amount of finance that may be necessary, will be provided by the sponsors of the project, either through the provision of equity or subordinated debt, and this is often a condition to the provision of finance by other sources. Where the banking or outside commercial finance for a project is provided from several sources, it is likely that there will be some element of co-ordination as between the facilities and as to the exercise of remedies on default and the sharing of security.

13.1.8 A lawyer's considerations

A lawyer who is advising upon a project finance transaction will have to consider the structural, commercial, and legal issues that arise in relation to the project itself, as well as those that concern its financing. This is especially the case given the dependency for the repayment and servicing of the finance upon the successful outcome of the project and the recourse to its assets and revenues. From a legal perspective, project finance involves an amalgam of the techniques and principles that are relevant to many of the other matters that are addressed in this book. In a sense, it amounts to the practical application of those techniques and principles. For instance, the underlying project will involve the application of contractual and proprietary principles, especially in considering the assets and the layers of contractual arrangements which concern the project and by which it is to be governed. The financing of the project will concern matters that relate to the provision of loan finance, usually through syndicated lending, but sometimes involving other methods such as a capital markets issuance, as well as relating the provision of the finance to the stages in which the project is undertaken, taking security over a range of assets

---

[1] The ECGD is referred to in Chap 16.

and hedging some of the finance risks through derivatives transactions. Almost inevitably, a project and its financing will necessitate a consideration of the principles of conflict of laws, except where there is an entirely domestic arrangement.

13.2 The Sponsors and the Project Vehicle

13.2.1 The sponsors

The sponsors are the commercial proponents of a project. They will usually comprise a consortium whose members represent interests in the various stages of the project as, for instance, in designing and constructing the project, in operating and maintaining the project facility once it is up and running, in supplying or taking materials or product to or from it, or in using the facility that is established by the project. The sponsors are likely to be large international corporate groups, acting through their respective subsidiaries.

13.2.2 The vehicle

As mentioned above, it is probable that the sponsors will form a vehicle or consortium arrangement of some description as the means by which they will act collectively. Various different types of mechanisms for achieving this may be considered, including a partnership[2] or a joint venture between the sponsors, a limited liability partnership (LLP),[3] and a European Economic Interest Group (EEIG),[4] but the usual vehicle will be a separate corporate entity, with its own legal personality, in which each sponsor holds shares.

13.2.3 Considerations as to the types of vehicle

There are various considerations that will be relevant in determining which type of collective mechanism (which will be referred to below in the generic sense of a 'vehicle') should be used. They will include the following.

---

[2] Under English law, it could be an ordinary partnership under the Partnership Act 1890 or a limited partnership under the Limited Partnerships Act 1907. In the former case, each partner is jointly liable for all the debts and obligations of the firm. In the latter case, there must be one or more general partners with unlimited liability but the other partners (called limited partners), who must not take part in management of the business, are only liable for the debts and liabilities of the firm up to the amount of their capital contributions.

[3] Under English law, pursuant to the Limited Liability Partnerships Act 2000. Under that Act, a limited liability partnership is a body corporate with a separate legal personality. It is liable to the same extent as any of its members for a wrongful act or omission of the member whilst acting in the course of the business of the LLP or with its authority.

[4] Which may be formed pursuant to the Council Regulation on the European Economic Interest Grouping (2137/85/EEC OJ L199/1 31/7/85). For the position in Great Britain, see also the European Economic Interest Grouping Regs (SI 1989/638), under which the EEIG has separate legal personality but each of its members is jointly and severally liable for its debts and obligations.

13.2.3.1 Licence requirements

The conditions upon which the licence or concession for the project is granted by the relevant State may prescribe the type of vehicle that may be used, perhaps by requiring that it should be locally incorporated or that it should be one or more of the sponsors acting directly. Less prescriptively, the conditions may set out other requirements concerning vehicle, such as the minimum amount of its capital, that it should be locally registered as a foreign corporation that is entitled to carry on business in the State, and, perhaps, that its members should meet certain requirements and that those members should guarantee its obligations under the licence or concession or arrange for bonding lines to be put in place to cover those obligations.

13.2.3.2 Establishment, status, and powers

Subject to those matters, the vehicle should be established or incorporated in a jurisdiction which will permit it to pursue its intended activities, where its continuance will not be jeopardised by precipitate action taken by the State which is outside its own control and in which shareholdings or ownership participations may be transferred without undue or onerous restrictions. It will also be necessary that the vehicle should be accorded legal recognition in each other jurisdiction in which it is to carry on its business and hold assets, particularly in relation to the project. There may be a risk, for instance, that a vehicle that is given the status of having a separate legal personality in one jurisdiction may be considered in a different jurisdiction to be nothing more than an unincorporated association or a partnership of the sponsors, or it may be ignored altogether. From a practical perspective, it is desirable that the rules of its law of establishment or incorporation which concern the vehicle's internal organisation and its decision-making processes should be straightforward and not unduly prescriptive, and that they should be recognised in other relevant jurisdictions. In that regard, the sponsors will wish to nominate the vehicle's management and other senior personnel, but they may have to accept a certain number of local employees, even at a senior level. Local employment laws will also have to be observed. Another practical consideration will be the ease with which the vehicle may be liquidated and wound up upon completion of the project or an earlier termination of the venture.

13.2.3.3 Structural separation

The sponsors will probably also wish to achieve a form of structural separation from the vehicle so that, as a matter of the general law of each of those jurisdictions, the sponsors will not be liable for its debts and obligations,[5] although the

---

[5] In English law, the concept of the corporate veil representing the separation of a company from its shareholders and that the latter should not be liable for the debts and liabilities of the former

general position may be overridden by express provisions in contracts to which one or more of the sponsors may be parties (for instance, relating to the obligations of the vehicle under the licence for the project and they may be contractors involved in carrying out aspects of the project) and many jurisdictions assert the right to pursue the officers, including shadow directors, and members of a corporation for unpaid tax liabilities or where their own default or dereliction of duty has contributed to a loss to creditors on the corporation's insolvency. Similarly, in accounting terms, the sponsors may wish to avoid a consolidation of the vehicle as a subsidiary undertaking in their respective consolidated balance sheets or the inclusion in their balance sheets of their interest in the vehicle as a participating interest.

13.2.3.4 On the other hand, the sponsors will wish to extract profits from the vehicle without undue restriction occasioned by the structure of the vehicle. They may also wish to off-set project expenditure against their own profits for tax purposes, which may be difficult to achieve where they have created a vehicle which is remote from them for accounting purposes. Where it is intended to obtain export credit support or grants or aid in support of the project, the vehicle will have to comply with any requirements that may be relevant.

13.2.4 Relationship between the sponsors

In addition to the issues described above concerning structural matters relating to the vehicle, the sponsors will also need to agree the more substantive matters of the relationship as between themselves and the tasks and responsibilities they will assume, as well as the approach that they wish to take relating to the project, even if, from the formal standpoint, those matters will be implemented through the auspices of the vehicle they have set up to represent them.

13.2.4.1 Agreement between the sponsors

Such things will be set out in one or more agreements between the sponsors. The contents of such agreements will cover the preliminary work to be done in assessing the viability of the project, including conducting feasibility and environmental studies, the work in preparing and submitting the bid or tender to the relevant authority which is to grant the licence or concession, negotiating and agreeing all of the necessary contractual arrangements for the project and its financing, establishing the project vehicle, the financial contributions that are to be made towards the costs of those matters, confidentiality and non-compete provisions, termination of the venture, withdrawal of a sponsor and bringing in new members of the

---

was originally recognised by the House of Lords in *Salomon v Salomon & Co Ltd* [1897] AC 22, although the veil may be pierced in various circumstances. This issue is explored further at para 13.7.4 below.

consortium, the allocation and extraction of profits from the project, and the financial and other support that each sponsor will make towards the project, as well as a timetable for contributing such support. Such support may include the provision of expertise or services and goods.

13.2.5 Financial support by the sponsors

Financial support by the sponsors may involve contributions to the capital of the vehicle, the provision of loans by the sponsors to the vehicle, or that the sponsors should guarantee certain of the debt provided to the vehicle by third parties, such as the sponsors' own banks, perhaps pending the sponsors making their own direct contributions at a later date. The banks and similar providers of finance for the project are likely to impose requirements concerning the amount, timing, and manner of financial support that should be provided by the sponsors. It is also likely that the banks will require that such contributions, to the extent that they have not been provided at the outset of the project, should be phased and relate to drawdowns of the finance provided by the banks or be available to meet costs and expenses that are not covered by the funds provided by the banks. The banks will require that loan contributions by the sponsors (or loans which they have guaranteed) should be subordinated in right of payment, after the entitlement of the banks to payment.

Where, or to the extent that, the sponsors' financial contributions (or funds that they have guaranteed) are not provided at the outset, the banks will wish to find ways by which they might seek to ensure that the contributions will be made. One method is by providing for the contributions to be made as conditions precedent to the right of the borrower to make drawings at correlative stages under the finance facility. That solution will not be of much help where the contributions, or some part of them, are intended to be provided after the finance has been drawn down in full or where the borrower is unable to make drawings because it is in default or, worse, has become insolvent and gone into liquidation. The financiers might seek to overcome those potential difficulties by taking direct covenants from the sponsors, to the effect that they will make their contributions at the agreed time and in the agreed manner. Such covenants might be contained in a separate agreement between the financiers and the sponsors, or the financiers might be added as parties to the agreement between the sponsors and the vehicle which provides for such contributions to be made. **13.2.5.1**

As a matter of English law, however, there could be difficulties in the enforcement by the financiers of such covenants. It is very unlikely that they would be susceptible to an order for specific performance, and it is difficult to envisage that the financiers would be awarded much by way of damages if the covenants were breached. Similarly, the vehicle (as the borrower) would be unlikely to achieve **13.2.5.2** very much on its own behalf, if the contributions were to be provided by way of loan, particularly if it was already insolvent.[6] On the other hand, if the contributions were to be provided by way of paying up partly paid shares in the vehicle, then the vehicle, or its liquidator, could enforce the obligation to make the contributions[7] and, subject to there being a power to do so in the company's memorandum or articles of association, which has not been countermanded by a resolution of its members,[8] security can be taken over the uncalled share capital of a company[9] but it cannot be taken over the members' undertaking to contribute if the company is a company limited by guarantee.[10]

13.3 The Licence

13.3.1 For the sake of convenience, the expression 'licence' will be used to connote both a licence and a concession, as they amount to much the same thing in practical terms. Whilst the expression refers to a licence in the singular, it is quite possible that it will be comprised in more than one instrument. The licence may take the form of legislation of the country where the project is to take place or, either additionally or as the licence in its own right, in some other form or set of documentation, most probably as authorised by legislation. Obviously, the legislation and the constitutional position must be checked to ensure that the relevant authority has the power to grant the licence and to undertake whatever commitments it is to undertake pursuant to the grant of the licence.

13.3.2 The bidding process

The grant of the licence will usually follow a competitive bidding or tendering process under which the authority which is to grant the licence will invite interested consortia of potential sponsors to submit bids after satisfying requirements for them to qualify as bidders. Such requirements may include providing evidence that the bidders will have sufficient resources to proceed with the bidding process (and the resulting project if a bid is successful) and the provision of a bid or tender bond by a financial institution which will be called if a bidder fails to proceed.

---

[6] Because the court would not order specific performance of the agreement to lend (see Chap 3) and the sponsors could probably argue that, as the borrower was already insolvent, they were entitled to anticipate its inability to repay and repudiate the agreement. A different view might be taken if they had caused the insolvency by refusing to provide their contributions.

[7] As to the liability of such shareholders as contributories of a company in a liquidation, see ss 74(1) and (2)(d) of the Insolvency Act 1986.

[8] *Re Mayfair Property Co, Barlett v Mayfair Property Co* [1898] 2 Ch 28.

[9] See the summary that is provided in *Halsbury's Laws of England* (4th edn, 2004 Reissue), Vol 7(2), at para 1528.

[10] *Re Irish Club Co Ltd* [1906] WN 127.

Apart from the apparent common sense of using a competitive process, the need for it may be dictated by a necessity to follow the World Bank's requirements for projects that it funds,[11] the World Trade Organisation's Agreement on Government Procurement of 1994, or the EU's public procurement requirements[12] (which, in the case of the EU's requirements, extend also to procurement by privately owned utilities). In addition, the EU's requirements concerning State aids may be relevant if a country within the EU (or one of its constituent elements) is to provide a subsidy or other assistance for the project.[13] The successful consortium will then be given the status of a preferred bidder and it will proceed to finalise the negotiations leading to the grant of the licence. Alternatively, the licensing authority may decide that it should continue to negotiate with more than one group, in which case the final negotiations will also involve choosing the consortium which is to be granted the licence and the elimination of the others.

13.3.3 Contents of a licence

Almost inevitably, the licensing process will reflect divergent approaches between the desire of the authority which is granting the licence to advance the public good at the least risk and expense to itself, on the one hand, and the commercial objectives of the sponsors and the need for them to meet the requirements of their financial funders, on the other hand. Indeed, the funders will be concerned with a great deal of the licence and its contents, as the viability of the project from the perspective of its commercial proponents and its funders is dependent upon the licence. Bearing that point in mind, there now follows an outline of the principal matters that will be addressed in the licence.[14] The entity which grants the licence is referred to as the 'licensor' and the project vehicle to which the licence is granted is referred to as the 'licensee'.

13.3.3.1 The basic details

The licence will contain a description and specification of the project, setting out details to identify the project and the relevant technical data, as well as the scope of the licensee's obligations. Environmental issues will also be addressed. The

---

[11] Entitled *Guidelines: Procurement Under IBRD Loans and IDA Credits*, which were published in May 2004 by the World Bank.

[12] Contained in two directives, being the Directive on the co-ordination of procedures for the award of public works contracts, public supply contracts, and public service contracts (2004/18/EC OJ L134/114 30/4/2004) and the Directive co-ordinating the procurement procedures of entities operating in the water, energy, transport, and postal services sector (2004/17/EC OJ L134/1 30/4/2004).

[13] State aids are addressed in Chap 16.

[14] In relation to PFI projects in the UK, much of the licensing process has been standardised under documentation produced by HM Treasury called *Standardisation of PFI Contracts*, the original version of which was published in 1999 and was updated in March 2007 (SoPC Version 4).

duration for which the licence is granted, or the method for determining it, will be set out. The site of the project and associated assets will be allocated and provision will be made for transferring or vesting title (or some lesser procedure) in the licensee. It may be necessary for the licence to provide for the provision of ancillary works or assets or other matters which are needed to make the project physically or economically viable (e.g. building approach roads to a bridge or an undertaking on the part of the licensor not to permit a competitive scheme that would detract from the usefulness of the project and the economic return generated by the project).

13.3.3.2 *Performance and maintenance requirements, royalties, fees and charges*

Where the licensee is to operate the completed project under a BOT, PPP, or similar concession, the licence (or perhaps some separate document) will specify the performance and maintenance requirements that must be met by the licensee and the method for calculating the remuneration or subsidy (if any) that is to be paid to the licensee under the licence, as well as specifying the criteria that must be met for return or handing over of the project facilities to the licensor (normally at no charge to the licensor) at the end of the concession, if such a return or handing over is envisaged by the licence. The licence (or such a separate document) may also limit any charges that the licensee may make to the public for the services it supplies or the use that the public makes of the project facility (e.g. toll charges). In some cases (e.g. a licence for the exploitation of oil, gas, or minerals, or a concession to operate a profitable infrastructure project), the licensee may be required to pay fees or royalties for the grant of the licence and the continued use of the concession contained within it.

13.3.3.3 *Allocation of risks*

Generally speaking, the licensor will seek to impose on the licensee all of the technical and commercial risks that may be inherent in the project, so that the licensee will suffer the consequences if anything goes wrong (or, at least, the licensee will have to guard itself against those risks by passing them on to its own contractors or by obtaining insurance cover). Because of the licensor's interest in the project and its assets, the licence will also lay down requirements, which the licensee must see are met, as to the insurance cover that should be in place during the various stages of the project, including as to the nature of the cover, the identity of the insurers and re-insurers, that the licensor's interest (amongst others) should be covered by the policies, and as to the loss payable provisions of the policies. Quite often there will be a requirement that local insurers should provide some part of the cover, in which case particular attention should be paid to the re-insurance of those risks. Insurance matters are referred to in more detail later in this chapter.

13.3.3.4 *Licensor's risks*

In some cases, however, the licensor may be prepared to accept and bear the consequences of certain of the risks associated with the project, particularly where it would be unreasonable or inappropriate to expect the licensee to accept them, such as in situations where the project is only marginally viable as a commercial or physical proposition, or it is not possible to obtain insurance cover for certain types of casualty. An example in the present day would be the risk of terrorist activity which destroys or damages the project or its assets. In such situations, the licence may provide for the licence to terminate, for the licensor to pay compensation or fees to the licensee, or the licence may be adjusted as, for instance, by extending its duration or reducing the fees or royalties that are payable by the licensee.

13.3.3.5 *Warranties and undertakings*

The licensee will be required to give warranties and undertakings as to how it will carry out the project and that it has adequate finance to complete the project. Supporting evidence will be required on these points. The licensor may stipulate that it should approve any contractors or sub-contractors that will work on the project, as well as the terms on which they will be engaged. There may also be requirements concerning the employment of local contractors and labour. The licence will probably contain limitations on its assignment or transfer by the licensee, and this must be considered in relation to the usual requirement of the project's financiers that they should have the benefit of security over the licensee's entitlement under the licence, as well as step-in rights in the event of a default by their borrower.

13.3.3.6 *Sponsors' undertakings*

As the licensee is the project vehicle and is really a creature of the consortium of the sponsors who won the bidding process, the sponsors may be required to give certain assurances and undertakings relating to themselves and the performance and observance of the terms of the licence by the licensee. This may include provisions limiting changes in the identity of the sponsors and concerning the ownership and continuance of the vehicle for the duration of the project. They may also be required to establish performance guarantees or bonds by acceptable banks or similar institutions.

13.3.3.7 *Termination*

Termination of the licence and its consequences should also be addressed. Termination may arise by effluction of time in accordance with the original grant, at an earlier point because of default on the part of the licensee, as provided in the licence, or because of the occurrence in the course of the licence of a *force majeure* event[15] as specified in the licence. As mentioned above, in the case of certain types of concession arrangement where the licence contemplates the return or handing over of the project assets at the expiry of the licence, the licence will specify the condition in which the project facility and its assets should be transferred or returned to the licensor. Where the licence is terminated early because of default by the licensee, the licence may provide for the licensor, or some other person nominated by it, to take over the project and its assets in place of the licensee, including a right to step in to contracts that have been entered into by the licensee with various contractors. The concept of stepping in to contracts is discussed in more detail below. The question which follows from this (in which the financiers will be particularly interested) is whether the licensor should pay any compensation to the licensee for depriving it of the benefit of the project, especially as the licensee may have incurred considerable expenditure and financial commitments prior to the time of termination. This should be addressed in the licence, including by providing a mechanism for computing a fair level of compensation that should be paid by the licensor and an allowance to it for the inconvenience of terminating the licence and having to make alternative arrangements. Sometimes the licence will provide that an expert or a tribunal should make the relevant calculations and determine the amounts that should be awarded. Such a mechanism can also be used to calculate adjustments to amounts payable under the licence to take account of matters for which the licence provides for price or royalty variations during the term of the licence (for example, a variation in the specifications for the project or where the licence permits a variation to take account of unforeseen circumstances).

13.3.3.8 *Governing law*

As a matter of its constitutional law, not to mention its national pride, the licence will probably be expressed to be governed by the law of the country concerned. Apart from ensuring that that law and its effect is understood when the licence is granted, this can obviously raise problems subsequently for the licensee, because of the risk that the law may be changed to suit the purposes of the licensor in its desired interpretation of the licence, that a programme of confiscation and renationalisation of assets in private hands occurs or that a change in the political regime occurs which might lead to a decision by the new regime to repudiate or renegotiate licences granted by its predecessor. This is one of the principal elements of what is called political risk. Some protection against the economic consequences of the intervention of political risk may be possible under specialist insurance cover, such as provided by the ECGD in the UK. Practical refuge may also be gained by sheltering behind the involvement in the financing of a project by international

---

[15] As to *force majeure* events, see Chap 1.

agencies and multilateral development banks, such as the World Bank, the IFC, or the EBRD, as it is generally considered inadvisable from a political or diplomatic perspective for a country to take action which endangers projects in which they have a financial interest.

13.3.3.9 *Disputes*

The licence should also provide a mechanism for the resolution of any disputes that may arise between the licensor and the licensee. A common method is to provide for arbitration by a panel of independent expert arbitrators, with the seat of the arbitration in a neutral country. The award may then be enforceable in pursuance of the New York Convention of 1958. The licensee may also be able to take advantage of a bilateral investment treaty between the State of the licensor and the licensee's own State. Arbitration and enforcement of an arbitral award may be available in pursuance of the treaty. These matters are discussed in Chapter 6.

13.3.4 Other related matters

Whilst they may not be dealt with in the licence, there may be additional issues that arise under the local law of the licensing country and which are associated with the grant of the licence and the implementation and exploitation of the project under the licence, as well as its financing. The licensee should see that such issues are properly considered and addressed. These matters will also be relevant to the financiers who are funding the project. For instance, there may be restrictions under local law concerning exchange controls, foreign remittances, the making of investments by foreign entities or their associates, and upon foreign currency payments. Local law may also have the effect of requiring that payments which are linked to the project and that revenues earned by the project should be denominated and paid in local currency, or that local currency should be converted into a foreign currency at a set rate and only processed by the central bank. There may be adverse tax consequences in relation to dividend and interest payments, including the imposition of withholding taxes. Labour and employment laws and laws concerning local contractors may be unfavourable or overly protective. It may be possible that some of these matters can be dealt with by obtaining waivers and consents from the relevant authorities. There remains the political risk that waivers and consents may be revoked or that new laws may be imposed during the term of the project. It is unlikely that a State would give an unequivocal commitment not to change its law but some lesser assurance might be sought.

13.4 The Contractual Elements of a Project

13.4.1 It is now appropriate to discuss the contractual documentation that is associated with a project. This will concern the contracts dealing with the construction phase of the project and the contracts relating to maintenance, operation, use, and exploitation of the project facilities once they have been constructed, including contracts for the supply of raw materials to be processed by the facility, contracts for the sale of its products, and, in the case of project facilities that comprise pipelines and transmission networks and PPP facilities, contracts for the use of the facility.

13.4.2 Interest of the financiers

Once again, the financiers who are providing the finance for the project will be interested in the contracts, as the project will depend upon the contracts and the financiers will wish to include the benefit of the contracts (or, at least, the principal contracts to which the vehicle is a party) within their security package. They will also wish to have (or to be able to nominate someone else to have) step-in rights to take over the vehicle's position under the contracts to which it is a party, should it default under those contracts or the finance documentation. The matters concerning security and step-in rights are discussed separately in this chapter. For the moment, it is sufficient to note that the contracts should permit such security to be taken and recognise that such step-in rights should be available.

13.4.3 Governing law

It is important that all such contracts should provide expressly for a governing law, but it must always be remembered that not all of the legal issues that may arise in the context of a contract will necessarily be governed by the chosen law. For instance, the rules of the forum that is hearing a claim may prevail over the chosen law, as may the public policy of that jurisdiction, and the rules of a jurisdiction that is closely connected with the subject matter of the contract may also have to be considered. See further the discussion of those matters in Chapter 4. In the text that follows, it will be assumed that English law will be applied in the consideration of the various issues that may arise.

13.4.4 The discussion below will look mainly at the matters that are relevant to the principal construction contract, but quite a number of those matters will be relevant to all of the various contracts. In the case of the contracts that are not concerned with the construction of the project, the discussion will just mention their principal features.

13.4.5 Construction contracts

The considerations relevant to construction contracts are as follows.

13.4.5.1 The framework

There are, typically, two types of alternative contractual structure that may be used. The first involves a 'turnkey' contract between the project vehicle and a main contractor, which may be a sponsor, under which the main contractor undertakes to build the project to the specifications and requirements as laid down by the contract and, upon practical completion of the project, to deliver it to the project vehicle. The main contractor would then engage sub-contractors, who may be other sponsors, for different aspects of the works and for the supply of materials, although the main contract would prescribe conditions as to who may be engaged and as to the terms of the sub-contracts. The alternative structure involves the project vehicle acting in the role of a main contractor and entering directly into contracts with the various contractors for the different aspects of the works and supply of materials. It is likely that the project vehicle would appoint a manager, probably a sponsor, to act on its behalf in the second type of situation.

13.4.5.2 Contractual chains

It is worth bearing in mind, however, that there is likely to be a chain of contracts, particularly in the first type of structure, but also in the alternative structure, under which sub-contractors, sub-sub-contractors and so on will be engaged under separate contracts by their immediate superior in the line to carry out certain parts of the works. The question arises as to the responsibility that a contractor has under such a contract. Clearly, there will be a responsibility to its direct contracting counterparty arising from the contractual relationship between them. Generally speaking, it is unlikely under English law that the contractor will assume responsibility, particularly for economic loss, to any party that is higher up in the chain of contracts.[16] This means that it is essential that each contractor, in the contract with its immediate counterparty, should assume responsibility for the work done by its own sub-contractors.

---

[16] It is unlikely that such responsibility could be asserted in either contract or tort. The immediate difficulty with a contractual claim would be that the contractor has not contracted with anyone higher in the chain. An attempt to argue that a person higher in the chain was intended to benefit from the contract and thus could rely upon it pursuant to s 1 of the Contract (Rights of Third Parties) Act 1999 is unlikely to succeed, unless the matter is expressly acknowledged in the contract: see the opinion of the Law Commission (*Privity of Contract* Report No 242 of 31/7/1996, para 7.18), which was quoted with approval by the Court of Appeal in *Laemthong International Lines Co Ltd v Abdullah Mohammed Fahem & Co* [2005] EWCA Civ, [2005] 1 Lloyd's Rep 688. The position in tort for economic loss was addressed by Lord Goff in *Henderson v Merrett Syndicates Ltd* [1995] 2 AC 145, at 195–196.

13.4.5.3 The various contracts and sub-contracts in either situation would be likely to follow industry-standard forms as used in international projects, but amended and tailored for the particular requirements of the project. The party to a contract which commissions the work to be done under it is usually referred to as the 'employer' and the party which undertakes to do the work is called the 'contractor'. Such contracts will contain provisions dealing with matters along the following lines.

13.4.5.3.1 The parameters The contract will set out the relevant design, engineering, and technical specifications that are required, with provisions for amendments. It will provide for the pricing of the work, usually on a fixed or inclusive price basis, but with adjustment mechanisms to take account of matters such as variations in the specifications, unforeseen ground or engineering risks, the risk of interruption due to the discovery of archaeological matters or the discovery of antiquities, the cost of obtaining some materials at prevailing market prices, and some adjustments or compensation arising from *force majeure* events. The contract will provide for payment to be made to the contractor by the employer at defined stages during the construction process, usually upon production to the employer of certificates given by an engineer or other suitably qualified expert, which certify that the relevant stage has been reached by the work done under the contract. It is likely that the contract will provide for retentions that are held back from payments to cover the cost of remedying defects that might subsequently come to light.

13.4.5.3.2 Practical completion The contract will provide for the date by which the works should be substantially completed, usually referred to as 'practical completion' (although the date may be delayed to take account of variations to the contract). Practical completion is a significant stage in the contract process, including for payment to the contractor. It is the point at which the work under the contract is substantially complete, although some subsidiary matters may still have to be finished. There will usually be testing and associated certification that practical completion has been reached, upon the satisfactory conclusion of which the finished work will be handed over to the employer under the contract and, at that point, the contract will provide that risk in what has been constructed or fabricated should pass to the employer. Prior to that point, the contractor will have arranged insurances to cover matters such as fire and physical damage, death and personal injury claims, and, if available, cover for contractual interruption. After practical completion, the employer will have to arrange the cover.

13.4.5.3.3 *Force majeure* The contract is likely to contain a *force majeure* clause. Such clauses are discussed in Chapter 1 of this book. As explained there, the effect of the operation of the clause in the particular circumstances of a case may be that the contract is terminated and abandoned or that extra time is given for the contract to be completed. The clause may also provide for compensation to be paid by the employer and other financial adjustments to be made between the parties so as to take account of the effect of the relevant event that has led to the operation of the clause.

13.4.5.3.4 Default The contract may seek to legislate for the consequences of a default by the contractor, both in terms of a financial detriment that it should suffer and the right of the employer to terminate the contract. The right of termination will be effective as a matter of general law, although the right to claim general damages for loss of the benefit of the contract will depend upon whether the grounds for termination amount to a repudiatory breach of the contract.[17] The imposition through the contract of a financial detriment to the contractor, such as requiring that the contractor should make a default payment to the employer (which is often referred to as a 'liquidated damages clause'), may be held to be unenforceable as an unlawful penalty, unless it can be shown that it was a genuine pre-estimate of loss. The issue of penalties is explored in Chapter 3. A way of overcoming these difficulties is through the opening of bonding or guarantee lines, under which a third party financial institution issues a bond or guarantee in favour of the employer as the beneficiary, which can be called by the making of a demand upon the issuer in the event of a default by the contractor as prescribed in the relevant instrument.[18] Construction contracts sometimes provide for the contractor to arrange for such instruments to be issued, but contractors would normally prefer not to have to do so because of the expense that is involved (the issuer will charge the contractor a fairly hefty fee by way of commission and it may require security) and, save in the case of fraud, the contractor has no opportunity to challenge the making of a demand under the instrument.[19]

13.4.5.3.5 Disputes Not surprisingly when one considers their subject matter and the opportunity (in a practical sense) for things to go wrong, construction contracts (and, indeed, many of the other contracts that are associated with a project) are redolent with the risk of disputes between the parties. It is common for such contracts to contain arbitration clauses under which disputes should be submitted to arbitration. Arbitration is a preferred method of adjudicating upon disputes in these types of case because the arbitral tribunal may comprise arbitrators chosen in accordance with the contract who have the technical expertise and experience to asses the situation, it can be seen as a neutral forum, its seat can be located in a neutral country, and the arbitration can be conducted under the procedures and rules of an arbitral body as specified in the contract or as otherwise

---

[17] See the discussion in Chap 1.
[18] As was the case in *Export Credits Guarantee Department v Universal Oil Products Co* [1983] 1 WLR 399.
[19] See the discussion in Chap 16.

decided upon by the arbitrators. In addition, in many cases the award will be enforceable under the provisions of the New York Convention of 1958.

13.4.6 Operating and maintenance contracts

The operating and maintenance contracts are concerned with the operation and maintenance of the finished project facility. The subject matter may be dealt with in one contract or in separate contracts. These contracts may be entered into at the inception of the project, with the intention that they will come into effect when the project facility has been constructed, or their parameters (including the requirements as to who would qualify to be appointed as the contractor) may be outlined at the outset of the project, but the contracts would then only be signed once the construction had finished. The contracts will specify the required standards for operation and maintenance of the facility, remuneration, duration, the effect of *force majeure*, termination for default, governing law, and dispute resolution.

13.4.7 Raw materials

It may be necessary for the project facility, once constructed, to be assured of a supply of raw materials for it to use in the production of the finished product. For instance, oil for a refinery, electricity or gas for a distribution network and so on. In such cases, a supply contract will be required. The quantity and security of supply, pricing, and duration of the arrangement will be important factors to be dealt with by such a contract.

13.4.8 Finished products or services

It may also be essential to address the use of the project facility and the sale or supply of its products or services, so as to be certain that it will produce profitable revenues. The financiers of the project will be particularly concerned to know that the project facility will produce sufficient revenues and in a predictable period to service and repay the debt.

13.4.8.1 Those objectives can be addressed if there are one or more contracts agreed (or, at least, provided for) at the outset of the project for the sale and purchase of goods or services that the finished project facility is to supply or, in the case of a facility that is to be used by others, for the use of specified proportions, amounts, or quantities of what the facility offers. Such a contract would specify the quantities, proportions, or amounts of the relevant goods, services, or usage that would be made available and purchased or used at specified dates or over specified periods, together with the mechanism for calculating the price, with the fall-back that if delivery was not taken at a specified time or over a specified period, or the facility was not used in accordance with the minimum contemplated usage, the contract would require that payment should be made as if the goods or services had been supplied or the requisite use had been made of the facility (sometimes referred to as 'take or pay contracts'[20]). The contract would specify quality and performance requirements that had to be met by the facility and would contain price adjustment mechanisms where those requirements were not achieved.

These types of consideration would be relevant to project facilities such as infra- 13.4.8.2
structure facilities (e.g. toll roads, tunnels, and bridges), pipelines, transmission networks, and various types of PPP facilities. Examples would include take or pay and off-take agreements, under which the purchaser agrees to purchase and take the specified quantities or pay as if it had taken them. Similar considerations would apply to throughput facilities (e.g. a gas or oil pipeline facility or an electricity distribution network) where, additionally, provision would have to be made for the consequences of loss or reduction in quantities in the course of transmission and mixing of entitlements as between several users. Under build-operate-transfer (BOT) infrastructure arrangements, the licensing authority may agree to pay for or guarantee a minimum usage of the facility (and revenues receipts) over periods whilst it is operated by (or on behalf of) the project vehicle, so as to ensure a sufficient revenue stream to compensate the vehicle, and provide a profit, for building the facility, operating it, and finally handing it over to the authority at the end of the licence.

Insurance arrangements are also important to a project and the facility that results 13.4.9
from it. As they are also important to the considerations of the financiers, they will be addressed separately below.

13.5 The Assessment of Risks in Financing a Project

It will be apparent from what has already been said that a bank or other financier 13.5.1
which is considering a proposal to provide finance for a project must consider the viability of the project as a technical and commercial proposition, as well as from a legal perspective, so as to obtain a clear view of where the risks may be which might imperil its success. This is not least the case because, as a general proposition, the financier will be looking to the project assets and the revenues that the project generates for payment. This flows from the concept that the sponsors as the commercial parties behind the project will not accept overall responsibility for payment in the same way as would an ordinary borrower (or a guarantor of the

---

[20] It has been held that the obligation to pay in default of or in lieu of taking the specified quantity could, in theory, amount to an unenforceable penalty. It would then depend, on the facts, whether the contract was commercially justifiable as a reasonable pre-estimate, at the time of contracting, of the consequences of the failure to take and thus a reasonable pre-estimate of the loss that would be caused: *M&J Polymers Ltd v Imerys Minerals Ltd* [2008] EWHC 344 (Comm).

borrower's obligations), bearing in mind that the actual borrower will be the project vehicle which is unlikely to have any resources or assets other than those associated with the project. In this sense, project finance involves a financier in making more of a commercial and technical assessment of the project than it might make as an ordinary lender where it will also have the benefit of a general right of recourse to a borrower (or a guarantor) of substance.

13.5.2 Covering the risks

In some situations, an apparent risk may be covered by an insurance policy (insurance matters are mentioned separately below) or by provisions in a contract or in the licence for the project which place the burden of a casualty, a default, or some other detrimental occurrence on an identified entity (assuming, of course, that such entity is properly bound). In some cases that entity may even be one or other of the sponsors or the licensor in relation to some specific obligation or risk that it has accepted. In other cases, however, the financier may find that the risk will fall ultimately on it and that there will be no practical avenue available to recoup its losses if the risk eventuates. Even in situations where a particular risk may be covered by a right of recourse against a particular contracting entity, that right will only be as good as the capacity of the entity to honour its obligations. If it defaults, there may be a right to pursue legal proceedings, but they may be protracted and uncertain and the entity may simply not have the resources to pay. Bearing those points in mind, it is now relevant to review some of the types of risk that might be associated with a project and its financing.

13.5.3 Background risks

For the reasons that have already been mentioned, it is imperative that the licence which has been granted is sufficient in its scope for the fulfilment of the project, and its continuance until the finance has been repaid, and that the burdens that the licence places on the project vehicle, as the licensee, are adequately covered in the arrangements that it enters into under the relevant project contracts. Similarly, it is necessary to ensure that the various matters that have been referred to already concerning the vehicle and the sponsors have been properly addressed.

13.5.4 Physical and technology risks

In relation to the project itself, there are physical risks which, if they occur, may destroy the project or prevent it from coming to fruition. In general, such risks should be covered by insurance (though it may not be possible to obtain cover for risks of inherent uncertainties in the project from the outset). On the other hand, insurance will not cover a failure which arises because the project was not commercially or technically feasible as, for instance, because there was an insufficient quantity of resources to be exploited by the project, where the technology that was to be used in developing the project was inadequate, or where the product or facility that eventuates from the project becomes out of date or is superseded by new technology before the project has run its full course.

Quite a number of these matters might be the subject of feasibility and technical **13.5.4.1** studies that were conducted or commissioned by the sponsors before the project was commenced, with reports being based on the outcome of those studies. To ensure that the financiers of the project are also entitled to the benefit of such reports, the authors should be required to include the financiers as addressees of their reports and to accept that the financiers may rely upon them. Such reports are not guarantees of success, however. They are really in the nature of opinions based on an assessment of the data gathered by the studies. Assuming that the studies were properly conducted and the reports based on them were reasonably prepared (e.g. without negligence), it is unlikely that there would be a right of recourse to the authors if matters turn out to be different from the predictions contained in the reports. Subject to any limitation of liability or recoverable loss that has been properly agreed, if the authors were negligent then damages may be recoverable for the loss that was foreseeable and which eventuated from the negligence but that may not be sufficient to see the financiers whole.[21]

13.5.5 Risks in construction and implementation and commercial risks

The construction and implementation of the project may run into difficulties. There may be delays or default in construction of the project and in the subsequent operation of the project facility, and the associated costs may increase. As mentioned above, those matters may be covered by specific rights of recourse against a contractor but the rights may turn out to be of little practical value. Worse still, the project may grind to a complete halt and be abandoned (for instance, due to the occurrence of a terminal event of *force majeure*). The conditions of the licence might be breached, giving the licensor the right to terminate or revoke the licence or to impose further conditions for its continuance, including an increase in royalties or fees payable by the licensee, or, in the case of a concession or service facility, a decrease in the subsidy or fees payable by the licensor. There may be sales difficulties with the products or services that are produced or supplied by the project facility, arising from a lack of demand or competition from other suppliers. There may be currency risks due to a mismatch between the currency or currencies in which the project facility receives its revenues and the currencies in which its debt or other expenditure is denominated. As previously

---

[21] As to recovery in the tort of negligence under English law, see Chap 9. The issues that would arise for a contractual claim, if one exists, are discussed in Chap 1.

mentioned, political risks may arise which lead to the project becoming unsustainable or uneconomic because of political intervention and a change of law.

13.5.6 Environmental risks

One particular matter which has become prominent in recent years concerns the risk of environmental damage (e.g. air or water pollution and contamination of land) associated with a project site or from the construction and operation of a project. This extends to the consequential responsibility placed upon those who may be connected with the site or the project for the damage that has been caused, including pre-existing damage to the site before the project was commenced. The damage may be to the land occupied by the project, it may be to water or air quality that is affected by the site or the project, and it may extend to other areas of land or sea and affect human beings, animals, crops, forests, and other things.

13.5.6.1 The responsibility arising from the connection with the site or the project may depend upon proof of fault, or it may be strict without the necessity of proving fault. Responsibility may relate only to damage that arose after acquisition of the project site, or it may include damage that occurred before the site was acquired for the purposes of the project. It may extend beyond those who directly caused the damage, as it may also be visited upon persons who have an interest in the project and its assets, including the project vehicle and the financiers who provided finance for the project. More immediately in the case of the financiers, responsibility may rest upon them through holding or enforcing a security interest over the project's assets and revenues and by the exercise of step-in rights. Even if a financier is not directly liable, it may be affected because of the economic consequences of liability being placed upon the project vehicle. The nature and extent of the liability of those concerned will depend upon the law of the relevant country,[22] but it may give rise to both criminal and civil liability and could include fines and penalties, the cost of remedying the damage, and compensation claims by those who have been affected. Some limited insurance cover may be available for the consequences of a catastrophic event, such as an explosion at the project facility, but it is unlikely that cover will be available for incipient or gradual damage to the environment.

---

[22] As to the position under English law, see Part IIA of the Environmental Protection Act 1990. For the position in the EU, see the Directive on the assessment of the effects of certain public and private projects on the environment (85/337/EEC OJ L175/40 5/7/1985, amended by 97/11/EC OJ L73/5 14/3/1997) and the Directive on environmental liability (2004/35/EC OJ L143/56 30/4/2004).

13.5.6.2 *The Equator Principles*

The Equator Principles[23] address the approach that should be taken by project financiers to the environmental and, additionally, social consequences of the projects they finance.

The principles are based on a set of performance standards for social and environ- **13.5.6.2.1**
mental sustainability of projects that were developed by the IFC. The principles were originally promulgated in 2003 and they were updated in 2006. They comprise a voluntary set of ten broad principles to which various financiers have subscribed in relation to projects that they finance with an individual capital cost of US$10 million or more. In specific terms, the subscribers undertake not to provide finance or undertake an advisory role for a project unless its sponsors are able to demonstrate that the project will be constructed and operated in accordance with sound social and environmental management practices.

The subscribers also agree that, depending upon the likely consequences of a **13.5.6.2.2**
project, they will impose requirements that must be fulfilled by those involved in the project and, in addition, that certain covenants will be imposed in their finance documents. This is achieved by determining into which of three categories a project will fall, so that the imposition of the requirements will depend upon the category into which the project has been placed.

The categories are as follows: **13.5.6.2.3**

Category A (High risk)	A project with the potential for significant adverse social or environmental consequences which are diverse, irreversible, or unprecedented.
Category B (Medium risk)	A project with the potential for limited adverse social and environmental consequences which are few in number, generally site specific, largely reversible, and readily addressed through mitigation measures.
Category C (Low or no risk)	A project with minimal or no social or environmental consequences.

There are no specific requirements for Category C projects. All Category A pro- **13.5.6.2.4**
jects must fulfil the following requirements, as must most Category B projects, particularly if they are located in non-OECD countries or are in OECD countries with low incomes. There must be:

(1) an environmental and social impact assessment of the project;
(2) an action plan and management system which addresses the matters raised by the assessment;

---

[23] The principles are set out at <http://www.equator-principles.com>.

(3) public consultation of communities that may be affected by the project;

(4) grievance procedures for communities that may be affected by the project;

(5) an independent expert review;

(6) independent monitoring; and

(7) annual reporting obligations by the financiers.

The following loan covenants on the part of the borrower should be contained in the finance documentation:

(1) to comply materially with applicable social and environmental laws, regulations, and permits;

(2) to comply materially with the action plan and the systems for monitoring and management;

(3) to provide regular reports on compliance with 1 and 2;

(4) decommissioning of the project facilities in accordance with an agreed plan.

It is also provided that there should be a materiality threshold before a breach of these covenants would amount to a default. If the borrower defaults, the lender should not immediately trigger enforcement action but the borrower should co-operate with the lender in taking steps to remedy the breach.

13.6 Insurance Arrangements

13.6.1 Because of the physical nature of a project, the insurance arrangements will be an important factor and one in which the financiers will be particularly interested. Commonly, a project should be covered for physical damage to or the destruction or loss of project assets, as well as providing cover for liability to third parties. It is essential that the true value of the assets should be covered by the policy, as a claim under a policy where the value is under-insured will be subject to reduction in proportion to the under-insurance, unless it has been agreed with the insurers that there should be an element of self-insurance (but that would not suit the financiers). Cover may be difficult to obtain, however, for loss arising from acts of war or terrorism. To a limited extent, cover may be available for environmental damage caused by an accident arising from damage to a physical asset. At least in the London market, it is difficult nowadays to obtain cover for business interruption and delays in start-up of the project or for loss arising from political risk (although some cover may be obtained against political risk under an ECGD policy relating to the supply or goods or services from the UK).

13.6.2 Physical damage and third party liability cover

Generally speaking, the physical damage and third party liability insurances cover should be arranged by the contractors in the period up to practical completion of the project. Thereafter, the cover should be arranged by the project vehicle (or by the sponsors acting on its behalf). It is relevant to consider with and through whom the cover should be arranged and who should be covered.

13.6.2.1 *Inception of the cover*

The financiers will require that the insurances should be arranged through brokers and with underwriters of international standing, often through the Lloyd's, the American or similar markets, and that such brokers and underwriters (together with the terms of the cover) should be approved by the financiers. However, the licence for the project may require that some of the cover should be placed with local insurers, in which case it is advisable that such cover should be re-insured through underwriters in an established market, with a 'cut-through' clause which gives a direct right to the primary insureds for payment by the re-insurers; thus, in effect, by-passing the local insurers in the payment of claims.

13.6.2.2 *Cover for the financiers*

In addition to the project vehicle and anyone else with an acceptable interest that wishes to be covered (for instance, the licensor and the sponsors, as well as the contractors), the financiers will insist that they should be covered. In this regard, it is best that the financiers are expressed to be covered as co-insureds under a composite policy, rather than as joint-insureds. The former acknowledges that the financiers have a different interest to that of the other persons covered by the policy, whereas in the case of the latter, they should have the same interest.[24] In traditional terms, the distinction is relevant to assessing the consequences where there has been non-disclosure or a breach of warranty, although that matter is usually now addressed explicitly, as mentioned below. In any event, it is not sufficient for the financiers merely to be named as the loss-payees under a policy if they are not also covered as insureds. If they are merely named as a loss-payee then they will have no direct contractual rights under the relevant policies and their entitlement to payment will be dependent upon there being a valid and enforceable claim by one of the named insureds. The financiers should also seek an undertaking from the insurers that they will not cancel a policy or allow it to lapse (for instance, because of non-payment of premium) without giving the financiers at least 30 days' prior notice and the opportunity to remedy whatever the problem may be.

13.6.3 Non-disclosure and breach of warranty

One of the principal features of an insurance policy is that a policy, being a contract *uberrimae fidei* (of the utmost good faith), may be avoided by the insurer for non-disclosure of a material fact or for breach of warranty in the proposal for the

---

[24] See Sir Wilfred Greene MR in *General Accident Fire and Life Assurance Corp v Midland Bank Ltd* [1940] 2 KB 388, at 404 and Staughton LJ in *New Hampshire Insurance Co v MBN Ltd* [1977] LRLR 25, at 56–57.

policy and the submission of claims may be subject to compliance with various strict conditions.[25]

13.6.3.1 The difficulty with this from the perspective of the financiers who might be involved in financing a project is that the arrangements for taking out insurances are not in their hands and they cannot be expected to supervise and vet those arrangements in great detail; nor will the financiers be aware of all the facts relevant to the risk that is to be insured. In the case of a project, the policies will be taken out by the contractors and the sponsors (the latter acting on behalf of the project vehicle). As protection against these difficulties, it used to be possible for financiers to obtain an endorsement to a policy, or direct confirmation from the insurers, to the effect that the insurers would not avoid the policy as against and to the detriment of the financiers, even where they might have done so as against the borrower or other insureds.

13.6.3.2 Such endorsements are more difficult to obtain these days. Even in cases where the financiers are named as co-insureds under a composite policy, insurers may now insist on having a right to avoid the policy as against all the insureds where there was material non-disclosure or a breach of warranty when the policy was incepted. One possible approach to this difficulty might be to obtain confirmation from the insurers of the specific matters that they require to be disclosed when the policy is taken out and their agreement that they will not seek to avoid the policy for non-disclosure of other matters. That would, at least, reduce the possible scope for avoidance of the policies. It may also be possible for a financier to obtain separate cover against avoidance of a policy, but that is expensive and not readily available.

13.6.4 Payment of claims

It is normal for a policy to provide that the proceeds of claims under third party liability cover will be paid to the relevant third parties (except where the insured has paid the third party, in which case the insurer will reimburse the insured), and the insurer will usually control the defence to any litigation or dispute as brought against the insured by a third party.[26] There is often debate, however, as to what should be provided in a policy (and in the financing documentation) as to the payment of claims under the policy for loss and physical damage to assets (and, if relevant, the proceeds of reimbursement of any third party liability claim for loss suffered by a third party which the insured has paid).

---

[25] See the discussion in Chap 11.

[26] Under s 1 of the Third Parties (Rights Against Insurers) Act 1930, a third party has a direct right against the insurer if the insured is insolvent.

Except in the case of a total loss which leads to abandonment of the project (where **13.6.4.1** the claim will be paid as a capital amount), the negotiating stance usually taken by the commercial parties and the licensor (and by the insurers as well) would be that the payments should be applied towards remedying the damage or in replacement or reinstatement of the loss (or in reimbursement of expenditure incurred for those purposes).[27] The financiers, on the other hand, are more likely to wish that the proceeds of a claim should be applied in reduction of the indebtedness due to them or, at least, that they should have the right to determine if the proceeds should be applied in remedying the loss or in repayment of the debt.

A compromise will usually be reached, which will be reflected in the loss payable **13.6.4.2** clauses in the policies, under which it is agreed that the proceeds of claims below a certain level may be applied in reinstatement or repair, and the financiers will have a discretion as to the destination of the proceeds of claims over that amount.[28] Such a compromise, however, must take into account the position of the project contractors and the licensor, who may have obligations and rights under the contracts or the licence, as the case may be, as to the deployment of the proceeds of claims for the purposes of repair and reinstatement of the project assets under the insurances.

13.6.5 Brokers' undertakings

The financiers will require that the brokers who arrange the insurances should undertake to them that they will arrange for loss payable clauses, in the agreed form, to be incorporated in the policies (the insurers may insist on a right of set-off for unpaid premiums), to arrange for notices of assignment to the financiers of the policies (such assignments being part of the security package taken by the financiers), that they will hold the slips and policy documents when issued to the order of the financiers, and that they will give the financiers notice of any non-payment of premiums due on the policies, any proposed changes to the terms or cover under the policies, and of any grounds on which the insurers might assert that the policies have lapsed or been avoided.

---

[27] A point which is sometimes overlooked is that under s 83 of the Fires Prevention (Metropolis) Act 1774, the insurer or any person interested in a building that is lost or damaged by fire is entitled to require that the insurance moneys should be applied in repair or reinstatement of the building. The section has general application throughout England: *Sinnott v Bowden* [1912] 2 Ch 414.

[28] This could lead to an issue as to whether the security that the financiers held over the benefit of the policies and claims payable under them was in the nature of a fixed or a floating charge, because of the element of freedom allowed to the chargee as to the disposition of the proceeds of a claim. Such freedom was found not to exist in *Re CCG International Enterprises Ltd* [1993] BCC 580 because it was held that the chargee was in complete control of the disposition of the proceeds of a claim under the policy.

13.6.6 Covenants in the finance documents

The various matters concerning insurances as discussed above will be reflected in covenants undertaken by the borrower in the facility or security documentation.

13.6.6.1 For instance, such covenants will require the borrower to ensure that the relevant cover is effected and maintained, to the extent it is available (perhaps worded as reasonably available) in the insurance markets, during the period of construction of the project and, thereafter, during the operation and use of the project facilities, in the insured amounts but subject to agreed deductibles (which amounts may be increased in accordance with an agreed mechanism), with the financiers covered as co-insureds and with the relevant loss-payee clauses indorsed on the policies, as well as to procure the requisite undertakings from the brokers.

13.6.6.2 The borrower will also be required to see that the insurances are effected through brokers and with insurers approved by the financiers and on terms approved by the financiers, to ensure that the premiums are paid when due, and to provide evidence thereof to the financiers (failing which the financiers will be entitled to pay them and claim reimbursement).

13.6.6.3 There will also be provisions as to the application of the proceeds of the payment of claims (which will also be addressed in the provisions relating to control accounts, as discussed below).

13.7 The Financing of a Project

13.7.1 Bearing in mind the matters that have already been discussed concerning a project and those concerned with a project, it is now appropriate to consider how the finance for a project might be documented and the issues that are likely to arise. Conflict of laws issues must also be borne in mind from the outset, as they are likely to be relevant at many levels of the financing package as, for instance, in relation to the contractual elements of the financing and when considering the security that will be taken.

13.7.2 Sources of finance

Syndicated lending (with facility and security agents acting on behalf of the lenders) remains the most common method for financing projects by commercial banks, but it should be also be appreciated that, save for relatively small and discrete projects, it is likely that there may be a number of possible sources of finance for a project, which might include not just private commercial finance but also finance provided by sources such as international agencies and development banks and export credit agencies. Some projects have been financed, or re-financed, using bonds issues and structured finance through securitisation programmes and the like. In addition, it is possible that different elements of the project will be financed separately and that finance facilities for the same integrated project may be furnished from more than one source.

13.7.3 Co-ordination and fair treatment

In all such cases, there must be co-ordination, by agreement between all concerned, of the overall project and its financing so as to ensure that the whole thing will come together as a completed whole, that payments of interest and repayments of debt will be shared out proportionately, and that, if there should be default, there will be a unified approach to the steps that should be taken to remedy the default or in the enforcement of the various financiers' rights and remedies. It follows that there should also be a sharing of the benefit of any security that is taken and of the benefit of any enforcement of the security, as it is unlikely that assets will be severable from the whole, particularly once the project has achieved a certain level of construction, or that one financier would be allowed by the others to enforce against the wishes of the majority or to achieve more than its fair share of the recoveries that were available on enforcement. These matters are discussed separately below.

What has just been said assumes an intention that each of the financiers should **13.7.3.1** rank on an equal basis with the other financiers in terms of the right to payment and in sharing the benefit of security. The position will be different, of course, if the intention is that there will be different rankings so that some financiers should rank behind others for payment and as to the benefit of security. In the latter situation, there will probably need to be priority arrangements concerning the security and subordination of payment rights.

13.7.4 Limited or non-recourse elements

As previously mentioned, an important factor in project finance is that it involves a measure of limited or nil recourse to the commercial sponsors and others involved in the project for repayment and servicing of the debt incurred in financing the project. This is an important consideration, given the large amounts that are likely to be involved and the financially tenuous position of the borrower because of its dependency upon the exploitation of the project's completed facilities for it to generate money to repay its debt.

13.7.4.1 *Sponsors' responsibility*

One qualification to the protection that the sponsors may desire is that the lenders may insist that the sponsors should accept responsibility for the completion of the construction phase of the project, so that if the project fails, the sponsors should accept some responsibility for the consequences. The extent of that responsibility will be a matter for negotiation. One possibility is that the sponsors should guarantee repayment of the finance, with the guarantee being retired or falling away if practical completion of the project is achieved. In the alternative, the lenders may be prepared to accept that they will have an indirect opportunity to recover from the sponsors where the project vehicle has rights to recover compensation from them should they default under the project contracts to which they are parties. The benefit of such rights should fall within the security package that is held by the lenders.

13.7.4.2 *Corporate structures*

A practical method by which the sponsors can achieve protection from liability is by the use of a corporate structure where the project vehicle, which is the borrower, is a separate legal entity so that, under normal principles of company law, the sponsors (who are likely to be its shareholders) will not be liable for its debts and obligations. There may be situations, however, where the commercial parties behind a vehicle may not escape legal responsibility for its debts and liabilities, either because the law of a relevant jurisdiction in which the entity is established or has a presence does not recognise the separation between the entity and its proprietors or shareholders, perhaps because of the nature of the vehicle,[29] or because in specific circumstances the law will pierce the corporate veil and impose criminal or civil liability upon those involved with a corporate vehicle due either to some element of fault or culpability on their part in the way that the vehicle's affairs have been conducted, or by imposing strict liability regardless of fault.

13.7.4.3 *Officers of the vehicle*

It is not just the shareholders or proprietors of a vehicle who may be at risk of having liability imposed upon them, as the law may also visit liability upon the directors and officers of a vehicle for criminal acts or for negligence, breach of duty, wrongful trading, and similar matters that have caused loss to the vehicle and its creditors, particularly at a time when the vehicle might have been insolvent.[30] It might be possible for such personnel to obtain insurance cover against civil liability, but such cover may not be sufficiently extensive to provide comprehensive protection and it is doubtful if cover will protect against criminal liability.

13.7.4.4 *Restrictions on recourse against the borrower*

With such considerations in mind, those who represent the borrower or who are involved with it are likely to press for a further element of protection in relation to

---

[29] As to the position under English law, see paras 13.2.2 and 13.2.3 above.

[30] For instance, under English law pursuant to s 214 of the Insolvency Act 1986. There are also prohibitions or limits on the extent to which a director of a company can be protected by the company directly or by insurance or an indemnity provided by a third party: see ss 232–239 of the Companies Act 2006.

the borrower's responsibility in paying and servicing its debt, through specific provisions that limit the borrower's own payment liability to the financiers.[31] This can be achieved under English law by a lender which takes security over a borrower's assets agreeing that it will limit its right of recourse or recovery to those assets and that it will not have any personal right of recovery against the borrower. It is also possible for a lender to agree that its rights to payment will be limited by certain conditions as, for instance, by being tied in to cash flow and other monetary sources available to it (e.g. compensation and insurance payments), so that its liability to make payment at any time will be dependent upon the available revenues and monetary amounts that it receives in a period preceding that time, with the payment of any amount that is not covered being deferred until the relevant conditions have been met.

By using a combination of those techniques, together with the benefits (such as **13.7.4.5** they may be) of the borrower having a separate legal personality, the concerns of those involved with the borrower in a project financing as to potential responsibility to the financiers for the borrower's payment obligations can be addressed or, at least, ameliorated as a matter of English law, although the position may not be as favourable under other legal systems. They may still find that they could be liable at general law in other respects, such as for wrongful trading when the company was insolvent.

13.7.5 The facility agreement

A project facility agreement will require quite a deal of adaptation from what would normally be found in a more straightforward loan facility. It would usually address the following additional matters.

13.7.5.1 Conditions precedent

The facility would contemplate phased drawings over the commitment period, tied in to the anticipated stages of the project. There would be a raft of initial conditions precedent to the availability of the facility in the first instance, covering matters such as the satisfactory provision, in a substantive sense, of documentation or evidence relating to feasibility studies for the project, environmental assessments and plans as required in accordance with the Equator Principles, the licence, the various project contracts, the agreement as to the sponsors' financial contributions, insurance coverage, establishment of bank accounts, security arrangements, tri-partite agreements as to the lenders' step-in rights concerning the licence and the project contracts, and co-ordination and security sharing arrangements with other financiers. For each particular drawing, there would be specific conditions

---

[31] See the discussion in Chap 3.

precedent relating to that drawing, such as the delivery of certificates from engineers confirming that the relevant stage in the construction or commissioning of the project had been achieved, and, where it was required, the contribution of specific amounts of debt or equity by the sponsors in relation to the amount borrowed under the facility.

13.7.5.2 *Payments and cash flows*

As a practical matter, it is very unlikely that the project will generate any funds to meet interest on the finance that is provided, or to repay the finance, until revenue is generated by the operation of the completed project facility. Interest on the amounts borrowed will have to be rolled-up (i.e. interest would accrue in the normal way, but payment of the interest would be deferred) or, alternatively, some part of the finance facility may be made available for drawing to meet interest payments. It would normally be anticipated that revenue receipts from the completed project would build up over time, so that repayment of the debt (and of rolled-up interest) would have to be deferred until funds in sufficiently large amounts have been generated from receipts.

13.7.5.2.1 To meet this, there would be a schedule of repayment dates and amounts linked to the original projections for income and capital receipts by the borrower (as the project vehicle) once the project had become operational. These would have to be adjusted under the agreement to take into account actual cash flows and receipts and the receipt of extraordinary items, such as under insurance policies (where the receipt was to be applied in reduction of the debt) and default or termination compensation that might be received under project contracts or the licence, as well as the acceleration provisions of the agreement consequent upon the occurrence of an event of default. The management of the borrower's cash flow (through the use of control accounts) for drawings, receipts, and expenditure is referred to further below.

13.7.5.3 *Covenants and undertakings*

The borrower would be required to give various covenants and undertakings relating to the project and its documentation. Some of these would be contained in the facility agreement, some in the security documentation, and some would be in both. They would include covenants to the following effect.

13.7.5.3.1 Limit on activities Because of its financial dependency on the project and the desire that it should not expose itself to risks and obligations arising outside activities connected with the project, the vehicle would be restricted in its activities to pursuing the project and operating the project facilities (and associated matters).

13.7.5.3.2 Financial ratios The vehicle would be required to ensure the maintenance of various financial ratios, the details of which would be negotiated (including, for instance, whether the secondly described ratio below would be based on a cash or accruals basis and what account should be taken of amounts standing in the control accounts), but would be likely to include matters along the following lines:

(1) a ratio of the net present value of anticipated future net revenues (that is, net of anticipated expenditure, excluding finance charges) that will be generated by the project, when compared against the principal amount of outstanding indebtedness of the borrower (excluding subordinated debt due to connected parties) as at certain dates;

(2) a ratio of net revenues in a defined period when compared with financing charges and repayments of principal that fall due in that period; and

(3) a ratio of equity contributions (including, for this purpose, subordinated debt) of the sponsors when compared with indebtedness due to the financiers (this last mentioned ratio may, instead, appear as a condition precedent to drawings).

13.7.5.3.3 Environmental and social matters There would be covenants as to environmental and social matters which, if the lenders have subscribed to the Equator Principles, would be as previously described.

13.7.5.3.4 Implementation of the project There would be a covenant to pursue the project in accordance with an agreed plan and projections, and a covenant not to terminate or abandon the project.

13.7.5.3.5 The project contracts and the licence There would be covenants relating to the project contracts and the licence, including to observe and comply with the vehicle's obligations under them, to enforce them, and not to agree any variation or termination of them without the prior consent of the lenders.

13.7.5.3.6 Insurances There would be requirements as to insurance cover and the maintenance of that cover, as previously mentioned.

13.7.5.4 Hedging

The borrower may be required to take out hedging arrangements, the benefit of which would be included in the security package. Such contracts might relate to hedging of currency exposures (for instance, the risk that arises where the currencies of revenue receipts are not the same as the currencies of debt service and other expenditure) and the risks associated with dealings in commodities (for instance, where the project vehicle in operating the completed project is buying or selling commodities and is exposed to increases or decreases in market prices).

13.7.5.5 Events of default

In addition to the usual provisions, the events of default provisions would include clauses concerning the failure or termination of the project or of a significant contract or of the licence, failure to complete the project by an end date, nationalisation or requisition of the project, the occurrence of *force majeure* events, default by the sponsors in the performance of their obligations or the insolvency of a sponsor or any change in the identity of the sponsors or in their shareholdings in the borrower, and any change of control of a sponsor, loss of insurance cover, and any other breach of the various covenants set down in the facility or security documentation (with an exception as to the consequences of a breach of the environmental covenants as referred to in the Equator Principles).

13.7.5.6 Bank accounts

The financing documentation would provide (in the facility agreement or in separate documentation) for the establishment of specific bank accounts relating to the borrower's receipts and expenditure. Various controls would be imposed as to payments into, and withdrawals and transfers from, the accounts. Such accounts are commonly referred to as 'control accounts'. In most cases the control accounts would be held with a bank in one of the international financial centres, but the borrower might also be permitted to maintain an account or accounts, not necessarily being control accounts, with a local bank in its place of operations, to deal with local currency expenditure and receipts.

13.7.5.6.1 The borrower would be prohibited from opening any other accounts. The control accounts would be held by the borrower with a named bank or banks (or changed to accounts with another bank approved by the financiers) and would be the subject of the financiers' security package.[32] The bank holding a control account would be required to acknowledge the financiers' security and to waive any rights that it might otherwise have of netting, set-off, or combination and consolidation of accounts. There would be arrangements for the control accounts to bear and accrue interest and, sometimes, for balances not immediately needed to be invested. There would probably be a requirement for some documentary evidence as to proper purpose, which must be presented to the bank before a withdrawal or transfer could be made from a control account.

---

[32] In this regard, conflict of laws issues should be addressed in terms of ensuring that the accounts may be opened and maintained in accordance with the agreed requirements, that the bank's rights of set-off and so on may be excluded, and that the benefit of the accounts would be susceptible to security in favour of the financiers. Under English law, if the borrower is given the right to make withdrawals or transfers from an account (even if under regulated conditions) then the security over the account is likely to be characterised as being a floating charge: see *Agnew v Inland Revenue Commissioner* [2001] UKPC 28, [2001] AC 710 and *National Westminster Bank PLC v Spectrum Plus Ltd* [2005] UKHL 41, [2005] 2 AC 680.

There will be different control accounts and arrangements concerning them, depending upon the type of project involved. As they concern the movement, use, and availability of money, the provisions that relate to them (particularly concerning the circumstances in which amounts may be withdrawn or transferred) tend to be heavily negotiated and, in consequence, complex.

13.7.5.6.2

The following is an abbreviated example of some types of control account (it is possible that the functions of some of these accounts may be divided up between yet more accounts):

13.7.5.6.3

(1) a disbursement account, into which would be paid amounts drawn down under the facility agreement, sponsors' contributions, and transfers from the capital proceeds account, and from which would be paid project and other authorised expenditure;

(2) a revenue proceeds account, into which would be paid operating revenues generated by the project, and from which may be paid amounts to meet operating expenditure and transfers to other accounts;

(3) a capital proceeds account, to receive compensation payments under the project contracts or the licence and the proceeds of insurance claims, and from which would be paid transfers to the debt payment account and transfers to the disbursements account to meet justified expenditure (for instance, authorised project expenditure and, where permitted, the cost of repairing damaged assets that were the subject of an insurance claim);

(4) a debt payments account, to receive amounts transferred from other accounts and to pay principal and interest when due, with a reserve being accumulated over time for that purpose (it may be agreed that periodic excess balances over the amount of a required reserve could be used to pay distributions to the sponsors or be invested).

13.8 Security

13.8.1 Co-ordination and sharing

Whether there is a number of different financing arrangements involving one project or just a single group of lenders within a syndicated facility, and assuming an intention that they should all be put on an equal footing as to rights to payment and the benefit of security, it follows (as previously mentioned) that there should be an orderly and fair distribution of payments to the financiers in the normal course of events. It also follows that there should be a sharing of the benefit (on a *pari passu* basis) of any security that is taken, as well as the benefit of any enforcement of the security, as it is unlikely that the project assets and revenues will be severable from the whole, particularly once the project has achieved a certain level of construction and, even more so, once the finished project has become operational. In addition, there should be a measure of collective agreement (represented by a system of majority voting by value of facility commitments) as to the circumstances in which default should be called and enforcement action taken. These matters will need to be dealt with by agreement as between the financiers of the project, it being preferable that such agreement (often called an 'inter-creditor agreement', which would deal, inter alia, with the sharing of receipts and the like both before and after default) should be finalised before the provision of any finance.

13.8.2 Taking the security

To assist in those matters, it would be best if the security were taken comprehensively on behalf of all the financiers. Under English law (where that is relevant), this can be achieved by using a security trustee, which would take the security on behalf of all the financiers, the security being expressed to secure all of the present and future indebtedness, both actual and contingent, that might be due to the financiers.[33] There would also be a parallel debt provision, by which the indebtedness that was due to the financiers would also be expressed to be due to the security trustee, to assist the security trustee in its recoveries.[34] The position may not be so straightforward in other jurisdictions which do not have the benefit of the common law system. It should always be remembered that under the principles as to conflict of laws, the relevant issues may be governed by the law that is directly relevant to the assets that are intended to fall within the security, rather than the law that the parties would like to choose, which may not have the necessary connection with the assets.

13.8.3 Comprehensive security

So far as possible, the security package should seek to cover the whole of the borrower's business and assets, both present and future, on a comprehensive basis. The extent to which this can be achieved will depend, once again, upon the application of the rules of the conflict of laws, so as to find the laws that will be applicable in determining questions relating to matters such as the assets that might be available as security, the liabilities that can be secured, the nature

---

[33] The representative capacity of a security trustee to hold security on behalf of the banks as its beneficiaries, as well as the right of the facility agent to bind the banks, was examined in *British Power & Energy Trading Ltd v Credit Suisse* [2007] EWCA 53. That case concerned a syndicated facility. This is subject, of course, to the terms of the facility agreement or other documentation under which the trustee is appointed to hold the security on behalf of the syndicate members, which may place restrictions upon the powers of the trustee.

[34] Such provisions go on to provide that, to the extent that the indebtedness is paid in the ordinary course, that will constitute a *pro tanto* reduction of the indebtedness that is due to the trustee.

of the security that may be taken, the procedures that should be followed in taking the security, in whose favour the security may be taken, the effect of the security (for instance, as against other creditors in an insolvency of the giver of the security and in determining priorities), the duration of the security, and the rights and procedures upon enforcement. Those issues are discussed further in Chapter 4.

For illustrative purposes, assuming that all those matters were governed by English law, then a comprehensive package of security could be taken by the security trustee, which would include the benefit to the borrower of the licence and the various project contracts to which it was a party (including any compensation that might be payable in the normal course or upon termination of the licence or a contract), the benefit of the insurances, revenues and other receipts of the project, the control accounts, the physical assets of the project, and the business, goodwill, and uncalled capital of the borrower. Not all of the security would be fixed security, as some of it would be characterised as only being a floating charge. The position concerning priorities under English law is difficult and floating charges suffer certain disadvantages in an insolvency of the chargor. Enforcement remedies under English law are fairly straightforward but are subject to various general restrictions. See further the discussion of these matters in Chapter 14.

13.8.4

13.9 Step-in Rights and Direct Agreements

13.9.1 The nature of step-in rights

Step-in rights are usually seen as being an adjunct to the financiers' security.[35] In summary, they enable a representative of the financiers, or someone else nominated by them (for instance, a receiver appointed on enforcement of the financiers' security[36] or a third party trade purchaser of the project), to take over (or step into) the position of the project vehicle under the licence or the project contracts. This will arise if there has been a default by the vehicle under the finance documentation or under those contracts or instruments (default under the latter would most probably amount to an event of default under the finance documentation in any case), so as to keep them on foot and to enable the project to continue. In effect, upon the exercise of the rights, the project vehicle's position is novated in favour of the entity that stepped into its place.

---

[35] The concept of 'step-in rights' also occurs in ss 72C–72E of the Insolvency Act 1986 and has a definition for the purposes of those sections in para 6 of Sched 2A to the Act. See further Chap 14.

[36] Such a receiver would not be acting as a representative of the financiers who appointed him; similarly as to the position of an administrator: see *Feetum v Levy* [2005] EWHC 349 (Ch), [2005] 1 WLR 2576 (upheld on appeal: *Cabvision v Feetum* [2005] EWCA Civ 1601, [2005] Ch 585).

13.9.2 When step-in rights arise

Step-in rights usually arise in pursuance of tri-partite agreements between the licensor or the relevant contractor, the vehicle, and the security trustee (or other representative of the financiers). They are entered into as one of the required sets of condition precedent documentation under the facility arrangements. Such contracts also provide an opportunity for the financiers to obtain direct undertakings from the contractors as to matters arising under their contracts. There is no hard and fast rule as to the contents of these agreements, but the types of matters dealt with by them are described below. They are usually subject to negotiation and it is quite possible that the contents of the agreements may differ depending upon which counterparty is involved.

13.9.3 The contents of a tri-partite agreement with the licensor

A tri-partite agreement with the licensor might cover the following matters.

13.9.3.1 The licensor would consent to the security that was to be taken by the financiers over the benefit of the licence. The licensor would agree that it would give a period of notice to the financiers before it terminated the rights of the project vehicle under the licence due to default or other stipulated grounds. The agreement may go on to provide that a representative of the financiers, or a third party nominated by them (and which conformed with grounds of approval being as laid down in the agreement), could be nominated within that period (or even beforehand, so as to cover the position where an event of default had occurred under the financing documentation) to step in and take over the benefit of the licence in place of the project vehicle. In addition, or in the alternative, the licensor (or its nominee) may be given the option, after it had served its notice, to become directly involved with the project as if it were the licensee.

13.9.3.2 In the case of step-in, the licensor might require that direct undertakings should be given to it by the financiers or the relevant third party, to the effect that they would abide by the terms of the licence when the step-in occurs. In addition, an undertaking may have to be provided by the party exercising the step-in rights, to cure any outstanding breaches of the licence up to that time. To cater for the case where the licensor became directly involved, it would be necessary to provide either for the continuance of the project and the financing arrangements, as well as passing through revenues received by the completed project to repay the debt or, alternatively, for the licensor to buy out the banks or come to some other acceptable arrangement for repayment of their finance.

13.9.4 The contents of a tri-partite agreement with a contractor

A tri-partite agreement with a contractor might cover the following.

The contractor would consent to the financiers taking security over the project **13.9.4.1**
vehicle's benefit of the underlying contract. The contractor would agree that it
would not terminate the underlying contract without giving the financiers a specified period of notice. It would also agree that the financiers could nominate a representative or an acceptable third party (acceptable, that is, on grounds laid down
in the tri-partite agreement) to step in to the underlying contract in place of the
project vehicle. The tri-partite agreement would specify whether the right to so
nominate was to be exercisable at any time (if so, the financiers may agree separately with the project vehicle not to exercise their right unless the vehicle had
defaulted under the relevant contract or an event of default had occurred), or only
on specific grounds or after the contractor had given a notice of its intention to
terminate. The agreement might also provide, in the case of a step-in by a nominee
acting for the financiers, that it could retire from the step-in on giving notice to
the contractor (in which case the project vehicle might resume its own position in
relation to the underlying contract or, more realistically, that the contract would
terminate). In return, the contractor might require that the financiers, should
they exercise their rights, would guarantee the payment of amounts falling due to
the contractor under the underlying contract after the time of the nomination,
and, perhaps as well, any outstanding and unpaid amounts due up to that time
(or, at least, within a certain period before that time).

The contractor may also be prepared to give direct undertakings to the financiers **13.9.4.2**
in the tri-partite agreement along the following lines: that it undertook and
acknowledged a duty of care towards them in the performance of its duties pursuant to the underlying contract; that it would duly perform the underlying contract; that it would obtain and maintain the insurances that were required by the
underlying contract (in conformity with the matters discussed above); and that, if
step-in occurred, it would make available to the financiers, or a person nominated
by them, all plans and technical information that related to the subject matter of
the underlying contract.

Part D: Secured Transactions, Equipment Finance, and Guarantees

of the guarantee and provisions to save the lender from a position under the guarantee.

Chapter 18 relates to the case for reform of secured transactions under English law. It discusses the reasons why reform is needed and then reviews a proposal that was put forward by the Law Commission to effect reform of the law.

Part D

SECURED TRANSACTIONS, EQUIPMENT FINANCE, AND GUARANTEES

Chapter 15 is concerned with secured transactions as understood under English law. It also examines certain matters that are similar to or associated with such transactions. After an introduction dealing with matters that are relevant in a general sense to secured transactions, it then moves to consider concepts of property, interests in property and dealings therein, future property and attachment of proprietary interests, accretions to and the proceeds of assets, the forms of security, floating charges, security in financial assets, security over intellectual property, security over credit balances, rights of set-off, Quistclose trusts, registration requirements for corporate security, priorities, subordination of unsecured debt, upsetting prior transactions, and enforcement of security.

Chapter 16 is concerned with equipment finance, sometimes called title finance. It examines the methods by which a financier might acquire title in equipment, the forms of transaction by which equipment is made available by the financier to its customer, the financier's statutory responsibilities for the equipment and the effectiveness of attempts to exclude or restrict that responsibility, the rights and obligations of the parties following a default by the customer, the effect of the customer's insolvency, the financier's rights against third parties, and insurance arrangements.

Chapter 17 concerns guarantees. It looks at the nature of a guarantee as contrasted with other types of instrument, preliminary matters in taking a guarantee, State guarantees under EC law, the types of guarantee, Export Credits Guarantee Department (ECGD) cover, the rights of the guarantor, reasons for the discharge of the guarantor, and provisions to save the beneficiary's position under the guarantee.

Chapter 18 relates to the case for reform of secured transactions under English law. It discusses the reasons why reform is needed and then reviews proposals that were put forward by the Law Commission to effect reform of the law.

14

SECURED TRANSACTIONS

14.1 Introduction and Preliminary Matters

14.1.1 The nature of security

Taking security involves the concept that one or more assets (in American terminology called 'collateral') is set aside or appropriated by the security giver to provide a security right or interest in favour of a creditor of the obligor, the security giver, or another debtor.[1] In the event of a failure in the fulfilment of the underlying obligation for which the security has been taken, the creditor may have recourse to the asset, usually by selling it (there are other methods of enforcement or realisation of security that will also have to be discussed), so that the proceeds of the sale or other method of enforcement can be applied towards satisfying the

---

[1] In this chapter, the expression 'creditor' or 'security taker' will be used to refer to the party that takes the benefit of security and the expression 'obligor' or 'security giver' will be used to describe the party that provides the security.

unfulfilled obligation. It is said that the creditor, through taking its security, acquires a 'proprietary' interest in the asset, that is, a right *in rem* in the asset. It is also possible, at least under English law, that the same asset may serve as security in favour of more than one creditor. Each such creditor may hold separate security from the obligor over the asset or the security may be held for them jointly, through a trustee acting on their behalf.

14.1.1.1 The asset (or assets) concerned may have some direct correlation to the finance provided by the creditor, because the finance was used to fund its purchase ('purchase money security'). Alternatively, the security may be more remote, in the sense that the obligor made it available as security for liabilities which were not directly associated with the finance provided for the acquisition of that particular asset. The distinction usually does not matter in English law, although it might be relevant to a priority race, as will be discussed at a later point in this chapter.

14.1.1.2 In terms of the assets which may form the subject matter of security, this chapter is concerned, by and large, with tangible personal property (e.g. goods) and intangible assets. Because of its entirely domestic nature under English law, the chapter will not be concerned with taking security over English real property, although much of the discussion is also relevant in the context of security over real property.

14.1.2 The equity of redemption

It is inherent in the concept of security that an obligor has an equity of redemption; that is, a right to redeem its security upon the payment or discharge of the liabilities covered by the security.[2] Subject to any agreement between the creditor and the obligor to the contrary, there is no equitable right to redeem in part only and the creditor is entitled to the whole of its security until it has been fully repaid.[3] Subject again to any agreement to the contrary, the obligor must tender unconditional and irrevocable payment or discharge in redemption of the secured liabilities.[4]

14.1.2.1 In equity, it is not permissible to prevent an obligor from redeeming its security; for instance, by providing that the security may never be redeemed. The obligor is entitled to redeem its security on payment or discharge of the secured liabilities and a provision which is intended to prevent that entitlement (called a 'clogg on

---

[2] As to the relationship between a contractual provision for redemption and the equitable right to redeem, especially in the context of contingent and future liabilities due to the mortgagee, see *Re Rudd and Son Ltd* (1986) 2 BCC 98,955 and *Law Debenture Trust Corp PLC v Concord Trust* [2007] EWHC 1380 (Ch).

[3] *Law Debenture Trust Corp PLC v Concord Trust* [2007] EWHC 1380 (Ch).

[4] Ibid.

the equity of redemption') is void and unenforceable.[5] The parties may agree that the right of redemption should be postponed for the period of the relevant facility,[6] provided that is not an unreasonably long period.[7] The position has been changed by legislation in relation to companies, which can issue perpetual debentures, including by way of security.[8]

14.1.3 The reasons for taking security

The principal reason for taking security over an asset is to provide the creditor with protection against the consequences of a default by the obligor or another debtor whose liabilities are covered by the security. The security provides the creditor with a right of recourse to the asset or its proceeds of realisation so as to meet the relevant liabilities. Although enforcement rights may arise in other circumstances, this is particularly relevant in a situation where the obligor or other debtor has become insolvent, so that it is unable to meet its obligations to its general body of creditors. Except where legislation has intervened to reduce its rights,[9] the creditor is able to stand outside the insolvency to the extent of its security and enforce that security for its own benefit. This is because the proprietary right of the creditor in the asset is paramount. The asset is treated as not forming part of the insolvent debtor's assets that are available to meet the claims of its unsecured creditors, except to the extent that there is any value left over once the liability covered by the security has been discharged.[10] Without the benefit of security, an ordinary creditor will find itself enmeshed in the mire of the insolvency, sharing with the other creditors on a *pari passu* basis in whichever of the debtor's free assets are available to meet their claims (that is, assets which are not subject to security or held on trust for a third party[11]).

---

[5] *Noakes & Co Ltd v Rice* [1902] AC 24; *Krelinger v New Patagonia Meat and Cold Storage Co Ltd* [1914] AC 25; *Jones v Morgan* [2001] EWCA Civ 995, [2002] 1 EGLR 125.

[6] *Teevan v Smith* (1882) 20 ChD 724; *Williams v Morgan* [1906] 1 Ch 804.

[7] *Morgan v Jeffreys* [1910] 1 Ch 620.

[8] S 739 of the Companies Act 2006, (previously s 193 of the Companies Act 1985). See *Knightsbridge Estates Trust Ltd v Byrne* [1940] AC 613.

[9] Principally with respect to making available for preferential creditors, unsecured creditors and the liquidator for his expenses, recoveries under floating charges, pursuant to ss, 40, 175 (2)(b), 176A, and 176ZA of the Insolvency Act 1986 and s 754 of the Companies Act 2006 (formerly s 196 Companies Act 1985). A floating charge holder also suffers certain disadvantages in an administration, such as under para 70 of Sched BI to the Insolvency Act 1986, which entitles the administrator to dispose of assets subject to a floating charge. The holders of both fixed and floating security are subject to a moratorium on their rights of enforcement in an administration of a corporate obligor pursuant to paras 43 and 44 of Sched 1 to the Insolvency Act 1986. Similar restrictions apply where a proposal has been made for a company voluntary arrangement of an obligor which is an eligible company pursuant to para 12 of Sched A1 to the Insolvency Act 1986.

[10] See the helpful summary provided by Lord Millett in *Buchler v Talbot* [2004] UKHL 9; [2004] 2 AC 298, at [51].

[11] As noted by Rose LJ (on behalf of himself, Saville and Millett LJJ) in *Re Bank of Credit and Commerce International SA (No 8)* [1996] Ch 245, at 256. Although the decision was the subject

The usual consequence is that very little is recovered by the unsecured creditors in satisfaction of what is owed to them.[12]

Table 14.1 The Order of Claims in an English Liquidation

1. Ownership of Assets, Fixed Security Over Assets, and Liquidation Set-off Rights
   Ownership e.g.:
      Conditional sale and Retention of title
      Hire-purchase
      Equipment leases
      Receivables purchases
      Quistclose claims [1970] AC 567
   Fixed Security e.g.:
      Legal mortgages
      Equitable mortgages
      Fixed equitable charges
      Pledges
      Liens
   Set-off in Winding up: Rules 2.85 and 4.90 Insolvency Rules 1986 (amended by SI 2005/527)
   Note:
   (i) Priority issues where there are competing claims
   (ii) Existing and future assets
2. Liquidation expenses: section 176ZA Insolvency Act 1986
3. Preferential creditors

   i.e.: Occupational pension scheme contributions, Employees' remuneration & coal and steel contributions
4. The prescribed part of floating charge recoveries for the benefit of unsecured creditors
   S 176A Insolvency Act
5. Floating charges over assets
   Note: Crystallisation of the charge may raise such a charge to Category 1 for some purposes, but not to defeat categories 2, 3 and 4
6. Unsecured creditors (other than preferential creditors and distribution of the prescribed part)
   Note: Possible ranking of certain unsecured creditors over subordinated creditors
7. Shareholders
   Note: Ranking of different types of shareholders
   Note: The above assumes:
   (i) the due registration of the security;
   (ii) that the security is not vulnerable under the relevant provisions of the Insolvency Act 1986 (e.g.: ss 238, 239, 245, and 423);
   (iii) that the security was given by a company.

14.1.3.1 Table 14.1 sets out the order of claims in an English winding up. It serves to demonstrate the value to a creditor of holding security or rights which have a

of an appeal to the House of Lords (decided at [1998] AC 214), this particular point was not controversial.

[12] As Lord Hoffmann explained in *Wight v Eckhardt Marine GmbH* [2003] UKPC 37; [2004] 1 AC 147, at [27], the liquidation of an insolvent company does not extinguish the debts due by an

similar effect, as well as indicating the relative rankings of claims. It might also provide a useful source of comparative reference for the reader whilst reading this chapter and considering the various issues and entitlements that may arise when the dead arm of insolvency, particularly liquidation, intervenes.

A subsidiary benefit in taking security is that it might give the creditor that has taken the security a priority right in the relevant asset which will rank ahead of, and may even defeat, the claim of another creditor in the same asset. In that sense, the creditor with priority may be able to desist from having to take enforcement action to recover funds or other facilities that it has provided to the debtor, or at least defer its decision to do so. This, of course, will depend upon the secured creditor being confident as to the adequacy of its security and its continued right of priority.[13] By way of example, the holder of a floating charge cannot be confident that it will prevail against the claims of third parties who acquire an interest in the charged assets.[14] Thus, an execution creditor will prevail against the interest of the holder of a floating charge, provided that the execution has been completed before the charge crystallises.[15]

14.1.3.2

In more general terms, a creditor which holds security may be willing to provide credit in circumstances where it might not be available on unsecured terms because the debtor is not considered to be a good risk. A creditor with security may also be more willing to continue providing credit to a debtor which finds itself in financial difficulties. Security is usually required to support financial rescues and work outs.[16]

14.1.3.3

Holding security, as one type of credit risk mitigation technique, may also lead to regulatory benefits for the creditor, particularly if it is a bank. The security may entitle the bank to ascribe a lower risk weighting to an exposure than would be the case if the exposure was unsecured. This is explained further in Chapter 2.

14.1.3.4

---

insolvent debtor to its creditors, but it has the practical effect that the creditors are confined in their remedies to lodging proofs of their claims against the debtor and receiving a *pari passu* dividend paid out of the available realised assets with respect to such claims.

13 For instance, it might lose its claim to priority for further advances that it makes once it has notice of another security over the same asset, pursuant to s 94 of the Law of Property Act 1925.

14 The position as to floating charges is discussed further below.

15 *Evans v Rival Granite Quarries Ltd* [1910] 2 KB 979.

16 One of the criticisms of administration as a regime that should lead to the rehabilitation of businesses in the UK, is that there is no statutory mechanism by which the administrator can raise fresh funds to support the business, such as by granting security over the company's assets which would take priority over the rights of existing secured creditors under security granted before the administration commenced. This is unlike the position under Chapter 11 of the US Bankruptcy Code, where so-called 'super priority' security can be conferred on creditors which are willing to provide such funding to the company.

14.1.4 The liabilities that may be covered by security

The liabilities that the security purports to cover will be determined as a matter of construction of the relevant security instrument or other agreement under which the security was created. Sometimes the security may only relate to a specific transaction or even, more concisely, to a particular debt that is due to the creditor. Once the relevant liability has been satisfied then the security will cease to be effective. The risk that arises in this respect is that, either by the debtor appropriating one or more particular payments against the secured liability or by the application of *Clayton's* case,[17] the secured liability will be treated as having been discharged and the creditor will find that it is unsecured for any other remaining or fresh liabilities of the debtor towards the creditor.

14.1.4.1   In the alternative, the security might be in the form of an 'all moneys' security, with the intention that it should cover all of the liabilities (present and future, actual or contingent[18]) of the obligor or other debtor to the creditor. Even so, the courts may find some limitation in the liabilities that are covered by the security. For instance, as a matter of construction the courts would be reluctant to find that the security was intended to cover indebtedness that was not originally incurred to the creditor but of which the creditor had taken an assignment from a third party, although it would appear that by the use of express wording such an eventuality might be covered in terms of the intended application of the security.[19] It is submitted, however, that as a matter of public policy such security should not be effective in an insolvency of an obligor, to the extent that it expressly purports to cover assigned debt that was previously unsecured. Otherwise, it could be employed as a device that might be entered into between an assignor (which had been an unsecured creditor of the debtor) and an assignee (which held security in a comprehensive form), by which the assignor received a payment from the assignee in return for the assignment, with the consequential effect of turning previously unsecured debt into secured debt held by the assignee, thereby subverting the general principle for the *pari passu* treatment of unsecured debts of an insolvent debtor.

---

[17] *Devaynes v Noble, Clayton's Case* (1816) 8 LJ Ch 256, 35 ER 767. See also Nourse J in *Re Quest CAE Ltd* (1985) 1 BCC 99,389, at 99,393.

[18] An example of a contingent liability is one that exists under a guarantee. Until there is a default, the guarantor has no actual monetary liability to make a payment. Once the default occurs and the guarantor becomes liable to pay, however, the liability will crystallise into an actual liability of the guarantor.

[19] See *Re Quest CAE Ltd* (1985) 1 BCC 99,389, which concerned the construction of an all moneys clause in a debenture and *Kova Establishment v Sasco Investments Ltd* [1998] 2 BCLC 83, which concerned the construction of a guarantee and a charge. See also *ING Lease (UK) Ltd v Harwoood* [2007] EWHC 2292 (QB), in which a similar approach was taken in construing a guarantee.

It is possible for a creditor to assign a liability that is due or owing to it, together   **14.1.4.2**
with an assignment of the security for such a liability, so long as there is no
contractual restriction that would prevent the assignment taking place and that
the liability is one that can be assigned as a matter of law. This is recognised by section 114 of the Law of Property Act 1925 and by the Third Schedule to the Act,[20]
which relate to transfers by way of deed of 'mortgages', which is defined to include
a mortgage or charge of any property for securing money or money's worth.[21]
'Property' is defined comprehensively to include any chose in action and any
interest in real or personal property. It is clear, therefore, that section 114 is
intended to apply to transfers by way of deed of security over all types of asset, with
a specific exception for transfers of security bills of sale over chattels.[22] Section 114
provides that an assignment by way of deed of a mortgage (as defined) is effective
to assign the rights and benefit of the transferor in the security and in the liabilities
that are secured by it, but this is expressly subject to the mortgagor's right of
redemption. Section 114 is a facilitative provision. It does not provide the only
method by which a transfer of security can take place.

Despite what has just been said concerning transfers of security, it is submitted   **14.1.4.3**
that it is not possible to take a bare assignment of security without also taking an
assignment of the liabilities to the transferor that were intended to be covered by
such security, even if the security document states that the chargee or mortgagee
under it includes the successors and assigns of the original beneficiary of the security. Accordingly, the transferee cannot rely upon the security to cover liabilities
that the debtor has incurred directly to the transferee as, for instance, liabilities
due or owing to the transferee prior to the assignment which were unsecured
at the time of the assignment. There are three reasons for this. First, if such an
assignment was possible then the effect would be that a previously unsecured
creditor would be elevated to the position of being a secured creditor and that
would have the effect of subverting the *pari passu* rules of insolvency as they
would relate to the position of unsecured creditors of the obligor that had created
the security.[23] Secondly, the granting of security for the liabilities that it is intended
to secure is a consensual act, which requires agreement between the parties. It
would be contrary to the requirement for such a consensus if liabilities that were

---

[20] As to the effect of s 114 of the Act in relation to transfers of registered and unregistered land,
see *Credit & Mercantile PLC v Marks* [2005] EWCA Civ 760, [2005] 1 WLR 3412 and *Paragon
Finance PLC v Pender* [2005] EWCA Civ 760, [2005] 1 WLR 3412.

[21] See s 205(1)(xvi) of the Act.

[22] The exception is contained in s 114(5) of the Act.

[23] This point was adverted to in *obiter* comments in the decision at first instance in *OBG Ltd
v Allan* [2001] Lloyd's Rep Bank 365, at 373. Although the case went on appeal to the Court of
Appeal ([2005] EWCA Civ 106, [2005] QB 762) and the House of Lords ([2007] UKHL 21), the
point did not arise in the appeals.

originally intended to be unsecured could effectively become secured without the consent of the debtor. Thirdly, the effect of the assignment would be to deny to the obligor the benefit of its equity of redemption upon the discharge of the liabilities that were originally secured by the security.

14.1.5 Non-recourse security

In the usual case, security is taken to support the primary obligation or personal covenant of the obligor to pay, perform, or be responsible for the relevant liabilities. A consequence of this is that if the security is insufficient to cover the liabilities, the obligor will remain liable for the deficiency under its personal obligation, although that may be of small comfort to a creditor which is faced with an insolvent obligor.[24] It is possible, however, for the parties to agree that the creditor will confine its right of recourse or recovery to the secured assets, so that it will not have any personal right of recovery against the obligor.[25] This model is sometimes used in project or property construction finance, under which the relevant financiers agree to take the risk that the project or property assets may not yield a sufficient value to see them whole. No doubt, the interest and fees that they charge for providing the finance will reflect that risk.

14.1.5.1 Other methods of non-recourse financing

There are other techniques by which finance might be provided on a non-recourse basis. Sometimes a transaction might involve a combination of them, together with the use of security without a personal covenant to pay. A brief description will now be given of such other techniques.

14.1.5.1.1 A fairly simple method of achieving an element of non-recourse financing is for the finance to be provided to a subsidiary company in a group, on the basis that the other members of the group, including its parent company, may rely on the normal principle of separate identity in company law, so that they should not be responsible for the borrower's debts and liabilities. However, there may be situations where the concept of separate identity may be overridden by statutory provisions. In addition, the directors and other officers of the borrower might find themselves being held responsible if it could be shown that they had engaged in fraudulent or wrongful trading.[26] It is also worth bearing in mind that the liabilities of a

---

[24] A secured creditor is entitled to value its security and prove in a liquidation as an unsecured creditor for any deficiency and it is also entitled to prove for a deficiency after it has realised its security: see Rules 4.75 (1)(e), 4.88, and 4.95 of the Insolvency Rules 1986.

[25] *Mathew v Blackmore* (1857) 1 H&N 762; *De Vigier v IRC* [1964] 1 WLR 1073; *Levett v Barclays Bank PLC* [1995] 1 WLR 1260, at 1271–1272.

[26] See ss 213 and 214 of the Insolvency Act 1986.

subsidiary may have to be included in the consolidated accounts for the parent
company and its group.

It is also possible for a lender to agree that a borrower's obligation to make repay- **14.1.5.1.2**
ment of its debt, and to pay its other obligations, should be limited by conditions
that are set out in the relevant credit agreement. For instance, the borrower's obligation to make payments might be made dependent upon meeting cash flow and
other conditions or the prior payment of other creditors.

In debt or receivables financing, the financier which purchases the debts might be **14.1.5.1.3**
prepared to do so on a non-recourse basis, so that if the underlying debtor defaults
in payment of the debts that have been purchased, the financier will suffer the
attendant loss. If the financier is not prepared to take that risk then it will require
a right of recourse against the seller.

14.1.6 Third party security

It is possible for a guarantor or other type of surety to give security in support of
its obligations under the guarantee or other relevant instrument. It follows from
what has been said above concerning non-recourse security that it is also possible
for a person to give security over its own assets for the performance of another's
(the debtor's) obligations by way of third party security without the giver of the
security undertaking a personal obligation by way of guarantee.[27] Security of the
latter type is often referred to as collateral or third party security.[28]

14.1.7 Security held by a trustee

Where the obligor has liabilities that are owed to several persons and it is not practical for each of them to take separate security then it would be useful if the security could be taken and held by one person on their joint behalves. The utility of
this would be further enhanced if that security could be held on behalf of the successors, transferees, and assigns for the time being of such persons, such as the
bond holders under a bond issue, where the identity of the bond holders is capable
of changing frequently during the lifetime of the issue, or the syndicate members
under a syndicate loan facility which contemplates the transference of participations in the facility from time to time by way of novation. This can be achieved
under English law by using a security trustee, which would take the security and

---

[27] *Re Conley* [1938] 2 All ER 127, in which it was held that the giver of the security would still
fall to be considered as a 'surety or guarantor' for the purposes of the forerunners of ss 239 and 340
of the Insolvency Act 1986 (persons who might be preferred under the provisions dealing with
preferences).

[28] See Rose LJ in *Re Bank of Credit and Commerce International SA (No 8)* [1996] Ch 245, at 254.
Although the decision was the subject of an appeal to the House of Lords (decided at [1998] AC
214) this particular point was not controversial.

hold it on trust on behalf of all the syndicate members or bond holders for the time being,[29] the security being expressed to secure all of the present and future indebtedness, both actual and contingent, that might be due to them.[30] To assist the trustee in pursuing recovery proceedings and in the enforcement of the security, the documentation under which the security is taken by the trustee is likely to contain a parallel debt provision, by which the indebtedness that was due to the financiers would also be expressed to be due to the security trustee.[31]

14.1.8 Intention to create security

The creation of security is a consensual act of the parties. English law does not automatically give a creditor security merely because it is a creditor or even a particular type of creditor, except in the case of certain creditors who may assert a possessory lien over goods (strictly speaking, this arises as an implied incident of the agreement under which possession of the goods was delivered to the lienee) or certain unpaid vendors of assets or purchasers of such assets who have pre-paid and are entitled to assert an equitable lien (where the lien arises by operation of law). Apart from those unusual cases, if the creditor is to take and hold security then it must obtain the obligor's agreement to give the security.[32] It follows that a prerequisite to the creation of security is that the parties (and, crucially, the obligor) should intend that security will be created. It will usually be fairly obvious that such was the intention of the parties although it is also possible that whilst the parties may intend to enter into a proprietary transaction other than by way of security, it may be characterised as being in the nature of a secured transaction.

---

[29] One of the basic requirements for the validity of a trust is that there should be certainty as to the composition of the class of beneficiaries under the trust. Notwithstanding the fluctuating nature of the bond holders or syndicate members under such a trust, it is submitted that the appropriate test as to certainty of the beneficiaries in such a situation is that laid down in *McPhail v Doulton* [1971] AC 424, namely, whether at any particular time that it was relevant to determine the identity of the beneficiaries, the trustee could say with certainty that any particular person was or was not a member of the class of beneficiaries.

[30] The representative capacity of a security trustee in holding security on behalf of the banks as its beneficiaries, was discussed in *British Power & Energy Trading Ltd v Credit Suisse* [2008] EWCA Civ 53. That case concerned a syndicated facility. This is subject, of course, to the terms of the trust deed or other documentation under which the trustee is appointed to hold the security on behalf of the syndicate members, which may place restrictions upon the powers of the trustee.

[31] Such provisions usually go on to provide that, to the extent that the indebtedness is paid in the ordinary course under the relevant financial documentation prior to default, such a payment will constitute a *pro tanto* reduction of the liability to make a payment that is due to the trustee.

[32] *Palmer v Carey* [1926] AC 703; *Swiss Bank Corp v Lloyds Bank Ltd* [1982] AC 584; *Edwards and Smith v Flightline Ltd; Re Swissair Schweizerische Luftverkehr AG* [2003] EWCA Civ 63, [2003] 1 WLR 1200. In none of those cases was it found that the facts supported an agreement to create security.

There are situations, however, where a transaction may have the superficial appearance of being in the guise of security but where, on closer examination, it turns out that the necessary intention was lacking, thereby leaving the creditor in an unsecured position. This difficulty is likely to arise where there has been an agreement that moneys should be set aside and only dealt with in a certain way,[33] but it may also arise in other situations as well, such as where there has been an agreement to similar effect concerning securities.[34] In *Palmer v Carey*[35] the Privy Council drew a distinction between two situations in determining if the necessary consensual intention existed for the creation of a proprietary interest by way of security. First, when there was merely an agreement that moneys or other property should be paid into an account or otherwise isolated and could not be dealt with by the payor or other similar person except in an agreed manner. In that situation, no security would arise because there was just a contractual arrangement restricting the use to which the moneys or other property could be put. Even though such a restriction might be protected by the grant of an injunction restraining its breach, it would not amount to the grant of a proprietary interest by way of security. Secondly, the alternative situation was where it was agreed that the moneys or other property should be treated as being security to repay the lender out of the fund that had been created. In other words, that it had been agreed that a proprietary interest in favour of the creditor should be created in the fund or other property, to which the creditor could look for payment and discharge of the liabilities due to it. In the second case, there would be an agreement for the creation of security. It should be noted, however, that even though there may be an agreement to create security, it will still be necessary to show that the relevant assets exist and have been appropriated to the security.[36]

14.1.9 Contractual impediments to the creation of security

A person might be precluded by a contractual undertaking that it has given from creating security. The undertaking may be in the form of a negative pledge which restricts that person from entering into transactions by way of security in favour of third parties. Alternatively, the undertaking may amount to a restriction in a contract upon dealing with the rights that arise in that person's favour under the contract. Each of those types of provision is discussed elsewhere in this book, so what follows is limited to a brief summary.

---

[33] As was the case in *Palmer v Carey* [1926] AC 703 and in *Edwards and Smith v Flightline Ltd; Re Swissair Schweizerische Luftverkehr AG* [2003] EWCA Civ 63, [2003] 1 WLR 1200.

[34] As in *Swiss Bank Corp v Lloyds Bank Ltd* [1982] AC 584.

[35] [1926] AC 703.

[36] *Mac-Jordan Construction Ltd v Brookmount Erostin Ltd* [1992] BCLC 350.

14.1.9.1 *Negative pledges*

Negative pledges are discussed in more detail in Chapter 3 and in Chapter 12.[37] A negative pledge is a contractual undertaking in an agreement or security document by which a party (A) to that agreement or document agrees with the other party (B) that A will not create security over its assets, or dispose of those assets, in favour of anyone else (C). In the present context, A as the party that has agreed to be bound by the negative pledge would be the obligor that wishes to create security, and C as the third party would be the creditor that is to receive such security. When considering the effect of a negative pledge, it is necessary to check carefully as to the types of transaction that fall within the overall compass of the clause. In addition, there might also be agreed exceptions to the restrictions contained in the clause, and the proposed transaction might come within a permitted exception.

14.1.9.1.1 Negative pledge clauses arise in three different contexts. First, such a clause might be contained in an unsecured facility or other credit or debt raising instrument (such as in the terms and conditions of a bond issue), by which A as the debtor agrees with B as the lender or lenders that it will not create security in favour of third parties such as C. The intention behind such a clause is to maintain the lender's *pari passu* unsecured position with respect to other claimants against the debtor and in the distribution of its assets, particularly in an insolvency of the debtor. Secondly, in a floating charge a negative pledge clause may be used to restrict the types of transaction that A as the chargor might otherwise be able to enter into within the general concept of the liberty to deal with the charged assets in the ordinary course of business. Thirdly, a negative pledge clause should invariably be contained in any security document by which it is intended to create fixed security, so that A as the chargor or mortgagor is precluded from engaging in any dealings with the assets that are the subject of the security. This is necessary to demonstrate that the security is not a floating charge.

14.1.9.1.2 The principal difficulty concerning negative pledges is in establishing the consequences, as against a third party such as C, where a person such as A breaches the clause and enters into a prohibited transaction in favour of the third party. This comes down to making a determination as to whether the third party is liable to B for the tort of inducing or procuring a breach of the contract between A and B. If so, the third party would be liable in damages (which may not be of much practical utility) but, more importantly, an injunction might be available to B so as to prevent C as the third party from relying upon the benefit of the transaction.[38]

---

[37] See also the author's article, 'Restrictions on Dealing with Assets in Financing Documents: Their Role, Meaning and Effect' [2002] JIBL 193.

[38] See Browne-Wilkinson J in *Swiss Bank Corp v Lloyds Bank Ltd* [1979] Ch 548.

For B to succeed against the third party, it is necessary (in addition to showing that the relevant person (A) had breached the negative pledge) to demonstrate that the third party (C) had the necessary knowledge of the contract and the relevant restriction, that it realised that the relevant person (A) would breach it, and that the third party (C) intended to cause the breach.[39] Such an intention will be lacking, for instance, if the third party had acted on legal advice to the effect that it would not be entering into a transaction which amounted to a breach of the restriction[40] or if it honestly believed that the relevant person (A) had received consent to enter into the transaction.[41]

14.1.9.2 Restrictions within a contract upon dealing with rights arising under the contract

Such restrictions would be relevant where an obligor wishes to create security over the benefit of contractual rights in its favour, such as a debt payable to it. It may be precluded from doing so by the terms of a restriction in the contract under which the right arises. These types of restriction are discussed in more detail in Chapter 12.[42]

When considering the effect of a contractual restriction, it is necessary to consider both the contractual rights to which it relates and the types of dealing with those rights that it prohibits or otherwise restricts. This will be a matter of construction of the contract.[43] For instance, a distinction might be drawn in the terms of the restriction between dealing with unearned rights (such as a right to be paid which will only arise after a service has been performed), which might be prohibited, and dealing with accrued rights that have been earned under the contract (for instance, a right to be paid because the service has been performed).[44] Similarly, a distinction might be drawn in the construction of the relevant wording between a statutory assignment, an equitable assignment, and a declaration of trust of a contractual right,[45] or between an assignment by way of mortgage and a charge. Thus, the clause may prevent one or more of those types of dealing but permit the others

14.1.9.2.1

---

[39] These aspects were explored by Lord Hoffmann in *OBG Ltd v Allan; Douglas v Hello! Ltd; Mainstream Properties Ltd v Young* [2007] UKHL 21.

[40] *Meretz Investments NV v ACP Ltd* [2007] EWCA Civ 1303.

[41] Which was the position on the facts in *Mainstream Properties Ltd v Young* [2007] UKHL 21.

[42] See also the author's article, in two parts, 'Contractual Restrictions on a Creditor's Right to Alienate Debts' at [2003] JIBL 1 and [2003] JIBLR 43.

[43] See Lord Browne-Wilkinson in *Linden Gardens Trust Ltd v Lenesta Sludge Disposals Ltd* [1994] AC 85.

[44] As, for instance, occurred in *R v Chester and North Wales Legal Aid Area Office (No 12), ex p Floods of Queensferry Ltd* [1998] 1 WLR 1496.

[45] *Don King Productions Inc v Warren* [2000] Ch 291; *Devefi Pty Ltd v Mateffy Pearl Nagy Pty Ltd* [1993] RPC 493, at 505 (Fed Ct of Aust); and *Barbados Trust Co Ltd v Bank of Zambia* [2007] EWCA Civ 148, [2007] 1 Lloyd's Rep 495.

to occur. From the perspective of a contracting party in whose favour the restriction applies, the more comprehensive the wording of the restriction, the less opportunity the other party will have to enter into dealings relating to its contractual rights. From the perspective of the latter party, it is best to ensure that the terms of the restriction are specifically confined to stated matters and that the relevant clause states what dealings are permitted.

14.1.9.2.2 Because the restriction upon dealing goes to the very heart of the contractual right that it affects and defines the freedom of the relevant party to deal with the right, a purported dealing in favour of a third party that offends against the restriction will be ineffective to confer a proprietary right upon the third party.[46] This will be the case, whether or not the third party was aware of the restriction or intended to cause a breach of it.

14.1.9.3 Other types of restriction

There may be other types of restriction, principally of a statutory nature, which may prevent a proprietary transaction from taking place, or place constraints as to the circumstances in which it can take place. An example of this is the prohibition upon a public company, or a subsidiary of such a company, giving financial assistance (including by way of giving a guarantee or security) in connection with an acquisition of shares in the public company.[47] Similarly, a public company may not give financial assistance in connection with an acquisition of shares in a private company, if that company is its parent company.[48] Another example concerns restrictions upon a company in entering into transactions with parties that are connected with it.[49] A further example concerns dealing in assets that are subject to regulatory restrictions upon transfer or acquisition of such assets, such as the shares in an authorised person which carry 'control' of the authorised person, under Part XII of the Financial Services and Markets Act 2000.

14.1.10 Conflict of laws and cross-border issues

A number of issues might arise which may involve cross-border elements and the associated considerations that arise in the subject of conflict of laws. They may include the matters already referred to above and other issues as well, such as

---

[46] See, for instance, the strict approach that was taken by the Court of Appeal in *Barbados Trust Co Ltd v Bank of Zambia* [2007] EWCA Civ 148, [2007] 1 Lloyd's Rep 495 as to the obligation to comply with the precise requirements of the relevant clause before an assignment of the lender's rights could take place.

[47] S 678 of the Companies Act 2006 (which prospectively replaces the more comprehensive prohibitions to be found in s 151 of the Companies Act 1985).

[48] S 679 of the Companies Act 2006.

[49] See the provisions concerning substantial property transactions contained in s 190 et seq of the Companies Act 2006 (which replace the provisions of s 320 et seq of the Companies Act 1985).

whether the relevant asset is capable of being taken as security, and if it is available as security, the liabilities that may be secured and the types of creditor that may hold security, the types of security that are available and the methods involved in taking the security, as well as the attendant procedures and formalities that must be observed (including, for instance, if it is necessary to notarise and register the security), the effectiveness of the security, the ranking and priority of different claimants in the same asset, the creditors which may have preferential claims in an asset, the right to enforce the security and the procedures for enforcement of the security, as well as the effect of an insolvency of the debtor.

Those various issues will be examined in this chapter under English law, and the **14.1.10.1** chapter will proceed on the basis that English law governs all of the aspects that are relevant to the subject matter. Nonetheless, conflict of laws considerations are bound to arise in transactions that have a cross-border element, particularly where the relevant asset is located in another jurisdiction. In such cases, one or more foreign laws may govern the various relevant issues and it would be necessary to take advice in the jurisdictions concerned. The conflict of laws and cross-border insolvency aspects are examined further in Chapters 4, 5 and 12. Reference should also be made to Chapter 17 where alternative systems for maintaining secured transactions are discussed. Although the discussion that is contained in this chapter concentrates on the way that English law analyses the issues and deals with them, the discussion may also serve to provide a point of reference for comparative purposes when conflict of laws and cross-border issues arise.

14.2 Concepts of Property, Interests in Property, and Dealings in Property: An Introduction

It is not really possible to comprehend the approach that English law takes to **14.2.1** secured and other forms of proprietary transaction without understanding the types of interest that may exist in property (or assets) under English law, as well as the difference between law and equity and the methods by which dealings in property may take place. At the risk of over-simplification of a complex area of study, there now follows a general description of those matters.

14.2.2 Concepts of property

If a person has an interest in an asset, by an ownership or a security right, then he is said to have a 'proprietary' interest in the asset. Traditionally, English law distinguishes between real property, which concerns land and certain interests in land, and personal property, which covers everything else (e.g. goods and all types of intangible assets). Somewhat confusingly, English law has also treated some interests in land as 'chattels real' and, thus, as being personal property (e.g. a tenant's rights under a lease). English law also distinguishes between tangible and intangible property. Tangible property includes all forms of real property, as well as goods (sometimes called chattels). These assets have a physical presence. Intangible property covers the remainder, being rights of various kinds which do not have a physical quality, but which the law recognises and protects, whose quality and value is protected by being able to sue so as to enforce the right (e.g. for payment of a debt) or to protect the right against misuse by others (e.g. intellectual property). Intangible property therefore includes choses in action (e.g. debts) and intellectual property.[50]

14.2.2.1 The above is the English law domestic classification of property and assets. Different concepts are employed in categorising assets where there is a foreign or extra-territorial element, involving issues outside the English domestic jurisdiction. This is the area of conflict of laws. The relevant categories in that situation are immovable property (i.e. land and interests in land) and movable property (i.e. the rest, which is split between tangible movables and intangible movables).

14.2.3 Legal and equitable interests in assets

English law distinguishes between legal and equitable interests in an asset. The distinction may be relevant to a security transaction for the following reasons. First, it will affect the method and structure of the transaction. Secondly, it will dictate the types of interest that may arise or be taken. Thirdly, it will be relevant to matters relating to attachment of the security to the relevant assets, as well as perfection and priority issues, and the enforcement of the security.

14.2.3.1 Legal interests

In the original understanding of English law there were only common law (or 'legal') interests, because only the common law existed. The common law recognised one ownership interest and that interest depended on the existence of the asset in the ownership of the owner. The transfer of ownership of land depended upon a formal conveyance of the title from the old owner to the new owner, and the transfer of ownership of goods usually depended upon an intention to transfer the property (ownership) in the goods usually, but not always, accompanied by the delivery of possession. The common law did recognise certain subservient interests in an asset, such as the rights of a tenant to occupy land and the rights of a bailee to possession of goods, but they were less than ownership and

---

[50] English law also recognises as a chattel a documentary intangible (i.e. the physical document comprising an instrument such as a bill of exchange) where the rights of the holder, including the right to enforce it, are encapsulated in the instrument, so that possession of the instrument represents the proprietary entitlement to it and the rights it represents. For practical purposes, this means negotiable instruments.

were limited. The common law was unable to recognise that the title in an asset might technically be held by one person but in reality or conscience he did so on behalf of a third party (e.g. because the third party was only an infant or a poor widow). On the other hand, the common law did recognise the concept of shared ownership of a legal interest, either as joint tenants or as tenants in common.

It should also be noted that the common law has never been able to recognise pro- **14.2.3.1.1** prietary interests in future property, including property yet to be acquired by the putative owner. It can only deal with what exists. Any transaction at common law concerning such future property could only give rise to a contractual obligation, for which damages could be awarded if the contract was breached. A claim for damages is not much use if the defendant has become insolvent.

The creation of security at common law followed the same rigid pattern as for **14.2.3.1.2** transfers of ownership. Security over land (before the 1925 property legislation) in essence involved a formal conveyance of the title by the obligor to the creditor. Discharge of the security required a formal re-conveyance back to the obligor once it had satisfied its obligations. At best, the obligor might be able to point to a contractual right to call for the re-conveyance, but it had no proprietary interest in the land in the meantime because it had given up its title. Having no propri- etary interest, the obligor was in a weak position.

The position was a little different with goods. Security could be created by mort- **14.2.3.1.3** gage but historically, as a matter of convenience, it was often done by means of a pledge, which involved giving possession to the creditor and regaining posses- sion once the debt had been paid off. In the case of a pledge, the common law was prepared to recognise two different legal interests, being that of ownership vested in the borrower (the 'pledgor') and the 'special property' of the security holder (the 'pledgee') in the goods. The common law also recognised a right of retention by way of a lien over goods, which was asserted to protect a debt due to the person holding the goods by the person who had delivered possession to him.

So far as concerned choses in action and other types of intangible property, the **14.2.3.1.4** common law was unable to recognise dealings ('assignments') in such assets, by way of outright transfer or security. Traditionally, such transactions could only take place in equity. This was rectified by section 1 of the Policies of Assurance Act 1867, which allowed for policies of life assurance to be assigned at law for the first time, section 1 of the Policies of Marine Insurance Act 1868 (now section 50 of the Marine Insurance Act 1906), which allowed for the assignment of marine policies, and section 25(6) of the Judicature Act 1873, which is now section 136 of the Law of Property Act 1925, which concerns assignment at law of all other forms of legal choses. There are strict formal requirements that must be met to obtain the benefit of the statutory provisions.[51] Although the effect of those statutory provisions was to impose upon the common law a system by which it would recognise assignments which met the requisite conditions, it also remained possible to effect transactions in equity to the same extent as had been the case before the passing of the statutes.[52]

14.2.3.2 Equitable interests

It was to overcome the rigidity of the common law that the separate and more flexible jurisdiction of equity was developed by the chancery courts. These courts (which historically operated separately from the jurisdiction at common law) were prepared to impose obligations upon the conscience of parties and also acted to overcome the rigid and formal requirements and restrictions of the common law. For instance, they regarded that as done which ought to be done. In consequence, there developed a recognition in equity of proprietary interests (called 'equitable' or 'beneficial' interests) which could be superimposed upon the simple legal title recognised at common law. In such a case, equity said that in addition to the underlying legal title held at common law, there was an equitable or beneficial title which the chancery courts would protect by directing the parties to take appropriate action, even by issuing restraining and other orders directed at action in the common law courts.

14.2.3.2.1 When there is an equitable interest there will also be an underlying legal interest in the asset. Usually, but not always (see Lord Browne-Wilkinson in *Westdeutsche Landesbank Girozentrale v Islington LBC*[53]), the holder of the legal interest will be forced by equity to hold his interest on trust for the benefit of the person entitled to the beneficial interest. In such a situation, the person holding the legal title is called the trustee and the person recognised in equity is called the beneficiary. Equity thus developed the concept of the trust. In its simplest form, the trust will be express where it is made clear that one person (the 'trustee') will hold the legal title in identifiable assets (the 'trust property') for one or more other people (the 'beneficiaries'). In other cases, equity will impose a trust where the circumstances require, such as by imposing an implied or constructive trust or a resulting trust. Since legislation in the second half of the 19th century,[54] the common law courts have also been given power to recognise and protect equitable interests and vice versa.

---

[51] It is interesting to note that the 1867 Act and the 1868 Act pre-dated the provision for the legal assignment of other choses that was provided for by s 25(6) of the Supreme Court of Judicature Act 1873.

[52] See Lord Macnaghten in *William Brandt's Sons & Co v Dunlop Rubber Co Ltd* [1905] AC 454, at 461.

[53] [1996] AC 669, at 706–707.

[54] Principally under the Judicature Act 1873.

Equity said that an obligor which had received credit and given a mortgage (the **14.2.3.2.2**
'mortgagor') had an equity of redemption which equity recognised as being a proprietary interest in the asset. The equity of redemption gave the mortgagor the
right to regain its legal title from the creditor (the 'mortgagee') upon discharge of
the secured liability. The chancery court would enforce that right against the
mortgagee, even to the extent of arranging for the re-conveyance to be executed if
the mortgagee refused to do so. Similarly, equity said that in the case of assets of a
special or unique character, where the remedies of the common law were inadequate if the other party failed to honour its contract to transfer the asset, then
equity would treat that as done which ought to be done and require fulfilment of
the contract. In the meantime, equity would recognise a proprietary interest in the
transferee.

Equity was also prepared to recognise the effectiveness of transactions in the whole **14.2.3.2.3**
or parts of choses in action and other types of intangible property. It did this by
the concept of an equitable assignment, to which it attached little in the way of
requirements for the observance of formalities, so long as the intention to assign
was clear (see Lord Macnaghten in *William Brandt's Sons & Co v Dunlop Rubber
Co Ltd*[55]). Such an assignment could be an outright transfer or by way of
mortgage.

Once equity had developed its concept of equitable proprietary interests, it then **14.2.3.2.4**
went on to develop its own concept of security. Such security might arise because
the subject of the security was an equitable interest (e.g. the equity of redemption
of the mortgagor or the right of a beneficiary under a trust). Alternatively, it might
arise because the security was over a common law interest in an asset, but had not
fulfilled all of the formal requirements for the creation of security at common law,
so long as enough had been done or agreed for equity to recognise the intended
consequences of the transaction. In addition, equity developed the charge, which
differs from other forms of security in that it does not involve a concept, however
notional, of a transfer of title, but simply a proprietary impediment upon the asset
for repayment of the secured obligation.[56]

Equity was also prepared to go a step further than the common law in relation to **14.2.3.2.5**
transactions concerning future property. As mentioned above, the common law is
only able to comprehend in a proprietary sense what exists. In certain circumstances,
however, equity is prepared to give proprietary recognition to the effectiveness of

---

[55] [1905] AC 454. But there must be, as a bare minimum, a sufficient outward evidence of an
intention to assign the relevant subject matter: see Blackburne J in *Finlan v Eyton Morris Winfield*
[2007] EWHC 914 (Ch); [2007] 4 All ER 143, at [33].

[56] See Atkin LJ in *National Provincial and Union Bank of England v Charnley* [1924] 1 KB 431,
at 449–450 and Lord Hoffmann in *Re Bank of Credit and Commerce International SA (No 8)* [1998]
AC 214, at 226.

contracts concerning future assets, by saying that a beneficial interest will attach to the property upon its acquisition, as if that interest had existed as from the time of contracting (see Lord Macnaghten in *Tailby v The Official Receiver*[57]). This can be very useful as a security device.

14.2.3.2.6 There are some further points which should be noted. First, that equitable interests cannot exist in a vacuum; there must always be an underlying legal title in an asset. Secondly, there cannot be equitable and legal interests all vested in one and the same person (i.e. without some other person with an intervening interest). In such a case, there will simply be one all-encompassing legal title.[58] Thirdly, that in an ordinary sale of goods transaction, the Sale of Goods Act 1979 provides a complete code for sales of goods, so that equitable interests will not arise as a normal consequence of the transaction.[59] Fourthly, that there cannot be several legal titles existing at the same time, except in the case of limited subservient entitlements, such as that of the lessee under a lease of land, the bailee of goods, and a pledgee or lienee of goods. Equity, however, has no such qualms and will merrily permit several equitable interests, as well as the underlying legal interest, to exist in the same asset. Fifthly, whilst it is perfectly possible to have equitable security over legal interests, it is not possible to have legal security over equitable interests. There is one possible exception to this that may arise under section 136 of the Law of Property Act 1925 in relation to assignments of equitable choses in action. Sixthly, that dealings in future property with a proprietary effect can only take place in equity. Seventhly, the 1925 property legislation did some funny things to real property, such as by inventing the curious security of a charge (which, hitherto, had only been an equitable security) by way of legal mortgage and then saying that there could be successive charges by way of legal mortgage over the same piece of land. It also left the legal title to the land in the mortgagor. Those heresies are confined to security transactions involving real property.

14.2.3.2.7 There is a final point to raise concerning the willingness of equity to recognise and enforce the outcome of an intended proprietary transaction, which will be returned to later in this chapter. It concerns the extent to which equity requires the giving of value by the person who seeks equity's assistance to recognise a transaction. Sometimes value is required and sometimes it is not required, depending upon the circumstances. Value in this context means real or substantial value, as opposed to the nominal value that is understood at common law as being required as the consideration to support a contract. Value, as understood in equity, may consist of a monetary amount, such as an outright payment or an advance by way of loan, or it might consist of some real detriment being suffered, such as the

---

[57] (1888) 13 App Cas 523.
[58] See *Re Bond Worth Ltd* [1980] Ch 228.
[59] See Atkin LJ in *Re Wait* [1927] 1 Ch 606, at 625–641.

promise to do something, giving up a benefit, or the deferment of a right. In determining if value is required, there are two of equity's famous maxims that are in play. One that has already been mentioned is that equity treats as done that which ought to be done. Another is that equity will not assist a volunteer (i.e. a person who has not given value).

14.3 The Concepts of Future Property and Attachment

In general terms, it is possible under English law to take security over just about every type of asset and interest in an asset. As has already been mentioned, English law is prepared to go even further and recognise the proprietary consequences of transactions involving future property, as well as the effect where an asset is converted into proceeds of sale or other products made from it. There are, however, certain limitations upon the breadth of those statements, as will be seen from the discussion that follows.

14.3.1

14.3.2 Future property

Future property may be defined as property (including an interest in property) that an obligor does not hold at the time that it purports to create security over it (or, indeed, when it enters into any other type of transaction concerning such property). The relevant assets may not yet exist or, whilst existing, they may not yet be owned by the obligor. Future property will include goods which the obligor will acquire in the future,[60] debts to become due to the obligor in the future,[61] dividends not yet declared,[62] copyright in works not yet written,[63] an expectancy under the will or intestacy of a living person,[64] and damages not yet sued for and awarded.[65]

It is sometimes difficult to be sure whether the subject matter of a purported dealing is presently existing property or future property by way of a mere expectancy, such as income that might be earned in the future from the use of existing property.[66]

14.3.2.1

---

[60] *Holroyd v Marshall* (1862) 10 HL Cas 191.

[61] *Tailby v Official Receiver* (1888) 13 App Cas 523. By contrast, a debt that has been incurred but is payable in the future is presently existing property.

[62] *Norman v Fed Comr of Taxation* (1963) 109 CLR 9.

[63] *Performing Right Soc Ltd v London Theatre of Varieties Ltd* [1924] AC 1; *Peer International Corp v Termidor Music Publishers Ltd* [2002] EWHC 2675 (Ch), [2004] RPC 22 (the case was subject to an appeal, which did not concern this point: [2003] EWCA Civ 1156, [2004] Ch 212).

[64] *Re Lind, Industrials Finance Syndicate Ltd v Lind* [1915] 2 Ch 345.

[65] *Glegg v Bromley* [1912] 3 KB 474.

[66] See, for instance, the different results (reached by majority decisions) in two Australian cases: *Norman v Fed Comr of Taxation* (1963) 109 CLR 9 and *Shepherd v Fed Comr of Taxation* (1965) 113 CLR 385.

An analogy has been drawn in Australian case law between the 'tree', which is existing property, and the 'fruit' that the tree may produce tomorrow, next year, or thereafter, which is future property.[67] The difference may be important for a number of reasons, including in determining the true subject matter of an assignment and whether the assignee is entitled to enforce the rights that have purportedly been assigned,[68] the extent of a prohibition on assignment and whether it catches what has purportedly been assigned,[69] the rights of set-off that may be enjoyed by the assignee,[70] the method of transfer that is employed, and whether value is required to support the transaction[71] and for priority purposes.[72] It may also be important in the context of the discussion, below, as to whether accretions to an asset might be caught within security that is taken over the asset.

14.3.2.2 Whilst the common law is unable to recognise the proprietary effect of transactions involving future property, equity is able to do so, provided that the conditions that it lays down are met. This was originally determined by the House of Lords in *Holroyd v Marshall*,[73] which held that an agreement that was intended to vest a proprietary interest in future property in a transferee (in that case, by way of security over future goods) could be effective to do so when the property came into existence in the hands of the transferor.

14.3.2.3 The concept of dealing with future property was developed further by the House of Lords in *Tailby v The Official Receiver*,[74] which was a case concerning an assignment of future book debts. It was held that equity will recognise the effect of an

---

[67] The analogy was drawn by Kitto J in *Shepherd v Fed Comr of Taxation* (1965) 113 CLR 385, at 396.

[68] See, for instance, *Batey v Jewson Ltd* [2008] EWCA Civ 18. In that case, if the assignment had only been of the proceeds of a claim (i.e. the fruit), rather than the right of action itself (i.e. the tree), then the assignee would have been unable to pursue the claim and assert it for the purposes of a set-off of a counterclaim that the assignee wished to establish as against the other party to the litigation. The assignor, having become insolvent and been struck off the register of companies, was not in a position to pursue the counterclaim.

[69] See, for instance, *R v Chester and North Wales Legal Aid Area Office (No 12), ex p Floods of Queensferry Ltd* [1998] 1 WLR 1496.

[70] *Batey v Jewson Ltd* [2008] EWCA Civ 18.

[71] As it is not possible to assign future property at law and value is required to support an equitable assignment of future property.

[72] For the purposes of the priority rule in *Dearle v Hall* (*Dearle v Hall, Loveridge v Cooper* (1828) 3 Russ 1), which concerns priorities as between competing assignments, it is not possible to give notice to a potential debtor of a debt that does not yet exist. See further the discussion of the rule in Chap 12.

[73] (1862) 10 HL Cas 191.

[74] (1888) 13 App Cas 523. See, in particular, the speech of Lord Macnaghten where the requirements are clearly set out. His Lordship also dispelled the red-herring linking the recognition of assignments of future property to a requirement that the transaction should be one that was capable of being the subject of a decree for specific performance, which had arisen from what had been said by Lord Westbury in *Holroyd v Marshall* (1862) 10 HLC 191, at 209 and 211.

agreement to assign future property, so that equity will treat the property as vesting in the intended transferee so long as the following conditions are met:

(1) the transaction is supported by valuable consideration given at or following the time of the agreement (i.e. past consideration is insufficient to support the agreement);[75]

(2) there is sufficient ascertainment in the identity of the relevant assets when they come into existence so that it is certain that they were intended to be caught by the agreement; and

(3) the intention between the parties at the time of their agreement is that immediately the assets came into existence in the hands of the putative transferor (and without further condition or the exercise of discretion on the part of the transferor) the intended proprietary interest should vest in the transferee. Such a transferee could be either an absolute purchaser or someone taking security. The security could be by way of fixed or floating security.

In *Re Lind*[76] it was said that the effect of the principle is that the interest of the intended transferee is treated as having been effective from the date of the agreement to assign and so will apply notwithstanding an intervening insolvency of the intended transferor which occurs after the date of the agreement to assign but before the asset comes into existence.[77] For the same reason, the attachment of the security to the asset when it comes into existence, where that occurs after the commencement of a compulsory winding up, will not be treated as a 'disposition' for the purposes of section 127(1) of the Insolvency Act 1986. For the purpose of meeting the time limit for registration under section 870 of the Companies Act 2006,[78] the relevant period commences to run from the date of the original agreement to

14.3.2.4

---

[75] The requirement for valuable consideration in equity is examined further below.

[76] [1915] 2 Ch 345. In *Peer International Corp and ors v Termidor Music Publishers Ltd & ors* [2002] EWHC 2675 (Ch), [2004] RPC 22 Neuberger J said, at [74]–[82], that he preferred the analysis in *Re Lind* to that of the Court of Appeal in *Collyer v Isaacs* (1881) 19 ChD 342, which had doubted that the agreement would be treated as effective, in a proprietary sense, as from the date of the agreement rather than the date the property came into existence. It should be noted that *Collyer v Isaacs* pre-dated the decision of the House of Lords in *Tailby v The Official Receiver*. See further the discussion by Meagher, Gummow & Lehane, *Equity: Doctrines and Principles* (4th edn, 2002), at paras 6-275 to 6-330.

[77] Where, however, the purported assignor subsequently becomes bankrupt and an asset arises in the course of the trustee in bankruptcy running the business, such an asset will vest in the trustee, despite an earlier purported assignment executed before the assignor became bankrupt: *Re Jones, ex p Nichols* (1882) 22 ChD 782. This is consistent with s 306 of the Insolvency Act 1986, by virtue of which property comprised in the bankrupt's estate vests in the trustee. The position may be different in a winding up, as the assets of the insolvent company do not vest in the liquidator unless the court, at his request, makes an order vesting the property in the liquidator pursuant to s 145(1) of the Insolvency Act 1986: see Lord Hoffmann in *Cambridge Gas Transportation Corp v Official Committee of Unsecured Creditors of Navigator Holdings PLC* [2006] UKPC 26, [2007] 1 AC 508 and Ramsey J in *Ruttle Plant Hire Ltd v Secretary of State for the Environment and Rural Affairs* [2007] EWHC 2870 (TCC).

[78] Formerly s 395(1) of the Companies Act 1985.

create the security, not the date that the security attaches to the asset upon its coming into existence.[79] It has also been said that a conditional agreement to give security would be treated as an agreement to give a floating charge and the agreement would be registrable.[80]

14.3.3 Attachment

An obligor may agree to create security over an asset but the security may not necessarily attach immediately to such asset, in the sense of the asset becoming subject to the security in a practical sense. For attachment to occur, the asset must be sufficiently identified and come into the ownership of the obligor, as well as being sufficiently identified for the purpose of the security. This is particularly relevant in the case where a debtor has agreed to give security over future assets (e.g. 'all debts which may become owing to me in the future' or 'the car that I will buy next week' or 'next year's wheat crop'). Until the relevant asset is in existence, is sufficiently identified for the purposes of the security, and is owned by the obligor, there is nothing on which the security can attach.[81] The same analysis will be relevant where the obligor owns an asset but does not identify it with sufficient certainty for security to attach to the asset.

14.3.3.1 Attachment is a different concept to enforcement. The consequence of attachment of security is that the creditor obtains a proprietary interest in the relevant asset which rests there until such time as the obligor defaults, following which the creditor can move to enforce the security and deprive the obligor of its interest in the asset. Obviously, enforcement cannot take place if the security has not attached to an asset, but the reverse is by no means true. It will be necessary to consider, however, if the foregoing distinction between attachment and enforcement is necessarily the case in relation to floating charges.

14.3.3.2 The rules for attachment differ as between goods and intangible property, so it will be necessary to look at them separately.

14.3.3.3 Goods

At general law, property (ownership) cannot attach in favour of a purchaser under a contract for the sale of the goods until the goods have been specifically ascertained and appropriated to the contract.[82] This is the consequence of section 16

---

79 *Independent Automatic Sales Ltd v Knowles* [1962] 1 WLR 974; *The Annangel Glory* [1988] 1 Lloyd's Rep 45.

80 See Lord Scott in *Smith (Administrator of Cosslett (Contractors) Ltd v Bridgend CBC* [2001] UKHL 58; [2002] 1 AC 336, at [63].

81 As discussed above, once the security has attached, it may be treated as having done so from the time of the agreement to give the security.

82 *Re Wait* [1927] 1 Ch 606; *Re London Wine Co (Shippers) Ltd* [1986] PCC 121; and *Re Goldcorp Exchange Ltd* [1995] 1 AC 74.

of the Sale of Goods Act 1979 and that consequence used to follow even where the goods formed part of a homogenous bulk[83] in the hands of the seller and it had been agreed that the purchaser's order would be satisfied out of that bulk. Until the specific goods to be supplied to the purchaser had been appropriated to the contract by being physically separated from the bulk, property could not pass to the buyer (nor did any interest in the bulk pass to the buyer), even if the buyer had paid for the goods that were to be purchased.[84] Accordingly, if the buyer has agreed to give security over the goods that it is to buy, the security cannot attach to the goods until the buyer's own interest in them has attached.

Similar consequences follow with respect to a purported transaction by way of security over unspecified goods or a portion of a homogenous bulk of goods already owned by the obligor.[85] The security cannot attach until the goods have been identified or, in the case of a bulk, the relevant portion has been identified and separated from the bulk. However, if the obligor agrees to give security over all of the goods it owns or all of its goods meeting a certain sufficient description to make them identifiable (e.g. every red car owned by the obligor), the security will attach to those goods when and if the obligor has ownership of goods that fall within the description.   **14.3.3.3.1**

The position at general law with respect to a transaction by way of a sale of goods   **14.3.3.3.2** that form part of a bulk was ameliorated by amendments to the Sale of Goods Act 1979 which were made in pursuance of the Sale of Goods (Amendment) Act 1995. The 1995 Act introduced changes to the rules in section 18 of the 1979 Act, as well as introducing new sections 20A and 20B and inserting a definition of 'bulk' into section 61(1) of the 1979 Act.[86] In summary, the consequences of those amendments are as follows. Under new rules 5(3) and 5(4) of section 18 (unless a different intention appears), where the contract is for the sale of part of a bulk and all other orders to be satisfied from the bulk have been fulfilled then the purchaser will become the owner of what remains (whether or not it has made any payment) provided that the quantity of the bulk has been reduced to no more than is sufficient to satisfy the purchaser's order.[87] Under section 20A (unless a contrary intention appears), where the buyer has made payment for all or some part of its order, which it has been agreed will be satisfied out of an identified bulk,[88] the buyer

---

[83] An appropriate definition of the concept of a bulk is that now contained in s 61(1) of the Sale of Goods Act 1979, which is set out below.

[84] *Re Wait* [1927] 1 Ch 606.

[85] Unless, perhaps, it is intended that the creditor should receive security over the relevant portion of each and every item comprised in the bulk: *Re London Wine Co (Shippers) Ltd* [1986] PCC 121.

[86] The definition provides that, 'bulk means a mass or collection of goods of the same kind which (a) is contained in a defined space or area; and (b) is such that any goods in the bulk are interchangeable with any other goods therein in the same number or quantity.'

[87] This might be characterised as a form of ascertainment by exhaustion.

[88] Such agreement being either at the time of contracting or by subsequent action by the parties.

obtains in consequence of that agreement a proportionate interest in the bulk, the proportion representing the ratio of its payment to the overall bulk. There are provisions in sections 20A and 20B to deal with a scaling down of the proportion where the bulk is insufficient for all the orders to be satisfied from it and also to impose a deemed consent to dealings in the bulk. It should be noted that these provisions only apply to transactions by way of sale of goods; they do not apply to a transaction by way of a purported grant of security over part of a bulk of goods.[89]

14.3.3.4 Intangible property

Once again, for security over intangible property to attach to the relevant assets, it is necessary that the obligor should own the property and that it is sufficiently identified for the purposes of certainty under the security. The position is different from that relating to goods, however, in a case where the interest over which ownership or security is asserted forms part of a bulk or fund of fungible property of the same kind, provided that the bulk or fund is itself sufficiently identified and that the intended proportionate interest is also clear. In such a case, it is possible to assert the relevant proprietary interest.[90] It is not clear if a claimant in such a bulk or fund holds its interest as a tenant in common with other claimants or on some other basis, particularly if the composition of the interests in the bulk or fund is changing from time to time. There are also likely to be difficulties where it transpires that the bulk or fund is insufficient to satisfy the claims of all of those interested in it. This issue is addressed further in Chapter 10.

14.3.4 Security bills of sale

Under section 5 of the Bills of Sale Act (1878) Amendment Act 1882, an individual is precluded from giving security over personal chattels[91] of which he was not the true owner at the time the security was taken.

14.3.5 Static and transient assets

English law permits security to be taken in both static assets, that is, assets which are intended to have a degree of permanence in the hands of the obligor, and (where the obligor is not an individual) in revolving or transient assets which of their nature are turned over or consumed by an obligor as part of its business. As will be discussed later in this chapter, the latter are best encompassed within a floating charge, whereas the former can be subject to either fixed or floating security.

---

[89] S 62(4) of the Sale of Goods Act 1979 provides that the provisions of the Act which concern contracts of sale of goods do not apply to security transactions.

[90] See *Hunter v Moss* [1994] 1 WLR 452; *Re Harvard Securities, Holland v Newbury* [1997] 2 BCLC 369; and *Re CA Pacific Finance Ltd* [2000] 1 BCLC 494. See further the discussion in Chap 10.

[91] See further below as to the meaning of 'personal chattels'.

14.4 An Asset, Accretions to and Substitutions for the Asset, and the Proceeds of Sale of the Asset

In the context of taking and holding security over an asset, it may be necessary to consider if the security will extend to accretions to the asset, such as income earned by the asset, as well as substitutions for the asset and the proceeds of sale of the asset. In one sense, the original asset and such accretions, substitutions, and proceeds are all distinct assets, but a question which arises is the extent to which a security interest in the original asset will extend to those other assets. These matters were considered by Arden LJ in *Buhr v Barclays Bank PLC*[92] and the conclusions which her Ladyship drew were as follows, although it is submitted that each of them would be subject to any express agreement to the contrary as agreed between the security giver and the security holder, save in so far as a bona fide purchaser might be affected.

14.4.1

14.4.2 Accretions and substitutions

Security over an asset, whether it be land, goods, or intangible property, carries with it an inherent security right in the fruits of the asset, that is, accretions to it, such as rent or income earned by the asset. The security will also extend to any asset which is substituted for the original asset, such as upon renewal of a leasehold interest that had been the subject of the security. To that extent, the mortgagor or chargor will be treated as a fiduciary which holds the benefit of the accretions or substitutions for the mortgagee or chargee.

14.4.3 Proceeds of sale of an asset

If with the consent of all the parties an asset is sold subject to the continuance of the mortgage or charge over the asset then the security will continue to exist over that asset. The security holder will not be entitled to claim that its security over that asset has been converted into security over the proceeds of sale (although it is submitted that this should not prejudice any security over the proceeds that the security holder may hold separately or additionally to the security over the asset that has been sold). If a mortgaged or charged asset is sold with the consent of the security holder, but on the basis that the asset will be sold free of the security, then the security will cease to exist over that asset. Instead, the security holder will be entitled to claim security in the proceeds of the sale. If the asset is sold without the security holder's consent,

---

[92] [2001] EWCA Civ 1223; [2002] BPIR 25. Lord Woolf LCJ and Tuckey LJ agreed. In reaching her conclusions, Arden LJ drew heavily upon commentary that had been provided by Professor Sir Roy Goode in *Commercial Law* (2nd edn, 1995) pp 667–688 and *Legal Problems of Credit & Security* (2nd edn, 1988) p 16.

it will be entitled, at its election, to continue to assert its security over the asset, or it will be entitled to treat its security as converted into security over the proceeds of sale. Of course, if its security was effectively overreached by the sale, as where the purchaser is entitled to assert priority, the security holder may be forced effectively to elect that its security should be converted to the proceeds. Where the security is converted to security in the proceeds of sale, the mortgagor or chargor will be treated as a fiduciary holding the proceeds for the security holder.

14.5 Forms of Security

14.5.1 A distinction is drawn in English law between possessory and non-possessory security. There are different forms of security that fall within those two types of security.[93] Some types of security arise at common law and some arise in equity. The position was summarised by Millett LJ in *Re Cosslett (Contractors) Ltd*[94] as follows:

> There are only four kinds of consensual security known to English law: (i) pledge; (ii) contractual lien; (iii) equitable charge; and (iv) mortgage. A pledge and a contractual lien both depend upon the delivery of possession to the creditor. The difference between them is that in the case of a pledge the owner delivers possession to the creditor as security, whereas in the case of a lien the creditor retains possession of goods previously delivered to him for some other purpose. Neither a mortgage nor a charge depends on the delivery of possession. The difference between them is that a mortgage involves a transfer of legal or equitable ownership to the creditor, whereas an equitable charge does not.

What follows will expand upon that summary. In addition to the forms of consensual security to which his Lordship made reference, it will also be relevant to refer to a form of non-consensual security, being the equitable lien.

14.5.2 Possessory security

There are two types of possessory security. They both concern tangible personal property, such as goods and documentary intangibles capable of transfer by delivery, including negotiable instruments, and they both arise at common law. They are the pledge and the contractual or possessory lien.

14.5.2.1 Pledges

A pledge involves the pledgor (the obligor) giving possession of the relevant property[95] to the pledgee (the creditor) as security for an obligation owed by the

---

93 The discussion that follows does not include maritime liens or statutory liens, such as that given to an unpaid seller of goods under ss 39(1)(a) and 41 of the Sale of Goods Act 1979.

94 [1998] Ch 495, at 508 (affd [2001] UKHL 58, [2002] 1 AC 336).

95 Which must be tangible personal property, such as goods or documentary intangibles. Accordingly, it is not possible to have a pledge of the owner's benefit of hire purchase agreements

pledgor to the pledgee.[96] A power of sale for enforcement of the security is an inherent consequence of the security.[97] There are two types of possession that may be taken to constitute the pledge. One type is actual possession, by which the pledgee obtains the physical control of the property.[98] The other type of possession is constructive possession, by which the person with possession of the property undertakes to hold the property for the pledgee by entering into an attornment in favour of the pledge,[99] under which it 'attorns' to the pledgee.

It is also possible to constitute a pledge of goods by the pledgee being given possession of the document of title to goods;[100] the only such document of title which is known to English law being the bill of lading.[101] This procedure is a valuable adjunct to the provision of finance by way of the issuance of a documentary letter of credit, in pursuance of which the issuing bank is presented with the bill of lading under the letter of credit and thereby obtains a pledge of the goods as security for reimbursement by its customer, being the party on whose behalf the letter of credit was opened. **14.5.2.1.1**

A trust receipt is a document that is executed by the pledgor in favour of the pledgee, under which the pledgor is allowed to take possession of the goods **14.5.2.1.2**

---

by a deposit of the agreements, and an agreement to do so will amount to a registrable charge: *Independent Automatic Sales Ltd v Knowles and Foster* [1962] 1 WLR 974.

96 Simply obtaining possession on its own is not sufficient without evidence of the intention to create a pledge. This is because possession may be taken for other reasons and so may not evidence the creation of a pledge. For instance, possession might be given to permit the goods to be retained and used, or possession may be taken as a consequence of the creditor enforcing its charge over the goods: *Re Cosslett (Contractors) Ltd* [1998] Ch 495 (upheld on appeal: [2002] 1 AC 336). Evidence that possession was given so as to create the pledge may be recorded in a memorandum, but care must be taken that the memorandum does not constitute an agreement to create a pledge, which might be taken to constitute a registrable bill of sale.

97 *Pothonier & Hodgson v Dawson* (1816) Holt 383; Cotton LJ in *Re Morritt, ex p Official Receiver* (1886) 18 QBD 222, at 232.

98 For example, *Wrightson v McArthur and Hutchinson (1919) Ltd* [1921] 2 KB 807, where the goods were contained in a separate room in a warehouse which contained no other goods and the pledgee was given the only keys to the room and a licence to enter and remove them. This should be contrasted with *Dublin City Distillery Ltd v Doherty* [1914] AC 823, where the key that was given to the creditor did not give it access, as a second key was also needed.

99 In theory, the debtor could itself attorn to the creditor to constitute a pledge but this would have to be accompanied by a surrendering of the obligor's ability to use and control the goods: *Dublin City Distillery Ltd v Doherty* [1914] AC 823. Furthermore, a written form of attornment by the obligor runs the risk of being categorised as an agreement to give a pledge which would amount to a bill of sale with the attendant requirements as to formalities and registration under the Bills of Sale Act (1878) Amendment Act 1882 or, if given by a company, registration as a company charge: *Re Townsend* (1886) 16 QBD 532, *Dublin City Distillery Ltd v Doherty*.

100 *North Western Bank Ltd v Poynter Son and Macdonalds* [1895] AC 56. The procedures for doing this are illustrated by *Lloyds Bank Ltd v Bank of America National Trust and Savings Assoc* [1938] 2 KB 147.

101 Not, for instance, a delivery warrant: *Dublin City Distillery Ltd v Doherty* [1914] AC 823. Nor will the deposit of hire purchase agreements constitute a pledge of the goods let on hire by the owner under the agreements: *Independent Automatic Sales Ltd v Knowles and Foster* [1962] 1 WLR 974.

subject to a pledge and sell them. By virtue of the arrangement, the pledgor obtains possession as trustee for the pledge and so acts on behalf of the pledgee and not on its own account. The consequence of this is that the security under the pledge continues until the goods are sold, when it transfers to the proceeds of sale.[102]

14.5.2.2 Contractual liens

A contractual or possessory lien depends upon the relevant creditor (the lienee) obtaining possession of goods which it may keep until it has been paid by the obligor (the lienor). Unlike a pledge, a lien does not give rise to a power of sale.[103] It is simply a right to detain the goods.[104] It arises in a context where the goods are delivered to the lienee for some purpose other than by way of security, such as for storage, carriage, or repair. A lien may be specific, where it relates to indebtedness incurred by the lienor to the lienee in relation to the particular goods concerned, or it may be a general lien, where the lienee is entitled to keep goods of the lienor for other types of indebtedness. It is possible for the parties to agree that a specific lien should be turned into a general lien. A lienee's rights are subject to ss 246 and 349 of and paragraphs 43(2) and 44 of Schedule B1 to the Insolvency Act 1986.

14.5.3 Non-possessory security

Non-possessory security may arise at common law or in equity. The security involves the creation of a proprietary right in the asset in favour of the creditor, but until enforcement action is taken the obligor is entitled to remain in possession of the relevant property. In each case, the security arises by virtue of the terms of the agreement between the parties and is dependent upon that agreement, as it is not constituted by the yielding of possession of the relevant asset by the obligor to the creditor.[105] The forms of non-possessory security are as follows.

---

[102] However, the right of the pledgee can be defeated by a dealing by the pledgor acting as a mercantile agent: *Lloyds Bank Ltd v Bank of America National Trust and Savings Assoc* [1938] 2 KB 147.

[103] It would appear that the validity of the lien will not be imperilled if the parties agree that the lienee should have a power of sale: see *Great Eastern Rly Co v Lord's Trustee* [1909] AC 109 and *Re Hamlet International PLC, Trident International Ltd v Barlow* [1999] 2 BCLC 506. It is submitted that the outcome of the latter case may be explained on the basis that the sale of the goods took place pursuant to a consent order of the court which, in its terms, permitted the lienee to have the proceeds of the sale if it was found that it had a valid lien in the first place. It is not immediately clear why, given that the lienor was a company in administration, the administrator did not invoke the provisions of what is now para 43 of Sched B1 to the Insolvency Act 1986.

[104] The very act of detention, however, has been held to amount to enforcement of security in the context of an administration of the lienor: see *Bristol Airport plc v Powdrill* [1990] Ch 744. See also *London Flight Centre (Stansted) Ltd v Osprey Aviation Ltd* [2002] BPIR 1115.

[105] *Re Cosslett (Contractors) Ltd* [1998] Ch 495 (upheld on appeal: [2002] 1 AC 336).

14.5.3.1 *Legal mortgage*

In technical terms (except in the case of land), a legal mortgage involves a formal conveyance or transfer of the mortgagor's (the obligor's) legal title in the relevant asset to the mortgagee (the creditor).[106] The mortgagor is protected by its equity or redemption, in consequence of which it is entitled to a re-conveyance or re-transfer of the property upon discharge of the security. The position is different for land as the security will be in the form of either a charge by way of legal mortgage or a demise for a term of years absolute.[107]

Where the property which is to be the subject of the security consists of a debt[108] or other legal chose in action[109] (and apart from the mortgage of a legal right that vests by registration in the appropriate register or a mortgage of a negotiable instrument, where additional action is needed[110]), a legal mortgage will take the form of an absolute written assignment of the chose under the hand of the mortgagor as the assignor,[111] of which written notice must be given to the debtor, under section 136 of the Law of Property Act 1925.[112] In this respect, it should be noted

14.5.3.1.1

---

106 It is arguable that it may be possible to assign an equitable chose in action pursuant to s 136 of the Law of Property Act 1925 because, whilst the section speaks of the assignment of a 'debt or other legal chose in action', it then contemplates that notice of the assignment might be given to a trustee: see Younger J in *Re Pain; Gustavson v Haviland* [1919] 1 Ch 38, at 44. The difference may not be material, in light of the outcome of *William Brandt's Sons & Co v Dunlop Rubber Co Ltd* [1905] AC 454 and *Three Rivers DC v Governor and Co of the Bank of England* [1996] QB 292.

107 See ss 85–87 of the Law of Property Act 1925 and s 51 of the Land Registration Act 2002. By virtue of the latter provision, a mortgage of registered land, upon registration, is a charge by way of legal mortgage.

108 It will still be a debt for this purpose even though litigation for its recovery was contemplated at the time of the assignment: *Camdex International Ltd v Bank of Zambia* [1998] QB 22.

109 Which may include a right of action in tort or contract if, prior to 1873, equity would have compelled the assignor to pursue the defendant for the benefit of the assignee: *Compania Colombiana de Seguros v Pacific Steam Navigation Co* [1965] 1 QB 101. In other words, the legal chose must be of a type that equity would have regarded as being assignable prior to 1873: *Tolhurst v Associated Portland Cement Manufacturers* [1903] AC 414, at 424; *G&T Earle (1925) Ltd v Hemsworth RDC* (1928) 140 LT 69.

110 For instance, shares in a company, where legal title vests upon being entered in the relevant register: *Torkington v Magee* [1902] 2 KB 636, so that it will be necessary in the case of a mortgage of shares in an unlisted company for the mortgagee to obtain the mortgage instrument, the share certificate, and the relevant share transfer instrument, the latter two of which must be submitted to the appropriate registrar so that the mortgagee can be entered in the register. The position as to shares in a listed company is referred to below. In the case of certain types of intellectual property, it will be necessary for the mortgagee to be registered on the statutory register (i.e. trade marks, patents, and registered designs). With respect to a mortgage of a negotiable instrument, it is necessary for the mortgagee to obtain possession (and, perhaps, endorsement) of the instrument, as well as obtaining execution of the mortgage instrument (as opposed to a pledge of the instrument, where possession (and, perhaps, endorsement) is required to constitute the pledge).

111 An assignment by way of deed, although not being under hand, will meet this requirement: *Marchant v Morton Down & Co* [1901] 2 KB 829. This is also subject to Reg 4(3) of the Financial Collateral Arrangements (No 2) Regulations 2003 (SI 2003/3226) as noted later in this chapter.

112 Or the equivalent under s 1 of the Policies of Assurance Act 1867, for policies of life assurance, and s 50 of the Marine Insurance Act 1906, for marine policies. As to the requirements of s 136, see Chap 12.

that the section requires that the assignment should be absolute and not conditional or incomplete,[113] it must be of the whole of the chose,[114] and it must not purport 'to be by way of charge only'. The effect of this is that the form of the mortgage by way of assignment, and the written notice of it, should be absolute and entirely unconditional, rather than expressed as being limited and only effective until the secured liabilities have been discharged, although it is acceptable for the mortgagee to agree with the mortgagor that the mortgagee will re-convey the chose back to the mortgagor once the secured liabilities have been discharged, thereby recognising the mortgagor's equity of redemption.[115] Whilst in a technical sense the mortgage effects a transfer of the mortgagor's rights, the latter retains its equity of redemption so that the mortgage will not affect the validity of the underlying chose that is assigned, nor its recoverability. Accordingly, if the subject of the assignment is the benefit of a contract for the rendering of work or services to the mortgagor and the contract is breached by the other contracting party, so that there is a claim for damages suffered by the mortgagor, the damages will be recoverable even though the breach occurred after the date of the mortgage. It is not a defence to the claim for damages that the mortgagee has suffered no loss. The damages will remain recoverable after a re-conveyance back following discharge of the mortgage.[116]

14.5.3.1.2 In contrast to certain forms of equitable transaction, to which further reference is made below, it is not necessary that the mortgage should be supported by valuable consideration.[117] Accordingly, a legal mortgage of a chose (or indeed, other types of property) may be taken as security for an existing debt, although the transaction may still be vulnerable under various provisions of the Insolvency Act 1986 that are concerned with the re-opening of prior transactions that might constitute a transaction at an undervalue or a preference.[118]

14.5.3.1.3 So long as there are not any impediments relating to the particular asset concerned, it is possible to take a legal mortgage over just about any type of existing legal property of an obligor. However, an individual who gives a mortgage (a security bill of sale) of personal chattels[119] must comply with the requirements of the

---

[113] *Re Williams, Williams v Ball* [1917] 1 Ch 1.

[114] *Jones v Humphreys* [1902] 1 KB 10.

[115] *Tancred v Delagoa Bay & East Africa Rly Co* (1889) 23 QBD 239; *Hughes v Pump House Hotel Co* [1902] 2 KB 190.

[116] *Bovis International Inc v Circle Limited Partnership* (1995) 49 Conv LR 12, [1995] NPC 128.

[117] *Nanney v Morgan* (1887) 37 ChD 346, at 352; *Re Westerton, Public Trustee v Gray* [1912] 2 Ch 104; *Walker v Bradford Old Bank Ltd* (1884) 12 QBD 511.

[118] Ss 238, 239, 339, and 340 of the Insolvency Act 1986.

[119] Strictly speaking, the expression 'bill of sale' is narrower than the concept of a mortgage and the expression 'personal chattels' is narrower than simply referring to goods. By virtue of s 3 of the 1882 Act, both expressions have the definitions given to them by s 4 of the Bills of Sale Act 1878. The consequence of this is that there are various exclusions from what might normally be thought

Bills of Sale Act (1878) Amendment Act 1882. That includes identifying correctly the mortgaged chattels under section 4 of the Act and meeting the requirements as to attestation and registration of the Bill, which must also contain a true statement of the consideration for which it was given, pursuant to section 8 of the Act. The form of the Bill must comply with the requirements of section 9 of the Act.[120] Otherwise it will be invalid, either absolutely, or as to the security contained within it. On a slightly more positive note, the difficulties that had previously existed with respect to an individual, who was a trader, in giving a mortgage of chattels of which he continued in possession, because of the reputed ownership provisions under section 38(c) of the Bankruptcy Act 1914 (and its predecessors), were repealed by the Insolvency Act 1985 (which was itself replaced by the Insolvency Act 1986).

A legal mortgage of a ship, or a share in a ship, must comply with the requirements of the Merchant Shipping (Registration etc) Act 1993, including as to registration of the mortgage in the register. An unregistered mortgage can only be equitable and will suffer in terms of priority as against other registered interests. The position is different for mortgages of aircraft, as a failure to register a mortgage under the Mortgaging of Aircraft Order 1972[121] is relevant to priorities but not the nature of the security.

14.5.3.1.4

14.5.3.2 *Equitable mortgage*

An equitable mortgage takes the form of an equitable transfer or assignment of the relevant property.[122] It may arise because:

(i) the subject matter of the security is equitable property (for instance, a mortgagor might wish to mortgage its equity of redemption or a person that has a beneficial interest may wish to give security over that interest);

(ii) the formalities that are required for a legal mortgage of legal property have not been fulfilled (for instance, where notice of an assignment of a chose in action has not been given to the debtor or where the security is by way of an uncompleted agreement to give a legal mortgage);

---

of as being included within a chattel mortgage, including mortgages of ships, goods in foreign parts or at sea, bills of lading, and the assets of companies, wherever incorporated (see also s 17 of the 1882 Act and *Slavenburg's Bank NV v Intercontinental Natural Resources Ltd* [1980] 1 WLR 1076). Aircraft are also excluded by virtue of Art 16(1) of the Mortgaging of Aircraft Order 1972 (SI 1972/1268). There is also an exemption for certain imported goods under s 1 of the Bills of Sale Act 1890.

[120] Which must be in the form of a deed of indenture: see the Schedule to the Act.

[121] SI 1972/1268.

[122] For a fuller discussion as to equitable assignments, which is also relevant in this context, see Chap 12.

(iii) the property is not transferable at law (as was the position prior to 1873 with respect to choses in action and remains the case with respect to an assignment of only part of a chose);[123] or

(iv) the form of transaction could not meet the requirements for a legal assignment (for instance, an assignment that is expressed to be by way of security until discharge of the secured obligations which is, in the words of section 136 of the Law of Property Act 1925, by way of charge only).

14.5.3.2.1 There is little that is required by way of formalities for an equitable mortgage, but it must at least be clear in the case of intangible property (and the same should apply to other types of property as well) that the mortgagor, as the equitable assignor, clearly intends the transaction to take place,[124] and that such intention is manifested in some outwardly observable manner.[125] There are, however, two further requirements that may have to be met in certain (but not all) circumstances. They concern the need for the security to be in writing and that the creation of the security should be supported by the giving of valuable consideration. Those two requirements, when they are applicable, will apply whether the transaction is in the form of an equitable mortgage or an equitable charge. The necessity to meet those requirements is discussed in Chapter 12. Although those passages address the assignments of debts, what is said there will also apply to taking security over both tangible and intangible property more generally. What follows is intended merely to provide a summary.

14.5.3.2.2 Writing is required where the subject matter of the security that is to be taken consists of an equitable interest in property.[126] An agreement in writing signed by both parties is also required for the creation of any security over an interest in land,[127] including by way of a deposit of title deeds.[128] For practical reasons, however, it is always sensible that the security should be in a written form, so that there can be no doubt as to the scope of the security and the relevant terms that should apply to it, as well as demonstrating that the obligor intended to create the security. It should also be noted that the powers of enforcement of security under section 101 of the Law of Property Act 1925 depend upon the security being in the form of a deed.

14.5.3.2.3 The question of value arises in connection with the taking of security for outstanding and unsecured liabilities that already existed at the time the security

---

[123] *Bank of Liverpool and Martins Ltd v Holland* (1926) TLR 29.

[124] See the famous statement of Lord Macnaghten in *William Brandt's Sons & Co v Dunlop Rubber Co Ltd* [1905] AC 454, at 462.

[125] See Blackburne J in *Finlan v Eyton Morris Winfield* [2007] EWHC 914 (Ch); [2007] 4 All ER 143, at [33].

[126] S 53(1)(c) of the Law of Property Act 1925.

[127] S 2 of the Law of Property (Miscellaneous Provisions) Act 1989.

[128] *United Bank of Kuwait v Sahib* [1995] 2 All ER 973.

was taken. The concept of value in equity means real and substantial value, such as the making of further advances or the suffering of a real detriment, such as giving up a right or postponing it for some meaningful period, such as a forbearance to sue for repayment of outstanding indebtedness.[129] Value is always required in connection with any proprietary dealing with future property.[130] Value is also required to support the giving of an equitable charge.[131] On general equitable principles, value is required in any other case where the security cannot be perfected by the creditor alone, in other words, where the obligor has not done all of those things which it alone could do and which are necessary to establish the security over the relevant property.[132] Even in cases where value is not required in an equitable sense to establish the validity of the security, the transaction may still be vulnerable under various provisions of the Insolvency Act 1986 that are concerned with the re-opening of prior transactions that might constitute a transaction at an undervalue or a preference.[133]

It is not possible for an individual to give a written form of equitable security, whether by way of equitable mortgage or equitable charge, over goods. This is because the statutory form that must be used is in the form of a legal mortgage.[134]

14.5.3.2.4

14.5.3.3 Equitable lien

An equitable lien arises by operation of law and does not depend upon the lienee gaining possession of the relevant property. In many senses, the consequence of such a lien is similar in effect to an equitable charge. However, because the lien arises by operation of law and so is not 'created' by the lienor, it is not a registrable charge for the purposes of section 860 of the Companies Act 2006.[135]

An equitable lien arises to secure to a vendor of property payment of the purchase price.[136] It will also arise to secure to a purchaser repayment of any part of the price already paid if the transaction fails to proceed to completion.[137] A person who

14.5.3.3.1

---

129 See *Glegg v Bromley* [1912] 3KB 474.
130 *Tailby v The Official Receiver* (1888) 13 App Cas 523.
131 *Re Earl of Lucan, Hardinge v Cobden* (1890) 45 ChD 470.
132 *Milroy v Lord* (1862) 4 De G F & J 264, in which it was established that equity would not perfect an imperfect gift. See also *Kekewich v Manning* (1851) 1 DM&G 176 and, more recently, *T Choithram International SA v Pagarani* [2001] 1 WLR 1 and *Pennington v Waine* [2002] EWCA Civ 227, [2002] 1 WLR 2075.
133 Ss 238, 239, 245, 339, and 340 of the Insolvency Act 1986.
134 See s 9 of and the Schedule to the Bills of Sale Act (1878) Amendment Act 1882.
135 Formerly s 395 of the Companies Act 1985. See *London and Cheshire Insurance Co Ltd v Laplagrene Property Co Ltd* [1971] Ch 499.
136 *Re Birmingham* [1959] Ch 523.
137 *Rose v Watson* (1864) 10 HL Cas 672; *Chattey v Farndale Holdings Inc* [1997] 1 EGLR 153, in which it was said that the principle did not depend upon the availability of specific performance.

extends credit which is used to pay the vendor is entitled to be subrogated to the seller's lien.[138] However, if the party that would be entitled to the lien agrees to take security for the relevant obligation, then the lien will not arise,[139] even if the security is or becomes unenforceable, for instance through failure to register in the Companies Registry.[140]

14.5.3.3.2 Generally speaking, an equitable lien can arise in relation to most types of property,[141] although it probably cannot arise under an ordinary contract for the sale of goods. This is because the Sale of Goods Act 1979 provides a complete code as to the passing of title, and equitable interests cannot arise in consequence of the contract.[142] However, where the contract is one for the building and supply of goods to a special order or specification, an equitable lien can arise, at least in favour of a purchaser which has prepaid and a person who has financed the purchaser.[143]

14.5.3.4 *Equitable charge*

An equitable charge (sometimes called a hypothecation[144]) differs from an equitable mortgage in that it does not involve the concept, however notional, of a transfer of title. Instead, it effects a proprietary impediment upon the asset by way of security for repayment and discharge of the secured obligation.[145] There are two types of equitable charge, namely, the fixed charge and the floating charge. The floating charge is dealt with separately below, so the present discussion will focus on the fixed charge.

14.5.3.4.1 A fixed equitable charge may be taken in the same circumstances in which an equitable mortgage may be taken, with respect to both present and future property, and the comments that are made above in relation to the requirements in taking an equitable mortgage (particularly as to need for writing and valuable

---

[138] *Orakpo v Manson Investments Ltd* [1978] AC 95.

[139] *Capital Finance Co Ltd v Stokes* [1969] 1 Ch 261; *London and Cheshire Insurance Co Ltd v Laplagrene Property Co Ltd* [1971] Ch 499.

[140] *Orakpo v Manson Investments Ltd* [1978] AC 95; *Capital Finance Co Ltd v Stokes* [1969] 1 Ch 261; *London and Cheshire Insurance Co Ltd v Laplagrene Property Co Ltd* [1971] Ch 499; *Burston Finance Ltd v Speirway Ltd* [1974] 1 WLR 1648. The position may be different if the security was invalid from the outset: *Nottinghamshire Permanent Benefit Building Soc v Thurstan* [1903] AC 6; *Orakpo v Manson Investments Ltd*.

[141] It applies to real property: *Rose v Watson* (1864) 10 HL Cas 672; *Re Birmingham* [1959] Ch 523; and personal property: *Re Stucley, Stucley v Kekewich* [1906] 1 Ch 67 (apart from goods).

[142] *Transport and General Credit Corp Ltd v Morgan* [1939] Ch 531.

[143] *Hewett v Court* (1983) 149 CLR 639; *International Finance Corp v DSNL Offshore Ltd* [2005] EWHC 1844 (Comm), [2007] 2 All ER (Comm) 305.

[144] *Lowe v National Insurance Bank of Jamaica* [2008] UKPC 26.

[145] See Atkin LJ in *National Provincial and Union Bank of England v Charnley* [1924] 1 KB 431, at 449–450; Slade J in *Re Bond Worth Ltd* [1980] Ch 228, at 250; and Lord Hoffmann in *Re Bank of Credit and Commerce International SA (No 8)* [1998] AC 214, at 226.

consideration) are also applicable to taking a fixed equitable charge.[146] There is no particular form that is required to create a charge, so long as the intention to do so is clear.[147] An agreement to create a trust over an asset as security for performance of an obligation will constitute security, most probably in the form of a charge (which might be either a fixed or floating charge, depending upon the circumstances).[148]

For most purposes, the distinction between a fixed equitable charge and an equit- **14.5.3.4.2** able mortgage is of little relevance, as they will each confer an effective form of equitable security, the consequences for priority purposes will be the same, and, provided the security document that is used is in the form of a deed, the same enforcement remedies will arise under section 101 of the Law of Property Act 1925. Indeed, the two are often conflated and referred to in the same way, even by statute.[149] In strictly technical terms, the discharge of a charge does not result in a re-conveyance or re-transfer of the secured property to the chargor as no convey-ance of title occurred when the charge was granted. In more practical terms, the distinction may have some relevance in considering the effect of taking security over a credit balance or other contractual right that is owed by the chargee to the chargor, which will be referred to at a later point in this chapter. It is also relevant where the subject of the security is a chose in action against a third party. As there is no transfer of the chargor's title in the chose, the chargor must remain as the person that should sue the third party for performance, and the chargor will also be the person who can grant a good discharge to the third party.[150] If the chargor refuses to co-operate then the chargee will need the assistance of the court to com-pel the chargor to act.[151] The distinction will also be important with respect to the remedy of 'appropriation' of financial collateral under Regulation 17 of the Financial Collateral Arrangements (No 2) Regulations 2003,[152] for the reasons discussed later in this chapter. As already noted, the distinction is relevant in determining if valuable consideration is required to support the giving of the rele-vant security.

---

[146] The giving of valuable consideration is a pre-requisite for an equitable charge: *Re Earl of Lucan, Hardinge v Cobden* (1890) 45 ChD 470.

[147] See Romer J in *Cradock v Scottish Provident Institutions* (1893) 69 LT 380, at 382 (affd (1894) 70 LT 718).

[148] See Slade J in *Re Bond Worth Ltd* [1980] Ch 228, at 250 and Jonathan Parker J in *Re ILG Travel Ltd* [1996] BCC 21, at 44–45.

[149] See s 861(5) of the Companies Act 2006 (formerly s 396(4) of the Companies Act 1985).

[150] This may be contrasted with the position where there has been an assignment by way of mortgage under s 136 of the Law of Property Act 1925 and, it would appear, where the assignment was equitable, at least if notice of the assignment was given to the debtor: *William Brandt's Sons & Co v Dunlop Rubber Co Ltd* [1905] AC 454; *Three Rivers DC v Governor and Co of the Bank of England* [1996] QB 292.

[151] A power of attorney taken under s 4 of the Powers of Attorney Act 1971 would be an alternative.

[152] SI 2003/3226.

14.5.3.5 Debenture

The expression 'debenture' is used in various different contexts in English law. For instance, in section 738 of the Companies Act 2006[153] it is defined to include 'debenture stock, bonds and any other securities of a company, whether or not constituting a charge on the assets of the company'. By contrast, in relation to the giving of security the expression is used to mean a security document by which a company gives comprehensive security for indebtedness due to a creditor such as a bank, such security being over all or substantially all of its assets. The security will normally be by way of a combination of fixed security over those assets that are susceptible to such security and floating security over the remainder of its assets.

14.6 Floating Charges

14.6.1 Introduction

It has already been seen that English law developed the concept that security could be taken over future assets, so that the assets would come within the security when they were acquired by the obligor. It then became necessary to consider if security could be taken, not just over assets that the chargor might wish to acquire from time to time, but also over assets (often the same assets as those that might be suitable candidates to fall within an after-acquired property clause in a security instrument) that it might wish to deal with, that is, dispose of or consume, in the course of its business, without the necessity of obtaining specific releases from the creditor each time a disposal or consumption was to take place. Taking the continuum of such types of asset from acquisition to disposal or consumption, in the context of their acquisition and use for the purposes of the chargor's business, it could be said that the assets were of a fluctuating or circulating nature. In other words, that they would be turned over in the course of the business, with the likelihood that assets would be acquired on a fairly repetitive basis to replace those that were, also repetitively, disposed of or consumed. If such assets were not available as security then a considerable portion of a company's current assets would be ignored in determining the availability of credit, and financiers might not be so willing to extend finance to the company to assist in the financing of the business. On the other hand, if such assets upon acquisition were tied up in a form of fixed security, without the right to deal with them and use them, then the company would be unable to carry on its business. The equitable floating charge was developed in the second half of the nineteenth century to permit incorporated business

---

[153] Formerly s 744 of the Companies Act 1985.

to give such security over assets which were of a fluctuating or circulating nature.[154]

14.6.1.1 The happy state of affairs under which the chargor is able to deal with the charged assets under a floating charge continues until such time as the right to do so is taken away. At that point, the charge is said to 'crystallise', when it becomes a fixed charge with respect to the assets then or thereafter within its compass. This is also called the process of 'crystallisation'.

14.6.1.2 A word of caution must be introduced at this point. Whilst it is helpful in understanding the historical development of the floating charge to describe the matter in the context of assets that typically are of a circulating or fluctuating character, that is not the determinative test for ascertaining in any particular case if a charge is a floating charge or a form of fixed security. As was made clear in the *Brumark* case (to which reference is made below) and other cases as well, what is important is whether the chargor is able to deal with the charged assets free of the security and as if they were its own, or whether, on the other hand, that liberty has been entirely removed so that the assets are subject to the real control of the chargee. It is only in the latter case that there will be fixed security. The reason why the requisite element of control is not present is usually because the assets are needed for use by the chargee in dealing with them in its business, and that is typified by assets that are characteristically of a circulating or fluctuating nature. Nonetheless, it is possible to take a form of fixed security over an asset that is normally associated with a floating charge, if the chargor's ability to deal with it is frozen. Similarly, it may be found that an asset that is usually associated with fixed security is subject only to a floating charge because the chargor has been given a liberty to deal with the asset.

14.6.1.3 Floating charges were developed as a form of corporate security.[155] Largely for historical reasons to do with the doctrine of reputed ownership in bankruptcy, which no longer applies, they were not available as a form of security that might be given by individuals.[156] In addition, as a consequence of legislation,

---

[154] As Lord Millett pointed out in *Agnew v Commissioner of Inland Revenue* [2001] UKPC 28, [2001] 2 AC 710, the earliest cases were *Re Panama New Zealand and Australian Royal Mail Co* (1870) LR 5 Ch App 318; *Re Florence Land and Public Works Co, ex p Moor* (1878) 10 ChD 530; *Re Hamilton's Windsor Ironworks, ex p Pitman & Edwards* (1879) 12 ChD 707; and *Re Colonial Trusts Corp, ex p Bradshaw* (1879) 15 ChD 465.

[155] Lord Hoffmann made a passing reference to this in *Aquachem Ltd v Delphis Bank Ltd* [2008] UKPC 7. The fact that the security was developed in a corporate context is clear in the famous statement that is taken from the judgment of Romer LJ in *Re Yorkshire Woolcombers' Association Ltd* [1903] 2 Ch 284, at 295, which is quoted below.

[156] See Lord Millett in *Agnew v Commissioner of Inland Revenue* [2001] UKPC 28; [2001] 2 AC 710, at [8]. Apart from personal chattels that are the subject of the Bills of Sale Act (1878) Amendment Act 1882, there would appear to be no reason why the courts should not now be able to recognise the ability of an individual to give a floating charge, particularly over business assets,

an individual cannot give a floating charge over most types of personal chattels.[157]

14.6.1.4   A valuable explanation of the historical development of the floating charge and of the essential nature of a floating charge, as compared with fixed security, was provided by Lord Millett in giving the advice of the Privy Council in *Agnew v Commissioner of Inland Revenue*,[158] often referred to as the *Brumark* case, after the name of the company which had given the security in that case. The advice that his Lordship delivered in that case should be regarded as required reading for anyone who wishes to study this subject.

14.6.2   The importance of the distinction between fixed security and floating charges

Before progressing further in examining the nature and characteristics of a floating charge, it is worth mentioning briefly the importance of the distinction between fixed security and floating charges. Many of the reasons for the distinction will be dealt with in more detail at a later stage, so what follows is by way of summary to give a general perspective. The discussion will begin by examining the advantages of taking floating security. It then turns to the disadvantages of such security. From the overall perspective of a creditor which wishes to take security, it has to be admitted that the advantages are outweighed by the disadvantages.

14.6.2.1   *Advantages*

In the first place, as adverted to above, a floating charge can be taken over fluctuating or circulating assets of a business in circumstances where it would not be possible, in a practical sense, for the assets to be the subject of fixed security, as the company would be unable to carry on its business if it was subject to the restrictions associated with giving fixed security. This is because it is of the essence of fixed security that the obligor cannot deal with the assets without the consent of the creditor, which means, for instance, that the obligor cannot have access to the secured assets to dispose of them and it cannot use the proceeds of such a disposition to make payments. In this sense, it might be said that the floating charge provides security where it might not otherwise be available, and it permits the

---

but it may now be too late for this development to occur. It should be noted that a general assignment by a trader of book debts, whether absolutely or by way of security, should be registered pursuant to s 344 of the Insolvency Act 1986.

[157] This is the consequence of ss 4 and 5 of the Bills of Sale Act (1878) Amendment Act 1882, to which there is an exception in s 6 of that Act (although the ambit of that exception is cut down by s 9 of the Act). Further exceptions arise with respect to agricultural assets under the Agricultural Credits Act 1928.

[158] [2001] UKPC 28, [2001] 2 AC 710.

company to carry on its business, and thus its ability to generate cash flow, for the benefit of all concerned.

Secondly, the presence of a floating charge as part of a package of comprehensive security over the whole or substantially the whole of a company's assets may permit the creditor to appoint an administrative receiver of the company and its assets.[159] An administrative receiver has considerable powers with respect to the management of the company and dealing with its assets.[160] The right to make such an appointment, however, has been curtailed by section 72A of the Insolvency Act 1986.[161] Where an administrative receiver is appointed, the creditor by doing so is able to defeat the subsequent appointment of an administrator[162] and the commencement of a moratorium with respect to an eligible company where there is a proposal for a voluntary arrangement of the company.[163] The creditor which holds a floating charge as part of a comprehensive package of security is also in a position, as the 'holder of a qualifying floating charge',[164] to appoint an administrator, which at least is useful in determining who should be appointed,[165] although the creditor cannot influence what should happen thereafter in the conduct of the administration.

14.6.2.1.1

14.6.2.2 *Disadvantages*

The disadvantages of a floating charge are all borne by the creditor which holds such a charge. The first and most general disadvantage is that because the chargor is permitted to deal with the assets in the ordinary course of its business, the chargee loses out, in a priority sense, to just about anyone else with whom the chargor deals with the charged assets in a proprietary sense. In effect, the chargor is entitled to confer on third parties rights in its assets that will prevail against the interest of the chargee. As will be seen from what is said below, the concept of dealing in the ordinary course of business has been developed rather liberally by the case law.

Secondly, for registration purposes, any floating charge is registrable under section 860 of the Companies Act 2006,[166] even where a fixed form of security over the same assets would not have been registrable. Failure to register has drastic consequences that affect the validity of the security.

14.6.2.2.1

Thirdly, there are a number of statutory provisions which confer priority on various persons with respect to floating charge assets and their proceeds of realisation,

14.6.2.2.2

---

[159] The definition of an 'administrative receiver' is contained in s 29(2) of the Insolvency Act 1986.

[160] See, for instance, s 42 of and Sched 1 to the Insolvency Act 1986.

[161] This is discussed further below.

[162] See paras 17(b), 25(c), and 39(1) of Sched B1 to the Insolvency Act 1986.

[163] See para 4(1)(c) of Sched A1 to the Insolvency Act 1986.

[164] Which is defined in para 14(3) of Sched B1 to the Insolvency Act 1986.

[165] See para 14 of Sched B1 to the Insolvency Act 1986.

[166] See s 860(7)(g) of the Act (formerly s 396(1)(f) of the Companies Act 1985).

ahead of the interests of the chargee (irrespective of whether the charge has crystal-lised). These are referred to in greater detail below.

14.6.2.2.3 Fourthly, the rights of the chargee suffer if the chargor is in administration or if a moratorium is in force with respect to a proposed voluntary arrangement of a chargor. If the chargor is in administration, the administrator has the right to deal with the charged assets as if they were free of the charge, although the chargor is given the same priority over assets acquired in substitution for the charged assets.[167] If a moratorium is in place, it is not possible to crystallise the charge nor to restrict the right of the chargor to dispose of the charged assets.[168] In addition, a provision in a floating charge is void if it provides that obtaining a moratorium or doing anything to that end will cause the charge to crystallise, lead to a restriction on the right of the chargor to dispose of charged assets, or be a ground for the appoint-ment of a receiver.[169]

14.6.2.2.4 Fifthly, under section 245 of the Insolvency Act 1986 floating charges are subject to an additional ground on which they might be avoided in the event that the chargor goes into winding up or administration, which does not apply to fixed security. Section 245 is addressed in further detail later in this chapter.

14.6.3 The nature of a floating charge

In two early cases, Lord Macnaghten provided explanations as to the nature of a floating charge. In *Governments Stock and Other Securities Investment Co Ltd v Manila Rly Co*[170] he said that:

> A floating security is an equitable charge on the assets for the time being of a going concern. It attaches to the subject charged in the varying condition in which it hap-pens to be from time to time. It is of the essence of such a charge that it remains dor-mant until the undertaking charged ceases to be a going concern, or until the person in whose favour the charge is created intervenes.

In *Illingworth v Holdsworth*[171] his Lordship contrasted a specific charge (a fixed security) with a floating charge and said:

> A specific charge, I think, is one that without more fastens on ascertained and defin-ite property or property capable of being ascertained and defined; a floating charge, on the other hand, is ambulatory and shifting in its nature, hovering over and so to speak floating with the property which it is intended to affect until some event occurs or some act is done which causes it to settle and fasten on the subject of the charge within its reach and grasp.

---

[167] See para 70 of Sched B1 to the Insolvency Act 1986.
[168] See para 13 of Sched A1 to the Insolvency Act 1986.
[169] See para 43 of Sched A1 to the Insolvency Act 1986.
[170] [1897] AC 81, at 86.
[171] [1904] AC 355, at 358. In the Court of Appeal, the case was called *Re Yorkshire Woolcombers' Association Ltd* [1903] 2 Ch 284, to which further reference is made below.

It is clear from what Lord Macnaghten said in the first of those cases that a floating charge is a present form of security which extends to the assets that come within its compass from time to time;[172] it is not an agreement to give future security.[173] It follows that the receipt of new assets within the charge after the commencement of winding up of the chargor is not invalidated as a new disposition in favour of the chargee by section 127(1) of the Insolvency Act 1986.[174] **14.6.3.1**

What is not very clear from the two statements is the extent of the interest of the chargee prior to crystallisation of the charge, bearing in mind the freedom of the chargor to deal with the assets as if they were free of the charge.[175] In the first of the two passages, Lord Macnaghten appears to be saying that the security can be treated as attaching to the assets that come within its compass from time to time. However, in the second of the two passages quoted above Lord Macnaghten appears to be saying that the charge does not attach to the charged assets until crystallisation, as he says that it does not 'settle and fasten on' the assets prior to that point. The preponderance of views is that whilst there is some form of security interest in the charged assets prior to crystallisation, it is not sufficient to be regarded as having attached to the assets. That is the reason why third parties can acquire superior rights in the charged assets and why the chargor is able to deal with the assets as if they were free of the charge and confer entitlements on third parties which may be by way of absolute ownership or otherwise take priority over the interest of the chargee.[176] **14.6.3.2**

It is possible to take a floating charge over the whole of a company's undertaking and assets or over only one asset or some part of its assets. It is common, but not necessary for its validity, that the instrument of charge will contain the power for the chargee to appoint a receiver of the charged property.[177] **14.6.3.3**

The relationship between the chargor and the chargee, which arises from the contractual agreement between them contained in the charge, governs much of the consequences of the security, including as to the circumstances in which the charge crystallises so that it attaches to the charged assets in the manner just described. This was made clear by Hoffmann J in *Re Brightlife Ltd*.[178] **14.6.3.4**

---

[172] See Kay LJ in *Driver v Broad* [1893] 1 QB 744, at 749 and the helpful analysis provided by Helsham CJ in Eq in *Re Margart Pty Ltd* (1985) 9 ACLR 269, at 271–273.

[173] Although it has been said that an agreement to give security in the future, in the event that certain conditions arise, might be considered to fall within the description of a 'floating charge' that is required to be registered under s 860 of the Companies Act 2000 (formerly s 395 of the Companies Act 1985): see Lord Scott in *Smith (Administrator of Cosslett (Contractors) Ltd) v Bridgend CBC* [2001] UKHL 58; [2002] 1 AC 336, at [63].

[174] See *Re Margart Pty Ltd* (1985) 9 ACLR 269.

[175] See further the commentary provided in Chap 13 of Gough, *Company Charges* (2nd edn, 1996).

[176] See, for instance, Fletcher Moulton and Buckley LJJ in *Evans v Rival Granite Quarries Ltd* [1910] 2 KB 979, at 994 and 999–1002, respectively.

[177] See *Re Cimex Tissues Ltd* [1994] BCC 626, at 634–635.

[178] [1987] Ch 200, at 212.

14.6.4 The essential characteristic of a floating charge

The most commonly quoted description of the usual characteristics of a floating charge was that provided by Romer LJ in *Re Yorkshire Woolcombers' Association Ltd*,[179] as follows:

> I certainly do not intend to attempt to give an exact definition of the term 'floating charge', nor am I prepared to say that there will not be a floating charge within the meaning of the Act [i.e. Section 14 of the Companies Act 1900], which does not contain all the three characteristics that I am about to mention, but I certainly think that if a charge has the three characteristics that I am about to mention it is a floating charge. (1) If it is a charge on a class of assets of a company present and future; (2) if that class is one which, in the ordinary course of the business of the company, would be changing from time to time; and (3) if you find that by the charge it is contemplated that, until some future step is taken by on or behalf of those interested in the charge, the company may carry on its business in the ordinary way as far as concerns the particular class of assets I am dealing with.

14.6.4.1   Despite the reticence shown by Romer LJ in providing an exact definition, it was confirmed by the Privy Council in the *Brumark* case and by the House of Lords in *Re Spectrum Plus Ltd*[180] that the essential hallmark or characteristic of a floating charge is the third of the three characteristics that were identified by Romer LJ, namely, the liberty of the chargor to deal with the charged assets in the ordinary course of business until the charge is crystallised.[181] As Lord Millett remarked in the *Brumark* case, the first two of the characteristics may typically be found in the case of a floating charge but are not an essential ingredient of such a charge and they may also be present in a fixed charge,[182] for instance, in a fixed charge over future property. Furthermore, it is possible to take a floating charge over a declining stock of assets, which is not being replenished. Cases which had been decided before the decisions of the Privy Council and the House of Lords on the basis that all three of the criteria had to be present before there could be a floating charge, and thus that an absence of either or both of the first two criteria meant that the security should be treated as a fixed charge, should now be regarded as having been incorrectly decided.[183]

14.6.4.2   Taking the decisions in the *Brumark* and *Spectrum Plus* cases together, the consequence is that only if the chargor has been effectively deprived in full and from the outset of the liberty to deal with the charged assets in a proprietary sense, so that

---

[179] [1903] 2 Ch 284, at 295.

[180] [2005] UKHL 41, [2005] 2 AC 680.

[181] See Lord Scott in *Re Spectrum Plus Ltd* [2005] UKHL 41; [2005] 2 AC 680, at [107]–[111].

[182] At [13].

[183] On this basis, it is submitted with respect that the decisions on this aspect of the Court of Appeal in *Re Atlantic Computer Systems PLC* [1992] Ch 505 and of Vinelott J in *Re Atlantic Medical Ltd* [1992] BCC 653 were incorrect.

the assets have truly been set aside as security for payment of the secured obligations, can it be said that there is a fixed charge. To achieve a fixed charge, the chargee has to be in control of the assets, so that the chargee must consent, within its discretion, to their release from the security before they can be dealt with by the chargor. In practice, the distinction in characterising the nature of the security comes down to a practical factual analysis in relation to the security, the assets concerned, and the means by which they can be exploited. It is also important to ensure that the restrictions from dealing that are contained in the security instrument have been followed through in practice and, to that extent, it is relevant to take into account the conduct of the parties subsequent to the creation of the charge.[184] The label ascribed by the parties to the security, whilst indicating their subjective intention, is not determinative of its nature, as it is a matter of determining the legal effect from the substance of the transaction.[185] Furthermore, as Hoffmann J had remarked in *In re Brightlife Ltd*[186] and Millett LJ had also said in *Re Cosslett (Contractors) Ltd*,[187] a partial restriction would not be a sufficient deprivation of the chargor's liberty to deal with the assets for there to be a fixed charge. In addition, a third party will only be affected by a partial restriction if, on normal principles, it was aware of the restriction and took its interest with the intention of causing the chargor to breach the restriction.

14.6.5 The liberty to deal

In light of its central importance in determining if security is by way of fixed or floating security, as well as the consequences of such a determination, it is necessary to consider the approach that the courts have taken in considering what is meant by the concept of the liberty to deal or, to describe it more fully, dealing in the ordinary course of business with the charged assets. Transactions that take place within the scope of the liberty to deal will have the effect of conferring on the third party that treats with the chargor either an outright ownership right or otherwise a right in the assets that takes priority over the interest of the chargee.

The concept has been given a wide and liberal meaning, bearing in mind the pro-   **14.6.5.1**
prietary consequences to third parties which deal with the company in reliance

---

184 See Lord Millett in the *Brumark* case at [2001] UKPC 28; [2001] 2 AC 710, at [48] and Lord Walker in *Re Spectrum Plus Ltd* [2005] UKHL 41; [2005] 2 AC 680, at [140].

185 See Lord Millett in the *Brumark* case at [2001] UKPC 28; [2001] 2 AC 710, at [31]–[32], and Lords Scott and Walker in *Re Spectrum Plus Ltd* [2005] UKHL 41; [2005] 2 AC 680, at [119] and [141], respectively. This point was taken to the opposite extreme in *The Russell Cooke Trust Co Ltd v Elliott* [2007] EWHC 1443 (Ch), in which it was held that a charge which was described as a floating charge was, nonetheless, a fixed charge because the chargor was effectively prevented by the charge instrument from being able to deal with the charged assets.

186 [1987] Ch 200, at 209.

187 [1998] Ch 495, at 510.

upon its liberty to deal with its assets. It refers to general concepts of carrying on business, not the particular business of the chargor.[188] It has been held that an unprecedented or exceptional transaction, in terms of the transactions usually entered into by the chargor, may still be within the ordinary course of business.[189] The fact that the directors may exceed their powers or that the transaction might amount to a preference of the chargee does not necessarily mean that it would fall outside what might be considered as being in the ordinary course of business.[190] A disposal of a substantial part of the chargor's assets, even by one transaction, may still be regarded as being in the ordinary course of business if it is not done with a view to the permanent cessation of the business.[191] However, if it is done with a view to the permanent cessation of the business of the company, that is, the company intends to cease business, it will be outside the ordinary course of business and it will cause the charge to crystallise.[192]

14.6.5.2 The following types of transaction involving charged assets have been held to fall within the ordinary course of business:

(1) disposals of assets whilst trading,[193] even if it is a quick sale to raise cash;[194]

(2) use of the proceeds of sale of assets to meet the expenses of the business;[195]

(3) the creation of rights of set-off, either arising as legal set-offs or equitable set-offs;[196]

(4) a sale and lease-back of assets;[197]

(5) the grant of fixed security over the assets;[198] and

(6) the grant of a limited floating charge,[199] but the grant of a general floating charge is not in the ordinary course of business.[200]

---

[188] Kay LJ in *Driver v Broad* [1893] QBD 744, at 748–749; *Ashborder BV v Green Gas Power Ltd* [2004] EWHC 1517 (Ch), at [227].

[189] See *Willmot v London Celluloid Co* (1886) 34 ChD 147; *Re Borax Co* [1901] 1 Ch 326.

[190] See *Willmot v London Celluloid Co* (1886) 34 ChD 147; *Ashborder BV v Green Gas Power Ltd* [2004] EWHC 1517 (Ch), at [227].

[191] See *Re Florence Land and Public Works Co, ex p Moor* (1878) 10 Ch D 530; *Hubbuck v Helms* (1857) 56 LJ Ch 536; *Re Borax Co* [1901] 1 Ch 326.

[192] See *Re Woodroffes (Musical Instruments) Ltd* [1986] Ch 366; *Re Real Meat Co Ltd* [1996] BCC 254.

[193] *Re Florence Land and Public Works Co, ex p Moor* (1878) 10 Ch D 530.

[194] *Hamer v London, City & Midland Bank Ltd* (1918) 87 LJKB 973.

[195] *Re Panama, New Zealand and Australian Royal Mail Co* (1870) 5 Ch App 318.

[196] *Biggerstaff v Rowatt's Wharf Ltd* [1896] 2 Ch 93; *Edward Nelson & Co Ltd v Faber & Co* [1903] 2 KB 367; *Rother Iron Works Ltd v Canterbury Precision Engineers Ltd* [1974] QB 1. The right of a third party to set-off a liquidated cross-claim that it has against the chargor will cease with respect to cross-claims that arise after the third party has received notice that the charge has crystallised: *Business Computers Ltd v Anglo-African Leasing Ltd* [1977] 1 WLR 578.

[197] *Reynolds Bros (Motors) Pty Ltd v Esanda Ltd* (1984) 8 ACLR 422.

[198] *Re Castell and Brown Ltd* [1898] 1 Ch 315; *Re Benjamin Cope & Sons Ltd* [1914] 1 Ch 800.

[199] *Re Automatic Bottle Makers* [1926] Ch 412.

[200] *Re Benjamin Cope & Sons Ltd* [1914] 1 Ch 800. It would appear that this point was overlooked by Morritt J in *Griffiths v Yorkshire Bank PLC* [1994] 1 WLR 1427.

14.6.6 Fixed v floating security in the context of particular transactions

It is relevant to consider what conditions or requirements may have to be fulfilled, in any particular case, so that the creditor can be sure that it has taken fixed security. This is particularly important if one takes into account the comparative advantages to a creditor of holding fixed security, as opposed to floating security. The question has arisen most strikingly in relation to security over book debts, but it could also arise in many other instances.

In theory, it should be possible to take fixed security over any asset,[201] but to achieve fixed security, the chargee has to be in control of the charged assets.[202] Control in this sense means that the chargee must be in the position that the assets can only be dealt with by the chargor if they have been released from the security with the consent of the chargee, which it should be at liberty to grant within its discretion on a case-by-case basis. Thus, a standing arrangement or understanding that assets will be released from the charge (with or without meeting certain requirements) will result in the security being in the nature of a floating charge rather than by way of fixed security. It must also be borne in mind that the question cannot be resolved simply by looking at the title in the asset, without also considering the constituent elements of the asset and its practical or commercial utility. Nor is the answer dictated by the label or form of the security; thus, a security which calls itself a legal mortgage or a fixed charge might turn out to be no more than a floating charge when it has been subjected to proper scrutiny.[203] The distinction in characterising the nature of the security will often come down to a factual analysis of the assets concerned, taking into account the true nature of the assets and the means by which they can be exploited and realised in a practical sense.

14.6.6.1

---

[201] A point that had initially been recognised by Slade J in *Siebe Gorman & Co Ltd v Barclays Bank Ltd* [1979] 2 Lloyd's Rep 142.

[202] It has to be the chargee that exerts control over the assets. It is not enough that the chargor has been deprived of control in its own right as, for instance, where the charged assets are subject to an external restriction, where control has been vested in a third party, or where there is joint control between the chargor and chargee: see, for instance, *Re ASRS Establishment Ltd* [2000] 2 BCLC 631, in which the Court of Appeal held that there could not be a fixed charge over the benefit of a bank account where, vis-à-vis the chargee, the chargor would have access to the relevant account, which was maintained with a third party, even though there were restrictions inherent in the nature of the account which precluded the company from unrestricted dealing with the account.

[203] It was on this issue that it is respectfully submitted that Slade J fell into error in *Siebe Gorman & Co Ltd v Barclays Bank Ltd* [1979] 2 Lloyd's Rep 142. He concluded that the necessary element of control over the proceeds of the collections of the charged book debts could be assumed to be in favour of the chargee because the parties had intended that the security should be by way of fixed charge. To put it colloquially, he put the cart before the horse.

14.6.6.2 *Book debts (receivables)*

Both the *Brumark* and the *Spectrum Plus* cases involved attempts to take fixed security over the present and future book debts of the chargor.[204] What follows applies the approach that was taken in those cases.

14.6.6.2.1   The essential nature of book debts as assets, in a practical and economic sense, rests in the ability to turn them into cash proceeds and to use such proceeds. This can be achieved by selling the debts or by getting in payment of the debts. That has to be borne in mind in characterising the nature of security over book debts and the necessity to take control of the debts and the practical utility that they represent. In both the *Brumark* case and the *Spectrum Plus* case it was said that it was not sufficient to draw a line between the debts in their uncollected state and the proceeds of their collection.[205] To achieve a fixed charge, the chargor has to be deprived from the outset of both the power to dispose of the debts before collection and the effective use of their proceeds after collection. The deprivation has to be enforced from the very beginning of the security. It matters not whether one views the book debts and their proceeds of collection as two separate assets or that one is the emanation of the other. In reality, the proceeds of collection are 'merely the traceable proceeds of the [debt] and represent its entire value'.[206] It makes no commercial sense to treat them separately, in the sense of attempting to isolate the debts from their proceeds of collection. What follows will assume that the chargor has been precluded from dealing with the book debts prior to their collection. It will concentrate on how the collection should be achieved and what should be done with the proceeds of the collection.

14.6.6.2.2   Where the chargee is a bank and is able to provide an account which the chargor can use to receive collections of the book debts, it is possible to achieve a fixed charge by requiring the chargor to collect payment of the debts through the account. However, it is not sufficient merely to provide that the chargor is obliged to collect the debts by paying them into its account with the chargee, if the chargor may then have effective use of the proceeds of collection by drawing on the account into which they had been paid.[207] Thus, in a case where the proceeds are paid into an overdrawn account, if that goes towards restoring the overdraft limit in consequence of which the chargor could make further withdrawals from the account, then there would not be an effective or practical limit to the chargor's

---

[204] A number of other cases also involved the same issue, including *Siebe Gorman & Co Ltd v Barclays Bank Ltd* [1979] 2 Lloyd's Rep 142 and *Re New Bullas Trading Ltd* [1994] 1 BCLC 485.

[205] As had been done erroneously by the Court of Appeal in ibid.

[206] Per Lord Millett in the *Brumark* case at [2001] UKPC 28; [2001] 2 AC 710, at [46].

[207] Which had been the view taken by Slade J in *Siebe Gorman & Co Ltd v Barclays Bank Ltd* [1979] 2 Lloyd's Rep 142.

ability to use the proceeds of collection. It follows that the proceeds must be paid into a blocked account to which the chargor is denied access, so that the balance on the account may only be released to the chargor on a case-by-case basis. The facts must substantiate that the account is blocked in practice and not just in theory. Hence, it is insufficient that the chargee simply reserves the right to block the account in the future. The necessary procedures can be achieved by using the model in the Irish case of *In re Keenan Bros Ltd*.[208] In that case, the chargor was obliged to collect payment of its receivables by paying them into a blocked account at the chargee bank, with the bank retaining complete discretion and day-to-day control over withdrawals from that account. *Keenan Bros* was referred to with approval in both the *Brumark* case and the *Spectrum Plus* case.

An alternative method would be for the debts to be assigned by way of mortgage **14.6.6.2.3** to the financier from the outset, with notice of the assignment being given to the debtors, such that the debtors would be directed to make payment directly to the financier. The financier would then collect payment itself and retain the proceeds as security or use them in discharge of the secured liabilities.[209] As Lord Millett pointed out in the *Brumark* case, this structure may not be commercially practical, unless the financier was able to undertake the administrative work of receiving and processing the payments.[210]

A further alternative, which might be useful if the financier is not a bank, is that **14.6.6.2.4** there would be an unnotified equitable assignment by way of mortgage of the debts. The assignor (i.e. the financier's customer) would declare itself to be the trustee of the financier for the purpose of collecting the debts, having been given the authority of the financier to do so on behalf of the financier. The assignor would be required to open a separate account at a bank into which the debts would be collected. The account would itself also be subject to a trust in favour of the financier, with notice given to the bank of the security. It would be necessary that all concerned should agree that no withdrawal could be made from the account without the financier's consent.

Whichever of the above methods is used, it is bound to be rather cumbersome. It **14.6.6.2.5** is also unlikely to appeal to the chargor/assignor because the chargor/assignor will not have ready access to the proceeds of collection of the book debts and so will be denied the economic use of the proceeds of collection of its receivables. Therein, of course, lies the basis of the decisions by the Privy Council and the House of Lords.

---

[208] [1986] BCLC 242.

[209] This alternative, and the one that is next mentioned, were canvassed briefly by Lord Hope in *Re Spectrum Plus Ltd* [2005] UKHL 41; [2005] 2 AC 680, at [54]. See also Lord Millett in the *Brumark* case at [2001] UKPC 28; [2001] 2 AC 710, at [17].

[210] Per Lord Millett in the *Brumark* case at [2001] UKPC 28; [2001] 2 AC 710, at [17].

14.6.6.2.6 A completely different method of structuring a receivables transaction, which will put a financier in a similar position to that in which it would have been had it been possible to take fixed security over the customer's book debts, would be for the financier to enter into a debt purchase transaction with its customer, such as a factoring, invoice discounting, or block discounting transaction. Such transactions involve the purchase by the financier of the customer's book debts and do not have to give way to the claims of a liquidator for liquidation expenses or the claims of the preferential creditors in an insolvency of the customer, nor will they suffer from the depredations inflicted on the realisations of assets subject to a floating charge pursuant to section 176A of the Insolvency Act 1986. In *Lloyds & Scottish Finance Ltd v Cyril Lord Carpets Sales Ltd*[211] the House of Lords held that the invoice discounting arrangement in that case was to be regarded as a purchase of the relevant debts, rather than a loan with security. As such, it did not constitute a registrable charge within the equivalent in Northern Ireland of section 860 of the Companies Act 2006.[212]

14.6.6.3 Other assets

Although the decisions in *Spectrum Plus* and *Agnew* were specifically concerned with transactions involving book debts or receivables, they have a wider implication, particularly in the emphasis that they place on three matters in distinguishing fixed from floating security. First, that the crucial matter in determining the character of the security lies in whether or not the chargee is in control of the assets so that the chargor has been fully deprived of the liberty to deal with the assets. Secondly, that the first two of the characteristics mentioned by Romer LJ in the *Yorkshire Woolcombers* case are not defining criteria, so that their presence or absence will not be conclusive. Hence, it is possible that a floating charge may be taken over a single or itemised asset or assets and such a charge may exist over a diminishing number of assets which may not be replenished. Thirdly, that it will not be sufficient to judge the first issue by looking at a particular asset in isolation and removed from its practical nature and utility, as well as its effective exploitation as an asset.

14.6.6.4 Plant and equipment

If it is wished to take fixed security over items of plant and equipment or similar types of 'fixed asset' (as described in accounting terms), it is suggested that it would not be safe to rely on cases[213] where it was held that if the charge covered

---

[211] [1992] BCLC 609.

[212] Formerly s 395 of the Companies Act 1985.

[213] Such as *National Provincial Bank of England Ltd v United Electric Theatres Ltd* [1916] 1 Ch 132 and *Re Cimex Tissues Ltd* [1994] BCC 626. Although the latter case referred to *Holroyd v Marshall* (1862) 10 HL Cas 191 as an early authority for the view that it was consistent with a fixed

specific plant or equipment which was itemised (or otherwise identified) in the security document then that was a sufficient indication of an intention to grant fixed security to be determinative, even though the chargor was given a limited licence to dispose of the assets, for instance if they were to be replaced. In *Re Cosslett (Contractors) Ltd*,[214] which was a case concerning equipment, Millett LJ had emphasised the importance of the control test as to dealings with the relevant equipment, that is, control in the hands of the chargee. On this basis, a fixed charge can only be taken if the chargor is precluded from disposing of the asset (in the sense of disposing of it or granting proprietary entitlements in it) without the permission of the chargee.[215] In this regard, it is relevant that quite a lot of computer and other electronic equipment has a relatively short life before it falls due for replacement and so it looks more like circulating assets than long-term permanent or semi-permanent assets, which adds further necessity to the requirement for control in the hands of the chargee.[216] It is also submitted that the chargor should be precluded from entering into other types of dealing in the asset, by way of bailment, which may affect, in a substantial sense, the entitlement to take possession of the asset or the long-term value of the asset. On the other hand, a permission that is given to the chargor to grant bailments at will, which can be immediately terminated, or relatively short-term periodic bailments, should not affect the nature of the security, because they do not threaten the chargee's interest to any material extent.

14.6.6.5 *Equipment leases or hire purchase transactions and rental payable under them*

The decisions in *Re Atlantic Computer Systems plc*[217] and in *Re Atlantic Medical Ltd*,[218] which each preceded the decisions in the *Brumark* case and the *Spectrum Plus* case, now stand in great doubt, particularly in relation to the charge over rentals under the security in those cases. In the *Atlantic Computers* case, the company was in the business of leasing equipment to end users. It obtained finance for the

---

charge that the chargor might have a limited licence to dispose of charge assets, it is submitted that the House of Lords in that case did not have this particular point in mind (after all, *Re Panama New Zealand and Australian Royal Mail Co* (1870) LR 5 Ch App 318, which came some years later, is generally regarded as the first case in which the concept of the floating charge was recognised). Furthermore, the grantor of the bill of sale in *Holroyd v Marshall* was an individual trader and not an incorporated entity.

[214] [1998] Ch 495 (affd at [2001] UKHL 58, [2002] 1 AC 336).

[215] The one possible qualification to this could be that the chargor might safely be given a licence to dispose of equipment once it has reached a state of such longevity that it has no value, provided that adequate precautions are in place to demonstrate that fact before a disposal takes place. This would be because the chargee would not be affected in a practical sense by such a disposition.

[216] See the approach taken in *Re GE Tunbridge Ltd* [1994] BCC 563.

[217] [1992] Ch 505.

[218] [1992] BCC 653.

cost of its acquisition of the equipment through entering, as hirer, into a hire purchase agreement or, as lessee, into a leasing agreement of the equipment, which it had already agreed to sub-hire or sub-lease to the end users. As security for the performance of its own obligations, it had given security to the financier over the benefit of the sub-leases, including the rentals payable to it thereunder. The sub-leases were identified in a schedule to the security. There was no contractual restriction as to the collection or use of such rentals by the company, at least prior to enforcement, and whilst the court noted that there was no specific permission given to the company as to the exercise by it of its rights under the sub-leases, there would appear to have been no specific conferral of control over those rights in favour of the chargee. The Court of Appeal held, nonetheless, that the company had given fixed security over both the sub-leases and the rental payable thereunder because the relevant assets were in existence and identified when the security was given and should therefore be distinguished from a floating charge where the charge was ambulatory and covered present and future assets. This analysis draws upon the first two of Romer LJ's characteristics in the *Yorkshire Woolcombers* case,[219] whilst saying little in relation to the third of those characteristics. The court noted specifically that its decision was not affected by the fact that the company had unrestricted access to the rentals and the use of their proceeds.

14.6.6.5.1 The position was almost the same in the *Atlantic Medical* case, except that the security extended to cover any future leases of the equipment and the rentals payable under such leases. Vinelot J followed the Court of Appeal in the *Atlantic Computers* case and held that the extension of the security to cover the future sub-leases was not material as they would be in replacement of the identified existing sub-leases and therefore amounted to much the same thing. He also held that it was not realistic to distinguish, for security purposes, between the sub-leases and the rentals payable under them, as in taking security over the benefit of the sub-leases the security would also attach to the rentals. The two were inextricably linked.

14.6.6.5.2 It may well be said that the Court of Appeal and Vinelott J failed to place sufficient weight on the importance of the rentals as representing much of the benefit of the sub-leases and as signifying the value of the company's rights in the sub-leases. In any event, the reasoning in these cases runs counter to the *Brumark* case and the *Spectrum Plus* case, where emphasis was placed on the third of Romer LJ's characteristics, rather than the first two of those characteristics, which were said to be inconclusive as tests. In addition, Millett LJ said in *Royal Trust Bank v National Westminster Bank PLC*,[220] when considering the position concerning rentals

---

219 [1903] 2 Ch 284.
220 [1996] BCC 613, at 619–620.

payable under such contracts, that such an arrangement would only constitute a floating charge. On this basis, it is submitted that the correct analysis is that there was only a floating charge over the rentals that were payable under the agreements and it might also be the case that the remaining benefit of those agreements was also only subject to a floating charge.

14.6.6.6 *Insurance policies*

The necessity of establishing control in the hands of the chargee will also apply to situations where it is desired to take fixed security over an insurance or assurance policy and any claim or proceeds of a claim made under the policy. This requirement was found to have been met in *Re CCG International Enterprises Ltd*,[221] where the charge required the chargor to take out and maintain the relevant policy and that the proceeds of any claim should, at the option of the chargee, be paid to the chargee or applied in re-instatement of the damaged property to which the claim related. The chargee was in control and could decide how it wished the proceeds of the claim to be applied. It would have been different if that option had rested in the chargor. It is not uncommon to find situations where the chargor is given such an option with respect to the proceeds of claims, either altogether or up to certain monetary levels. It is submitted that such situations would result in there being only a floating charge over the policy and claims under it, even in cases where the total claim exceeded the stipulated level, because the claim is one chose in action and indivisible. In line with the *Brumark* case and the *Spectrum Plus* case, the chargee must be in control of the policy and claims made and payable under it, if it wishes to take fixed security, including both its uncollected state and its proceeds of collection or recovery.[222]

14.6.6.7 *Shares in a company*

It might be tempting to treat the taking of security over share capital as simply involving the grant of a legal or equitable interest in the title in the relevant shares and, therefore, that all that is necessary to achieve a form of fixed security over the shares would be to prevent dealings in that title. It is submitted that such an approach would be erroneous, as it ignores the essential nature of the asset and what it represents, which must also be taken into account in determining if fixed or floating security has been taken over the shares.

---

[221] [1993] BCC 580.

[222] There must be a query, in this regard, as to the effect of s 83 of the Fires Prevention (Metropolis) Act 1774, which provides that the proceeds of any claim arising from a fire causing damage to a building shall be applied in re-instatement and repair of the building, if so requested by any person interested in the building. This must detract from the chargee's control as to the application of such proceeds.

14.6.6.7.1 Lord Hoffmann, in delivering the advice of the Privy Council in *Cambridge Gas Transport Corp v The Official Committee of Unsecured Creditors of Navigator Holdings PLC*,[223] described the legal nature of shares in a company. He said that the 'classic definition' had been provided by Farwell J in *Borland's Trustee v Steel Brothers*,[224] 'a share is the interest of the shareholder in the company measured by a sum of money, for the purpose of liability in the first place [i.e. the liability to pay calls of partly paid or nil-paid share capital], and of interest in the second'. In the case of fully paid shares, there is no question of liability, so the question comes down to the interest under the second limb. Lord Hoffmann then said:

> So a share is the measure of the shareholder's interest in the company: a bundle of rights against the company and the other shareholders. As against the outside world, that bundle of rights is an item of property, a chose in action. But as between the shareholder and the company itself, the shareholder's rights may be varied or extinguished by the mechanisms provided by the articles of association or the Companies Act.

14.6.6.7.2 In reality, the most important of the rights that are encompassed within a share are to receive dividends, either by way of the distribution of income or of capital, to vote as a shareholder, and to require that the affairs of the company are properly conducted in accordance with the memorandum and articles of association. As those matters represent the essence of the asset, it is submitted that effective fixed security cannot be taken without the control of those rights being surrendered to (or at least under the control of) the chargee. Simply preventing dealings with the title in the shares, without also taking account of those other aspects within the scope and coverage of the security, would not be sufficient to constitute fixed security over the shares. Accordingly, the security should provide that the rights attached to the shares, particularly to vote and to receive dividends, should be vested directly in the security holder and would be exercisable by it (which would follow if the security holder became registered as the legal holder of the shares) or, otherwise, that those rights were held by the chargee on trust for the benefit of the chargee, to be held and exercised in accordance with the chargee's instructions. It is respectfully submitted that the decision in *Arthur D Little Ltd v Abelco Finance LLC*[225] was incorrect in failing to give sufficient weight to those factors.

14.6.6.7.3 There is a practical problem, however, in meeting those requirements. It arises as follows. Where the effect of taking security over the shares in a company might be that the security holder holds or controls the majority of the voting rights and such like in the company, the security holder could find that the company will be

---

223 [2006] UKPC 26; [2007] 1 AC 508, at [26].
224 [1901] 1 Ch 279, at 288.
225 [2002] EWHC 701 (Ch), [2003] Ch 217.

treated as being its 'subsidiary'[226] or 'subsidiary undertaking'.[227] That risk can be overcome by providing that, prior to enforcement of the security or except to preserve its value, the relevant rights are held for, and are exercisable for the benefit of, the giver of the security.[228] Of course, if those matters are accommodated by the security then there must be a real risk that the security would only amount to a floating charge.

14.6.6.8 *Contractual rights*

Similarly, if security is to be taken over other types of intangible rights, such as contractual rights, the chargee should ensure that the chargor cannot deal with those rights and their constituent elements without the chargee's consent, and that the chargee will be fully entitled to receive and control the fruits or the proceeds of those rights and other entitlements relating to them.

14.6.6.9 *Intellectual property*

There may also be difficulties associated with taking fixed security over intellectual property, particularly if the chargor is permitted to continue in the exploitation of the rights concerned, such as by granting licences to third parties or, indeed, if the structure requires that an exclusive licence back should be granted to the giver of the security by the party taking the security.[229] An exclusive licence will usually be granted where the security has taken the form of an absolute or legal assignment by way of mortgage of the rights concerned, such a mortgage having the consequence that the legal title in the rights is vested in the mortgagee. That may have the effect of depriving the mortgagor of the right to assert the rights in infringement proceedings and to deal with them by granting licences, unless the mortgagee joins in the proceedings and in the granting of licences. To avoid such difficulties, the mortgagee may grant an exclusive licence to the mortgagor for the period of the security or, at least, until its enforcement.

From a security perspective, however, the granting of an exclusive licence may **14.6.6.9.1** have unfortunate consequences in terms of ascertaining whether only a floating charge has been granted. This is because an exclusive licence has the effect that the licensee is granted the exclusive right to exploit the licensed rights to the exclusion of the licensor during the period of the licence. Even where there is not a

---

[226] See s 1159 of the Companies Act 2006 (formerly s 736 of the Companies Act 1985).

[227] See s 1162 of the Companies Act 2006 (formerly s 258 of the Companies Act 1985).

[228] See para 7 of Sched 6, and para 8 of Sched 7, to the Companies Act 2006 (formerly s 736A(7) of, and para 8 of Sched 10A to, the Companies Act 1985).

[229] As is likely to be the case where the security takes the form of an assignment of the relevant intellectual property. An exclusive licence will usually be granted back to enable the assignor/mortgagor to continue using and exploiting the rights and to enable it to take proceedings in defence of the rights.

requirement for the grant of an exclusive licence, such as where the security is by way of equitable mortgage or charge, if the security giver is permitted to carry on with the exploitation of the relevant rights as if it were the owner of them then there is a real risk that the security may be characterised as only being by way of a floating charge.

14.6.6.10 Real property

Given its permanent and enduring nature, the ownership of real property (whether it be a freehold or a leasehold interest) is a prized form of ownership under English law and, accordingly, such an asset should be a suitable subject over which fixed security may be taken. However, commercial, farming, and other types of investment property is often leased out on leases of varying length and, indeed, a tenant under a lease is recognised as capable of having a legal estate in land which is separate and distinct from the estate in fee simple.[230] A sub-lease has the same consequences with respect to the head lease out of which it has been granted. Section 99 of the Law of Property Act 1925 expressly recognises and authorises the power of a mortgagor to grant leases (or sub-leases) for substantial periods, subject to any contrary provision in the mortgage instrument. With that in mind, it is not uncommon to find in a mortgage of an interest in land (strictly speaking, such an instrument is called a legal charge) where the interest is not held for investment purposes (investment purposes in this sense principally comprising the granting of leases) to find that the security document forbids the mortgagor from granting leases, no doubt because a lease of any substantial period would have a detrimental effect on the value of the reversionary interest.

14.6.6.10.1 A question must therefore arise as to the effect on a mortgagee's security where the mortgagor has the right to enter into leases or sub-leases or, indeed, licences, except where the tenant or licensee can be dispossessed of its occupation quickly and without difficulty. Whilst in theory the freehold or leasehold interest of the grantor of the lease or licence is separate from the interest that arises under the lease or the right of occupation under the licence, the practical or economic effect of a lease or licence upon the value of the grantor's reversion could be substantial. The difficulty arises most acutely where the interest that is to be mortgaged is held for investment purposes, because the whole reason why the mortgagor as owner holds its interest is to rent it out and derive an income from it. Indeed, a substantial part of the value of the interest may lie in its suitability to be used for that purpose.

14.6.6.10.2 It is submitted that the answer to the dilemma may be found in the point that has just been made, bearing in mind that the question must be examined by

---

230 See s 1 of the Law of Property Act 1925.

818

considering where the practical value and utility of the asset lies. The point of holding investment property is that the asset should be exploited by entering into leases. If, by so doing, the value of the holding is preserved or even enhanced, rather than diminished, then the legal estate of the mortgagor over which the security is taken should be recognised as a valuable asset in itself, which is not imperilled by the granting of leases. On the other hand, if the grant of a lease means that the value of the reversionary interest is undermined (for instance, because the grant is for such a long period that, as a result of the grant, there would be little value left in the reversion) then that should be a matter that needs to be controlled by the mortgagee so that it can be confident that it has a fixed security interest. The cautious approach, however, would be to prevent the mortgagor from having the right to grant leases or licences without the mortgagee's consent, with the mortgagor having to rely upon the mortgagee to take a common-sense approach in deciding if it will grant consent when an application is made to it for consent.

14.6.7 Crystallisation

The right of the chargor to deal with the charged assets under a floating charge continues until such time as the right to do so is taken away. At that point, the charge is said to 'crystallise', when it becomes a fixed charge with respect to the assets then or thereafter within its compass.[231] This is also called the process of 'crystallisation'. The consequence is that the chargor is no longer authorised to deal with the charged assets. If the security is comprehensive this has the practical effect that the chargor can no longer carry on its business.

14.6.7.1 The circumstances in which crystallisation may occur

In principle, a floating charge will crystallise in accordance with the terms of the agreement contained in the charge, which will be those implied by law in consequence of that agreement (unless inconsistent with the express terms of that agreement[232]), together with any additional grounds that may have been specifically agreed.[233]

The grounds that are implied by law are as follows. First, the winding up of the chargor, whether it is a compulsory winding up or a solvent or insolvent voluntary winding up.[234] It is the making of the winding-up order or the passing of the

14.6.7.1.1

---

[231] *NW Robbie & Co Ltd v Witney Warehouse Co Ltd* [1963] 1 WLR 1324; *Re The Real Meat Co Ltd* [1996] BCC 254.

[232] There must be an overt and real inconsistency. The implied grounds will not be treated as overridden simply because there are also express terms which do not also contain the grounds that would be implied: see *Re The Real Meat Co Ltd* [1996] BCC 254, at 261.

[233] *Re Brightlife Ltd* [1987] Ch 200.

[234] *Re Panama New Zealand and Australian Royal Mail Co* (1870) LR 5 Ch App 318; *Evans v Rival Granite Quarries Ltd* [1910] 2 KB 979; *Re Crompton & Co. Ltd* [1914] 1 Ch 954.

resolution to wind up which causes the charge to crystallise on this ground, not action preliminary thereto.[235] Secondly, the appointment by the chargor of a receiver and other action to enforce the security.[236] It should be noted that the appointment of a receiver by another creditor will not cause the charge to crystallise unless it also provides another of the grounds for the charge to crystallise.[237] Thirdly, the company permanently ceasing to carry on business, to the extent not already encompassed within the other two grounds.[238] A company will not necessarily cease its business simply because another creditor takes enforcement action, such as by appointing a receiver or because an administrator has been appointed. The receiver (if he has power to do so) or administrator may decide to continue the business.[239]

14.6.7.1.2　　It is now clear that a charge will also crystallise on any additional grounds that are specified in the charge, such as pursuant to events of default-type provisions.[240] The charge may require that the chargee should give notice to the chargor that the charge has crystallised following upon the occurrence of such an event, or it may provide, just as effectively, that the charge will crystallise automatically.[241]

14.6.7.1.3　　Obviously, an automatic crystallisation clause is not in the interests of the chargor, which should resist the inclusion of such a clause in the charging instrument. An automatic crystallisation clause does not advance the interests of the chargee as against creditors that enjoy a statutory right of priority against the chargee, because those rights apply even if the charge has crystallised. Nonetheless, it may be helpful in defeating the claim of an execution creditor,[242] and it may also prevent the chargor from disposing of charged assets to the detriment of the chargee. Care should be taken, however, in being over-zealous in the drafting of an automatic crystallisation clause. This is because of the risk that the charge might crystallise on obscure grounds without the chargee realising that it has done so. That could lead to arguments that the chargee has waived its right to rely on the clause or that it is estopped from doing so. It is best that the clause should be limited, so that it operates to provide protection in situations where the interests of

---

[235] *Re Victoria Steamboats Co* [1897] 1 Ch 158; *Stein v Saywell* (1969) 121 CLR 529.

[236] *Evans v Rival Granite Quarries Ltd* [1910] 2 KB 979.

[237] *Re Woodroffes (Musical Instruments) Ltd* [1986] Ch 366; *Re The Real Meat Co Ltd* [1996] BCC 254.

[238] *Re Woodroffes (Musical Instruments) Ltd* [1986] Ch 366; *Re The Real Meat Co Ltd* [1996] BCC 254.

[239] *Re Woodroffes (Musical Instruments) Ltd* [1986] Ch 366; *Re The Real Meat Co Ltd* [1996] BCC 254.

[240] *Re Brightlife Ltd* [1987] Ch 200.

[241] *Re Manurewa Transport Ltd* [1971] NZLR 909; *Re Brightlife Ltd* [1987] Ch 200.

[242] An example can be drawn from *Evans v Rival Granite Quarries Ltd* [1910] 2 KB 979, where the execution creditor prevailed against assets that were only subject to an uncrystallised floating charge.

the chargee in charged assets might be at risk of being jeopardised, such as in execution proceedings.

14.6.8 Priorities

It is relevant to consider how the interest of a chargee under a floating charge might fare vis-à-vis the interests of third parties, such as those that enter into transactions with the chargor concerning the charged assets. The discussion as to priorities will be divided into three parts. The first part will describe the position with respect to transactions with third parties that the chargor enters into prior to the crystallisation of a floating charge. The second part will discuss the position where such transactions occur after the charge has crystallised. The third part will address statutory priorities that arise in favour of certain prescribed classes of third parties.

It is always open to private parties to enter into a priority agreement, by which **14.6.8.1** they agree as to the ranking of their respective interests, which will override the outcome that would otherwise apply as a matter of general law.[243] If they do so, however, they must be mindful of the decision in *Re Portbase Clothing Ltd*,[244] to which reference will be made after the discussion concerning statutory priorities.

14.6.8.2 Transactions that take place before crystallisation

So long as such transactions fall within the inherent authority of the chargor under a floating charge to deal with the charged assets in the ordinary course of business, third parties which take under them will prevail as against the interest of the chargee. If such a third party is an outright purchaser then it will acquire ownership of the asset free of the charge. If it takes fixed security, or a limited second floating charge, its security will rank ahead of the interest of the chargee under the floating charge, including as to the consequences of enforcement of the third party's security. This will be the case even if the third party had notice of the existence of the floating charge, as such notice on its own does not serve to negative the inherent ability of the chargor to deal with the assets as if they were free of the charge.[245] In similar vein, an execution creditor which completes its execution against the charged assets before the charge crystallises will take free of the charge.[246] Similarly, rights of set-off for claims that have accrued before crystallisation will be enforceable notwithstanding the charge.[247]

---

[243] *Cheah Theam Swee v Equiticorp Finance Group Ltd* [1992] 1 AC 472.
[244] [1993] Ch 388.
[245] *English & Scottish Mercantile Investment Co v Brunton* [1892] 2 QB 700; *Re Castell & Brown Ltd* [1898] 1 Ch 315.
[246] *Evans v Rival Granite Quarries Ltd* [1910] 2 KB 979.
[247] *Biggerstaff v Rowatt's Wharf Ltd* [1896] 2 Ch 93; *Edward Nelson & Co Ltd v Faber & Co* [1903] 2 KB 367; *Rother Iron Works Ltd v Canterbury Precision Engineers Ltd* [1974] QB 1.

14.6.8.2.1 There is an important qualification to what has just been said, which concerns the effect of a negative pledge provision in the floating charge.[248] Under such a provision, the chargor will undertake in favour of the chargee that the chargor will not enter into certain types of transaction with third parties concerning the charged assets without the prior consent of the chargee. Such transactions are likely to include the granting of security to third parties and other types of transaction, such as receivables sales, that are primarily in the nature of raising finance or which have the effect of reducing the overall value of the charged property. Clearly, such a restriction will have contractual effect as between the chargor and the chargee, but it will not serve to turn the charge into a fixed charge.[249] The important question is the effect that it might have on the validity and enforceability of the interest purportedly acquired by the third party that is concerned in an impugned transaction.

14.6.8.2.2 In answering that question, it must be remembered that the assumption which is inherently associated with a floating charge is that the chargor has the right to deal with the charged assets as if it were the outright owner of them, so long as the transaction is of a type that would fall within the very general concept of the ordinary course of business as it has been interpreted by the case law. A third party which deals with the chargor is generally entitled to rely on that assumption. To upset the transaction, the chargee must displace the assumption, which will not be an easy burden. The answer lies in considering the basis upon which a third party can be made responsible for participating in a transaction which amounts to a breach of the contract between the chargor and the chargee; in other words, whether the third party was guilty of the tort of inducing or procuring a breach of the contract. If the third party has taken its interest without notice of the restriction then it cannot be so liable.[250] It will not be affected by the restriction and will take its interest free of the effect of the restriction.[251] Even if it had notice of the restriction, the third party will only be affected by it if the third party intended to cause the chargor to breach the restriction.[252] Thus, if the third party believed that the chargor had the chargee's consent to enter into the transaction, or if it acted on an erroneous view of the legal position, it will have a defence and should be able

---

[248] Negative pledges are referred to earlier in this chapter. For a more detailed discussion concerning negative pledges, see Chap 3.

[249] See *Re Brightlife Ltd* [1987] Ch 200.

[250] For the reasons advanced in Chap 3 actual notice of the restriction is required. Furthermore, notice (including constructive notice) of the existence of a security does not give notice of its contents: *Wilson v Kelland* [1910] 2 Ch 306; *Siebe Gorman & Co Ltd v Barclays Bank Ltd* [1979] 2 Lloyd's Rep 142. The foregoing may need to be qualified if details of a negative pledge associated with a floating charge become a registrable matter under s 860 of the Companies Act 2006. This has been foreshadowed by a draft statutory instrument which was circulated by the Department for Business, Enterprise and Regulatory Reform at the end of 2007.

[251] *English & Scottish Mercantile Investment Co v Brunton* [1892] 2 QB 700.

[252] *OBG Ltd v Allan; Douglas v Hello! Ltd; Mainstream Properties Ltd v Young* [2007] UKHL 21.

to take free of the restriction.[253] However, if the third party knew of the restriction and can raise no such defence, the chargee should be able to obtain an injunction (subject to the usual discretionary defences) to restrain the third party from asserting or relying upon the benefit of the transaction that it has entered into with the chargor.[254] If the charge has not crystallised when the injunction is sought, the chargee would be seeking to protect its contract and to restrain the third party from relying upon its tortious action in procuring the chargor to breach its contractual obligations to the chargee. If the charge has crystallised, the chargee would also be seeking to protect its entitlement and assert priority under its fixed charge.

If a transaction takes place which is outside the ordinary course of business then it will be a question of competing priorities, as between the interest of the chargee and that of the third party taking under the transaction. If the party to the transaction had notice (including constructive notice) of the existence of the floating charge then it is submitted that the interest of such a party would defer to that of the chargee, because that party should be aware that the chargor had no authority to enter into the transaction and, accordingly, that the transaction amounted to a breach of the contractual authority of the chargor. That would certainly be the position if the transaction followed upon a decision to cease business, thereby causing the floating charge to crystallise.[255]   **14.6.8.2.3**

At this point, it is necessary to mention the decision of Morritt J in *Griffiths v Yorkshire Bank PLC*.[256] It was held in that case that where a second general floating charge crystallised before an earlier floating charge, the interest of the holder of the crystallised charge would have priority over the interest of the holder of the earlier charge, which crystallised later. This was because the second charge had become a fixed charge before the first charge had done so, and thus was to be treated as if it were the first in time. It is submitted, with respect, that this conclusion was incorrect. This is because the granting of the second general floating charge fell outside the ordinary course of business and so the chargor did not have authority to grant the second general floating charge;[257] nor had the holder of the first charge consented to the granting of the second charge. On that basis, the rights and interest of the holder of the second charge should have been subject to those of the holder of the first charge and the crystallisation of the second charge should not have affected the outcome.   **14.6.8.2.4**

---

[253] *OBG Ltd v Allan; Douglas v Hello! Ltd; Mainstream Properties Ltd v Young* [2007] UKHL 21; *Meretz Investments NV v ACP Ltd* [2007] EWCA Civ 1303.

[254] *Swiss Bank Corp v Lloyds Bank Ltd* [1979] Ch 548.

[255] *Re The Real Meat Co Ltd* [1996] BCC 254. In that case, not only was the purchaser under the transaction affected by knowing that the charge had crystallised but so also was the bank which lent the money to fund the purchaser and took security over the purchased assets for its loan. The consequence was that the holder of the crystallised charge took priority over both the purchaser and the bank.

[256] [1994] 1 WLR 1427.

[257] *Re Benjamin Cope & Sons Ltd* [1914] 1 Ch 800.

14.6.8.3 Transactions that take place after crystallisation

Upon crystallisation of the charge, the liberty of the chargor to deal with the assets is withdrawn. As between the chargor and the chargee, the chargor no longer has authority to enter into any transactions on its own account with third parties concerning the charged assets. The interest of the chargee becomes that of the holder of a fixed equitable charge over any assets that then or thereafter come within the compass of the charge. The position as between the chargee and any third party that purportedly acquires an interest in the charged assets thereafter becomes a matter of priorities between competing interests. The general priority rules (which are referred to later in this chapter) should apply, with the following modifications.

14.6.8.3.1 Where the third party had acquired an interest in a charged asset prior to crystallisation that prevailed against the charge at that time, the interest will continue to prevail notwithstanding that the charge has crystallised. Accordingly, if that interest could have been enforced by an order for specific performance, the fact that the charge has crystallised (for instance, by the appointment of a receiver) should not affect that interest.[258] The position regarding an option to purchase charged assets that had been granted by the chargor to a third party prior to the crystallisation of the charge but had not been exercised prior to the crystallisation was addressed in an Irish case, in which it was held that the optionee had only a contractual right and had not acquired a proprietary right that would prevail as against the crystallised charge.[259]

14.6.8.3.2 Where the third party acquired an interest which would be subject to the charge if the third party had notice of the charge when it acquired its interest, it is submitted that the third party will not be defeated by knowledge of the charge if it was only aware (including due to having constructive notice, for instance, by registration of the charge) that the charge was a floating charge and did not know that it had crystallised. This would be because the knowledge it possessed was that the chargor had authority to deal with the assets and that entitled it to assume that it could safely deal with the chargor. This would be relevant, for instance, in the application of the rule in *Dearle v Hall*,[260] under which a claim by a subsequent purchaser or incumbrancer may be denied the benefit of the rule, and so unable to assert priority over a prior interest, if the subsequent party had notice of the prior interest at the time that it gave value for its interest. It is submitted that the third party would not be defeated on that ground if it only knew that the charge was a floating charge and did not know that it had crystallised.

---

[258] *Freevale Ltd v Metrostore (Holdings) Ltd* [1984] Ch 199.
[259] *Re Tullow Engineering (Holdings) Ltd* [1990] 1 IR 452.
[260] *Dearle v Hall, Loveridge v Cooper* (1828) 3 Russ 1.

The position with respect to set-offs that a third party may wish to assert against the chargor (and, thus, the chargee) depends upon the nature of the set-off and whether the claim of the chargor against the third party falls within the assets subject to the charge. In this discussion, it will be assumed that the latter does fall within the charged assets. The position is as follows. The right of the third party to plead the set-off of a liquidated cross-claim as a legal set-off will cease with respect to cross-claims that arise after the third party has received notice that the charge has crystallised.[261] Rights of equitable or transaction set-off that arise in consequence of a transaction that existed between the chargor and the third party prior to crystallisation of the charge will continue to be available to the parties.[262]

14.6.8.4 *Statutory priorities*

There are a number of statutory provisions which confer priority on various persons with respect to floating charge assets and their proceeds of realisation, ahead of the interests of the chargee (irrespective of whether the charge has crystallised[263]). In summary, they are as follows:

(1) in a liquidation of the chargor, the expenses of the winding up will enjoy priority, in so far as the assets available to the general body of creditors are insufficient to meet such expenses;[264]

(2) preferential creditors of the chargor have a claim on such assets either ahead of the rights of the chargee or to the extent that the assets available to general creditors are insufficient to meet the claims of the preferential creditors;[265] and

(3) a prescribed part of such assets have to be set aside to meet the claims of unsecured creditors of the chargor.[266]

---

[261] *Business Computers Ltd v Anglo-African Leasing Ltd* [1977] 1 WLR 578.

[262] Ibid.

[263] This is because the provisions refer to 'a charge which, as created, was a floating charge'. See, for instance, the definition of 'floating charge' in s 251 of the Insolvency Act 1986.

[264] S 176ZA of the Insolvency Act 1986, which came into force on 6 April 2008. As to the expenses that qualify for such priority, see Rules 4.218 and 4.218A–4.218E of the Insolvency Rules 1986. These provisions have the effect of overcoming the consequences of the decision in *Buchler v Talbot* [2004] UKHL 9, [2004] 2 AC 298, which itself had reversed the decision of the Court of Appeal in *Re Barleycorn Enterprises Ltd* [1970] Ch 465.

[265] See s 754 of the Companies Act 2006 (formerly s 196 of the Companies Act 1985) and ss 40 and 175(2)(b) of the Insolvency Act 1986. The list of preferential debts is set out in Sched 6 to the Insolvency Act 1986. As to s 754 of the 2006 Act and s 40 of the 1986 Act, see *Griffiths v Yorkshire Bank PLC* [1994] 1 WLR 1427 and, taking a contrary view, *Re H&K Medway Ltd* [1997] 1 WLR 1422.

[266] See s 176A of the Insolvency Act 1986. The Insolvency Act 1986 (Prescribed Part) Order 2003 (SI 2003/2097) sets out the way in which the prescribed part is to be calculated. The High Court has held that s 176A applies only for the benefit of creditors who hold no security at all, so that a secured creditor cannot participate as an unsecured creditor with respect to that part of its claim that is not effectively covered by its security: see *Re Permacell Finesse Ltd* (ChD, Birmingham, 30/11/2007, unreported) and *Re Airbase Services (UK) Ltd* [2008] EWHC 124 (Ch).

These provisions only affect the entitlement of the floating charge holder. Subject to what is said next concerning the decision in *Re Portbase Clothing Ltd*,[267] they do not affect the right of a holder of fixed security in the charged assets.[268]

14.6.8.4.1 The position becomes more complicated where either a fixed security is expressed to rank behind a floating charge or if there is a priority agreement between the holder of the fixed security and the holder of the floating charge to that effect. Chadwick J in *Re Portbase Clothing Ltd*[269] held that, in either case, this would affect the rights of the two securities in a proprietary sense, so that the statutory priority of the preferential creditors over the floating charge would also prevail over the security held under the fixed charge. This was because the fixed charge was subordinate to the floating charge which was itself subordinate to the claims of the preferential creditors.[270] The same consequence should follow with respect to the priority entitlements that are statutorily conferred by sections 176ZA and 176A of the Insolvency Act 1986.

14.6.8.4.2 His Lordship did suggest that it might be possible to avoid this consequence if the agreement did not purport to govern the priorities of the two securities but, instead, provided that the fixed chargee would hold any recoveries it received on enforcement of its security on trust for the benefit of the other chargee. There is a risk, however, that the agreement to hold its recoveries on trust might imply an agreement by the fixed chargee as to the underlying security. It is suggested that a safer course would be that the fixed chargee, rather than agreeing to hold its recoveries on trust, should simply agree to pay to the other chargee an amount equivalent to whatever it received under its security. Of course, the other chargee would be taking a risk that the fixed chargee might default in the observance of its obligation, particularly should it have become insolvent in the meantime.

14.7 Taking Security Over Shares and Other Financial Securities

14.7.1 The types of financial securities over which security may be taken are numerous and may encompass shares in public companies, including listed and unlisted companies, and shares in private companies, as well as bonds and other debt instruments, government securities, and units in collective investment funds and other types of funds. Sometimes such securities may be held directly by the person that is to give

---

[267] [1993] Ch 388.

[268] *Re Lewis Merthyr Consolidated Collieries Ltd, Lloyds Bank Ltd v The Company* [1929] 1 Ch 498.

[269] [1993] Ch 388. In reaching his conclusion, Chadwick J followed and applied the decision of Nicholson J in the Victorian (Australia) case of *Waters v Widdows* [1984] VR 503.

[270] Morritt J in *Griffiths v Yorkshire Bank PLC* [1994] 1 WLR 1427 disagreed with the approach taken in the *Portbase* case, and said that an agreement as to priorities would not have the proprietary effect contemplated by Chadwick J in the *Portbase* case.

the security and sometimes they may be held on its behalf by an intermediary, in which case it is likely that the entitlement will be held as part of a pool of like securities or entitlements that is held by the intermediary for a number of people. There may or may not be a physical instrument representing the relevant securities. Where there is no instrument at all, the securities are said to be 'dematerialised', in the sense that the entitlements in the securities are represented by entries recorded in electronic registers. Even if there is an instrument, it may be isolated and removed from circulation so that dealings in it and the recording of entitlements in it may take place again through electronic means, in which case it is said that the instrument is 'immobilised'.

If security is to be taken, particularly over shares in a company, it is necessary to check that there are no provisions in the memorandum and articles of association of the issuer (or its other constitutive documents) or in any other relevant agreement (such as a shareholders' agreement) which would restrict the right of the security giver to create the security or which might restrict the enforcement of the security. Care needs to be taken to check both of those points because a permission to create security over securities may not necessarily imply a right for the securities to be sold upon enforcement of the security. It is also possible that a condition might be imposed as part of any relevant permission, which might have the effect that a purchaser of the securities would be required to accept restrictions concerning the securities, including as to its right to transfer them. **14.7.1.1**

There may also be competition law aspects that should be considered, both in terms of taking the security and in the disposal of the shares upon exercise of the security. If the company operates in the regulated sector, there could also be regulatory matters that would be relevant. **14.7.1.2**

There is a further point which concerns listed securities. The City Code on Takeovers and Mergers contains requirements as to building stakes or interests in the share capital of listed companies. Under Rule 9 of the Code, if a person acquires 30 per cent or more of the voting capital, or in any class of its share capital, it is required to make a mandatory bid for the company, unless a waiver has been granted by the UK Panel on Takeovers and Mergers. This requirement might be relevant both in terms of taking security and with respect to its enforcement. **14.7.1.3**

14.7.2 Equitable interests in shares

Section 126 of the Companies Act 2006[271] provides that:

> No interest of any trust, expressed, implied or constructive, shall be entered on the register of members of a company registered in England and Wales or Northern Ireland, or be receivable by the registrar.

---

[271] Formerly s 360 of the Companies Act 1985.

This is often extended by the articles of association to any other type of equitable interest that might arise in the company's shares. The statutory provision, and probably its extension via the articles, has obvious consequences in terms of priorities, because it means that it is not possible to protect beneficial interests by serving notice of them on the company or its registrar. In terms of priorities, the safest course is for the security holder to perfect a legal mortgage and be registered as the holder of the shares.[272]

14.7.3 Certificated securities and physical instruments

If the financial security is directly held by the obligor that is to give security over its entitlement and that entitlement is represented by a certificated security or physical instrument, then it will be necessary to determine if title passes by physical delivery of the certificate or instrument or if title passes by entries made in a register.

14.7.3.1 If the instrument is in bearer form, then it is likely that the instrument is negotiable and, accordingly, that title will pass by delivery of the instrument. Similarly, if title in the instrument passes by endorsement together with delivery then it is likely to be a negotiable instrument.[273] Such a document is sometimes called a documentary intangible. Title is represented by the instrument, including title in the payment and other rights encapsulated by the instrument. Examples of such instruments include bills of lading, bills of exchange, promissory notes, certificates of deposit, and bearer bonds. In such a case, security may be taken in a possessory form, by pledge or lien, where the creditor obtains possession of the instrument (endorsed in blank, if necessary). Alternatively, security may be taken in a non-possessory form, but that is much more risky, as the obligor has been left armed with the instrument and can confer a superior title on an innocent third party who obtains the instrument without notice. A middle ground, which has no particular advantage over the use of possessory security, is to take security by way of mortgage or charge but also to take possession of the instrument by way of perfection of the security.

14.7.3.2 If the transfer of the entitlement represented by the instrument requires registration in a register that is kept by or on behalf of the issuer, the instrument would not be negotiable. A typical example would be the shares in an English private company. In such a case, it is not possible to have an effective pledge or lien over

---

[272] See *Société Générale de Paris v Walker* (1885) 11 App Cas 20. Where there has been underhand dealings, it might be possible to obtain a 'stop notice' issued by the court and then served on the company, the effect of which is to prevent the company from registering a transfer for a limited period pending an application to the court for an injunction, but this is of limited effect: *Re Holmes* (1885) 29 ChD 786.

[273] As to negotiable instruments, see the discussion in Chap 10.

the instrument and the entitlements that it represents.[274] Worthwhile security can only be taken in the form of a mortgage or charge. A legal mortgage requires that the mortgagee is registered as the holder of the relevant entitlement. An equitable mortgage requires an agreement that the entitlement should be transferred, together with the means to obtain the transfer, such as an executed form of share transfer and the relevant share certificate. Technically, a charge does not require the executed share transfer, but it is sensible to obtain it for ease of perfecting and enforcing the security, should that be necessary.

14.7.4 Uncertificated securities

Such securities are most likely to be issued by listed companies, sovereign or governmental issuers, supra-national bodies, and similar institutions. Typical examples would include debt securities held through the Euroclear or Clearstream systems in Brussels and Luxembourg and securities held through the CREST system in the UK. The discussion that follows will concentrate on the CREST system.

14.7.4.1 The CREST system

The Uncertificated Securities Regulations 2001[275] provide the legislative basis for the establishment and operation of the CREST system, under which rules and conditions have been formulated for the operation of the system. The operator of the system is CRESTCo. In summary of a rather complex system, the operator maintains a computerised system in which are recorded entitlements in dematerialised securities issued by eligible issuers, which are mostly UK incorporated issuers, but also include foreign issuers (the discussion will assume that the securities have been issued by a UK issuer). The system maintains accounts to record entitlements of its participating members in the relevant securities. Such members may be direct users, who have direct computerised access to the system, or sponsored members who connect to the system via a direct user. Whichever type of member it may be, the system will record entitlements credited to its account. Members may hold a recorded entitlement for themselves or on behalf of one or more third parties, in which case the member would be acting as an intermediary on behalf of the third parties.

A member's account in the system will distinguish between each issue of securities that are held in the member's account. For each such issue, the account will also distinguish between securities that the member holds for itself and those that it holds for other persons, where it is acting as an intermediary. It is also possible for the account to designate securities that are held under escrow, where a transaction

14.7.4.1.1

---

[274] The effect of attempting to obtain such security is merely to create a pledge or lien over the piece of paper, but not the rights to which it refers.

[275] SI 2001/3755 (as amended). The regulations were made under s 207 of the Companies Act 1989 and continue pursuant to ss 783–788 of the Companies Act 2006.

cannot take place without the authority of the designated 'escrow agent', being another member of the system.

14.7.4.1.2 The eligible securities of an issuer may be held in dematerialised form through the CREST system or in certificated form outside the system. The recorded holder of a security has the right to require that a security be removed from the system and re-issued in certificated form, or that the opposite should occur, by surrendering the certificated form of the security (together with a form of transfer) so that it is credited in dematerialised form to a member's account in the system. Whichever form is used, the relationship between the issuer (if it is a UK issuer) and the registered holder remains the same and, in that sense, the CREST system does not act as an intermediary (unlike the position with Euroclear and Clearstream).[276] It is simply acting as a system for recording the legal position as between the issuer and the account holder. Legal ownership of the securities rests in whoever is recorded as owner, either through the system or in physical records kept by the issuer or its registrar. Where a security is held through the system, a back-up record will be kept by the issuer or its registrar (which will be notified by the system of any transfers), but it is the entitlement as recorded in the system which is decisive of legal ownership.

14.7.4.1.3 A legal mortgage of uncertificated securities in the CREST system can be accomplished by a transfer to the account of the mortgagee, if it has an account in the system. Any other form of transfer within the system will only achieve a form of equitable security and no notice of any trust can be entered on the system. Where the security giver is a member of the system, it can transfer the charged securities to its escrow account, by way of charge. Alternatively, where the chargor is not a member of the system, it could instruct its intermediary to transfer the securities to the intermediary's escrow account. The consequence of this is that the securities cannot be transferred from the escrow account without an instruction from the designated escrow agent, which would be the chargee (if it is a member of the system) or (if the chargee is not a member of the system) a member acting as its agent.

14.7.4.1.4 The alternative procedure to taking security over uncertificated securities in the CREST system, particularly shares, is for the securities to be taken out of the system so that they are converted into certificated securities and then made subject to the more traditional methods for establishing security as described earlier.

14.7.5 The Financial Collateral Arrangements (No 2) Regulations 2003[277]

These Regulations purport to implement in the UK the EC Directive on financial collateral arrangements.[278] The Regulations apply where each of the parties to a

---

[276] The position is different for securities issued by non-UK issuers.

[277] SI 2003/3226. In force 26/12/2006.

[278] Directive 2002/47/EC OJ L168/43 27/6/2002. At the time of writing, discussions were taking place within the EC as to the possibility of amending the Directive.

financial collateral arrangement is a 'non-natural person' (i.e. not an individual).[279] The Regulations have the effect of modifying certain formalities and requirements of the law in the UK with respect to such an arrangement, extending the rights of a recipient under such an arrangement by way of security to the use and appropriation of financial collateral, and providing a conflict of laws rule where financial collateral is held through an intermediary. The latter aspect is discussed in Chapter 10.

14.7.5.1 Definitions

The definitions that are used in the Regulations will be found in Regulation 3. Those that are of particular relevance in the context of secured transactions are summarised as follows.

'Financial collateral' is either 'cash' or 'financial instruments'. 'Cash' is basically **14.7.5.1.1** the credit balance, in any currency, on an account or a similar claim for repayment. 'Financial instruments' is widely defined to include shares in companies,[280] bonds and similar debt instruments tradeable on the capital market, and other types of securities and financial instruments and claims and rights derived therefrom.

A 'financial collateral arrangement' is either a 'title transfer financial collateral **14.7.5.1.2** arrangement' (where there is an outright transfer of title in the relevant financial collateral, with an obligation to re-transfer equivalent collateral at a later time) or a 'security financial collateral arrangement'. The latter is a secured transaction over financial collateral by way of pledge, lien, mortgage (whether legal or equitable), fixed charge, or a certain type of floating charge. That type of floating charge must be one where the collateral is under the possession or control of the chargee but where the chargor has a right to substitute assets within the charged financial collateral and to withdraw financial collateral whose value is in excess of the secured obligations.

A 'close-out netting provision' is a provision for netting or set-off that is contained **14.7.5.1.3** in a financial collateral arrangement or an arrangement of which a financial collateral arrangement forms a part or any similar legislative provision, under

---

279 In this respect, it is arguable that the Regulations go further than merely implementing the Directive, because the Directive requires that at least one of the parties should be a specially designated type of entity (basically (a) a public authority; (b) a central bank, multilateral development bank, the IMF, BIS, or EIB; (c) a financial institution subject to financial supervision; or (d) a central counterparty, settlement agent or clearing house): see Art 1(2). As the Regulations were made pursuant to s 2(2) of the European Communities Act 1972, it is questionable if they were validly made, at least in so far as they go further than the Directive requires or permits.

280 Once again, the Regulations depart from the text of the Directive. The Regulations encompass all types of shares in companies, including private and unlisted companies. However, it appears from the definition of 'financial instruments' in Art 2(1) of the Directive that shares in a company should be tradeable on the capital market, which would exclude shares in a private or unlisted company.

which upon the occurrence of an 'enforcement event' (which is widely defined) either (a) the obligations of the parties are accelerated or terminated with a balance sum due which represents the estimated current value or replacement cost, or (b) an account is taken of the parties' obligations and a balance sum is due one way or the other.

14.7.5.1.4 'Equivalent financial collateral' means, for cash, the same amount in the same currency, and, for financial instruments, means (unless otherwise specified in the arrangement) instruments of the same issuer, amount, currency, class and description.

14.7.5.2 Modifications to formal and registration requirements under English law

The Regulations make the following modifications to the requirements of English law relating to formalities and registration, in so far as financial collateral arrangements are concerned:

(1) With respect to guarantees, the requirement as to writing and the necessity for a signature under section 4 of the Statute of Frauds 1677 shall not apply (Regulation 4(1)).

(2) With respect to dealings in equitable interests, the requirement as to writing and the necessity for a signature under section 53(1)(c) of the Law of Property Act 1925 shall not apply (Regulation 4(2)).

(3) With respect to an absolute assignment of a chose in action, the requirement that the assignment should be signed by the assignor or his agent under section 136 of the Law of Property Act 1925 shall not apply (Regulation 4(3)).

(4) The obligation to register security under section 860 of the Companies Act 2006[281] shall not apply (Regulation 4(3)).

(5) The obligation to file information relating to charges under section 4 of the Industrial and Provident Societies Act 1967 shall not apply.

14.7.5.3 Modifications to English insolvency law

The Regulations make the following modifications to the provisions of English insolvency law under the Insolvency Act 1986 (the 'Act'), in so far as financial collateral arrangements are concerned:

(1) The restrictions on enforcement of security in an administration and to the appointment of a receiver[282] do not apply, nor may the administrator deal with the charged property[283] (Regulations 8 (1) and (2)).

---

[281] Formerly s 395 of the Companies Act 1985.
[282] Under, respectively, paras 43(2), 44, 41(2) to the 1986 Act.
[283] Under paras 70 and 71 of Sched B1 to the 1986 Act.

(2) The provisions concerning the effect of a moratorium for an eligible company that is the subject of a proposal for a voluntary arrangement, as they relate to disposals of charged property and enforcement of security,[284] shall not apply (Regulation 8(5)).

(3) Section 127 of the 1986 Act shall not apply to avoid any disposition under such an arrangement or to prevent a close-out netting provision from taking effect (Regulation 10(1)).

(4) Section 88 of the 1986 Act shall not apply to any transfer of shares under such an arrangement (Regulation 10(2)).

(5) Section 176A of the 1986 Act shall not apply with respect to any floating charge within a security financial collateral arrangement (Regulation 10(3)).

(6) Section 178 of the 1986 Act shall not apply with respect to any such arrangement (Regulation 10(4)).

(7) Section 245 of the 1986 Act shall not apply to any floating charge within a security financial collateral arrangement (Regulation 10(5)).

(8) Section 754 of the Companies Act 2006[285] shall not apply to any floating charge within a security financial collateral arrangement (Regulation 10(6)).

(9) A close-out netting provision is to take effect notwithstanding the winding up, administration, or voluntary arrangement of a party, provided that the party asserting the provision lacked notice or awareness that the proceedings had been commenced or were pending when it entered into the financial collateral arrangement or when the relevant secured obligations arose (Regulation 12).

(10) A party entering into a financial collateral arrangement or taking possession or control of such collateral will not be affected, as against third parties, by the making of a winding-up order against, or the appointment of an administrator of, a party to the arrangement on the day such events took place, if the first mentioned party was not aware (or should not have been aware) of them (Regulation 13).

14.7.5.4 *The right to use and appropriate financial collateral*

Part 4 of the Regulations makes provision for the holder of security under a security financial collateral arrangement to use and dispose of the collateral before enforcement of the security and to enforce its security by way of appropriation of the collateral, if the terms of the arrangement permit it to do so (and subject to those terms).

Under Regulation 16, the right of use and disposal prior to enforcement is exercisable by the security holder as if it were the outright owner of the collateral,

14.7.5.4.1

---

[284] Under, respectively, paras 20 and 12(1)(g) of Sched A1 to the Insolvency Act 1986.
[285] Formerly s 196 of the Companies Act 1985.

but there is an obligation to replace what has been used and disposed of prior to the due date for performance of the secured obligations, by transferring back to the other party equivalent financial collateral to that which was used, or (if permitted by the terms of the arrangement) by setting-off the value of what has been used against the secured obligations. In one sense, the provider of the collateral is taking a risk by permitting the security holder to use and dispose of the collateral, as the obligation to restore equivalent collateral is merely a personal obligation of the security holder. The risk can be minimised if it is also provided that a failure by the security holder to do so will result in an automatic set-off of the value of the collateral against the secured obligations. The risk is not entirely removed, however, as the collateral provider will suffer to the extent that the value of the collateral exceeds the amount of the secured obligation.

14.7.5.4.2 Under Regulation 17, if the security is by way of a legal or equitable mortgage (and, thus, not merely by way of charge), the security holder may exercise a power of appropriation of the collateral, without having to obtain an order for foreclosure from the court.[286] This provision may be used to provide a solid legal basis for appropriation in the case where security has been taken over 'cash', as discussed below. Under Regulation 18, a security holder which exercises such a power must value the collateral in accordance with the provisions of the security and, in any event, in a commercially reasonable manner. It must account to the mortgagor for any balance, being the amount by which the value exceeds the secured obligations. The mortgagor remains liable for any difference if the balance is in the other direction.

14.8 Taking Security over Intellectual Property

14.8.1 When considering assets that might fall within the compass of security, a creditor will usually think of tangible assets (land or goods) and intangible assets in the nature of choses in action (debts or receivables). It might also be relevant for the creditor to consider the obligor's intellectual property (IP). Pure IP differs from other types of intangible rights because, whilst being intangible property, it is largely constituted by a monopoly in its use and exploitation. Although the rights in IP may be asserted against third parties, their essence is in protecting that

---

[286] A question has arisen as to what is required to constitute an 'appropriation' of the collateral for the purposes of Art 17. In *Alfa Telecom Turkey Ltd v Cukurova Finance International Ltd*, which was a case in the British Virgin Islands that was decided in 2007 (in which expert evidence was given by Sir Ross Cranston, who was then a Professor of Law and a QC and is now a High Court judge, and Lord Millett, a retired Law Lord), it was said that the concept of appropriation under Art 17 required that the legal title in the collateral should be vested in the security taker. It is understood that an appellate court has since reversed the decision and that a further appeal may be pending to the Privy Council.

monopoly and exploiting the rights associated therewith, rather than simply being founded upon a chose in action. The IP rights concerned relate to trade marks, patents, registered designs, copyright, unregistered design rights, and database rights.

At the same time, it may also be relevant to think of other rights and assets (which could be tangible or intangible) which are associated with or similar to IP rights or which may have been derived by the application or exploitation of IP rights. Accordingly, it may be advisable to deal with physical assets which represent the physical embodiment or use of the relevant right and rights derived from the exploitation or use of IP rights. An important point to note from this is that in attempting to deal with one aspect, it may be necessary to deal separately with a related aspect and not to confuse the two. By way of two examples, a contrast can be made between the bare IP right and a licence that is granted or received to use that right. A contrast may also be made between the IP right and a physical asset made from using it or to which the IP right is applied. **14.8.1.1**

A distinction which also needs to be made is between pure IP rights and rights that have similar characteristics but which may not be susceptible to the usual forms of dealing with property rights. This will be relevant to rights associated with confidential information, business reputation (including a right to sue for passing off), and know-how. There is a right to protect them, such as by preserving them from disclosure or from wrongful interference, but it is not a transferable right. It may not be possible to take security over such rights except in the sense of including them within a general charge over the undertaking and goodwill of the business of the chargor or by taking security over the benefit of claims for damages where such rights have been infringed. **14.8.1.2**

Some businesses are almost entirely dependent upon their IP, such as those which rely upon brand names, copyright, or patents. The value of IP lies in the ability of the holder to exploit its monopoly right (either by its own use or by licensing others to do so), although the accounting profession has wrestled with how such value should be defined and recorded (if at all) for accounting purposes. The value of IP and associated rights may, however, be more apparent than real. Even if a business considers itself to be the owner of the IP, it may lose its monopoly right as, for instance, by a failure to exploit the right, by a failure to keep its registration of the right up to date, by expiry of a statutory right, or due to a challenge to the essential validity of the right.[287] There may also be an issue as to the true ownership of the IP rights. For instance, if the rights were created under contract by a contractor rather than by an employee acting within the course of his employment, the rights **14.8.1.3**

---

[287] For instance, that a patent may be challenged on the basis that, when granted, it was not novel or that it did not involve an inventive step.

may have vested in the contractor rather than the person who engaged the contractor.[288] In such a case, it will be necessary to ensure that the contract provides adequately with respect to the rights. These issues as to ownership and value and as to the strength of IP and associated rights will also be relevant to a creditor in assessing the strength of the borrower's business and the reliance to be placed upon its IP and associated rights as security.

14.8.1.4 From a different perspective, it may also be necessary for a creditor to consider the strength of its borrower when the borrower is dependent upon the ability to use an IP right which is licensed to it by a third party. If the licence is taken away then the borrower's business may collapse. In addition, the licence will have to be examined to determine if it permits the borrower to grant security over its rights under the licence and, if it does, if there are any restrictions upon transferring the benefit of the licence if the security is enforced. In similar vein, it will be necessary to determine if the licence might be revoked upon a change in ownership or control of the borrower.

14.8.1.5 In seeking to take security over IP rights, the creditor will consider the usual forms of security (i.e. legal mortgage, equitable mortgage, fixed charge, and floating charge) but some situations will call for one type of security rather than another. Traditionally, many creditors have been content that IP rights should be swept-up in the generality of a floating charge. This may occasionally be the correct approach where the IP has little real value. For more valuable IP rights, it would be appropriate for the creditor to seek specific, fixed security, even by way of legal mortgage,[289] but the difficulties in doing this, in terms of vesting control in the creditor (as discussed earlier in this chapter), must be borne in mind. A legal mortgage would involve a full assignment to the creditor of all of the relevant rights, subject to a right of redemption. A full assignment may also expose the creditor to certain risks and involve it in the on-going matters needed to maintain and exploit the IP right (e.g. in granting licences, suing infringers, and maintaining registrations). Accordingly, the creditor may find that it has to grant an exclusive licence back to the borrower to enable the borrower to act of its own volition but, as noted earlier, this may imperil the nature of the mortgage as fixed security.

14.8.2 Taking security over statutory IP rights in the UK

Some IP rights exist by virtue of registration of the owner of the right. Other IP rights, whilst existing under statute, do not have a registration system. For the sake of simplicity, the following refers to domestic UK law, without reference to the

---

[288] See, for instance, s 11(2) of the Copyright, Designs and Patents Act 1988 and contrast that with Regs 14 and 15 of the Copyright and Rights in Databases Regs 1997 (SI 1997/3032).

[289] Particularly in relation to copyright and unregistered design rights, for the purposes of preserving priority.

expanded position under EC law. IP rights that exist in the UK by virtue of registration are trade marks (under the Trade Marks Act 1994, the 'TMA'), patents (under the Patents Act 1977, the 'PA'), and registered designs (under the Registered Designs Act 1949, the 'RDA'). Those that exist under statute but do not have a registration system are copyright (under the Copyright, Designs and Patents Act 1988, the 'CDPA'), unregistered design rights (also under the CDPA) and database rights (under the Copyright and Rights In Database Regulations 1997[290]).

14.8.2.1 *Registered rights*

A trade mark is personal property[291] capable of continued existence, subject to the periodic renewal of its registration and the requirements as to use. It may be the subject of security, which may be registered,[292] and (save for the effect of prior knowledge) priority is by date of registration.[293] A patent is granted for a period of 20 years, subject to payment of the necessary fees for continued registration in that period. It is personal property and security may be taken over a patent, but it must be in writing signed by both parties.[294] Subject to prior knowledge, priority is by date of registration.[295] A registered design is personal property and is valid for 25 years, subject to payment of renewal fees. It can be the subject of security.[296] For security purposes, there is a requirement for writing[297] and, for priority purposes, the security should be registered.[298]

14.8.2.2 *Unregistered rights*

Copyright, unregistered design rights, and database rights, whilst existing by virtue of statute, do not have a registration system. Copyright exists, in most cases, for the life of the author etc. plus 70 years. It is personal property that is capable of assignment in writing, including the assignment of future copyright.[299] There is no system for the protection of priority and, accordingly, the general rules should apply, so that equitable interests will rank in accordance with the date of their creation and the holder of a legal interest should take free of a prior equitable interest of which it had no knowledge. Unregistered design rights exist for a duration of either 10 years from first manufacture of the article incorporating the design or 15 years from creation. They are personal property and are capable of

---

290 SI 1997/3032.
291 TMA, s 22.
292 TMA, ss 24 and 25.
293 TMA, s 25(3).
294 PA, s 30.
295 PA, s 33.
296 RDA, s 19.
297 RDA, s 20.
298 RDA, s 19.
299 CDPA, ss 90 and 91.

assignment in writing.[300] Database rights exist for a period of 15 years from compilation or publication. They are personal property capable of assignment in the same way as copyright.

14.8.3 Companies Act registration

As is generally the case, any floating charge is registrable, whatever the subject matter of the security. Security that is given by a company by way of fixed security over goodwill or any 'intellectual property' must be registered with the Companies Registry.[301] 'Intellectual property' is defined for this purpose to be any patent, trade mark, registered design, copyright, or design right, as well as any licence under or in respect of any such right.[302]

14.9 Taking Security over Book Debts

14.9.1 The issues that arise in taking security over book debts (or trade debts or receivables, to use more modern terms) have already been addressed, so they will simply be summarised at this point. Subject to any impediment that may be placed upon the ability of the security giver to create the security, particularly under a contractual restriction affecting its ability to dispose of its rights, it should be possible to create security over both present and future book debts. The most important issue that is likely to arise concerns whether the security that is to be taken will be by way of fixed security (i.e. legal or equitable mortgage or fixed equitable charge) or by way of floating charge. That will depend upon the nature and extent of the control that is vested in the creditor with respect to dealings with the debts in their uncollected state and as to the procedures for collection and access to the proceeds of collection.

14.9.2 If security is to be taken by way of legal mortgage then the requirements of section 136 of the Law of Property Act 1925 must be observed. Otherwise, the procedures in taking the security will be less rigid, but it may be necessary for the security taker to provide value to support the taking of the security. Any security over book debts that is given by a company will have to be registered under section 860 of the Companies Act 2006.[303] If an individual who is engaged in business gives security over his book debts then in most cases it should be registered pursuant to section 344 of the Insolvency Act 1986.

---

[300] CDPA, ss 222 and 223.

[301] S 860 of the Companies Act 2006 (formerly ss 395 and 396 of the Companies Act 1985).

[302] S 861(4) of the Companies Act 2006 (formerly s 396(3A) of the Companies Act 1985). Curiously, database rights are not included in the definition.

[303] Formerly s 395 of the Companies Act 1985.

14.10 Taking Security over Credit Balances and Other Obligations Owed by a Creditor

A dilemma that has arisen concerns whether security can be taken by a creditor **14.10.1** over the benefit of an obligation that the creditor owes to the debtor (sometimes referred to as a 'charge back'). The creditor may wish to take security over the obligation so as to secure a debt or some other liability, particularly a contingent liability, that is owed by the debtor or a third party to the creditor. In the hands of the debtor, the obligation of the lender is an asset, being a claim (a chose in action) that the debtor has against the creditor.[304] It may be of considerable value and of good quality. On normal principles, there should be no difficulty in the asset (that is, the benefit of the claim) being provided as security to a third party for a liability that is owed to the third party.[305] The problem arises where the security is to be provided to the person against whom the claim is enforceable. In effect, that person is seeking to take security over its own liability. In traditional terms, this has been the subject of set-off of one claim against the other, rather than the taking of security.

Two examples will serve to illustrate the type of claim or asset that might be involved. **14.10.1.1** The first is the credit balance on an account that the debtor may have with a bank which, in turn, may wish to take security over that credit balance. The second is the benefit of a life policy issued by a life company and held by the debtor. The life company may have provided credit to the policy holder or some other party (for instance, by way of a loan to purchase a house) and wish to take security over the policy.[306]

14.10.2 The reasons for taking security

There are various reasons why the creditor (the bank or the life company in the two examples given above) may wish to take security, rather than being content to rely upon its rights of set-off. In the first place, a right of set-off may not exist as, for instance, where the credit balance or life policy is intended to stand as security for the obligations that are owed by a third party to the creditor, without the person holding the balance or policy incurring a personal liability by way of guarantee which could be the subject of a set-off.[307] Secondly, set-off may not be available

---

[304] See *Foley v Hill* (1848) 2 HL Cas 28.

[305] See Lord Hoffmann in *Re Bank of Credit and Commerce International SA (No 8)* [1998] AC 214, at 226–227.

[306] In this example, the problem is likely to surface if the life company seeks to assign the loan and the 'security' that it holds for the loan, as a claim to set-off cannot be assigned.

[307] That was the position in *Tam Wing Chuen v Bank of Credit & Commerce Hong Kong Ltd* [1996] BCC 388 and in *Re Bank of Credit and Commerce International SA (No 8)* [1998] AC 214. The unusual feature in each case was that because the bank was insolvent, it did not wish to assert a right of set-off against the credit balance over which it purported to hold security.

in an insolvency of one or other (or both) of the parties because the insolvency proceedings might take place in a foreign jurisdiction which does not permit such a set-off.[308] Thirdly, set-off may not be available to cover the type of liability which is intended to be secured or there may be practical difficulties in establishing and quantifying the claims and their relative amounts for the purposes of the set-off. Fourthly, set-off requires mutuality as between the holders of the respective cross-claims at the time the set-off is asserted. Mutuality will be lost if one of the claims has been assigned prior to the time that it is wished to assert or apply the set-off, with the consequence that the assignee will be unable to rely upon the set-off that the assignor might have enjoyed.[309] This will be a particular problem in an insolvency of the assignor, if it continues to be liable on the claim due by it.[310]

14.10.2.1 Set-off as a topic in its own right is addressed separately below.

14.10.3 The conceptual impossibility argument

The dilemma referred to above was addressed initially by Millett J in *Re Charge Card Services Ltd*,[311] in which his Lordship held that it was a conceptual impossibility for a party to take security over its own obligation.[312] This was because the taking of security would theoretically involve a re-assignment back to the security taker of its own obligation, which would have the effect of discharging that obligation. Clearly, that would not be what the parties had intended to achieve. He held that an attempt to take a charge in such circumstances would amount to no more than an agreement for contractual set-off which would cease to apply in the liquidation of one (or both) of the parties. It is interesting to note, in passing, that his Lordship applied this analysis even though the security would, if valid, have been by way of charge, rather than an assignment by way of legal or equitable mortgage.

14.10.3.1 The view that was taken in the *Charge Card* case was overturned ultimately by the decision of the House of Lords in *Re Bank of Credit and Commerce International SA (No 8)*,[313] in which the leading speech was delivered by Lord Hoffmann, with

---

[308] As is demonstrated by the lack of insolvency set-off in Luxembourg, as discussed in *Re Bank of Credit and Commerce International SA (No 10)* [1997] Ch 213.

[309] Although the obligor should be able to assert the set-off for its own benefit, particularly where it can rely upon equitable or transaction set-off: *Business Computers Ltd v Anglo-African Leasing Ltd* [1977] 1 WLR 578.

[310] *Re City Life Assurance Co; Stephenson's Case* [1926] 1 Ch 191, at 214.

[311] [1987] Ch 150, at 175–176 (the case was the subject of an appeal, which did not deal with this aspect: [1989] Ch 497).

[312] This view was followed in the single judgment of the Court of Appeal (of which Millett LJ was a member) in *Re Bank of Credit and Commerce International SA (No 8)* [1996] Ch 245, at 257–262.

[313] [1998] AC 214. It might be argued that the decision on this aspect was merely *obiter*, as the House dismissed the appeals to it by deciding that, in any event, the two sets of depositors would not be able to force the liquidators to return the deposits or to apply the rules of insolvency set-off,

whom the other Law Lords who sat on the appeal agreed. Lord Hoffmann said that the conceptual impossibility argument was misconceived and that it was possible to take the security. In passing, his Lordship remarked that the law should not deny the use of a form of security which was seen to have practical utility in the banking and commercial community. In arriving at his conclusion, his Lordship looked at the essential characteristics of security. The person taking the security only has a limited entitlement in the asset that is the subject of the security, being the right to resort to it to satisfy the liability secured by it. The giver of the security retains its equity of redemption, which is its entitlement to have the asset fully restored to it when the liability has been discharged. The only difference between a creditor seeking to take security over its own liability and taking security over any other type of asset was in the method of enforcement of the security, as in the former case it will take place by a book entry, by which the asset would be appropriated against the amount of the secured liability. In all other aspects, the rights and consequences attached to the security would be the same. In particular, given the presence of the equity of redemption, there would not be a merger of interests, as the giver of the security retains its interest, but subject to the security. The consequence of this is that taking security over a deposit does not effect an outright re-assignment of the liability that the deposit represents. The security giver's equity of redemption serves as the point of distinction and prevents a merger of the interests from taking place.

Lord Hoffmann's analysis is based on the security being in the form of a charge. As previously discussed, the creation of a charge does not involve any concept of a conveyance or transfer of title in the charged asset and that is the clearest method of avoiding the conceptual impossibility argument. However, the analysis that his Lordship employed should also apply if the security is in the form of a legal or equitable mortgage, given the importance that he attached to the continued presence of the equity of redemption which prevents the merger of the interests of the parties and of the underlying security with the liability it secures. **14.10.3.2**

It is apparent from what he said that Lord Hoffmann saw no difficulty in the method of enforcement of this type of security being by way of application of the deposit against the secured liability, without the necessity of having recourse to the traditional methods of enforcement of security, such as by sale or (with a court order) foreclosure. He did not explain how this might be different from the **14.10.3.3**

---

because the liquidators were not obliged to repay the deposits, due to the 'flawed asset' provisions, and because there was no mutuality between the claims due to the company in liquidation (the bank) and the claims due by it to the depositors, who were not the borrowers and had not undertaken a personal liability for payment of the claims due by the borrowers to the bank. However, the issue currently under discussion was raised and fully argued in the appeals and formed part of reasons for the decision to dismiss the appeals and, on that basis, should be regarded as being a binding authority of a unanimous decision by the House.

position when a right of set-off is exercised, which achieves the same thing. It might be argued, in consequence, that his Lordship impliedly invented a new method for enforcing security, which would apply to this type of security. However, it is submitted that the same method of enforcement would apply if a third party took security over a deposit. It is hardly likely that the third party would have to sell the deposit to realise its security. In reality, it would simply require that the amount of the deposit should be paid to it, which it would then apply against the outstanding secured liability.

14.10.3.4   Lord Hoffmann declined to say if the credit balance on a bank account might be a 'book debt' and, therefore, if security over it might constitute a charge that should normally be registered under section 860 of the Companies Act 2006.[314] He did refer to the view taken in *Northern Bank Ltd v Ross*[315] (which, in turn, had relied on what his Lordship had said previously on the subject[316]) which suggested that it was unlikely that the security would be considered to be a charge on book debts. Of course, if the security is only a floating charge then it will normally be registrable, whatever its subject matter.[317] However, whether or not security over a bank balance would normally be registrable under section 860, it will not be registrable if the security comprises a 'security financial collateral arrangement' over 'cash' under the Financial Collateral Arrangements (No 2) Regulations 2003, for the reasons referred to earlier.

14.10.4 Insolvency set-off

A question that remains outstanding concerns the relationship between a charged deposit or similar asset of the type just discussed and the rules as to insolvency set-off, which are discussed below; in particular, as to whether the deposit or similar asset (for convenience, the 'asset') must be brought into the account for the purposes of those rules, where the secured liabilities consist of one or more liabilities (including contingent liabilities) that are owing by the security giver to the security holder. The question is likely to arise where the security holder wishes to keep the asset separate and thus to sit on its security until it can be sure that all of the liabilities that are covered by its security have crystallised, matured, and been dealt with and discharged to its satisfaction. This would be relevant if those liabilities remain contingent so that the actual amount of them may not be known when the liquidator or trustee of the security giver wishes to apply the rules. The security holder might be faced with an attempt by the liquidator or trustee to place an

---

[314] Formerly s 395 of the Companies Act 1985.

[315] [1990] BCC 883.

[316] In *Re Brightlife Ltd* [1987] Ch 200 and in *Re Permanent Houses (Holdings) Ltd* (1989) 5 BCC 151.

[317] See s 860(7)(g) of the Companies Act 2006 (formerly s 396(1)(f) of the Companies Act 1985).

estimated value on the liabilities for the purposes the application of the rules of insolvency set-off.

There are four principles that are in play in considering this question. The first is that a security holder is not obliged to enforce its security, even after default in observance of the secured liabilities; it is entitled to sit on its security until the secured liabilities have been discharged in full, including any contingent liabilities.[318] Pending the discharge of such liabilities, the property covered by the security is detached from the fund of assets that is available in the insolvency of the security giver, although this is subject to the effect of any statutory requirements to the contrary.[319] Secondly, a secured creditor has an option with respect to a bankruptcy or winding up of its debtor. The security holder can stay outside it and rely upon its security. Alternatively, it can surrender its security and participate in the insolvency as a creditor. It is also entitled to prove for any deficiency between the amount due to it and the value of its security.[320] Thirdly, there is the security giver's equity of redemption, but that right can only be exercised if all of the secured liabilities have been discharged.[321] Fourthly, there are the rules of insolvency set-off, which are mandatory and cannot be contracted out of by private agreement or arrangement between the parties.[322] They are also self-executing and do not depend upon the creditor lodging a proof in the bankruptcy or winding up, despite the wording used in the legislative provisions.[323] The asset would normally fall to be taken into account in the application of those rules, if no issue arose as to the effect of the security that had been taken.

14.10.4.1

It is submitted, somewhat tentatively, that the rules of insolvency set-off should prevail in resolving the question.[324] The rules should be seen as creating an exception to the detached right that a security holder has in its security. As is explained below, the courts have given a wide interpretation to the concept of 'mutual credits, mutual debts or other mutual dealings' as between the parties which gives rise to the operation of the rules. That wording is intended to refer to the existence of mutual cross-obligations from which the claims to be set off arose, howsoever they might have arisen. This would appear to be capable of encompassing the type of arrangement under which the security exists, bearing in mind that the point of the rules is to achieve finality in establishing the state of the account between the parties.

14.10.4.2

[318] See *China and South Sea Bank Ltd v Tan* [1990] 1 AC 536.

[319] See Lord Millett in *Buchler v Talbot* [2004] UKHL 9; [2004] 2 AC 298, at [51].

[320] See Rules 4.75 (1)(e), 4.88, and 4.95 of the Insolvency Rules 1986.

[321] See *Re Rudd and Son Ltd* (1986) 2 BCC 98,955 and *Law Debenture Trust Corp PLC v Concord Trust* [2007] EWHC 1380 (Ch).

[322] See the discussion on insolvency set-off below.

[323] See Lord Hoffmann in *Stein v Blake* [1996] AC 243, at 253.

[324] Support for this view may be gained from Dillon LJ in *MS Fashions Ltd v Bank of Credit and Commerce International SA* [1993] Ch 425, at 446 and from Jonathan Parker J in *Re ILG Travel Ltd* [1996] BCC 21, at 46–48.

14.10.5 'Flawed asset' provisions

A 'flawed asset' provision is one which provides that a liability due by A to B (for instance, a liability of A as a bank to repay a deposit that has been placed with it by B) may be withheld and will not fall due for payment or discharge whilst any liability remains outstanding that is owing and undischarged by B (or a third party) to A. It will probably also provide for A to have the right to set off one liability against the other once they have both been fully established. Such provisions were developed with a view to overcoming the difficulty created by the decision in the *Charge Card* case. Although they could not, in themselves, enable A to treat the deposit placed with it as security, it was intended that they might have much the same effect, as A would wish to retain the deposit and refuse to repay it whilst any liability which the deposit 'secured' remained outstanding and unsatisfied, particularly where the outstanding and unsatisfied liability was that of a third party.

14.10.5.1 Such a provision was considered by the Court of Appeal in *Re Bank of Credit and Commerce International SA (No 8)*,[325] whose judgment was the subject of an appeal to the House of Lords, as discussed above. Lord Hoffmann simply agreed with what had been said by the Court of Appeal on this aspect and did not add any additional commentary.[326] In this case, it was held that the depositor had no personal liability to the bank. The deposit was simply intended to 'secure' the obligation of a third party to the bank. The Court of Appeal said that such a provision was a purely contractual arrangement. It could not give rise to any proprietary interest in favour of the bank. Subject to the point as to the effect of the rules of insolvency set-off (as mentioned below) the court went on to say, however, that the effect of the provision was that the bank could not be forced to return the deposit whilst any liability of the third party remained outstanding. This was despite the fact that the bank was in liquidation. In a case where it was the depositor that was insolvent, rather than the bank, the court thought it would be likely that the depositor's trustee or liquidator would wish to come to an arrangement with the bank, by which the bank would apply the deposit, so that the insolvency practitioner could obtain any balance remaining for the benefit of the depositor's general body of creditors.

14.10.5.2 The Court of Appeal did indicate, however, that if the 'flawed asset' deposit was intended to 'secure' an obligation of the depositor to the bank (whether directly incurred or by way of guarantee) then the rules of insolvency set-off might apply. To that extent, the bank might find that the deposit would be taken into account and applied in striking a balance under the rules as to insolvency set-off, if the account that was taken for that purpose was based on an estimate of the relevant obligation owing to the bank.

---

[325] [1996] Ch 245, at 262–263.
[326] [1998] AC 214, at 225.

In view of the decision of the House of Lords that true security can be taken over   **14.10.5.3**
such a deposit, it is unlikely that a creditor would now need to rely on a 'flawed
asset' provision.

14.11 Set-off

Set-off is the means by which opposing cross-claims between parties are applied   **14.11.1**
or netted against each other to arrive at a net balance that is payable one way or the
other. Whilst it is not, strictly speaking, a matter of security, the subject of set-off
is important and relevant in the context of this chapter because it can be very similar in its consequences to holding security. In practical terms, it can amount to
pretty good 'security'. This is because set-off can have the effect of reducing the
risk exposure that a creditor has towards its counterparty, particularly in the event
of a default by, or an insolvency of, the counterparty. There are, in addition, a number
of other benefits that may accrue to a creditor which has a right of set-off. These
include, first, the ease of valuation of the benefit it enjoys from the set-off; secondly, the ease with which a set-off can be exercised under contractual set-off and
insolvency set-off, by a simple application of one claim against the other; and,
thirdly, regulatory benefits which may allow a bank to treat the risk exposure referable to its counterparty as the net balance after taking into account the set-off,
rather than the gross figure of its exposure before such an account is taken. In a
more commercial context, set-off may have the effect of providing an abatement
in the price of goods and services that have been supplied, so as to accommodate
the loss because of defective performance. It may also avoid the necessity of pursuing separate proceedings for recovery of the cross-claim.

In discussing the subject, it is necessary to distinguish between rights of set-off   **14.11.1.1**
that are exercisable before the insolvency of one of the parties (or both of them)
and the position as to mandatory insolvency set-off that arises in the winding
up or bankruptcy of a party (and sometimes in the administration of a party).
It will also be necessary to refer to the consequences where a party assigns a claim
which would otherwise have been subject to a set-off between the original
parties.

14.11.2 Pre-insolvency set-off

Outside the context of insolvency, the matters for examination concern the right
of a party to assert, as against the other party, a legal set-off, an equitable set-off,
and a contractual set-off, as well as its right to rely on a contractual provision
which denies to the other party the right to exercise a set-off. It will also be
necessary to consider the special rules that apply in the case of negotiable
instruments.

14.11.2.1 *Legal set-off*[327]

Legal set-off is a procedural device that arises in litigation for the convenience of avoiding a multiplicity of suits.[328] It allows the defendant in the proceedings to plead in its defence the cross-claim that it has against the claimant. It is not necessary that there should be any connection between the claim and the cross-claim. The set-off may only be asserted, however, if the cross-claim is both liquidated (or capable of precise calculation or valuation) and due at the times when the defence is filed and when judgment is given.[329] It is also necessary that the claim and the cross-claim should be between the same people and in the same right, that is, a requirement for mutuality as between the parties to the set-off.[330]

14.11.2.1.1 When considering the parameters in which legal set-off may take place, it could be said that the set-off is wide in one sense and narrow in another. It is wide in the sense that there need be no connection between the claim of the claimant in the proceedings and the cross-claim of the defendant, provided the requirement for mutuality is met. It is narrow in the sense that the cross-claim must be liquidated or capable of precise calculation and it must be due at the time it is asserted and when judgment is given.

14.11.2.2 *Equitable set-off*

There are at least three different types of equitable set-off that might be relevant in a commercial context. They are transaction set-off, set-off as between a claim and cross-claim at a beneficial level which would not be available at law, and the set-off that is available to a debtor whose debt has been assigned. It is also important to consider the circumstances in which a right to equitable set-off may be denied.

14.11.2.2.1 Transaction set-off[331] Transaction set-off, which arises as a defence to a claim in litigation, is wide and narrow in the opposite way to legal set-off. It is

---

[327] See Hoffmann LJ in *Aectra Refining & Marketing Inc v Exmar NV* [1994] 1 WLR 1643, at 1649–1653; Lord Hoffmann in *Stein v Blake* [1996] AC 243, at 251; and Clarke LJ in *Glencore Grain Ltd v Agros Trading Co Ltd* [1999] 2 Lloyd's Rep 410, at 415–417.

[328] The procedural nature of this type of set-off is relevant in the context of conflict of laws, as discussed at Chap 4.

[329] It is still possible to plead the set-off even though the amount of the cross-claim might be disputed, in which case the court will have to determine the correct amount: *Aectra Refining & Marketing Inc v Exmar NV* [1994] 1 WLR 1643.

[330] A lack of mutuality at a beneficial level will prevent the set-off: see Sir George Jessell MR in *Re Whitehouse & Co* (1878) 9 ChD 595, at 597. Parke B in *Briscoe v Hill* (1842) 10 M&W 735, at 738, said that it is not possible to plead a joint liability against a several debt because the debts were not due in the same right.

[331] As to a legal right of set-off and the distinction between that and equitable or transaction set-off, see Hoffmann LJ in *Aectra Refining & Marketing Inc v Exmar NV* [1994] 1 WLR 1643, at 1649–1653; Clarke LJ in *Glencore Grain Ltd v Agros Trading Co Ltd* [1999] 2 Lloyd's Rep 410, at 415–417; Buxton LJ in *Smith v Muscat* [2003] EWCA Civ 962; [2003] 1 WLR 2853, at [37]–[45]; and *Benford Ltd v Lopecan SL* [2004] EWHC 1897 (Comm), [2004] 2 Lloyd's Rep 618.

wide in the sense that the cross-claim does not have to be for a liquidated amount, as it can include a claim for damages to be assessed.[332] It is narrow in the sense that it would be manifestly unjust to refuse to allow the set-off and there must be an inseparable connection between the claim and the cross-claim, as they must arise out of the same course of dealings and transactions.[333] The requirement for an inseparable connection can be met even though the claim and the cross-claim arise under different contracts; indeed, it has been said that two claims under the same contract may not be sufficiently connected to meet the requirement.[334]

Transaction set-off will usually arise where the original claim is for a liquidated sum and the set-off is in respect of an unliquidated cross-claim for damages. Nonetheless, the right to equitable set-off can also be asserted where both the claims are for unliquidated damages.[335]   **14.11.2.2.1.1**

It has been said that a claim to transaction set-off goes to 'impeach' the original claim and so it is a substantive defence, rather than being merely procedural. This also has implications for the treatment of the two claims as a matter of conflict of laws.[336]   **14.11.2.2.1.2**

It has also been said that a claim for abatement of the price of goods or services for breach of warranty is a form of transaction or equitable set-off[337] although, strictly speaking, such a claim arises at common law as, for instance, under section 53(1)(a) of the Sale of Goods Act 1979.   **14.11.2.2.1.3**

14.11.2.2.2 Equitable set-off at the beneficial level   This type of set-off arises where set-off would not be available between claims at common law, because the claims are not as between the same parties. It is allowed as a form of equitable set-off where, at the beneficial level, the claims are really between the same parties.[338] For instance, it would arise where A is indebted to B and C is indebted to A, but where B is acting as trustee of C with respect to the debt due to B by A. A set-off would not be available at common law, but it would arise in equity.

The onus is on the person that wishes to assert the set-off to establish the true relationship as between the trustee and the beneficiary. It is not sufficient for that   **14.11.2.2.2.1**

---

[332]   The amount of the cross-claim must then be assessed as part of the proceedings.
[333]   See Potter LJ in *Bim Kemi AB v Blackburn Chemicals Ltd* [2001] EWCA Civ 457, [2001] 2 Lloyd's Rep 93.
[334]   See Potter LJ in the *Bim Kemi* case.
[335]   See Potter LJ in the *Bim Kemi* case, at [21]–[23].
[336]   See the discussion at Chap 4.
[337]   See Hoffmann LJ in *Aectra Refining & Marketing Inc v Exmar NV* [1994] 1 WLR 1643, at 1648–1649.
[338]   *Cochrane v Green* (1860) CB (NS) 448; *Thornton v Maynard* (1875) LR 10 CP 695; *Bhogal v Punjab National Bank* [1988] 2 All ER 296.

person simply to assert that one of its counterparties is acting as a trustee, if it cannot establish that the trustee is acting for the other counterparty.[339]

14.11.2.2.3 Set-off in the context of assignment or security The issue that arises at this point is the effect that an assignment of a debt may have on the rights to set-off that a debtor had or would have enjoyed against the assignor, and whether the debtor can assert those rights against the assignee. In other words, whether the debtor can continue to assert, as against the assignee, a set-off that it would have been entitled to assert against its original creditor, in the situation where its debt has been assigned so that, at least superficially, the element of mutuality has been broken. This matter is addressed in Chapter 12. The discussion there is equally applicable in the context of security being taken over the debt. Indeed, *Business Computers Ltd v Anglo-African Leasing Ltd*,[340] which is one of the leading cases, concerned the effect on the debtor's rights of set-off following upon its receipt of a notice of the crystallisation of a floating charge, the event of crystallisation being treated for these purposes as being equivalent to an assignment of the debt.

14.11.2.2.4 Denying equitable set-off It would appear that a claim to equitable set-off cannot be asserted by a defendant where the claim against the defendant arises from the defendant's wrongful action, such as due to its wrongful conversion of goods or breach of a statutory obligation.[341] It has also been held that where money is paid to a person in the position of a trustee or fiduciary, to be used for a specific purpose and the purpose cannot be achieved, then (in the absence of an agreement to the contrary) that person will not be allowed to set-off against its obligation to refund the money some other claim that it may have against the original payer of the money.[342]

14.11.2.3 Contractual set-off

It is open to the parties to an agreement to provide for the availability of set-off by either or both of them in circumstances that would not arise as a legal or equitable set-off. For instance, they may agree that the set-off might be applied outside the parameters of litigation, so that a party could advance its right to set-off to a contractual date for payment under a contract, rather than having to wait for litigation to be commenced. If one of the parties is a bank, they might agree that it would be entitled to exercise a right or set-off outside the confines that normally apply to the implied right that a banker has to combine accounts (see below).

---

339 *Bhogal v Punjab National Bank* [1988] 2 All ER 296; *Saudi Arabian Monetary Agency v Dresdner Bank AG* [2004] EWCA Civ 1074, [2005] 1 Lloyd's Rep 12.

340 [1977] 1 WLR 578.

341 See Lords Hoffmann and Scott in *Smith (Administrator of Cosslett (Contractors) Ltd v Bridgend CBC* [2001] UKHL 58; [2002] 1 AC 336, at [34]–[36] and at [76]–[78], respectively.

342 *Re Niagara Mechanical Services International Ltd* [2001] BCC 393.

The parties could also agree that the set-off might be applied to claims that would arise in different countries or as between claims in different currencies.[343]

It is also possible for them to agree that one of them could set-off against the other a claim due to one of them by a third party, such as another company in the same group as one of the contracting parties. However, if it is sought to apply a set-off against a claim made by the third party, that party would have to agree. Thus, A and B may agree that A could set-off a debt due to it by C against a debt due to B by A. However, A and B could not agree, without C's agreement, that A could avoid having to pay a debt due by it to C by setting-off a debt due by B to A. Of course, it is perfectly possible for a number of parties to enter into a multilateral agreement providing for netting and set-off on a multilateral basis between them all as, for instance, by having a settlement of debts on a periodic basis through a clearing house or central body and establishing an ultimate balance due as between the participants.

14.11.2.3.1

Under English domestic insolvency law, contractual rights of set-off cease to be available upon the bankruptcy or liquidation of one of the parties to the contract,[344] because the mandatory rules of insolvency set-off apply, whatever the contract might provide.[345] However, there are statutory savings for the settlement of market contracts and the operation of the rules of recognised investment exchanges and clearing houses pursuant to sections 158 and 159 of the Companies Act 1989,[346] as well as other savings under the Financial Markets and Insolvency (Settlement Finality) Regulations 1999[347] and, with respect to close-out netting, under the Financial Collateral Arrangements (No 2) Regulations 2003.[348]

14.11.2.3.2

A contractual set-off agreement may be valuable, however, in the context of a cross-border insolvency of a party within the EC. Article 6 of the EC Insolvency Regulation,[349] which is repeated in the relevant EC legislation concerning insolvent credit institutions[350] and insurance undertakings,[351] provides for the

14.11.2.3.3

---

[343] In which case it would be necessary to provide for a mechanism for calculating the conversion of one currency into another so as to achieve the set-off.

[344] And, in limited circumstances, an administration of a party.

[345] *National Westminster Bank Ltd v Halesowen Presswork and Assemblies Ltd* [1972] AC 785; *British Eagle International Airlines Ltd v Cie Nationale Air France* [1975] 1 WLR 758; *Re Maxwell Communications Corp PLC (No 2)* [1993] 1 WLR 1402.

[346] And, pursuant thereto, the Financial Markets and Insolvency Regs 1991 (SI 1991/880).

[347] SI 1999/2979.

[348] SI 2003/3226.

[349] The Regulation on insolvency proceedings (EC1346/2000 OJ L160/1 30/6/2000). Art 6 is discussed in Chap 5.

[350] Art 23 of the EC Directive on the reorganisation and winding up of credit institutions (EC 2001/24 OJ L125 5/5/2001). The Directive has been implemented in the UK by the Credit Institutions (Reorganisation and Winding Up) Regs 2004 (SI 2004/1045).

[351] EC Directive on the reorganisation and winding up of insurance undertakings (EC 2001/17 OJ L110 20/4/2001). The Directive has been implemented in the UK by the Insurers (Reorganisation and Winding Up) Regs 2004 (SI 2004/353, as amended by SI 2004/546).

preservation of rights of set-off where the law that governs the insolvent debtor's claim would permit the set-off, despite the opening of insolvency proceedings under the law of a Member State which might not acknowledge such rights. In addition, the validity and effectiveness of a netting agreement to which an EC or EEA insolvent credit institution is a party, is governed by the law that governs the agreement.[352]

14.11.2.4 *The banker's right of set-off*

By virtue of the relationship between banker and customer, the banker has a right in certain situations to combine or net the balances on the separate accounts that it holds for a customer so as to achieve a net balance due one way or the other. Although there is some doubt as to the basis of the right, it is submitted that it arises as a form of implied right of contractual set-off. This is because it springs from the contractual relationship between the parties and it is a right in favour of the bank, which it can determine to exercise if it wishes, rather than an automatic and continuous netting that arises in favour of both parties.[353]

14.11.2.4.1 This form of set-off should be distinguished from the situation that arises on a single running account, to which debit and credit entries are made on a continuous basis as, for instance, on an overdraft account. The making of the debit and credit entries to the account does not give rise to the operation of set-off; rather, there is a single relationship with a balance being struck from time to time to show what is due one way or the other.[354]

14.11.2.4.2 The implied right of the bank to combine accounts arises where the balance on each account is due and payable, as would be the case between two current accounts.[355] It will not arise whilst the customer's liability to the bank is contingent or payable in the future,[356] nor where one account is a current account and the other is a deposit or term account,[357] at least until the accounts have reached maturity or where the bank has an express right to combine the accounts. In light of the decision of the House of Lords in *Miliangos v George Frank (Textiles) Ltd,*[358] to the effect that a debt in a foreign currency may properly be treated as a debt and is no longer to be treated as a claim for a mere commodity, it should now be possible for a bank to set off balances in different currencies.

---

[352] Art 25 of EC 2001/24.

[353] See, for instance, Lord Denning MR in *National Westminster Bank Ltd v Halesowen Presswork and Assemblies* Ltd [1971] 1 QB 1, at 34 and Buckley J in *Re EJ Morel Ltd* [1962] Ch 21, at 31.

[354] See Buckley LJ in *National Westminster Bank Ltd v Halesowen Presswork and Assemblies Ltd* [1971] 1 QB 1, at 46, and Millett J in *Re Charge Card Services Ltd* [1987] Ch 150, at 174.

[355] *Garnett v McKewan* (1872) LR 8 Ex 10.

[356] *Jeffryes v Agra & Masterman's Bank* (1866) LR 2 Eq 674.

[357] *Bradford Old Bank v Sutcliffe* [1918] 2 KB 833.

[358] [1976] AC 443.

The implied right to set-off depends upon mutuality as between the entitlement **14.11.2.4.3**
in the accounts. Accordingly, if the accounts are maintained in the same name
but the bank is on notice that the beneficial entitlement in one of the accounts
rests in a third party, the bank will not be entitled to combine the accounts.[359]
By contrast, if the bank can demonstrate that an account, although maintained
in the name of one person, is held beneficially for another customer, it should
be able to set-off the entitlement on that account against a liability of that
customer to the bank, but the onus rests on the bank to demonstrate the
connection.[360]

14.11.2.5 Precluding the exercise of rights to set-off

Just as it is possible to enhance or create rights of set-off by contract, so it is also
possible by contract to reduce or withdraw those rights,[361] although this is subject
to certain statutory limitations which will be mentioned. As a matter of interpretation, the intention to preclude or limit the exercise of the right must be clearly
expressed. Accordingly, an agreement that required payment to be made 'without
any deduction'[362] or 'without discount'[363] were held not to preclude the exercise of
a right of set-off, as was an agreement that a party's payment obligations were
unaffected 'by any matter whatsoever'.[364]

As with a contract which confers rights of set-off, an agreement that precludes or **14.11.2.5.1**
restricts the exercise of such rights will cease to have effect upon the bankruptcy or
liquidation of one of the parties.[365]

14.11.2.5.2 Statutory limitation There are two areas of potential statutory
limitation to the effectiveness of a contractual provision that purports to preclude
a party from asserting a right of set-off (a 'no-set off clause'). The first arises under
the Unfair Contract Terms Act 1977 (UCTA) and the other arises under the
Unfair Terms in Consumer Contracts Regs 1999[366] (UTCCR).

14.11.2.5.3 UCTA More detailed discussions of UCTA will be found in
Chapters 9 and 15. What follows here is intended to provide a summary of the
provisions of UCTA that are of immediate relevance to the present discussion.

---

[359] *Barclays Bank Ltd v Quistclose Investments Ltd* [1970] AC 567.
[360] *Saudi Arabian Monetary Agency v Dresdner Bank AG* [2004] EWCA Civ 1074, [2005] 1
Lloyd's Rep 12.
[361] *Coca-Cola Financial Corp v Finsat International Ltd* [1998] QB 43; *John Dee Group Ltd v
WMH (21) Ltd* [1998] BCC 972; *International Lease Finance Corp v Buzz Stansted Ltd* [2004]
EWHC 292 (Comm).
[362] *Connaught Restaurants Ltd v Indoor Leisure Ltd* [1994] 1 WLR 501.
[363] *Compania Sud Americana de Vapores v Shipmair BV, The Teno* [1997] 2 Lloyd's Rep 289.
[364] *BOC Group plc v Centeon LLC* [1999] 1 All ER (Comm) 970.
[365] *National Westminster Bank Ltd v Halesowen Presswork and Assemblies Ltd* [1972] AC 785.
[366] SI 1999/2083.

14.11.2.5.3.1 Section 3 of UCTA provides that where a contracting party is dealing as a consumer[367] or on the other party's standard terms of business,[368] that other party cannot by a contractual term exclude or restrict his own liability for breach of the contract, nor purport to render no performance at all or a substantially different performance than was reasonably to be expected under the contract, except (in either case) in so far as the term satisfies the requirement of reasonableness in section 11 of UCTA. This is supplemented by section 13(1) of UCTA, the salient part of which provides as follows,

> To the extent that this Part of this Act [which includes both section 2 and section 3 of the Act] prevents the exclusion or restriction of any liability it also prevents—
>
> (a) making the liability or its enforcement subject to restrictive or onerous conditions;
> (b) excluding or restricting any right or remedy in respect of the liability, or subjecting a person to any prejudice in consequence of his pursuing any such right or remedy;
> (c) excluding or restricting rules of evidence or procedure . . .

14.11.2.5.3.2 In *Stewart Gill Ltd v Horatio Myer & Co Ltd*[369] the Court of Appeal held that paragraph (b) applied to a no set-off clause which prevented the exercise by a customer of a right of equitable set-off or counterclaim in an instalment payment contract, where faulty goods had been supplied. The customer had wished to set off its counterclaim for the loss it had suffered due to the goods being defective, against the instalments that it was due to pay under the contract. It was held that the right of set-off or counterclaim was a right or remedy that the customer would normally have been entitled to assert against the supplier. The clause prevented it from exercising the right. It would also subject the customer to prejudice, in that the clause would have the effect of forcing the customer to pursue its claim against the supplier separately, rather than being able to use the more effective and immediate right of set-off. An attempt by the supplier to limit or restrict its liability for the defective goods would have fallen within section 3 of UCTA. Accordingly, section 13 was engaged and the anti-set-off clause could only be saved if it met the requirement of reasonableness. That requirement had not been satisfied, as it could not be reasonable to prevent the customer in any and all circumstances from seeking to assert a right of set-off including, for instance, where it might have made an over-payment under an earlier instalment.

14.11.2.5.3.3 It is possible that much the same approach might be taken towards a no set-off clause which related to a cross-claim that a party might wish to assert concerning

---

[367] As to dealing as a consumer, see s 12 of UCTA and *R&B Customs Brokers Co. Ltd v United Dominions Trust Ltd* [1988] 1 WLR 321.

[368] As to dealing on standard terms of business, see *St Albans City and District Council v International Computers Ltd* [1996] 4 All ER 481.

[369] [1992] QB 600.

loss due to the negligence of the other party. Section 2 of UCTA applies to attempts by a contractual provision (or by a non-contractual notice) to limit or exclude liability for negligence. Assuming that the liability does not concern death or personal injury, any such provision (or notice) will only be effective if it satisfies the requirement of reasonableness in section 11 of UCTA.

On the other hand, in *Governor & Co of the Bank of Scotland v Singh*[370] it was held that section 3 (and therefore section 13) of UCTA would not normally apply to a no set-off clause in a guarantee that operated against the guarantor. This was because a guarantee is usually a form of unilateral contract under which it was the guarantor that had contractual obligations to the lender. The lender had no contractual obligations to the guarantor. It was, accordingly, difficult to see how a no set-off clause could be said to fall within section 3, as there were no obligations of the lender towards the guarantor under the contract which could be excluded, restricted, or abrogated.

14.11.2.5.3.4

It was also said in the same case that, assuming sections 3 and 13 of UCTA were engaged, a no set-off clause might, nonetheless, satisfy the requirement of reasonableness under section 11 of UCTA, which had to be judged by the circumstances as at the time the guarantee was entered into. The purpose of a no set-off clause in a guarantee was to ensure that the guarantor's payment obligations, which arose because of the borrower's default in making payment, could not be deferred or diminished by disputes concerning a cross-claim that the guarantor might allege it had against the lender (in that case, the cross-claim was for 'reflective loss' arising from the economic loss suffered by the guarantor due to the failure of the principal debtor which, it was alleged, was the fault of the lender). The lender wants its money, which it should have received from the borrower, without further delay. It was significant in that case that the clause did not prevent the guarantor from pursuing a claim separately if it wished to do so and so, in that sense, the clause did not have the effect of excluding or restricting the lender's liability. For the same reason, such clauses are not subject to the strict rules that are applied to the construction of exclusion clauses.[371]

14.11.2.5.3.5

By reference to the guidance given in Schedule 2 to UCTA,[372] the clause was held to be reasonable. The guarantor had received independent legal advice on the meaning and effect of the document and, through its control of the principal debtor, it wanted the debtor to be able to borrow from the lender, which could only be achieved if it gave the guarantee. The guarantor knew that the guarantee

14.11.2.5.3.6

---

[370] Unreported, HHJ Kershaw QC, sitting in the High Court in Manchester, 17/6/2005.

[371] See the approach taken by Parker LJ in the Court of Appeal in *Continental Illinois National Bank & Trust Co of Chicago v Papanicolaou* [1986] 2 Lloyd's Rep 441, at 444.

[372] As to the relevance of which outside the express circumstances where the schedule applies, see Stuart-Smith LJ in *Stewart Gill*, n 369 above, at 608.

would cover the borrowing. It could control the amount of the debt that was guaranteed. In so far as the clause prevented the guarantor from purporting to set off a reflective loss claim, it was likely that such a claim would be brought at a time when the guarantor had lost its control of the borrower because of the latter's insolvency and it was not unreasonable for the lender to seek to protect itself in that situation.

14.11.2.5.4 UTCCR Regulation 4(1) of UTCCR provides that 'The Regulations apply in relation to unfair terms in contracts concluded between a seller or supplier and a consumer'. A consumer is defined by Regulation 3(1) to be a natural person who is acting outside his trade, business, or profession, whereas a seller or supplier is a natural or legal person acting for the purposes of his or its trade, business, or profession. Regulation 5(1) provides that: 'A contractual term which has not been individually negotiated shall be regarded as unfair if, contrary to the requirement of good faith, it causes a significant imbalance in the parties' rights and obligations arising under the contract, to the detriment of the consumer.' It should be noted that the reference in Regulation 5(1) is to the rights and obligations arising under the contract itself. Regulation 5(5) provides that Schedule 2 to the regulations gives a non-exhaustive indication of unfair terms. Paragraph 1(b) of that Schedule includes a no set-off clause that applies with respect to a total or partial non-performance or inadequate performance by the seller or supplier of any contractual obligation.

14.11.2.5.4.1 The regulations will apply to the provisions of standard form contracts for the provision of financial services to consumers. Accordingly, a no set-off clause in such a contract, by which the consumer was denied the opportunity to assert a set-off against a debt due to the provider of the services would be caught by the regulations. In *Governor & Co of the Bank of Scotland v Singh*,[373] however, it was held that the regulations would not normally apply in the context of a guarantee given by an individual with respect to a facility provided by a bank to the principal debtor. The characteristic of the guarantee was that it was the guarantor who was undertaking obligations under the contract towards the lender, rather than the other way around. Hence, the effect of the no set-off clause could not be said to be causing any significant imbalance in the parties' rights and obligations arising under the contract, because the obligations under that contract only went in one direction, from the consumer towards the lender. Whilst paragraph (b) of Schedule 2 was intended to catch no set-off clauses, it applied in the context of attempts to limit or exclude a consumer's rights or remedies with respect to breaches by a seller or supplier of its obligations to the consumer under the contract. On the same basis, as already mentioned with respect to section 3 of UCTA, there were no

---

[373] Unreported, HHJ Kershaw QC, sitting in the High Court in Manchester, 17/6/2005.

relevant obligations of the beneficiary towards the guarantor under the contract which would be affected by the clause.

14.11.2.6 *Negotiable instruments*

Because of the special character of a negotiable instrument and the fact that it is treated as being equivalent to cash, it is not possible for a party that is liable on the instrument to set off an unliquidated cross-claim that it may have against its obligation to make payment on the instrument, even if the cross-claim relates to the underlying transaction and is against an immediate party to the instrument.[374] Nonetheless, it should be possible to set off a liquidated cross-claim arising on a total or partial failure of consideration or fraud relating to the underlying transaction, except against a holder in due course of the instrument.[375]

It has been suggested that a party which is liable on a negotiable instrument might be entitled to assert a legal set-off against a holder of the instrument if it is sued by the holder on the instrument,[376] but this would appear to be contrary to the general approach that is taken towards such an instrument.[377]

14.11.2.6.1

It has also been suggested that, in an exceptional case, a defendant which has been sued on a negotiable instrument and is unable to assert its cross-claim by way of set-off might be entitled to obtain a stay on enforcement of a judgment on the instrument, pending the hearing of its cross-claim,[378] but that has been doubted.[379]

14.11.2.6.2

It should at least be possible to assert a cross-claim so as to resist a petition for winding up that is presented on the basis of non-payment of a negotiable instrument.[380]

14.11.2.6.3

14.11.3 Insolvency set-off

This type of set-off applies in the bankruptcy or winding up of a party and, sometimes, in an administration of a party,[381] where there are outstanding cross-liabilities as between the insolvent debtor and its creditor. The effect of the set-off is that a balance should be struck as at the date of the making of the bankruptcy or winding-up order or the date of the resolution to wind up, which will result in either a net amount due to the creditor, for which it can prove in the insolvency,

---

374 *Nova (Jersey) Knit Ltd v Kammgarn Spinnerei GmbH* [1977] 1 WLR 713.

375 Ibid; *Cebora SNC v SIP (Industrial Products) Ltd* [1976] 1 Lloyd's Rep 271.

376 See Hirst J in *Hongkong & Shanghai Banking Corp v Kloeckner & Co AG* [1990] 2 QB 514, at 524.

377 See Waller LJ in *Safa Ltd v Banque du Caire* [2000] 2 Lloyd's Rep 600, at 606.

378 *Barclays Bank Ltd v Aschaffenburger Zellstoffwerke AG* [1967] 1 Lloyd's Rep 387.

379 *Cebora SNC v SIP (Industrial Products) Ltd* [1976] 1 Lloyd's Rep 271.

380 *Re Bayoil SA* [1999] 1 WLR 147.

381 The provisions as to set-off in administration are to be found in Rule 2.85 of the Insolvency Rules 1986. They only apply if the administrator is to make a distribution pursuant to para 65 of Sched B1 to the Insolvency Act 1986. The provisions of Rule 2.85 correspond to those contained in Rule 4.90 of the Insolvency Rules 1986, so the commentary will concentrate on the latter rule.

or a net sum payable by the creditor to the insolvent estate.[382] It has also been held that the balance should be struck notwithstanding that one of the parties may hold security from the other for the debt due to the security holder.[383]

14.11.3.1 The rules of insolvency set-off in bankruptcy and winding up are mandatory and self-executing,[384] even if the other party does not lodge a proof of debt, and it is not possible to contract out of them.[385] Their effect is extensive, being wider in scope than both the rules as to legal set-off and those for transaction set-off, as they apply to all claims as between the parties and not just those that would ground an entitlement to assert either a legal set-off or a transaction set-off.

14.11.3.2 The rules of insolvency set-off depend, however, upon mutuality of what is due at the beneficial level as between the parties to the set-off,[386] so that, for instance, an assignment by one of the parties of its claim against the other before the commencement of its insolvency will destroy the mutuality of the claim as between the original parties,[387] although the debtor whose debt has been assigned may be entitled to assert its original rights of set-off against the assignee. If there is, separately, a debt due by the assignee to the insolvent debtor whose debt has been assigned, that can give rise to a set-off provided that the assignee did not acquire the debt after the winding up or with knowledge that the winding up was pending.[388] Subject to some rather difficult and imprecise qualifications, it has been suggested that mutuality would also be destroyed where the creditor has assigned the debt due to it by way of mortgage or has charged it by way of fixed charge.[389]

14.11.3.3 The rules as to bankruptcy set-off are contained in section 323 of the Insolvency Act 1986. The rules as to set-off in a winding up are contained in Rule 4.90 of the Insolvency Rules 1986. Prior to 2005, they were to substantially the same effect. Rule 4.90 was effectively replaced by a new rule in 2005,[390] and much of the previous difficulty in interpretation of the old rule, particularly as to the determination

---

[382] See Hoffmann LJ, sitting at first instance, in *MS Fashions Ltd v Bank of Credit and Commerce International SA* [1993] Ch 425 (affd [1993] Ch 439) and Lord Hoffmann in *Stein v Blake* [1996] AC 243.

[383] See Jonathan Parker J in *Re ILG Travel Ltd* [1996] BCC 21, at 46–48.

[384] There is a substantial departure from this principle in respect of set-off in an administration, as the rules will only apply if the administrator decides to make a distribution, as mentioned above.

[385] *National Westminster Bank Ltd v Halesowen Presswork and Assemblies Ltd* [1972] AC 785. See also Lord Hoffmann in *Stein v Blake* [1996] AC 243, at 253. This does appear to be contrary to the express wording of the statutory provisions, which speak of the set-off arising where the creditor proves or claims to prove in the bankruptcy or winding up. This is also subject, however, to the discussion above as to a cross-border insolvency in an EC context.

[386] As to which, see *Re West End Networks Ltd, Secretary of State v Frid* [2004] UKHL 24, [2004] 2 AC 506.

[387] *Re City Life Assurance Co; Stephenson's Case* [1926] 1 Ch 191, at 214.

[388] Rule 4.90(2)(d) of the Insolvency Rules 1986.

[389] See Derham, *The Law of Set-Off* (3rd edn, 2003) at paras 11.25–11.36.

[390] In consequence of the Insolvency (Amendment) Rules 2005 (SI 2005/527).

of what might be 'due' as between the parties, was addressed by the new rule. However, the wording of section 323 of the Insolvency Act 1986 was not changed and so it is necessary to provide a summary of the law as it has developed in relation to the old provision. The new form of Rule 4.90 reflects much of what the case law had eventually determined was the position under the old wording. Rule 4.90 is set out at a later point in this discussion.

14.11.3.4 *Set-off in bankruptcy*

Section 323 provides as follows:

(1) This section applies where before the commencement of the bankruptcy there have been mutual credits, mutual debts or other mutual dealings between the bankrupt and any creditor of the bankrupt proving or claiming to prove for a bankruptcy debt.

(2) An account shall be taken of what is due from each party to the other in respect of the mutual dealings and the sums due from one party shall be set-off against the sums due from the other.

(3) Sums due from the bankrupt to another party shall not be included in the account taken under subsection (2) if that other party had notice at the time they became due that a bankruptcy petition relating to the bankrupt was pending.

(4) Only the balance (if any) of the account taken under subsection (2) is provable as a bankruptcy debt or, as the case may be, to be paid to the trustee as part of the bankrupt's estate.

Section 323, which concerns set-off in bankruptcy, is a re-enactment of the rules that had applied under section 31 of the Bankruptcy Act 1914. It requires an account to be taken of what is 'due' as between the bankrupt and the creditor arising from the 'mutual credits, mutual debts or other mutual dealings' between the parties prior to the commencement of the insolvency proceedings (the commencement of the bankruptcy being the date of the bankruptcy order). It has been held that 'mutual credits, mutual debts or other mutual dealings' has an extended meaning referring to the existence of mutual cross-obligations from which the claims to be set-off arose, howsoever they had arisen.[391]

14.11.3.4.1

The principal difficulty that had arisen under the section concerned unquantified or contingent and unascertained liabilities of the bankrupt to the other party which had existed before the bankruptcy but had not crystallised into an actual liability for an ascertained amount prior to the bankruptcy. It was unclear whether such claims should be taken into account as being due in computing the set-off and, if so, how that should be done. At the same time, it had been decided that contingent and unascertained claims due to the insolvent debtor by the other party could not be taken into account if they had not crystallised and matured

14.11.3.4.2

---

[391] See Lord Hoffmann in *Re West End Networks Ltd, Secretary of State v Frid* [2004] UKHL 24; [2004] 2 AC 506, at 514–515.

into quantified liabilities before the end of the bankruptcy.[392] This is changed in the new form of Rule 4.90.

14.11.3.4.3 In a series of decisions, particularly in the period since the mid-1980s, the courts have held that it is not necessary that the debt or other obligation of the insolvent debtor which is to be set-off should have been actually due and payable as well as quantified prior to the date of the commencement of the bankruptcy or winding up. Lords Hoffmann and Millett have played a significant role in those decisions. It has been held that it is sufficient that there had been a liability at that date which had crystallised into an actual monetary claim after the commencement of the insolvency proceedings or which could otherwise be anticipated and valued.[393] It was also possible to take into account events that had occurred after the date of the commencement of the insolvency to ascertain the correct amount of the liability.[394]

14.11.3.4.4 By way of example, the principles established in those cases have applied where there was a pre-existing contract which was breached after the commencement of the insolvency proceedings.[395] The principle has also applied where a guarantor has claimed an indemnity from an insolvent debtor with respect to a payment made under a guarantee, where the guarantee had been given before the debtor's insolvency, even though the payment under it was made after the commencement of the insolvency proceedings.[396] Of course, the surety must have a claim which it could prove in the debtor's insolvency but for the set-off, so if the surety has not made any payment under its guarantee then the rule against doubt proof would operate to preclude the surety submitting a proof and so the set-off could not arise.[397]

14.11.3.5 *Set-off in a winding up*

As already said, much of the case law on insolvency set-off is now reflected in the new form of Rule 4.90, which concerns set-off in a winding up. The Rule provides as follows:

> (1) This Rule applies where, before the company goes into liquidation there have been mutual credits, mutual debts or other mutual dealings between the company and any creditor of the company proving or claiming to prove for a debt in the liquidation.

---

[392] See Lord Hoffmann in *Stein v Blake* [1996] AC 243, at 253.

[393] See Millett J in *In re Charge Card Services Ltd* [1987] Ch 150; Lord Hoffmann in *Stein v Blake* [1996] AC 243; and Lord Hoffmann in *Re West End Networks Ltd, Secretary of State v Frid* [2004] UKHL 24, [2004] 2 AC 506.

[394] Sometimes referred to as the 'hindsight principle'. Lord Hoffmann explained the application of the principle in *Wight v Eckhardt Marine GmbH* [2003] UKPC 37, [2004] 1 AC 147.

[395] *In re Asphaltic Wood Pavement Co Ltd* (1885) 30 ChD 216.

[396] *In re Moseley-Green Coal and Coke Co Ltd* (1865) 12 LT (NS) 193. See also Lord Hoffmann in *Re West End Networks Ltd, Secretary of State v Frid* [2004] UKHL 24, [2004] 2 AC 506.

[397] See *Re Fenton* [1931] 1 Ch 85 and Lord Hoffmann in *Re West End Networks Ltd, Secretary of State v Frid* [2004] UKHL 24, [2004] 2 AC 506.

(2) The reference in para. (1) to mutual credits, mutual debts or other mutual dealings does not include—

    (a) [debts arising under obligations incurred after the creditor knew of the summoning of a meeting of creditors or the presentation of a petition for winding up];

    (b) [debts arising under obligations incurred with notice of steps for a preceding administration of the debtor];

    (c) [debts arising under obligations incurred in such an administration];

    (d) [debts acquired by assignment or otherwise after the winding up or preceding administration began or which were acquired with notice of steps to achieve such a winding up or administration].

(3) An account shall be taken of what is due from each party to the other in respect of the mutual dealings, and the sums due from one party shall be set-off against the sums due from the other.

(4) A sum shall be regarded as being due to or from the company for the purposes of para. (3) whether—

    (a) it is payable at present or in the future;

    (b) the obligation by virtue of which it is payable is certain or contingent; or

    (c) its amount is fixed or liquidated, or is capable of being ascertained by fixed rules or as a matter of opinion.

(5) Rule 4.86 [which provides for estimation of the value of an obligation] shall also apply for the purposes of this Rule to any obligation to or from the company which, by reason of its being subject to any contingency or for any other reason, does not have a certain value.

(6) Rules 4.91 to 4.93 [which provide for converting debts in foreign currencies, periodical payments and interest] shall apply for the purposes of this Rule . . .

(7) Rule 11.13 [which provides a discounting factor to be applied in ascertaining the value of future debts] shall apply for the purposes of this Rule to any sum due to or from the company which is payable in the future.

(8) Only the balance (if any) of the account owed to the creditor is provable in the liquidation. Alternatively, the balance (if any) owed to the company shall be paid to the liquidator as part of the assets except where all or part of the balance results from a contingent or prospective debt owed by the creditor and in such a case the balance (or that part of it which results from the contingent or prospective debt) shall be paid if and when that debt becomes due and payable.

(9) In this Rule, 'obligation' means an obligation however arising, whether by virtue of an agreement, rule of law or otherwise.

The previous law as to the expansive interpretation of the words, 'mutual credits, mutual debts or other mutual dealings' will continue to apply to those words as used in paragraph 1, so that the Rule will apply to the existence of mutual cross-obligations from which the claims to be set-off arose, howsoever they may have arisen.   **14.11.3.5.1**

Paragraph (2) is wider than the equivalent provision in section 323(3) of the Insolvency Act 1986.[398] In particular, section 323(3) does not contain any equivalent to paragraph 2(d) of Rule 4.90.   **14.11.3.5.2**

---

[398] Which, in any event, refers only to the creditor having notice of a pending bankruptcy petition concerning the insolvent debtor.

14.11.3.5.3 Paragraphs (4) and (9) emphasise the width in scope of the claims and liabilities that should be taken into account. It should be noted that paragraph (4) makes it clear that, unlike the old law, contingent and future claims due to the insolvent company by the other party should be taken into account. Paragraphs (5), (6), and (7) make provision as to the methods of valuing contingent and future claims and claims in foreign currencies. This might lead to an injustice if it eventuates, particularly after the winding up has been completed, that an incorrect valuation was placed on a claim.

14.12 *Quistclose* Trusts

14.12.1 The *Quistclose* case

The decision of the House of Lords in *Quistclose Investments Ltd v Rolls Razor Ltd*[399] caused quite a stir. The leading speech in the case was delivered by Lord Wilberforce. In his decision, Lord Wilberforce recognised the possibility of the co-existence of legal and equitable remedies to protect a lender for the repayment of its loan. In addition to the right to sue at law for the repayment of the loan, a lender which had provided funds to a borrower to be used for some specific purpose might also be able to pray in aid the law of trusts for the lender's protection in the event that the proceeds of the loan could not be used for that purpose. Such protection might be valuable in the event of the insolvency of the borrower.

14.12.1.1 In the *Quistclose* case, the loan had been provided to enable a company to pay its shareholders a dividend which had been declared but which the company did not have the funds to pay. Before the date for payment of the dividend, the company went into voluntary liquidation, which meant that the dividend could not lawfully be paid. Although there was no evidence that the parties to the transaction had contemplated that their arrangements would constitute anything other than the usual relationship of debtor and creditor, the lender sought to recover its loan by asserting that the proceeds of the loan, which had been paid into a separate account at the borrower's bank, were held on trust for the lender.

14.12.1.2 Lord Wilberforce spoke of such arrangements giving rise in equity 'to a relationship of a fiduciary character or trust, in favour, as a primary trust, of the [shareholders] and, secondarily, if the primary trust fails, of the [lender]'. In the event that the primary trust is carried out and the proceeds of the loan are used for the agreed purpose for which they were provided, then the lender would simply be left with its common law rights as a creditor to sue for repayment of the loan if it was not repaid. In the event of the borrower's insolvency, the claim for repayment

---

[399] [1970] AC 567.

would suffer along with all the other claims of the unsecured creditors. If the primary trust could not be achieved and failed, so that the moneys were not applied for the relevant purpose, then the secondary trust would protect the lender, which could achieve repayment as the beneficial owner of the funds. Not only is this a valuable right in the event of the borrower's insolvency but it might also prevail over the competing interests of third parties who are on notice of the lender's rights, as indeed was the case in the *Quistclose* case where the bank, which was holding the funds, was denied a right of set-off against those funds for its exposure to the company on facilities it had provided.

14.12.2 Other cases

The decision in the *Quistclose* case has been followed and applied in numerous cases, not just in relation to loans of money but also in connection with other payments made for some specific purpose. For instance, in *Carreras Rothman Ltd v Freeman Mathews Treasure Ltd*,[400] the *Quistclose* case was invoked in relation to a payment made by a recipient of advertising services to the provider of those services, so as to enable the services provider to meet disbursements owing by it to third parties for work done in advertising the products of the services recipient. The services provider became insolvent before the money had been applied and the liquidator asserted that the money was part of the insolvent's estate, available to meet the claims of the general body of its creditors. The services recipient was able to rely upon the *Quistclose* case to defeat the liquidator, although it is not entirely clear if it did so to force the funds to be used for payment of the third parties' claims (of which it had taken an assignment) or for repayment to it of the funds on the basis that they had not been used for the agreed purpose for which they had been provided.

14.12.3 The type of trust

Trusts along the lines of the authority in the *Quistclose* case are sometimes referred to as 'Quistclose Trusts', as if they were a special class of trust. This reflects the difficulties that have been experienced in seeking to fit this type of trust within the established and orthodox categories of trust as traditionally understood by English law. Not the least of those difficulties concerns the manner of classifying the trusts that are said to arise and, indeed, if it is correct to say that such arrangements could give rise to any trusts at all. For instance, it is often a hard, if not impossible, task to locate sufficient evidence of any form of intention held by the relevant parties that would support the trusts and beneficial interests that are said to arise from the expression of some particular purpose for which the funds

---

[400] [1985] Ch 207.

are to be used.[401] If there are trusts then it may be questionable whether they are express or implied trusts, whether there is one trust or two trusts, if there is one trust, whether it has one or two limbs, whether in their primary form such trusts are for the benefit of identifiable beneficiaries or are for some purpose, how the interest arises under the secondary limb or trust, and the nature of the rights enjoyed by the potential beneficiaries under the two trusts or limbs, particularly in the period before it is certain if the primary trust or limb will be carried out.

14.12.3.1 Although Lord Wilberforce in the *Quistclose* case said that the primary trust that he described was in favour of the shareholders to whom the dividend was payable, the language that he used and some of the subsequent cases would appear to indicate that such a primary trust might be described as a type of purpose trust. Indeed, Sir Robert Megarry V-C in *In re Northern Developments (Holdings) Ltd*[402] seems to have identified the arrangements in that case as giving rise to a purpose trust which was enforceable by identified individuals, even though the beneficial interests under either trust or limb might not have vested but were held in suspense pending the outcome of the arrangements.[403] In *Re EVTR*[404] the Court of Appeal was willing to accept that there was a primary trust of the proceeds of a loan 'for the purchase of equipment'. This is troubling because it is a fairly elementary principle of the law of trusts that, with very limited exceptions, it is not possible to have private purpose trusts.

14.12.4 The questionable need for protection

It is questionable if lenders and other providers of funds really need the protection that the *Quistclose* case purports to give them. The *Quistclose* case is seen as furnishing a form of quasi-security as protection to an otherwise unsecured lender against the default of a borrower, where the lender has parted with its funds before they are needed for the requisite purpose. However, in devising unsecured loan facilities, lenders and their lawyers are quite familiar with employing structures which ensure that the funds can only be drawn down at the time they are required for application for the purpose identified in the facility. If the borrower is unable to meet the stipulated requirements then the funds will not be provided and the lender will still have its money. A similar device could be also be used in other forms of transaction. Furthermore, the law already provides protection for those lenders who wish to be protected from an insolvency of a borrower. The lenders could take security for repayment. That could have been done in the *Quistclose* case, where the lender could have taken security over the balance standing to the

---

[401] See, for instance, the difficulties that were encountered in *Re Goldcorp Exchange Ltd* [1995] 1 AC 74 and in *Re Farepak Food and Gifts Ltd* [2006] EWHC 3272 (Ch), [2007] 1 BCLC 1.

[402] Unreported, 6/10/1978.

[403] See also the discussion by Peter Gibson J in the *Carreras Rothmans* case [1985] Ch 207, at 222.

[404] [1987] BCLC 646.

credit of the account at Barclays Bank, although it must be conceded that such security would probably only have been by way of floating charge. Following the decision of the House of Lords in *Re Bank of Credit and Commerce International SA (No 8)*,[405] security could now also be taken by a bank lender where the proceeds of the loan had been credited to an account with the bank itself. It is also possible for the provider of the funds, including a provider who has provided the funds, otherwise than by way of loan, to gain protection before the funds have been used, by stipulating expressly for the funds from the outset to be impressed with a trust in its favour pending disbursement of the funds as the provider of the funds has approved.[406] A further possibility is that a recipient of funds can declare itself to be the trustee of them under an express trust.[407]

14.12.5 Sufficient intention or purpose

There is also a difficulty in ascertaining when the intention or purpose of the arrangement has been defined with sufficient precision so as to invoke the aid of the *Quistclose* case. Lord Wilberforce made it clear that there must be a 'specific purpose' underlying the intended use of the money. The difficulty which then arises is to understand the point at which an arrangement will be incapable of identification with sufficient precision for the *Quistclose* case to apply. In the *Quistclose* case the purpose was specific enough for the protection to follow. It must be questionable, however, if the purpose of using funds for the purchase of equipment in *Re EVTR* was sufficiently specific to deserve the favourable result given to the lender of the funds in that case. On the other hand, in *Re Challoner Club Ltd*[408] it was held that funds provided by the members of a club to its directors, to be used for the purpose of safeguarding its future, was too imprecise as a purpose to prevent the funds from falling into the hands of the club's liquidator.[409]

14.12.6 Acceptance of the principle

Notwithstanding the various doubts that have arisen following the decision in the *Quistclose* case, it has to be admitted that a number of eminent judicial minds have accepted that trusts of the type described in the *Quistclose* case can exist, although there remains uncertainty as to the basis of the principles it established. Such a body of judges is headed by Lord Wilberforce, Lord Millett,[410] and Lord

---

[405] [1998] AC 214.

[406] See, for instance, the example given by Lord Millett of the solicitor in *Twinsectra Ltd v Yardley* [2002] UKHL 12; [2002] 2 AC 164, at [99].

[407] As was done in *Re Kayford Ltd* [1975] 1 WLR 279. See also *OT Computers Ltd v First National Tricity Finance Ltd* [2003] EWHC 1010 (Ch), at [14]–[16].

[408] The Times, 4/11/1997.

[409] See also *Re Holiday Promotions (Europe) Ltd* [1996] BCC 671.

[410] See *Twinsectra Ltd v Yardley* [2002] UKHL 12, [2002] 2 AC 164.

Browne-Wilkinson,[411] and also includes Sir Robert Megarry, Sir Christopher Slade,[412] and Mr Justice Gummow in Australia.[413] There have been a number of attempts by academics to provide an analysis of the *Quistclose* case and the principles that flow from it.[414]

14.12.7 Lord Millett's analysis

Lord Millett provided a useful analysis of the *Quistclose* case in *Twinsectra Ltd v Yardley*.[415] Lord Millett said in the *Twinsectra* case that the beneficial interest in the funds should be considered, even if not expressed by the parties as such, as remaining from the outset in the lender or provider of the funds, so that the borrower or recipient is simply a trustee holding the funds for such a lender or provider of funds on a resulting trust, with a power or duty to disburse the funds in the circumstances contemplated by the arrangements agreed between them. On this basis, the third parties who were intended to receive the funds would not acquire any beneficial or other enforceable interest in them until such time as the funds had been disbursed to them. Lord Millett's analysis provides a much needed rationale for this area of the law, although it has to be said that it is at variance with the views expressed in some of the other cases mentioned above. A difficulty that arises in Lord Millett's analysis would concern the situation where the provider of the funds became insolvent and went into liquidation before the funds had been used for the agreed purpose. At that point, the authority of the borrower to disperse the funds would cease, despite the fact that the borrower had borrowed the funds and had contracted for the right to use them.

14.12.8 Money received when the recipient has stopped trading

A different line of authority, but one which might also be raised in conjunction with a *Quistclose* case argument, is based upon what was said in *Neste Oy v Lloyds Bank PLC*.[416] In that case it was held that where money is received by a company under a contract for the provision of goods or services at a time that it has decided to cease trading it cannot, in conscience, retain that money and should return it (assuming that it is unable or unwilling to perform the contract). A constructive trust would be imposed on the money to protect it. The decision has been highly controversial and it has been doubted.[417]

---

[411] See *Westdeutsche Landesbank Girozentrale v Islington LBC* [1996] AC 669, at 707–708.
[412] See *R v Common Professional Examination Board, ex p Mealing-McCleod*, The Times 19/4/2000.
[413] See *Re Australian Elizabethan Theatre Trust* (1991) 102 ALR 681.
[414] See William Swaddling (ed), *The Quistclose Trust: Critical Essays* (Hart, 2004).
[415] [2002] UKHL 12; [2002] 2 AC 164, at [52]–[103].
[416] [1983] 2 Lloyd's Rep 658.
[417] See the discussion by Mann J in in *Re Farepak Food and Gifts Ltd* [2006] EWHC 3272 (Ch); [2007] 1 BCLC 1, at [37]–[40].

14.13 Company Registration Requirements

Part 25 of the Companies Act 2006 (the 'Act') deals with the requirement for the   **14.13.1**
registration of company charges, that is, security given by companies.[418] Part 25
largely re-enacts the previous provisions of Part XII of the Companies Act 1985,[419]
although the legislature could not resist the temptation needlessly to re-order the
provisions and scatter them around, rather than leaving them in the same order
in which they had previously appeared. An earlier attempt in the Companies Act
1989 at amending and modifying the provisions of Part XII of the Companies Act
1985 never came into force.[420] The proposals that the Law Commission put forward for a more radical shake-up of the system have also fallen by the wayside.[421]

Chapter 1 of Part 25 (being sections 860 to 877 of the Act) deals with the require-   **14.13.1.1**
ments for the registration of charges created by companies that are registered in
England and Wales or Northern Ireland. Chapter 2 contains the provisions for
companies that are registered in Scotland.[422] Chapter 3 contains various powers
for making secondary legislation. The discussion that follows will concentrate on
the provisions of Chapter 1 of Part 25, with some additional reference to Chapter 3
of Part 25 at the end. It will also be necessary to refer to section 1052 of the
Companies Act 2006, which concerns security over property in the UK which is
given by a registered overseas company.

14.13.2 The obligation to register

Section 860 (1) of the Act[423] requires that if a company that is registered in England
and Wales or in Northern Ireland[424] creates a registrable charge (the categories of
such charges is addressed below) then the charge, together with the prescribed

---

[418] At the time of writing, it was anticipated that Part 25 would be brought into force on
1/10/2009. For the purposes of the current discussion, Part 25 will be treated as being in force, with
appropriate cross-referencing to the previous provisions in Part XII of the Companies Act 1985,
which were to remain in force until Part 25 took effect.

[419] Which, in turn, replaced the corresponding provisions of s 95 et seq of the Companies Act
1948. The legislative history of these provisions goes back to s 14 of the Companies Act 1900,
which was extended by s 10(1)(e) of the Companies Act 1907 and further extended by s 43(1) of
the Companies Act 1928 and s 79 of the Companies Act 1929 to what was pretty much the same as
the present legislation. The 1948 Act, which replaced the previous legislation was, in turn, replaced
by the 1985 Act.

[420] See ss 92–104 of the Companies Act 1989.

[421] These are described in Chap 17.

[422] The failure by a Scottish company to comply with the registration requirements of Chapter 2
would be a matter that was justiciable before the English courts: *Arthur D Little Ltd v Ableco Finance
LLC* [2002] EWHC 701 (Ch), [2003] Ch 217.

[423] Formerly s 395(1) of the 1985 Act.

[424] See s 861(5) of the Act.

particulars of the charge,[425] must be delivered to the Registrar of Companies within a set period.[426] The period is, essentially, 21 days from the date of creation of the charge, which is extended if the charge is created outside the UK.[427] The delivery should be effected by the company or, pursuant to section 860(2),[428] it may be effected by any other person interested in the charge, such as the chargee, being the person with the greatest practical interest in ensuring that the statutory requirements are fulfilled. Section 866 of the Act contains provisions which contain limited alternatives relating to charges created outside the UK or charges created over property situated outside the UK.[429] Section 867 of the Act contains provisions that relate to charges created in, or over property situated in, Scotland or Northern Ireland.[430]

14.13.2.1 Section 862 of the Act[431] requires that if a company acquires property that is already subject to a registrable charge, it must deliver a copy of the charge, together with the prescribed particulars, to the Registrar of Companies within the prescribed period.[432] Failure to meet this requirement is an offence on the part of the company and its officers, punishable by a fine.

14.13.2.2 For the purposes of Chapter 25 of the Act, section 861(5) of the Act provides that the expression 'charge' also includes a mortgage.[433]

14.13.2.3 For convenience, the process of delivering the charge and the prescribed particulars to the Registrar of Companies will be referred to below as 'registering' the charge, although the statutory obligation is merely to make the delivery.

14.13.3 The consequences of a failure to register

Subject to the court permitting late registration pursuant to section 873 of the Act (which is dealt with below), the civil law consequence[434] of a failure to register a

---

[425] I.e. a form setting out various brief particulars of the chargor, the chargee, the date of the charge, the liabilities secured under the charge and a description of the charge and the charged property, previously known as 'Form 395'. In December 2007 the Department for Business, Enterprise and Regulatory Reform circulated a draft statutory instrument which, if implemented, would also provide for registration under s 860 of the Companies Act 2006 of the details of a negative pledge relating to a floating charge.

[426] Ss 875–877 (formerly ss 406–488 of the 1985 Act) additionally make provision for the company to maintain its own register of charges and to keep copies and allow inspection thereof.

[427] S 870(1) of the Act (formerly ss 395 and 398(2) of the 1985 Act).

[428] Formerly s 399(1) of the 1985 Act.

[429] Formerly ss 398(1) and (3) of the 1985 Act.

[430] Formerly s 398(4) of the 1985 Act.

[431] Formerly s 400 of the 1985 Act.

[432] As set out in s 870(2) of the Act (formerly ss 400(2) and (3) of the 1985 Act).

[433] Formerly s 396(4) of the 1985 Act.

[434] The criminal law consequence of a failure to comply is dealt with in ss 860 (4) and (5) of the Act (formerly s 399(3) of the 1985 Act).

charge as required by section 860(1) within the requisite period is set out in section 874 of the Act.[435] It provides that the unregistered charge is void, with respect to the assets covered by the charge, as against a liquidator, administrator, or 'creditor' of the company, but that is to be without prejudice to any relevant contract. The money secured by the unregistered charge becomes immediately payable. The effect of the section is to avoid the unregistered charge as from the date when the security was created and not just from the date of the liquidation or administration.[436]

A 'creditor' for the purposes of the section, that is, a creditor against whom the unregistered charge is void, means a creditor with a proprietary interest in the charged assets, namely, a secured creditor or an execution creditor.[437] This is because unsecured creditors have no proprietary entitlement in the assets before the onset of an insolvency of the chargor, and their interests are represented by the liquidator or administrator in the liquidation or administration of the chargor. **14.13.3.1**

In *Smith (Administrator of Cosslett (Contractors) Ltd) v Bridgend CBC*[438] the House of Lords considered what was meant when the section said that the unregistered charge was void as against a liquidator or administrator of the company. The wording meant that the charge was void as against the company in liquidation or administration, as represented by that person. The intention was to protect the interests of the company, so that the charged assets would be available to the company and its creditors as if the charge did not exist. One result of this was that the liquidator or administrator was entitled to pursue the invalidity on behalf of company, including the right of the company to bring an action for conversion against the chargee which had wrongly enforced the void security and disposed of the charged assets. **14.13.3.2**

Where the charged property consists of debts that have been assigned to the chargee under an unregistered charge, and the chargor goes into liquidation or administration, the chargee is not entitled to receive the debts because they are treated as being the unencumbered property of the chargor. This also has the effect that the chargee cannot demand payment of the debts and the debtor is entitled to rely on the section to refuse to pay the chargee and, instead, to account to the chargor.[439] **14.13.3.3**

---

[435] Formerly s 395 of the 1985 Act. The effect of these provisions may be contrasted with the position that applies under s 8 of the Bills of Sale Act (1878) Amendment Act 1882 with respect to security given by an individual over personal chattels, by virtue of which unregistered security is void for all purposes with respect to the assets comprised in the security.

[436] *Paul & Frank Ltd v Discount Bank (Overseas) Ltd* [1967] Ch 348, at 362 and *Orion Finance Ltd v Crown Financial Management Ltd* [1996] BCC 621, at 633.

[437] See Lord Brightman, sitting in the Court of Appeal, in *Re Ashpurton Estates Ltd* [1983] Ch 110, at 119, relying upon the earlier decision of the Court of Appeal in *Re Ehrmann Brothers Ltd* [1906] 2 Ch 697.

[438] [2001] UKHL 58, [2002] 1 AC 336.

[439] *Orion Finance Ltd v Crown Financial Management Ltd* [1996] BCC 621, at 631–635.

Otherwise, the debtor would be at risk of being in double jeopardy in being obliged to pay both the liquidator or administrator of the chargor, as well as the chargee.

14.13.3.4 It should be noted that a purchaser of charged assets is not entitled to rely on the section to assert the invalidity of the security.[440] That deficiency would have been cured by the amendments to the companies charges registration regime that were contemplated by the Companies Act 1989.[441]

14.13.4 The categories of registrable charge

Section 860(7) of the Act[442] provides that the categories of registrable charge are as follows:

(a) a charge on land or any interest in land, other than a charge for any rent or other periodical sum issuing out of land,[443]

(b) a charge created or evidenced by an instrument which, if executed by an individual, would require registration as a bill of sale,

(c) a charge for the purposes of securing any issue of debentures,[444]

(d) a charge on uncalled share capital of the company,

(e) a charge on calls made but not paid,

(f) a charge on book debts of the company,[445]

(g) a floating charge on the company's property or undertaking,

(h) a charge on a ship or aircraft, or any share in a ship,

(i) a charge on goodwill or any intellectual property.[446]

14.13.4.1 Before discussing some of the individual paragraphs in the section, it must be remembered that security which amounts to a 'security financial collateral arrangement' for the purposes of the Financial Collateral Arrangements (No 2) Regulations 2003[447] is exempt from the registration requirements under section 860 of the Act.[448] This is discussed above.

14.13.4.2 Security over goods

In relation to paragraph (b), see the earlier discussion in this chapter concerning bills of sale. Essentially, the paragraph applies to security which is given over personal chattels, that is, most situations where non-possessory security is given over goods.

---

[440] A point that was overlooked in *E Pfeiffer Weinkellerei-Weineinkauf GmbH v Arbuthnot Factors Ltd* [1988] 1 WLR 150.

[441] See s 399(1)(a) of the Companies Act 1985, as inserted by s 95 of the Companies Act 1989.

[442] Formerly s 396(1) of the 1985 Act.

[443] See also ss 861(1) and (2) (formerly s 396(3) and 396(1)(d) of the 1985 Act).

[444] See also ss 863, 864 and 865 (formerly ss 397, 399 and 402 of the 1985 Act).

[445] See also s 861(3) (formerly s 396(2) of the 1985 Act)

[446] For the definition of 'intellectual property' see s 861(4) (formerly s 396(3A) of the 1985 Act).

[447] SI 2003/3226.

[448] Reg 4(4) of the Regulations.

It has been suggested that the paragraph would still apply to security over future personal chattels, even though section 5 of the Bills of Sale Act (1878) Amendment Act 1882 provides that a bill of sale over such chattels is void, save as against the grantor.[449] The conclusion that was drawn was that the security would still be a bill of sale within the meaning of that Act, which required registration, albeit that the security over the future chattels would be void. A failure to register would render the bill of sale void with respect to the personal chattels concerned, even as against the grantor of the security.[450]

14.13.4.3 *Security over book debts*

Paragraph (f) relates to charges on 'book debts', which is a rather antique phrase that should have been updated, but it persists in the legislation. The case law has established that the phrase should be interpreted in accordance with accounting practice and that it was intended to refer to both present and future book debts.[451] It refers to debts that could or would in the ordinary course of business be entered into well-kept books of that business,[452] whether or not they were actually entered in the books of the chargor.[453] It does not, however, include the benefit of a contract which would not, without more, give rise to a book debt or would only do so on the happening of a contingency, such as the benefit of an insurance policy.[454]

The question has arisen as to whether a charge over the benefit of a bank account **14.13.4.3.1** would amount to a charge on a book debt. In a series of cases involving the construction of the expression 'book debts' in security instruments, rather than its use in the legislation, but where the expression has been construed in accordance with accounting practice, the courts have concluded that the balance on a bank account would not be a book debt but, rather, would be considered to be 'cash at bank' and thus would appear under a different category of the assets of a company.[455]

14.13.4.4 *Floating charges*

Paragraph (g) requires that any floating charge should be registered. This is irrespective of whether or not the security would have been registrable had it been by

---

449 See Sir Nicholas Browne-Wilkinson V-C in *Welsh Development Agency v Export Finance Co Ltd* [1990] BCC 393, at 410–411.

450 S 8 of the 1882 Act.

451 *Independent Automatic Sales Ltd v Knowles and Foster* [1962] 1 WLR 974; *Paul & Frank Ltd v Discount Bank (Overseas) Ltd* [1967] Ch 348.

452 *Shipley v Marshall* (1863) 14 CBNS 566.

453 *Independent Automatic Sales Ltd v Knowles and Foster* [1962] 1 WLR 974.

454 *Paul & Frank Ltd v Discount Bank (Overseas) Ltd* [1967] Ch 348.

455 *Re Brightlife Ltd* [1987] Ch 200; *Re Permanent Houses (Holdings) Ltd* (1989) 5 BCC 151; *Northern Bank Ltd v Ross* [1990] BCC 883. The latter case was referred to with apparent approval by Lord Hoffmann in *Re Bank of Credit and Commerce International SA (No 8)* [1998] AC 214, at 227. In the *Northern Bank* case, uncollected cheques and outstanding amounts due from credit card companies were held to be book debts.

way of fixed charge, in other words, even if the charged assets are not mentioned in one of the other paragraphs of section 860(7) of the Act. Lord Scott in *Smith (Administrator of Cosslett (Contractors) Ltd) v Bridgend CBC*[456] ventured the view that an agreement to give a charge on the occurrence of an uncertain future event over assets that would then be identified would amount to an agreement to give a floating charge which, in itself, would require registration.[457]

14.13.4.5 *Security not requiring registration*

Subject to the point that has just been made concerning floating charges and security for an issue of debentures, security over the shares in a company (other than within paragraphs (d) or (e)), and security over a bank balance or ordinary contractual rights (where such contractual rights do not amount to book debts, an interest in land, or rights with respect to intellectual property) does not fall within the registrable categories. In addition, possessory security by way of pledge or lien is not registrable, because it would not amount to a bill of sale under the 1882 Act. On the other hand, a written agreement to give such security might amount to a charge and would be registrable.[458] An equitable lien, which arises by operation of law, is not registrable, as it is not security that is 'created' by the company.

14.13.4.5.1 Apart from possessory security and equitable liens, it is difficult to understand why there should be any exemptions from the requirement for registration, as the whole point of having a registration system is so that third parties which wish to deal with a company can make a search at the Companies Registry and discover the true state of affairs, including as to whether the company has given security to other persons.

14.13.4.5.2 As mentioned above, security which arises under a security financial collateral arrangement does not require to be registered, assuming it would otherwise have been registerable.

14.13.5 The register of charges

Section 869 of the Act[459] provides for the register of charges for each company, which must be maintained by the Companies Registry. The register contains the brief particulars that have to be delivered when the charge instrument is delivered under section 860 or section 862 of the Act. The register may be searched by the public. Neither the charge instrument, nor a copy of it, is placed on the register nor, indeed, retained within the Companies Registry. Provided that the statutory requirements have been met as to delivery of the charging instrument and accompanying

---

[456] [2001] UKHL 58; [2002] AC 336, at [63].
[457] His Lordship returned to this theme, in passing, in *National Westminster Bank PLC v Spectrum Plus Ltd* [2005] UKHL 41; [2005] 2 AC 680, at [107].
[458] *Re Townsend* (1886) 16 QBD 532; *Dublin City Distillery Ltd v Doherty* [1914] AC 823.
[459] Formerly s 401 of the 1985 Act.

particulars, the Registrar must issue a certificate of registration, which must state the amount secured. Issuance of the certificate is conclusive evidence that the statutory requirements have been met[460] even if, as a matter of fact, there has been some defect.[461]

Section 871 of the Act[462] provides that if a receiver of a company's property is **14.13.5.1** appointed, by either the court or under a security instrument, the person who obtained the court appointment, or who appointed the receiver under the security, must notify the Registrar of Companies of the appointment within seven days after the appointment. Upon relinquishing his appointment, if appointed under a security instrument, the receiver must notify the Registrar of that fact. It is an offence if those requirements are not met.

Section 872 of the Act[463] provides for the Registrar to enter a note on the register **14.13.5.2** of the satisfaction, in whole or in part, of the amount secured by, or the assets comprised within, a registered charge.

14.13.6 Late registration

Section 873 of the Act[464] provides for the court to grant permission for the late registration of a charge or for the rectification of the register where there has been an omission or mis-statement. What follows will concentrate on applications for late registration.[465]

The court is given a wide power of discretion to permit late registration.[466] There **14.13.6.1** are limits, however, as to the circumstances in which the court will be prepared to exercise its discretion.[467] In the first place, the court will not look favourably on an application where there has been knowing delay in seeking relief after the failure to register has been discovered.[468] Secondly, the court will refuse to permit registration where proceedings for winding up have been commenced when the application is made for permission.[469] Where winding-up proceedings were imminent at the

---

[460] S 869(6)(b) (formerly s 401(2)(b) of the 1985 Act).

[461] *Re CL Nye Ltd* [1971] Ch 442.

[462] Formerly s 405 of the 1985 Act.

[463] Formerly s 403 of the 1985 Act.

[464] Formerly s 404 of the 1985 Act.

[465] As to the rectification of an error, see *Igroup Ltd v Ocwen* [2003] EWHC 2431 (Ch), [2004] 1 WLR 451.

[466] *Re Braemar Investments Ltd* [1989] Ch 54.

[467] In addition to the grounds now mentioned, it is submitted that permission would be refused where there had been a deliberate decision by the chargee not to register when it knew that the charge should be registered: this can be inferred from *Barclays Bank PLC v Stuart Landon Ltd* [2001] EWCA Civ 140; [2002] BCC 917, at [16].

[468] *Re Ashpurton Estates Ltd* [1983] Ch 110. On this point, it might be argued that the court was unduly sympathetic in *Re Fablehill Ltd* [1991] BCC 590.

[469] *Re Ashpurton Estates Ltd* [1983] Ch 110. In that case, the court also refused permission where the insolvency proceedings had been commenced whilst an appeal against a refusal to grant

time of the application, but had not yet been commenced, that fact was a relevant factor for the court to consider but the court should still be prepared to grant permission unless it was certain that a later application to have the permission set aside (as shortly to be referred to) was bound to succeed.[470]

14.13.6.2　If the court grants permission for late registration, it will normally provide in its order that the late registration is to be without prejudice to the interests of third parties that have been acquired in the charged assets prior to the date that late registration takes place.[471] However, if a third party took its interest on the basis that its rights would be postponed behind those of the unregistered charge, then an exception will be made to make it clear that the rights of such a person will remain postponed behind the charge.[472] Similarly, if a person who is responsible for the failure to register the charge has itself obtained an interest in the charged property, that person's interest should be postponed behind the charge.[473]

14.13.6.3　If permission is given at a time when winding-up proceedings are imminent, then the court will normally require that its order may be challenged by an unsecured creditor or the liquidator if liquidation of the chargor occurs within a set period after the late registration is achieved.[474] The point of this is to permit such a creditor to show that it gave credit to the company, having searched, believing that its property was unencumbered. It also permits the liquidator to challenge the order on the basis that there were no proper grounds for permitting late registration, such as because the liquidator can establish that there had been a deliberate decision not to register the charge in the first place.[475]

14.13.7 The power to make secondary legislation

Chapter 3 of Part 25 of the Companies Act 2006, comprising sections 893 and 894 of the Act, contains provisions to permit secondary legislation to be made dealing with the effect of a registration in another register and the ability to make amendments to Part 25.

14.13.7.1　Under section 893 of the Act, secondary legislation may be made as to the sharing of information between the Companies Registry and other registries, including foreign registries, the consequence of which could be that charges that are registered in such other registries need not be registered separately in the Companies Registry.

---

permission was pending. As to the position where an administrator had been appointed, see Millett J in *Re Barrow Borough Transport Ltd* [1990] Ch 227.

470　*Re Ashpurton Estates Ltd* [1983] Ch 110; *Re Braemar Investments Ltd* [1989] Ch 54; *Barclays Bank PLC v Stuart Landon Ltd* [2001] EWCA Civ 140, [2002] BCC 917.
471　*Re Ashpurton Estates Ltd* [1983] Ch 110, at 122–124.
472　*Barclays Bank PLC v Stuart Landon Ltd* [2001] EWCA Civ 140, [2002] BCC 917.
473　*Re Fablehill Ltd* [1991] BCC 590.
474　This is the so-called 'Re Charles' order: *Re RL Charles & Co* [1935] WN 15.
475　*Barclays Bank PLC v Stuart Landon Ltd* [2001] EWCA Civ 140, [2002] BCC 917.

In such instances, there would be a cross-reference made in the Companies Registry to the registration in the other registry. Examples of where this might occur would be registration of a legal charge in the Land Registry or of security in the specialist registries dealing with ships, aircraft, or intellectual property.

Under section 894 of the Act, secondary legislation could enable amendments to be made to the provisions of Part 25. It is submitted, however, that this would not enable a wholesale change to be made to the system for the registration of charges as it presently applies.

14.13.7.2

14.13.8 Security given by a registered overseas company

Section 1052 of the Companies Act 2006 reflects a welcome change from the position that had applied previously with respect to security given by foreign companies.

Under section 409 of the Companies Act 1985, if a company that was incorporated outside Great Britain, which had established a place of business in England and Wales, gave a charge of a registrable category over property in England and Wales (or acquired property subject to such a charge), the charge had to be registered as if it had been given by an English company. The section applied whether or not the company had registered as an 'overseas company' under Part XXIII of the 1985 Act and it applied with respect to property which was in England and Wales when the charge was created, or which came within that jurisdiction subsequently.[476] The establishment of a place of business in England and Wales was a question of fact to be assessed as at the time the charge was created and implied a place of establishment of some permanence,[477] which it might be difficult to ascertain.

14.13.8.1

Because of the difficulties in knowing if the charge had to be registered, the practice had developed, in cases where the chargor was a foreign company and there was a possibility of the charged assets being or coming within the jurisdiction, of sending the charge to the Companies Registry, together with an attempt at supplying the relevant prescribed particulars, in the hope that this would satisfy the requirements of section 409 (commonly referred to as a 'Slavenburg registration'). It was intended that section 409 of the 1985 Act would cease to apply when section 1052 of the 2006 Act came into force.

14.13.8.2

Under section 1052 of the 2006 Act, secondary legislation may provide that a charge given by a registered overseas company[478] over property in the UK may have to be registered. The secondary legislation will provide for the security that is registrable, the consequences of a failure to register and the provisions of Part 25

14.13.8.3

---

[476] *Slavenburg's Bank NV v Intercontinental Natural Resources Ltd* [1980] 1 WLR 1076.

[477] *Re Oriel Ltd* [1986] 1 WLR 180.

[478] That is, a company that has registered particulars under s 1046(1) of the Act.

of the Act that will apply. At the time of writing, no relevant secondary legislation had been prepared.

14.13.9 Re-characterisation

Re-characterisation is the process by which a transaction that has the superficial appearance of being in one form is treated, as a matter of law, as being of a different type. In the context of financing and similar transactions, the issue that arises is whether a transaction by which a financier or other type of creditor obtains a proprietary interest in an asset in the form of what appears to be outright ownership of the asset, is nonetheless treated as having provided credit on the basis of only having security over the asset, so that its apparent outright proprietary interest is held as security, to which the recipient of the credit has an equity of redemption. The issue is pertinent in English law because of the traditional tolerance that the courts have shown in addressing the matter, although there appears in more recent times to have been a change in judicial approach.[479] This subject is discussed in more detail in Chapter 12, as well as in Chapter 15, and the reader is referred to the discussion in those places for further reference.[480]

14.13.9.1 If a proprietary transaction is re-characterised as being, in reality, a form of security, then it would be necessary to consider if it amounts to a charge that should have been registered under section 860 of the Act. Assuming that it was not registered, the consequences will be as mentioned above.

14.14 Priorities

14.14.1 In English law it is possible for several people to claim proprietary interests in the same asset, whether by way of ownership or security. This arises from the fact that legal and equitable interests may exist in an asset, that there may be more than one equitable interest subsisting at the same time, and that transactions may take place

---

[479] Two decisions in the Court of Appeal and two in the House of Lords serve to illustrate the change in judicial attitudes. The high water mark of a tolerant and laissez-faire approach is illustrated by the decision of the Court of Appeal in *Welsh Development Agency v Export Finance Co Ltd* [1992] BCLC 148. The tide was on the turn only a few years later in the decision of the Court of Appeal in *Orion Finance Ltd v Crown Financial Management Ltd* [1996] BCC 621, particularly in the discussion of Millett LJ, at 626–627. His Lordship was much more definite in delivering the advice of the Privy Council in *Agnew v Inland Revenue Commissioner* [2001] UKPC 28, [2001] AC 710. The approach that he took there was approved by the House of Lords in *Smith (Administrator of Cosslett (Contractors) Ltd) v Bridgend CBC* [2001] UKHL 58, [2002] AC 336 and in *National Westminster Bank PLC v Spectrum Plus Ltd* [2005] UKHL 41, [2005] 2 AC 680.

[480] See also the Australian case of *Beaconwood Securities Pty Ltd v Australia and New Zealand Banking Group Ltd* [2008] FCA 594, which concerned the effectiveness and characterisation of title transfer provisions in securities lending transactions. The court held that they did not amount to secured transactions.

at law or in equity.[481] Accordingly, it is possible that different types of interest may exist in the same asset, which may or may not naturally be in harmony (e.g. legal v equitable, equitable v equitable, security v security, purchaser v security, and purchaser v purchaser). The parties may have agreed as to the order in which their respective interests will rank under a priority agreement and such an agreement will normally bind them to what they have agreed.[482] In other situations, however, there may be a need to resolve the disharmony between the competing interests, which English law achieves through its priority rules. The rules are of a somewhat piecemeal nature and tend to depend upon some general rules and the nature of the particular asset concerned. Nonetheless, the concept of notice (including constructive notice) is an important part of the rules.

The rules are fairly straightforward if there is a specialist registration system for the particular type of asset involved. This is the case with land, ships,[483] aircraft,[484] and some types of intellectual property.[485] In general, priorities are determined by date of registration or notification of an interest on the register. In some instances, that might be defeated by an equity that has priority, as, for instance, one of which a party has notice. In addition, if none of the competing interests have been properly registered or notified then it will be necessary to fall back on the general principles. What follows will concentrate on the position for the general body of assets where no specialist register exists. **14.14.1.1**

It should be noted that each of the rules that follow is subject to the special rules that apply in the case of further advances, which are discussed below. **14.14.1.2**

14.14.2 Some general principles

There are some general principles, or themes, which appear when looking at the priority rules, which will now be described, although it must be borne in

---

[481] Note, however, that if there is only one person with an interest in an asset, that interest can only be the full comprehensive legal title, as it is not possible to have a separate legal and equitable title vested in one person if there is no other person with an interest in the asset: see Viscount Radcliffe in *Commissioner of Stamp Duties (Qld) v Livingstone* [1965] AC 694, at 712; Slade J in *Re Bond Worth Ltd* [1980] Ch 228 and Lord Browne-Wilkinson in *Westdeutsche Landesbank Girozentrale v Islington LBC* [1996] AC 669, at 706.

[482] *Cheah Theam Swee v Equiticorp Finance Group Ltd* [1992] AC 472. See also s 94(1)(a) of the Law of Property Act 1925.

[483] For mortgages in statutory form, priority is regulated by date of registration in the British Ship Register: para 8 of Sched 1 to the Merchant Shipping Act 1995. This is subject to the earlier filing of a priority notice under that para. Notice of an earlier unregistered mortgage will not defeat the statutory priority: *Black v Williams* [1895] 1 Ch 408.

[484] Priority of mortgages is by date of registration at the Aircraft Registry: Art 14 of the Mortgaging of Aircraft Order 1972 (SI 1972/1268). This is subject to the earlier filing of a priority notice under that article. Notice of an earlier unregistered mortgage will not defeat the statutory priority: Art 14(4).

[485] I.e. trade marks, patents, and registered designs, as previously described.

mind that they may be overtaken by specific rules that apply to particular types of assets.

14.14.2.1 *The role of notice*

The most important of the general principles concerns the effect upon a party if it has notice, including constructive notice (such as in consequence of registration of security at the Companies Registry), of an incompatible interest that is earlier in time to its own interest. Generally speaking, such notice will serve to defer the interest of the later party behind that of the earlier interest. This matter is discussed in Chapter 12, to which the reader is referred for further guidance.

14.14.2.2 *Purchaser for value of the legal estate*

Where a person (or a trustee acting on his behalf) acquires the legal estate in an asset and does so for value and without having notice (including by virtue of constructive notice) of an earlier equitable interest in the asset,[486] the legal estate will prevail over the equitable interest.[487] This does not apply, however, in relation to debts and similar choses in action.[488] It would appear that the relevant time for determining if a party had notice of an earlier interest is at least the time when the purchaser gave value. The position is not entirely clear if the purchaser (i.e. an outright purchaser or a mortgagee) acquires notice of an existing equitable interest in the interval between giving value and then acquiring the legal title. It would appear that if the earlier equitable interest exists otherwise than under a trust, the purchaser (provided that it is not a mortgagee) can rely upon the doctrine of *tabula in naufragio* and take free of the equitable interest.[489] However, if the earlier equitable interest is that of a beneficiary under a trust, the conveyance of the legal title will involve a breach of trust upon which the purchaser cannot rely.[490]

14.14.2.2.1 To that qualification there is a separate further exception in relation to the acquisition of a legal estate in shares, through becoming registered as the shareholder. If the purchaser both provided its consideration and acquired the share certificate and a valid transfer form duly executed by the existing registered holder without having notice of an existing beneficial interest in the shares, the purchaser will prevail over the earlier beneficial interest (howsoever it exists), even if the purchaser

---

486 If the purchaser is using a trustee to acquire for him then both the purchaser and the trustee must be without notice.

487 See *Pilcher v Rawlins* (1872) LR 7 Ch App 259; *Macmillan Inc v Bishopsgate Investment Trust (No 3)* [1995] 1 WLR 978, at 1,000 (the case was subject to an appeal that did not deal with this issue: [1996] 1 WLR 387).

488 See Phillips J in *E Pfeiffer Weinkellerei-Weineinkauf GmbH v Arbuthnot Factors Ltd* [1988] 1 WLR 150, at 161.

489 *Macmillan Inc v Bishopsgate Investment Trust (No 3)* [1995] 1 WLR 978, at 1,002–1,003.

490 *Harpham v Shacklock* (1881) 19 ChD 207; *Macmillan Inc v Bishopsgate Investment Trust (No 3)* [1995] 1 WLR 978, at 1,003–1,004.

acquired notice in the intervening period before it became registered as the holder of the shares.[491]

It would also appear to be the case that a purchaser who acquired a good legal title having done so for value and without notice of an existing beneficial interest can pass on that title to a sub-purchaser that does have notice of the beneficial interest, provided the sub-purchaser is not involved in a fraud or has otherwise participated in a breach of trust involving the original transfer to the first purchaser.[492]

14.14.2.2.2

14.14.2.3 *The* nemo dat *rule*

The other side of the coin to the rule favouring a bona fide purchaser of the legal estate, is the rule encapsulated in the Latin maxim, '*nemo dat quod non habet*', namely, that a person cannot confer a better estate than he possesses. Accordingly, a person without a legal estate cannot confer such an estate on someone else. There are certain exceptions to the rule. The most important relate to goods and the exceptions contained in the Sale of Goods Act 1979, the Factors Act 1889, and Part III of the Hire Purchase Act 1964. More generally, there is an exception where a person is conferred with actual or apparent authority by the true owner to deal with the owner's title.

14.14.2.4 *Competing equitable interests*

In a competition as between equitable interests, the starting point is the general rule that where the equities are equal, the first in time should prevail.[493]

Under the doctrine of *tabula in naufragio*, the holder for value of a later equitable interest in tangible property[494] which gets in the legal estate can overreach an earlier equitable interest, provided it did not have notice of the earlier equitable interest when it gave value for the acquisition of its own equitable interest.[495] For the reasons already stated, this does not apply if the earlier equitable interest was that of a beneficiary under a trust and the holder of the later interest knew of it at the time it acquired the legal estate. Nor does it apply in favour of a mortgagee, because of section 94(3) of the Law of Property Act 1925.[496]

14.14.2.4.1

---

[491] *Dodds v Hills* (1865) 2 H&M 424; *Macmillan Inc v Bishopsgate Investment Trust (No 3)* [1995] 1 WLR 978, at 1,003–1,004.

[492] *Wilkes v Spooner* [1911] 2 KB 473.

[493] See Phillips J in *E Pfeiffer Weinkellerei-Weineinkauf GmbH v Arbuthnot Factors Ltd* [1988] 1 WLR 150, at 161–163 and Mummery J in *Compaq Computer Ltd v Abercorn Group Ltd* [1991] BCC 484, at 497–502.

[494] This rule does not apply to choses in action, because the rules for choses are entirely derived from the equitable rules as to competitions between equitable interests, for the reasons explained by Phillips J in *E Pfeiffer Weinkellerei-Weineinkauf GmbH v Arbuthnot Factors Ltd* [1988] 1 WLR 150, at 161.

[495] *Bailey v Barnes* [1894] 1 Ch 25; *McCarthy & Stone Ltd v Julian S Hodge & Co. Ltd* [1971] 1 WLR 1547, at 1,555–1,556.

[496] See *McCarthy & Stone Ltd v Julian S Hodge & Co Ltd* [1971] 1 WLR 1547, at 1,556; *Macmillan Inc v Bishopsgate Investment Trust (No 3)* [1995] 1 WLR 978, at 1,002.

14.14.2.4.2 There is a series of cases where the holder of a prior equitable interest in tangible property has been held to have lost its priority to the holder of a subsequent equitable interest because the merits of the holder of the subsequent interest were greater than those of the earlier interest.[497] Some of the cases are based on a concept of 'negligence' or 'postponing conduct' on the part of the earlier holder, the consequence of which is that the subsequent holder was misled into believing that the earlier interest did not exist, as, for instance, where title deeds were left available to a mortgagor so that it could represent that the property was unencumbered,[498] where the prior holder has postponed its interest by waiver,[499] or where the prior holder was a mere volunteer and the subsequent holder gave value and had no notice of the earlier interest.[500]

14.14.2.5 *The purchase money security interest*

There is a special rule to protect the position of someone who advances money for the purchase of an asset on the basis of an agreement, on which the advance is made, that it will be given fixed security by the borrower over that asset to secure the advance. Such security is sometimes referred to as a 'purchase money security' and the interest of the holder of the security as a 'purchase money security interest'. The holder of such security will enjoy priority over an earlier general security interest which would catch the relevant asset by way of an after-acquired property clause. This will be the result even if the purchase money security holder knew of the earlier interest, provided that it was unaware of any negative pledge which prevented the chargor from giving the purchase money security.[501]

14.14.2.6 *Floating charges*

The position as to floating charges has already been discussed. By way of general summary, if security is held by way of a floating charge then essentially it will concede priority to almost every other competing interest in the assets covered by the charge, so long as such an interest was acquired in circumstances that were within the ordinary course of business of the chargor (which is a concept that has been interpreted very widely) and before the charge crystallised.[502] Even after crystallisation, the holder of the charge must defer to a number of other interests that are preferred before it by statute.

---

[497] The cases are discussed by Meagher, Gummow and Lehane, *Equity: Doctrines and Remedies* (4th edn, 2002), at paras 8-030 to 8-080.

[498] *Farrand v Yorkshire Banking Co* (1888) 40 ChD 182; *Walker v Linom* [1907] 2 Ch 104.

[499] *Fung v Tong* [1918] AC 403.

[500] *Taylor v London and County Banking Co* [1901] 2 Ch 231.

[501] See Lord Oliver in *Abbey National Building Society v Cann* [1991] 1 AC 56, at 89–93 and Jonathan Parker LJ in *Whale v Viasystems Technograph Ltd* [2002] EWCA Civ 480.

[502] This is subject to the holder of the competing interest not having notice of a negative pledge which prevented the chargor from creating that interest.

If the competing interest was acquired after the charge had crystallised then the position is assessed by treating the charge as a fixed equitable charge from the time of crystallisation. However, for the purpose of determining if the holder of the other competing interest had notice of the crystallised charge, it is notice of the fact of crystallisation that is the relevant issue as, otherwise, such a holder will only have notice of a floating charge and the apparent entitlement of the chargor to deal with its assets in the ordinary course of its business. It may also be arguable that if the chargee permits the chargor to continue to deal with the charged assets after the charge has crystallised, the chargee may be precluded from denying the chargor's entitlement to do so.

14.14.2.7 *Priority agreements*

As mentioned above, the parties with competing interests in an asset may agree as to the order in which their respective interests will rank under a priority agreement, and such an agreement will normally bind them to what they have agreed.[503] The parties to such an agreement should bear in mind the potential pitfall of the decision in *Re Portbase Clothing Ltd*[504] which has been previously discussed. In that case it was held that where, by agreement, the fixed chargee conferred priority upon a floating chargee, the preferential creditors could assert their statutory priority ahead of both charges. Presumably the same result would apply in favour of the liquidator for his liquidation expenses under section 176ZA of the Insolvency Act 1986 and the right of unsecured creditors under section 176A of the Insolvency Act 1986.

14.14.3 Goods

Turning now to priorities concerning competing interests in goods (except for ships and aircraft where the interests are registered on the relevant register and other than where one such interest is by way of a floating charge) the starting point is the '*nemo date*' rule outlined above. An example of this rule is to be found in *The Shizelle*[505] which was a case concerning a ship that fell outside the regime for the registration of ships. It was held that where a legal mortgage had been granted, the owner (having, via the mortgage, divested itself of the legal title in the vessel) could not confer a later legal interest by way of sale. Accordingly, a later purchaser took subject to the mortgage, even though he was unaware of the mortgage and, in fact, could not have discovered it.

---

[503] *Cheah Theam Swee v Equiticorp Finance Group Ltd* [1992] AC 472. See also s 94(1)(a) of the Law of Property Act 1925.
[504] [1993] Ch 388.
[505] [1992] 2 Lloyd's Rep 444.

14.14.3.1 There are exceptions to the *nemo date* rule in the Sale of Goods Act 1979 and the Factors Act 1889,[506] as well as in Part III of the Hire Purchase Act 1964 in relation to motor vehicles. Further difficulties can arise for an owner of goods in relation to the rights of lien holders and the loss of title through goods becoming fixtures and incorporated in land or where the goods are mixed with or incorporated into other goods. These matters are discussed in Chapter 15.

14.14.3.2 The next rule is that a bona fide purchaser (a purchaser being a person who has given value, who could be an outright purchaser or a person taking security) of the legal estate in goods, who takes without notice of an earlier equitable interest, will prevail. Here, constructive notice would be relevant.

14.14.3.3 In the absence of the application of the previous rules, priority will be governed by the residual rules, of which the most salient is likely to be that the first in time will prevail, unless it is defeated by a purchase money security interest.

14.14.4 Debts

The position as to competing priorities in debts is discussed in Chapter 12.

14.14.5 Further advances

The above has referred to the priority position of the holder of security for securing a fixed sum or advance. There are special rules to deal with priorities where the holder of a fixed security with priority learns, before it makes a further advance, of another fixed security or purchase interest in the charged assets,[507] which will now be discussed.

14.14.5.1 Section 94(3) of the Law of Property Act 1925 abolished the old general law concept of 'tacking', under which a person with security for a specific advance might in certain limited circumstances have been able to use its security to cover further indebtedness of a borrower.[508] The previous concept of tacking was replaced by section 94(1) of the Law of Property Act 1925, which provides that the holder of

---

[506] I.e. s 24 of the Sale of Goods Act 1979 and s 8 of the Factors Act 1889 (a further disposition by a seller who remains in possession), and s 25(1) of the Sale of Goods Act and s 9 of the Factors Act (a disposition by a purchaser or a person who has agreed to buy and obtained possession).

[507] What follows does not deal with the priority of the proprietor of a registered charge over registered land, to which the provisions of s 49 of the Land Registration Act 2002 apply.

[508] As, for instance, used to be case under the rule in *Hopkinson v Rolt* (1861) 9 HL Cas 514. It has been held, however, that s 94(3) did not also have the effect of abolishing the doctrine of *tabula in naufragio* in cases that did not involve a mortgagee. Under that doctrine, the holder of an equitable interest in a tangible asset that was second in time could, by getting in the legal interest, over-reach an earlier equitable interest of which the holder had no notice at the time it acquired its own equitable interest: see *McCarthy & Stone Ltd v Julian S Hodge & Co Ltd* [1971] 1 WLR 1547, at 1556.

a prior ranking security will continue to enjoy priority over a subsequently rank-ing security for any further advance it makes if it meets any one of three condi-tions, namely:

(a) that it was unaware of the other security at the time of making the advance;
(b) if the security instrument obliges it to make the further advance; or
(c) if there is an agreement between the security holders which continues the pri-ority of the prior security holder.

14.14.5.2

There are a number of difficulties in the application of the section.

14.14.5.2.1

First, section 94(1) refers to further 'advances' that are made by the prior ranking security holder. It is not clear if this would also cover other financial accommoda-tion that is granted by it or other obligations that become due to it by the chargor. Nor is it clear if the section would apply where the security secures a guarantee in circumstances where advances were being made to a third party in reliance upon the guarantee.

14.14.5.2.2

Secondly, it is uncertain if the priority would be lost only if the prior security holder had actual notice of the subsequent security or if constructive notice would be sufficient. It is submitted that the latter construction would be unjust, as it would, for instance, have the consequence that the security holder would have to conduct a search each time it wished to make an advance in case a later security had been registered at the Companies Registry.

14.14.5.2.3

Thirdly, the provision in section 94(1) that refers to an obligation to make the further advance provides for the obligation to be contained in the security instru-ment itself, not just somewhere else, and it must be an obligation to make the fur-ther advance, not simply a discretion to do so. Hence, if an event of default has occurred and the lender has the contractual right to refuse to make an advance, there will not be an obligation to make the advance.

14.14.5.2.4

Fourthly, if the prior security holder cannot claim the benefit of protection under section 94(1) then the risk that the prior security holder has of losing its priority for further advances may be accentuated by the operation of the rule in *Clayton's* case.[509] Accordingly, if the borrower makes payments into its account, such payments would have the effect under the rule of paying off the indebtedness incurred on that account before the prior security holder received notice of the later security.[510] This can be overcome by the prior security holder ruling off the account and opening a new account from which further advances are made and into which repayments are credited.

---

[509] *Devaynes v Noble, Clayton's Case* (1816) LJ Ch 256, 35 ER 767.
[510] This was the position under the general law before s 94: see *Deeley v Lloyds Bank Ltd* [1912] AC 756.

14.14.5.2.5 Finally, section 94(1) only applies to a situation where there are competing securities. It does not apply if the later interest is that of a purchaser. This final situation was addressed, however, by Slade J in *Siebe Gorman & Co Ltd v Barclays Bank Ltd*.[511] His Lordship held that it would be inequitable to allow the security holder to assert its priority for advances it made with notice of the purchaser's interest, to the detriment of the purchaser, when it had not been obliged to make those advances. It is not clear what the position would be if the security holder was obliged to make the further advances despite having notice of the subsequent interest. It had been held at common law[512] that the further advances would not have priority, although it would appear to follow from Slade J's reasoning in the *Siebe Gorman* case that the security holder should be able to assert its priority for further advances made in those circumstances.

14.15 Subordination

14.15.1 Introduction

Subordination is a process by which an unsecured creditor (or creditors) agrees to subordinate its right to payment by a debtor, particularly in an insolvency of the debtor, behind the claims of one or more other unsecured creditors. The subordinated creditor is often referred to as the 'junior creditor' and the indebtedness due to the junior creditor (including principal and interest) is referred to as the 'junior debt'. The other creditors in whose favour the subordination exists are called the 'senior creditors' and their debt is referred to as the 'senior debt'.

14.15.1.1 Subordination has the effect that if there are any assets of the debtor available for distribution to unsecured creditors, the junior creditor will only be entitled to receive and retain payments in the distribution with respect to the junior debt once the senior creditors have been paid out in full for the senior debt. Accordingly, it is not a matter that concerns rights in security or of regulating such rights. By contrast, an agreement as to priorities concerns the competing interests of secured creditors under their respective securities and how those interests should rank. Although subordination does not involve matters of security, it is still a matter of relevant interest and it is convenient to discuss it at this point.

---

[511] [1979] 2 Lloyd's Rep 142. The case is famous for dealing with the question whether it was possible for a fixed charge to be taken over a company's book debts. It is not so well known for its decision on the issue presently under discussion. The effect of the decision on this point meant that the bank really obtained a pyrrhic victory, as nearly all of the benefit of having a fixed charge was lost to the priority gained by the purchaser of the relevant debts, as the vast majority of the outstanding indebtedness secured to the bank had arisen after the bank received notice of the assignment.

[512] *West v Williams* [1899] 1 Ch 132.

If the junior creditor agrees to put its claims with respect to the junior debt behind those of all the other creditors of a debtor (except, perhaps, other subordinated creditors) then the consequence will be that its junior debt will have the appearance of a form of quasi-equity, ranking just ahead of the claims of the shareholders in a winding up of the debtor. It is not correct, however, to treat subordinated debt as being assimilated to equity, for a number of reasons. In the first place, because it is debt that still ranks ahead of the claims of the shareholders in a distribution upon winding up of the debtor. Secondly, subordinated debt can carry a contractual right to interest, whereas dividends can only be paid out of distributable profits and certain reserves. Thirdly, a repayment of subordinated debt does not amount to a reduction of a company's capital, which can only be achieved in accordance with the requirements of the Companies Act 2006. Fourthly, subordinated debt can be issued at a discount, whereas share capital cannot be issued at a discount.[513] Fifthly, the tax treatment of interest that is payable on subordinated debt is likely to be different to that which applies to dividends on shares. Finally, to the extent that the company is a worthwhile and profitable enterprise, the shareholders are likely to make a greater return upon their investment than the holders of debt. For that reason, there is an incentive to keep the number of shareholders limited by arranging for funding via a subordinated debt issue.

14.15.1.2

Subordinated debt may comprise loans as well as capital markets debt issues. It is often used to provide a part of private equity financing, as one or more of the layers of debt to fund the acquisition. The thought is that some investors will be prepared to take a greater level of risk in return for more profitable rewards via higher interest rates on the debt. If they do so then that will encourage others to provide funding that is less risky, although the safer debt does not carry such a high return. The sense of such freestyle thinking has been sorely tested by the crisis in the world's financial markets in the second part of 2007. Subordinated debt may also be used as a method of providing funds within a group of companies, as an alternative to the parent company injecting the funds through a subscription of share capital. Subordination also occurs in some forms of guarantee, by which the guarantor agrees not to compete with the creditor by proving in the winding up of the primary debtor, and to subordinate its claims against the primary debtor behind those of the creditor. This is particularly important if the guarantee does not cover the whole of the indebtedness of the primary debtor to the creditor. Subordinated debt may also be issued for regulatory purposes, as it may qualify as part of regulatory capital in computing capital adequacy ratios and requirements.

14.15.1.3

The subordination may be in favour of all of the debtor's other creditors or only one or a particular class of them. The former is likely to be the case when subordination

14.15.1.4

---

[513] S 580 of the Companies Act 2006 (formerly s 100 of the Companies Act 1985).

is used to achieve a regulatory capital requirement or in situations where it is wished to encourage third parties to grant credit to the debtor, whereas the latter is more likely to occur in private financing transactions where it is simply a matter of ranking the claims of the various debt holders.

14.15.1.5 Something similar to subordination can be achieved through the use of a corporate group structure. In such a structure, debt could be raised by a parent company which is then passed down to its subsidiary, either by a subscription for shares in the subsidiary or by making a subordinated loan to the subsidiary. By virtue of the legal distinction between the two entities, the creditors of the subsidiary would have a first claim against it before the claim of the parent. Assuming that the only asset of the parent was its investment in the subsidiary, the debt of the parent would, in a practical sense, be dependent upon receipts from the subsidiary which, in turn, would only be payable after the subsidiary's own creditors had been satisfied. By process of similar reasoning, lenders to a subsidiary company will rank ahead of the claims of the parent company as a shareholder in the subsidiary.

14.15.2 Types of subordination arrangement

There are two principal methods of achieving a subordination as between creditors of the same debtor. Sometimes a combination of these methods might be appropriate as, for instance, by providing for the junior creditor to turn over to the senior creditor any rights it has and any payment it receives, so as to cover the possibility that the contingent debt method fails (whether wilfully or otherwise) to achieve what is required.

14.15.2.1 As a preliminary matter, it is also necessary to determine which of the indebtedness that might be owing to the junior creditor should be treated as junior debt. This will not cause a difficulty where the junior debt is to comprise all such indebtedness. The position will be more problematic where only part of that indebtedness is to be treated as junior debt. In such a case it will be necessary to ensure that the junior creditor is not unduly favoured in receiving payments of its unsubordinated debt and that junior debt cannot surreptitiously be paid in the guise of being unsubordinated debt.

14.15.2.2 Turnover subordination and subordination trusts

The first method is often referred to as 'turnover subordination'. Under it, the junior creditor agrees to account to the senior creditor, or to turn over to the senior creditor, the benefit it has of the junior debt in specified circumstances, particularly if the debtor has become subject to insolvency proceedings. This may be achieved by a purely contractual arrangement, but the senior creditor will then be taking the risk that the contractual arrangements will wither in an insolvency of the junior creditor. For that reason, the senior creditor would usually prefer that the arrangement should take the form of a subordination trust, by which the junior creditor undertakes to hold its rights and any payment that it receives on trust for the senior creditor. An example of such a trust can be seen in *Re British and Commonwealth Holdings PLC (No 3)*.[514] Where the junior debt is comprised in a bond issue, then the trustee for the bond holders can be joined in the arrangement, so that the trust deed will provide that its obligations under the subordination trust, including as to making distributions, will take precedence over those in favour of the bond holders. It is advisable that the senior creditor should possess authority, preferably in the form of a power of attorney, to take action on behalf of the junior creditor with respect to the junior debt, including lodging proofs and pursuing claims. If the senior creditors comprise all of the other unsecured creditors of the debtor then the trustee or junior creditor can be directed to make payment to the liquidator of the debtor for distribution by him amongst the senior creditors. Similarly, a subordination trust could be in favour of a trustee on behalf of the senior creditors in a case where there were more than one such creditor.

14.15.2.3 Contingent debt subordination

By this method, it is a term of the contract under which the junior debt arises, usually reinforced by agreement between all the parties, that in the event that the debtor is subject to insolvency proceedings, the junior debt will only be payable to the junior creditor if the senior creditor has been paid out in full. The junior creditor will also usually agree not to claim against the debtor or prove in its insolvency whilst any amount of the senior debt remains outstanding. An example of this type of subordination will be found in *Re Maxwell Communications Corp PLC (No 2)*,[515] where the relevant governing law of the jurisdiction concerned was unable to accommodate a subordination trust. This method of subordination is not suitable where there are unsecured creditors of the debtor who are not senior creditors. This is because the effect of the arrangement is not to direct the junior creditor's share to the senior creditors but, in effect, to swell the pot that is available for distribution to all the unsecured creditors other than the junior creditor. In consequence, it will usually also have the effect of prolonging the subordination of the junior creditor's claims.

14.15.2.4 Situations outside the insolvency of the debtor

Strictly speaking, subordination looks to the situation that will apply in the debtor's insolvency. For practical reasons, however, it might be desirable to extend any restrictions and turn over obligations that apply with respect to payments that fall due to the junior creditor so that they, or something to similar effect, will also

---

[514] [1992] 1 WLR 672.
[515] [1993] 1 WLR 1402.

apply even when the debtor has not entered insolvency proceedings. Accordingly, a well drafted subordination agreement will impose various tests and conditions that have to be met in the ordinary course before the debtor may make, or the junior creditor is entitled to receive or retain, payments of interest, fees and the like, and repayments of principal. Such tests will usually address:

(i)   the debtor's solvency at the time the payment falls due;

(ii) that there are sufficient reserves which are held by the debtor and available to pay the indebtedness due to the senior creditors as measured and projected over a certain period of time; and

(iii) that there has been no actual or anticipated default by the borrower in meeting its obligations under the relevant agreements between it and the senior creditors.

14.15.2.5   It is also desirable to ensure that in a financial re-construction of the debtor and its liabilities, the position of the junior creditor is carried through into the new arrangements. It may also be necessary to consider the ability of the junior creditor to vote as a separate class and to provide that it should vote in accordance with the directions of the senior creditors.

14.15.3 Legal issues that arise in connection with subordination

There are a number of legal issues that arise in connection with subordination arrangements, which will now be discussed. Some of these issues concern matters that relate to the relationships that will exist between the junior creditor, the debtor, and the senior creditor; others would arise in an insolvency of the debtor; and yet others of them concern issues that might arise in an insolvency of the junior creditor. One consequence of this is the necessity to keep in mind when considering these issues the possibility that either or both of the debtor and the junior creditor might enter insolvency proceedings which may remain current.

14.15.3.1 Pari passu *distribution in a winding up of the debtor*

It is rather surprising that until comparatively recently, English law had not managed to determine if subordination arrangements might offend against the fundamental principle in a winding up or bankruptcy, which requires the distribution of a insolvent debtor's available assets on a *pari passu* basis amongst the debtor's unsecured creditors. This is encapsulated in sections 107 and 328(3) of the Insolvency Act 1986 and in Rule 4.181 of the Insolvency Rules 1986 and is usually referred to as the '*British Eagle*' principle. An arrangement which would have the consequence of subverting that principle is void.[516] It had been argued that the

---

[516] *British Eagle International Airlines Ltd v Cie Nationale Air France* [1975] 1 WLR 758. Reference should also now be made to the decision of the High Court of Australia in *International*

intended effect of a subordination was to subvert the principle and was therefore ineffective, because the subordination had the effect that the junior creditor would rank behind the senior creditors in a winding up or bankruptcy of the debtor, rather than equally with them.

A series of cases beginning in the early 1990s has now established the validity of the concept of subordination in English law.[517] Two early cases, which actually concerned issues arising in schemes of arrangement, so were not of binding authority in relation to a bankruptcy or winding up, were the decisions of Vinelott J in *Re British and Commonwealth Holdings PLC (No. 3)*[518] and *Re Maxwell Communications Corp. PLC (No.2)*.[519] In the first of those cases, his Lordship upheld the validity of a subordination trust. In the second case, his Lordship upheld the validity of a contingent debt subordination. More recently, both types of subordination arrangement have been held valid in a winding up of a debtor in *Re SSSL Realisations (2002) Ltd; Manning v AIG Europe Ltd*.[520] The essential reasoning of those cases is that the *British Eagle* principle is intended to prevent the debtor agreeing with one or a few of its creditors to an arrangement which is for the benefit of that one or few creditors but not for the equal benefit of all of its creditors. The principle does not prevent an arrangement by which one or a few creditors agree with the debtor to postpone their rights behind those of other creditors. Put more colloquially, if a junior creditor is silly enough to agree to postpone its rights behind the claims of other creditors then that should be its lookout and no one else's problem.

14.15.3.1.1

14.15.3.2 *Insolvency set-off as between the insolvent debtor and the junior creditor*
As previously explained, the rules as to insolvency set-off are mandatory in the bankruptcy or winding up of a debtor and they may also come into play in the administration of the debtor, where the administrator proposes to make a distribution to creditors. The question which arises at this point is whether the rules apply where the junior creditor has a liability to the debtor which, but for the subordination, would be taken into account for insolvency set-off purposes. If the

---

Air Transport Association v Ansett Australia Holdings Ltd [2008] HCA 3, in which the outcome in the *British Eagle* case was distinguished because the scheme that was considered by the House of Lords had been subsequently amended, so that the High Court was able to find that the amended scheme did not infringe the *pari passu* rule.

517 A little earlier, subordination arrangements had been held valid in Australia: *Horne v Chester & Fein Property Developments Pty Ltd* (1987) 5 ACLC 245. See also *Re NIAA Corporation Ltd* (1994) 12 ACLC 64 and *United States Trust Co of New York v Australia & New Zealand Banking Group Ltd* (1995) 17 ACSR 697.

518 [1992] 1 WLR 672.

519 [1993] 1 WLR 1,402.

520 [2004] EWHC 1760 (Ch), [2005] 1 BCLC 1 (Lloyd J), upheld [2006] EWCA Civ 7, [2006] Ch 610.

set-off is not available then the junior creditor will be forced to pay its liability and it will be unable to reduce the amount of that liability by reference to the set-off. The question assumes that at the time the bankruptcy or winding up commences, the subordination remains in place because the senior creditors have not been paid out.

14.15.3.2.1 In the case of a subordination trust, where the junior creditor has effectively disposed of its rights in the junior debt outright, there will be no mutuality as between the junior creditor and the debtor on which the set-off could be based. The junior creditor would be forced to pay to the liquidator or trustee in bankruptcy the full amount of its liability to the debtor (assuming that its amount is determined). It is submitted that the same consequence should follow if the trust is over all of the junior debt, albeit limited as to the amount recoverable by the senior creditor under it.

14.15.3.2.2 Where the subordination is achieved through the means of a contingent debt arrangement, without the back-up of a subordination trust, it is theoretically arguable that the set-off would apply, because contingent liabilities may still be taken into the account for the purposes of the set-off. However, it would then be necessary to put a value on the contingent debt for the purpose of taking the account of the respective amounts to be set off. If the senior debt will not be paid out in full then nothing will be payable by the insolvent debtor with respect to the contingent debt, so that no value should be placed on it. The practical consequence would be that there would be nothing available to be set off. The junior creditor would be obliged to pay to the liquidator or trustee in bankruptcy the debt that it owes to the insolvent debtor and no set-off would be available to it to reduce that payment.

14.15.3.2.3 By way of extra precaution, it would be sensible in the subordination arrangements to provide that the junior creditor should account to the senior creditors for the benefit it receives in any set-off that is applied.

14.15.3.3 *Participation of the junior creditor in the prescribed part of floating charge property*

Section 176A of the Insolvency Act 1986 provides for a prescribed part of the recoveries under a floating charge to be made 'available for the satisfaction of unsecured debts.' Under a subordination trust, the junior debt should still qualify to be taken into account under the section as an unsecured debt, and the junior creditor would be required to hold the benefit of any amount it received pursuant to the operation of the section for the senior creditors. The position is not so clear in relation to a contingent debt subordination, because it is arguable that there is no debt due by the debtor to the junior creditor which would qualify to be taken into account for the purposes of the section.

14.15.3.4 Subordination trusts by way of security

This issue concerns whether a subordination trust constitutes a form of third party security that is given by the junior creditor to the senior creditors, over the junior debt, as security for the payment of the senior debt. If so, then the further question that arises is whether the security is registrable as a charge under section 860 of the Companies Act 2006.[521] If the charge is registrable, and it is not registered, then it will be void in the liquidation or administration of the junior creditor, and it will also be void as against other secured creditors of the junior creditor. Whether or not the charge is registrable, it might also infringe the terms of a negative pledge which the junior creditor has agreed in favour of a third party. In addition, if the trust constitutes security that has been given by the junior creditor, it would be subject to the restrictions and other provisions that would apply to such security in an administration of the junior creditor or if a proposal has been made for a company voluntary arrangement of the junior creditor.[522]

It is possible that a trust which a person declares over the benefit of an asset might be absolute, in the sense that it confers a sole beneficial ownership of the trust property in favour of the beneficiaries and, accordingly, that the trustee gives up all its real rights in the trust property. Alternatively, such a trust might be held to be by way of charge, even by way of floating charge, because the trustee has not given up all of its interest in the trust property.[523] It is also important to remember that in English law security may be given to secure the obligations of a third party without the security giver undertaking a personal obligation to pay the liability for which the security has been given. The essential question in resolving this issue is whether the person that declares the trust (in this case the junior creditor) retains an interest in the trust property (the junior debt) by way of an equity of redemption, or whether it has completely passed all of its entitlement, in a beneficial sense, to the beneficiary or beneficiaries (in this case, the senior creditors). **14.15.3.4.1**

In the context of a subordination trust, it is unlikely that a junior creditor would give up all of its entitlement in the junior debt, even to the extent of parting with its interest in the debt once the senior creditors had been paid out in full. Accordingly, it is strongly arguable that the trust would not be absolute but by way of security, because the junior creditor retained an equity of redemption in the trust property. In *Re SSSL Realisations (2002) Ltd; Manning v AIG Europe Ltd*[524] it appears to have been accepted that such an arrangement might constitute security that is given by the junior creditor except where, as in that case, the junior **14.15.3.4.2**

---

521 Formerly s 395 of the Companies Act 1985.
522 See para 12(1) of Sched A1, and paras 43 and 44 of Sched B1, to the Insolvency Act 1986.
523 See Slade J in *Re Bond Worth Ltd* [1980] Ch 228, at 247 and Jonathan Parker J in *Re ILG Travel Ltd* [1996] BCC 21, at 44–45.
524 [2004] EWHC 1760 (Ch); [2005] 1BCLC 1 (Lloyd J), at [49]–[51], upheld [2006] EWCA Civ 7; [2006] Ch 610, at [122].

creditor was itself indebted to the senior creditor and the subordination arrangements were part and parcel of the means by which that indebtedness was to be paid. That would not be the position in the usual case.

14.15.3.4.3 If the subordination trust is a form of security, then it will be registrable under section 860 of the Companies Act 2006 if it falls into any of the following three categories:

    (i) it is a charge for securing an issue of debentures[525] (which would be the case if the senior debt is a bond issue or some other form of capital markets transaction);

    (ii) it is a charge on a 'book debt';[526] or

    (iii) it is a floating charge.

It is unlikely that the charge would be a floating charge, given the strict controls that would usually be found in the documentation as to the exercise of the junior creditor's rights in relation to the junior debt. It might well be a charge on a book debt if the charge is over the junior creditor's rights in the junior debt. There would not be a charge on a book debt if the charge was simply over the proceeds of payment of the debt once received by the junior creditor,[527] although it is doubtful if a well advised senior creditor would be content to rely on such a limited form of security. The right of a creditor to receive dividends in the bankruptcy or liquidation of an insolvent debtor is probably not a debt,[528] so a charge over that right should not be considered to be a charge on a book debt.

14.15.3.5 The British Eagle *principle in the insolvency of the junior creditor*

In *Re SSSL Realisations (2002) Ltd; Manning v AIG Europe Ltd*[529] it was also argued that the agreement by the junior creditor to the subordination arrangements might offend against the *British Eagle* principle in relation to a bankruptcy or winding up of the junior creditor. The argument was put on the basis that by agreeing that its rights to payment by the debtor would be restricted, the junior creditor had prejudiced its own creditors by making one of its assets unavailable in its own insolvency. The argument was rejected. The *British Eagle* principle relates to arrangements which have the effect of putting the claims of certain unsecured creditors of an insolvent debtor, without their consent, behind the claims of other unsecured creditors of that insolvent debtor. The principle has nothing to

---

[525] S 860(7)(c), formerly s 396(1)(a) of the Companies Act 1985.

[526] S 860(7)(f), formerly s 396(1)(e) of the Companies Act 1985.

[527] *Re SSSL Realisations (2002) Ltd; Manning v AIG Europe Ltd* [2004] EWHC 1760 (Ch); [2005] 1BCLC 1 (Lloyd J), at [52]–[54], upheld [2006] EWCA Civ 7; [2006] Ch 610, at [122].

[528] See s 325(2) of the Insolvency Act 1986 and Rule 4.182(3) of the Insolvency Rules 1986.

[529] [2004] EWHC 1760 (Ch), [2005] 1BCLC 1 (Lloyd J), upheld [2006] EWCA Civ 7, [2006] Ch 610.

do with the availability or quality of the assets of the insolvent debtor to meet those claims. In effect, the fact that the asset was impaired by the subordination arrangements agreed by the junior creditor with the senior creditors was not relevant to the application of the *pari passu* principle. It is worth noting that a similar point was considered by Peter Gibson J in *Carreras Rothman Ltd v Freeman Mathews Treasure Ltd*,[530] which concerned a company that was in liquidation and which, in relation to a debt that was owed to it, had agreed before the commencement of the liquidation to give up that debt (i.e. to give up the asset being the debt due to it) in return for its former debtor participating in the establishment and funding of a *Quistclose* trust arrangement (see the decision of the House of Lords in *Barclays Bank Ltd v Quistclose Investments Ltd*[531]) in favour of certain debtors of the company.

14.15.3.6 Disclaimer of a subordination arrangement as an unprofitable contract in the insolvency of the junior creditor

This issue, which particularly concerns the contingent debt aspects of a subordination, was explored by Lloyd J at first instance and by Chadwick LJ in the appeal in *Re SSSL Realisations (2002) Ltd; Manning v AIG Europe Ltd*.[532] The explanation that follows is taken from the judgments of Lloyd J and Chadwick LJ, the latter upholding the judgment of the former.

14.15.3.6.1

The right to disclaim onerous property is exercisable by a trustee in bankruptcy[533] and by a liquidator.[534] The provisions concerning bankruptcy are in much the same terms as those for winding up, so the discussion will concentrate on the provisions that apply in a winding up, principally section 178 of the Insolvency Act 1986. The effect of a disclaimer by a liquidator is that the rights and liabilities of the company in liquidation with respect to the relevant contract or asset are terminated, so that the company will be released from having to make further performance of its obligations under the contract or with respect to the asset. A counterparty that is adversely affected by the disclaimer is given a right to prove for the loss or damage that it sustains, but that will usually be of little real benefit. There is a saving provision as to the associated liabilities of a third party, which has given rise to difficulties in areas such as guarantees of property leases that have been disclaimed.[535]

---

[530] [1985] Ch 207.

[531] [1970] AC 567.

[532] [2004] EWHC 1760 (Ch); [2005] 1BCLC 1, at [56]–[71] (Lloyd J), upheld [2006] EWCA Civ 7; [2006] Ch 610, at [33]–[54].

[533] Under s 315 of the Insolvency Act 1986.

[534] Under s 178 of the Insolvency Act 1986.

[535] See *Hindcastle v Barbara Attenborough* [1997] AC 70; *Active Estates v Parness* (2002) 36 EG 147; *Scottish Widows v Jane Tripipatkul* [2003] EWHC 1874 (Ch).

14.15.3.6.2 Section 178(3) of the Insolvency Act 1986 defines 'onerous property' to mean (a) an unprofitable contract or (b) other property which is unsaleable or not readily saleable or which has onerous liabilities attached to it. In light of the definition of 'Property' in section 436 of the Act, Lloyd J came to the view that something could only qualify as property within (b) if it involved some element of benefit or entitlement for the person holding it. The obligations of a junior creditor are unlikely to fit that requirement. That view was approved by Chadwick LJ. Accordingly, section 178 should only apply in the case of a subordination by the junior creditor if its liquidator could establish that the relevant subordination arrangement was an unprofitable contract for the junior creditor.

14.15.3.6.3 In relation to the concept of an unprofitable contract, Lloyd J referred to the decision of Chesterman J in the Supreme Court of Queensland, Australia, in *Transmetro Corporation Ltd v Real Investments Pty Ltd*[536] in which his Honour, in considering a similar legislative provision, had said that an unprofitable contract was one which imposed on the company in liquidation continuing financial obligations without sufficient reciprocal benefits. It must give rise to prospective liabilities. A contract is not unprofitable merely because it is financially disadvantageous or because the company could have made a better bargain. Contracts that will delay the winding up, which will have to be performed over a substantial period of time and which will involve irrecoverable expenditure are unprofitable. This was approved by Chadwick LJ who referred to the decision in the *Transmetro* case, together with a series of other Australian cases which supported the view taken in that case.[537]

14.15.3.6.4 Chadwick LJ also referred to a summary of the purposes for which the power to disclaim is conferred on a liquidator, which had been provided by Professor Sir Roy Goode.[538] They were, first, to enable the liquidator to bring the liquidation to an end without being held up by continuing obligations under unprofitable contracts,[539] and secondly, in an insolvent liquidation to avoid the continuance of liabilities which would be payable as expenses of the liquidation to the detriment of unsecured creditors.

14.15.3.6.5 On the facts of the case, Chadwick LJ upheld the finding by Lloyd J that the subordination arrangements entered into by the junior creditor did not amount to an unprofitable contract. Although it was disadvantageous to the interests of the junior creditor's own creditors, it did not impose continuing financial

---

[536] (1999) 17 ACLC 1314.

[537] Namely the decisions of Santow J in *Global Television Pty Ltd v Sportsview Australia Pty Ltd* (2000) 35 ACSR 484; Hodgson J in *Rothwells Ltd v Spedley Securities Ltd* (1990) 8 ACLR 783; and Young J in *Dekala Pty Ltd v Perth Land & Leisure Ltd* (1989) 12 ACLR 585.

[538] *Principles of Corporate Insolvency Law* (3rd edn, 2005), at para 6-20.

[539] See also Lord Millett in *Re Park Air Services PLC* [2000] 2 AC 172, at 184.

obligations on the junior creditor, it did not give rise to prospective liabilities to be performed by the junior creditor, it did not involve expenditure by the junior creditor, nor did it require performance over a substantial period of time. Furthermore, the junior creditor had obtained its reciprocal benefit from the senior creditor in consideration of entering into the subordination arrangement.

Chadwick LJ did go on to say, however, that he could envisage circumstances where a subordination arrangement might fall to be considered as an unprofitable contract because future obligations that had to be performed under it were such as to impede the liquidator in realising the junior creditor's property and paying a dividend to its creditors within a reasonable time. He gave as an example a situation (which would be rare) where a junior creditor in a solvent liquidation might be required to provide cash cover against a future obligation it might have to the senior creditor in an amount that was not then capable of being quantified. His Lordship also said that a provision which prevented the junior creditor from proving in the debtor's liquidation might be considered as an unprofitable contract if the facts were such that there was a prospect that at some future date the senior creditor would be paid off so that the restriction on proving would have the effect that the junior creditor had been prevented from proving in the debtor's liquidation for the junior debt.

14.15.3.6.6

14.15.3.7 *Administration of the junior creditor*

If the junior creditor enters administration then the various restrictions that apply to the enforcement of security and pursuing creditors' rights in such an administration will apply.[540] This will act as a restriction on the action that the senior creditors may take against the junior creditor. Similar restrictions will apply in the case of the moratorium that arises where a proposal has been made for a voluntary arrangement of an eligible company, should the junior creditor be such a company.[541]

14.15.3.8 *The junior creditor as a surety*

Where a subordination trust constitutes a form of third party security, as discussed above, then the junior creditor might be seen as taking on the mantle as a surety for the senior debt. The analogy is less clear in a purely contingent debt arrangement but it is not entirely fanciful. In either case, it is possible that the junior creditor might be able to argue, in principle, that the subordination arrangements were only intended to apply with respect to the circumstances as they existed at the time it entered into the subordination arrangements. Just as a surety is entitled to insist that the underlying agreement as between the creditor and principal

---

[540] See, for instance, paras 43 and 44 of Sched B1 to the Insolvency Act 1986.
[541] See para 12 of Sched A1 to the Insolvency Act 1986.

debtor, and security and other suretyships, should not be changed or abrogated to the potential detriment of the surety, so also the junior creditor might be entitled to insist that the terms and conditions of the senior debt (and other matters relevant to it) should not be changed or released without its consent. This could be relevant to matters such as the amount and maturity date of the senior debt and other financial conditions that relate to it, as well as other matters that might be material to it, such as the continued existence of guarantees and of subordination arrangements entered into by other junior creditors. If changes occur without the consent of the junior creditor then the junior creditor might be entitled to say that it has been discharged (either in whole or in part) from the obligations and restrictions that apply with respect to it and the junior debt under the subordination arrangements.

14.15.3.8.1 In an attempt to defeat any arguments of that nature which the junior creditor might raise, it would be advisable to include in the subordination arrangements provisions that are similar to those usually found in well drawn forms of guarantee, by which the guarantor effectively consents to changes and amendments, as well as the discharge of security and other sureties, and confirms that its liability under the guarantee will continue unaffected by the occurrence of any such matters.[542] Of course, the junior creditor may not wish to concede a wide amount of liberty in that regard and a negotiated position may have to be found.

14.16 Upsetting Prior Transactions Entered into by an Obligor

14.16.1 The Insolvency Act 1986 (the 'Act') provides a number of grounds upon which a transaction which had been previously entered into by an obligor might be upset. All but one of them arises in the context of the liquidation, bankruptcy or administration of the obligor, where the liquidator, trustee, or administrator is given the right to challenge the transaction. The discussion that follows will concentrate on the grounds upon which a transaction might be challenged, but it is important to bear in mind that there are also other provisions of the Act under which liability may be imposed upon the directors and others concerned with an insolvent company in relation to misfeasance and other wrongful action on their part which may have caused loss to the company and its creditors.[543] For simplicity, the discussion will concentrate on the grounds for upsetting transactions entered into by a corporate obligor, but there are similar provisions that apply in the case of an individual.

---

542 See generally the discussion in Chap 16.
543 See ss 206–214 of the Insolvency Act 1986.

14.16.2 Avoidance of dispositions of property in a compulsory winding up

Section 127(1) of the Act[544] provides that where a company is being wound up by the court, a disposition by a company of its property (and any transfer of its shares or alteration in the status of its members) made after the commencement of its winding up is void unless validated by the court.[545] A disposition would include a payment or the granting of any interest in property of the company, whether outright or by way of security.[546] For this purpose, the winding up is deemed to have commenced on the date on which the petition for winding up was presented or, if earlier, the date of the passing of a resolution for winding up. A number of points arise in considering section 127(1).

A payment into a company's overdrawn account with its bank constitutes a disposition in favour of the bank for the purposes of section 127(1).[547] This is in contrast to a payment into a bank account that was in credit.[548] When a bank honours a cheque drawn by a company on its account with the bank, where the account is in credit, that is a disposition by the company in favour of the payee but the bank will not incur liability under section 127(1) for acting in accordance with its mandate. The same would probably apply if the account was overdrawn.[549]

14.16.2.1

The following principles should apply when the court is deciding if it should grant a validation order:[550]

14.16.2.2

(i) the court has a discretion, which is at large;
(ii) the basic principle underlying the purpose of the section is that of achieving a *pari passu* distribution as between all of the unsecured creditors of the insolvent company for the benefit of the general body of creditors and to prevent the dissipation of the company's assets contrary to that purpose;[551]
(iii) the court should ensure that the interests of the unsecured creditors are not prejudiced;

---

[544] For bankruptcy see s 284 of the Insolvency Act 1986.

[545] The position is far less severe with respect to a company that is in voluntary winding up which has not been converted into a compulsory winding up: see ss 87 and 88 of the Act.

[546] But it must be property in which the company has a beneficial interest: *Re Margart Pty Ltd* (1985) 9 ACLR 269; *Re Branston & Gothard Ltd* [1999] BPIR 466. The receipt by the chargee of the proceeds of a disposition of charged property would not amount to a disposition in favour of the chargee because of the chargee's pre-existing equitable interest in the proceeds: *Re Margart Pty Ltd*.

[547] *Re Gray's Inn Construction Co Ltd* [1980] 1 WLR 711.

[548] *Re Barn Crown Ltd* [1995] 1 WLR 147.

[549] *Hollicourt (Contracts) Ltd v Bank of Ireland* [2001] Ch 555.

[550] These principles were set out in *Rose v AIB Group (UK) PLC* [2003] EWHC 1737, [2003] 1 WLR 2791, which drew upon *Re Gray's Inn Construction Co Ltd* [1980] 1 WLR 711 and *Denney v John Hudson & Co Ltd* [1992] BCLC 910.

[551] See also Lightman J in *Coutts & Co v Stock* [2000] 1 WLR 906, which was approved by the Court of Appeal in *Hollicourt (Contracts) Ltd v Bank of Ireland* [2001] Ch 555.

(iv)   except unusually where it was in the interests of creditors generally, the court should not validate a transaction which would have the effect of one pre-liquidation creditor being paid off in full where other creditors would only receive a dividend; and

(v)   a disposition carried out by the parties in good faith at a time when they were unaware that a petition had been presented might be validated unless there were grounds for thinking that the transaction was an attempt to prefer the disponee ('prefer' in this sense not having its technical meaning under the Act but, rather, something generally having the effect of circumventing the *pari passu* rule). In this regard, however, good faith by itself is not sufficient to justify validation.

There are two further requirements that should be met. First, that the parties were acting in the ordinary course of business and secondly, that the relevant transactions were likely to be for the benefit of the creditors generally. The second point demonstrates that the decision of the Court of Appeal in *Re Gray's Inn Construction Co. Ltd*[552] should not be taken as authority that a court will always validate payments made into an overdrawn bank account where the payments were apparently in the ordinary course of business.

14.16.2.3   The claim by a liquidator for recoupment of an invalid payment or other disposition is in the nature of a restitutionary claim, as section 127(1) does not provide a statutory right to recover assets that have been wrongfully disposed of by the company.[553] As the claim is restitutionary in nature, the recipient of a disposition may be able to assert a defence based upon a change of its position. Such a defence would be available where the recipient was unaware or had genuinely overlooked the fact, when it changed its position, that the payment might be invalid or where it had acted upon an assurance from the liquidator that he would not claim against the recipient.[554]

14.16.2.4   It has been suggested that if the claim which is pursued by the liquidator relates to property which had been the subject of an uncrystallised floating charge when it was disposed of then the charge will apply to what is recovered by the liquidator under section 127(1) of the Act.[555] It is submitted, with respect, that this is incorrect, at least in the situation where the original disposition was absolute and fell within the broadly understood concept of being in the ordinary course of the

---

[552] [1980] 1 WLR 711.

[553] *Hollicourt (Contracts) Ltd v Bank of Ireland* [2001] Ch 555; *Rose v AIB Group (UK) PLC* [2003] EWHC 1737, [2003] 1 WLR 2791.

[554] Such a defence may be difficult to make out on the facts: *Rose v AIB Group (UK) PLC* [2003] EWHC 1737, [2003] 1 WLR 2791.

[555] *Mond v Hammond Suddards* [1996] 2 BCLC 470. The point was accepted on appeal: *Re RS&M Engineering Co Ltd, Mond v Hammond Suddards* [2000] Ch 40, at 50.

company's business. If so, then the charge would have ceased to apply to the relevant property at the time the disposition took place. As has been seen above, the claim of the liquidator is restitutionary in nature and does not automatically give a full right to recovery. Defences, such as based upon a change of position, may be asserted to defeat the claim or, alternatively, the court may validate the disposition. Accordingly, whilst the word 'void' is used in the section, the consequence is not to treat the disposition as being void *ab initio* so that the disposition is treated as never having occurred with the consequence that the property must be returned *in specie*, but merely to give the liquidator a claim which he can pursue. The claim vests in him. The chargee has no right to bring the proceedings, nor can it compel the liquidator to bring them. If he does pursue the claim, he does it for the benefit of the general body of the company's unsecured creditors and not to restore to the company the property, nor to restore to the chargee the charged property, as if it had never been the subject of the original disposition.

14.16.3 Transactions at an undervalue

Section 238 of the Act[556] concerns transactions at an undervalue that a company may have entered into at a relevant time prior to its entry into winding up or administration. The liquidator or administrator is given power to challenge any such transaction. Section 238 is addressed in more detail in Chapter 16 and the reader is referred to the discussion in that chapter for a fuller explanation of the section.

14.16.3.1 By way of brief summary, the section applies if the debtor company has entered into a transaction at an undervalue at a 'relevant time' (which, essentially, is a period of two years prior to the onset of the insolvency proceedings,[557] provided that the company met the relevant insolvency tests when the transaction occurred or became insolvent in consequence of the transaction). The court has a wide amount of discretion as to the order that it might make if such a transaction has occurred.[558]

14.16.3.2 A transaction at an undervalue entered into by a debtor company is defined to be one which meets either of the following tests:

(a) the [debtor] company makes a gift to [another] person or otherwise enters into a transaction with that person on terms that provided for the company to receive no consideration, or

---

[556] The comparable section for bankruptcy is s 339 of the Insolvency Act 1986. Similar provisions will also be found in s 423 of that Act (transactions defrauding creditors), which applies to both companies and individuals.

[557] The period of two years is laid down in s 240 of the Act, but note also the alternative period provided in s 240(1)(c) and (d) (to which the solvency tests do not apply). The period is five years for insolvent individuals: see s 341 of the Act.

[558] The powers of the court to make an order are discussed below.

(b) the [debtor] company enters into a transaction with that [other] person for a consideration the value of which, in money or money's worth, is significantly less than the value, in money or money's worth, of the consideration provided by the company.

14.16.3.3 The court may not make an order, however, if it can be shown that the debtor company entered into the transaction:[559]

(a) . . . in good faith and for the purpose of carrying on its business, and
(b) at the time it did so there were reasonable grounds for believing that the transaction would benefit the company.

14.16.3.4 Giving security

There has been some debate as to whether the giving of security could ever amount to a transaction at an undervalue. In *Hill (as Trustee in Bankruptcy of Nurkowski) v Spread Trustee Co Ltd*,[560] which was a case that concerned section 423 of the Act but in which the same two limbs of the definition are used, the Court of Appeal held that the giving of security without the receipt of any consideration in return will fall within the first limb of the definition. In that case, security had been given for an existing debt. There had been no consideration provided to the security giver for doing so, such as by way of a forbearance in suing for the debt.

14.16.3.4.1 With respect to the second limb of the definition, Millett J in *Re MC Bacon Ltd*[561] said that the granting of security could not constitute a transaction at an undervalue within the second limb. This was because the granting of the security did not deplete the debtor company's assets nor diminish their value. The debtor retained the right to redeem, sell, or remortgage the charged assets. All it lost in giving the security was the ability to apply the assets otherwise than in satisfaction of the secured debt. That was not something which was capable of valuation in monetary terms and was not customarily disposed of for value.

14.16.3.4.2 The view that had been taken by Millett J was contradicted by Arden LJ in *obiter* comments in *Hill (as Trustee in Bankruptcy of Nurkowski) v Spread Trustee Co Ltd*.[562] Her Ladyship expressed the view that the granting of security by the debtor could amount to a transaction at an undervalue within the second limb of the definition. She said that the definition did not necessarily require that there should be a diminution in the debtor's assets or in their value, nor did it require that there was a grant of proprietary rights by the debtor. A grant by the debtor

---

[559] It should be noted that there is no equivalent provision in s 339 of the Act in relation to insolvent individuals.

[560] [2006] EWCA Civ 542; [2006] BCC 646.

[561] [1990] BCC 78, at 91–92, [1990] BCLC 324, at 340–341. The view expressed by Millett J was approved by Balcombe LJ in the Court of Appeal in *Menzies v National Bank of Kuwait SAK* [1994] BCC 119, at 129.

[562] [2006] EWCA Civ 542; [2006] BCC 646, at [138].

of other rights could be considered as falling within the definition and so could constitute the giving of consideration by the debtor. In any event, she considered that the grant of security might involve a disposition of property rights by the debtor. Whilst the grant of security does not involve an outright transfer of ownership in assets so as to deprive the debtor of its physical connection with them (although a legal or equitable mortgage does involve a notional transfer of title, subject to the debtor's equity of redemption), it does involve the granting of a right of recourse to the assets and a commensurate granting of priority in the assets over the claims of other creditors of the debtor.[563] There was no reason why the value of the right to have such recourse and to such priority should be left out of the account in determining if there had been a transaction at an undervalue.

If the view expressed by Arden LJ is correct then a rather curious consequence   **14.16.3.4.3** could follow. This consequence is that the security might be capable of challenge under section 238 when it is not possible, or it is more difficult, to mount a successful challenge under section 239, which is the section that is more appropriately tailored to challenging the validity of security. For instance, the security may have been granted outside the more limited time period that might apply under section 239, or it may not be possible to establish the necessary motive on the part of the company in terms of the desire to prefer the recipient of the security. In that regard, the task of the liquidator or administrator is easier under section 238 than under section 239. Under section 239, the liquidator or administrator has the task of showing that the requisite desire existed on the part of the company. Under section 238, the liquidator or administrator has to establish that a transaction at an undervalue took place but it is then for the person that is seeking to uphold the transaction to defend it by showing that in entering into the transaction the company did so both (i) subjectively in good faith and for the purpose of carrying on its business, and (ii) objectively, in that that there were reasonable grounds to believe the transaction would be for the company's benefit.

14.16.4 Preferences

Section 239 of the Act[564] concerns preferences that a company may have given in favour of another person at a 'relevant time' prior to its entry into winding up or administration. The liquidator or administrator is given power to challenge any such preference and the court is given a wide discretion as to the order which can

---

[563] As to the consequences of granting security, Arden LJ referred to what was said by Lord Hoffmann and Lord Millett in *Buchler v Talbot* [2004] UKHL 9; [2004] 2 AC 298, at [29] and [51], respectively.

[564] The comparable section for bankruptcy is s 340 of the Insolvency Act 1986.

be made to restore the position to what it would have been had the preference not been given.[565]

14.16.4.1 There are three essential ingredients that must be established by the liquidator or administrator before an order may be made. First, that the preference was given by the company at a relevant time. Second, that what occurred constituted a preference in favour of another person. Thirdly, that the company was influenced by a desire to prefer the beneficiary of the preference. Each of those requirements will now be examined.

14.16.4.2 *Relevant time*

Subject to meeting the insolvency tests, a relevant time can be any of three possible periods. First, it is a period of two years prior to the onset of the insolvency proceedings, if the person preferred was connected with the company.[566] Secondly, it is a period of six months before the onset of the insolvency proceedings.[567] Thirdly, it is the preliminary period before the appointment of an administrator.[568] However, it will only be a relevant time in either of the first two situations if the company was insolvent (i.e. unable to pay its debts within the meaning of section 123 of the Insolvency Act 1986) at the time the preference was given, or became insolvent in consequence of the giving of the preference.[569]

14.16.4.3 *A preference*[570]

A company gives a preference in favour of another person if:

(a) that [other] person is one of the company's creditors or a guarantor or surety of any of the company's debts or other liabilities, and

(b) the company does anything or suffers anything to be done which (in either case) has the effect of putting that person in a [better position than he would otherwise have endured in an insolvent liquidation of the company].

14.16.4.3.1 It is a question of fact as to whether or not the relevant person has been put in a better position than it was in before the relevant act was done. It follows that there cannot be a preference in favour of someone who was not an existing creditor, guarantor, or surety. Hence, the granting of security to a new lender will not amount to a preference. In addition, on the basis that it would not put the lender in a better position than it was in beforehand, the granting of security simply to cover a new facility that is made available by an existing lender should also be safe,

---

565 The powers of the court to make an order are discussed below.
566 S 240(1)(a) of the Act. The test for connection is contained in s 249 of the Act.
567 S 240(1)(b) of the Act.
568 S 240(1)(c) and (d) of the Act.
569 S 240(2) of the Act.
570 S 239(4) of the Act.

so long as the facility does not amount to a re-financing of existing indebtedness and the security does not extend to cover the existing indebtedness.

Examples where a person would be put in a preferential position would include repayment of existing indebtedness of the company, the granting of security for existing indebtedness, repaying a creditor so as to relieve a guarantor of exposure under the guarantee, and any other act which has the effect of putting an existing creditor in a better position than it would be in should the company go into insolvent liquidation.

14.16.4.3.2

The fact that the act was done pursuant to a court order does not prevent it from being a preference.[571]

14.16.4.3.3

14.16.4.4 Influenced by a desire[572]

The court may only make an order if the company, in giving the preference, was 'influenced by a desire' to achieve the result mentioned in (b) above (i.e. to put the other person in that better position). This will be presumed (unless the contrary is proved) where the other person was connected with the company.[573] This matter should be judged at the time the preference occurred[574] and there must probably have been some contemplation that the company may not be able to pay its debts. It is the subjective desire of the company which is relevant, not that of the recipient of the preference, although it might be possible to infer the desire from the relevant circumstances.[575] Because the company must have been influenced by the desire, there must be a positive desire to prefer, although it need not be the only or predominant intention of the company; it can be one of the factors that influenced the company.[576] A decision that is taken for proper commercial considerations should be contrasted with one that was intended to put the other party in a preferred position.[577] An intention to keep the support of the company's bank by giving it security may not amount to a desire to prefer the bank.[578]

14.16.5 Sections 238 and 239: remedies

Each of sections 238 and 239 of the Act provides that the court may make such order as it thinks fit to restore the position to what it would have been but for the impugned transaction or giving of the preference. Section 241 of the Act[579]

---

571 S 239(7) of the Act.
572 S 239(5) of the Act.
573 S 239(6) of the Act.
574 *Wills v Corfe Joinery Ltd* [1997] BCC 511.
575 *Re Fairway Magazines Ltd* [1992] BCC 924.
576 *Re MC Bacon Ltd* [1990] BCC 78.
577 *Re Fairway Magazines Ltd* [1992] BCC 924.
578 *Re MC Bacon Ltd* [1990] BCC 78.
579 The comparable section for bankruptcy is s 342 of the Insolvency Act 1986.

amplifies upon this by setting out a non-exhaustive list of the orders that the court may make. The remedies available under sections 238 and 239 are without prejudice to any other remedies that might be available at general law.[580]

14.16.5.1 It is clear that the power of the court is discretionary and that the court is given a wide discretion as to the orders that it might make, although the court should not act oppressively or unreasonably.[581] The court should take into account whether it would be appropriate to make an order that would have extra-territorial effect.[582] It has been held that the circumstances may justify the court in making no order at all.[583]

14.16.5.2 The court might order monetary compensation or a reversal of the transaction and appropriate compensatory adjustments for any compensation that had been received.[584] In relation to a transaction or preference which had the effect of releasing or discharging a surety, the court is specifically given the power to reinstate the surety's obligations.[585]

14.16.5.3 *Third parties*

Section 241(2) of the Act provides that the order that the court makes may affect a third party or property of a third party, even if the third party was not the direct party to an impugned transaction or the direct recipient of a preference. It goes on, however, to provide a defence to a third party with a derivative, rather than direct, connection with an impugned transaction or preference, if it acted in good faith and for value. The onus is on the defendant to make out the defence.[586] There are several further factors which must be taken into account in relation to such a defence.[587]

14.16.5.4 *Secured parties*

The question arises as to whether the recovery that a liquidator or administrator might make under section 238 or section 239 would be subject to security that had been given by the company prior to the onset of the insolvency proceedings. At the outset, the question must be distinguished from the position where property which is the subject of proceedings brought by the insolvency official was

---

[580] S 241(4) of the Act.

[581] See Sir Donald Nicholls V-C in *Re Paramount Airways Ltd* [1993] Ch 223, at 239.

[582] *Re Paramount Airways Ltd* [1993] Ch 223; *Re Unigreg Ltd* (unreported, 12/2/2004, Judge Weeks QC sitting in the High Court).

[583] *Singla (Trustee of Brown) v Brown and Malden-Browne* [2007] EWHC 405 (Ch), [2007] BPIR 424.

[584] *Re Thoars (Decd), Ramlort Ltd v Reid* [2004] EWCA Civ 800, [2004] BPIR 985.

[585] S 241(1)(e) of the Act.

[586] *Re Sonatacus Ltd* [2007] EWCA Civ 31, [2007] BCC 342.

[587] See ss 241(2A) to (3C) of the Act.

disposed of by the debtor company at a time when it was within the compass of fixed security and such disposition was without the security holder's consent. In such a case, the property might continue to be the subject of the security, on the basis as discussed earlier in this chapter. In such a case, the proceedings brought by the insolvency official should not overreach the security holder's interest under its pre-existing security. On the other hand, if the property was only subject to an uncrystallised floating charge at the time of its disposition, and the disposition was by way of absolute transfer, then it would have ceased to be subject to the charge at the time of the disposition, provided the disposition fell within the broadly understood concept of being in the ordinary course of business.

Bearing those points in mind, the question might become whether the benefit of the recovery by the liquidator or administrator in proceedings brought under the sections would fall within the compass of pre-existing security where the security contains an after-acquired property clause which, in its terms, seeks to catch such benefit. Generally speaking, the answer to the question should be that the benefit of the recovery by the insolvency official would not be caught by the pre-existing security, particularly where the recovery is seen as being compensatory, such as where the defendant is required to make a payment to redress any unfair benefit it had received under the impugned transaction. This is because the right of action is vested in the insolvency official. The proceedings are brought by him for the benefit of the general body of unsecured creditors. The recoveries are held by the insolvency official for the benefit of the general body of creditors,[588] which should be seen as being distinct from the property rights of the company prior to the onset of the insolvency proceedings.

14.16.5.4.1

Some qualification may have to be made to that analysis, however. As mentioned above, it has been held that, amongst the armoury of orders that are available, the court might require that a previous transfer of property by the debtor should be reversed, so that the property is revested in the debtor. This is recognised by section 241(1)(a) of the Act, which includes amongst the orders that the court may make, an order that any property which the company had transferred should be vested in the company. In such a case, it might be arguable that the effect of the vesting in the company is that its property is restored to it *in specie*, so that it resumes its ownership of the property as if the impugned transaction had not taken place.[589] Alternatively, it might be argued that the vesting has the effect of conferring a property right on the company. Thus, the vesting might be seen either as restoring the situation to that which existed before the impugned original

14.16.5.4.2

---

588 *Re Yagerphone Ltd* [1935] 1 Ch 392; *Re MC Bacon Ltd* [1991] Ch 127, at 137.
589 See *NA Kratzmann Pty Ltd v Tucker* (1968) 123 CLR 295 for a similar view that has been taken in Australia.

transfer by the company, so that the asset would be subject to the security that had then existed, or the vesting might be seen as having the effect of conferring a property right on the company which would then fall under the after-acquired property clause in the security. However, those arguments must still be viewed in light of the fact that the order of the court revesting the property only occurs in consequence of the pursuit of a right of action that is settled on the insolvency official for the benefit of the general body of the debtor's creditors. The right is not exercisable by or for the benefit of the security holder. In policy terms, it is difficult to see how it would be correct to finish up with the result that the outcome of the proceedings should benefit the security holder.

14.16.6 Transactions defrauding creditors

Section 423 of the Act concerns transactions at an undervalue that a debtor has entered into to defraud or prejudice one or more of its creditors. That section is supported by further provisions in sections 424 and 425 of the Act. Section 423 applies to both company debtors and individual debtors and it applies whether or not insolvency proceedings have been commenced against the debtor. There is no necessity to show that the debtor was insolvent at the time of the relevant transaction and there are no time limits in terms of when the transaction took place.[590] The court has a wide discretion in the orders it may make to restore the position to what it would have been had the transaction not occurred and to protect the interests of persons who were victims of the transaction. This is amplified in section 425 of the Act, which also provides for certain defences that are available to third parties.

14.16.6.1 The ingredients of the section are that there should have been (i) a transaction at an undervalue that was entered into by the debtor, (ii) which was entered into for a relevant purpose, and (iii) which has been to the actual or potential prejudice of one or more victims, by whom or on whose behalf a claim is brought under the section. Those ingredients will now be examined.

14.16.6.2 *Transaction at an undervalue*

The expression 'transaction at an undervalue' as used in section 423 of the Act is, essentially, the same as that used in section 238 of the Act, with the additional ground of a transaction that was entered into in consideration of marriage or a civil partnership.[591]

---

[590] Although the Limitation Act 1980 will apply: see *Hill (as Trustee in Bankruptcy of Nurkowski) v Spread Trustee Co Ltd* [2006] EWCA Civ 542, [2006] BCC 646; *Giles v Rhind* [2008] EWCA Civ 118.

[591] S 423(1) of the Act.

14.16.6.3 *Purpose*

Section 423(3) of the Act provides that the court may only make an order if the court is satisfied that the purpose of the debtor in entering into the transaction at an undervalue was either:

(a) [to put] assets beyond the reach of a person who is making, or may at some time make, a claim against [the debtor], or
(b) [otherwise to prejudice] the interests of such a person in relation to the claim which he is making or may make.

The purpose must have been a real or substantial purpose but it need not be the only or dominant purpose for the transaction.[592] Arden LJ made a number of further comments as to the concept of purpose as it is relevant to section 423 in *Hill (as Trustee in Bankruptcy of Nurkowski) v Spread Trustee Co Ltd*.[593] Her Ladyship said that it was not necessary to show that the purpose of the debtor could be achieved by entering into the transaction. Similarly, the debtor might have the necessary purpose even though he was mistaken in believing that he could achieve that purpose by entering into the transaction. It was the entry into the transaction, not the outcome of the transaction itself, which must have the necessary purpose. The concept of purpose would not be satisfied by evidence that the debtor only had a mere hope, but it would be sufficient to show a positive intention, which substantially motivated the debtor in entering into the transaction. **14.16.6.3.1**

14.16.6.4 *Victims*

Proceedings under section 423 might be instituted by either an insolvency official or a 'victim' of the transaction.[594] Such proceedings are brought on behalf of all of the victims of a transaction,[595] although it is still possible for proceedings to be brought if there is only one victim, such as where its security has been adversely affected by the transaction.[596] A victim of the transaction is a person who is, or is capable of being, prejudiced by it.[597] A person may be a victim of a transaction, and thus a person whose interests may be protected by an order under section 423(5), even though the debtor's purpose in entering into the transaction, as referred to in section 423(3), may not have been to prejudice that person but, rather, someone else; indeed the debtor may have been unaware of the victim when the transaction was entered into.[598]

---

[592] *Inland Revenue Commissioners v Hashmi* [2002] EWCA Civ 981, [2002] BCC 943.
[593] [2006] EWCA Civ 542; [2006] BCC 646, at [102].
[594] This is subject to s 424(1) of the Act in a case where the debtor is subject to insolvency proceedings.
[595] S 424(2) of the Act.
[596] *National Westminster Bank PLC v Jones* [2001] EWCA Civ 1541, [2002] 1 BCLC 55.
[597] S 423(5) of the Act.
[598] See Arden LJ in *Hill (as Trustee in Bankruptcy of Nurkowski) v Spread Trustee Co Ltd* [2006] EWCA Civ 542; [2006] BCC 646, at [101].

14.16.7 Avoidance of floating charges

Section 245 of the Act applies to floating charges.[599] It gives the liquidator or administrator of a debtor company the right to challenge (in whole or in part) a floating charge that was given by the company, if the charge was created at a 'relevant time' prior to the onset of the relevant insolvency proceedings. It should be noted, at the outset, that section 245 of the Act does not apply to a floating charge which is within a security financial collateral arrangement, as discussed earlier in this chapter.[600]

14.16.7.1 Relevant time

There are three alternative periods in which a 'relevant time' might have occurred in relation to the granting of the charge.[601] Where the charge was created in favour of a person that is connected to the company,[602] a relevant time can be any time within a period of two years prior to the onset of the insolvency proceedings.[603] Where the chargee was not a connected person, a relevant time can be any time within a period of one year before the onset of the insolvency proceedings, provided that the debtor company was either then insolvent or it became insolvent in consequence of the transaction under which the charge was created. Whether or not the chargee was connected to the company, a charge will also be created at a relevant time if it was created in the preliminary period before an administrator was appointed.

14.16.7.2 The invalidity[604]

If the floating charge was created at a relevant time then it is invalid except to the extent of:

 (a) the value of so much of the consideration for the creation of the charge as consists of money paid, or goods or services supplied, to the company at the same time as, or after, the creation of the charge,
 (b) the value of so much of that consideration as consists of the discharge or reduction, at the same time as, or after, the creation of the charge, of any debt of the company, and
 (c) [interest thereon].

14.16.7.3 Points arising

Unlike the position under section 239 of the Act, there is no need for the insolvency official to prove any intention to prefer the interests of the chargee. In other

---

599 I.e. a charge which was created as a floating charge, even if it has crystallised: see s 251 of the Act.
600 See Reg 10(5) of the Financial Collateral Arrangements (No 2) Regs 2003 (SI 2003/3226).
601 Ss 245(3) and (4) of the Act.
602 The test for connection is contained in s 249 of the Act.
603 As defined in s 245(5) of the Act.
604 S 245(2) of the Act.

words, to the extent that the charge secures a pre-existing liability of the chargor to the chargee, the charge is invalid. Nor can the charge be saved by a defence like that which is provided in section 238(5) for transactions at an undervalue (i.e. bona fide intention and reasonable belief of benefit to the company). On the other hand, the charge is only invalid under the section to the extent that it secures such pre-existing indebtedness; it is not invalid under section 245 with respect to any value provided at the same time as, or after, its creation.

Cases decided under predecessor legislation had taken a liberal view as to the **14.16.7.3.1** saving condition that the secured value should have been contemporaneous or subsequent to the granting of the charge. It had been held that the requirement would be taken as met, even if the value was provided before the charge was created, provided that the value was provided in consideration of an agreement that the charge would be provided.[605] That view no longer applies. The requirement is now that the charge should truly be contemporaneous with, or precede, the giving of value by the chargee, although it might be permissible to save a later formal security document which merely implements a preceding, but enforceable, charge.[606]

The value of goods or services supplied is their monetary value at the time of **14.16.7.3.2** supply to the company, taken as the amount which could reasonably have been obtained for their supply in the ordinary course of business on the same terms.[607] It should be noted that the money or the goods and services must be paid or supplied to the company, hence a charge to secure an advance to a third party would not be saved. However, it is legitimate for the charge to secure a payment made to a third party on behalf of the company, if the company was indebted to the third party, as that would be done in discharge of the indebtedness of the company to the third party.

The charge can legitimately cover money lent for a re-financing or discharge of **14.16.7.3.3** existing indebtedness of the company. It is submitted, however, that this must be the re-financing or discharge of indebtedness due to a third party and not to the lender itself, as that would not constitute the provision of new value to the company.[608]

The effect of the section is to avoid the charge, not any debt obligation purport- **14.16.7.3.4** edly secured under it, so that the section cannot be relied upon to challenge a repayment of the debt.[609]

---

[605] *Re Columbian Fireproofing Co Ltd* [1910] 1 Ch 758.
[606] *Re Shoe Lace Ltd, Power v Sharp Investments Ltd* [1993] BCC 609.
[607] S 245(6) of the Act.
[608] See *Re GT Whyte & Co Ltd* [1983] BCLC 311.
[609] *Mace Builders (Glasgow) Ltd v Lunn* [1987] Ch 191.

14.16.7.3.5 Section 245 represents a rare situation where the rule in *Clayton*'s case[610] may be applied for the advantage of a bank.[611] By the application of the rule, indebtedness on a running account that was existing at the time the charge was taken can be treated as discharged by payments that are made into the account, whereas drawings from the account after the charge was taken are treated as effectively secured under the charge and will not be treated as paid off until all of the old debt has been repaid.

14.16.8 Extortionate credit transactions

Section 244 of the Act[612] concerns extortionate credit transactions. It gives a liquidator or administrator the power to challenge such a transaction (whether it remains current or has terminated) if it was entered into by the debtor company within a period of three years preceding the onset of the relevant insolvency proceedings.[613] The court is given a number of wide powers to re-order or otherwise qualify the transaction, an obligation under it or any relevant security, or to require payments to be made to the insolvency official or for accounts to be taken.[614] The burden is on the person defending the transaction to show that it was not extortionate.[615] Because of the language that it used, it is submitted that the court could re-open a transaction and review the effect of the transaction with reference to the position at the outset of the transaction or with respect to the effect of changes in an interest rate or other matters which came into effect or occurred after the date on which the transaction took effect.[616]

14.16.8.1 Section 244(3) provides that:

. . . a transaction is extortionate if, having regard to the risk accepted by the person providing the credit—

(a) the terms of it are or were such as to require grossly exorbitant payments to be made (whether unconditionally or in certain contingencies) in respect of the provision of credit, or

(b) it otherwise grossly contravened ordinary principles of fair dealing.

---

[610] *Devaynes v Noble, Clayton's Case* (1816) LJ Ch 256, 35 ER 767.

[611] See *Re Yeovil Glove Co Ltd* [1965] Ch 148.

[612] The comparable provision for individuals will be found in s 343 of the Act.

[613] S 244(2) of the Act. A challenge to a transaction may be mounted under this section concurrently with a challenge under s 238 of the Act: see s 244(5) of the Act.

[614] S 244(4) of the Act.

[615] S 244(3) of the Act.

[616] This is different from the position under comparable provisions that used to apply under ss 137 and 138 of the Consumer Credit Act 1974 (now repealed), where the position had to be judged primarily as at the time the transaction was entered into: see *Paragon Finance plc v Staunton* [2001] EWCA Civ 1466; [2002] 1 WLR 685, at [63]–[66]; *Broadwick Financial Services Ltd v Spencer* [2002] EWCA Civ 35; [2002] 1 All ER (Comm) 446, at [48]–[56].

The concept of an extortionate credit transaction was considered by the Court of **14.16.8.2**
Appeal in *Paragon Finance plc v Staunton*.[617] That was a case which concerned
comparable provisions in what was then sections 137 and 138 of the Consumer
Credit Act 1974 (now repealed). The court quoted from Professor Sir Roy Goode's
book, *Consumer Law and Practice*,[618] that:

> the concepts of extortion and unconscionability are very similar. 'Extortionate', like
> 'harsh and unconscionable', signifies not merely that the terms of the bargain are
> stiff, or even unreasonable, but that they are so unfair as to be oppressive. This carries
> with it the notion of morally reprehensible conduct on the part of the creditor in tak-
> ing grossly unfair advantage of the debtor's circumstances.[619]

14.17 Enforcement of Security

14.17.1 Determining whether to enforce and the position before enforcement

The rights and duties of a secured creditor in relation to the enforcement of its
security are grounded in equity. Assuming that the right to enforce has arisen due
to the default of the obligor,[620] the creditor is then entitled to determine in its own
interests when and how it wishes to enforce its security, and, if the security involves
more than one item of property, the order in which it will enforce its security over
those items of property.[621] The security holder is under no obligation to preserve
the security prior to the exercise of its enforcement rights.[622] If the obligor is
unhappy with the situation and the delay in the enforcement of the security, it can
either exercise its right of redemption, pay off the outstanding liability, and retrieve
the security, or it can apply to the court for an order for sale of the property.[623]
The obligor's right of redemption was mentioned earlier in this chapter.

There are statutory limitations upon the right of enforcement of security where
the obligor is in administration[624] or, if it is an eligible company, where proposals **14.17.1.1**
have been made for a voluntary arrangement concerning it.[625]

Prior to the right to enforcement arising, generally speaking the security holder
does not have rights to intervene in relation to the secured property, unless it can **14.17.1.2**

---

[617] [2001] EWCA Civ 1466, [2002] 1 WLR 685.

[618] At para 47.26.

[619] See also Sir John Donaldson MR in *Wills v Wood* [1984] CCLR 7.

[620] For instance, by the obligor failing to meet a lawful demand for repayment: *Bank of Baroda v Panessar* [1987] Ch 335. See further Chap 3.

[621] *Farrar v Farrars Ltd* (1888) 40 LR 40 ChD 395; *China and South Sea Bank Ltd v Tan* [1990] 1 AC 536.

[622] *AIB Finance Ltd v Alsop (Debtors)* [1998] 2 All ER 929.

[623] S 91 of the Law of Property Act 1925. See *Palk v Mortgage Services Funding PLC* [1993] Ch 330.

[624] See para 43(2) of Sched B1 to the Insolvency Act 1986 (which is extended to the period pre-liminary to the appointment of the administrator by para 44 of that Schedule).

[625] See para 12(1)(g) of Sched A1 to the Insolvency Act 1986. There are also limits under con-sumer protection legislation, where the security giver is an individual.

show that the sufficiency of its security was threatened. However, there is no legal restriction on the security holder from doing so if it is given the appropriate power by the security instrument. Accordingly, it would be entitled to require that an option should be exercised if the benefit of the option formed part of the security. It would be a matter of interpretation to see if the parties had agreed that the security holder should have such a right.[626]

14.17.1.3 Where the security holder's consent was required before the obligor could take certain action with respect to the secured property prior to the enforcement of the security then, in the absence of a contractual provision to the contrary, the security holder is entitled to have regard to its own interests, rather than those of the obligor, in deciding if it should grant its consent.[627]

14.17.1.4 The methods of enforcement that exist under English law, at least in theory, are foreclosure, the application of financial collateral under a security financial collateral arrangement, and the application of cash balances, taking possession of the secured property, the exercise of a power of sale, the appointment of an administrator, and the appointment of a receiver. Each of those methods of enforcement will now be looked at in turn.

14.17.2 Foreclosure

Foreclosure is the most ancient of the powers of enforcement, although it rarely arises and so it is more of a theoretical than real power of enforcement. It is the method by which the obligor's equity or redemption is closed out or, in effect, extinguished, so that the creditor becomes the full and unencumbered owner of the property.[628] Once the foreclosure has been completed, the creditor loses its right to pursue the obligor for the debt that was secured on the property, unless it gives up its rights and allows the foreclosure to be re-opened, which the security holder cannot do if it has sold the property.[629] Foreclosure is only available where the security is a legal mortgage[630] or an equitable mortgage which can be perfected by being turned into a legal mortgage pursuant to an agreement by the mortgagor to give a legal mortgage.[631] It is not available to enforce a pledge of goods,[632] nor to enforce an equitable charge or an equitable mortgage which cannot be turned into a legal mortgage.[633]

---

[626] See *Citibank NA v MBIA Assurance SA* [2007] EWCA Civ 11, [2007] 1 All ER (Comm) 475, which followed *Wise v Landsell* [1921] 1 Ch 420 and *Nelson v Hannam* [1943] 1 Ch 59.

[627] *Starling v Lloyds TSB Bank PLC* [2000] Lloyd's Rep Bank 8.

[628] See *Silberschildt v Schiott* (1814) 3 Ves&B 45; *Le Gros v Cockerell* (1832) 5 Sim 384; *Carter v Wake* (1877) 4 ChD 605; and *Re Farnol Eades Ervine & Co* [1915] 1 Ch 22.

[629] *Lockhart v Hardy* (1846) 9 Beav 349.

[630] *General Credit and Discount Co v Glegg* (1883) 22 ChD 549.

[631] *Perry v Keane, Perry v Partridge* (1836) 6LJCh 67; *Cox v Toole* (1855) 20 Beav 145.

[632] *Carter v Wake* (1877) 4 ChD 605.

[633] *Tennant v Trenchard* (1869) 4 Ch App 537; *Re Owen* [1894] 3 Ch 220.

Foreclosure requires an order of the court which extinguishes the obligor's equity **14.17.2.1**
of redemption, which will not be given without allowing the obligor time to pay,
failing which the order will be made absolute and the equity of redemption will be
extinguished.[634] The court can order the property to be sold in any foreclosure
action,[635] which is what it would normally do.

14.17.3 Application of financial collateral

A legal or equitable mortgagee of financial collateral under a security financial
collateral arrangement may appropriate the collateral by way of enforcement, if
the security instrument permits it to do so. This has been discussed earlier in this
chapter.

14.17.4 Application of cash balances

Where security has been taken over the benefit of a bank account, that is, the cash
balance on the account, then if the cash balance comprises financial collateral
under a security financial collateral arrangement, and that arrangement is by way
of legal or equitable mortgage, it should be possible to appropriate it by the method
just referred to (provided that the security instrument permits such action). In the
alternative, the appropriation could be effected at common law. This method of
enforcement was acknowledged by Lord Hoffmann in *Re Bank of Credit and
Commerce International SA (No 8)*,[636] which was a case where the cash balance
arose on an account that was held with the security taker.

It is submitted that where the bank account over which security has been taken is **14.17.4.1**
held with a third party, the security would be enforced by requiring the third party
to pay the balance to the security taker, which would then effect the application as
the final step in the enforcement. The same analysis should also apply in the case
of any other debt that is the subject of security, where the security holder obtains
payment of it and then applies that payment in satisfaction of the secured
liability.

14.17.5 Taking possession

The right to take possession is usually associated with a mortgage of land, by
which the mortgagee becomes entitled to collect the rents on the property. It
also applies to other types of property, although the right to take possession
of goods under a security bill of sale given by an individual is restricted.[637]
For instance, the right to take possession of the mortgagor's business has been

---

[634] *Platt v Mendel* (1884) 27 ChD 246.
[635] S 91(2) of the Law of Property Act 1925.
[636] [1998] AC 214.
[637] See s 7 of the Bills of Sale Act (1878) Amendment Act 1882.

permitted where the security extended to the business.[638] At common law, the right to take possession by implication of the security only arises if the security is by way of legal mortgage. It does not extend to equitable mortgages or charges.[639] This problem can be overcome by an express provision in the security instrument. Possession may not be taken of a dwelling house without a court order.[640]

14.17.5.1 A security holder which goes into possession undertakes onerous duties with respect to the secured property and, for that reason, it is generally considered best not to go into possession. By going into possession, the security holder assumes a duty to take reasonable care of the property and to protect and exploit it, maximising the return but without taking undue risks.[641] For example, the security holder has a duty, albeit limited,[642] to execute repairs to real property and is liable for waste, that is, destruction or damage to the property.[643] The security holder is liable to account for both the income it receives from the property whilst in possession as well as what it would have received but for its wilful default or negligence in failing to exploit the property.[644] A security holder in possession of land may find itself responsible for environmental liabilities.

14.17.6 The power of sale

When examining the right of a security holder to sell the secured assets by the exercise of its power of sale, a distinction needs to be drawn between the right of a pledgee to sell the goods that are subject to the pledge, and the position as it relates to non-possessory security.

14.17.6.1 Pledges

A pledgee has a power of sale at common law which is an inherent incident of the security.[645] The duties as to the exercise of the power are pretty much the same as those that apply to a sale under non-possessory security.[646]

---

638 *Chaplin v Young* (1863) 33 Beav 330.

639 *Western Bank Ltd v Schindler* [1977] Ch 1.

640 S 36 of the Administration of Justice Act 1970.

641 *Silven Properties Ltd v Royal Bank of Scotland PLC* [2003] EWCA 1409, [2004] 1 WLR 997.

642 *Perry v Walker* (1855) 3 Eq Rep 721; *Silven Properties Ltd v Royal Bank of Scotland PLC* [2003] EWCA 1409, [2004] 1 WLR 997.

643 *Millett v Davey* (1862) 9 Jur NS 92.

644 *Chaplin v Young* (1863) 33 Beav 330; Rigby LJ in *Gosling v Gaskell* [1896] 1 QB 669, at 691 (approved on appeal at [1897] AC 575).

645 *Pothonier & Hodgson v Dawson* (1816) Holt 383; Cotton LJ in *Re Morritt, ex p Official Receiver* (1886) 18 QBD 222, at 232.

646 See the Privy Council in *The Odessa* [1916] 1 AC 145, at 159.

14.17.6.2 *Non-possessory security*

The position at common law as to an implied power of sale under non-possessory security was not very satisfactory.[647] To overcome those difficulties, it became common to include an express power of sale and to take a power of attorney from the security giver, so that an equitable security holder could convey the legal title.[648] The position is now dealt with by statute. Section 101(1)(i) of the Law of Property Act 1925 provides for an implied power of sale of any secured property[649] under any mortgage or charge[650] which has been made by deed. The right to exercise the implied power is regulated by section 103 of the Act, but this is usually overcome by express wording, as permitted by section 101(3) of the Act. It is also possible to apply to the court for an order for sale under section 91 of the Act.

The effect of the exercise of the statutory power of sale is provided for in section 104 of the Act. In effect, the sale overreaches any interests that were subordinate to those of the security holder which has exercised the power of sale, but the sale will be subject to interests which had priority over the interest of that security holder. Section 105 provides for the disposition of the proceeds of the sale.

14.17.6.2.1

14.17.6.3 *Duties in exercising the power of sale*

The security holder in exercising its power of sale is subject to important equitable duties.[651] The duties are owed to the security giver and others interested in the equity of redemption, such as other security holders of the property and, perhaps, guarantors.[652] The first is the duty to act in good faith so as not deliberately to set out to injure the mortgagor.[653] The second duty is to obtain a proper price, being the fair or true market value of the property at the time of sale.[654] In meeting that duty, the security holder must take proper care, such as by fairly and properly advertising the property, to obtain the best price reasonably obtainable at the date of the sale. Accordingly, the security holder may not act in a way which unfairly

---

[647] The power did not exist for a legal mortgage of land, because of the right to apply for an order for foreclosure. It did exist in relation to mortgages of personal chattels: see Cotton LJ in *Re Morritt, ex p Official Receiver* (1886) 18 QBD 222, at 233.

[648] It remains possible to take an express power of sale: *The Maule* [1997] 1 WLR 528.

[649] See the definition of 'mortgage' and 'property' in ss 205(1)(xvi) and (xx) of the Act.

[650] A 'mortgage' is defined to include a charge: see s 205(1)(xvi) of the Act. A similar construction applies to the expression 'mortgagee'.

[651] The duties are equitable rather than arising at common law: *China and South Sea Bank Ltd v Tan* [1990] 1 AC 536. The duties are comprehensively summarised in *Silven Properties Ltd v Royal Bank of Scotland PLC* [2003] EWCA 1409, [2004] 1 WLR 997.

[652] *Downsview Nominees Ltd v First City Corp* [1993] AC 295; *Burgess v Auger* [1998] BCLC 478; *Barclays Bank PLC v Kingston* [2006] EWHC 533, [2006] 2 Lloyd's Rep 59.

[653] *Downsview Nominees Ltd v First City Corp* [1993] AC 295.

[654] *Cuckmere Brick Co Ltd v Mutual Finance Ltd* [1971] Ch 949.

prejudices the security giver by selling hastily at a knock-down price.[655] On the other hand, the security holder is entitled to accept a firm offer to purchase, rather than having to wait so as to see if a higher, but uncertain, offer will materialise.[656] The security holder is entitled to sell the property in its existing state and, accordingly, there is no duty to improve the property or take other action to make it more saleable.[657] The security holder is obliged to ensure that any extra potential improvement that might be available for increasing the value of the property is properly advertised so as to influence the sale price, but the security holder is not obliged to undertake action to make the improvement.[658] If the security giver wishes to obtain greater protection than the foregoing then it must stipulate for that expressly in the security instrument.[659]

14.17.7 Appointment of an administrator

The 'holder of a qualifying floating charge' may appoint an administrator of a corporate debtor.[660] Such a holder is, essentially, a secured creditor which holds comprehensive security (by one or more instruments) over the whole or substantially the whole of the debtor's assets, where such security includes a floating charge and the charge instrument purports to give the holder the power to appoint an administrator or an administrative receiver, or states that the relevant statutory provision applies to it.[661] There are various restrictions and procedures that must be followed in making the appointment (including as to giving notice to the holder of a prior floating charge and the charge must have become enforceable)[662] and the appointor must indemnify a person whom it has wrongly appointed.[663]

14.17.7.1 Despite the power of appointment that is vested in the security holder, the administrator is an officer of the court[664] and must perform his duties for the statutory purposes as laid down.[665] Accordingly, he does not owe his duties to the appointor and the latter cannot give instructions to the administrator. Thus, the ability to appoint an administrator might be thought to be of limited benefit to a security holder. However, the security holder can choose the administrator and the

---

655 See Sir Donald Nicholls V-C in *Palk v Mortgage Services Funding PLC* [1993] Ch 330, at 337–338.

656 *Meftah v Lloyds TSB Bank PLC* [2001] 2 All ER (Comm) 741.

657 *Silven Properties Ltd v Royal Bank of Scotland PLC* [2003] EWCA 1409, [2004] 1 WLR 997.

658 *Cuckmere Brick Co Ltd v Mutual Finance Ltd* [1971] Ch 949; *Silven Properties Ltd v Royal Bank of Scotland PLC* [2003] EWCA 1409, [2004] 1 WLR 997.

659 Ibid, at [18].

660 Para 14(1) of Sched B1 to the Insolvency Act 1986.

661 Paras 14(2) and (3) of Sched B1 to the Insolvency Act 1986.

662 See paras 7–9 and 15–20 of Sched B1 to the Insolvency Act 1986.

663 Para 21 of Sched B1 to the Insolvency Act 1986.

664 Para 5 of Sched B1 to the Insolvency Act 1986.

665 Para 3 of Sched B1 to the Insolvency Act 1986.

appointment does allow an insolvency practitioner to take charge of the debtor company, which may lead to a more realistic appraisal and order of its affairs than the company's own management might have been able to achieve. The administrator might also be able to achieve a sale of the business of the company as a going concern, especially with the co-operation of the security holder. In fact, a practice has developed of so-called 'pre-packaged' administrations, under which the sale of the business and assets of the debtor company is organised in advance of the appointment of the administrator, who then effects the sale shortly after his appointment, with the co-operation of the security holder which appointed him. A word of caution must be sounded at this point. As mentioned above, the administrator has statutory duties, he is an officer of the court, and he must conduct the administration for the statutory purposes. He must therefore ensure that the transaction is one which it is proper for him to enter into on behalf of the company.

14.17.8 Appointment of a receiver

A receiver may be appointed by the court under section 37 of the Supreme Court Act 1981 but that is unusual.[666] Such a receiver must act fairly as an officer of the court.[667] Such appointments at the behest of a security holder are rare and will not be explored further.

By far the greater number of appointments of receivers are made by security holders pursuant to their security, which will be the subject of the remaining discussion. There are two types of such receiver, being the receiver appointed over specific assets, and a receiver and manager who is appointed under comprehensive security given by a company, called an 'administrative receiver'.
14.17.8.1

The power to appoint a receiver is limited by the provisions of the Insolvency Act 1986 which deal with administration. Essentially, any receiver who is in office must vacate his office if an administrator is appointed.[668] Furthermore, the appointment of a receiver would amount to an act in enforcement of security, which is prohibited where a company is in administration, unless the administrator consents or the court permits,[669] neither of which would be likely. However, if an administrative receiver is in office then it is not possible for a company to go into administration, unless the security holder who appointed the administrative
14.17.8.2

---

[666] In *Masri v Consolidated Contractors International Co SAL* [2008] EWCA Civ 303, [2008] 2 Lloyd's Rep 128, the Court of Appeal considered the situation where the court might appoint a receiver by way of equitable execution of a debt, including foreign debts and debts that might arise in the future which related to an asset.

[667] *Re Newdigate Colliery Ltd* [1912] 1 Ch 468.

[668] Para 41 of Sched B1 to the Insolvency Act 1986.

[669] Para 43(2) of Sched B1 to the Insolvency Act 1986. The prohibition is extended to the period that is preliminary to the appointment of the administrator: see para 44 of the Act.

receiver consents[670] (at which point the administrative receiver would have to vacate office).

14.17.8.3 A person who appoints, or who obtains a court appointment of, a receiver must give notice of the appointment to the Registrar of Companies within seven days of the appointment.[671] When the receiver ceases to act, he must give notice of that fact to the Registrar.[672]

14.17.8.4 Receivers of specific assets

Section 101(1)(iii) of the Law of Property Act 1925 provides that a security holder under security made by deed may appoint a receiver. This is regulated by section 103 of the Act which, in turn, is usually overcome by an express provision in the security instrument, in accordance with section 101(3) of the Act. A receiver appointed under the statute is expressed by section 109(3) of the Act only to be a receiver of income. Accordingly, it is common in security instruments to use section 101(3) to extend the powers of the receiver so that he can manage the charged property and sell it. In the alternative, the security instrument might contain an express power of appointment of a receiver, as well as a statement of his powers. It should be noted that section 109(2) of the Act provides that the receiver is deemed to be the agent of the security giver, which alone is responsible for the receiver's acts and omissions, unless the security instrument provides otherwise. It would be a very rare security instrument which so provided. There is usually an express statement in the security instrument that the receiver acts as the agent of the security giver.

14.17.8.4.1 Essentially, this type of receiver is appointed to take possession of and manage the specific assets subject to the security and to receive the income from them, with the principal intention of selling the assets. The receiver may be appointed irrespective of whether the security giver is a corporate entity or an individual.

14.17.8.5 Administrative receivers

Administrative receivership only applies where the security giver is a company. The definition of an administrative receiver will be found in section 29(2) of the Insolvency Act 1986. It has a certain resonance with the definition of the holder of a qualifying floating charge. An administrative receiver is a receiver and manager appointed under comprehensive security over the whole or substantially the whole of the company's property, where such security comprises, or at least includes, a floating charge, no matter how insignificant the floating charge might be as a part of the overall package of security.[673] By the appointment of an administrative

---

[670] Para 39(1) of Sched B1 to the Insolvency Act 1986.
[671] S 871(1) of the Companies Act 2006 (formerly s 405(1) of the Companies Act 1985).
[672] S 871(2) of the Companies Act 2006 (formerly s 405(2) of the Companies Act 1985).
[673] *Re Croftbell Ltd* [1990] BCLC 844.

receiver, the secured creditor can prevent the appointment of an administrator of the company.[674]

The right to appoint an administrative receiver has been curtailed by legislation, which will be discussed at a later stage.

14.17.8.5.1

14.17.8.5.2 The role and powers of an administrative receiver

An administrative receiver acts as the agent of the company until it goes into liquidation.[675] In that role, he has extensive powers to manage and realise the business and assets of the company.[676] In effect, his powers override the management functions of the directors, although technically they remain in office with responsibilities under the Companies Acts and some very limited power to bring proceedings, so long as that does not impinge on the assets that are subject to the security.[677] The administrative receiver is personally liable on any contract that he enters into in carrying out his functions, unless the contract otherwise provides (as it will almost invariably do).[678] He is also liable for existing contracts of employment that he 'adopts'.[679]

As the administrative receiver acts as the agent of the company, the person who appointed him is not responsible for his acts and defaults, unless the appointor intervenes in the receivership, such as by giving the receiver instructions as to the conduct of the receivership.[680] Despite the fact that he is the agent of the company and not the agent of the security holder which appointed him, the receiver owes his primary duty to the appointor, to realise the assets, and pay off the secured debt.[681] The company, on whose behalf he acts, has no right to say who should be appointed, to dismiss the receiver, or to give him instructions.[682] In a sense, this leads to something of a split personality.

14.17.8.5.2.1

---

674 Paras 17, 25, and 39 of Sched 1 to the Insolvency Act 1986.

675 S 44(1)(a) of the Insolvency Act 1986. Because he acts as its agent and the company alone is responsible for his actions, the receiver should not normally be made liable under a third party costs order for unsuccessful litigation which the receiver had caused the company to bring: *Dolphin Quays Developments Ltd v Mills* [2007] EWHC 1180 (Ch), [2007] 4 All ER 503 (upheld [2008] EWCA Civ 385, but with less emphasis on the importance of an element of impropriety or unreasonableness as a necessary factor in deciding if the order should be made).

676 S 42(1) of the Insolvency Act 1986.

677 *Newhart Developments Ltd v Co-operative Commercial Bank Ltd* [1978] QB 814; *Tudor Grange Holdings Ltd v Citibank NA* [1992] Ch 53; *GE Capital Finance Ltd v Sutton* [2004] EWCA Civ 315, [2004] 2 BCLC 662.

678 S 44(1)(b) of the Insolvency Act 1986. He is entitled to an indemnity out of the assets of the company for that liability: s 44(1)(c).

679 S 44(1)(b) of the Insolvency Act 1986. Again, he has an indemnity as just mentioned.

680 *American Express International Banking Corp v Hurley* [1985] 3 All ER 564.

681 *Re B Johnson & Co (Builders) Ltd* [1955] Ch 661; *Gomba Holdings UK Ltd v Homan* [1986] 1 WLR 1301; *Downsview Nominees Ltd v First City Corp Ltd* [1993] AC 295; *Medforth v Blake* [2000] Ch 86; *Silven Properties Ltd v Royal Bank of Scotland PLC* [2003] EWCA 1409, [2004] 1 WLR 997.

682 See Rigby LJ in *Gaskell v Gosling* [1896] 1 QB 669, at 692 (approved [1897] AC 575); *Silven Properties Ltd v Royal Bank of Scotland PLC* [2003] EWCA 1409, [2004] 1 WLR 997.

14.17.8.5.2.2 The position of the receiver concerning existing contracts[683] that were in place prior to his appointment reflects a combination of factors: first, his position as the agent of the company; secondly, the fact that he is appointed under security that is or has become fixed security; thirdly, his primary duty to manage that security so as to pay off the secured debt. The consequence of this is that, generally speaking, the receiver is not bound by such contracts and can cause the company to breach them by not performing them.[684] Whilst the company may incur a liability in damages due to the breach, the receiver will not be personally liable for causing or procuring a breach of contract.[685]

14.17.8.5.2.3 Notwithstanding what has just been said, a receiver will be bound by an interest that ranks ahead of the security under which he was appointed.[686] In addition, it has been said that he may not seriously damage the goodwill of the company if there might be a surplus of assets after the security has been discharged or if the security does not extend to all of the assets of the company and his actions might impair the ability of the company to continue to trade with its other assets.[687] It has also been said that if a pre-existing contract were of a type that would normally be susceptible to an order for specific performance, then the court may be willing to make such an order, even though the receiver does not wish to perform the contract, unless the receiver has decided to end the business.[688] It is submitted that this ignores the interest of the security under which the receiver was appointed. By ordering performance of the contract, the company will probably have to use charged assets over which the security holder has a paramount claim.

14.17.8.5.2.4 The agency of the administrative receiver ends if the company goes into liquidation.[689] This means that he can no longer run the business of the company. Nonetheless, the receiver remains in possession of the assets over which he was appointed. The loss of his agency to act on behalf of the company does not mean that he becomes the agent of the appointor.[690] He remains in possession of the secured assets and is entitled to sell the assets in the realisation of the security

---

[683] Except, as already mentioned, existing employment contracts that he 'adopts'.

[684] This should be contrasted with the position of an administrator: see *Astor Chemicals Ltd v Synthetic Technology Ltd* [1990] BCC 97.

[685] *Airlines Airspares Ltd v Handley Page Ltd* [1970] Ch 193; *Welsh Development Agency v Export Finance Co Ltd* [1992] BCLC 148.

[686] *Freevale Ltd v Metrostore (Holdings) Ltd* [1984] Ch 199.

[687] See *Airlines Airspares Ltd v Handley Page Ltd* [1970] Ch 193, at 198 and *Astor Chemicals Ltd v Synthetic Technology Ltd* [1990] BCC 97, at 105.

[688] *Land Rover Group Ltd v UPF (UK) Ltd* [2002] EWHC 3183 (QB), [2003] 2 BCLC 222. The approach in that case should be contrasted with that taken in *Re Trans Tec Automotive (Campsie) Ltd* [2001] BCC 403.

[689] S 44(1)(a) of the Insolvency Act 1986.

[690] *Gosling v Gaskell* [1897] AC 575.

under which he was appointed.[691] The receiver may also continue litigation which had been commenced before the liquidation, whether it had been commenced by the company or by the receiver.[692]

14.17.8.6 *The duties of a receiver*

The duties of a receiver in the exercise of his powers were reviewed in *Silven Properties Ltd v Royal Bank of Scotland PLC*[693] and what follows is largely a distillation of the decision in that case. A receiver has duties in equity, not common law.[694] The duties are owed to the security holder who appointed him, as well as to the security giver and others with an interest in the equity of redemption, but the duty to the security holder to bring about a repayment of the secured debt is paramount.[695] Accordingly, the receiver's powers of management are not exercised for the benefit of the security giver but, rather, for the benefit of the security holder and are ancillary to that paramount obligation. If the receiver does breach his duty, that does not give rise to a claim in damages but, rather, to a duty to account. On the same basis as the duty of a security holder in exercising the power of sale, a receiver when selling property is obliged to take care to obtain the best price reasonably obtainable at the time of sale,[696] but he is entitled to sell the property as he finds it without a duty to make any improvement or to await an increase in value.[697]

There are two important statutory duties of a receiver which must not be overlooked. Under section 40 of the Insolvency Act 1986, if the company is not in the course of liquidation, the receiver must apply recoveries out of assets subject to a floating charge (as taken) in payment of preferential creditors, ahead of the claims of the security holder. In addition, under section 176A of that Act, the receiver must set aside the prescribed part from the recoveries under such a charge to meet the claims of unsecured creditors. **14.17.8.6.1**

14.17.9 Curtailment of the right to appoint an administrative receiver

Section 72A of the Insolvency Act 1986 provides that, with certain exceptions, an administrative receiver may not be appointed under security taken on or after the

---

[691] *Gosling v Gaskell* [1897] AC 575; *Sowman v David Samuel Trust Ltd* [1978] 1 WLR 22.

[692] *Mills v Birchall* [2008] EWCA Civ 385, at [27].

[693] [2003] EWCA 1409; [2004] 1 WLR 997, at [21]–[29].

[694] *Medforth v Blake* [2000] Ch 86; *Raja v Austin Gray* [2002] EWCA Civ 1965, [2003] BPIR 725.

[695] *Downsview Nominees Ltd v First City Corp* [1993] AC 295; *Burgess v Auger* [1998] BCLC 478; *Barclays Bank PLC v Kingston* [2006] EWHC 533, [2006] 2 Lloyd's Rep 59.

[696] *Downsview Nominees Ltd v First City Corp* [1993] AC 295; *Medforth v Blake* [2000] Ch 86; *Raja v Austin Gray* [2002] EWCA Civ 1965, [2003] BPIR 725.

[697] *Garland v Ralph Pay & Ransom* [1984] 2 EGLR 147; *Routestone Ltd v Minories Finance Ltd* [1997] BCC 180; *Meftah v Lloyds TSB Bank PLC* [2001] 2 All ER (Comm) 741.

date that the section came into force, which was 15 September 2003.[698] There is no restriction upon appointments made under security granted before that date.

14.17.9.1 There are a number of exceptions to section 72A, where it remains possible to appoint an administrative receiver under security taken after the above-mentioned date. These are contained in sections 72B to 72H of the Act.[699] The exceptions apply to the following situations: capital market arrangements (section 72B); public–private partnerships (section 72C); utility projects (section 72D); urban regeneration projects (section 72DA); project finance (section 72E); financial markets charges (section 72F); registered social landlords (section 72G); and protected railway, transport, and water companies (section 72GA). It is intended to mention some of those exceptions below.

14.17.9.2 Capital market arrangements (section 72B)

This exception is discussed at some length in Chapter 12. By way of summary, the exception applies to the appointment of an administrative receiver under an agreement that is or forms part of a 'capital market arrangement' which involves an actual or expected debt of at least £50 million (in any currency) and an arrangement for the issue of a capital market investment. The expressions 'capital market arrangement' and 'capital market investment' are defined in Schedule 2A to the Act.

14.17.9.3 Public–private partnerships (section 72C)

This exception applies to the appointment of an administrative receiver of a project company of a public–private partnership project which includes step-in rights.

14.17.9.3.1 A public–private partnership project is defined in the section as a project under which either:

(a) the resources [for the project] are provided partly by one or more public bodies and partly by one or more private persons, or
(b) [the project] is designed wholly or mainly to assist a public body to discharge a function.

14.17.9.3.2 The expression 'resources' is given a widely inclusive definition in Schedule 2A to the Act and that schedule also defines the expression 'public body'. There is no statutory definition of function but it probably means a function which the relevant public body was established or exists to perform.

---

[698] The Insolvency Act 1986, Section 72A (Appointed Date) Order 2003 (SI 2003/2095).
[699] S 72H of the Act provides that additions, deletions, and amendments to the exceptions may be made by secondary legislation.

The meaning of 'project' is left undefined, although it will be noted that it is used **14.17.9.3.3** in conjunction with the concepts of 'project company' and 'public–private partnership project'. In *Feetum v Levy*,[700] which was a case concerning the exception in section 72E but which would also be relevant in the present context, Lewison J, whilst declining to provide a complete definition of the word as it is used in these sections of the Act, said that the meaning of 'project' was not limited just to construction and engineering operations. It would also include the scheme in that case where the relevant company had entered into an agreement to purchase IT rights, which it intended to exploit.

A 'project company' is, essentially, a company which is dedicated to the project. In **14.17.9.3.4** more detail, it is defined in paragraph 7 of Schedule 2A for the purposes of the exceptions contained in section 72C and other sections, as follows:

(1) . . . a company is a 'project company' of a project if—
    (a) it holds property for the purpose of the project,
    (b) it has sole or principal responsibility under an agreement for carrying out all or part of the project,
    (c) it is one of a number of companies which together carry out the project,
    (d) it has the purpose of supplying finance to enable the project to be carried out, or
    (e) it is the holding company of a company within any of paragraphs (a) to (d).
(2) But a company is not a 'project company' of a project if—
    (a) it performs a function within sub-paragraph (1)(a) to (d) or is within sub-paragraph (1)(e), but
    (b) it also performs a function which is not—
        (i) within sub-paragraph (1)(a) to (d),
        (ii) related to a function within sub-paragraph (1)(a) to (d), or
        (iii) related to the project.
(3) For the purpose of this paragraph a company carries out all or part of a project whether or not it acts wholly or partly through agents.

'Step-in rights' in relation to a project are defined in paragraph 6 of Schedule 2A **14.17.9.3.5** for the purposes of this and other exceptions, as follows:

(1) . . . a project has 'step-in rights' if a person who provides finance in connection with the project has a conditional entitlement under an agreement to—
    (a) assume sole or principal responsibility under an agreement for carrying out all or part of the project, or
    (b) make arrangements for carrying out all or part of the project.
(2) In sub-paragraph (1) a reference to the provision of finance includes a reference to the provision of an indemnity.

In considering the definition of 'step-in rights' it should be noted that the word **14.17.9.3.5.1** 'agreement' is given a widely inclusive meaning in Schedule 2A, to include

---

700 [2005] EWHC 349 (Ch), [2005] 1 WLR 2576 (upheld on appeal: *Cabvision v Feetum* [2005] EWCA Civ 1601, [2005] Ch 585).

'an agreement or undertaking effected by (a) contract, (b) deed, or (c) any other instrument intended to have effect in accordance with' the law of any jurisdiction. It should also be noted that the definition requires that it is the person who provides the finance (including by the provision of an indemnity) who must have the conditional entitlement to assume the relevant responsibility or make the arrangements. A 'person' is defined in Schedule 2A to include a partnership or another unincorporated group of persons, so a syndicate of lenders could be considered to be a person which has provided the finance. However, it is not so clear that a security trustee, which simply held the security on behalf of the syndicate, would be considered to be such a person, although perhaps a facility agent acting as agent within the authority of the syndicate might be considered sufficient to meet the requirement.[701]

14.17.9.3.5.2 In *Feetum v Levy*, it was argued that the security holder (whose security was to secure an indemnity within sub-paragraph (2) of the definition of 'step-in rights') had the relevant entitlement by virtue of its right under the security either to appoint an administrative receiver of the project company or to appoint an administrator of the company. That argument was dismissed by the judge. If an administrative receiver was appointed, he would be acting as the agent of the company, as expressly provided in the security document (and, incidentally, as also provided by section 44(1)(a) of the Insolvency Act 1986). As such, the receiver would not be acting on behalf of the security holder but on behalf of the project company, and it would be up to the receiver to decide whether and how he should act. Similarly, an administrator would not be acting on behalf of the secured creditor who appointed him but would act on behalf of the company pursuant to his statutory powers. Hence, it could not it be said that the receiver or the administrator was assuming responsibility on behalf of the secured creditor to carry out the project, nor could the appointment of either of them be tantamount to the secured creditor making arrangements for carrying out the project.

14.17.9.4 Project finance (section 72E)

This exception permits the appointment of an administrative receiver of a project company of a project which is a 'financed project' and includes step-in rights. As to the concepts of a 'project company', a 'project', and 'step-in rights', see the discussion above concerning section 72C of the Act. See also that discussion as to the meaning of 'agreement', which is used in the definition that is about to be mentioned.

14.17.9.4.1 Section 72E provides that:

> a project is 'financed' if under an agreement relating to the project a project company incurs, or when the agreement is entered into is expected to incur, a debt of at least £50m for the purpose of carrying out the project.

---

[701] See the distinction between the role of a security trustee and a facility agent that was drawn in *British Energy Power & Trading Ltd v Credit Suisse* [2007] EWCA Civ 53.

14.17.9.4.2 It should be noted that in paragraph 5 of Schedule 2A to the Act, it is provided that the debt of £50 million:

(a) may be incurred at any time during the life of the . . . financed project, and

(b) may be expressed wholly or partly in foreign currency (in which case the sterling equivalent shall be calculated as at the time when the project begins).

14.17.9.4.3 Guidance as to the components of the definition of 'financed project' was provided by Lewison J in *Feetum v Levy*.[702] His Lordship said, first, that although the debt must be incurred by a project company, it need not necessarily be incurred by the project company over which the administrative receiver is appointed. Secondly, that the debt must be incurred under an agreement relating to the project, but not necessarily the agreement under which the administrative receiver is appointed. Thirdly, as to the requirement that a debt of at least £50 million is incurred (or, when the agreement is entered into, is expected to be incurred) under an agreement relating to the project, his Lordship said that, as a matter of construction of the statutory wording, the 'agreement' had to be the same agreement under which the debt was incurred, or, alternatively, was expected to be incurred, so as to finance the project. Fourthly, his Lordship distinguished between hope and the more objective concept of an expectation, the latter being what was required if there was to be an expectation of incurring a debt of at least £50 million under the relevant agreement. An expectation depends on the likelihood of meeting the conditions to its fulfilment. He also noted that the section requires an expectation that 'at least' £50 million will be borrowed, rather than 'up to' a figure, even if higher. Whilst a borrower might initially have hoped that it could borrow above the figure of £50 million, there would not be the requisite expectation if, in fact, it had realistically been entitled under the agreement to borrow only a lower sum because of circumstances that were known or appreciated at the time.

---

702 [2005] EWHC 349 (Ch), [2005] 1 WLR 2576 (upheld on appeal: *Cabvision v Feetum* [2005] EWCA Civ 1601, [2005] Ch 585).

15

EQUIPMENT FINANCE

15.1 Introduction

15.1.1 A broad outline

This chapter is concerned with the methods of title finance that might be employed by a financier[1] in financing business equipment that is intended to be used by its

---

[1] The terms 'financier' and 'customer' will be used in this chapter, to indicate the parties which, respectively, supply the finance and which receive that finance under an equipment financing transaction. They may be compared with the lender and the borrower in a loan transaction.

customer for commercial purposes.[2] The term 'equipment' refers to goods that are of a relatively high value and which are intended to have a degree of long-term use in a business. The expressions 'plant and machinery' might sometimes also be used to describe them. The term is used in distinction to goods that amount to stock-in-trade or raw materials, which are of a transitory nature and are intended, as stock, for re-sale or, as raw materials, to be used and consumed in a process of manufacture to produce stock for sale or for some other purpose of the business. Nonetheless, the concept of the retention or reservation of title that is part and parcel of the title finance of equipment may also be relevant where a supplier of stock or raw materials grants credit to it customer.

The forms of equipment finance, or title finance, with which this chapter is con-   **15.1.1.1**
cerned involve the financier in acquiring the ownership of the relevant equipment, the possession and use of which is then made available to the customer on
instalment payment terms, usually over a period of years. It may or may not
involve the customer ultimately in acquiring the ownership of the asset, once it
has paid off the finance. In economic terms (and, indeed, in its accounting treatment) the financing will have similar characteristics to lending money so as to
provide the finance for the acquisition by the borrower of an asset, with the borrower giving security over the relevant asset. This is because the real commercial
interest of the financier in an equipment financing transaction is to obtain repayment of the capital and costs that it has expended, together with a rate of return
representing an interest factor as its profit.[3] As protection against the risk of default
by the customer, the financier retains its title in the asset, so that it can repossess
and sell the asset should the customer default. Despite the economic view of such
transactions, the legal approach that is taken under English law is to treat them

---

[2] Accordingly, it will not address the financing of consumer equipment under consumer credit
agreements or consumer hire agreements. Whilst consumer financing will usually involve the same
or similar structures as are used in business financing, such as hire or lease agreements, hire purchase
agreements, and conditional sale agreements, the Consumer Credit Acts 1974 and 2006 provide
special rules that govern the rights and remedies of the parties, as well as imposing certain formal
requirements. The Acts concern such matters as the form and content of the agreements, the procedures for execution of the agreements, cooling-off periods and enforcement upon default, as well
as imposing connected lender liability upon a financier in relation to the equipment that has been
financed. Consumers may also enjoy protection against unfair terms pursuant to the Unfair Terms
in Consumer Contracts Regs 1999 (SI 1999/2083).

[3] The true economic nature of this real interest has been recognised in cases where the financier
has sued a third party in conversion, because the customer has wrongly disposed of the goods to the
third party. Rather than awarding damages for the whole market value of the goods at the time the
wrongful conversion took place (which would be the usual measure of damages: see Lord Nicholls
in *Kuwait Airways Corp v Iraqi Airways Co* [2002] UKHL 19; [2002] 2 AC 883, at [67]), the courts
have assessed the damages by reference to the more limited but true economic loss suffered by the
financier, as reflected in the outstanding amount of finance it had provided: see *Wickham Holdings
Ltd v Brooke House Motors Ltd* [1967] 1 WLR 295 and *VFS Financial Services (UK) Ltd v Euro
Auctions (UK) Ltd* [2007] EWHC 1492 (QB).

as a form of transaction by way of the supply of goods. The obligations, rights, and remedies of the parties are dictated by that characterisation, rather than with reference to the intention that they should be regarded as a method of providing finance with attendant security in case of default.[4]

15.1.1.2 The types of transaction that are used in equipment financing by way of title finance are conditional sale, hire purchase and finance lease. Each of those transactions will be described more fully in this chapter, so only a brief description will be given at this stage. A conditional sale agreement involves the financier in agreeing (in a fully committed sense) to sell the equipment to the customer, and the customer (in the same sense) agreeing to buy it, but the agreement provides that the title in the goods will not pass to the customer, and so will remain vested in the financier, until the customer has paid the full amount of all instalments due under the agreement. A hire purchase agreement provides for the customer, as hirer, to hire the equipment for the period of the finance. At the conclusion, once the hirer has paid all the instalments that fall due for payment under the agreement, the hirer has the right to exercise an option to purchase the goods and so acquire title in them. Until that time, the financier remains as the owner of the goods and the customer is merely a hirer of the equipment. A finance lease provides for the customer to have the use and possession of the goods during their substantive useful life, during which time instalments of rental will be paid, but the customer will not become the owner. The goods will usually be sold, scrapped, or otherwise disposed of at the end of the lease.

15.1.1.3 Title finance is not the only method by which finance may be provided by a financier for the acquisition of equipment. It can also be provided by way of loan, with or without security being taken over the equipment (and, indeed, other assets as well). If the security over the equipment is given by an individual then it will have to meet the rigorous requirements (including as to registration in the Bills of Sale Registry and as to formalities of the security instrument and its execution) of the Bills of Sale Act (1878) Amendment Act 1882 which, as a practical matter, it is very difficult to achieve. It is not possible for an individual to create floating charge security over equipment.[5] If the security is given by a company, it will need to be registered in the Companies Registry.[6] Such security given by a company will be

---

[4] Hence, they are not registrable in England as charges under Chap I of Part 26 of the Companies Act 2006 (formerly Chap I of Part XII of the Companies Act 1985). This is different, for instance, to the approach that applies under Art 9 of the Uniform Commercial Code in the USA, where they are treated as giving rise to a security interest that is a registrable transaction. It is interesting to note that English law takes a similar and strictly legalistic approach to transactions that provide finance by way of the purchase of book debts (receivables), by preferring the legal form over the economic substance of the transaction: see *Lloyds and Scottish Finance Ltd v Cyril Lord Carpets Sales Ltd* [1992] BCLC 609 (despite the date of the report, the case was actually decided in 1979).

[5] This is because of the combined effect of ss 4 and 5 of the 1882 Act.

[6] Under Chap I of Part 26 of the Companies Act 2006 (formerly Chap I of Part XII of the Companies Act 1985).

by way of a floating charge, unless the creditor can demonstrate that it has control of the equipment so that the debtor is precluded from being able to deal with it in the ordinary course of business.[7]

It is also possible that the supplier of the equipment might itself be willing to provide credit, by giving time to pay. In such a case, the supplier could protect itself, if it so wished, by retaining the title in the goods until it had been paid, and it can achieve this by using one of the types of transaction that will be described in this chapter. Usually, however, the supplier would prefer not to grant credit for an extended period, so it is more likely that the finance that is needed to enable the customer to obtain the use and possession of the equipment would be provided by a financier, by means of the financier acquiring ownership of the goods from the supplier and then making them available to the customer.

15.1.1.4

15.1.2 Accounting treatment

The accounting treatment of the customer's interest in an equipment or title financing transaction differs from its legal treatment. In essence, for accounting purposes the goods are treated as if they belonged to the customer and the finance element is treated as if it were a loan. This is because the accounting treatment is concerned with the economic substance of the transaction. It assumes that the long-term risks and benefits associated with the goods will reside in the customer and that the customer has really borrowed the funds necessary for it to acquire the goods. This is demonstrated by the definition of a finance lease that appears in International Accounting Standard 17: 'A finance lease is a lease that transfers substantially all of the risks and rewards incidental to ownership of an asset. Title may or may not eventually be transferred [to the customer].'

15.1.3 Taxation

Generally speaking, the usual principle that is followed when considering the tax consequences of a transaction is that only expenditure of a day-to-day or revenue nature should be taken into account as a deduction from receipts in computing the profits of a business. The expenditure associated with the acquisition of new equipment (in UK tax terms, referred to as 'plant and machinery') would not usually fall within that description. Instead, the depreciation of the asset over its life might be considered to be an allowable deduction against income in computing profits. If a business is liable to tax on a capital gain then in the unlikely event that

---

[7] In accordance with the tests laid down by Millett LJ in *Re Cosslett (Contractors) Ltd* [1998] Ch 495 (upheld and approved in *Smith (Administrator of Cosslett (Contractors) Ltd) v Bridgend CBC* [2001] UKHL 58, [2002] 1 AC 336), by the Privy Council in *Agnew v Inland Revenue Commissioner* [2001] UKPC 28, [2002] 2 AC 710 and by the House of Lords in *Re Spectrum Plus Ltd* [2005] UKHL 41, [2005] 2 AC 680.

the equipment appreciates in value during its life, the initial cost of acquisition might be taken into account in computing the capital gain for tax purposes. However, some jurisdictions do allow account to be taken of the costs of acquisition of equipment. This is because it is thought to be desirable that businesses should be encouraged to acquire new equipment, so that they may develop and prosper. Accordingly, businesses in such jurisdictions may be permitted to claim an allowance for the acquisition costs of new equipment, which may be offset against receipts in calculating taxable profits. Sometimes the whole cost of the equipment might be allowed as a deduction against income in the year the equipment was acquired. In other instances the cost might have to be spread out to give proportionate deductions over two or more years.

15.1.3.1 In the UK, allowances which relate to the original cost of equipment are spread over a number of years and may be claimed as deductions against income in calculating taxable profits, under the Capital Allowances Act 2001 (as amended, particularly by the Finance Act 2006). What follows is intended to provide a brief overview of the position in the UK, in what is a highly technical and specialist area. Needless to say, there are a great many complexities in the system which it is not possible to address in the description that follows.

15.1.3.2 A portion of the acquisition cost of plant and machinery may be deducted by way of an allowance in each year over the life of the asset. The allowances that can be claimed are available at set percentages of the acquisition cost, calculated on a reducing balance basis, with the percentages depending upon whether the assets for which the allowances are claimed are 'long life assets' (i.e. with an expected useful economic life of 25 years or more) or are other assets. The annual percentage for long life assets is 10 per cent per year and for other assets it is 20 per cent per year.[8]

15.1.3.3 The UK regime also permits the customer under an equipment finance transaction, rather than the financier, to be treated as if it had made the expenditure for acquisition of the equipment, even though title may not pass to it for some time or, in a leasing transaction, where it may not pass at all. Where the taxpayer customer has acquired title in the asset outright from the beginning then its cost of acquisition is relatively simple to calculate. Similarly, it can easily be treated for tax purposes as having done so if it has entered into a conditional sale agreement. Where, on the other hand, the customer has entered into a hire purchase transaction or a lease (that is, a lease which is treated as a 'long funding lease'), the qualifying expenditure that applies in calculating the amount on which the relevant percentages is based is the present value at the outset of the total amounts payable

---

[8] For equipment acquired prior to the tax year 2008/09, the percentages were 6% and 25% respectively.

under the financing agreement, less the financier's finance charges (e.g. the interest element). The latter may also be claimed as normal deductible expenses in each year in which they are incurred. A long funding lease is, essentially, a lease that is a finance lease for accounting purposes and which is of more than five years in duration. By contrast, a 'short lease' does not meet those requirements. Under a short lease, the allowances calculated on the acquisition cost of the equipment may be claimed by the lessor and, depending upon the commercial arrangement between them, the benefit (or some part of it) could then be passed on to the customer in computing the lease rentals that are payable by the customer under the lease.

15.1.4 Conflict of laws and the Cape Town Convention

This chapter is concerned with equipment financing as a matter of English law. Where the assets are not situated in England and in other cross-border situations, the position may be different and the principles as to conflict of laws will be relevant. Those principles are addressed in Chapter 4.

Because of its potential importance to the financing of equipment and the protection of the financier's interest, however, it is relevant at this point to consider the Cape Town Convention of 2001 on international interests in mobile equipment, which was drawn up under the auspices of UNIDROIT. If the UK adopts the Convention then it will import some significant changes to the approach that is taken in English law in relation to matters such as priorities of interests and the remedies that are available on default under title financing transactions that concern such equipment. A general description of the Convention was provided in Chapter 4.   **15.1.4.1**

The Convention is intended to apply to three types of asset, namely, (a) airframes, aircraft engines, and helicopters; (b) railway rolling stock; and (c) space assets.[9] The Convention provides a number of general rules in the abstract. It is made applicable on a practical level to each of the separate categories of asset by the adoption of the Convention for the relevant category of assets through the use of protocols. A protocol may also provide specific rules that vary from the general rules contained in the Convention as, for instance, has been done in the case of assets within category (b). To date, protocols have been signed for the assets in categories (a) and (b), but not (c). The Cape Town Protocol of 2001 applies in the case of category (a). The Luxembourg Protocol of 2007 applies in the case of category (b). At the time of writing, the UK had not ratified the Convention nor the two Protocols.[10]   **15.1.4.2**

---

⁹ Art 2(3) of the Convention.
¹⁰ Copies of the Convention and the two Protocols, together with official commentary, are available on the UNIDROIT website, <http://www.unidroit.org>.

15.1.4.3 The Convention aims to facilitate the acquisition and financing of items of mobile equipment which are of large value by providing for the creation of an international interest in the equipment (an object). That interest would be recognised in each contracting state that ratifies the Convention. The equipment must be uniquely identifiable and there must be an appropriate connection of the debtor (but not necessarily the creditor) with a Contracting State.[11] The international interests in the equipment to which the rules of the Convention apply are a security interest and an interest that is vested in a person who is a seller under reservation of title or a lessor of the equipment.[12] In the case of aircraft objects, this is extended by the Cape Town Protocol to outright transfers. An international interest in an object extends to the proceeds of that interest.[13] Characterisation of an interest is to be determined by the applicable law.[14]

15.1.4.4 The Convention provides for the possibility of adopting a range of basic default remedies and insolvency-related remedies, as well as a means of obtaining speedy interim relief pending a final determination of the merits of a claim in the equipment.[15] It also provides for the establishment of an international registry, operated and available for searching electronically, through which international interests of an owner and financier can be registered. By that means notice of their interests will be given to third parties and priorities can be protected against subsequent interests, whether registered or unregistered. Registered interests will also be effective in insolvency proceedings concerning the relevant debtor.[16] The Convention also provides rules for perfection of such interests, as well as basic default remedies. In addition, it contains provisions that relate to the assignment of associated rights to the international interest, such as to payment by the debtor.[17]

15.1.4.5 The Luxembourg Protocol contains some variations from the scheme of the Convention as applied under the Cape Town Protocol for aircraft objects. For example, there is an additional alternative concerning insolvency proceedings and there is provision for the continued availability of railway rolling stock which is required for services of public importance. It is also possible for the owner of

---

[11] Art 2(2) of the Convention specifies the requirement as to identification. Art 3 contains the requirement as to the situation of the debtor, which is to be determined in accordance with Art 4.

[12] Arts 2(1) and 2(2) of the Convention.

[13] Art 2(5) of the Convention. 'Proceeds' is defined in Art 1(w) to mean 'money or non-money proceeds . . . arising from the total or partial loss or physical destruction of the object or its total or partial confiscation, condemnation or requisition'.

[14] Art 2(4) of the Convention. Art 5(3) provides that the applicable law is to be the domestic rules of the law that should be applied by virtue of the conflict of laws rules of the *lex fori*.

[15] Default remedies are contained in Arts 8–15 of the Convention and matters relating to perfection and priority of interests and the effect of insolvency are dealt with in Arts 18–30 of the Convention.

[16] The registration system is dealt with in Arts 16 and 17 of the Convention.

[17] Arts 31–36 of the Convention.

rolling stock which is not subject to any financing to place a record of its interest on the register, so as to give notice to third parties. The Protocol also applies to all types of rolling stock (including locomotives, carriages and wagons, city centre trams, and light rail systems, as well as high speed and freight rolling stock), whether or not it is intended for use in cross-border travel. This is because of the ease with which rolling stock can, in practice, be moved from one country to another. Thus, it will be possible to record interests in the international register even where there may not be a local register in which a purely domestic interest could be registered.

Contracting states to the Cape Town Convention are permitted to enter declarations or reservations relating to registrable non-consensual interests in equipment, the priority of certain unregistered interests, and the protection of national interests arising under purely internal transactions.[18]   **15.1.4.6**

15.1.5 Covenants and undertakings in the financing documentation

The financing documentation will contain covenants and undertakings on the part of the customer. Many of them will be similar to what will be found in an ordinary form of loan agreement, including provisions as to payments and the like.[19] Other covenants will relate more specifically to the use, upkeep, and repair of the equipment and to insurance cover,[20] as well as dealing with the circumstances in which the customer would be entitled to part with possession of the equipment by delivering it to third parties. It is also likely that there will be events of default-type provisions, which will be intended to permit the financier to terminate the financing and repossess the equipment should a stipulated event occur. The documentation will also need to refer to the arrangements under which the financier is to acquire title to the equipment, which are likely to be found in the conditions precedent clauses. It is also likely that the customer will be required to confirm that it has inspected the equipment and that it is fit for purpose and of satisfactory quality.

15.1.6 The Sale of Goods Act 1979

There will be frequent references to the Sale of Goods Act (the Act) in this chapter. The Act was a consolidation of the Sale of Goods Act 1893,[21] as it had been amended from time to time. The 1979 Act has itself been subject to various amendments, including those under the Sale of Goods Act (Amendment) Acts of 1994 and 1995. Much of the relevant case law that will be mentioned in this

---

18 Arts 39 and 40 of the Convention.
19 See further Chap 3.
20 The insurance aspects are dealt with later in this chapter.
21 The formal date of the Act is inaccurate, as it was not actually passed by Parliament until 1894.

chapter concerned the original Act, but is equally relevant to the 1979 Act, as amended. For convenience of reference, the section numbers of this legislation that are used in this chapter will be those of the 1979 Act, as amended.

15.1.7 Chapter plan

The discussion in this chapter will proceed by examining the methods under which the financier may acquire property (i.e. title or ownership) in the equipment. It will move on to describe the methods by which possession, and sometimes ownership, may be conferred by the financier upon the customer. It will then examine the statutory obligations that the financier assumes in relation to equipment that it finances, before looking at the remedies that may be available to the financier should the customer default in the performance of its obligations. It will also consider the protections that may be available to the customer in such a situation and the position should the customer go into administration. It will then discuss the financier's rights in the equipment as against third parties and conclude with a brief description of the insurance arrangements that are usually put in place concerning the equipment.

15.2 Acquisition by the Financier of Title in the Equipment

15.2.1 Assuming that the manufacturer or a commercial supplier is not financing the acquisition of the equipment by the customer, by granting time to pay through credit terms, there are two potential sources from which an external financier might acquire title (or, in terms of the expression that is used in the Sale of Goods Act 1979, 'property') in the equipment. By far the most common source is a purchase of the equipment from the manufacturer or a supplier of the equipment. Less commonly, the equipment might be sold to the financier by the customer itself as a method of raising cash. This is done by means of a sale of the equipment by the customer to the financier and a grant back to the customer, under deferred payment terms, of the right to maintain possession of the equipment (and ultimately, perhaps, a right in the customer to regain title in the equipment) under one or other of the title finance transactions that will be explored in this chapter. Each of those methods by which the financier obtains title and allows possession to the customer will now be discussed, beginning with transactions under which the customer purports to sell the equipment to the financier.

15.2.2 Acquisition of title from the customer

Under this type of transaction, the customer (being, or claiming to be, the owner of the equipment) contracts to sell the equipment to the financier, but to retain the possession of the equipment. In formal terms, there is likely to be an agreement for sale of the equipment to the financier, with a cash price to be paid to the customer, and an agreement under which the customer is allowed possession of the equipment (perhaps with the right to regain ownership) on deferred or instalment payment terms, by way of conditional sale, hire purchase, or lease. There are three potential pitfalls for a financier in such an arrangement.

15.2.2.3 Re-characterisation

The first potential pitfall is that the transaction, when taken as a whole, might be re-characterised as one that involves the provision of finance by way of loan, with the transfer of title being seen as involving a charge or mortgage in favour of the financier, to act as security against the risk of default in repayment of the finance.[22] This problem may arise where the transaction provides that the customer may regain its title under a conditional sale agreement or a hire purchase agreement. It is not so likely to be a cause of concern if the customer only has a right to possession under a lease, without the possibility of regaining its title. Where the problem arises, the most important consequence is that the security should be registered at the Companies Registry or, if it was given by an individual, in the Bills of Sale Registry. A failure to meet either of those requirements will lead to the security being invalid, to a greater or lesser extent.[23]

Re-characterisation may arise on two possible grounds. First, because the transaction as portrayed in the documents is seen as a sham, that is, as a deliberate attempt to cloak its true nature as a secured loan. This type of attack in financing transactions was more common in the days of legislation that has now been repealed, such as the Moneylender Acts of 1900 to 1927. An example arose in *North Central Wagon Finance Co Ltd v Brailsford*.[24] Attacks on this basis are not common these days in relation to equipment finance transactions. **15.2.2.3.1**

If the transaction is to be challenged then the more likely argument that might be mounted is that, as a matter of the proper construction of the transaction (but without casting aspersions upon the honesty of the parties), the substance of the transaction when taken as a whole should be characterised by the court as being a secured transaction, rather than that represented by its form as described by the parties. In essence, the court will be engaged in an exercise to determine if the proprietary interest that was conferred upon the financier was a limited interest which would expire upon repayment of the finance it had extended, rather than **15.2.2.3.2**

---

[22] See the discussion on this issue at Chap 12.

[23] Under s 8 of the Bills of Sale Act (1878) Amendment Act 1882, the unregistered security is void. Under s 874 of the Companies Act 2006 (formerly s 395(1) of the Companies Act 1985), the unregistered security is avoided against the liquidator, administrator, and secured creditors of the company.

[24] [1962] 1 WLR 1288.

an outright acquisition of an unencumbered title. As a corollary to answering that question, it will be necessary to determine whether the customer, when it transferred the interest to the financier, retained an equity of redemption, so that it would become the full and unencumbered owner of the asset once the finance had been repaid. Unfortunately, as Millett LJ observed in *Orion Finance Ltd v Crown Financial Management Ltd*,[25] there is no one single criterion which can be employed to determine how the answers to those questions should be found and, thus, how the transaction should be characterised. An example of a case where a transaction was re-characterised is *Curtain Dream PLC v Churchill Merchanting Ltd*,[26] in which a sale of goods by the customer to a finance house and its resale back by the finance house to the customer on credit terms was held to give rise to a loan with security.[27] It was held that the two parts of the transaction had to be looked at together. Neither would have occurred without the other. That interdependence between them served to demonstrate that the financier had only acquired an interest in the goods that was defeasible upon payment. The other side of the coin was that the customer only agreed to create a proprietary interest in favour of the financier on the basis that it would regain its full ownership of the goods once the finance had been repaid. As the security had not been registered, it was held to be invalid against another secured creditor, as well as the administrative receiver who had been appointed by that other secured creditor.

15.2.2.4 Fraud

The second potential pitfall arises from the risk of fraud, because the alleged ownership of the goods that are to be sold to the financier by the customer is fictitious. Such a fraud might be perpetrated where the financier is unable to conduct a full investigation of the customer's title in the goods before it proceeds with the transaction. An example is to be found in *Associated Japanese Bank (International) Ltd v Credit du Nord SA*,[28] in which it was discovered that goods that were meant to be the subject of a sale and leaseback transaction did not exist. The customer was a fraudster, who pocketed the capital sum received on the alleged sale to the financier and then failed to pay the lease rentals. A guarantee that had been given of the customer's obligations under the lease was held to be unenforceable, either because of a mistake as to the subject matter of the transaction that had been guaranteed or because it was a pre-condition of the guarantee that there was a genuine lease of the goods to the customer.

---

[25] [1996] BCC 621, at 626.

[26] [1990] BCC 341.

[27] Some care must be taken in placing too much reliance on this case, however, as it appears that an appeal against the decision might not have proceeded in light of the outcome of the decision of the Court of Appeal in *Welsh Development Agency v Export Finance Co Ltd* [1992] BCC 270. See, in particular, the remarks of Staughton LJ at 301.

[28] [1989] 1 WLR 255.

15.2.2.5 *Customer remaining in possession*

The third potential pitfall arises because the customer remains in possession of the goods that have been sold to the financier, or regains possession at some point following the sale. If the customer (or its agent) subsequently disposes of the goods to a third party which is acting in good faith and without notice of the financier's interest, under a sale, pledge, or other disposition, the latter can acquire a good title (which will defeat the claim of the financier) pursuant to the operation of section 24 of the Sale of Goods Act 1979 or section 8 of the Factors Act 1889. Those sections contain one of the exceptions to the principle of *nemo dat quod non habet*, which is reflected in legislative form in section 21 of the Sale of Goods Act 1979.[29]

Section 24 of the 1979 Act provides as follows (section 8 of the 1889 Act is in similar terms):

    15.2.2.5.1

> Where a person having sold goods continues or is in possession of the goods or the documents of title to the goods, the delivery or transfer by that person or by a mercantile agent acting for him of the goods or documents of title under any sale, pledge or other disposition thereof [or under any agreement for sale, pledge or other disposition thereof—section 8] to any person receiving the same in good faith and without notice of the previous sale, has the same effect as if the person making the delivery or transfer were expressly authorised by the owner of the goods to make the same.

In relation to the bona fides of the person to whom the sale etc. is made, it should be noted that section 61(3) of the 1979 Act provides that:

    15.2.2.5.2

> A thing is deemed to be done in good faith within the meaning of this Act when it is in fact done honestly, whether it is done negligently or not.

An example of the risk to a financier that arises under section 24 is to be found in the decision of the Court of Appeal in *Michael Gerson (Leasing) Ltd v Wilkinson*.[30] That case involved a transaction for a sale of goods by the customer to the first financier and a leaseback of the goods to the customer, which had remained in possession and then purported to sell them to another financier. The second financier successfully argued that it had obtained a good title under section 24.

    15.2.2.5.3

15.2.2.6 *Motor vehicles*

A similar problem may arise under section 27 of the Hire Purchase Act 1964 (as amended). Section 27 provides that if the goods consisted of a motor vehicle which was the subject of a conditional sale or hire purchase agreement then a private third party purchaser, who has purchased the vehicle from the original hirer or buyer (or from an intermediate trade or finance purchaser), will be able to

---

[29] Further exceptions are contained in s 25(1) of the Sale of Goods Act 1979 and s 9 of the Factors Act 1889, to which reference is made in relation to conditional sale agreements, below, and in s 27 of the Hire Purchase Act 1964, which will shortly be mentioned.

[30] [2001] QB 514.

obtain good title if he acquired the vehicle in good faith and without notice of the hire purchase or conditional sale agreement.

15.2.3 Acquisition of title from the manufacturer or supplier

In diagrammatic form, the sequence of transactions that gives rise to an acquisition of title in the equipment by the financier from the supplier or manufacturer and the passing to the customer of the right to possession and use of the equipment by the customer on deferred payment terms might be represented as in Figure 15.1.

15.2.3.1 This structure is sometimes referred to as giving rise to a 'tri-partite' transaction or relationship, although that can be misleading if it is taken to imply that there is a contractual relationship as between the three parties. The transaction, taken overall, arises in the following way. Essentially, the financier acquires ownership of the equipment from the manufacturer or a commercial supplier. This will usually occur in consequence of initial discussions between the customer and the manufacturer or supplier. The customer will indicate that it cannot pay for the goods outright and the supplier or manufacturer will also indicate that it cannot provide credit by supplying on instalment payment terms (or that it is unwilling to do so on terms that are acceptable to the customer). In consequence, the financier will purchase the goods from the manufacturer or supplier instead. The financier will enter into an agreement with the customer, by which it agrees to grant the customer possession of the goods for the duration of the deferred payment period. Under a conditional sale agreement, the agreement reflects an intention from the outset that the customer will acquire title in the goods at the end of that period, once it has paid the full amount due to the financier. Under a hire purchase agreement, the customer is given an option to purchase the goods at the conclusion of the agreement, which is exercisable once all the instalments of the deferred consideration due by the customer to the financier have been paid. Under a lease, the customer pays rentals over the period of the agreement but merely has a right to

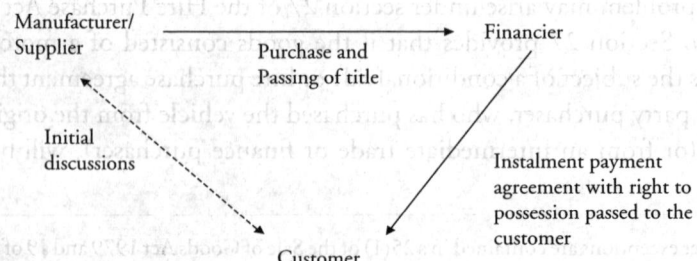

Figure 15.1 The tri-partite transactions

possession of the goods during the term of the agreement, without either the right or an option to acquire ownership of the goods.

15.2.3.2 *The relationship between the financier and the supplier or manufacturer*

It has been held that, in the normal course, the manufacturer or supplier is not to be regarded as the agent of the financier, except perhaps in acting in a mechanical manner in making delivery of the goods to the customer on behalf of the financier. Accordingly, the manufacturer or supplier does not have authority to contract on behalf of the financier.[31] Similarly, the financier will not be bound by statements made by the supplier or manufacturer as to the suitability, fitness for purpose, or quality of the goods, or as to the pricing of the goods under the arrangements between the financier and the customer.[32] However, it has also been held that the financier might be estopped from denying that the supplier or manufacturer had authority to act on its behalf where the financier had adopted what the manufacturer or supplier had done or had otherwise acted in such a way that an implication to that effect could reasonably be drawn from its conduct.[33]

15.2.3.3 *The relationship between the customer and the supplier or manufacturer*

The other side of the coin is that, in the usual case, the customer only contracts with the financier and not also with the manufacturer or supplier. On an historical analysis, the ordinary consequence of this at common law was that the customer could not acquire any direct contractual rights against the manufacturer or supplier, which might have been valuable in relation to terms concerning the quality and fitness for purpose of the goods. Under traditional principles, the customer could not argue that it was entitled to enforce the contract between the financier and the manufacturer or supplier, even if it was intended to benefit from the contract, because of the doctrine of privity of contract.[34] Faced with this, the customer might these days seek to overcome those difficulties in the following ways. First, the customer could insist upon entering into a direct warranty agreement with the manufacturer or supplier, which will often be the case in relation to high value items, such as aircraft. Secondly, the financier might be prevailed upon by the customer to contract with the manufacturer or supplier on its own behalf and, with respect to the benefit of the warranties in the contract concerning the goods, as agent or trustee on behalf of the customer.[35] Thirdly, the customer might be able

---

[31] *Shogun Finance Ltd v Hudson* [2003] UKHL 62, [2004] 1 AC 919.
[32] *Branwhite v Worcester Works Finance Ltd* [1969] 1 AC 552.
[33] *Lease Management Services Ltd v Purnell Secretarial Services Ltd* [1994] Tr LR 337.
[34] The doctrine of privity of contract is addressed in Chap 1.
[35] See *New Zealand Shipping Co Ltd v AM Satterthwaite & Co Ltd (The Eurymedon)* [1975] AC 154 and *Port Jackson Stevedoring Pty Ltd v Salmond and Spraggon (Australia) Pty Ltd (The New York Star)* [1981] 1 WLR 138. Clauses under which a party to a contract acts as an agent in obtaining protection for a third party, when used in a contract for the carriage of goods by sea, are often referred

to take advantage of the benefit of the sale agreement between the supplier or manufacturer and the financier by relying upon the Contracts (Rights of Third Parties) Act 1999, unless its right to do so has been disapplied by, or is otherwise inconsistent with, the terms of the contract.[36] Fourthly, the customer might take an assignment of the financier's rights against the supplier or manufacturer.

15.2.2.3.1 The problem with relying upon the last of those methods, namely, an assignment of the financier's rights, is that under the law as it relates to assignments, an assignee cannot obtain or enforce better rights than those that were enjoyed by the assignor, so that the assignee cannot recover to a greater extent than the assignor could have done had it not assigned its rights.[37] If the assignor would not have suffered any loss that relates to the rights that have been assigned then, in the absence of the assignment, it would only have been entitled to nominal damages. The assignee cannot be in a better position. Those principles might apply in the context of an equipment finance transaction in the following way. The financier will usually seek to pass the risk relating to the fitness and quality of the goods to the customer and thereby limit its liability and any loss associated with the goods. If the financier is successful in achieving that result[38] then the consequence will be that the financier (having no real economic interest in the goods) will not suffer any loss that, in turn, it could recover from the manufacturer or supplier of the goods. In the result, an assignment of its rights would be of little real value. If the financier is unsuccessful in limiting its liability then the customer is unlikely to need the assignment because it will have a direct claim against the financier.

15.2.3.4 The manufacturer's or supplier's liability to the customer in tort

It is also worth noting that the customer is unlikely to have a claim in the tort of negligence against the manufacturer or supplier based upon a claim for economic or financial loss arising because a defective product is of unsatisfactory quality or not fit for purpose.[39] Generally speaking, claims for damages in tort caused by defective products have been confined to personal injury caused by the defective product[40] or for damage that has been caused by the defective product to other

---

to as 'Himalaya clauses' after the name of the vessel that was involved in *Adler v Dickson* [1955] 1 QB 158.

[36] For the reasons that are explained further below, it might be to the advantage of the financier to ensure that the customer could rely on the Act and thereby be entitled to enforce the contract between the financier and the manufacturer or supplier, because that might help to justify (for the purpose of satisfying the requirement of reasonableness in the Unfair Contract Terms Act 1977) a limitation or exclusion of the financier's potential liability to the customer for the fitness or quality of the goods.

[37] *Dawson v Great Northern & City Ry Co* [1905] 1 KB 260.

[38] A question that is addressed further below.

[39] This discussion does not cover the possibility of claims by consumers under consumer protection legislation, such as the Consumer Protection Act 1987.

[40] *Donoghue v Stevenson* [1932] AC 562.

property,[41] although both manufacturers and distributors have been found liable in such cases.[42] Claims have not been allowed for economic or financial loss suffered by the user of the product because the product was defective.[43] Furthermore, the duty of care is not absolute, as it might be under a contractual duty. The duty is only to exercise reasonable care with respect to the use for which the product was intended by the manufacturer.[44] In addition, the duty will not extend to injury or damage that is suffered if the product is used with knowledge of the defect[45] or, perhaps, where there has been the opportunity for an intermediate inspection before use.[46]

15.3 Conditional Sale Agreements

The essence of a conditional sale agreement is that the parties agree that the buyer **15.3.1** (being, in the case of an equipment financing transaction, the customer) will purchase the goods from the seller (i.e. the financier) on deferred payment terms, but that the seller will remain as the owner until the seller has been paid. Accordingly, ownership will not pass to the buyer until the seller has received payment in full from the buyer.[47] The agreement will usually provide that the seller may determine the agreement and repossess the goods if the buyer defaults under the agreement, particularly in making payment. From its outset, the agreement is still a binding agreement for the sale and purchase of the goods, under which the buyer is obliged to pay for the goods and the seller is obliged to pass title in the

---

[41] There may also be a problem in identifying whether the damage has been suffered by the thing supplied or other property, particularly where the thing supplied has been incorporated in another object or has been used as a constituent in making a new thing: *Bacardi-Martini Beverages Ltd v Thomas Hardy Packaging Ltd* [2002] 2 Lloyd's Rep 379, which can be contrasted with *Nitrigin Eireann Teoranta v Inco Alloys* [1992] 1 WLR 498.

[42] *Donoghue v Stevenson* concerned the liability of a manufacturer. *Watson v Buckley Osborne Garrett & Co Ltd* [1940] 1 All ER 174 concerned a distributor.

[43] See, for instance, *Simaan General Contracting Co v Pilkington Glass Ltd* [1988] QB 758; Lord Bridge in *Murphy v Brentwood DC* [1991] 1 AC 398, at 475; and *Hamble Fisheries v Gardner* [1999] 2 Lloyd's Rep 1. In the latter case, it was said by Tuckey LJ (at 7) after a review of the cases that a duty of care not to cause economic loss may arise in an exceptional case that is akin to contract, save for a lack of consideration, if there has been a clear assumption of responsibility on the part of the manufacturer, although even that would be hard to establish in a case of mere silence rather than one of a misrepresentation, and reliance would have to be shown.

[44] See Lloyd LJ in *M/S Aswan v Lupdine Ltd* [1987] 1 WLR 1, at 23.

[45] *Grant v Australian Knitting Mills Ltd* [1936] AC 85; *Gledhill v Liverpool Abattoir Ltd* [1957] 1 WLR 1028.

[46] See Lord Atkin in *Donoghue v Stevenson* [1932] AC 562, at 599.

[47] Under s 38(1) of the Sale of Goods Act 1979, the seller is treated as remaining unpaid until it has received full and unconditional payment and the fact that the buyer, strictly speaking, may not be in default does not change this: see Diplock LJ in *Ward (RV) Ltd v Bignall* [1967] 1 QB 534, at 550.

goods once it has been paid in full, in accordance with the provisions of the contract.[48]

15.3.1.1 This is consistent with section 17 (1) of the Sale of Goods Act 1979,[49] which provides that 'property' (the term that the Act uses to mean title) is to pass under an agreement for sale of the goods at the time that the parties intend it to pass. Section 17(2) then provides that in ascertaining their intention, regard should be had to the terms of the contract, the conduct of the parties and the circumstances of the case. Section 19 of the Act then provides that under the contract the seller may reserve its title[50] until payment, with a right to repossess and re-sell the goods should the buyer default in making payment.[51] Because the seller remains as the owner of the goods until payment, the goods will not form a part of the assets of the buyer that are available for its general body of creditors, should it become insolvent and pass into bankruptcy or liquidation before it has paid for them.[52]

15.3.2 Credit sale

The position under a conditional sale agreement should be contrasted with that which arises under a credit sale agreement, pursuant to which title will pass immediately upon contracting, provided that the goods are ascertained, in a deliverable state and are owned by the seller, notwithstanding that the time for payment or delivery (or both) has been delayed. This follows from the rebuttable presumption to that effect which arises under section 18, rule 1 of the Act.[53]

---

48 As to the obligation to pass title at the time agreed under the contract, see s 12 of the Sale of Goods Act 1979, but note that in an exceptional case the contract may be taken to provide an additional obligation upon the seller that it should have title from the outset of the transaction and not just at the time that title is to pass under the contract: see *Barber v NWS Bank PLC* [1996] 1 WLR 641.

49 The Act provides a comprehensive code as to the passing of title in the normal course under a sale of goods contract and an equitable title cannot pass merely by virtue of the sale: see Atkin LJ in *Re Wait* [1927] 1 Ch 606, at 625 to 641, approved by the Privy Council in *Re Goldcorp Exchange Ltd* [1995] 1 AC 74. As Aitkin LJ (at 636) made clear, however, it is still possible for the owner of goods to create other types of interest, such as under security, outside the confines of a sale of goods contract or as an express term of the contract.

50 It is essential that this is done by a reservation of the seller's full property in the goods and not by an expression that the seller is to retain 'equitable and beneficial ownership' of the goods, as the latter implies a transfer of ownership to the buyer and a grant back of a charge to the seller to secure payment: see *Re Bond Worth Ltd* [1980] Ch 288.

51 The right of repossession is subject to the restrictions that apply in an administration of the buyer: see para 43(3) of Sched B1 to the Insolvency Act 1986 and the definition of 'hire-purchase agreement' in para 111(1) of that Schedule. A similar difficulty can arise pursuant to a moratorium under a company voluntary arrangement of an eligible company: see para 12(1)(g) of Sched A1 to the Insolvency Act 1986.

52 *McEntire v Crossley Bros Ltd* [1895] AC 457.

53 In *Ward (RV) Ltd v Bignall* [1967] 1 QB 534 it was said that it was not difficult to displace the presumption.

15.3.3 The effect of sub-sales

A problem for the seller which can arise under a conditional sale agreement is that the interest of the seller in the goods, as owner, may be defeated by a sub-sale (or other dealing) by the buyer to a third party before the buyer has paid for the goods and thus before the contractual date for passing of title. This can arise either because of an express or implied authority that is given to the buyer to enter into a sub-sale,[54] or by virtue of the operation of section 25(1) of the Sale of Goods Act 1979 and section 9 of the Factors Act 1889.[55]

Section 25(1) provides as follows (section 9 of the 1889 Act is in similar terms):   **15.3.3.1**

> Where a person having bought or agreed to buy goods obtains, with the consent of the seller possession of the goods or the documents of title to the goods, the delivery or transfer, by that person or by a mercantile agent acting for him, of the goods or documents of title, under any sale, pledge, or other disposition thereof [or under any agreement for sale, pledge or other disposition thereof—section 9], to any person receiving the same in good faith and without notice of any lien or other right of the original seller in respect of the goods, has the same effect as if the person making the delivery or transfer were a mercantile agent in possession of the goods or documents of title with the consent of the owner.

Under section 2 of the Factors Act 1889, a mercantile agent who is in possession   **15.3.3.1.1**
of goods or their documents of title with the consent of the owner, if acting in the ordinary course of business of a mercantile agent, is able to pass a good title to a third party, provided that the third party acts in good faith and without notice that the agent does not have authority to act. The combined effect of these provisions is that provided the buyer who has possession sells in circumstances that are consistent with those in which a mercantile agent might sell, the sub-buyer will obtain a good title if it acted in good faith and without notice of the interest of the original seller.[56]

15.3.4 Retention of title agreements

For comparative purposes, it is appropriate at this point to mention the law that has developed in relation to retention of title clauses in commercial sales agreements concerning the sale on deferred payment terms of stock-in-trade and raw materials. Much of that law is also relevant to matters that may arise under conditional sales agreements which concern equipment. Retention of title clauses have a number of common features with equipment finance title arrangements by way of conditional sale, including the reservation of title in the seller until payment by

---

[54] See *Four Point Garage Ltd v Carter* [1985] 3 All ER 12 and *Fairfax Gerrard Holdings Ltd v Capital Bank PLC* [2007] EWCA Civ 1226.
[55] *Lee v Butler* [1893] 2 QB 318.
[56] *Newtons of Wembley Ltd v Williams* [1965] 1 QB 560.

the buyer. They also differ from a conditional sale agreement in a practical sense, because they usually involve the supply of a number of items of relatively less individual value over a period of time, often on a repeat basis, with shorter credit periods in which payment is to be made.

15.3.4.1 The essential validity of such retention of title clauses is supported by section 19 of the Sale of Goods Act 1979, in the same way in which that section applies to conditional sale agreements involving equipment finance.[57] By extension of that principle, it has been held that a retention of title clause may validly and effectively provide that title in the goods is not to pass until both the price for the specific goods and all debts and other obligations of the buyer to the seller have been discharged.[58] On normal principles, unless the terms of the agreement provide otherwise, the seller is not entitled to repossess the goods until the credit period has expired and the buyer has defaulted in its obligations.[59]

15.3.4.2 Where the goods are intended to be stock for resale by the buyer, the seller realistically has to accept that its proprietary interest in the goods will be defeated by a sub-sale,[60] provided that under the terms of the sub-sale the title has passed to the sub-purchaser and has not been reserved pending payment by the sub-purchaser.[61] It has also been held that if the goods begin to undergo a process of manufacture, even if they retain much of their original qualities and substance, the title of the seller in the original goods will be lost and will not be treated as inherently carrying over into the product nor, indeed, the proceeds of sale of the product.[62] However, if the goods retain their original identity and can easily and without

---

[57] The starting point in terms of the case law on these types of arrangement is usually taken to be the decision of the Court of Appeal in *Aluminium Industrie Vassen BV v Romalpa Aluminium Ltd* [1976] 1 WLR 676, hence the expression 'Romalpa clause' that is often ascribed to the clause under which it is agreed that title is retained in the seller until payment. Some care must be taken with that case, however, in so far as it also decided that the seller's title in the original goods could extend to products of manufacture in which the original goods had been used and to the proceeds of re-sale of the original goods or of such products. This is because the Court of Appeal's approach was based on the concept of a fiduciary relationship as between the buyer and the seller, under which the buyer owed fiduciary obligations to the seller with a duty to account to the seller. This, in turn, was said to have arisen from a supposed bailment of the goods under the original sales agreement. That analysis (which was based upon an unfortunate concession in argument) has been rejected in subsequent cases. See, for instance, *Re Bond Worth Ltd* [1980] Ch 288 and *Borden (UK) Ltd v Scottish Timber Products Ltd* [1981] Ch 25.

[58] *Armour v Thyssen Edelstahlwerke AG* [1991] 2 AC 339.

[59] *Hendy Lennox (Industrial Engines) Ltd v Grahame Puttick Ltd* [1984] 1 WLR 485.

[60] Because there is an express or implied right to re-sell (*Four Point Garage Ltd v Carter* [1985] 3 All ER 12 and *Fairfax Gerrard Holdings Ltd v Capital Bank PLC* [2007] EWCA Civ 1226) or due to the operation of s 25(1) of the Sale of Goods Act 1979 and s 9 of the Factors Act 1889.

[61] *Re Highway Foods International Ltd* [1995] BCC 271.

[62] *Borden (UK) Ltd v Scottish Timber Products Ltd* [1981] Ch 25; *Re Peachdart Ltd* [1981] Ch 131. For the reasons expressed above, this is in spite of the view that was taken in *Aluminium Industrie Vassen BV v Romalpa Aluminium Ltd* [1976] 1 WLR 676, based upon the mistaken concept of an alleged fiduciary relationship as between the buyer and the seller.

causing damage be detached from any other item to which they may have been attached by the buyer then the seller's title will remain until payment, unless a third party has acquired title in the composite item to which they were so attached.[63]

It is perfectly possible for the contract between the seller and the buyer of the original goods to provide expressly that the seller should be the owner of any products that are made from the original goods and, if those products are sold, of the proceeds of sale of the products. Assuming that no other supplier whose goods have been used has a similar claim (which would give rise to other complications), such a provision will confer upon the seller a proprietary interest in the products when they are made, and that interest could, in theory, be that of an outright owner of the goods.[64] However, if the interest is defeasible upon payment by the buyer, as is almost certain to be the case where the seller is only looking for the payment due on the original goods, then it will be held as security for payment and will constitute a registrable charge and the usual consequences will follow if the security has not been registered.[65] A similar analysis will apply where the contract purports to confer upon the seller an interest in the proceeds of sale of the original goods or of products made by using the original goods.[66]

15.3.4.3

15.4 Hire Purchase Agreements

Hire purchase was developed to overcome the difficulty that the ownership of the seller in the goods under a conditional sale agreement might be defeated by a disposition of the goods by the buyer under section 25(1) of the Sale of Goods Act 1979 or section 9 of the Factors Act 1889. Under a hire purchase agreement, there is a hiring of the goods by the owner (the financier) to the hirer (the customer) for the instalment period during which hire is payable, although the agreement is likely to provide that the owner may determine it and repossess the goods if the hirer defaults in its obligations under the agreement. The hirer is also given an option in the agreement to purchase the goods, which may be exercised at the conclusion of the hiring. In the meantime, ownership of the goods remains vested

15.4.1

---

[63] *Hendy Lennox (Industrial Engines) Ltd v Grahame Puttick Ltd* [1984] 1 WLR 485.

[64] See Robert Goff LJ in *Clough Mill Ltd v Martin* [1985] 1 WLR 111, at 119.

[65] *Re Peachdart Ltd* [1981] Ch 131; *Clough Mill Ltd v Martin* [1985] 1 WLR 111.

[66] *Pfeiffer (E) Weinkellerei-Weineinkauf GmbH v Arbuthnot Factors Ltd* [1988] 1 WLR 150; *Tatung (UK) Ltd v Galex Telesure Ltd* (1989) 5 BCC 325; *Compaq Computer Ltd v Abercorn Group Ltd* [1991] BCC 484. On the other hand, if the buyer assigns to the seller the right to receive payment under the sub-sales as the consideration payable by the buyer under the original contract, that would be an outright conferral of such a right and would not be a grant of security: *Re Marwalt Ltd* [1992] BCC 32; *Associated Alloys Pty Ltd v ACN001452106 Pty Ltd* [2000] HCA 25, (2000) 171 ALR 56.

in the owner. The hirer is not obliged to exercise the option and become the owner. Prior to doing so, the hirer merely has a right to possession under the agreement. The consequence of this is that until the option is exercised, the hirer is not a person who has bought or agreed to buy the goods for the purposes of section 25(1) of the Sale of Goods Act 1979 and section 9 of the Factors Act 1889, so the sections will not apply.[67] This should be contrasted with an agreement under which the supposed hirer is obliged from the outset to complete the agreement and become the owner, which will amount to a conditional sale agreement.[68]

15.4.2 The option to purchase

The option to purchase may be expressed in either of two forms. First, it may be a positive option, in the sense that the hirer must give notice to the financier at the end of the hiring, once it has paid the full amount of hire, if it wishes to exercise the option and purchase the goods. It must also pay a fee to exercise the option as provided for in the agreement. This is the safest method of protecting the financier's interest whilst any amount remains outstanding under the agreement. In the alternative, the option may be expressed in a negative sense. Under this method, the agreement would provide that the hirer will acquire ownership of the goods if it should complete the agreement by paying all amounts of hire, but that it will have the right to return the goods beforehand and cease paying hire if it does not wish to become the owner.[69]

15.4.2.1 If the latter form is used (i.e. the form containing the negative option), the agreement must provide the hirer with a realistic opportunity to decide that it does not wish to keep the goods at the end of the hiring, so that it will return them to the owner. For instance, if the agreement provides that the hirer must pay all amounts due under the agreement and that it will become the owner unless it opts to return the goods at the conclusion of the hiring, that would not amount to a realistic option, as it is very unlikely that a hirer would decide to return the goods if, in effect, it has paid the full amount due.[70]

---

67 *Helby v Matthews* [1895] AC 471.

68 *Lee v Butler* [1893] 2 QB 318.

69 *Helby v Matthews* [1895] AC 471.

70 *Forthright Finance Ltd v Carlyle Finance Ltd* [1997] 4 All ER 90. This should be contrasted with the agreement in *Helby v Matthews* [1895] AC 471, where the hirer was given the right to return the piano at any time during the hiring, whereupon the hirer would be released from any obligation to pay further amounts of hire that would have fallen due after the date upon which the goods were returned. Phillips LJ in *Forthright Finance Ltd v Carlyle*, at 98, declined to indicate whether, in the case of the positive option type of agreement, the option fee had to be an amount that was not just a nominal figure, so as to demonstrate that the decision to exercise the option was commercially realistic. However, Buckley J in *Close Asset Finance Ltd v Care Graphics Machinery Ltd* [2000] CCLR 43 held that the inclusion of an option to buy at a nominal fee after payment of the final instalment indicated that the agreement was a hire purchase agreement and not a conditional sale agreement.

15.5 Finance Leases

Under a lease of equipment, the customer pays rentals over the period of the **15.5.1**
agreement but merely has a right to possession of the goods during the term of
the agreement, without either the right or an option to acquire ownership of
the goods. Once again, the agreement containing the lease is likely to provide
that the lessor may determine the lease and repossess the goods if the lessee defaults
in the performance of its obligations under the lease. There are two types of
lease that are commonly in use. They are the finance lease and the operating
lease.

A finance lease involves the lessee in taking (in an economic and practical sense) **15.5.2**
substantially all of the risks and rewards incidental to ownership of an item of
equipment. It will usually be for a lengthy duration. An operating lease is of a
shorter duration. Under it, the substantial body of the risks and rewards associated
with the goods remains held by the lessor as owner of the goods.[71] This chapter
will be concerned with finance leases rather than operating leases.

Rental under a finance lease may be payable by equal instalments over the period **15.5.3**
of the lease. Alternatively, the lease may provide for different amounts to be paid
at different times and there may even be a large amount (a 'balloon payment')
payable at the end of the lease. Quite often, the duration of the lease will be for a
substantial primary period, during which the finance provided by the financier
will be recouped. The leasing of the equipment may then be continued by the lessee for a secondary period at a lesser rental (usually only a nominal amount) until
such time as the lessee decides to end the lease, at which point the equipment may
be scrapped or sold.

15.6 The Financier's Statutory Responsibility
for the Equipment

One of the consequences of the legal character of equipment, or title, finance is **15.6.1**
that the financier is regarded as a supplier of the equipment to the customer, in the
guise of a seller under a conditional sale agreement, the owner that is hiring the
goods to the hirer under a hire purchase agreement, or the lessor of goods under
an equipment lease. This brings into play some important statutory responsibilities that are imposed upon those who supply goods with respect to, inter alia,

---

[71] Examples of finance leases will be found in *Lombard North Central PLC v Butterworth* [1987]
QB 527 and *On Demand Information PLC v Michael Gerson (Finance) PLC* [2001] 1 WLR 155
(Court of Appeal) and [2002] UKHL 13, [2003] 1 AC 368 (House of Lords).

the title in the goods and their quality and fitness for purpose.[72] The statutory responsibilities are additional to any express or implied contractual obligations that the financier might undertake by virtue of the other provisions of the agreement between the financier and the customer.[73]

15.6.1.1   The discussion that follows will describe the statutory responsibilities. Further on, the chapter will examine the extent to which the liability of the financier can be excluded or limited by provisions to that effect in the contract between the financier and the customer. The discussion will assume that the relevant equipment that is subject to a financing has been specifically identified, so that questions of sale, hiring, or leasing of goods by description or sample will not be relevant.[74]

15.6.1.2 The legislation

There are four statutes that are relevant to this discussion. They are:

(1) the Sale of Goods Act 1979 as amended (the SGA), which is relevant to conditional sale agreements;

(2) the Supply of Goods (Implied Terms) Act 1973 as amended (the SGITA), which is relevant to hire purchase agreements;

(3) the Supply of Goods and Services Act 1982 as amended (the SGSA), which is relevant to leases; and

(4) the Unfair Contract Terms Act 1977 as amended (the UCTA) which is relevant to attempts that might be made to limit or exclude the financier's liability under those other statutes.[75]

15.6.2 Implied terms as to title, freedom from encumbrance, and quiet possession: conditional sale and hire purchase agreements

Section 12 of the SGA contains terms that are to be implied in a contract for the sale of goods (including conditional sale agreements). They concern the right of

---

[72]   There are also statutory provisions that deal with the sale and supply of goods by sample or description. As almost invariably an equipment finance transaction as between the financier and the customer is concerned with specifically identified goods, those provisions will not be mentioned in this discussion.

[73]   As occurred, for instance, in *Barber v NWS Bank PLC* [1996] 1 WLR 641 (an independent agreement as to the financier's title in the goods subject to a conditional sale agreement) and *Purnell Secretarial Services Ltd v Lease Management Services Ltd* [1994] Tr LR 337(representations and warranties by the financier under an equipment lease agreement as to the functions that the equipment could perform). Although not involving a finance transaction, *St Albans CDC v International Computers Ltd* [1996] 4 All ER 481 provides another example of such obligations arising (suitability of software supplied on a computer disk for the task it was meant to perform).

[74]   Such matters would otherwise arise under ss 13 and 15 of the SGA, ss 9 and 11 of the SGITA, and ss 8 and 10 of the SGSA.

[75]   In consumer transactions, there would also be a number of other relevant pieces of legislation, such as the Unfair Terms in Consumer Contracts Regs 1999 (SI 1999/2083), the Consumer Protection (Distance Selling) Regs 2000 (SI 2000/2334), and the Sale and Supply of Goods to Consumer Regs 2002 (SI 2002/3045).

the seller to sell the goods, that the buyer will have quiet possession of the goods, and that the goods will be free from charges and encumbrances. As section 8 of the SGITA is to much the same effect in relation to hire purchase agreements, the discussion will concentrate upon section 12 of the SGA.

Section 12 of the SGA provides as follows: **15.6.2.1**

(1) In a contract of sale, other than one to which subsection (3) below applies, there is an implied term on the part of the seller that in the case of a sale he had a right to sell the goods, and in the case of an agreement to sell he will have such a right at the time when the property is to pass.

(2) In a contract of sale, other than one to which subsection (3) below applies, there is also an implied term that—

  (a) the goods are free, and will remain free until the time when the property is to pass, from any charge or encumbrance not disclosed or known to the buyer before the contract is made, and

  (b) the buyer will enjoy quiet possession of the goods except so far as it may be disturbed by the owner or other person entitled to the benefit of any charge or encumbrance as disclosed or known.

(3) This subsection applies to a contract of sale in the case of which there appears from the contract or is to be inferred from its circumstances an intention that the seller should transfer only such title as he or a third person may have.

(4) In a contract to which subsection (3) above applies there is an implied term that all charges or encumbrances known to the seller and not known to the buyer have been disclosed to the buyer before the contract is made.

(5) In a contract to which subsection (3) above applies there is also an implied term that none of the following will disturb the buyer's quiet possession of the goods, namely—

  (a) the seller;

  (b) in a case where the parties to the contract intend that the seller should transfer only such title as a third person may have, that person;

  (c) anyone claiming through or under the seller or that third person otherwise than under a charge or encumbrance disclosed or known to the buyer before the contract is made.

(5A) As regards England and Wales and Northern Ireland, the term implied by subsection (1) above is a condition and the terms implied by subsections (2), (4) and (5) above are warranties.

(6) [not relevant].

It will be seen that section 12(1) provides for a term that is to be implied in a contract of sale, except where section 12(3) applies. The term has the status of a condition, as opposed to a mere warranty.[76] The condition is to the effect that the seller had the right to sell the goods and that the seller will have that right at the time property in them is intended to pass under the contract. A failure to meet the condition will entitle the buyer to reject the goods and sue for damages, even where **15.6.2.2**

---

[76] The term is a condition by virtue of s 12(5A) of the Act.

the buyer has been in possession of the goods for a substantial period before it discovers the breach.[77] The condition relates both to the transfer of title in the goods to the buyer and to other reasons why the seller might be unable to sell them.[78] In relation to the transfer of title in the goods, the condition requires that the seller should itself transfer a good title or, by the time of contracting, have arranged for another person to do so. An obvious difficulty for the seller in meeting the condition is the situation where, unbeknown to it, the goods are owned by a third party.

15.6.2.2.1 It is not clear in the case of a conditional sale agreement whether the seller must be in the position from the outset of being able to vest title in the buyer or whether it is sufficient that this in fact happens by the time that property was intended to pass under the agreement. It is possible, although not yet decided, that provided the buyer does not take action to reject the goods before the time that title is to pass to it, the seller will be able to cure any breach that has occurred and meet its obligation by ensuring that the buyer does get title at the appropriate time, such as by buying in the title from a third party ('feeding the title').[79] The position will be different if the seller expressly undertakes that at the time of contracting it is the owner of the goods, such as by stipulating that it will remain as the owner until the buyer has paid the full price. In such a case, it will be in breach of that undertaking and the buyer will be entitled to reject the goods, even if the seller manages to get in the title before the date that title is to pass to the buyer.[80]

15.6.2.3 Section 12(2) also applies where section 12(3) does not apply. It is difficult to see what section 12(2) adds to the effect of section 12(1). Section 12(2) imports an implied term into the contract, which has the status of a warranty.[81] A breach of the warranty will give rise to a claim for damages by the buyer. One part of the warranty is to the effect that the goods will be free from charges and encumbrances in favour of third parties, at both the time of contracting and when property is to pass, except those that were disclosed or otherwise known to the buyer when the contract was made. The second part contains an implied warranty for quiet possession of the goods by the buyer, except where disturbed by the seller or pursuant to a charge or encumbrance of which the buyer was aware when it contracted.

---

[77] This is because the essence of the seller's obligation under a sale of goods contract is to ensure that title passes to the buyer in accordance with the contract. See *Rowland v Divall* [1923] 2 KB 500 and, in similar circumstances where there was an express term of the contract, *Barber v NWS Bank PLC* [1996] 1 WLR 641. It should also be noted that the right of rejection for breach of the condition under s 12 is not one that may be lost by virtue of the operation of s 15A of the Act.

[78] For instance, because the sale would be in breach of a third party's intellectual property rights: see *Niblett Ltd v Confectioners' Materials Ltd* [1921] 3 KB 387. Given the importance of such rights, particularly IT rights, this is an important consideration when entering into a contract.

[79] See Pearson J in *Butterworth v Kingsway Motors Ltd* [1954] 1 WLR 1286, at 1291.

[80] *Barber v NWS Bank PLC* [1996] 1 WLR 641, which was a case concerning equipment finance by way of a conditional sale agreement.

[81] See s 12(5A).

15.6.2.4

Sections 12(1) and 12(2) do not apply to a contract of sale to which section 12(3) applies.[82] Section 12 (3) applies where it appears from the contract or from its circumstances[83] that the seller will only transfer such title as it or a third person may have. This means that it is possible for the seller to protect itself from undertaking the onerous obligations that would arise in pursuance of section 12(1), by stipulating in the contract that the buyer will only obtain such title as the owner or a named third party may have. This has obvious advantages for a financier selling under a conditional sale agreement, where the financier may not be absolutely sure of the title that it will acquire from a manufacturer or supplier. It would also appear from the wording of section 12(1) that by using this means the financier can limit its liability as to other reasons why it may not be able to sell the goods to the customer.

15.6.2.4.1

Where section 12(3) applies, sections 12(4) and 12(5) import implied terms on the part of the seller, which have the status of warranties[84] and so will give rise to a claim for damages by the buyer, if they are breached by the seller. Under section 12(4), the implied term is that the seller disclosed to the buyer all charges and encumbrances that were known to the seller and unknown by the buyer as at the time of contracting. Under section 12(5), the implied term is that the buyer's quiet possession of the goods will not be disturbed by the seller, any third party from whom it was intended that title would pass to the buyer, and any person claiming under the seller or such a third party, except pursuant to a charge or encumbrance that was disclosed to the buyer prior to contracting.

15.6.3 Implied terms as to possession, freedom from encumbrance and quiet possession: lease agreements

Section 7 of the SGSA contains terms on the part of the lessor that are to be implied into an equipment lease agreement. Under section 7(1), there is an implied condition that the seller will have the right to transfer possession of the goods to the customer for the duration of the lease. Under section 7(2), there is an implied warranty that the customer will have quiet possession of the goods for that period, save in consequence of action taken by the lessor or by a person pursuant to a charge or encumbrance that was disclosed or known to the customer before the contract was made.

15.6.4 Implied terms as to satisfactory quality and fitness for purpose

Section 14 of the SGA, section 10 of the SGITA, and section 9 of the SGSA contain implied terms that the goods will be of satisfactory quality and, in defined circumstances, reasonably fit for a particular purpose. They apply where the seller of

---

[82] There is an apparent conflict between the effect of s 12(3) of the SGA and s 6 of the UCTA, which is discussed below in relation to s 6 of the UCTA.

[83] Such as where a bailiff is selling goods.

[84] See s 12(5A).

the goods, the owner of goods that are hired under a hire purchase agreement, or the lessor of goods that are leased, sells, hires, or leases the goods in the course of a business. The requirement as to acting in the course of a business has been construed widely in this context[85] and is bound to be met where the seller, owner or lessor is a financier.

15.6.4.1 It should be noted that the implied terms are conditions and not just mere warranties. However, section 15A of the SGA[86] provides that if the effect of a breach of the conditions in section 14 is so slight that it would be unreasonable to allow the buyer to reject the goods then, so long as the buyer is not dealing as a consumer, the breach should only be treated as a breach of warranty for which damages would be awarded. It should also be noted that the right to reject goods for breach of a condition may be lost under section 35 of the SGA where the buyer is deemed to have accepted them.[87]

15.6.4.2 The implied terms may be annexed to a contract by usage.[88] They may also apply where the seller is acting as the agent of another.[89]

15.6.4.3 The provisions of section 10 of the SGITA and section 9 of the SGSA are almost the same as those in section 14 of the SGA, so the provisions of section 14 of the SGA will be referred to below. It is convenient to examine the two implied terms in section 14 separately.

15.6.5 Satisfactory quality

The relevant provisions of section 14 of the SGA dealing with the implied term for satisfactory quality are as follows:

(2) Where the seller sells goods in the course of a business, there is an implied term that the goods supplied under the contract are of satisfactory quality.

(2A) For the purposes of this Act, goods are of satisfactory quality if they meet the standard that a reasonable person would regard as satisfactory, taking account of any description of the goods, the price (if relevant) and all the other relevant circumstances.

(2B) For the purposes of this Act, the quality of goods includes their state and condition and the following (among others) are in appropriate cases aspects of the quality of the goods—

(a) fitness for all the purposes for which goods of the kind in question are commonly supplied,

---

[85] See *Stevenson v Rogers* [1999] QB 1028 and *Feldarol Foundry PLC v Hermes Leasing (London) Ltd* [2004] EWCA Civ 747, (2004) 101(24) LSG 32. This should be contrasted with the approach that has been taken towards to the expression 'Deals as consumer' in the Unfair Contract Terms Act 1977: see *R&B Customs Brokers Co Ltd v United Dominions Trust Ltd* [1988] 1 WLR 321 and *Stevenson v Rogers*.

[86] See also s 11A of the SGITA and s 10A of the SGSA.

[87] See *Truk (UK) Ltd v Tokmakidis GmbH* [2000] 1 Lloyd's Rep 543.

[88] S 14(4) of the SGA.

[89] S 14(5) of the SGA.

    (b) appearance and finish,
    (c) freedom from minor defects,
    (d) safety, and
    (e) durability.
(2C) The term implied by subsection (2) above does not extend to any matter making the quality of goods unsatisfactory—
    (a) which is specifically drawn to the buyer's attention before the contract is made,
    (b) where the buyer examines the goods before the contract is made, which that examination ought to reveal, or
    (c) in the case of a contract for the sale by sample, which would have been apparent on a reasonable examination of the sample.

15.6.5.1 These provisions replace those which used to apply under previous legislation, under which the goods had to be of 'merchantable quality'.[90] It will be seen that the scheme of the provisions is that sub-section (2) lays down the implied term, that the goods that are supplied under the contract are of satisfactory quality. Sub-section (2A) then prescribes the standard that is required in meeting the term, and sub-section (2B) provides a non-exhaustive list of particular matters going to the state and condition of the goods that may be taken into consideration in determining if that standard has been met. Sub-section (2C) sets out circumstances in which the implied term will not apply. The implied term is to be judged at the time the goods are supplied under the contract.

15.6.5.2 The implied term covers 'the goods supplied under the contract' and not just the goods that are sold. This would extend to containers, packaging, and other things with which or in which the goods are sold. It would include items, like containers, that remained the property of the seller and had to be returned.[91]

15.6.5.3 The standard of satisfactory quality that is required under sub-section (2A) is to be judged on objective grounds by reference to what a reasonable person would regard as satisfactory, taking into account any description of the goods, the price (if relevant), and other relevant circumstances. The description could include a standard of quality or performance, for instance that the goods were 'high quality' or 'standard'. Alternatively, the goods might be described as 'scrap'. The list of the particular aspects of the state and condition of the goods in determining their quality, as set out in sub-section (2C), is not intended to be exhaustive and could be overruled in a particular case by the description of the goods as contained in the contract. It should also be noted that the fitness test in this sub-section (in contrast to that contained in section 14(3)) is that the goods should be fit for all the purposes for which goods of that kind are commonly supplied and not just one of those purposes.

---

[90] The change was effected by the Sale and Supply of Goods Act 1994.
[91] *Gedding v Marsh* [1920] 1 KB 668; *Wilson v Rickett Cockerell & Co Ltd* [1954] 1 QB 598.

15.6.5.4 Under sub-section (2C), the implied term will not apply to any matter which (a) was specifically drawn to the buyer's attention before the contract was made, (b) should have been revealed by an examination of the goods which the buyer made before the contract, or (c) would have been apparent on a reasonable examination of a sample, where the contract was for the sale by sample. With respect to (a), it is not clear how precise the disclosure should have been. It is also unclear if the disclosure must be by the seller or if it would be sufficient that the disclosure was made by a third party, such as by the manufacturer. With respect to (b), it should be noted that this exception will only apply if the buyer has actually conducted an examination before the contract is made, rather than applying should the buyer (in theory) have examined the goods. It is possible, however, that if the buyer is realistically invited to conduct an examination and declines to do so, the buyer might be taken to have waived its right to rely upon the implied condition under sub-section (2). The position is not clear where the buyer only conducts a cursory examination, because the exception only applies to what 'that examination ought to reveal', rather than what a well conducted examination should reveal.[92]

15.6.5.5 The application of the implied term under sub-section (2) in the case of an equipment finance transaction can be seen from the facts of *Feldarol Foundry PLC v Hermes Leasing (London) Ltd*.[93] In that case, an expensive sports car, which was the subject of a hire purchase agreement, was found to be of unsatisfactory quality, due to defective steering and brakes, even though the car could have been repaired for a relatively small cost. The car was unsafe and was not free from minor defects.

15.6.5.6 It has also been said that, whilst a computer program or software is not 'goods' within the definition of that word in section 61 of the SGA, a physical device onto which it had been encoded was goods.[94] If that device was sold or hired for the purpose of using the program or software so encoded on it and the program or software was defective, so that the intended purpose of acquiring and using the software or program could not be achieved, the goods would be of unsatisfactory quality (and might also be unfit for a particular purpose) within section 14 of the SGA, section 10 of the SGITA, and section 9 of the SGSA, and damages would be assessed on that basis, rather than by reference to the relatively modest value of the device on its own.

---

[92] Nonetheless, in *Thornett & Fehr v Beers & Son* [1919] 1 KB 486, a cursory examination was held to be sufficient to engage the exception, with respect to matters that a more thorough examination would have revealed.

[93] [2004] EWCA Civ 747, (2004) 101(24) LSG 32.

[94] See Sir Iain Glidewell in *St Albans CDC v International Computers Ltd* [1996] 4 All ER 481, at 493.

15.6.6 Fitness for a particular purpose

The relevant provisions of section 14 of the SGA dealing with the implied term that the goods will be fit for a particular purpose are as follows:

(3) Where the seller sells goods in the course of a business and the buyer, expressly or by implication, makes known—
  (a) to the seller, or
  (b) [consumer contracts involving a credit-broker],

any particular purpose for which the goods are being bought, there is an implied term that the goods supplied under the contract are reasonably fit for that purpose, whether or not that is a purpose for which such goods are commonly supplied, except where the circumstances show that the buyer does not rely, or that it is unreasonable for him to rely, on the skill or judgment of the seller [or credit-broker].

In summary, the implied term will arise where the buyer makes known to the seller a particular purpose for which the buyer is buying the goods. The term is that the goods supplied under the contract are reasonably fit for that purpose. The term will not be implied, however, where the circumstances show either that the buyer does not rely on the skill or judgment of the seller or that it would be unreasonable for the buyer so to rely. Thus, where the customer (as the buyer) has formed its own judgment as to the suitability of the goods, or where it possesses sufficient technical expertise to form such a judgment, an obligation by way of an implied term under this section should not arise against the financier (as the seller).   **15.6.6.1**

Once again, it is the goods that are supplied that must be fit for the purpose, not just the goods that are being bought. The term only requires that the goods should be 'reasonably fit' for the purpose; the test is to an objective rather than an absolute standard. This is probably measured by asking what a reasonable buyer would expect from the goods so as to meet that standard. The particular purpose must be communicated to the seller. It is not entirely clear at what point a purpose is sufficiently particular to distinguish it from the purposes for which goods are commonly used, as referred to in section 14(2B)(a). It would appear that goods may be unfit where there is a latent defect which was unknown at the time of delivery. The question as to whether the goods meet the required standard of fitness for purpose is to be judged at the date of delivery of the goods. The issue as to reliance is judged as at the date of the contract.   **15.6.6.2**

15.7 Exclusion or Limitation of a Financier's Liability Concerning the Equipment

Given the potential risk to a financier from both express terms of the contract and from the implied statutory terms as to the goods, as described above, the financier may well wish to draft its way out of the problem by seeking in the contract to   **15.7.1** exclude or limit its liability arising from those terms. The approach that should be taken to the construction of clauses in a contract that seek to limit or exclude a party's liability in contract or in tort is discussed in Chapter 9, which also contains a general review of the Unfair Contract Terms Act 1977 (UCTA), to which further reference is made below.

15.7.2   Assuming that, as a matter of construction, the clause applies to limit or exclude the financier's potential liability, the next issue is whether it is caught by the UCTA. The relevant sections of the Act that might be relevant are sections 3, 6, 7, 11, and 13, which are discussed below. In general terms, the Act may either preclude the financier from being able to limit or exclude its liability, or subject an attempt at doing so to the threshold that the attempt will only be effective if the provision which contains the limitation or exclusion meets the requirement of reasonableness that is laid down by section 11 of the Act. It should be noted that section 10 of the Act prevents the evasion of the Act by the use of a secondary contract. It should also be noted that an attempt by a contractual term to exclude or restrict liability arising from a misrepresentation will fall within the ambit of section 3 of the Misrepresentation Act 1967 and will only survive if the term satisfies the requirement of reasonableness in section 11 of the UCTA.[95]

15.7.3 Cross-border and conflict of laws considerations

In the context of equipment finance which involves cross-border transactions and considerations relating to conflict of laws, there are two preliminary matters which may need to be addressed, so as to determine if the UCTA is relevant.

15.7.3.1 *International supply contracts*

The first of those preliminary matters concerns section 26 of the UCTA. Section 26 has the effect that the Act does not apply to 'international supply contracts' which, by virtue of sub-section (3), includes a sale of goods contract or a contract of hire purchase or lease of goods that, in each of those cases, meet the following requirements. The contract must be made between parties whose place of business (or, if they do not have a place of business, their habitual residences) are in the territories of different States. One of the following conditions, as contained in sub-section (4), must also be met:

(a) the goods in question are, at the time of the conclusion of the contract, in the course of carriage, or will be carried, from the territory of one State to the territory of another; or

(b) the acts constituting the offer and acceptance have been done in the territories of different States; or

---

[95] S 3 of the Misrepresentation Act is addressed in Chap 9. S 11(3) of the UCTA is addressed in Chap 9.

    (c) the contract provides for the goods to be delivered to the territory of a State other than that within whose territory those acts were done.

It has been held that paragraph (c) requires that the goods should be delivered out of one State and to a different State, even where the place of delivery might be a State that was not one where the acts of offer and acceptance of the contract had taken place.[96]

15.7.3.2 Choice of law clauses

The second preliminary point arises in consequence of section 27 of the UCTA. Section 27 concerns the effect of choice of law clauses. Sub-section (1) has the effect that the Act will not apply if, apart from an express choice of law, the governing law of a contract would be the law of some country other than a constituent part of the UK. Sub-section (2) concerns the reverse situation. The Act will still apply to a contract which contains a foreign governing law clause where either (or both) (a) the governing law appears to have been chosen so as to evade the Act, or (b) one of the parties, who was habitually resident in the UK, dealt as a consumer[97] in making the contract and he or others on his behalf took the essential steps in the UK for making the contract.

15.7.4 Section 3 of the UCTA: liability arising in contract

Section 3 is one of the sections of the UCTA that would be relevant to an attempt by a financier to escape from or restrict its obligations under the implied terms that arise by virtue of the SGA, the SGIT, and the SGSA. It would also be relevant to an attempt by the financier to escape from or restrict a liability that might arise independently of the implied terms.[98]

15.7.4.1 Section 3 of the UCTA provides that, where a contracting party (the customer) is dealing as a consumer or on the other party's standard terms of business, that other party (the financier) cannot by a contractual term exclude or restrict his own liability for breach of the contract, nor purport in pursuance of such a term to render no performance at all or to render a substantially different performance from what was reasonably to be expected under the contract, except in so far as the term satisfies the requirement of reasonableness in section 11 of the Act. By way of example, the section has been applied to a case where a financier's standard terms included an exclusion clause which excluded liability for misrepresentations that had been made about the relevant goods,[99] and to a case where a supplier

---

[96] *Amiri Flight Authority v BAE Systems PLC* [2003] EWCA Civ 1447, [2003] 2 Lloyd's Rep 767.

[97] The concept of dealing as a consumer is examined below.

[98] As, for instance, was the case in *Purnell Secretarial Services Ltd v Lease Management Services Ltd* [1994] Tr LR 337.

[99] Ibid.

of software purported to limit its liability for breach of an implied term as to the fitness and quality of a computer program to a maximum amount.[100]

15.7.4.1.1 It will be seen from the above that the section only applies if either (1) the party against whom the relevant provisions are relied upon (that is, the customer) was dealing as a consumer in entering into the contract, or (2) if the party relying upon those provisions (that is, the financier) is dealing on its written standard terms of business (whether or not the other party was acting as a consumer). It is necessary to consider each of those possibilities in turn.

15.7.4.2 *Dealing as a consumer*

Section 12 of the UCTA spells out what is meant by the phrase 'deals as consumer' when it is used in the Act. The phrase is used in sections 6, 7, 13, and 27 of the Act, as well as in section 3.

15.7.4.2.1 Section 12 provides as follows:

> (1) A party to a contract 'deals as consumer' in relation to another party if—
>> (a) he neither makes the contract in the course of a business nor holds himself out as doing so; and
>> (b) the other party does make the contract in the course of a business; and
>> (c) in the case of a contract governed by the law of sale of goods or hire-purchase, or by Section 7 of this Act, the goods passing under or in pursuance of the contract are of a type ordinarily supplied for private use or consumption.
>
> (1A) But if the first party mentioned in subsection (1) is an individual paragraph (c) of that subsection must be ignored.
>
> (2) But the buyer is not in any circumstances to be regarded as dealing as consumer—
>> (a) if he is an individual and the goods are second hand goods sold at public auction at which individuals have the opportunity of attending the sale in person;
>> (b) if he is not an individual and the goods are sold by auction or by competitive tender.
>
> (3) Subject to this, it is for those claiming that a party does not deal as consumer to show that he does not.

15.7.4.2.2 It has been held that a company may still be considered as a person dealing as a consumer for the purposes of the UCTA where the relevant transaction is merely incidental to the carrying on of a business and there has not been a sufficient degree of regularity for the activity concerned to have become an integral party of the business.[101]

---

100 *St Albans City and District Council v International Computers Ltd* [1996] 4 All ER 481

101 *R&B Customs Brokers Co Ltd v United Dominions Trust Ltd* [1988] 1 WLR 321. The approach taken to s12 of the UCTA should be distinguished from that which applies concerning the issue of whether a seller sells in the course of a business for the purpose of s 14 of the SGA: see *Stevenson v*

15.7.4.3 *Written standard terms of business*

It has been held that the use of a standard form put forward by a trade association or a similar body can be treated as being a party's standard terms of business if that party 'invariably or at least usually' contracts on those terms.[102] It has also been held that that there could still be standard terms of business where there had been some negotiation of the provisions of a contract, if the terms remained effectively the same, which is a question of fact.[103] Whilst there will often be negotiation of the provisions of an equipment finance agreement dealing with commercial matters, it is less usual for the remaining provisions to be negotiated to any great extent and they are often accepted without dissent. Accordingly, there must be some risk that the provisions on which the financier relies might be held to be its written standard terms of business if the document, although subject to some negotiation, is based upon its own standard form or the commonly used standard forms in its industry.

Assuming that one or other (or both) of the above requirements are satisfied, it then falls to be considered whether the relevant term in favour of the financier satisfies the requirement of reasonableness, which will be dealt with separately below. It will be noted that, in common with other sections of the UCTA, it is the term itself which must satisfy the requirement of reasonableness, not its application to the particular circumstances.[104] Hence, a term which has the effect of absolving a financier from rendering any performance under the contract, or which excludes any and all liability for breach, will be inherently unreasonable, no matter what may be the particular circumstances in which it has been invoked.[105]

15.7.4.3.1

15.7.5 Section 6 of the UCTA: The statutorily implied terms under a conditional sale or hire purchase agreement

Section 6 of the UCTA is aimed directly at attempts to exclude or restrict the liability of a seller (under a conditional sale agreement) or an owner (under a hire purchase agreement) with respect to the terms that are to be implied by, inter alia, sections 12 and 14 of the SGA and sections 8 and 10 of SGITA. In examining the effect of section 6, it is easiest to distinguish contracts where the customer has

---

Rogers [1999] QB 1028 and *Feldarol Foundry PLC v Hermes Leasing (London) Ltd* [2004] EWCA Civ 747, (2004) 101(24) LSG 32.

[102] *British Fermentation Products Ltd v Compair Reavell Ltd* [1999] 2 All ER (Comm) 389, at [46].

[103] Nourse LJ held in *St Albans City and District Council v International Computers Ltd* [1996] 4 All ER 481, at 491, that it was a question of fact whether there had been a dealing, i.e. a contracting, on one of the party's standard terms and that there could still be standard terms even if there had been prior negotiations, so long as the terms remained effectively untouched by the negotiations.

[104] See Stuart Smith LJ in *Stewart Gill Ltd v Horatio Myer & Co Ltd* [1992] QB 600, at 608.

[105] For a recent decision on this point, see *Regus (UK) Ltd v Epcot Solutions Ltd* [2008] EWCA Civ 361.

dealt as a consumer, from those where it has not done so. The concept of dealing as a consumer is examined above.

15.7.5.1 Where the customer has dealt as a consumer, none of the statutorily implied terms that are attributed to the seller or owner may be excluded or restricted.[106]

15.7.5.2 In other cases, the implied terms under section 12 of the SGA and section 8 of the SGITA cannot be excluded or restricted. However, the implied terms under section 14 of the SGA and section 10 of the SGITA may be excluded or restricted by a term in the contract, provided that the term which contains the exclusion or restriction satisfies the requirement of reasonableness that is contained in section 11 of the UCTA.[107]

15.7.5.3 A question arises at this point as to the uneasy relationship between the exception that is contained in section 12(1) of the SGA, where section 12(3) applies instead (and, respectively, the exception to section 8(1) of the SGITA in the circumstances where section 8(2) of the SGITA applies), on the one hand, and section 6(1) of the UCTA. It will be recalled that in section 12(1) of the SGA it is provided that the implied term (which is a condition of the contract) that the seller has the right to sell the goods does not apply where section 12(3) applies. Section 12(3) applies in a case where it appears from the contract or the circumstances that the seller only intended to transfer such title as he or a third party may have, in which case certain lesser warranties will be implied. It may be argued that a contract which purports to disapply section 12(1) by providing that the seller will only transfer such title as he or a third party may have, amounts to an attempt to exclude or restrict the seller's liability for matters which section 6(1) provides cannot be excluded or restricted. It is not easy to reconcile the apparent inconsistency. The answer, although it is not very satisfactory, appears to be that a provision in the contract that the seller (or the owner, in the case of hire purchase) will only transfer such title as it or a third party may have, will be acceptable, as it takes advantage of a permissible alternative that is provided by the SGA. However, an attempt to exclude or restrict such liability as the seller may have under section 12, after taking into account the exception that is allowed in consequence of section 12(3), would not be permissible and would fall foul of section 6(1) of the UCTA.

15.7.6 Section 7 of the UCTA: The statutorily implied terms under a lease agreement

The position concerning attempts to exclude or restrict liability under the statutorily implied terms relating to lease agreements is a little different than that which applies for sales and hire purchase agreements. Section 7 of the UCTA addresses

---

[106] See ss 6(1) and 6(2) of the UCTA.
[107] See ss 6(1), 6(2), and 6(3) of the UCTA.

attempts to exclude or restrict liability of a lessor under the implied terms that arise in consequence of, inter alia, sections 7 and 9 of the SGSA.

In the case of liability that arises under the implied terms contained in section 7 of the SGSA (right to transfer possession and such like), such liability can only be excluded or restricted if the relevant term satisfies the requirement of reasonableness.[108] The position is the same whether or not the customer has dealt as a consumer.

15.7.6.1

With respect to liability that arises under the implied terms contained in section 9 of the SGSA (quality and fitness), the position depends upon whether the customer has dealt as a consumer. If it has so dealt, liability cannot be excluded or restricted.[109] Otherwise, liability can be excluded or restricted if the relevant term satisfies the requirement of reasonableness.[110]

15.7.6.2

15.7.7 Section 13 of the UCTA: alternative means of escaping from liability

Section 13 of the UCTA contains provisions which are intended to prevent a party from escaping from its liability or which make it difficult to enforce such a liability. For present purposes, the salient part of section 13(1) provides as follows:

> To the extent that this Part of this Act [which includes all of the preceding sections] prevents the exclusion or restriction of any liability it also prevents—
>
> (a) making the liability or its enforcement subject to restrictive or onerous conditions;
> (b) excluding or restricting any right or remedy in respect of the liability, or subjecting a person to any prejudice in consequence of his pursuing any such right or remedy;
> (c) excluding or restricting rules of evidence or procedure;
>
> And (to that extent) Ss [6 and 7] also prevent excluding or restricting liability by reference to terms and notices which exclude or restrict the relevant duty or obligation.

The precise ambit of this section is not entirely clear. However, it is clear that paragraph (a) would catch contractual provisions that limit the period in which a claim may be brought or which require conditions to be fulfilled before it could be brought. This would include, for instance, onerous requirements as to serving a notice of a defect where goods were faulty.

15.7.7.1

In *Stewart Gill Ltd v Horatio Myer & Co Ltd*[111] the Court of Appeal held that paragraph (b) applied to an anti-set-off clause which prevented the exercise by a customer of a right of equitable set-off or counterclaim in an instalment payment

15.7.7.2

---

108 S 7(4) of the UCTA.
109 S 7(2) of the UCTA.
110 S 7(3) of the UCTA.
111 [1992] QB 600.

contract, where faulty goods had been supplied. The customer had wished to set off its counterclaim for the loss it had suffered due to the goods being defective, against the instalments that it was due to pay under the contract. It was held that the right of set-off or counterclaim was a right or remedy that the customer would normally have been entitled to assert against the supplier. The clause prevented it from exercising the right. It would also subject the customer to prejudice, in that the clause would have the effect of forcing the customer to pursue its claim against the supplier separately, rather than being able to use the more effective and immediate right of set-off. An attempt by the supplier to limit or restrict its liability for the defective goods would have fallen within section 3 of the UCTA. Accordingly, section 13 was engaged and the anti-set-off clause could only be saved if it met the requirement of reasonableness. That requirement had not been satisfied, as it could not be reasonable to prevent the customer in any and all circumstances from seeking to assert a right of set-off including, for instance, where it might have made an over-payment under an earlier instalment.

15.7.8 Section 11 of the UCTA: the requirement of reasonableness

It will be seen from the above that attempts by a contractual term to exclude or restrict liability may founder altogether or, in other cases, will only succeed if the term meets the requirement of reasonableness. Section 11 of the UCTA sets out the formulation of that requirement.[112] The party relying upon the contract term has the onus of showing that the requirement of reasonableness has been met.[113]

15.7.8.1 With respect to a contract term, section 11(1) provides that the test is whether:

> The term shall have been a fair and reasonable one to be included having regard to the circumstances which were, or ought reasonably to have been, known to or in the contemplation of the parties when the contract was made.

15.7.8.1.2 It is the incorporation of the term in the contract that must satisfy the requirement of reasonableness. The relevant time to assess if that requirement has been met is the time of contracting, so it is not relevant to judge the matter at the time of a later breach of the contract or by reference to the way the term has operated in relation to the specific facts of the case,[114] except, perhaps, if those facts should have been in the parties' contemplation when the contract was made. The relevant circumstances must have been known to or in the contemplation of both of the parties, not just the party seeking to rely upon the clause.

---

[112] It should be noted that s 2 of the UCTA, which concerns liability in negligence, catches not just contractual terms that purport to exclude or restrict liability, but also attempts to do so by virtue of a non-contractual 'notice', which is defined in s 14 of the Act. S 11(3) addresses the requirement of reasonableness in relation to such a notice.

[113] S 11(5) of the Act.

[114] See Stuart-Smith LJ in *Stewart Gill Ltd v Horatio Myer & Co Ltd* [1992] QB 600, at 608.

Section 11(2) makes provision for certain guidelines, which are set out in Schedule 2 to the Act, to which regard should be had in assessing the reasonableness of a term. Whilst the guidelines, strictly speaking, are expressed only to be relevant with respect to sections 6 and 7 of the Act,[115] they are generally taken as being relevant in providing guidance as to the application of the reasonableness test in relation to other provisions of the Act as well.[116] The guidelines are as follows:

(a) the strength of the bargaining positions of the parties relative to each other, taking into account (among other things) alternate means by which the customer's requirements could have been met;

(b) whether the customer received an inducement to agree to the term, or in accepting it had an opportunity of entering into a similar contract with other persons, but without having to accept a similar term;

(c) whether the customer knew or ought reasonably to have known of the existence and extent of the term (having regard, among other things, to any custom of the trade and any previous course of dealing between the parties);

(d) where the term excludes or restricts any relevant liability if some condition is not complied with, whether it was reasonable at the time of the contract to expect that compliance with that condition would be practicable;

(e) whether the goods were manufactured, processed or adapted to the special order of the customer.

It is submitted that, in the context of equipment financing, where the customer has selected the goods that were to be supplied by the manufacturer or the supplier to the financier and thence to the customer, paragraph (e) above might be modified or applied by reference to the fact that the financier acquired the goods from the manufacturer or the supplier at the request of the customer, and that it was the customer who chose them. In this regard, it should be borne in mind that the financier would profess to have no skill in the selection and could be taken to have been reliant upon the customer in that regard. However, that argument might be seen as being inconsistent with the fact that the financier contracts as a supplier of goods, rather than a lender of money. As a supplier of goods, it may be argued that it should accept the usual responsibilities which go with that role.[117]

Section 11(4) makes provision for contractual terms or notices which seek to restrict the liability of a person to a specified sum of money, in which case regard should be had to the resources that the person could have expected to be available

---

[115] And they are not an exhaustive list: see for instance the further tests outlined by Potter LJ in *Overseas Medical Supplies Ltd v Orient Transport Services Ltd* [1999] 2 Lloyd's Rep 273, at 276–277.

[116] See Stuart-Smith LJ in *Stewart Gill Ltd v Horatio Myer & Co Ltd* [1992] QB 600, at 608.

[117] See the approach taken in *Purnell Secretarial Services Ltd v Lease Management Services Ltd* [1994] Tr LR 337, to which further reference is made below.

to him to meet the liability if it arose and how far it was open to him to obtain insurance cover.[118]

15.7.8.4 The position as to reasonableness will vary from one set of circumstances to another, so the decisions in the cases which depend on factual matters must be regarded with caution. Nonetheless, the following cases do give some flavour of the attitude that has been taken. In *St Alban's City and District Council v International Computers Ltd*[119] and in *Salvage Association v Cap Financial Services*[120] provisions in relation to the supply of computer software which limited liability to an aggregate amount, were held not to be reasonable. In *Purnell Secretarial Services Ltd v Lease Management Services Ltd*[121] it was held that an exclusion clause in a financier's standard leasing terms, which excluded liability in a comprehensive fashion for any liability or obligation that the financier might otherwise have had under the contract, including for misrepresentations that had been made by it about the relevant goods, was unreasonable. The financier had argued that it was only a financier and did not have expertise in practical matters concerning the goods. That defence failed, in part on the basis that it had contracted as a supplier of goods and so it must accept the responsibilities that went with such a role.

15.7.8.4.1 In *Stewart Gill Ltd v Horatio Myer & Co Ltd*[122] a clause which precluded a purchaser from setting off a claim for damages against the payment of the price for the supply and installation of equipment was held to be unreasonable, within the context of section 13(1)(b) of the Act. However, clauses precluding the exercise of a right of set-off have also been upheld: *Schenkers Ltd v Overland Shoes Ltd*,[123] *Surzur Overseas Ltd v Ocean Reliance Shipping Co Ltd*,[124] *Skipskredittforeningen v Emperor Navigation*,[125] *WRM Group Ltd v Wood*,[126] and *Governor & Co of the Bank of Scotland v Singh*.[127]

15.7.8.4.2 It is also submitted that an equipment financier may be able to justify the reasonableness of an exclusion or modification of its liability to the customer under the statutorily implied terms relating to the quality and fitness of the goods where it can show that the customer had a sufficient remedy which it could enforce directly against the manufacturer or supplier of the goods. Such a result could be achieved

---

[118] The availability of insurance cover would be a relevant factor under s 11(1) as well: see Lord Griffiths in *Smith v Eric S Bush* [1990] 1 AC 831, at 858. But the actual existence or otherwise of insurance cover is irrelevant: see *Flamar Interocean Ltd v Denmac Ltd* [1990] 1 Lloyd's Rep 434.

[119] [1996] 4 All ER 481.

[120] [1995] FSR 654.

[121] [1994] Tr LR 337.

[122] [1992] QB 600.

[123] [1998] 1 Lloyd's Rep 498.

[124] [1997] CLY 906.

[125] [1998] 1 Lloyd's Rep 66.

[126] [1998] CLC 189.

[127] Unreported. HHJ Kershaw QC, sitting in the High Court in Manchester, 17/6/2005.

with the aid of the Contracts (Rights of Third Parties) Act 1999, by providing expressly in the contract between the supplier or manufacturer and the financier that the customer was a person which it was intended should be entitled to enforce the contract for its own benefit with respect to the terms in that contract which related to the quality and fitness of the goods.

Such an argument would only be likely to succeed, however, if it could be shown **15.7.8.4.2.1** that the customer was provided with an adequate remedy for its own protection. Thus, the subject matter of the terms enforceable against the supplier or manufacturer should be at least as extensive as those that would have applied as between the financier and the customer. Further, if it was anticipated at the time of entry into the equipment finance transaction that the supplier or manufacturer was not financially sound, then it could hardly be reasonable (having regard to the circumstances) that the customer should be deprived of its remedy against the financier and left to rely upon a less certain remedy against the supplier or manufacturer. In addition, if the terms of the exclusion applied to a situation where the customer might otherwise have been entitled to terminate the finance transaction due to a breach of an implied condition as to fitness or quality, then it might be arguable that the term was unreasonable, notwithstanding the fact that the customer might have a claim against the supplier or manufacturer. This is because the customer's third party claim against the manufacturer or supplier would only sound in damages, as it is difficult to conceive that the customer would be able to effect a termination of the contract between the supplier or manufacturer and the financier to which it was not a party. Perhaps the way of dealing with this point would be for the financier to undertake to the customer that, if the customer required it to do so, the financier would exercise its right to terminate the contract between it and the manufacturer or supplier (but without prejudice to the right of the customer to claim damages against the supplier or manufacturer) and, at the same time, that the equipment finance contract would also be treated as terminated.

It should also be noted that the courts have been reluctant, in general, to intervene **15.7.8.4.3** and hold unreasonable a provision which excludes or restricts the liability of a person in situations involving a transaction between experienced commercial parties of equal bargaining power and adequate resources. They have regarded such provisions as representing an agreed allocation of risk in which the courts should not interfere. Chadwick LJ reflected this approach when he said the following in *Watford Electronics Ltd v Sanderson CFL Ltd*:[128]

> Where experienced businessmen representing substantial companies of equal bargaining power negotiated an agreement, they may be taken to have had regard to the matters known to them. They should, in my view, be taken to be the best judges of

---

[128] [2001] EWCA Civ 317; [2001] 1 All ER (Comm) 696, at [63].

the commercial fairness of the agreement which they have made; including the fairness of each of the terms of that agreement.[129]

15.8 The Right of the Financier to Terminate Due to the Customer's Default

15.8.1 It is convenient to consider this aspect on two alternative bases: first, on the basis that the relevant agreement is a conditional sale agreement; secondly, on the basis that the agreement is either a hire purchase agreement or a finance lease. Whichever of those alternatives is relevant, it is important to bear in mind that a title financier which provides equipment finance by one of those methods, that is, other than by way of lending the finance and taking security over the goods as security for the loan, is to be treated as a supplier of goods rather than simply as a lender of money. The remedies available to such a title financier upon the default of its customer, therefore, will be to terminate the agreement and repossess the goods, provided the grounds exist to justify such a termination to take place, and to claim damages for breach of the agreement, whether the agreement has been terminated or not. The entitlement to damages will depend upon which form the agreement has taken, and it will also involve establishing the correct measure of damages to which the financier is entitled.[130]

15.8.1.1 This should be contrasted with the remedies of a lender that has taken security over the goods to secure repayment of the loan. Provided the grounds to demand repayment have arisen,[131] the lender can enforce the security, and if there is a shortfall remaining after enforcement has taken place, it may sue the borrower in debt for a liquidated sum equal to the balance.

15.8.2 The deprivation principle[132]

Before examining the remedies that may be available to the financier, it is necessary to consider whether the expressed right of the financier to terminate an equipment

---

[129] See also Clarke LJ in *National Westminster Bank PLC v Utrecht-America Finance Co* [2001] EWCA Civ 658; [2001] 3 All ER 733, at [57] to [62] and Tucker LJ in *Granville Oil and Chemicals Ltd v Davies Turner & Co Ltd* [2003] EWCA Civ 570; [2003] 2 Lloyd's Rep 356, at [31].

[130] It is respectfully submitted that this cardinal point was overlooked in the approach that was taken in *Protea Leasing Ltd v Royal Air Cambodge Co Ltd* [2002] EWHC 2731 (Comm), in which the relevant agreements for the financing of three aeroplanes, which were described as finance leases, were treated as being the same as financing transactions in which the financier was entitled to stipulate for and receive repayment of the finance it had provided should default occur and the agreements be terminated. Damages were assessed on that basis. In addition, no point was taken that the agreements were, in reality, conditional sale agreements, as there was an obligation on the 'lessee' to purchase the aeroplanes.

[131] See *The Angelic Star* [1988] 1 Lloyd's Rep 122 and *Cryne v Barclays Bank* [1978] BCLC 548.

[132] This principle is also discussed in Chap 11.

finance agreement and to repossess the goods on grounds that are set out in the agreement when the customer is insolvent, might infringe a general legal principle that applies in insolvency (taking that term in a broad sense). In this regard, it is relevant to bear in mind that the written grounds for termination may include an event such as the commencement of insolvency proceedings or some other indication that the customer is insolvent, even where a default in payment may not have occurred.

In particular, the question arises as to whether the apparent right to terminate a transaction on such grounds might infringe the public policy principle against contracts which have the effect of depriving an insolvent person of its assets in consequence of its insolvency (referred to as the 'deprivation principle'). In this context, the asset of the customer would be seen as its contractual right to possession of the goods for their effective life and, in the case of conditional sale and hire purchase, its expectancy of ownership of the goods.

15.8.2.1

In *Money Markets International Stockbrokers Ltd v London Stock Exchange Ltd*[133] Neuberger J, after a review of the case law, provided a useful summary of his conclusions concerning the deprivation principle.[134] He confirmed that the principle is based on the common law rule of English public policy, that the assets of an insolvent should be available to meet the claims of its creditors on a *pari passu* basis, which also underlay the basis of the decision of the House of Lords in the *British Eagle* case.[135] For these purposes, his Lordship did not draw any distinction between the various types of insolvency proceedings that might arise under English law. The principle has been applied where the effect of a contract has been that, upon its insolvency, the insolvent has been deprived of an asset, either by its passing back to the person from whom its ownership had been acquired[136] or by its being confiscated. His Lordship acknowledged, however, that there are circumstances in which the principle does not apply (for instance, in relation to forfeiture provisions in leases of land), and that there are no very coherent criteria which determine when the principle does apply and when it does not apply.

15.8.2.2

Neuberger J then set out ten propositions that could be derived from the case law on the subject.[137] They were as follows:

15.8.2.2.1

(1) A person cannot validly arrange his affairs so that what is already his own property becomes subject to being taken away in the event of his insolvency;

---

[133] [2002] 1 WLR 1150.

[134] At [116]–[118].

[135] *British Eagle International Airlines Ltd v Cie Nationale Air France* [1975] 1 WLR 758. It reflects the legislative provisions which are now to be found in ss 107 and 328(3) of the Insolvency Act 1986 and Rule 4.181 of the Insolvency Rules 1986.

[136] For example, in *Fraser v Oystertec plc* [2003] EWHC 2787 (Ch), [2004] BCC 233 the transferee of a patent was required by the contract to re-transfer it to the transferor upon the transferee's insolvency.

[137] At [118].

(2) Subject to the first proposition, the transfer of an asset for an interest coming to an end on the transferee's insolvency (or on some other event) is apparently effective even if the transferee is insolvent;

(3) Subject to the following propositions, the transfer of an asset on the condition that the asset will revest in the transferor in the event of the transferee's insolvency is generally invalid;

(4) A proviso in a lease for determination, ie. for forfeiture or re-entry, even in the event of the lessee becoming insolvent, is enforceable where the lessee is insolvent;

(5) In deciding whether a deprivation provision exercisable other than on insolvency offends against the principle, one is primarily concerned with the effect of the provision and not with the intention of the parties, but it may be that, if the deprivation provision is exercisable for reasons which are not concerned with the owner's insolvency, default or breach, then its operation will not be within the principle;

(6) However, if the intention of the parties when agreeing the deprivation provision was to evade the insolvency rules, then that may invalidate a provision which would otherwise have been valid, and if the intention of the parties was not to evade the insolvency laws, the court will be more ready to uphold the deprivation provision if it provides for compensation for the deprivation.

(7) The court will scrutinise with particular care a deprivation provision which would have the effect of preferring the person to whom the asset reverts or passes, as against other unsecured creditors of the insolvent person whose estate is deprived of the asset pursuant to the provision;

(8) Where the deprivation provision relates to an asset which has no value, or which is incapable of transfer, or which depends on the character or status of the owner, then it will normally be enforceable on insolvency;

(9) A deprivation provision which might otherwise be invalid in light of the principle may be held to be valid if the asset concerned is closely connected with or, more probably, subsidiary to a right or other benefit in respect of which a deprivation provision is valid;

(10) If the deprivation provision does not offend against the principle, then (subject to there being no other objection to it) it will be enforceable against a trustee in bankruptcy or on a liquidation just as much as it would have been enforceable in the absence of an insolvency.

15.8.2.2.2 From those propositions, it is possible to draw some themes and further arguments which would be relevant in assessing if a termination provision in an equipment finance transaction that comes into play on the customer's insolvency might fall foul of the deprivation principle.

15.8.2.2.2.1 First, the principle does not apply to leases of land, even though the effect of such a lease is to confer on the tenant an interest in the land. An analogous view might be taken of an equipment finance transaction, especially as the law generally assumes that an interest in land is of greater importance than possessory interests in goods.

15.8.2.2.2.2 Secondly, and as will be seen below, a customer under an equipment finance transaction is given a right, albeit a limited right, to challenge the termination of its right to possession, by seeking relief against forfeiture. There is no overriding reason why the customer (through its liquidator) should be given any further right to challenge the effectiveness of a termination provision by being able to resort to the deprivation principle.

Thirdly, a termination provision does not contravene the doctrine against penalties,[138] so it will not be struck down as an unenforceable penalty, and thus it is not to be regarded as being inequitable or contumacious in that sense.

15.8.2.2.2.3

Fourthly, a special rule is provided in the case of administration and some company voluntary arrangements, by which an equipment financier is denied the right to repossess its goods.[139] As Parliament has not seen fit to extend that protection to a company in liquidation (or an individual in bankruptcy), there is no good reason to do so by the application of a principle of public policy.

15.8.2.2.2.4

Fifthly, there is a large number of cases where buyers of goods and hirers or lessees under hire purchase or lease agreements have been deprived of possession in reliance on a termination provision, in which an argument based on the deprivation principle has played no part in the court's reasoning. Indeed, as mentioned below, an unpaid seller is given a statutory right of termination under sections 48(3) and 48(4) of the Sale of Goods Act 1979.

15.8.2.2.2.5

Sixthly, however, the intention of the parties is not conclusive in determining if the deprivation principle should apply, but if their intention in agreeing to the presence of the termination provision in their agreement was to evade the insolvency laws that will be relevant, particularly if the consequence of the operation of the provision was to put the person who benefits from it in a better position than other unsecured creditors. It is difficult to escape from the conclusion that a provision which allows a financier to terminate an equipment finance transaction due to the customer's insolvency does put the financier in a better position than it would otherwise be in due to the customer's insolvency.

15.8.2.2.2.6

15.8.3 The financier's remedies under a conditional sale agreement

Under section 48(4) of the Sale of Goods Act 1979, where the seller of goods has an express right under the contract, should the buyer default, to repossess the goods and re-sell them, and it exercises that right, then the original contract is 'rescinded', that is, terminated *ab initio*.[140] This is without prejudice to the seller's

---

[138] *Transag Haulage Ltd v Leyland Daf Finance PLC* [1994] 2 BCLC 88.

[139] See, respectively, paras 43(3) and 111(1) of Sched B1 to the Insolvency Act 1986, and paras 12(g) and 1 of Sched 1A to that Act.

[140] *Ward (RV) Ltd v Bignall* [1967] 1 QB 534. Under s 48(3) of the Act, the seller can achieve the same consequences where the buyer is in default in payment but the seller does not have the express right to repossess and re-sell, if it gives the buyer reasonable notice to pay which is not met.

right to claim damages as well. In this situation, the seller may rely upon its contractual right of termination for breach without having to establish if such a breach amounts to a repudiatory breach of contract by the buyer.[141] Of course, the parties are free in their contract to vary the statutory right of the seller, by providing for a more limited right to terminate, or by providing for the giving of notice and the elapse of grace periods before the right to terminate may be exercised. They may also agree to limit the damages that the seller can recover following termination, so that they are less than those that would be available at general law.[142]

15.8.3.1 In *Ward (RV) Ltd v Bignall*[143] the Court of Appeal held that the claim for damages of an unpaid seller which had exercised a right of termination upon the buyer's default in making payment, was a claim for damages under sections 48(3) or (4) of the Sale of Goods Act 1979, rather than simply for the price.[144] Such damages should be measured as the difference between the contract price of the goods, after giving allowance for the amount already paid under the contract, and the value of the goods at the time of termination (or presumably, if later, as at the date of repossession. In *Ward v Bignall*, the purchaser never took possession). This assumes that there is a market for the goods to be re-sold and that the seller will not suffer by selling such goods instead of other goods that it had in stock or readily available to fulfil the new customer's order.[145] It is not clear if an allowance should also be given in the case of an instalment sale contract, when calculating the damages payable by the customer, for the benefit achieved by the notional acceleration of

---

[141] In *More OG Romsdal Fylkesbatar AS v Demise Charters of the Ship 'Jutunheim'* [2004] EWHC 671 (QB), [2005] 1 Lloyd's Rep181, it was suggested in argument that it would be necessary to show that the parties had agreed, expressly or impliedly, that an obligation to make timely payment was of the essence of the contract, before a seller could terminate a contract of sale for non-payment of an instalment of the price. This was because of s 10(1) of the Sale of Goods Act 1979. Cooke J said, however, that an express right of termination for non-payment in the contract would amount to a sufficient indication that prompt payment was of the essence of the contract so as to satisfy that requirement. Regrettably, his Lordship did not refer to ss 48(3) and 48(4) of the Act, which allow the seller to terminate the contract and repossess the goods for non-payment where either the seller has expressly reserved that right or, if not, by service of a reasonable notice requiring payment.

[142] It has been held, however, that clear words are needed to rebut the presumption that a contracting party does not intend to abandon any rights that it may have at general law arising from a breach of contract: see Lord Diplock in *Gilbert-Ash (Northern) Ltd v Modern Engineering (Bristol) Ltd* [1974] AC 689, at 717, quoted with approval by Lord Goff in *Stocznia Gdanska SA v Latvian Shipping Co* [1998] 1 WLR 574, at 585.

[143] [1967] 1 QB 534.

[144] Under s 49 of the Act, the unpaid seller may sue for the price but this is on the basis that it has affirmed, rather than terminated, the contract.

[145] See the discussion below concerning *In re Vic Mill Ltd* [1913] 1 Ch 465; *Interoffice Telephones Ltd v Robert Freeman Co Ltd* [1958] 1 QB 190; and *Robophone Facilities v Blank* [1966 1 WLR 1428. If the goods are unique then it may be the case that there would not be a readily available market for them: *Lazenby Garages Ltd v Wright* [1976] 1 WLR 459 and Treitel, *The Law of Contract* (11th edn) at p 955.

the payment of the price, but that would appear to follow from the nature of the claim as one for damages for the loss the seller has suffered.[146]

The allowance to be given for the amount already paid prior to termination follows the facts in *Ward v Bignall*, where a partial down-payment had been made. It is also in accordance with the case law which has held that instalments of the purchase price paid before termination should be refunded, subject to the seller's right of set-off for its claim in damages, because the effect of the termination of the contract is to release the seller from its primary obligation to sell the goods and pass title, so that there is a total failure of consideration.[147] Such an allowance does not have to be given if the contract is not just for the sale of goods but also involves the supply of services, which had been supplied (in whole or in part) prior to the date of termination.[148]

15.8.3.1.1

There is a quandary as to the position where the seller makes a profit on re-sale. This might arise because the value of the goods has increased (an unlikely scenario, except in times of rampant inflation or in the case of goods that are unique and for which there are more buyers than sellers), or because the price achieved on re-sale, when added to what the seller had already received from the buyer, yields an overall profit. Robert Goff LJ suggested in *Clough Mill Ltd v Martin*[149] that in such circumstances, in a case where the contract had not been terminated, the seller might be bound by an implied term of the contract to account to the buyer for any such profit. Where the contract had terminated, his Lordship conceded that the seller would have to pay back to the buyer what had already been paid because there had been a total failure of consideration. With respect, it is submitted that the first part of that analysis is incorrect. As has already been mentioned, if the seller exercises its right to repossess and re-sell the goods, that has the effect that the contract is terminated *ab initio* (in contrast to the position where another type of contract is terminated in consequence of a repudiatory breach, as the termination is only prospective and not retrospective, so that certain provisions of the contract might survive the termination[150]). Any implied term to account would not survive the *ab initio* termination of the contract. Thus, the position

15.8.3.2

---

[146] *Ward v Bignall* concerned a contract where the price was payable in full on the date of contracting.

[147] See Dixon J in *McDonald v Dennys Lascelles Ltd* (1933) 48 CLR 457, at 476–478; *Dies v British and International Mining and Finance Corporation Ltd* [1939] 1 KB 724; and *Rover International Ltd v Cannon Film Ltd* [1989] 1 WLR 912, per Kerr LJ, at 928–932, and per Dillon LJ, at 935–937.

[148] See *Hyundai Heavy Industries Co Ltd v Papadopoulos* [1980] 1 WLR 1129 and *Stocnia Gdanska SA v Latvian Shipping Co* [1998] 1 WLR 604.

[149] [1985] 1 WLR 111, at 117.

[150] See Lord Diplock in *Moschi v Lep Air Services Ltd* [1973] AC 331, at 350; Sir Owen Dixon in the High Court of Australia in *McDonald v Dennys Lascelles Ltd* (1933) 48 CLR 457, at 476–477; Lord Brandon in *Bank of Boston Connecticut v European Grain & Shipping Ltd* [1989] AC 1056, at 1098–1099.

should be that in all cases of a pure sale of goods transaction, the amount that had already been paid to the seller would have to be refunded, but the seller could set off against the refund any damages (computed in the manner referred to above) that it had suffered because of the buyer's breach of contract. The seller would be entitled to pursue a claim for damages for any remaining loss after setting off the refund. If the seller had made an overall profit then it should be entitled to keep whatever was left after the refund had been made.

15.8.3.3 In passing, it should be noted that the parties may be entitled in their contract to adopt the Uniform Law on the International Sale of Goods 1964. This can be done as a matter of English law pursuant to the Uniform Law on International Sales Act 1967 if the parties are in different contracting States at the time of contracting and had they intended to treat the contract as one for the sale of goods. In fact, only the UK and six other States qualify, so the Uniform Law is of little practical utility. If the Uniform Law applies then the measure of damages available to the seller upon termination for breach would fall to be assessed under Articles 84 to 89 of the Uniform Law.

15.8.4 The financier's remedies under a hire purchase or finance lease agreement

There has been quite an amount of case law on the rights of a financier to terminate a hire purchase or finance lease agreement and the consequences of such a termination, including the effect of provisions in such agreements that stipulate the amount recoverable upon termination for breach and whether they should be struck down as being a penalty.[151] In the absence of a provision which allows the financier to terminate the agreement for breach by the customer, the right of termination will only arise if the breach amounts (or is correctly anticipated to amount) to a repudiation by the customer of the agreement. Thus, a failure by the customer to pay one or even a few instalments might not be treated as a repudiatory breach, although the financier can recover the unpaid instalments as a debt.[152] An express right to terminate for breach by the customer will permit the financier to terminate the agreement and repossess the goods, and will not be considered to be an unenforceable penalty.[153] It is not enough, of itself, to permit the financier to treat the breach as a repudiatory breach of contract.[154]

---

[151] See, for instance, the discussion in *Lombard North Central PLC v Butterworth* [1987] QB 527. That case concerned a finance lease but the Court of Appeal made it clear that the same approach applied to finance leases and to hire purchase agreements. Similarly, in *Robophone Facilities Ltd v Blank* [1966] 1 WLR 1428 the Court of Appeal was concerned with a lease but it applied the earlier case law relating to hire purchase agreements.

[152] *Financings Ltd v Baldock* [1963] QB 104.

[153] *Transag Haulage Ltd v Leyland Daf Finance PLC* [1994] 2 BCLC 88.

[154] See, for instance, *Financings Ltd v Baldock* [1963] QB 104 and *Capital Finance Co Ltd v Donati* (1977) 121 SJ 270.

It is possible for the parties to stipulate in the contract that the obligation to make payment of each instalment should be treated as a condition of the contract, such as by virtue of a 'time of the essence' provision.[155] Breach of such a condition would amount to a repudiatory breach. Otherwise, it will be a matter to be decided upon the facts of the particular case if the actual or anticipated breach by the hirer (or, more probably, a continued series of breaches) should be treated as a repudiatory breach of the contract.[156]

15.8.4.1

By and large, a provision in such an agreement which stipulates for the amount payable on a termination is likely to be viewed by the courts as amounting to a penalty and will be unenforceable.[157] This has sometimes been because the relevant provision made no attempt to differentiate between the consequences of a termination due to a repudiatory breach of the agreement, such as a breach of a condition of the agreement, and termination for some lesser reason.[158] Where the agreement has been terminated following a contractual right to terminate in circumstances where the default of the hirer did not amount to a repudiatory breach, it has been held that the financier should only be entitled to receive the outstanding and unpaid amount that had fallen due for payment prior to the time of termination.[159] In other cases the provision has been struck down because, although the right to terminate had arisen following upon a repudiatory breach and thereby the financier had become entitled to general damages for loss of bargain, the amount stipulated to be payable in the agreement failed to reflect the true economic position at the time of breach. In other words, the stipulated amount did not represent a reasonable pre-estimate by the parties, as at the original time of contracting, of the likely loss that the financier would suffer in consequence of the breach and termination of the contract at the time it occurred.[160]

15.8.4.2

It appears, however, that the agreement can validly stipulate for the amount that should be payable if the lessee or hirer exercises a voluntary right to terminate.[161] This is because the amount that is payable is seen as legitimate consideration

15.8.4.2.1

---

[155] See *Lombard North Central PLC v Butterworth* [1987] QB 527.

[156] As, for instance, was held to be the case in *Yeoman Credit Ltd v Waragowski* [1961] 1 WLR 1121 and *Overstone Ltd v Shipway* [1962] 1 WLR 117.

[157] Although Diplock LJ in *Robophone Facilities Ltd v Blank* [1966] 1 WLR 1428, at 1446–1448 cautioned against finding the imposition of a penalty. His view did not gain support from Lord Denning MR nor Harman LJ, who also sat in that case.

[158] See, for instance, *Financings Ltd v Baldock* [1963] QB 104 and *Capital Finance Co Ltd v Donati* (1977) 121 SJ 270.

[159] See, again, *Financings Ltd v Baldock* and *Capital Finance Co Ltd v Donati* where the courts held that the failure to pay one or two instalments in a long-term instalment payment agreement did not amount to a repudiatory breach, even though there was a contractual right to terminate and repossess the goods.

[160] As, for instance, in *Bridge v Campbell Discount Co Ltd* [1962] AC 600; *Anglo Auto Finance Co Ltd v James* [1963] 1 WLR 1042; and *Lombard North Central v Butterworth* [1987] QB 527.

[161] See *Bridge v Campbell Discount Co Ltd* [1962] AC 600.

for the exercise of a contractual right that is conferred upon the customer, rather than as an attempt at prescribing in the contract for assumed damages that would be payable for the loss suffered in consequence of a breach of contract.[162]

15.8.4.3 A guide to the measure of damages that will be awarded by the court to the financier upon termination following a repudiatory breach by the hirer or lessee was provided by the Court of Appeal in *Overstone Ltd v Shipway*,[163] which was a case concerning a hire purchase agreement. The court held that the finance company could recover the amount of unpaid instalments up to the time of termination and, as general damages, the minimum residual amount that the hirer would have been obliged to pay had the agreement continued, after giving allowance for the value of the goods at the time of termination and a rebate for the notional accelerated early payment of such residual amount. If the financier would have been responsible under the contract for maintenance and repair costs then there should be an allowance for the fact that the financier will be relieved of that burden over the unexpired period.[164] Furthermore, if the contract contemplated that the equipment would have a residual value at the end of the hiring, an allowance should be given for that value, expressed as a depreciation factor.[165]

15.8.4.4 There is a further factor to be taken into account in the assessment of damages. It concerns the circumstances in which it is correct to take into account the future rentals that would have been payable by the hirer but for the termination of the agreement. It is legitimate to take this into account if the financier has really lost that income stream, which will be the case if it could not find another customer to enter into a replacement contract to replicate the income stream. If, however, it was possible to find such a customer to whom it could have supplied the equipment on similar terms then, subject to what follows, the financier would have a duty to mitigate its loss by entering into an agreement with the replacement customer. The financier would not be obliged to mitigate in such a situation if it can show that it would have done business with the replacement customer in any event, and so it could have maintained contracts at the same time with the original customer and the new customer. This would follow if it has sufficient resources

---

[162] As *Bridge v Campbell Discount Co Ltd* demonstrates, the court may strain to find that the relevant party did not intend to exercise its right to terminate and thus relieve it from paying the sum stipulated, in a situation where it would have to pay less as damages for a wrongful repudiation of the contract.

[163] [1962] 1 WLR 117. See also the reference to the 'balance sheet' approach in calculating the benefits and losses arising on termination of a contract, as outlined by Mance LJ in *Cine Bes Filmcilik Ve Yapimcilik v United International Pictures* [2003] EWCA Civ 1669; [2004] 1 CLC 401, at [9]–[21].

[164] See Diplock LJ in *Robophone Facilities Ltd v Blank* [1966] 1 WLR 1428, at 1444.

[165] See again Diplock LJ in ibid.

available to it, in terms of funding and equipment, to meet both contracts at the same time.[166]

15.9 The Customer's Protection: To Seek Relief Against Forfeiture

Because the customer is not a mortgagor or chargor with respect to the goods under an equipment financing transaction, it does not have an equity of redemption which can be asserted to protect it once the financier has begun to exercise its rights following a default by the customer. Instead, it has available the lesser right to seek equitable relief against forfeiture by applying to the court for the granting of such relief. **15.9.1**

15.9.2 The jurisdiction to grant relief

The basis on which the court may grant such relief at the application of the customer was addressed by the Court of Appeal in *On Demand Information PLC v Michael Gerson (Finance) PLC*,[167] following the earlier decision of the House of Lords in *Shiloh Spinners Ltd v Harding*[168] (which involved the more traditional area of application of the jurisdiction to leases of land). In principle, the court will have jurisdiction in equity to grant relief in cases where the applicant for relief seeks to protect a proprietary or possessory right in an asset,[169] where the right of forfeiture is essentially to secure the payment of money or the performance of another obligation which can be attained when the matter comes before the court.[170] This will include a customer under a conditional sale agreement,[171] a hire purchase agreement,[172]

---

[166] See *Interoffice Telephones Ltd v Robert Freeman Co Ltd* [1958] 1 QB 190 and *Robophone Facilities Ltd v Blank* [1966 1 WLR 1428. The same principle applies in relation to contracts for the sale of goods: *In re Vic Mill Ltd* [1913] 1 Ch 465, which was discussed in the *Interoffice Telephones* case.

[167] [2001] 1 WLR 155. The decision was reversed on the facts, as to the grounds for exercise of the discretion to grant relief, by the House of Lords: [2002] UKHL 13, [2003] 1 AC 368.

[168] [1973] AC 691.

[169] Dillon LJ in *BICC PLC v Burndy* [1985] Ch 232, at 251–252, recognised that such relief might be available where it was sought to protect a proprietary or possessory right.

[170] The Court of Appeal in the *On Demand Information* case came to the view that relief could not be granted because the goods had been sold, pursuant to a consent order, with the proceeds of sale being held pending the decision of the court. Hence, possession of the goods could not be restored to the lessee. The House of Lords reversed that decision by holding, in effect, that the proceeds could be taken to represent the goods.

[171] See Romer LJ in *Stocklosser v Johnson* [1954] 1 QB 476, at 502. It is submitted that, on its facts, *More OG Romsdal Fylkesbatar AS v Demise Charters of the Ship 'Jutunheim'* [2004] EWHC 671 (QB), [2005] 1 Lloyd's Rep 181 (in which the jurisdiction to grant relief was acknowledged, although relief was refused in the exercise of the court's discretion) was really a case of conditional sale.

[172] *Transag Haulage Ltd v Leyland Daf Finance PLC* [1994] 2 BCLC 88.

and a finance lease agreement.[173] It is also clear that the court will not be able to grant relief in relation to a time charter or a 'wet lease' where the owner remains in possession of the vessel or the goods and so is really providing services rather than granting possession of the goods to the customer.[174]

15.9.3 Exercise of the court's discretion

Whilst the court may have jurisdiction to grant relief, it is still a matter for the court to determine, in its discretion, if it is appropriate for the relief to be granted on the facts of the case. Lord Wilberforce in the *Shiloh Spinners* case[175] identified the following matters that would be relevant in determining if the discretion should be exercised in favour of granting relief: (a) the conduct of the applicant for relief; (b) whether its default was wilful and the gravity of the breach; and (c) the disparity in the value of the relevant asset against the damage caused by the breach. Knox J in *Transag Haulage Ltd v Leyland Daf Finance PLC*,[176] which was a case concerning a hire purchase agreement, put the matter slightly differently when he identified the following three tests for deciding if relief should be granted:

(1) whether, if relief is granted, the financier will be deprived of the economic benefits that it had bargained for under the agreement;
(2) whether, if relief is not granted, the financier would receive an economic windfall by being allowed to continue with its repossession; and
(3) whether the hirer's conduct, including during the continuance of the agreement, disentitled it to relief.

15.9.3.1 In the *Transag* case, Knox J granted relief against forfeiture. This was because the financier's right to repossess did not arise due to a breach of the agreement by the hirer but because of an event of default provision in the agreement which permitted the financier to repossess the goods if the hirer went into administrative receivership, which event had occurred. The receiver had tendered all that remained owing under the agreement. The goods were worth substantially more than the amount that had been tendered, so the financier would enjoy a windfall if it was allowed to continue with the repossession. By contrast, in the *Jutunheim* case,[177] Cooke J declined to exercise his discretion in favour of the charterer and so he refused to grant the relief that had been sought. The charterer's breaches had been deliberate. Although the charter hire instalments had eventually been paid,

---

[173] *On Demand Information PLC v Michael Gerson (Finance) PLC* [2001] 1 WLR 155 (Court of Appeal) and [2002] UKHL 13, [2003] 1 AC 368 (House of Lords).

[174] See the decision of the House of Lords in *The Scraptrade* [1988] 2 Lloyd's Rep 253 and *Sport International Bussum BV v Inter-Footwear Ltd* [1984] 1 WLR 776.

[175] [1973] AC 691, at 723–724.

[176] [1994] 2 BCLC 88.

[177] *More OG Romsdal Fylkesbatar AS v Demise Charters of the Ship 'Jutunheim'* [2004] EWHC 671 (QB), [2005] 1 Lloyd's Rep 181.

the charterer had been persistently late in paying all of the instalments that had fallen due before the owner had taken action to terminate the agreement and the charterer had not paid in full. The attitude of the charterer which underlay the breaches gave rise to a continuing cause for concern. It was likely that there would be further breaches in the future if relief was granted.

15.10 Administration and Making Proposals for a Voluntary Arrangement of the Customer

The discussion that follows will concentrate upon the effect of an administration, **15.10.1** or the making of a proposal for a voluntary arrangement, upon the rights of a financier under an equipment finance transaction, as well as the effect of an administration or the making of such a proposal on the equipment that is the subject of such transaction. It is not proposed to comment more generally on the process of an administration or a voluntary arrangement and the means by which they might come about. For the purposes of the following discussion, it is assumed that the customer is a company that is subject to English insolvency law.

By way of the history of the relevant legislation, Schedule B1 to the Insolvency Act **15.10.1.1** 1986 contains the provisions that relate to an administration of a company. Schedule B1 was inserted into the 1986 Act by virtue of the Enterprise Act 2002. It came into effect on 15 September 2003 with respect to companies that entered administration after that date.[178] It replaced the provisions relating to administration that had previously been contained in Part II of the Insolvency Act 1986. Schedule A1 to the Insolvency Act 1986 contains the provisions that concern the effect of proposals for the voluntary arrangement of a company. It was inserted into the Act by the Insolvency Act 2000. It came into effect on 1 January 2003.[179]

15.10.2 Administration

There are two features of administration that are of relevance to the present discussion. The first concerns the right of an equipment financier to repossess its equipment when its customer is in administration. The second concerns the right of the administrator to dispose of such goods.

15.10.2.1 Repossession

As with the regime that had previously existed under the Insolvency Act 1986, paragraph 43 of Schedule B1 to the Act provides for there to be a moratorium

---

[178] The Enterprise Act 2002 (Commencement No 4 and Transitional Provisions and Savings) Order 2003 (SI 2003/2093).

[179] The Insolvency Act 1986 (Amendment) (No 3) Regs 2002 (SI 2002/1990).

whilst a company is in administration. The moratorium prevents, inter alia, the enforcement of security over its assets,[180] the repossession of goods in its possession which are subject to a 'hire purchase agreement', and the entry into possession of its premises by its landlords, unless permission is given to take such action as described below. There is also a moratorium (in the absence of such permission) upon any person instituting or continuing other legal process (including legal proceedings, execution, distress, and diligence). The moratorium upon enforcement action and the like are each advanced to cover situations where an appointment is pending, either by the court pursuant to paragraph 10 of Schedule B1 or out of court pursuant to paragraphs 14 or 22 of Schedule B1.[181] A 'hire purchase agreement' is defined to include a conditional sale, chattel leasing, or retention of title agreement.[182] Goods will be treated as being in the company's possession under a hire purchase agreement where it has bailed them to a sub-lessee or a sub-hirer.[183]

15.10.2.1.1 In each case, the creditor affected may seek permission from the administrator or the court to take the relevant action. In *Re Atlantic Computer Systems plc*,[184] the Court of Appeal gave guidance as to the considerations that should apply if such permission was sought by a secured creditor or the owner of goods under the original provisions that contained the moratorium in the 1986 Act. The court said that in considering the application for permission, the rights of the secured creditor or the owner should be balanced against the purposes of the administration. Such persons should not be made to suffer simply for the benefit of the company and its unsecured creditors, especially in a case where the realistic purpose of the administration was to achieve a more advantageous realisation of the company's assets than would be obtained in a winding up. In the *Atlantic Computer Systems* case, the court granted permission to secured creditors to enforce security and to equipment financiers to repossess their goods, because the administration was really a means of achieving a winding up of the company's affairs, rather than enabling it to survive in business. A different view was taken in *Re David Meek Plant Ltd*[185] in which repossession was refused in relation to goods that were essential to the continued business of the company. Any loss that the relevant financiers would suffer was limited to the diminution in the value of the goods during the period of the administration. The period of the administration was likely to be relatively

---

[180] As to the width of the concept of enforcement of security, see *Bristol Airport plc v Powdrill* [1990] Ch 744. See also *London Flight Centre (Stansted) Ltd v Osprey Aviation Ltd* [2002] BPIR 1115.
[181] Para 44 of Sched B1 to the Act.
[182] Defined in para 111(1) of Sched B1 to the Act.
[183] *Re Atlantic Computer Systems plc* [1992] Ch 505.
[184] [1992] Ch 505.
[185] [1993] BCC 175.

short and those financiers who wished to repossess their goods would be able to do so when the administration ended.

In the view of the Government when the new provisions that are now contained in Schedule B1 to the Act were being debated in Parliament, the balancing test under the principles established in *Atlantic Computer Systems* would continue to apply under the new legislation.[186] It is submitted, however, that the court's approach in that case may not be followed with respect to a request for permission under the new legislation, even in a situation where the relevant objective within the purpose of the administration is under Schedule B1 paragraph 3(1)(c), that is, for realising the company's property to make a distribution to one or more secured or preferential creditors. This is because there is an emphasis placed by paragraph 3 upon the interests of the creditors as a whole ahead of those of a secured creditor. Paragraph 3(2) also provides that, even in a situation where the objective of the administration is to make distributions to the secured creditors, the interests of the creditors of the company as a whole are not to be unnecessarily harmed. Curiously, paragraph 3 does not mention the position of the owner of goods under a hire purchase agreement (as defined) but such a person will probably be taken as falling within the same downtrodden grouping as the secured creditors in this regard, given that their interests are assimilated in other respects.

15.10.2.2 Disposal of the equipment by the administrator

There are similar provisions in Schedule B1 to the original provision in the 1986 Act concerning the ability of an administrator to dispose of assets subject to security or of goods which are subject to a hire purchase agreement (as defined). With respect to assets of the company subject to a floating charge,[187] the administrator may dispose of them or take other action concerning them free of the charge, and the chargee will have the same priority in property acquired directly or indirectly in consequence of the disposal.[188] There is no explicit requirement that the administrator's action should be taken in aid of the purpose of the administration. As to assets of the company subject to fixed security or goods in its possession which are subject to a hire purchase agreement, the administrator may apply to the court for permission to dispose of such assets or goods, but the court may only give its permission if it thinks that the disposal would be likely to promote the purpose of the administration.[189] The net proceeds of the disposal and any difference between that amount and the net amount that would have been achieved on a sale at market value[190]

---

[186] HL Official Report (Enterprise Bill) 29/7/2002 Cols 791–792.

[187] A 'floating charge' is defined by para 111(1) of Sched B1 to the Act to be a floating charge as at its creation.

[188] Para 70 of Sched B1 to the Act.

[189] Paras 71 and 72 of Sched B1 to the Act.

[190] 'Market value' is defined in para 111(1) of Sched B1 to the Act.

must be applied in discharging the amount outstanding under the security or owing under the agreement.

15.10.2.2.1 Notwithstanding the above, it is interesting to note that paragraph 73 of Schedule B1 states that the administrator's proposals for achieving the purpose of the administration may not include any action which, inter alia, affects the right of a secured creditor to enforce its security (except with the creditor's consent). As it relates to the rights of secured creditors, the purport of that provision might be considered as being inconsistent with the above-mentioned provisions as to selling assets subject to floating charges or fixed security. Any such sale would, of its nature, prevent the security holder from enforcing his security. The sale therefore could not be foreshadowed within the administrator's proposals. The secured creditor might well feel entitled to ask why the sale was to take place if it had not been anticipated, even if only generally, in the administrator's proposals in the first place. It should be noted that the provision makes no reference to the rights of owners of goods subject to a hire purchase agreement (as defined) so, presumably, the administrator may include plans as to their goods within his proposals.

15.10.3 Making a proposal for a company voluntary arrangement

If a company which is the subject of a proposal for a voluntary arrangement is an 'eligible company' then a moratorium, which is similar to that relating to a company in administration, may be imposed pursuant to the provisions of Schedule A1 to the Insolvency Act 1986. An eligible company is one which meets the requirements contained in Part 1 of the Schedule. In summary, the company must meet two of the qualifying conditions to be a 'small company' under the Companies Acts,[191] and not fall within one of the exclusions contained in Part 1. The moratorium will be achieved if the directors of the company follow the procedures laid down in Part II of the Schedule, by filing the documents relevant to the proposal with the court. The duration of the moratorium is for an initial period of up to 28 days,[192] but it may be extended for up to a further two months.[193]

15.10.3.1 During the period of the moratorium, no steps may be taken, inter alia, to enforce security over the company's assets or to repossess goods subject to a 'hire purchase agreement'.[194] There are also provisions dealing with disposal of assets that are subject to security or a hire purchase agreement.[195] It is also worth noting that the Schedule contains special provisions relating to floating charges.[196]

---

[191] S 382 of the Companies Act 2006 (formerly s 247 of the Companies Act 1985).
[192] Para 8 of Sched A1 to the Act.
[193] Para 32 of Sched A1 to the Act.
[194] Para 12(1) of Sched A1 to the Act. A 'hire purchase agreement' is defined in para 1 of the Schedule and has the same meaning as under Sched B1 in relation to administration.
[195] Para 20 of Sched A1 to the Act.
[196] Paras 13 and 43 of Sched A1 to the Act.

15.11 The Financier's Rights Against Third Parties

15.11.1 Priority rights

In some instances, it may be possible for an equipment financier to protect its priority rights by registering its interest in an appropriate register. This is the case with ships above a certain size and aircraft, where the financier can be registered as the owner in the appropriate registry. When it comes into force, registration of the financier's interest against the relevant assets may also give protection pursuant to the regime to be established under the Cape Town Convention, as noted earlier in this chapter.

In other cases, the financier will need to rely on the protection that is afforded to it by the general law. Assuming that property was duly vested in it in the first place, the financier's basic position is that its ownership of the goods cannot be lost, because of the principle of *nemo dat quod non habet*, as enshrined in section 21 of the Sale of Goods Act 1979. The principle is to the effect that an apparent transferor without title (such as the customer under an equipment finance transaction) cannot confer a better title on a third party. As has already been seen, the principle is subject to the exceptions that are contained in sections 24 and 25 of the Sale of Goods Act 1979, and the corresponding provisions in sections 8 and 9 of the Factors Act 1889. In addition, the owner might lose its title under a conditional sale agreement if it has authorised the buyer, either expressly or impliedly, to re-sell the goods.[197] There is no reason to think that the same conclusion would not be drawn where a financier has conferred authority upon a customer to dispose of the goods that are the subject of a hire purchase or lease agreement, although it is unlikely to arise in practice. It is also provided in section 23 of the Sale of Goods Act 1979 that a seller of goods which has a voidable title can confer a good title on a buyer provided that the seller's title has not been avoided before the time of the sale.[198] There is a further exception in favour of a private purchaser who buys a motor vehicle in good faith without notice of a defect in the seller's title, which is to be found in section 27 of the Hire Purchase Act 1964.[199]

15.11.1.1

---

[197] See *Four Point Garage Ltd v Carter* [1985] 3 All ER 12 and *Fairfax Gerrard Holdings Ltd v Capital Bank PLC* [2007] EWCA Civ 1226.

[198] A voidable title may arise, for instance, because of a mistake in a sale agreement which entitled the seller to avoid the buyer's title. This should be distinguished from the position where the transaction was void from the outset so that the buyer obtained no title at all: see *Shogun Finance Ltd v Hudson* [2003] UKHL 62, [2004] 1 AC 919.

[199] It was this section which provided the background to *Forthright Finance Ltd v Carlyle Finance Ltd* [1997] 4 All ER 90; *Shogun Finance Ltd v Hudson* [2003] UKHL 62, [2004] 1 AC 919; and *GE Capital Bank Ltd v Rushton* [2005] EWCA Civ 1556, [2006] 1 WLR 899. The latter case contains an interesting analysis of the concept of when a person 'carries on a business' for the purposes of s 29(2) of the Act.

15.11.2 The rights of a repairer

The customer may have given the goods to a third party to repair them. In such a case, the repairer (the lienee) may wish to assert a possessory lien over the goods for the cost of the repairs, if it has not been paid. The assertion of such a lien would be inconsistent with the ownership of the goods by the equipment financier, particularly where the financier wishes to repossess the goods. In consequence of the decision of the Court of Appeal in *Tappenden v Artus*,[200] the lienee's interest should prevail over that of the financier as the owner of the goods, provided that the lienee meets the following conditions. First, that at the time it received the goods for repair from the customer, the customer was lawfully in possession of the goods with the consent of the financier. Secondly, that the delivery of the goods by the customer to the repairer was to carry out repairs that were reasonably incidental to the use of the goods by the customer for a purpose sanctioned by the owner. Thirdly, that the repairer was not on actual notice that the customer had no authority to allow the lien to be created.

15.11.2.1 In line with the third of those conditions, it is common for an equipment financier to insist that the goods should carry a notice, to the effect that the goods are owned by the financier, that the customer has possession of them pursuant to the relevant agreement, and that the customer has no authority to permit any liens to be created over the goods. It is, of course, another matter to prove that the notice was adequately affixed in a legible form when the goods were delivered to the repairer.

15.11.2.2 It should be noted that the rights of a lienee as against the customer may be defeated if the customer enters administration. This is because of the moratorium against the enforcement of security over the company's property where the company is in administration.[201] For this purpose, an asset that has been leased to the company is treated as being its property,[202] and the same consequence should follow if the asset is the subject of a conditional sale or hire purchase agreement. The assertion of a lien (that is, of the right to maintain possession as lienee) amounts to the enforcement of security.[203] The result is that the lien cannot be asserted without the permission of the administrator or of the court.

15.11.3 Sub-bailees

If the customer is given authority to grant possession of the goods to a third party (a sub-bailee) then the financier as owner will be bound by the terms agreed between the customer and the sub-bailee if the financier agreed, expressly or

---

200 [1964] 2 QB 185.
201 See para 43(1) of Sched B1 to the Insolvency Act 1986.
202 *Bristol Airport plc v Powdrill* [1990] Ch 744.
203 Ibid; *London Flight Centre (Stansted) Ltd v Osprey Aviation Ltd* [2002] BPIR 1115.

impliedly, to those terms. In such a case, there will be a relationship between the owner and sub-bailee of bailor and bailee, and the sub-bailee will owe duties towards the owner that are those of a bailee of the goods. The owner will not be bound by the terms agreed by the customer if the owner has not so agreed to them.[204]

15.11.4 Fixtures

The owner of goods which become annexed as a fixture to the land of another (such as a building) will lose its ownership of them, because they cease to be goods and become part of the land to which they have been affixed. Whether goods which are affixed to land will lose their independent identity and become a fixture, and so part of the land, depends upon the object and purpose of the annexation and if they can be removed without doing irreparable damage to the land (or building). If the object and purpose of the affixation was the permanent and substantial improvement of the land, the goods will have become a fixture. If the goods were only attached for a temporary purpose or for their further use and enjoyment as goods then they will retain their identity and not become part of the land.[205]

Nonetheless, if the financier has retained its title in the goods and has reserved the right to enter upon the customer's land so as to sever and remove the goods upon the customer's default, the financier's right of entry will give it an equitable right in the land. That right will prevail against the ownership rights of the customer in the land, as well as against the rights of a subsequent equitable encumbrancer of the land, such as an equitable mortgagee.[206] As against such persons, the financier will be entitled to enter on the land, so that it can sever the goods from the land and then remove them.[207]

15.11.4.1

15.11.5 Unauthorised mixing with or incorporation in another asset

The difficult and rather undeveloped area of English law concerning the consequences of the mixing of goods, the incorporation of one chattel in another, and the consequences where a new product is made using goods which lose their independent identity, was reviewed by Moore-Bick J in *Glencore International*

---

204 *KH Enterprise (cargo owners) v Pioneer Container (owners)* [1994] 2 AC 324.

205 *Leigh v Taylor* [1902] AC 157; *TSB Bank PLC v Botham* [1995] EGCS 3 (Jacob J) and [1996] EGCS 149 (Court of Appeal).

206 But not a bona fide purchaser of the legal estate in the land taking for value and without notice.

207 *Re Samuel Allen & Sons Ltd* [1907] 1 Ch 575; *Re Morrison Jones & Taylor Ltd* [1914] 1 Ch 50; *Melluish (Inspector of Taxes) v BMI (No 3) Ltd* [1996] AC 454

AG v Metro Trading International Inc.[208] His Lordship's conclusions may be summarised as follows.[209]

15.11.5.1 First, if goods are delivered by a person who owns them (A) to another (B) for storage and are mixed lawfully by the recipient B with goods of the same kind (commingling) which belong to one or more third parties and cannot be separately identified, then, in the absence of an agreement to the contrary, A and the third parties will each have an interest in common in the mixed bulk in the respective proportions of their contributions to the whole bulk. The proportions will vary to reflect additions and depletions from the bulk.[210] This principle will also apply if some of the mixed bulk was supplied by B, being the person entrusted with the storage, who will also be treated as a contributor. However, if the intention of A and the other third party contributors, if any, was that the person who received the goods should treat them as his own then he will become the owner of them.[211]

15.11.5.2 Secondly, if goods are delivered by A to B and, without authority, are commingled by B with his own goods of the same type, such that they cannot be separately identified, the mixture will be held in common between A and B. A will be entitled to withdraw a quantity equal to his contribution, with any doubt being resolved in his favour. A may also have a claim for damages against B.[212]

15.11.5.3 Thirdly, where goods are delivered by A to B with the intention that B will use them, together with his own goods, to make a new product (blending), the parties are free to decide which of the two of them should own the resultant product.[213] In the absence of such an agreement, the usual consequence is that title in A's goods should pass to B and that B will be the owner of the product.[214] The effect of a supposed agreement between A and B may not be so easy to determine if goods of third parties are also involved.

---

[208] [2001] 1 Lloyd's Rep 284, at [153]–[185].

[209] The position where the goods retain their separate identity and can be removed without causing loss or damage to other goods to which they were attached is not addressed below. It was addressed in *Hendy Lennox (Industrial Engines) Ltd v Grahame Puttick Ltd* [1984] 1 WLR 485 and is referred to at para 15.3.4 above.

[210] *Mercer v Craven Grain Storage Ltd* [1994] CLC 328.

[211] *South Australian Insurance Co v Randell* (1869) LR 3 PC 101. This will be the position where original goods are sold under retention of title, under which the buyer will become their owner upon payment. It would be inconsistent with that arrangement that the parties could intend that the seller would be the outright owner of any product that the buyer makes by using the original goods and a contractual arrangement which purports to have that effect would be a charge: see *Clough Mill Ltd v Martin* [1985] 1 WLR 111 and the discussion at para 15.3.4 above.

[212] *Indian Oil Corp Ltd v Greenstone Shipping SA, the Ypatianna* [1988] QB 345.

[213] See Robert Goff LJ in *Clough Mill Ltd v Martin* [1985] 1 WLR 111, at 119.

[214] As noted at para 15.3.4 above, this will be the position under a sale of goods contract where title is retained pending payment.

Fourthly, if a wrongdoer takes goods belonging to two or more other innocent **15.11.5.4**
persons and blends them for his own purposes, so that a different product results,
the innocent contributors will become owners in common in the blended product.[215]
The proportions of their respective entitlements will depend upon the quantity
and the value of what they each contributed.[216] The wrongdoer will also be liable
in damages for any loss suffered by the innocent contributors. A similar outcome
will apply where the wrongdoer blends his own goods with those of an innocent
contributor, with any doubt being resolved in favour of the innocent contributor,
who will also be entitled to damages.[217]

Fifthly, if it is not feasible to divide the resultant product that has been made by **15.11.5.5**
the wrongdoer between the wrongdoer and an innocent contributor then a different outcome will be required, which may mean that the innocent contributor will
be held to own the whole of the product.[218]

15.11.6 A claim in conversion

In cases where the third party cannot establish that it has acquired ownership or a
valid right to possession of the goods (or products made from or incorporating
them), the financier will have a claim against the third party in conversion under
the Torts (Interference With Goods) Act 1977, where it can be shown that the
third party has acted, even if innocently,[219] in a manner that is inconsistent with
the right of the financier to possession of the goods.[220] That right to possession will
exist where either the financier has the right to immediate possession by having
the right to repossess the goods or where the third party has acquired possession in
circumstances that are repugnant to the financier's rights.[221] An owner of goods

---

[215] Which would include blending of entirely different goods and blending of different grades or
quality of the same type of goods so that the respective contributions cannot be separated from the
resultant blend (e.g. different grades of oil).

[216] This is derived from the speech of Lord Millett in *Foskett v McKeown* [2001] 1 AC 102, at
131–133.

[217] To this extent, Moore-Bick J felt that he was not obliged to follow Bovill CJ in *Spence v Union
Marine Insurance Co Ltd* (1868) LR 3 CP 427, at 437–438 and Lord Moulton in *Sandeman & Sons v
Tyzack and Branfoot Steamship Co Ltd* [1913] AC 680, at 694–695, preferring the approach of Joyce
J in *Re Oatway* [1903] 2 Ch 356, at 359 and Lord Millett in *Foskett v McKeown* [2001] 1 AC 102.

[218] As was done in the Canadian case of *Jones v De Marchant* (1916) 28 DLR 561 (the case of the
fur coat wrongfully made by a man for his mistress, using 18 of his wife's beaver skins and 4 of his
own. The wife was held to be the owner of the coat, her interest prevailing over that of the mistress,
who was a volunteer and to whom the coat had been given by the miscreant husband). An alternative approach would be to require the product to be sold and the proceeds of sale divided between
the rival claimants.

[219] *Fine Art Society v Union Bank of London Ltd* (1886) 17 QBD 705.

[220] If sought, the court has a discretion under s 3(1) of the Torts (Interference With Goods) Act
1977 to order delivery up of the goods, although this would be an unusual remedy.

[221] See the helpful summary provided by Mummery LJ in *MCC Proceeds Inc v Lehman Bros
International (Europe)* [1998] 4 All ER 675, at 685–686.

who does not have an immediate right to possession of them also has a right to sue a third party for damage to the goods which will affect the owner's enjoyment of the reversionary interest in the goods.[222] If the third party, in the mistaken but honest belief that it had acquired a good title in the goods, has improved the goods then it is entitled to an allowance for the value added to the goods by virtue of the improvement.[223]

15.11.6.1 In *Wickham Holdings Ltd v Brooke House Motors Ltd*,[224] the Court of Appeal held that damages in conversion in a claim where the goods had been the subject of a hire purchase agreement should be assessed by reference to the true loss that the financier had sustained. That loss was referable to its true economic interest and the amount that it would have received had the hirer completed the agreement and acquired the title in the goods. In reality, the financier had a limited interest rather than an unlimited interest, and so damages should not be assessed on the basis of the value of the goods as if it had a full interest. That analysis did not change if the financier had terminated the hirer's right to possession.

15.11.6.2 The analysis in the *Wickham Holdings* case may appear to be inconsistent with what Lord Nicholls said in *Kuwait Airways Corp v Iraqi Airways Co*.[225] Lord Nicholls, who gave the leading speech in that case, said that the normal measure of damages in a claim in conversion was the market value of the goods at the time of conversion, as that would usually be taken to represent the loss that the claimant had suffered. However, His Lordship also said that the foregoing was the general rule, to which there might be an exception depending upon the facts of the particular case. He also expressly approved the decision in the *Wickham Holdings* case, which recognised the proposition that the claimant should not be compensated for a loss that it had not suffered. The High Court, after reviewing the position, has since held that the approach that was taken in the *Wickham Holdings* case should continue to be applied in the case of an owner of goods who was suing a third party in conversion, where the goods had been subject to a hire purchase agreement.[226]

15.11.6.3 Although the *Wickham Holdings* case concerned a hire purchase agreement, it is submitted that the same approach in a claim for conversion should be taken in cases concerning misappropriated goods that are the subject of a conditional sale agreement or a finance lease. In each case, the financier's real interest is a limited economic interest, which it will obtain if it receives the full amount it would have

---

[222] See Longmore LJ in *HSBC Rail (UK) Ltd v Network Rail Infrastructure Ltd* [2005] EWCA Civ 1437; [2006] 1 WLR 643, at [19]–[22].
[223] S 8 of the Torts (Interference With Goods) Act 1977.
[224] [1967] 1 WLR 295.
[225] [2002] UKHL 19; [2002] 2 AC 883, at [67].
[226] *VFS Financial Services (UK) Ltd v Euro Auctions (UK) Ltd* [2007] EWHC 1492 (QB).

received had the agreement run its full course. The position would be otherwise where the goods were the subject of an operating lease. This is because, in that situation, the owner does have a real economic interest in the residual value of the goods beyond its interest under the lease. In cases where the *Wickham Holdings* approach is followed, presumably some discount should be allowed for the fact that, had the agreement run its full course, the claimant would have received its money over a period of time, whereas damages fall to be assessed at the earlier date of conversion. In addition, in a hire purchase agreement, some fairly small element of what the claimant might have received under the agreement may represent the discretionary element of the option to purchase and that should also be deducted in the computation of loss.

15.12 Insurance Arrangements

Insurance arrangements concerning equipment will be an important factor in a **15.12.1** financing transaction and one in which a financier will be particularly interested where the asset is of any appreciable value. A fairly normal requirement is that the equipment should be covered for physical damage to it and its destruction or loss, as well as providing cover for damage or injury caused to third parties by the equipment and its use. It is essential that the true value of the equipment should be covered by the policy, as a claim under a policy where the value is under-insured will be subject to reduction in proportion to the under-insurance, unless it has been agreed with the insurers that there should be an element of self-insurance (which would not suit the financier). Cover may be difficult to obtain, however, for loss arising from acts of war or terrorism.[227]

15.12.2 Physical damage and third party liability cover

Generally speaking, the physical damage and third party liability insurances cover should be arranged by the customer. It is relevant to consider with whom and through whom the cover should be arranged, as well as who should be covered. The financier will require that the insurances should be arranged through brokers and with underwriters of international standing, often through the Lloyds market, and that such brokers and underwriters (together with the terms and extent of the cover) should be approved by the financier. In addition to the customer, the financier should insist that it is covered by the insurances.

It is best that the financier is expressed to be covered as a co-insured under a com- **15.12.2.1** posite policy, rather than as a joint-insured. The former acknowledges that the

---

[227] For shipping, this aspect will often be covered by a protection and indemnity club of which the customer is a subscriber.

financier has a different interest from that of the other persons covered by the policy, whereas in the case of the latter, it is necessary that they should have the same interest.[228] In traditional terms, the distinction is relevant to assessing the consequences where there has been non-disclosure or a breach of warranty, although that matter is usually now addressed explicitly, as mentioned below. In any event, it is not sufficient for the financier merely to be named as the loss-payee under a policy if it is not also covered as an insured. If it is merely named as a loss-payee then it will have no direct contractual rights under the policy and its entitlement to payment will be dependent upon there being a valid and enforceable claim by the customer as the named insured. The financier should also seek an undertaking from the insurers that they will not cancel a policy or allow it to lapse (for instance, because of non-payment of premium) without giving the financier at least 30 days' prior notice and the opportunity to remedy whatever the problem may be.

15.12.3 Non-disclosure and breach of warranty

One of the principal features of an insurance policy is that a policy, being a contract *uberrimae fidei* (of the utmost good faith), may be avoided by the insurer for non-disclosure of a material fact in the proposal for the policy or for a breach of warranty. The submission of claims may also be subject to compliance with various strict conditions. The difficulty with this from the perspective of a financier is that the arrangements for taking out the insurance cover will be in the hands of the customer and the financier will not usually be in a position to supervise and vet those arrangements in great detail; nor will the financier be aware of all the facts relevant to the risk that is to be insured. As protection against these difficulties, it used to be possible for a financier to obtain an endorsement to a policy, or direct confirmation from the insurers, to the effect that the insurers would not avoid the policy as against and to the detriment of the financier, even where they might have done so as against the customer.

15.12.3.1 Such endorsements are more difficult to obtain these days. Even in cases where the financier is named as a co-insured under a composite policy, insurers may now insist on having a right to avoid the policy as against all the insureds where there has been a breach of warranty or there was material non-disclosure when the policy was incepted. One possible approach to this difficulty might be to obtain confirmation from the insurers of the specific matters that they require to be disclosed when the policy is taken out, and their agreement that they will not seek to avoid the policy for non-disclosure of other matters. That would, at least,

---

[228] See Sir Wilfred Greene MR in *General Accident Fire and Life Assurance Corp v Midland Bank Ltd* [1940] 2 KB 388, at 404 and Staughton LJ in *New Hampshire Insurance Co v MBN Ltd* [1977] LRLR 25, at 56–57.

reduce the possible scope for avoidance of the policies. It may also be possible for a financier to obtain separate innocent owner's cover against avoidance of a policy.

15.12.4 Payment of claims

It is normal for a policy to provide that the proceeds of claims under third party liability cover will be paid to the relevant third parties (except where the insured has paid the third party, in which case the insurer will reimburse the insured) and the insurer will usually control the defence to any litigation or dispute as brought against the insured by a third party.[229] There is often debate, however, as to what should be provided in a policy (and in the financing documentation) as to the payment of claims under the policy for loss and physical damage to the equipment (and, if relevant, the proceeds of reimbursement of any third party liability claim for loss suffered by a third party which the insured has paid).

Except in the case of a total loss or destruction of the equipment (where the claim will be paid as a capital amount), the negotiating stance that is usually taken by the customer would be that the payments should be applied towards remedying the damage or in replacement or reinstatement of the loss (or in reimbursement of expenditure incurred for those purposes). The financier, on the other hand, is more likely to wish that the proceeds of a claim should be applied in reduction of the outstanding finance due to it or, at least, that it should have the right to determine if the proceeds should be applied in remedying the loss or in effective repayment of the finance it has extended. A compromise will usually be reached, which will be reflected in the loss payable clauses in the policies, under which it is agreed that the proceeds of claims below a certain level may be applied in reinstatement or repair, and the financier will have a discretion as to the destination of the proceeds of claims over that amount.

15.12.4.1

15.12.5 Brokers' undertakings

The financier will require that the brokers who arrange the insurances should undertake to it that they will arrange for loss payable clauses, in the agreed form, to be incorporated in the policies (the insurers may insist on a right of set-off for unpaid premiums), that they will hold the slips and policy documents when issued to the order of the financier, and that they will give the financier notice of any non-payment of premiums due on the policies, of any proposed changes to the terms or cover under the policies, and of any grounds on which the insurers might assert that the policies have lapsed or been avoided.

---

[229] Under s 1 of the Third Parties (Rights Against Insurers) Act 1930, a third party has a direct right against the insurer if the insured is insolvent.

15.12.6 Insurance covenants in the financing documentation

The various matters concerning insurances as discussed above will be reflected in covenants undertaken by the customer in the financing documentation. For instance, such covenants will require the customer to ensure that the relevant cover is effected and maintained, to the extent it is available (perhaps worded as reasonably available) in the insurance markets, during the period of the financing, in the insured amounts but subject to agreed deductibles (which amounts may be increased in accordance with an agreed mechanism), with the financier covered as a co-insured, and with the relevant loss-payee clauses indorsed on the policies, as well as to procure the requisite undertakings from the brokers. The customer will also be required to see that the insurances are effected through brokers and with insurers approved by the financier and on terms approved by the financier, to ensure that the premiums are paid when due and to provide evidence thereof to the financier (failing which the financier will be entitled to pay them and claim reimbursement). There will also be provisions as to the application of the proceeds of the payment of claims.

16

GUARANTEES

16.1 Introduction

In a number of legal systems, particularly civil law systems, guarantees are seen as **16.1.1**
a type of non-proprietary security. The common law does not share that view but,
instead, regards them as a form of contractual undertaking by the guarantor to be

answerable for the performance of the debtor's obligations. As such, they represent an unsecured obligation on the part of the guarantor or surety, which is additional or supplementary to the primary obligations of the debtor, which may themselves be unsecured or protected by security that the debtor has given. It is, of course, possible for the guarantor to give security for the performance of its obligations under the guarantee and, indeed, it is also possible for a person to give security for the performance of the debtor's obligations by way of third party security without that person undertaking a personal obligation by way of guarantee.[1]

16.1.2   The primary focus of this chapter will be on guarantees but it will also be relevant to refer to other types of instruments and undertakings, such as under demand bonds, performance bonds, and indemnities, which can also give a creditor the right to have recourse to a third party where the debtor fails to perform. This chapter is concerned with guarantees that are given by commercial parties in a business context, so it will not examine the additional issues that would arise if the guarantee was given outside that context.[2]

16.1.3   The principal reason for a creditor obtaining a guarantee or a similar instrument or undertaking is to spread the credit risk, so that it will have another party to which it may look for performance should the debtor default. If the creditor is a bank then there may also be a regulatory benefit to the bank if the exposure risk associated with the guarantor for capital adequacy purposes is better than that which attaches to the debtor. To the extent that the guarantee covers the risk, the exposure will be measured by reference to the guarantee and the guarantor rather than the borrower.

16.1.4   As a matter of English law, the rights and liabilities of the parties under a guarantee and under similar instruments or undertakings rests primarily in contract, with certain associated equitable rights (such as rights of contribution and subrogation) that the guarantor will enjoy because of its obligations as a surety. The contractual basis of a guarantee is a fundamental aspect in defining the obligations of a guarantor and in understanding the nature of the relationship that exists between the guarantor and the creditor which is the beneficiary of the guarantee.

---

[1] *Re Conley* [1938] 2 All ER 127, in which it was held that the giver of the security would still fall to be considered as a 'surety or guarantor' for the purposes of the forerunners of ss 239 and 340 of the Insolvency Act 1986 (persons who might be preferred under the provisions dealing with preferences).

[2] For instance, the developments in the law concerning undue influence that may be exerted where a woman guarantees the business liabilities of her husband, the requirements that arise under the Consumer Credit Acts 1974 and 2006, and the possibility, which remains a moot point, as to whether a guarantee that is given by a 'consumer' may fall within the purview of the Unfair Terms in Consumer Contracts Regs 1999 (SI 1999/2083) with respect to their requirements concerning unfair terms and that written contracts should use plain and intelligible language: see *Governor & Co of the Bank of Scotland v Singh* (unreported 17/6/2005, HHJ Kershaw QC sitting in the High Court in Manchester).

Generally speaking, English law has sought to protect guarantors by taking the view that the guarantor is entitled to expect that its contractual position and the rights it enjoys will not be interfered with except if it has consented to such interference. It does not take much on that basis to find a defence at general law for a guarantor, which is why the standard forms of guarantee that are taken by banks from guarantors have such voluminous contents which seek to cover any arguments that a guarantor may raise and which attempt, in consequence, to prevent such defences from being successful. The courts have also been prepared to bolster the position of guarantors by the approaches that they have taken to the construction of guarantees, although there has not been an overall consistency in this and, recently, the courts have tended to take a more even-handed approach. In some cases, the courts have said that any ambiguity should be construed against the beneficiary of a guarantee and in favour of the guarantor[3] or, perhaps more generously, on a fair but strict reading of the wording in the guarantee.[4] If the guarantee has been drafted by the beneficiary, which will usually be the case, the *contra proferentem* rule will be applied to resolve any ambiguity.[5] However, if the contract is clear, the court should not strain to place an interpretation on it that was not intended.[6] In other cases, the courts have said that a guarantee should be viewed as a commercial document and given a sensible interpretation, but against the background that it was a standard form document put forward by the creditor (if such be the case) and that the guarantor was likely to have been influenced by the continuing availability to it of such rights as it may have enjoyed by giving the guarantee, such as by virtue of rights of subrogation and contribution.[7]

16.1.5

For ease of reference in this chapter, the parties that are likely to be involved will be referred to mostly as (i) the 'creditor', being the beneficiary under the guarantee or similar instrument or undertaking and the party which has extended credit or to whom the underlying relevant obligations are owed; (ii) the 'debtor', being the party that received the credit and owes the underlying obligation to pay or perform that obligation; and (iii) the 'guarantor' or 'surety', being the third party which has given the guarantee or similar instrument or undertaking to the creditor. A guarantee is one type of suretyship, which is an expression that connotes the general concept that a person assumes, in a commercial sense, a secondary or accessory liability for the performance of a debtor's obligations even though, as between the surety and the creditor, the surety's obligations may sometimes, but not necessarily, be expressed to be those of a primary obligor.

16.1.6

---

3 For example, Hilbery J in *Eastern Counties Building Society v Russell* [1947] 1 All ER 500, at 503.

4 *First National Finance Corp v Goodman* [1983] BCLC 203.

5 E.g. the Court of Appeal in *Eastern Counties Building Society v Russell* [1947] 2 All ER 734, at 736 and 739, and *Barclays Bank Ltd v Thienel* (1980) 247 EG 385.

6 *Tam Wing Chuen v Bank of Credit and Commerce Hong Kong Ltd* [1996] 2 BCLC 69.

7 *Barclays Bank PLC v Kingston* [2006] EWHC 533 (QB), [2006] 2 Lloyd's Rep 59.

16.2 The Nature of a Guarantee

16.2.1 What the guarantor has guaranteed will be determined as a matter of construction of the contract. Sometimes the guarantee will be in the form of an 'all moneys' guarantee, and will cover all of the liabilities (present and future, actual or contingent) of the debtor to the creditor.[8] On other occasions, the guarantee may only relate to a specific transaction or even, more concisely, to a particular instalment that is payable by the debtor.[9] Generally speaking, however, the guarantor will be presumed to have intended to guarantee all of a debtor's liabilities with respect to the transaction or transactions that have been guaranteed, rather than just a specific instalment payable under a transaction.

16.2.1.1 It is a different matter as to proving those liabilities. It has been held, for instance, that (in the absence of very clear words to the contrary) a judgment or arbitral award against the principal debtor, in proceedings to which the guarantor was not a party, will not bind the guarantor. The guarantor is entitled to have the extent of the liabilities proved in direct proceedings against it.[10]

16.2.2 The following propositions are derived principally from the speech of Lord Diplock in *Moschi v Lep Air Services Ltd*.[11] A guarantee is in the nature of a secondary, or contingent, suretyship obligation, under which the guarantor undertakes to ensure that the debtor will perform its obligations.[12] The liability of the guarantor crystallises into an actual liability upon a failure of the principal debtor to pay its indebtedness when due, as the guarantor has correspondingly failed to ensure the proper performance by the debtor of its obligations. Furthermore, the liability of the guarantor is limited to the enforceable liabilities of the debtor that the guarantor has agreed to guarantee,[13] so that the guarantor will not be liable for any

---

[8] Even so, the court may find some limitation in what is covered. For instance, the courts will be reluctant to find that the guarantor intended to be liable in respect of indebtedness that was not originally incurred to the creditor but of which the creditor has taken an assignment from a third party, although it would appear that by the use of express wording such an eventuality could be covered: see *Kova Establishment v Sasco Investments Ltd* [1998] 2 BCLC 83. See also *ING Lease (UK) Ltd v Harwoood* [2007] EWHC 2292 (QB). A similar approach has been taken in construing an all moneys clause in a debenture: *Re Quest CAE Ltd* (1985) 1 BCC 99,389.

[9] See the explanation provided by Lord Reid in *Moschi v Lep Air Services Ltd* [1973] AC 331, at 344–345. See also *Hyundai Heavy Industries Co Ltd v Papadopoulos* [1980] 1 WLR 1129. As Lord Reid explained, if the liability of the guarantor is limited to a specific instalment under an instalment payment contract and the contract is terminated before the instalment became payable then it is arguable that the guarantor will have no liability.

[10] *Re Kitchen* (1881) 17 ChD 668; *Bruns v Colocotronis, The Vasso* [1979] 2 Lloyd's Rep 412; *Sabah Shipyard (Pakistan) Ltd v Islamic Republic of Pakistan* [2007] EWHC 2602 (Comm).

[11] [1973] AC 331, at 347.

[12] Sometimes referred to as 'see to it' guarantees.

[13] As to the position regarding the debtor's obligation to pay interest if the debtor is in liquidation, see s 189 of the Insolvency Act 1986 and Rule 4.93 of the Insolvency Rules 1986 (for bankruptcy,

obligations of the debtor that fall outside the ambit of what has been guaranteed;[14] nor will the guarantor be liable if the debtor is not liable as, for instance, if the creditor does not have an enforceable right against the debtor.[15] On the other hand, if the debtor repudiates the contract and the creditor accepts the repudiation so that the contract is brought to an end and the debtor is made liable for the loss the creditor has suffered in consequence of the termination of the contract, the guarantor will similarly be treated as being liable for those consequences. Furthermore, if a liquidator or trustee in bankruptcy disclaims a lease or other onerous property or an unprofitable contract under section 178 or section 315 of the Insolvency Act 1986, as the case may be, the liability of a guarantor with respect to the transaction is preserved.[16]

Curiously, it has been said that the liability of the guarantor upon default by the debtor will sound in damages for breach of contract, rather than in debt for the amount equivalent to what the debtor should have paid, with the consequence that the creditor will be put to proof of its loss and under a duty to mitigate its loss. Nonetheless, the computation of the loss recoverable from the guarantor should amount to the same thing as the amount recoverable from the debtor, particularly if the guarantee contains an undertaking by the guarantor to pay should the debtor default in making payment.[17] A conclusive evidence clause will be of assistance to the creditor in establishing the amount of the guarantor's liability, as it is taken to be conclusive evidence of the liability, save where an error is manifest on the face of the certificate.[18]

16.2.3

---

see ss 322(2) and 328(4) of the Insolvency Act 1986 and Rule 6.113 of the Insolvency Rules 1986). A guarantee of the debtor's obligation to pay interest will not cover interest from the date of the commencement of the debtor's liquidation or bankruptcy: *Re Moss* [1905] 2 KB 307, which can be circumvented by a direct obligation upon the guarantor to pay interest on the amount falling due under the guarantee: *Re Fitzgeorge* [1905] 1 KB 462. As to the guarantor's right to prove in the debtor's winding up for interest paid by the guarantor, see *Re Empire Paper Ltd* [1999] BCC 406.

[14] In *ST Microelectronics NV v Condor Insurance Ltd* [2006] EWHC 977 (Comm), [2006] 2 Lloyd's Rep 525 it was held that a guarantor would not be liable where the creditor advanced money or supplied goods or services on terms that the money was to be repayable or the price was to be payable immediately or at some earlier time than the original credit period that had been agreed. This was because the transaction was not that which was guaranteed.

[15] *Coutts & Co v Browne-Lecky* [1947] KB 104, which concerned an unenforceable loan to a minor. The particular difficulty in that case would now be overcome by s 2 of the Minors Contracts Act 1987. Another example of the principle will be found in *Heald v O'Connor* [1971] 1 WLR 497, which concerned a transaction involving unlawful financial assistance.

[16] By ss 178(3) and 315(3) of the Insolvency Act 1986. In relation to the effect upon a guarantor of a disclaimer of a lease, see *Hindcastle Ltd v Barbara Attenborough Associates Ltd* [1997] AC 70 and *Scottish Widows PLC v Tripipatkul* [2003] EWHC 1874 (Ch), [2004] BCC 200.

[17] See the explanation of this point by Professor Sir Roy Goode in *Commercial Law* (3rd edn, 2004) at pp 814–815.

[18] *Bache & Co (London) Ltd v Banque Vernes et Commerciale de Paris SA* [1973] 2 Lloyd's Rep 437; *Van Der Merwe v IIG Capital LLC* [2007] EWHC 2631 (Ch). In the latter case, it was said (at [44]) that if the consequence was that the guarantor made an overpayment, the guarantor would be

16.2.4 It also follows from the nature of a guarantee that the guarantor is only liable in respect of the obligations that it has guaranteed, taking into account the risk it assumed in giving its guarantee. If those obligations and the risks and security associated with those obligations have been changed or abrogated by agreement between the creditor and the debtor without the guarantor's consent, then the guarantor is entitled to say that the resultant new situation is not what it guaranteed and that, depending upon the circumstances, it has been discharged in whole or in part. That issue will be discussed later in this chapter.

16.3 The Nature of First Demand Instruments and Indemnities

16.3.1 First demand instruments

In contrast to the nature of a guarantee as outlined above, if the undertaking of the guarantor or surety is in the nature of an independent first demand obligation then it may exist independently of the underlying contract between the debtor and the creditor, the liability to pay a liquidated sum would arise upon the making of a simple demand by the creditor (accompanied perhaps, depending upon the requirements set out in the relevant instrument, by specified documentation), the issuer of the undertaking would not be concerned to check if the debtor had breached the underlying contract, except where the issuer was on notice of fraud or, perhaps, illegality;[19] nor would the validity of the issuer's obligations be affected by a variation of the underlying contract between the debtor and the creditor.[20] Traditionally, such types of undertaking have been issued by banks, insurance companies, and similar types of institution, rather than by ordinary guarantors, and have been in the form of well-known types of independent instrument.[21]

16.3.1.1 An example of such an instrument is the standby letter of credit. This type of instrument originated in the USA as a means of avoiding regulatory restrictions in the issuance by banks of guarantees across state lines. They are now used

---

entitled to a refund of the excess from either the creditor or the debtor. The decision in the *Van Der Merwe* case was upheld on appeal: [2008] EWCA Civ 542. In the appeal, the position concerning the right to seek a refund for an overpayment was not so clear, although it was suggested that if the debtor failed to seek a refund, the guarantor might be subrogated to the debtor's right to seek it: see [2008] EWCA Civ 542, at [22]–[27].

[19] *Mahonia Ltd v JP Morgan Chase Bank* [2003] EWHC 1927, [2003] 2 Lloyd's Rep 911.

[20] See the well-known description by Lord Denning MR of the issuer's obligations under a performance bond in *Edward Owen Engineering Ltd v Barclays Bank International Ltd* [1978] QB 159, at 171. See also *Marubeni Hong Kong & South China Ltd v The Mongolian Government* [2005] EWCA Civ 395, [2005] 1 WLR 2497.

[21] *Esal (Commodities) Ltd v Oriental Credit Ltd* [1985] 2 Lloyd's Rep 546; *IE Contractors v Lloyds Bank Plc* [1990] 2 Lloyd's Rep 496; and *Gold Coast Ltd v Caja de Ahorros del Mediterraneo* [2001] EWCA Civ 1086, [2002] 1 Lloyd's Rep 617.

throughout the world in a wide range of finance and other transactions which require reliable independent assurances of payment. They are usually issued on the basis that they will be subject to either the International Standby Practices (currently ISP98) or the Uniform Customs and Practice for Documentary Credits (currently UCP600), each promulgated by the International Chamber of Commerce (the ICC). Under a standby letter of credit, the issuer undertakes to pay the beneficiary up to the maximum amount stated, upon presentation to the issuer of the documentation stated in the instrument. That documentation will usually include a written demand, stating that the primary obligor is in default. The principle of the autonomy of the instrument, and the issuer's obligations under it, from the underlying commercial transaction to which it relates, is enshrined in both ISP98 and UCP600.

Outside the context where a traditional form of independent instrument is issued **16.3.1.2** by a bank or a similar institution, the law would require a clear indication in the instrument that it was intended to create an independent undertaking rather than being of a secondary nature, which would be the usual presumption.[22] In *Van Der Merwe v IIG Capital LLC*[23] it was held that the presumption had been overcome where each of the following factors was present in the relevant instrument (although the judge declined to say whether the absence of any of them would have led to a different result):

(1) a conclusive evidence clause, by which a certificate given by the creditor would be conclusive evidence of the amount due under the instrument;

(2) that the liabilities which were guaranteed were stated to include not just the moneys that were actually due, owing, or payable by the debtor to the creditor, but also moneys 'expressed' to be due, owing, or payable by the guarantor;

(3) that the obligation of the guarantor was said to be that of a primary obligation and not merely that of a surety; and

(4) that the guarantor's obligation was stated to be payable on demand.

With respect, some care should be taken in placing too much reliance upon this decision.[24] It is a first instance decision and cuts across the more conservative

---

[22] Lord Denning MR in *Stadium Finance Ltd v Helm* (1965) 109 SJ 471; Lord Jauncey in *Trafalgar House Construction (Regions) Ltd v General Surety & Guarantee Co Ltd* [1996] AC 199, at 208; Carnwath LJ in *Marubeni Hong Kong & South China Ltd v The Mongolian Government* [2005] EWCA Civ 395, [2005] 1 WLR 2497; and Gloster J in *Canmer International Inc v UK Mutual Steamship Assurance Association (Bermuda) Ltd, the MV 'Rays'* [2005] EWHC 1694 (Comm); [2005] 2 Lloyd's Rep 479, at [43]–[50].

[23] [2007] EWHC 2631 (Ch).

[24] However, the decision was upheld by the Court of Appeal: [2008] EWCA Civ 542. It is understood that leave was granted for the case to be taken on appeal to the House of Lords, in view of its general importance.

approach taken by the Court of Appeal, as seen in *Marubeni Hong Kong & South China Ltd v The Mongolian Government*.[25] In that case, the court emphasised the importance of the type of institution that normally entered into first demand instruments and distinguished that from the usual situation under which an ordinary guarantee is given. In addition, of the four cumulative factors in the *Van Der Merwe* case which were held to be sufficient, taken together, to overcome the usual presumption and turn the instrument into a first demand guarantee, at least three (i.e. those numbered (1), (2), and (4) above) will normally be found in ordinary types of guarantee. They have not, until this case, been held sufficient to convert an ordinary guarantee into a first demand instrument. The other factor was unusual but it hardly seems sufficient to have tipped the balance. A well advised guarantor will seek to ensure, however, that such wording does not appear in the guarantee that it gives.

16.3.1.3 It is clear under English law that a bank or similar institution which has issued such an independent first demand undertaking must pay in accordance with the terms of the instrument unless it has knowledge of fraud on the part of the beneficiary.[26] The relevant date as at which it must have the knowledge is the date it intends to make payment to the beneficiary and it must be clear knowledge.[27] If the bank's customer (i.e. the person on whose behalf the bank issued the instrument) wishes to obtain an injunction to restrain the bank from making payment under the instrument, it must show that it is 'seriously arguable' on the material available that the only realistic inference that could be drawn was that the beneficiary could not honestly have believed in the validity of its demand or presentation for payment.[28] There has been some debate as to whether the test of 'seriously arguable' should also apply to a defence raised by a bank in a case where the beneficiary is seeking summary judgment against the bank and the bank wishes to plead a defence based on the fraud of the beneficiary or a misrepresentation by the beneficiary in obtaining the issuance of the instrument. The alternative test is at a lesser threshold of a 'realistic prospect of success'. The lower threshold was put forward by Waller LJ in *Safa v Banque du Caire*[29] but that was rejected by Mance LJ in *Solo Industries UK Ltd v Canara Bank*[30] who said that a higher standard was required which was consistent with demonstrating an 'established fraud'.

---

[25] [2005] EWCA Civ 395, [2005] 1 WLR 2497.

[26] See Lord Denning MR in *Edward Owen Engineering Ltd v Barclays Bank International Ltd* [1978] 1 QB 159, at 171.

[27] *United Trading Corp v Allied Arab Bank Ltd* [1985] 2 Lloyd's Rep 554.

[28] See Ackner LJ in the *United Trading* case, at 560–561, where a contrast is drawn with the position for obtaining interim relief in the USA.

[29] [2000] 2 Lloyd's Rep 600.

[30] [2001] EWCA Civ 1059, [2001] 1 WLR 1800.

16.3.2 Indemnities

Another method that is used in attempting to overcome some of the difficulties associated with a guarantee, particularly those which have the effect of limiting the guarantor's liability to such of the corresponding obligations that are enforceable against the debtor, is by expressing the guarantor's obligations as an indemnity rather than simply as a guarantee. An indemnity is said to be a form of independent and primary obligation and so is not secondary to, nor dependent upon, the liability of the debtor.[31] In addition, an indemnity is not subject to the requirements of section 4 of the Statute of Frauds 1677.

The difference between a guarantee and an indemnity, especially when it is only given orally, is often difficult to discern. Dealing with such a situation, Lord Esher MR in *Sutton and Co v Grey*[32] said that the difference lay in whether the person who gave the undertaking was interested in the underlying transaction to which it formed a part. If so then it would be construed as an indemnity. If, however, he did not have an interest and was solely connected with the transaction by his undertaking then it would be construed as a guarantee. Vaughan Williams LJ in *Harburg India Rubber Comb Co v Martin*[33] expressed the matter a little differently, in saying that an indemnity would only arise where the interest of the person giving the undertaking was central to the transaction, in which the giver played a real part. If his interest was merely peripheral to the transaction then the undertaking would be considered to be a guarantee. The difference between the two approaches was considered by Smith LJ in *Pitts v Jones*.[34] Her Ladyship preferred the approach taken by Vaughan Williams LJ, which she followed. She expressed the matter as follows:[35]

16.3.2.1

> Instead of asking whether or not the promisor had had any interest in the transaction, the court should ask what was the object of the contract or transaction and if the promisor's obligation to pay arose as an incident to the central object of the contract or transaction, that obligation would be an indemnity, whereas if it was the central obligation of the contract or transaction, it would be a guarantee . . . In short, it appears that [Vaughan Williams LJ] was saying that Lord Esher's formulation should not be taken literally. Not every interest in the transaction would serve to take the promise out of the statute; there had to be more than a motive for offering the promise; there had to be a real interest in the subject matter of the contract. If the promisor had no real interest in the subject matter of the contract but only a motive for offering his promise, the promise would be a . . . guarantee.

---

31 *Yeoman Credit Ltd v Latter* [1961] 1 WLR 828 and *Goulston Discount Co Ltd v Clark* [1967] 2 QB 493.
32 [1894] 1 QB 285, at 288.
33 [1902] 1 KB 778, at 783–786.
34 [2007] EWCA Civ 1301.
35 At [31].

16.3.3 Many forms of guarantee obtained by banks contain an additional provision which provides for an indemnity to be given by the guarantor, with the intention that if the guarantee does not provide the appropriate recourse to the guarantor then the indemnity will do so. Such a provision would be along the lines that the guarantor will indemnify and hold harmless the creditor for any loss that it may suffer in consequence of the debtor failing to make payment in full to the creditor even though the purported obligations of the debtor may be unenforceable and irrecoverable from the debtor.

16.3.3.1 The effectiveness of such an indemnity, however, is not altogether clear and is open to some doubt. In two cases where the indemnity was contained within an overall contract of guarantee, the Court of Appeal read down the indemnity and gave it no further effect than the guarantee, on the basis that it was insufficiently distinct from the guarantee.[36] At the very least, it appears necessary that the document should make it clear that the obligations under the indemnity are primary and distinct from those under the guarantee, although simply stating that a guarantor should be treated as a primary obligor and not merely as a surety will be insufficient in itself to constitute an indemnity.[37] It must also be doubtful on general principles relating to the effect of an unlawful transaction, if an indemnity would be enforced against the guarantor or surety in circumstances involving an illegal underlying transaction where the creditor was aware of the facts giving rise to the unlawfulness.

16.3.3.2 Care should also be taken in drafting the indemnity to ensure that it is not limited in its application simply to the loss that the creditor would suffer if the underlying transaction were unenforceable against the debtor. If drafted in that fashion, the creditor may be unable to recover the full amount of its exposure because it may have been unable to recover very much from the debtor even if the debtor's obligations had been enforceable, because of the debtor's impecuniosity. The indemnity should therefore make it clear that it covers the full amount that the debtor would have been liable to pay had the underlying transaction been enforceable.

16.3.4 There is also doubt as to the remedy that would be available to the creditor, as the beneficiary of an indemnity, on enforcement of the indemnity.[38] Obviously, the

---

[36] *Western Credit Ltd v Alberry* [1964] 1 WLR 945 and *Stadium Finance Co Ltd v Helm* (1965) 109 SJ 471.

[37] *Heald v O'Connor* [1971] 1 WLR 497. However, the importance of expressing the obligation of the indemnifier as that of a principal obligor is demonstrated by *MS Fashions Ltd v Bank of Credit and Commerce International SA* [1993] Ch 425 (Hoffmann LJ sitting at first instance), sub nom *MS Fashions Ltd v Bank of Credit and Commerce International SA (No 2)* [1993] 3 All ER 769 (CA). See also *TS & S Global Ltd v Fithian-Franks* [2007] EWHC 1401 (Ch).

[38] For interesting discussions of this subject, see A Berg, 'Rethinking Indemnities' in (2002) 9 JIBFL 360 (Part 1) and 403 (Part 2), and R Zakrzewski, 'The Nature of a Claim on an Indemnity' (2006) Journal of Contract Law 1.

beneficiary would wish to claim recovery of a liquidated sum, equivalent to the amount owing by the debtor (or which would be owing if it were recoverable) and outstanding interest thereon. The Court of Appeal has been prepared to take that approach and treat the claim under an indemnity as a claim for a liquidated sum,[39] subject to the creditor establishing the amount that would notionally have been due from the debtor in consequence of its default and the termination of the relevant agreement.[40]

However, the House of Lords held in *Firma C-Trade SA v Newcastle Protection and Indemnity Association, The Fanti*[41] that at common law a claim under an indemnity gives rise to an unliquidated claim for damages and not for a liquidated sum in debt, because the obligation of an indemnifier is to keep the beneficiary harmless against loss. Such loss has to be established and proved and will be subject to the duty to mitigate the loss. Furthermore, as a matter of construction, it is presumed in the absence of clear words to the contrary that an indemnity should not cover loss which the beneficiary suffers as a result of its own negligence or other breach of duty.[42]   **16.3.4.1**

There is an exception to the severity of these rules, however, where the indemnity   **16.3.4.2**
is intended to provide protection against a liability of the beneficiary to a third party. In equity, following upon the Judicature Acts, there may be an equitable right in the beneficiary to compel payment under the indemnity of the amount properly due to the third party without the beneficiary having first to pay the third party, unless this right is contractually overridden.[43] Of course, it would still be necessary for the beneficiary to establish that the amount claimed was properly due to the third party.

16.4 Consideration and the Intention to Contract

As a guarantee is based in contract, it will be necessary to establish that there was   **16.4.1**
an intention to contract and that the guarantee was supported by consideration or is in the form of a deed. It is not necessary that the consideration should be set out in the guarantee,[44] but if the document does state the consideration it is not permissible to lead evidence of any other consideration.[45] As with any contract, past consideration will not be sufficient to support the guarantee.

---

[39] *Yeoman Credit Ltd v Latter* [1961] 1 WLR 828; *Goulston Discount Co Ltd v Clark* [1967] 2 QB 493; and *Royscott Commercial Leasing Ltd v Ismail* (unreported 29/4/1993).
[40] Ibid.
[41] [1991] 2 AC 1.
[42] *Smith v South Wales Switchgear Ltd* [1978] 1 WLR 165.
[43] *Firma C-Trade v Newcastle Protection and Indemnity Association, The Fanti* [1991] 2 AC 1, at 28 (per Lord Brandon) and at 35–36 (per Lord Goff).
[44] S 3 of the Mercantile Law Amendment Act 1856.
[45] *Oldershaw v King* (1857) 2 H&N 517.

16.4.2 In a number of cases, such as those concerning so-called 'comfort letters', the courts have held on the facts that there was no intention to contract or to create mutual relations and so there was not an enforceable contractual obligation on the part of the alleged guarantor.[46] Hence, a statement by a parent company in relation to credit extended to its subsidiary that, 'it is our policy to ensure that the business of [the debtor] is at all times in a position to meet its liabilities to you under [the credit agreement]' was held to be just a statement of the present intention of the parent at the time it was written and did not give rise to a contractual obligation on the part of the parent to ensure that the subsidiary would have funds to pay the creditor.[47] Furthermore, a clear indication in a document that no liability was accepted by the writer would mean that there was no binding promise to be liable for the debtor's obligations, despite wording in the document which might otherwise have given rise to liability.[48] It has also been held that an agreement entered into by a company remained the obligation of the company alone and did not also import a liability on the part of the directors that the company would fulfil that undertaking, despite wording in the undertaking that the directors would also be liable and the fact that the document was signed on the company's behalf by one of its directors, because there was no evidence that the directors intended to incur any personal liability.[49]

16.4.3 Nonetheless, a statement of fact that is made by a third party to a creditor and on which the creditor relies in extending credit may give rise to a tortious claim for damages against the third party if it is wrong. Such a claim might be based in deceit or for negligent misrepresentation. It might also give rise to a claim under a collateral contract.

16.5 Other Preliminary Issues in Taking a Guarantee

16.5.1 In addition to the requirements as to consideration and intention to contract, there are a number of other preliminary issues that may arise in taking a guarantee and which, if not correctly satisfied, may mean that the guarantee cannot be enforced against the guarantor.

---

[46] For instance, *Kleinwort Benson Ltd v Malaysia Mining Corp Bhd* [1989] 1 WLR 379; *Re Atlantic Computers PLC; National Australia Bank Ltd v Soden* [1995] BCC 696; *Carlton Communications PLC v The Football League* [2002] EWHC 1650 (Comm); and *Manches LLP v Freer* [2006] EWHC 991 (QB).

[47] *Kleinwort Benson Ltd v Malaysia Mining Corp Bhd* [1989] 1 WLR 379.

[48] *Re Atlantic Computers PLC; National Australia Bank Ltd v Soden* [1995] BCC 696.

[49] *Manches LLP v Freer* [2006] EWHC 991 (QB), in which *Young v Schuler* (1883) 11 QBD 651 and *VSH Ltd v BKS Air Transport Ltd* [1964] 1 Lloyd's Rep 460, were distinguished because in those cases the director had intended to be personally bound. See also Lord Brandon in *Elpis Maritime Co Ltd v Marti Chartering Co Inc (The Maria D)* [1992] 1 AC 21, at 28.

16.5.2 The Statute of Frauds

One such matter arises under section 4 of the Statute of Frauds 1677, which provides (with the spelling in modern form) as follows:

> No action shall be brought whereby to charge the defendant upon any special promise to answer for the debt, default or miscarriages of another person . . . unless the agreement upon which such action shall be brought or some memorandum or note thereof shall be in writing and signed by the party to be charged therewith or [by] some other person thereunto by him lawfully authorised.

The section only applies if there is a secondary liability, that is, under a guarantee, rather than to obligations in the nature of a primary liability,[50] such as under an indemnity.[51] It is also provided by legislation that the section does not apply in relation to a financial collateral arrangement.[52] In terms of its formal requirements, the section requires, first, that the agreement containing the guarantee, or some memorandum or note thereof, should be in writing and, secondly that the agreement, note, or memorandum should be signed by the guarantor or by his lawfully authorised agent.

The policy of the section[53] is to protect people from being held liable on informal communications made without sufficient deliberation upon the wisdom in giving a guarantee. It was also intended to protect them against such informal communications being expressed ambiguously or being given in consequence of a fraud perpetrated by the recipient. It was consistent with that policy that where there was an offer in writing by the guarantor which was verbally accepted, there was a sufficient note or memorandum. The requirement for a signature was by way of authentication of the instrument, so as to give authenticity to the instrument.[54] It has been held that there will be sufficient writing if the guarantee is contained in an email but that the email must contain a signature, such as by typing the name of the sender at the foot of the email by way of an intended signature.[55] **16.5.2.1**

In *Actionstrength Ltd v International Glass Engineering In.Gl.En. SpA*[56] the purported beneficiary of an oral guarantee sought to argue that the guarantor should be estopped from pleading the statute in denying the validity of the guarantee **16.5.2.2**

---

[50] *Harburg India Rubber Comb Co v Martin* [1902] 1 KB 778.

[51] See Lord Esher MR in *Sutton & Co v Grey* [1894] 1 QB 285, at 288; Vaughan Williams LJ in *Harburg India Rubber Comb Co v Martin* [1902] 1 KB 778, at 783; and Smith LJ in *Pitts v Jones* [2007] EWCA Civ 1301, at [21].

[52] Reg 4(1) of the Financial Collateral Arrangements (No 2) Regs 2003 (SI 2003/3226).

[53] See the review in *Mehta v J Pereira Fernandes SA* [2006] EWHC 813 (Ch), [2006] 1 WLR 1543.

[54] See Lord Chelmsford LC and Lord Westbury in *Caton v Caton* (1867) LR 2 HL 127, at 139–140 and 143, respectively.

[55] *Mehta v J Pereira Fernandes SA* [2006] EWHC 813 (Ch), [2006] 1 WLR 1543. See also now the Electronic Communications Act 2000.

[56] [2003] UKHL 17, [2003] AC 541.

because, to the guarantor's knowledge, the beneficiary had relied upon the guarantee in extending credit to the principal debtor. The beneficiary failed in its argument because to have allowed the argument would have resulted in a direct contradiction of the import of the statute. It is almost inherent in any transaction involving a guarantee that the beneficiary will have relied upon the guarantee in providing funds or credit to the principal debtor, so there was nothing unusual or exceptional in this case upon which the beneficiary could ground its argument for an estoppel. The House of Lords left open the possibility, however, that in an appropriate case a beneficiary might be able to rely upon an estoppel in a situation where it might otherwise be defeated by the statute. This might cover situations where the beneficiary had acted in reliance upon a representation by the guarantor to the effect that it would not invoke the statute, that the statute did not apply, or that it would confirm the guarantee in writing or in cases where the guarantor had made some payment in affirmation of the alleged guarantee.

16.5.3 General issues

In common with general contractual principles, a guarantee may be vitiated in consequence of pleas of *non est factum*,[57] mistake,[58] the failure of a condition precedent to the application of the guarantee,[59] undue influence of individuals,[60] and misrepresentation by the creditor, including by conduct.[61] A claim in fraudulent misrepresentation (and probably a claim under section 2(1) of the Misrepresentation Act 1967[62]) relating to matters concerning the debtor, such as its character of creditworthiness, would have to be based upon a written representation, signed by the representor.[63]

16.5.4 Non-disclosure

In contrast to a contract of insurance, where there is an obligation of disclosure of all material facts in pursuance of the duty of utmost good faith owed by the insured to the insurer, there is no general obligation of disclosure that is owed by

---

57 *Lloyds Bank PLC v Waterhouse* (1991) 10 TrLR 161.

58 *Associated Japanese Bank (International) Ltd v Credit du Nord SA* [1989] 1 WLR 255, where the possibility was discussed in relation to both common mistake and unilateral mistake.

59 Ibid. In *TCB Ltd v Gray* [1987] Ch 458 it was argued that it was a condition precedent that the creditor would take valid collateral security. The argument was dismissed because no such agreement could be substantiated and was contradicted by a clause in the guarantee which specifically consented to a failure by the creditor to take or perfect security.

60 *Barclays Bank PLC v O'Brien* [1994] 1 AC 180 and *Royal Bank of Scotland plc v Etridge* [2002] 2 AC 773.

61 *Geest PLC v Fyffes PLC* [1999] 1 All ER (Comm) 672.

62 *UBAF Ltd v European American Banking Corp* [1984] QB 713.

63 S 6 of the Statute of Frauds Amendment Act 1828.

the creditor to the guarantor in taking the guarantee.[64] There is an obligation upon the creditor, however, to disclose to the guarantor matters that have been agreed between the creditor and the debtor which make the terms of the debtor's obligations materially different in a potentially disadvantageous way from what the guarantor might naturally expect to be the case.[65] The duty only relates to matters that have been agreed between the creditor and the debtor that affect the legal relationship between them, so it does not impose an obligation on the creditor (except if responding to a specific enquiry made by the prospective guarantor, in which case the answer must be true and not misleading[66]) to disclose facts known to the creditor that relate to the risk that is being undertaken by the guarantor, such as facts concerning the state of the debtor's account,[67] serious financial difficulties that affect the customers,[68] that the debtor's account could be operated by her husband, who was an undischarged bankrupt,[69] or that the creditor had suspicions that the debtor had been acting in a fraudulent manner.[70]

16.5.5 Corporate matters

Generally speaking, for a guarantor which is a company incorporated under one of the Companies Acts, it can be assumed that the guarantor will have the necessary corporate power to give a guarantee and that a person dealing in good faith with the board of directors of such a company may safely rely upon the board's powers to bind the company.[71] For other types of entity, the same assumptions cannot safely be made. Thus, if the giving of a guarantee is *ultra vires* such an entity, then it may be unlawful and thus unenforceable against the guarantor.[72]

Notwithstanding the comfort just expressed in relation to companies that are incorporated under the Companies Acts, where the directors of a company are deciding if the company should give a guarantee, they must act in the best interests of the company in accordance with their fiduciary duties,[73] subject to the right

16.5.5.1

---

[64] *Geest PLC v Fyffes PLC* [1999] 1 All ER (Comm) 672.

[65] *Levett v Barclays Bank PLC* [1995] 1 WLR 1260; *Far Eastern Shipping PLC v Scales Trading Ltd* [2001] 1 All ER (Comm) 319.

[66] *National Westminster Bank Ltd v Cond* (1940) 46 Com Cas 60.

[67] *Hamilton v Watson* (1845) 12 Cl & Fin 109.

[68] *Lloyds Bank Ltd v Harrison* (1925) 4 LDB 12.

[69] *Cooper v National Provincial Bank Ltd* [1946] KB 1.

[70] *National Provincial Bank of England Ltd v Glanusk* [1913] 3 KB 335.

[71] Ss 35 and 35A of the Companies Act 1985 (ss 39 and 40 of the Companies Act 2006).

[72] See, for instance, *Credit Suisse v Allerdale Borough Council* [1997] QB 306, where it was found that an English local authority did not have power to give the guarantee, which was *ultra vires* and void. For a foreign entity, conflict of laws issues would have to be considered in determining the powers of an entity under the law of its place of incorporation or establishment. See Chap 4.

[73] See now the modified formulation of the duty in s 172 of the Companies Act 2006.

of the shareholders to ratify the acts and decisions of the directors.[74] If the creditor is on notice, which could include constructive notice, of a breach of the directors' duties in deciding that their company should give a guarantee, then the creditor will be affected by the breach and, in consequence, be unable to rely upon the guarantee.[75]

16.5.6 Partnerships

The execution by one partner, purportedly on behalf of the partnership, of a guarantee of a third party's liabilities can give rise to particular difficulties, as it would not usually fall within the partnership business and thus within the authority of a partner to bind the firm under section 5 of the Partnership Act 1890. However, the guarantee would bind the firm if it had been authorised by all of the partners or if it was given in pursuance of, and was incidental to, a transaction which the partnership had authorised.[76]

16.5.7 Transactions at an undervalue

Allied to the considerations concerning the giving of a guarantee by a company is the effect of section 238 of the Insolvency Act 1986,[77] which concerns transactions at an undervalue entered into by a company at a 'relevant time' before the onset of its administration or winding up.[78] If such a transaction has occurred, the court (on the application of the administrator or liquidator of the company) has a wide discretion as to the order which can be made for restoring the position to what it would have been had the transaction not taken place.[79] A relevant time is a time within two years prior to that onset, if the company was insolvent (i.e. unable to pay its debts within the meaning of section 123 of the Insolvency Act 1986[80]) at the time of the transaction or became insolvent in consequence of the

---

[74] In circumstances where insolvency is in prospect, the duty includes taking account of the interests of the company's creditors and a breach of their duty in such circumstances cannot be overcome and ratified by the shareholders: see the summary provided by Sir Andrew Morritt V-C in *Bowthorpe Holdings Ltd v Hills* [2002] EWHC 2331 (Ch); [2003] 1 BCLC 226, at [50]–[52]. This is recognised by s 172(3) of the Companies Act 2006.

[75] *Rolled Steel Products (Holdings) Ltd v British Steel Corp* [1986] Ch 246.

[76] *Governor and Company of the Bank of Scotland v Henry Butcher & Co* [2003] EWCA Civ 67, [2003] 2 All ER (Comm) 557.

[77] The equivalent section for individuals is s 339 of the Insolvency Act 1986. Similar provisions will also be found in s 423 of that Act (transactions defrauding creditors), which applies to both companies and individuals.

[78] In more detail, see s 240 of the Insolvency Act 1986.

[79] Which is amplified by s 241 of the Insolvency Act 1986. As to the orders that the court might make, see *Re Thoars (Decd)* [2004] EWCA Civ 800, [2004] BPIR 985. It should be noted that the defence that is available to third parties under s 241(2) is not available to a counterparty to the impugned transaction, so it could not be relied upon by the creditor which received the impugned guarantee.

[80] S 240 of the Insolvency Act 1986.

transaction.[81] A 'transaction' is widely defined to include a gift, agreement or arrangement.[82]

A transaction at an undervalue is one where either:[83]   **16.5.7.1**

(i) the company made a gift to another person or entered into a transaction with that other person on terms that provided for the debtor to receive no consideration, or

(ii) the company entered into a transaction with that other person for a consideration the value of which, in money or money's worth, is significantly less than the value, in money or money's worth, of the consideration provided by the insolvent company.

The test under paragraph (i) is fairly obvious and involves the company in making   **16.5.7.2**
a gift or receiving no consideration in return for entering into the impugned transaction. It is most likely to arise where the company disposed of an asset (including by making a payment) as a gift or otherwise undertook an obligation for which it received no consideration.[84]

The test under paragraph (ii) involves a comparison, to be made in monetary terms, of the consideration provided by the company as against what it received for entering into the transaction, including what it received from an overall and wider transaction of which the particular transaction to which it was a party formed an integral part.[85] The test is to be assessed as at the time the transaction was entered into by the company. There is no hard and fast test as to what would constitute a significant imbalance in the respective elements of the consideration provided and received by the company; it will depend upon the facts of the particular case.

It has also been said that there is no necessity for a transaction at an undervalue   **16.5.7.3**
to include a transfer or diminution in the value of the company's assets as an

---

[81] Insolvency is presumed, unless the contrary is shown, where the company entered into the transaction with a person who is connected with the company: s 240(2) of the Insolvency Act 1986.

[82] S 435 of the Insolvency Act 1986.

[83] S 238(4) of the Insolvency Act 1986.

[84] An example of a transaction for which no consideration was received will be found in *Hill (as Trustee in Bankruptcy of Nurkowski) v Spread Trustee Co Ltd* [2006] EWCA Civ 542, [2006] BCC 646, in which security was given by a debtor to secure his existing indebtedness when there was no compelling reason for him to give the security.

[85] *Re MC Bacon Ltd* [1991] Ch 127 and *Phillips v Brewin Dolphin Bell Lawrie Ltd* [2001] 1 WLR 143. The consideration need not be precisely measured if that is not realistically possible: *Re Thoars (Decd)* [2004] EWCA Civ 800, [2004] BPIR 985. It is the true worth of the consideration that must be valued: *Phillips v Brewin Dolphin* and some limited element of hindsight may be involved in ascertaining the effect of uncertain events at the time of the transaction: *Phillips v Brewin Dolphin* and *Re Thoars; Reid v Ramlort* [2002] EWHC 2416 (Ch), [2003] 1 BCLC 499. The company may receive consideration under the transaction from more than one source, not just the person to whom it provided its consideration: *Phillips v Brewin Dolphin*.

immediate consequence of its entry into the transaction.[86] It follows that an unfavourable undertaking by the insolvent company, by which it undertook obligations to a counterparty under the transaction, such as under a guarantee, could amount to a transaction that was capable of being impugned under the section.

16.5.7.4 If there has been a transaction at an undervalue, the transaction will be saved if the court is satisfied that the insolvent company:[87]

(a) entered into the transaction in good faith and for the purpose of carrying on its business, and

(b) at the time it did so there were reasonable grounds for believing that the transaction would benefit the company.

It will be seen from this that a transaction which has been impugned as falling within the parameters of an undervalue transaction can only be saved if the requirements of both of those paragraphs are met, to be judged as at the time of entering into the transaction. It is for those who wish to resist an order being made under section 238 to establish the grounds upon which the transaction is saved.[88] The first requirement is subjective, based upon the concept of the transaction being entered into by the company in good faith and for the purpose of carrying on its business. The second requirement is objective, based on showing that there were reasonable grounds for believing that the transaction would be beneficial to the company.

16.5.7.5 It is submitted that the giving of a guarantee could fall within section 238, although a liquidator or administrator of the guarantor might find it difficult to establish the necessary ingredients to bring a claim. It is unlikely that the giving of the guarantee would be by way of gift, and the guarantor will probably have received some consideration, even if it is only of a nominal value. Any attack on a guarantee under the section is likely, therefore, to be based on an allegation that the value of the consideration that the guarantor received for giving the guarantee was significantly less than the value of the consideration that the guarantor provided. Assessing the relative values of the consideration given and received by the guarantor will not be an easy exercise, bearing in mind that the assessment must be made as at the time the guarantee was given and should be done on a commercial basis by ascribing value to the consideration provided and received.

---

[86] In *obiter* comments, Arden LJ said in *Hill (as Trustee in Bankruptcy of Nurkowski) v Spread Trustee Co Ltd* [2006] EWCA Civ 542; [2006] BCC 646, at [138], when commenting on the corresponding provisions in s 423 of the Act, that a transaction at an undervalue could occur without the necessity for a transfer or diminution in the value of assets. In that case, her Ladyship was referring to the giving of security as being capable of being a transaction at an undervalue within the test under para (ii) above.

[87] S 238(5) of the Insolvency Act 1986. This saving is not replicated in s 339 of the Act.

[88] *Re Barton Manufacturing Co Ltd* [1999] BCLC 740.

As to the value of the consideration provided by the guarantor, that will depend **16.5.7.6** upon factors such as the likelihood that the debtor will default and that the creditor would have recourse to the guarantee, the likely extent of any claim upon the guarantor, and what other resources would be available to the creditor, including from security provided by the debtor and claims against co-sureties. The value of the consideration received by the guarantor should take into account whatever benefit it received from the overall transaction of which the guarantee forms a part. If they were not taken into account in assessing the value of the consideration it provided (i.e. as counterbalances to the amount of its likely exposure under the guarantee), the prospective (but realistic) value of the rights of the guarantor against the debtor and the contribution from co-sureties and subrogation to security provided by the debtor should be included in the computation of the value of the consideration it received.

Despite the apparent difficulties in making those assessments, there will be cases **16.5.7.7** where a challenge should succeed because there was no good or sufficient commercial benefit to the guarantor in giving the guarantee, when measured against the risk it had undertaken in giving the guarantee (taking into account the indemnity from the debtor and rights of contribution and subrogation). This should be judged from the perspective of the guarantor taken as a separate entity in its own right, in giving the guarantee. An example where such a situation may arise would be where the guarantee was given by a company in support of the obligations of a sister company or a parent company in the same group as the guarantor, if there was no trading or financial dependency of the guarantor upon the other company, nor any other realistic and commensurate benefit that it would derive or protections that it would receive in consequence of giving the guarantee.[89] In such circumstances, it is unlikely that the guarantee could be saved by reliance upon the saving provision, as it is difficult to envisage how either of the two requirements in the saving provision would be met.

16.6 State Guarantees

There may be particular considerations if a guarantee is provided by a State or **16.6.1** government (or a sub-division thereof). In the first place, it is necessary that the guarantee should be given within the requirements and constraints of the law of the relevant State, including its constitutional and administrative law. Such matters may affect the underlying right for the guarantee to be given as well as the

---

[89] On the other hand, a parent company might have good reason to guarantee the obligations of its subsidiary because of the benefits it would hope to derive from the continuing activities of its subsidiary.

procedure that must be observed and the authority of the relevant person to execute it on behalf of the guarantor.

16.6.2 State aids within the EU

Secondly, within the rules as to State aids under EU law, there are limits on the powers of EU Member States and their respective entities to give guarantees. Articles 87 to 89 of the Treaty of Rome form part of the competition law chapter of the Treaty and regulate the giving by EU Member States of 'State aids' to undertakings[90] engaged in business of any kind within the EU.[91] These articles are supplemented by a procedural Council Regulation.[92] Articles 87 to 89 are intended to prevent Member States from distorting competition within the EU by giving financial grants or other financial benefits to particular companies or industries, in a manner which confers an unfair competitive advantage on them, relative to their rivals and is liable to affect trade between Member States. Aid which is liable to distort competition and to affect trade between Member States will generally be regarded as compatible with the common market, and permitted to be granted, only where it contributes to the attainment of some other policy objective recognised by the EC Treaty.

16.6.2.1 The State aid provisions deal separately with 'existing aids' and with 'new aids'. Under Article 88, paragraphs 1 and 2, existing aids (effectively those which pre-date the coming into force of the State aids provisions with respect to the relevant State[93]) are permitted to remain in place, subject to the possibility of investigation by the EC Commission, and, if appropriate, the adoption by the Commission of a formal decision declaring the aid to be incompatible with the common market, prohibiting its continuation.

16.6.2.2 In contrast, a Member State will generally be required to obtain the consent of the EC Commission to the grant of a new aid. Article 88, paragraph 3, requires the Member State formally to notify the EC Commission of its proposal to grant new aid. The Member State is then generally required to wait for up to two months before granting the aid, in order to enable the Commission to examine whether the proposed aid raises doubts as to its compatibility with the common market. In that event, the Commission will open formal investigative proceedings, and the Member State will be required to defer the grant of the aid pending the outcome

---

[90] The State aid rules may apply to the giving of aid by a Member State to its own State-owned undertakings, but this text focuses on the application of the rules to the giving of aid to private sector undertakings.

[91] Similar rules apply under the EEA Agreement and under agreements between the EU and various third countries (e.g. Turkey).

[92] 659/99/EC OJ [1999] L83/1.

[93] For the initial members of the EEC, 1 January 1958 and for the UK, 1 January 1973.

of those proceedings. If the Commission does not identify grounds to open a formal investigation, or does not reply to the Member State's notification at all, the Member State may give the Commission prior notice of its intention to grant the aid, and may then proceed to do so.[94] The aid, once granted, may fall to be reviewed, at a later stage, under the rules governing existing aids. If a Member State wrongfully fails to notify a proposed new aid to the EC Commission and obtain approval for it, the aid will be unlawful and the recipient may be required to repay it (either at the suit of a third party in the national courts, or pursuant to an infringement decision adopted by the EC Commission).

Case law of the European Court of Justice and the Court of First Instance makes clear that the State aid rules apply not only to financial grants given by the Member State itself, but to all financial benefits, whatever their legal form, given out of State resources.[95] Thus, aid given by a local authority or a publicly funded body (e.g. the Arts Council) will fall to be examined as State aid.[96] In addition, aid in the form of tax concessions available only to particular companies, or companies engaged in a particular industry, will be examined as State aid.[97] Case law also makes clear that where a public body enters into a commercial transaction with a private sector company (e.g. the subscription for shares of the company, the lending of money to the company, or the guaranteeing of the company's debts in favour of a third party), the transaction will be treated as State aid if the transaction is made otherwise than on arm's length terms which satisfy a 'market investor test'—that is, if the public body accepted commercial terms which a private investor seeking normal commercial returns would have found unacceptable.[98] In such a case, the amount of the aid is generally equivalent to the difference between the value of the terms which the public body accepted and the terms which a market investor would have expected to receive for undertaking similar obligations. Difficult questions of valuation arise where the public sector effectively rescues an insolvent company by a transaction of a kind which no private sector investor would have been willing to contemplate at all.

16.6.2.3

---

[94] Articles 2–4 of the Procedural Regulation.

[95] *Amministrazione delle Finanze v Denkavit Italiana* Case 61/79, [1980] ECR 1205; *Banco Exterior de Espana v Ayuntamiento de Valencia* Case C-387/92, [1994] ECR I-877; *Sloman Neptun v Bodo Ziesemer* Cases C-72 and 73/91, [1993] ECR I-887; see also, the Court of Appeal in *R v Attorney General ex p ICI* [1987] 1 CMLR 72.

[96] *Intermills v Commission* Case 323/82, [1984] ECR 3809; *Pigs and Bacon Commission v McCarren* Case 177/78, [1979] ECR 2161.

[97] *Banco Exterior de Espana v Ayuntamiento de Valencia* Case C-387/92, [1994] ECR I-877; *FFSA v Commission* Case T-107/95, [1997] ECR II-229; *Germany v Commission* Case C-156/98, [2000] ECR I-6857.

[98] *Belgium v Commission (Meura)* Case 234/84, [1986] ECR 2263; *Belgium v Commission (Boch No 2)* Case 40/85, [1986] ECR 2321; *Air France v Commission (CDC-P)* Case T-358/94, [1996] ECR II-2109; *Cityflyer Express v Commission* Case T-16/96, [1998] ECR II-757.

16.6.2.4 It is clear from what is said above that, where a public sector body guarantees a debtor's obligations to its creditor, it is necessary to examine whether the transaction may entail State aid to one or more of the parties, by failing to conform to 'market investor' principles. For example, as to whether the guarantor undertook obligations without securing the fee a private guarantor would have expected for undertaking similar obligations; or whether the debtor thereby secured a financial benefit, by securing more favourable borrowing rates (by virtue of the creditor's entitlement to resort to the guarantor for payment) than it could otherwise have secured without paying a fee commensurate with the normal market cost of such a guarantee. If so, then the guarantee entails an element of aid to the debtor and, prima facie, falls to be examined by reference to the substantive criteria of Articles 87 to 89 and, if necessary, notified in advance to the EC Commission for approval.

16.6.2.5 In order to avoid a deluge of notifications of insignificant aid, the EC institutions adopted a Regulation,[99] to provide an exemption from the normal state aids rules for *de minimis* aid.[100] The Regulation provides that aid measures should be deemed not to amount to aid for the purposes of Article 87 of the EC Treaty if the total aid granted to any one enterprise does not exceed EUR100,000 over any period of three years. The Regulation also provides for the calculation of the amount of aid granted in tranches or otherwise than via a cash grant. A separate Regulation[101] similarly exempts certain aids given to small and medium-sized enterprises from the State aid rules.

16.6.2.6 The EC Commission has published a notice,[102] outlining how it would generally expect to assess aid in the form of guarantees. The notice does not detract from the rules on notification of proposed aids, as outlined above. The notice makes clear that, if a guarantee is given by a public body out of State resources, it will amount to State aid to the borrower whose obligations are guaranteed, if the borrower benefits from better borrowing terms, or the ability to borrow more, without paying a commensurate premium; the guarantee may also amount to aid to the lender (the beneficiary of the guarantee), if the State guarantees an existing loan, made on terms which did not already reflect the benefit to the lender of the guarantee. The notice also provides guidance as to how the amount of any aid will be assessed. It makes clear that there is no obligation to notify aids which do not favour particular companies or industries, or which do not affect trade between Member States. The notice also outlines the consequences of non-compliance with the notification

---

[99] 69/2001/EC OJ [2001] L10/30.

[100] Separate rules and exemptions apply to particular industrial sectors: for example, agriculture, fisheries, aquaculture, and transport; and to aid for export-related activities.

[101] 20/2001/EC OJ [2001] L10/33.

[102] Commission Notice on the application of Articles 87 and 88 of the EC Treaty to State aid in the form of guarantees, OJ [2000] C71/14.

rules (in terms of obligations to repay aid already granted, and the potential illegality of the instruments whereby aid is granted).

Generally speaking, the only person with standing to apply to the EC Commission **16.6.2.7** for State aid clearance is the Member State. Private sector beneficiaries may not apply for State aid approval. Nonetheless, in view of the consequences for private parties of a Member State's non-compliance with the formal notification requirements in respect of new aid, it is common in commercial transactions entailing potential State aid, for the private parties to require sight of the Member State's application for State aid approval, and of any ensuing correspondence with the EC Commission. This should enable the parties to satisfy themselves that the Member State has made full disclosure of the proposed transactions and their consequences to the EC Commission, so as to ensure that any approval granted by the EC Commission is not open to challenge as having been based on false or incomplete information. Where the EC Commission approves aid by reference to a particular set of facts (e.g. as to the purpose for which the aid is to be given, or the extent of the guarantor's exposure), it will be necessary to seek further approval if there is a material change in circumstance (e.g. if the aid funding is to be used for a different purpose or the amount of the guaranteed liability is to be altered).

16.7 The Types of Guarantee

16.7.1 Specific and continuing guarantees

A guarantee may be of a specific obligation or transaction, which has already been mentioned, or it may be a continuing guarantee for all of the debtor's liabilities from time to time. A guarantee of a specific obligation or transaction will be discharged when the debtor ceased to be liable, such as by the debtor paying off and performing its obligation or obligations to the creditor[103] or by the creditor releasing the debtor, except where the creditor reserves its rights against the guarantor.[104] The effect of a continuing guarantee is that, subject to the effect of the service of a notice of discontinuance by the guarantor upon the creditor, the guarantor will be liable for the ultimate balance due by the debtor to the creditor, notwithstanding the fluctuating balance of account between the debtor and creditor or any temporary nil or credit balance of the amount due by the debtor to the creditor. The effect of a notice of discontinuance is to crystallise the liabilities of the debtor that are the subject of the guarantee, as explained further below.

---

[103] For example, *Western Credit Ltd v Alberry* [1964] 1 WLR 945. If the payment by the debtor is subsequently set aside as a preference under s 239 of the Insolvency Act 1986, the court has the power to reinstate the guarantor's liability under s 241(1)(e) of that Act.

[104] *Greene King PLC v Stanley* [2001] EWCA Civ 1966, [2002] BPIR 491.

16.7.2 Demand guarantees

A guarantee may provide that the guarantor will guarantee the debtor's obligations and pay to the creditor the amount thereof upon demand made by the creditor. The purpose of such a provision is to prevent the limitation period under the Limitation Act 1980[105] running against the creditor until such time as a demand has been made on the guarantor.[106] Otherwise the limitation period under the guarantee will run from the time of the debtor's default, being the date on which the cause of action will have accrued against the guarantor because the guarantor will have defaulted in its own 'see to it' obligations under the guarantee. However, if the liability of the guarantor is expressed to be that of a principal debtor then it appears that, even if its obligations are expressed to be on demand, a demand under the guarantee may not be necessary for the cause of action to accrue against the guarantor, so the limitation period would begin to run from the date of the debtor's default.[107] This is because the effect of the 'principal debtor' wordings is to create a primary liability, so that the debt will not be treated as contingent upon the making of a demand.

16.7.3 Limited guarantees

A guarantee may be limited as to time, the amount guaranteed, or the total amount of the guarantor's liability under the guarantee.

16.7.3.1 A guarantee that is limited as to time will usually provide that it is only valid with respect to demands made under it before a stated date. The point of such a provision is to enable the guarantor to ascertain with certainty when it may consider itself as under no further liability, except with respect to any demand made before that date.[108]

16.7.3.2 A guarantee that is limited as to the amount that has been guaranteed contains a danger to the creditor if it is a guarantee of the obligations of the debtor under an overdraft or similar type of running account because the effect of the rule in

---

105 If the guarantee is in the form of a simple contract, the limitation period is six years from the date the cause of action accrues against the guarantor: s 5 of the Limitation Act 1980. If the guarantee is in the form of a deed, the period is 12 years: s 8(1) of that Act.

106 *Bradford Old Bank Ltd v Sutcliffe* [1918] 2 KB 833.

107 *MS Fashions Ltd v Bank of Credit and Commerce International SA* [1993] Ch 425 (Hoffmann LJ sitting at first instance), sub nom *MS Fashions Ltd v Bank of Credit and Commerce International SA (No 2)* [1993] 3 All ER 769 (CA). See also *TS&S Global Ltd v Fithian-Franks* [2007] EWHC 1401 (Ch).

108 This has given rise to difficulties with suretyships (in particular, first demand bonds and similar instruments) that have been given in favour of States or their entities, where the beneficiary has threatened to make a demand unless the issuer agrees to extend the period of its undertaking. Care is needed if an extension is to be granted, so as not to endanger the surety's rights against the debtor and other sureties.

Clayton's case[109] may be to treat payments into the debtor's account with the creditor as paying off the amount that was guaranteed. A guarantee that is limited as to the amount of the debtor's liability can also cause problems to the creditor with respect to the lodging of proofs in the liquidation of the debtor, because the guarantor will be entitled, after meeting its liability under the guarantee,[110] to prove for the amount in the debtor's liquidation. Such a proof will serve to diminish the assets of the debtor that are available to meet the creditor's own proof in a case where there is an unsatisfied residual liability owed by the debtor to the creditor.

The problems just referred to can be overcome by expressing the guarantee to be a continuing guarantee for all of the debtor's liabilities to the creditor but with a limitation as to the total amount recoverable from the guarantor. **16.7.3.3**

16.7.4 Conditional guarantees

A guarantee may be conditional, in the sense that the effectiveness of the guarantee and the liability of the guarantor thereunder may be subject to the satisfaction of a condition precedent.[111] One such condition may be that the guarantee will also be executed jointly by other guarantors, that other guarantees will be taken, or that the creditor will take security from the debtor. The general principle is that a purported guarantee will not be binding on any of the intended guarantors unless it is executed by all of them, as it is a condition precedent to the liability of any of them that all will execute and be bound by the guarantee.[112] Similarly, if the parties agreed that the creditor would take other guarantees or security, the fulfilment of that requirement may amount to a condition precedent to the liability of the guarantor under the guarantee.[113] However, the parties may agree in the guarantee that a particular guarantor will be bound despite the failure of the other intended guarantors to execute the guarantee or of the creditor to take the other

---

[109] *Devaynes v Noble, Clayton's Case* (1816) 8 LJ Ch 256, 35 ER 767. See also Nourse J in *Re Quest CAE Ltd* (1985) 1 BCC 99,389, at 99,393.

[110] The rule in insolvency against double proofs prevents the guarantor from proving before it has met its own liability to the creditor. Prior to meeting that requirement, it is the creditor who has the right to prove: *Re Fenton* [1931] 1 Ch 85. If the guarantee is of the whole debt then the creditor retains the right to prove in the debtor's insolvency for the whole debt unless the guarantor has paid in full. If the guarantee is limited to only part of the debt then once the guarantor has met its liability, it is entitled to prove in the debtor's liquidation, to the exclusion of the creditor's previous right with respect to that part of the debt: per Vaughan Williams J in *Re Sass* [1896] 2 QB 12, at 15.

[111] *Associated Japanese Bank (International) Ltd v Credit du Nord SA* [1989] 1 WLR 255. See also *TCB Ltd v Gray* [1987] Ch 458, where the existence of the alleged condition precedent was not substantiated and was, in fact, contradicted by the provisions of the guarantee.

[112] *James Graham & Co (Timber) Ltd v Southgate Sands* [1986] QB 80, at 94.

[113] But a mere expectation, even a shared expectation, that the creditor would obtain such additional guarantees or security will not operate as a condition precedent to the guarantor's liability. There must be an agreement between the creditor and the guarantor that the creditor would obtain such guarantees or security: *Capital Bank Cashflow Finance Ltd v Southall* [2004] EWCA Civ 817, [2004] 2 All ER (Comm) 675. This is similar to the approach taken in *TCB Ltd v Gray* [1987] Ch 458.

guarantees or such security. If there is a provision to that effect then the guarantor will then be bound despite such a failure arising.[114]

16.8 ECGD Cover

16.8.1 Reference has already been made of the distinction that should be drawn between guarantees and other types of suretyship instruments, such as first demand instruments issued by banks and similar institutions and indemnities. The attributes of such instruments has also been described. There is another type of instrument that should be mentioned in the context of the promotion of the international sale of goods and services by UK exporters, which relates to the guarantees that are issued by the Export Credits Guarantee Department (ECGD).[115] The ECGD was originally established in 1911 and is a department of the UK Government. It currently derives its powers from the Export and Investment Guarantees Act 1991. It issues both guarantees and insurance policies.

16.8.2 There are four types of guarantee that are issued by the ECGD under facilities granted by the ECGD in favour of approved banks operating from a UK branch, although not necessarily having their head office in the UK.

16.8.2.1 One facility (the Supplier Credit Financing Facility) covers financial accommodation that is provided by a bank to a UK exporter and is related to contracts for the sale or supply of goods or services to foreign purchasers. The accommodation takes the form of a purchase by the bank from the exporter of bills of exchange or promissory notes drawn on the foreign purchaser as the means of payment by the purchaser under the sale or supply contract.[116] The guarantee covers payment of the bills or notes.[117] The ECGD may insist on having a right of recourse against the exporter, should the guarantee be called, if the exporter is in default in its obligations under the export contract.

16.8.2.2 A second facility (the Buyer Credit Facility) covers financial accommodation provided by a bank to foreign customers of UK exporters or suppliers, to finance high value export, construction, project, or consultancy contracts, and covers repayment of the finance by the foreign customer. In essence, the bank provides finance to the

---

[114] *Governor and Company of the Bank of Scotland v Henry Butcher & Co* [2003] EWCA Civ 67, [2003] 2 All ER (Comm) 557.

[115] For a fuller description, see the ECGD's website at <http://www.ecgd.gov.uk>.

[116] There is a variant of this facility under which there are direct bank to bank arrangements without the use of bills or notes.

[117] There is an illustration of such an ECGD guarantee in *Credit Lyonnais Bank Nederland NV v Export Credits Guarantee Department* [1996] 1 Lloyd's Rep 200 (the case was the subject of an ultimate appeal to the House of Lords, reported at [2000] AC 486, but the appeal did not concern this issue).

foreign customer which is used to pay the UK supplier, either by direct payment to the supplier from loan drawdowns or to reimburse payments made directly by the customer to the supplier. The guarantee covers the foreign customer's repayment obligations to the bank. There is a risk to the UK supplier if the foreign customer's refusal to repay relates to a default by the supplier in its contract with the customer, as the ECGD (by virtue of a separate agreement between the ECGD and the supplier) has a right of recourse against the customer for any corresponding claim by the bank against the ECGD guarantee.[118] A third facility (the Lines of Credit Facility) concerns credit provided by a bank to a foreign borrower which is used to pay a UK exporter of goods or services under a series of contracts. The borrower's obligations to repay the bank are guaranteed by ECGD. The fourth facility (the 'Project Financing Facility') is intended for project finance loans in excess of £20 million, where there is substantial reliance on the project assets and revenues and only very limited recourse to others such as the project sponsors of a government. The guarantee will cover commercial risks and can also include political risks.

To complete the picture, there are three types of insurance policy that are issued by the ECGD, usually in conjunction with its issuance of a guarantee, being an Export Insurance Policy to a UK exporter covering specific commercial and political risks giving rise to non-payment by a foreign buyer, a Bond Insurance Policy to cover unfair calls under bonds, and an Overseas Investment Insurance Policy in respect of political risks concerning investments in developing countries. **16.8.3**

16.9 Rights of the Guarantor as a Surety

By virtue of being a surety, a guarantor is entitled to various rights as against the debtor and other co-sureties, as well as being subrogated to the rights of the creditor against the debtor and to security held by the creditor. These rights arise as a matter of general law and, with respect to its rights of subrogation and to contribution, under section 5 of the Mercantile Law Amendment Act 1856. A guarantor also has a right to determine its liability under a continuing guarantee. These various rights will now be examined. **16.9.1**

16.9.2 Indemnity by the debtor

As against the debtor, the surety[119] is entitled to be indemnified by the debtor for the liability that the surety has incurred to the creditor and, even before a demand

---

118 An example of this will be found in *Export Credits Guarantee Department v Universal Oil Products Co* [1983] 1 WLR 399.

119 Which would include a person who has given a third party charge to secure the performance of the debtor's obligations: *Re Conley* [1938] 2 All ER 127; *Piers v Piers* (1750) 1 Ves Sen 521; *Re Pittortou* [1985] 1 WLR 58.

has been made upon the surety, the surety is entitled to a declaration that the surety should be exonerated from liability by the debtor and that the debtor is obliged to perform its obligations to the creditor.[120] It has been held, however, that the right to the indemnity will not arise where the surety undertook its obligations voluntarily and not at the request of the debtor.[121] The surety is entitled to recoupment[122] under its indemnity for each payment it made and for which it had an accrued liability in consequence of the debtor's default or under the express terms of the suretyship, even if a demand had not been served on the surety by the creditor before the surety made the payment.[123]

16.9.3 Subrogation

A surety is entitled to be subrogated to the creditor's rights against the debtor and to the benefit of any security held by the creditor for the debtor's obligations.[124] This includes the right to sue the debtor in the creditor's name[125] and to prove in its insolvency and a right to the benefit of any security held for the guaranteed obligations[126] at the time the suretyship was undertaken or which was taken subsequently and whether or not the surety knew of the security.[127] For this purpose, the guaranteed debt is treated as remaining outstanding even though the surety has paid off the debt.[128] The right to enforce subrogation arises on payment but not before[129] and whether or not the debtor concurred in the surety giving its guarantee. The surety is subrogated in the same degree to the rights of the creditor, so it will enjoy the same level of priority as that held by the creditor.[130] However, if the surety has guaranteed the whole of the debtor's indebtedness, even if there is a limit on the guarantor's total liability, the right to enforce subrogation will only

---

[120] *Thomas v Nottingham Incorporated Football Club Ltd* [1972] Ch 596. However, the debtor cannot be forced to pay the creditor before the due date for payment.

[121] *Owen v Tate* [1976] QB 402. This should not prejudice the surety's right of subrogation to the creditor's rights against the debtor.

[122] I.e. principal plus interest running from the date of the surety's payment: *Re Fox, Walker & Co ex p Bishop* (1880) 15 ChD 400.

[123] *Thomas v Nottingham Incorporated Football Club Ltd* [1972] Ch 596.

[124] S 5 of the Mercantile Law Amendment Act 1856.

[125] However, the right of subrogation does not mean that the cause of action to which the surety is subrogated is vested in a proprietary sense in the surety: *Re Ballast PLC, St Paul Travelers Insurance Co Ltd v Dargan* [2006] EWHC 3189 (Ch).

[126] Including, to the extent of the surety's right to contribution, security given by co-sureties: Lord Blackburn in *Duncan Fox & Co v North and South Wales Bank* (1880) 6 Ch App 1, at 19; *Re Parker, Morgan v Hill* [1894] 3 Ch 400.

[127] *Forbes v Jackson* (1882) 19 ChD 615.

[128] S 5 of the 1856 Act. Such security should be in the same form and condition as it was originally taken: *Forbes v Jackson* (1882) 19 ChD 615.

[129] *Re Howe, ex p Brett* (1871) 6 Ch App 838.

[130] See, for instance, *Re Lamplugh Iron Ore Co Ltd* [1927] 1 Ch 308, with respect to preferential debts.

arise once that indebtedness has been paid off in full.[131] By contrast, where the guarantee was for a stated amount of the indebtedness, the right to enforce subrogation, on a pro rata basis, will arise once the surety has met its obligations with respect to that part of the debt,[132] unless the surety and the guarantor have agreed that the right should be postponed.

16.9.4 Contribution

At general law[133] and by virtue of section 5 of the Mercantile Law Amendment Act 1856, a surety has a right to claim contribution from co-sureties for the same debt[134] where the surety has paid (or is required to pay[135]) more than its share of the commonly guaranteed and outstanding liability of the debtor[136] and it is not able or feasible to recover in full from the debtor.[137] The right arises even though the surety was unaware of its co-sureties,[138] whether or not they had undertaken their obligations to the creditor before or after the surety gave its own suretyship and whether they are bound severally or jointly and severally and by the same or different instruments.[139] The right will arise before a demand has been made on the surety if it has paid an ascertained and guarantee liability, so long as it was not acting officiously or voluntarily.[140]

The right will only arise where the co-sureties had a common liability for the same debt as the surety. Thus, if the co-sureties are liable for different debts of the debtor[141] or for separate parts of a debt but not the same parts of a debt as that for which the surety is liable,[142] the right to contribution will not arise.

16.9.4.1

Unless the sureties have agreed otherwise between themselves, the usual presumption is that they intended to bear the burden of their suretyships on an equal footing, so that a surety can recover by way of contribution from the co-sureties an amount

16.9.4.2

---

[131] *Re Sass* [1896] 2 QB 12.

[132] *Goodwin v Gray* (1874) 22 WR 312; *Re Sass* [1896] 2 QB 12.

[133] *Deering v Earl of Winchelsea* (1787) 2 Bos & Pul 270.

[134] That is, third parties who are sureties for the same debt, whether under guarantees or other instruments of an accessory nature, and even though, as between the creditor and such co-sureties, the latter may be expressed as being primary obligors.

[135] *Stimson v Smith* [1999] Ch 340.

[136] That is, more than the surety's proportionate share of the whole of the commonly guaranteed and outstanding liability, not just more than its share of a partial amount of that liability: *Stirling v Burdett* [1911] 2 Ch 418.

[137] *Hey v Carter* [1935] Ch 397.

[138] *Deering v Earl of Winchelsea* (1787) 2 Bos & Pul 270, *Craythorne v Swinburne* (1807) 14 Ves 160.

[139] See Peter Gibson LJ in *Stimson v Smith* [1999] Ch 340, at 348.

[140] *Stimson v Smith* [1999] Ch 340.

[141] *Deering v Earl of Winchelsea* (1787) 2 Bos & Pul 270.

[142] *Pendlebury v Walker* (1841) 4 Y&C Ex 424.

sufficient to restore the equal balance between them,[143] but the recovering surety must bring into hotchpot (by bringing it into the account) the benefit of security or other benefits it held from the debtor.[144] Where the sureties have different limits on liability under their respective suretyships, they will only be liable to contribute in proportion to those limits.[145] If one of the co-sureties is insolvent then the proportionate liability to make contribution is calculated as between the solvent sureties, ignoring the insolvent surety.[146] However, the solvent sureties will then have a right to prove in the insolvent surety's liquidation for the extra burden they have been forced to undertake.[147]

16.9.4.3 A claim for contribution should be made by joining each of the sureties and the debtor to the action, except in the case of a surety which is clearly insolvent.[148]

16.9.5 Discontinuance

A guarantor under a continuing guarantee of an uncommitted facility, such as an overdraft facility, has a right to determine its on-going liability by serving a notice of discontinuance or revocation upon the creditor.[149] This is because the consideration is not entire, as the creditor is not obliged at any time to extend further credit to the debtor and it may increase or decrease the facility it has given to the debtor or refuse to make further credit available. In effect, consideration for the continued applicability of the guarantee to further advances and credit is provided each time the creditor makes an advance or extends other credit to the debtor on the faith of the guarantee.[150]

---

[143] *Hampton v Minns* [2002] 1 WLR 1, in which it was held that the usual presumption would apply even though the two guarantors held unequal proportions of the share capital of the debtor company.

[144] *Berridge v Berridge* (1890) 44 ChD 168.

[145] *Ellesmere Brewery Co v Cooper* [1896] 1 QB 75.

[146] *Lowe v Dixon* (1885) 16 QBD 455.

[147] The difficulty of determining the situation where more than one, or indeed all, of the sureties is insolvent is demonstrated by *Brown v Cork* [1986] PCC 78.

[148] *Hey v Carter* [1935] Ch 397.

[149] In the absence of a stipulation in the guarantee dealing with the matter, it is not clear as to who should serve the notice in the case of guarantors who are jointly or jointly and severally liable under the guarantee. It may be that all of them should give notice if they all wish to be relieved of their continuing liability, as it is arguable that the service of a notice by only one guarantor will not determine the liability of the other guarantors. This is by analogy to a case where the creditor received notice of the death of one co-surety (which relieved his estate of continuing liability) but that did not affect the continuing liability of the other sureties: *Beckett v Addyman* (1882) 9 QBD 783. As to the effect of the creditor receiving notice of the death of a surety under a continuing guarantee, see para 16.10.4 below.

[150] *Coulthart v Clemenston* (1879) 5 QBD 42 and *Lloyds v Harper* (1880) 16 ChD 290. An alternative explanation is based on the inequity of holding the guarantor bound when the creditor has the liberty of deciding if it will extend further credit to the debtor: see James LJ in *Lloyds v Harper*, at 314.

The position is different if the creditor is obliged to the surety to continue making credit available under a committed facility, as where the guarantee is expressed as being given in consideration of the creditor agreeing to make the facility available to the debtor. In such a case, unless the guarantee provides to the contrary, the guarantor cannot determine its liability under the guarantee.[151] **16.9.5.1**

In the absence of a provision as to the length of the notice that should be given, the guarantor under a continuing guarantee may determine its liability at any time by giving notice to that effect to the creditor. If the guarantor does so, it will remain liable under the guarantee for the obligations of the debtor that were incurred up to the time the notice was given, but it will not be liable for any further liabilities of the debtor that were incurred after that date.[152] It has been said that where the guarantee prescribes a period of notice that must be given by the guarantor before the discontinuance will be effective, the guarantor will remain liable for any guaranteed liabilities incurred by the debtor to the creditor in the period before the expiration of the notice.[153] It has also been held that if there is a notice period in a case where the liability of the guarantor under the guarantee is dependent upon the making of a demand upon the guarantor, then the guarantor will be released entirely unless a demand has been made upon it prior to the expiration of the notice period.[154] As to the effect of a notice period generally, it is difficult to reconcile the finding that the guarantor remains liable with respect to further advances or credit provided to the debtor in the notice period with the fact that the creditor has no obligation to make the advances or extend the credit to the debtor in the notice period. The guarantor is entirely at the mercy of the creditor during the notice period, which appears to be rather inequitable. **16.9.5.2**

A guarantor which has served a notice of discontinuance on the creditor may be able to take advantage of the rule in *Clayton's* case[155] as to the extent of its residual liability upon the discontinuance becoming effective. As stated above, the guarantor will be liable for the guaranteed liabilities of the debtor that have accrued up to the date on which the discontinuance becomes effective. If those liabilities have been incurred by the debtor on a running account between it and the creditor, under which withdrawals are debited to the account and payments in are credited **16.9.5.3**

---

151 *Lloyd's v Harper* (1880) 16 ChD 290.

152 *Coulthart v Clementson* (1879) 5 QBD 42; *Silverburn Finance (UK) Ltd v Salt* [2001] EWCA Civ 279, [2001] 2 All ER (Comm) 438.

153 The point was debated but not finally determined by the Court of Appeal in *Lloyd's v Harper* (1880) 16 ChD 290. The Court of Appeal in *National Westminster Bank PLC v Hardman* [1988] FLR 302 treated the notice period as effective, subject to the point as to the making of a demand upon the guarantor.

154 *National Westminster Bank PLC v Hardman* [1988] FLR 302, but this would appear to be contrary to *Bank of Credit and Commerce International SA v Simjee* [1997] CLC 135.

155 *Devaynes v Noble, Clayton's Case* (1816) 8 LJ Ch 256, 35 ER 767.

to the account (such as would be the case in relation to an overdraft facility maintained on a current account) then, in the absence of any appropriation by the debtor as to the way in which credits should be dealt with, the credits will be treated as paying off (in historical order) the remaining guaranteed liabilities of the debtor so that, eventually, all those liabilities will be treated as paid off. This will be the case notwithstanding that the debtor may have been incurring new liabilities to the creditor after the date of the discontinuance and that the overall debit balance on the account may have remained unchanged or even increased.

16.9.5.4 To overcome the problem which arises by the application of *Clayton*'s case, upon the discontinuance becoming effective, the creditor should rule off the old account that it maintains for the debtor which is covered by the guarantee and open a new account for the debtor, upon which all further transactions should take place. The effect of this is that the guaranteed debit balance on the old account will remain and will not be treated as reduced by the application of the rule in *Clayton*'s case.[156] Well drawn forms of guarantee usually provide for such procedures to be followed.

16.10 Discharge of the Guarantor

16.10.1 There are a number of grounds at common law on which the liability of a guarantor under a guarantee may be discharged or reduced. The grounds include the following, which concern the consequences of the payment or discharge by the debtor or the guarantor of the guaranteed liabilities, the determination of continuing guarantees, the invalidity of the debtor's purported obligations to the creditor, changes in the identity of the debtor or the guarantor, and conduct by the creditor which is adverse to the rights and interest of the guarantor. A guarantor may also be discharged on equitable grounds that relate to the conduct of the creditor, which will be examined separately.

16.10.2 Performance by and discharge of the debtor

The guarantor is discharged if the debtor pays or otherwise performs or discharges its obligations in full to the creditor,[157] including where the debtor exercises a right of early termination so that the extent of its ultimate obligations are less than they would have been had it elected to continue with the underlying transaction.[158]

16.10.2.1 The usual example of performance by the debtor will be where the debtor actually pays the creditor but payment could also arise by virtue of a set-off between

---

[156] *Re Sherry* (1884) 25 ChD 692; *Westminster Bank Ltd v Cond* (1940) 46 Com.Cas 60.
[157] *Silverburn Finance (UK) Ltd v Salt* [2001] EWCA Civ 279, [2001] 2 All ER (Comm) 438.
[158] *Western Credit Ltd v Alberry* [1964] 1 WLR 945.

cross-claims as between the debtor and the creditor[159] as, for instance, in an insolvency of either the debtor or the creditor. Whether the debtor has performed and discharged its obligations will depend upon the terms of the contract between the debtor and the creditor and if the method of payment effects a full discharge of the debtor's obligations. If the debtor owes obligations to the creditor on more than one account, only one of which is guaranteed, it will be a question of whether a payment by the debtor is appropriated to the guaranteed account. In the absence of express agreement, that will depend upon the appropriation of the payment by the debtor or, failing that, of the creditor,[160] or, in the case of a running account where there has been no appropriation by the debtor or the creditor, by the application of the rule in *Clayton's* case.[161] In a winding up of the debtor, the dividend payable to the creditor must be applied rateably to all of the debts due by the debtor to the creditor. If the guarantor is insolvent and the creditor proves in the guarantor's bankruptcy or winding up, the creditor must give credit for any amounts it has received from the debtor in reduction of its indebtedness to the creditor if such amounts have been received prior to the date on which the creditor lodges its proof.[162]

16.10.3 Payment by the guarantor

Payment by the guarantor will discharge the guarantor to the extent of the payment.[163] At general law and outside the context of an insolvency of the debtor, such a payment will also have the effect of discharging the debtor to the extent of the payment.[164] To overcome that consequence in a situation where the guarantee is limited or the creditor has been unable for some other reason to recover the whole indebtedness in full, many forms of guarantee contain a provision which entitles the creditor to place any payment received from the guarantor in a suspense account pending receipt by it of the full debt. Whilst held in suspense, the

---

[159] *Hyundai Shipbuilding and Heavy Industries Co Ltd v Pournaras* [1978] 2 Lloyd's Rep 502; *Aurora Borealis Compania Armadora SA v Marine Midland Bank NA, The Maistros* [1984] 1 Lloyd's Rep 646. However, the guarantee can overcome this by requiring the guarantor to pay the creditor in full irrespective of counterclaims and claims to set-off as between the creditor and the debtor: *Hyundai Shipbuilding and Heavy Industries Co Ltd v Pournaras, Hyundai Heavy Industries Co Ltd v Papadopoulos* [1979] 1 Lloyd's Rep 130 (CA) (approved [1980] 1 WLR 1129 (HL)). In addition, it has been held that a guarantor which has given the creditor a mortgage cannot resist enforcement of the mortgage on a failure of the debtor to pay the principal debt on the ground that the debtor has a larger cross-claim for unliquidated damages against the creditor: *National Westminster Bank PLC v Skelton* [1993] 1 All ER 242; *Ashley Guarantee PLC v Zacaria* [1993] 1 WLR 62.

[160] *Kinnaird v Webster* (1878) 10 ChD 139.

[161] *Devaynes v Noble, Clayton's Case* (1816) 8 LJ Ch 256, 35 ER 767.

[162] *Re Blakeley* (1892) 9 Morr 173; *Re Houlder* [1929] 1 Ch 205.

[163] Even if the payment is funded by a loan from the creditor to the guarantor: *Brown Shipley & Co Ltd v Amalgamated Investment (Europe) BV* [1979] 1 Lloyd's Rep 488.

[164] Although as between the guarantor, on the one hand, and the debtor and co-sureties, on the other hand, the payment does not have that effect: s 5 of the Mercantile Law Amendment Act 1856.

payment is not treated as being applied in reduction of the debtor's liability, which has the effect of allowing the creditor to pursue the debtor and any other co-surety for the full amount of the debt, so as to maximise the chances of recovering what is due to it.[165] Such a provision, however, will be ineffective in the winding up of the guarantor, and the payment will have to be brought into the account as between the two of them.

16.10.3.1　As previously explained, in the insolvency of the debtor, a partial payment by the guarantor under the guarantee is not treated as payment by the debtor until the guarantor has paid the full amount for which it is liable.[166] In consequence, the creditor retains its right to prove in the insolvency of the debtor for the whole amount of the guaranteed debt. However, if only part of the debt has been guaranteed then the guarantor will be entitled to prove in the debtor's insolvency once it has met the whole of its obligations under the guarantee, unless the guarantor has agreed otherwise, such as by use of the suspense account wording referred to above.[167]

16.10.4　Determination of the guarantee

The position as to a guarantor's right to serve notice discontinuing its liability under a continuing guarantee has already been mentioned. The death or insanity of the guarantor does not, of itself, operate to determine a guarantee. However, a continuing guarantee of an uncommitted facility will be determined as regards new liabilities undertaken by the debtor from the time when the creditor received notice of the death[168] or insanity.[169] The making of a winding-up order or a bankruptcy order against the guarantor will also have the practical effect of limiting a continuing guarantee of an uncommitted facility, because the creditor will only have a right to prove in the guarantor's liquidation or bankruptcy for the actual or contingent liabilities of the guarantor that had been incurred prior to the date on which the guarantor went into liquidation or commenced bankruptcy.[170] It is also possible, with respect to both guarantees of specific obligations and continuing

---

[165] *Commercial Bank of Australia v Official Assignee of the Estate of Wilson* [1893] AC 181.

[166] However, if the obligation of the guarantor is expressed to be that of a primary or principal debtor, it would appear that the payment would have the effect of reducing the indebtedness of the real debtor, because the real debtor and the guarantor are treated as being joint debtors for the same debt: *MS Fashions Ltd v Bank of Credit and Commerce International SA* [1993] Ch 425 (Hoffmann LJ sitting at first instance), sub nom *MS Fashions Ltd v Bank of Credit and Commerce International SA (No 2)* [1993] 3 All ER 769 (CA).

[167] The point being to prevent the surety competing with the creditor in extracting as much as possible by way of dividend in the debtor's insolvency.

[168] *Bradbury v Morgan* (1862) 1 H&C 249.

[169] *Bradford Old Bank Ltd v Sutcliffe* [1918] 2 KB 833.

[170] See Rule 13.12 of the Insolvency Rules 1986 as to the debts that are provable in a winding up and s 382 of the Insolvency Act 1986 for the debts that are provable in a bankruptcy.

guarantees, that a liquidator or trustee in bankruptcy of a guarantor might seek to disclaim the obligations of the guarantor under, respectively, sections 178 and 315 of the Insolvency Act 1986, on the basis that the guarantee constitutes an unprofitable contract.[171]

16.10.5 Invalidity of the underlying obligations

It has already been mentioned that, by virtue of the nature of a guarantee, the invalidity of the debtor's purported obligations or the discharge by operation of law of the debtor's liabilities will result in a commensurate discharge of (or lack of coverage by) the guarantee. There are, however, various qualifications that must be made to that statement. As previously discussed, a suretyship by way of indemnity or independent primary obligation may survive the unenforceability or discharge of the debtor's obligations. Section 2 of the Minors Contracts Act 1987 overcomes the problem where a guarantee is given of the unenforceable obligations of a minor (that is, which are treated as unenforceable because of the debtor's minority).[172] Generally speaking, the insolvency of the debtor should not affect the liability of the guarantor to the creditor. Furthermore, it is specifically provided that the discharge of a bankrupt does not affect the liability of a surety for the bankrupt's debts.[173] There are savings for the liabilities of third parties, such as guarantors, where a liquidator or trustee disclaims the obligations of a debtor in liquidation or bankruptcy.[174] There are, however, particular difficulties with respect to a guarantee of interest expressed to be payable by an insolvent debtor.[175]

16.10.6 Changes in identity

Changes in the identity of the debtor or the creditor will, in general, mean that a guarantee will not apply to liabilities incurred by the debtor after the date of the change, in the absence of agreement[176] to the contrary[177] or an Act of Parliament which provides for the guarantee to apply to such liabilities.[178] For instance,

---

[171] The meaning of an 'unprofitable contract' was discussed in *Re SSSL Realisations (2002) Ltd* [2004] EWHC 1760 (Ch), [2005] 1 BCLC 1 (Lloyd J), sub nom *Manning & Ors (Liquidators of SSSL Realisations (2002) Ltd) v AIG Europe (UK) Ltd* [2006] EWCA Civ 7, [2006] Ch 610 (CA).

[172] Thereby reversing the effect of the decision in *Coutts & Co v Browne-Lecky* [1947] KB 104.

[173] S 281(7) of the Insolvency Act 1986.

[174] Ss 178(4) and 315(3) of the Insolvency Act 1986. See *Hindcastle Ltd v Barbara Attenborough Associates Ltd* [1997] AC 70 and *Scottish Widows PLC v Tripipatkul* [2003] EWHC 1874 (Ch), [2004] BCC 200.

[175] See para 16.2.2 above.

[176] Usually to be found in a well drawn guarantee, but it could be covered by agreement at the time the change occurs, provided such a contemporaneous agreement is supported by consideration or is made by way of deed.

[177] *First National Finance Corp Ltd v Goodman* [1983] BCLC 203.

[178] Note, however, the conflict of laws issue that arises where the guarantee is not governed by English law. It is a matter for the governing law to determine the circumstances in which a guarantee

a guarantee of the liabilities of an individual will not cover liabilities incurred by him on behalf of a partnership of which he later became a member,[179] and a continuing guarantee of the liabilities of a partnership will not apply to liabilities incurred after there has been a change in the composition of the partnership.[180] A guarantee of the liabilities of a named individual or company will not cover the debts of a related company nor a company to which the debtor's business is transferred on a reconstruction or amalgamation.[181] A change in the identity of the creditor (for instance, on an amalgamation or merger of the creditor with another entity) means that a continuing guarantee will not apply to future liabilities incurred by the debtor.[182] On the other hand, a change in the shareholding, control, or name of a debtor or creditor company should not affect the liability of the guarantor.[183]

16.11 Equitable Grounds for Discharge of a Guarantor

16.11.1   Before embarking upon a discussion of the equitable grounds upon which the conduct of the creditor may adversely affect its claim against a guarantor, it is important to make the point that, in the absence of an agreement with the guarantor to the contrary, the creditor is under no obligation to the guarantor to take action against the debtor or to enforce the security it holds; nor is it under any duty as to the order in which it enforces any particular elements of its security. That is the case even if it is foreseeable that a loss might be suffered because of a delay in realising security in a falling market.[184]

16.11.1.1   However, once the creditor takes action to enforce security, the creditor[185] is obliged to achieve a proper price[186] on the realisation of the security. If it fails to

---

would be discharged (see Art 10 of the Rome Convention and, at common law, *Wight v Eckhardt Marine GmbH* [2003] UKPC 37, [2004] 1 AC 147), so an Act of the UK Parliament on such a matter may be ineffective if the governing law is not English law.

179   *Leatherley v Spyer* (1870) LR 5 CP 595.

180   S 18 of the Partnership Act 1890.

181   *First National Finance Corp Ltd v Goodman* [1983] BCLC 203. See, however, Part VII of the Financial Services and Markets Act 2000.

182   *First National Finance Corp Ltd v Goodman* [1983] BCLC 203. For instance, if the creditor is a partnership, a continuing guarantee will not cover liabilities incurred by the debtor after a change in the composition of the partners: s 18 of the Partnership Act 1890. For partnerships and other types of entity see, however, Part VII of the Financial Services and Markets Act 2000.

183   *First National Finance Corp Ltd v Goodman* [1983] BCLC 203.

184   *China and South Sea Bank Ltd v Tan* [1990] 1 AC 536, in which it was said that the relationship between the creditor and guarantor is purely equitable and that the creditor does not owe a duty of care at common law to the guarantor. See also the discussion in *Silven Properties Ltd v Royal Bank of Scotland plc* [2003] EWCA Civ 1409, [2004] 1 WLR 997.

185   And a receiver appointed by it: *Burgess v Auger* [1998] 2 BCLC 478; *Cohen v TSB PLC* [2002] 2 BCLC 32.

186   That is, the true market value: *Skipton Building Society v Stott* [2001] QB 261.

do so then the guarantor is entitled to a *pro tanto* reduction in its liability under the guarantee to reflect the loss that it suffers in consequence of the creditor's failure.[187] This reflects the position as between a mortgagee or a receiver appointed by it and the mortgagor.[188] On the same basis, the creditor (and a receiver appointed by it) has a duty to the guarantor to act in good faith in the manner in which it enforces its security[189] and in its management of the security once in possession and pending its realisation.[190] It has been said that a guarantor should only be entitled to the benefit of such duties if it has a realistic interest in the equity of redemption in the security. A guarantor would not have such an interest in circumstances where it had made no payment to the creditor, the claim of the creditor against the guarantor was statute barred, and there was no evidence that a sale at a proper value would have left any surplus for the benefit of the guarantor.[191]

16.11.2 Conduct of the creditor

Subject to what is said at 16.11.1 and to the effect of a saving provision as mentioned at 16.12, a guarantee may be discharged, or the guarantor's liability may be reduced, on equitable principles[192] as a result of conduct by the creditor that is adverse to the guarantor's interests. This is in addition to the grounds for discharge that may arise at common law, as previously stated. Such conduct relates to situations where the creditor varies the time for payment by the debtor or releases the debtor, or, to the prejudice of the guarantor in the exercise of its rights to indemnification by and recovery from the debtor, otherwise varies the agreement between the creditor and the debtor, or where the creditor prejudices the guarantor's rights to be subrogated to the rights of the creditor against the debtor and to security that the creditor holds or to contribution from co-sureties. In some cases, the guarantor will be wholly discharged by such conduct, whilst in other cases its liability will be reduced *pro tanto* to the loss it has suffered as a consequence of what has occurred. These matters will now be examined.

16.11.3 Releases of the debtor and giving time for payment

A binding and unconditional release by the creditor of the debtor will have the effect of wholly releasing the guarantor.[193] In addition, where the creditor agrees

---

[187] *Skipton Building Society v Stott* [2001] QB 261; *Barclays Bank PLC v Kingston* [2006] EWHC 533 (QB), [2006] 2 Lloyd's Rep 59.

[188] *Cuckmere Brick Co Ltd v Mutual Finance Ltd* [1971] Ch 949 and *Silven Properties Ltd v Royal Bank of Scotland plc* [2003] EWCA Civ 1409, [2004] 1 WLR 997, where it was held that a receiver was under a similar duty to the mortgagor as that owed by the mortgagee.

[189] *Downsview Nominees Ltd v First City Corp* [1993] AC 295.

[190] *Medforth v Blake* [2000] Ch 96.

[191] *Burgess v Auger* [1998] 2 BCLC 478.

[192] *China and South Sea Bank Ltd v Tan* [1990] 1 AC 536.

[193] *Mahant Singh v U Ba Yi* [1939] AC 601, at 606–607.

with the debtor to vary the time for payment of the debtor's obligations, that will wholly release the guarantor.[194] This covers both the giving of extra time to the debtor[195] and an agreement to accelerate the date for payment by the debtor,[196] and the principle will apply even if, in fact, the guarantor suffers no detriment.[197]

16.11.3.1   On the other hand, the guarantor will remain bound if there is no binding agreement between the creditor and the debtor to give the debtor extra time to pay,[198] if the creditor simply delays in enforcing payment or security it holds,[199] if the debtor decides of its own volition to tender early payment of part of the indebtedness,[200] or where the creditor terminates the contract between it and the debtor because of the latter's wrongful repudiation of the contract.[201] In addition, where there is a continuing guarantee which relates to a series of separate obligations of the debtor, a variation in the time for payment by the debtor with respect to one such obligation will not affect the liability of the guarantor for the other guaranteed obligations of the debtor.[202] The same conclusion should follow with respect to a continuing guarantee in the case of a release of one such obligation of the debtor.

16.11.3.2   The guarantor will remain bound, however, if the creditor merely agrees not to sue the debtor or to give it time whilst reserving, either expressly or impliedly,[203] its rights against the guarantor, whether or not the guarantor is aware of, or has consented to, the reservation.[204]

---

[194] Including in consequence of a composition achieved by a voluntary arrangement between the debtor and its creditors, to which the creditor is bound: see Chadwick LJ in *Johnson v Davies* [1999] Ch 117. Subject to using appropriate wording, the effectiveness of provisions in a guarantee which are designed to preserve the liability of the guarantor in such a situation can be gauged by the approach taken in *Lombard Natwest Factors Ltd v Koutrouzas* [2002] EWHC 1084 (QB), [2003] BPIR 444, where a surety remained bound because of protective wording in the guarantee despite an individual voluntary arrangement which effected a modification of the obligations of a co-surety. An obligation upon the creditor, within the voluntary arrangement, that the creditor will not call a guarantee which covers the debtor's obligations is *prima facie* enforceable by the debtor, but, depending upon the facts, the creditor may be entitled to challenge the arrangement as being unfairly prejudicial to the creditor: *Prudential Assurance Co Ltd v PRG Powerhouse Ltd* [2007] EWHC 1002 (Ch).

[195] *Polak v Everett* (1876) 1 QB 669; *Rouse v Bradford Banking Co Ltd* [1894] AC 586.

[196] *ST Microelectronics NV v Condor Insurance Ltd* [2006] EWHC 977 (Comm), [2006] 2 Lloyd's Rep 525.

[197] *Polak v Everett* (1876) 1 QB 669.

[198] *Clarke v Birley* (1889) 41 ChD 422.

[199] *Carter v White* (1883) 25 ChD 666; *China and South Sea Bank Ltd v Tan* [1990] 1 AC 536.

[200] *ST Microelectronics NV v Condor Insurance Ltd* [2006] EWHC 977 (Comm), [2006] 2 Lloyd's Rep 525.

[201] *Moschi v Lep Air Services Ltd* [1973] AC 331.

[202] *Bingham v Corbitt* (1864) 34 LJQB 37 and *Croydon Commercial Gas Co v Dickinson* (1876) 2 CPD 46. See also *Bank of Baroda v Patel* [1996] 1 Lloyd's Rep 391.

[203] *Finley v Connell Associates* [1999] Lloyd's Rep PN 895.

[204] *Kearsley v Cole* (1846) 16 M&W 128; *Bateson v Gosling* (1871) LR 7 CP 9; *Cole v Lynn* [1942] 1 KB 142; *Greene King PLC v Stanley* [2001] EWCA Civ 1966, [2001] BPIR 491.

16.11.4 Other dealings with the debtor

Dealings of this type include: an agreement to re-finance the debtor's obligations to the creditor;[205] an agreement to extend a facility at an increased rate of interest;[206] an agreement to consolidate the drawings under a loan facility which would then be subject to common interest periods;[207] where there was a guarantee of drawings on a particular account, the opening of a second account to which payments by the debtor were credited whilst the guarantee remained current;[208] and a variation of the permitted use of a property under a guaranteed lease.[209] The devil is in the detail, however, in attempting to discern whether the effect of a variation has been to release the debtor (or to change the time for payment), on the one hand, and other types of variation whose effect may be less drastic, on the other hand.

A variation of the underlying obligations under a specific contract between the debtor and the creditor that have been guaranteed will have the effect that the guarantor will be released from the guarantee unless the guarantor has consented to the variation,[210] or unless it is self-evident that either the variation could only be beneficial to the surety or that its effect was insubstantial to the risk undertaken by the guarantor. The possible effect of the variation is to be judged objectively as at the time it occurred, and the mere possibility of detriment that is not insubstantial will lead to the discharge of the guarantor. A variation which might be beneficial or detrimental to the guarantor, depending upon the eventual outcome of the facts, will not escape the severity of the operation of the rule.[211] **16.11.4.1**

There are a number of qualifications that must be made to what has just been said. If the variation is not binding upon the creditor or is otherwise ineffective, the principle will not apply.[212] If the guarantee covers a number of separate and distinct contracts or obligations of the debtor and the variation only affects one such contract or obligation, the guarantor will remain liable under the guarantee with **16.11.4.2**

---

[205] *Marubeni Hong Kong & South China Ltd v The Mongolian Government* [2004] EWHC 472 (Comm), [2004] 2 Lloyd's Rep 198 (affd [2005] EWCA Civ 395, [2005] 1 WLR 2497) and *Triodos Bank NV v Dobbs* [2005] EWCA Civ 630, [2005] 2 Lloyd's Rep 588.

[206] *Burnes v Trade Credits Ltd* [1981] 1 WLR 805.

[207] *Credit Suisse v Allerdale Borough Council* [1995] 1 Lloyd's Rep 315 (affd [1997] QB 306), but it was found that the guarantor had consented to the variation.

[208] *National Bank of Nigeria Ltd v Awolesi* [1964] 1 WLR 1311. The position would have been different if the guarantor had served notice of discontinuance prior to the opening of the second account: see para 16.9.5 above.

[209] *Howard de Walden Estates Ltd v Pasta Place Ltd* [1995] 1 EGLR 77.

[210] Which may be done prospectively in the guarantee or at the time of the variation.

[211] *Holme v Brunskill* (1878) 3 QBD 495, which was the subject of a lengthy examination by Cresswell J in *Marubeni Hong Kong & South China Ltd v The Mongolian Government* [2004] EWHC 472 (Comm), [2004] 2 Lloyd's Rep 198 (affd [2005] EWCA Civ 395, [2005] 1 WLR 2497).

[212] *Egbert v National Crown Bank* [1918] AC 903.

respect to the contracts or obligations that were not varied.[213] Similarly, if the guarantee does not relate to specific contracts or obligations of the debtor but more generally to its obligations from time to time or to some more generally described course of dealing between the debtor and the creditor, the guarantor will remain liable despite a variation in a contract between the debtor and the creditor provided, in a situation concerning a course of dealings, that the guaranteed liabilities fall within the course of dealings.[214]

16.11.5 Default by the creditor

A similar approach will be taken where the creditor fails to perform the contract between it and the debtor, if that contract is the subject of the guarantee,[215] or if the creditor breaches a requirement of the guarantee. The guarantor will be discharged from its liability under the guarantee, unless the guarantor has consented to what has occurred or unless it is self-evident that either the failure or breach could only be beneficial to the guarantor or that its effect was insubstantial to the risk undertaken by the guarantor.[216] However, if the guarantee does not relate specifically to the contract between the debtor and the creditor that has been breached, as where the contract simply falls within an overall guaranteed course of dealing, or if the guarantee is of all the debtor's liabilities from time to time, without distinguishing in any particular way between them, a breach by the creditor of a contract between it and the debtor will not have the effect of releasing the guarantor, unless the breach is so serious as to amount to a repudiatory breach of contract.[217]

16.11.6 Loss of rights of subrogation

As previously explained, on payment of the guaranteed debt, the guarantor is entitled to be subrogated to the benefit of any security that has been taken by the creditor from the debtor or from co-sureties[218] and to have the benefit of the security transferred to it, whether such security was in existence at the time the guarantee was given or was taken subsequently. The creditor is required to hand over the security in the condition that it was originally taken by the creditor and on the basis that the creditor has done all that was necessary to perfect the validity of the

---

213 *Skillett v Fletcher* (1867) LR 2 CP 469; *Croydon Commercial Gas Co v Dickinson* (1876) 2 CPD 46; and *Midland Motor Showrooms Ltd v Newman* [1929] 2 KB 256.

214 *Egbert v National Crown Bank* [1918] AC 903.

215 As in *Watts v Shuttleworth* (1861) 7 H&N 353.

216 *Holme v Brunskill* (1878) 3 QBD 495; *Egbert v National Crown Bank* [1918] AC 903.

217 *National Westminster Bank PLC v Riley* [1986] BCLC 268 (where the bank wrongfully dishonoured two direct debits on the debtor's account, there being an all moneys guarantee); *Wardens etc of Mercers of the City of London v New Hampshire Insurance Co Ltd* [1992] 1 WLR 792.

218 *Duncan, Fox & Co v North and South Wales Bank* (1880) 6 App Cas 1, *Smith v Wood* [1929] 1 Ch 14.

security.[219] The guarantor will be discharged, either in whole or in part, if those requirements are not met,[220] unless the guarantor has given its consent to what has (or has not) occurred.[221]

What is not clear is the extent to which the guarantor is discharged in such cir- cumstances.[222] The position appears to be that if the grant of the security was a requirement of the contract between the creditor and the debtor or was a condition of the guarantee then a discharge or alteration in the security or a failure to take or perfect it without the guarantor's consent will lead to the discharge of the guarantor in full. In other circumstances, the impugned action or omission by the creditor will lead to a reduction in the guarantor's liability, which will be *pro tanto* to the loss in the value of the security occasioned by the creditor's action or omission.[223]

16.11.7 Release of co-sureties

The release of a co-surety without the guarantor's consent will lead to a discharge of the guarantor or to a *pro tanto* reduction in the liability of the guarantor, depending upon the circumstances. However, there will be no such discharge if, when giving the release, the creditor reserved its remedies against the guarantor or if it merely covenanted not to sue the co-surety[224] or gave it time to pay.[225] Subject to that qualification, if the guarantor is bound either jointly[226] or jointly and severally[227] with the co-surety then the release of the co-surety will have the effect of discharging the guarantor in full.[228] Where the guarantor is only severally bound[229] and there was no such condition to its giving the guarantee, a release of a co-surety will only affect the liability of the guarantor to the extent that the guarantor's right of contribution from such co-surety is affected.[230] In addition, and as previously discussed, if it is a condition of the guarantor executing the guarantee that another

---

[219] But the creditor will not be responsible for a decline in the value of the security and has no duty to preserve that value: *China and South Sea Bank Ltd v Tan* [1990] 1 AC 536.

[220] For instance, because the creditor has released the security, in whole or in part.

[221] *Wulff v Jay* (1872) LR 7 QB 756; *China and South Sea Bank Ltd v Tan* [1990] 1 AC 536.

[222] *Skipton Building Society v Stott* [2001] QB 261.

[223] *Carter v White* [1884] 25 ChD 666; *Taylor v Bank of New South Wales* (1886) 11 App Cas 596; *Skipton Building Society v Stott* [2001] QB 261.

[224] *Commercial Bank of Australia v Wilson & Co's Estate* [1893] AC 181.

[225] *Kearsley v Cole* (1846) 16 M&W 128.

[226] That is, where the guarantors are only bound jointly so that all must be sued together.

[227] That is, where the guarantors agreed to be bound on a joint and several basis, so that each may be sued separately or jointly, at the option of the creditor. The distinction between joint and joint and several liability has been modified by s 3 of the Civil Liability (Contribution) Act 1978.

[228] *Ward v National Bank of New Zealand* (1883) 8 App Cas 755; *Mercantile Bank of Sydney v Taylor* [1893] AC 317.

[229] That is, as opposed to joint liability, so that it may be sued separately.

[230] *Ward v National Bank of New Zealand* (1883) 8 App Cas 755.

guarantor will also execute it or give a separate guarantee, and such condition is
not met, then the guarantor will not be liable.

16.12 Saving Provisions

16.12.1 Each of the equitable grounds for discharge of the guarantor, or for a reduction in
its liability, is subject to the agreement or consent of the guarantor that such matters will not have an adverse effect on the guarantor's liability. In consequence of
such an agreement or consent, the position of the creditor is preserved and thus its
right of recourse as against the guarantor remains, provided, of course, that the
wording of the agreement or consent covers the situation.[231] The agreement or
consent of the guarantor may be given at the time of the proposed action by the
creditor. Alternatively, and more usually, such an agreement or consent is likely to
be prospective and contained within the terms of the guarantee.[232]

16.12.2 At first blush, it might be thought that such provisions in a guarantee would be
susceptible to challenge under sections 2 and 3 of the Unfair Contract Terms Act
1977. It is submitted, however, that those sections would not apply to savings
provisions which have the effect of negating the equitable protections that otherwise would protect a guarantor. Sections 2 and 3 of the Act concern attempts to
exclude or restrict liability for breach of common law duties and attempts to evade
or modify a contractual obligation that would otherwise be owed. The creditor
does not commit such a breach or evade its common law and contractual duties to
the guarantor in the situations now under discussion. The protections in favour of
the guarantor arise in equity[233] and do not create corresponding duties at common law that are owed by the creditor to the surety.[234] The use of savings provisions simply overcomes the right of the guarantor to say that it has been released
from its own obligations, or that its liability has been reduced.[235]

---

231 *Perry v National Provincial Bank of England* [1910] 1 Ch 464. In this regard, the courts have
often found that the wording that has been used to protect the creditor does not cover the situation
which has occurred; see, for instance, *Barclays Bank PLC v Kingston* [2006] EWHC 533 (QB),
[2006] 2 Lloyd's Rep 59.

232 An example of such a prospective agreement in the context of the effect of a voluntary
arrangement between a debtor and its creditors will be found in *Prudential Assurance Co Ltd v PRG
Powerhouse Ltd* [2007] EWHC 1002 (Ch).

233 *Watts v Shuttleworth* (1860) 5 H&N 235; *China and South Sea Bank Ltd v Tan* [1990] 1
AC 536.

234 Ibid. In so far as the decision of the Court of Appeal in *Standard Chartered Bank v Walker*
[1982] 1 WLR 1410 decided that a creditor or mortgagee might owe duties in tort to the debtor or
the guarantor, that decision is inconsistent with the law as enunciated in *China and South Sea Bank
Ltd v Tan* and cannot stand: see *Silven Properties Ltd v Royal Bank of Scotland plc* [2003] EWCA Civ
1409, [2004] 1 WLR 997.

235 See the discussion, as to s 3 of the 1977 Act, in *Governor & Co of the Bank of Scotland v Singh*
(unreported 17/6/2005, HHJ Kershaw QC sitting in the High Court in Manchester). If the relevant

Nonetheless, there is a limit as to the scope and effectiveness of provisions in a **16.12.3**
guarantee which purport prospectively to preserve the guarantor's liability notwithstanding a variation in the terms of the agreement between the creditor and
the debtor. Where the creditor seeks to rely on such a provision, it will only be
effective, and so the surety will only remain liable, if the underlying contract as
varied 'remains a contract within the purview of the original guarantee'.[236] A new
agreement between the creditor and the debtor which truly 'replaced' the original
agreement, in the sense that it was a different agreement and covered additional
matters to those covered under the original agreement, would not be considered
to be a protected variation of the original agreement. Two points follow from
this.[237] First, it is necessary to distinguish between a true variation of an existing
obligation, on the one hand, and, on the other, entering into what is in fact a different obligation even though it may purport to be no more than a variation. That
may be a difficult task and will depend upon the facts of the case, so it is not possible to draw a hard and fast line, but a court is likely to take a fairly conservative
approach. Secondly, if it is provided as a condition of the power to vary that the
guarantor should not be liable, following a variation, for a greater sum than would
have been the position had there been no variation, that might justify a wider
construction of the power to vary than might otherwise be permitted.[238]

---

provision goes further and does seek to excuse the creditor from its contractual obligations towards
the surety then ss 2 and 3 of the Act may apply.

[236] See Longmore LJ in *Triodos Bank NV v Dobbs* [2005] EWCA Civ 630, [2005] 2 Lloyd's Rep
588, applying a test propounded in Rowlat, *Law of Principal and Surety* (5th edn, 1999 at para 4-72)
which repeated the test as contained in an earlier edition of that work, which had been approved by
Lord Atkin in *Trade Indemnity Co Ltd v Workington Harbour and Dock Board* [1937] AC 1, at 21
and had been applied by Bingham J in *Polaris Steamship Co SA v A Tarricone Inc, The Nefeli* [1986] 1
Lloyd's Rep 339 and by Cresswell J in *Melvin v Poseidon, The Kalma* (unreported 18/6/1999).

[237] As outlined by Longmore LJ in *Triodos Bank NV v Dobbs* [2005] EWCA Civ 630, [2005] 2
Lloyd's Rep 588.

[238] Which might provide an explanation for the result on the facts in *British Motor Trust Co
Ltd v Hyams* (1934) 50 TLR 230, although the reasoning of Branson J in that case was doubted by
Longmore LJ in *Triodos Bank NV v Dobbs* [2005] EWCA Civ 630, [2005] 2 Lloyd's Rep 588.

17

THE REFORM OF THE ENGLISH LAW OF SECURED TRANSACTIONS

17.1 Introduction

There have been various suggestions since the early 1970s that English law concerning secured transactions should be reviewed and reformed, commencing with the recommendations made in the Crowther Committee Report in 1971.[1] The Companies Act 1989 made provision for some limited amendments and modifications to be made to the system for the registration of company charges but those amendments were never brought into force and will lapse in consequence of the Companies Act 2006. The late Professor Aubrey Diamond also made suggestions for reform of the law in 1989.[2] The Final Report of the Company Law Review Steering Group made some preliminary proposals for reform but also

17.1.1

---

[1] See Parts IV and V of the *Report of the Committee on Consumer Credit*, CMND 4596.
[2] AL Diamond, *A Review of Security Interests in Property* (1989, HMSO, London).

recommended that further work should be carried out.[3] To that end, the Law Commission published a *Consultation Paper* in 2002,[4] which was followed by a *Consultative Report* in 2004[5] and, in the end, by a *Final Report* in 2005.[6] The latter contained the Law Commission's considered proposals for reform of the law concerning transactions involving corporate security and sales of receivables. Although the last of those documents was stated to be a final report, the Law Commission did envisage that it might conduct further work in areas where it had not recommended reform in its report, as will be referred to further below. One significant area that was left out of the Law Commission's recommendations concerned secured transactions involving individuals, which would have to await consideration at a later date.

17.1.2 The Law Commission's proposals were put forward on the assumption that the legislation to implement the reforms would be formulated in regulations that would be made under powers that would be contained in what was to become the Companies Act 2006. Drafts of such regulations were prepared by the Law Commission. Although such powers were provided for in an initial draft of the legislation in its passage through Parliament, they were removed at an early stage, as support for substantial reform had disappeared. It now appears that the proposals may never be implemented. Nonetheless, they (and the Law Commission's earlier work) are worthy of consideration, because they are the most thoroughly documented attempts at making suggestions for the reform of English law in the field of secured transactions.

17.1.3 An important point that must be made initially is that the relevant subject matter for discussion is not confined just to secured transactions as understood in a narrow sense. It also extends to other forms of proprietary transaction (often referred to as 'quasi-security'), particularly those entered into as a method of financing or granting credit, which have similar consequences to a secured transaction but which the law has hitherto considered as not being by way of security. In a practical sense, there is a large degree of overlap in the economic effect, as well as in the nature and characteristics, that such transactions have as between themselves and with secured transactions. In addition, there may sometimes be a conflict between different interests claiming under them. It would not be sensible to undertake a review of the law without taking such transactions into account.

---

[3] See Chap 12 of *Modern Company Law for a Competitive Economy: Final Report* (2001 URN 01/942).

[4] *Registration of Security Interests: Company Charges and Property other than Land*, Consultation Paper No 164 (July 2002, TSO, London).

[5] *Company Security Interests, a Consultative Report*, Consultation Paper No 176 (August 2004, TSO, London).

[6] *Company Security Interests: Final Report*, Law Com No 296 (August 2005, Cm 6654, TSO, London). Copies of the three documents published by the Law Commission are available at its website: <http://www.lawcom.gov.uk>.

The plan of this chapter is to begin by examining the case for reform and then to describe the proposals that were originally envisaged by the Law Commission, as well as the recommendations contained in its *Final Report*.[7] The chapter will end with some concluding remarks on the benefit of having a new system in this area of the law.

17.1.4

17.2 Examining the Case for Reform

English law concerning secured transactions and other similar transactions has been built up over the centuries. It is largely based on case law, with some statutory intervention, particularly in relation to the imposition of requirements for the registration of certain types of security and as to the effect of insolvency on transactions. The Law of Property Act 1925 (and the Land Registration Act 2002 and its predecessor legislation) also plays an important role concerning land law and in relation to matters such as assignments of choses in action, tacking of further advances, and the enforcement of security. The law also reflects the division between legal and equitable interests and the different approaches that are taken at law and in equity in relation to the creation and the consequences of proprietary transactions.

17.2.1

Given its background and the way it has developed, the law in this area is of a somewhat piecemeal nature. It lacks a coherent and uniform set of rules, which leads to complexity and the fact that different results may follow depending upon matters such as the form and characterisation of a transaction (rather than its practical or economic substance), the type of assets and interests that may be involved in the transaction, and the number of parties who may assert an entitlement in those assets or interests or be affected by the transaction.

17.2.2

The piecemeal nature of the law in this area is not a good reason to change the law, however, if it works satisfactorily in practice and if it can be understood and applied without giving rise to injustice or unpredictable consequences. Because of the inherent difficulty of the subject matter and the number of different people who might be interested in the outcome of one or more sets of transactions, any system of law in this area is bound to be complex. There must always be a risk that changing an established system, particularly by way of radical reform,

17.2.3

---

[7] Due to the size of the subject, this chapter will not deal with the conflict of laws issues that may arise in some secured transactions with a cross-border element. The Law Commission did raise such issues in its *Consultation Paper* of 2002 (at paras 5.87–5.120) and in its *Consultative Report* of 2004 (at paras 3.343–3.363), as well as in a discussion paper that it prepared in October 2003. It eventually decided not to pursue them in any detail. Such issues will be relevant where there is a cross-border aspect to a transaction, such as where one or more of the parties to the granting of security is outside England, or the asset over which the security is to be taken is situated outside England.

may not necessarily lead to a more straightforward and simple set of rules, or mean that every aspect will be covered by a new system to the satisfaction of all concerned.

17.2.4 On the other hand, if the case for reform is made out then it would be unsatisfactory to leave things as they are simply because of a conservative reluctance to countenance change. One considerable advantage in considering the possibility of reform and how it might be implemented in English law is that other common law systems in North America and New Zealand have already paved the way and would appear successfully to have implemented comprehensive codes that function satisfactorily.

17.2.5 A useful way of deciding if there is a case for reform is to look at some of the difficulties and other complexities that arise under the present system. What follows will contain a brief review of some of the more obvious problems which can be seen in more detail in the discussion in other chapters in this book, particularly Chapter 14, which concerns secured transactions; Chapter 15, which concerns equipment financing; and Chapter 12, which concerns loan transfers and assignments of debts.

17.2.6 The review will begin with some general considerations concerning the multiplicity of interests in assets that may exist under English law. It will then discuss the difference between fixed and floating charges and the distinction that is drawn between transactions which fall to be treated as forms of security on the one hand, and other forms of proprietary transaction that may be entered into in the context of a financing but which are not considered to be by way of security. The review will then mention the rules for registration of security before moving to the priority rules which apply if there are competing interests in the same asset. The review will attempt to demonstrate that there is a good case for reform.

17.3 The Multiplicity of Interests and Forms of Transaction under English Law

17.3.1 One present difficulty concerns the multiplicity of interests and forms of transaction that may arise in secured and other forms of proprietary transaction. For instance, a transaction may take the form of a legal or equitable transfer or a legal or equitable mortgage or an equitable charge, which itself may be a fixed or a floating charge. In some situations, such as that relating to an unpaid vendor, a lien may arise by operation of law, with similar features to an equitable charge.[8]

---

[8] Note, however, the different position concerning an unpaid seller of goods under ss 41–43 of the Sale of Goods Act 1979.

It is also possible that a security transaction involving physical assets such as goods, **17.3.2**
their documents of title,[9] or documentary intangibles may take the form of a
pledge or a contractual lien, which are common law forms of security that depend
upon the creditor having 'possession'. Such possession may be constituted by
actual[10] or constructive[11] possession. Furthermore, a pledgee may release the
goods or their documents to the pledgor under the mechanism of a trust receipt,
without destroying the pledge.[12] However, an agreement to give possessory security runs the risk that it may be considered as an equitable charge with the consequence that it would be a registrable transaction.[13]

If the subject matter of the security is land then there is the further complexity that **17.3.3**
was introduced in the 1925 legislation. The legislation provided for the concept
of a charge, which historically was an equitable form of security, by way of legal
mortgage. It also allowed for the possibility of a succession of such securities.
Before 1925, it was not possible to have a series of successive legal interests existing
at the same time in the same asset, which essentially remains the case for assets
other than land.

If the subject matter of the security or transfer is only an equitable or beneficial **17.3.4**
interest then the form of the security or transfer can only be an equitable form.[14]
On the other hand, and subject to two qualifications, a transfer of, or security
over, a legal interest in existing property can be by way of either a legal transaction
or an equitable form of transfer or security. The first qualification is that a sale of
goods (as opposed to security created by a company over goods) is usually comprehended only at law, as the Sale of Goods Act 1979 provides a comprehensive
code for such transactions.[15] Secondly, the law cannot deal in a proprietary sense
with a transfer of only part of an asset (including by way of security), whereas
equity can understand that concept. In any event, future property can only be the
subject of an equitable proprietary transaction,[16] and if there has already been a
legal dealing with an asset then any further dealings by the original owner must be
equitable, subject as mentioned above in the case of real property.

---

9 *North Western Bank v Poynter* [1895] AC 56 and *Lloyds Bank Ltd v Bank of America National
Trust & Savings Association* [1938] 2 KB 147.
10 E.g. *Wrightson v McArthur* [1921] 2 KB 807.
11 E.g. where a person with possession attorns to the creditor. Such an attornment may even be by
the debtor itself: see *Martin v Reed* (1862) 11 CBNS 730; Willes J in *Meyerstein v Barber* (1866) LR 2
CP 38, at 52; and Lord Parker in *Dublin City Distillery Co Ltd v Doherty* [1914] AC 823, at 852.
12 See, for instance, *Lloyds Bank Ltd v Bank of America National Trust & Savings Association*
[1938] 2 KB 147.
13 *Dublin City Distillery Co Ltd v Doherty* [1914] AC 823.
14 With the possible exception of an assignment under s 136 of the Law of Property Act 1925,
where it may be possible to have an absolute assignment of a beneficial interest in a chose in action.
15 See Atkin LJ in *Re Wait* [1927] 1 Ch 606.
16 See Lord Macnaghten in *Tailby v The Official Receiver* (1888) 13 App Cas 523.

17.3.5 Generally speaking, legal forms of transaction will involve formalities that are not required in equity.[17] Nonetheless, value (in an equitable sense, i.e. real value and not just the nominal consideration to support a simple contract) may sometimes be required to support an equitable transaction[18] which should not be necessary in the case of a legal transaction.[19] In addition, the nature of the transaction may, sometimes but not always, be relevant in determining priorities if there are rival claimants competing to assert their respective interests in an asset.

17.3.6 Surely it would be far simpler to have one general form of security interest for all non-possessory security transactions and to clarify the position as to the requirements for possessory security.

17.4 Fixed v Floating Charges

17.4.1 Recent case law[20] has reinforced the distinction between fixed and floating security and the necessity for the security holder to have sufficient control of the assets within the security if it is successfully to assert that it holds fixed security. Pious labels and expressions of intention are insufficient; there must be actual control. Obtaining and keeping control may be impractical and the requirement for control may extend beyond the asset in its simple form. This is demonstrated by the problems in taking a fixed charge over book debts, because of the necessity for the chargee to control not just the debts in their uncollected state, but also the process of their collection and what happens to the proceeds of collection. It is not yet clear just how far the implications of this will extend, but there must now be a serious risk that in many situations the security that is taken will only qualify to be considered as a floating charge. The consequences to the security holder if it merely has a floating charge will concern matters such as priorities and the ranking of the entitlements in an insolvency of the chargor.

17.4.2 In terms of priorities, third party purchasers and others who acquire an interest, including by way of security, will rank ahead of the floating chargee if they dealt

---

[17] For instance, the formalities required by s 136 of the Law of Property Act 1925 in relation to absolute assignments that are recognised at law, as opposed to assignments in equity (see Lord Macnaghten in *William Brandt's Sons & Co v Dunlop Rubber Co Ltd* [1905] AC 454, at 461–462), but care should be taken that s 53(1)(c) of that Act is not overlooked if there is to be a disposition of an equitable interest.

[18] For instance, to support an assignment of future property (*Tailby v The Official Receiver* (1888) 13 App Cas 523) or an equitable charge (*Re Earl of Lucan, Hardinge v Cobden* (1890) 45 ChD 470).

[19] Care must be taken, however, in ensuring that the transaction may not be set aside under transaction avoidance provisions in the Insolvency Act 1986, if there has been no value or insufficient value.

[20] *Agnew v Inland Revenue Commissioner* [2001] UKPC 28, [2001] AC 710 and *National Westminster Bank PLC v Spectrum Plus Ltd* [2005] UKHL 41, [2005] 2 AC 680.

with the chargor in the ordinary course of business, which is a concept that has been given a wide definition by the courts. Attempting to prevent such transactions from taking place by the use of negative pledge provisions are unlikely to be of much use. On an insolvency of the chargor, the floating chargee will find itself ranking behind the claims of the liquidator for liquidation expenses and of the preferential creditors, and it will also suffer the indignity of watching as a proportion of the recoveries from its security are set aside for unsecured creditors pursuant to section 176A of the Insolvency Act 1986. A floating charge is also vulnerable in the first one or two years of its life to attack under section 245 of the Insolvency Act 1986, except for new value advanced on or after the granting of the charge.

There is a case for abolishing the distinction between fixed and floating security **17.4.3** and for providing, instead, for the specific circumstances in which third parties may safely acquire business assets. If the concept of the floating charge was abolished then it would be necessary to draft new provisions in place of the existing statutory provisions that apply to floating charges in an insolvency of the chargor, but that should not be an insuperable difficulty. For instance, it could be provided that new value was required to support security over the trading assets that were for business use (i.e. assets that were of a revolving or transitory nature, held for the purpose of consumption or sale in the business), and that liquidation expenses and preferential creditors would have a prior right in business assets in an insolvency. Provisions could also be drafted along similar lines to cover the situation that presently obtains under section 176A of the Insolvency Act 1986.

17.5 Security v Other Transactions, the Risk of Re-characterisation, and the Difficulties with Rights and Remedies

17.5.1 The distinction

There is a rather fine distinction that is made in English law between transactions by way of security and other transactions of a proprietary nature which, for practical and economic purposes, have much the same effect as a secured transaction but which the law treats as something other than a secured transaction.[21] The distinction applies, in particular, to finance or credit transactions that involve an assignment of debts or receivables[22] and title retention devices concerning goods, such as retention of title (ROT), conditional sale, hire purchase (HP), and finance leasing.

---

[21] Contrast the position with the accounting treatment of such transactions. See, for instance, SSAP 21, FRS 5, IAS 17, and IAS 39.

[22] Including assignments where the assignor remains at risk for any default by the debtors, through recourse arrangements.

None of them are treated as giving rise to security. In each of those cases, however, the finance or credit is extended to the recipient customer on the basis that the creditor will have proprietary protection by way of ownership of the relevant assets, which will put it ahead of the unsecured creditors of the customer if there should be a default or insolvency of the customer.

17.5.1.1 The distinction is particularly important when determining if the transaction may be registrable as a charge or as a security bill of sale.[23] Indeed, in the cases of an assignment of debts or receivables or of an ROT transaction, the assignment or transaction may have the substantive appearance of being a floating charge but, because it is not by way of security, it will not suffer from the disadvantages that are inherent in a floating charge.[24] That is rather anomalous.

17.5.1.2 The distinction may also have significance for priority and similar purposes; for instance, where a third party may seek to assert a derivative interest acquired in reliance upon the transaction, where a third party may mistakenly believe that it has taken security over assets which it turns out were not owned by the chargor or mortgagor, or where it is argued that the granting of security was in breach of a negative pledge.[25]

17.5.1.3 In policy terms, the fact that such financing transactions, although having much the same proprietary consequences as actual security, do not have to be registered means that those who conduct searches in the register of charges will not discover the true state of affairs and might erroneously believe that the entity with which they are dealing owns the assets that are in its apparent possession or control when that is not the case.

17.5.2 Characterisation

Generally speaking, the approach that the courts have taken in characterising transactions[26] to determine if they are by way of security or if they are some other

---

[23] However, just to confuse matters further, a general assignment of book debts by a trader who is an individual is registrable under s 344 of the Insolvency Act 1986, whether it is by way of security or an outright transfer by way of sale.

[24] Had the transaction in *Lloyds & Scottish Finance Ltd v Cyril Lord Carpet Sales Ltd* [1992] BCLC 609 been characterised as a charge, it would almost inevitably have been a floating charge, given the almost total lack of control the was exercised by the financier over the underlying pool of assigned debts. As it was found to be an absolute sale, there was no need for the control mechanisms that would have been necessary to establish a fixed charge.

[25] As in *Welsh Development Agency v Export Finance Co Ltd* [1992] BCLC 148.

[26] In the absence of an argument that the transaction was a sham, deliberately designed to cloak its true nature. See, for instance, *North Central Wagon Finance Co Ltd v Brailsford* [1962] 1 WLR 1288. Challenges on this basis are now rare in the field of financing transactions and unlikely to succeed, as they are tantamount to an allegation of a deliberate attempt to mislead. A fairly recent case involving sham transactions is *Kensington International Ltd v Republic of the Congo* [2005] EWHC 2684 (Comm), [2006] 2 BCLC 296.

type of transaction, has been to seek the true nature of the transaction as that contained in the contractual documentation. In doing so, the courts have tended to honour the form of the transaction as that of a sale of the relevant asset or as a supply of goods, being that which the parties expressed as their intention in the documentation, rather than giving weight to the economic and practical outcome or real substance of the transaction, as a method for the provision of secured finance.[27] The high water mark of this approach was reached by the Court of Appeal in *Welsh Development Agency v Export Finance Co Ltd*.[28] The court was strongly influenced by the expressed intention of the parties and the description that they gave to the transaction in the documentation. It held that the transaction was by way of a sale of goods, rather than as a form of financing secured on receivables generated by the customer's business, which was the real economic substance of what had been achieved. The approach taken by the Court of Appeal should be contrasted with the more pragmatic and realistic view that was taken by Sir Nicholas Browne-Wilkinson V-C at first instance, who held it to be a transaction by way of lending with security.[29]

There is a cloud on the horizon, however. The liberal approach to characterisation might now be subject to review in light of the stricter approach to that issue that has been in evidence in recent cases. In those cases, the judges have played down the importance of an expressed subjective intention in favour of deciding the nature of the transaction as a pure matter of law.[30]

17.5.2.1

Even with the benefit of the traditionally liberal approach to characterisation, it is often unclear where the distinction should lie when looking at the facts of any particular set of circumstances. For instance, there are cases where an assignment

17.5.2.2

---

[27] See, for instance, the approaches taken by Lord Herschell LC in *McEntire v Crossley Bros Ltd* [1895] AC 457, at 463–466; by the Court of Appeal in *Re George Inglefield Ltd* [1933] 1 Ch 1; by the House of Lords in *Lloyds & Scottish Finance Ltd v Cyril Lord Carpet Sales Ltd* [1992] BCLC 609; and by the Court of Appeal in *Welsh Development Agency v Export Finance Co Ltd* [1992] BCLC 148.

[28] [1992] BCLC 148.

[29] *Welsh Development Agency v Export Finance Co Limited* [1991] BCLC 936. In *Curtain Dream plc v Churchill Merchanting Ltd* [1990] BCLC 925 a transaction by way of sale of goods with a hire purchase back of the goods was held to constitute a charge over the goods, but the judgment in that case was given before the decision of the Court of Appeal in the *Welsh Development Agency* case.

[30] See Lord Millett (giving the advice of the Privy Council) in *Agnew v Inland Revenue Commissioner* [2001] UKPC 28; [2001] AC 710, at [31]–[32]; Lords Hoffmann and Scott (in the House of Lords) in *Smith (Administrator of Cosslett (Contractors) Ltd) v Bridgend CBC* [2001] UKHL 58; [2002] AC 336, at [40]–[42] and at [53]; and Lord Walker (in the House of Lords) in *National Westminster Bank PLC v Spectrum Plus Ltd* [2005] UKHL 41; [2005] 2 AC 680, at [141]. Both the *Agnew* case and the *Spectrum Plus* case involved the issue of whether an admitted security was by way of fixed or floating charge. The *Cosslett* case, on the other hand, involved the question of whether the transaction was by way of security or was some other type of transaction. Both Lord Hoffmann and Lord Scott in *Cosslett* expressly approved the approach that had been taken by Lord Millett on this issue in the Privy Council in the *Agnew* case.

of debts or receivables was held to be by way of outright transfer, and thus not being by way of security, and other cases where such an assignment was held to be by way of security.[31]

17.5.2.3   Another example where there has been confusion concerns ROT transactions. Whilst a simple retention or reservation of the 'property' (to use the concept of title as employed in the Sale of Goods Act 1979) in the goods supplied will be effective and will not be considered as creating security, an attempt to retain the 'equitable and beneficial ownership' in the goods was held to constitute a registrable charge.[32] Even with the correct drafting, the seller still has to establish that it was its terms of sale, containing the ROT clause, that governed the transaction, which is not always an easy task, especially where the buyer had its own form of purchase order. That may lead to a 'battle of the forms'. The seller will also be faced with the practical difficulty, if it wishes to enforce its rights of repossession, in identifying its own goods, if they have been muddled up with other goods owned by the buyer or third parties. Further, and despite the decision of the Court of Appeal in *Aluminium Industrie Vassen BV v Romalpa Aluminium Ltd*,[33] attempts by suppliers in their documentation to claim ownership in the products made from the goods originally supplied, or in the proceeds of sale of such original goods or products, have almost invariably been held to constitute registrable security and they have then been struck down for want of registration.[34]

17.5.3 Rights and remedies

In relation to title finance or credit transactions by way of ROT, conditional sale, HP, and finance leasing, issues also arise as to the respective rights, obligations, and remedies of the parties concerning both the subject matter of the transaction and in relation to the consequences of a default by the customer. If such transactions were, instead, expressly entered into by way of loan or the provision of credit with security being taken over the asset, the usual consequence would be that the lender would not be responsible at the outset for the state or condition of the goods, nor would it give any undertaking as to good title. The position of the parties on default would be governed by the rules that apply to recovery of an outstanding debt, and any enforcement of the security would be subject to the debtor's

---

[31] Compare *Re Marwalt Ltd* [1992] BCC 32, where the assignment was held to be absolute and not by way of security, with *Orion Finance Ltd v Crown Financial Management Ltd* [1996] BCC 621 where the assignment was held to be by way of security. The discussion by Millett LJ in the latter case served as a warning that the approach to characterisation might change.

[32] *Re Bond Worth Ltd* [1980] Ch 288.

[33] [1976] 1 WLR 676.

[34] See, for instance, *Re Bond Worth Ltd* [1980] Ch 288 and *Borden (UK) Ltd v Scottish Timber Products Ltd* [1981] Ch 25.

equity of redemption (and its corresponding right to any surplus on sale following repossession) and its obligation to make up any shortfall.[35]

On the other hand, a title financier is to be treated as a supplier of goods rather than as a lender of money. As such, it has imposed upon it[36] obligations as to its title in the goods (or, more correctly, its right to sell or supply them)[37] and as to their quality and fitness for purpose.[38] The remedies available to such a title financier/supplier of goods upon the default of its customer will be to terminate the agreement and repossess the goods, provided the grounds exist to justify such a termination,[39] and to claim damages for breach of the agreement. The entitlement to damages will depend upon which form the agreement has taken and it will involve establishing the correct measure of damages to which the financier is entitled.[40] There will also be the question, which was raised by Robert Goff LJ in *Clough Mill Ltd v Martin*,[41] as to the entitlement to any surplus that might be achieved upon a re-sale of the goods that had been the subject of a conditional sale or ROT agreement.[42]

17.5.3.1

From the customer's perspective, as it is not a borrower that has given security, it will not have an equity of redemption and so it will not have the right to pay off the finance and keep possession of the goods should the financier take action to repossess the goods. Instead, it will have the more precarious and far less certain course of making an application to the court for the equitable remedy of relief against forfeiture which, being a discretionary remedy, may not be granted, especially if

17.5.3.2

---

[35] See Romer LJ in *Re George Inglefield Ltd* [1933] Ch 1, at 28. This assumes, of course, that it was not a transaction in which it had been agreed that the lender would confine its recovery to the security and therefore would not have recourse to the borrower for any shortfall: see *Mathew v Blackmore* (1857) 1 H&N 762 and *De Vigier v IRC* [1964] 1 WLR 1073.

[36] Subject to attempts to exclude liability, which must run the gauntlet of the Unfair Contract Terms Act 1977 and the Unfair Terms in Consumer Contracts Regs 1999 (SI 1999/2083).

[37] See s 12 of the Sale of Goods Act 1979 (SGA), s 8 of the Supply of Goods (Implied Terms) Act 1973 (SGITA), and s 7 of the Supply of Goods and Services Act 1982 (SGSA). This could extend to infringement of intellectual property rights in the goods: see *Niblett Ltd v Confectioners Materials Co Ltd* [1921] 3 KB 387.

[38] SGA, ss 14(2) and (3); SGITA, ss 10(2) and (3); and SGSA, ss 9(2) and (5).

[39] In relation to hire purchase agreements and finance leases, see *Financings Ltd v Baldock* [1963] QB 104; *Capital Finance Co Ltd v Donati* (1977) 121 SJ 270; and *Lombard North Central plc v Butterworth* [1987] QB 527. For conditional sale and ROT agreements, see ss 48(3) and (4) of SGA.

[40] In relation to a conditional sale or ROT agreement, see ss 48(3) and (4) of SGA and *RV Ward Ltd v Bignall* [1967] 1 QB 534. In relation to hire purchase and finance leases, see *Overstone Ltd v Shipway* [1962] 1 WLR 117 and *Lombard North Central plc v Butterworth* [1987] QB 527. In assessing damages it is also necessary to bear in mind the possibility that the financier may have to mitigate its loss by reference to the market for alternative customers: see *In re Vic Mill Ltd* [1913] 1 Ch 465; *Interoffice Telephones Ltd v Robert Freeman Co Ltd* [1958] 1 QB 190; and *Robophone Facilities Ltd v Blank* [1966] 1 WLR 1428.

[41] [1985] 1 WLR 111.

[42] The approach taken by Robert Goff LJ is questionable in light of s 48(3) of SGA and the decision of the Court of Appeal in *RV Ward Ltd v Bignall* [1967] 1 QB 534.

the customer's conduct during the course of the transaction has been less than exemplary.[43]

17.5.4 Reform

In light of the various difficulties, it would make sense to recognise that the transactions referred to above are really a form of lending money or granting credit on the security of the accompanying assets. They should be treated as secured transactions, and the rights and remedies of the parties should be expressed so that they correspond to those that apply in the case of a secured transaction.

17.6 Registration of Security

17.6.1 The current system for the compulsory registration of security[44] is hardly perfect and clearly is in need of reform. There are legislative provisions that concern security created by companies and other provisions that deal with security created by individuals. This analysis will concentrate on the legislation for the registration of corporate security, with a brief mention at the end of the position as it relates to individuals.

17.6.2 Corporate security

Chapter I of Part 25 of the Companies Act 2006 (formerly Chapter I of Part XII of the Companies Act 1985) provides for the registration in England and Wales of charges[45] given by companies.[46] It is not all charges, however, that are registrable, but only those that fall within the prescribed categories as set forth in section 860(7) of the 2006 Act. There are some notable omissions from the list, including fixed charges over contractual rights, if they are not book debts,[47] and most types of charges over securities, investments, and bank accounts.[48] However, any floating

---

[43] See *Shiloh Spinners Ltd v Harding* [1973] AC 691; *Transag Haulage Ltd v Leyland Daf Finance plc* [1994] 2 BCLC 88; *On Demand Information plc v Michael Gerson (Finance) plc* [2001] 1 WLR 155 (CA) and [2003] 1 AC 368 (HL); and *More OG Romsdal Fylkesbatar AS v The Demise Charterers of the Ship 'Jotunheim'* [2004] EWHC 671 (Comm), [2005] 1 Lloyd's Rep 181.

[44] What follows is concerned with the system of compulsory registration of security. In addition, there are specialist registries for the registration of security over particular types of asset, which are important for priority purpose. These include the registries to do with land, ships, and aircraft, and the intellectual property registers for trade marks, patents, and registered designs.

[45] For definitional purposes, 'charge' includes mortgage (s 861(5) of the Companies Act 2006).

[46] As previously mentioned, the amendments that were proposed to be made by the Companies Act 1989 never came into force.

[47] See *Paul and Frank Ltd v Discount Bank (Overseas) Ltd* [1967] Ch 348.

[48] See now the Financial Collateral Arrangements (No 2) Regs 2003 (SI 2003/3226) but the case law had established that much the same applied as a consequence of the statutory wording, particularly as to what constituted a book debt.

charge and any charge to secure an issue of debentures is registrable, whatever the subject matter of the security.

The list of registrable charges also contains some fairly quaint and rather out-of-date language. For instance, a fixed charge over goods will be registrable if it falls within the description of being, 'a charge created or evidenced by an instrument which, if executed by an individual, would require registration as a bill of sale'. That led a judge in one case to consider if a fixed charge over future goods may not be registrable.[49] Possessory security, such as a pledge, is not a bill of sale and so it is not registrable. A charge on 'book debts' is registrable, but the meaning of that expression is far from clear and has bedevilled many attempts at providing an explanation. As mentioned earlier, any floating charge and any charge to secure an issue of debentures is registrable,[50] even if the charge would not have been registrable in other circumstances. Taking this a stage further, Lord Scott suggested in *Smith (Administrator of Cosslett (Contractors) Ltd) v Bridgend CBC*[51] that a conditional agreement to give security over unspecified assets in the future would be considered to be an agreement to give a floating charge and would fall within the requirements for registration of a floating charge. The time limit for registration would run from the date of the original agreement and not the subsequent date upon which the agreement became unconditional when the relevant condition had been fulfilled.

17.6.2.1

Sections 860(1) and 870(1) of the 2006 Act require that the original and the prescribed particulars of a registrable charge must be submitted to the Registrar of Companies within 21 days of the creation of the charge.[52] The civil consequence of a failure to comply with those requirements is that the charge will be void against a liquidator or administrator of the chargor[53] and any 'creditor' of the chargor, which has been interpreted to mean other secured creditors of the chargor.[54] On the other hand, section 869(6) of the 2006 Act provides that the issuance by the Registrar of Companies of a certificate of registration is to be conclusive evidence that the requirements of the Act have been met. Accordingly, even if there

17.6.2.2

---

[49] See Sir Nicholas Browne-Wilkinson V-C in *Welsh Development Agency v Export Finance Co Ltd* [1990] BCC 393, at 409–411.

[50] With the possible exception of a floating charge over financial collateral if it falls within para (d) of the definition of a 'security interest' in Reg 3 of the Financial Collateral Arrangements (No 2) Regs 1999 (SI 2003/3226).

[51] [2001] UKHL 58; [2002] AC 336, at [59]–[64]. His Lordship returned to this theme in *National Westminster Bank PLC v Spectrum Plus Ltd* [2005] UKHL 41; [2005] 2 AC 680, at [107].

[52] As an equitable lien is not created, but arises by operation of law, it is not registrable.

[53] I.e. the charge is avoided as against the company in liquidation or administration, as represented by its liquidator or administrator: *Smith (Administrator of Cosslett (Contractors) Ltd) v Bridgend CBC* [2001] UKHL 58, [2002] 1 AC 336.

[54] See Romer LJ in *Re Ehrmann Bros Ltd* [1906] 2 Ch 697 and Lord Brightman in *Victoria Housing Estates Ltd v Ashpurton Estates Ltd* [1983] Ch 110.

has been some irregularity concerning compliance with the statutory require-ments, the issuance of the certificate will be conclusive.[55] In addition to the civil consequence of a failure to register, there are also criminal penalties that may be imposed upon the company and its officers.[56] As there is a 21-day time limit in which to comply with the need to submit the relevant items to the registrar,[57] there is always the possibility that anyone who conducts a search during that period may not discover that a charge has been taken, as the lodgement of the charge instrument and its prescribed particulars may not have been made before the search is carried out.

17.6.2.3   A significant omission from the list of those who may take the point of non-registration is outright purchasers of the relevant charged assets. The legislation does not have the effect of invalidating an unregistered charge over an asset as against a purchaser of the asset. It has been held, however, that a debtor whose debt had been assigned by way of a registrable charge that had not been registered could take the point concerning a failure to register the charge.[58] This was despite the fact that such a debtor would hardly be described as a creditor of the chargor and does not fall within the list of the other persons mentioned in section 874(1) of the 2006 Act as one against whom the unregistered charge is avoided.

17.6.2.4   It is possible for the chargee to apply to the court for permission under section 873 of the 2006 Act to seek late registration, but if permission is given the court's order will usually provide that the late registration will be subject to the rights of any third party, including purchasers, which have arisen in the meantime. Various dif-ficulties in making an application will arise if the chargor is then insolvent or likely to become insolvent.

17.6.3   Security given by an individual

The position concerning the registration of security given by an individual is even more quixotic.[59] Essentially, non-possessory security given by an individual over goods[60] has to be registered under the Bills of Sale Act (1878) Amendment Act 1882.[61] The Act goes on to prescribe the form of the security, as well as matters

---

[55] *Re CL Nye Ltd* [1971] Ch 442.

[56] Ss 860(4) and (5) of the 2006 Act.

[57] Sometimes referred to as the 'invisibility period'.

[58] *Orion Finance Ltd v Crown Financial Management Ltd* [1996] BCC 621, at 631–635.

[59] It was initially to get around the severity of the operation of the Bills of Sale legislation that financing by way of conditional sale came into being. An early example is *McEntire v Crossley Bros* [1895] AC 457.

[60] More correctly, 'personal chattels' as defined by s 4 of the Bills of Sale Act 1878, but there are several exceptions contained in both that definition and in the definition of a 'bill of sale' in s 4 (e.g. ships and foreign goods).

[61] The Bills of Sale Act 1878 requires (subject to certain exceptions) the registration of an absolute bill of sale that is given by an individual by way of the transfer in writing of his property in the goods.

concerning its execution and registration within seven clear days, the requirements for the security to set out the consideration for which it was given, and that the goods which comprise the security must be itemised in a schedule to the instrument. An individual may not give security over future goods, and the powers of enforcement of the security are limited. A failure to meet the Act's requirements is likely to have drastic consequences; for instance, if the security document does not follow the prescribed form it is void. It is very difficult to be sure that the requirements of the Act have been met, and many security instruments have fallen foul of the Act.[62] A further consequence of the 1882 Act is that an individual is precluded from giving a floating charge over goods.

Section 344 of the Insolvency Act 1986 provides that any general assignment or charge given by an individual trader of his book debts must be registered as if it were a bill of sale. There is an exception for assignments of specific debts. If a registrable assignment or charge is not registered then it will, as to uncollected book debts, be void against the individual's trustee in bankruptcy. It should be noted that the section applies to both outright assignments by way of sale, and to assignments and charges by way of security. **17.6.4**

17.7 Priorities

The priority rules that apply where there are competing interests in the same asset are complicated and tend to be of a piecemeal nature, although the parties can enter into an agreement to resolve the competition and so agree the order in which their respective interests will rank.[63] It is important to bear in mind that priority issues may arise between competing security claimants, between competing purchasers, or any mixture thereof. **17.7.1**

The priority rules have been addressed elsewhere in this book and it is not feasible here to attempt much more than a brief summary of some of the issues that arise. By way of general comment, there is certainly nothing that is straightforward about the rules, although the effect upon a party if it has notice of an earlier interest **17.7.2**

---

62 A difficulty that was recognised by Lord Macnaghten in *Thomas v Kelly & Baker* (1888) 13 App Cas 506, at 517.

63 *Cheah Theam Swee v Equiticorp Finance Group Ltd* [1992] 1 AC 472. However, the parties to such an agreement should bear in mind the potential pitfall of the decision in *Re Portbase Clothing Ltd* [1993] Ch 388 in which it was held that where by agreement the fixed chargee conferred priority upon a floating chargee, the preferential creditors could assert their statutory priority ahead of both charges. Presumably the same result would apply in favour of a liquidator for liquidation expenses and the right of unsecured creditors under s 176A of the Insolvency Act 1986. As to an agreement regulating the priority for further advances, see s 94(1) of the Law of Property Act 1925 and s 49 of the Land Registration Act 2002.

when it acquired its own interest or gave value for that interest looms large in most discussions concerning priorities. For this purpose, notice would usually include constructive notice, the boundaries of which are not precise.

17.7.3 Where there is a specialist register which provides for the relevant asset, as is the case with land, ships, aircraft, and some types of intellectual property,[64] the starting point is that priorities will normally be determined by the date of notification or lodgement of the interest with the registry or entry of the interest in the register. Notice of a prior interest may, in some cases, serve to defeat that priority. Other complications may arise in the case of interests that are not registrable or which are protected by some other means, as, for instance, with overriding interests in land. The registration system will not help with competitions between interests that have not been registered.

17.7.4 In cases where a specialist register is not relevant, the priority rules often depend on the nature of the particular asset that is involved and the types of competing interest that are fighting for priority. Thus, the rules that apply to competing interests in choses in action are, in practice, different to those that apply to goods. Another rule applies in favour of the holder of a purchase money security interest.[65] When a floating charge is involved, the counterparty to a transaction that is entered into by the chargor in the ordinary course of business should usually take priority over the interest of the chargee, although the position becomes more opaque if the charge has crystallised.

17.7.5 A further complication arises where a lender with established priority makes further advances, as it is at risk of losing its priority for the further advances, unless it can bring itself within certain narrow areas of protection.[66] Once again, it is not easy to unravel the particular boundaries of the rules that apply in this situation and *Clayton's* case[67] can appear like a thief in the night to steal away such priority as might have been available to the lender for its established priority.

17.7.6 When all of those various matters are taken into account, it is submitted that the present law concerning priorities is in need of reform, to remove the inconsistencies and vagaries of the law, and to establish a more orderly and common pattern of priorities.

---

[64] I.e. trade marks, patents, and registered designs.

[65] See Lord Oliver in *Abbey National Building Society v Cann* [1991] 1 AC 56, at 89–93 and Jonathan Parker LJ in *Whale v Viasystems Technograph Ltd* [2002] EWCA Civ 480.

[66] See s 94 of the Law of Property Act 1925 and *Siebe Gorman & Co Ltd v Barclays Bank Ltd* [1979] 2 Lloyd's Rep 142.

[67] *Devaynes v Noble, Clayton's Case* (1816) LJ Ch 256.

17.8 The Law Commission's Proposals in 2002 and 2004

The Law Commission's original proposals, as put forward in its *Consultation Paper* in 2002, were modified by its *Consultative Report* in 2004. As so modified, they contemplated a fundamental reform of the law relating to secured transactions and many types of quasi-security transactions. In framing its proposals, the Law Commission drew heavily upon the models that had been developed in North America and New Zealand, principally as contained in Article 9 of the American Law Institute's Uniform Commercial Code (as revised in 1999) (the UCC).[68] New Zealand had been the last of those jurisdictions to adopt the model that had originally been formulated in the USA and then adopted in Canada. As previously mentioned, the proposals were put forward in the expectation that they would initially be implemented for security given by companies. The Law Commission envisaged that reform of the law relating to security given by individuals would be implemented at a later stage.   **17.8.1**

The modified proposals as represented by the *Consultative Report* in 2004 went further than the Law Commission's final proposals in its *Final Report* of 2005. It is intended at this stage to describe the broad outline of the proposals as put forward in 2004. At a later stage, the discussion will move to describing the less extensive final proposals.   **17.8.2**

Before outlining the proposals, it may be helpful to summarise some of the terminology that is used in Article 9 of the UCC. That terminology was used by the Law Commission in its proposals in 2002 and 2004 for the new English system.   **17.8.3**

Term	Summarised meaning
Security Interest	The security/title protection of the financier/creditor in the relevant collateral
Collateral	The asset(s) over which security/title protection is to subsist
Secured Party	The party which holds the security interest (irrespective of form) and so usually provides the finance
Debtor	The borrower or other obligor which creates the security interest in favour of the secured party
Security Agreement	The relevant documentation recording the agreement by which the security interest is to be given
Financing Statement	The form that is filed in the relevant registry giving brief details of the transaction

---

[68] See also the Personal Property Security Acts of the various Canadian provinces and of New Zealand. It is also worth noting that UNCITRAL put forward a legislative Guide on security interests for adoption by States (a draft of which was set out in the UNCITRAL *Yearbook*, Vol XXXVI, 2005, documents A/CN.9/WG.VI/WP.21 and Addenda 1–5).

Term	Summarised meaning
Attachment	Attachment of a security interest is when, as between the secured party and the debtor, the security interest attaches to the asset. For this to occur, there must be (1) a security agreement pursuant to which the relevant collateral is sufficiently identified, (2) value given, and (3) rights of the debtor in the collateral
Perfection	Perfection of a security interest is when the security interest has attached to the collateral and all steps have been taken (by filing or by obtaining possession/possession and control) to make the security interest enforceable in the insolvency of the debtor and effective against third parties
Inventory	Stock and raw materials, being goods which are held for sale or other disposition or to be used up in a business, such as in a process of manufacture
Equipment	Goods other than inventory

17.8.4 What now follows is a distillation of the Law Commission's proposals as represented by its paper in 2004. The proposals were to the following effect.

17.8.4.1 The rather complicated and confusing system which currently applies in England for the registration of corporate security should be replaced by a more comprehensive system of notice-filing of most types of secured transactions and quasi-security transactions or, alternatively, taking possession and control of the collateral. This would be much along the lines that apply in the USA under Article 9 of the UCC, and in Canada and New Zealand. The filing would be at a central registry. The concepts of attachment and perfection of a security would be central in understanding the system.

17.8.4.2 Transactions having a security nature, in a practical sense, should be characterised and identified by their substance rather than their form, so that the system would apply to both security in a narrow sense and to many types of quasi-security, such as ROT and equipment title finance (e.g. conditional sale, HP, leasing (where the lease was for more than one year) and consignments/sale and return transactions) and to receivables finance (i.e. transfers of 'accounts', defined to cover book debts and other receivables, such as by way of factoring, invoice, and block discounting, but not transfers of loan participations). Unlike the North American schemes, there would be no special arrangements for 'chattel paper', which would be subsumed within the general arrangements for transfers of accounts.

17.8.4.3 All such transactions would be regarded as being tantamount to the conferral upon the creditor of a security interest in the relevant collateral. This would also have the advantage of ending the debate as to the characterisation of transactions, and the risk that a transaction which might have been intended by the parties to be otherwise than a form of security might be re-characterised as a registrable charge.

A filed security interest in goods could extend into products made from or incorporating the goods and to proceeds of sale of the goods or their products.

17.8.4.4

In contrast to the present system of requiring the registration of specifically identified types of security transactions (e.g. charges over book debts, charges on land, charges to secure an issue of debentures, charges which, if given by an individual, would require registration as a bill of sale, charges over intellectual property, and floating charges), the new scheme would work on the basis that it applied comprehensively to all forms of transaction, with certain limited exceptions.

17.8.4.5

A simple form of financing statement, giving brief details of the transaction (such as the names of the parties and a description of the collateral) would be filed, without the need or requirement for submitting the relevant security instrument. The system for filing and searching would be electronic and open on a 24-hour basis. Filing would be made electronically and searching could be done on-line.

17.8.4.6

Possessory securities would not need to be filed (e.g. pledges of and liens over goods and documentary intangibles).

17.8.4.7

Similarly, it would not be necessary to file for security in financial assets having a quasi-possessory nature. This would cover security over bank accounts, where the secured party controlled the account, and other financial collateral such as shares, bonds, and other financial assets where the secured party was registered as the holder of the security or recorded electronically as such, or otherwise had possession or control over the asset (see also in this connection the EU Financial Collateral Directive,[69] implemented in the UK by the Financial Collateral Arrangements (No 2) Regulations 2003[70]). Special rules would be required to set out the necessary elements for possession and control to exist over such assets.

17.8.4.8

The principal rule for priorities would be that they would be governed by the order of filing of details concerning the security or, for possessory and quasi-possessory security, taking effective possession or control. There would also need to be other rules to deal with particular situations (e.g. for priorities as between two unfiled security interests). Purchasers and security holders would be able to rely on the priority rules, so that a purchaser in good faith would take free of an unperfected security interest. The current risk as to an 'invisibility period' (i.e. the period of up to 21 days in which a charge might be registered) would disappear.

17.8.4.9

It would be possible, with the debtor's consent, to file ahead of a proposed transaction to ensure priority ('pre-filing').

17.8.4.10

---

[69] EC 2002/47 OJ L168/43, 27/6/2002.
[70] SI 2003/3226.

17.8.4.11 Special priority would be accorded to purchase money security interests, i.e. security taken over an asset or a quasi-security in such an asset, other than investment property, to secure finance provided for the acquisition of the asset (a PMSI). The PMSI would rank ahead of a general security interest over after acquired property that might have been granted at an earlier date. Where the collateral was inventory, the PMSI would have priority if it was perfected and notice of it was given (before the debtor acquired the collateral) to any other holder of a filed security interest in the collateral. For equipment and other types of collateral, the PMSI would gain priority if it was perfected within ten days of the debtor's acquisition of the collateral. It would be possible for a PMSI to be extended into proceeds of a subsequent sale of the collateral. If that conflicted with another security interest in the proceeds that had been protected by filing then that other security interest should be entitled to priority.

17.8.4.12 Filing and priorities for assets dealt with on specialist registers would be governed by the system for the relevant register (e.g. land, ships, aircraft, and intellectual property).

17.8.4.13 The current 21-day time limit for registering company security would go, but where a filing was not made before the commencement of insolvency proceedings, the relevant secured transaction would be ineffective in the insolvency. A similar position would apply with respect to the interests of execution creditors.

17.8.4.14 A query was raised as to whether floating charges would continue as such. The Law Commission did not recommend their abolition, but envisaged that the distinction between them and fixed security would effectively disappear. Under the new scheme, it would be possible for a debtor to dispose of ordinary course of business assets to purchasers, whatever the nature of the security. If floating charges were abolished or became redundant, it would mean that consequential changes would have to be made to the various provisions in insolvency law which concern floating charges, such as those relating to the position of the liquidator for liquidation expenses, the position of preferential creditors, and the position of unsecured creditors under section 176A of the Insolvency Act 1986, as well as the provisions of section 245 of the Act which concern the potential invalidity of a floating charge.

17.8.4.15 Sales of trading assets in the ordinary course of business to purchasers would take priority over a security interest in the assets unless the purchaser had express knowledge of a negative pledge which prevented the sale.

17.8.4.16 The remedies and rights upon default and as to enforcement of security and quasi-security would be codified and standardised, so as not to depend upon the peculiarities of the form of the transaction. This would be a useful method of dealing with the difficulties adverted to earlier in this chapter concerning the position following upon a default in equipment finance transactions. Due to their nature, however, the standardised rules would not apply to receivables purchase transactions.

Filing for security given by foreign companies would be required for assets situated within the jurisdiction, irrespective of whether or not the chargor was registered as a foreign company, thereby overcoming the problem associated with the necessity to make *Slavenburg*[71] registrations. **17.8.4.17**

17.9 The Proposals in the Law Commission's Final Report of 2005[72]

The Law Commission's final proposals, as contained in its *Final Report*, were not as far reaching as its earlier proposals. Essentially, its final proposals were limited to recommending a new system to cover corporate security in a narrow sense, together with certain sales of receivables by companies. Title finance transactions, such as ROT, conditional sale, HP, and equipment leases, were not to be included within the new system. The final report made no recommendation for the standardisation of rights and remedies upon default; nor did it purport to regulate the form or the content of security interests and transactions. Non-possessory security could continue to be taken by way of a legal mortgage (or, in the case of land, a legal charge) or an equitable mortgage or as an equitable charge. A charge could be either fixed or floating. Possessory security would continue to be held in the form of a pledge or a contractual lien, and equitable liens could arise by operation of law. **17.9.1**

The final proposals were accompanied by a set of draft regulations, which the Law Commission entitled the 'Company Security Regulations'. They are to be found in Appendix A to its *Final Report*. **17.9.2**

The Law Commission also recommended that further consideration should be given in the future to reform in three areas that were not included in its final proposals, namely: **17.9.3**

(1) whether the reform of the law of secured transactions should extend to security and receivables sales involving unincorporated businesses, sole traders, consumers, and unregistered companies;

(2) whether title finance transactions should become a registrable form of transaction; and

---

[71] A reference to attempts to register security given by foreign companies, in light of the decision in *Slavenburg's Bank NV v Intercontinental Resources* [1980] 1 WLR 1076.

[72] The *Final Report* contains a valuable and lengthy description of the factors that the Law Commission took into account in making its recommendations, to which reference should be made for further guidance.

(3) if there should be a statutory restatement of the law of secured transactions dealing with such matters as the creation and attachment of security interests, the rights and duties of the parties to such transactions, and the consequences of default and the remedies that would be available upon enforcement.

17.9.4 A summary of the major matters covered in the Law Commission's *Final Report* is as follows.

17.9.4.1 Security, in the traditional sense, that is given by a company would be within the new scheme. It would continue to be possible for companies to give floating charges.

17.9.4.2 Sales of receivables by a company would also be within the new scheme. For this purpose, a receivable would be defined as a monetary obligation, whether or not earned by performance, which arises from the sale or supply of goods or services (other than insurance services) or from the sale of energy or brokerage fees. Certain transactions would be excluded from the concept of a 'sale' of receivables, including a sale of an insignificant portion of the seller's total portfolio of receivables, a sale which was part of the sale of a business, an assignment as the consideration for the satisfaction of a pre-existing debt, an assignment to facilitate collection of the receivables, and an assignment of a right to payment in favour of a person to whom performance of the matching obligation had been delegated.

17.9.4.3 There would be special provisions concerning financial collateral (such as the benefit of bank accounts, money market deposits, shares, and debt securities). This would have to take into account the provisions of the Financial Collateral Arrangements (No 2) Regulations 2003,[73] which implement the Directive on Financial Collateral Arrangements.[74] The provisions of the scheme to deal with this matter were complex and cannot be summarised conveniently in this chapter, other than to say that much would depend upon a creditor having possession or control (or both) of the relevant collateral.

17.9.4.4 Reverting to the position for assets other than financial collateral, the primary requirement under the new scheme would be that the security, or sale of receivables, would constitute a registrable transaction, which would involve lodging the relevant details ('filing') at the Companies Registry. The responsibility for filing would fall upon the security holder or assignee. There would be no penalty upon

---

[73] SI 2003/3226. Such provisions include Reg 4(4) which provides that a security financial collateral arrangement (which is defined in Reg 3) or any charge arising thereunder, shall not be registrable under the provisions of Part 25 of the Companies Act 2006 (and its predecessor under the Companies Act 1985). It should be noted that a security financial collateral arrangement may include certain types of floating charge.

[74] EC 2002/47 OJ L168/43 27/6/2002.

the company or its officers for a failure to file. The register of charges and sales of receivables would be maintained by the Registrar of Companies.

Filing (or registration, to give it another name) would be by way of filing a finan- 17.9.4.5
cing statement, and giving brief details of relevant matters such as the parties and a description of the affected assets (the collateral). Filing and searching would be carried out electronically.

If the security taker had possession of goods or documentary intangibles by way 17.9.4.6
of pledge or contractual lien, that would also be an alternative to filing. Similarly, an alternative to filing would exist for financial collateral, if the security taker had obtained possession or control of the collateral.

There would be no strict time limits for filing or for taking possession or control 17.9.4.7
but a failure to do so would render the security or assignment ineffective in the liquidation or administration of the company and as against execution creditors.

It would be possible to file a financing statement in advance of taking security, so 17.9.4.8
as to gain and protect priority.

A failure to file or to take possession or control would also have priority conse- 17.9.4.9
quences as against third parties claiming an interest in the collateral. The system would contain a scheme for priorities. As a consequence of the reforms, the risk to third parties of an 'invisibility period' would disappear.

In a little more detail, the principal rules for priorities would be as follows (bearing 17.9.4.10
in mind that there would be certain specific rules for particular situations):

(1) an agreement between the competing parties as to priorities would be binding upon them;
(2) where interests were registered on a specialist register (i.e. land, ships, aircraft, and some types of intellectual property), priority would be dealt with by the rules relevant to that register;
(3) there would be special rules for priorities in financial collateral;
(4) a registered interest would have priority over an unregistered interest;
(5) in general, a purchaser of an asset would take subject to a registered interest but not an unregistered interest of which it did not have notice. If the registered interest was that of a floating charge, a transferee of the collateral in the ordinary course of business and without actual notice of a relevant negative pledge (there would be no system for registering negative pledges) would take free of the charge;
(6) as between registered interests, priority would be by the first to file, which would be a useful rule for the holder of an interest where the filing was made in advance of the date on which the interest was obtained;

(7) as between unregistered non-possessory interests, priority would be by the date of creation or sale of the interests;

(8) as between a charge and a possessory interest by way of pledge, priority would be determined by the relative dates of filing of the charge and the date of the creation of the possessory interest. There would also be a specific provision dealing with the effect of a trust receipt;

(9) as between a charge and a possessory interest by way of contractual lien, priority would be determined by the relative dates of the filing of the charge and the later of the date of the agreement for the lien and the date on which the lienee obtained possession. A lien arising by operation of law (for example, an unpaid vendor's lien) would have priority over both registered and unregistered charges;

(10) a transferee of security would have the same priority as the transferor enjoyed;

(11) a charge over or sale of a supporting obligation (e.g. a mortgage) has the same priority as the charge or sale of the principal obligation (e.g. the mortgage debt) that it supports;

(12) the right of a chargee to the proceeds of collateral, where the collateral is the subject of a fixed charge, would have the same priority as that fixed charge;

(13) priority would apply to cover all advances, including further advances (defined in a wide sense), with some qualification in favour of execution creditors; and

(14) there would be no special rule in favour of the holder of a purchase money security interest.

17.9.4.11 Provisions in the scheme would deal with the position of an 'account debtor' vis-à-vis a purchaser of the receivable or a person who had taken security over the receivable. An account debtor would be the person who was obliged to pay the receivable. Those provisions would deal with the account debtor's rights of set-off and provide it with protection in terms of the person to whom it should make payment of the receivable. Somewhat more controversially, the scheme would also provide that an assignment of a receivable, or the taking of security over the receivable, could occur notwithstanding a prohibition against such a transaction in the underlying contract under which the receivable arose.

17.9.4.12 The scheme would apply to companies incorporated in England and Wales, irrespective of the location of the relevant collateral. However, the scheme would acknowledge conflict of laws principles where the collateral was located in another jurisdiction, as, for instance, in matters relating to the validity of a transaction and issues concerning priorities.

17.9.4.13 For foreign companies and Scottish companies, the scheme would apply with respect to security that was taken over collateral located in England and Wales, irrespective of whether or not the company was registered or had a place of business in England and Wales. The scheme would not, however, apply to sales of receivables by such companies, even if the *lex situs* of the receivables was English law.

17.10 Concluding Remarks

At the time of writing, it looked unlikely that reform along the lines outlined above would occur. The early part of this chapter presented a case for reform of the law, by reference to a number of the difficulties that presently arise under the existing law. There have been calls for reform going as far back as the Crowther Committee in 1971. The Law Commission's modified proposals in 2004 represented an attempt to put forward a comprehensive scheme for corporate security that would, with some exceptions, have covered the field for many types of secured transactions and quasi-security transactions. The proposals drew heavily on the examples provided by the models developed and operating successfully in the common law jurisdictions in North America and New Zealand, the latter being a common law jurisdiction which, historically, has been particularly close in its characteristics to the practice of the law in England. An English system based on such models would benefit from the experience gained in those jurisdictions and would not be an attempt to re-invent the wheel.   **17.10.1**

It is submitted that such a scheme would have been beneficial to the development of the law in England and Wales. Almost inevitably, there would be some matters to be sorted out in the fine-tuning of the legislation that implemented the scheme. Allowances would also have been required so as to ensure that the introduction of a new system did not imperil the rights and obligations of parties under existing transactions that were current when the system was introduced. Overall, however, the concept of a comprehensive system covering nearly all financial and credit transactions having a proprietary nature would lead to more certainty and less inconsistency of outcome than obtains under the existing system based on various historical peculiarities as they have developed in the law. There is a symmetry in treating all proprietary transactions which have the substantive effect of a financing or credit transaction in the same way.   **17.10.2**

The idea of a simple method of notice filing (including the ability to file in advance of the conclusion of a transaction), with exceptions for cases where the creditor had obtained possession and control of the relevant assets, has many attractions. It would provide the basis of an effective method of protection for a creditor and for determining priorities. The arbitrary consequences under the present system of failing to meet the 21-day limit for lodging the charge and the prescribed particulars, and the uncertainties inherent in making an application for late registration, would be removed. Filing and searching would have become simple and easy   **17.10.3** to achieve. The register would provide a more accurate picture than is presently available to those who wish to search, particularly if one bears in mind the types of non-possessory security and other types of transaction which presently escape the requirements for registration. A person intending to deal with a debtor could easily discover if the debtor had already given security or entered into a receivables assignment or an ROT or title finance transaction with a third party which might defeat or otherwise come ahead of the security that such a person was intending to take. An ROT creditor or a title financier would be able to extend its claim to include products and proceeds, protect itself by filing, and discover what other transactions the debtor had entered into which might be adverse to its interests.

17.10.4 The scheme represented by the final proposals of the Law Commission in its *Final Report* was not as extensive as that originally envisaged in its earlier papers. Nonetheless, it would have been better to adopt the final proposals than to leave the law in its present unreformed state. Consistently with a preference for the comprehensive scheme as put forward in 2004, it would be desirable to include in any scheme the three additional matters that the Law Commission in its *Final Report* recommended should receive further consideration. By way of reminder, those matters were to extend the scheme to include individuals and other types of entity not covered by the scheme as presently envisaged, to include ROT and title finance transactions, and to set out a statutory restatement of the law covering matters such as the rights, duties, and remedies of the parties to a transaction.

INDEX